Graphics and Multimedia for the Web with Adobe Creative Cloud

Navigating the Adobe Software Landscape

Jennifer Harder

Apress®

Graphics and Multimedia for the Web with Adobe Creative Cloud: Navigating the Adobe Software Landscape

Jennifer Harder
Delta, BC, Canada

ISBN-13 (pbk): 978-1-4842-3822-6   ISBN-13 (electronic): 978-1-4842-3823-3
https://doi.org/10.1007/978-1-4842-3823-3

Library of Congress Control Number: 2018963115

Copyright © 2018 by Jennifer Harder

This work is subject to copyright. All rights are reserved by the Publisher, whether the whole or part of the material is concerned, specifically the rights of translation, reprinting, reuse of illustrations, recitation, broadcasting, reproduction on microfilms or in any other physical way, and transmission or information storage and retrieval, electronic adaptation, computer software, or by similar or dissimilar methodology now known or hereafter developed.

Trademarked names, logos, and images may appear in this book. Rather than use a trademark symbol with every occurrence of a trademarked name, logo, or image we use the names, logos, and images only in an editorial fashion and to the benefit of the trademark owner, with no intention of infringement of the trademark.

The use in this publication of trade names, trademarks, service marks, and similar terms, even if they are not identified as such, is not to be taken as an expression of opinion as to whether or not they are subject to proprietary rights.

While the advice and information in this book are believed to be true and accurate at the date of publication, neither the authors nor the editors nor the publisher can accept any legal responsibility for any errors or omissions that may be made. The publisher makes no warranty, express or implied, with respect to the material contained herein.

Managing Director, Apress Media LLC: Welmoed Spahr
Acquisitions Editor: Natalie Pao
Development Editor: James Markham
Coordinating Editor: Jessica Vakili

Cover image designed by Freepik

Distributed to the book trade worldwide by Springer Science+Business Media New York, 233 Spring Street, 6th Floor, New York, NY 10013. Phone 1-800-SPRINGER, fax (201) 348-4505, e-mail orders-ny@springer-sbm.com, or visit www.springeronline.com. Apress Media, LLC is a California LLC and the sole member (owner) is Springer Science + Business Media Finance Inc (SSBM Finance Inc). SSBM Finance Inc is a **Delaware** corporation.

For information on translations, please e-mail rights@apress.com, or visit http://www.apress.com/rights-permissions.

Apress titles may be purchased in bulk for academic, corporate, or promotional use. eBook versions and licenses are also available for most titles. For more information, reference our Print and eBook Bulk Sales web page at http://www.apress.com/bulk-sales.

Any source code or other supplementary material referenced by the author in this book is available to readers on GitHub via the book's product page, located at www.apress.com/978-1-4842-3822-6. For more detailed information, please visit http://www.apress.com/source-code.

Printed on acid-free paper

Contents

About the Author xxi

About the Technical Reviewers xxiii

Acknowledgments xxv

■Part I: Welcome to the Adobe Creative Cloud. Where Should You Begin? 1

■Chapter 1: Entering the Software Maze or Labyrinth 3

Where Should You Begin? 3

    How Will You Get to Your Destination? 5

    A Visual Map of How the Creative Cloud Software Works 6

    Choosing the Smallest Number of Adobe Software Programs to Accomplish Your Goals 6

    Basic Web File Formats for Images and Multimedia 9

Summary 11

■Part II: Working with Photoshop to Create Web Graphics and Animations 13

■Chapter 2: Getting Started 15

Working with Your RAW and Layered Files 17

Creating a New File 23

Image Files from Other Adobe Programs 28

Summary 30

■Chapter 3: Color Choices: CMYK, RGB, Grayscale, and Index 31

Adjusting the Image Size and Resolution 42

Summary 46

iii

Chapter 4: Saving or Exporting Your Files for the Web 47

Option 1: File ➤ Save As... 48

- Bitmap (BMP) 50
- JPEG 52
- PNG 55
- CompuServe GIF 55
- Photoshop PDF 61

Option 2: File ➤ Export ➤ Quick Export as PNG 65

- JPEG 66
- GIF 67
- SVG 68

Options 3: File ➤ Export ➤ Export As... 68

- PNG 68
- JPEG 71
- GIF 72
- SVG 73

Option 4: File ➤ Export ➤ Save for Web (Legacy) 74

- GIF 78
- JPEG 82
- PNG-8 83
- PNG-24 85
- WMBP 86

Additional Options That You Can Use to Export Files for the Web 88

- Artboards 88
- Layer Comps 90
- Layers 92

Summary 93

Chapter 5: Actions to Speed up File Conversion and Slicing Tools 95
Actions to Speed up the File Conversion Process 95
- Automate Batch Actions 106
- Automate Droplet Actions 107
Slicing Tools 110
- Use the Slice and Slice Select Tool 110
- Layer-based Slices 119
- Exporting Slices 120
Zoomify an Image 124
Summary 126

Chapter 6: Tools for Animation 127
GIF (animated) (.gif) 129
The Timeline Panel 129
- Adding a Frame 131
- Adding, Altering, and Removing Frames 133
- Add Layer Style Effects and Turn Them On or Off in the Frame Sequence 135
- Tweening Layers in the Timeline 140
- Export Animated GIF 143
Summary 143

Chapter 7: Tools for Video 145
Video Setup Tips 146
Video Timeline 149
- Layers in the Timeline 151
- Other Layer Properties 155
- Smart Object Layers 157
- Adding Video Layers 158
- Interpret Footage 171

CONTENTS

Playing and Previewing Video 174

Working with the Timeline and Playhead 175

Adding Background Audio 184

Rendering the Video 186

Saving the Original File 187

Summary 187

■Chapter 8: Other Miscellaneous Items in Photoshop That You Can Use for Web Design 189

Libraries CC 189

Extraction of Code from Layers 190

Web Fonts and SVG Fonts 191

Filter for Repeating Backgrounds 192

New to Photoshop CC 2018 Paint Symmetry 194

Web Styles 196

Color Blindness Proofs 197

Summary 200

■Chapter 9: Putting It into Practice with Photoshop CC 201

Exporting Images for a Gallery 201

Exporting a GIF Animation 206

Exporting a JPEG Poster Image for Your Movie for the Web 209

Rendering Your Movie 212

Summary 219

■Part III: Working with Illustrator to Create Web Graphics 221

■Chapter 10: Getting Started with Illustrator CC 223

Working with RAW and Layered Files (AI, EPS, PDF) 225

Creating a New File 228

RAW File Types 232

Summary 237

Chapter 11: Color Choices: CMYK, RGB, and Grayscale 239

Working with Color 239

- Copying CMYK Graphics to an RGB Document 242
- Color Panel 243
- Swatches Panel 245

Other Panels for Working with Color 246

- Color Guide Panel 247
- Adobe Color Themes Panel 248
- Gradient Panel 248
- Transparency Panel 249
- Appearance Panel 250

Summary 251

Chapter 12: Saving or Exporting Your Files for the Web 253

Option 1: File ➤ Save As or File ➤ Save a Copy 254

- Adobe PDF (.pdf) 254
- SVG (.svg) and SVG Compressed (.svgz) 259

Option 2: File ➤ Export ➤ Export for Screens 264

- Artboards Tab 265
- PNG 270
- PNG 8 270
- JPEG 272
- SVG 274
- PDF 275
- Assets Tab 276

Option 3: File ➤ Export ➤ Export As 283

- Bitmap 283
- JPEG 284
- PNG 285
- SVG 285
- CSS 286

CONTENTS

Option 4: File ➤ Export ➤ Save for Web (Legacy) 290
    GIF 292
    JPEG 293
    PNG-8 and PNG-24 293

Summary 295

■Chapter 13: Actions to Speed up File Conversion and Slicing Tools 297

Using Scripts 297

Actions to Speed up the File Conversion Process 298
    Actions Panel 298

Automate Batch Actions 303

Slicing Tools 306
    Use the Slice and Slice Select Tools 307
    Object ➤ Slice Options 310
    Align Slices 311
    Slice Options 312
    Delete All Slices 316
    Lock Slices 316
    Hide Slices 316
    Save Your Slices for the Web 316

Creating Image Maps 319

Summary 321

■Chapter 14: Tools for Animation and Video 323

Tools for Animation 323
    SVG Interactivity Panel 323

Copying Illustrations to Photoshop (Vector Smart Objects) 330
    Rasterize Smart Objects 332
    Puppet Warp Tool 333

Tools for Video 337
    New Layout for Film and Video 337
    Adding 3D Images 338

Summary 340

Chapter 15: Other Miscellaneous Items in Illustrator That You Can Use for Web Design 341

Library CC 341

Web Fonts and SVG Fonts 342

Creating Swatch Patterns 344

Graphic Styles for Buttons and Rollovers 356

Symbols Panel for Web Symbol Creation 357

Color Blindness Proofs 359

Summary 360

Chapter 16: Putting It into Practice with Illustrator CC 361

Exporting Images for an Instructional Webpage 361

    Create a Custom Action 363

Exporting an SVG File 368

Summary 378

Part IV: Working with Animate to Create Animations, Movies, and HTML5 Canvas 379

Chapter 17: Getting Started with Animate CC 381

Getting Started 383

    Differences and Similarities Between Animate and Character Animator CC 384

    Setting up the Workspace 384

    Create a New FLA Document 386

What Is HTML5 Canvas? 390

    HTML5 Canvas Can Draw Text 390

    HTML5 Canvas Can Draw Graphics 391

    HTML5 Canvas Can Be Animated 391

    HTML5 Canvas Can Be Interactive 391

    HTML5 Canvas Can Be Used in Games 391

CONTENTS

Working with RAW Files 391

    Properties Panel 392

    Timeline Panel 394

    Library Panel 394

    Tools Panel 395

    FLA Conversions ActionScript to HTML5 396

Summary 398

■Chapter 18: Color Choices: RGB 399

Adding Color to the Stage 399

The Tools Panel Stroke and Fill 400

Properties Panel 401

Color Panel 402

    Gradient Fills 403

    Bitmap Fills 405

Swatches Panel 406

Info Panel 407

Summary 407

■Chapter 19: Importing Your Artwork 409

Importing Files to the Stage or Library Panels 409

    Import an Image Sequence 410

    Export Images from an External Library 411

    Importing Illustrator and Photoshop Files with Their Elements or Effects Intact 411

    Animate CC Effects 436

Import Other Graphic File Formats 456

Summary 457

■Chapter 20: Import Your Audio and Video 459

Import Audio 459

    Sound Effect Settings 462

    Sync Setting 464

    Repeat Sound 466

Import Video 466
    Components and Component Parameters 467

Summary 472

Chapter 21: Working with the Timeline Panel 473

Working with the Timeline Panel 473
    A Review of Layers 473
    New Layers 475
    Folders 476
    Hide and Show Layers and Folder 476
    Lock Layers and Folders 477
    Layer Outlines 477
    Advanced Layer Settings 479
    Layer Depth Panel 480
    Layer Types 485

The Parts of the Timeline 488
    Frames Types 491

Easing for Classic, Shape, and Motion Tweens 500
    Shape Tween Easing 500
    Classic Tween Easing 502
    Motion and Camera Tween Easing 504

Camera Tool 508

Bone Tools 511
    Bone Tool and Armature Easing 511
    The Bind Tool 516

Frame Picker Panel 519

Scene Panel 520

Summary 521

Chapter 22: Exporting Your Files to the Web 523

Saving or Exporting Your Files for the Web 523

Option 1: File ➤ Export ➤ Export Image 525
- GIF 528
- JPEG 530
- PNG-8 and PNG-24 530

Option 2: File ➤ Export ➤ Export Image (Legacy) 531
- SWF Movie (removed in CC 2019) 532
- JPEG 532
- GIF 533
- PNG 534
- SVG 535

Option 3: File ➤ Export ➤ Export Movie 537
- SWF Movie 537
- JPEG 537
- GIF 538
- PNG 538

Option 4: File ➤ Export ➤ Export Video 539
- Tips for Controlling the Audio in Video When Exporting to MOV 540

Option 5: File ➤ Export ➤ Export Animated GIF 541

Option 6: File ➤ Publish Settings HTML5 Canvas 542
- Publish Settings 544
- Dissecting the Canvas HTML5 File 558

Other Export Options from the Symbols in the Library Panel 558
- Export PNG Sequence 559
- Generate Sprite Sheet 559
- Generate Texture Atlas 562

Other Web Export Options 563
- AIR Options 563
- Projector 567
- WebGL 567

Summary 569

Chapter 23: Other Miscellaneous Items in Animate that You Can Use for Web Design 571

Edit ➤ Preferences 571

Actions, Code Snippets, and History Panels 573

Actions Panel 573

Code Snippets Panel 574

History Panel 578

CC Libraries 581

Patterns for Paint Brush and Pen Tools 582

3D in Animations 591

Web Fonts 592

The Dangers of Flashing Graphics 595

Summary 596

Chapter 24: Putting It into Practice with Animate CC 597

Create an Animated GIF 597

Export your GIF Animation 599

Create a Video (.mov) File 603

Creating a Storyboard 604

Pre-Plan Your Video Settings 606

Reviewing the Files 606

Exporting the Video 607

Opening in Adobe Media Encoder 608

Create an HTML5 Canvas Animation 608

Publish HTML5 Canvas and OAM File 610

Summary 612

Part V: Working with Media Encoder to Create Audio and Video Files 613

Chapter 25: Getting Started with Media Encoder 615

Getting Started 615

Looking at the Setup of Media Encoder CC and Queue 620

    Set up a Workspace 621

Media Browser Panel 626

Queue Panel 630

    Format Options 632

    Preset Options 633

    Output File Options 634

    Status Options 634

    Interpret Footage 634

Watch Folders Panel 636

Encoding Panel 636

Preset Browser Panel 636

    Preset Menu Options 638

Summary 640

Chapter 26: Working with Your RAW Video Files (AVI and MOV) 641

Working with Your RAW Files (AVI or MOV) 641

    Audio Video Interleave 642

    QuickTime File Format 642

Convert Video with Export Settings 642

    Export Settings Dialog Box 644

    Combine Video (Stitch Clips) 676

WebM and Ogg 677

Summary 678

Chapter 27: Working with Your RAW Video Files and Converting Them to Audio 679

Convert Audio to (Export Settings) 679
- MP3 680
- Waveform Audio (.wav) 686
- Theora Ogg (.ogg) 690
- Working with Audio Files That Are Audio 3GA 690

Summary 690

Chapter 28: Working with Your RAW Video Files and Converting Them to an Image Sequence 691

Convert to Other Web Formats (Image Sequence) 691
- Bitmap Sequence Export settings 692
- JPEG Sequence Export Settings 696
- PNG Sequence Export Settings 697
- GIF (Static) Image Sequence Export Settings 699
- Animated GIF 700

Summary 703

Chapter 29: Putting It into Practice with Media Encoder CC 705

Create a Video MP4 File 705
Create an Audio MP3 File and a WAV File 724
Summary 729

Part VI: Working with Dreamweaver: Adding Images, Animations, and Multimedia to HTML5 Pages 731

Chapter 30: Getting Started with Dreamweaver CC 733

Entering the Maze's Center 733
Differences and Similarities Between Dreamweaver and Muse 734
Setting up in Dreamweaver 736
- Toolbar Overview 740

CONTENTS

What is HTML5 (.html)? 747
Import and Save Your File to Your Site 752
Files Panel 755
Fixing Errors 756
Summary 756

Chapter 31: Working with Images and Tags 757

Adding More Images to the Folder 760
Inserting Images on an HTML Page 762
    Insert Panel 762
    Working with SVG Images 768
    Properties Panel 769
Adding Images Inside Various Tags 775
    A Bit of HTML History 776
    <div> Tags 777
    Sematic Elements 779
    Are Tables Obsolete in Web Design? 790
    Image Maps <area> and <map> Tags 793
    The <picture> and <source> Element 796
    The <details> and <summary> Elements 797
    The <dialog> Element 798
    The <menu> and <menuitem> Elements 798
Inserting Images Favicons into Your Browser's Tab 798
HTML5 and the Snippets Panel 799
Summary 800

Chapter 32: Working with CSS 801

CSS Inline Internal or External Styles? 801
    Inline CSS 801
    Internal CSS 804
    External CSS 821

CONTENTS

What Is CSS3? 827
- Applying CSS to the <img> Tag 828
- Should You Add Background Images to Form Elements? 830
- CSS3 Borders 830
- Rounded CSS3 Borders 831
- Outline CSS2 833
- CSS3 box-decoration-break 834
- Adding CSS3 Filters and Shadows 834
- Image Masking in CSS3? 838
- Adding Custom Images to Bullets 838

Creating CSS Animation Transitions and Transforms 840
- CSS3 Animations 841
- CSS Transitions and Transitions Panel 844

CSS Transforms 2D and 3D: It's All About Perspective 853
- 2D Transform 854
- 3D Transform 856

Summary 859

Chapter 33: Working with Images for Mobile Web Design 861

CSS Floats 861
- z-index 864
- Clip 864

Responsive Media Queries and the View Port 865

Image Slices and Mobile Devices 870

Media Queries (Mobile-First) 872
- Scaling Images 875
- Scaling a div with a Background Image 876
- Loading a Different Image Based on Media Queries 877

Column Count 878

CSS for Print with CSS Designer Panel 878

Summary 879

Chapter 34: What Is JavaScript? 881

Creating a New JavaScript File 883

Insert Rollover Images 885

Behaviors Panel 888

    Additional Behaviors 892

JavaScript and the Snippets Panel 894

Print Preview 897

Summary 898

Chapter 35: Working with Bootstrap, Templates, Library Items, and the Assets Panel 899

Bootstrap 899

Working with Templates, Library Items, and the Assets Panel 905

    Templates 905

    Library Items 917

Summary 927

Chapter 36: Working with Video, Audio, and Animations 929

Inserting HTML5 Video 930

    Streaming and Embedded Video or Have The Video On Your Own Site? 930

    Setup and Testing 931

    The Track Tag 935

    Mobile and Video Scaling 936

    Can You Insert Video into a Background Using CSS? 936

Inserting HTML5 Audio 936

    Setup and Testing 936

    Can You Insert Audio into a Background Using CSS? 940

    Audio CSS Aural 940

Insert a Canvas Element 940

    Importing Animate Canvas into Dreamweaver 941

    Canvas Element Created Without Animate 942

Insert Animated Composition or OAM 944

Inserting Flash SWF and Flash Video 947

Insert Plug-in 948

Summary 948

Chapter 37: Additional Options to Apply Images in Dreamweaver 949

Target Attributes 949

Graphs and Charts 951

Web Fonts 952

CC Libraries Panel 958

Dreamweaver ➤ Extract PSD 958

Summary 960

Chapter 38: Final Testing, Getting Ready to Upload Your Site 961

Edit ➤ Preferences of Browsers 961

Validation Options and Uploading Site 963

    Site Reports Panel 964

    Link Checker Panel 964

    Validation Panel 965

    Output Panel 967

    Local and Remote Sites 967

    Manage Site 968

Check Advanced Settings 972

Uploading Site to Remote Server 972

Summary 976

Chapter 39: Putting It into Practice with Dreamweaver CC 977

Adding Images to Web Pages Review 977

Carousel Gallery (Bootstrap) 979

Video with Channel Changer 986

Summary 989

Part VII: Further Dreamweaver Integration with Other Adobe Products for Websites 991

Chapter 40: What Other Programs That Are Part of Adobe Creative Cloud Can I Use to Display My Graphics or Multimedia Online? 993

Additional Creative Cloud Software for Your Projects 993

What Additional Adobe Creative Cloud Software Can You Use to Display Graphics or Multimedia Online? 994

    Adobe InDesign CC 994

    Adobe Experience Design 994

    Adobe Portfolio 995

    Adobe Spark: Storytelling with Audio and Video 996

    Exporting to Phone GAP Build 997

Test Your Knowledge Quiz 997

Summary 1000

Index **1001**

About the Author

Jennifer Harder has worked in the graphic design industry for over ten years. She has a degree in graphic communications and is currently teaching Acrobat, InDesign, and Dreamweaver courses at Langara College. As a freelancer, Jennifer frequently works with Adobe PDFs and checks them before they go to print or are uploaded to the web. She enjoys talking about Adobe software and her interests include writing, illustration, and working on her websites.

About the Technical Reviewers

Logan West is the Assistant Director of Marketing and Communications at Fordham University. Logan joined Fordham after working with the University of Minnesota, Duluth, as their web manager and multimedia designer. During his time in higher education, Logan has focused on two university-wide redesigns, playing an active member as a designer and brand manager.

Logan holds two bachelor's degrees in graphic design and German studies from the University of Minnesota, Duluth, and is currently pursuing his master's degree in media management at Fordham University.

Breanna Craven is a visual problem solver and digital and web designer. She's worked remotely and in-house with industry-leading tech firms and consultant agencies on projects for web-related design, defining brands and the user experience. Design and layout are central in my career and what I do. I care deeply about creating useful and beautiful designs that help people and businesses make a difference. I enjoy being involved in the full process and touch on many aspects of web from sketching to design, and even front-end WordPress development. I am currently based in Duluth, Minnesota, after four years leading the design and creative direction at Faster Solutions Inc. Connect with her through LinkedIn.

Acknowledgements

For their patience and advice, I would like to thank the following people; without them, I could never have written this book. My parents for encouraging me to read large computer textbooks that would one day inspire me to write my own books. My dad for talking the time to shoot video footage with me at the Loafing Shed Glass Studio and Gallery in Surrey, British Columbia, Canada. Glass artist Robert Gary Parkes, owner of the Loafing Shed, and his apprentice, Jay, for their permission to shoot video and their time and demonstration of the beautiful art and history of glass blowing. My friend Osvaldo DeSouza; with his musical composition talents, he created the background music for my video. My program coordinator at Langara College, Raymond Chow, whose knowledge of video rendering and working in the movie industry helped me to compile the video and understand the importance of preplanning the script so I could tell a story. I am grateful for the time he took to proofread select chapters on video creation. My printing boss, Eddie, at Pender Copy Ltd. for his inspiration and encouraging me to write this book.

At Apress, I would like to thank Natalie and Jessica for showing me how to layout a professional textbook and pointing out even when you think you've written it all, there's still more to write. Also thanks to the technical reviewers Logan West and Breanna Craven for taking the time to review my chapters and their encouraging comments. And the rest of the Apress team—thank you for printing this book and making my dream a reality. I am truly grateful and blessed.

PART I

Welcome to the Adobe Creative Cloud. Where Should You Begin?

CHAPTER 1

Entering the Software Maze or Labyrinth

Where Should You Begin?

Adobe Creative Cloud is an amazing collection of software that allows you to render your thoughts in a digital or physical form. Whether the artist has been in the graphics industry for one year or fifty, and whether creating a layout for a book, designing a painting for a gallery, creating an animated video, editing sound, or creating a three-dimensional form—all of this is possible.

However, if you haven't upgraded your Adobe software skills for a while, or you are just starting to use the Creative Cloud, the various software choices can look intimidating. It's very much like entering a maze or labyrinth, as seen in Figure 1-1.

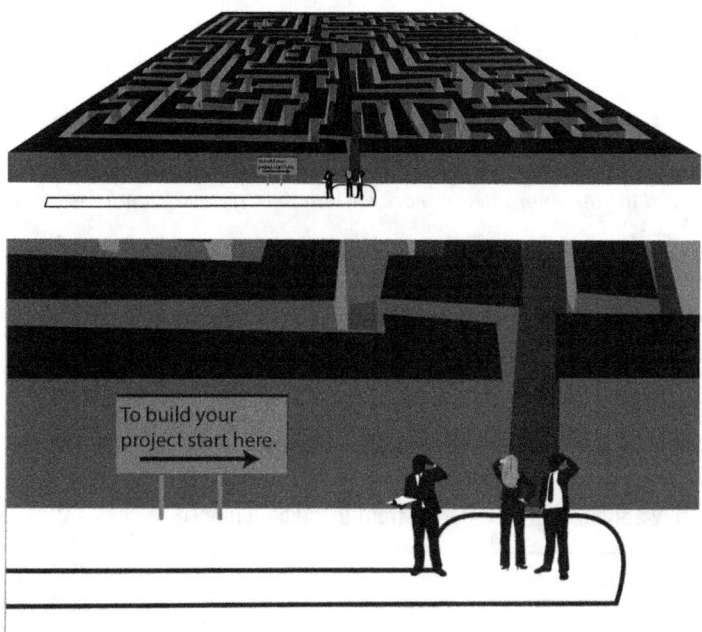

Figure 1-1. A representation of a maze or labyrinth that some designers in a company have encountered

In this book, you focus on how to work with graphics images, animations, video, and audio that will be added to a mobile-friendly website. As you progress through the book, your initial perception of what an animation is may change. Let's start by looking at some of the Creative Cloud console software apps, as seen in Figure 1-2.

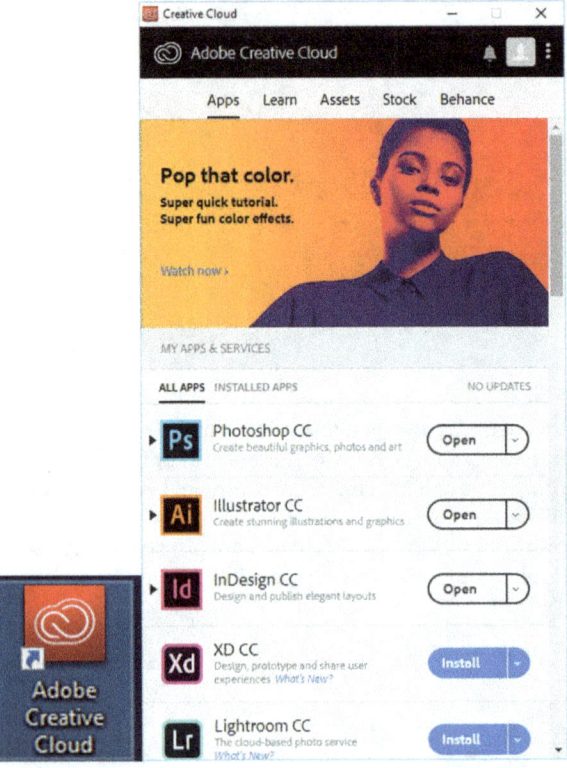

Figure 1-2. *A view of the Adobe Creative Cloud icon (left) and some of the software found in the Adobe Creative Cloud console that you can download to your computer or work with in the Creative Cloud*

Take the time to scroll through the list in the Apps tab and see all the software that is available. The amount of software can appear overwhelming to a first-time Adobe user.

■ **Note** While this chapter does not contain any assignments, it assumes that you have Adobe Creative Cloud installed on your computer, and that the icon is on your desktop or in the top menu bar. You can double-click the icon to open the application console and see the software available for download. The screenshots in this book are from a Windows 10 computer, so they may appear slightly different from those on a macOS.

CHAPTER 1 ■ ENTERING THE SOFTWARE MAZE OR LABYRINTH

How Will You Get to Your Destination?

I teach Adobe Dreamweaver at a college. You'll be looking at Dreamweaver in Part 6 of the book, which is where you add your multimedia to various web pages. I don't teach my students how to use Photoshop or basic HTML coding; so before they come to my Dreamweaver class, I expect that they have taken a few introductory courses on web coding and Photoshop. This is to ensure that when they start adding images to HTML5 web pages, they know which file formats are acceptable for a website. However, not everyone comes to my class with the same level of skills or knowledge about image formats. If they haven't learned the basics, they are overwhelmed by choices when new concepts, like video and animation, are presented. I think this same feeling applies when you look at how Adobe Creative Cloud uses its various software for website creation, as seen in Figure 1-3.

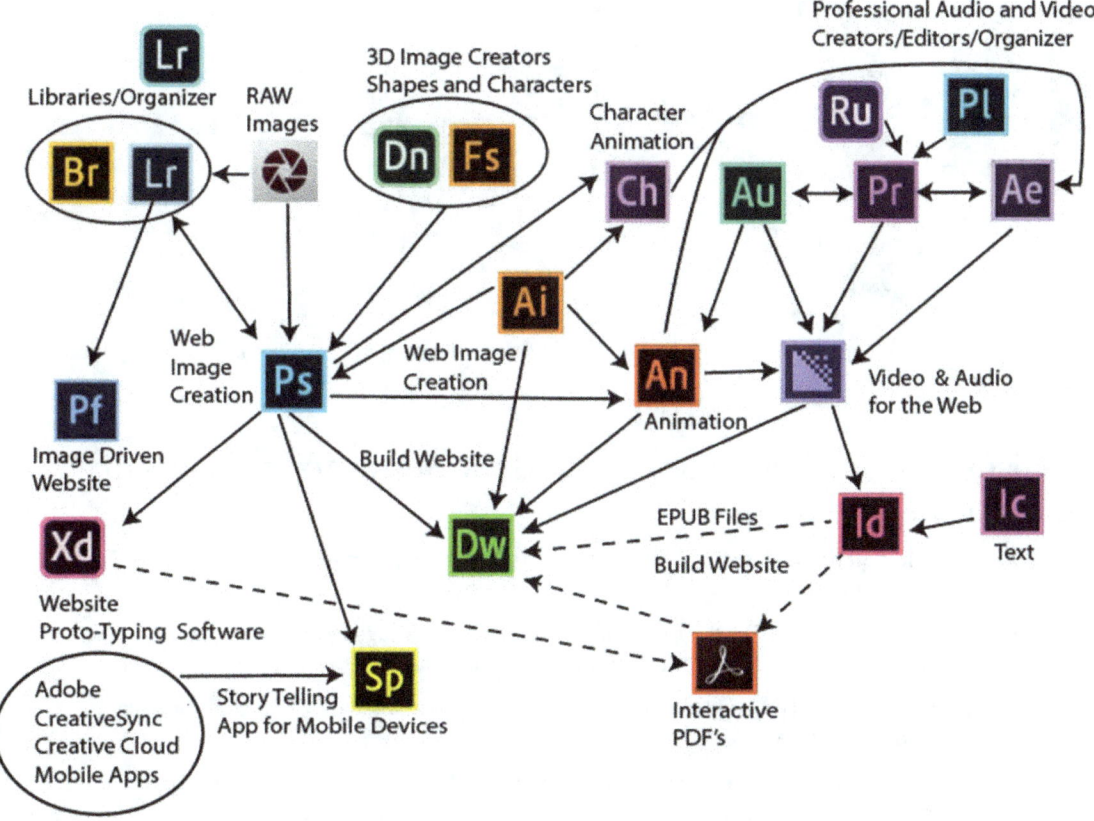

Figure 1-3. *A diagram describing how a company with many employees with a variety of skills might use all the Adobe Creative Cloud software to build a website*

5

A Visual Map of How the Creative Cloud Software Works

Let's look at the diagram in Figure 1-3. If these are the operations for creating a website in Adobe Creative Cloud CC 2019 software, you can see there is a lot going on. However, in smaller companies, or if you are a student, you may be more familiar with one program than another. I'll guess that even some veteran Adobe designers have never seen some of these software icons before. If some of the software is unfamiliar to you, take a moment to click the What's New link in your Creative Cloud console and read up on what the software is used for. Refer to Figure 1-3 to compare icons.

So, at this point, you might ask, "Do I need to learn all of this software to build a website?" No. To build a website that you can add multimedia to, let's narrow the selection to the five core programs that I discuss in this book (see Figure 1-4).

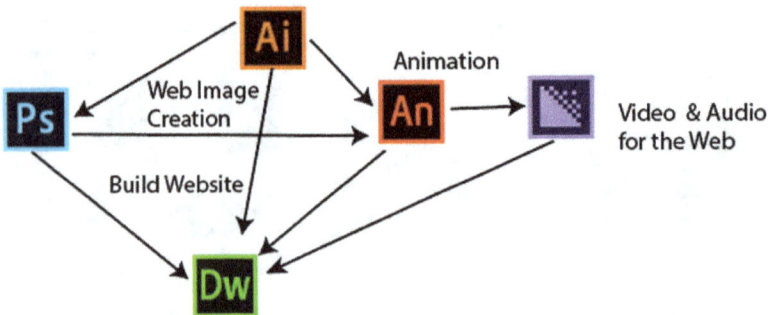

Figure 1-4. *A diagram of the five core programs: Photoshop CC, Illustrator CC, Animate CC, Media Encoder CC, and Dreamweaver CC*

Choosing the Smallest Number of Adobe Software Programs to Accomplish Your Goals

From a web design point of view, the following describes what these programs are used for (see Figures 1-3 and 1-4 for a review of the icons).

- **Photoshop CC (Ps):** Used for creating and editing still images from a camera, scanning or drawing from your imagination, creating simple animations and videos.
- **Illustrator CC (Ai):** Used for drawing images using vector (scalable) shapes for stills or animation frames.
- **Animate CC** and **Mobile Device Packaging (An)** (formerly known as Flash): Used for creation of HTML5 animation and movies with or without audio.
- **Media Encoder CC:** Used for formatting and basic movie creation to the correct web video or audio format. For more advanced editing of video clips, a program like Premiere Pro CC (Pr) or After Effects CC (Ae) is used before formatting in Media Encoder. For audio, use Audition CC (Au).

- **Dreamweaver CC (Dw)**: Used for creating a website with pages that include text, images, and other types of multimedia. (I will not focus on Muse CC(Mu) for this book, because while you can use it to initially build simple websites, once it is brought into Dreamweaver CC for a more complex task, you cannot return to Muse. If you attempt this, it may corrupt or render the files useless. Also Muse is no longer part of the Creative Cloud package.)

■ **Note** If you are skilled in any of the software shown in Figure 1-3, feel free to use it along with the projects discussed in later chapters. If you have used Project Felix (Fe), please note that it was rebranded as Dimension CC (Dn) for the 2018 version (see Figure 1-5).

Figure 1-5. *Project Felix (Fe) is now Dimensions (Dn)*

Each part of this book focuses on a core Adobe Creative Cloud software as it relates to graphics and multimedia.

- Part 2: Photoshop
- Part 3: Illustrator
- Part 4: Animate
- Part 5: Media Encoder
- Part 6: Dreamweaver
- Part 7: Looks briefly at software that you can use to further enhance your web design experience, such as InDesign's EPUB files and interactive PDFs. The versions of software I used were CC 2018 and 2019.

Once you narrow down the software that you will use, the maze looks less complicated (as shown in Figure 1-6).

CHAPTER 1 ■ ENTERING THE SOFTWARE MAZE OR LABYRINTH

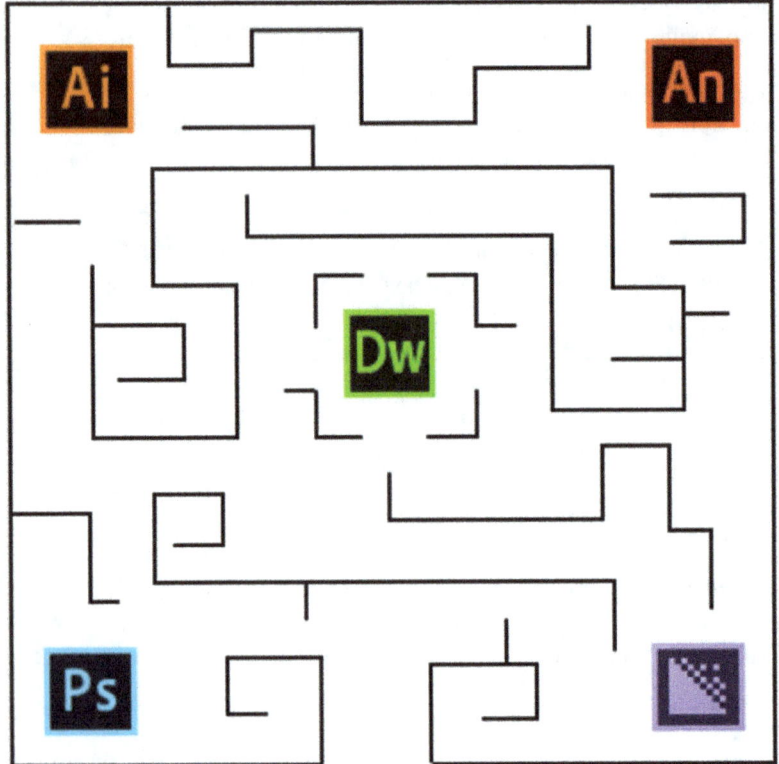

Figure 1-6. *A simplified maze with a less complicated layout*

You can see your destination or goal in the center of the maze: Dreamweaver. However, the path still takes several twists and turns. Why?

The twists and turns represent choices that you must make when deciding which web format to choose for your final multimedia files in Dreamweaver. Poor format choices mean wrong turns and usually cause you to retrace your steps. Good choices lead you to getting your project done on time. At the start of each of the book parts—on Photoshop, Illustrator, Animate, and Media Encoder, you see a graphic representing the software, or in the maze, a junction point (see Figure 1-7).

CHAPTER 1 ■ ENTERING THE SOFTWARE MAZE OR LABYRINTH

Figure 1-7. *Workers in a company trying to decide what file format choices to use while in the "software maze"*

You can choose any of the following file formats or paths that this software offers. However, if you don't understand why you are using a format, you may be making a poor or uninformed choice.

Basic Web File Formats for Images and Multimedia

Let's take a moment to briefly look at some of the main file formats that you might encounter. You will look at them in more detail in each chapter.

- **Bitmap (.bmp)**: A bitmap file can be used for web or print. You often see this format when you scan a file with a copier or scanner. However, due to its large file size, it is not generally used on the Internet.

- **JPEG, or Joint Photographic Experts Group (.jpg)**: Supports 24-bit color. A file format with a compression algorithm that reduces the file sizes of bit-mapped images using a "lossy" compression method. The quality of a JPEG degrades with each successive save of a "copy." Logos that contain type can appear grainy. Since it can support a wide range of colors, this file type is ideal as pictures on the web or those sent as email attachments. They do not support transparency, but you can add a matte color to the file if you have a solid background of a similar color on your site.

9

- **PNG, or Portable Network Graphics (.png)**: A bit-mapped image format that employs lossless data compression. It is sometimes used instead of GIF files. It can support a wider range of colors like a JPEG. However, unlike a JPEG, it can also support transparency, and its compression for the web is sometimes cleaner than a JPEG. It cannot be used for animation unless combined with additional CSS or JavaScript coding in an HTML file. PNG has lately been found more often on the web than in the past. It comes in two types: 8-bit (supports full transparency or full opaque) and 24-bit (multilevel transparency or semi-transparency). If you are not sure if your browser will support PNG, choose the GIF file format.

- **GIF, or Graphic Interchange Format (static and animated) (.gif)**: A bit-mapped file format that is found on the web. It displays a maximum of 256 colors (Index mode), which is ideal for websites and solid-colored logos and can have transparency or a solid color added. However, unlike JPEG and PNG files it is not ideal for reproducing photos or some gradients which may appear grainy. It can also be used to create simple animations for banners or backgrounds.

- **SVG, or Scalable Vector Graphics (.svg)**: This is based on the XML coding vector image format for two-dimensional graphics, with support for interactivity and animation. It is also used to create new color-based web fonts, as you will see in later chapters. Vector images can be scaled to any size and keep their basic form without losing quality, whereas JPEGs, GIFs, and PNGs appear pixilated when scaled up.

- **Canvas**: While this is not an actual file format, it can be combined within an HTML5 file as a <canvas> tag or element to create a still image or animation. It can appear slightly bitmapped if scaled incorrectly.

- **PDF, or Portable Document Format (.pdf)**: Developed by Adobe Systems and read by Adobe Acrobat Reader. This file has become the standard used by most print houses and websites. It's able to have text, color, vector and bitmap images, and contain multiple pages. It can be viewed independently from the original layout program (e.g., Microsoft Word and InDesign). Its file size is relatively low. If you have Adobe Acrobat Distiller, you can convert most files to a PDF. Visually, you cannot see the file unless you download it so that it can be viewed in your browser or in Acrobat Reader.

- **Video files (.mp4, .webm, .ogg/.ogv)**: There are three video files that are recognized for use on the Internet; however, MP4 is recognized by most current browsers.

- **Audio files (.mp3, .wav, .ogg)**: There are three audio files that are for use on the Internet; however, MP3 and WAV are recognized by most current browsers.

- **Interactive PDF (.pdf) and EPUB (.epub)**: While the PDF is typically a static document, you can use a program like Adobe InDesign or Adobe Acrobat to make it interactive, such as a slideshow or a form. EPUBs can be created using Adobe InDesign; however, you need a specific reader on your computer or smartphone to view the file. EPUBs cannot be viewed in Adobe Acrobat Reader or previewed without a specific extension in the browser. An EPUB format is a package or mini website in the way that a ZIP file contains a collection of compressed files. I briefly discuss these types of files in Part 7 of the book; they are not created with the five Adobe programs that you use in this book.

In addition to file types that you can export, you will look at various color spaces in each chapter. When working on the web, it is important that you use images that are in RGB (red, green, blue) mode or Index mode, but not CMYK (cyan magenta, yellow, black) mode for our web project. For example, a JPEG image can be saved as RGB or CMYK; however, if the JPEG is not converted and saved as RGB, its colors may not appear correctly when viewed in a browser, and its file size may be larger than expected. Each Adobe software program looks at how to convert a file to the correct color spaces.

Summary

In this chapter, you looked briefly at the several types of graphic software for developing a website available in the Creative Cloud suite. At first glance, the choices appear overwhelming—until you narrow it down to five core software choices: Photoshop, Illustrator, Animate, Media Encoder, and Dreamweaver. Once you choose a program, however, you need to choose which type of file format to export your multimedia to the web.

In Chapter 2, the first stop in the software labyrinth is Adobe Photoshop CC, where you discover how to create graphics and video for a website.

PART II

Working with Photoshop to Create Web Graphics and Animations

CHAPTER 2

Getting Started

In Part 2, you are going to start with a review of some Adobe Photoshop CC basics. Along the way, you are going to look at the variety of menu options within the program that you can use to export images and GIF animations, and render video for your website. In this chapter, you will set up your workspace.

Note This chapter does not have any actual projects; however, you can use the files in the Chapter 2 folder to practice opening and viewing for this lesson. They are at `https://github.com/Apress/graphics-multimedia-web-adobe-creative-cloud`.

Symbolically, entering the maze is like starting a project. If you're planning on having a website rich with images, likely your first destination will be Photoshop CC (see Figure 2-1).

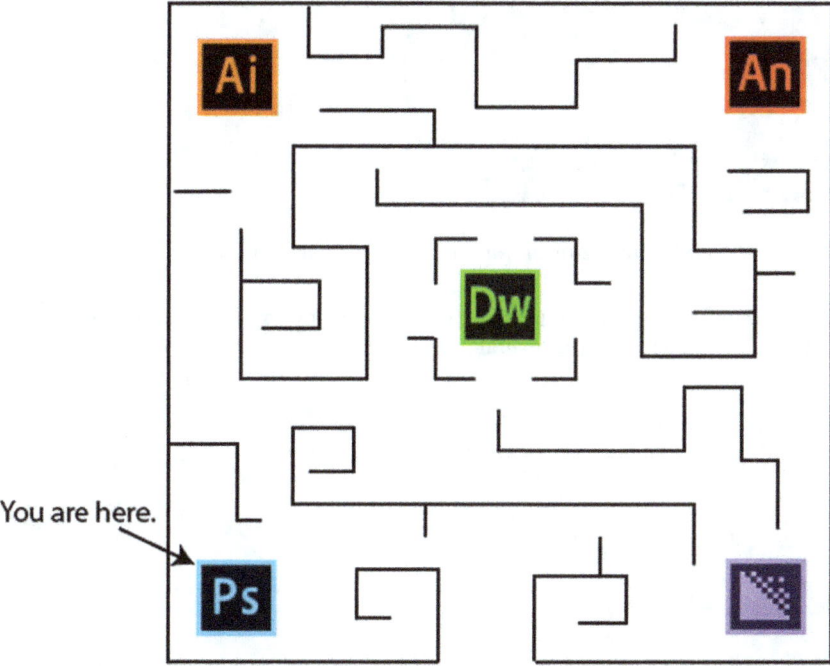

Figure 2-1. *This is a representation of where you currently are in the software maze*

CHAPTER 2 ■ GETTING STARTED

If you have never used Photoshop before on a project, or you are a beginner, I recommend reading a book like *Photoshop CC Classroom in a Book* by Andrew Faulkner (Adobe Press, 2018) where you get a basic overview of the program and many of its tools. You can also check out Photoshop's Learn panel, which has step-by-step tutorials on various projects, as shown in Figure 2-2.

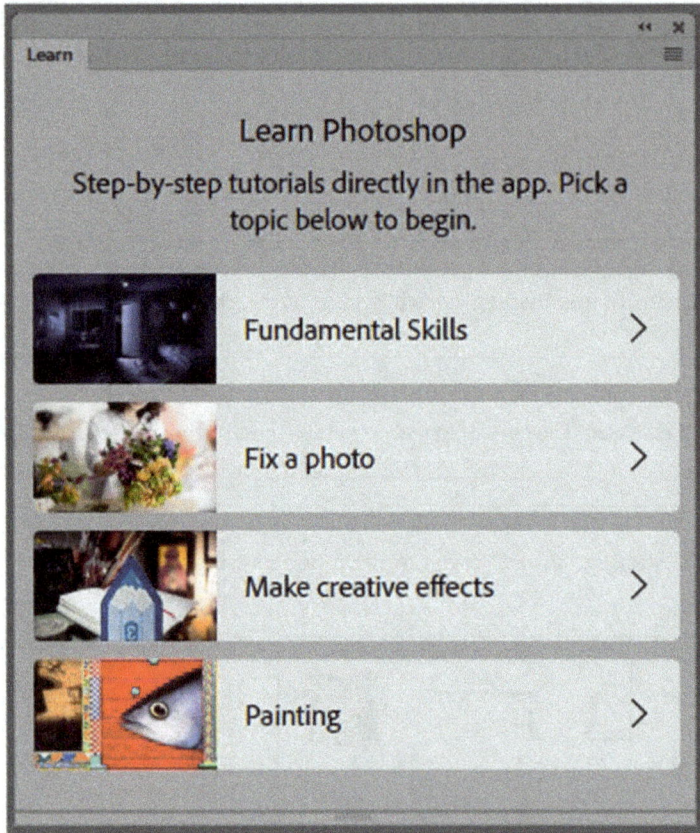

Figure 2-2. *The learn panel has easy step-by-step tutorials for the beginner Photoshop user*

In this book, you will work with some graphics that are already created, and then save them to the web. As you can see in Figure 2-3, we will be looking at several image formatting choices.

16

Figure 2-3. *Here you see a junction or point of decision within Photoshop. What is the correct type of file format to use for a specific project?*

Working with Your RAW and Layered Files

Let's begin by opening Photoshop CC. I am working with the CC 2019 version. If you do not have Photoshop on your computer, but you do have the Creative Cloud application, click the Install button beside the Photoshop icon (see Figure 2-4), and follow the instructions on how to install the program.

CHAPTER 2 ■ GETTING STARTED

Figure 2-4. The Install button that is found beside the Creative Cloud software on the Creative Cloud console

■ **Note** Before you install any Adobe program, make sure that your computer meets the system requirements; otherwise, the install may fail. For more information on Photoshop requirements check https://helpx.adobe.com/photoshop/system-requirements.html.

If you already have Photoshop CC installed on your computer, double-click on the icon. Or, in the Creative Cloud application, click Open to launch the program, as shown in Figure 2-5.

Figure 2-5. You can open Photoshop CC from the Creative Cloud application by clicking the Open button

Once Photoshop opens, set up your workspace so that yours is the same as mine.
I chose Graphic and Web in the Workspace icon (in the upper right), as seen in Figure 2-6.

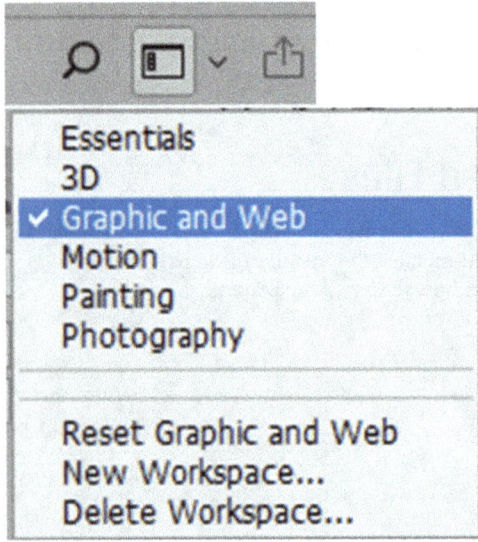

Figure 2-6. Choose the Graphic and Web workspace from the Workspace drop-down menu

18

CHAPTER 2 ■ GETTING STARTED

If you have already used the Graphic and Web workspace, you can choose Reset Graphic and Web from the menu to return the workspace to its default settings.

Or, if you prefer, you could work with the Essentials workspace since it offers the full range of tools in the Tools panel, as seen in Figure 2-7.

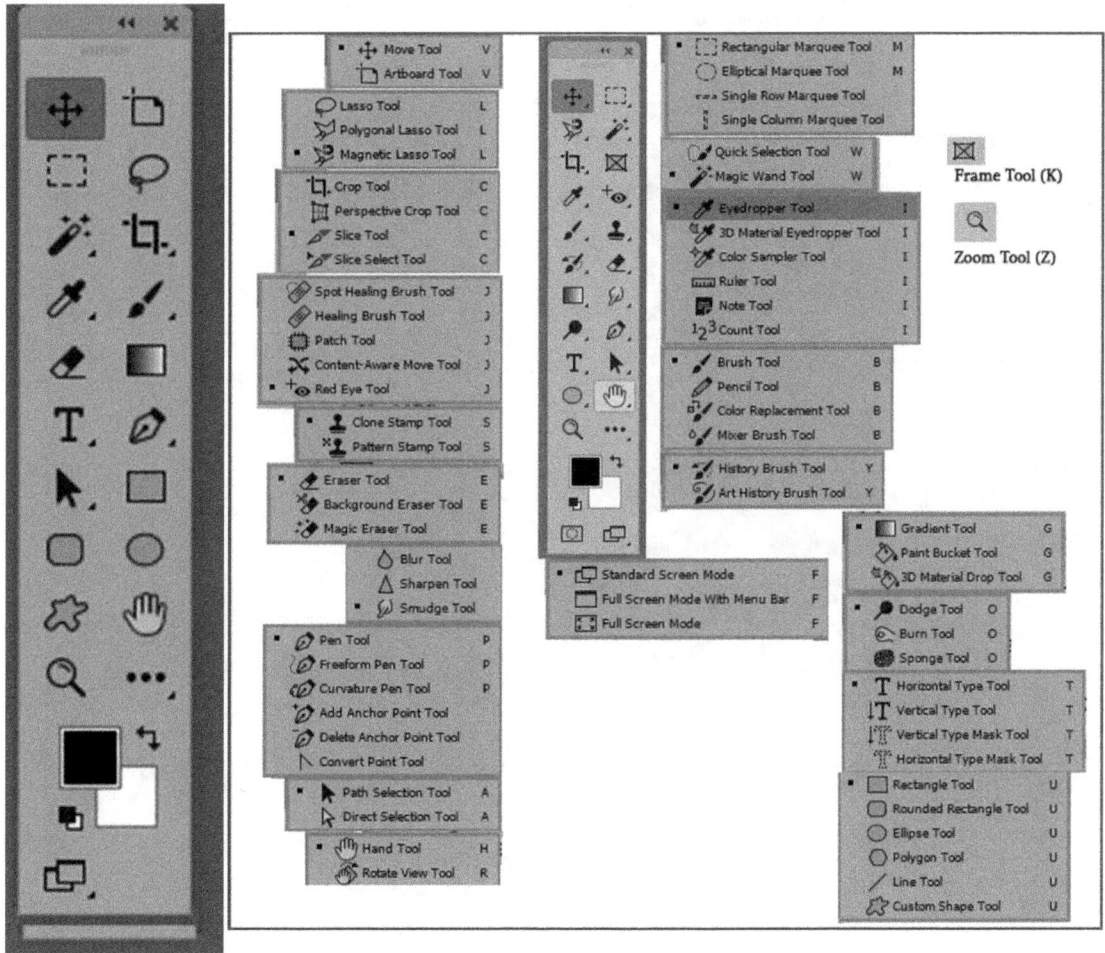

Figure 2-7. *Comparison of the Tools panel in in the Graphic and Web workspace vs. the Essentials workspace, which has more tool options available.*

■ **Note** If you notice that your toolbar does not have all the tools you require, you can click the Edit Toolbar icon. This will allow you to add more or all tools back onto the tool panel, as seen in Figure 2-8 and Figure 2-9.

19

CHAPTER 2 ■ GETTING STARTED

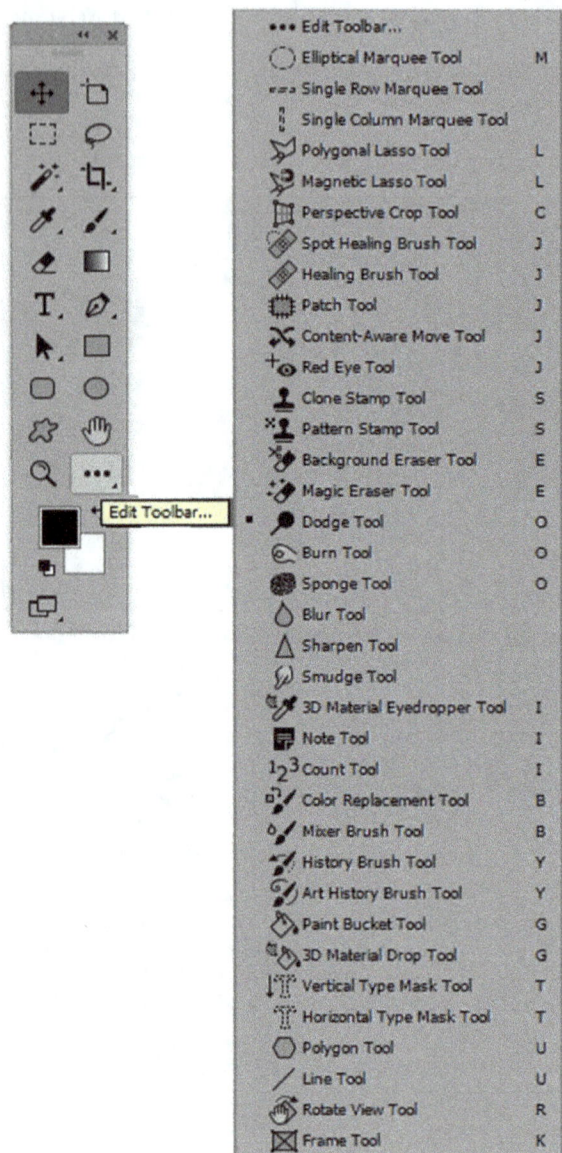

Figure 2-8. *By clicking the Edit Toolbar icon, you can add tools to customize your tool selection*

Clicking the Edit Toolbar icon opens the Customize Toolbar dialog box so that you can drag tools from Extra Tools on the right to the left into the toolbar; as you do so, the toolbar updates. You can also group tools together by hovering an extra tool over a current tool in the toolbar when a blue line appears under the other tool, as seen in Figure 2-9.

CHAPTER 2 ■ GETTING STARTED

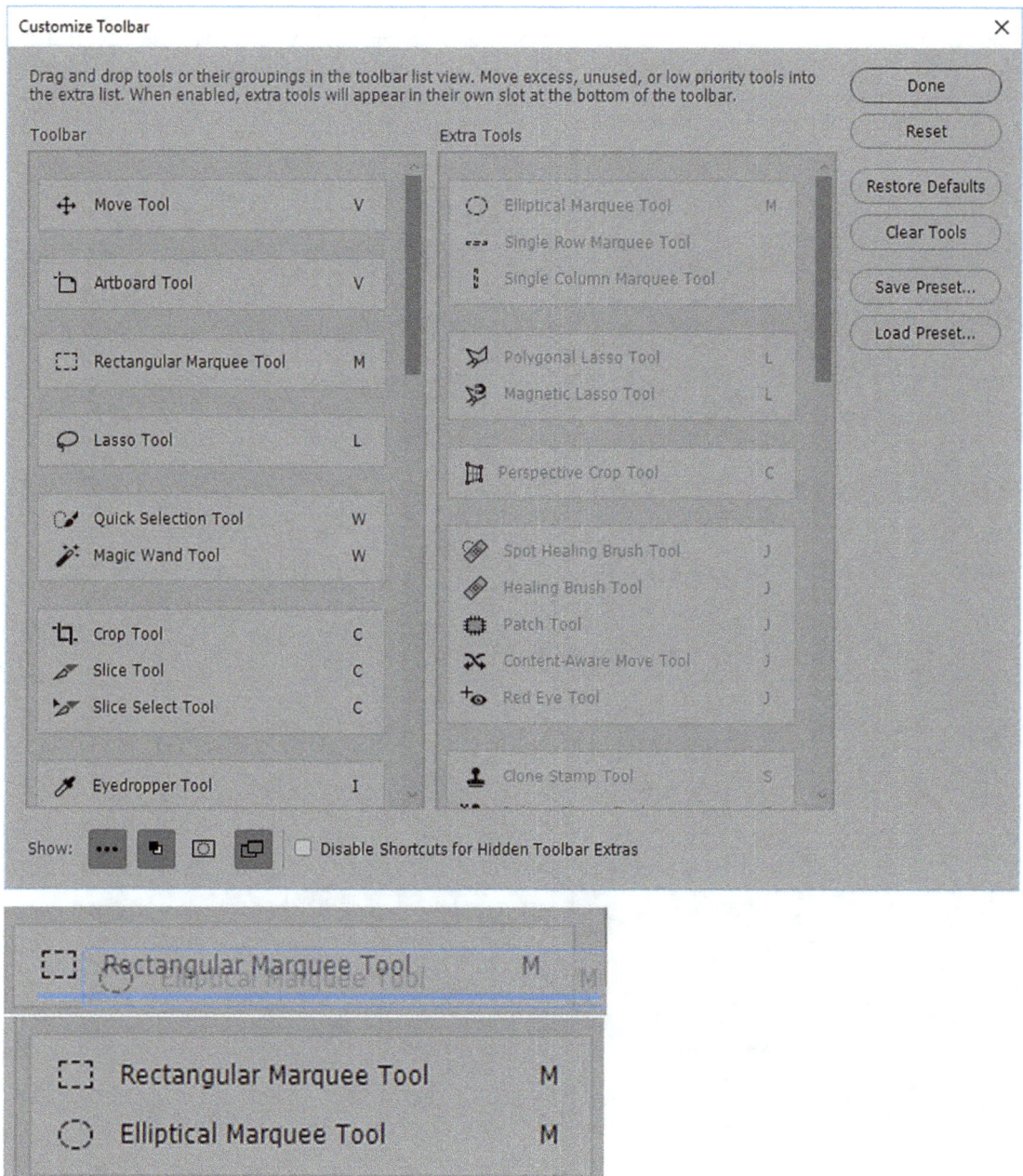

Figure 2-9. *The Customize Toolbar dialog box allows you to add or remove tools from your tools panel and preview it at the same time*

21

CHAPTER 2 ■ GETTING STARTED

You can also remove tools by dragging them back to the Extra Tools side. Or you can choose restore defaults to add all tools, or clear tools to remove all tools. Likewise, you can load presets that others created or save your own presets. When you have added the tools you require, click Done, or Cancel to exit without making any changes.

Your layout should now look something like Figure 2-10.

Figure 2-10. *The Graphics and Web workspace layout*

If you prefer another workspace for your web design, you can always choose a different one or create your own custom workspace (New Workspace) as seen in Figure 2-6.

22

CHAPTER 2 ■ GETTING STARTED

Creating a New File

If you want to create a new file, choose File ➤ New, as seen in Figure 2-11.

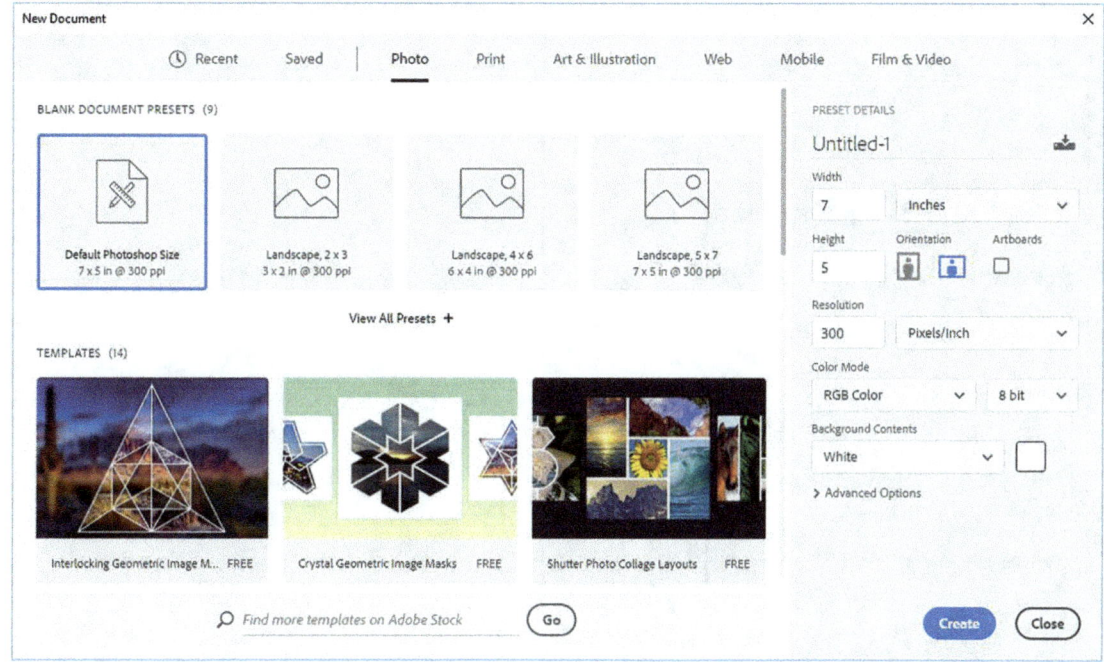

Figure 2-11. *The New Document dialog box with the Photo tab options selected*

Photoshop CC has organized many of its standard layouts as tabs so that you can easily choose a layout for your project, whether for photos, print, web, mobile or film and video. You can create your own custom sizes. You can use an artboard, where you have two or more layered layouts display (see the Layers panel when a file is open) within one .psd file. However, when you begin creating a file that you are planning to use for the web, make sure that the color mode is set to RGB Color, as seen in Figure 2-12. You'll learn more about color in Chapter 3.

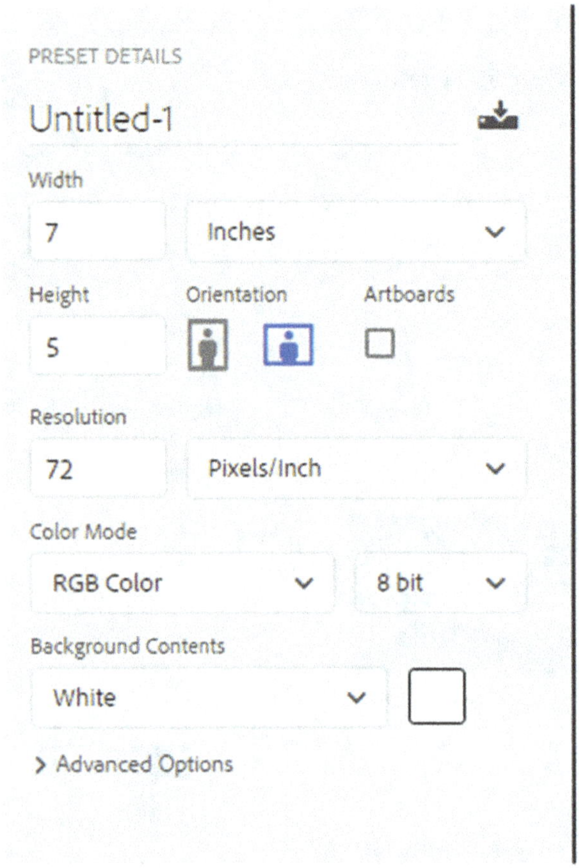

CHAPTER 2 ■ GETTING STARTED

Figure 2-12. The New Document dialog box preset details with the color mode set to RGB 8-bit color

■ **Note** If you are not sure of the exact dimensions the images that you are planning to create for the web, you can always keep your file at 300 pixels/inch so that your original graphic has the highest resolution. You can always scale down to a low-res copy later when you export your image. It is more difficult to scale a file back up to high-res due to loss of image quality. However, if you know the exact size, set the resolution to 72 pixels/inch, which is generally the accepted resolution for most images on the web.

When you have the correct settings, click the Create button on the bottom right of the New Documents dialog box, as seen in Figure 2-13. Your new file will open.

CHAPTER 2 ■ GETTING STARTED

Figure 2-13. *Click the Create button so that Photoshop can create your new file with your preferred settings. The Close button will close the dialog box and no new file will open.*

At this point, you begin to add Layers via the Layers panel, as seen in Figure 2-14, and design your artwork using one or more of the tools in the Tools panel.

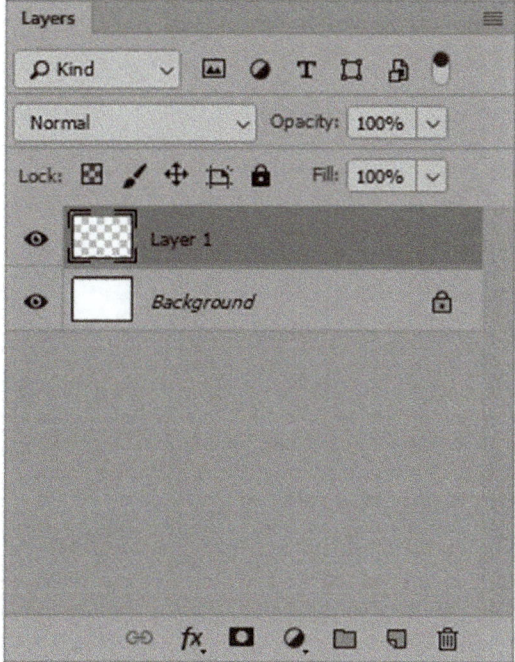

Figure 2-14. *A background default layer and now a new layer has been added to the newly created Photoshop file by clicking the New Layer icon on the bottom right near the Trash icon*

While you can always create your files directly in Photoshop CC, you may have collected or acquired your original images in other file formats. Here I have listed some of the ones you will likely encounter. In the main menu, go to File ➤ Open.

- **Bitmap (.bmp)**: This file is often created when you scan a file with your office scanner. It is common in Windows-compatible computers. While it can be used on the web, the file size is often quite large, so it's better to save a copy in a file format suited for the web.

- **TIFF (.tif,.tiff)**: Often, graphic artists will save a final single layered piece of artwork as a TIFF file. These files are considered images that do not lose quality (lossless) as copies are saved from them. They retain their original size; no compression of data occurs.

25

- **Photoshop PSD (.psd, .pdd, .pstd)**: While creating your graphics, you may save your files with multiple layers. Photoshop PSD files allow you to retain these layers, effects, and masks. After you save and close the file, you can always come back another day and continue to edit it until you are ready to export a flattened copy to the web.
- **Large document format (.psb)**: Sometimes the file size of a layered file can become very large such as over 2GB. Layered files over this size are often saved as a .psb known as a Photoshop Big to preserve the file quality.
- **Camera RAW or digital negative (.dng)**: A camera raw image file is in a camera-specific proprietary format that is essentially a "digital negative," with no filtering, white balance adjustments, or other in-camera processing. You need the Camera Raw program plugin to install with Photoshop CC to view these files. Refer to Figure 2-15.

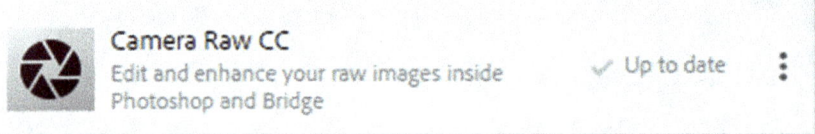

Figure 2-15. *This is how the Camera Raw CC program should appear in your Creative Cloud console so that you know it is operating correctly*

This is not to be confused with a Photoshop RAW (.raw) file for transferring images between applications and computer platforms. While they can be a larger file size, they only contain one layer.

- **JPEG files from a camera (.jpg, .jpeg, .jpe)**: Some cameras only create JPEGs. Since it comes directly from the camera, it is the original and has not lost quality yet. If it is altered or subsequent JPEG images are saved from it, they will be of lower quality.

While these are all good file formats for your original files (except for the bitmap and JPEG files), you cannot display the other formats in most browsers.

Note that Photoshop can open many other file formats, including video (see Figure 2-16).

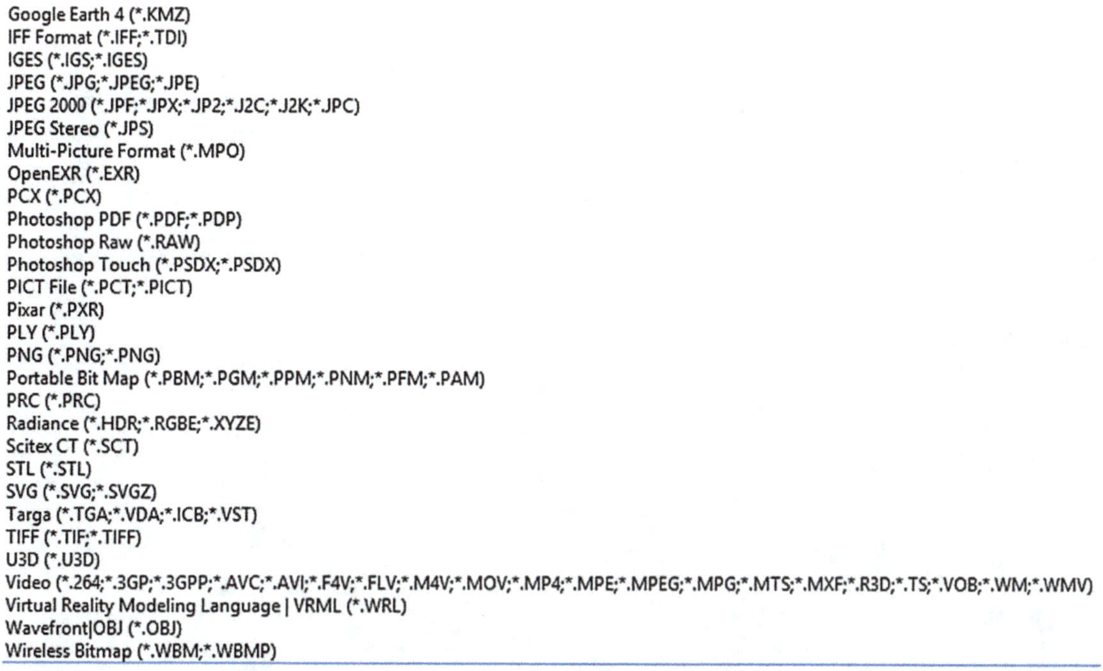

CHAPTER 2 ■ GETTING STARTED

```
Google Earth 4 (*.KMZ)
IFF Format (*.IFF;*.TDI)
IGES (*.IGS;*.IGES)
JPEG (*.JPG;*.JPEG;*.JPE)
JPEG 2000 (*.JPF;*.JPX;*.JP2;*.J2C;*.J2K;*.JPC)
JPEG Stereo (*.JPS)
Multi-Picture Format (*.MPO)
OpenEXR (*.EXR)
PCX (*.PCX)
Photoshop PDF (*.PDF;*.PDP)
Photoshop Raw (*.RAW)
Photoshop Touch (*.PSDX;*.PSDX)
PICT File (*.PCT;*.PICT)
Pixar (*.PXR)
PLY (*.PLY)
PNG (*.PNG;*.PNG)
Portable Bit Map (*.PBM;*.PGM;*.PPM;*.PNM;*.PFM;*.PAM)
PRC (*.PRC)
Radiance (*.HDR;*.RGBE;*.XYZE)
Scitex CT (*.SCT)
STL (*.STL)
SVG (*.SVG;*.SVGZ)
Targa (*.TGA;*.VDA;*.ICB;*.VST)
TIFF (*.TIF;*.TIFF)
U3D (*.U3D)
Video (*.264;*.3GP;*.3GPP;*.AVC;*.AVI;*.F4V;*.FLV;*.M4V;*.MOV;*.MP4;*.MPE;*.MPEG;*.MPG;*.MTS;*.MXF;*.R3D;*.TS;*.VOB;*.WM;*.WMV)
Virtual Reality Modeling Language | VRML (*.WRL)
Wavefront|OBJ (*.OBJ)
Wireless Bitmap (*.WBM;*.WBMP)
```

Figure 2-16. *File format options found when choosing File ➤ Open*

Or if you choose File ➤ Open As, you will see the Camera Raw option for opening the files shown in Figure 2-17.

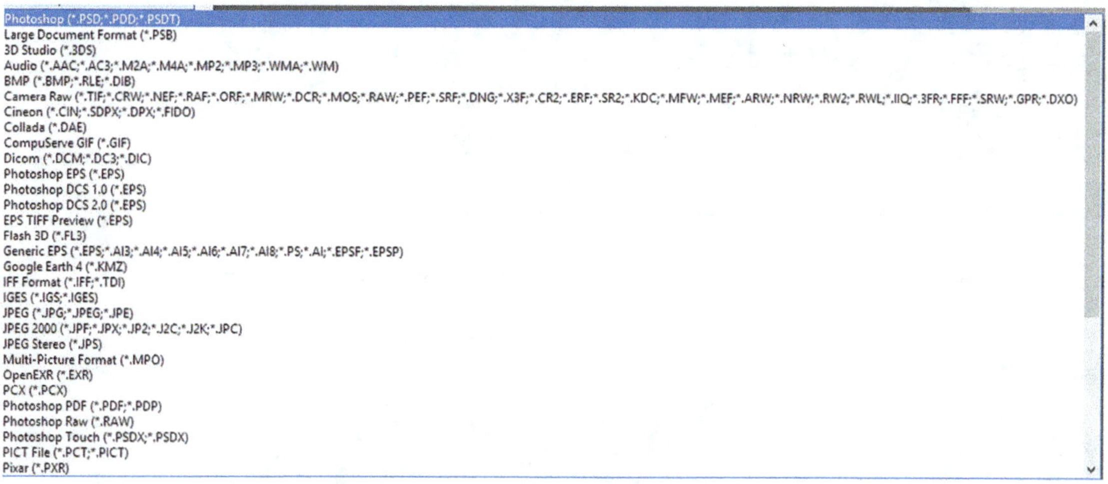

```
Photoshop (*.PSD;*.PDD;*.PSDT)
Large Document Format (*.PSB)
3D Studio (*.3DS)
Audio (*.AAC;*.AC3;*.M2A;*.M4A;*.MP2;*.MP3;*.WMA;*.WM)
BMP (*.BMP;*.RLE;*.DIB)
Camera Raw (*.TIF;*.CRW;*.NEF;*.RAF;*.ORF;*.MRW;*.DCR;*.MOS;*.RAW;*.PEF;*.SRF;*.DNG;*.X3F;*.CR2;*.ERF;*.SR2;*.KDC;*.MFW;*.MEF;*.ARW;*.NRW;*.RW2;*.RWL;*.IIQ;*.3FR;*.FFF;*.SRW;*.GPR;*.DXO)
Cineon (*.CIN;*.SDPX;*.DPX;*.FIDO)
Collada (*.DAE)
CompuServe GIF (*.GIF)
Dicom (*.DCM;*.DC3;*.DIC)
Photoshop EPS (*.EPS)
Photoshop DCS 1.0 (*.EPS)
Photoshop DCS 2.0 (*.EPS)
EPS TIFF Preview (*.EPS)
Flash 3D (*.FL3)
Generic EPS (*.EPS;*.AI3;*.AI4;*.AI5;*.AI6;*.AI7;*.AI8;*.PS;*.AI;*.EPSF;*.EPSP)
Google Earth 4 (*.KMZ)
IFF Format (*.IFF;*.TDI)
IGES (*.IGS;*.IGES)
JPEG (*.JPG;*.JPEG;*.JPE)
JPEG 2000 (*.JPF;*.JPX;*.JP2;*.J2C;*.J2K;*.JPC)
JPEG Stereo (*.JPS)
Multi-Picture Format (*.MPO)
OpenEXR (*.EXR)
PCX (*.PCX)
Photoshop PDF (*.PDF;*.PDP)
Photoshop Raw (*.RAW)
Photoshop Touch (*.PSDX;*.PSDX)
PICT File (*.PCT;*.PICT)
Pixar (*.PXR)
```

Figure 2-17. *File format options found when choosing File ➤ Open As*

For more information on other formats, visit https://helpx.adobe.com/photoshop/using/file-formats.html.

CHAPTER 2 ■ GETTING STARTED

Image Files from Other Adobe Programs

Your image files might originally come from Adobe programs like Illustrator CC (.ai and .eps files), Lightroom CC (Camera Raw), Dimension CC to create 3D shapes (.png or .psd), Fuse CC to create 3D characters as (.obj and .png) files, and Adobe Acrobat PDFs. All of these files can be opened and saved as pixeled raster images within Photoshop.

For example, in Illustrator CC, you can File ➤ Open and save a copy as a pixilated image or as a smart object that can be in a layer and later scaled. You can choose File ➤ Open As Smart Object. Find an Illustrator (.ai) file in your open dialog box and click Open to see the dialog box, as seen in Figure 2-18.

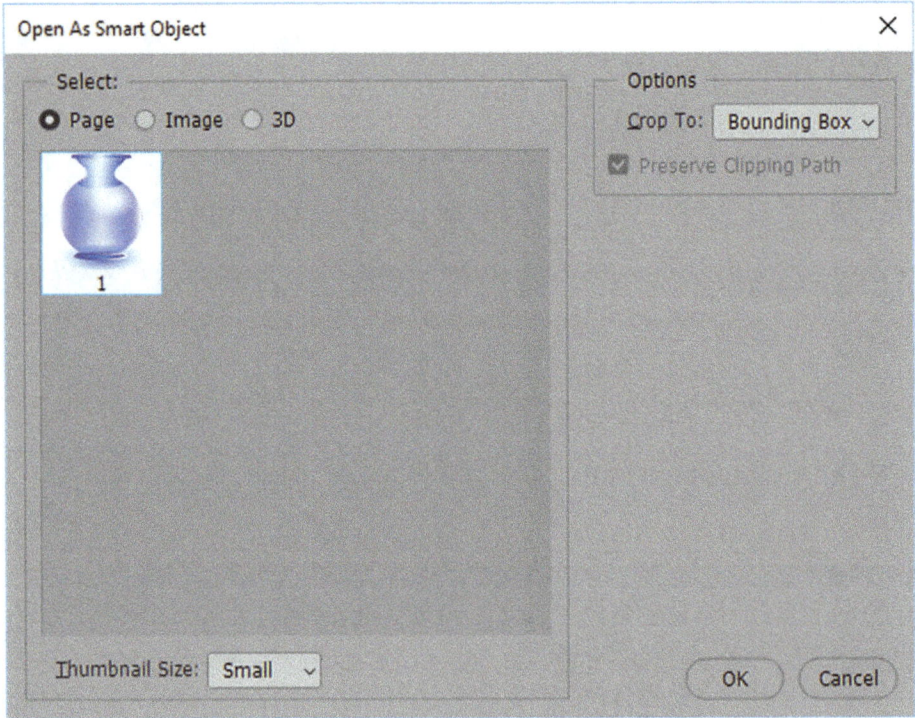

Figure 2-18. File formatting options found when choosing File ➤ Open As Smart Object

Click OK and then choose Duplicate Image to create a copy, as seen in Figure 2-19.

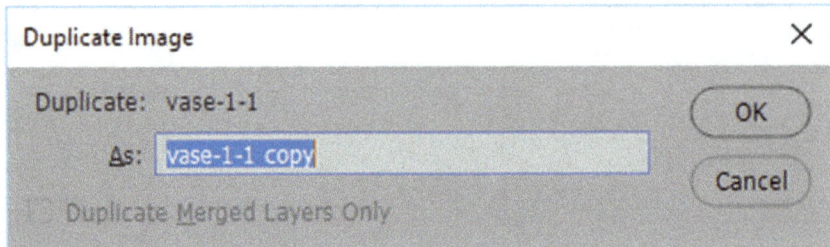

Figure 2-19. Create a duplicate copy of the Smart Object from the Illustrator file

28

Then save the new file as a PSD, or select the smart object layer and then drag it into your new file. Be careful not to edit the original smart object by double-clicking on the layer, which will open the smart object layer in a new window or in the Illustrator CC. Refer to Figure 2-20.

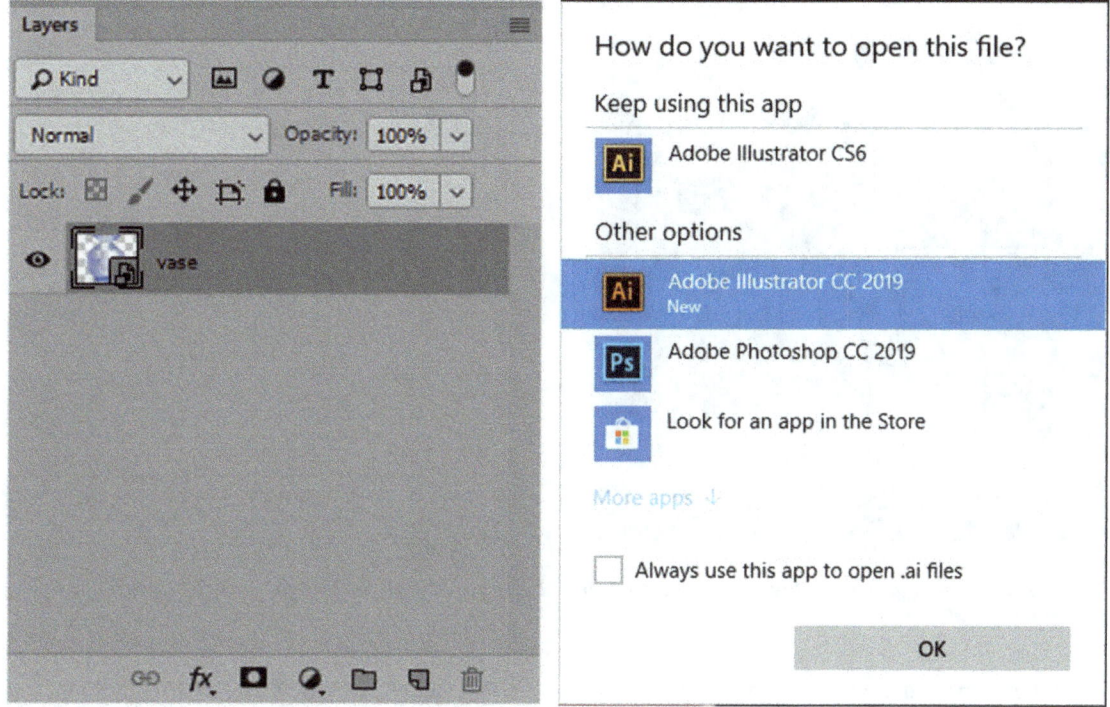

Figure 2-20. *The Smart Object is displayed in the Layers panel. If you by mistake, double-clicking the Illustrator layer may give the following warning*

If you get a warning message from Illustrator CC, just click Cancel to prevent the file from opening, and return to Photoshop CC.

In Photoshop, you can make further outward adjustments to the Smart Object by using masks, layers, effects, blending modes, or tools to alter color and shape. You can also Edit ➤ Transform to resize the image without it losing quality because it is a Smart Object. As seen in Figure 2-21.

CHAPTER 2 ■ GETTING STARTED

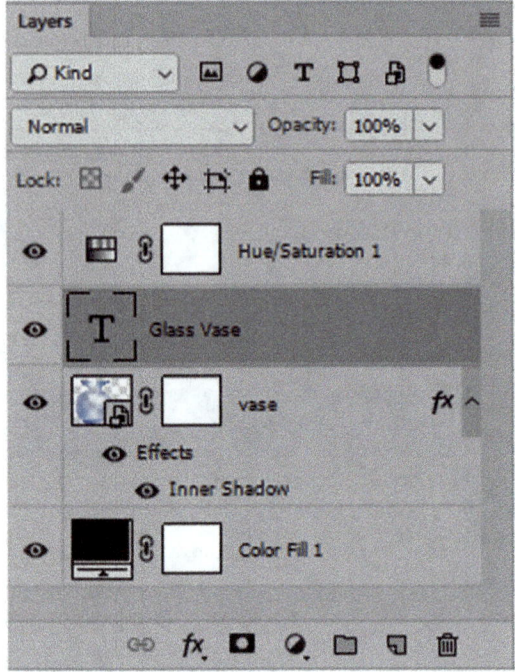

Figure 2-21. *The smart object layer is displayed in the Layers panel with additional masks, outward effects, and layers applied*

When you are done, you can save any open file by selecting File ➤ Save, and then File ➤ Exit exit to Photoshop CC or keep Photoshop open for the next chapter.

Summary

In this chapter, you looked at how to set up a workspace in Photoshop. You also looked at some of the different image file formats that you can open within the Photoshop program. You can either create your own files with Photoshop or work with images that come from another source, such as another Adobe program like Illustrator, or from a camera, scanner, or another client. In the next chapter, we explore the correct color choices for your web design projects.

CHAPTER 3

Color Choices: CMYK, RGB, Grayscale, and Index

In this chapter, you explore some of the color options that are available and that are appropriate to use for your web projects.

> **Note** This chapter does not have any actual projects; however, you can use the files in the Chapter 3 folder if you do not have any file examples of your own to practice opening and viewing for this lesson. They are at https://github.com/Apress/graphics-multimedia-web-adobe-creative-cloud.

When you are working with files, you want to make sure that the file that will be part of the website is in the correct color mode. If you are starting with a new piece of artwork, you need to consider what is required to achieve optimum quality. When you create a new file in Photoshop (File ➤ New), you want to make sure that your starting file is saved as RGB, which is the color channel of the monitor on which you will view the website while building it. Refer to Figure 3-1.

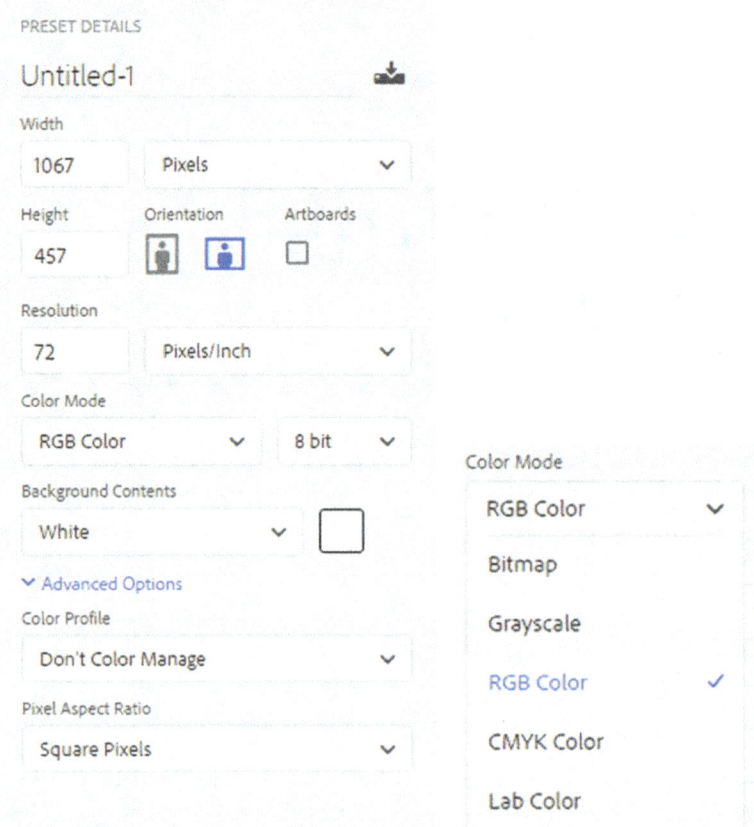

Figure 3-1. *Choosing the correct RGB color mode in the File ➤ New dialog box*

The following are other available color mode options:

- **Bitmap**: A low-res one-color file, often black and white, that can be used for simple line drawing. This is not the same as a (.bmp) file, which can have many colors.

- **Grayscale**: An image that has many shades of gray; good for black and white photography, you can have this color format on the web, but there are more options in Photoshop if you save as RGB.

- **CMYK**: This is best for print work. After you create an RGB image, you can always change a copy of the file to CMYK if you need to create promotional material. However, be aware that CMYK does not allow many filter options from the main menu, as seen in Figure 3-9.

- **Lab**: This is the widest range of color, and some of the larger file formats you receive from clients may be set to this mode. To keep your files small and manageable, you can always create a copy and set it to RGB. Lab is useful for print materials.

You also want to set the bit depth. The greater amount of the bits the bigger the file size. Unless you are working on something that requires high resolutions like a project that will also be printed or for gaming keep the bit amount small. For the web, I generally leave my bit size at 8-bit, as seen in Figure 3-2.

CHAPTER 3 ■ COLOR CHOICES: CMYK, RGB, GRAYSCALE, AND INDEX

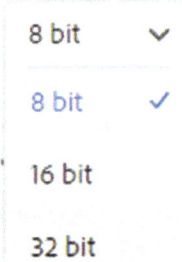

Figure 3-2. *Choose a bit-depth of 8 bit, 16 bit, or 32 bit*

In the lower-right side of the New Document dialog box, you will notice a tab called Advanced Options. If you are not sure how the color profile of your image will be used, leave it at the Don't Color Manage setting; otherwise, you can use Working RGB: sRGB IEC61966-2.1, which is the profile of some digital camera images, as seen in Figure 3-3.

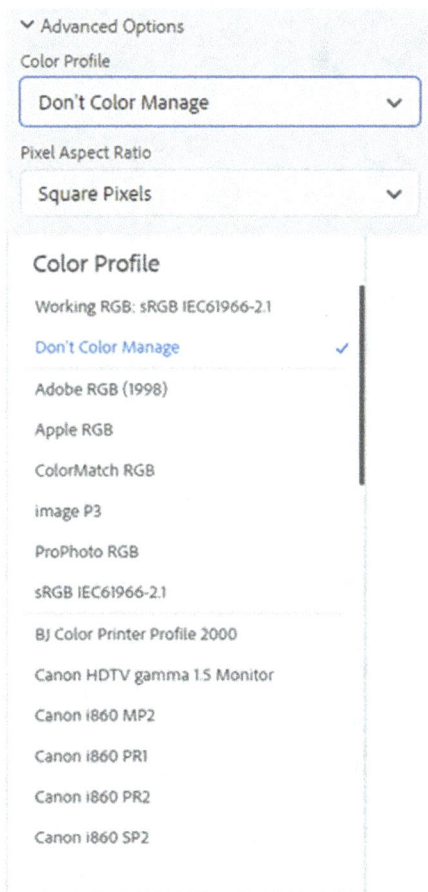

Figure 3-3. *Looking at the advanced color profile options under Advanced Options*

33

Another advanced option is Pixel Aspect Ratio. I recommend leaving it as Square Pixels.

■ **Note** If you need to open a file (File ➤ Open) from a client and you are not sure of the image's color profile, you can find it under Edit ➤ Assign Profile. The radio button that is highlighted is the current profile of that image, but you can change it to another, if necessary. Just remember that changing the profile may alter color settings within the file, and it may not display as it did before. If this is a concern while previewing the file, it is better to work on a copy of the original. Refer to Figure 3-4.

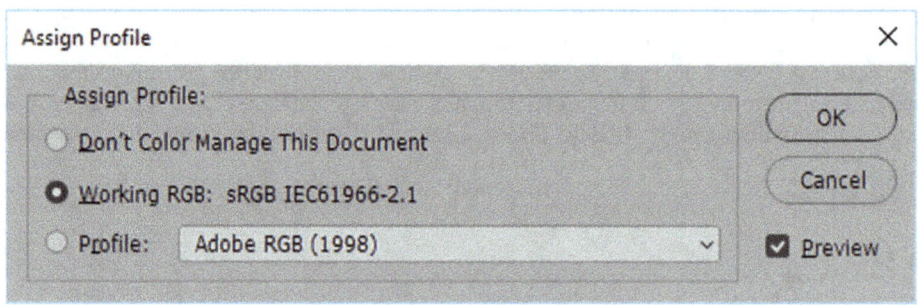

Figure 3-4. *Checking the Assign Profile of an image*

If your opened image is in a color profile that is not RGB, you can change it at Image ➤ Mode. Choose RGB Color, as seen in Figure 3-5.

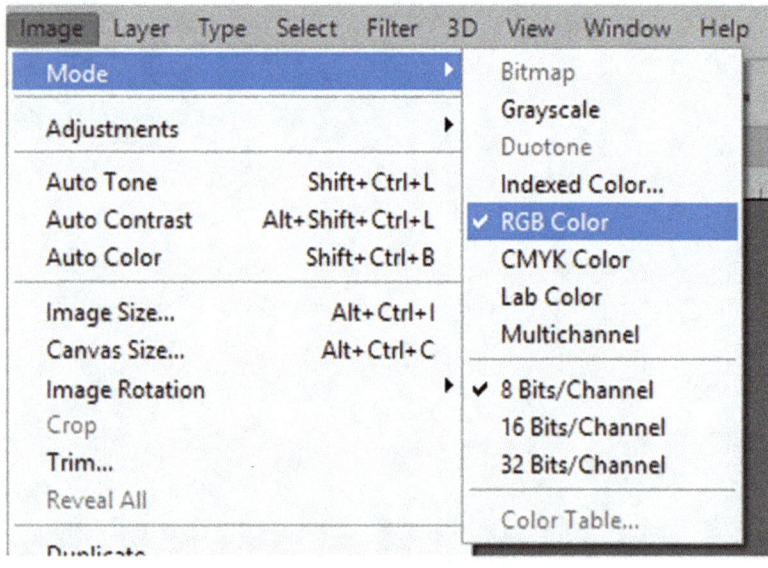

Figure 3-5. *Change your mode to RGB color if not already set*

CHAPTER 3 ■ COLOR CHOICES: CMYK, RGB, GRAYSCALE, AND INDEX

You can also adjust the color settings. This automatically converts the file to Working RGB: sRGB, unless you have set a custom profile under Edit ➤ Color Settings, as seen in Figure 3-6.

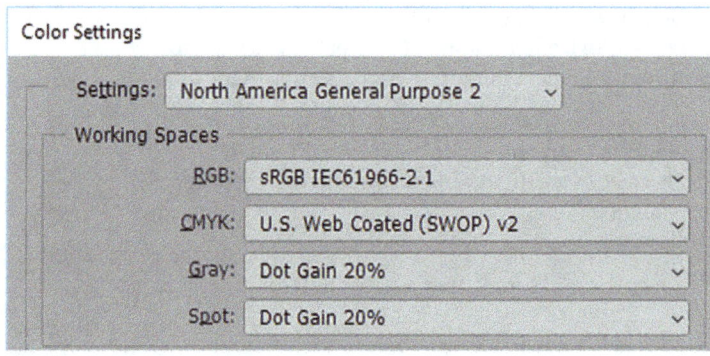

Figure 3-6. *The current color setting preferences*

You can tell that the mode of the file has changed by looking at the area on top of where the name of file is located, as seen in Figure 3-7.

Figure 3-7. *The color mode has been changed from CMYK to RGB*

Make sure that if you want to preserve the original's color and bits, work on a copy. Go to Image ➤ Duplicate, as seen in Figure 3-8.

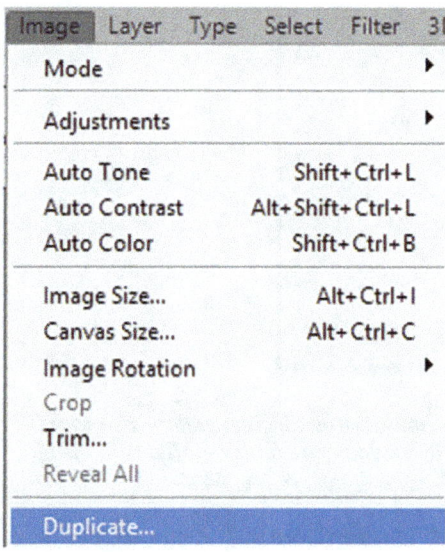

Figure 3-8. *To preserve the original image, always work with a duplicate file*

35

Figure 3-5 shows some other color modes.

- **Duotone**: This is generally used for print work and is for two color jobs. It can appear like grayscale or sepia tone found in old photos. In addition, you could add a second color, such as blue or yellow, for an interesting effect. Other options within this mode are monotone (1-color), tritone (3-color), and quadtone (4-color). If you want to keep this effect for an image on your website, remember to save a copy of the original in RGB mode.

- **Index Color**: This is an 8-bit image that can only contain 256 colors of RGB. Called a CLUT, or color look up table, it is used for GIF image file formats and keeps the images small, as you will see in later chapters. This mode can be viewed on the web and is best for logos, but not photographs.

- **Multichannel**: With 256 levels of gray per channel, this mode is best for print and not the web.

■ **Note** One benefit of working in RGB mode vs. CMYK is that you have access to more of the Photoshop filters and 3D options, as seen in Figure 3-9.

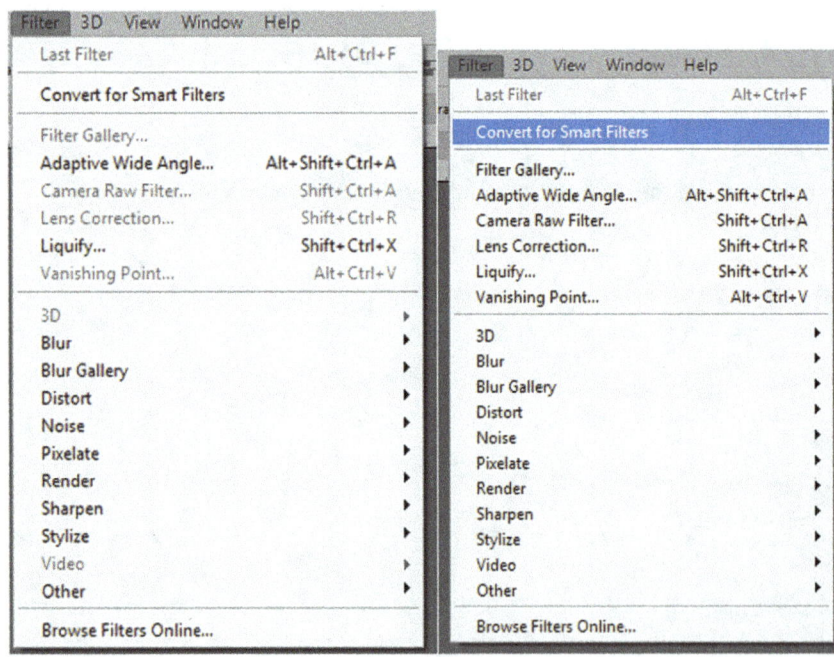

Figure 3-9. *Compare the options of CMYK to RGB color mode. See how 3D and the filter gallery are grayed out with no access in CMYK mode, but are available in RGB mode when you work with your filters in the file.*

■ **Note** When you open a GIF file in Photoshop, you may notice that it has an Index Color mode, as seen in Figure 3-10. That mode is within the RGB color platform, which is OK; you do not need to change it back to RGB.

CHAPTER 3 ■ COLOR CHOICES: CMYK, RGB, GRAYSCALE, AND INDEX

Figure 3-10. GIF image are in the Index Color mode

From looking at modes, the best color mode options for an image on the web are RGB, Index, Grayscale, and Bitmap (for simple black-and-white line drawings).

As you progress through the book to Part 6, you will look at some other color spaces, such as HEX color, RGBA, and HSLA, which you can use on your website in Dreamweaver CC. If you need to find a HEX color in an image in Photoshop, you can click your foreground or background color in the Tools panel, and use the color picker and eyedropper to determine the HEX color code, which is a six-digit code of numbers and letters that begins with the # symbol, as seen in Figures 3-11 and 3-12.

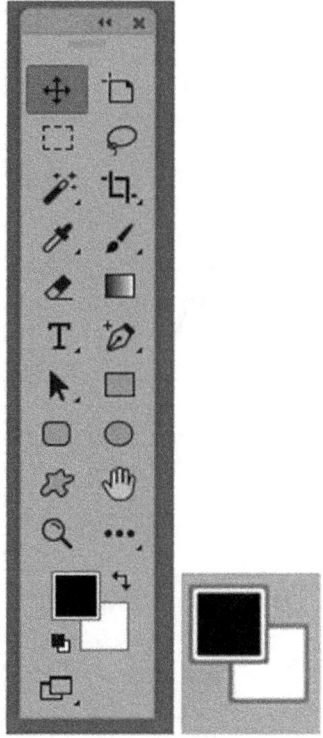

Figure 3-11. In the Tools panel, click either the foreground or background color to bring up the Color Picker dialog box

CHAPTER 3 ■ COLOR CHOICES: CMYK, RGB, GRAYSCALE, AND INDEX

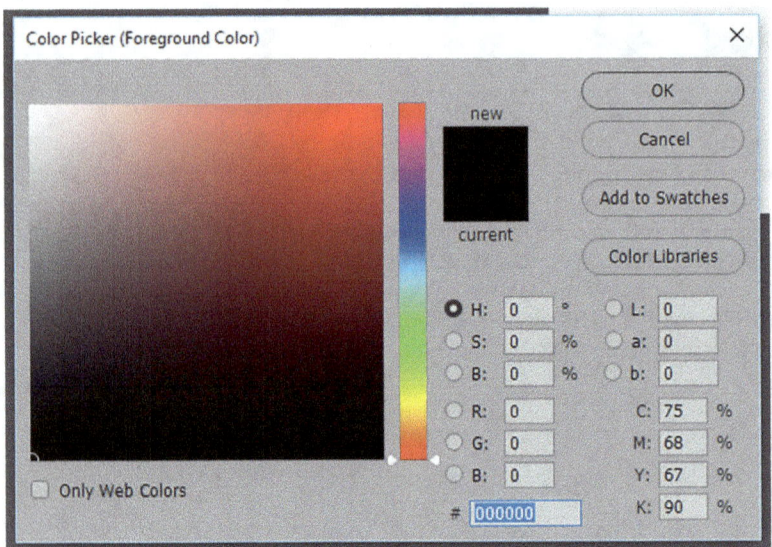

Figure 3-12. *The Color dialog box allows you to work with colors in different modes, including Hex color (#), found at the bottom of the dialog box*

■ **Note** Even though you are in RGB mode in the color picker, you can use other modes, like HSB (hue saturation brightness), Lab, and CMYK to match equivalent colors for other projects.

If you check Only Web Colors (see Figure 3-13), you will only see HEX color options, which reduce the number of color options. However, these days, most computer screens and mobile devices can handle a wide range of colors, so I often leave that unchecked.

38

CHAPTER 3 ■ COLOR CHOICES: CMYK, RGB, GRAYSCALE, AND INDEX

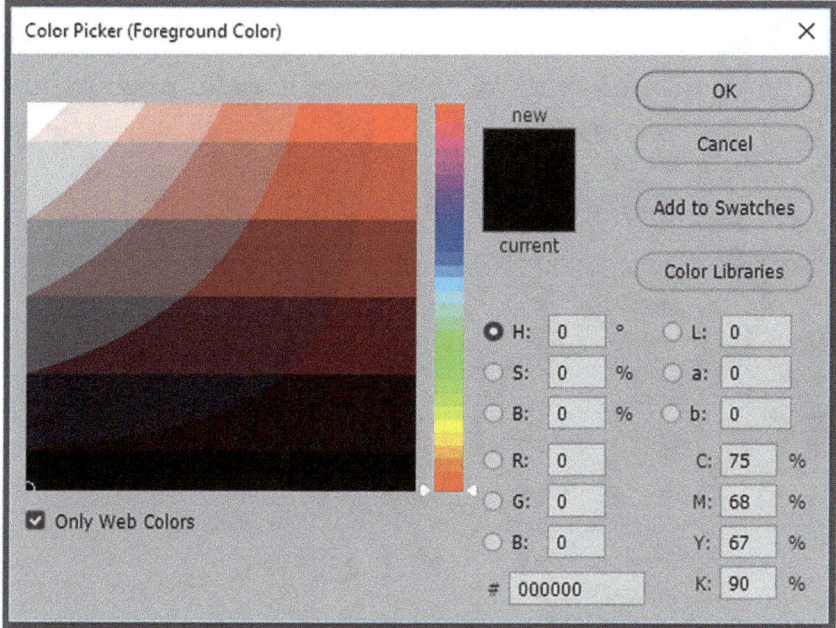

Figure 3-13. The Color dialog box viewing only web-safe colors

This setting is helpful if you are working with GIF images since they only include 256 colors; for example, if your client needs to convert their logo to a specific web-safe color.

You can further adjust and work with color by using the Color panel, as seen in Figure 3-14.

CHAPTER 3 ■ COLOR CHOICES: CMYK, RGB, GRAYSCALE, AND INDEX

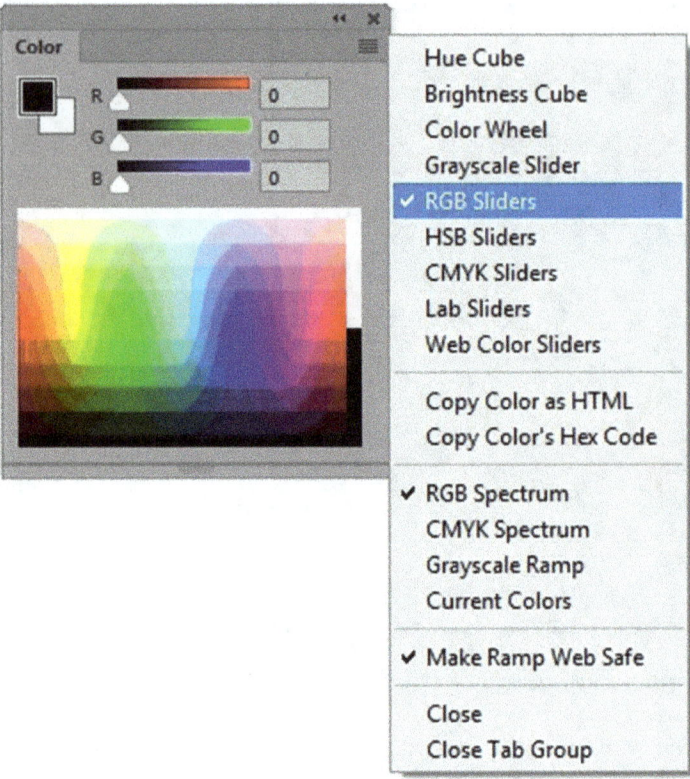

Figure 3-14. *The Color panel to create additional colors*

Settings like RGB Sliders and RGB Spectrum ensure that you are only looking at RGB color options. Make Ramp Web Safe is good for working with files that are saved as GIFs, which you'll look at in the next chapter.

■ **Note** If you need you need to know the HTML or hex code of the current color, select Copy Color as HTML or Copy Color's Hex Code, and then paste the information into a program like Notepad++ or Dreamweaver CC. A text version of the code will appear in the file; for example: color="#b73f3f".

Colors that you create that appear in the foreground or background of the Tools panel can be saved as swatches. Save specific colors in the Swatches panel, as seen in Figure 3-15.

Figure 3-15. *The Swatches panel allows you to add specific colors from the foreground or background to your set by clicking a New Swatch icon or choosing New Swatch from the panel's menu*

The Swatch panel also allows you to load or replace swatches that are specific to the web spectrum. You can use the menu to reset the Swatches panel; however, be aware that any swatches that you do not save under Save Swatches will be lost.

One final panel that can be used to work with color is the Extension Adobe Color Themes panel, where you can explore and create assorted color combinations, as seen in Figure 3-16.

CHAPTER 3 ■ COLOR CHOICES: CMYK, RGB, GRAYSCALE, AND INDEX

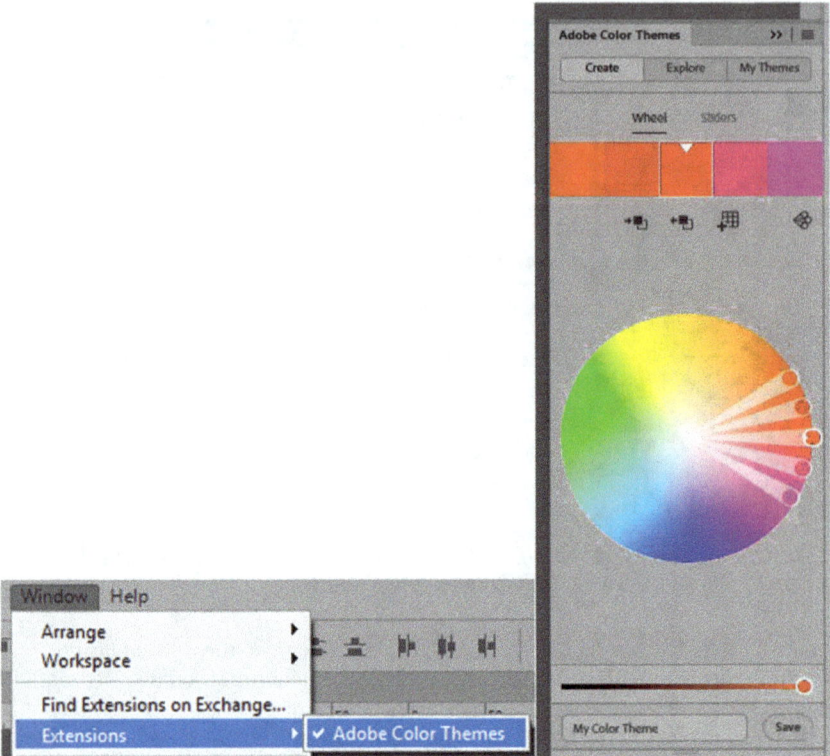

Figure 3-16. *The Adobe Color Themes panel assists in finding complimentary colors for your themes*

Adjusting the Image Size and Resolution

As a last step before exporting your image to a web format, you can adjust its final size and resolution by going to Image ➤ Image Size.

Figure 3-17 shows the vase_image.psd image to set a final size for the image and resolution before exporting.

CHAPTER 3 ■ COLOR CHOICES: CMYK, RGB, GRAYSCALE, AND INDEX

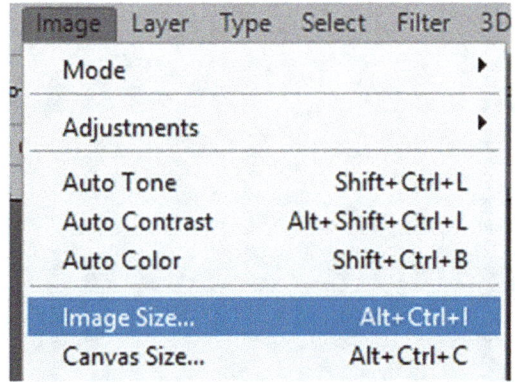

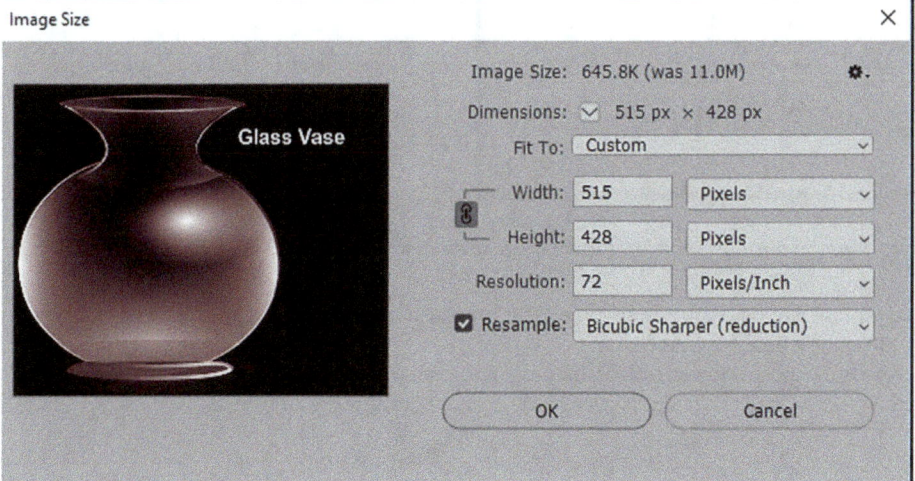

Figure 3-17. The Image Size dialog box to reduce the image size and resolution

If you are reducing the image, a resample setting of Bicubic Sharper (reduction) is the best setting for an image that will become smaller with a lower resolution as seen in Figures 3-17 and 3-18.

43

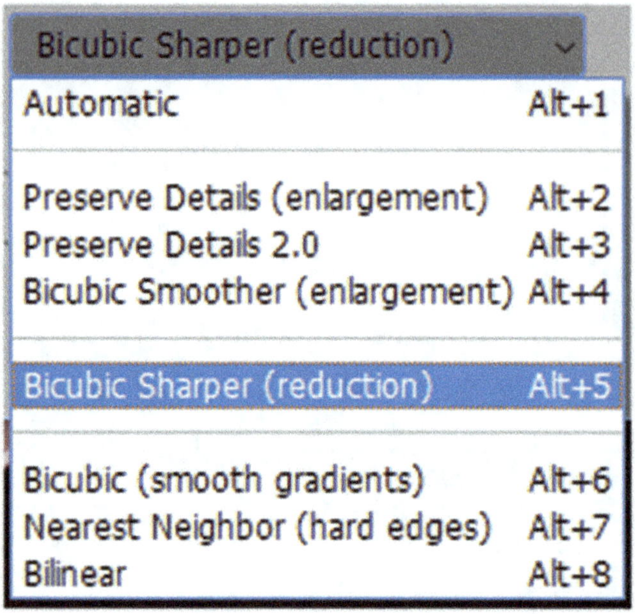

CHAPTER 3 COLOR CHOICES: CMYK, RGB, GRAYSCALE, AND INDEX

Figure 3-18. Various resample options found in the Image Size dialog box

Much of this resampling can be done when you export the file, as you will see in the next chapter where we look at the resample setting in more detail.

If you want to crop the image's canvas, rather than make the resolution smaller, go to Image ➤ Canvas Size (see Figure 3-19).

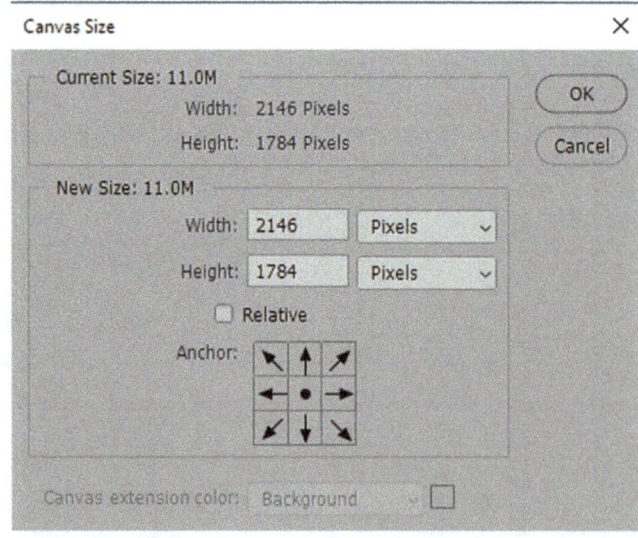

Figure 3-19. In the Canvas Size dialog box, you can reduce or increase the size of the image's canvas

44

CHAPTER 3 ■ COLOR CHOICES: CMYK, RGB, GRAYSCALE, AND INDEX

You can also use the Crop tool found in Tools panel. Its settings are in the Options panel. The crop options are seen in Figure 3-20.

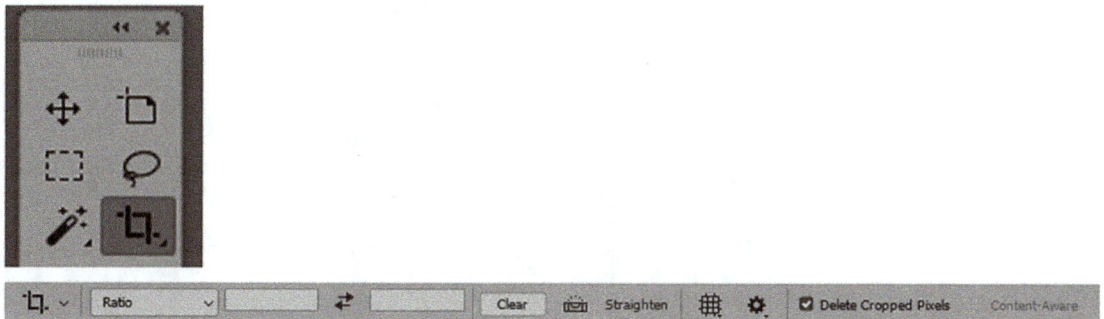

Figure 3-20. In the Canvas Size dialog box, you can reduce or increase the size of the image's canvas

Use the handles on the Crop tool to size the image. Alternatively, choose a ratio option from the control panel to adjust the size to get a specific width and height, as seen in Figure 3-21.

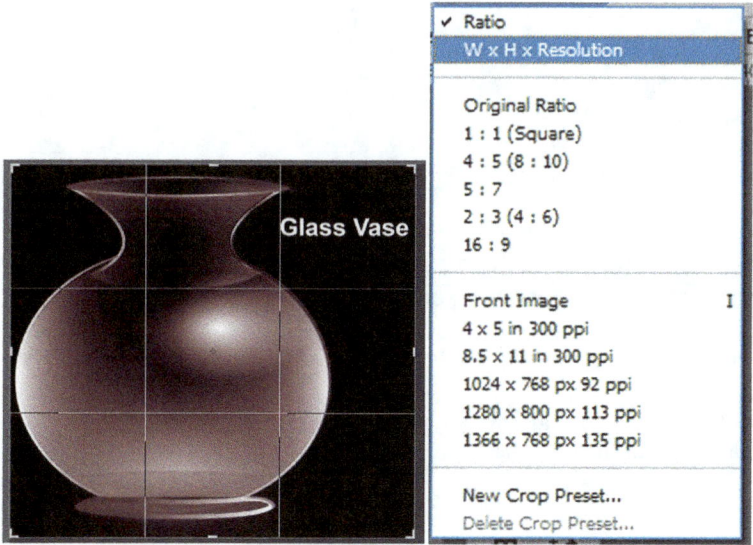

Figure 3-21. In the Canvas Size dialog box, you can reduce or increase the size of the image's canvas and choose where to affect the resolution

If you don't want to use the Crop tool, either right click on the image and choose cancel from the pop-up menu, as seen in Figure 3-22. Or click the cancel current crop operation symbol that will appear in the control panel. And then choose another tool from the panel.

45

CHAPTER 3 ■ COLOR CHOICES: CMYK, RGB, GRAYSCALE, AND INDEX

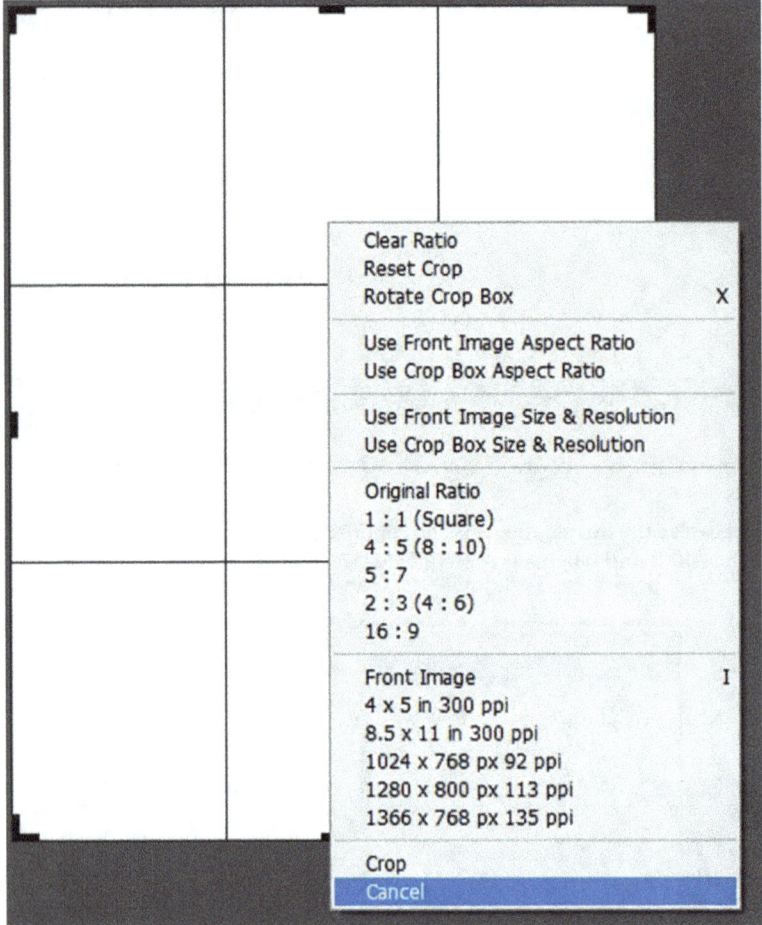

***Figure 3-22.** How to stop the cropping action by right-clicking on the crop*

When you are done looking at color choices, you can save any open file with File ➤ Save. File ➤ Exit to exit Photoshop CC, or keep Photoshop open for the next chapter.

Summary

In this chapter, you looked at some of the color choices and modes that are available to prepare images for your website. Some modes are better for print, like CMYK and Duotone; others, like RGB and Index, are meant for the web. You also took a look at how to further adjust the size and resolution of an image before export.

In Chapter 4, you look at how to make further adjustments or optimize your image files during export. Photoshop CC gives you several menu options for export, but figuring out which method is best for your workflow can be a challenge if you have many files to work with and multiple conversions to make.

CHAPTER 4

Saving or Exporting Your Files for the Web

In this chapter, you are going to explore some of the many ways that are available to you to export your images for the web using Photoshop. Adobe has a variety of ways to do this; some of the options appear to overlap, so at times, it can get confusing to know which options are best for your project.

Note This chapter does not have any actual projects; however, you can use the files in the Chapter 4 folder to practice opening and viewing for this lesson. They are at https://github.com/Apress/graphics-multimedia-web-adobe-creative-cloud.

At this point in building your website using Photoshop CC, you probably have designed some artwork for your website; perhaps graphic buttons, images for a gallery, or a patterned background. After you have designed your artwork for your website, you want to start saving it for the web. Photoshop offers several ways to export your web-ready files. If you need a more detailed description of each of these file types, refer to Chapter 1. Table 4-1 describes which file formats are available under the various File menu options.

Table 4-1. *Export Options Available in Photoshop CC Under the File menu. (For more information, go to the section listed above each file.)*

File Format	(Option 1) File ➤ Save As	(Option 2) File ➤ Export ➤ Quick Export as PNG*	(Option 3) File ➤ Export ➤ Export As	(Option 4) File ➤ Export ➤ Save For Web (Legacy)
Bitmap (.bmp)	✓			
WBMP or Wireless Bitmap (.wmb, .wbmp)				✓
JPEG (.jpg, .jpeg, .jpe)	✓	✓(when Export preferences are altered)	✓	✓
PNG (8 and 24)(.png)	✓	✓(default)	✓	✓
GIF (static and animated) (.gif)	✓(static)	✓(static, when Export preferences are altered)	✓(static)	✓(static and animated)
SVG(.svg)		✓(when Export preferences are altered)	✓	
Photoshop PDF (.pdf)	✓			

CHAPTER 4 ■ SAVING OR EXPORTING YOUR FILES FOR THE WEB

■ **Note** One file type not discussed in Chapter 1 was WBMP or Wireless Bitmap (.wmb, wbmp). WBMP images are monochrome (black and white) so that the image size is kept to a minimum. A black pixel is denoted by 0 and a white pixel is denoted by 1. For colored images, Wireless Application Protocol (WAP) supports the PNG format. This type of graphic is used in mobile computing devices.

As you can see, Photoshop CC offers at least four ways to save your files for the web. Later in this chapter, we will look at a few more hidden export features.

For now, let's look at the four main options; refer to Table 4-1 if you need to compare information.

Option 1: File ➤ Save As…

File ➤ Save As… is probably the fastest option to use if you only have one or two images to add to your website (see Figure 4-1).

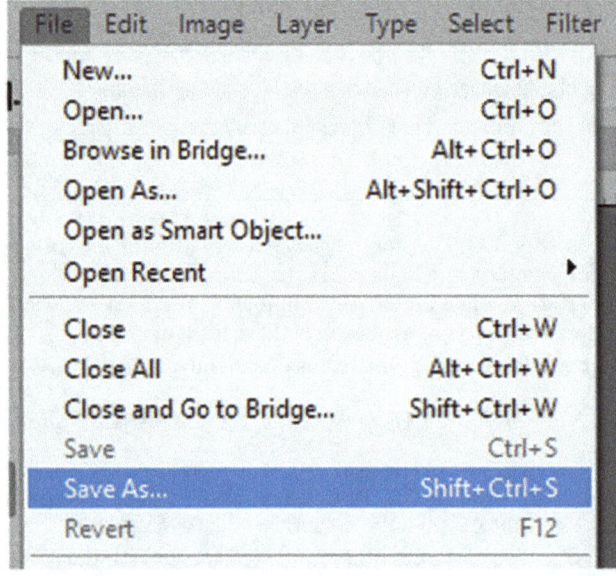

Figure 4-1. *Photoshop allows you to save a copy of your artwork in another format using File ➤ Save As*

You are then presented with options from the Save as type drop-down menu in the Save As dialog box, as seen in Figure 4-2.

48

CHAPTER 4 ■ SAVING OR EXPORTING YOUR FILES FOR THE WEB

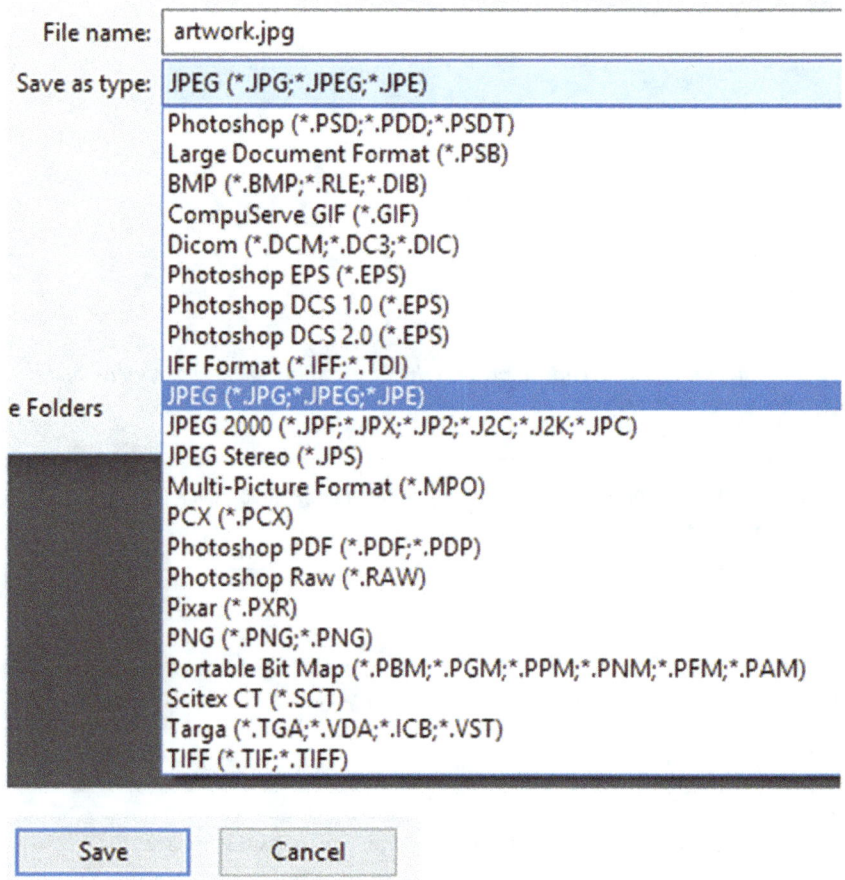

Figure 4-2. *The options found in File ➤ Save As in the Save as type drop-down menu*

However, as you see in Figure 4-2, you can't adjust or preview initial settings for that file until you click the Save button. Depending on the file format, only then are you able to click the preview check box in that particular file format's dialog box. Whatever format type you choose, you can't switch to another file format to compare both of your options at the same time.

To avoid overwriting your current file, if it's in the same folder, select As a Copy in Save Options. Depending on the file type chosen, some options are not available. You can also confirm the color profile for this file as well. When done, click the Save button to save your file, or Cancel to exit, as seen in Figure 4-3.

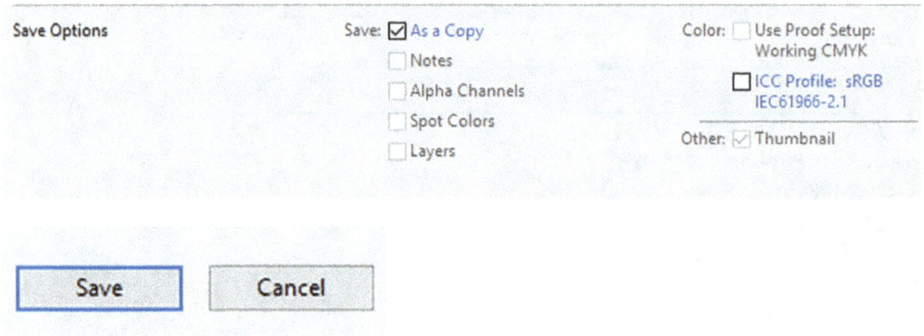

CHAPTER 4 ■ SAVING OR EXPORTING YOUR FILES FOR THE WEB

Figure 4-3. Before you save a file, you can save as a copy to prevent the file from being overwritten, as well as choose a color profile if it has not already been set

■ **Note** You may get a Warning button (see Figure 4-4) if your file contains layers. If you click it, it states that the file must be saved as a copy, which flattens that copy.

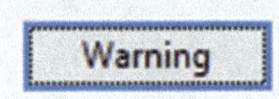

Figure 4-4. Click the Warning button if you are worried that your file may have issues before you save

Next are some settings that may appear for each web file format when you click the Save button.

Bitmap (BMP)

A bitmap, which is common to Windows computers, can be a created from a scan with your home or office scanner. It also can be used on a website. Often, its file size is large. Generally, when a person builds a website, they want to keep the images small so that they upload quickly. If you want to save a file as a .bmp file, you can adjust the setting in the BMP Options dialog box. Figures 4-5 and 4-6 show basic and advanced modes; use the button to toggle between the two.

CHAPTER 4 ■ SAVING OR EXPORTING YOUR FILES FOR THE WEB

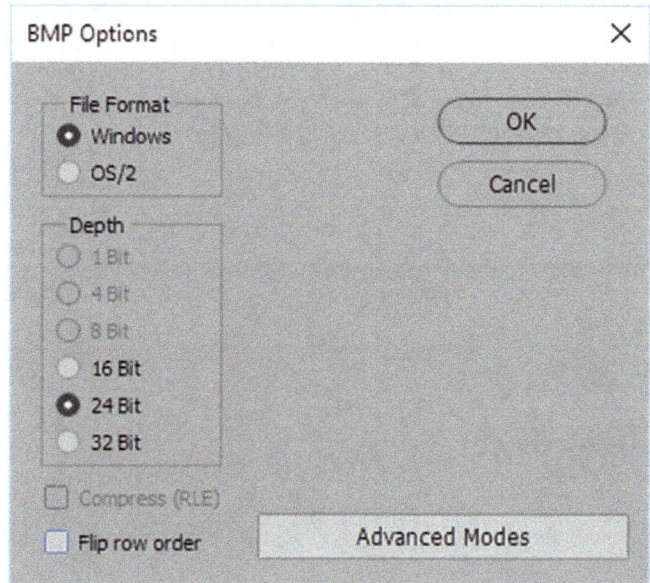

Figure 4-5. *BMP Options dialog box Basic Modes, use lower toggle button to see advanced modes*

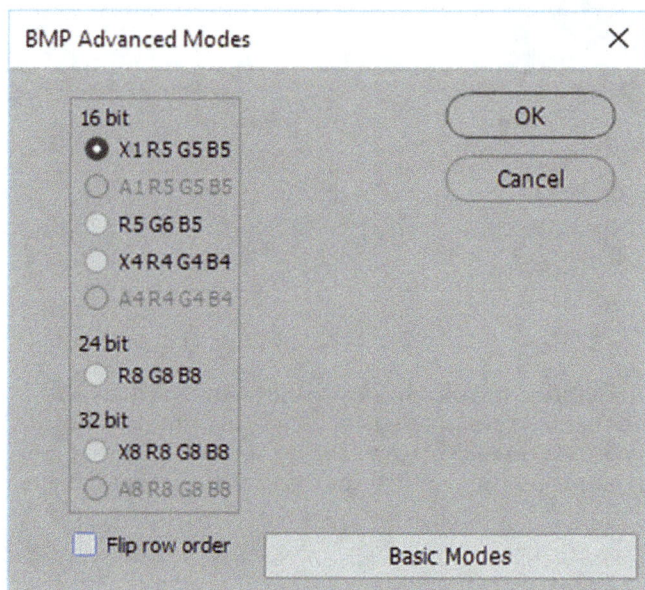

Figure 4-6. *BMP Options dialog box Advanced Modes use lower toggle button to return to basic modes*

51

The BMP file options have a toggle that you can use to set in either Basic Modes or Advanced Modes. In Basic Modes, you can set the file format to Windows or OS/2. You can also adjust the bit depth to 16, 24, or 32. Note that because I used the .bmp file extension, Compress (RLE) is unavailable. The "Flip row order" box refers to how the encoding is written, either from bottom to top or in reverse. According to Adobe, "Advanced Modes are most relevant to game programmers and others using DirectX."

JPEG

When you save your file as a (.jpg), the JPEG Options dialog box allows you to alter your setting while previewing your image, as seen in Figure 4-7.

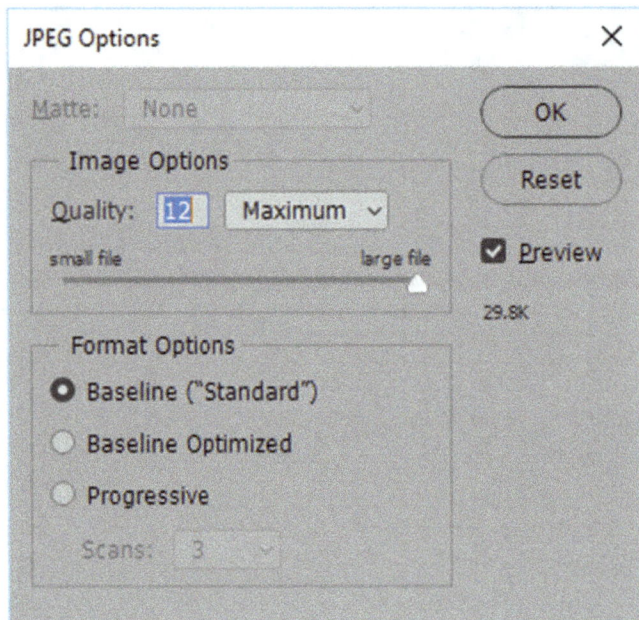

Figure 4-7. *Options in the JPEG Options dialog box*

If the image (.psd) has more than one layer with some transparent areas in the image, and there is no background (Layer 0), then the Matte background option is available; otherwise, it is set at the default None, so its unavailable. For color options, you can choose the current Foreground or Background colors that are in your Tools panel. You can also choose White, Black, 50% Gray, or Netscape Gray, which is about 25% gray (see Figure 4-8).

CHAPTER 4 ■ SAVING OR EXPORTING YOUR FILES FOR THE WEB

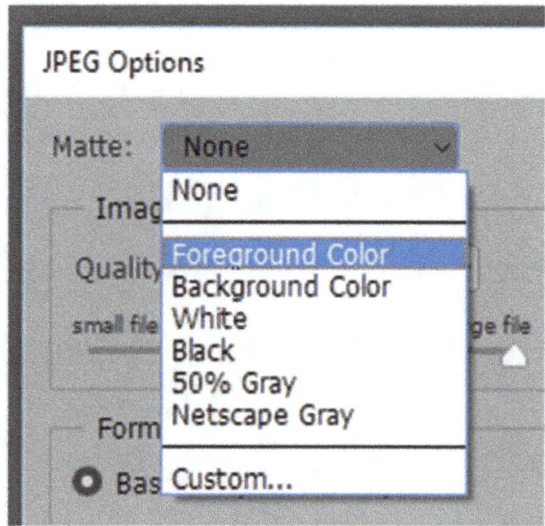

Figure 4-8. Matte color options when available

Custom brings up the Color Picker window, where you can choose whatever color you want. When it opens, it shows the last color that you picked in the list (in this case, Netscape Gray). Figure 4-9 shows the options.

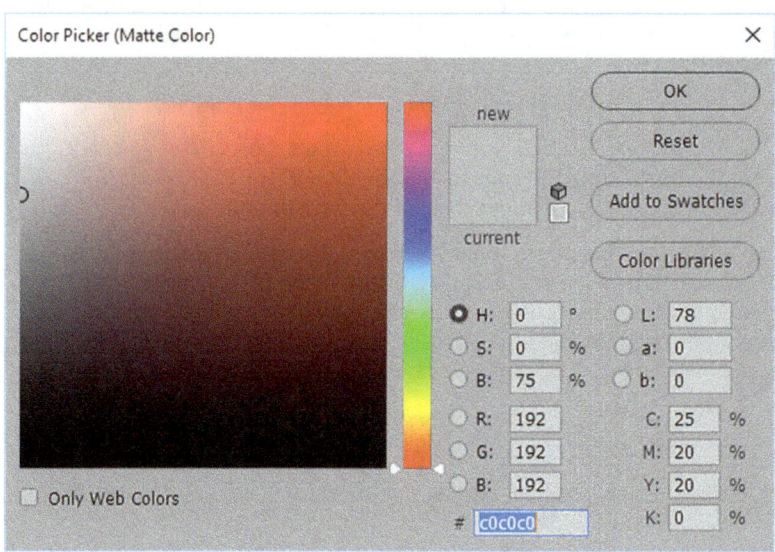

Figure 4-9. Choose a custom color using the Color Picker

Image Options refer to the quality of the image. You can either adjust the quality by typing a number quality from 0 to 12, by choosing a setting from the drop-down menu (Low, Medium, High, or Maximum), or by dragging the slider between the small file and the large file. Whatever option you choose, the number box, drop-down menu, and slider all reflect the changes, as seen in Figure 4-10.

53

CHAPTER 4 ■ SAVING OR EXPORTING YOUR FILES FOR THE WEB

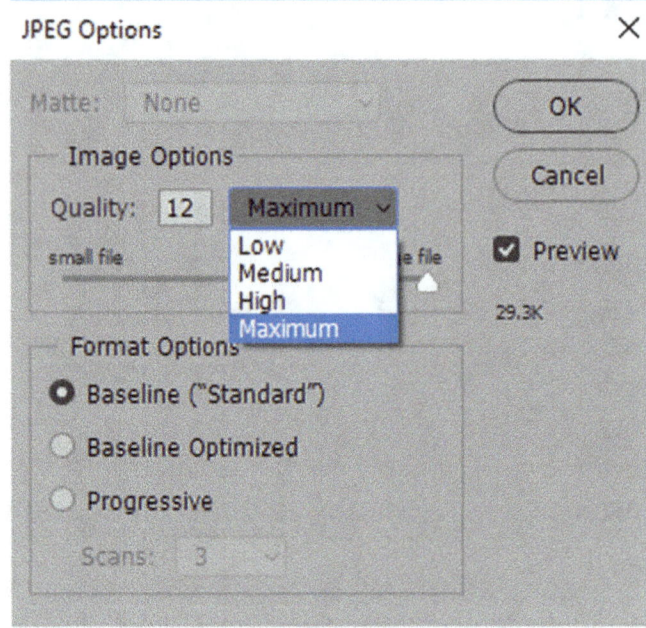

Figure 4-10. *Choose an image quality setting*

The number 0 results in a low, grainy image, while a high number like 12 results in a larger image with maximum quality. The size of the file can be seen in the Preview setting.

You can also choose Format Options.

- **Baseline ("Standard")**: Recognized by most web browsers and good for photos that need decent quality. It is supported by all browsers.

- **Baseline Optimized**: Similar to standard but compresses the file a little more. Depending on the image, the quality is indistinguishable from baseline standard.

- **Progressive**: Creates an image that displays gradually as it downloads. It appears as if the image is rendered as scan lines (like in the days of the old-fashioned tube TVs). At first, the browser quickly shows a reduced quality image of half the scan lines while it resolves the complete image. You can set between three and five scans to take place in this setting: however, with a fast Internet connection, this setting is not used as often.

■ **Note** According to Adobe, some browsers do not support progressive JPEGs, so if you want to use this setting, run a test first.

CHAPTER 4 ■ SAVING OR EXPORTING YOUR FILES FOR THE WEB

PNG

The PNG is considered a good compromise between a JPEG and a GIF since it can be used for photos that retain good color quality and can maintain transparency. However, you will notice that if you use the File ➤ Save As option for your image, you do not have access to the preview or transparency in PNG Format Options. Refer to Figure 4-11.

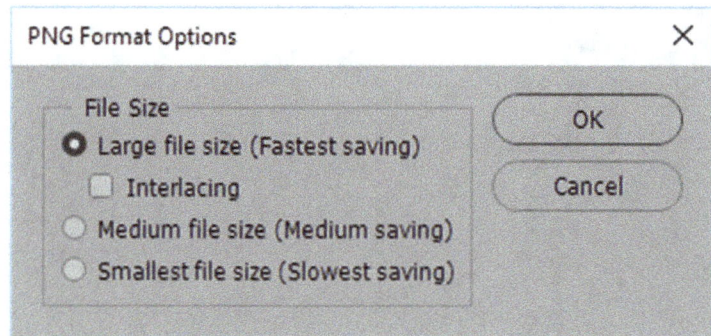

Figure 4-11. *PNG Format Options dialog box for File ➤ Save As*

The following are available.

- **Large file size (Fastest saving)**: Less compression is applied, so it saves faster.

- **Interlacing**: Similar to the Progressive option in the JPEG setting. The image loads in parts, gradually becoming clearer with each scan.

- **Medium file size (Medium saving)**: Some compression is applied, so it saves more slowly than large.

- **Smallest file size (Slowest saving)**: More compression is applied to the file and it may take longer to save.

Unlike the JPEG dialog box, you won't know how small your file will be until after it is saved.

CompuServe GIF

Because GIFs only use 256 indexed RGB colors, they are best for items that contain solid areas of graphics, such as logos or cartoon illustrations. The fewer the number of colors, the smaller the file size. Photos do not always reproduce at the best quality in a GIF. You can preview a GIF behind the dialog box, and a color lookup table is produced for the GIF. If a color cannot be reproduced, it is dithered to simulate the color. You can also reach this same dialog box via Image ➤ Mode ➤ Indexed Color, but that will affect the current image and not a copy. Either way, you may be asked to flatten the image if you have not already done so. Click OK. Refer to Figure 4-12.

55

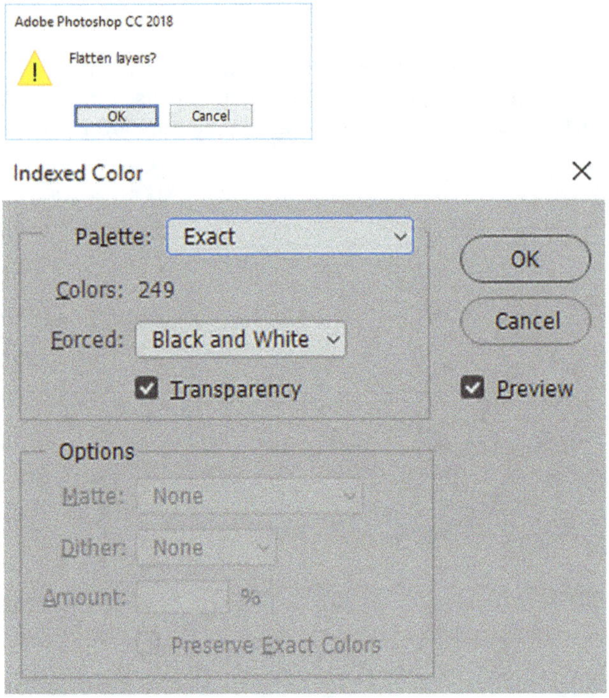

CHAPTER 4 ■ SAVING OR EXPORTING YOUR FILES FOR THE WEB

Figure 4-12. Index color options as seen in the Indexed Color dialog box

You can control the number of colors that the file has by using the Palette drop-down menu to set the colors that best represent the image, as seen in Figure 4-13.

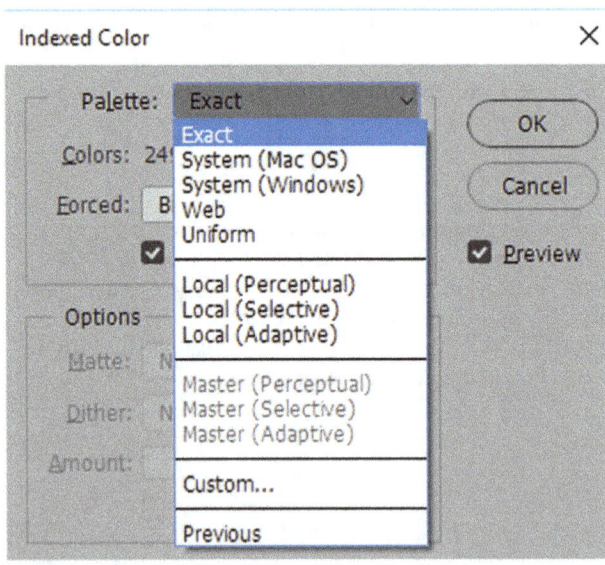

Figure 4-13. Choose an option from the Palette drop-down menu

CHAPTER 4 ■ SAVING OR EXPORTING YOUR FILES FOR THE WEB

The following options are from the Palette drop-down menu.

- **Exact:** Shows the current number of colors. Some files will have less than 256 colors.
- **System (Mac OS):** 256 colors for a macOS system palette.
- **System(Windows):** 256 colors for a Windows system palette.
- **Web:** 216 colors, also known as Restrictive. This compensates between Mac and PC computer monitors. If your image does not have 216 colors, the number of colors may be lower.
- **Uninform:** Type your own setting into the Colors area.
- **Local (Perceptual):** Creates a custom pallet of color that gives priority to the colors that the human eye has greater sensitivity to, or that are more pleasing. (Master refers to a master palette that you may have created earlier).
- **Local (Selective):** Similar to Perceptual, but also favors the broad range of continuous colors and the preservation of colors on the web. This usually produces an image with the greatest color integrity.
- **Local (Adaptive):** Samples colors that appear most commonly in the image. Images with a majority of red have a greater concentration of red shades.
- **Custom:** Allows you to create a custom pallet in the Color Table dialog box at Image ➤ Mode ➤ Color Table, as you can see in Figure 4-14.

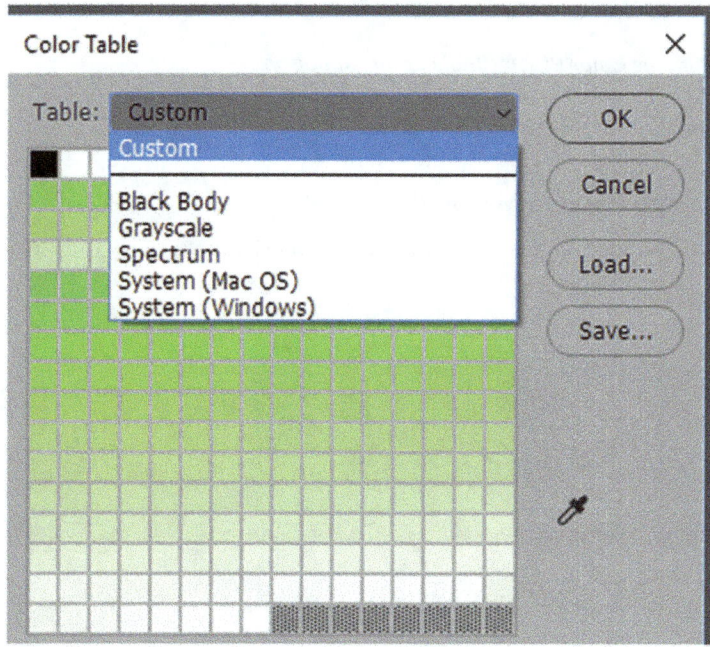

Figure 4-14. *A color table with different options appears when you choose Custom from the Indexed Color Palette*

57

CHAPTER 4 ■ SAVING OR EXPORTING YOUR FILES FOR THE WEB

You can click a color block and then edit it in the color picker, as seen in Figure 4-15. You can then save or load a table. It is saved as an .act file.

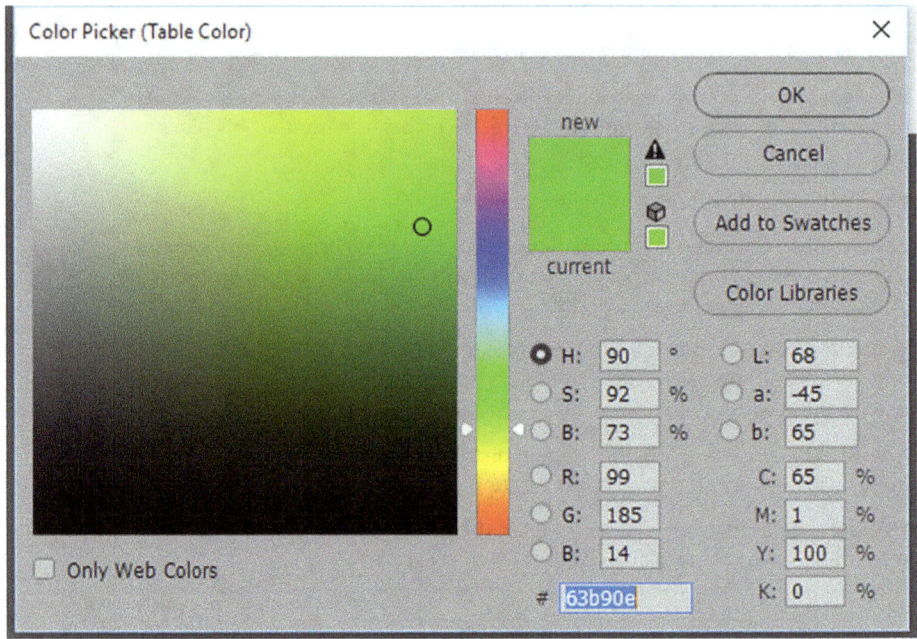

Figure 4-15. *Accessing the color picker from the Color Picker (Table Color) dialog box*

The Color Table's Eyedropper tool (on the right in Figure 4-14) allows you to sample colors. The following continues from the drop-down palette menu Figure 4-13.

- **Previous**: A custom pallet from a previous conversion.
- **Colors**: Determines the exact number of colors in the image, as seen in Figure 4-16.

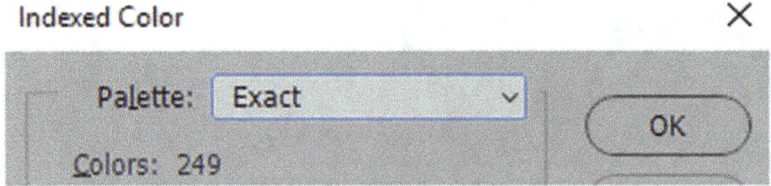

Figure 4-16. *The exact number of colors in the GIF image*

- **Forced**: This includes specified colors to be included in the conversion, such as black and white, primaries (red, green, blue, cyan, magenta, yellow, black and white), Web (216 web safe color), or your own custom colors that you can sample using the Color Picker when you click a color, as seen in Figure 4-17.

CHAPTER 4 ■ SAVING OR EXPORTING YOUR FILES FOR THE WEB

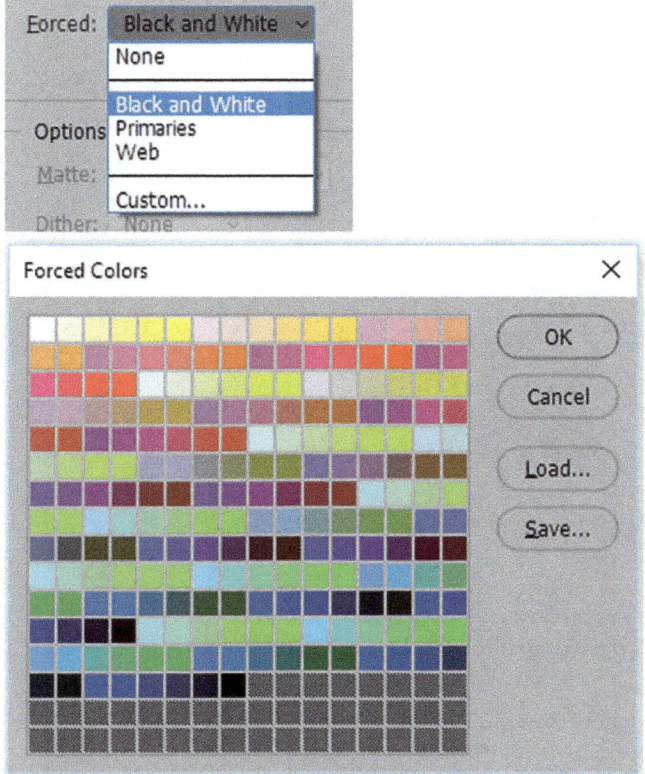

Figure 4-17. *Forcing specific colors in the GIF image*

The Transparency option lets you determine if the image contains transparency. If it is unchecked, the image is filled with a matte color of choice (see Figure 4-18).

Figure 4-18. *Choose Transparency if you want your GIF image to have a transparent background*

Let's look at the Options section of the Indexed Color dialog box. If the original image has transparent areas, more than one layer, and no background (Layer 0 or turned off), the Matte background option is available; otherwise; it is default at None, so unavailable. As with JPEG images, earlier similar color settings are available. Refer to Figure 4-19.

59

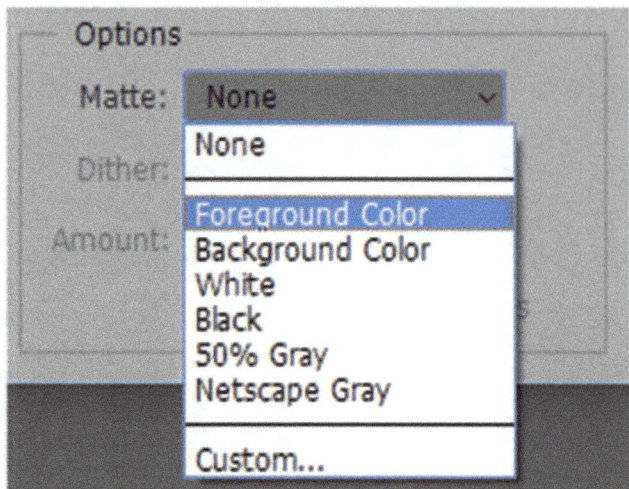

Figure 4-19. *This Matte drop-down menu can only be accessed if your background is transparent and your file has more than one layer*

- **Custom**: Brings up the color picker so you can choose your own color. The custom color or any Matte option will then blend into the area where the transparency once was.
- **Dither**: When you reduce the number of colors, the image may not blend well. You can use the options shown in Figure 4-20 to adjust this.

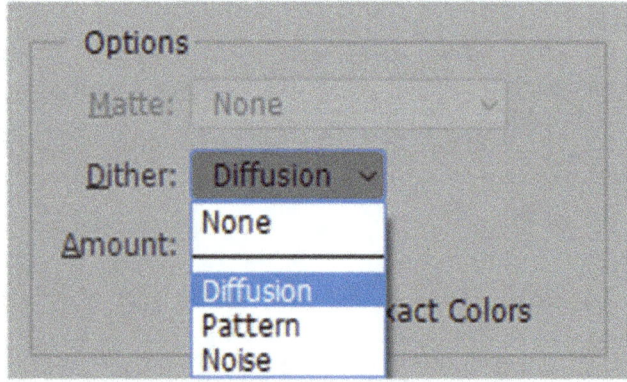

Figure 4-20. *Options for setting the amount of dither*

- **None**: The default for no dither.
- **Diffusion**: A random structure dither that is good for preserving delicate details and text in logos.
- **Pattern**: A halftone-like square pattern.

CHAPTER 4 ■ SAVING OR EXPORTING YOUR FILES FOR THE WEB

- **Noise**: Reduces the edge pattern if you are working with edges if you plan to slice your image for an HTML background with a <div> tag or within a table. (You will look at slices in Chapter 5.)
- **Amount**: You can adjust the amount of dither by percentage. Refer to Figure 4-21.

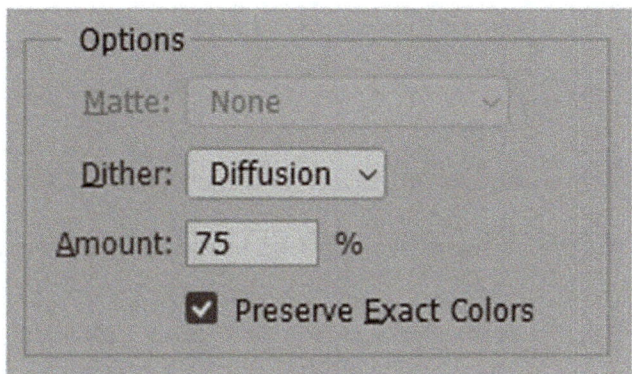

Figure 4-21. *Options for setting the dither by percentage to refine the amount*

- **Preserve Exact Colors**: This preserves the colors in the table from dithering.

Photoshop PDF

A PDF does not preview unless you click the file link on a web page and it is downloaded into the browser. You may want to save some images as a PDF by using Photoshop rather than placing them in a program like Adobe InDesign CC and then saving the file as a PDF. Either way, make sure that Acrobat DC Pro is installed on your computer so that you can use the distiller to create the PDF. Refer to the program icons shown in Figure 4-22.

Figure 4-22. *The Acrobat Pro DC and Acrobat Distiller icons; to create a PDF, these two programs should be installed on your computer*

When you save the file as a Photoshop PDF, you receive the alert shown in Figure 4-23.

CHAPTER 4 ■ SAVING OR EXPORTING YOUR FILES FOR THE WEB

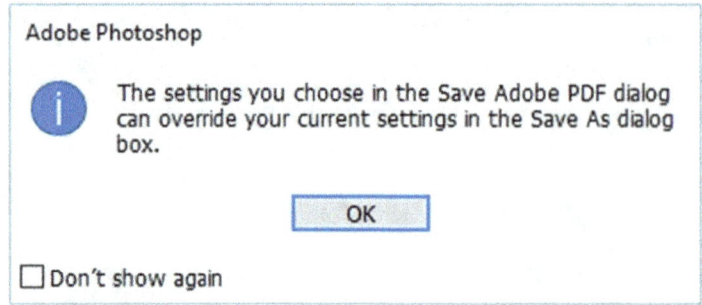

Figure 4-23. *The Photoshop alert you may receive when you choose to create a PDF*

Click OK and continue to the next dialog box. If you have used a program like Adobe InDesign CC, you will find the export setting familiar.

Here you are presented with various tabs, including Presets, Standards, and Compatibility, which you can choose from the drop-down menus. Refer to Figure 4-24 to see the assorted options and click the tabs on the left to get an overview of these settings.

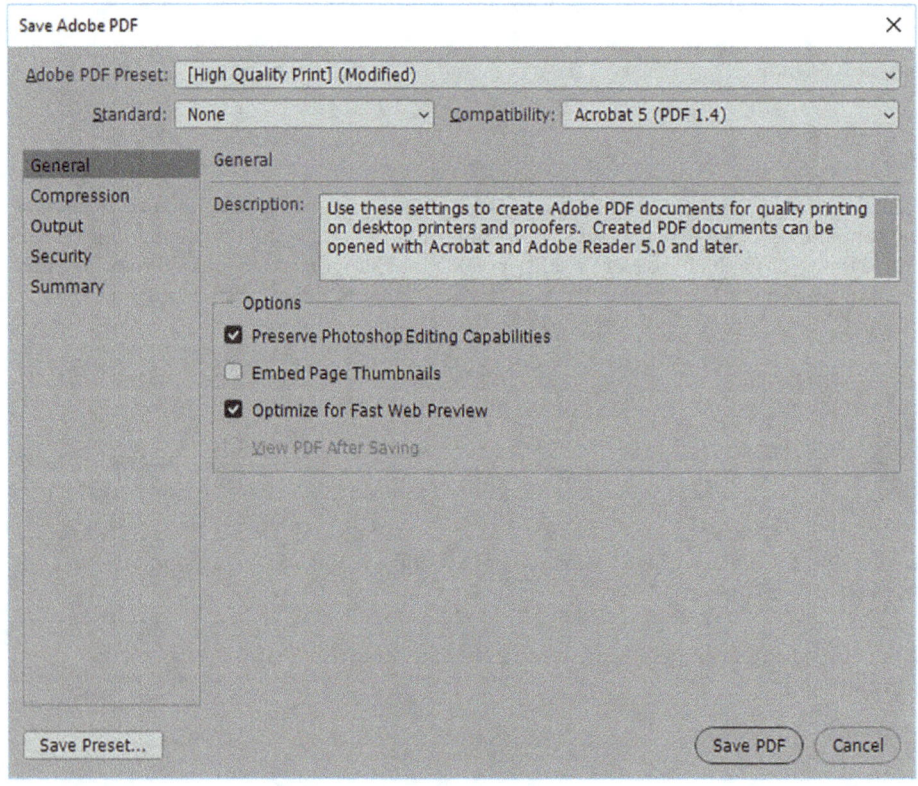

Figure 4-24. *Setting for the Save Adobe PDF dialog box*

CHAPTER 4 ■ SAVING OR EXPORTING YOUR FILES FOR THE WEB

- **General**: The main settings that allow you to preserve the file should you want to edit it again in Photoshop, embed a thumbnail, optimize for fast web preview, or view the PDF after saving.
- **Compression**: Distinct options for down sampling images and adjusting image quality within the PDF. Refer to Figure 4-25.

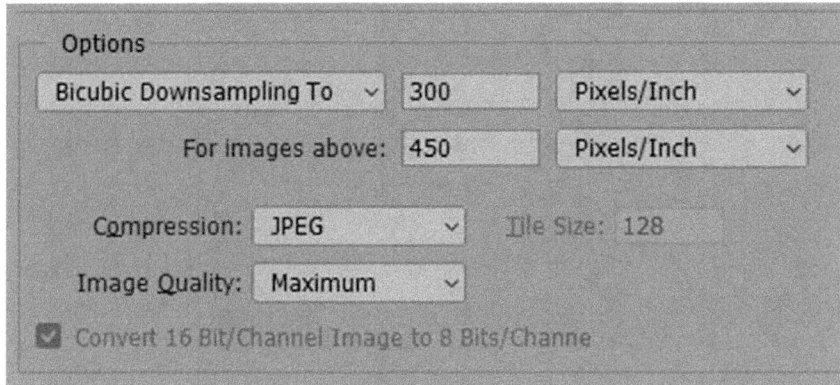

Figure 4-25. *Compression options for the Save Adobe PDF dialog box*

- **Output**: Deals with color and file conversion, as seen in Figure 4-26.

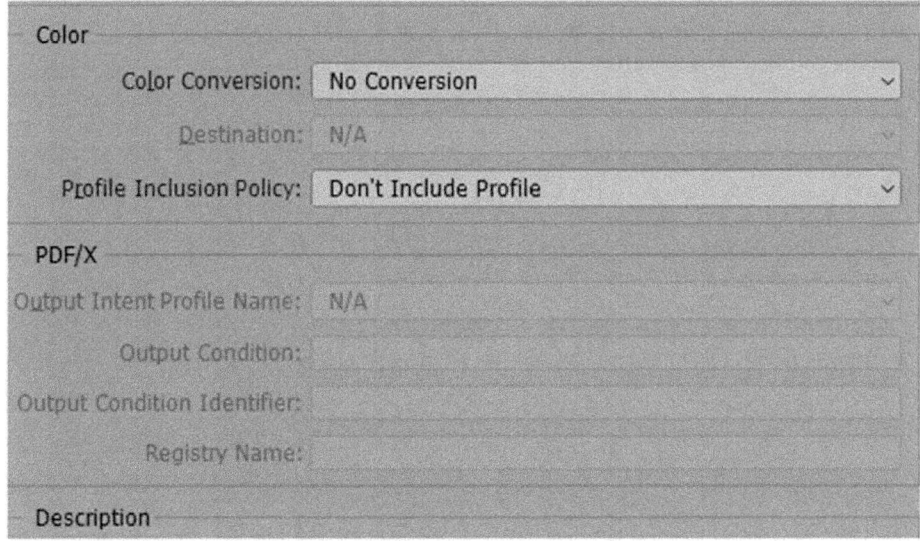

Figure 4-26. *Output options for the Save Adobe PDF dialog box*

Security: Sets security features for an image so that users who don't know the password can't open, print, or edit it, including those with screen readers. If you don't want security, leave these settings unchecked. Refer to Figure 4-27.

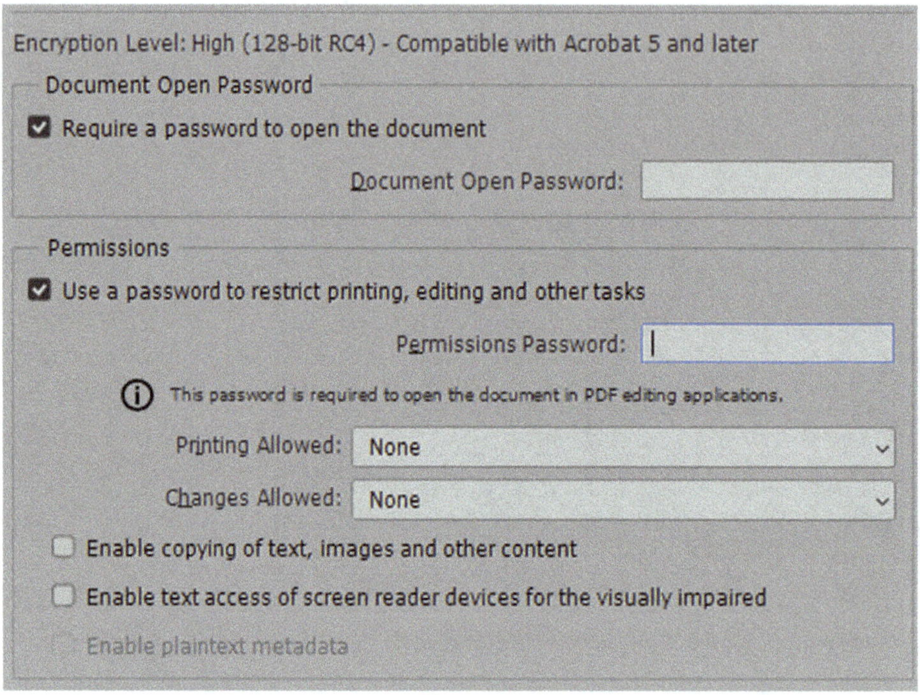

CHAPTER 4 ■ SAVING OR EXPORTING YOUR FILES FOR THE WEB

Figure 4-27. *Security options for the Save Adobe PDF dialog box*

- **Summary**: Lists all the settings and any warnings that may need to be corrected before pressing OK. Refer to Figure 4-28.

CHAPTER 4 ■ SAVING OR EXPORTING YOUR FILES FOR THE WEB

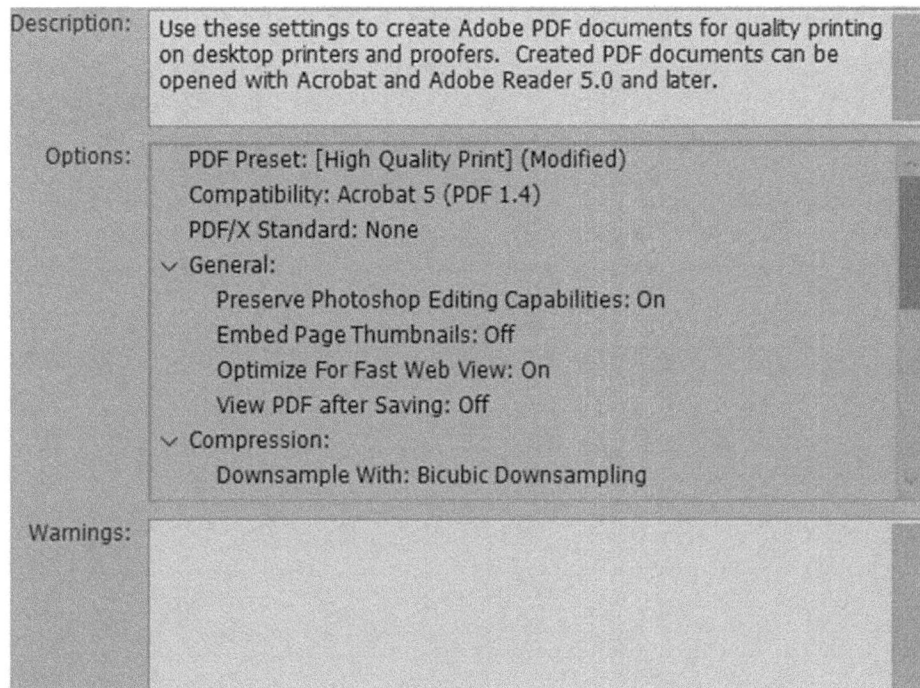

Figure 4-28. *Summary options for the Save Adobe PDF dialog box*

Once you have set your settings, click the Save PDF button in the bottom right of the dialog box (see Figure 4-24). A PDF is created, which you can view in Adobe Acrobat Pro DC or Reader.

Option 2: File ➤ Export ➤ Quick Export as PNG

You can use this option if you want to save a PNG file quickly without going through a dialog box: File ➤ Export ➤ Quick Export as PNG.

This option is only for PNG files. You cannot save the file in any other settings, and it only saves the file as a .png. Personally, I don't like this because it does not provide a dialog box to choose settings if each image is slightly different.

If you want to know what the Quick Export setting is, you can check it under File ➤ Export ➤ Export Preferences. This opens the Preferences Export tab, where you can view or alter the settings. Refer to Figure 4-29.

65

CHAPTER 4 ■ SAVING OR EXPORTING YOUR FILES FOR THE WEB

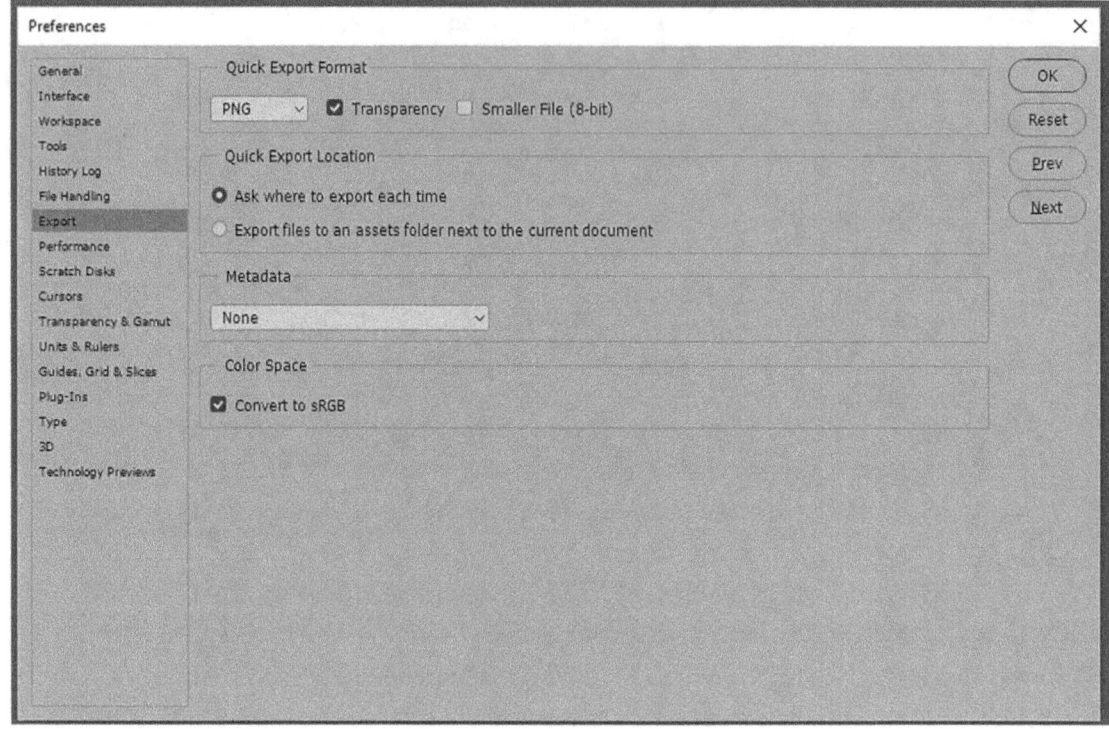

Figure 4-29. PNG preferences in the Quick Export Format option

Unlike in Option 1, however, you can choose if the PNG is transparent or not. Also, you can set the file to a smaller 8 bit or leave it at the larger size. Other options include the export location, metadata, and color space of sRGB. Click OK if you want to save the preference changes.

■ **Note** If you find you work more with JPEGs, GIFs, or SVGs, you can change the quick export to one of those options and it will reflect in the Quick Export instead of PNG. However, you can only use them one at a time. I find the options a bit limiting when working with more than one file type.

JPEG

If you are in the Export options and you switch to JPEG, you can only set the quality by number. Options like standard and progressive are not available. You can set the export location, metadata, and sRGB color space, however. Refer to Figure 4-30.

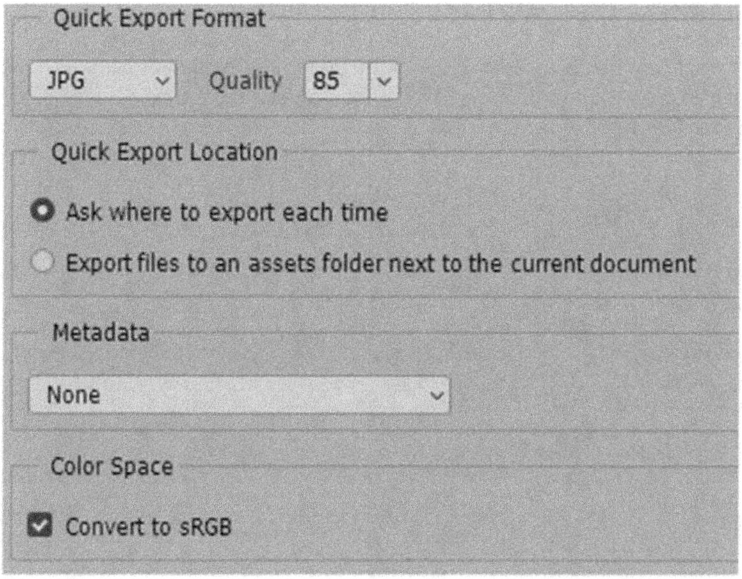

CHAPTER 4 ■ SAVING OR EXPORTING YOUR FILES FOR THE WEB

Figure 4-30. *JPEG preferences for the Quick Export Format option*

GIF

In the Quick export options you can switch to GIF, however there is no option to allow part of the GIF to remain transparent. Also, you cannot look at the color palette here. You can set the export location, metadata, and sRGB color space, however. Refer to Figure 4-31.

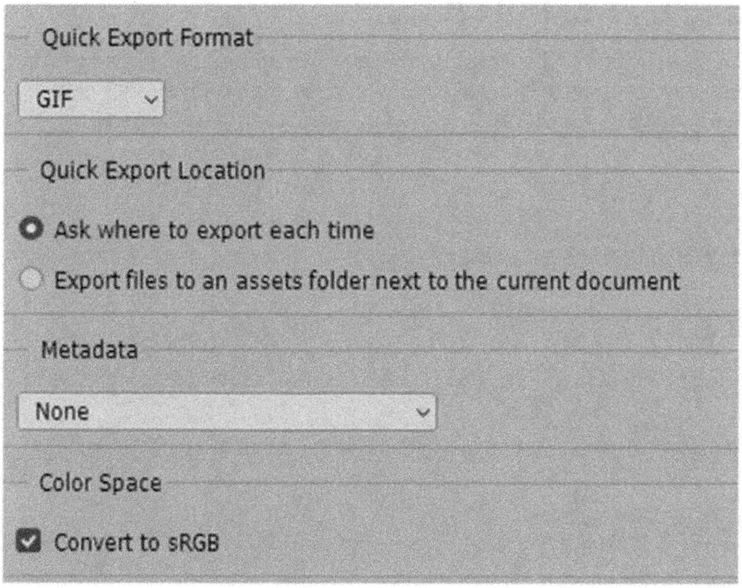

Figure 4-31. *GIF Preferences for the Quick Export Format option. You cannot set transparency here.*

67

SVG

SVG is a scalable graphic format. You can keep the vector-like shape of the image so that it does not become pixelated when scaled larger, as the other bitmap images would be. You can set the export location, metadata, and sRGB color space. Refer to Figure 4-32.

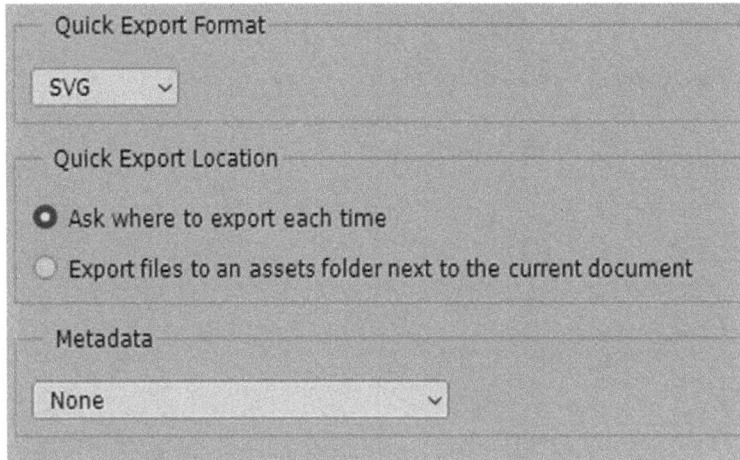

Figure 4-32. *SVG Preferences for the Quick Export Format option*

Quick Export Format is quick, but not always the best because it does not give all the options to format the images, or the option to preview your changes.

Options 3: File ➤ Export ➤ Export As…

The next option to look at is the Export As dialog box. This example allows you to control and preview your settings at the same time. As you can see, many of the options that are within the Export Preference settings can be found here. You can create several images with different scaling sizes and unique suffix names.

PNG

Choose PNG from the File Settings Format menu, as seen in Figure 4-33.

CHAPTER 4 ■ SAVING OR EXPORTING YOUR FILES FOR THE WEB

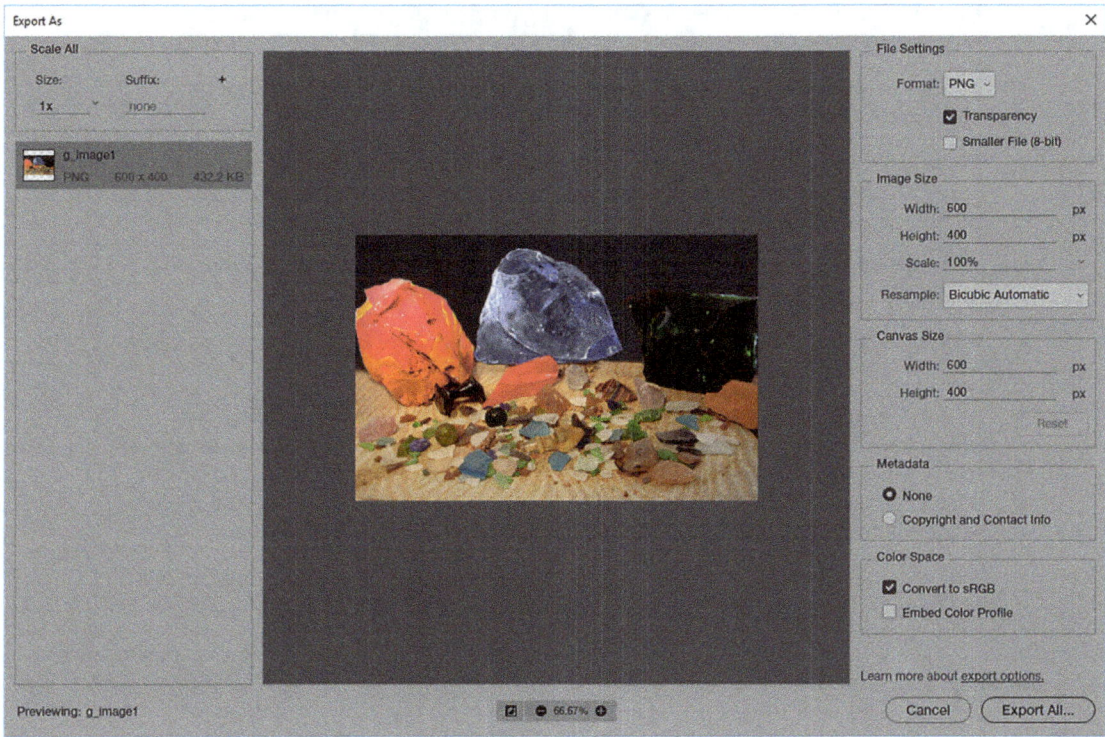

Figure 4-33. *PNG settings in the Export As dialog box*

- **File Settings**: Format: PNG or select another from the menu, set transparency, and set a smaller file size.

- **Image Size**: You can scale the original size of the image by width, height, and percentage, and the way that the pixels resample. Refer to Figure 4-34.

Figure 4-34. *Image resample options in the drop-down in the Export As dialog box*

69

- **Bicubic**: Examines the values of surrounding pixels. Using complex calculations, Bicubic produces smoother tonal gradations than Nearest Neighbor or Bilinear.

- **Bicubic Automatic**: Chooses the resampling method based on the document type and whether the document is scaling up or down.

- **Bicubic Sharper**: Reduces the size of an image based on bicubic interpolation with enhanced sharpening. This option maintains the detail in a resampled image. If Bicubic Sharper over-sharpens some areas of an image, try using Bicubic.

- **Bicubic Smoother**: Produces smoother results when enlarging images based on bicubic interpolation.

- **Bilinear**: Adds pixels by averaging the color values of surrounding pixels. It produces medium-quality results.

- **Nearest Neighbor**: A fast but less-precise method that replicates the pixels in an image. Used with illustrations containing edges that are not anti-aliased to preserve hard edges and produce a smaller file. It has been known to produce jagged effects, which becomes apparent when you distort or scale an image or perform multiple manipulations on a selection of the graphic.

- **Preserve Details**: A type of noise reduction for smoothing out noise as you upscale the image.

In this dialog box, you can also adjust canvas size separate from the image size, the metadata, and the color space. Refer to Figure 4-35.

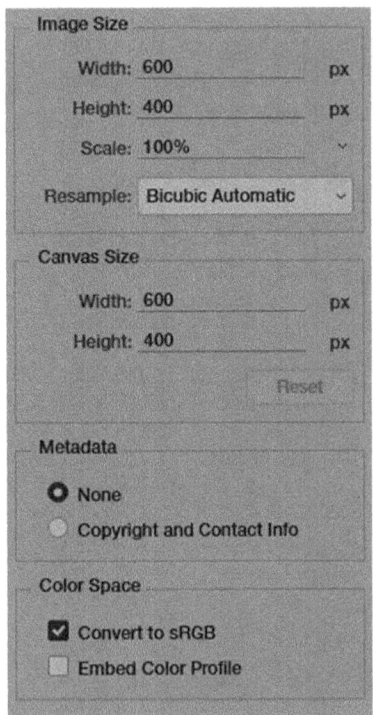

Figure 4-35. Examples of PNG settings in the Export As dialog box

CHAPTER 4 ■ SAVING OR EXPORTING YOUR FILES FOR THE WEB

JPEG

The JPEG format has a similar setting to PNG; however, you cannot adjust the matte background settings. Refer to Figure 4-36.

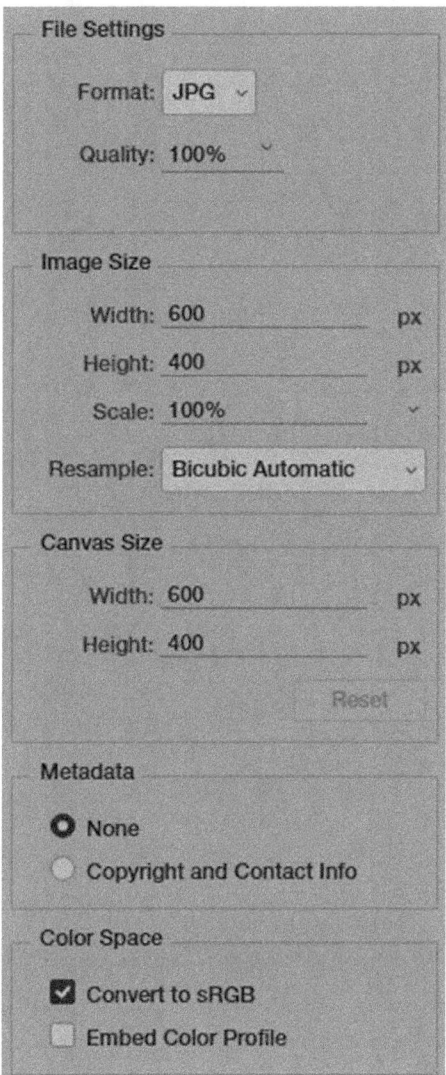

Figure 4-36. *Examples of JPEG settings in the Export As dialog box*

71

CHAPTER 4 ■ SAVING OR EXPORTING YOUR FILES FOR THE WEB

GIF

The GIF format has setting similar to PNG; however, you cannot adjust the transparency or matte background settings. Refer to Figure 4-37.

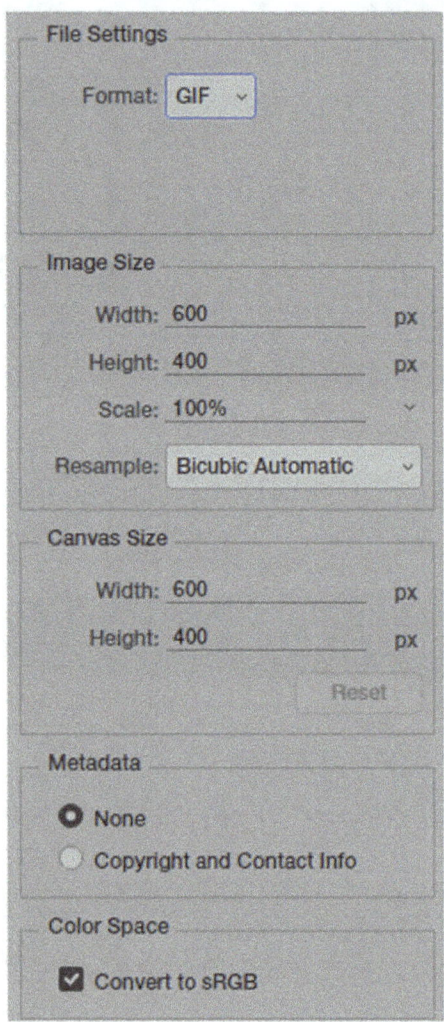

Figure 4-37. *Examples of GIF settings in the Export As dialog box*

CHAPTER 4 ■ SAVING OR EXPORTING YOUR FILES FOR THE WEB

SVG

SVG has settings similar to a PNG file; however, you cannot control the color profile as you can with the others. Refer to Figure 4-38.

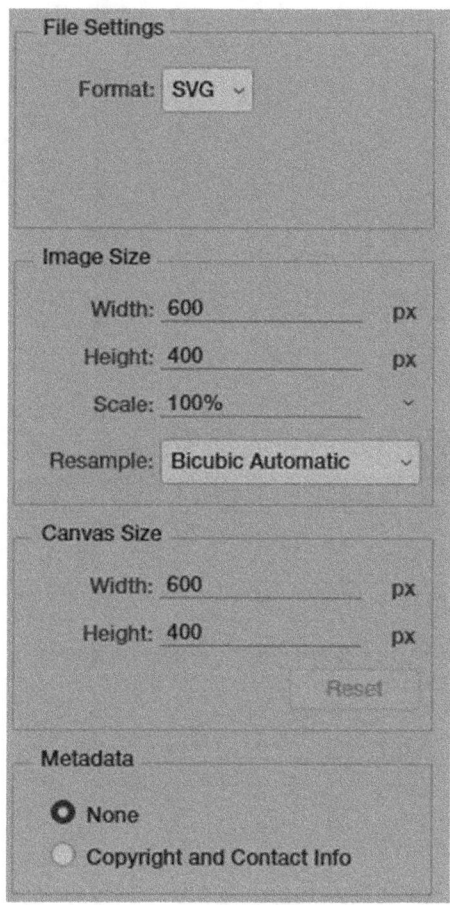

Figure 4-38. *Examples of SVG settings in the Export As dialog box*

When done, you can set more than one size for the same file on the left with the plus (+) icon. Next, choose Export All from the bottom of the dialog box, and then choose a folder to save the sizes in. The suffix that is added to the file lets you know which size was chosen. Use the Trash icon to remove sizes. Refer to Figure 4-39.

CHAPTER 4 ■ SAVING OR EXPORTING YOUR FILES FOR THE WEB

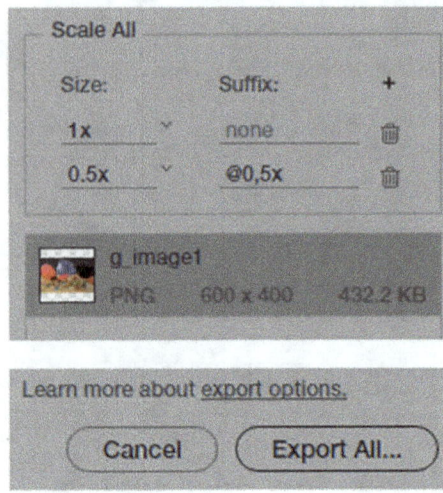

Figure 4-39. *Add sizes and then choose Export All to save the new web files*

Option 3's File ➤ Export ➤ Export As has a better preview option than Option 1's File ➤ Save As, but it does not allow you access certain matte and transparency options that you might need for some image projects. Is there a way to have it all for your raster images?

Option 4: File ➤ Export ➤ Save for Web (Legacy)

Personally, Option 4 is my favorite method to use when it comes to saving files for the web. It offers the most options when it comes to working with GIF files. Refer to Figure 4-40.

74

CHAPTER 4 ■ SAVING OR EXPORTING YOUR FILES FOR THE WEB

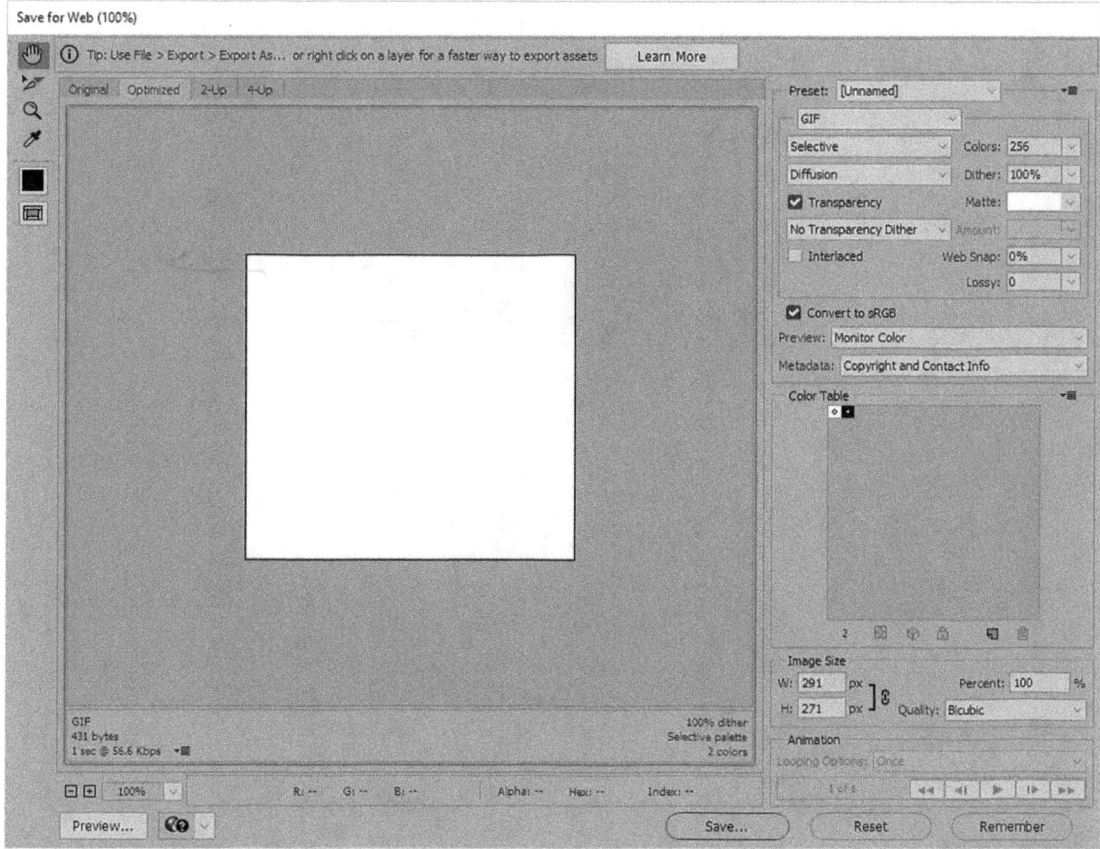

Figure 4-40. *The Save for Web (Legacy) dialog box*

The Save for Web (Legacy) dialog box has been used in many versions of Photoshop. It's similar to Export ➤ As, but it has many more options, including allowing you to save a GIF with transparency or as an animation, as you can see in the lower-right animation panel. You can even access the color table as you would using File ➤ Save As ➤ GIF. What's so wonderful about this layout is that you can use it to compare up to four layouts of the same image in different file formats or settings, and then you can choose which graphic adjustment looks best and uses the least amount of kbps (kilobytes per second). While size may not matter for viewing on your home computer, consider how fast the graphics load on a smaller device, like a tablet or smartphone. Refer to Figure 4-41.

CHAPTER 4 ■ SAVING OR EXPORTING YOUR FILES FOR THE WEB

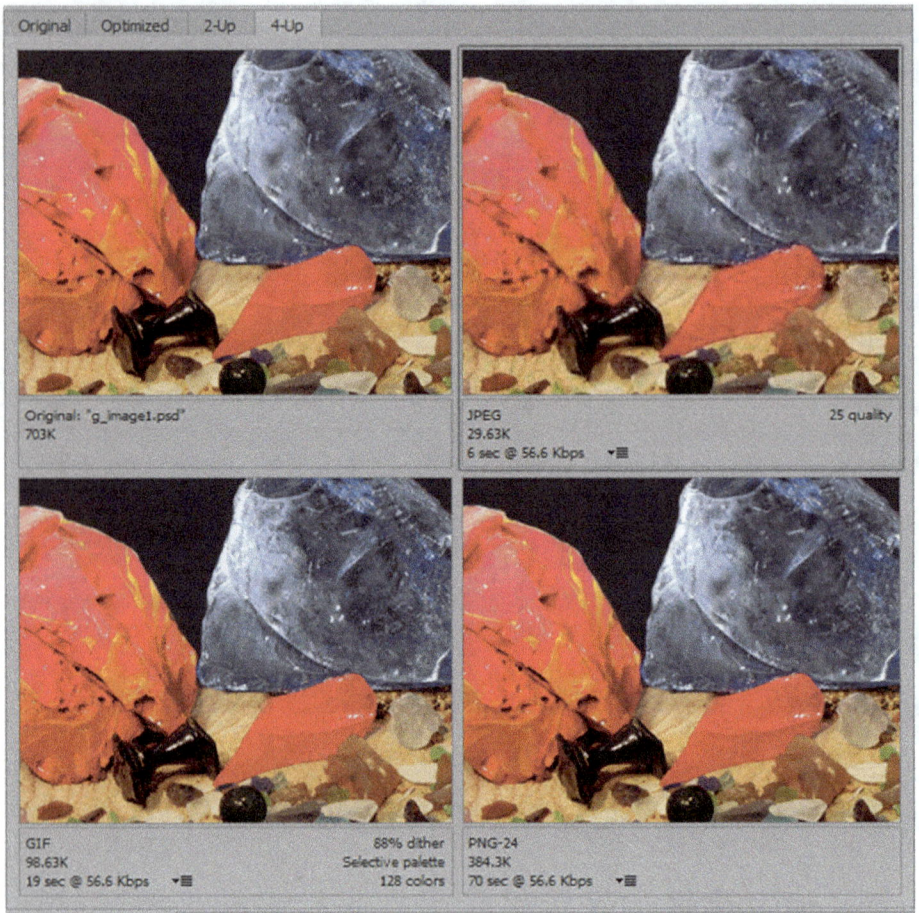

Figure 4-41. *The Save for Web (Legacy) dialog box lets you view four settings at once: Original, JPEG, GIF and PNG*

On the left side are a few tools. Refer to Figure 4-42.

- The **Hand tool (H)** allows you to move to the different selections and moving all image previews in the tabs at the same time.

- The **Slice Select tool (C)** allows you to select slices in an image and edit them if you created any earlier using the slice tool. You'll look more at this tool later in Chapter 5.

- The magnifying glass, or **Zoom tool (Z)**, allows you to Zoom in on an area so that you can compare all images and their colors in that area at the same time.

- The **Eyedropper tool (I)** allows you to select a color in the image and then check it in the Eyedropper Color pallet. Once you know the color, you can then use this color for a pallet background color, or add it to swatches, or check Color Libraries.

- The last tool is **Toggle Slices Visibility (Q)**, where you can turn the slices preview on or off as you preview an image.

CHAPTER 4 ■ SAVING OR EXPORTING YOUR FILES FOR THE WEB

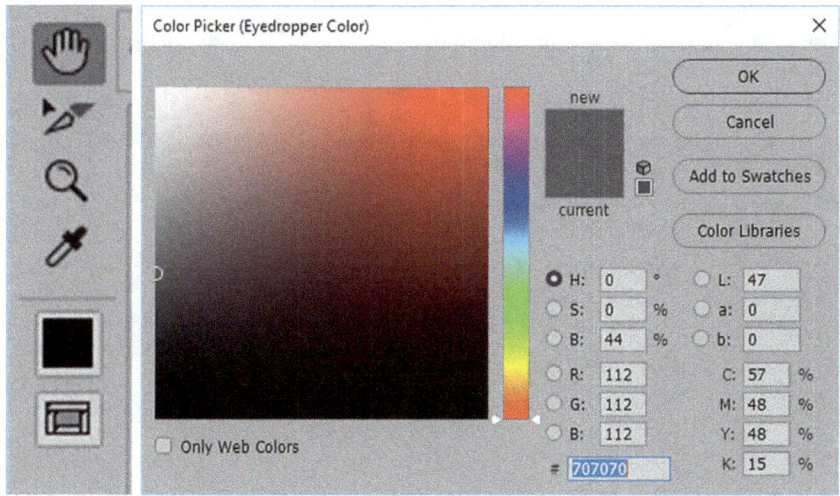

Figure 4-42. *The Save for Web (Legacy) tools to work with your image file*

Moving over to the right, there are several different presets that you can choose from or make your own. While you can work with most web bit-map file formats. The only file format that you cannot preview in this area are SVGs, which are vector. If you are working with SVGs, refer to Option 3: Export As settings. Refer to Figure 4-43 for the presets.

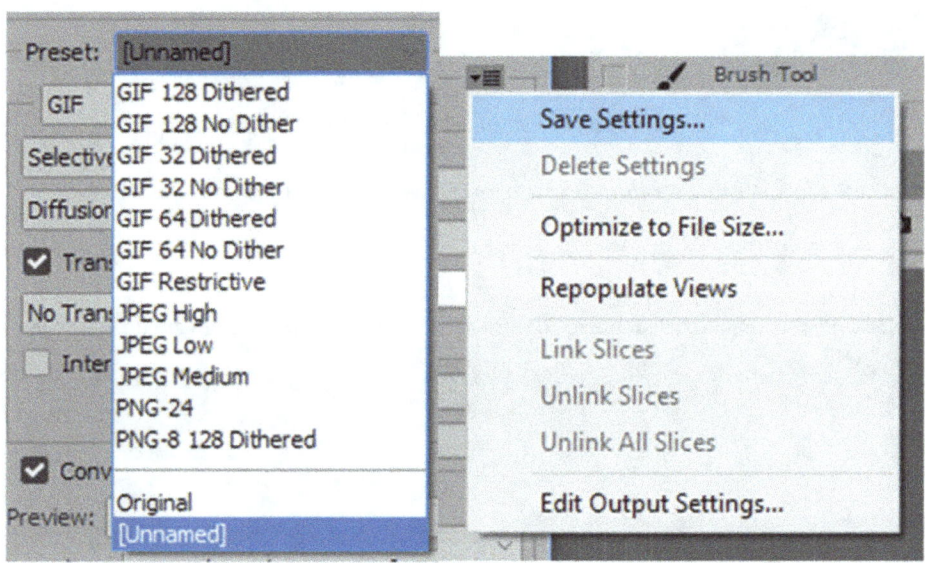

Figure 4-43. *There are many presets you can choose from or you can create your own*

77

CHAPTER 4 ■ SAVING OR EXPORTING YOUR FILES FOR THE WEB

In the menu, you can save settings and optimize file size, as well as link and unlink slices.

In the Color Table options (see Figure 4-44), you can add new colors, delete, edit, and sort colors so that you have the optimum quality and file size.

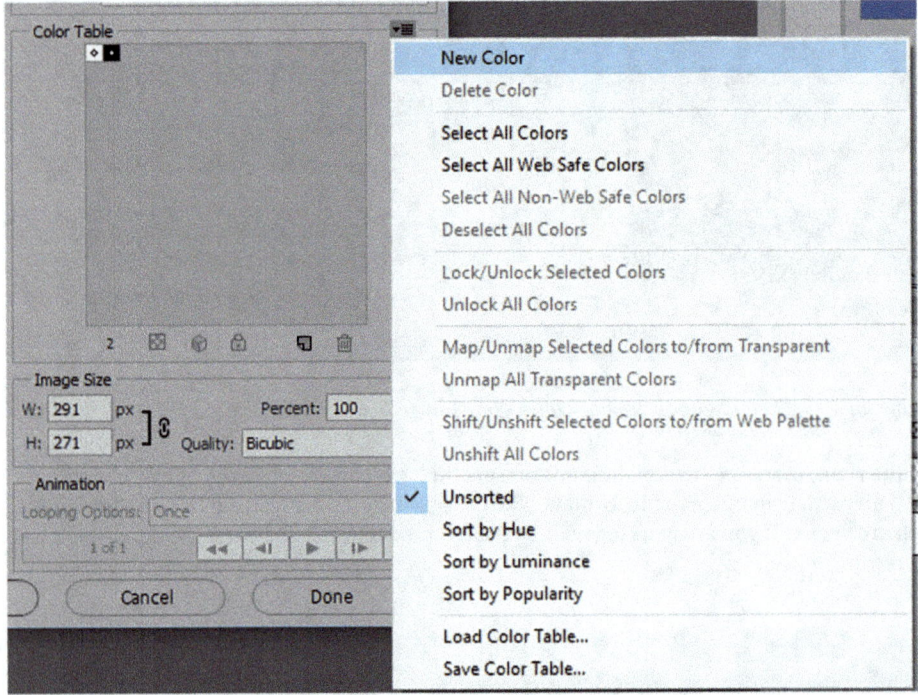

Figure 4-44. *The Save for Web dialog box allows you to sort colors for some files for optimum quality*

Let's now look at the file formats that we can work with for the web, and review some of their options.

GIF

While you can use several presets that are available to GIFs, as seen in Figure 4-43, you can create your own settings. Refer to Figure 4-45.

CHAPTER 4 ■ SAVING OR EXPORTING YOUR FILES FOR THE WEB

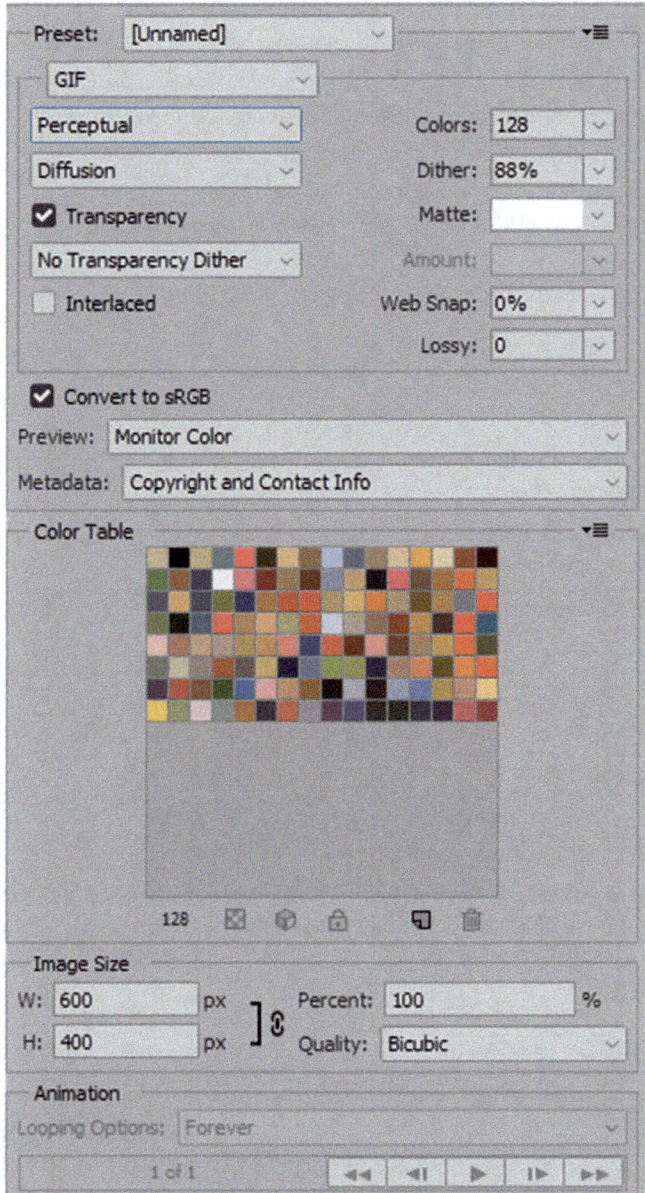

Figure 4-45. *The Save for Web (Legacy) dialog box setting for a static GIF file*

In the next drop-down menu (color reduction algorithm), whatever option you choose will alter the color amount.

- **Perceptual**: Creates a custom palette of color that gives priority to the colors that the human eye has greater sensitivity to, or that are most pleasing.

79

- **Selective**: Similar to Perceptual, but also favors the broad range of continuous colors and the preservation of colors on the web. It usually produces an image with the greatest color integrity.

- **Adaptive**: Samples colors that appear most commonly in the image. Images with a majority of red have a greater concentration of red shades.

- **Restrictive (Web: 216 colors)**: Compensates between Mac and PC computer monitors. If your image does not have 216 colors, they are removed. Sets Colors to Auto.

- **Custom**: You can create a custom pallet in the Color Table dialog box. Sets Colors to Auto.

- **Black and White**: Sets the colors to black and white. Sets Colors to Auto.

- **Grayscale**: All the shades of gray. Sets Colors to Auto.

- **System (Mac OS)**: There are 256 colors for a macOS system palette. Sets Colors to Auto. The color table differs by operating system.

- **System(Windows)**: There are 256 colors for a Windows OS system palette. Sets Colors to Auto. The color table differs by operating system.

The following are in the Specify the Dither Algorithm drop-down menu.

- **No dither**: The default for no dither or none.

- **Diffusion**: A random structure dither that is good for preserving minute details and text in logos.

- **Pattern**: A halftone-like square pattern.

- **Noise**: This reduces the edge pattern if you plan to slice up your image for an HTML background with <div> tag or within a table. (You will look at slices later in chapter 5.)

- **Dither**: You can adjust the amount of dither by percentage. Check whether you want transparency and then choose the type of dither, which is like the other dither setting but for transparent sections in the Specify transparency Dither Algorithm drop-down menu.

    - No Transparency Dither
    - Diffusion Transparency Dither
    - Pattern Transparency Dither
    - Noise Transparency Dither

- **Amount**: You can adjust the amount of transparency dither by percentage. If you are not using a transparent background, set a matte color that fills in the transparent area, which can be the same as the background color for your site or whatever color you choose. Do this in Other, which brings up the color picker. Refer to Figure 4-46.

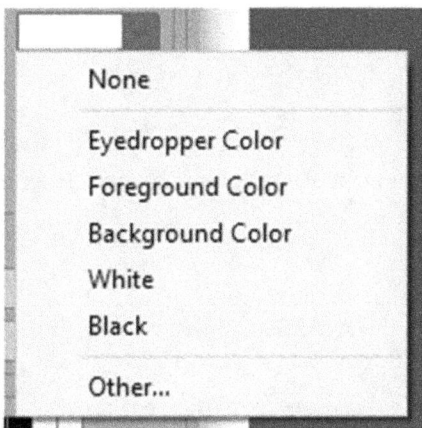

Figure 4-46. *The Save for Web (Legacy) dialog box setting for matte color background*

- **Interlaced**: Similar to the Progressive option in the JPEG setting. The image loads in parts, gradually becoming clearer with each scan.
- **Web Snap**: Snaps close colors to web pallet based on tolerance.
- **Lossy**: Controls the amount of file compression for that specific file format.
- **Covert to sRGB**: Makes sure the file is in the correct sRGB setting.
- **Preview**: Displays how the colors appear in monitors or screens.
- **Metadata**: Sets information on the file, such as copyright and contact information.
- **Color Table**: Shows which colors are currently in the table. You can edit these settings.
- **Image Size**: Allows you to adjust the size of the image using pixels in a uniform proportions (linked), separately (unlink), or by percentage, and sets the quality.

The following are from the quality (resampling method) drop-down menu:

- **Nearest Neighbor**: A fast but less-precise method that replicates the pixels in an image. Used with illustrations containing edges that are not anti-aliased to preserve hard edges and produce a smaller file. It has been known to produce jagged effects, which becomes apparent when you distort or scale an image, or perform multiple manipulations on a selection of the graphic.
- **Bilinear**: Adds pixels by averaging the color values of surrounding pixels. It produces medium-quality results.
- **Bicubic**: Exams of the values of surrounding pixels. Using complex calculations, Bicubic produces smoother tonal gradations than Nearest Neighbor or Bilinear.
- **Bicubic Smoother**: For enlarging images based on Bicubic interpolation but designed to produce smoother results.
- **Bicubic Sharper**: Reduces the size of an image based on bicubic interpolation with enhanced sharpening. This option maintains the detail in a resampled image. If Bicubic Sharper over sharpens some areas of an image, try using Bicubic.

CHAPTER 4 ■ SAVING OR EXPORTING YOUR FILES FOR THE WEB

You can also preview a GIF animation and choose the amount of time it loops. We look at this setting in more detail in Chapter 6.

JPEG

JPEG has some similar settings to GIF in this dialog box. You will only note the different settings here. Refer to Figure 4-47.

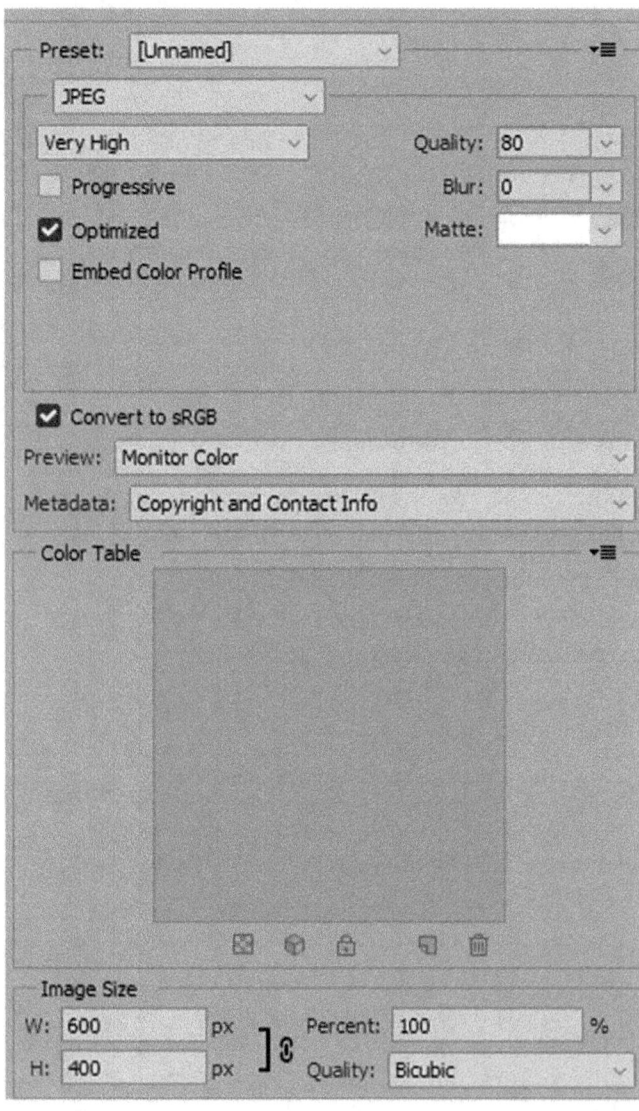

Figure 4-47. *The Save for Web (Legacy) dialog box JPEG setting*

You can either set the quality via the drop-down menu (Low, Medium, High, Very, High, or Maximum) or in the Quality text box by typing or using the slider. They all reflect the results of the change. Refer to Figure 4-48.

Figure 4-48. *The Save for Web dialog box setting JPEG quality control*

- **Progressive**: Refers to how the quality becomes greater with multiple passes or scans.
- **Blur**: Can be adjusted to reduce artifacts or graininess in a photograph, though the image may not appear as sharp and clear as it was before.
- **Matte**: Since JPEGs cannot have transparency, adding a matte background to match your website's solid background is an appropriate choice in an area you would normally consider transparent.
- **Embed Color Profile**: Allows you to include color information with the file (ICC Profile).

As with GIFs, you can make sure they are set to sRGB, view a preview, and set the metadata. You cannot use the Color Table because the file is in RGB and not indexed. Digital Photos in the JPEG format use many more colors, so there would be too much color information to include in a color table.

Like the GIF files, you can also adjust the size and quality of the image with various settings.

PNG-8

This file format for 8-bit files has many of the same settings as a GIF file (refer to this area if you are unsure what an unfamiliar setting does). You will look at only the different ones here. Refer to Figure 4-49.

CHAPTER 4 ■ SAVING OR EXPORTING YOUR FILES FOR THE WEB

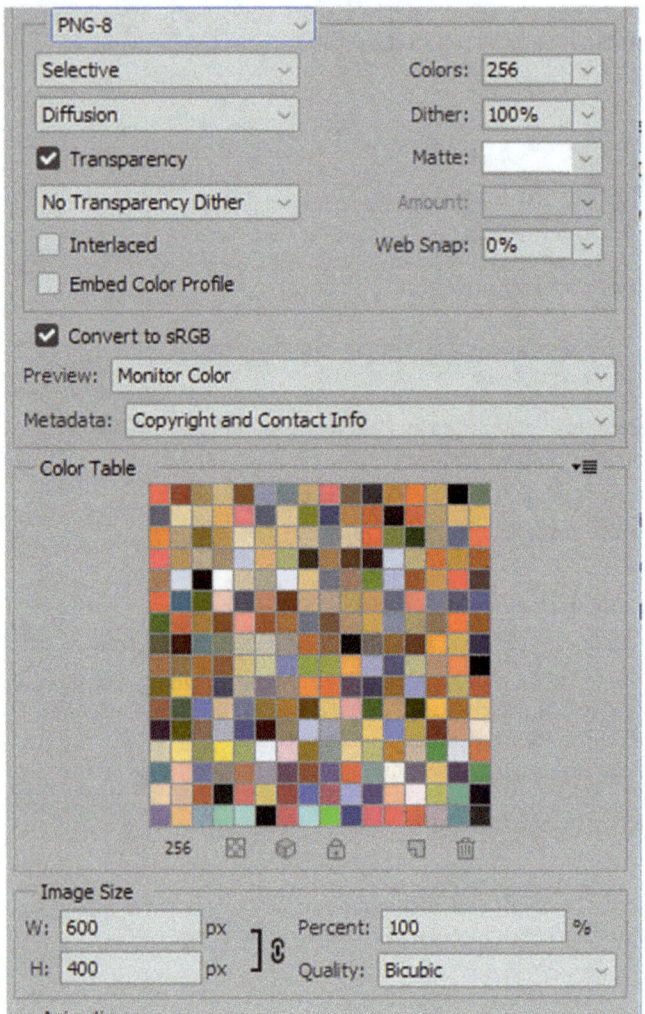

Figure 4-49. *The Save for Web (Legacy) dialog box setting PNG-8*

Like GIFs, you can set transparency and work with the Color Table.

- **Embed Color Profile**: Allows you to include color information with the file (ICC Profile).

■ **Note**   Unlike GIFs, you cannot set lossy compression, and you must use the other settings to reduce the file size. Like GIFs and JPEGs, you can adjust the image size and its quality with the settings in the lower right.

CHAPTER 4 ■ SAVING OR EXPORTING YOUR FILES FOR THE WEB

PNG-24

PNG (24 bit) has fewer settings than PNG-8 because it is a higher-quality file. Many of the settings are like the GIF; however, I will only note the different ones here. Refer to Figure 4-50.

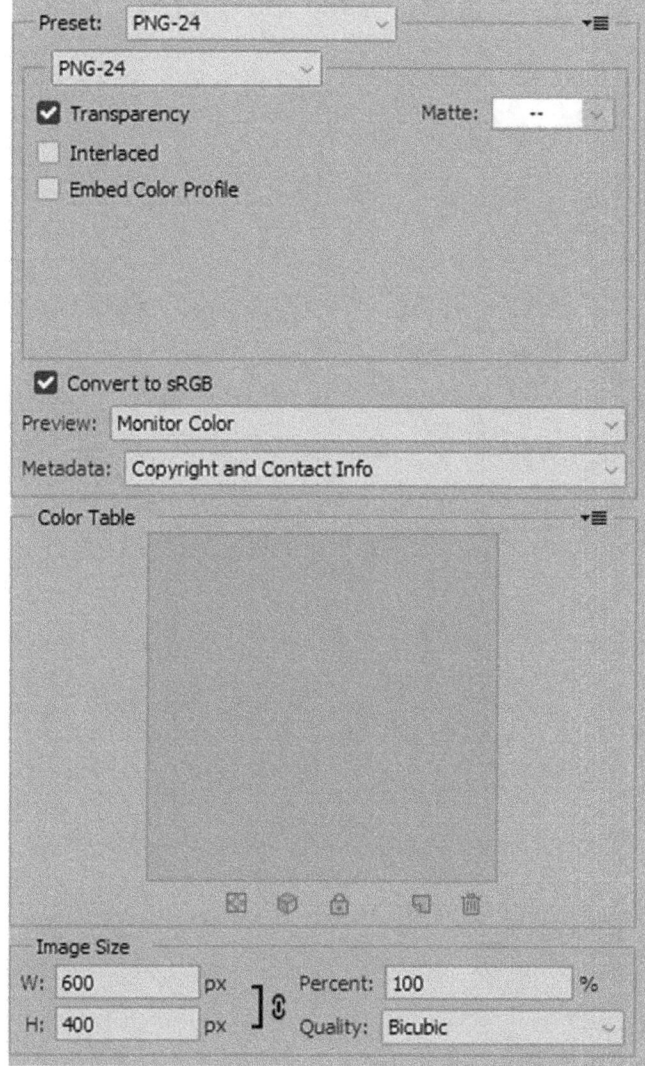

Figure 4-50. *The Save for Web (Legacy) dialog box setting PNG-24*

PNG-24 files can contain varying degrees of transparency (0–100%) that you built in your original file. Matte is not available if transparency is checked, since it blends into the web background.

As with the PNG-8, you can embed the color profile, preview, and add metadata. Because PNG-24 uses a large number of colors, like a JPEG, you cannot use the color table to check the colors. Like the other formats, you can still use the Image Size area to adjust the size and quality.

85

CHAPTER 4 ■ SAVING OR EXPORTING YOUR FILES FOR THE WEB

WMBP

WBMP is a file format that you haven't worked with yet. WBMP, or Wireless Bitmap (.wmb, wbmp), images are monochrome (black and white) so that the image size is kept to a minimum. A black pixel is denoted by 0 and a white pixel is denoted by 1. For colored images, Wireless Application Protocol (WAP) supports the Portable Network Graphics (PNG) format. This type of graphic is used for mobile computing devices. Refer to Figure 4-51.

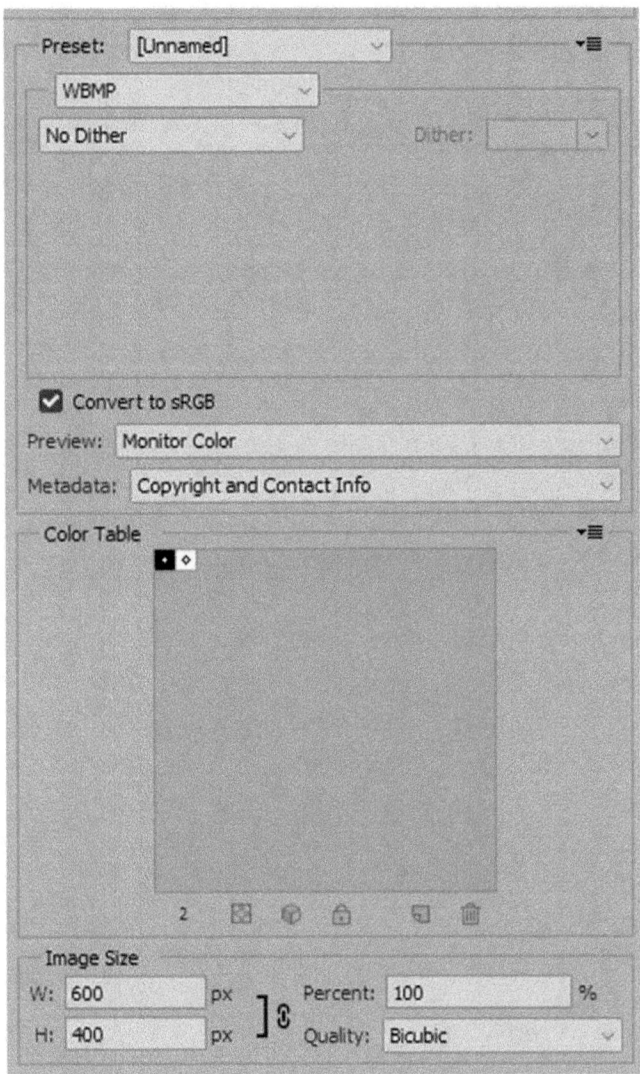

Figure 4-51. *The Save for Web (Legacy) dialog box setting WBMP*

There are few similar settings that you can adjust, such as dither, but since it is black and white, the image can look very grainy and low quality.

86

CHAPTER 4 ■ SAVING OR EXPORTING YOUR FILES FOR THE WEB

The other things you can do in this dialog box are preview the image in the browser of your choice, and then save the files in the correct folders. Refer to Figure 4-52.

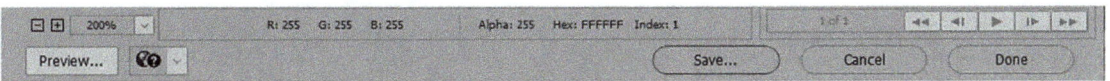

Figure 4-52. *When you have completed the setting for your images, you can either preview or save them*

When you click Save, you are presented with options, such as those seen in Figure 4-53.

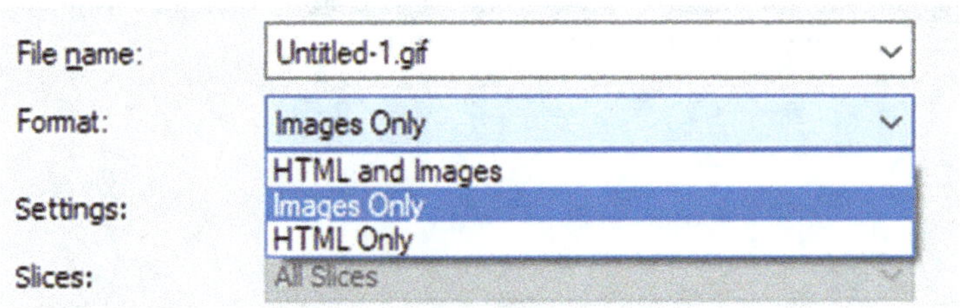

Figure 4-53. *Options when you save your image*

- **HTML and Images**: This is an option if you are working with slices and you want to keep the shape of the page as you have in Photoshop. You could bring this file into Adobe Dreamweaver and continue to edit the layout.

- **Images Only**: Best if you are only working with single images and will add them to Dreamweaver wherever they are required.

- **HTML Only**: Use the basic layout you created and exclude the images. I don't use this option often because I prefer to create my layout using Dreamweaver; however, if you're working in a group, check with your team what method they prefer for their workflow.

- **Settings**: I usually leave the settings at default. However, you can choose custom, background image, XHTML, or more advanced custom settings. Refer to Figure 4-54.

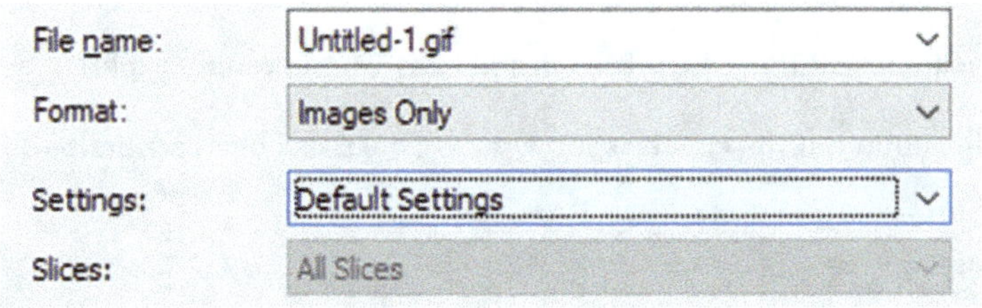

Figure 4-54. *Options for when you save your image and default or custom settings*

If your file has slices, you can choose to export all the slices or only the User(created) or Slices (user and auto) that were selected. You'll look at slices in Chapter 5.

Additional Options That You Can Use to Export Files for the Web

Depending on how you have built your original file, it may contain one of the items discussed in the following sections.

Artboards

You can either create an artboard when you start a file (File ➤ New) or while building it. In the Layers panel, in the upper-side menu, choose New Artboard. You can then use the Properties panel to modify it further.

Artboards are great if you must design layouts for multiple devices and want to store them all in one file. Each artboard is like a folder that contains a collection of layers. Refer to Figure 4-55.

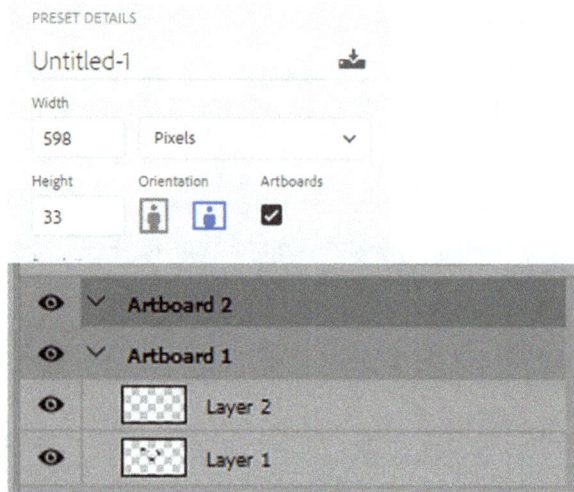

Figure 4-55. *How multiple artboards could appear in the Layer panel if the option is checked when you create a new document*

To Export you your artboards, you can choose File ➤ Export ➤ Export As (all artboards will be exported in the file).

The web files that you can export include BMP, JPEG, PDF, PNG-8, and PNG-24; you cannot export as a GIF or SVG using this option.

Artboards To Files provides exporting options if you check Export Options, but the choices are limited. Refer to Figure 4-56.

CHAPTER 4 ■ SAVING OR EXPORTING YOUR FILES FOR THE WEB

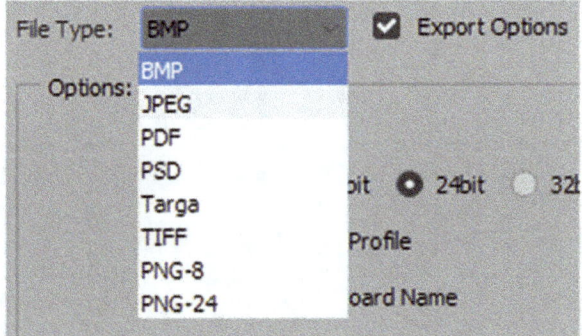

Figure 4-56. *Options for the Artboards To Files dialog box*

89

CHAPTER 4 ■ SAVING OR EXPORTING YOUR FILES FOR THE WEB

■ **Note** Artboards To PDF has the exact same layout; however, you can only choose a PDF file type.

When you have adjusted the settings, click the Run button so that you can save the files.
For more information on working with artboards, check out
`https://helpx.adobe.com/photoshop/using/artboards.html`.

Layer Comps

Sometimes a designer has multiple variations of a similar file. In this case, they might want to create a layer comp and store them all in one file. In the Layer Comps panel, you can store various states for your clients to view, such as layer visibility (visible or invisible), layer position within the document, and layer appearance (styles and blending mode). Refer to Figure 4-57.

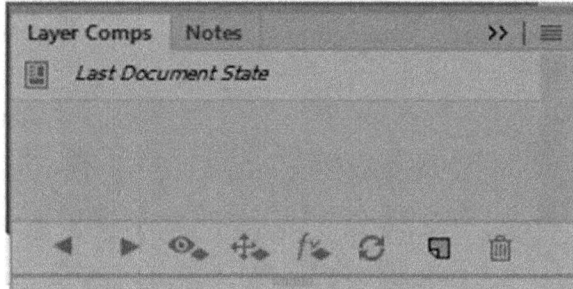

Figure 4-57. *The Layer Comps panel*

If you want to export your layer comps for the web, you can select File ➤ Export ➤ Layer Comps To Files or Layer Comps To PDF. Refer to Figure 4-58.

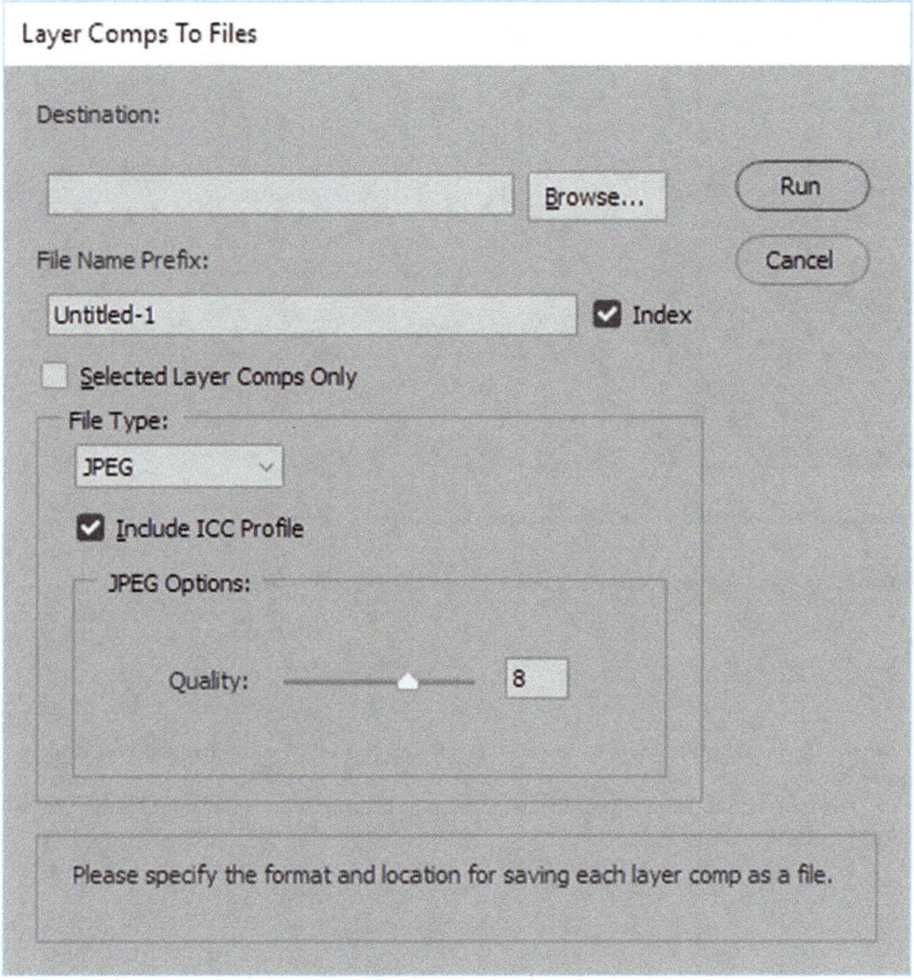

Figure 4-58. The layer comps settings are similar to artboards

However, as you can see, some options for export are limited, and you cannot export as a GIF or SVG using this option.

Note To export a layer comp as a PDF, the file must be saved first. The History panel has an item similar to Layer Comps called Snapshot (camera icon). Snapshots cannot be saved once the file is saved closed. If you want to save a snapshot rather than a layer comp, you can use the Create New Document from the current state icon. Refer to Figure 4-59.

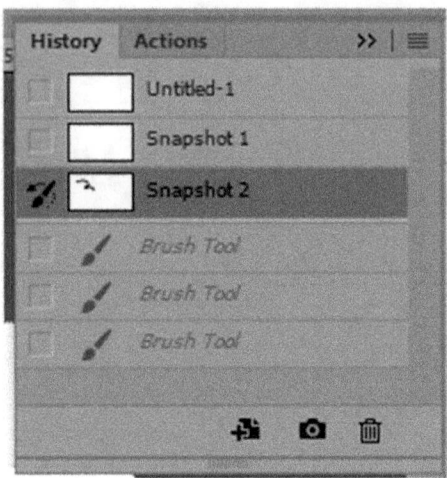

Figure 4-59. *Example of using a snapshot in the History panel*

For more information on layer comps, refer to https://helpx.adobe.com/ca/photoshop/using/layer-comps.html.

Layers

Most .PSD or Photoshop documents contain one or more layers. If you can't find your Layers panel, look under Window menu ➤ Layers.

If you just have a document with multiple graphic layers, such as buttons, you can use File ➤ Export ➤ Layers to Files. Refer to Figure 4-60.

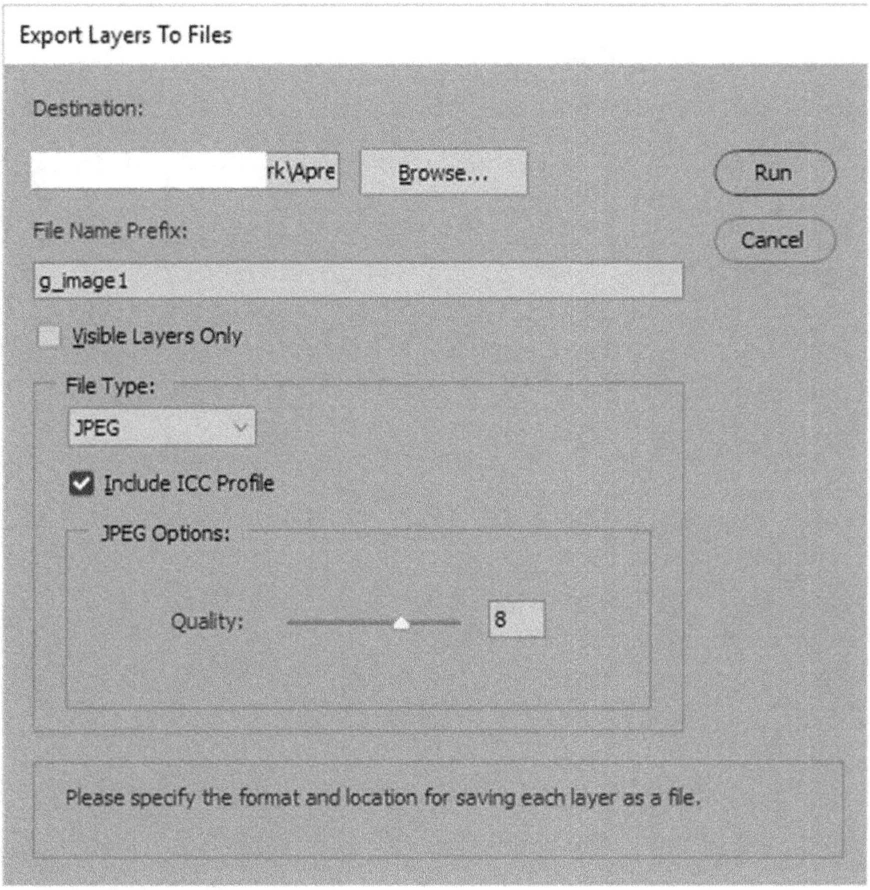

Figure 4-60. Export Layers To Files

As you can see, some options for export are limited, and you cannot export as a GIF or SVG using this option.

> **Note** A final option available for exporting options is File ➤ Generate ➤ Image ➤ Assets. You can use this with the Layers panel to further generate images that are JPEG, PNG, or GIF. To do this, you have to name each layer in a specific way, which can get quite complicated. If this is an option you are interested in, for more information visit https://helpx.adobe.com/photoshop/using/generate-assets-layers.html.

Summary

This chapter covered a lot of ground as it relates to exporting images in the correct file formats. Depending upon your workflow, you may prefer some options over others; the choice is up to you. In the next chapter, you look at some of the tools used in Photoshop CC to speed up automation in exporting and slicing images.

CHAPTER 5

Actions to Speed up File Conversion and Slicing Tools

In this chapter, you continue to explore some of the many ways to you to export your images for the web using Photoshop. You will look at some related action tools that can help speed up the export process should you have a lot of images that require similar formatting. Later in the chapter, you look at how to slice images and how to zoom in closer to images.

> **Note** This chapter does not have any actual projects; however, you can use the files in the Chapter 5 folder to practice opening and viewing for this lesson. They are at `https://github.com/Apress/graphics-multimedia-web-adobe-creative-cloud`.

Actions to Speed up the File Conversion Process

If you have a lot of files that you save in a certain format for the web, you can use the Actions panel. Refer to Figure 5-1.

CHAPTER 5 ACTIONS TO SPEED UP FILE CONVERSION AND SLICING TOOLS

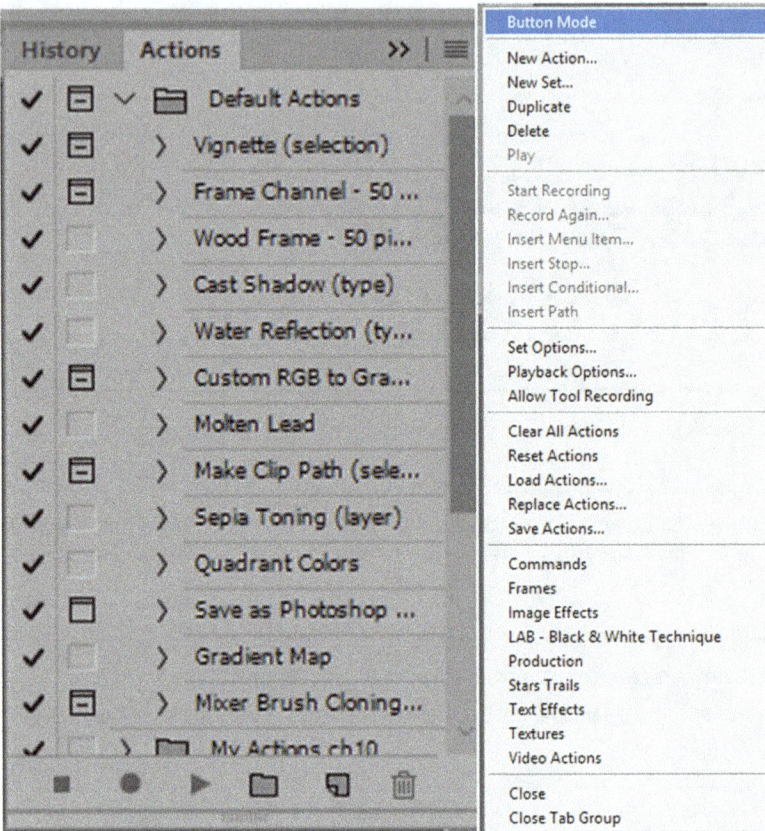

Figure 5-1. Speed up your export file conversion using the Actions panel

For example, let's say you have several photos that you want to set to a specific file size and save them as JPEGs. I'll explain the steps to go about doing this.

With your Actions panel open and no other files open, click the folder called Create new set. Refer to Figure 5-2.

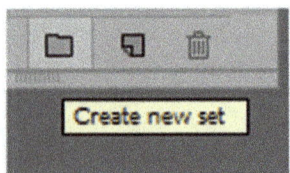

Figure 5-2. Create a new action set

Call the new set Images for the Web and click OK. Refer to Figure 5-3.

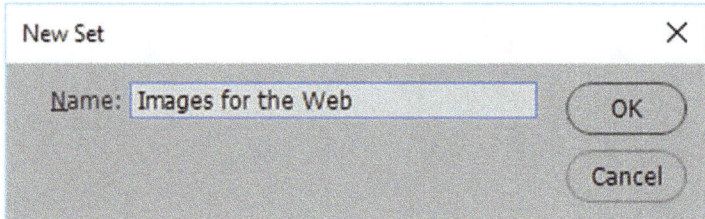

Figure 5-3. *Give the new set a name*

At this point, it is a blank folder that you will add an action set to, as seen in Figure 5-4.

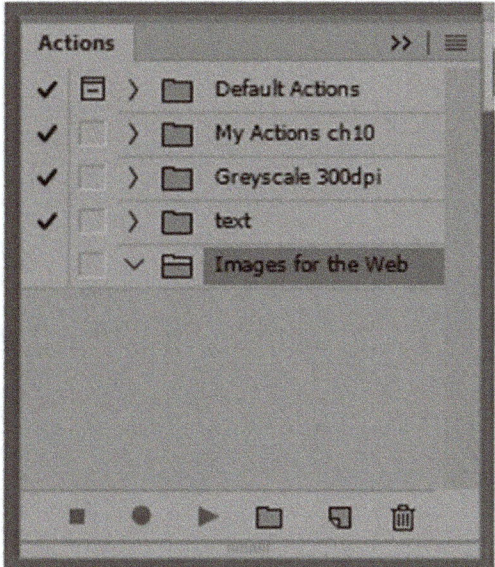

Figure 5-4. *An empty actions set folder*

While the folder is open, click the Create New Action button next to the Folder icon. Save the action as Save JPEG Photos, as seen in Figure 5-5.

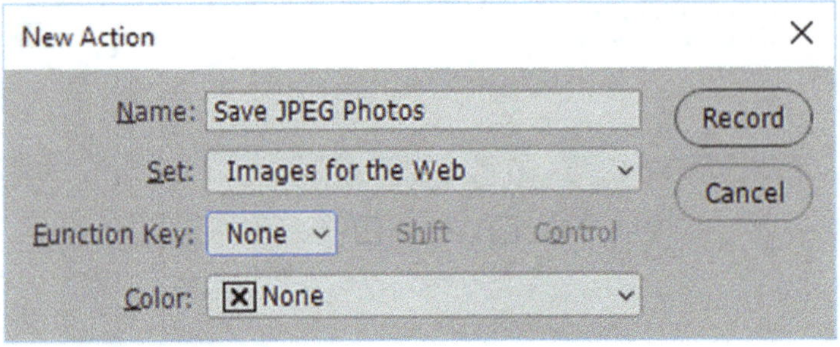

CHAPTER 5 ACTIONS TO SPEED UP FILE CONVERSION AND SLICING TOOLS

Figure 5-5. Adding a new action

Alternatively, you can also move the action to another set, give it a key function, and give the action a color for better identification. For now, leave the settings as is and click the Record button.

You will now notice that the little red Record button is on in the Actions panel. You can begin recording your actions as you move along, as seen in Figure 5-6.

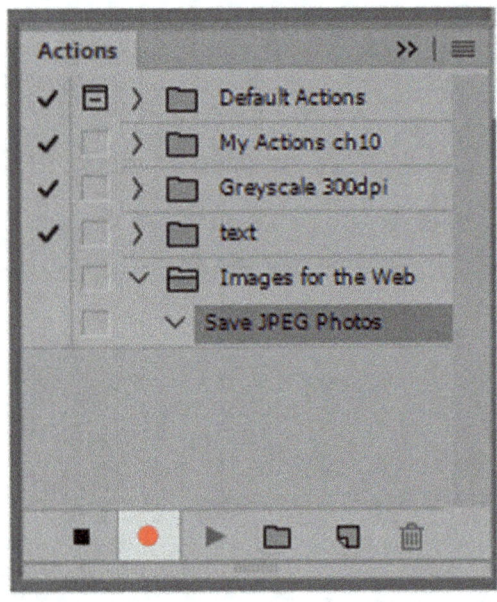

Figure 5-6. The red record circle in the actions panel is on

If at any time you wish to stop recording, click the square icon to the left. If you make a mistake in an action, you can now use the Trash icon to remove it. You can then resume by clicking the Record button and redoing the actions.

Afterward, to test an action, click the triangle (play) to the right of the Record button. Right now, nothing will happen until you add another action in Photoshop.

Go to File ➤ Open and locate a folder that contains the image or an image that you want to convert.

Select the file and click the Open button. The Actions panel has saved this action, as seen in Figure 5-7.

98

CHAPTER 5 ACTIONS TO SPEED UP FILE CONVERSION AND SLICING TOOLS

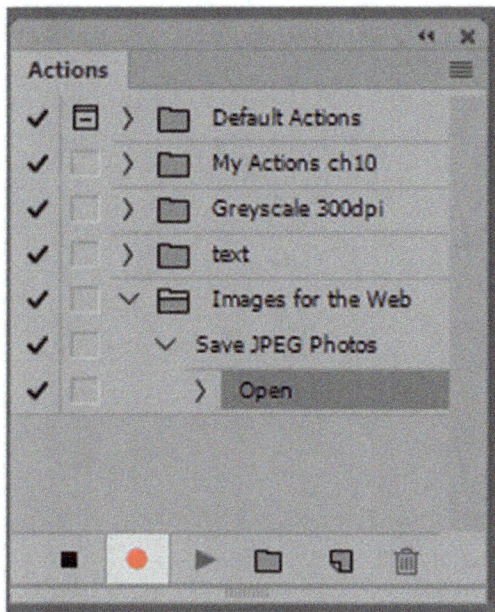

Figure 5-7. *The red record circle in the actions panel is on and has recorded an action of opening a file*

Now choose Image ➤ Duplicate from the main menu so that you don't override the original file. Refer to Figure 5-8.

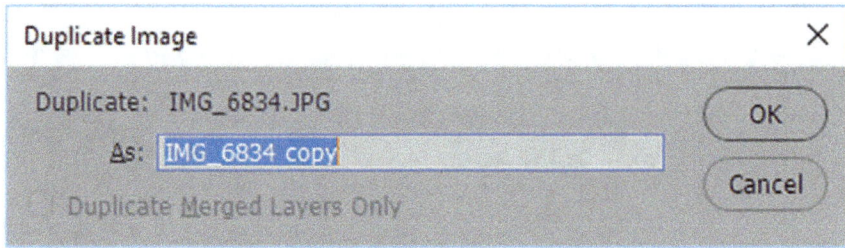

Figure 5-8. *Duplicate the image*

A new action has been added, as seen in Figure 5-9.

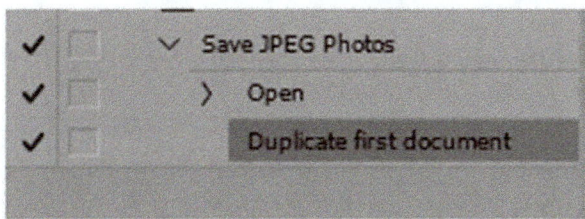

Figure 5-9. *The action duplicating the image has been added*

99

At this point, you may want to do some work or a minor color correction to the document that might be different for each file. Turn off the recording in the Actions panel. In the Action menu, select Insert Stop. Refer to Figure 5-10.

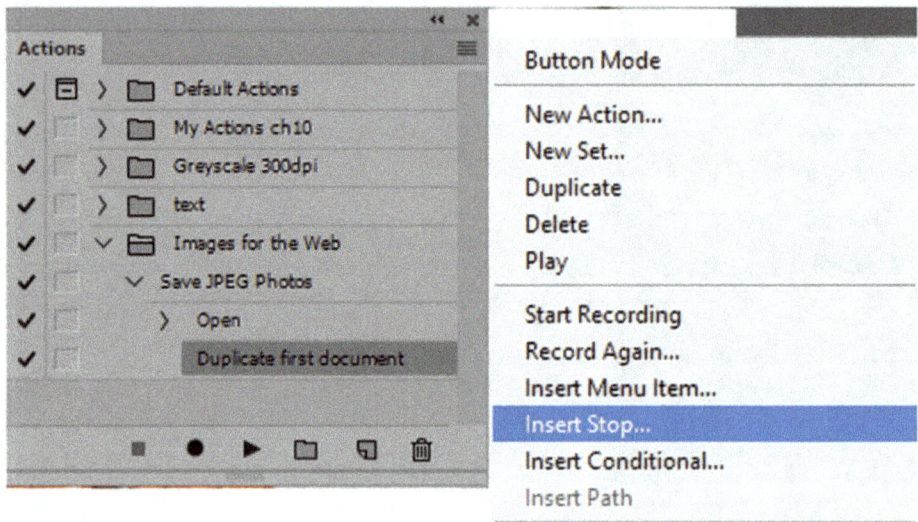

Figure 5-10. *Insert a stop when you need to do some custom actions to your file*

Type a message that reminds you why you have stopped, as seen in Figure 5-11.

Figure 5-11. *The message added to the stop as a reminder*

Check Allow Continue at the bottom of the dialog box, and then click OK on the right.
Now click the Record button in the Actions panel to continue creating the steps, as seen in Figure 5-12.

CHAPTER 5 ACTIONS TO SPEED UP FILE CONVERSION AND SLICING TOOLS

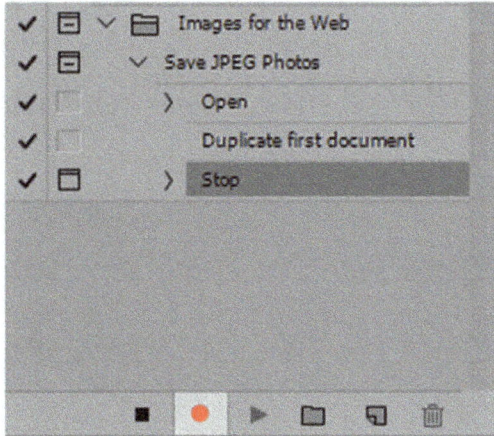

Figure 5-12. *Continue recording*

In the main menu, choose Image ➤ Image Size.

Set the image size at whatever you require for your website images. In my case, the photos are for a gallery, so I made sure that it was set to 72 pixels/inch, as seen in Figure 5-13.

Figure 5-13. *Set a specific image size for all images*

■ **Note** Your image may vary in size, depending upon your layout. You may also have to add actions, depending on how you set up your layers or blends.

When you're done with the Image Size dialog box, click OK. This action is now added to the Actions panel, as seen in Figure 5-14. If at any time you need to adjust the action, you can double-click it to open that dialog box and adjust the setting again to refine it.

101

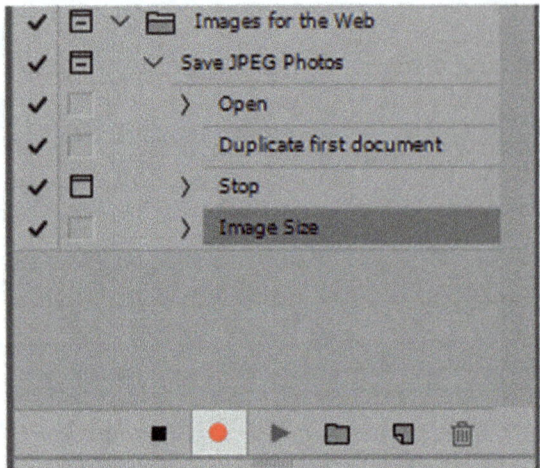

Figure 5-14. Add the image size setting while recording

Go to File ➤ Save As and save the new image as a JPEG with a new name in the folder of your choice, as seen in Figure 5-15.

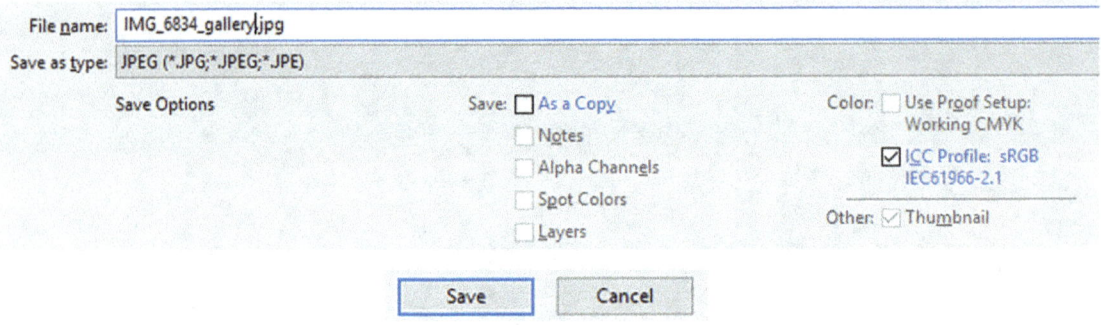

Figure 5-15. Save the file as a JPEG

When done, click the Save button to save the file. The JPEG options will appear. Choose your optimum file size and quality while watching the preview for changes as seen in Figure 5-16.

CHAPTER 5 ACTIONS TO SPEED UP FILE CONVERSION AND SLICING TOOLS

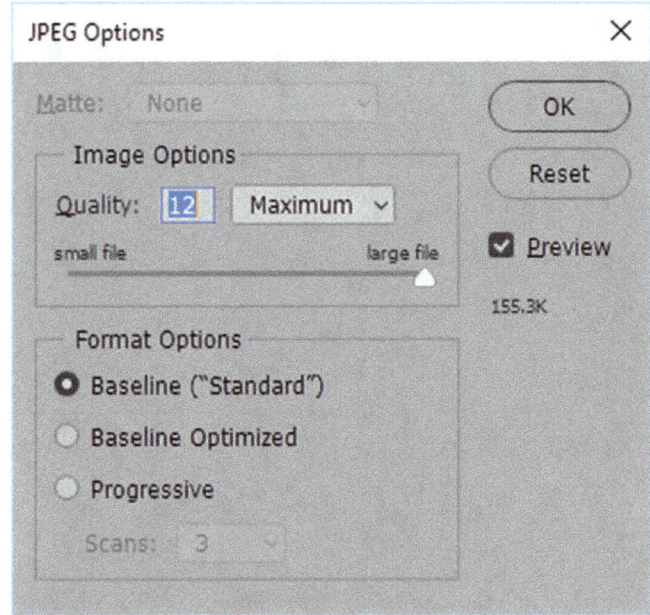

Figure 5-16. Set the JPEG option settings

When done, click OK. The Save action should now be added, as seen in Figure 5-17.

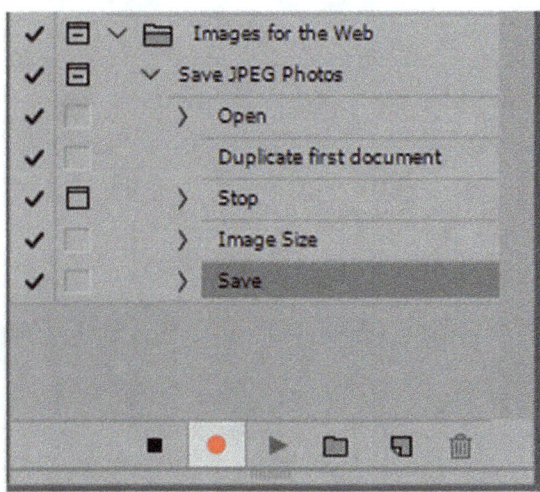

Figure 5-17. The Save action has been added to the Actions panel

At this point, you could stop the actions and play them, or add a recording of File ➤ Close to close the files. Refer to Figure 5-18.

103

CHAPTER 5 ■ ACTIONS TO SPEED UP FILE CONVERSION AND SLICING TOOLS

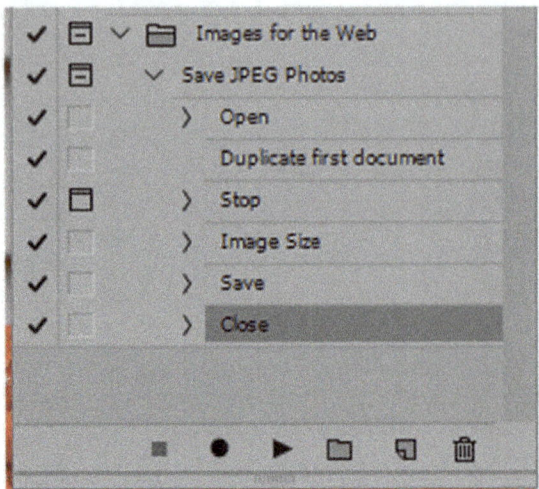

Figure 5-18. Add a file close action to close a saved file

When you click the Stop Record icon, you have a complete action. Now close all the open files. With no files open in Photoshop, test the action to see if it works by clicking the Play button, as seen in Figure 5-19.

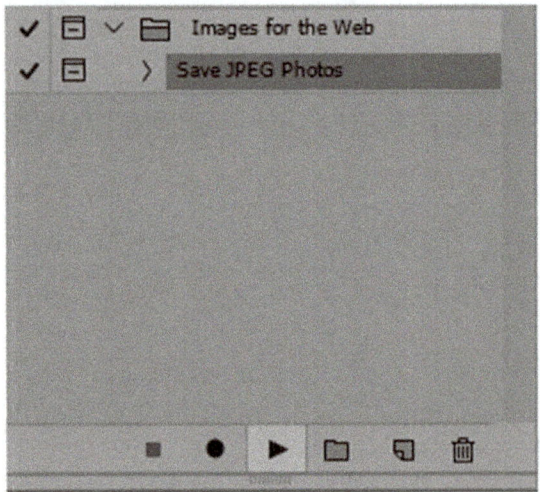

Figure 5-19. Play the action in the Actions panel to test it

You will notice at this point that the actions always pick the same image and override it, which may not be what you want. Refer to Figure 5-20.

104

CHAPTER 5 ■ ACTIONS TO SPEED UP FILE CONVERSION AND SLICING TOOLS

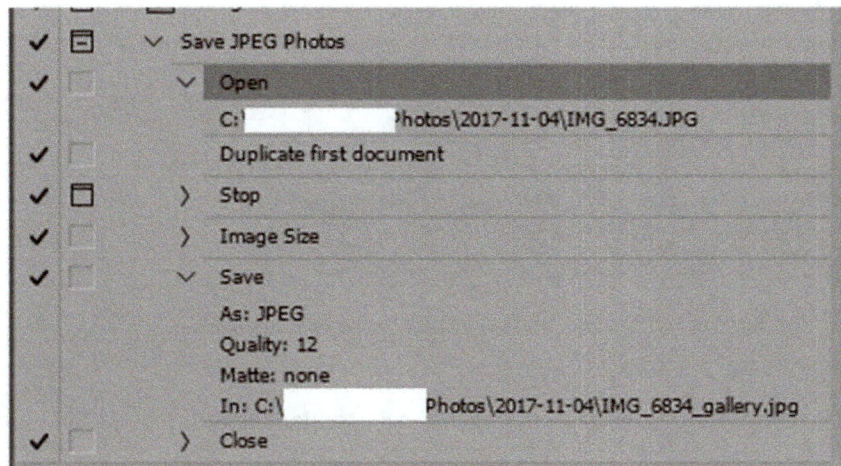

Figure 5-20. The same image is being picked; you must correct the action

You need to be able to open the folder so that you can pick a new image and save the new file with a new name.

So, click Toggle dialog on/off for both the Open and the Save As actions, and run the action again. Refer to Figure 5-21.

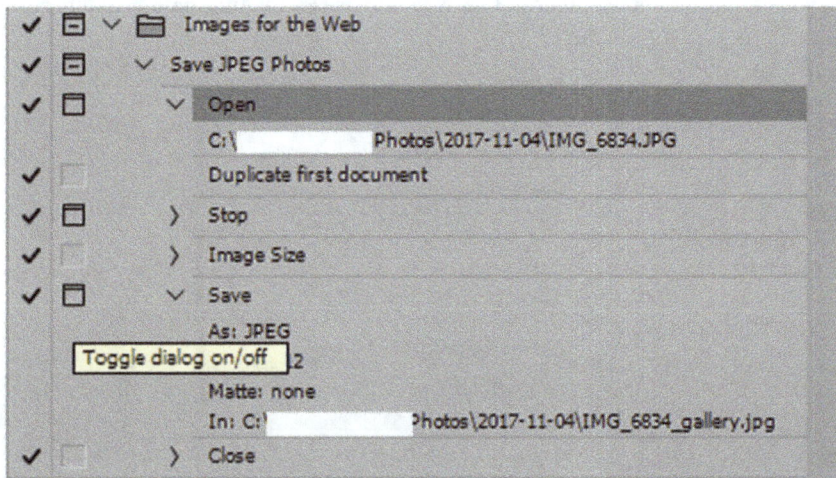

Figure 5-21. Make sure that the Open and Save dialog boxes open so that you can open, and then save the images with a new name

This makes the dialog box open before going to the next step.

You could also toggle on the Image Size dialog if you think there would be image size differences; however, do not this right now because it will only slow you down. Run the action with the Open and Save dialog boxes open so that you can make the selection of your images.

105

As you can see, once set up, this is much faster than having to select same folder, duplicate the image, and then find the menu to adjust the images size with the same changes each time. Also, if you are working with CMYK images, you could add another action to convert the image to RGB, as seen in Figure 5-22.

Figure 5-22. *There are many options that you can choose from when creating actions, such as mode conversion or file type*

The files can export in another setting by using one of the other export options that you looked at in Chapter 4.

Opening the file one at a time and saving change it to other file formats like GIF, PNG, PDF, or SVG by altering the action steps slightly and create another action for your set. You can then save that action within your set and use it for future projects.

Automate Batch Actions

While the above action steps are helpful and OK for a few images a day, what if you have over 20 images that need to be adjusted for a gallery, or even more for an e-commerce website?

There are two ways that you can automate the process. One way is to use File ➤ Automate ➤ Batch, as seen in Figure 5-23.

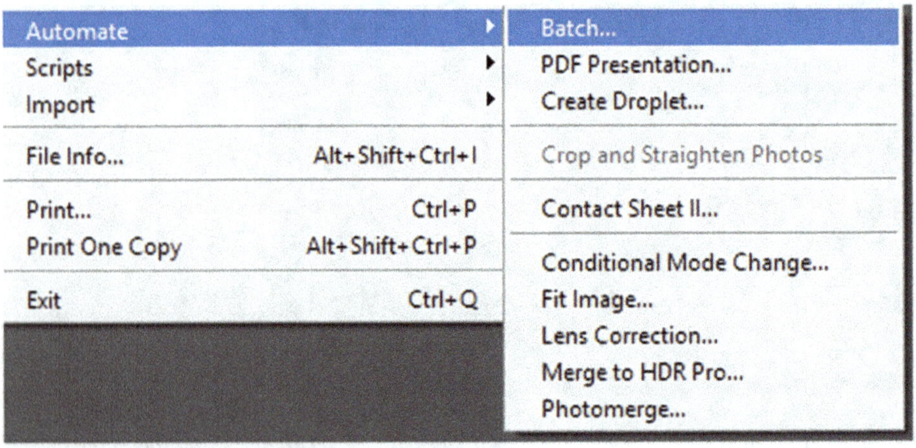

Figure 5-23. *Automate contains two ways to speed up the image conversion process*

In the Batch dialog box, you can reuse the actions that you just created within sets, and override settings such as folder destination, file naming conventions, length of numbering (2–4), and how the file extension displays (uppercase or lowercase). Refer to Figure 5-24.

CHAPTER 5 ■ ACTIONS TO SPEED UP FILE CONVERSION AND SLICING TOOLS

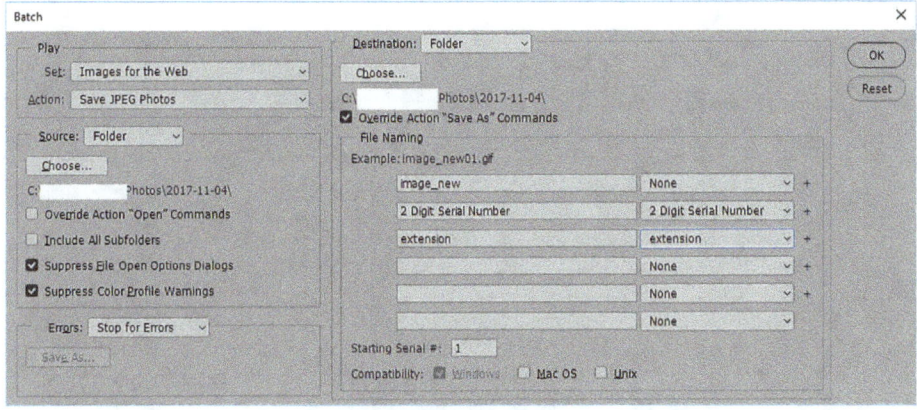

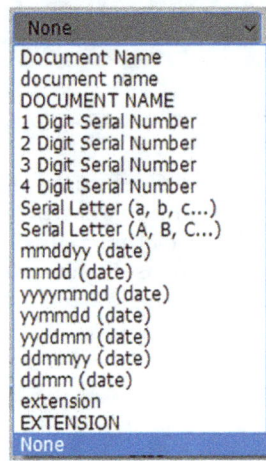

Figure 5-24. *Use the Batch dialog box to speed up your actions*

With a setting of None, you can set your own custom file names. If you use this setting, make sure to check Override Action "Save As" Commands. The example displays how the first one will appear.

If the batch runs into errors with the actions, it stops or logs the errors. You can also set the starting numbering sequence and choose a compatibility mode based on the computer that is being used.

When you click OK, the batch starts the actions and runs through the steps. Based on the actions you choose, the procedure will run faster or slower, but it is faster and more organized than having to open and duplicate each image one at a time. The new images will appear in the folder.

Automate Droplet Actions

The third way to automate your actions is if you want to create an icon to drop image files on that functions like an action, you can do so using a script called File ➤ Automate ➤ Create Droplet, as seen in Figure 5-25.

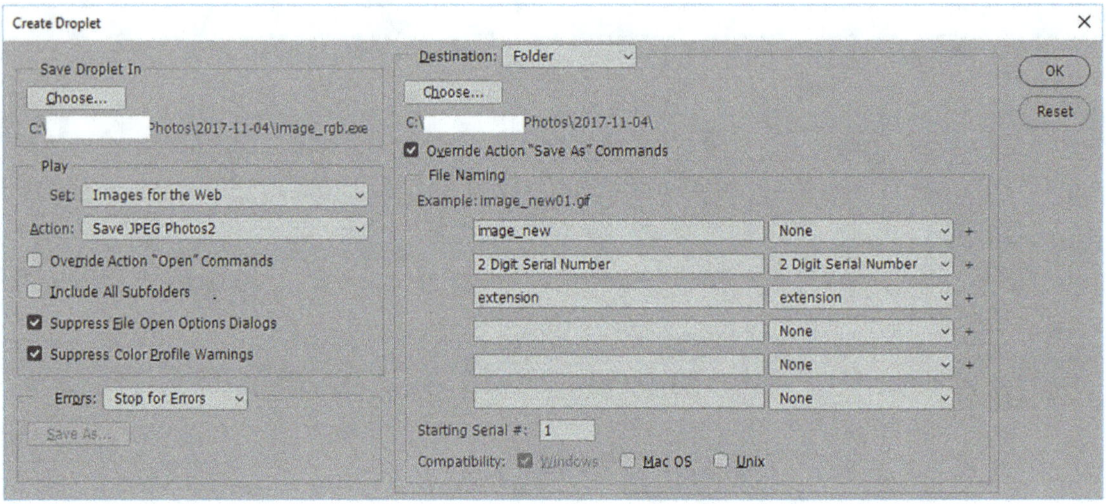

CHAPTER 5 ■ ACTIONS TO SPEED UP FILE CONVERSION AND SLICING TOOLS

Figure 5-25. *Use the Create Droplet dialog box to speed up your actions*

The Droplet dialog box looks very similar to the Batch dialog box; the only difference is that rather the doing the collecting through Photoshop, you just drop the image onto the icon. This is great if you have a few last-minute images that you need to quickly format. The droplet appears as an external (.exe) file.

During set up, make sure to select Override Action "Save As" Commands.

When you click OK, a droplet icon is created, as seen in Figure 5-26.

Figure 5-26. *Droplet icon*

Drop an image file onto it and see what happens.

■ **Note** With droplets, you may want to remove the Open setting because you are dropping one file at a time onto the icon. The Open option confuses the actions and slows down automation. Rather than delete it from the original action, Save For JPEG, in the panel, create a duplicate of the action and click the name to rename it Save For JPEG2. Then, select the Open action and click the Trash icon to remove it. Refer to Figure 5-27.

108

CHAPTER 5 ACTIONS TO SPEED UP FILE CONVERSION AND SLICING TOOLS

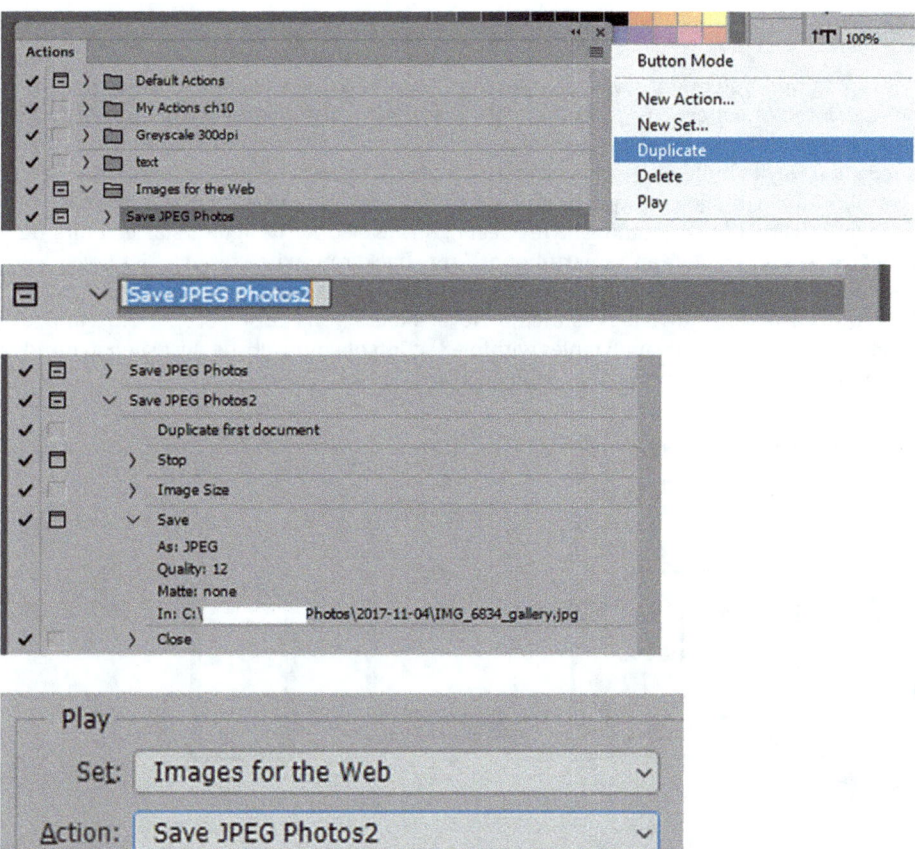

Figure 5-27. *Creating an alteration to the actions for the Droplet*

You can then resave the droplet with the new action and test.
Now the open action is removed and the only time the dialog box opens is when it is time to save.

■ **Note** While this is not part of any project in the book, File ➤ Automate ➤ PDF Presentation allows you to save multiple graphics as an interactive or moving PDF slide presentation, like what can be created in Adobe InDesign or Adobe Acrobat. You can then view the file in Acrobat Reader as a PDF file.

As you can see, there are many ways to work with actions to speed up your creation of graphics for the web.

109

Slicing Tools

When you export files for the web, you might save many photos or graphics that will appear somewhere in an HTML file on a solid-colored or patterned background; however, there are times when you might want an image to appear in a background that repeats in more <div> tags or in a table. In the past, tables rather than <div> tags were the accepted way to build website.

In Photoshop, you slice up an image into squares and rectangles, and then insert each part into the background cells of the table using CSS (Cascading Style Sheets); however, once designers started building layouts for multiple devices, such as tablets and smartphones, large background images in tables began to fall out of favor. The table could not flex and break to conform to the background movements; however, changes could be done with ease using <div> tags elements. Nevertheless, you can still use the Slice tool to create background images for <div> tags or small tables within a section of your website. Just keep in mind how your site's design may have to break or transition with each device (see Figure 5-28).

Figure 5-28. *Slicing up a graphic-rich website for a desktop display may look great, but how will this layout display for a tablet or a smartphone in portrait view?*

Unlike tables, you can float divs over other divs, so less slicing is required.

When you design a layout for more than one device, bear in mind that for tablets and smartphones, you may want to reduce the amount of graphics on your site for faster download. You'll look at media queries in Part 6.

Use the Slice and Slice Select Tool

Let's look at a slice layout I created in the Chapter 5 folder for a webpage on a desktop computer. Later, we will use a flexible layout that will not require slicing, but it will give you a rough idea of where slicing in today's website layouts succeeds and fails, and what you can salvage from a Photoshop sliced layout and later use in Dreamweaver again.

Using guides (View ➤ New Guide), you can layout where each slice is and how large. Refer to Figure 5-29.

CHAPTER 5 ■ ACTIONS TO SPEED UP FILE CONVERSION AND SLICING TOOLS

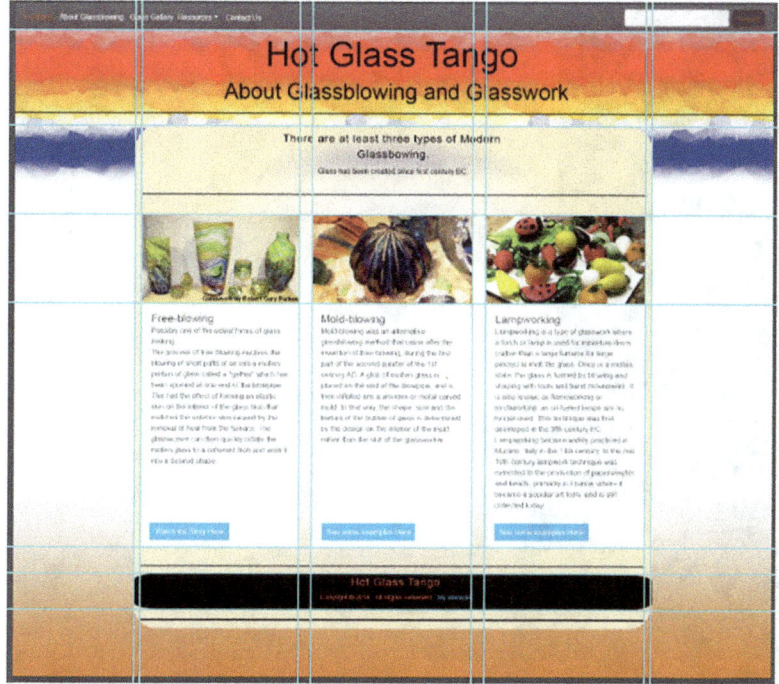

***Figure 5-29.** Arranging where to slice by creating guides first*

The Slice tool (C) is found docked under the Crop tool. It can marque around a section within the guides and create a user slice. It appears in blue (see Figure 5-30).

111

CHAPTER 5 ■ ACTIONS TO SPEED UP FILE CONVERSION AND SLICING TOOLS

Figure 5-30. *Creating a user slice (blue) using the Slice tool and auto slices (gray)*

Depending on where you create a slice, more slices will be generated around it. The generated slices are known as *auto slices*, which appear in a gray color.

Different icons and colors dictate what kind of slice it is.

- **Slice lines**: These define the boundary of the slice. Solid lines indicate that the slice is a user slice or layer-based slice; dotted lines indicate that the slice is an auto slice.

- **Slice colors:** Differentiates user slices and layer-based slices from auto slices. By default, user slices and layer-based slices have blue symbols, and auto slices have gray symbols and often a link icon. The File ➤ Export ➤ Save For Web (Legacy) dialog box uses color adjustments to dim unselected slices. These adjustments to appearance are for display purposes only and do not affect the color of the final image. By default, the color adjustment for auto slices is twice the amount of that for user slices.

- **Slice numbers:** Numbers are from left to right and top to bottom, beginning in the upper-left corner of the image. If you change the arrangement or number of slices, every slice number is updated to reflect the new order. Refer to Figure 5-31.

CHAPTER 5 ■ ACTIONS TO SPEED UP FILE CONVERSION AND SLICING TOOLS

Figure 5-31. *Close up of numbered user slice (blue) and auto slices (gray)*

■ **Note** For further alterations to slice color, go to Edit ➤ Preferences ➤ Guides Grids and Slices, where you can alter the line color and hide/show the slice number. Refer to Figure 5-32.

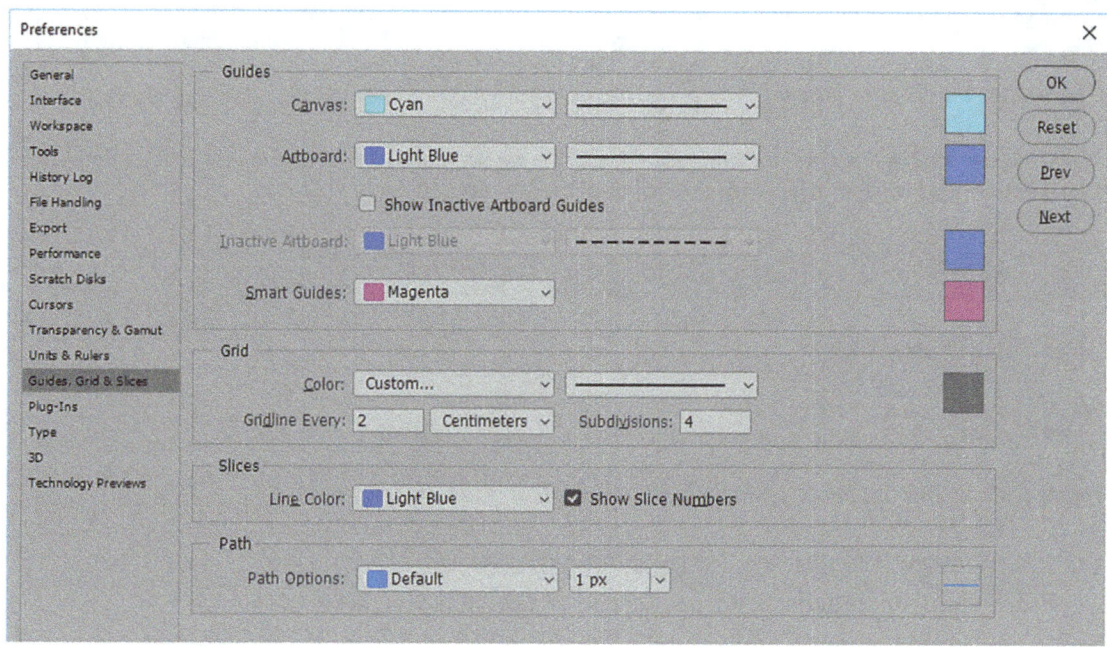

Figure 5-32. *You can adjust your default color preference for your slices in the Preferences dialog box in the Guides, Grids & Slices tab*

- **Slice badges:** The following badges, or icons, indicate certain slice types.
    - User or auto slice has image content. Refer to Figure 5-33.

Figure 5-33. *User or auto slice with image content*

113

- User slice has no image content. You cannot add this badge to an auto slice. It first must be promoted to a user slice. Refer to Figure 5-34.

Figure 5-34. *User or auto slice with no image content*

- Slice is layer-based. Refer to Figure 5-35.

Figure 5-35. *Slice is layer-based*

Slices can also be layer based when created with the Layers panel. You can further alter the information of the slice for the Slice tool selected in the Options panel, as seen in Figure 5-36.

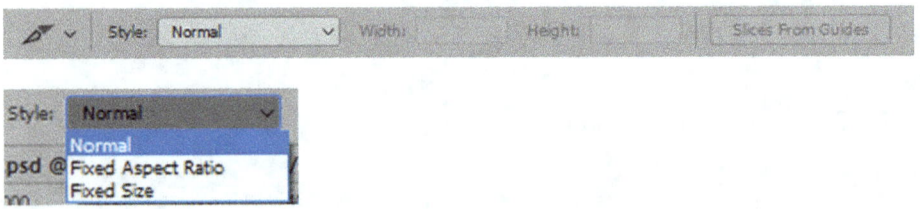

Figure 5-36. *Further options are available for the Slice tool in the Options panel*

- **Normal**: Uses whatever slice proportions you drag out.
- **Fixed Aspect Ratio**: Uses a height-to-width ratio. You can enter whole numbers or decimals for the aspect ratio. If you want your height to be twice as tall as the width, enter Width: 1 and Height: 2.
- **Fixed Size**: Enter the slices height and width in whole number pixels.

With the Slice tool, you can alter the size as you Shift-drag (to keep square) or Alt/Option-drag to draw from the center.

Slices can be altered using the Slice Select tool (C) (see Figure 5-28). With this tool, slices can be moved, resized, or aligned with other slices.

The Slice Select tool allows you to promote (bring forward or backward), divide (shift selecting two or more; and right-clicking allows you to choose to combine slices), and align slices. Refer to Figures 5-37 and 5-38.

CHAPTER 5 ACTIONS TO SPEED UP FILE CONVERSION AND SLICING TOOLS

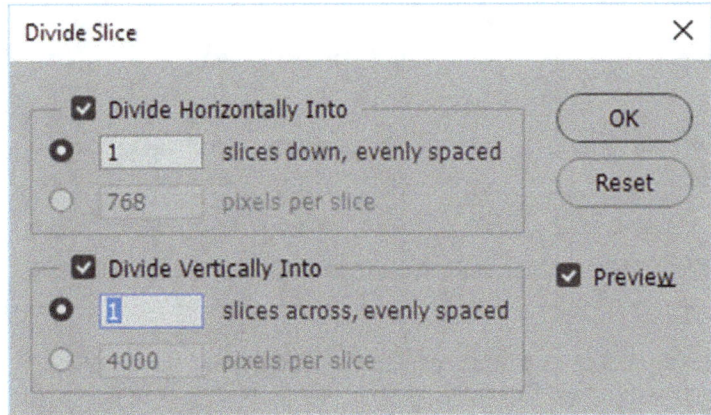

Figure 5-37. *Dividing slices using the divide slice dialog box*

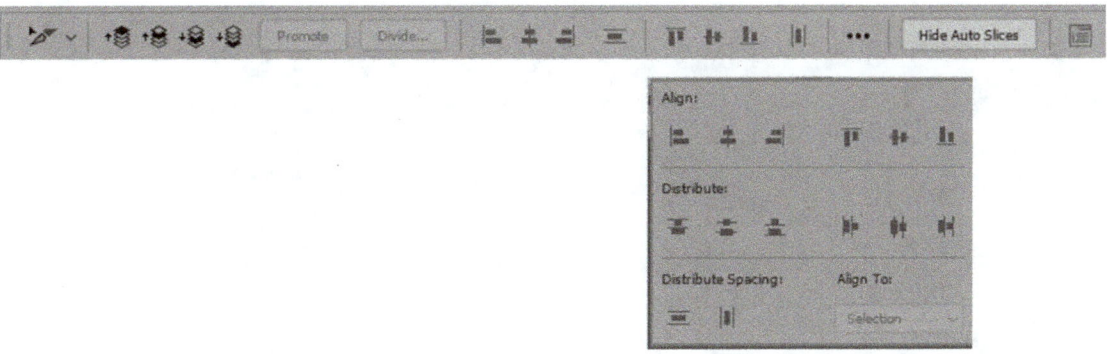

Figure 5-38. *The Options panel for the Slice Select tool*

When two or more cells are selected, you can use the alignment tools adjust the cells. The following are the options from left to right.

- Align top edges
- Align vertical centers
- Align bottom edges
- Align left edges
- Align horizontal centers
- Align right edges
- Distribute top edges
- Distribute vertical centers
- Distribute bottom edges

115

- Distribute left edges
- Distribute horizontal centers
- Distribute right edges

You can hide or show slices by clicking the Hide/Show Auto Slices toggle button, which makes auto slices easier to view.

■ **Note** If you want to show or hide all slices while working, you can also choose View ➤ Show ➤ Slices.

Clicking the File icon (Slice option) at the end of the Options panel, or double-clicking the Slice Select tool, allows you to set further options, such as the image's defaults.

- **Name:** Rename the slice, as seen in Figure 5-39.

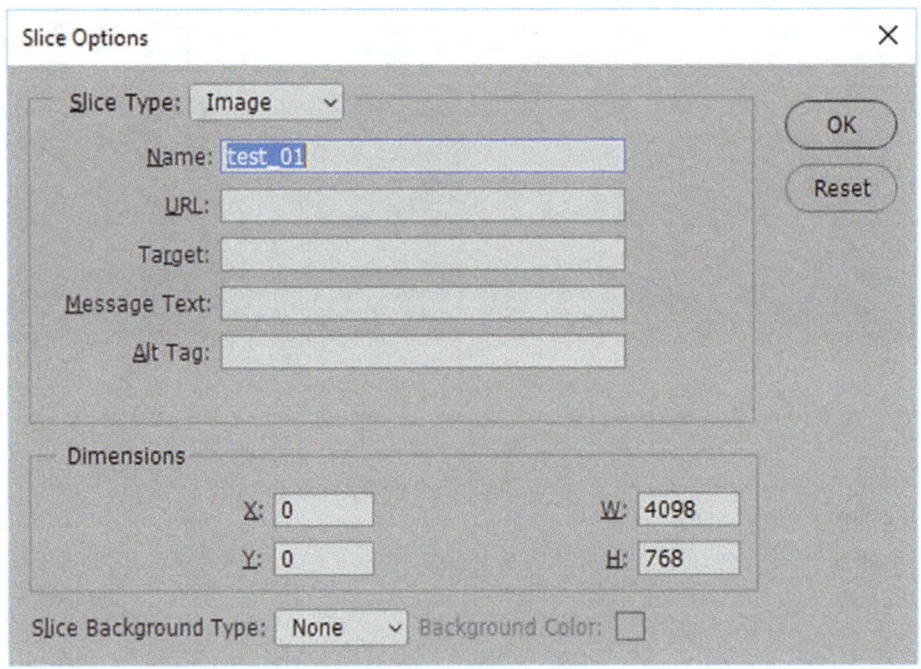

Figure 5-39. *The Slice Options dialog box for the Slice Select tool*

- **URL (website link):** The entire area of the slice becomes a link.
- **Target**: This determines how the webpage opens in a browser; the following are your options.
    - **_blank**: Opens a linked file in a new window or tab and leaves the original webpage open.
    - **_self**: Opens the linked document in the same frame in which it was clicked (this is the default).

CHAPTER 5 ■ ACTIONS TO SPEED UP FILE CONVERSION AND SLICING TOOLS

- **_parent**: Displays the linked file in its own parent frameset. Do not use this option unless the file contains a frame. The link is considered a child, and it appears in the parent frame.

- **_top**: Replaces the entire browser window with the linked file, removing all the current frames. The name must match a frame in the HTML file for this to work. When the link is clicked, the specified file appears in a new frame.

- **Message Text**: Changes the default message in the text rather than showing the default URL link.

- **Alt tag**: Refers to alternate text, and acts as a tool tip until the image downloads. Alt tags are important for people with visual impairment and require a screen reader as part of accessibility to the web; websites should be for everyone.

■ **Note** You can edit this information for any slice, including auto slices (linked), before you export in the Save for Web (Legacy) dialog box (see Figure 5-40). This is done when you double-click a slice using the Slice Select tool. If you do not complete these settings in Photoshop, you can always adjust them later in Dreamweaver CC.

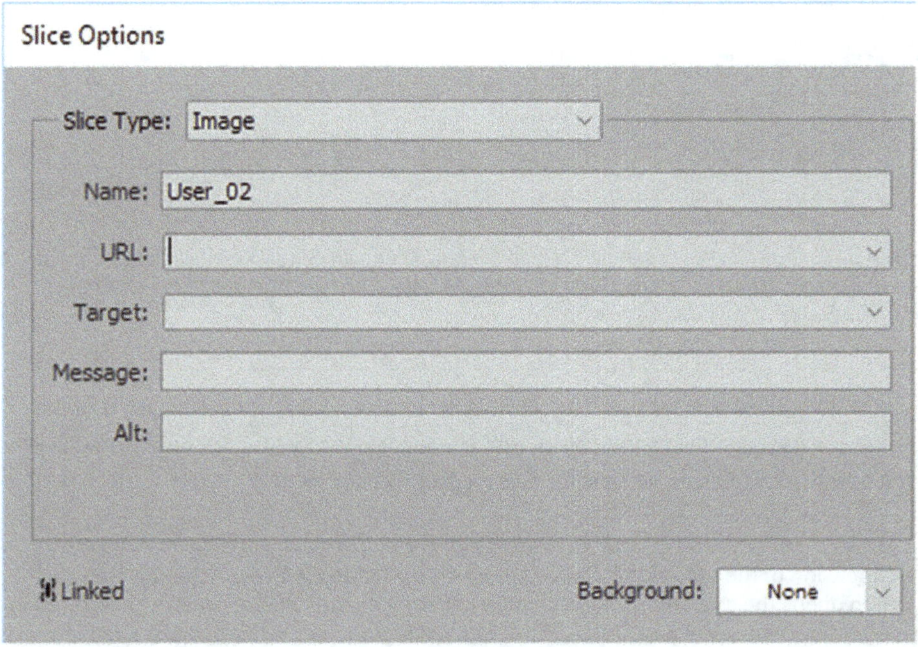

Figure 5-40. *How slice options appears in the Save for Web legacy dialog box when an image slice is click on*

If the area is a CSS (Cascading Style Sheet) solid color background or text, you can exclude that part of the image, which is Slice Type: No Image. The graphics within this slice are not exported when you choose File ➤ Export ➤ Save for Web (Legacy). Also, you cannot name these slices. Refer to Figure 5-41.

CHAPTER 5 ■ ACTIONS TO SPEED UP FILE CONVERSION AND SLICING TOOLS

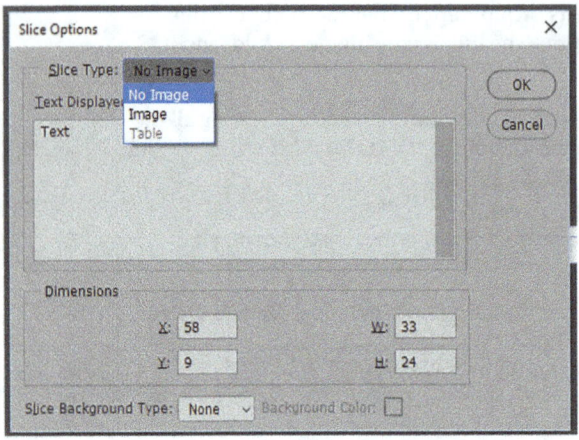

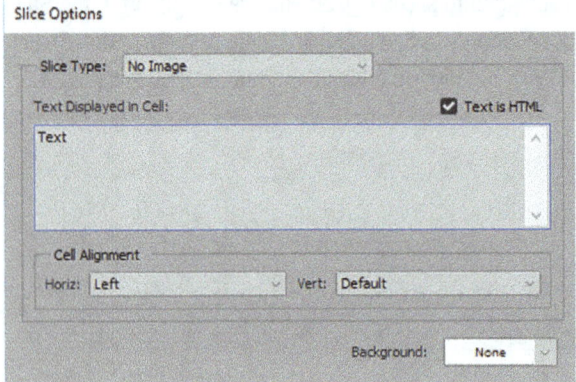

Figure 5-41. *When you don't want a slice to export, set it to No Image in your Slice Options dialog box. You can also add text. the upper screenshot shows working on the layer slice. The lower screenshot shows how the slice options appear in the Save for Web dialog box.*

■ **Note** The Slice Type: Table option is not accessible. This may be because Adobe is encouraging users to use CSS options with <div> tags rather than tables. Soon, I show you another way to adjust for CSS and avoid using tables during the final HTML output in the Save for Web (Legacy) dialog box.

You can set the dimension of the slice and the background type color to fill any transparent areas in the file. The Other option opens the color picker for custom color choices. You cannot preview this color in Photoshop, only in the browser, since it is part of the HTML file that is generated with the image. Refer to Figure 5-42.

CHAPTER 5 ■ ACTIONS TO SPEED UP FILE CONVERSION AND SLICING TOOLS

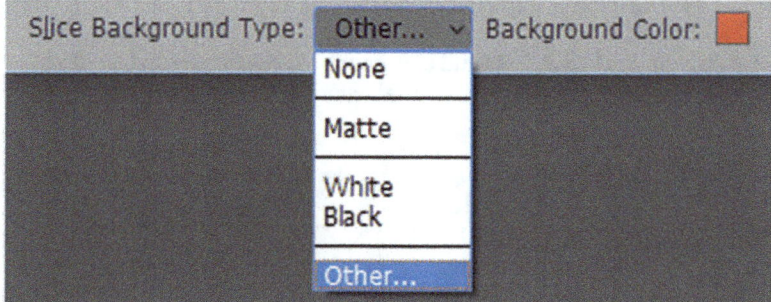

Figure 5-42. *Alter the slice background type color in the slice options dialog box*

Each time you draw a slice, it is numbered and auto slices around it renumber to match the flow. Sometimes subslices generate, which overlap. This can get confusing. If you don't keep track, and the image requires many slices, you may need to clear the slices from the page and start over again. Select View ➤ Clear Slices and begin to slice again.

Remember to be accurate. You can add guides to an image, select the Slice tool, and click Slices From Guides in the Options bar. Refer to Figure 5-43.

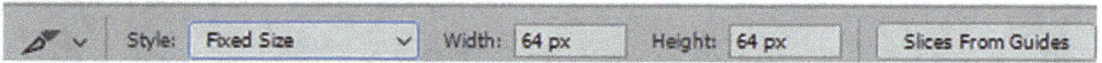

Figure 5-43. *Slices from guides are a faster way to add slices to your file*

When you create slices from guides, any existing slices are deleted, and the new ones replace them.

If you create additional slices, use View ➤ Snap To, which aligns a new slice to a guide or another slice in the image.

Layer-based Slices

A layer-based slice encompasses all the pixel data in the selected layer. If you move the layer or edit the layer's content, the slice area automatically adjusts to reflect the pixels that were added or removed. A layer-based slice must conform to the layer, so it is not as versatile as a user-based slice; however, you can change a layer-based slice to a user slice via the Promote button in the Control panel. Refer to Figure 5-44.

Figure 5-44. *Layer-based slices can be promoted to user-based slices*

You can create a layer-based slice by selecting Layer ➤ New Layer-Based slice; just be aware that it may override other slices.

A layer-based slice is tied to the pixel content of the selected layer, so the only way to move, combine, divide, resize, and align it is to edit the layer or convert it to a user slice.

Likewise, all auto slices in an image are linked and share the same optimization settings. To create different optimization settings for an auto slice, you need to select it with the Slice Select tool and click Promote to make it a user slice.

119

CHAPTER 5 ■ ACTIONS TO SPEED UP FILE CONVERSION AND SLICING TOOLS

Exporting Slices

When you are done slicing up your page, you can save the file and choose the specific file formats for each slice using File ➤ Export ➤ Save for Web (Legacy). Use the Optimize Tab window, as seen in Figure 5-45.

Figure 5-45. *Select user slices and alter the file format*

The Slice Select tool allows you to choose how each slice is treated to get the optimum quality and lowest file size. Areas of solid colors might be the best set for GIF files, while areas that have a lot of color or photographs should be saved as JPEGs or PNGs. If you need to turn the slices turn off and on, you can click the Toggle Slices Visibility icon (Q) beneath the Eyedropper tool.

Slices from Tables to div Tags, Generating Cascading Style Sheets

So that you use <div> tags rather than tables, let's look at hidden settings that you may be unaware of. Go to the Preset menu of the dialog box. Choose Edit Output Settings, as seen in Figure 5-46.

120

CHAPTER 5 ■ ACTIONS TO SPEED UP FILE CONVERSION AND SLICING TOOLS

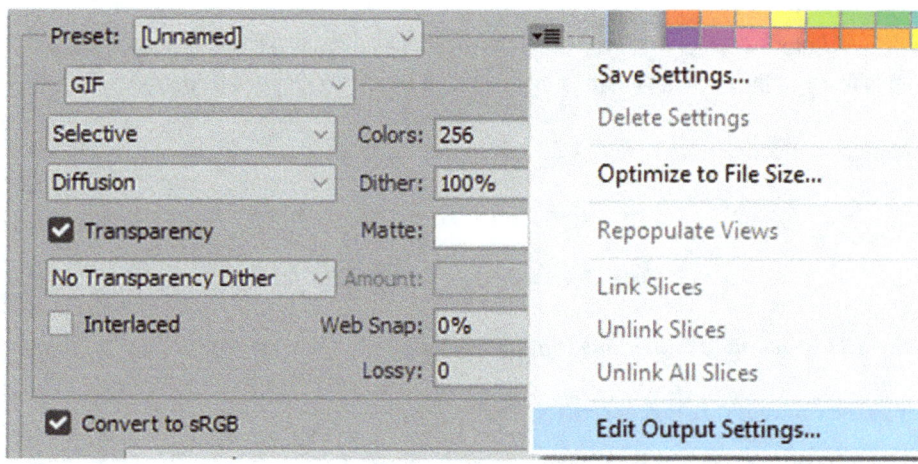

Figure 5-46. *Edit the output settings of your HTML*

In the HTML tab, check Output XHTML. Alternatively, you can select XHTML from the Settings dropdown menu, which checks this setting for you; however, you will be making changes in another tab within this dialog box, so the settings will register as Custom. Refer to Figure 5-47.

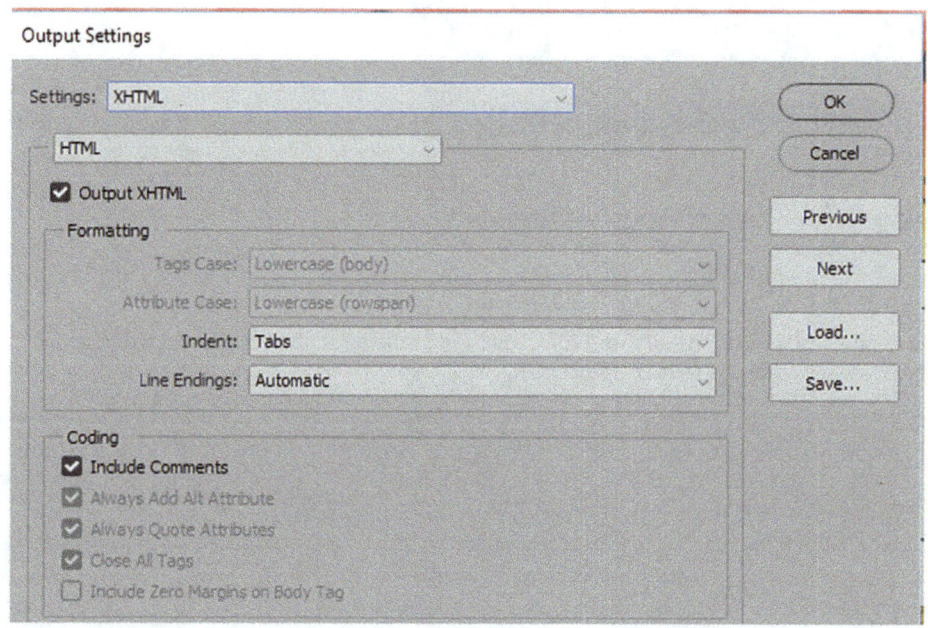

Figure 5-47. *Edit your HTML output settings by choosing Output XHTML in the HTML Tab*

121

■ **Note** If you don't check Output XHTML, when you bring the file into a program like Dreamweaver CC, you may receive a warning in line 1 of the document stating that the head has not been properly declared. Refer to Figure 5-48.

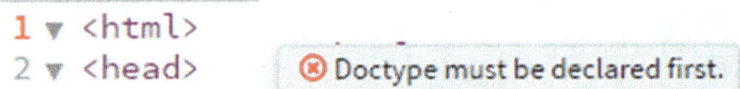

Figure 5-48. Avoid the doctype warning by checking Output XHTML

Here is how it appears when XHTML is checked.

```
<!DOCTYPE html PUBLIC "-//W3C//DTD XHTML 1.0 Transitional//EN" "http://www.w3.org/TR/xhtml1/DTD/xhtml1-transitional.dtd">
<html xmlns="http://www.w3.org/1999/xhtml">
```

This time, there is no warning.
Next, from the drop-down menu, choose Slices, as seen in Figure 5-49.

Figure 5-49. Choose Slices from the drop-down menu to adjust the next setting

Rather than the default Slice Output Generate Table, which has fallen out of favor with web designers, select the Generate CSS radio button, as seen in Figure 5-50.

CHAPTER 5 ■ ACTIONS TO SPEED UP FILE CONVERSION AND SLICING TOOLS

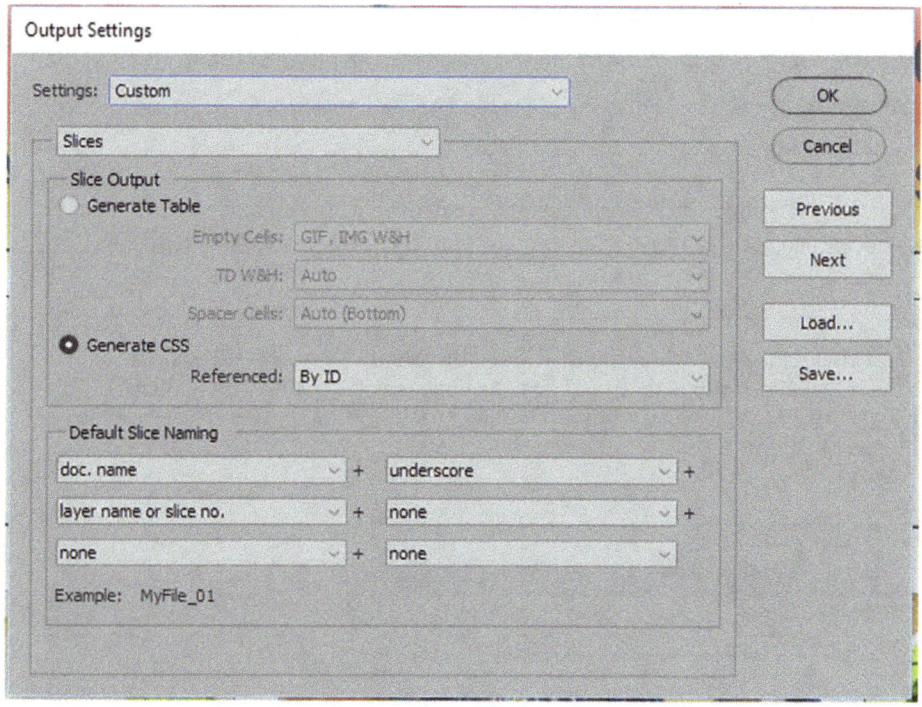

Figure 5-50. Choose that slices generate with CSS

The Referenced settings allow you to reference the CSS by ID tag, inline, or by class. Refer to Figure 5-51.

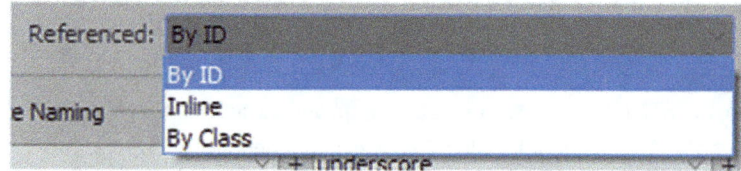

Figure 5-51. Choose a setting for your CSS

The following are descriptions.

- **By ID**: Generates an ID tag for each slice that is unique, but keeps the CSS separate in the head section.
- **Inline**: Puts all the code directly into the body. I do not recommend this setting because it makes the code cluttered and difficult to alter if you must adjust later in Dreamweaver.
- **By Class**: Generates a unique class for each slice, but only one main <div> tag. Like ID, this setting keeps the CSS separate in the head section. Personally, this appears to be the best setting because it keeps the code looking the cleanest, and it is easiest to edit.

123

I left all other settings in the drop-down menu at the default.

- **Background**: Refers to how the background is handled with an image or color.
- **Saving Files**: Takes care of the filename and the file extension is saved.

Click OK to exit this dialog box.

■ **Note** If you like these settings, you can save them as a preset so that they are available to you next time for another project.

Back in the Save for Web dialog box, when you click Save, the various file format slices are saved and numbered with the HTML file. If you plan to only save the images, you can reassemble them in Dreamweaver CC in an HTML5 file. Since you adjusted the CSS, choose HTML and Images. Leave the settings at Custom. Refer to in Figure 5-52.

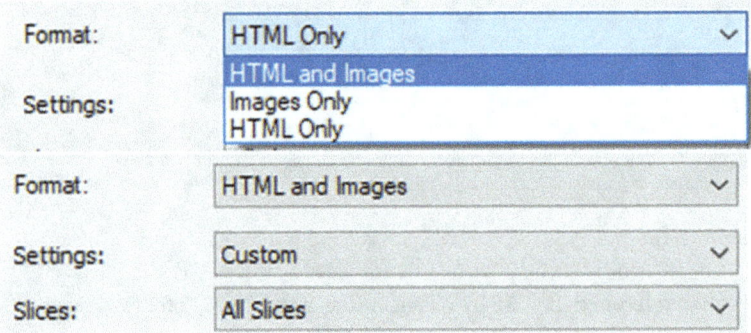

Figure 5-52. Choose HTML and Images when you save if you want to generate both at the same time

■ **Note** Depending on the slice setup, the HTML file that was generated from your slices might appear as if you were creating rollover images or buttons. Also, the HTML coding that was generated for the slices was not a version of HTML5. If you were not planning to create rollovers, but only graphics for your div, I recommend using this XHTML file as a starting point and only copy the parts of the code that you need into your HTML5 file and external CSS file, which you create in Dreamweaver CC. In addition, you can re-create rollovers in Dreamweaver with or without slices, which you look at in Part 6 of the book.

Zoomify an Image

One other unique way you can work with images for a webpage is to select File ➤ Export ➤ Zoomify.

Adobe, in collaboration with a company called Zoomify, created an effortless way to create a basic HTML page with a feature that allows you to zoom in on an image. The dialog box is shown in Figure 5-53.

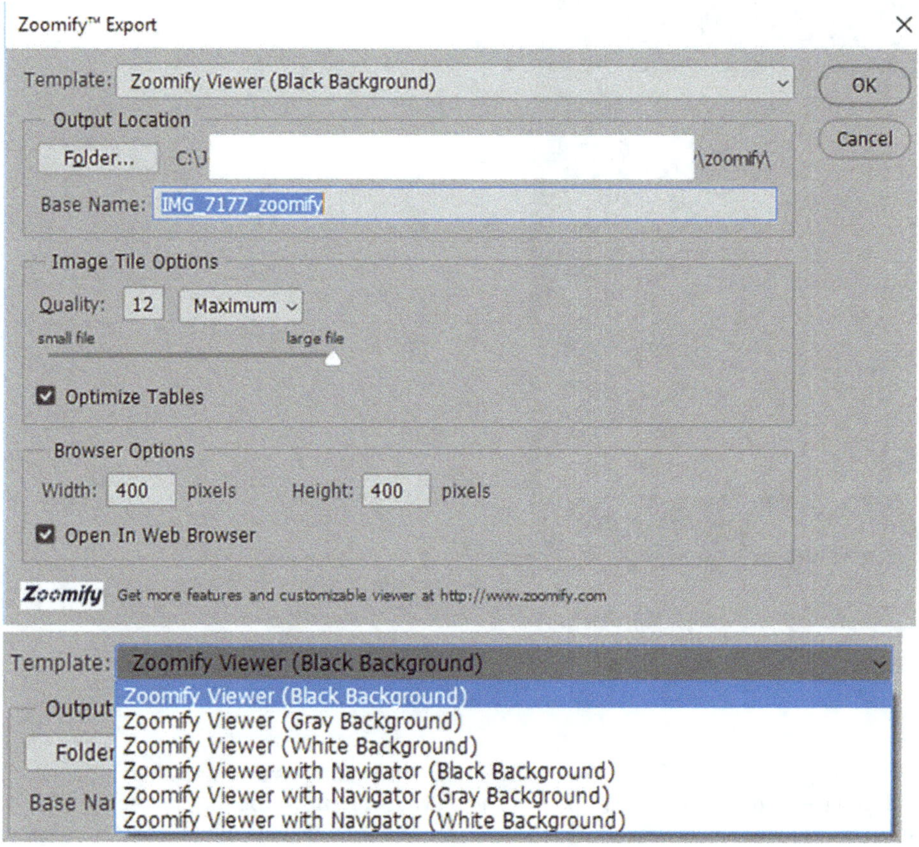

***Figure 5-53.** Options in the Zoomify dialog box*

Zoomify appears to work with only JPEG images. You can choose from various base templates for the background. Once you have set the folder location, you can name the file, set the JPEG image quality, and set the browser width and height of the zoom area. When you click OK. Photoshop generates several files in a folder containing tiled images, an XML file, a JavaScript (.js) file, and an HTML page.

You can open the HTML file in Dreamweaver to edit the HTML for your own project. This is a useful option if you need to have a page on your site with a detailed image or map that the user needs to examine up close by pressing the plus (+), minus(–), or reset (Z) keys. Refer to Figure 5-54, an example found in the Chapter 5 folder.

CHAPTER 5 ■ ACTIONS TO SPEED UP FILE CONVERSION AND SLICING TOOLS

Figure 5-54. Zoom in and out of an image with Zoomify

Summary

This chapter covered a lot of ground as it relates to exporting images, including using automation, slicing, and single images that you can zoom in and out of. Depending on your workflow, you may prefer some options over the others; the choice is up to you. In the next chapter, you look at some of the tools for creating basic animations in Photoshop CC using the Timeline panel.

CHAPTER 6

Tools for Animation

This chapter focuses on one specific file format: the GIF animation. As you saw in Chapters 4 and 5, GIF files are static images used for illustrations or logos; however, unlike the other image formats you have read about so far, they can also be used to create small animations within Photoshop CC and used on a website in several diverse ways, which you explore in Part 6.

■ **Note** This chapter does not have any actual projects; however, you can use the files in the Chapter 6 folder to practice opening and viewing for this lesson. They are at `https://github.com/Apress/graphics-multimedia-web-adobe-creative-cloud`.

Let's look at how to create a GIF animation. Animations in Photoshop, for the most part, appear like a collection of layers that are in a sequence or order. Each layer is void of movement until they are added to frames that are programed to move in a sequence, one after the other. Until then, there is no animation (see Figure 6-1).

CHAPTER 6 ■ TOOLS FOR ANIMATION

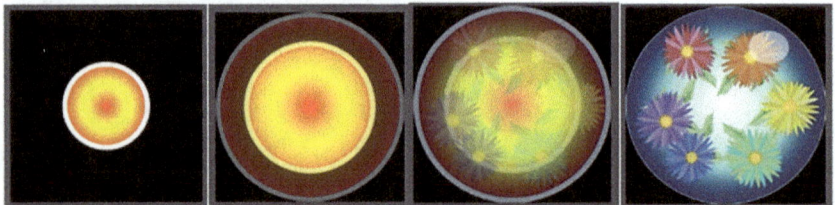

Figure 6-1. *Layers in the Layers panel can be used to create a GIF animation that appears to transform in size, position, opacity, and color effects*

You don't have to go to animation school to become an animator in Photoshop CC. Creating a basic animation just requires a bit of drawing skill, imagination, and creativity. A GIF animation also can take up very little space or can be very subtle, such as appearing somewhere behind text in the background of a website. Let's look at ways that you can accomplish a GIF animation.

GIF (animated) (.gif)

With your Layers panel and Photoshop tools, you may have designed backgrounds, part of a banner as an advertisement, or a procedural animation for a client's website. Once you have the layers and parts of your design to your liking, you can add movement. At this point, you might wonder if you need to export the layers and create the animation in a program like Adobe Animate CC (formerly Flash). Not necessarily. If you are comfortable designing animations with Animate CC, do it that way. You will look at that option in Part 4; however, if you are new to Animate CC, you can create a very simple animation to suit your purposes without leaving Photoshop CC.

For now, let's locate the Timeline panel in the main menu.

The Timeline Panel

The Timeline panel is a long horizontal panel that allows you to preview all your frames in an animation. It has two options in its drop-down button: Create Frame Animation and Create Video Timeline (see Chapter 7). You can choose which one you want to use. Let's look at Create Frame Animation first. Refer to Figure 6-2.

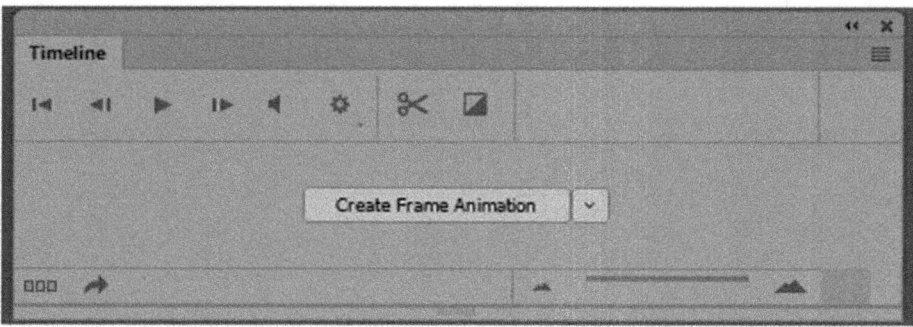

Figure 6-2. *The Timeline panel in Create Frame animation mode before the setting has been clicked*

If the Timeline panel appears at the bottom of the page, you can drag it out by its upper tab and place it somewhere else on the screen, so that it does not block your image.

Note Until the Create Frame Animation button is clicked, both panels' menu options appear for the video and frame; once the button is clicked, only those options for the frame or video are available.

Click the Create Frame Animation button to start your GIF animation.

The Timeline panel changes and gives you one starting frame to begin with. The layers that you have turned on or off in the Layers panel dictate the way that the first frame appears. Refer to the GIF animation start file and Figure 6-3.

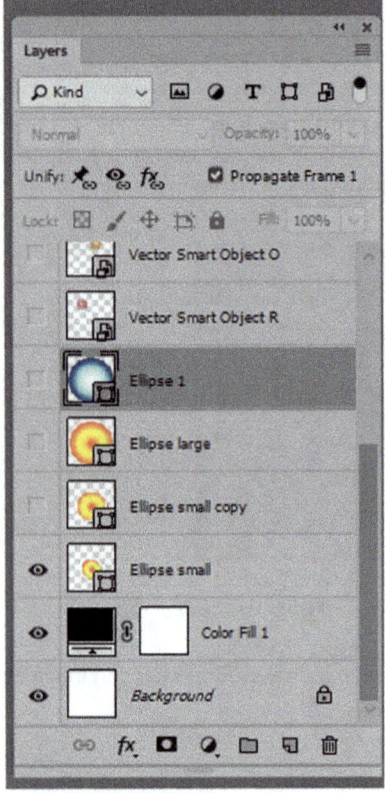

Figure 6-3. *A preview of the first frame of the animation in the Timeline panel based on which layers are selected*

You'll also notice that the Timeline panel's submenu has now changed to reflect the fact that you are creating a frame animation. Refer to Figure 6-4.

CHAPTER 6 ■ TOOLS FOR ANIMATION

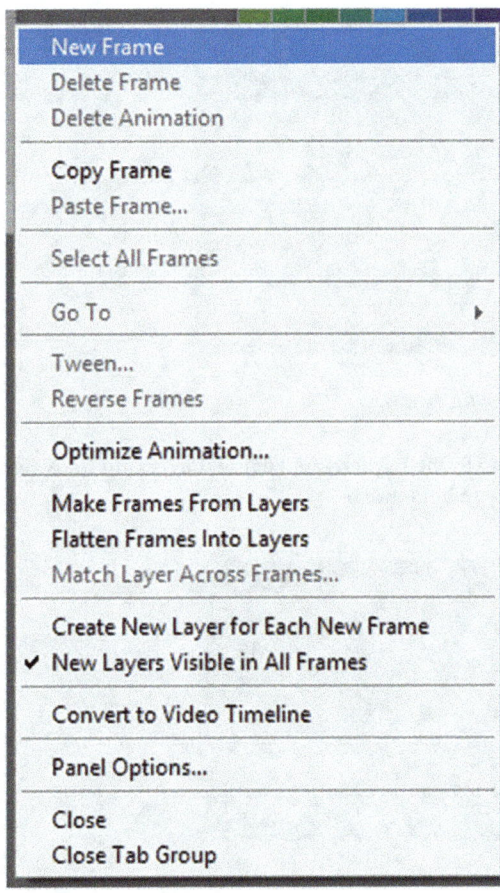

Figure 6-4. Menu options for the Frame Animation Timeline panel

Adding a Frame

An animation cannot take place unless you create another frame. This is done either via the menu (New Frame), or on the bottom edge of the panel, click the Duplicate Selected Frames icon. Refer to Figure 6-5.

Figure 6-5. Duplicate Selected Frames icon

CHAPTER 6 ■ TOOLS FOR ANIMATION

Once you have two frames, your play features become accessible. Refer to Figure 6-6.

Figure 6-6. *When you add a new frame, it is a duplicate of the first frame*

To alter the second frame, you need to change something in the Layers panel while the second frame is selected. You can do this by turning on or off a layer eye, as seen in Figure 6-7.

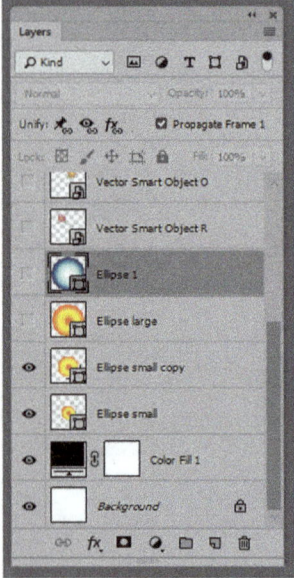

Figure 6-7. *When a layer eye is turned on or off in the Layers panel, this alters the selected frame*

132

CHAPTER 6 ■ TOOLS FOR ANIMATION

When you have more than one frame selected (using the Shift key), you can use this icon to create the same number of frames of the same kind. For example, if you have three frames in a sequence, you can select them all and press the Duplicate Selected Frames icon and the three frames will be duplicated. This brings you to a total of six frames, as seen in Figure 6-8.

Figure 6-8. *Creating repeating frames in the Timeline panel*

A frame can be deleted by selecting it, and then choosing Delete Frames from the menu or by clicking the Trash icon (delete selected frames) in the Timeline panel. If you don't like your entire animation, you can choose Delete Animation from the menu, which resets you back to the first frame. Refer to Figures 6-3 and 6-9.

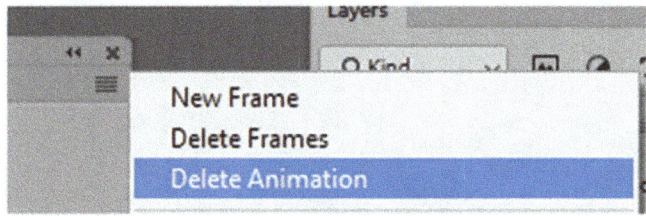

Figure 6-9. *Choose Delete Animation if you want to set the animation back to the first frame*

Adding, Altering, and Removing Frames

Assuming that you currently have only one frame in your animation, you now want to alter the second frame. Using the Layers panel, you can do one of several things.

If you have already set up movement with the layers, you can choose from the Make Frames From Layers menu. This adds all the layers as separate frames into the timeline and overrides the current frame, as seen in Figure 6-10.

Figure 6-10. *All layers are added as frames to the animation*

133

This may not be what you want. You may need to delete a few frames or turn off a few layer eyes in each frame to get the desired result.

Choose Layers and turn them on or off while a frame is selected, and then move to the next frame and do the same thing. Refer to Figure 6-11.

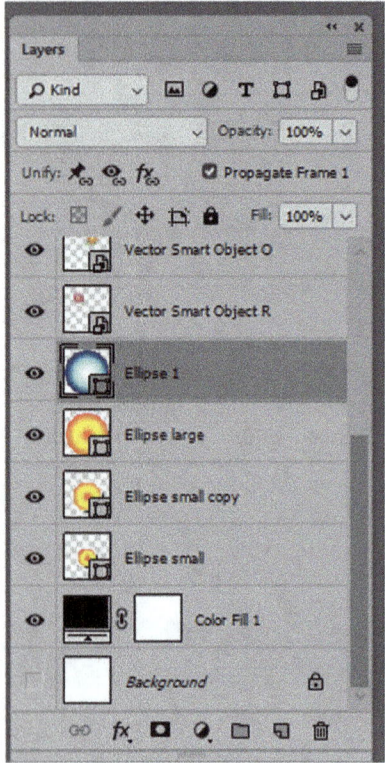

Figure 6-11. Notice how the layers and frames have been organized into a timeline animation with four frames

■ **Note** If required for your animation, while on a Layer using the Move Tool found in tools panel, Nudge with your keyboard's arrow keys or move the object around while the tool is selected on the Layer for a specific frame. This alters the position of a shape on a layer for that frame, but not for another frame in the sequence, as seen in Figure 6-12. Clicking back to a previous frame, the shape will be back in its original position on the layer.

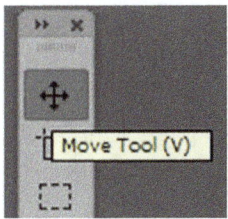

Figure 6-12. *Objects on layers can be moved to a new position and not effect a previous frame*

Notice that I added a fifth frame to show how the object moved on the layer. If I select frame 4, the object moves back to its original location on the layer. For now, I will remove frame 5 by clicking the Trash icon and returning it to the way it appeared in Figure 6-11.

Add Layer Style Effects and Turn Them On or Off in the Frame Sequence

Optionally, frame 5 could have effects(fx) or layer styles added to a layer while in frame 4 No effects would appear or they would be turn off in the layer panel. Refer to Figure 6-13 if you want to add this option to your animation.

CHAPTER 6 ■ TOOLS FOR ANIMATION

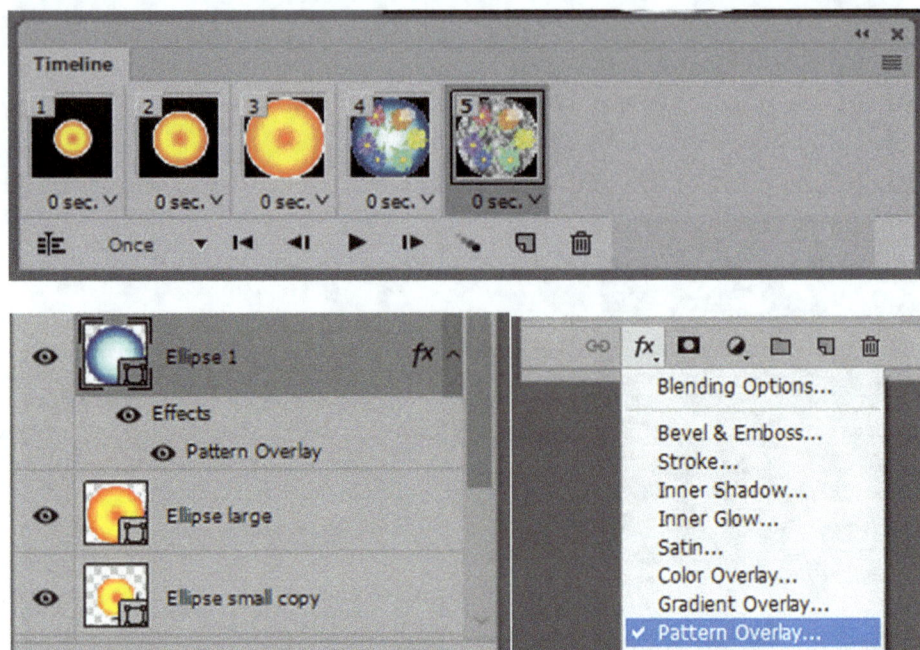

Figure 6-13. *An effect or layer style like "Pattern Overlay" could be added to a layer in one frame, but not be present in a previous frame*

Likewise, layer fill or adjustment layers could be turned on or off in sequence, as seen in Figure 6-14.

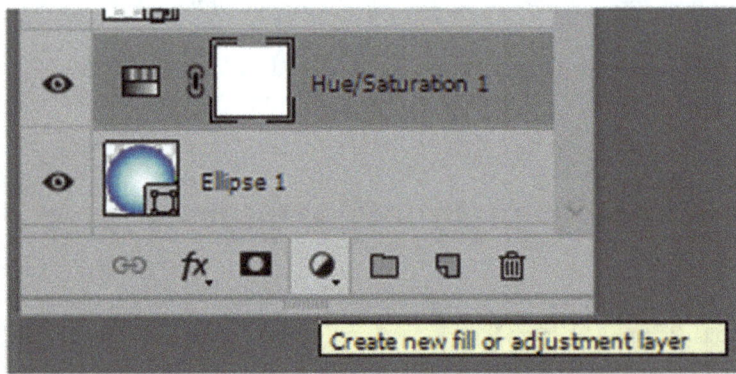

Figure 6-14. *Add a layer fill or adjustment layer to alter color in a specific frame*

At this point, you may want to preview or play your GIF animation. Click the play animation arrow to see how it runs (see Figure 6-15).

CHAPTER 6 ■ TOOLS FOR ANIMATION

Figure 6-15. *The play and preview features of the animation in the Timeline panel*

The arrows on the left move you back to the first frame or previous frame, and the arrow on the right moves to the next frame.

Click the square icon to stop the animation. Refer to Figure 6-16.

Figure 6-16. *The play icon turns into a stop icon*

You can also choose the number of times that you want the animation to run; see the drop-down menu in Figure 6-17.

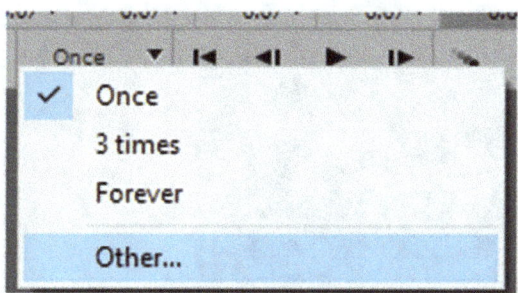

Figure 6-17. *Choose how long you want the animation to play*

- **Once**: The default; the animation plays one time.
- **3 times**: The animation plays three times.
- **Forever**: The animation never stops.
- **Other**: You can set the number of times that you want the animation to play, as seen in Figure 6-18.

CHAPTER 6 ■ TOOLS FOR ANIMATION

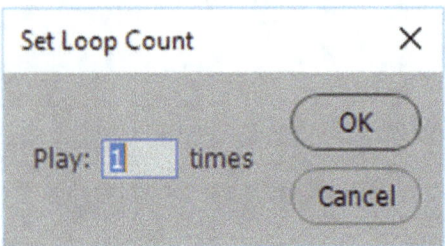

Figure 6-18. Choose the number of times you want the animation to play

For each frame, you can also set the duration with the little down arrow or leave it at the default time of 0 seconds. Refer to Figure 6-19.

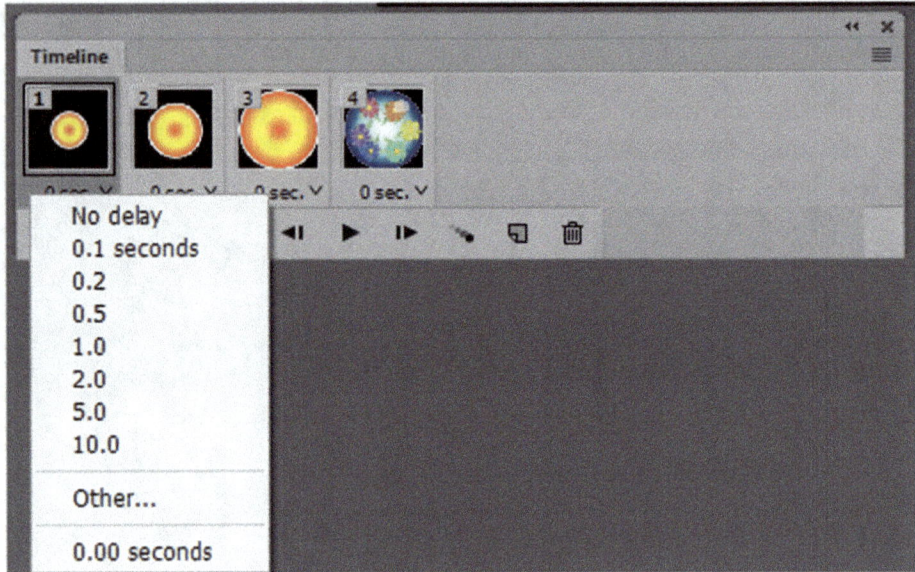

Figure 6-19. Set custom durations of time for each frame

If you want your animation to play in reverse order, select all or some frames, and from the Timeline panel, choose Reverse frames. This places the frames in reverse order in the Timeline panel, as seen in Figure 6-20.

CHAPTER 6 ■ TOOLS FOR ANIMATION

Figure 6-20. *Reverse the order of the frames*

To undo this right away, choose Edit ➤ Undo Reverse Frames.

To make frames match each other, choose Match Layer. Here you can choose how you want the layers to match to give them a similar look in their layer's position, visibility, and style, as seen in Figure 6-21. You can check or uncheck the areas you want to affect.

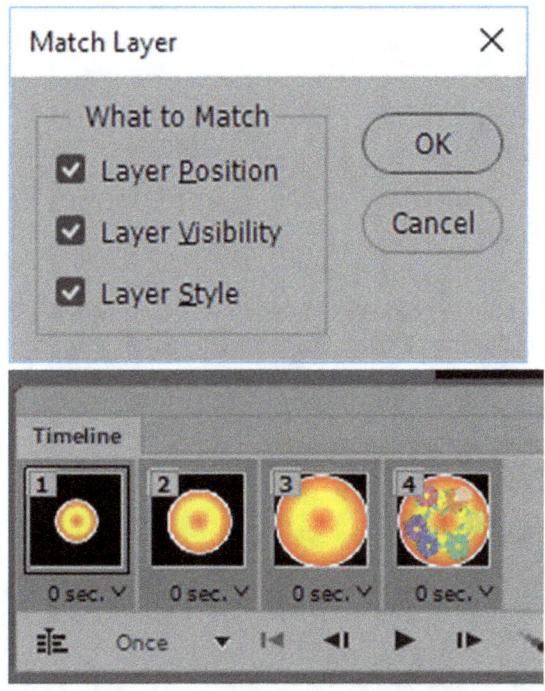

Figure 6-21. *Match layers so they have similar effects*

■ **Note** If you want to convert any frames into actual layers, from the Timeline panel's menu, choose Flatten Frames into Layers. This adds those frames to the Layers panel and is a quick way to keep a setting in an animation (see Figure 6-22).

139

CHAPTER 6 ■ TOOLS FOR ANIMATION

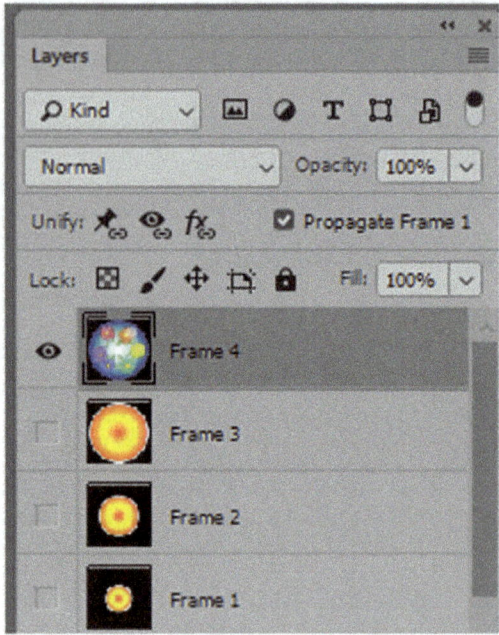

Figure 6-22. Flattening frames into layers

Tweening Layers in the Timeline

When you played the animation seen in Figure 6-15, it was a bit choppy. How can you make a smoother transition between the layers? In Adobe Animate CC, there is an option called tweening, which allows you to create additional transitory frames that give a smoother appearance of gradual change. The change might involve movement, opacity, or various effects. Select the frames that you want to tween, as seen in Figure 6-23.

Figure 6-23. Select the two layers that you want to create a transition tween

Choose Tween from the Timeline menu, or choose the Tween Animation Frames icon from the panel, which creates the tween. Figure 6-24 shows the dialog box.

140

CHAPTER 6 ■ TOOLS FOR ANIMATION

Figure 6-24. *Select the two layers that you want to create a transition tween*

Different types of tween effects can be accomplished by selecting one, two, or all frames at once. If you select two frames, for example, you can enter the number of frames you want to transition between them. When one frame is selected, you have access to Tween With: First Frame, Next Frame, Previous Frame, or Last Frame. This makes a smooth transition if you are planning to do some looping in the timeline of the GIF animation. For example, the last frame blends into the first when you tween the last frame. Refer to Figure 6-25.

141

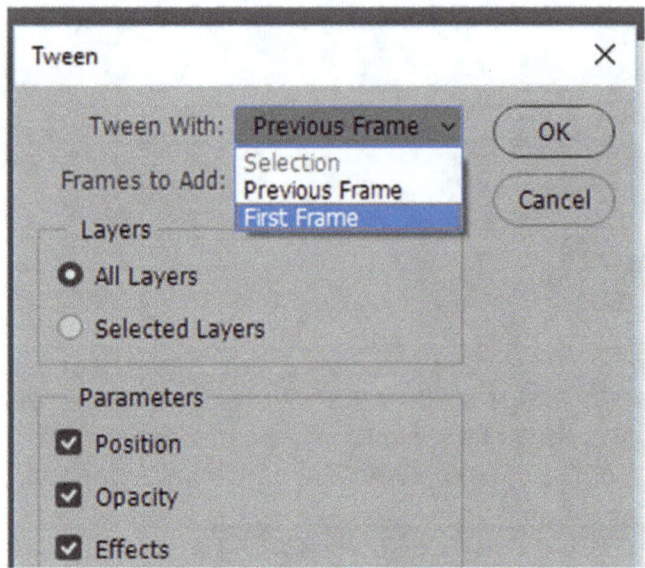

Figure 6-25. *The first frame tweens with the last*

For layers, you can choose the tween to happen on all layers or on selected layers.

If you have selected all the parameters, Photoshop will adjust for all of them or only the ones being used, and reflect the selected frames.

For a smoother appearance, continue to tween frames with choppy transitions before you export. You can also continue to alter the tween frames with the layers for an even smoother appearance. You can see my final example in this chapter's GIF Animation folder, which may look slightly different from Figure 6-26.

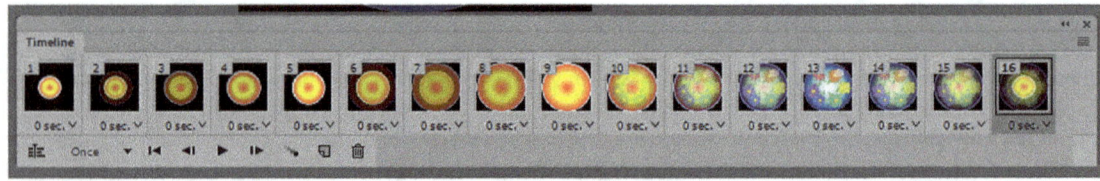

Figure 6-26. *A GIF animation with several tween layers*

Once you have tested your animation and it plays to your liking, make sure that you save the PSD file that you created it, in case you need to return to it or alter it later. Note that you can further optimize the animation using this option, but be aware that it may alter the quality of the image, so make sure to run a test on a copy first. Refer to Figure 6-27.

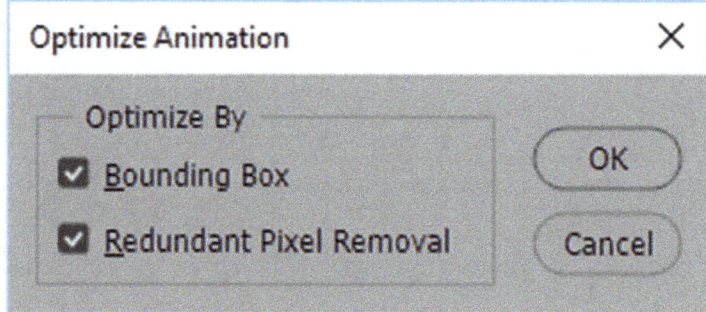

Figure 6-27. *Optimize the animation by bounding box or by removing redundant pixels*

Export Animated GIF

Now it's time to export. Go to File ➤ Export ➤ Save for Web (Legacy).

The Save for Web dialog box automatically recognizes that you are creating a GIF animation, because now the animation portion of the box is editable, as seen in Figure 6-28.

Figure 6-28. *You can now review and test the animation one more time before exporting it*

At this point in the dialog box as you did earlier in Chapter 4 with your static GIF you can spend time adjusting the quality of the file.

In the right column the bottom of the Animation area allows you to preview the animation and confirm the looping options. When done, click the Save button to save the GIF with the format of image only as you did in Chapter 4 with static GIFs with an image only format. When the file is saved it will be a single file containing the animation frames.

For an interesting tutorial on how to create a flowing water GIF animation, visit https://helpx.adobe. com/photoshop/how-to/make-animated-gif.html.

■ **Note** A GIF animation does not contain audio. You need to create a video timeline if you want sound in your animation. You look at video with audio in the next chapter.

Summary

This chapter explored how to create a simple GIF animation that can be placed on a webpage. These types of animations can be used as background, behind text, or as part of the text, such as a bullet on a webpage. While there are a lot of creative things that you can do with GIF animations, they unfortunately don't contain audio, and their quality is not always the best for photos. You will look at how to create a video with audio in the next chapter.

CHAPTER 7

■ ■ ■

Tools for Video

In this chapter, you are going focus on one specific file format for export: the MP4 video. So far in Photoshop, you have been working with static images, except for the GIF animation. However, while you can do some creative things with GIF animation frames, you cannot add audio to your animation, and GIF animations often have a posterized appearance when photographs such as a JPEG files are added as layers. Since you cannot animate a JPEG file, the choice is to create a video for your website.

This chapter explores the basic tools that are found in the Video Timeline panel. If you have used programs like Premiere Pro or After Effects, some of these video features might be familiar to you, and you can use what you know here in Photoshop CC. If you've never used those programs, that's OK; either way, you will be able to create a video that you can share with your clients on their websites.

■ **Note** This chapter does not have any actual projects. If you have RAW video of your own, make sure that it is in a MOV, AVI, or MP4 format for decent quality. However, you can use the files in the Chapter 7 folder if you do not have any file examples of your own to practice opening and viewing for this lesson. They are at https://github.com/Apress/graphics-multimedia-web-adobe-creative-cloud.

In Chapter 6, you looked at how to create an animation using frames.

If you are working with an existing animation that has frames, you can choose from the Timeline panel's Convert to Video Timeline menu, or click the Convert to Video Timeline icon at the bottom of the Timeline panel. Refer to Figure 7-1.

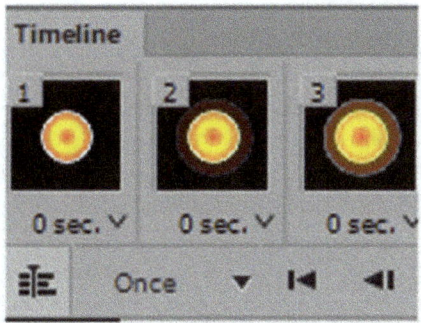

Figure 7-1. *Convert a frame animation to the Video Timeline with the icon on the lower left of the timeline*

CHAPTER 7 TOOLS FOR VIDEO

Video Setup Tips

Alternatively, if you are creating a new PSD file, you want to create a preset video file size (film and video), whatever size your RAW footage (AVI, MOV, MP4) was shot at, or a custom planned size for final web video for your site, as seen in Figure 7-2.

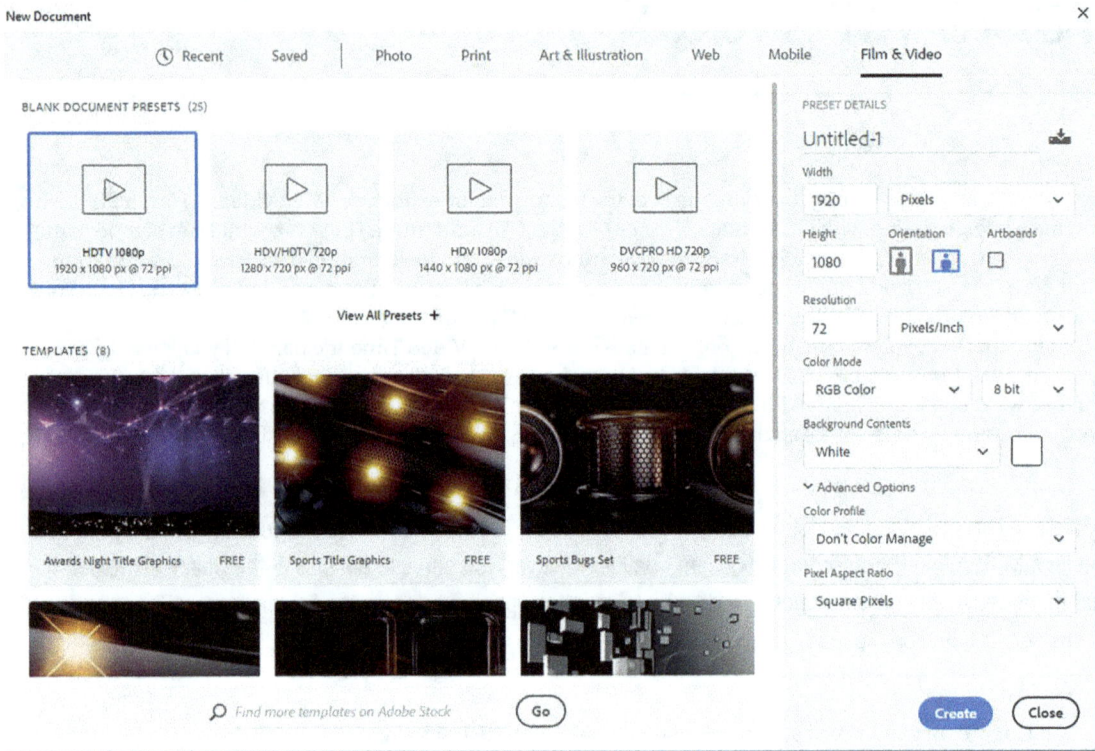

Figure 7-2. Choosing the correct file size for your video

View All Presets shows you more options.

Creating a Video in Photoshop is the one project that takes the most planning. The following are some tips to remember when planning to create a video.

- Make sure that you have a camera that can shoot at a decent resolution so that your images are clear for the viewer. Canon digital cameras can shoot in high definition and are great if you are on a budget and can't afford additional movie equipment or a professional camcorder. Some tablets and smartphones can also shoot adequate video for a website. Just remember, higher quality video means that you can use the footage for other non-web projects later. To be sure of the quality, run a few test videos to see what your video looks like under the conditions you will be shooting in. Review the video portion of your camera's manual if you need to adjust settings or lens focus.

- Shoot in landscape view, not in portrait view, especially when you are using a smartphone.

146

- Bring a tripod to keep your video stable, but for action shots, a steady hand (make sure the image stabilization setting is on) while panning and zooming may be just fine.

- Look for repetitive actions if you missed the action the first time you filmed it, or have a co-worker film the same action with their camera from another angle.

- Make sure that your audio is clear if it is part of the video when you use your digital camera. You may have to record the audio separately if you are doing narration. Smartphones often have audio recording apps that you can use for recording your voice or music in a quiet room. Later, you can convert these files to an MP3 format and add it to your video.

- Before you start shooting, plan a storyboard or sketch out your scenes for your video. What is the story you are trying to tell your viewers? It's OK to shoot extra footage, but you need to have a direction and goal for your storyline that will fit the time frame you intend. You want to account for time for things like the intro scene, voice over to match the action, and end credits.

- If you are shooting footage in a public area or a client's workplace, make sure that you have their permission to shoot video in that location and that the people acting in the video are OK with you shooting their action or voices. Get a media release (this might include a generic form they can download or you email to them). Get a signature that you have as a record.

- Always bring along an extra set of batteries for your camera. Video recording takes up more power than taking a still picture.

- Make sure that the end credits acknowledge all who contributed to the video or any audio that you did not create yourself.

- Make sure that you have adequate storage space on your computer and external drive so that you can work with your edited footage and your computer does not crash.

- As a novice, be realistic in your goals when it comes to creating your first video. You will not become Steven Spielberg overnight, so keep your effects simple until you have the time to master your skills. You can find special effects in the world around you, such as fire, steam, and smoke, which are difficult to create even in Photoshop.

- Listen for sounds in your immediate environment that you can record and use for other projects. If you can't create your own background music, or don't have a contact who can, visit this website for more resources: https://creativecommons.org/about/program-areas/arts-culture/arts-culture-resources/legalmusicforvideos/.

- Have fun and enjoy the process of shooting video; look for creative ways to tell the story through the lens.

To build a web video, I chose my size based on the size of most of my footage. My smaller Canon camera shot at 640×480 with a resolution of 72 dpi. Some of my footage was originally in AVI at 30 frames per second (fps) and some in MOV format at 24 fps (a second Canon camera at 1920×1800), but I converted to the same file format, size ratio, and 30 fps using Adobe Media Encoder (see Part 5). I also removed the audio from the videos. You do not have to do these steps before bringing your files into Photoshop CC because you can open MOV and AVI files and work with them right away.

Photoshop CC accepts the following RAW video formats: .264, .3gp, 3gpp, .avc, .avi, .f4v, .flv, .mov, .mp4, .mpe, .mpeg, .mpg, .mts, .mxf, .r3d, .ts, .vob, .wm, and .wmv.

CHAPTER 7 ■ TOOLS FOR VIDEO

■ **Tip** If the audio in your video does not relate to the story, and you want to add your own music and narration over top, then it is a good idea to remove the audio with Media Encoder before you create your video in Photoshop. Refer to the "Video Setup Tips" section in this chapter for a link to Creative Commons.

In addition, film from different cameras or video files from clients may not have the same ratio scale as your set video area. In my case, the MOV video files did not fit the same scale as the AVI format. I also have files that were created in the animation program, Animate CC, and had to be formatted in Media Encoder before being added to Photoshop CC. You'll look at how to adjust these properties and crop in Media Encoder in Part 5.

Nevertheless, you can use this extra footage area to your advantage. If your RAW video is larger than your intended size, use the extra area and pan or move the video around using keyframes so that the action is more centered. Extra size on the left and right is an useful if you could not center the scene while shooting as seen in Figure 7-3. You'll look at keyframes and how they relate to video layers shortly.

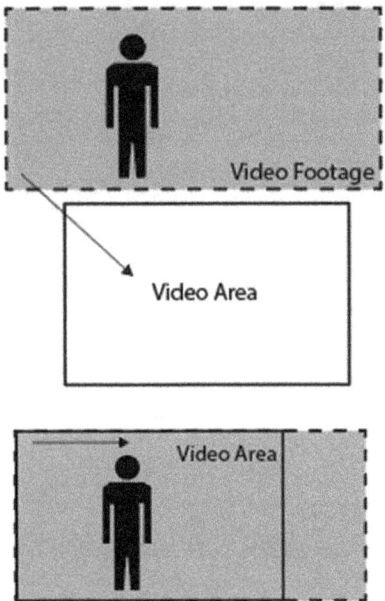

Figure 7-3. *When the footage area is larger than the video area, you can always move the video layer to center the action without leaving a gap on the sides*

Once you have all your video ready, you can begin. I spent time reviewing my footage and made a rough timeline with notes in Excel so that I could judge what footage to use for the timeline and in what order—basically, I created a verbal storyboard. It saves time if you must replace or add footage. While you can use Photoshop to do some trimming for you, using Media Encoder CC (see Part 5) to remove large unnecessary parts saves me time when working in Photoshop. You can use the files in the video footage folder for this chapter if you don't have any to practice with. For now, just use this chapter to understand the basics of the Video Timeline tool. You will create a basic video in Chapter 9 and put it into Dreamweaver in Part 6.

CHAPTER 7 ■ TOOLS FOR VIDEO

Video Timeline

Go to the Timeline and choose the Create Video Timeline button that appears as an option in the center of the drop-down menu. Refer to Figure 7-4.

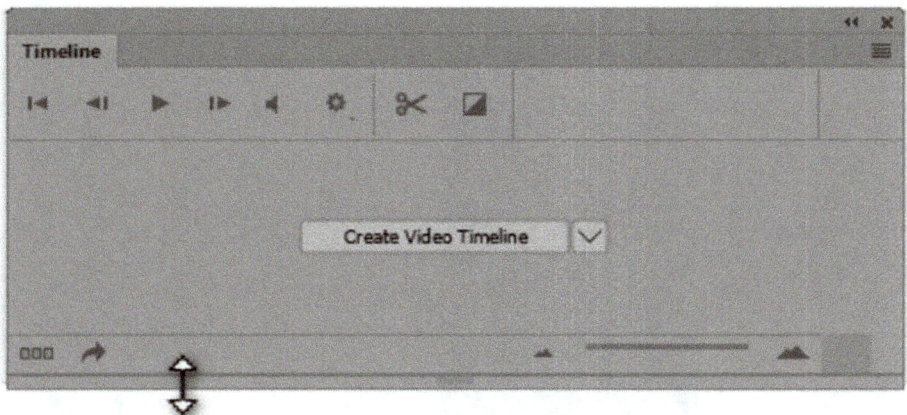

Figure 7-4. *Click Create Video Timeline to begin creating your video and scale the Timeline panel to fit your screen area*

You can scale the Timeline panel by dragging its sides and bottom when the white arrow-shaped icon appears.

Upon clicking the video option, you are presented with a new default selection of layers and frames in the Timeline panel. Refer to Figure 7-5.

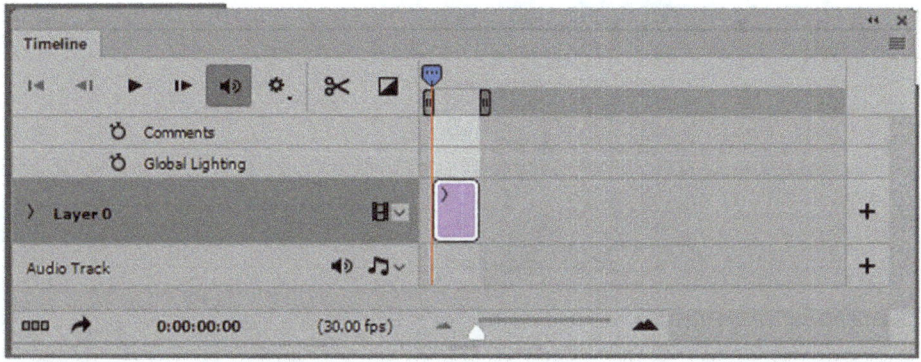

Figure 7-5. *How the timeline appears when you start a new file and currently have added no video. The background layer becomes layer 0.*

You'll notice that the Video Timeline layout and menu is different than the frame animation you saw in Chapter 6.

149

CHAPTER 7 ■ TOOLS FOR VIDEO

■ **Note** If you do not see the comments and global lighting options, you can turn them on in the Timeline menu in Show ➤ Comments Track and Show ➤ Global Lighting Track. You'll look at what these are later in the chapter. Refer to Figure 7-6.

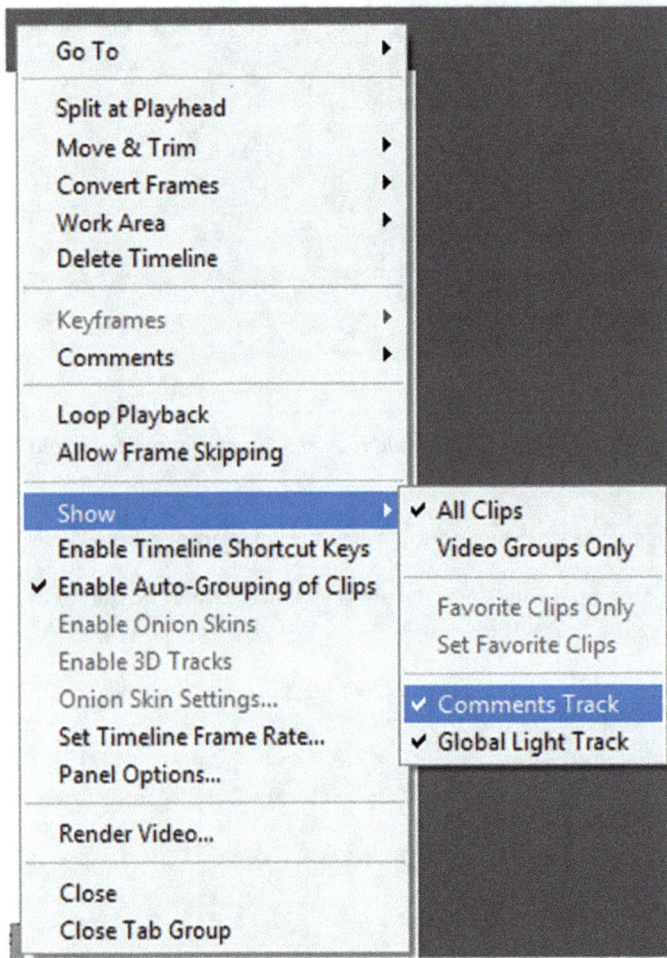

Figure 7-6. *The Timeline menu, where you can add comments and global lighting to the timeline*

As with the frames in Chapter 6, the Layers panel works closely with the Video timeline. Anything that appears in the timeline can also be found in the Layers panel with a matching name, as seen in Figure 7-7.

150

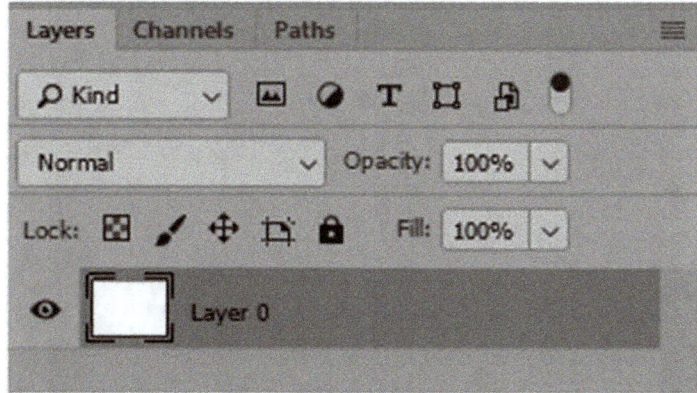

Figure 7-7. *The Layers panel with one layer that was formerly the background is now layer 0*

If you rename the layer, it changes in the Timeline panel.

The background layer becomes layer 0 when you convert to a video timeline. This way, even the background layer is editable and can be adjusted in various scenes as required.

■ **Caution** You can revert to a frame animation with the Convert to Frame Animation icon (see Figure 7-8), but be aware that certain changes that you make may not be preserved during transition, such as audio or some effects; so do any changes on a copy of the original.

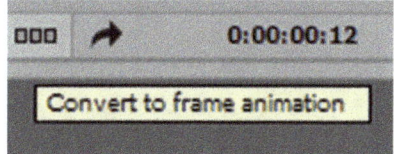

Figure 7-8. *The Convert to Frame Animation button allows you to return to a frame animation*

As mentioned, if you have ever worked with Premiere Pro CC, After Effects CC, or even Animate CC, the arrangement of the timeline will look familiar to you.

Let's take some time to look at the features of this part of the Timeline panel.

Currently, our file 640×480 at 72 dpi has no video in it; only one layer.

Layers in the Timeline

A layer appears as a purple rectangle in the Timeline panel. It is not a video layer, but it does have a small default amount of time attached to it; about 3 or 4 seconds. Every time you add a layer to the Layers panel, it adds that layer and its name to the Timeline panel. Refer to Figure 7-9.

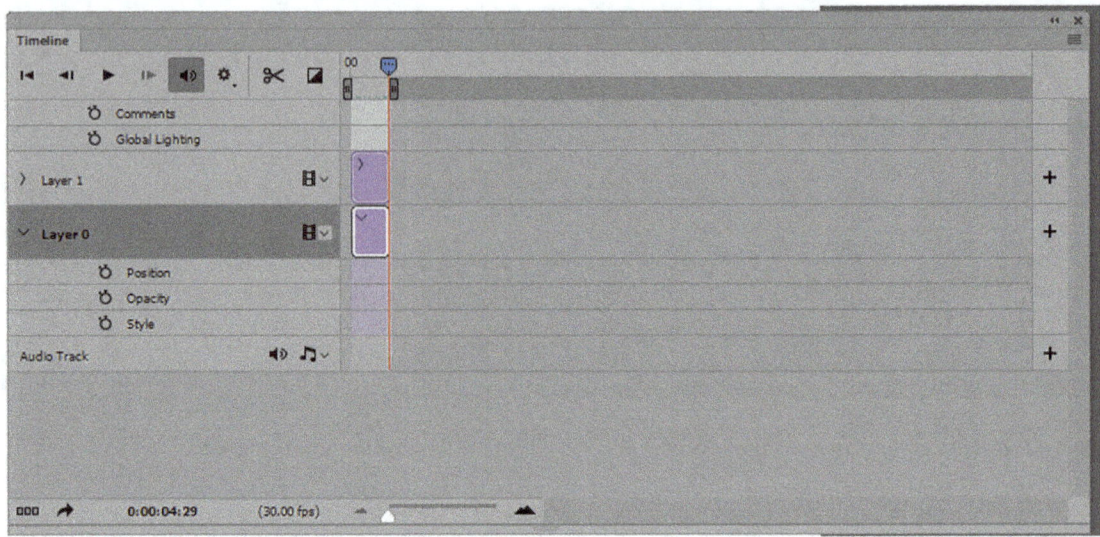

***Figure 7-9.** How layers appear in the Timeline panel*

Depending on where the blue playhead is located, the track (layer) starts at that location expanding the timeline.

As with an animated frame, a layer track can have its position opacity and style altered by using keyframes, as seen in Figure 7-10.

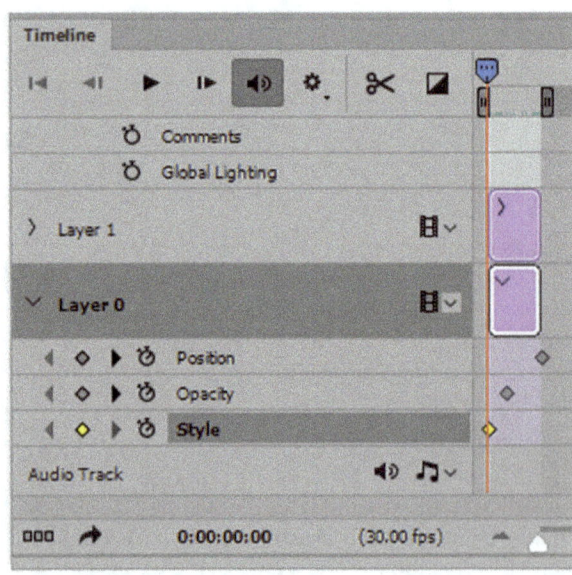

***Figure 7-10.** Adding keyframes to the timeline*

Keyframes are a point of transition. By opening the layer's options using the arrow and the blue scrubber playhead, you can then set a keyframe point where various transitions happen. For example, if you set a keyframe for a layer and then make an opacity change from that key point to the next or the end of the video, that change will happen. You should at least have two keyframes as a starting point, and then an ending point so that the transition works correctly.

■ **Note** You cannot transform a layer with keyframes. You see how to do that with Smart Objects shortly.

The keyframes that appear as yellow diamonds are called *linear interpolation*. You can check this when you right-click them, as seen in Figure 7-11.

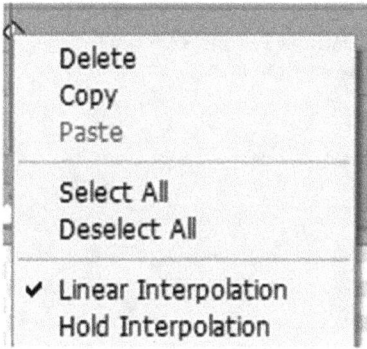

Figure 7-11. The keyframe selected is currently linear

■ **Note** Interpolation is also known as tweening. It is the process of filling in unknown values between two known values. Examples would be the morphing of a red object on the left into a blue object on the right. In digital video and film, interpolation usually means generating new values between two keyframes; you saw an example of tweening in the frame animation timeline in Chapter 6.

There are two types of interpolation.

- **Linear (diamond shape)**: Evenly changes the animated property from one keyframe to another. (The one exception is the Layer Mask Position property, which switches between enabled and disabled states abruptly.) In Figure 7-12, it may appear as yellow or gray, depending on if it is selected or not, or if an actual transition is preset, if not the diamond appears smaller.

Figure 7-12. Various linear keyframes in different states

- **Hold (square shape):** Maintains the current property setting. This interpolation method is useful for strobe effects, or when you want layers to appear or disappear suddenly. A red or yellow arrow can also be a hold if found with a linear interpolation combination, as seen in Figure 7-13.

Figure 7-13. *Various hold interpolation keyframes in different states*

Notice that by clicking the Clock icon for each layer's properties, you can add a yellow diamond at the playhead line point. This sets the points for when each event occurs on a keyframe. Further points can be added by clicking the diamond next to the clock. You can move from keyframe to keyframe with the left and right arrows. If you click the clock again, it permanently removes all existing keyframes for that track's properties as seen in Figure 7-14. To undo this right away, choose Edit ➤ Undo right away.

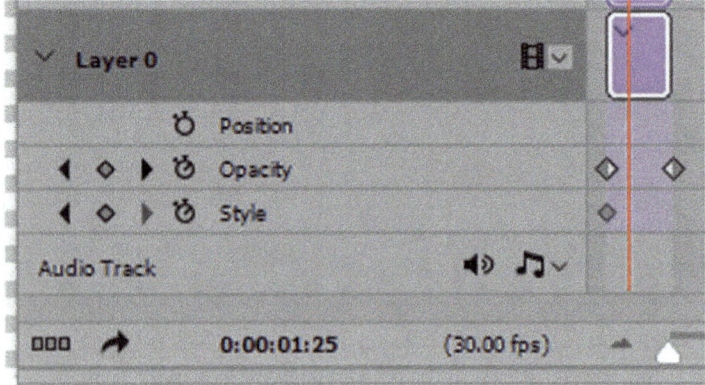

Figure 7-14. *Using the clock to add or remove keyframes from the track*

You can delete, copy, or paste a keyframe by right-clicking and choosing it from the pop-up menu (see Figure 7-11) or from the Video Timeline menu, as seen in Figure 7-15.

CHAPTER 7 ■ TOOLS FOR VIDEO

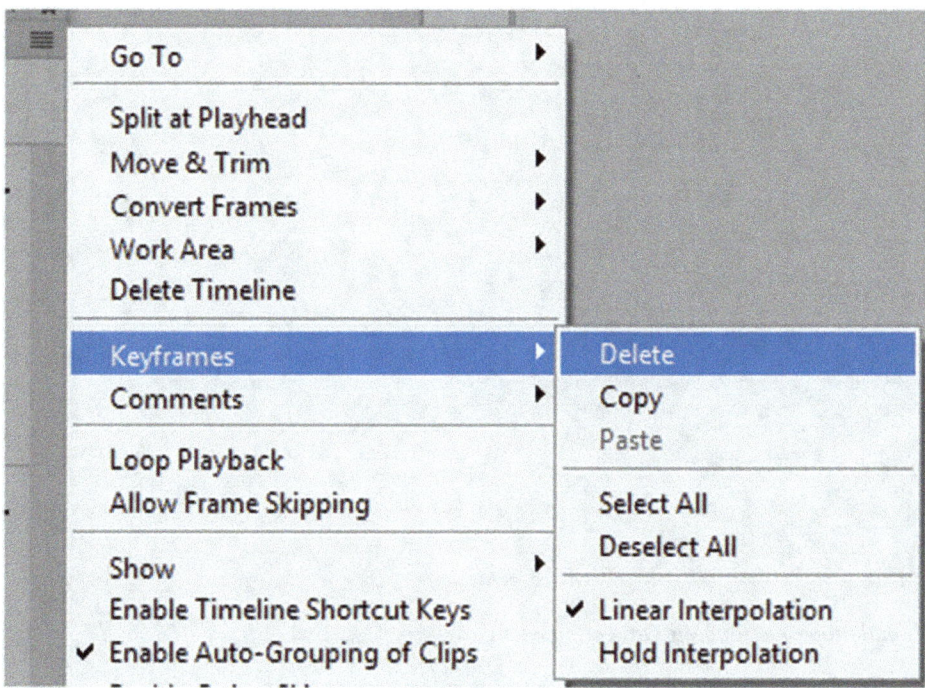

Figure 7-15. *The Timeline menu allows you to add or remove keyframes*

While selected as a diamond shape keyframe, the interpolation is linear interpolation, but you can switch it to hold interpolation, which is a square. For now, leave them at the default linear.

Animation of a keyframe requires that you have at least two keyframes to animate that property; otherwise, any changes made last for the entire layer video clip.

If a property is not turned on, it contains no keyframes.

If you click, a keyframe with your mouse and drag, you can move the keyframe to a new location on the video clip timeline.

Other Layer Properties

Other types of layers, such as fill or adjustment layers, can have properties added to their tracks. The same is true for vector-shaped layers. A vector mask or layer mask can be altered, as seen in Figure 7-16.

155

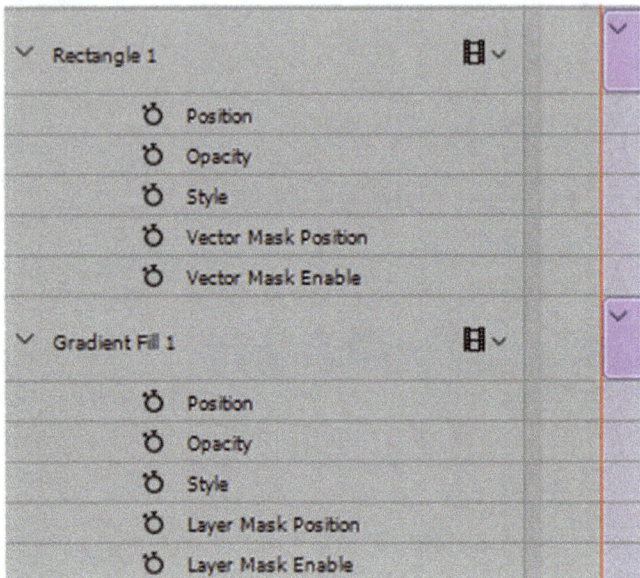

Figure 7-16. *Additional properties for vector and adjustment layers*

You can add this same mask setting to a non-video layers (purple) by adding a mask and a vector mask to the layer, and then edit them, as seen in Figure 7-17.

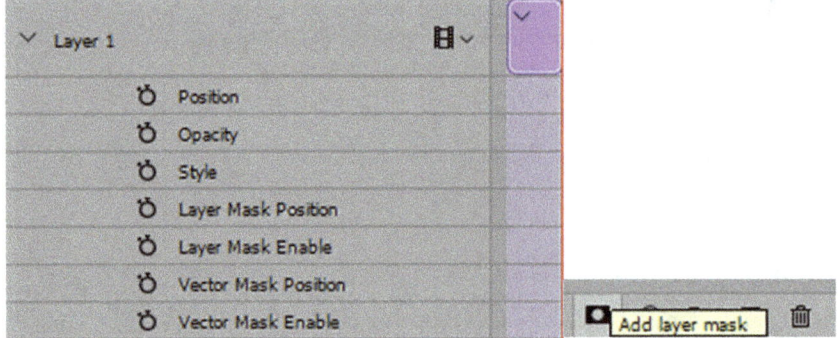

Figure 7-17. *Adding vector and layer masks to a layer in the Layers panel gives you access to the properties for the track*

A Type layer can also have Transform and Text Warp properties added, as seen in Figure 7-18.

CHAPTER 7 ■ TOOLS FOR VIDEO

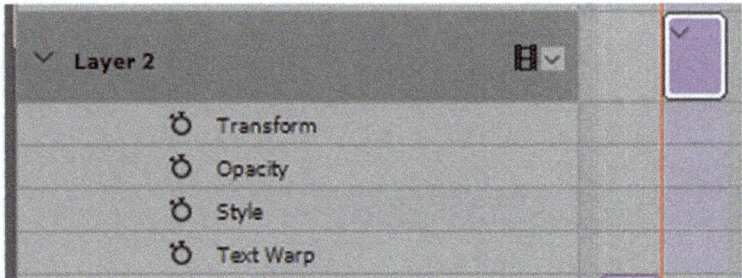

Figure 7-18. Type layers have the Transform and Text Warp properties

■ **Note** With the type, you have access to the Transform properties, but the with the layers, so far, you cannot. If you want to transform a non-video layer (purple) or even a video layer (blue) you need to make into a Smart Object (also purple).

Smart Object Layers

In the Layers panel, right-click a layer and choose Convert to Smart Object, as seen in Figure 7-19.

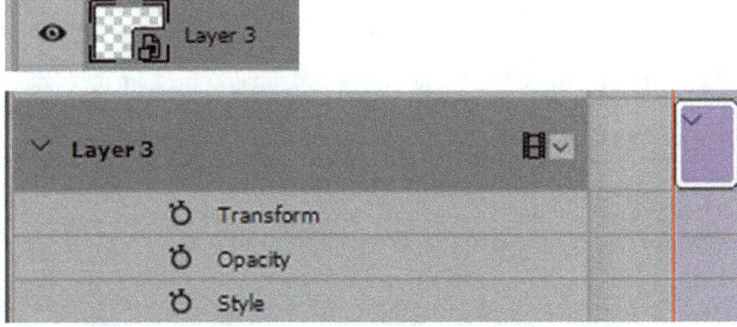

Figure 7-19. The layer is now a Smart Object, and you have access to the Transform properties

Transform and position are the same. When clicked, a Smart Object opens a PSB file that can have a timeline within it, as well as other layers blending and masks.

■ **Tip** if you are going to transform a mask, make sure that it is inside a Smart Object for the animation; otherwise, it might not scale accurately during the transform.

157

Adding Video Layers

At this point, you might want to import a video or add other photos to your Layers panel.

You can add video layers by going to Layer ➤ Video Layers ➤ New Video Layer from File..., as seen in Figure 7-20.

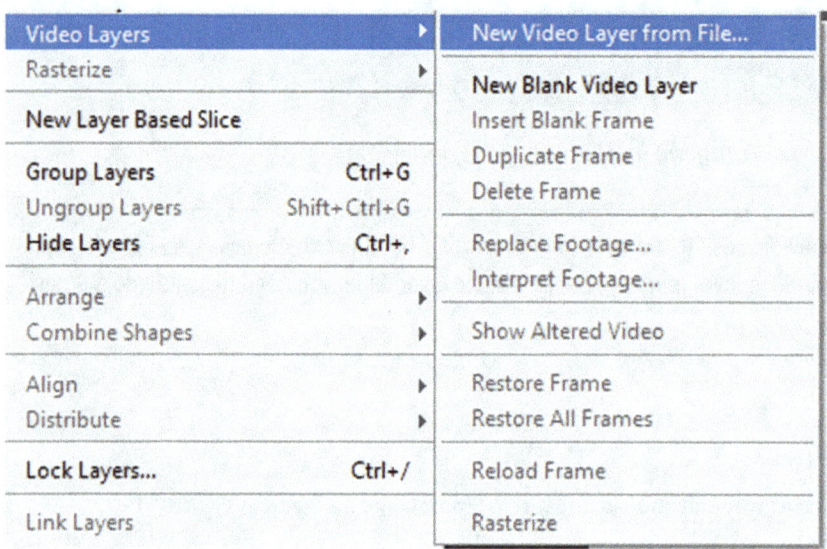

Figure 7-20. *Import a video layer*

Locate a video file like an AVI, MOV, or MP4 or any graphic image sequence (image1.jpeg, image2.jpg, and so on) listed in the format options.

This allows you to add a new graphic or video clip to your Layers panel and Video Timeline panel.

- **New Blank Video Layer:** Adds a new layer to your Layers panel and to the Video Timeline panel. The layers (video or non-video) in the timeline are also known as *tracks*. A blank video layer can act as a placeholder until you are able to add the actual track.

Notice that a new video layer is added to the Layers panel and to the Video Timeline panel. Refer to Figure 7-21.

CHAPTER 7 ■ TOOLS FOR VIDEO

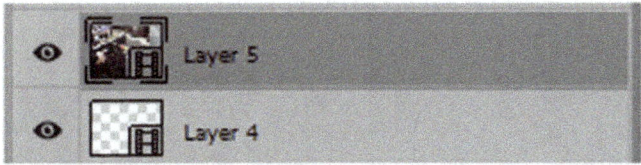

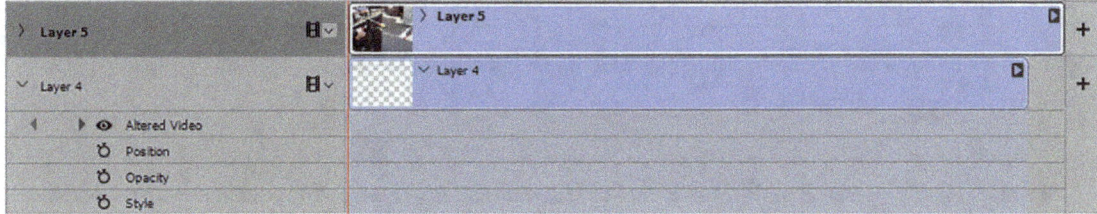

Figure 7-21. *A blank video layer and a video layer can be added to the Timeline panel and the Layers panel*

You can tell that it is a video layer because it has a little Film icon on the preview of the layers' thumbnail image. Video layers, whether they contain content or not, are blue with a play arrow. A non-video layer is purple with a play arrow, except for fills and adjustment layers.

If you click the arrow, it reveals two settings: video and audio. Video shows the current duration and speed of that track, which you can alter via drop-down sliders, as seen in Figure 7-22.

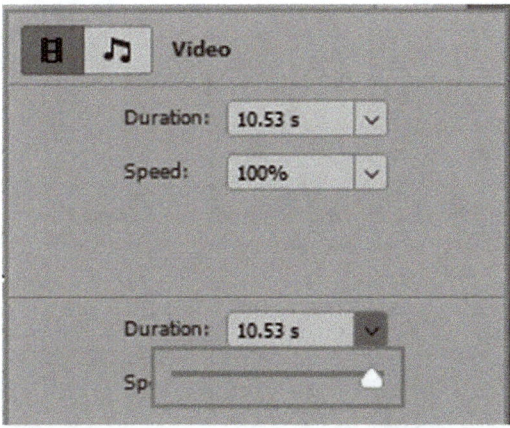

Figure 7-22. *Alter the speed and duration for the track*

Altering the speed of the track 100% or lower, slows it down; higher than 100% speeds it up. This can affect the duration. So, the track may be longer or shorter than the original time. Likewise, you can alter the duration of the track by holding your cursor over the front end or back end of your track. Your cursor will change into a prong-like icon, and then you can drag to remove footage from the front or the back of your track, as seen in Figure 7-23.

159

CHAPTER 7 ■ TOOLS FOR VIDEO

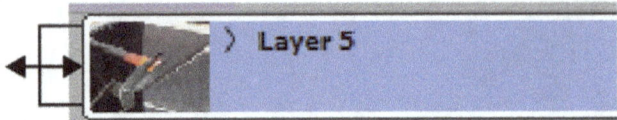

Figure 7-23. *Alter the duration of a track while in the timeline*

■ **Note** This removal does not affect the original footage, and you can always pull it back to the original size to reset it.

The audio option is found in the Music tab. If a video has audio, you can alter the volume or cause the sound to fade in or out at the end. While you can remove the audio before bringing your file into Photoshop using Adobe Media Encoder, you can choose Mute Audio to turn off the sound in that track; you can turn it on again if required. Refer to Figure 7-24.

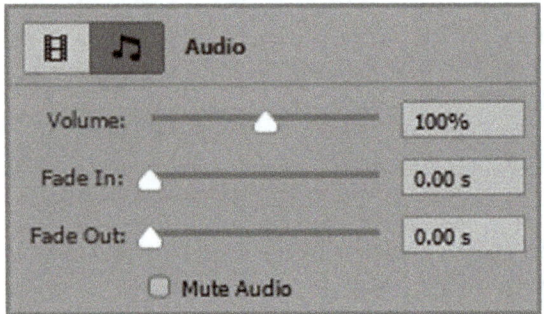

Figure 7-24. *Alter the audio for your video track*

As with the frame animation and non-video layers, each video layer in the timeline can be altered by position, opacity, and style (inner glow, drop shadow) by using the keyframes, as seen in Figure 7-25.

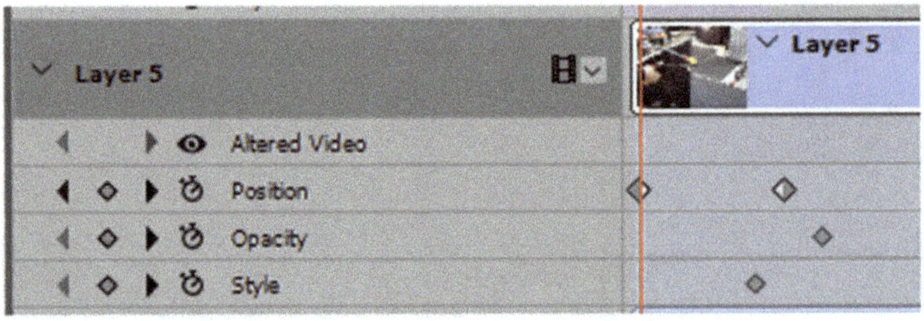

Figure 7-25. *Properties of a video track*

If you are using a blank video layer on top of a video layer to paint over an area, you can turn on and off the altered video eye to check your alterations that can be made with a Clone or Brush tools. To see where and how points along the track have been altered refer to Figure 7-26 and move the blue playhead to those areas.

160

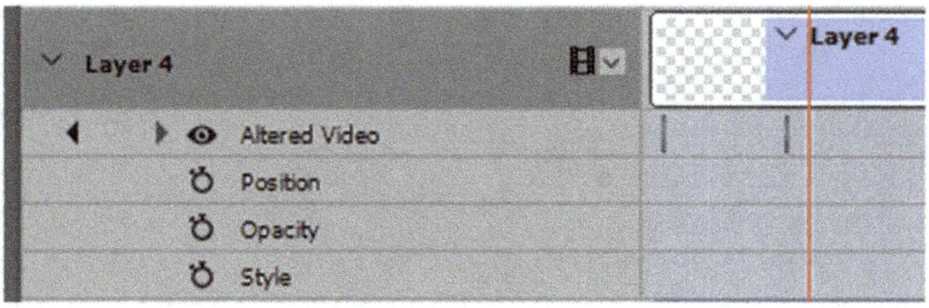

CHAPTER 7 ■ TOOLS FOR VIDEO

Figure 7-26. Properties of an altered blank video track

For more information on how to paint an altered video layer with the Clone stamp, Pattern stamp, Healing brush, or Spot Healing brush, visit https://helpx.adobe.com/photoshop/using/painting-frames-video-layers.html.

The brush only paints one frame at a time, so if you have mass areas of video that need coverage, you need to determine the best workflow to efficiently accomplish these changes. Perhaps a Smart Object is a better solution for areas that change little, such as an annoying glare in the corner of the frame.

To restore an altered video track, choose Layer ➤ Video Layers ➤ Restore Frame (while highlighted frame is selected using the playhead and mouse arrow) or Layers ➤ Video Layer ➤ Restore All Frames.

Video Groups

You can also add video layers via the timeline if you want to keep them all in one video group (folder) or track. This is good if you want one video to play after another without a transitional break. Click the plus (+) icon to add the video to the group, as seen in Figure 7-27.

Figure 7-27. Videos play one after the other in a video track

■ **Note** If you discover that you put the wrong video into the video layer, you can always select that layer track (white outline) and choose Layer ➤ Video Layers ➤ Replace Footage. Find the correct video and click Open, which automatically updates that layer with the correct video. Also, since the video is linked, if the original video is removed after the PSD file is closed from the folder, a warning icon or message will appear, as seen in Figure 7-28. You can also use the Replace Footage option to relink the video.

161

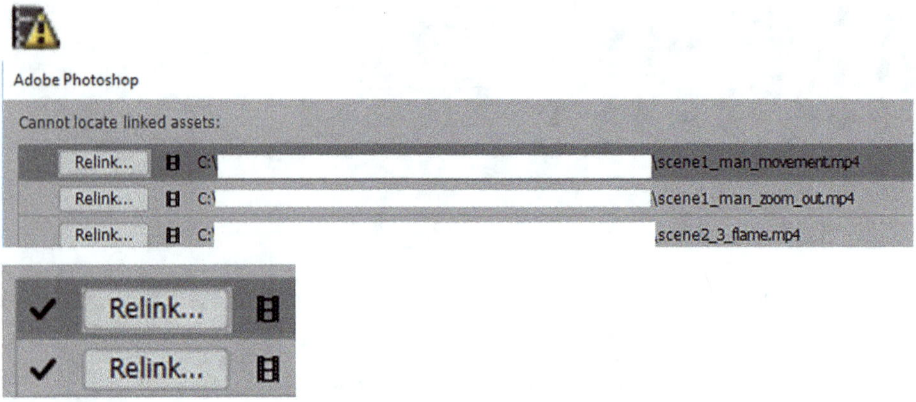

CHAPTER 7 ■ TOOLS FOR VIDEO

Figure 7-28. Video link is broken and you need to updated it

When one video is relinked, if other missing links are found in the same folder, they automatically relink. To confirm, click OK in the dialog box.

Video layers and non-video layers can be part of the same video group if you plan one to lead into the other without a transitional break.

Using Layers That Are Not Part of a Video Group

Layers within the Video Timeline panel can be moved up or down when you drag the video clip into another group. Refer to Figure 7-29.

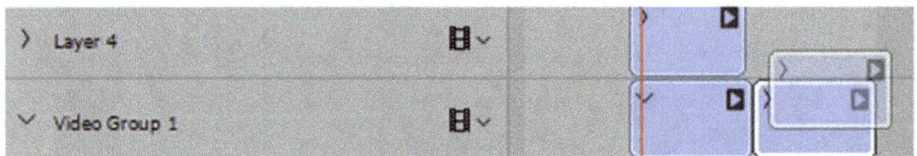

Figure 7-29. Moving a video from one group to another

To move outside the group, use the Layers panel to drag the video into its own layer track. To drag one or more video clips on the same layer timeline, Shift-click to select each movie clip and then drag upward to appear in above another video or downward to appear below a video that now overlaps it. Refer to Figure 7-30.

162

CHAPTER 7 ■ TOOLS FOR VIDEO

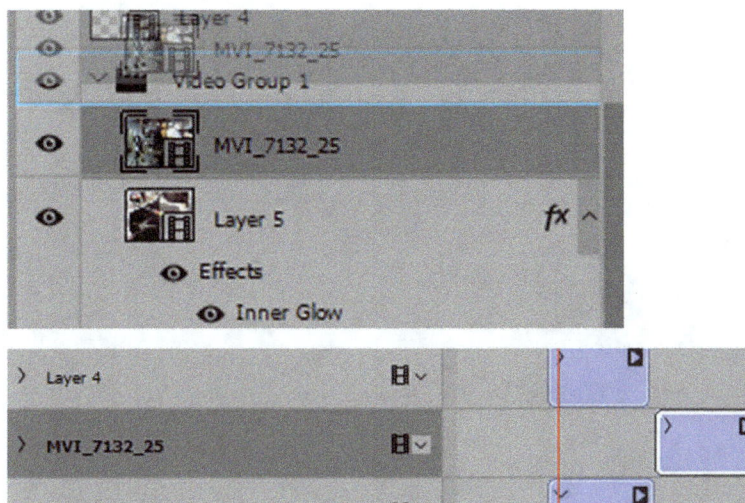

Figure 7-30. *Moving a video out of a group so that it is on its own layer in the timeline*

Remember, only when a movie clip is selected (white outline) can you alter its properties. Clicking blank areas in the timeline where the movie clip is not playing leaves properties like blends, opacities, and fills unavailable.

Convert Video Layers to Smart Objects

Video layers can be edited further when converted to Smart Objects. In some cases, you may need to do this if the orientation of the video is wrong, or you need to transform or scale the video so that two videos can play side by side, like a split screen. Like any other Smart Object layer, it is editable and could have a mask applied. To convert a video layer to a Smart Object, in the Layers panel, right-click a layer and choose Convert to Smart Object. The video clip will have a purple color in the timeline, indicating that it is a Smart Object with a video inside. Refer to Figure 7-31.

163

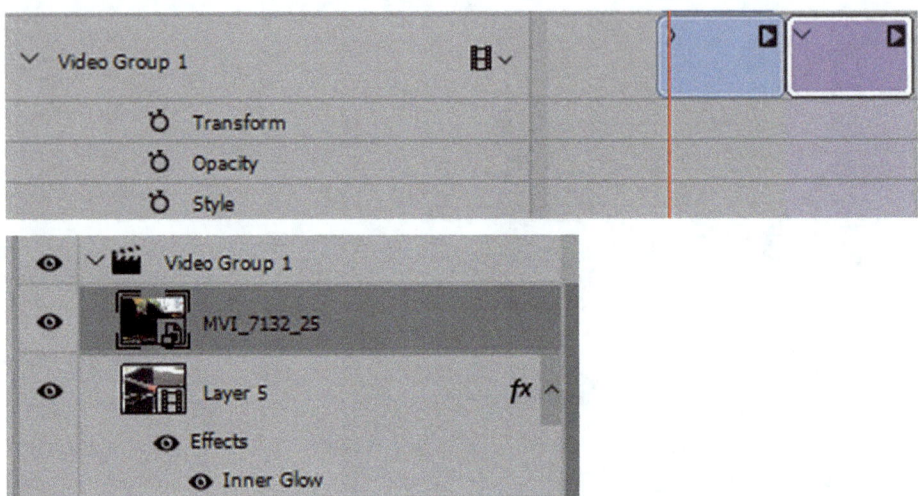

Figure 7-31. The video becomes a Smart Object, but can still be on the same track

You can still edit the video by double clicking it in the Layers panel, this bring up a PSB file that you can alter and then save changes and close. The alterations will be reflected in the Layers panel and Timeline panel.

The Smart Object's Play icon allows you to do something different. By right-clicking the Smart Object or Play icon in the track, you can choose several types of motion combinations, such as pan & zoom and rotate. Refer to Figure 7-32.

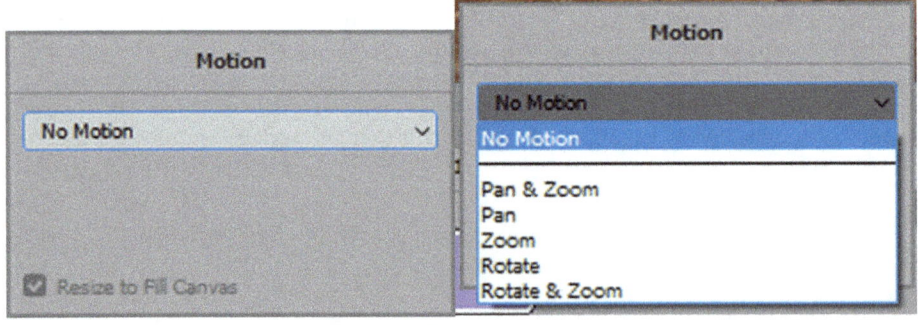

Figure 7-32. Adding motion to a Smart Object layer in the timeline

The default is No Motion. Each motion option (see Figure 7-33) gives various pan, zoom, or rotate settings. It also allows you to resize to fill canvas; this setting, when enabled, ensures that the clip is the same size as your Photoshop canvas during the motion.

CHAPTER 7 ■ TOOLS FOR VIDEO

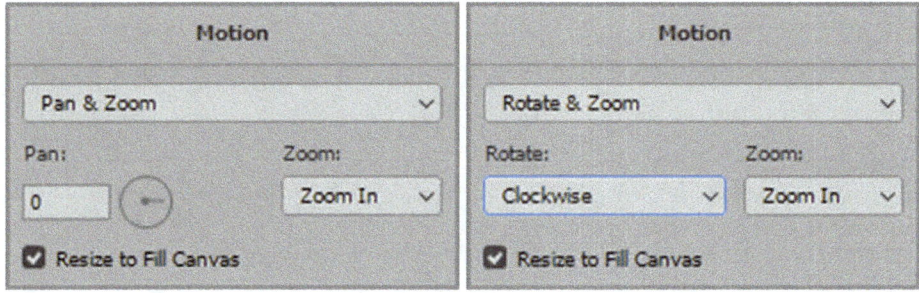

Figure 7-33. *Motion choices for your Smart Object*

If you don't want to use the preset motion settings, you can use keyframes to alter the point of zoom, pan, or rotation. To do this when you are over a selected Smart Object with the blue handle playhead, use the menu option Edit ➤ Free Transform to alter the width and height of the Smart Object for the current keyframe that will appear as a transform in the timeline panel.

■ **Note** Once the video clip is converted to a Smart Object, it cannot be returned to a video clip unless you undo the video change right away in the History panel (see Figure 7-34) or delete that layer from the Layers panel and add a new video.

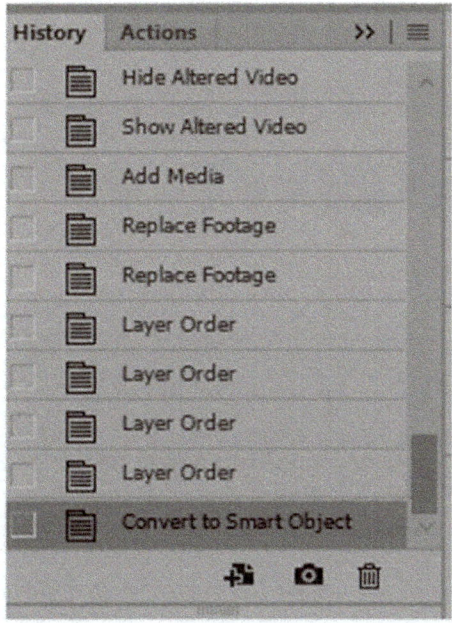

Figure 7-34. *Undo a Smart Object video layer right away in the History panel if you want it to return to being a video before making further changes*

165

CHAPTER 7 ■ TOOLS FOR VIDEO

Delete Timeline

If you want to want to remove the entire timeline in the Video Timeline menu, choose Delete Timeline. Refer to Figure 7-35.

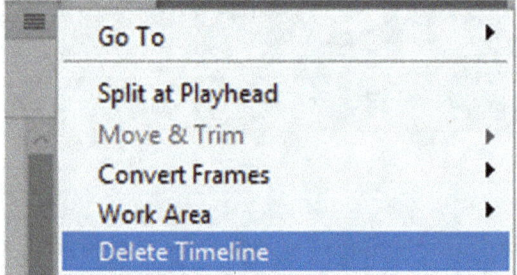

Figure 7-35. *Delete the entire timeline to start over again*

Delete Track

If you need to delete a layer or track at any time, refer to Figure 7-36. Click the arrow next to the layer's Film icon and select Delete Track.

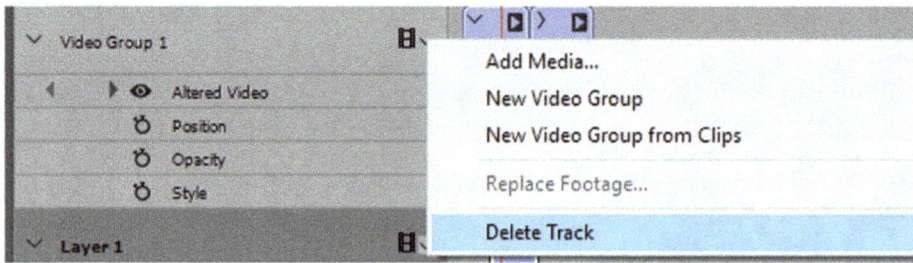

Figure 7-36. *Delete the entire track*

This removes the movie layers from the Layers panel as well.

Select Transition and Drag to Apply

When video layers, Smart Objects, or type layers are on their own tracks, you can blend one into another overlapping track by using various fade-in or fade-out sequences. Refer to Figure 7-37.

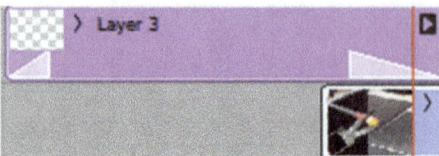

Figure 7-37. *Fade in or fade out to create a transition between video or Smart Objects*

166

CHAPTER 7 ■ TOOLS FOR VIDEO

You can set various transitional blends using the half-square icon in the video timeline between movies by choosing a transition and dragging that blend onto the selected movie clip's start or end. Move it around on the clip to set the duration. Refer to Figure 7-38.

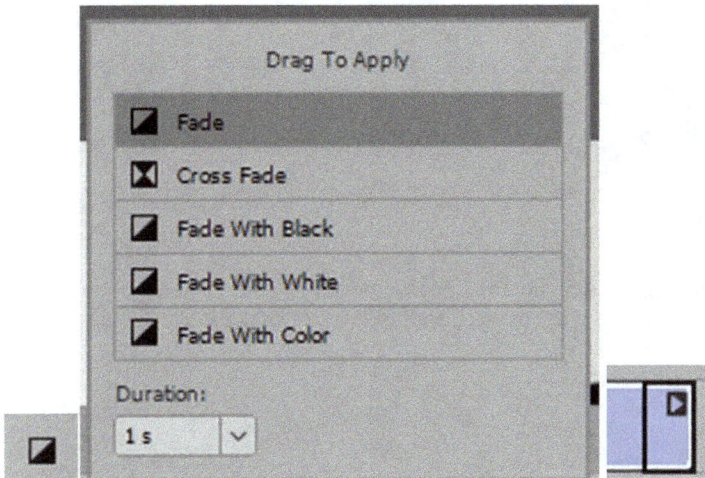

Figure 7-38. Choose a transition and drag it onto the track either at the start or the end

If you want the transition to be a default of one second, leave it at the current setting or while on the video track drag with the prong-like trim cursor to the end of the white transition ramp in or out to make it longer or shorter. Refer to Figure 7-39.

Figure 7-39. Drag the white transition fade on the video clip to shorten or lengthen it

- **Fade:** Causes the fade to be a gradual opacity change that makes the upper clip slowly disappear, revealing the lower clip; it can fade in or out, depending on where it is placed on the video track. **Cross Fade:** Works when two videos are in the same track group; then, you can overlap them. This takes up less space if you have many clips to cross fade. Refer to Figure 7-40.

Figure 7-40. Example of a cross fade

167

If you want to set a custom color from the color picker, choose Fade With Color; otherwise, it fades in black or white. Refer to Figure 7-41.

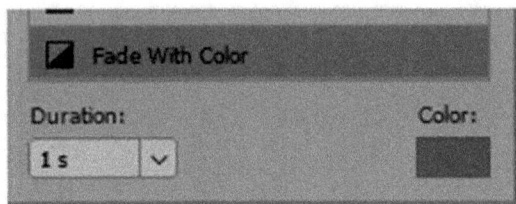

Figure 7-41. *Choose Fade With Color for a specific color*

If you need to alter or remove the fade, right-click the transition in the movie clip. Then choose a different transition from the drop-down menu and enter a new duration time, or click the Trash icon to delete, as seen in Figure 7-42.

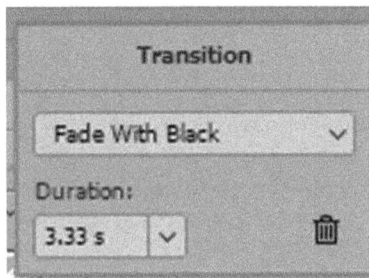

Figure 7-42. *Edit or remove the transition*

Split Video Clips

There may be parts in the middle of your video footage that you want to remove because you do not want it to be part of the final video. You can use the blue scrubber playhead to find a point in your track and split it.

- **Split the Playhead:** Scissor icon or found in the timeline's menu in the Video Timeline panel. Splits the video into two parts in the timeline when you place the playhead at the point you want to split. In Figure 7-43, the video appears on two layers in the Layers panel and as two parts in the Video Timeline.

CHAPTER 7 ■ TOOLS FOR VIDEO

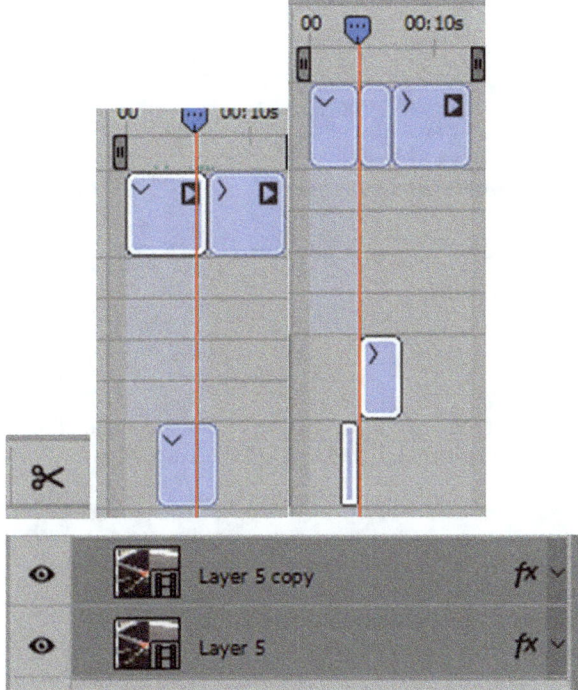

Figure 7-43. *Splitting the video into two parts*

You can then drag the split video to another location ion the timeline, and even collapse or expand it on either end to repeat or remove more footage.

■ **Note** You must be on a select area (white outline) of a video for this to work.

Trim Movie

If you would rather trim part of the footage than use the prong-shaped icon to clip the beginning or end, you can move your playhead to a point on a selected movie layer. Then choose Trim Start at Playhead or Trim End at Playhead, as seen in Figure 7-44.

169

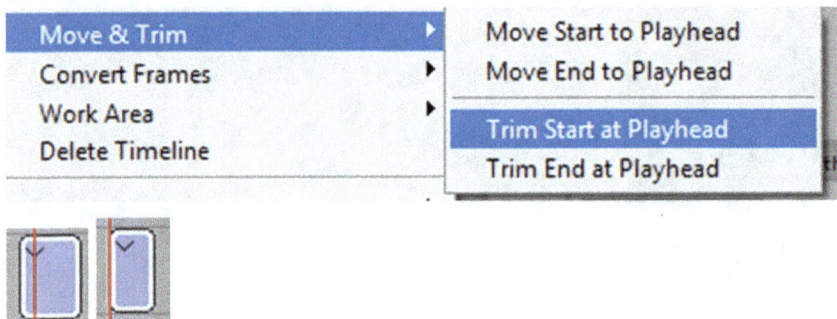

Figure 7-44. Trimming using the playhead

This shaves off part of the movie at this point. Move Start to Playhead and Move End to Playhead allow you to align a track to a specific point in the timeline using the playhead; this is easier than dragging the track.

Convert Frames

After you have completed the video, if you need to make a copy of each layer in a duplicate file (don't override the original), in the Video Timeline panel, choose Convert Frames. There are three settings, as seen in Figure 7-45.

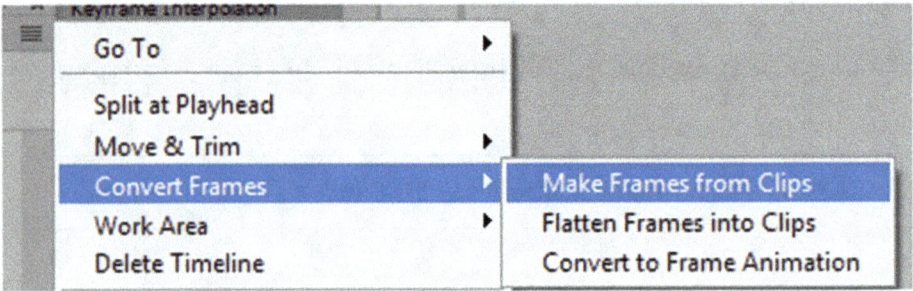

Figure 7-45. Convert Frames options

- **Make Frames from Clips:** Make the movie frames single clips on the timeline from separate layers. This only works if the video is first flattened into clips.

- **Flatten Frames into Clips:** This makes all the frames separate layers for clips in the Layers panel. And then as separate layers in the timeline, you can drag selected frames and order them onto one layer in the timeline as a video group to create a frame-by-frame animation. This is useful if you need to alter each frame to add or remove something from the scene. Examples are a floating orb or some item that added by creating a drawing first.

- **Convert to Frame Animation**: This converts back to the animation timeline; in doing so, you lose important data. If you do this by accident, make sure to hit Cancel in the warning box, or go back in your History panel to before this setting, as seen in Figure 7-46.

CHAPTER 7 ■ TOOLS FOR VIDEO

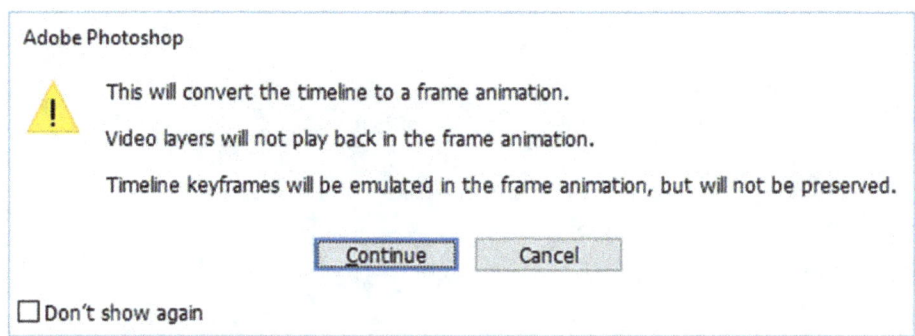

Figure 7-46. Warning for converting the timeline to a frame animation

Video and 3D Graphics

You can also add 3D effects to your layers.

- **3D object or camera position**: Use the 3D position or camera tools to move the model or 3D camera over a duration of time. Photoshop can tween frames between position or camera movements to create smooth motion effects.

- **3D render settings**: Alter render modes with the ability to tween transitions between some render modes. For example, change gradually from vertices mode to wireframe to simulate the sketching-in of a model's structure.

- **3D cross section**: Rotate an intersecting plane to display a changing cross section over time. Change cross section settings between frames to highlight different model areas during an animation.

In high-quality animations, you can render each animation frame using the Render options in the Render Video dialog box (see the "Rendering the Video" section in this chapter).

■ **Tip** You can create examples of faux 3D using a 2D photo, known as a 2.5D Parallax Effect, by cutting out the people or objects from the photo image, then fill in the gaps with the stamp tool where the people were. When the foreground object is separated from the background layer this gives the appearance when movement is added that the people or objects are alive and gives depth, bringing the scene to life. You often see this effect used in historical documentary videos where black-and-white pictures that are then colorized of an event when no video footage at that time was available. For more information on 3D, visit https://helpx.adobe.com/photoshop/using/creating-3d-objects-animations-photoshop.html#create_3d_animations_. For a basic example of 2.5D Parallax, check out my example in the Chapter 7 folder.

Interpret Footage

You can specify how Photoshop interprets the alpha channel (transparency) and frame rate of the video you've opened or imported. Go to Layer ➤ Video Layer ➤ Interpret Footage. Refer to Figure 7-47.

171

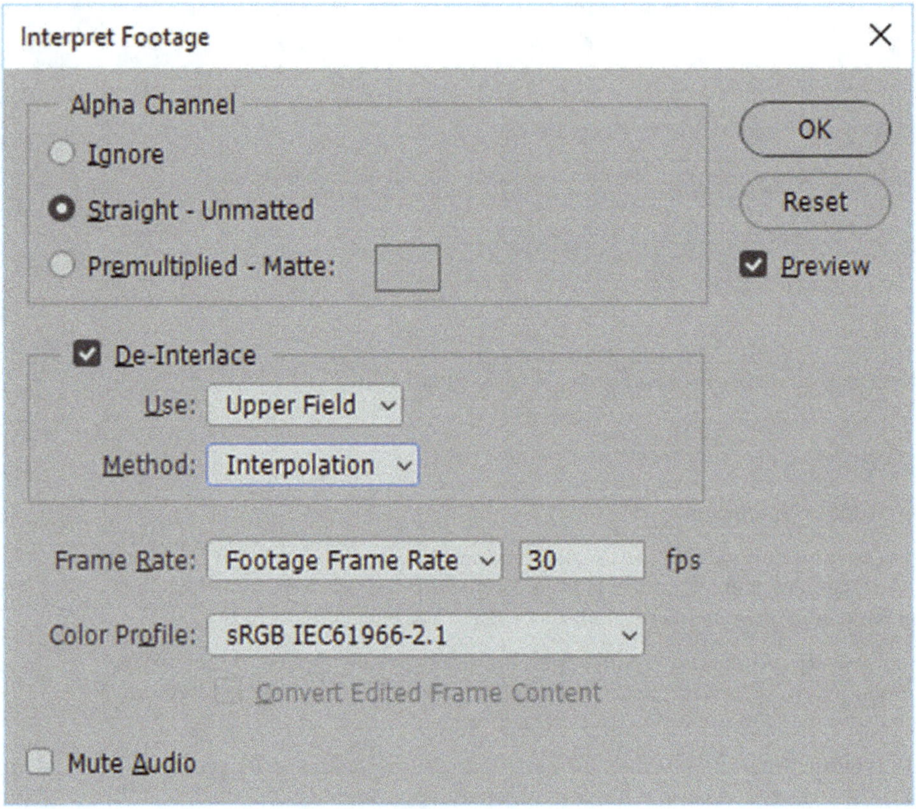

Figure 7-47. Interpret imported video footage

Alpha Channel

An example of an alpha channel is what you see when actors stand in front of a green or blue screen. The green background is not recognized as part of the scene; it is replaced by a different background that is digitally inserted later. If the imported video contains no alpha channel, this area is unavailable and ignored.

If an alpha channel is used in an image, there are two common representations available: straight (unassociated or unmatted) alpha, and premultiplied (associated or matted) alpha. When Premultiplied-Matte is selected, you can specify the matte color with which the channels are premultiplied or blended.

If an incorrect alpha color is chosen, ghosting or halos around objects can occur. When choosing the correct matte color, make sure to preview first. Blue or green are the common colors to use when shooting subjects who will be superimposed on a background or video footage. For more information, visit https://en.wikipedia.org/wiki/Alpha_compositing and https://helpx.adobe.com/photoshop/using/importing-video-files-image-sequences.html.

De-Interlace

This feature affects how the video renders. Sometimes it can affect the quality of the video with scaling or blurring, so it is important to preview and test your video to get the optimum quality. Interlacing is a technique developed for transmitting television signals using limited bandwidth. In an interlaced system, only half the number of horizontal lines or fields for each video frame is transmitted at a time.

CHAPTER 7 ■ TOOLS FOR VIDEO

Fields are upper (odd-numbered lines) or lower (even-numbered lines). The upper is usually drawn first on the screen from top to bottom in one pass, then the lower field. This is typical of the older analog system. However, with digital, you can use interlace or non-interlace. De-Interlace converts interlaced fields into non-interlaced, progressive-scan frames. This option is useful for clips that you want to play in slow motion or in freeze frame. This option discards one field (retaining the dominant field you specified for the project in the Fields setting in the dialog box). Then it interpolates the missing lines based on the lines in the dominant field (upper or lower). If you want to create more advanced interpolation, it is better to use Adobe Premiere Pro. For a visual example refer to Figure 7-48.

Figure 7-48. *How interlace(left) and de-interlaced footage might appear*

For more information on de-interlacing, visit https://en.wikipedia.org/wiki/Deinterlacing and https://helpx.adobe.com/premiere-pro/using/interlacing-field-order.html.

Frame Rate

You can adjust the number of frames per second at the current frame rate of the footage or whatever frame rate you choose. Just be aware that adjusting the frame rate slows down, speeds up, or makes the video appear choppy; so if you do not want this effect, leave the video at the Footage Frame Rate (default). Often, old film footage runs at about 24 frames per second, while newer digital film runs at about 30 frames per second. Your digital camera may have more than one option. To convert older film into the new digital format, technically, six new frames must be created for the speed to be compensated; this is where interlacing appears to fill in the gaps. Refer to Figure 7-49 for frame rate options.

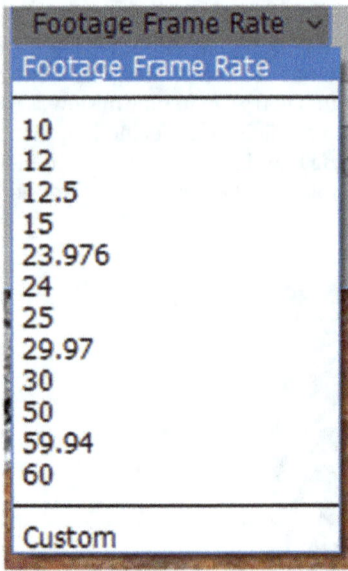

Figure 7-49. *Frame rate options*

Other Settings

Color Profile color-manages the frames or images in a video layer.

Mute Audio turns off the sound in the video. If you don't mute the audio here, you can always change it in the timeline (as you saw earlier when you looked at track settings).

Playing and Previewing Video

As with the Animation Frames timeline, there is a Play feature in the upper left so that you can play/stop your video timeline or move to the first, previous, or next frame. Refer to Figure 7-50.

Figure 7-50. *Play settings*

Before playing the video, you can turn the entire video's audio on or off in the timeline preview. Refer to Figure 7-51.

Figure 7-51. *Turn sound on or off*

CHAPTER 7 ■ TOOLS FOR VIDEO

You can also adjust the preview resolution for the entire video with the Widget icon, and add a loop playback. You can also select loop playback to play the video again from the Timeline menu, as seen in Figure 7-52.

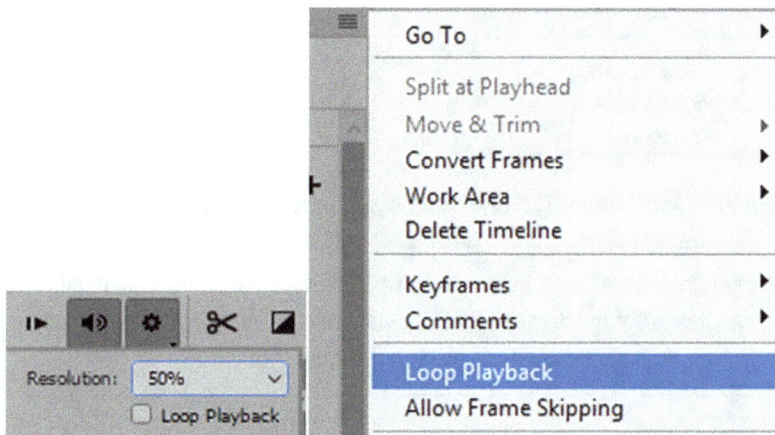

Figure 7-52. Set preview resolution and loop playback in the Widget icon

■ **Note**   Allow Frame Skipping (see Figure 7-52) refers to skipping uncashed frames (not fully loaded in to Random Access Memory (RAM)) to achieve real-time playback. If you find that your video still skips with this setting selected, it may mean that either Photoshop does not have enough RAM and or your computer requires more RAM.

Working with the Timeline and Playhead

The gray handles at the beginning and end of the timeline show the duration of the current video timeline; 00 is the beginning. You can drag the start or end frame to the left to shorten the length of the video, or to the right to lengthen it. Once it reaches the full length of the video it stops, and you can drag no further to the right unless you add more footage. Refer to Figure 7-53.

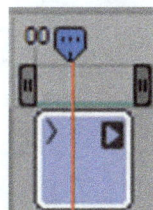

Figure 7-53. Drag the timeline handles to lengthen or shorten the video overall

175

CHAPTER 7 ■ TOOLS FOR VIDEO

You can further adjust the heads using the Video Timeline menu by selecting Work Area ➤ Set Start at Playhead or Set End at Playhead. Remember that the playhead is the blue triangular slider head that you can move back and forth along the timeline. Refer to Figure 7-54.

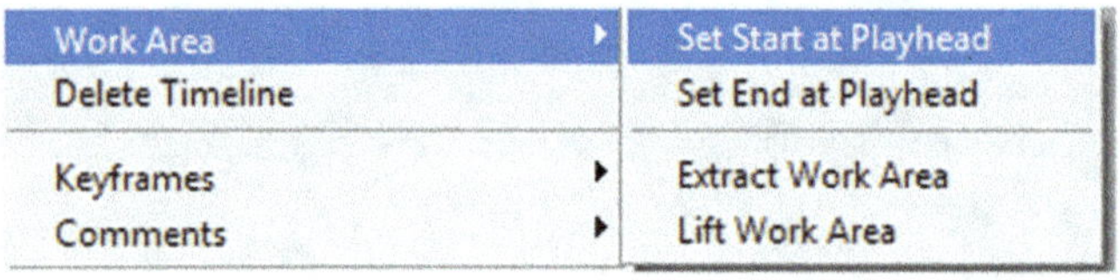

Figure 7-54. Adjust when the video starts and ends using Work Area settings in the timeline

■ **Note** Extract Work Area allows you to remove an area from a video or blank video keyframe split it onto two lines. Use the beginning and ending handles to set the duration that you want to remove. The playhead must be within the handles. Then choose Work Area ➤ Extract Work Area, as seen in Figure 7-55.

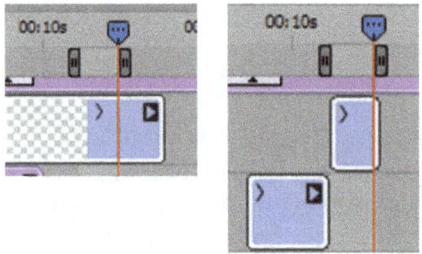

Figure 7-55. Extract a work area is very similar to split video clips

■ **Note** Now that the area is extracted, the remainder is divided on two layers.

- **Lift Work Area**: Works on the same principle as Extract Area except rather than compress the video layers after removing, it leaves a gap in the area that was removed, as seen in Figure 7-56.

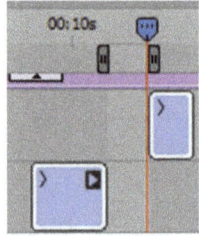

Figure 7-56. Lift a work area is very similar to split video clips

176

CHAPTER 7 ■ TOOLS FOR VIDEO

Both appear to work best with Smart Object and blank video layers. You want to move the gray handles back to the start and the end of the video so that all the tracks can play.

Continue Working with the Playhead to Edit Video

You can drag the blue playhead with the red line and "scrub" over the timeline to slowly preview the movement of your video. The playhead moves along when you click the Play button. You can also move around the playhead by using the Video Timeline menu. Go To ➤ Time lets you choose a point in the timeline or a frame, or move to the start of or the end of the work area. Refer to Figure 7-57.

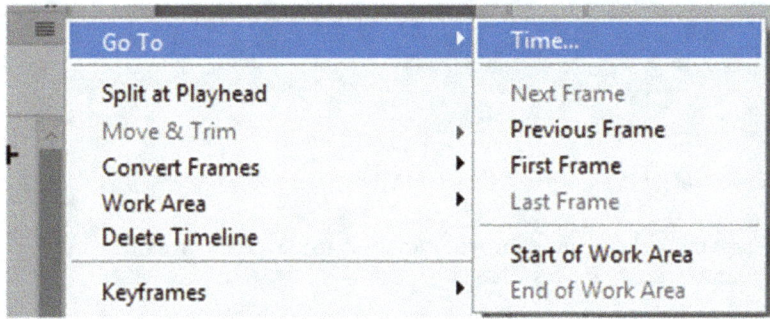

Figure 7-57. *Use the Timeline menu to navigate to a specific point in the timeline*

If you want to add more keyframes to your video timeline, you need to add a longer video. While on a blank or altered video layer choose Layer ➤ Video Layer ➤ Insert Blank Frame. Or drag the timeline portion of that layer forward to make the timeline longer by using the prong icon.

Likewise, you can use Layer ➤ Video Layer ➤ Delete Frame from a blank or altered video layer, or drag the tracks timeline portion backward to make the timeline shorter.

Frames can also be duplicated. Select Layer ➤ Video Layer ➤ Duplicate Frame if that frame of the altered video contains content; if not, this feature will not work. Refer to Figure 7-58.

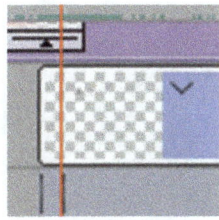

Figure 7-58. *Frames can be duplicated in blank altered video layers that contain content*

Other options are Layer ➤ Video Layers, Restore Frame, Restore All Frames, and Reload Frames.

177

Adjust Frame Rate

In the Timeline panel, the duration of the video and its frames per second (fps) are shown on the lower left. If you need to alter fps for the whole video, you can do so in the Timeline panel's Timeline Frame Rate dialog box, as seen in Figure 7-59.

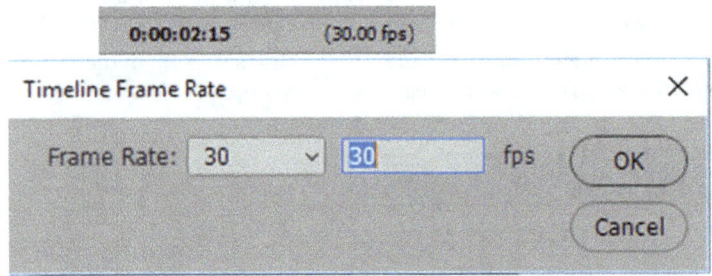

Figure 7-59. Adjust the timeline frame rate for the video

If you need to zoom in on different tracks in the timeline, you can do so using the slider, as seen in Figure 7-60. Left makes the timeline smaller; right makes it larger.

Figure 7-60. Zoom in or out in the timeline to look at tracks

Adding Comments

While building your video, you might want to add comments (see Figure 7-61) in case you need to give your original PSD file to another editor who might use the file in a program like After Effects and needs to continue where you left off.

Figure 7-61. Adding comments

For example, while on a blank video layer, you can select it and choose Comments ➤ Edit Timeline Comment from the Video Timeline panel's menu. Enter a comment in the dialog box, as seen in Figure 7-62.

CHAPTER 7 ■ TOOLS FOR VIDEO

Figure 7-62. *Adding comments to your video*

Click OK to save the comment.

You can also choose to export all comments as HTML or text, if required for other work.

The comment is visible as a yellow square on the top of your timeline if you choose Show ➤ Comments Track from the Video Timeline panel's menu, as seen in Figure 7-63.

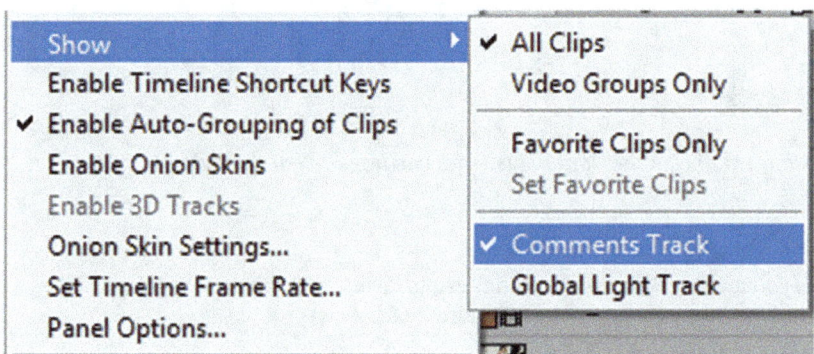

Figure 7-63. *Viewing the comments track*

The comment itself is not actually on the layer but on its own track and keyframe, so if you delete the track, you delete the original comments. So be aware of this. You can edit a comment by right-clicking it and choosing Edit Comment from the pop-up menu. Refer to Figure 7-64.

179

CHAPTER 7 ■ TOOLS FOR VIDEO

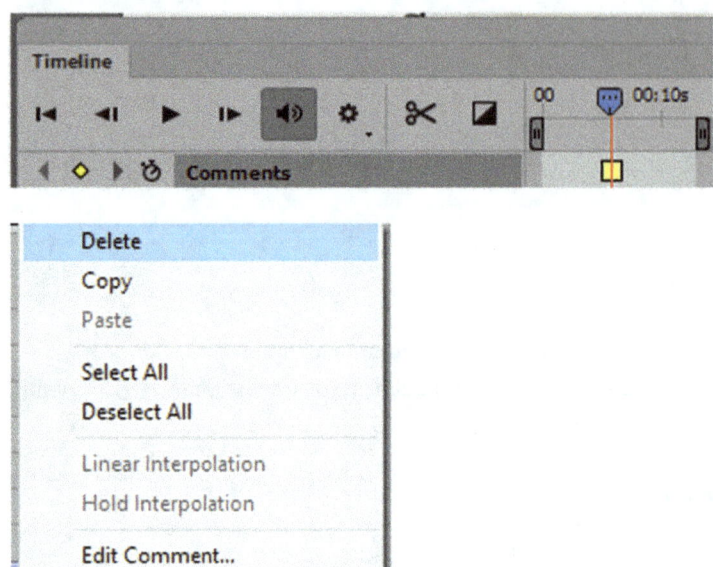

Figure 7-64. *The keyframe (yellow square) in the Comments Track can be edited or deleted*

Hide or Show Tracks

While working on the timeline, you may want to show or hide certain layers or tracks, as you saw with the comments clip. Refer to the Timeline menu area, as seen in Figure 7-65.

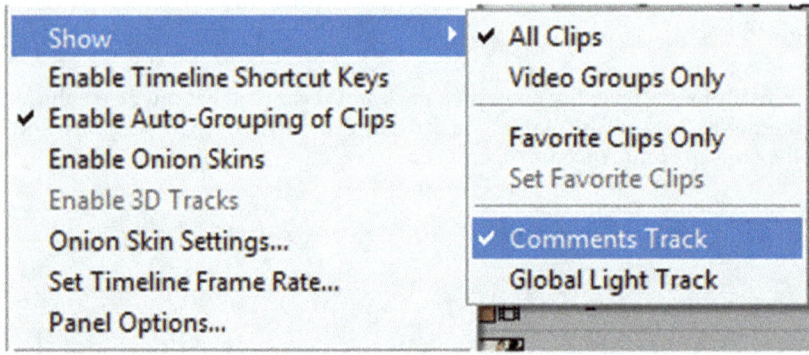

Figure 7-65. *Hide or show certain clips in the timeline*

All Clips is the default setting; however, if you only want the video group to show, select Video Groups Only. In Figure 7-66, Smart Objects and all no-video layers are hidden.

180

CHAPTER 7 ■ TOOLS FOR VIDEO

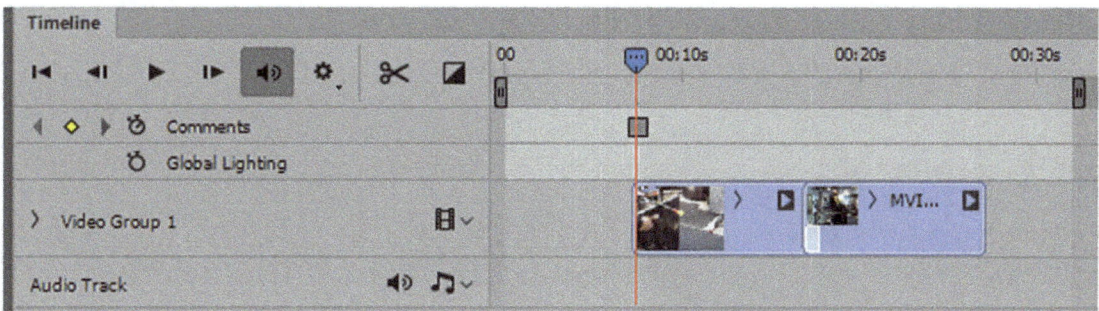

Figure 7-66. Hide or show select clips in the timeline

- **Favorite Clips Only:** To show only a select subset of layers, first set them as favorites in the Timeline panel.

- **Set Favorite Clips:** Select one or more layer tracks from the Timeline panel, then choose Show ➤ Set Favorite Layers from the menu.

- **Global Light Track:** Displays keyframes where you set and change the master lighting angle for layer effects, or styles such as Drop Shadow, Inner Shadow, and Bevel and Emboss. Refer to Figure 7-67.

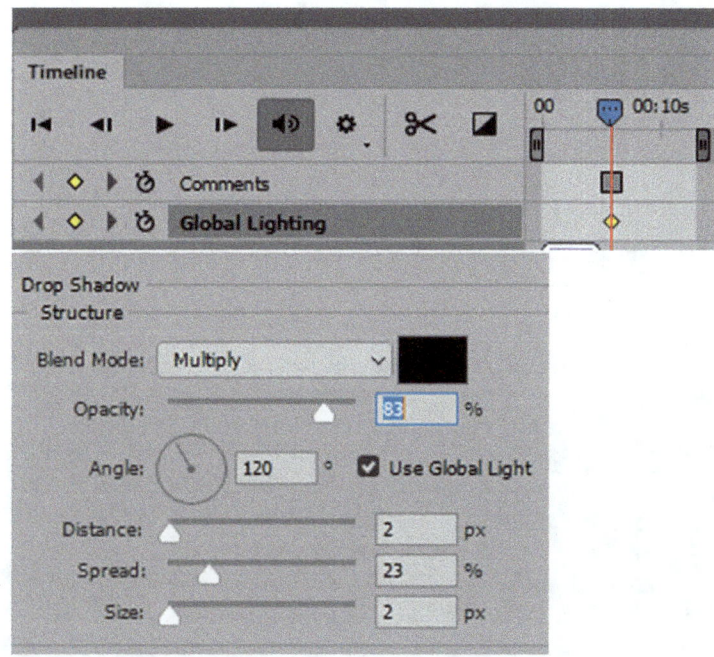

Figure 7-67. Different layers may have global lighting that you want to control in one keyframe to keep consistent with other layers with the same FX settings

181

CHAPTER 7 ■ TOOLS FOR VIDEO

Other Settings in the Timeline Menu

Figure 7-68 shows other settings in the Video Timeline panel's menu.

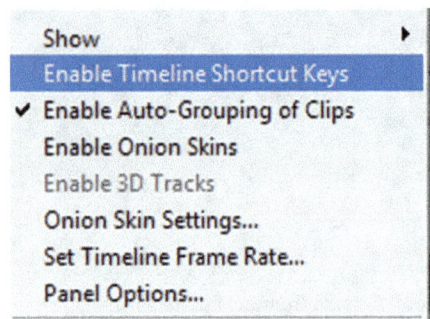

Figure 7-68. Additional timeline menu settings

- **Enable Timeline Shortcut Keys:** If you have created shortcut key from Edit ➤ Keyboard Shortcuts (see Figure 7-69), you could use them when this selection is checked.

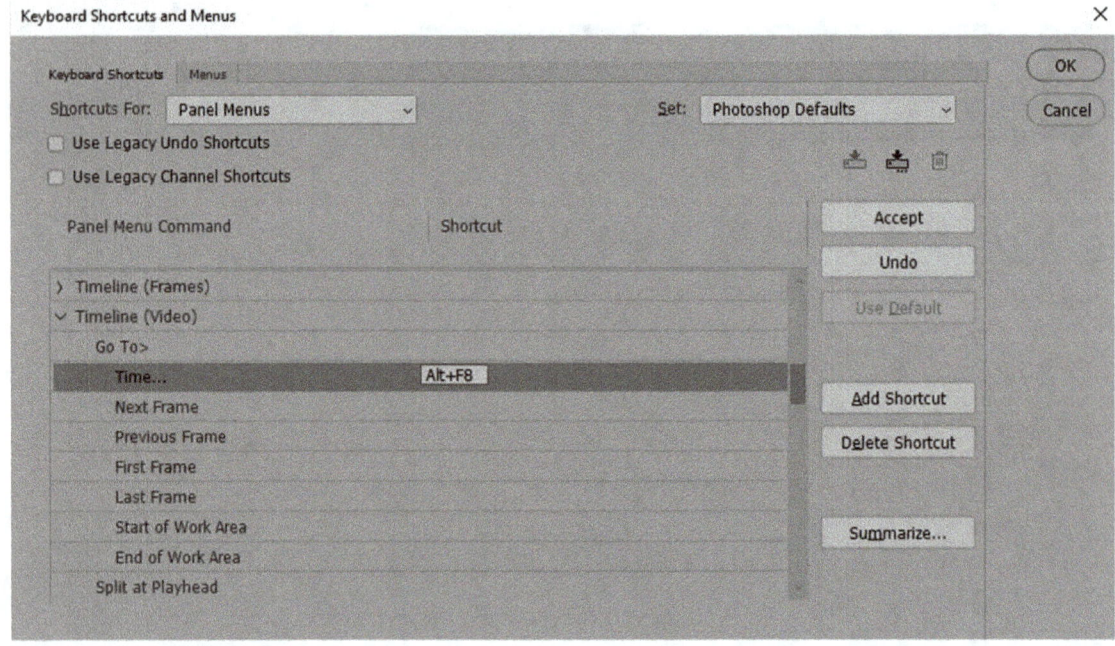

Figure 7-69. Keyboard shortcuts

- **Enable Auto-Grouping of Clips:** This is set as default and allows the movie clips to be grouped together.

182

CHAPTER 7 ■ TOOLS FOR VIDEO

- **Enable Onion Skins:** Use this feature if you are creating a type of hand-drawn stop motion animation. This makes the video slightly blurry so that you can see how different layers interact. It does not affect the actual video; it is only to help you preview the video during editing. If you need to adjust the options, go to Onion Skin Options.

- **Enable 3D Tracks:** If the layers contain 3D graphics, this area is enabled; otherwise, it is unavailable. For more information, refer to the "Video and 3D Graphics" section in this chapter.

- **Onion Skin Options:** If you have enabled onion skinning, you see whatever settings you applied here, as seen in Figure 7-70.

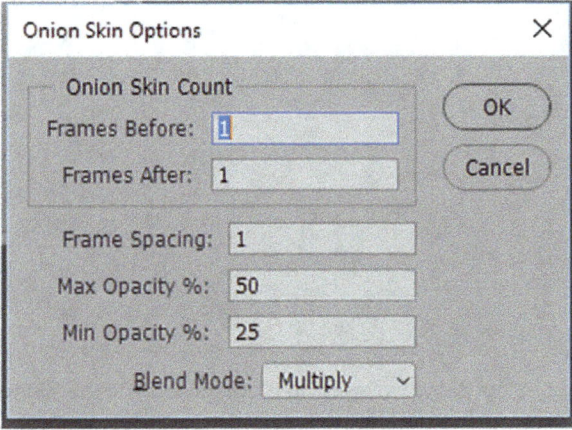

Figure 7-70. Onion Skin Options dialog box

- **Onion Skin Count:** Refers to the number of previous and forward frames displayed in the preview. You can enter the Frames Before (previous frames) and Frames After (forward frames) values in the text boxes.

- **Frame Spacing:** The number of frames between the displayed frames. For example, a value of 1 displays consecutive frames, and a value of 2 displays strokes that are two frames apart.

- **Max Opacity:** Enter a percentage of opacity for the frames immediately before and after the current time.

- **Min Opacity:** Enter a percentage of opacity for the last frames of the before and after sets of onion-skin frames.

- **Blend Mode:** Sets the appearance of the areas where the frames overlap. Multiply is the default but you can set it to Normal, Screen, or Difference for previewing.

- **Set Timeline Frame Rate:** Sets the frame rate for the movie. Refer to Figure 7-59 for a visual example.

- **Animation Panel Options:** This controls the way that you view the timeline icons at small or large sizes. You can also set this for the animation timeline. Refer to Figure 7-71.

183

CHAPTER 7 ■ TOOLS FOR VIDEO

Figure 7-71. Options for the Timeline panel and set units

Adding Background Audio

The final track is the audio track, which is always found below the video layers. It is not referring to the sound that comes with each movie clip but is rather a separate track or tracks for background music or voice-overs, which you can optionally choose to add. Refer to Figure 7-72.

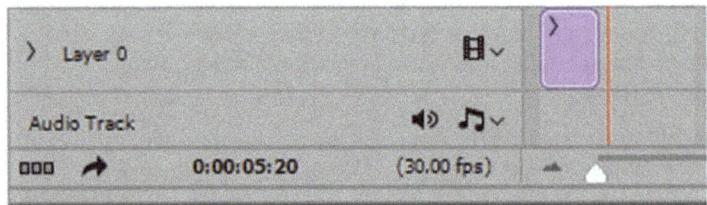

Figure 7-72. The area in the timeline to add the audio track

Click the drop-down arrow near the music notes and choose Add Audio…, as seen in Figure 7-73.

CHAPTER 7 ■ TOOLS FOR VIDEO

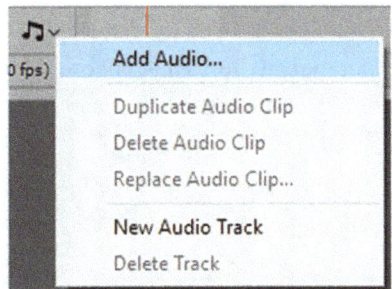

Figure 7-73. Add an audio track

You could also click the plus (+) symbol on the right of the Video Timeline panel audio track.

Search through the formats of audio and video for only the audio portion and choose an MP3 or WAV file. Also check which alternate formats Photoshop will accept before you click the Open button. Photoshop does not accept 3GA smartphone audio. I will show you how to get around this in Media Encoder in Part 5. When the audio is added, it appears as a green symbol with a play arrow. Refer to Figure 7-74.

Figure 7-74. Sound added to an audio track

As with other clips, you can turn off the sound; duplicate, delete, or replace it; or add another audio track. If you have more than one audio track (New Audio Track), you can add or delete one of them by choosing Delete Track, and the track will be removed. As with video, you can adjust the volume and have the sound fade in and out, or you can mute it. Refer to Figure 7-75.

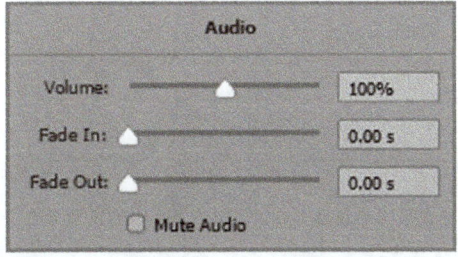

Figure 7-75. Adjust the audio track

■ **Note** If you have more than one track or your audio is spread out, you need to drag the track to the location. Unlike layers, sounds do not appear in the Layers panel; if you decide to add a sound between two other sounds, you may need to spend more time organizing and adjusting your sound order. If you need to edit your audio, use a program like Adobe Audition CC first.

CHAPTER 7 ■ TOOLS FOR VIDEO

Rendering the Video

When you are done creating your video, it's time to make the video ready for the web. To do this, choose Export ➤ Render Video, or from the Video Timeline panel, choose Render Video, or use the Arrow icon (Figure 7-76) at the bottom of the Video panel.

Figure 7-76. *Click to bring up the Render Video dialog box*

Here you can review many of the export options, including frame rate and range of frames for export, if you only want part of the video; interpret the quality of 3D objects; or alpha channel. Photoshop uses Adobe Media Encoder to do the rendering, which you look at in more detail in Part 5 to render your video as an MP4 (H.264) video file. You might have the other options, such as DPX, QuickTime, or Photoshop Image Sequence, but for the web, choose MP4(H.264). You can also choose the location to save the file and check Create New Subfolder if you want the video to appear in a new folder within the current folder. When you are ready, click Render, as seen in Figure 7-77.

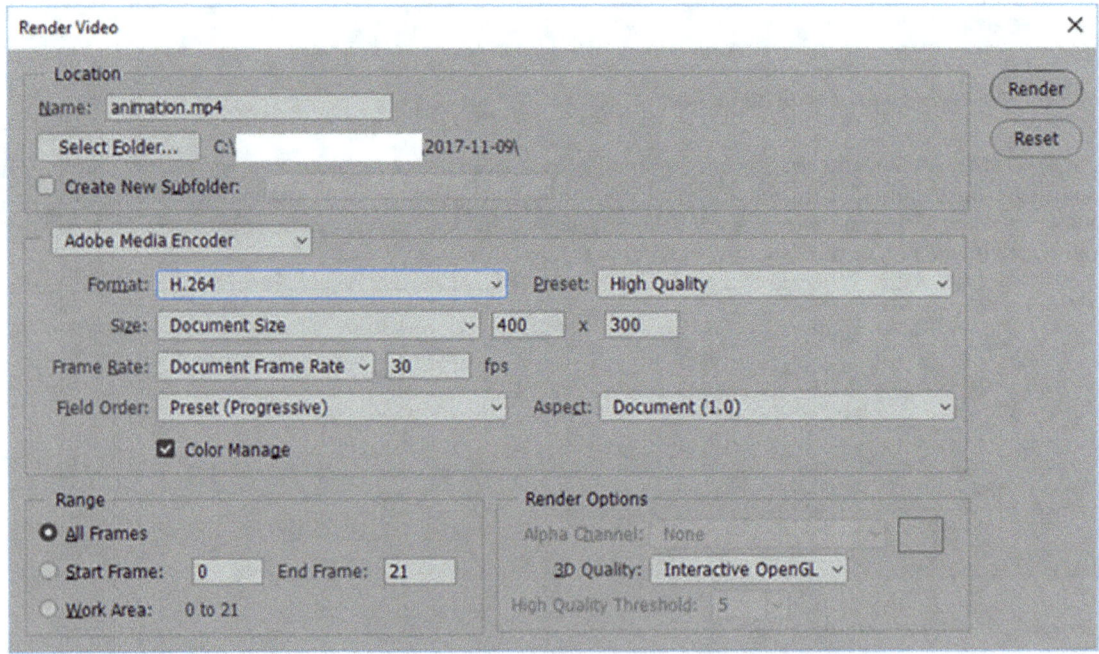

Figure 7-77. *Render to create your MP4 file*

■ **Caution** If your video is small (like the examples in this chapter), rendering your file on the main computer drive is fine. However, if you plan to render a large video file, as I show in Chapter 9, I recommend saving. Larger renderings take time and have the potential of crashing, or at the very least, slowing down your computer.

186

The Photoshop Image Sequence option lets you render individual frames in image formats such as JEPG, bitmap, TIFF, and PNG, which you could use for animation or print-related projects. Refer to Figure 7-78.

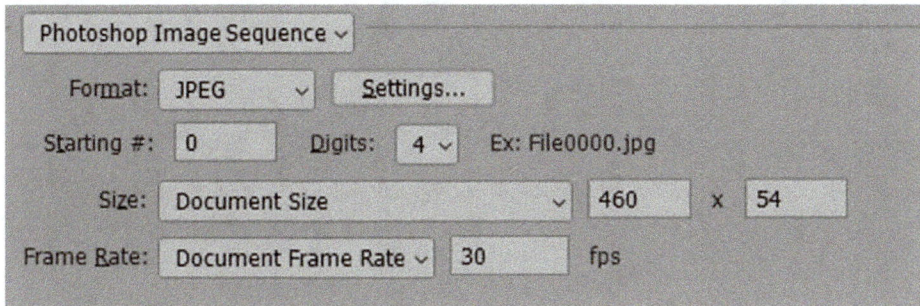

Figure 7-78. *Photoshop Image Sequence setting for render*

Remember, if you choose image sequence, it will produce a lot of individual frames; so it may be best to select a range rather than all in your render settings.

Saving the Original File

Your RAW video file can be saved as a PSD so that you can go back and alter it at any time. Just make sure to keep your video files in the same folder so that the link does not break.

When you are done, you can close the Timeline panel either by clicking the X in the upper right, or choose Close in the Video Timeline panel. Close Tab Group is used only if you have another panel docked with the timeline. Refer to Figure 7-79.

Figure 7-79. *Close the Timeline panel when not in use*

Summary

This chapter explored how to work with Video Timeline panel tools for the web and how to render an MP4 file. You'll practice this again in Chapter 9, but in the next chapter, you take a short detour to see which miscellaneous tools Photoshop has to offer for web design.

CHAPTER 8

Other Miscellaneous Items in Photoshop That You Can Use for Web Design

This chapter focuses on a few of the lesser-known panels and menu features that you can use as part of building image files for your multimedia website or web design workflow.

> **Note** This chapter does not have any actual projects; however, you can use the files in the Chapter 8 folder to practice opening and viewing for this lesson. They are at `https://github.com/Apress/graphics-multimedia-web-adobe-creative-cloud`.

Libraries CC

The Libraries panel was introduced with Creative Cloud. In Photoshop CC, you can store colors and images that you use in projects in a library. You can then move over to a program like Dreamweaver CC, and the colors will appear there so that you can refer to them during your project, as seen in Figure 8-1.

CHAPTER 8 OTHER MISCELLANEOUS ITEMS IN PHOTOSHOP THAT YOU CAN USE FOR WEB DESIGN

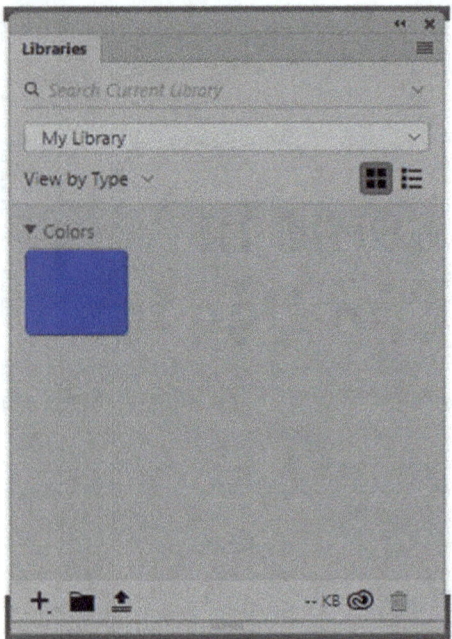

Figure 8-1. *Use the Libraries panel to move color and images to the Libraries panel in another Adobe program*

Extraction of Code from Layers

In the Layers panel, layers in your files might have CSS information or SVG data that you can later use when designing your website or when placing items. Right-clicking a layer allows you to use the Copy CSS and Copy SVG options, as seen in Figure 8-2.

Figure 8-2. *Extract CSS or SVG information from your layers*

You can then open a text-editing program like Notepad++, paste the information into it, and examine the contents before copying the data that you need into a CSS file in Dreamweaver CC.

There is another option. When you save the file as a PSD, you can use Dreamweaver CC's Extract panel and the Creative Cloud to get important data out of the file to work with Dreamweaver.

CHAPTER 8 ■ OTHER MISCELLANEOUS ITEMS IN PHOTOSHOP THAT YOU CAN USE FOR WEB DESIGN

Web Fonts and SVG Fonts

Many of the web fonts that Adobe supplies are in the Character panel's Type tool (see Figure 8-3).

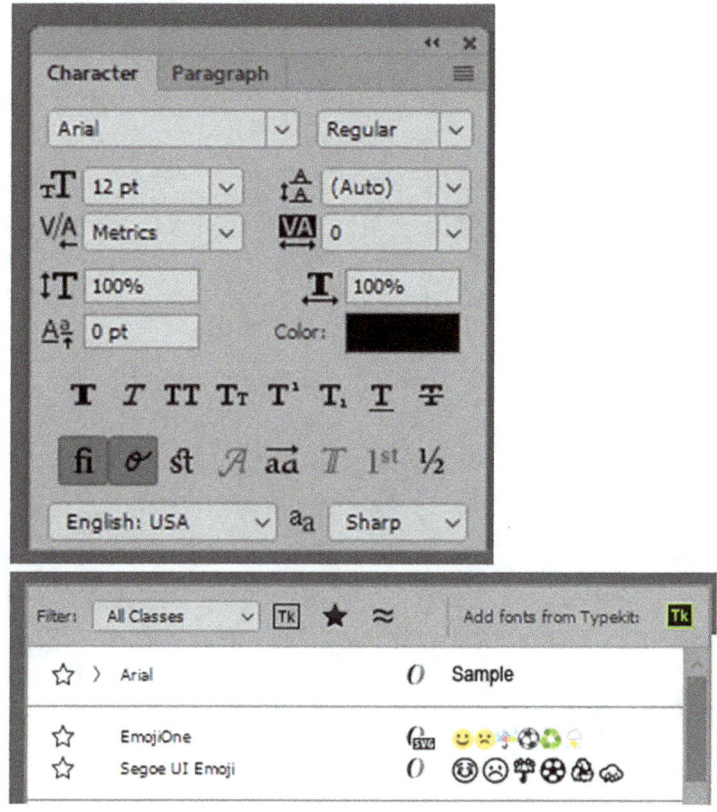

Figure 8-3. *Access Adobe Fonts or Typekit via the Character panel or Control panel when the Type tool is selected*

You can use colorful SVG fonts, like EmojiOne, from the Options panel.
You can view all the options and varieties in the Glyphs panel as well, as seen in Figure 8-4.

191

CHAPTER 8 ■ OTHER MISCELLANEOUS ITEMS IN PHOTOSHOP THAT YOU CAN USE FOR WEB DESIGN

Figure 8-4. SVG fonts

It's like having free clip art! For more information, visit `https://helpx.adobe.com/photoshop/using/svg-fonts.html` and `https://helpx.adobe.com/typekit/using/ot-svg-color-fonts.html`.

Filter for Repeating Backgrounds

Photoshop has many filters; however, my favorite is at Filter ➤ Other ➤ Offset. I use this often for repeating backgrounds. To start, create a square image, then place all the foreground items on a flattened layer that you want to repeat. Refer to Figure 8-5.

CHAPTER 8 ■ OTHER MISCELLANEOUS ITEMS IN PHOTOSHOP THAT YOU CAN USE FOR WEB DESIGN

Figure 8-5. *Create a repeating background with shapes*

Then use the Offset filter to adjust the horizontal and vertical pixel settings. For undefined areas, wrap around and preview the results. This ensures that the background tiles correctly, as seen in Figure 8-6.

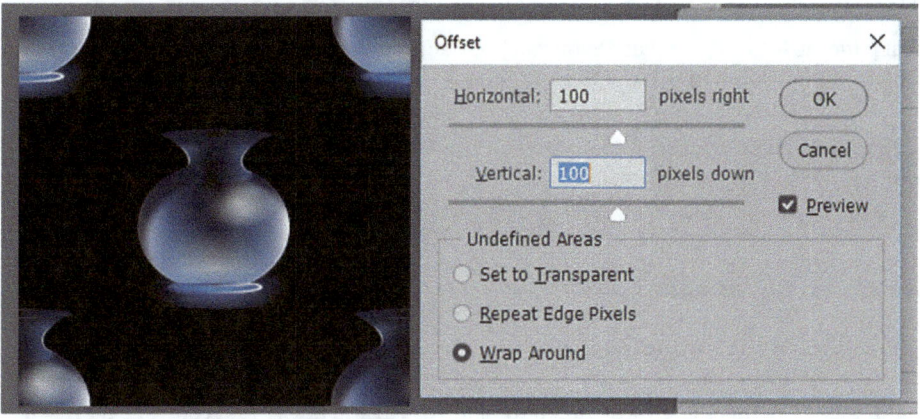

Figure 8-6. *Alter using the Offset filter*

Then, click OK. Later you can add images or shapes to any blank gaps, or use the Stamp tool to correct seams that are running down the center of the image, as seen in Figure 8-7. Refer to the repeating background image PSD in the Chapter 8 folder. You can then use one of the options from Chapter 4 to export the file in your desired format.

193

CHAPTER 8　OTHER MISCELLANEOUS ITEMS IN PHOTOSHOP THAT YOU CAN USE FOR WEB DESIGN

Figure 8-7. *The final pattern*

You can use this with CSS in Dreamweaver to create a repeating background for webpages.

New to Photoshop CC 2018 Paint Symmetry

Another way to repeat patterns is to use the Paint Symmetry option, which is by default in an off state for the brush, pencil, and eraser in the Tools panel. Refer to Figure 8-8.

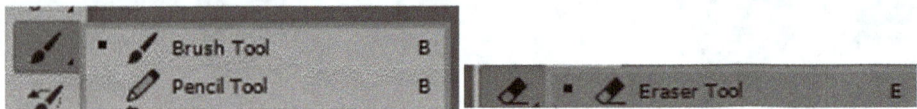

Figure 8-8. *The Tools panel brush and eraser tools*

If you cannot locate this option, go to Edit ➤ Preferences ➤ Technology Previews, and select Enable Paint Symmetry (see Figure 8-9). Note this is the path for version CC 2018. However in CC 2019 this link has been removed from the preferences and by default part of the brush and eraser tool control panel as in Figure 8-10.

CHAPTER 8 ■ OTHER MISCELLANEOUS ITEMS IN PHOTOSHOP THAT YOU CAN USE FOR WEB DESIGN

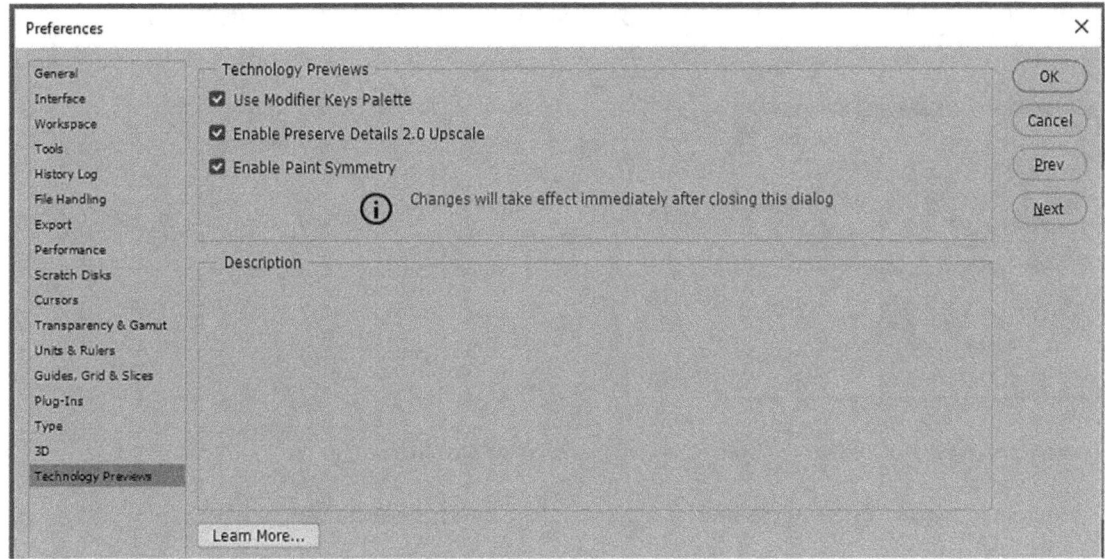

Figure 8-9. Enable Paint Symmetry option in Preferences

Select and click OK to exit the preferences. This adds a new option to your Options panel. It looks like a butterfly, as seen in Figure 8-10.

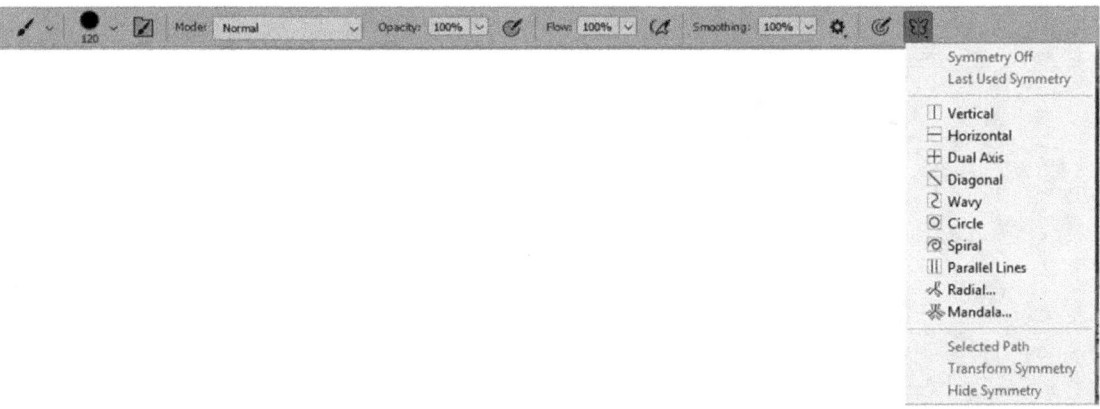

Figure 8-10. Paint Symmetry tool options allow you to reflect pattern

195

CHAPTER 8 ■ OTHER MISCELLANEOUS ITEMS IN PHOTOSHOP THAT YOU CAN USE FOR WEB DESIGN

By choosing from various symmetry paths, you can create all types of interesting repeating shapes, as seen in Figure 8-11.

Figure 8-11. *A pattern created with the Paint Symmetry New Dual Axis option*

Just make sure to turn off the Symmetry option while you are doing your regular painting.

Web Styles

The Styles panel (see Figure 8-12) offers web-friendly styles that you can add to your graphic buttons.

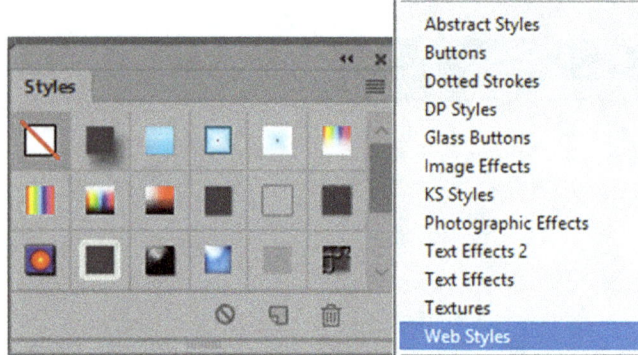

Figure 8-12. *Web Styles you can add to your buttons*

If you have not already added these styles to your list, Photoshop may ask (see Figure 8-13) if you want to replace or append these styles and add them to the current list.

CHAPTER 8 ■ OTHER MISCELLANEOUS ITEMS IN PHOTOSHOP THAT YOU CAN USE FOR WEB DESIGN

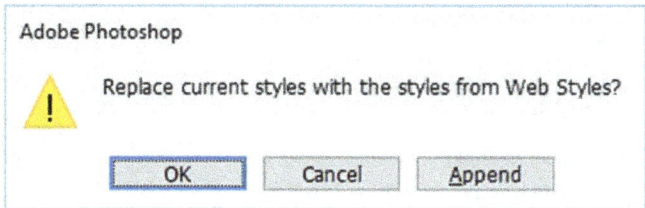

Figure 8-13. *Append or replace current styles*

Once added, they can be applied to a vector shape layer to create a button, as seen in Figure 8-14.

Figure 8-14. *Applying a style to a shape to create a glass-like button graphic*

■ **Note** As with the Swatches panel, you can reset the Styles panel; but any unsaved custom styles will be lost if not saved.

Color Blindness Proofs

Color Blindness Proofs is a feature that most Photoshop users likely do not know exists, but it's been around for several versions. While only eight percent of the world is color blind, it important to recognize that we all see color differently and not everyone can tell the difference between red, green, and blue, and some people can only see shades of black and white. You can preview your images to see how a person with protanopia (red loss) and deuteranopia (green loss) might see your images. Go to View ➤ Proof Setup. Refer to Figure 8-15.

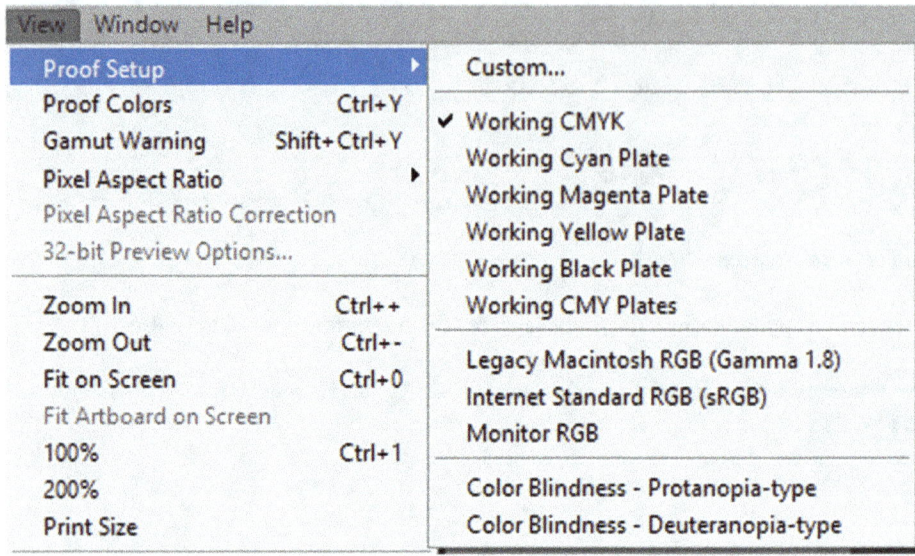

Figure 8-15. Color Blindness Proofs settings

To return to normal settlings, choose View ➤ Proof Colors.

■ **Note** Tritanopia (blue loss) and monochromacy (all color loss) are not very common, so there isn't a proof for those types of color blindness. However, you could use a curves adjustment layer (see Figure 8-16) to alter the amount of blue in the blue channel, or use the black and white adjustment layer for grayscale (see Figure 8-17).

CHAPTER 8 ■ OTHER MISCELLANEOUS ITEMS IN PHOTOSHOP THAT YOU CAN USE FOR WEB DESIGN

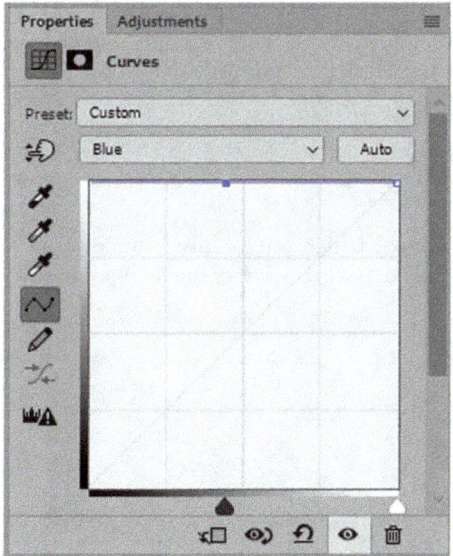

Figure 8-16. *Use the curve properties to remove blue from an image to see how things might look for a person with tritanopia*

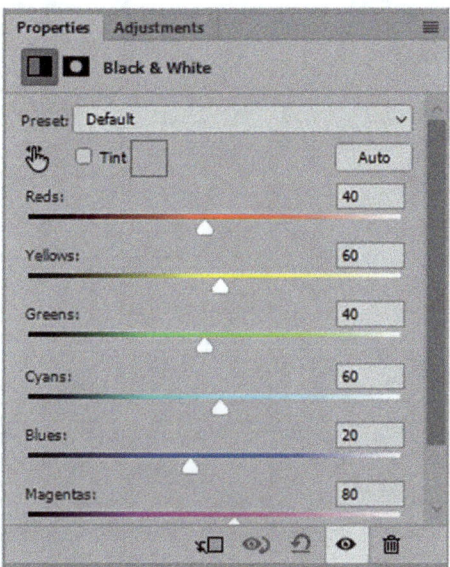

Figure 8-17. *Use Black & White properties to remove all color from an image to see how this might look for a person with monochromacy*

199

While you can't compensate for all color issues on your website, if you want to reach a wide audience, it's important to see how people with color blindness view your website in areas where color is a part of searching, choosing information (e.g., clothing), or doing an important task (e.g., filling out a form).

To learn more about color blindness, visit `https://en.wikipedia.org/wiki/Color_blindness`.

Summary

This chapter explored some tools that you might not have been aware of, which you can use to build your website. In the next chapter, you work on a few images and video files that will be part of the final project in the Dreamweaver multimedia website.

CHAPTER 9

Putting It into Practice with Photoshop CC

In this chapter, you review how to create images for a gallery, GIF animation, and video with an image poster for your website.

> **Note** This chapter has projects that are in four folders. You can use the files in the Chapter 9 folder to practice opening and viewing for this lesson. They are at https://github.com/Apress/graphics-multimedia-web-adobe-creative-cloud.

In this chapter, you will create four items for a website known as Hot Glass Tango. This site tells the story (through images, animation, video, and audio) of how handmade glass items are created. The multimedia items that you create in this chapter and other "Putting It into Practice" chapters are used to finish the final website in Part 6 of this book.

Exporting Images for a Gallery

In Chapter 4, you looked at how to export images for a gallery. In Chapter 5, you looked at how to use actions and automation to speed up that process. In this chapter, there is a folder called Gallery Images that contains about 11 PSD files (g_image1.psd, g_image2.psd, etc.) that you will use to create a final gallery in Dreamweaver in Part 6.

An image gallery is composed of images that are JPEG, PNG, or GIF files. If the image is a logo or illustration with not much photographic content or major gradient transitions, then saving the image as a static GIF is OK. However, if the image contains a lot of color or photographs, then it is better to use a JPEG or a PNG image. PNG and JPEG are comparable in quality for photographs; however, in photographic images that you want a lot of detail, I find that JPEG is the best option. Nevertheless, if download time is a concern, the choice is up to you. You may have to compare different formats of them side by side, using the 2-up or 4-up tabs as in the Save for the Web (Legacy) dialog box in Chapter 4.

Ensuring that you have scalable images that can look good in a large or small format is also important. In some cases, you want to create images in one or more sizes, as you saw in Chapter 4's Option 3 File ➤ Export As. In my case, if you look at g_image1.psd, I created the canvas size at about 400×600 pixels. Look at Figure 9-1, which is an average size for a website; it could be easily viewed on a desktop or tablet. And if I apply CSS, it can be scaled down to smartphone size.

CHAPTER 9 ■ PUTTING IT INTO PRACTICE WITH PHOTOSHOP CC

Figure 9-1. *The first image that appears in my gallery of glass*

Each PSD file has several custom layer adjustments, so creating an action set for these steps other than to set a similar image size would not be practical. However, if all of the images in your gallery only have minor color adjustments that were consistent throughout, then creating actions or a batch action may be the best workflow for you.

However, since you only have 11 images, to get the optimum quality, you will create a simple action called Export For Web that brings up the File ➤ Export ➤ Save For Web (Legacy) dialog box so that you can make minor adjustments to each file as you go along.

With your first image opens (g_image1.psd), go to the Actions panel and choose your images for the web folder set. Refer to Chapter 5, if you can't remember how to work with Actions panel. Refer to Figure 9-2.

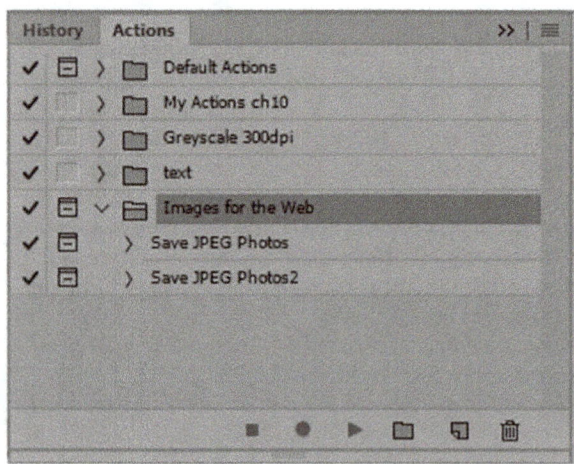

Figure 9-2. *Creating another action for your set*

Click the Create New Action button at the bottom of the dialog box.
Name the new action **Export for Web** and click Record, as seen in Figure 9-3.

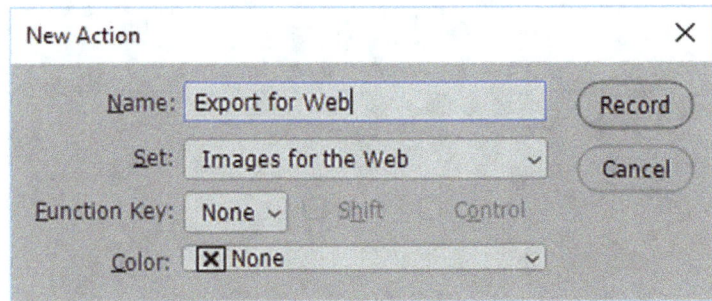

Figure 9-3. Creating a new action

The Record icon is now on. It appears as a red circle, as seen in Figure 9-4.

Figure 9-4. The actions are recording

Now go to File ➤ Export ➤ Save For Web (Legacy) dialog box. Refer to Figure 9-5.

CHAPTER 9 ■ PUTTING IT INTO PRACTICE WITH PHOTOSHOP CC

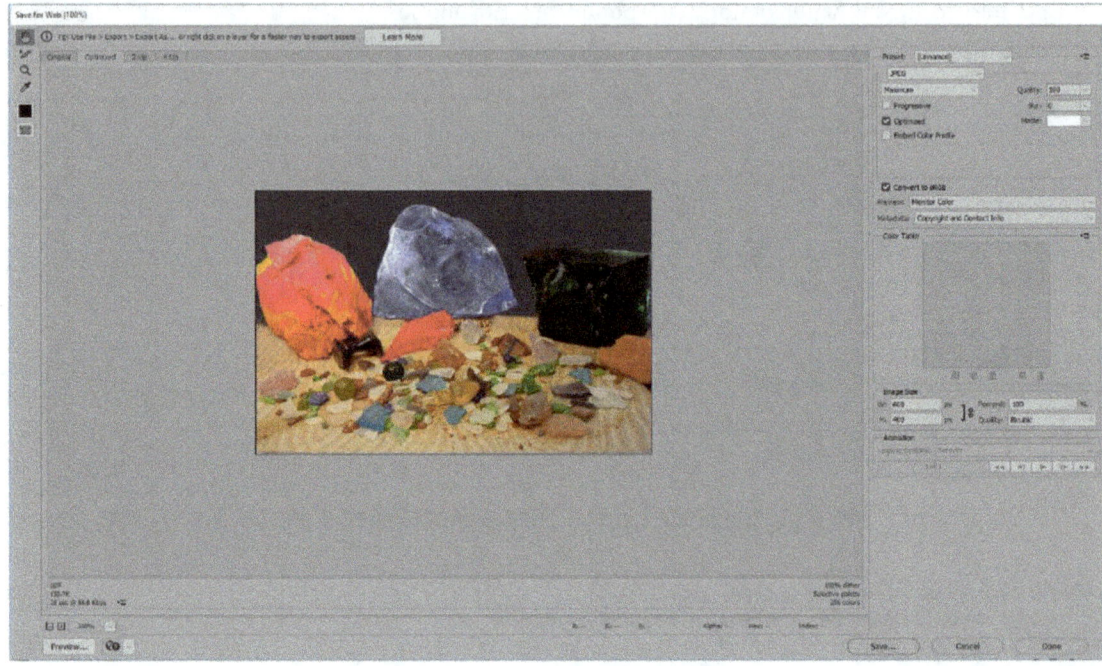

***Figure 9-5.** The Save for Web dialog box*

At this point, you could choose a preset as a JPEG, PNG, or a GIF once you are content with the settings (I chose JPEG Maximum, optimized).

Now choose Save at the bottom of the dialog box. Refer to Figure 9-6.

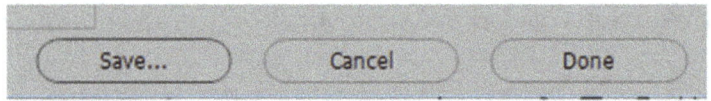

***Figure 9-6.** Click Save so you can export your image for the gallery*

If you have a website started, save this image into the Images folder; if not, save it in your current folder or your choice location.

Name the file. Make sure that the Format setting is Images Only and that Settings is Background Image, as seen in Figure 9-7.

File name:	g_image1b.jpg		Save
Format:	Images Only		Cancel
Settings:	Background Image		
Slices:	All Slices		

***Figure 9-7.** Naming file and saving as images only*

204

CHAPTER 9 ■ PUTTING IT INTO PRACTICE WITH PHOTOSHOP CC

Click Save.

The file is saved in the folder and the dialog box will close. An export action is added to the Actions panel. Refer to Figure 9-8.

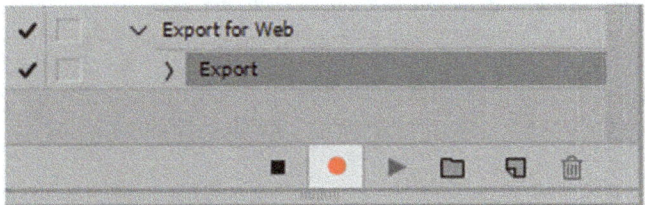

Figure 9-8. *Another step is added to the Actions panel*

You can now press the square Stop icon (on the left) to stop the action.

Look at Figure 9-9. If you explore the export action by clicking the toggle arrow, you see that there are a lot of settings.

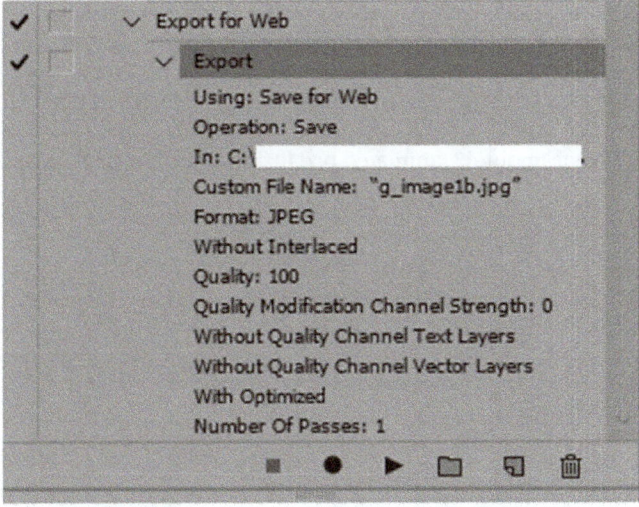

Figure 9-9. *Many setting have been applied to the action*

These are all recorded so that you do not have to make the same adjustments each time.

To make sure that the dialog box opens when you play the action, click the squares (toggle dialog on/off) icons near the check box, as seen in Figure 9-10.

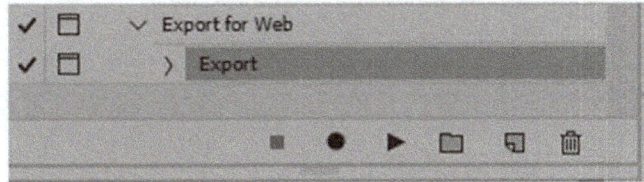

Figure 9-10. *Turn on the settings that allow the window dialog box to open*

CHAPTER 9 ■ PUTTING IT INTO PRACTICE WITH PHOTOSHOP CC

You can close the first image, and then select File ➤ Open to open g_image2.psd

This time, you just need to just select the Export for Web action from the Actions panel, and press Play for the action to play again. You can always make different adjustments or keep the same settings. In the dialog box, click Save and give this file a new name in your images folder. The action always keeps its original settings for each new file. However, if you keep the same image open and play it again, it uses the most recent setting in the export; so make sure to close the PSD files without saving changes and open it again to keep original export settings.

Take some time to save the 11 images as either JPEGs or PNGs for the gallery by using the action. You could speed up the process even further by creating a batch action or even a droplet, as in Chapter 5, if you had more image files to work with.

Now let's move on to the second project.

Exporting a GIF Animation

In Chapter 6, you looked at some of the basic steps to create a simple GIF animation that could be used for instructional purposes or as a beautiful ever-looping picture for a webpage. In other cases, you may want a very subtle change to take place in the background of your website, such as a slight graphic background shift.

In Chapter 8, you looked at some miscellaneous tools that can be used for the web; one that is very useful is the offset filter for repeating backgrounds. You can create a repeating background, but you can also animate it and use CSS to make it only repeat on the x or y axis to create a division on the page or appear as a stripe across the top of the page. From a design point of view, I do not recommend covering the entire page with a repeating animated GIF because this would look gaudy; however, if done correctly, it can add interest to your website.

Let's look at the GIF Animation folder and the background3_animated.psd file in your Chapter 9 folder. Refer to Figure 9-11.

Figure 9-11. *This gradient looks fractured like hot glass that is gradually cooling*

In the Layers panel in Figure 9-12, you can see a pattern that I created using a gradient and filters such as crystalize and offset. This is to give the look of hot glass.

CHAPTER 9 ■ PUTTING IT INTO PRACTICE WITH PHOTOSHOP CC

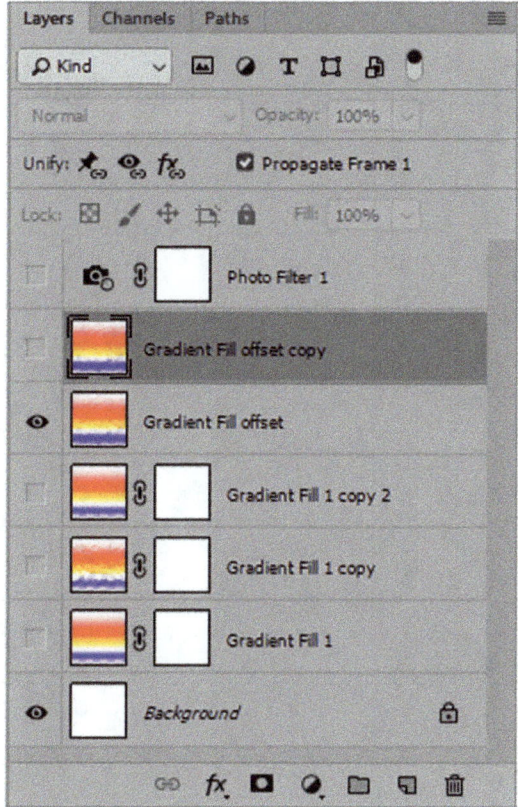

Figure 9-12. *The Layers panel contains different gradients and layers for the GIF frame animation*

■ **Note** In my original file, when I used the offset filter, it left a small seam down the middle that I had to use the Clone Stamp tool in the Tools panel to correct. I also set undefined areas of the offset filter to wrap around. In this case, the filter work is done for you.

Play the animation using the timeline, and you will notice a gradual change in color. To make it look as if this was done gradually, I used tweening between a starting and ending frame, and added an adjustment layer photo filter to make it appear like the glass is cooling. Refer to Figure 9-13.

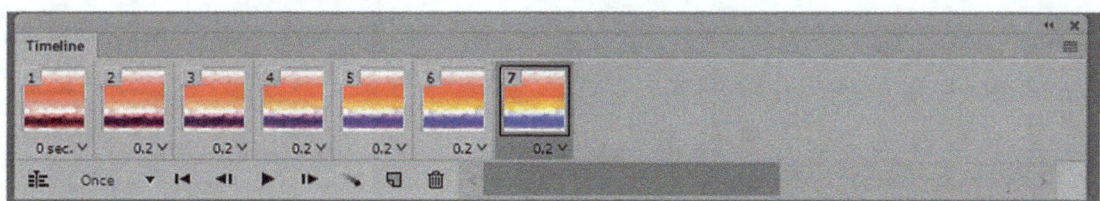

Figure 9-13. *Timeline for the GIF animation*

207

CHAPTER 9 ■ PUTTING IT INTO PRACTICE WITH PHOTOSHOP CC

In this file, I added some transparent areas into the layers so that you have the option to blend my animation on top of other backgrounds.

There is a time delay for each frame, and the animation is set to play once.

Once the animation is complete, and you have previewed it using the Timeline's play features, choose File ➤ Export ➤ Save for the Web (Legacy).

Refer to Figure 9-14 for all the settings.

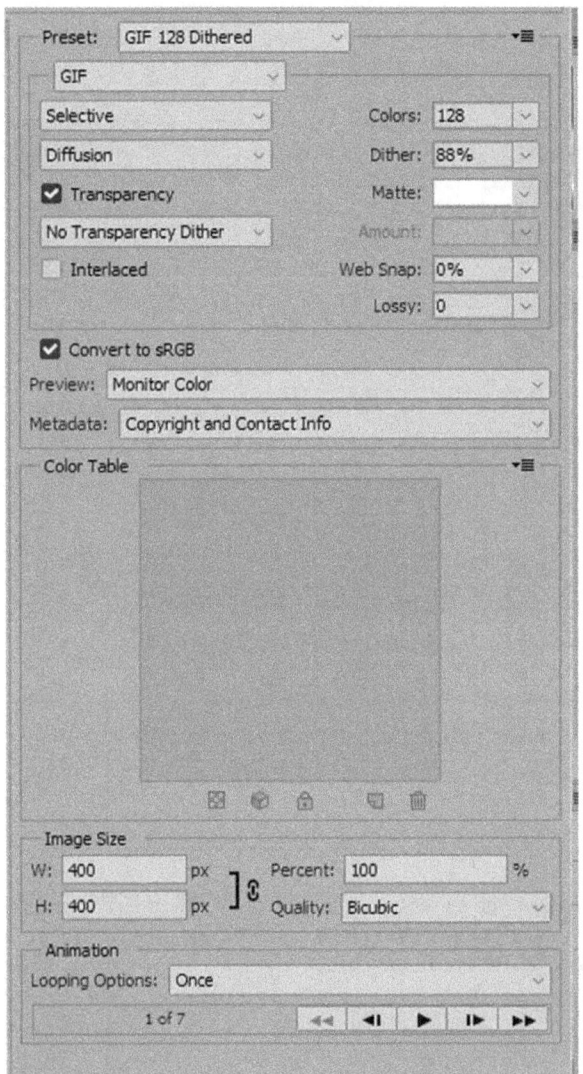

Figure 9-14. *Settings for the GIF animation*

Transparency is optional; in my case, the background is white, so you could leave it unchecked. Choose a white matte. At this point, you could play the animation again to test it or adjust the looping. Click Save the bottom of the dialog box. Refer to Figure 9-15.

208

CHAPTER 9 ■ PUTTING IT INTO PRACTICE WITH PHOTOSHOP CC

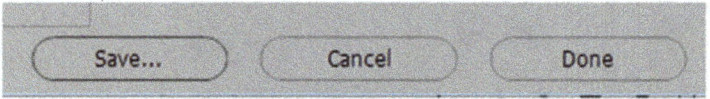

Figure 9-15. Click Save to save the animation

This brings up an area for you to save your file. The format is Images Only and the settings should be Background Image, as seen in Figure 9-16.

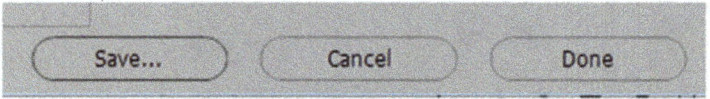

Figure 9-16. Save the animation in your website's Images folder

Find your website's Images folder and save it there with the other gallery images. Close the original PSD file without saving any changes.

■ **Note** Although this image contained gradients, they were distinct enough that the quality of the image did not deteriorate when you saved it as a GIF animation. There was no option to save it as a JPEG or PNG since these formats cannot be animated.

Now that you have completed the second project, let's look at project number three: the video poster.

Exporting a JPEG Poster Image for Your Movie for the Web

When you create a video for the web, it's a good idea to have a cover page so that your audience will know what the video or movie is about; this is also known as a poster. Rather than let your video decide which frame the audience should see, a poster allows you to create a custom starting frame that gives information about a select scene in the movie. A poster can be a GIF, JPEG, or PNG file and it will always be the first thing the audience sees before the movie loads or starts. Let's look at the Movie Poster folder and the poster_cover.psd file, as seen in Figure 9-17.

209

CHAPTER 9 ■ PUTTING IT INTO PRACTICE WITH PHOTOSHOP CC

Figure 9-17. *This is the poster for the movie Hot Glass Tango*

The Layers panel (see Figure 9-18) shows that the file has a background image and a Smart Object layer that is an illustration created in Illustrator CC.

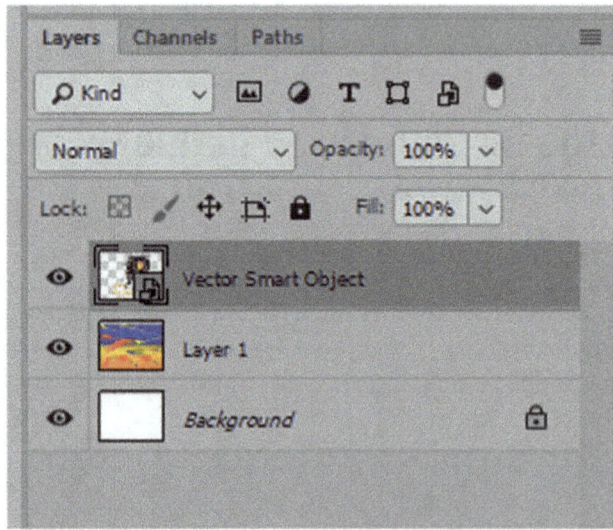

Figure 9-18. *The Layers panel for the video poster*

210

CHAPTER 9 ■ PUTTING IT INTO PRACTICE WITH PHOTOSHOP CC

The poster must be the exact same size as the final video; otherwise, distortion occurs and there is a size change when you click Play for the HTML5 video on your website.

In this case, it is 640 × 480 pixels.

You can now export the poster for the web, by selecting File ➤ Export ➤ Save for the Web (Legacy). You can save it as a JPEG or PNG because this is a colorful poster. Choose JPEG High with Quality set at 60, and check the Optimized box. Refer to Figure 9-19.

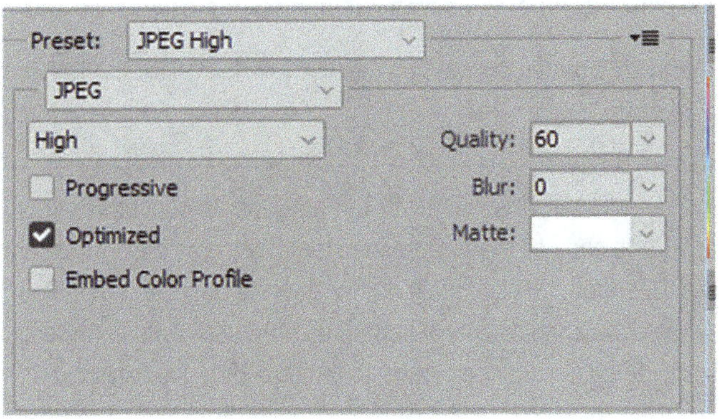

Figure 9-19. Setting for the poster in the Save for Web dialog box

When done, click Save, as seen in Figure 9-20.

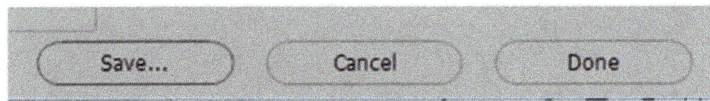

Figure 9-20. Save the poster image for the video

Save your poster in your Images folder so that you can link it in Part 6 for your video in Dreamweaver. Refer to the settings in Figure 9-21.

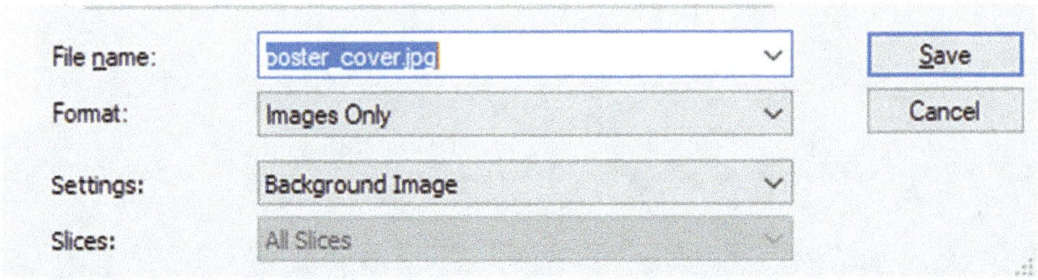

Figure 9-21. Save the poster image in the Images folder of your website

When done, close the PSD file without saving changes. You will now move on to the fourth and final project: rendering the video.

211

CHAPTER 9 ■ PUTTING IT INTO PRACTICE WITH PHOTOSHOP CC

Rendering Your Movie

The last item you need to work on in Photoshop CC is rendering the video. If you have created your own video for a project with your footage, use it in these final steps; otherwise, follow along with the video I have created.

Open the Movie folder's Movie_Glass_Tango_Part2.psd file. The file is linked to quite a few MP4 and MP3 files, so it may take a few moments to open. Also, you may get an alert saying that the files have become unlinked, as seen in Chapter 7, where I talk about video groups. You may need to relink the files; those that are in the same folder will automatically relink.

Make sure that the Timeline and Layers panels are opened so that you can see how I laid out the file and the links.

■ **Note** This assignment has a lot of video files. To make the video about 17 minutes and 30 seconds long, some clipping was done. Before rendering, make sure to copy all the files to an external drive so that you do not crash your computer during the rendering process. Open the PSD file again on the external drive, and then you render from it as an MP4 on the external drive as well. You can always copy the final MP4 back onto your home computer later when you combine it for the website in Part 6; otherwise, refer to the final MP4 file I created if you don't want to attempt rendering right now.

When the file is open, in the Timeline, go to the first frame (see Figure 9-22) using First Frame button; the preview screen is white.

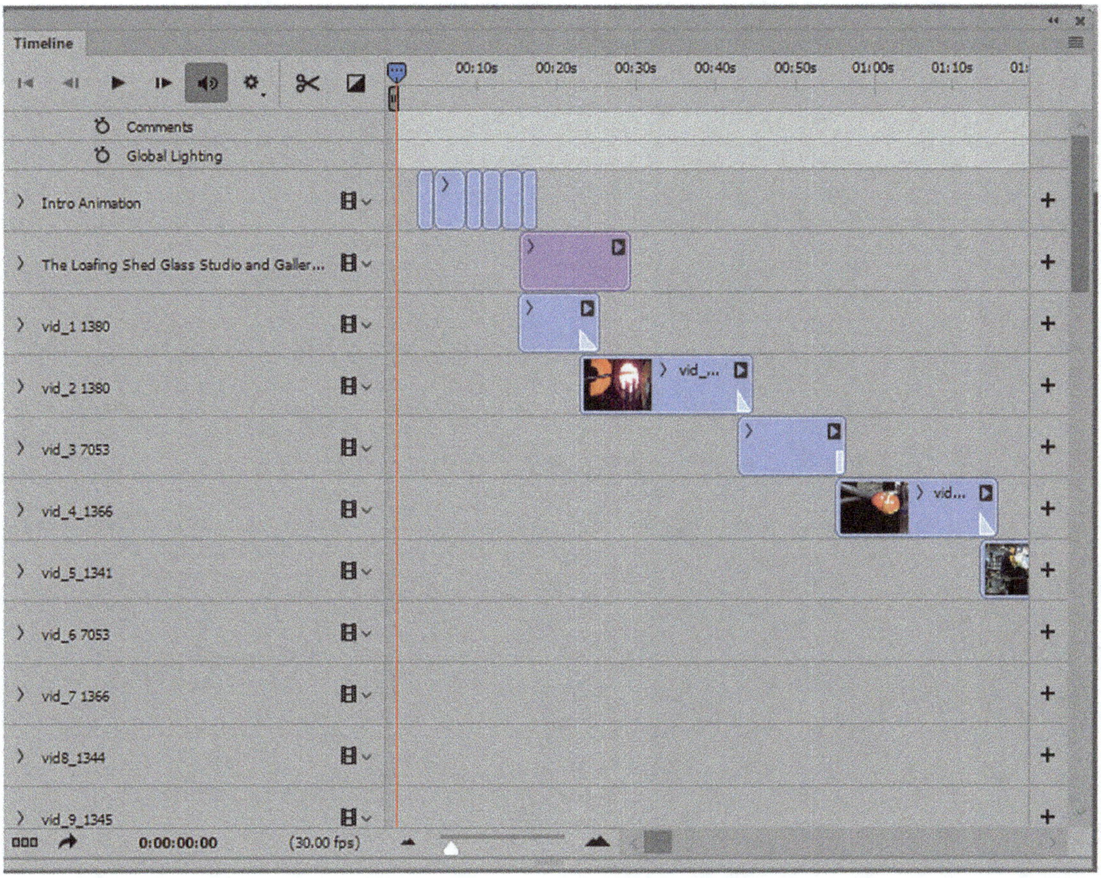

CHAPTER 9 ■ PUTTING IT INTO PRACTICE WITH PHOTOSHOP CC

Figure 9-22. *The Timeline panel with many tracks*

As you move around the timeline, use the scrollers and make the track bigger and smaller with the zoom. Notice how I grouped some tracks, such as my intro animation and final credits into video groups. Other videos kept on their own tracks so that I could add a fade transition. Some tracks contain keyframes to keep the image centered while the action in the video is happening. Refer to Figure 9-23.

Figure 9-23. *Keyframes to adjust position were added to some tracks*

213

CHAPTER 9 ■ PUTTING IT INTO PRACTICE WITH PHOTOSHOP CC

As you move to the next track, you move downward in the Layers panel. First layers or tracks should be on top so that they can be blended into the next scene, which is lower in the Layers panel. Keep this in mind when you organize your own video. Refer to Figure 9-24.

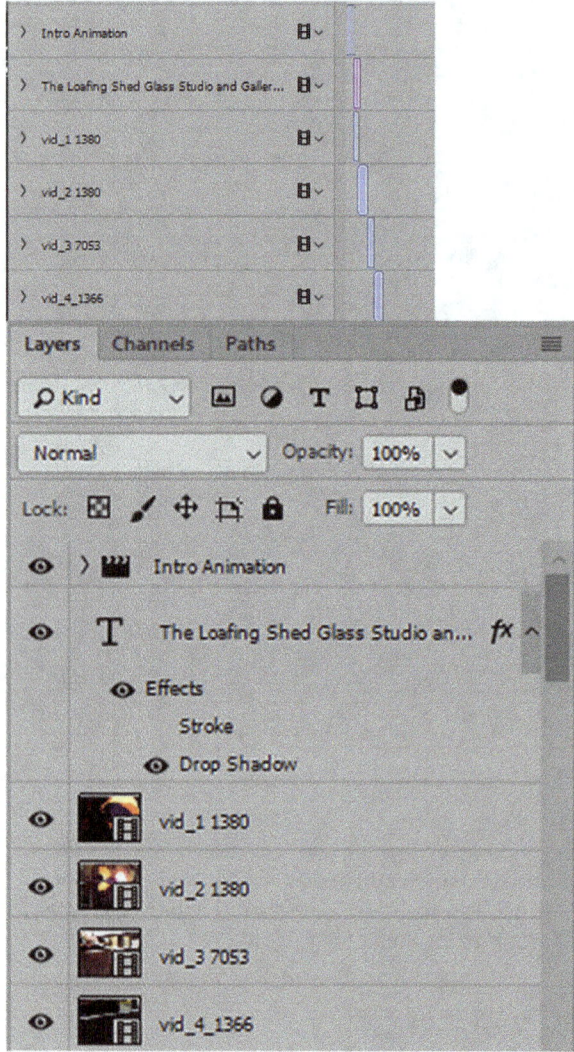

Figure 9-24. *As the video moves along, you move to lower tracks or layers to reveal them*

In the Glass Tango video, I also added a text layer that is seen on top of video footage. A text layer could have a text watermark that is seen throughout the footage. Refer to Figure 9-25.

CHAPTER 9 ■ PUTTING IT INTO PRACTICE WITH PHOTOSHOP CC

Figure 9-25. *Adding a text layer over the video footage*

Once I added the video layers, I dragged each track to the correct location in the video timeline before adding the transitions and audio. Often, you have to use the Play button several times to watch the video and stop the play head to make corrections as you go along. In this case, the video is set up for you, so use it as a guide for your future videos.

The videos that you create for the web likely will not have this much footage; possibly only 1 to 5 minutes in length. However, if you think your video will be longer than 20 minutes, a program like Premiere Pro and Adobe After Effects are better options for building longer stories with additional special effects.

■ **Note** I named each layer/track with the same name as my linked footage; this way, I can always return to my original AVI or MOV files (not supplied in the lesson) so that I can re-render them as MP4 files in case I need to make an adjustment.

Finally, at the end of the video Timeline panel, I added the audio tracks. In my case, I had three audio tracks. I removed the audio from my MP4 files because most of the dialog did not relate to the story. Refer to Figure 9-26.

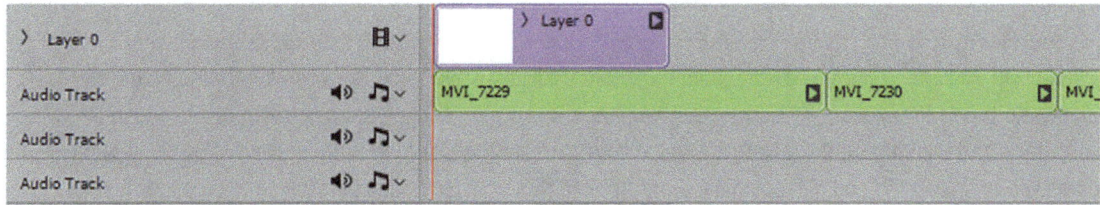

Figure 9-26. *This file has three audio tracks*

I cannot name each audio layer separately to identify it; however, I can give a unique name to my audio files, like sound_name or voice, so that I know what is happening and can then refer to the original files.

The audio does not show up in the Layers panel, only in the video timeline.

The top audio track has my intro music, sound effects, and final credits music. The audio often butts up right beside the next, so you may have to use your play head to determine where you want the audio and then drag the track to the new location, as seen in Figure 9-27.

Figure 9-27. *You may need to move the audio by dragging it to a new location*

215

Be careful not to drag the sound beyond the range of the video tracks or layers; this increases the file's length with no video footage. Refer to Figure 9-28.

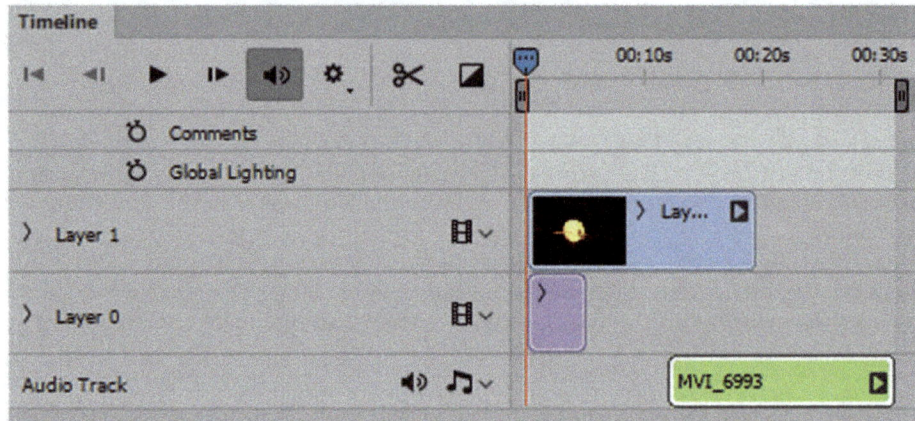

Figure 9-28. Don't move the audio beyond the bounds of the movie or it will increase its length with no footage present

The next audio track I added was my voice. I kept it at 100% volume so that you can hear me narrate the actions of the people creating the glass vase (Robert Gary Parkes and his apprentice, Jay). Your video may not contain narration, but you might use this track as an area to dub in another language, or the thoughts or backstory of a character as they are doing some action, or someone who is not yet in the scene or who left the scene; this is known in the movie industry as split edits, or J cuts and L cuts.

■ **Note** In Photoshop CC, you cannot split the audio from the video track to work with them separately. You can do this in Premiere Pro CC, however. An alternative option in Photoshop is to import the video into the audio track and then import the video as a video layer and set the sound to mute audio. Media Encoder also allows you to split audio and video as two separate files that you can add separately in Photoshop. Refer to Figure 9-29.

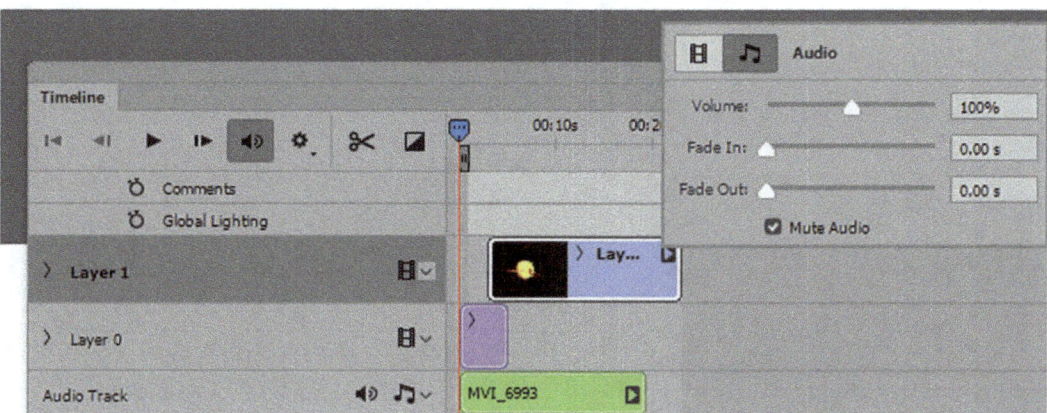

Figure 9-29. An alternative way to do an audio video split edit

The Lower audio track in my Hot Glass Tango video is the background music. If you listen to most commercials or movies, when the actors are not talking, or even sometimes when they are talking, music is often quietly playing in the background; usually, at a lower volume than the voices speaking.

Background music enhances the scene and often adds excitement and sets the mood. I find it beneficial when there are gaps in dialog to keep the flow of the story so that the silence is not tedious. Nevertheless, there are times where silence is good and gives a transitional break. You can always fade or overlap sound so that you go from music to silence at key moments.

Once you have previewed the video and adjusted the audio tracks to the correct location, it's time to render the video.

■ **Note** For your own personal video, make sure to save any changes you have made to your PSD file as you go. Do not save mine. Instead, work on a copy so that you do not accidently adjust the original file.

At this point, make sure that you are working with all files on the external drive, and then in the Timeline panel, choose the Render Video icon, or File ➤ Export ➤ Render Video. Refer to Figure 9-30.

Figure 9-30. Render the video

Refer to the steps in Chapter 7 regarding rendering video (see Figure 9-31).

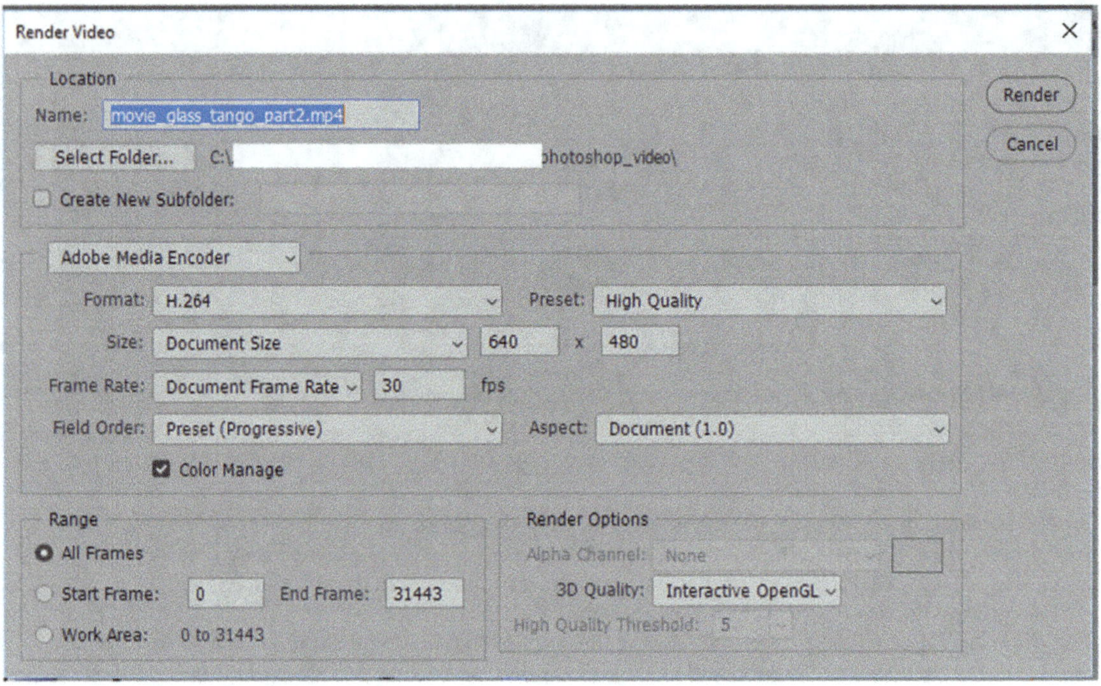

CHAPTER 9 ■ PUTTING IT INTO PRACTICE WITH PHOTOSHOP CC

Figure 9-31. Render Video dialog box

You can select a folder and create a subfolder, or render into the same folder as your files. Just make sure that with each new render, you delete any old files that you do not want to save.

In my case, the program is rendering with Adobe Media Encoder CC. I have it installed on my computer from the Creative Cloud. You will look at this program more closely in Part 5; otherwise, I keep the format at H.264 (MP4) and the document size at 640×480, and the frame rate at 30 fps. All other settings are the same as what's seen in Figure 9-30. I kept the preset at high quality, but for your video, you may want to choose medium or low quality, depending on your audience. Refer to Figure 9-32.

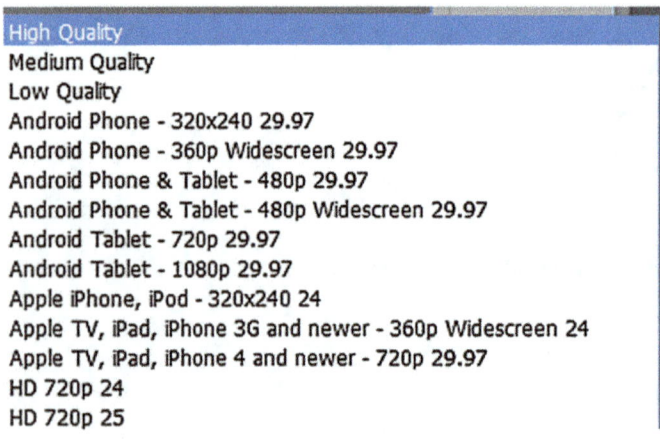

Figure 9-32. There are many preset options to choose from on the Preset drop-down list

218

There are presets that give a variety of frame rates and varying dimensions. Just be careful to choose the correct width, height, and frame rate for your video in the preplanning stages; otherwise, you may get some unexpected results or grainy footage if you upscale, change the field order, or adjust the aspect ratio.

Media Encoder can determine the dimensions and frame rate of your raw video files before you bring them into Photoshop. You'll look at how to check this in Part 5.

For the range, render all frames (see Figure 9-30); however, you may want to render only part. If you know which frame a scene and audio starts and stops, you should be able to do this successfully.

In this case, you do not touch the render options because you have no 3D graphics or alpha channels.

When done, press the Render button on the right of the dialog box. The video will begin to render into the folder in your external drive.

Rendering may take a few minutes or an hour, depending on the size of the video and how fast your computer is. If you have another computer, do some other work while the rendering is happening.

■ **Tip** It's a bad idea to render, check email, and download files at the same time on one computer. Also, it's good to have a backup battery connected to your computer in case there is an electrical surge or power outage that happens while the rendering is taking place. Having your files corrupted or destroyed when the power goes out, is a real time waster for everyone, especially on a tight deadline.

Once the file has rendered, you should find it in the folder you assigned for output. You can preview it in your computer's media player. At more than 17 minutes, my file is a little over 806MB, which is probably the largest size limit I would want for an HTML5 video file that streams online. As for duration, it's as long as I would want to hold the audience's attention.

When you are done looking at Movie_glass_tango_part2.psd, be careful that you do not save the original file. Close the file. Refer to Figure 9-33.

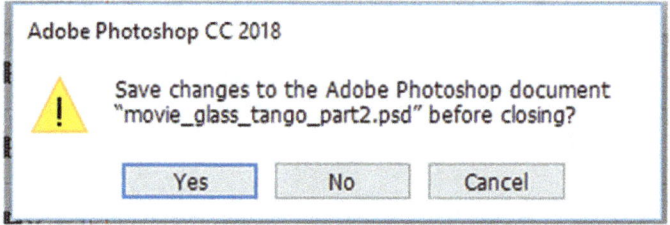

Figure 9-33. *Do not save changes to the original PSD video file*

You have now completed the final project in Photoshop CC.

Summary

In this chapter, you reviewed how to create images, GIF animations, a poster image, and video for the Hot Glass Tango website. This chapter concludes your study of Photoshop. At this point, review any areas of Part 2 that you don't understand so that you feel comfortable with working with your own graphics in Photoshop.

In Part 3, you journey to the next junction point in the software maze: Adobe Illustrator CC. You'll discover how it can be used to create web graphics.

PART III

Working with Illustrator to Create Web Graphics

CHAPTER 10

Getting Started with Illustrator CC

In Part 2, you traveled through the symbolic maze as you worked with Photoshop to create graphics for the web. Now you are going to travel to the next junction point, known as Adobe Illustrator CC. Refer to Figure 10-1.

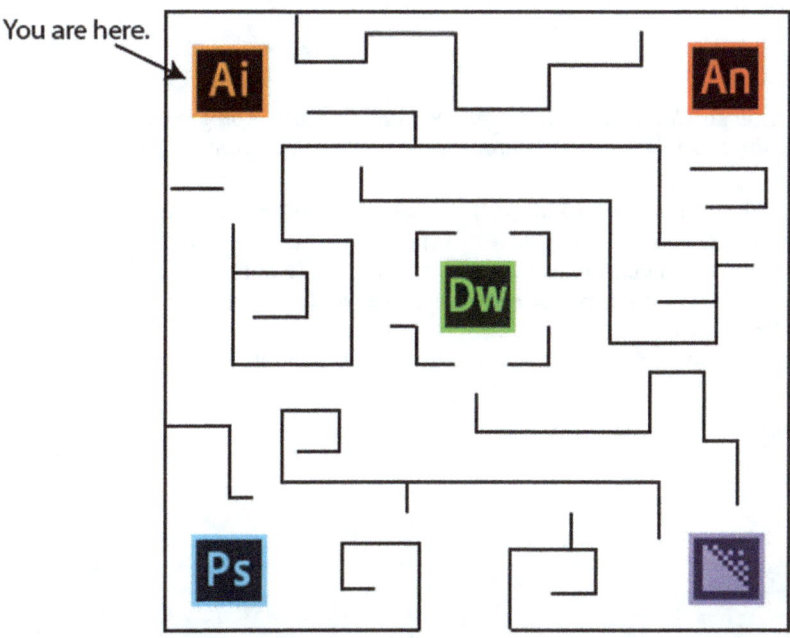

Figure 10-1. *After working with Photoshop, you now begin exploring Illustrator CC*

■ **Note** This chapter does not have any actual projects; however, you can use the files in the Chapter 10 folder to practice opening and viewing for this lesson. They are at https://github.com/Apress/graphics-multimedia-web-adobe-creative-cloud.

When I think of Illustrator, I think of it as a drawing program that I use to create hand-drawn sketches from pictures that I scanned or for tracing over photographs that I want to use for an illustrated book. However, if you look at the diagram (see Figure 10-2), you can see that the graphics you create for print can just as well be formatted for the web. They can be formatted in several ways, so that they can be imported into other Adobe products, like Photoshop (Smart Object Layers) and Animate (Symbols), which you'll look at in Part 4.

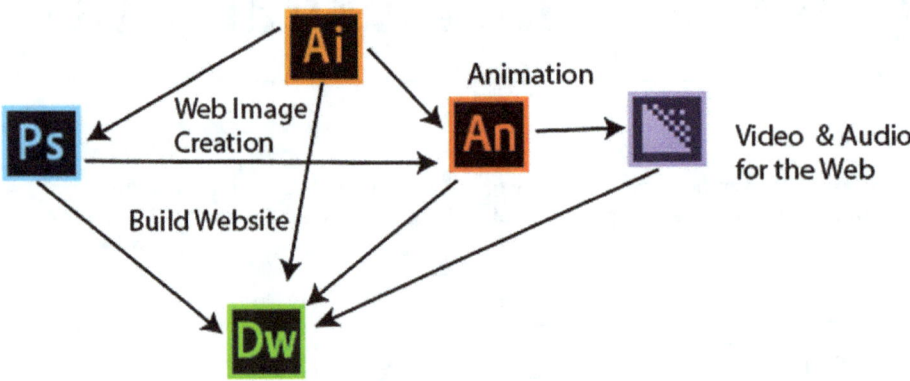

Figure 10-2. *Graphics that are drawn in Illustrator can be exported into other Adobe programs like Photoshop, Dreamweaver, and Animate so that you can continue your multimedia project*

In this chapter, you begin by setting up your workspace. If you have never used Illustrator, I recommend reading a book like *Adobe Illustrator CC Classroom in a Book* by Brian Wood (Adobe Press, 2017), where you get a basic overview of the program and many of its tools. You can also check out Illustrator's Learn panel, which has step-by-step tutorials on various projects. In Part 3, you work with graphics that are already created and then save them for the web.

As you can see in Figure 10-3, we look at several formatting choices throughout this section.

CHAPTER 10 ■ GETTING STARTED WITH ILLUSTRATOR CC

Figure 10-3. *Here you can see a junction or point of decision within Illustrator. What is the correct type of file format to use for a specific project?*

Working with RAW and Layered Files (AI, EPS, PDF)

Let's begin by opening Illustrator CC. If you do not have it on your computer, but you do have the Creative Cloud, click the Install button (see Figure 10-4) and follow the instructions on how to install the program.

Figure 10-4. *Click the Install button when you want to install an Adobe program like Illustrator from the Creative Cloud*

225

> **Note** Before you install an Adobe program, make sure that your computer meets the system requirements; otherwise, the installation may fail. For more information, see `https://helpx.adobe.com/illustrator/system-requirements.html`.

If you already have Illustrator CC installed on your computer, from your desktop, double-click the icon. In the Creative Cloud, click Open to launch the program, as seen in Figure 10-5.

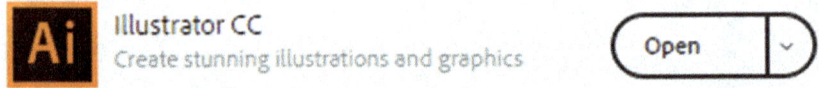

Figure 10-5. Click Open to open the Illustrator program

Once Illustrator CC opens, you can set up your workspace so that yours appears the same as mine. I chose the Web workspace from the Workspace icon in the upper right, as seen in Figure 10-6.

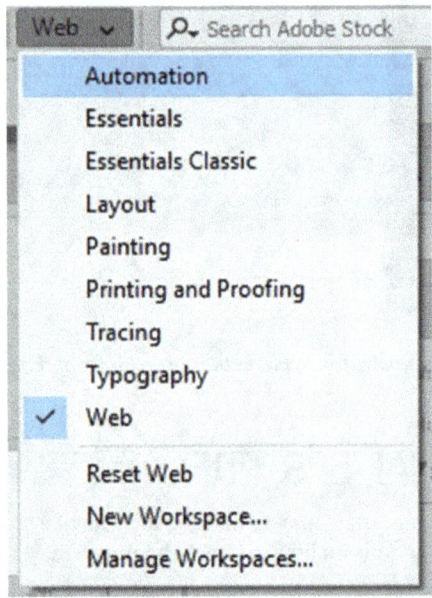

Figure 10-6. Choose Web in the Workspace tab in in Illustrator

Equally, you could work with the Essentials Classic workspace since it also offers a full range of tools in the Tools panel, as seen in Figure 10-7.

CHAPTER 10 ■ GETTING STARTED WITH ILLUSTRATOR CC

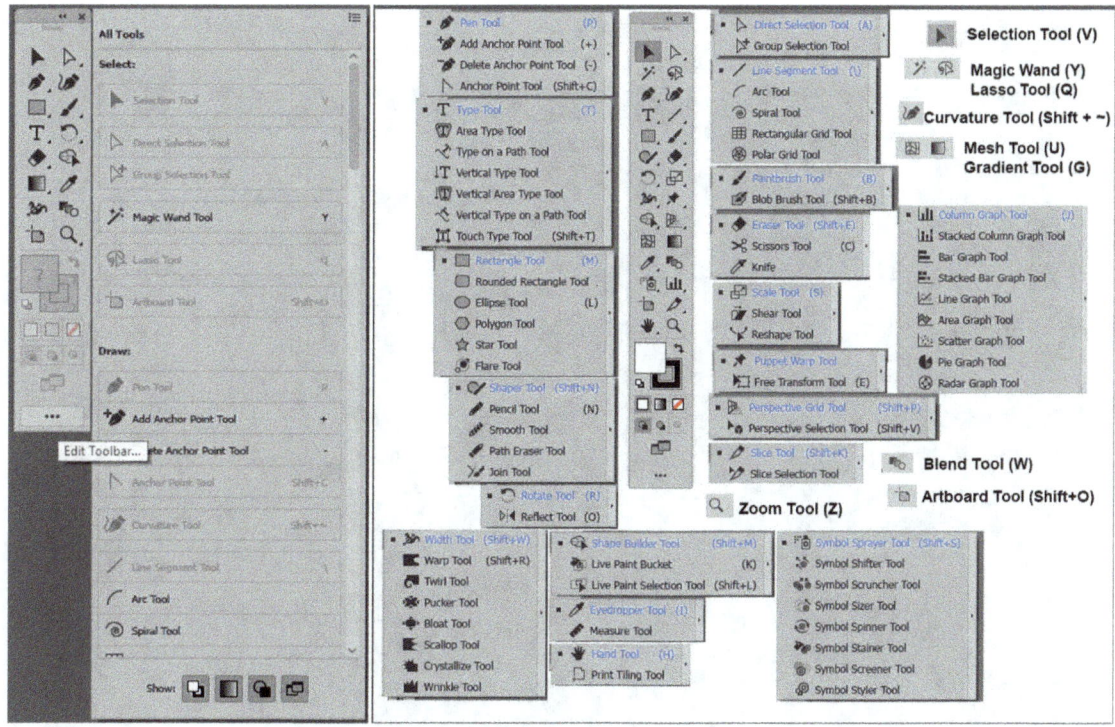

Figure 10-7. *The Essentials Classic workspace offers all tool, while web limits the amount of tools*

As seen in Figure 10-7 Photoshop's and Illustrator's Tools panels look similar, you can customize the Illustrator Tools panel as you did with Photoshop, this time using the (...) edit tool bar icon at the bottom of the panel.

In Part 3, you look at some of the panels available in the Automation workspace. If you prefer another workspace for your web design workflow, you can always choose a different one or create your own custom workspace (New Workspace), as seen in Figure 10-6.

Your workspace should now look similar to Figure 10-8.

227

CHAPTER 10 ■ GETTING STARTED WITH ILLUSTRATOR CC

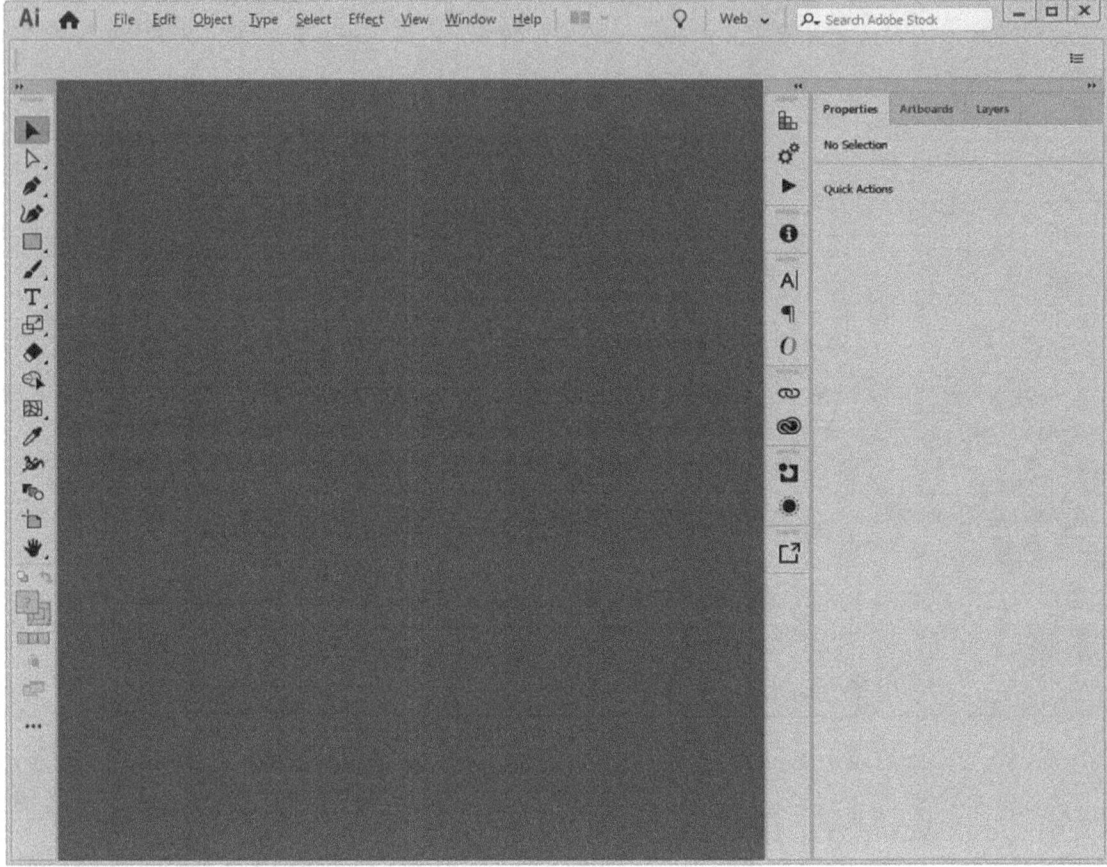

Figure 10-8. *The Web workspace*

If you prefer that your Tools panel is two columns, make sure to drag the panel out from the left to undock it, and then click the double arrows in the upper part of the Tools panel to make it two columns, as seen in Figure 10-7.

Creating a New File

If you want to create a new file, choose File ➤ New from the main menu. See Figure 10-9 for the dialog box.

CHAPTER 10 ■ GETTING STARTED WITH ILLUSTRATOR CC

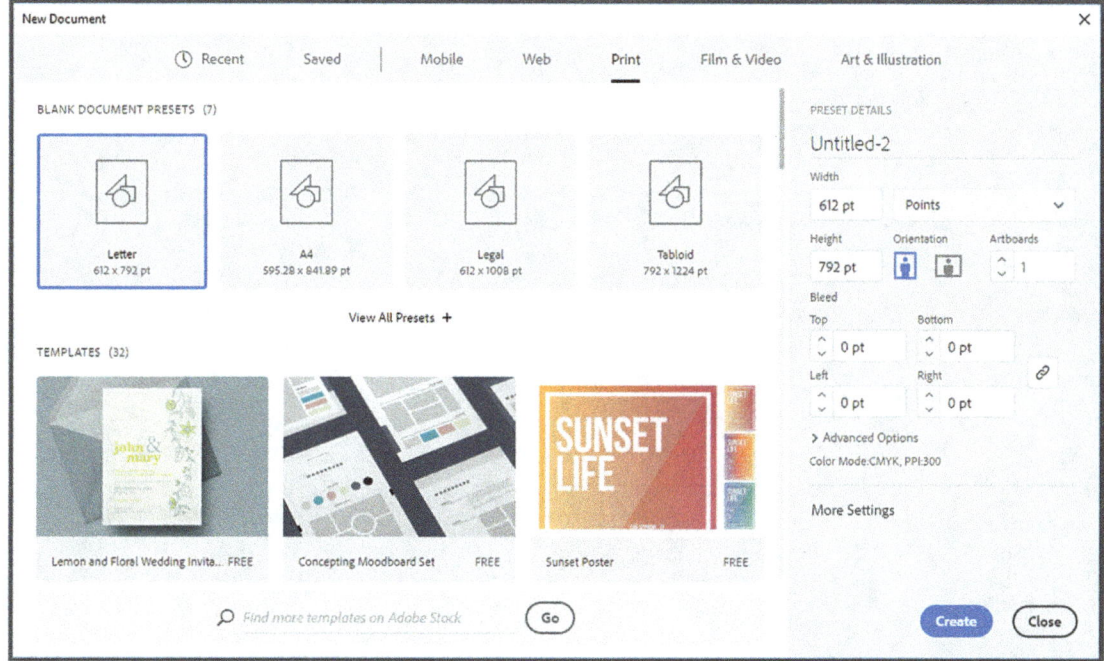

Figure 10-9. *The New Document dialog box*

To keep consistency across the Creative Cloud programs, Illustrator like Photoshop, has organized many of its standard layouts into tabs so that you can easily choose a layout for your project whether for the web, mobile, or film and video. You can even create your own custom sizes. Like Photoshop, you can use an artboard in which you can have more than one type of layout in a project; however, when you begin creating files that you are planning to use for the web, make sure that the color mode is set to RGB Color (see Figure 10-10) in the Advanced Options drop-down menu. I'll discuss color more in Chapter 11.

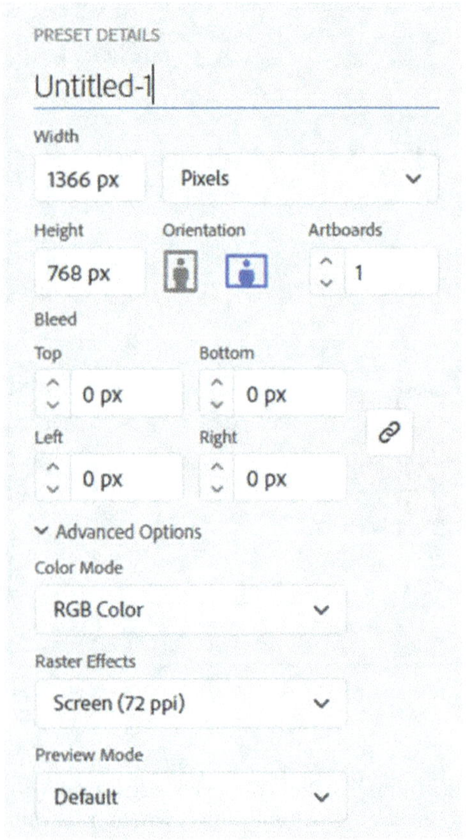

CHAPTER 10 ■ GETTING STARTED WITH ILLUSTRATOR CC

Figure 10-10. When working on illustrations for the web, make sure that the color mode is already set to RGB color

---

■ **Note** If you are not sure about size of the items that you are planning to create for the web, you can always keep your file at 300 pixels/inch (PPI). Unlike the raster images that you created in Photoshop, the graphics in Illustrator are vector; so if you keep the original AI or EPS file, the images will never degrade and they can be scaled to any size; however, if you know the exact size of your layout, such as when you are building a mockup for a website, use the Web tab to autoset the resolution to 72 pixels/inch (PPI), which is generally the acceptable resolution for most images on the web. Then, click the Create button, as seen in Figure 10-11. Whatever setting you chose, your new file will now open.

Figure 10-11. Use the Web tab in the New Document dialog box to choose a preset layout, and then click Create to create a new file

If the preset is not to your liking, you can adjust the color mode and resolution in the Advanced Options tab. However, unlike in Photoshop, you can only choose three raster effects or resolutions:

- Screen (72 ppi)
- Medium (150 ppi)
- High (300 ppi)

You can find more settings under the More Settings button in the New Document dialog box, as seen in Figure 10-12.

Figure 10-12. The More Settings button in the New Document dialog box

When you click the button, the More Setting dialog box opens, as seen in Figure 10-13.

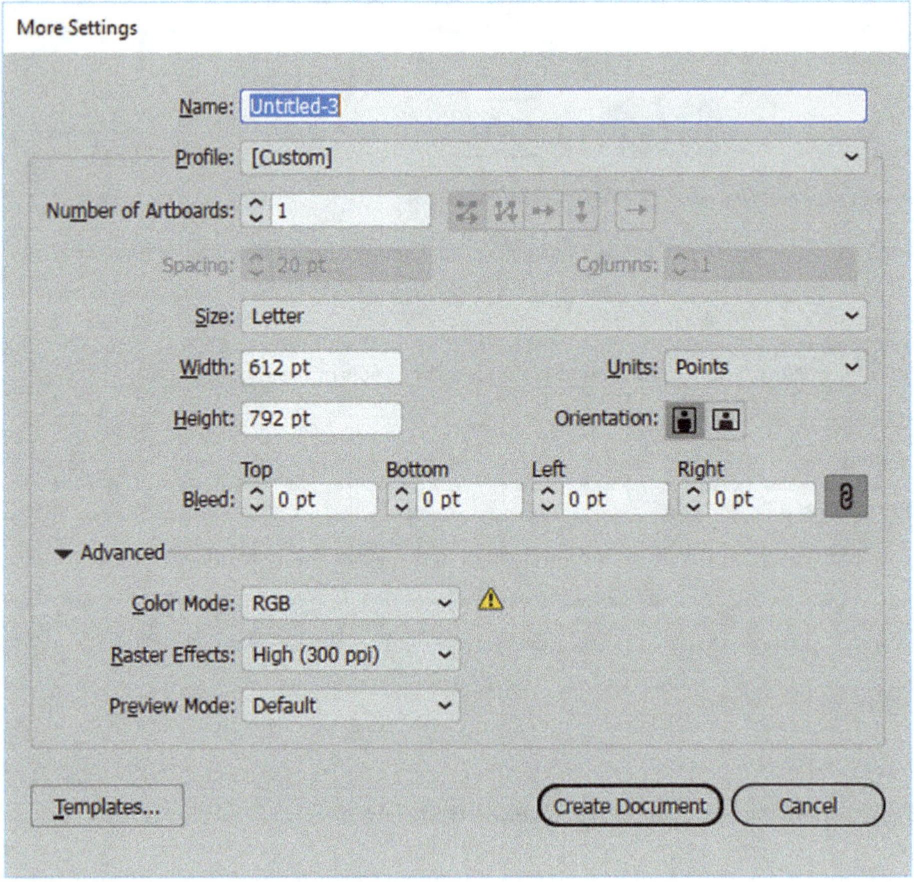

CHAPTER 10 ■ GETTING STARTED WITH ILLUSTRATOR CC

Figure 10-13. The More Settings dialog box

Here, most of the settings are like what you saw in Figure 10-9, but you can also adjust bleed, access templates, and adjust artboard spacing and columns. When you are done, either click Create Document or click Cancel to return to the New Document dialog box. Clicking Create Document creates a new blank Illustrator file.

You can always create your files directly in Illustrator CC, or you may have collected or acquired your original images in other file formats that you want to place within your new document so that you can trace the images. Others you can open directly in Illustrator. I have listed some you will likely encounter. In the main menu, go to File ➤ Open or to File ➤ Place.

RAW File Types

The following are raster images that may have been created in a program like Photoshop. You may want to use them for tracing the graphic (Image Trace). You may want to use the pen tool. But ultimately, if you continue to work with illustrated files in Illustrator, you have to save them in another vector format.

You can select File ➤ Place within an Illustrator document as a link for tracing.

- **Bitmap (.bmp)**: This file is often created when you scan a file with your office scanner. It is common to Windows-compatible computers. While it can be used on the web, the file size is often quite large, so it's best to save in a file format that is better suited for the web.

- **TIFF (.tif, .tiff)**: Often graphic artists save a final single-layered piece of artwork as a TIFF file, which are considered images that do not lose quality "lossless" as copies are saved from them, and they retain their original size; no compression of data occurs.

- **Photoshop PSD (.psd, .pdd)**: When creating your graphics, you may save your files in multiple layers. Photoshop PSD files allow you to retain layers, effects, and masks. After you save and close a file, you can always come back to continue to edit until you are ready to export a copy to the web.

There are many other raster graphics, including JPEGs, PNGs, and GIFs (discussed in Part 2) that can be placed directly into an Illustrator (.ai) file and onto separate layers in the Layers panel. This is often a better method than opening these files directly because you can move an image around in a file, or scale an image without altering the original. This is in the Links panel, as seen in Figure 10-14.

Figure 10-14. You can check which raster images are linked in the Links panel and where they are in the Layers panel

If you decided to embed an image within a document by using the Links panel, a graphic symbol will appear, as seen in Figure 10-15.

CHAPTER 10 ■ GETTING STARTED WITH ILLUSTRATOR CC

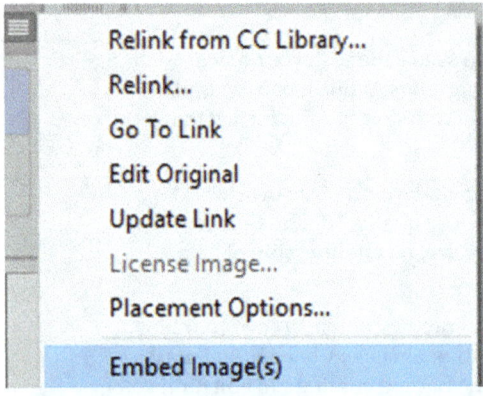

Figure 10-15. You can check which raster images are linked or embeded in the Links panel

To unembed the image right away, choose Edit ➤ Undo or from the Links menu (Unembed...) so that you can save the image as a PSD file or Tiff in a folder. The recreated image will now return to being a linked file and is now separate and in no way linked to the original you first placed.

Depending on the file format, if raster files are chosen using File ➤ Open, you may be able to choose further import settings. A Photoshop file is imported in Figure 10-16.

CHAPTER 10 ■ GETTING STARTED WITH ILLUSTRATOR CC

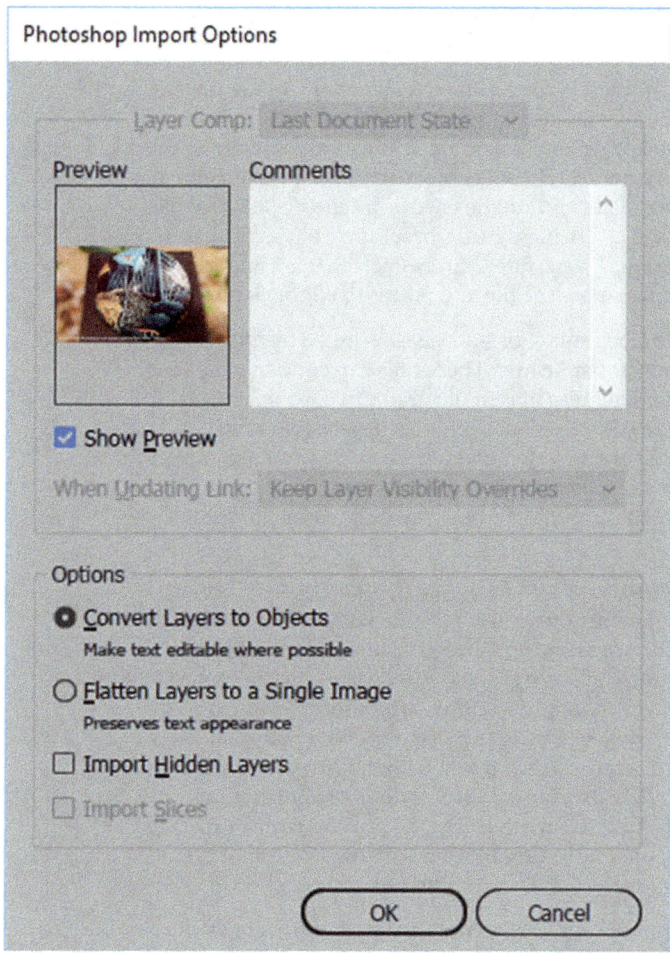

***Figure 10-16.** Example of what options are available if you import a Photoshop file*

You can

- **Convert Layers to Objects**: This is good if you want to keep text editable
- **Flatten to a Single Image**: Preserves text appearance
- **Import Hidden Layers** and **Import Slices**: If there are any in the original PSD

Make sure that you are working on a backup file so that you do not alter the original in some way.

In other instances, if you open a JPEG, no dialog box will appear, and the file is opened directly in Illustrator. That is why the File ➤ Place option may be best way to persevere the original artwork. It all depends on what you are trying to accomplish.

235

Alternatively, the following are commonly seen vector formats that you may acquire for original artwork from a client.

- **Adobe Illustrator (.ai, .ait)**: A proprietary file format developed by Adobe Systems for representing single-page vector-based drawings in the EPS and PDF formats. The .ai filename extension is used by Adobe Illustrator. While it can contain only one page, it can have multiple artboards. When it is saved with an .ait extension, it is known as an Adobe Illustrator template and can be used as a starting point for files that have certain similar designs (e.g., business cards, brochures, packaging, and logos). This format preserves various layers, filters, and effects that are applied to graphics within the file, and you can close the file and return to editing it further.

- **Adobe PDF (.pdf)**: The Portable Document Format was developed by Adobe Systems, and it is read by Adobe Acrobat Reader. These files can contain raster and vector images and text. You can open these files in Illustrator to copy out vector graphics, but be aware that due to compression, things like layer order or the integrity of the text may be altered or converted to outlines. Once you have copied the graphics that you want from a PDF file, it is best to save the new file as an AI or EPS file so that the integrity of the graphics and text are maintained for future projects.

- **Encapsulated Postscript** and **Illustrator EPS (.eps, .epsf, .ps)**: The EPS format preserves many of the graphic elements that you can create with Adobe Illustrator, which means that EPS files can be reopened and edited as Illustrator files (AI). Because EPS files are based on the PostScript language, they can contain both vector and bitmap graphics. If your artwork contains multiple artboards, these artboards are preserved in the EPS format. However, be aware that depending on what types of filters and effects were used to create the file, the EPS file size may be smaller or larger than an AI file when saved. Also, older EPS files do not support some Illustrator features, so it might be best to save any artwork you copy from an EPS as an AI file. For more information on how to save this type of artwork, visit `https://helpx.adobe.com/illustrator/using/saving-artwork.html`.

- **Enhanced metafile (.emf)**: Some CD and DVDs contain vector clip art in this format. Widely used by Windows applications as an interchange format for exporting vector graphics data. Illustrator may rasterize some vector data when exporting artwork to EMF format.

- **Windows metafile (.wmf)**: Some CD/DVDs that contain vector clip art in this format. An intermediate exchange format for 16-bit Windows applications. The WMF format is supported by almost all Windows drawing and layout programs; however, it has limited vector graphics support, and wherever possible, EMF format should be used in place of WMF format or saved as an EPS or AI file when working on your project.

Note Illustrator can open many other file formats, including AutoCAD and SVG files that can contain vector shapes, but unlike Photoshop, it cannot open video files. Refer to Figure 10-17.

CHAPTER 10 ■ GETTING STARTED WITH ILLUSTRATOR CC

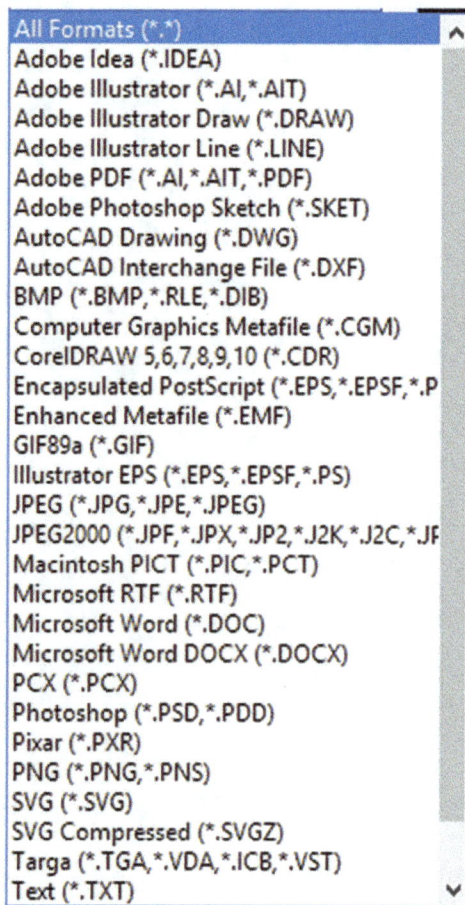

Figure 10-17. There are many file formats that Illustrator can open or link to

For more information on other formats you might encounter, visit https://helpx.adobe.com/illustrator/kb/supported-file-formats-illustrator.html.

When you are done, you can save any open file as an AI or EPS for now. Then select File ➤ Close and File ➤ Exit to leave Illustrator CC, or you can keep Illustrator and the files open for the next chapter.

Summary

In this chapter, you started to explore Illustrator CC and some of the file formats that you can work with or save your artwork as. In the next chapter, you look at some of the color mode choices and determine which ones are correct for your web design projects.

CHAPTER 11

Color Choices: CMYK, RGB, and Grayscale

In this chapter, you are going to look at how to work with color and choose the correct color choices in Illustrator CC.

> **Note** This chapter does not have any actual projects; however, you can use the files in the Chapter 11 folder to practice opening and viewing for this lesson. They are at `https://github.com/Apress/graphics-multimedia-web-adobe-creative-cloud`.

Working with Color

In Photoshop, you want to make sure that the files that will be part of the website are in the correct color mode—especially, if you are creating a fresh piece of artwork. In File ➤ New, you want to make sure that your starting file is saved as RGB, which is your monitor's color channel. In Advanced Options, choose RGB Color under the Color Mode, as seen in Figure 11-1.

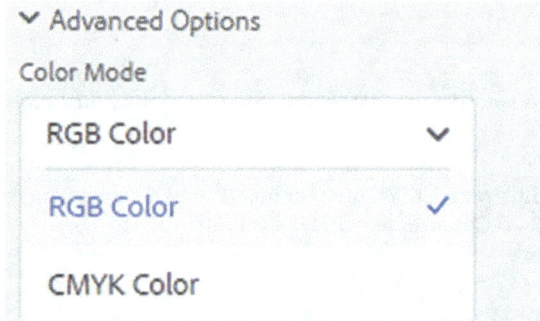

Figure 11-1. Choose RGB for the web images and not CMYK, which is for print

CHAPTER 11 ■ COLOR CHOICES: CMYK, RGB, AND GRAYSCALE

When you create a custom layout or choose the Print tab and set the color mode to RGB, some layouts show an alert, as seen in Figure 11-2.

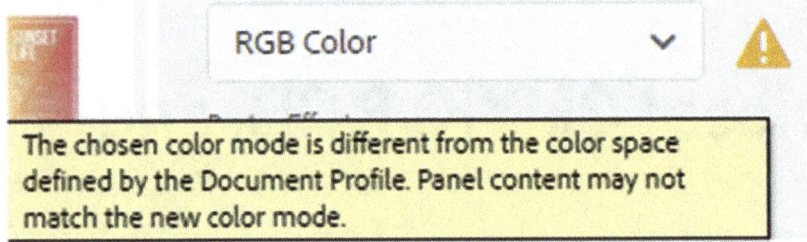

Figure 11-2. Some presets show an alert if you choose RGB color from the New Document dialog box

This simply means that your Color panel many not match the original presets or the swatches or colors modes in these panels and may not be set to RGB color mode when you click Create. It should appear as RGB; otherwise, you can alter it yourself in the Color panel, as seen in Figure 11-3.

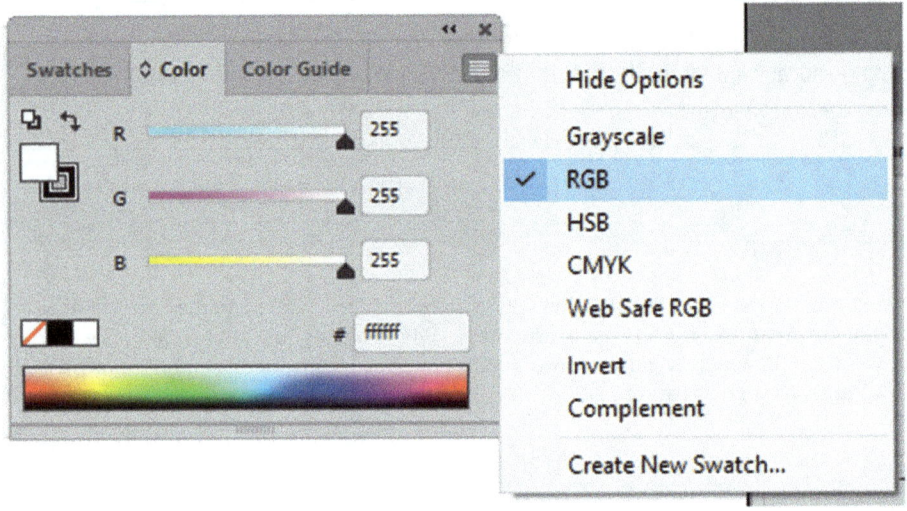

Figure 11-3. To make sure your Color panel is the same as your documents color mode, change it in the Color panel menu

If you want to check or convert an opened existing Illustrator CMYK document to RGB, you can change the mode by selecting File ➤ Document Color Mode ➤ RGB Color, as seen in Figure 11-4.

CHAPTER 11 ■ COLOR CHOICES: CMYK, RGB, AND GRAYSCALE

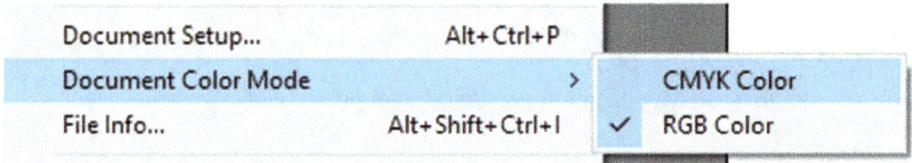

Figure 11-4. Change the document color mode to RGB if it is CMYK

Be aware that there may be a color shift, so if you are using some files for print later, always work with a copy before adjusting the color mode.

You can also make further adjustments, as seen in Figure 11-5, to the RGB settings under Edit ➤ Color Settings.

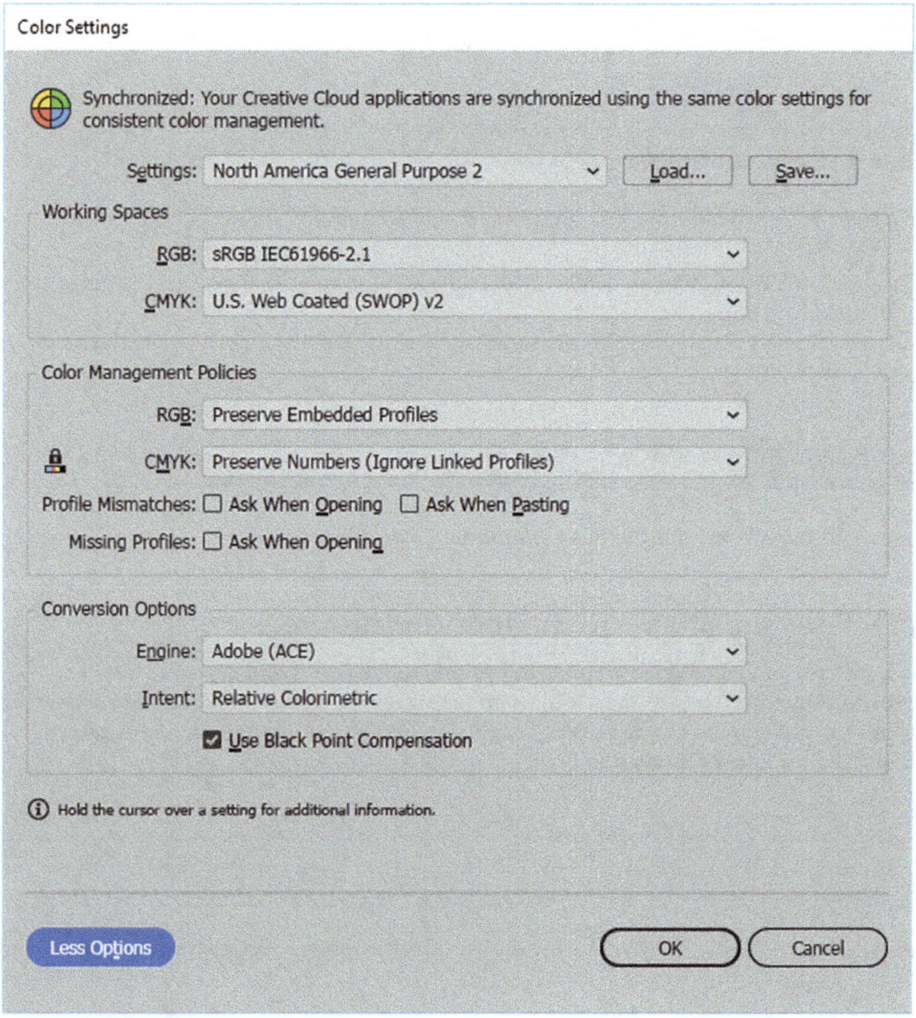

Figure 11-5. Alter color settings

CHAPTER 11 ■ COLOR CHOICES: CMYK, RGB, AND GRAYSCALE

Here you can review your current color spaces, if you don't want to make any changes, click Cancel; otherwise, make an adjustment, and to save it, click OK. In this case, the color space of sRGB is good for the website projects, so you don't need to change it.

If, for some reason, the files that you have acquired contain no color profile, you can set one using Edit ➤ Assign Profile. Refer to Figure 11-6.

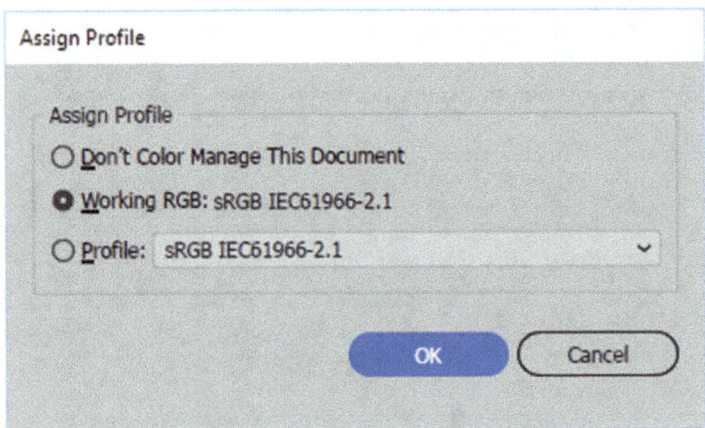

Figure 11-6. Assign a color profile if your AI or EPS document does not have one

Generally, for the web, the RGB profiles are left at the default sRGB, so you can leave these settings as is and click Cancel to exit the dialog box.

You can see your document's color settings because they show at the top of your artwork in the name tab area of each file. Refer to Figure 11-7.

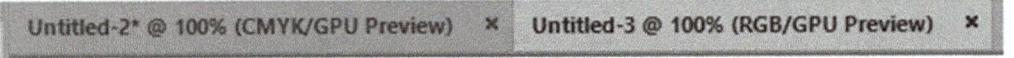

Figure 11-7. Color modes are displayed along with the file name of a document

Copying CMYK Graphics to an RGB Document

If you think that you may have copied a vector graphic into your RGB file that originally came from a document that was in CMYK mode, you can select it by marqueeing it with the Selection tool (V) in the Tools panel. This selects the entire item and makes the conversion for just that graphic shape, as seen in Figure 11-8. Go to Edit ➤ Edit Colors ➤ Convert to RGB.

CHAPTER 11 ■ COLOR CHOICES: CMYK, RGB, AND GRAYSCALE

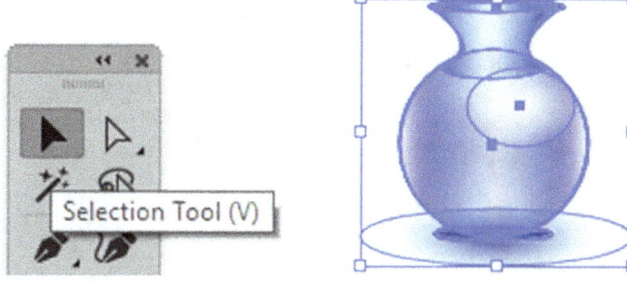

Figure 11-8. *Use the Selection tool to select an illustration and convert it to RGB mode if you suspect it is not RGB*

This ensures that the graphic shape added to the RGB AI or EPS file is in RGB color mode.

■ **Note** In an RGB mode file, CMYK conversion is unavailable. If you are in a CMYK file, Convert to RGB is unavailable. Refer to Figure 11-9.

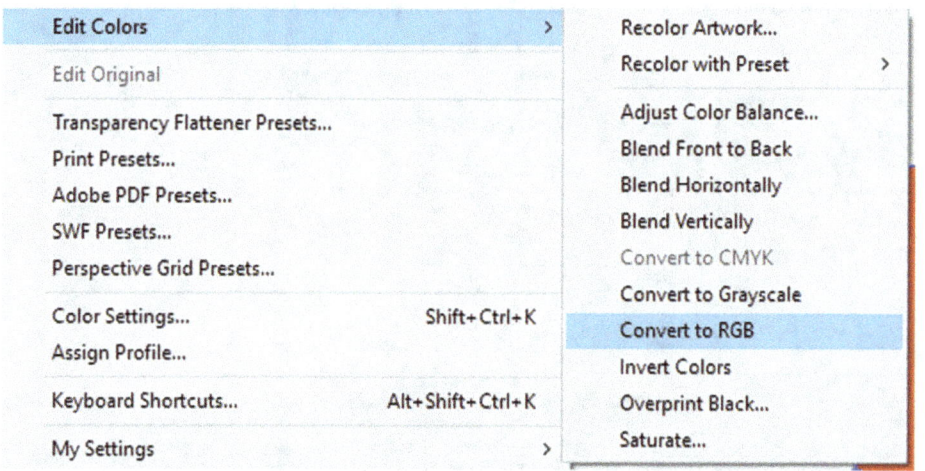

Figure 11-9. *Features of the Edit Colors CMYK are unavailable if in RGB mode*

You can also convert your item to a grayscale color, but it is still in an RGB mode format in your file. There is no actual grayscale color mode in Illustrator.

Color Panel

If, at any time, you need to adjust your Color panel from RGB to CMYK, Grayscale, HBS (Hue Brightness Saturation), or Web Safe RGB, you can do it in the menu, as seen in Figure 11-10. In no way does this alter your document current color mode of RGB.

243

CHAPTER 11 ■ COLOR CHOICES: CMYK, RGB, AND GRAYSCALE

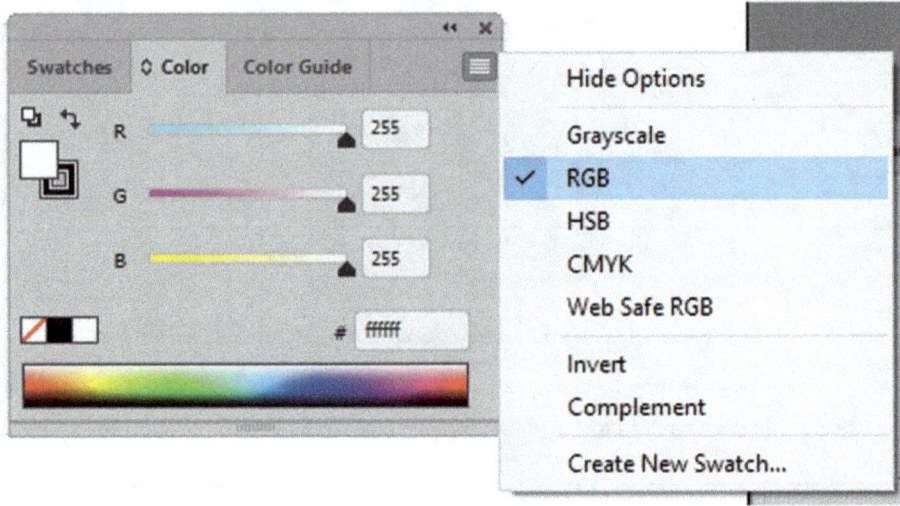

Figure 11-10. Changing the color mode display in the Color panel

Choosing to see and use colors in the Color panel as Grayscale or are Web Safe RGB is good if you plan to output a logo as a GIF or a website's preliminary design, as seen in Figure 11-11.

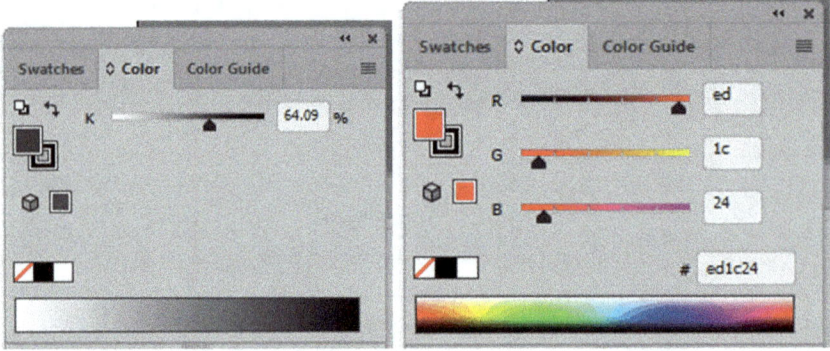

Figure 11-11. Grayscale and Web Safe RGB setting in the Color panel

You can then edit these colors in the Color Picker (see Figure 11-12) when you click the fill or stroke of a shape in the Color panel or in the Tools panel.

244

CHAPTER 11 ■ COLOR CHOICES: CMYK, RGB, AND GRAYSCALE

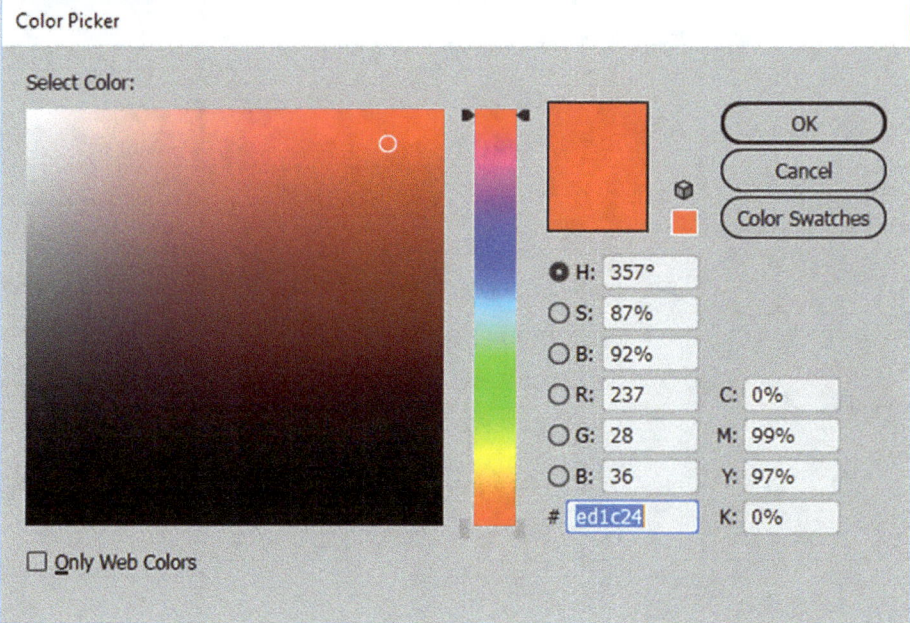

Figure 11-12. Choose a color for shape using the Color Picker found when clicking a color in the tool panel

As you can see, it is almost identical to the one used in Photoshop in Chapter 3. You can also choose Only Web Colors. You can view by color swatches by clicking that button to toggle between it and the current color models.

Swatches Panel

You can save specific colors as swatches that appear in the Tools panel, and drag or add them to your Swatches panel from the Swatches menu as a new swatch or within a new color group folder. Refer to Figure 11-13.

245

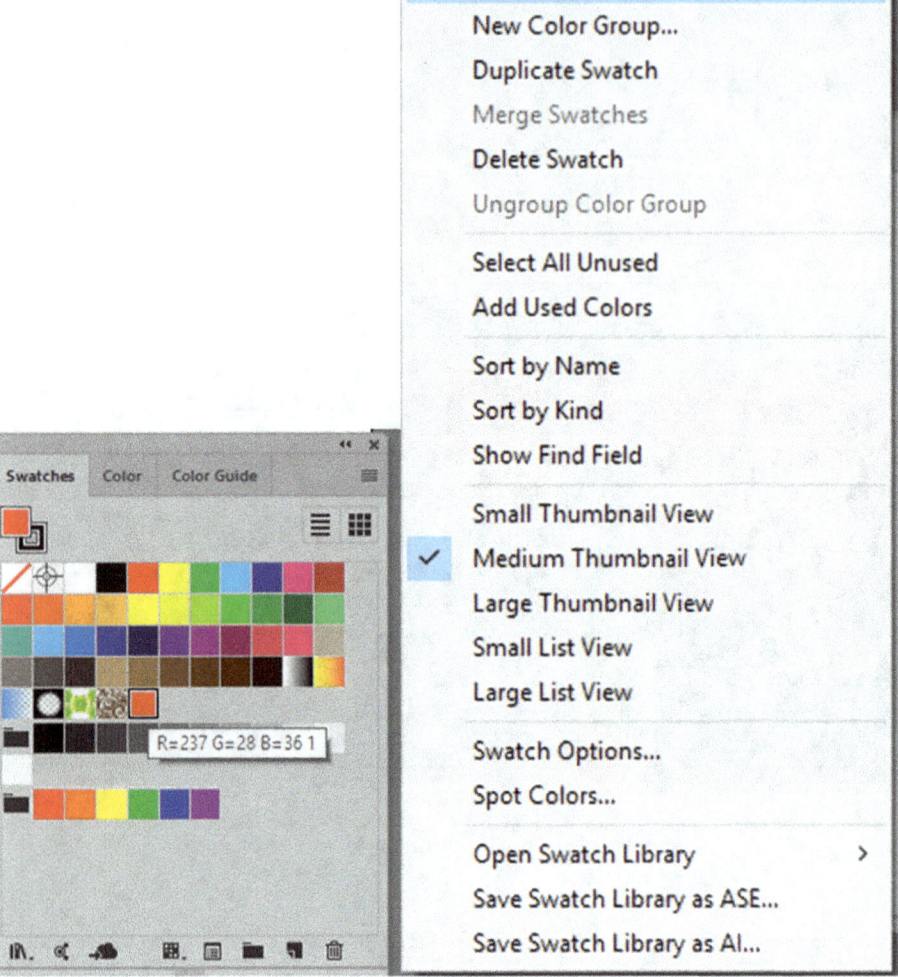

Figure 11-13. Add your new RGB swatch so that you can use it for other shapes later on

When you create new swatches, they are saved within your document. You can save them as a swatch library or open them from other AI or ASE documents from the Swatches menu, as seen in Figure 11-13.

Other Panels for Working with Color

Though not part of the main discussion of this book, there are a few other panels in Illustrator that you can use while working with color. I will briefly mention a few that you may want to use for your projects.

CHAPTER 11 ■ COLOR CHOICES: CMYK, RGB, AND GRAYSCALE

Color Guide Panel

The Color Guide panel is used to apply color to, edit, or recolor your shapes. Refer to Figure 11-14.

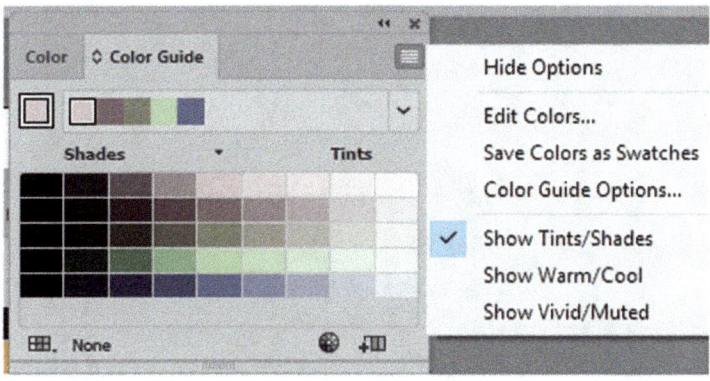

Figure 11-14. *Use the Color Guide to adjust colors for complex shapes*

Clicking the lower Edit or Apply Colors icon (color wheel) on the panel allows you to access the Recolor Artwork dialog box.

You can save these colors as swatches in the Swatches panel for later use.

247

CHAPTER 11 ■ COLOR CHOICES: CMYK, RGB, AND GRAYSCALE

Adobe Color Themes Panel

As in Photoshop, you can work with color in the Color Themes panel, where you can explore and create assorted color combinations (see Figure 11-15).

Figure 11-15. The Adobe Color Themes panel assists in finding complimentary colors for your themes

Gradient Panel

The Gradient panel (see Figure 11-16) allows you to add colors with color stops when creating a gradient for your shape. Likewise, you can use the Gradient tool (G) in the Tools panel to alter the gradient or add it to the Swatches panel. This panel has been updated in CC 2019 with the new free form gradient options.

CHAPTER 11 ■ COLOR CHOICES: CMYK, RGB, AND GRAYSCALE

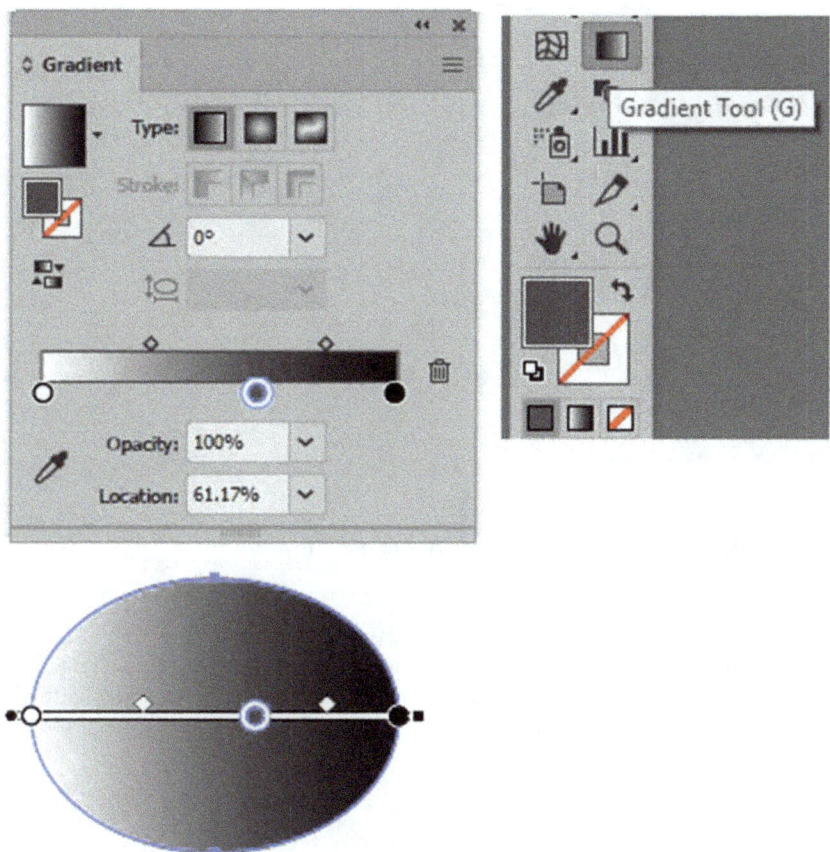

Figure 11-16. *Use the Gradient panel to add a gradient to your shape*

Gradients can be linear, radial, or freeform, and have a differing opacity and locations at each point on the slider. Gradients also work with the Mesh tool (U), which is to the left of the Gradient tool in the Tools panel.

Transparency Panel

The Transparency panel has many blending, opacity, and mask features. If you compare the Photoshop Layers panel to the Illustrator Layers panel, you notice that it does not have effects, masks, or blending modes that you can apply each layer. Rather, you must use either the Effect Filters panel or the Transparency panel, and apply them to the selected object. Refer to Figure 11-17.

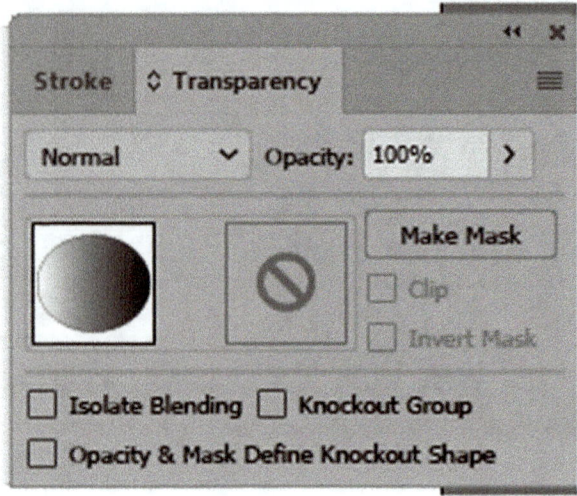

Figure 11-17. The Transparency panel has many blending, opacity and mask features

Appearance Panel

Once you apply different effects and gradients to an object, you can alter their order or add more using the Appearance panel. By adding or altering alternate fills, strokes, and effects, these can later be added to the Window Graphic Styles panel, which like the Swatches panel, can be used as library to store all the graphic styles that you create in your file. Refer to Figure 11-18.

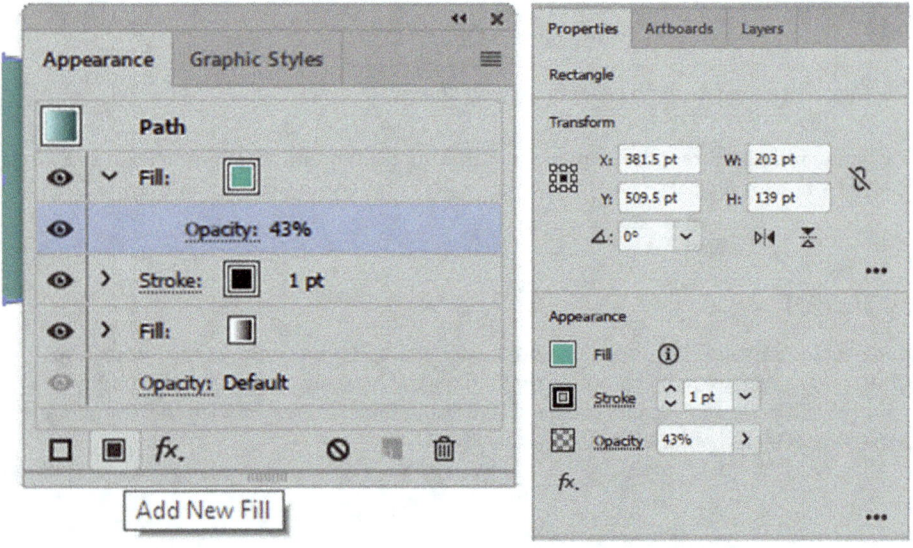

Figure 11-18. The Appearance panel and Properties panel allow you to alter your fills and strokes to create a variety of colors and effects (FX)

You will look at the Graphic Styles panel and other related panels in more detail in Part 3.

For now, take some time to review these panels and see how you can use them for your own projects.

Note that many of these panels' settings can be accessed through the Properties panel when a vector graphic is selected.

Summary

In this chapter, you looked at the two color mode settings: RGB and CMYK. You also saw how to emulate grayscale color. You looked at some of Illustrator's settings and panels, and saw how they allow you to effect and control your RGB colors.

In the next chapter, you discover how to use Illustrator's export settings to save your graphics for the web.

CHAPTER 12

Saving or Exporting Your Files for the Web

In this chapter, you are going to look at how to export files for the web using in Illustrator CC.

> **Note** This chapter does not have any actual projects; however, you can use the files in the Chapter 12 folder to practice opening and viewing for this lesson. They are at https://github.com/Apress/graphics-multimedia-web-adobe-creative-cloud.

At some point, you probably have designed some artwork for your website, whether it was graphic buttons, images for a gallery, or a patterned background. After you designed your artwork for your website, you want to start saving it for the web. Rather than bring it into Photoshop to export, Illustrator CC also offers several ways to export your web-ready files. If you need a more detailed description of each of these file types, refer to Chapter 1.

For this chapter, refer to Table 12-1.

Table 12-1. *Export Settings in Illustrator CC*

File Format	(Option 1) File ➤ Save As File ➤ Save a Copy	(Option 2) File ➤ Export ➤ For Screens	(Option 3) File ➤ Export ➤ Export As	(Option 4) File ➤ Export ➤ Save For Web (Legacy)
Bitmap (.bmp)			✔	
JPEG (.jpg, .jpeg, .jpe)		✔	✔	✔
PNG (8 and 24)(.png)		✔	✔	✔
GIF (static and animated) (.gif)				✔(static only)
SVG (.svg)	✔	✔	✔	
Illustrator PDF (.pdf)	✔	✔		

As you can see, Illustrator CC offers at least four separate ways to save web files. Let's look at each way. Refer to Table 12-1 if you need to compare information.

Option 1: File ➤ Save As or File ➤ Save a Copy

If you compare the options that are available to you in Illustrator CC (File ➤ Save As or File ➤ Save a Copy) to the options in Photoshop CC (see Chapter 4), you notice that there are a lot fewer options for files that you can save for the web. Refer to Figure 12-1.

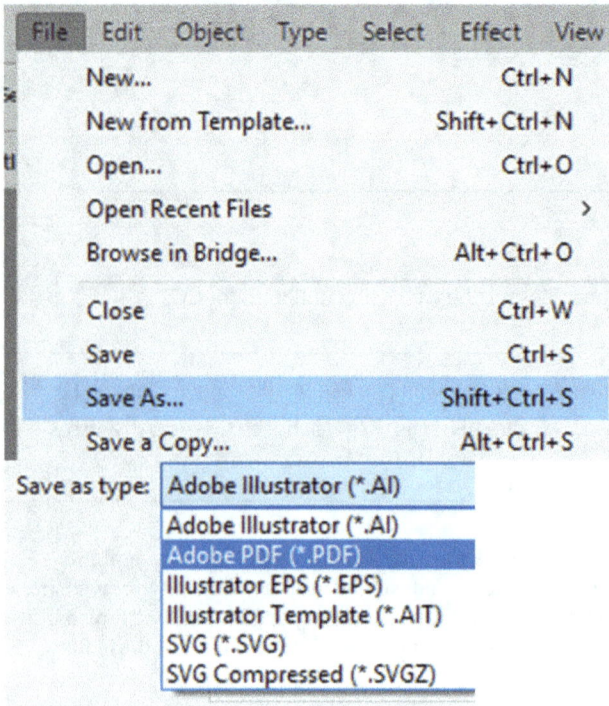

Figure 12-1. *Save, Save As, and Save a Copy have fewer web options than Photoshop*

Unlike Photoshop, whose focus is on creating raster or pixilated graphics, Illustrator's main purpose is to create graphics that are scalable or vector. About a decade ago, files that were scalable for viewing on a website were still in their infancy and slowly being adopted by web developers; so Illustrator was not considered the go-to for creating web graphics.

The main types of files that you can use on the web that contain vector elements are Adobe PDF, SVG, and SVG Compressed. Let's take a moment to look at their settings through Illustrator.

Adobe PDF (.pdf)

Although a PDF does not preview unless you click the file link on a webpage and it downloads onto the browser, you may want to save some images as a PDF by using Illustrator, rather than spend time placing them in a program like Adobe InDesign CC and then saving the file as a PDF. Either way, make sure that Acrobat DC Pro is installed on your computer so that you can use the Distiller to create the PDF. Refer to the icons in Figure 12-2.

CHAPTER 12 ■ SAVING OR EXPORTING YOUR FILES FOR THE WEB

Figure 12-2. *Make sure that Acrobat Pro and its Distiller are installed on your computer if you want to create PDFs with Illustrator*

When you choose this file format, you are presented with various tabs; many are familiar to you because they are like the ones in Photoshop. There are various presets, standards, and compatibilities that you can choose from drop-down menus. Refer to Figure 12-3 to see the General tab.

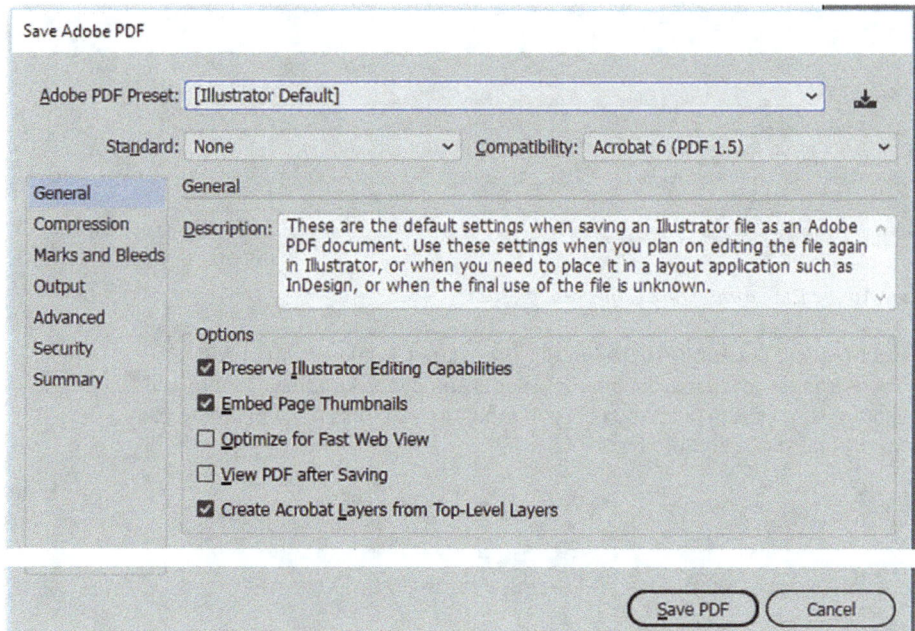

Figure 12-3. *The Save Adobe PDF dialog box General tab*

- **General:** The main settings that allows you to keep a standard and compatibility setting. Preserve the file should you want to edit it again, embed a thumbnail, optimize for fast web preview, view the PDF after saving, or retain layers for your PDF.

- **Compression:** Assorted options for downsampling bitmap images within the vector file. You can also compress text and line art. Refer to Figure 12-4.

255

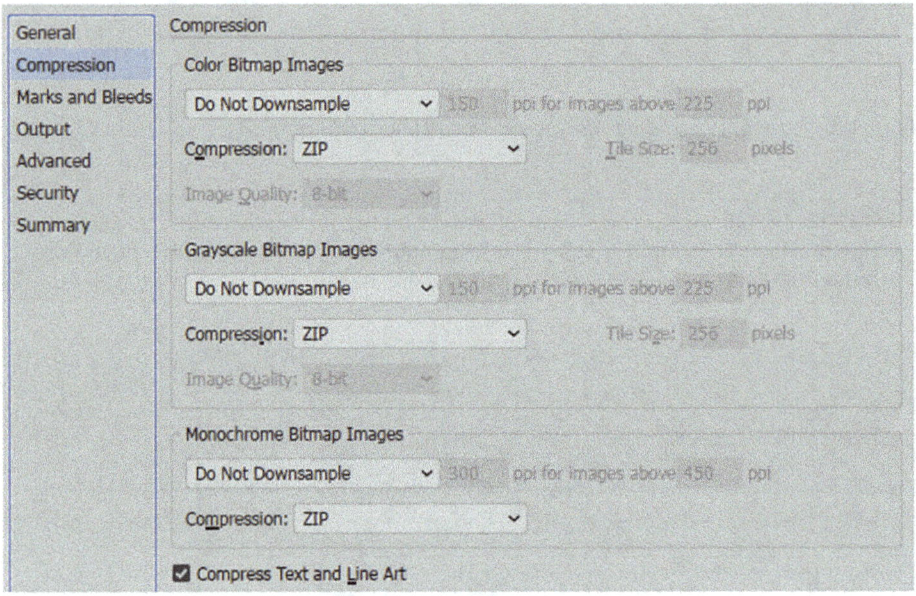

CHAPTER 12 ■ SAVING OR EXPORTING YOUR FILES FOR THE WEB

Figure 12-4. The Save Adobe PDF dialog box Compression tab

- **Marks and Bleeds:** Like Adobe InDesign CC, Illustrator CC allows you to add trim marks to your images for items like business cards and flyers. You may want to add these as part of your online portfolio or if you prefer to skip this area and create your own custom trim marks. Refer to Figure 12-5.

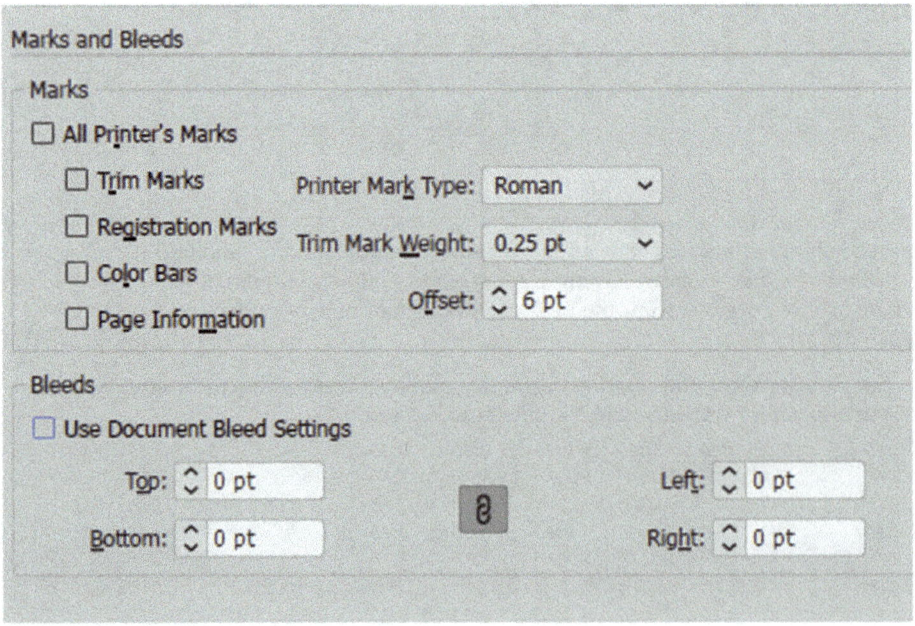

Figure 12-5. The Marks and Bleeds tab in the Save Adobe PDF dialog box

- **Output:** This tab deals with color and file conversion. Hovering over a filed item will give you a description of that setting in the field below. Refer to Figure 12-6.

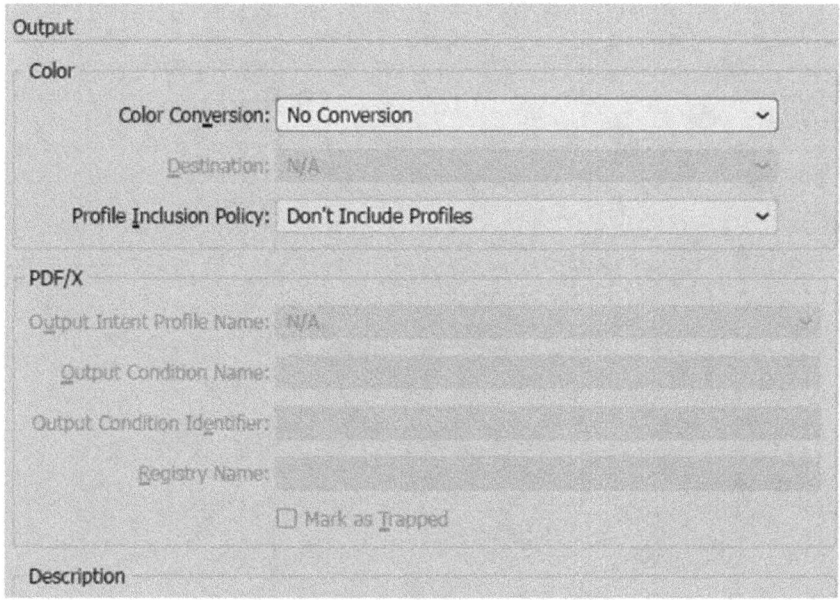

Figure 12-6. *The Output tab in the Save Adobe PDF dialog box*

- **Advanced:** This area deals with font subsets and handling transparency when the file is printed for older PDF compatibility; otherwise, it is unavailable. Refer to Figure 12-7.

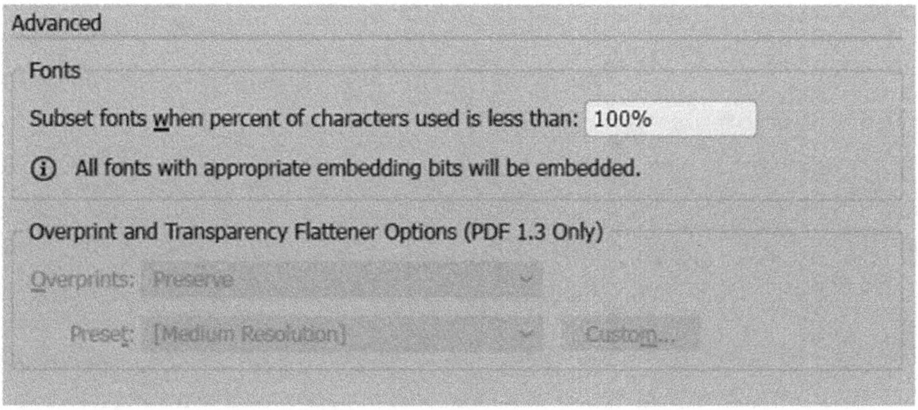

Figure 12-7. *The Advanced tab in the Save Adobe PDF dialog box*

CHAPTER 12 ■ SAVING OR EXPORTING YOUR FILES FOR THE WEB

- **Security:** Sets security features for an image so that users who don't know the password can't open, print, or edit it. Refer to Figure 12-8.

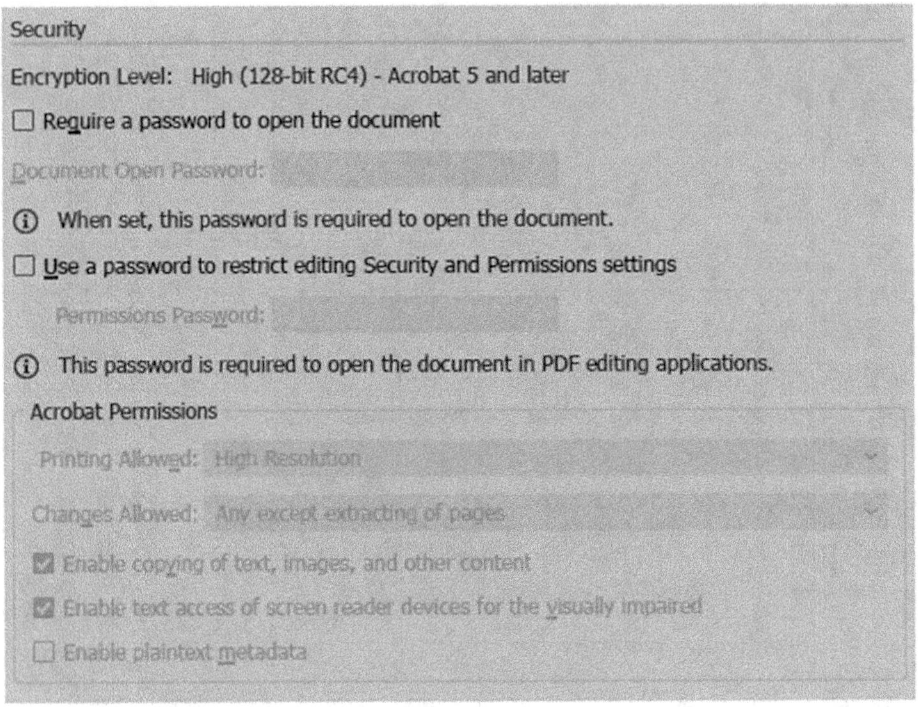

Figure 12-8. The Security tab in the Save Adobe PDF dialog box

- **Summary:** Lists all the settings that were made, as well as any issues or warning during creation. Refer to Figure 12-9.

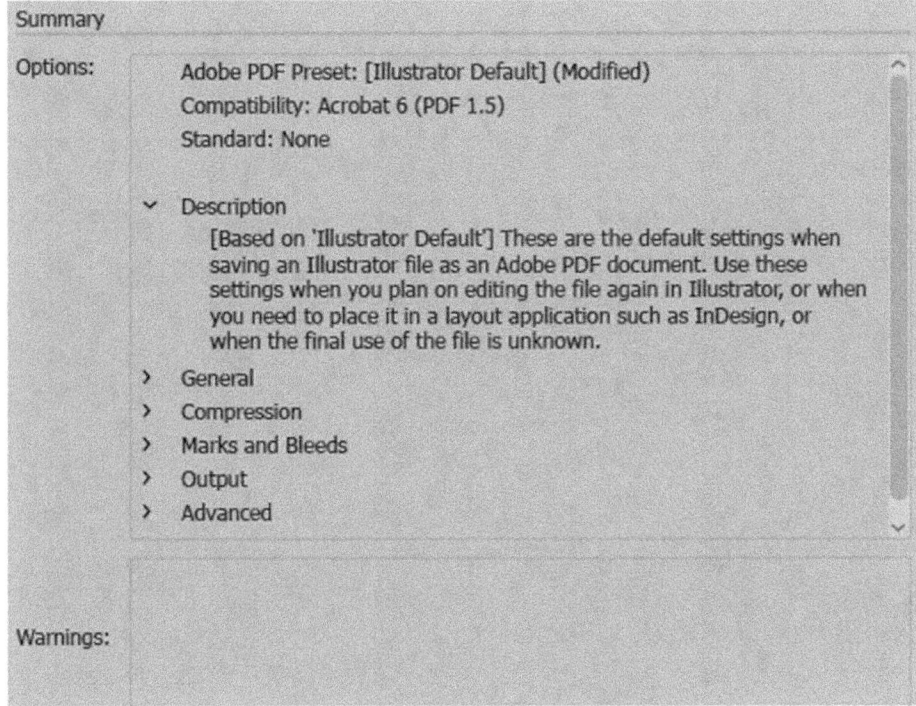

Figure 12-9. The Summary tab in the Save Adobe PDF dialog box

If you plan to save the PDF, click the Save PDF button, as seen in Figure 12-3, or click Cancel to exit.

SVG (.svg) and SVG Compressed (.svgz)

Scalable Vector Graphics, as you saw in Chapter 1, are based on an XML coding vector image format for two-dimensional graphics with support for interactivity and animation. As you saw in Chapter 8, they can also be used to create colorful fonts and fonts for the web. Vector images can be scaled to any size and keep their basic form without losing quality, whereas JPEGs, GIFs, and PNGs appear pixilated when scaled up. SVGs are generally considered "lossless," or don't compress; however, an SVGZ or compressed SVG can be 20% to 50% of the original size.

Both options will get you to the SVG Options dialog box, as seen in Figure 12-10 with the More Options button pressed to expand the box.

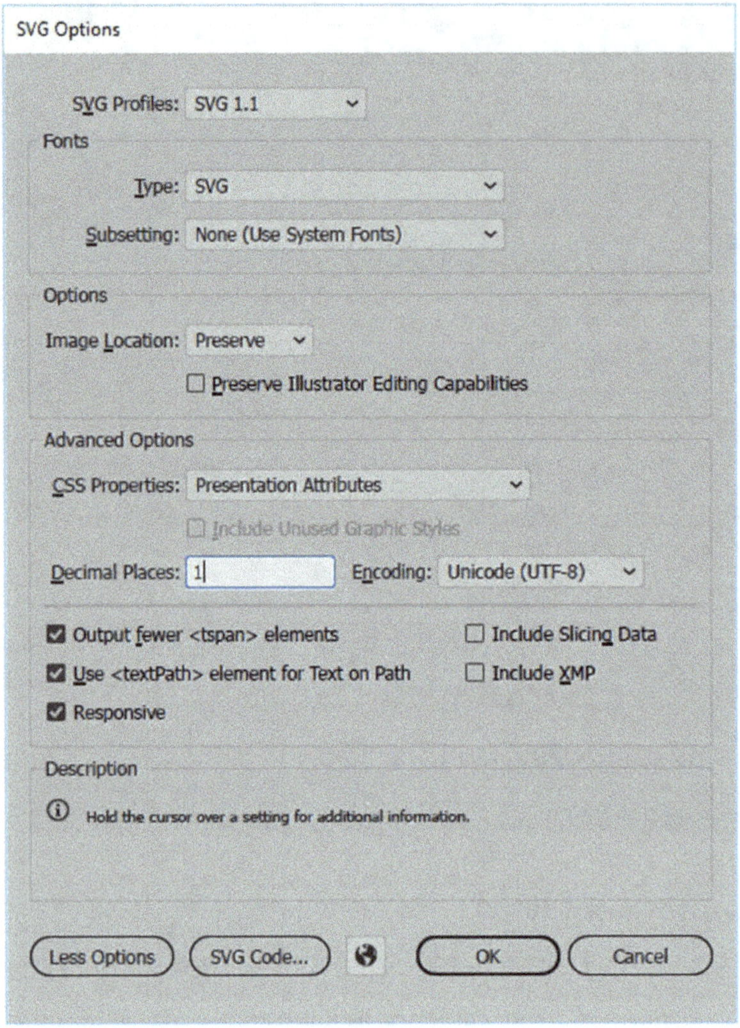

CHAPTER 12 ■ SAVING OR EXPORTING YOUR FILES FOR THE WEB

Figure 12-10. SVG Options dialog box

■ **Note** If you want to work with more than one file format at a time, choose Export for Screens, which looks at Option 2 in this chapter.

- **SVG Profiles**: SVG has various presets that you can use based on your compression settings. Refer to Figure 12-11.

CHAPTER 12 ■ SAVING OR EXPORTING YOUR FILES FOR THE WEB

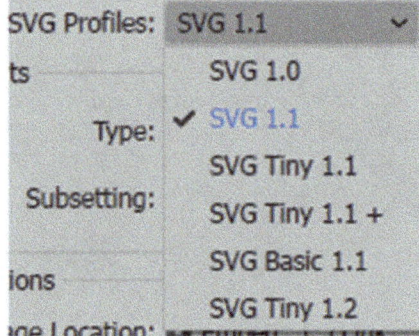

Figure 12-11. Profile settings in the SVG Options dialog box

- **Fonts:** If your SVG file contains fonts, you can set them to either Type: SVG or a graphic outline. Outlines make the text non-editable later. Subsetting allows only some or all font characters or glyphs to be loaded into the file, as seen in Figure 12-12.

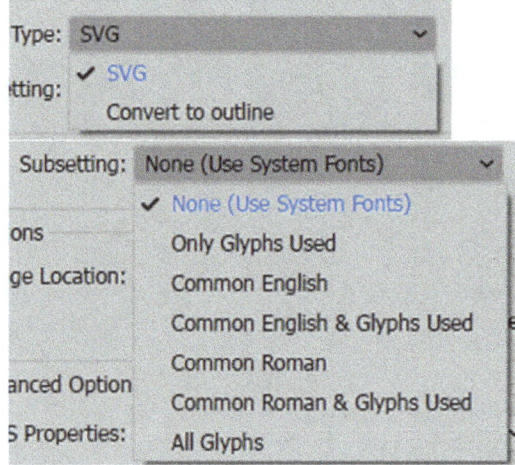

Figure 12-12. Font settings in the SVG Options dialog box

If you choose Use System Fonts, the user's computer interprets how the fonts appear when viewed on screen. A setting like All Glyphs should retain the shape of the font that you used in the file.

- **Options:** Determines if images are preserved embedded or linked to the file. You can also set whether Illustrator can continue to edit the file after it has been saved as an SVG. Refer to Figure 12-13.

261

CHAPTER 12 ■ SAVING OR EXPORTING YOUR FILES FOR THE WEB

Figure 12-13. *Option settings in the SVG Options dialog box*

- **Advanced Options:** When the More Options button is pressed, you see these additional options. Refer to Figure 12-14.

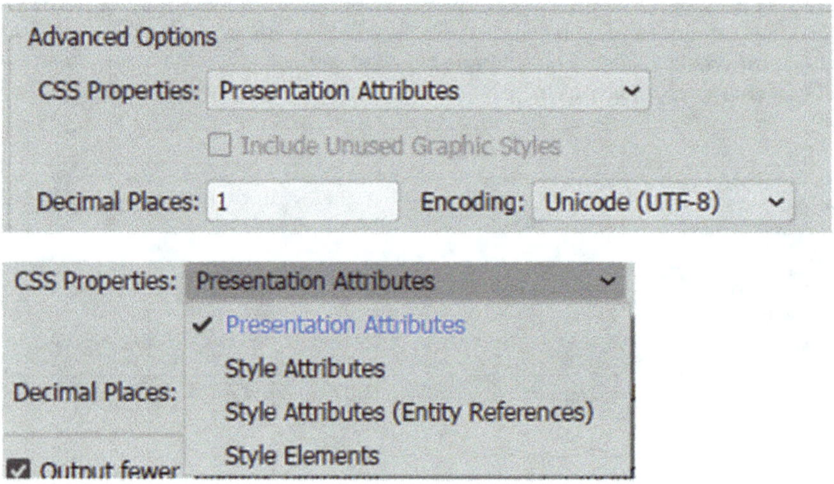

Figure 12-14. *Advanced settings in the SVG Options dialog box*

- **CSS Properties**: Refers to how the Cascading Style Sheets styles within the code; for a more detailed description, you can hover over each one and view the definition in the lower description area of the dialog box.

- **Decimal places**: Refers to how precise the vector is in the artwork. You can set it from 1 to 7; a higher value results in a larger file.

- **Encoding:** Refers to the type of coding used for the SVG file. The default is Unicode (UTF-8).

A few more options in this dialog box are presented in Figure 12-15. Hovering over them provides a description in the lower part of the dialog box.

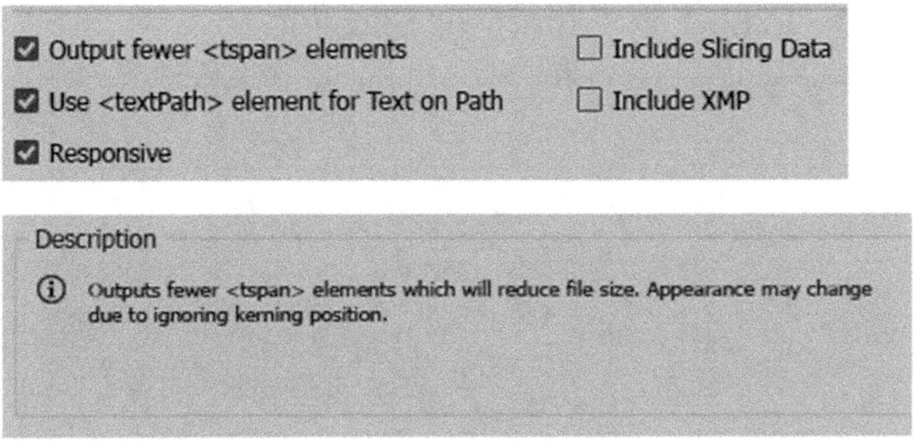

CHAPTER 12 ■ SAVING OR EXPORTING YOUR FILES FOR THE WEB

Figure 12-15. Advanced settings in the SVG Options dialog box

- **Selecting Output fewer <tspan> elements**: Reduces the file size, but it may alter the image slightly.
- **Use <textPath> element for Text on Path**: Preserves text on a path; otherwise, it is written as a <text> element. This keeps the XML code more compact, but it may not accurately preserve the appearance.
- **Responsive**: Allows the CSS to make the SVG image scalable in the browser. This is a good option for scalable websites.
- **Include Slicing Data**: If the image included slices, the location and optimization settings are preserved.
- **Include XMP**: Allows the SVG to include important metadata like author, date created, and date modified. Some of this information is found in your original AI file when you go to File ➤ File Info.
- **Less Options**: Hides the advanced features. You can use a text editor, like Notepad++ or Dreamweaver, to edit your SVG code. Refer to Figure 12-16.

Figure 12-16. SVG Options dialog box lower buttons

- **Globe icon**: Allows you to preview the image in a browser. Click OK if you want to save the file as an SVG or SVG compressed; click Cancel to exit the dialog box.

263

CHAPTER 12 ■ SAVING OR EXPORTING YOUR FILES FOR THE WEB

Option 2: File ➤ Export ➤ Export for Screens

Illustrator CC has a new way to export your web files, known as the Export for Screens dialog box, as seen in Figure 12-17.

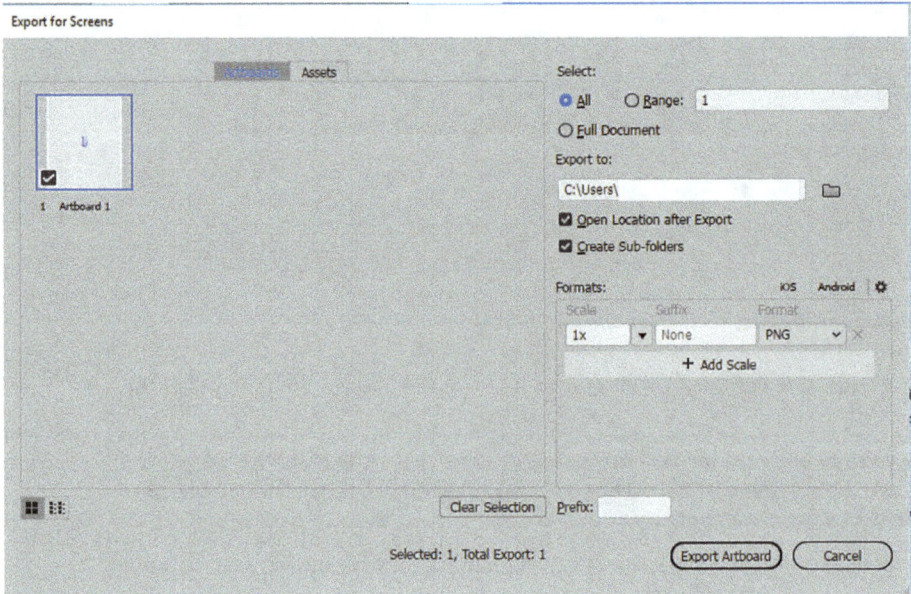

Figure 12-17. *Export for Screens dialog box: artboard settings*

The Export for Screens dialog box has two tabs for working with your images: Artboards and Assets. Refer to Figure 12-17 and Figure 12-18.

264

CHAPTER 12 ■ SAVING OR EXPORTING YOUR FILES FOR THE WEB

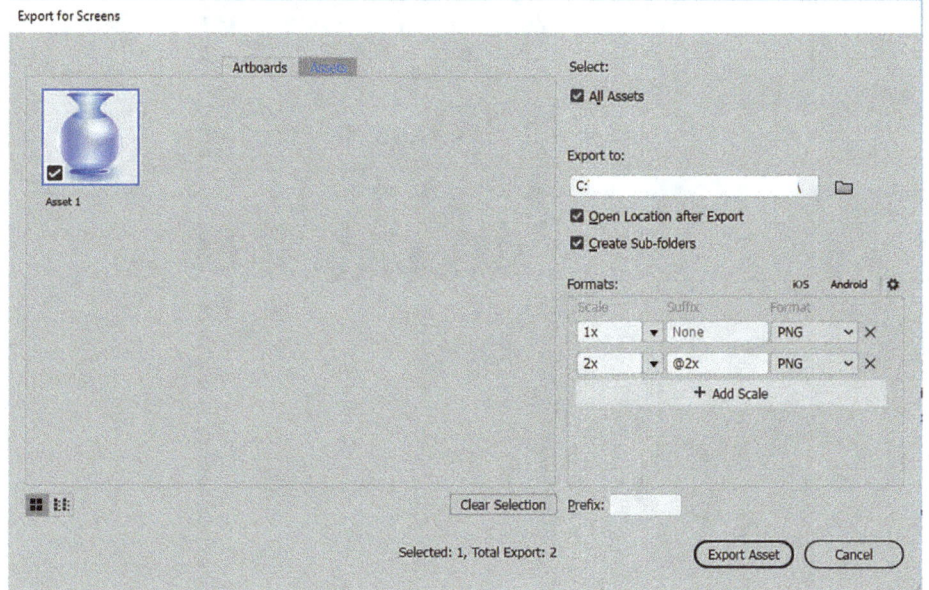

Figure 12-18. Export for Screens dialog box: Assets settings

Artboards Tab

Artboards are set when you create a new PSD or AI file, as seen in Figure 12-19.

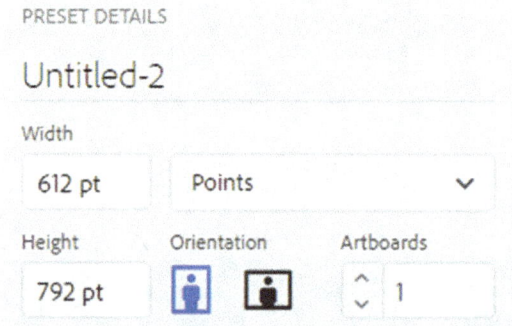

Figure 12-19. When you create a new file, choose the number of artboards that you require

An Illustrator AI file can contain multiple artboards of varying sizes. Refer to Figure 12-20.

265

CHAPTER 12 ■ SAVING OR EXPORTING YOUR FILES FOR THE WEB

Figure 12-20. *Two artboards in one file*

This is good for when you must create several layouts for a client and want to keep the layouts in a single file for organization and comparison. You can edit these artboards in the Tools panel by clicking the Artboard tool (Shift+O) and using the tools in Artboard mode, as seen in the Control panel. Refer to Figure 12-21.

CHAPTER 12 ■ SAVING OR EXPORTING YOUR FILES FOR THE WEB

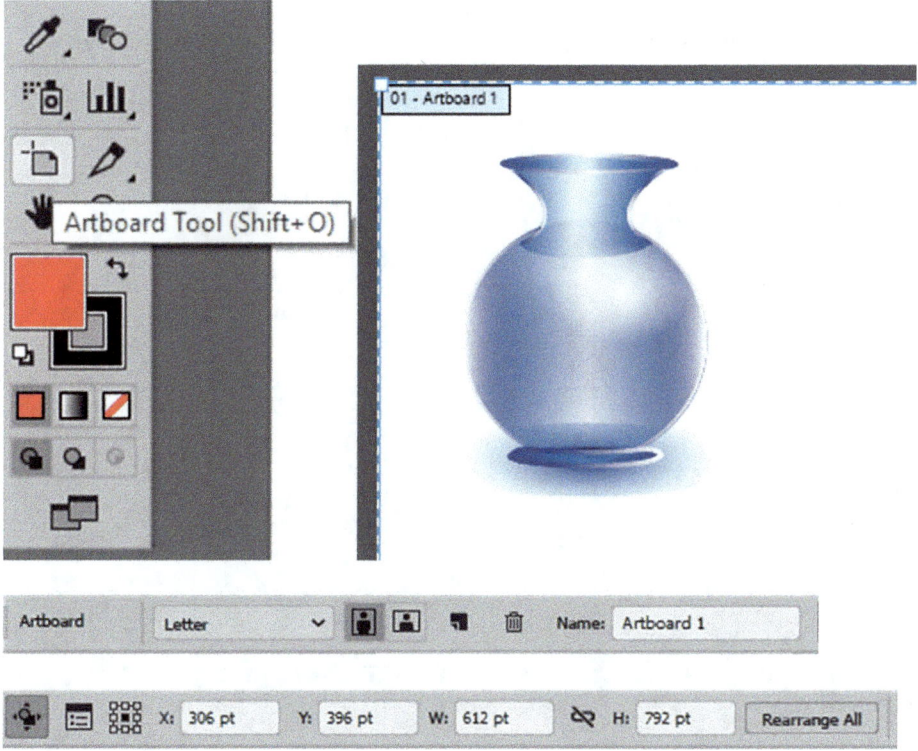

Figure 12-21. *Enter Artboard mode with the Artboard tool and use the Control panel to edit the artboard sizes*

To exit Artboard mode, click the Hand tool (H) in the Tools panel.

You can further organize your artboards using the Artboards panel; it is separate from the Layers panel. As seen in Figure 12-22.

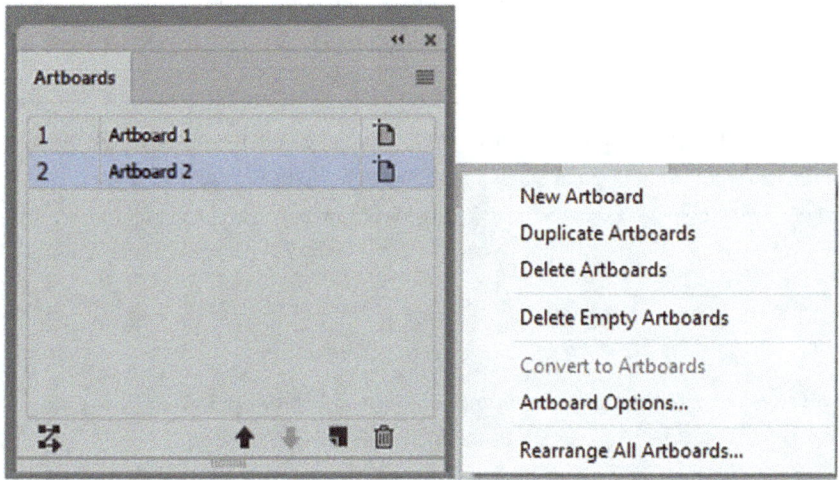

Figure 12-22. *The Artboards panel and its menu options*

267

CHAPTER 12 ■ SAVING OR EXPORTING YOUR FILES FOR THE WEB

You can add, duplicate, delete, and rearrange artboards using this panel.

Let's go back to Export for Screens dialog box, as seen in Figure 12-23. When working with artboards that you want to export, make sure that the Artboards tab is selected in the upper left preview.

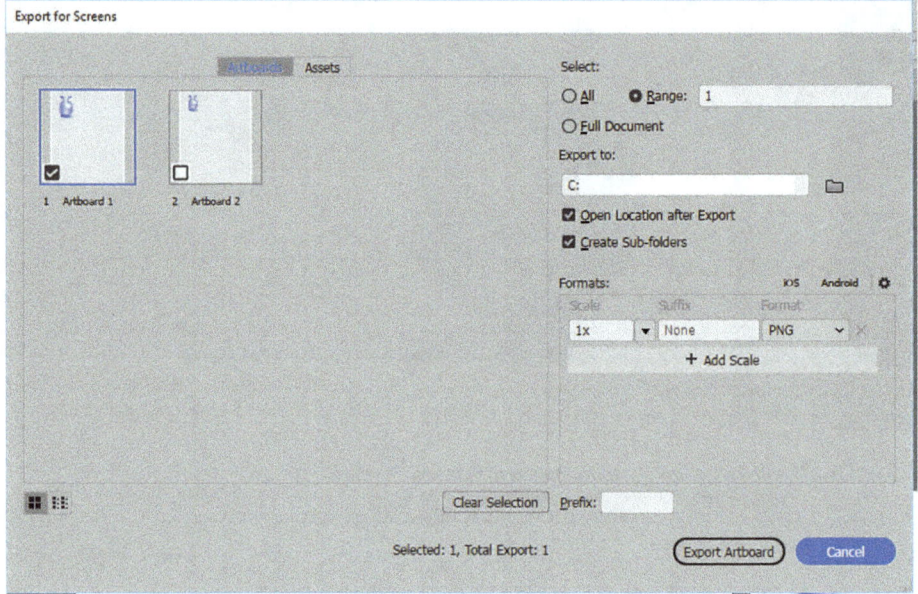

Figure 12-23. *The Export for Screens dialog box with two artboards*

Here you can choose which artboards you want to export.

- **All**: Everything in the preview is selected or checked
- **Range**: Only one or some are checked, but not all
- **Full document**: Where all artboards and their items are selected collectively

If you want to deselect all artboards, click the Clear Selection button in the lower area of the dialog box.

■ **Note** If you have many artboards that you need to view all at once, you can adjust the preview size of the artboards with the buttons in the lower left from large to small thumbnail view. Refer to Figure 12-24.

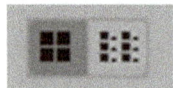

Figure 12-24. *Adjust how you view the artboard with the thumbnail buttons Export for Screens dialog box*

CHAPTER 12 ■ SAVING OR EXPORTING YOUR FILES FOR THE WEB

You can then browse for an export location, set whether the folder opens after export, and create a subfolder within that folder.

For file formats available to export from artboards are PNG, JPEG, SVG, and PDF.

As you saw in Chapter 4, each of these file formats have various settings of higher or lower quality; however, when applying these settings in Illustrator CC, you find that they are in a slightly different location.

You can set the scale size for each one and in various formats for export at the same time. Refer to Figure 12-25.

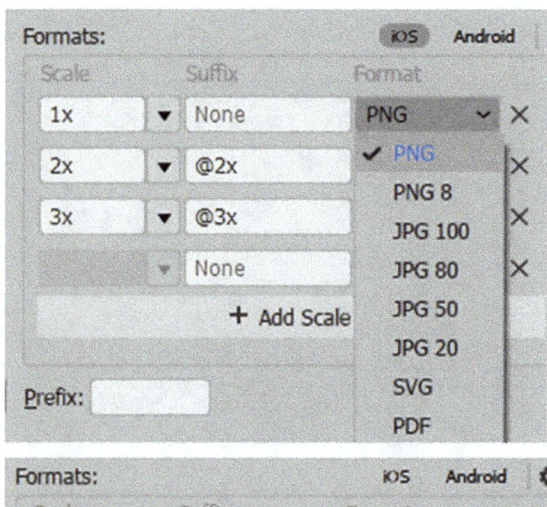

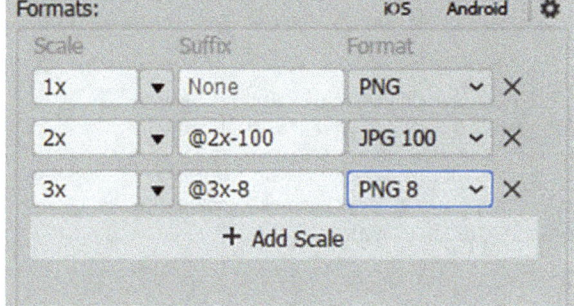

Figure 12-25. *Set and export several sizes, suffixes, and formats at once*

You can add more by clicking Add Scale, or remove by clicking the X on the right.

Suffix refers to the scale and the format you set and uses that to create a unique name for your file. You can also choose whether the file is for iOS or Android devices, clicking on this setting will add more formats to the list and allow you adjust the formats.

Prefix refers to text added to the front of the file name or each file create. If you don't want a prefix, then leave this area blank.

If you need to refine the settings for your file formats you can adjust them in the widget icon in the Format area.

■ **Note** Many of these settings are like the ones seen in Chapter 4.

CHAPTER 12 ■ SAVING OR EXPORTING YOUR FILES FOR THE WEB

PNG

This is the same as PNG-24. Refer to Figure 12-26.

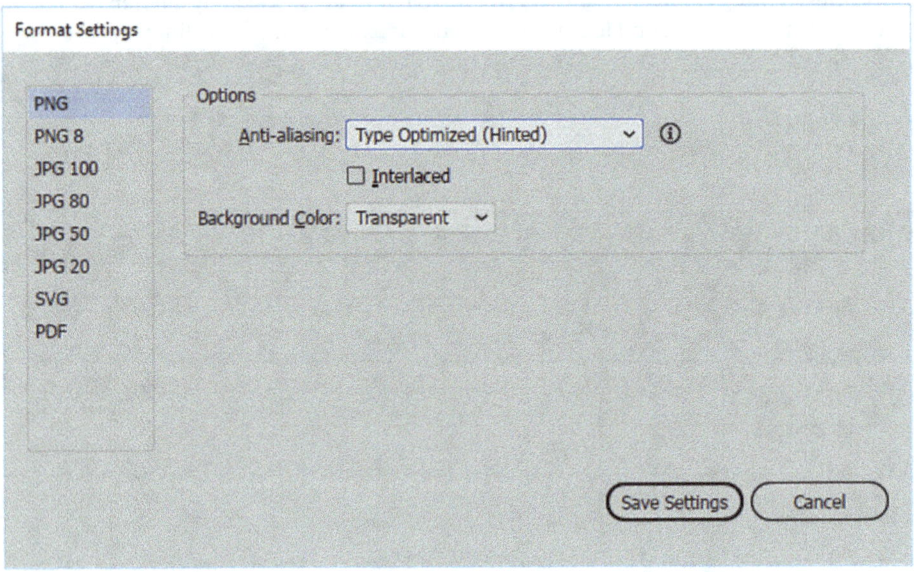

Figure 12-26. Advanced Format settings for PNG files

- **Options**: Anti-aliasing choices are None; Type Optimized (Hinted), which is best for text; and Art Optimized (Supersampling) focuses on the art, but text anti-aliasing is not honored.
- **Interlaced**: Refers to how the image loads and becomes clearer with each scan. You can set the background color here to transparent, black or white.

If you want to set your PNG background to a different custom color, you will need to use a PNG 8.

PNG 8

In this dialog box in Illustrator CC, PNG 8 has many settings similar to a GIF file. Note that the Export for Screens option does not allow you to save a GIF file. You need to use a different dialog box for that when you use Save for Web (Legacy). For now, refer to Figure 12-27.

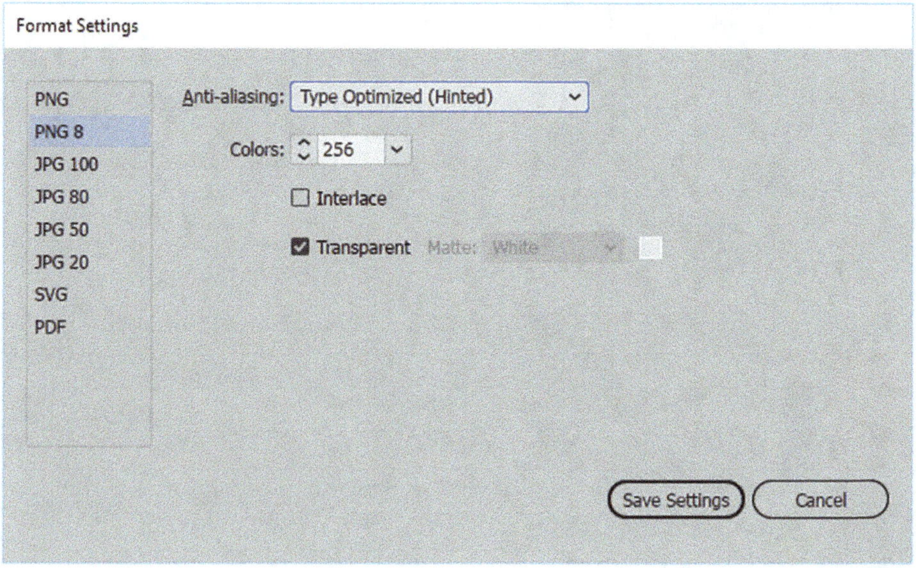

CHAPTER 12 ■ SAVING OR EXPORTING YOUR FILES FOR THE WEB

Figure 12-27. Advanced format settings for PNG-8 files

As you saw with PNG, you can set the anti-aliasing and interlace; however, here you are limited to 256 colors. You can still set the background as transparent, but with PNG-8, you can also choose a matte background to replace the transparency with either white, black, or other, which brings up the color picker so that you can choose a custom color (see Figure 12-28).

271

CHAPTER 12 ■ SAVING OR EXPORTING YOUR FILES FOR THE WEB

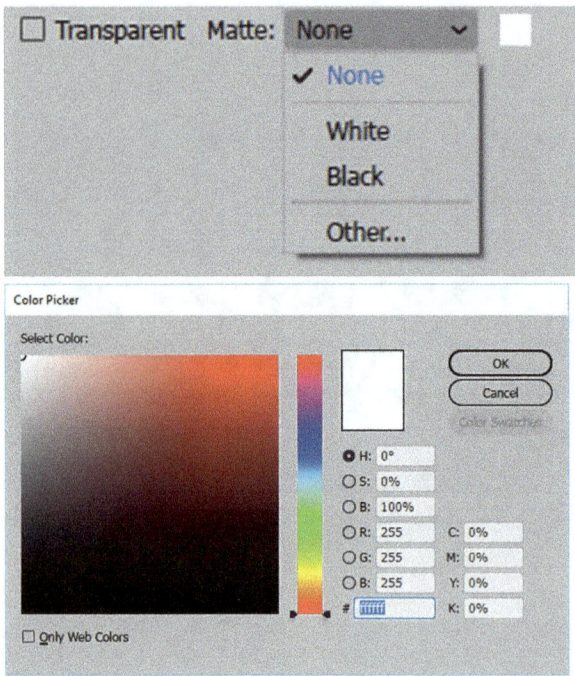

Figure 12-28. Advanced format settings for PNG-8 files allow you to choose a custom matte background color if you unselect transparent using the color picker

JPEG

Whether you choose JPG 100, JPG 80, JPG 50 or JPG 20, you are presented with the same options for compression and profile. The only difference is that the numbers refer to the quality of the compression; 100 is the highest quality and 20 is the lowest quality. Refer to Figure 12-29.

CHAPTER 12 ■ SAVING OR EXPORTING YOUR FILES FOR THE WEB

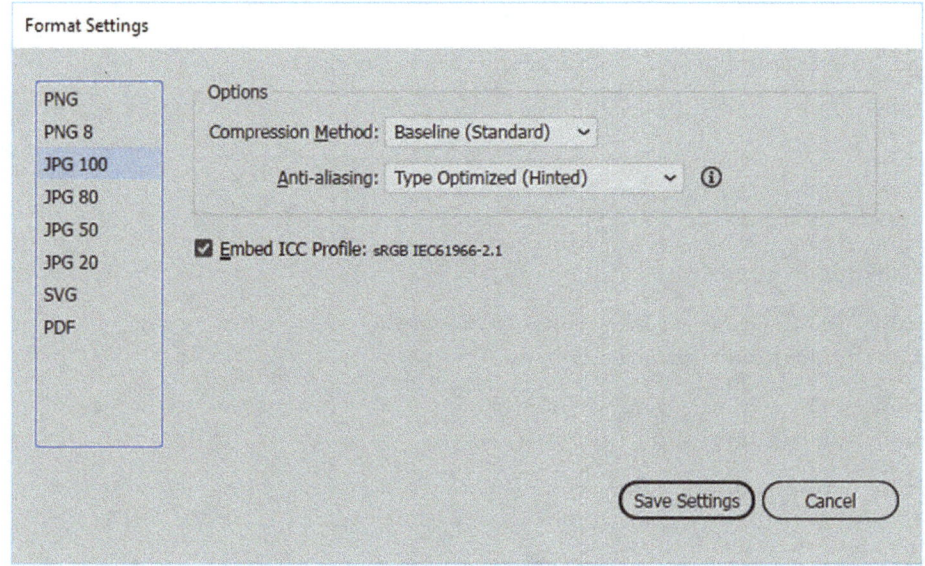

Figure 12-29. Advanced format settings for JPG 100, 80, 50, 20

As you saw in Photoshop CC, the following are compression methods.

- **Baseline ("Standard"):** Recognized by most web browsers. Good for photos that need decent quality.

- **Baseline Optimized:** Compresses the file a little more. Depending on the image, quality is indistinguishable from baseline standard.

- **Progressive:** Creates an image that displays gradually as it downloads. It appears as if the image is rendered as scan lines (like old-fashioned TVs). The browser shows a reduced quality image of half the scan lines while it resolves the complete image. You can set between three and five scans to take place on this setting (see Figure 12-30); however, with a fast Internet connection, this setting is not used as often.

Figure 12-30. Progressive compression method and scan range

■ **Note** According to Adobe, some browsers do not support progressive JPEGs, so if you use this setting, run a test first.

Refer to the PNG settings in this Option 2 section for the anti-aliasing options.
A JPEG is embedded with the ICC profile of sRGB, if checked.

273

CHAPTER 12 ■ SAVING OR EXPORTING YOUR FILES FOR THE WEB

SVG

You can set your exported artboards with the SVG setting, as seen in Figure 12-31.

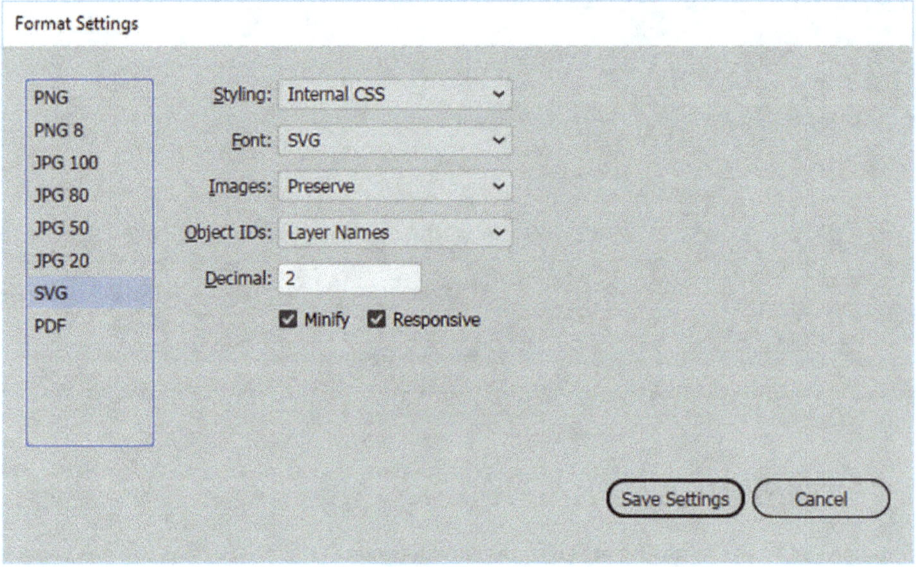

Figure 12-31. Advanced format settings for SVG

Here you see many of the settings that are available in Option 1 File ➤ Save As and saved as an SVG. Refer to this area in Option 1 for clarification on each setting, but note that they have been arranged in a slightly different order then what is seen in Format Settings dialog box in Figure 12-31.

You can adjust how the SVG is internally styled, how to handle fonts and images, the internal object IDs, the precision of the vectors (decimal), and compression (minify). Responsive allows the CSS to make the SVG image scalable in the browser.

■ **Note** If any of these items in the Format Settings dialog box SVG tab are unfamiliar to you, you can hover over them with your mouse to get a hint, as seen in Figure 12-32.

Figure 12-32. Hover over a field in the dialog box to get a hint

CHAPTER 12 ■ SAVING OR EXPORTING YOUR FILES FOR THE WEB

PDF

This option allows you to make some quick choices on how to save your files for PDF. Refer to Figure 12-33.

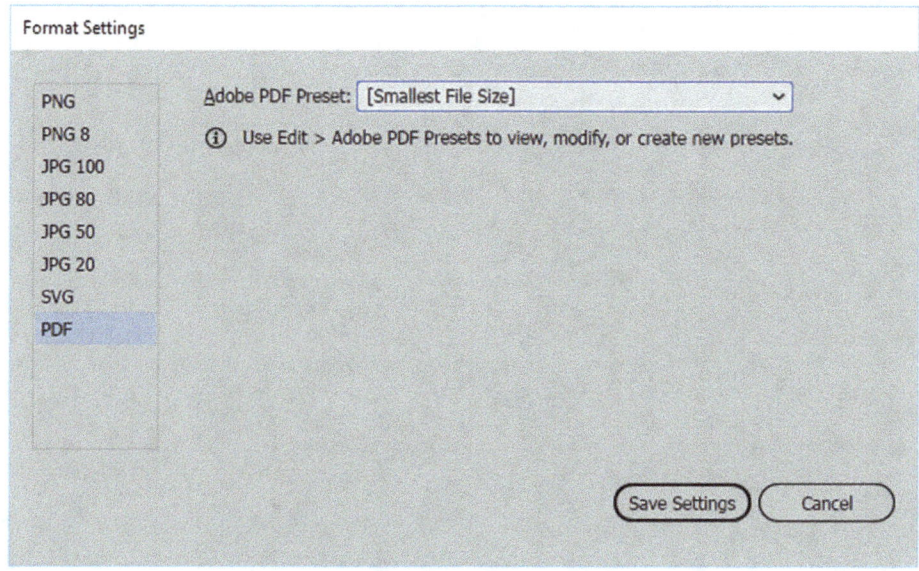

Figure 12-33. Save your artboards as PDF settings

If you need to save your PDF for the web, File ➤ Save As (Option 1) is a much better option because you can adjust the settings more accurately.

If you need to save your new setting, click the Save Setting button; otherwise, click Cancel. Just be aware that if you create new files with different settings in a different project, check this area first to avoid applying any unwanted settings in your a new project.

Once you have organized all the settings in the Export for Screen dialog box, you can click the Export Artboards button, which saves them in the folder that you chose earlier. Refer to Figure 12-34.

Figure 12-34. Save your artboards as a PDF

275

CHAPTER 12 ■ SAVING OR EXPORTING YOUR FILES FOR THE WEB

Assets Tab

The other tab option in the Export for Screens dialog box is the Assets tab.

Assets refer to individual objects or a group of several objects that are all on one artboard or are on several artboards. If you are working with more than one artboard, you need to add the objects to the Asset Export panel. Refer to Figures 12-35 and 12-36.

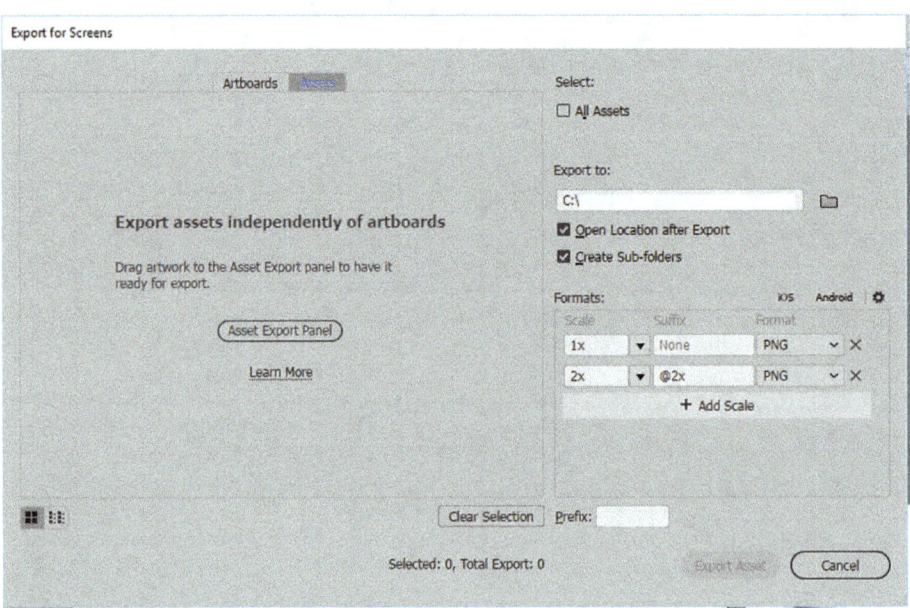

Figure 12-35. *Export for Screens Assets tab*

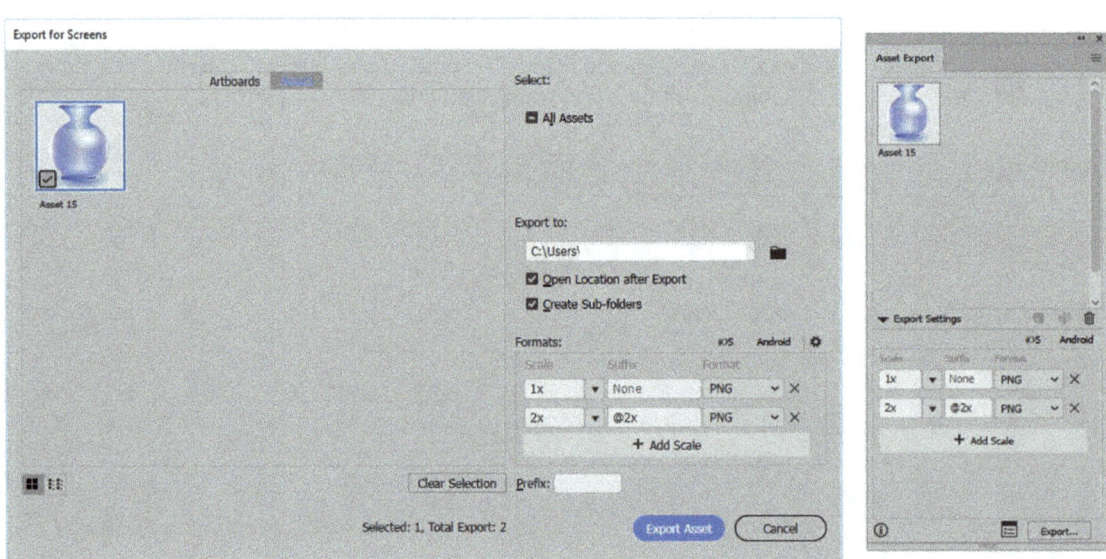

Figure 12-36. *Export for Screens on the Assets tab with an asset added from the Asset Export panel*

CHAPTER 12 ■ SAVING OR EXPORTING YOUR FILES FOR THE WEB

Assets can be objects (vector shapes) or many objects that are grouped together (Object ➤ Group) that you want to export as one image. You would choose to do this to keep the final file smaller rather than have all the extra blank space that a full artboard takes up. This is good for small objects and buttons on a webpage.

Most of the other settings on the Artboards tab are the same as the Assets tab. Refer to the "Artboards Tab" section.

However, there are a few differences when only some objects are selected the select will appear as a dash and when all are selected it appears as a check, as seen in Figure 12-37.

Figure 12-37. Some or all assets are selected

Also, the button in the lower right has changed to Export Asset, and you can save your assets to the folder of your choice.

There are two other related ways that you can convert your objects' assets.

File ➤ Export Selection

When an object is selected on an artboard with the Selection tool (V), choose File ➤ Export Selection to add that asset to the Selection options of the Export for Screens dialog box and to the Asset Export panel, as seen in Figure 12-38.

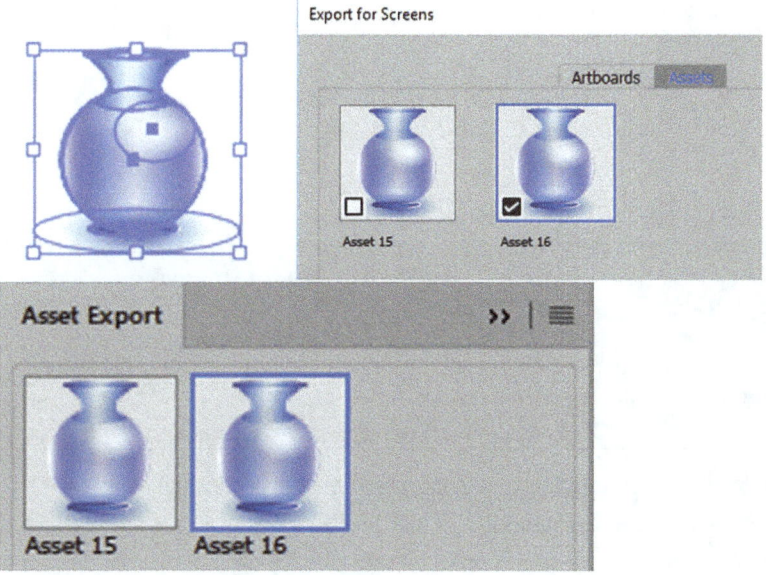

Figure 12-38. Adding selections as an asset for export

277

CHAPTER 12 ■ SAVING OR EXPORTING YOUR FILES FOR THE WEB

However, as you continue to do this, you might notice that you have more assets than objects on the artboard. What's going on here?

Asset Export Panel

To add assets, you can select and drag them into the Asset Export panel.
If you want to remove one, select it and click the Trash icon. Refer to Figure 12-39.

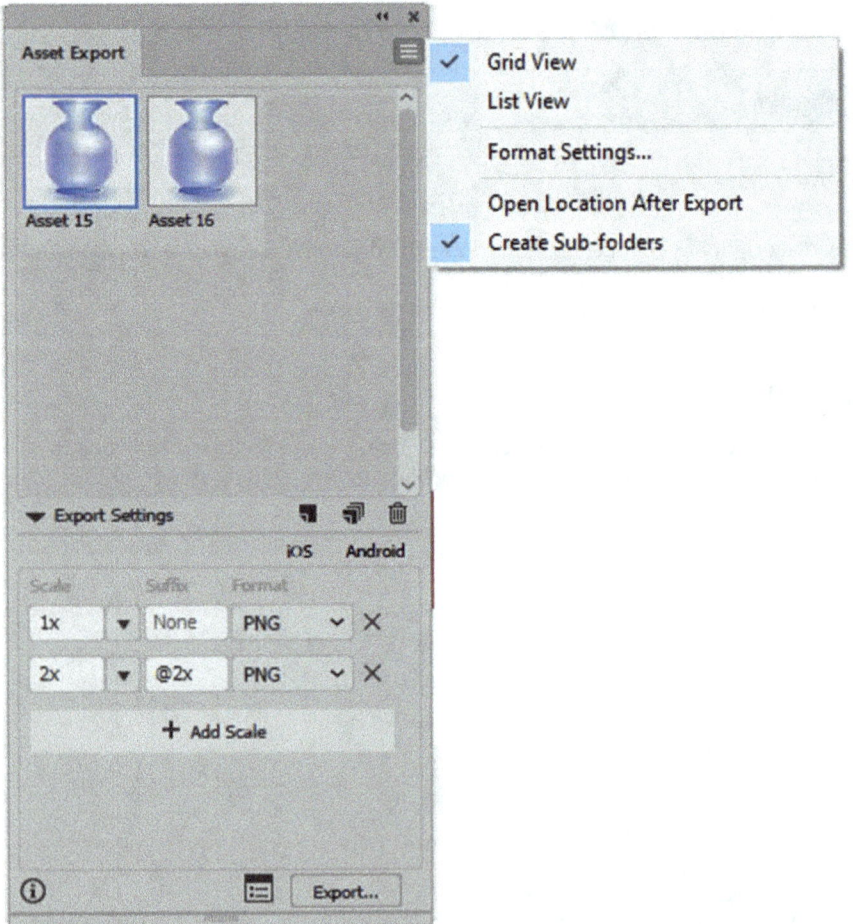

Figure 12-39. Adding and trashing assets in the Asset Export panel

■ **Note** If no assets appear, you can drag or Alt-drag them into this preview area, or click the new Assets button when an object or shape is selected. Refer to Figures 12-39 and 12-40.

278

CHAPTER 12 ■ SAVING OR EXPORTING YOUR FILES FOR THE WEB

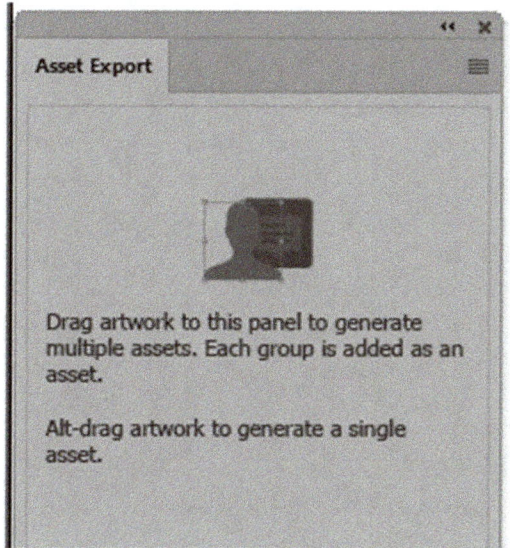

Figure 12-40. *Adding assets to the Asset Export panel*

In the Export Assets panel, you can rename by clicking the asset name, as seen in Figure 12-41.

Figure 12-41. *Renaming an asset the Asset Export panel*

Type the new name, and then click outside the asset to confirm.

In the lower portion of the panel, you find the same export setting as you saw in the Export for Screens dialog box. Refer to Figure 12-42.

279

CHAPTER 12 ■ SAVING OR EXPORTING YOUR FILES FOR THE WEB

Figure 12-42. *Set your export settings in Asset Export panel before you go to Export for Screens*

When an asset is selected, you can use the Information (I) icon to see the number of objects selected or exported. The square icon launches the Export for Screen dialog box, and the Export button determines which folder the file is exported to. The Asset Export panel also allows you to access file settings in its Format Settings menu, as seen in Figure 12-39. As well as open the export folder after export.

■ **Note** You can also right-click on an object that is not yet in the Asset Export panel and choose Export Selection to add it to the Asset Export panel, as seen in Figure 12-43. Alternatively you can use the icons in the Asset Export panel.

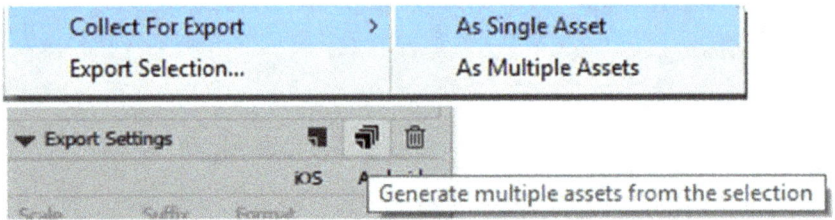

Figure 12-43. *Collect for Export, a selected object on an artboard*

When you choose Collect for Export ➤ As Single Asset, if one or more objects are selected, they are placed in the Asset Export panel together.

When you choose Collect for Export ➤ As Multiple Assets, if one or more objects are selected, they are placed in the Asset Export panel separately, as seen in Figure 12-44.

CHAPTER 12 ■ SAVING OR EXPORTING YOUR FILES FOR THE WEB

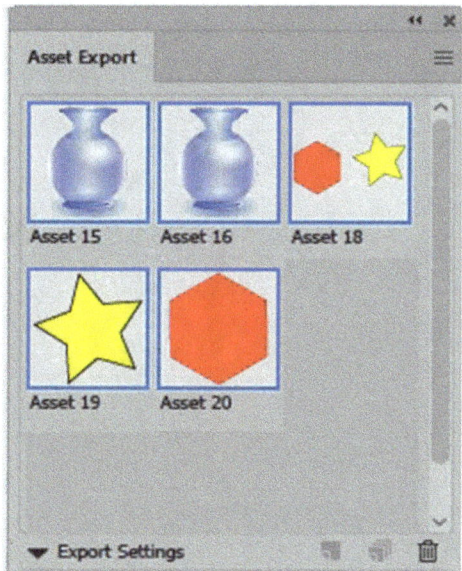

Figure 12-44. *Collect for Export: a selected object on an art board either as single or multiple*

Layers Panel: Collect for Export

You can find another icon on the Layers panel called Collect for Export, as seen in Figure 12-45.

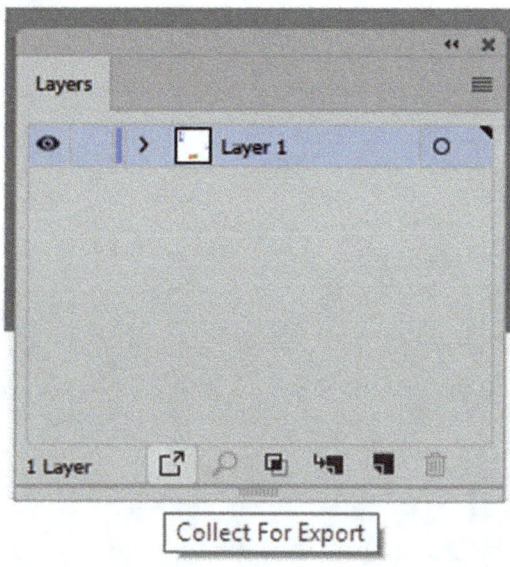

Figure 12-45. *Collect for Export on a layer in the Layers panel*

Because all the artboard items are (in this case) on one layer, all the objects are collected as a single asset in the Asset Export panel, as seen in Figure 12-46.

281

CHAPTER 12 ■ SAVING OR EXPORTING YOUR FILES FOR THE WEB

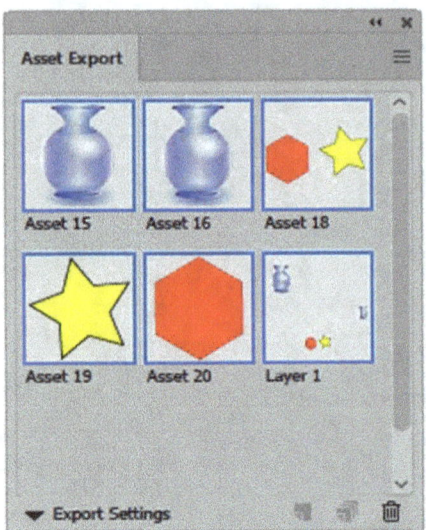

Figure 12-46. Collect for Export on a layer in the Layers panel and add to the Asset Export panel

■ **Note** If there are multiple layers in a file, then those assets on another layer disappear in the Asset Export panel if the layer eye is turned off. So be aware of this if part of an image goes missing during export, as seen in Figure 12-47.

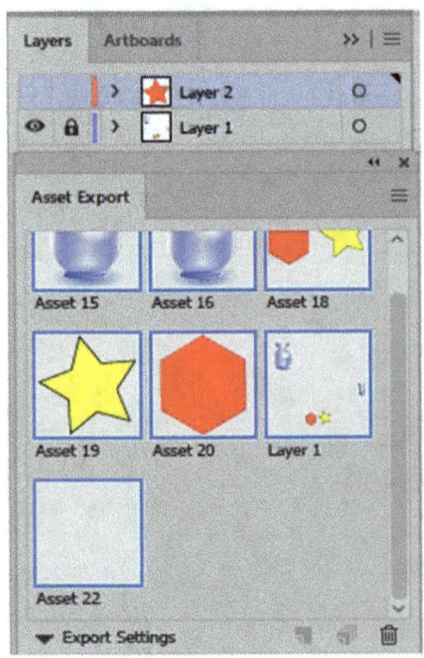

Figure 12-47. Assets can be turned on or off via the Layers panel

CHAPTER 12 ■ SAVING OR EXPORTING YOUR FILES FOR THE WEB

As you can see the Asset Export panel is very useful in organizing which shapes or objects you want to save for the web.

Option 3: File ➤ Export ➤ Export As

As with Photoshop CC, you can export the following web file formats, either as one artboard or all artboards within the file. Export As is good when you are working with single images or artboards, rather than multiple assets with in a file. In the Export As dialog box, choose the location that you want to save the file and the Save as type format, and then click Export to open that specific file format's dialog box. Refer to Figure 12-48.

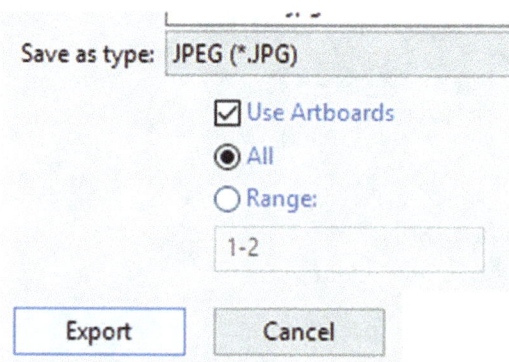

Figure 12-48. *Choose how to export the file, then click export*

Bitmap

Bitmap (.bmp) images can be saved for the web, but often their file size is quite large, so other file sizes are generally recommended. Export As is the only way that you can save a bitmap file from Illustrator CC. Save it with an RGB setting and a resolution of 72 ppi, as seen in Figure 12-49.

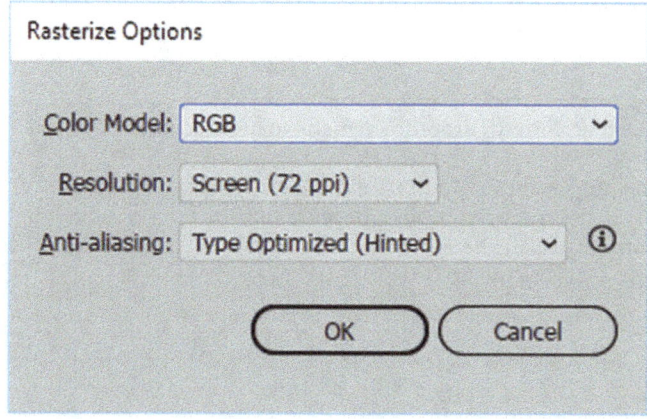

Figure 12-49. *Rasterize options for a bitmap file*

283

JPEG

The JPEG Options dialog box is very similar to Export for Screens, and most of the settings are the same; however, here you can control things like the color mode, as RGB, CMYK, or grayscale. You have this option here because you may want to export a CMYK version of the image for a print project. When you are exporting for screens, as you did earlier, RGB is the only choice you should use. Refer to Figure 12-50.

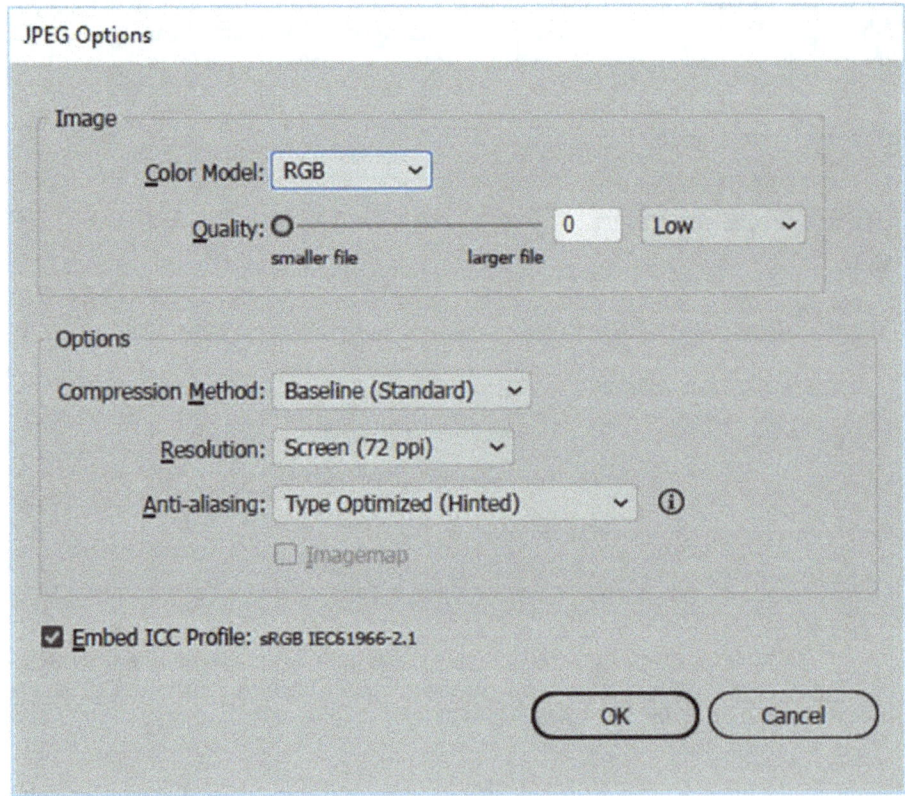

Figure 12-50. Rasterize options for a JPEG file

You can also adjust the quality with the slider, text box, or drop-down menu to more accurate levels of compression.

In the options you can control compression, the resolution 72, 150 or 300 or other custom resolution. In the Export for Screens dialog box (see Option 2) 72 dpi is the only option because the files are viewed on the Internet. Anti-aliasing type and ICC Profile options can also altered. Image map is currently unavailable, but you can easily create these in Dreamweaver as you will see in Part 6.

CHAPTER 12 ■ SAVING OR EXPORTING YOUR FILES FOR THE WEB

PNG

PNG Options is also very similar to the Export for Screens dialog box. The only difference is that you can alter the resolution to 72 ppi, 150 ppi, 300 ppi, or other. In the Export for Screens dialog box (see Option 2), 72 dpi is the only option because the files are viewed on the Internet. Refer to Figure 12-51.

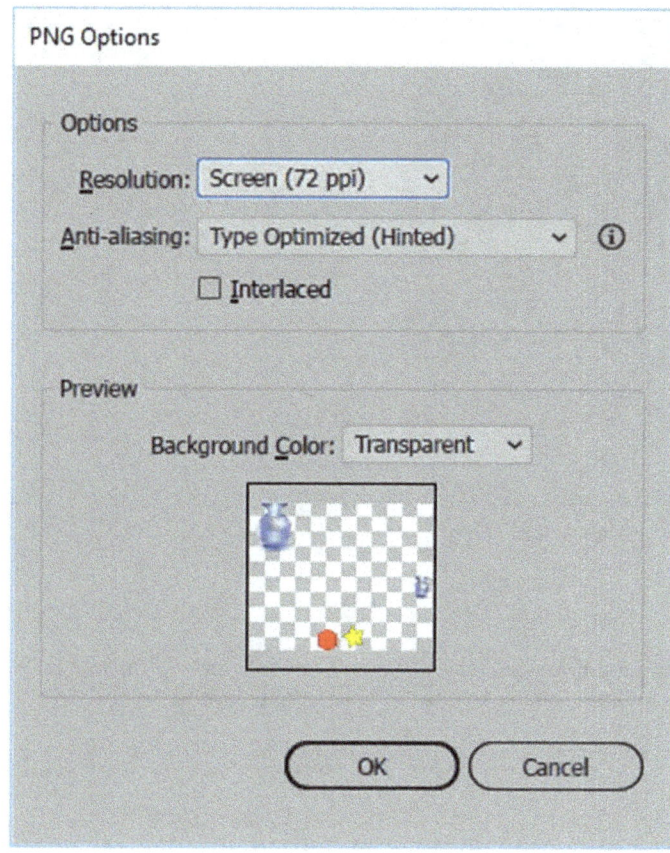

Figure 12-51. *Rasterize options for a PNG file*

SVG

SVG Options' settings are similar to Export for Screens (see Option 2) and Save As in Option 1. Please refer to these sections for a more detailed description of the settings. Refer to Figure 12-52.

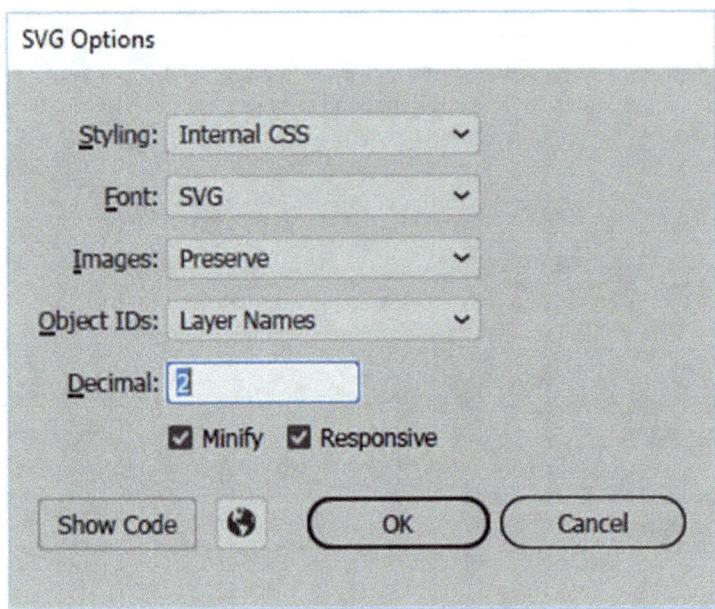

Figure 12-52. SVG Options dialog box

If any setting is unfamiliar to you, hover over a word for a hint.

CSS

Although CSS is not a graphic file, you can save many Cascading Style Sheet settings from your Illustrator files from the CSS Export Options dialog box for later use in Dreamweaver. Refer to Figure 12-53.

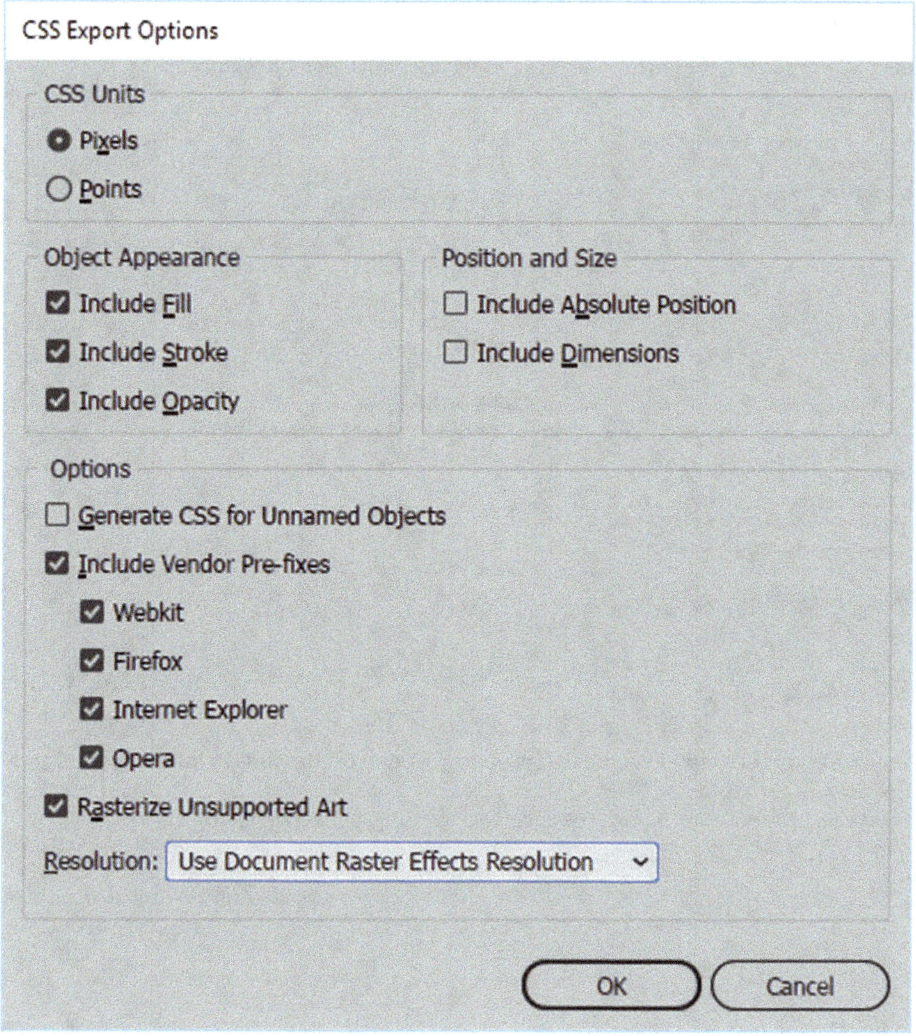

Figure 12-53. CSS Export Options

Many of these settings refer to settings found in your SVG file, or could be used for styling images or items used in animation that you create with CSS in a program like Dreamweaver CC. Often, images with gradients or special filters require vendor prefixes. Some artwork may be rasterized because not all browsers support special effects in the same way. If you need to adjust the resolution setting, you can choose Other from the drop-down menu and set a different resolution.

CSS Properties Panel

If your AI file contains CSS properties, they are in the CSS Properties panel. Refer to Figure 12-54.

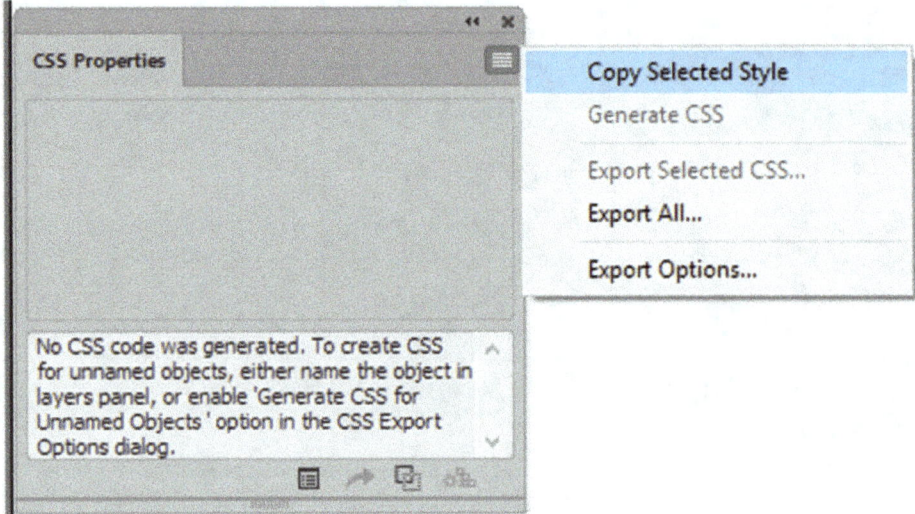

Figure 12-54. CSS Properties panel and its menu

You can reach the export options either via the CSS properties menu or the icons in the lower portion of the panel.

If there are no valid CSS properties to export, you receive a warning, as seen in Figure 12-55.

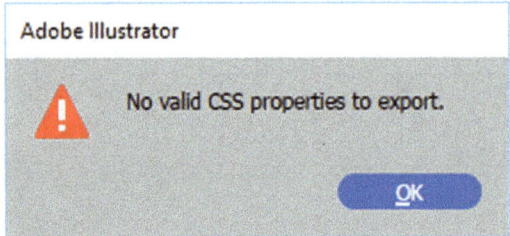

Figure 12-55. CSS Properties panel warning when no CSS present

CSS properties generally work best with text formatting. Refer to Figure 12-56.

CHAPTER 12 ■ SAVING OR EXPORTING YOUR FILES FOR THE WEB

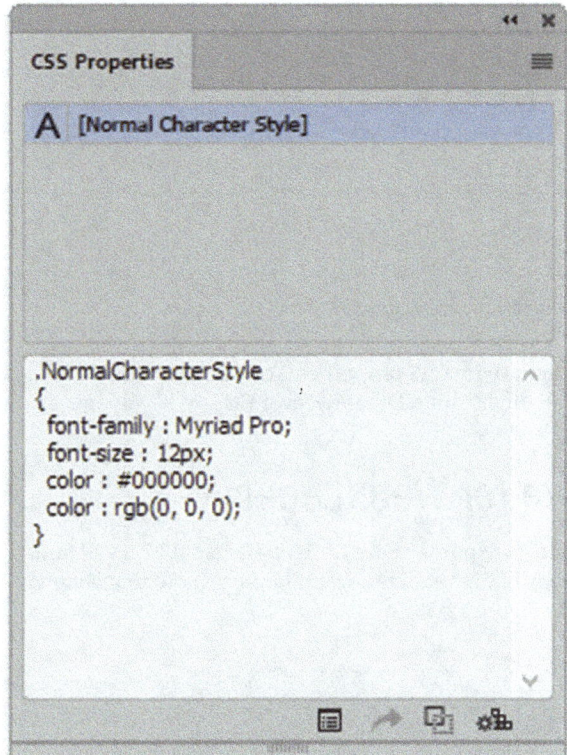

Figure 12-56. *CSS Properties allows you to copy CSS from text*

However, when you go to the Export Options dialog box and select Generate CSS for Unnamed Objects, you can now get the CSS from the objects selected on your artboard. Refer to Figure 12-53 and Figure 12-57.

CHAPTER 12 ■ SAVING OR EXPORTING YOUR FILES FOR THE WEB

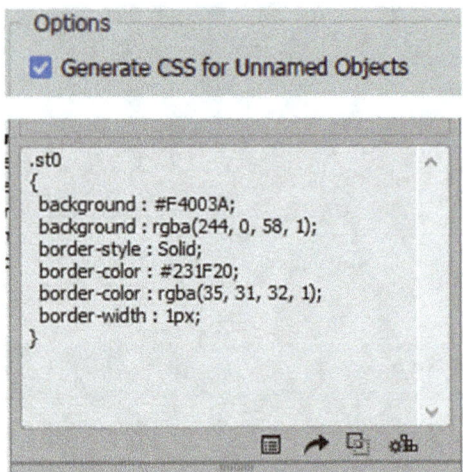

Figure 12-57. CSS Properties allows you to copy CSS objects on the artboard

Illustrator CC generates a temporary class for all items with CSS properties. You can then either export the CSS via the panel or copy and paste the information directly into Dreamweaver CC.

Option 4: File ➤ Export ➤ Save for Web (Legacy)

The final way that you can export files for the web is File ➤ Export ➤ Save for Web (Legacy). You will find this same option in Photoshop CC (see Chapter 4). Many of the settings are similar, so refer to that chapter for a more detailed explanation of the settings; also see Figure 12-58.

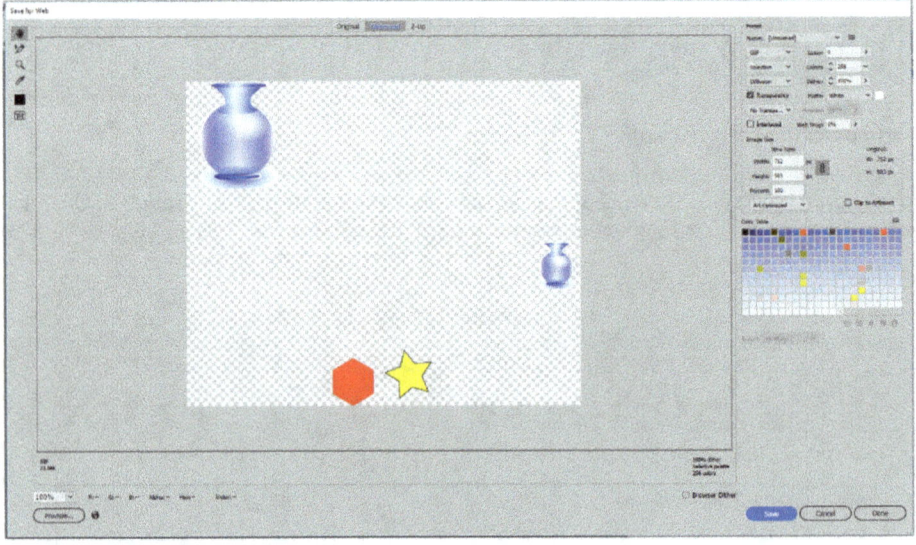

Figure 12-58. Save for Web (Legacy) dialog box

CHAPTER 12 ■ SAVING OR EXPORTING YOUR FILES FOR THE WEB

■ **Note** Save for Web Legacy only views the first artboard unless you uncheck check Clip to Artboard in the settings. Only then can you view all objects on all artboards. Refer to Figure 12-59.

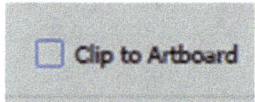

Figure 12-59. Keep this unchecked if you have to view all artboards at once

Also, this dialog box does not have the 4up option as Photoshop CC so you can only compare up to two settings at a time.

Illustrator has several presets that you can choose from, but you can create your own custom settings. Refer to Figure 12-60.

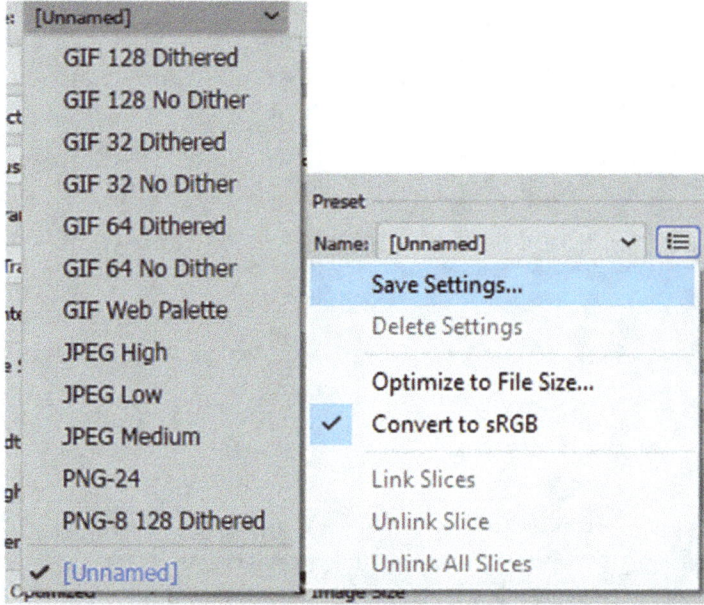

Figure 12-60. Choose a preset setting or save your own for another project

You can also save your custom settings. You can adjust for all raster images (GIF, JPEG, and PNG); however, for SVG you must use the Export As or Export for Screens options.

291

GIF

This is the only way that you can export a GIF file format out of Illustrator CC, as seen in Figure 12-61.

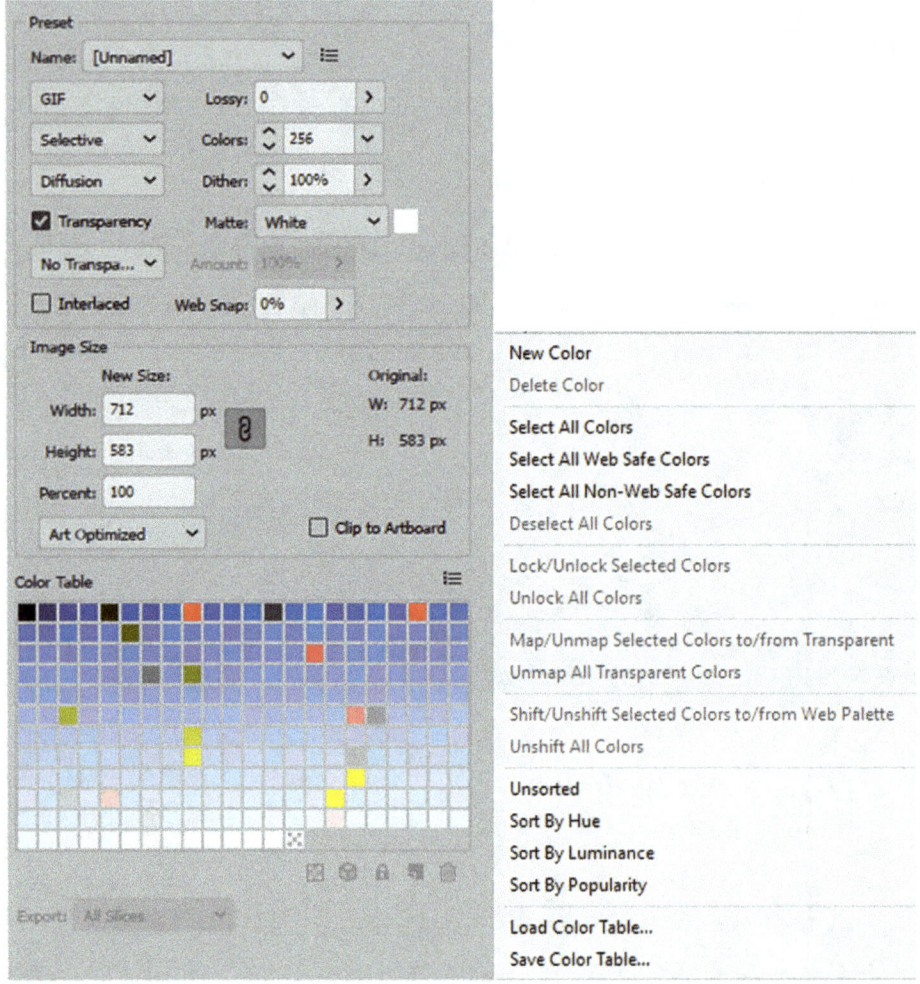

Figure 12-61. *Example setting for a GIF image in the Save for Web dialog box*

Most settings are the same as Photoshop CC Save for Web (Legacy) so refer to Chapter 4 for a more detailed explanation. As with Export for Screens option you can set Image Size to None, Art, or Text Optimized.

The Color Table for GIFs has the same setting as the dialog box in Photoshop CC; however, you will notice that there is no option for animation since you can only create stationary GIF image graphics from Illustrator CC and must use Photoshop or Adobe Animate CC for animation creation.

CHAPTER 12 ■ SAVING OR EXPORTING YOUR FILES FOR THE WEB

JPEG

Most settings are the same as Photoshop CC's Save for Web (Legacy), so refer to Chapter 4 for a more detailed explanation. As with the Export for Screens option, you can set Image Size to None, Art, or Text Optimized. Refer to Figure 12-62.

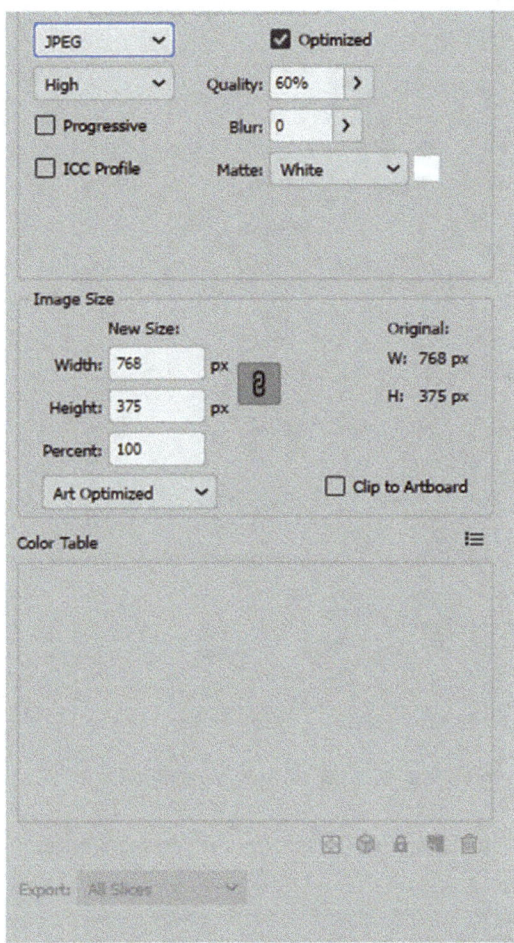

Figure 12-62. *Example of setting for a JPEG image in the Save for Web dialog box*

PNG-8 and PNG-24

Most settings are the same as Photoshop CC's Save for Web (Legacy), so refer to Chapter 4 for a more detailed explanation. As with the Export for Screens option, you can set Image Size to None, Art, or Text Optimized. Refer to Figure 12-63.

293

CHAPTER 12 ■ SAVING OR EXPORTING YOUR FILES FOR THE WEB

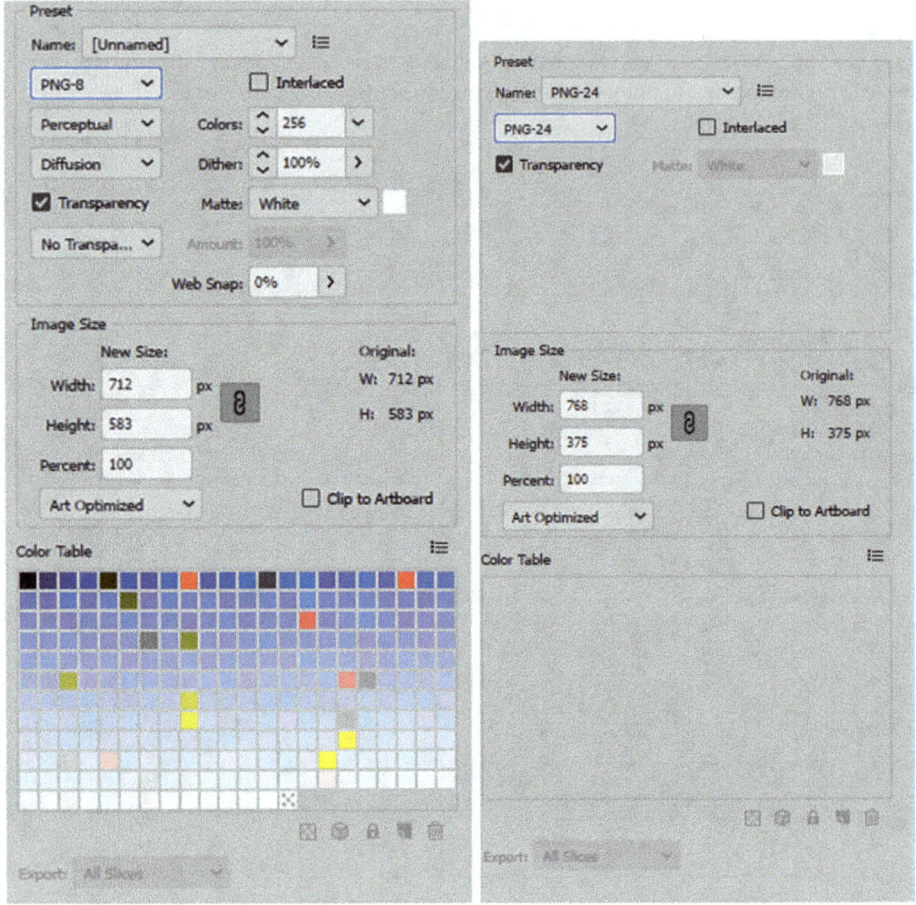

Figure 12-63. *Example settings for a PNG-8 and PNG-24 image in the Save for Web dialog box*

Browser Dither (at the bottom of the dialog box) shows how graphics appear in some browsers. Refer to Figure 12-64.

Figure 12-64. *Use Browser Dither to check your graphics, and then click Save to export them*

When you are done, save your file. You look at creating slices in Illustrator in Chapter 13. If your file contains no slices, this area of the dialog box is unavailable.

When you save, notice that only Save as type: Images Only is available, not HTML or Images and HTML. You look at how to get around this issue when you explore slices in Chapter 13. Refer to Figure 12-65.

294

CHAPTER 12 ■ SAVING OR EXPORTING YOUR FILES FOR THE WEB

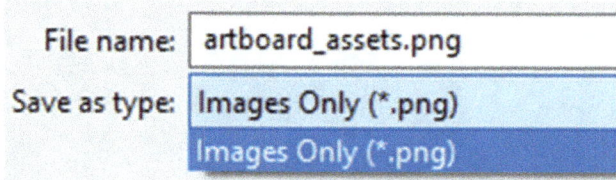

Figure 12-65. *When you save, Images Only is the only option*

Summary

In this chapter, you reviewed four possible ways to save Illustrator images for the web. Some options may work better for your workflow than others, so the choice is up to you. You also discovered how to work with the Asset Export and CSS Properties panels.

In the next chapter, you look at some ways that Illustrator can speed up the export process. You also look at how to create slices.

295

CHAPTER 13

Actions to Speed up File Conversion and Slicing Tools

In this chapter, you look at how to use scripts, along with the Actions panel and batch actions, to speed up your workflow. Then you look at slicing tools and image maps for the web using Illustrator CC.

■ **Note** This chapter does not have any actual projects; however, you can use the files in the Chapter 13 folder to practice opening and viewing for this lesson. They are at https://github.com/Apress/graphics-multimedia-web-adobe-creative-cloud.

Using Scripts

Like Photoshop, Illustrator CC comes with a few basic scripts (File ➤ Scripts ➤ SaveDocsAsPDF or SaveDocsAsSVG. You can use these to save some file formats for the web. Refer to Figure 13-1.

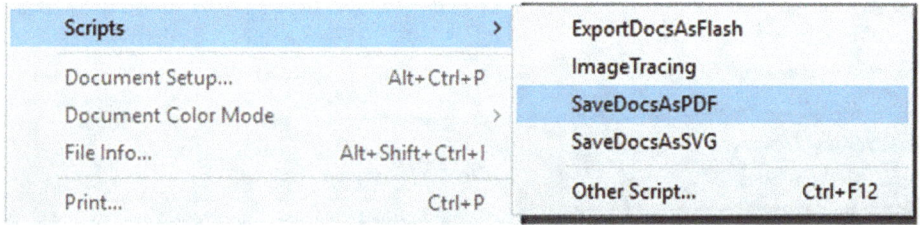

Figure 13-1. *Basic scripts that you can use to save documents either in the PDF or SVG format*

These scripts allow you to quickly save a PDF or SVG file into a selected folder; however, there are no options to allow you to adjust settings, so I do not recommend this option if you need your files to have specific adjustments before exporting.

Actions to Speed up the File Conversion Process

Like Photoshop CC, the Actions panel is available in Illustrator CC. It comes with some default or prebuilt actions that you can use for files for the web, or you can create your own.

Actions Panel

If you look though some of default actions, you might encounter some prebuilt action time-savers, such as

- Save For Web GIF 64 Dithered
- Save For Web JPG Medium
- Save For Web PNG 24
- All of these take you to the File ➤ Export ➤ Save For the Web (Legacy) dialog box, where you can adjust your settings before saving. Refer to Figure 13-2.

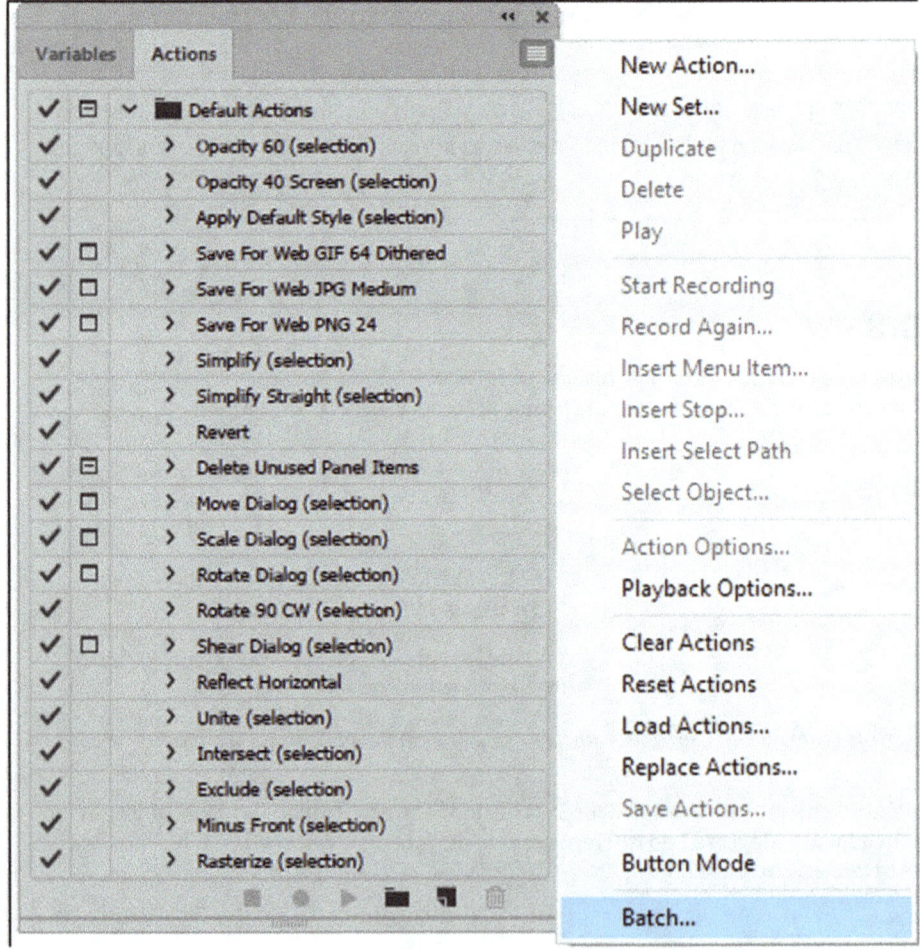

Figure 13-2. *The Actions panel in Illustrator*

CHAPTER 13 ■ ACTIONS TO SPEED UP FILE CONVERSION AND SLICING TOOLS

■ **Note** As with Photoshop CC, you can access the Actions panel menu to clear, reset, load, save or even replace actions. Actions that are not saved cannot be reloaded and will be lost from the list.

If you open one of the arrows beside the actions, you see the steps that were recorded. You can play them any time that you want to convert your file, as you did in Chapters 5 and 9. Refer to Figure 13-3.

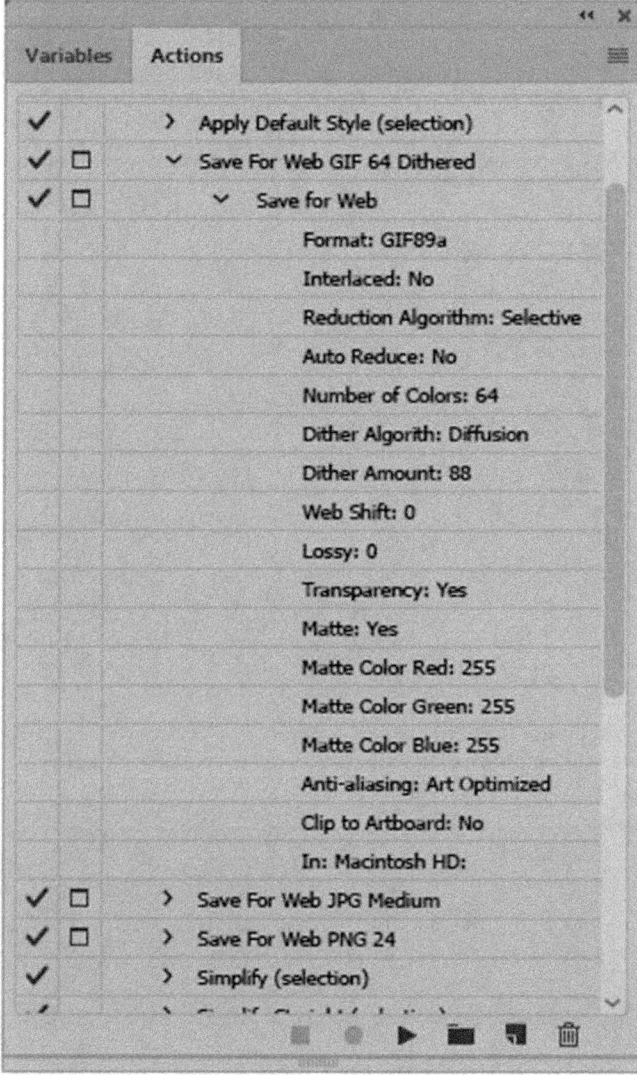

Figure 13-3. *The default actions have settings that are already saved for you*

299

CHAPTER 13 ■ ACTIONS TO SPEED UP FILE CONVERSION AND SLICING TOOLS

Create a New Action

As you saw with Photoshop CC, you can create a new set of actions by clicking on the folder in the lower bar of the panel, as seen in Figure 13-4.

Figure 13-4. Create a new action set

Since you don't have an action to save an SVG file, let's add that; name the set Save SVG File, as seen in Figure 13-5.

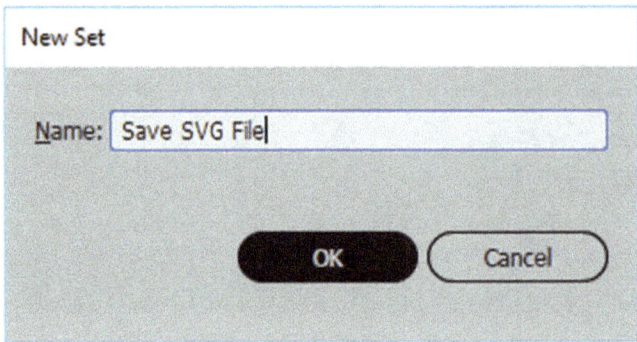

Figure 13-5. Give the new set a name

Then click OK.

I created the new set to keep the new action separate from my default actions.

While an AI file is open, click the Create New Action button. Save the action as Save SVG, as seen in Figure 13-6.

300

CHAPTER 13 ACTIONS TO SPEED UP FILE CONVERSION AND SLICING TOOLS

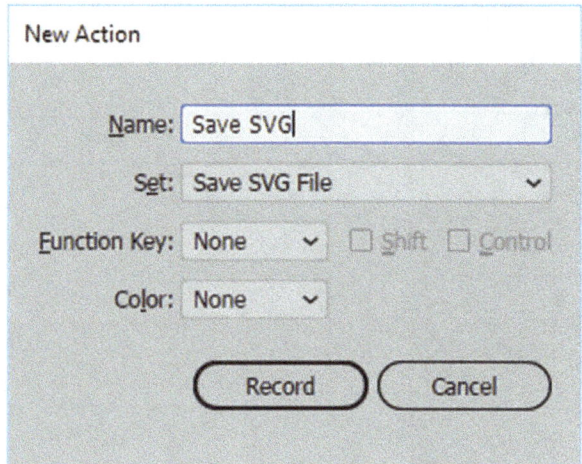

Figure 13-6. Name the new action

Alternatively, you can also move the action to another set. Give it a key function and give the action a color for better identification. For now, leave the settings as is, and click the circle Record icon, as seen in Figure 13-7.

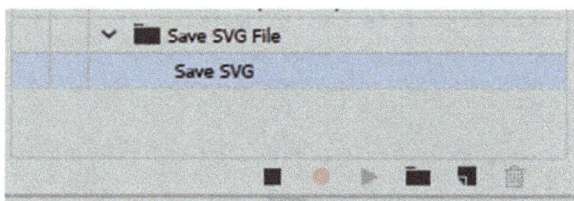

Figure 13-7. Click the Record icon to begin recording the action

You now notice that the little red Record button is on, and you can begin recording your actions as you move along. If at any time you wish to stop recording, click the square icon to the left. If you make a mistake in an action, you can use the Trash icon on the right to remove it. You can then resume by clicking the Record button and redoing the actions. Afterward, to test an action, click the triangle (play) to the right. Right now, nothing will happen until you do another action in Illustrator.

With your AI file open, you can choose File ➤ Export ➤ Export As and choose SVG as the file type, and click Export.

Then set the settings in the SVG options dialog box. Refer to Figure 13-8.

301

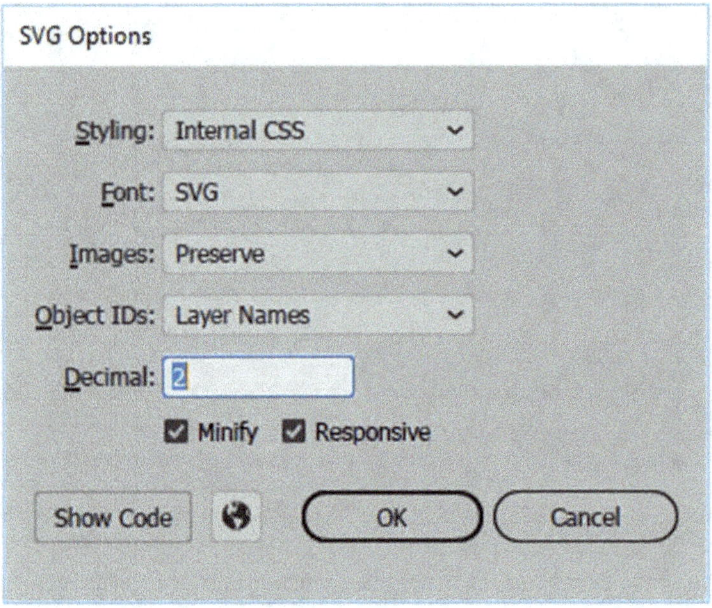

CHAPTER 13 ACTIONS TO SPEED UP FILE CONVERSION AND SLICING TOOLS

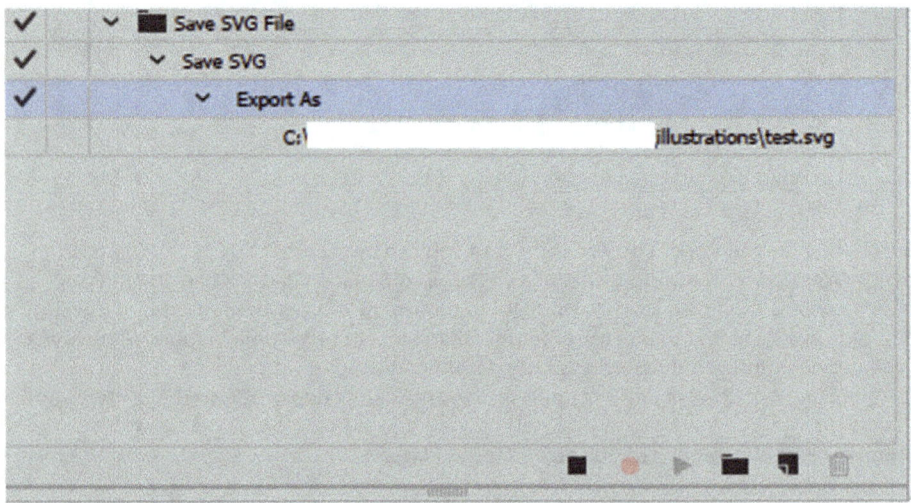

Figure 13-8. Choose settings in the SVG Options dialog box

Click OK to save the file in a folder; those actions should be recorded. Refer to Figure 13-9.

Figure 13-9. The action now appears in the Actions panel

Now click the Stop icon to stop the recording to complete the action and make sure that the Export As window (the toggle on and off dialog icon) opens, in case you need to adjust your settings during the action for different file. Refer to Figure 13-10.

CHAPTER 13 ■ ACTIONS TO SPEED UP FILE CONVERSION AND SLICING TOOLS

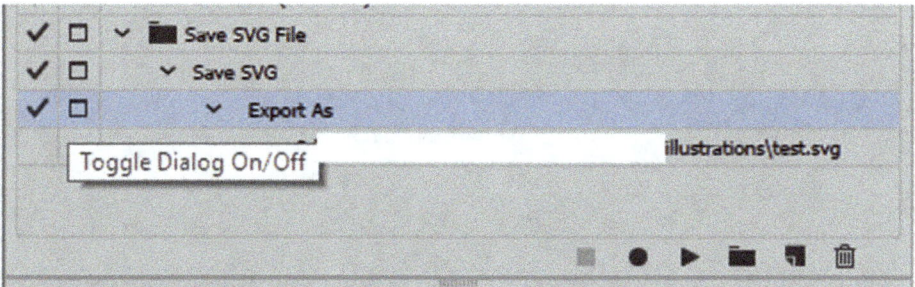

Figure 13-10. Add to the action the option for the dialog box to open

■ **Note** You can also insert stops if you want to record a message to remind you of a step. In the Actions menu, choose Insert Stop and enter a message, and then click OK. The stop is inserted into the action.

Open another AI or EPS file in Illustrator to test the action to see if it works. Do this by clicking the Play button.

While this is good for one image at a time, it would not make the process much faster if you have several images and then need to export another folder, since it goes to the same folder each time. To get around this, you need to create a batch.

Automate Batch Actions

As you saw in Photoshop, you can batch files. While the Actions panel is OK for a few images a day, what if you have over 20 images that need to be adjusted for a gallery or an e-commerce website?

The Batch option is not in the main menu. You need to use the Actions panel menu. Refer to Figure 13-2, where you see the Batch option at the bottom of the Actions panel's menu.

With the new action set, select Choose Batch, as seen in Figure 13-11.

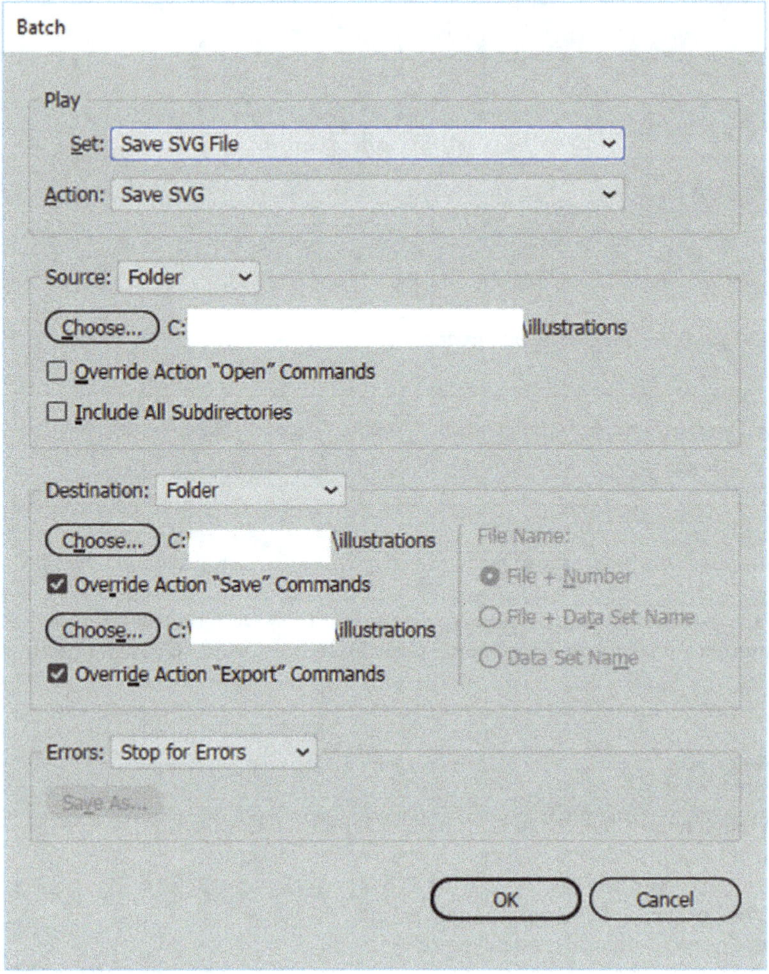

CHAPTER 13 ■ ACTIONS TO SPEED UP FILE CONVERSION AND SLICING TOOLS

Figure 13-11. *The Batch dialog box for Illustrator*

As with Photoshop CC, the Illustrator Batch feature allows you to choose a set of actions and the actions within the set. You can also choose a folder or data set as a source for where the file came from and a destination folder, if different from where the files will be saved or exported. Also, you can override these commands to be different than the actions. If you do not choose a different folder, you can choose to save and close from the Destination drop-down menu.

■ **Note** If the Source drop-down menu is set to Data Sets (it is assumed that your file contained data sets and you are working from one file), use the Batch command to populate a template for data-driven graphics with different sets of data. You can give the output file from those sets a file name and number or data set name. This sets an option for generating file names from the original document when overriding Save and Export commands. However, with Folder as the Source option, this area is unavailable. Refer to Figure 13-12.

304

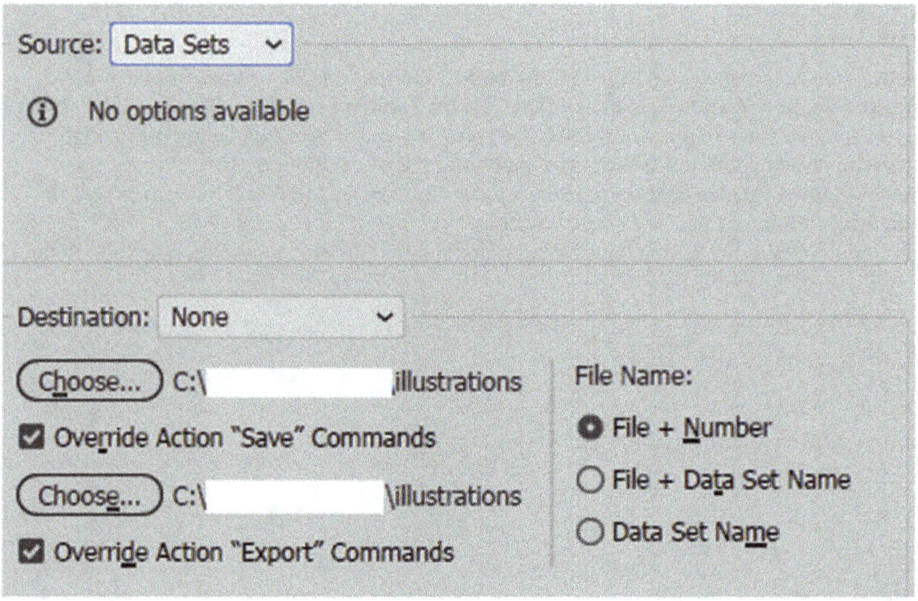

CHAPTER 13 ■ ACTIONS TO SPEED UP FILE CONVERSION AND SLICING TOOLS

Figure 13-12. Setting data sets in the Batch dialog box

For now, leave both the source and destination options as a folder, as seen in Figure 13-11.
You can then make sure that the file will stop for errors if there is an error during the batch process. Refer to Figure 13-13.

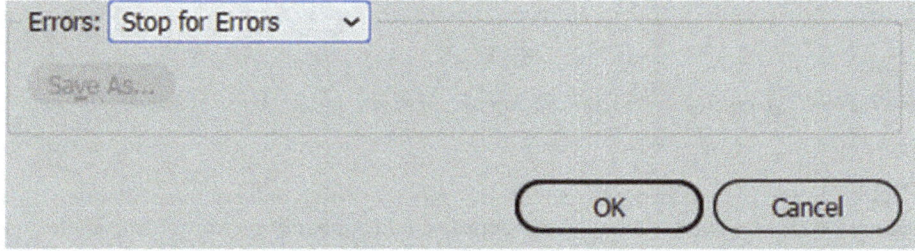

Figure 13-13. The batch process stops for errors if there is an issue with the file

Click OK to start the batch action.
You can save, export, and open each file's settings, one at a time, and adjust the settings if required. As you can see, Illustrator actions are more simplified than Photoshop CC, but they can be just as efficient when working with the conversion of more than one image for the web.

■ **Note** There is no automate droplet available in Illustrator as there is in Photoshop CC.

305

CHAPTER 13 ACTIONS TO SPEED UP FILE CONVERSION AND SLICING TOOLS

Slicing Tools

As you saw in Chapters 4 and 5, when you save files for the web in Photoshop CC, you might save many photos or graphics that will appear somewhere in an HTML file on a solid background. However, they are times when you might want an image to appear in the background of one or more <div> tags or in a table. In Illustrator, you can use the same principles to slice up a background that can later be saved for the web.

If you wish to review some of the basic ways to slice, refer to Chapters 4 and 5. In Illustrator, you will look at where you can find similar features and compare them.

Slices are best suited to backgrounds that have been created using File ➤ New and the Web tab. Refer to Figure 13-14.

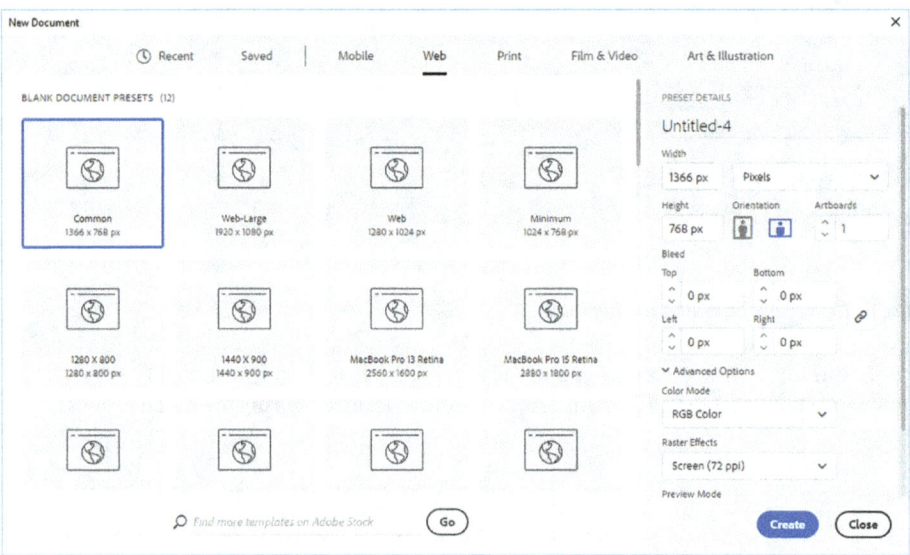

Figure 13-14. *Choose the Web tab when you create a new document that you plan to use as a layout for your website*

You can also create your own custom layout or create more than one artboard for different planned layout sizes. I've attached a slice example on how a large webpage could appear if you were slicing a selected area of a page. See slice_example_ill.ai and refer to Figure 13-15 for this part of the chapter.

CHAPTER 13 ■ ACTIONS TO SPEED UP FILE CONVERSION AND SLICING TOOLS

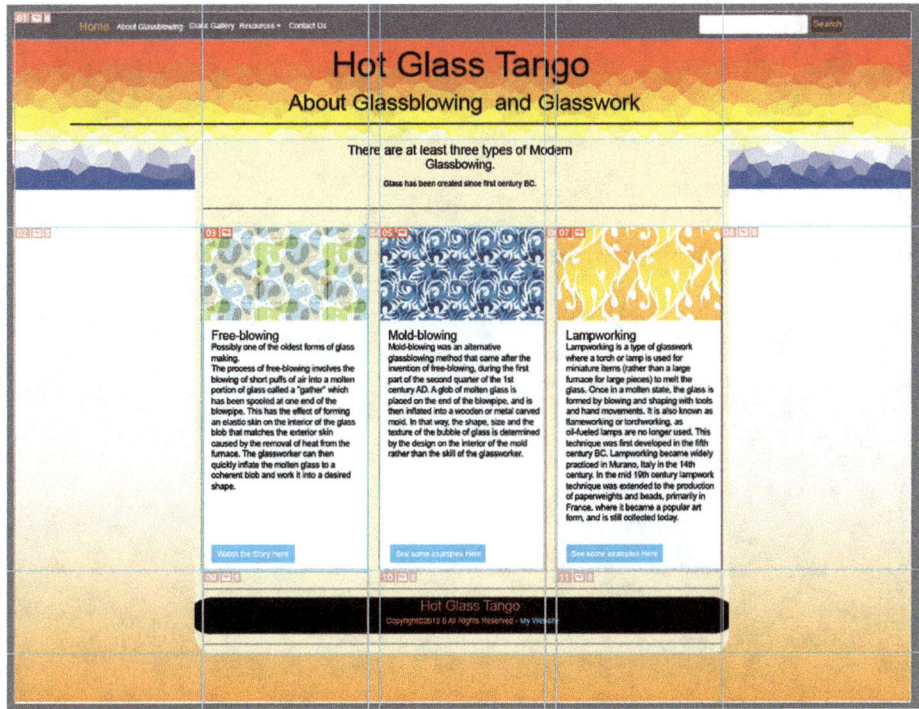

Figure 13-15. A webpage with areas that have been sliced

Here you can lay out your background image or sections with guides and use the Slice (Shift+K) tool and Slice Selection tool found in the Tools panel to carve the page up. Refer to Figure 13-16.

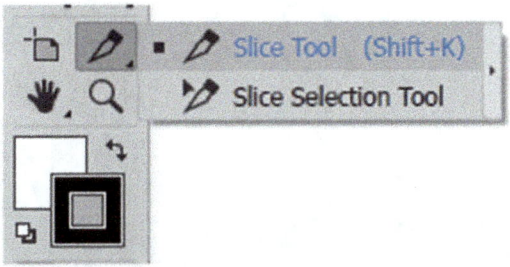

Figure 13-16. Use the Slice tool to create slices from your website

Use the Slice and Slice Select Tools

Using guides, you can lay out where each slice will be and how large it is. In the Web workflow, the Slice tool, which is docked beside the Artboard tool, can marque around a section within the guides and create a user slice (see Figure 13-17) to the right in bright red or a layer-based slice in faded red. Depending on where you create a slice, more slices will be generated around it. The generated slices are known as auto slices and subslices (faded red) when they overlap, and they cannot be selected.

307

CHAPTER 13　ACTIONS TO SPEED UP FILE CONVERSION AND SLICING TOOLS

Figure 13-17. Example of user and auto slices on a page

The Slice tool will allow you to create slices, whereas the Slice Selection tool allows you to move and size the slices. You can see user, or layer-based, slices and which layers they are on in the Layers panel (see Figure 13-18).

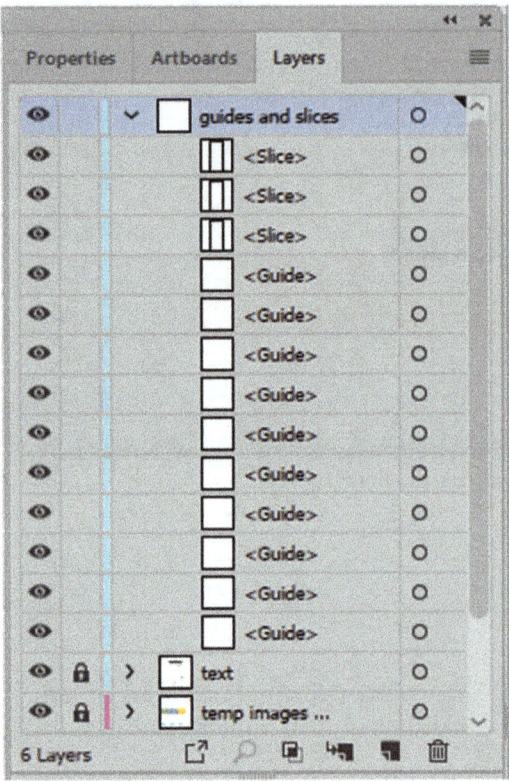

Figure 13-18. Example or auto or layer-based slicing in the Layers panel

Like any user slice or layer-based slice, it can be moved and resized as you would a vector object. Different icons and colors dictate what kind of slice it is.

- **Slice lines:** Define the boundary of the slice. Solid lines indicate that the slice is a user slice or layer-based sliced; lighter solid lines indicate that the slice is an auto slice.

308

CHAPTER 13 ACTIONS TO SPEED UP FILE CONVERSION AND SLICING TOOLS

- **Slice colors:** Differentiates user slices from auto slices. By default, user slices and layer-based slices have blue symbols, and auto slices have gray symbols and often a link icon when viewed in the Save for Web (Legacy) dialog box. Normally on the artboard, they appear in the default red color and not always with link icon while working on the artboard. The Save For Web (Legacy) dialog box uses color adjustments to dim unselected slices. These adjustments are for display purposes only and do not affect the color of the final image. By default, the color adjustment for auto slices is twice the amount of that for user slices. Refer to Figure 13-19.

Figure 13-19. How slices appear in the Save for Web (Legacy) (01,02) and on the artboard (07,06)

- **Slice numbers:** Numbers are from left to right and top to bottom, beginning in the upper-left corner of the image. If you change the arrangement or the number of slices, every slice number is updated to reflect the new order.

Note For further alterations to slice color, go to Edit ➤ Preferences ➤ Slices for Windows, and Illustrator ➤ Preferences ➤ Slices for macOS. You can alter the line color and hide/show the slice number. Click OK to confirm changes. Refer to Figure 13-20.

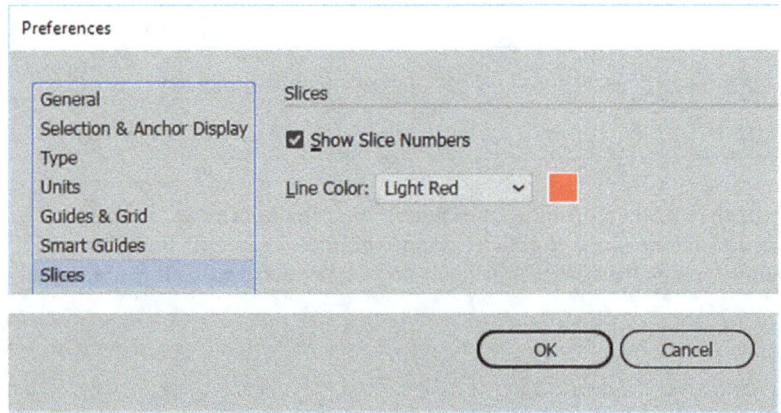

Figure 13-20. If you don't like the default color of the slices, alter it here as well as show or hide the slice numbers

Object ➤ Slice Options

To work with slices to add, duplicate, combine, divide, or delete them, you need to go to Object ➤ Slice, as seen in Figure 13-21.

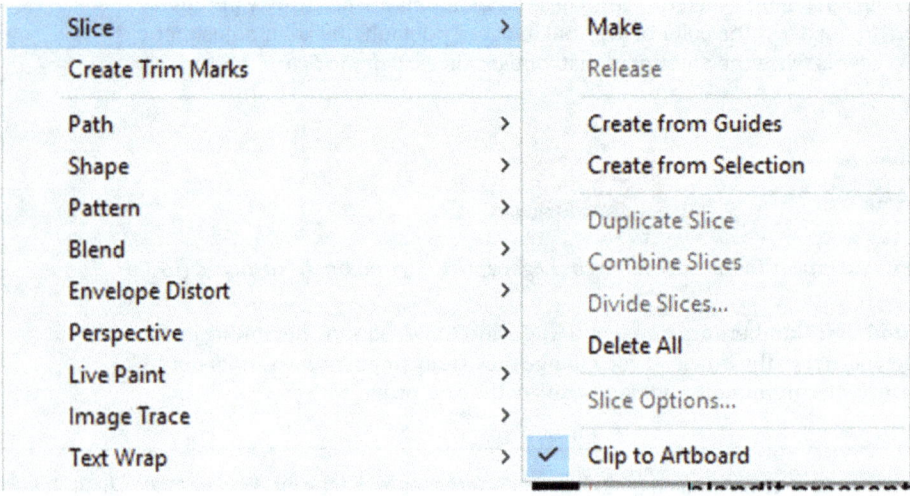

Figure 13-21. *There are more options for working with slices in the Object ➤ Slices main menu*

In this area, you can make or release a slice to its own sublayer. You can create a slice from guides or a selection when an object on the artboard is selected.

■ **Note** The Create from Guides feature overrides all current slices and slice numbers with any new slices created based on the guides.

When a slice is selected with the slice select tool in the Tools panel, you can duplicate, combine, divide, or delete all slices. The Clip to Artboard feature forces the slices to stay within the artboard's boundaries.

The Divide Slice dialog box allows you to divide slices vertically and horizontally, either by number or by pixel. Refer to Figure 13-22.

CHAPTER 13 ■ ACTIONS TO SPEED UP FILE CONVERSION AND SLICING TOOLS

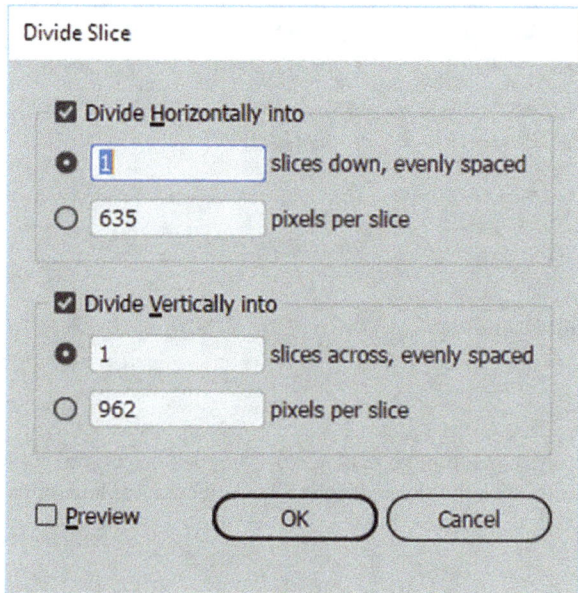

Figure 13-22. The Divide Slice dialog box

Align Slices

To align slices, Shift-select with the Slice Selection tool. You can then use the Align panel. Refer to Figure 13-23.

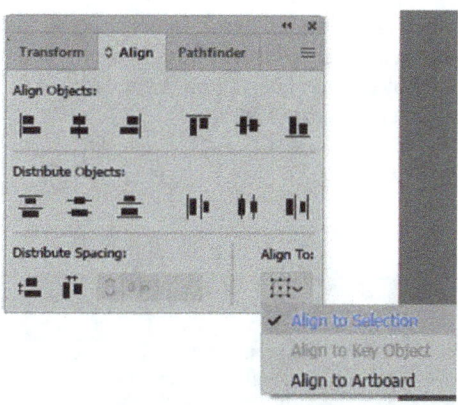

Figure 13-23. Use the Align panel to align your slices as you would align objects

To change the stacking order of the slices in the Layers panel, either rearrange the layers or choose Object ➤ Arrange, as seen in Figure 13-24.

311

Arrange	>	Bring to Front	Shift+Ctrl+]
Group	Ctrl+G	Bring Forward	Ctrl+]
Ungroup	Shift+Ctrl+G	Send Backward	Ctrl+[
Lock	>	Send to Back	Shift+Ctrl+[
Unlock All	Alt+Ctrl+2	Send to Current Layer	

Figure 13-24. *Send slices forward or back as you would objects*

You can send the slices forward or backward in sublayer order.

Slice Options

To get to the slice options, while the slices is selected, you can either go to Object ➤ Slice ➤ Slice Options. Or, while in the Save for Web(Legacy) dialog box, double-click the slice with the Slice Selection tool. Refer to Figures 13-25 and 13-26.

Figure 13-25. *Use the Slice Selection tool to gain access to the Slice Options dialog box*

Image

Image is the Default Slice Type in Slice Options. In Slice Type, the Image option is a user slice for images. You can see its icon is a picture. When Auto (gray) there is a link icon. Auto Slices cannot be edited or selected while working on the artboard. You can only edit auto slices by double-clicking on them with the slice select tool if you are in the Save For Web (Legacy) dialog box. Refer to Figure 13-26.

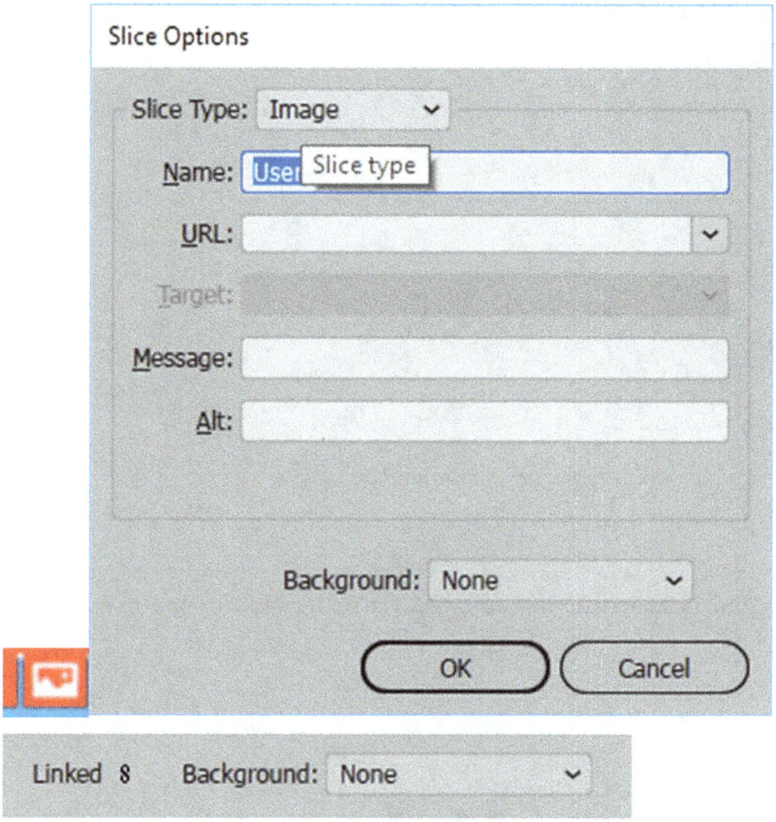

CHAPTER 13 ■ ACTIONS TO SPEED UP FILE CONVERSION AND SLICING TOOLS

Figure 13-26. *Setting for the Slice Options for the image slice*

In Slice Type, select Image if you want the slice area to be an image file in the resulting webpage. If you want the image to have an HTML link, enter a URL and target in the drop-down menu. Like Photoshop CC, you have the options of blank, self, parent, and top. For more information on those, refer to Chapter 5.

You can also specify that a message appear in the browser's status area when the mouse is positioned over the image, alternative text (alt) that appears when the image is not visible, and a background color for the table cell or <div> tag.

Background color options include None, Matte, Black, and White. Eyedropper Color and Other let you choose custom colors from the color picker. Refer to Figure 13-27.

313

CHAPTER 13 ■ ACTIONS TO SPEED UP FILE CONVERSION AND SLICING TOOLS

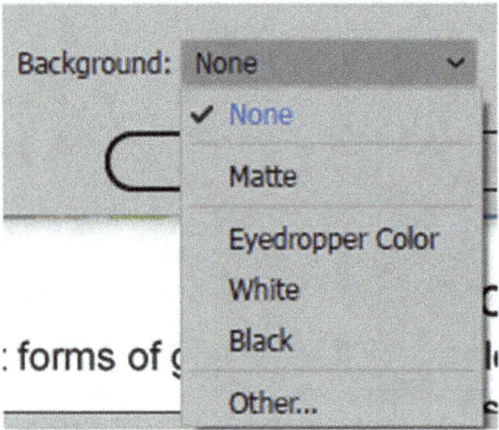

Figure 13-27. Choose none or a color background from the background options

No Image

A slice with No Image is excluded from the images that are exported. The No Image icon appears as a crossed-out box. Refer to Figure 13-28.

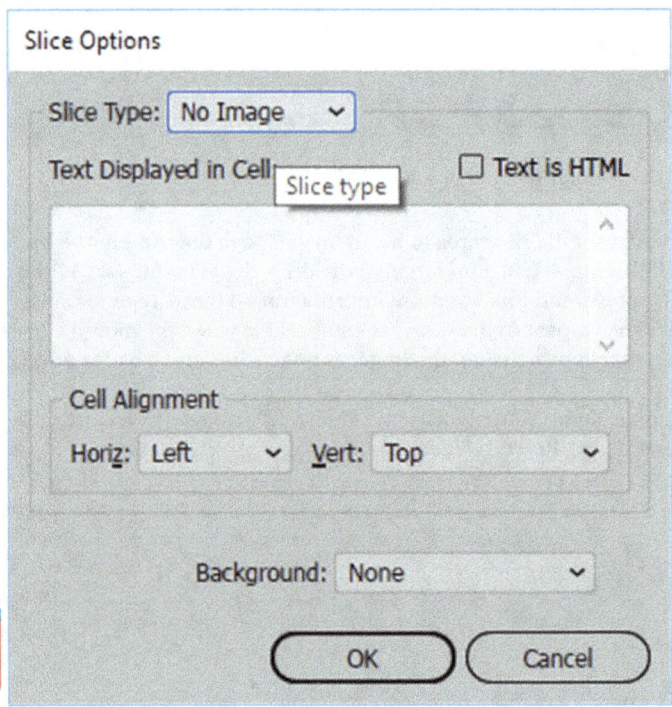

Figure 13-28. Select a slice and choose No Image if you do not want it to export that slice

314

CHAPTER 13 ■ ACTIONS TO SPEED UP FILE CONVERSION AND SLICING TOOLS

Select No Image if you want the slice area to contain HTML text and a background color in the resulting webpage. Enter the text you want in the Text Displayed in Cell text box, and format the text using standard HTML tags.

Take care not to enter more text than can be displayed in the slice area. If you enter too much text, it will extend into neighboring slices and affect the layout of your webpage. However, because you cannot see the text on the artboard, this will not be apparent until you view the webpage in a browser or in Dreamweaver CC.

Set the Horiz and Vert options to change the alignment of text in the table cell. Later, you can use CSS in Dreamweaver to alter the layout and change the table to <div> tags.

HTML Text

HTML Text is available only when you created the slice by selecting a text object box and chose Object ➤ Slice ➤ Make. Refer to Figure 13-29.

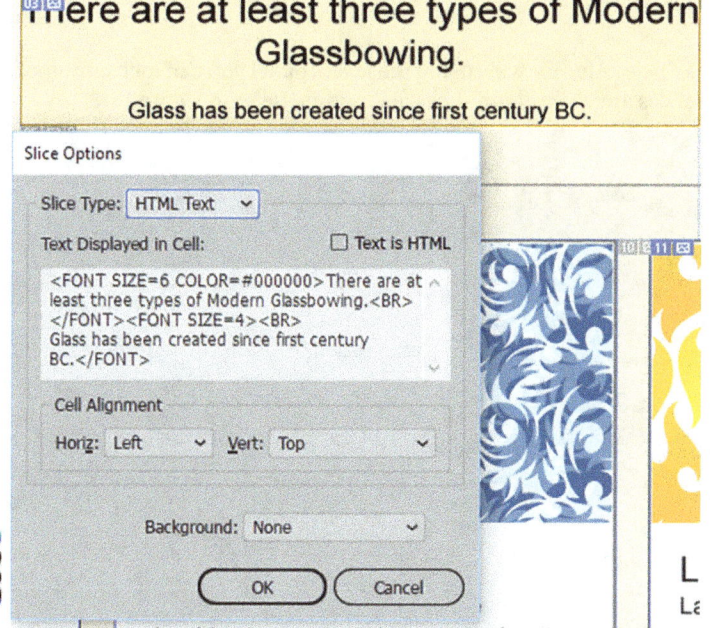

Figure 13-29. *Select a text box area that you can transform into a slice, and then set it to Slice Type: HTML Text*

The Illustrator text is converted to HTML text with basic formatting attributes in the resulting webpage. To edit the text, update the text in your artwork on the artboard. Set the Horiz and Vert options to change the alignment of text in the table cell. You can also select a background color for the table cell. Later, you can use CSS in Dreamweaver to alter the layout and change the table to <div> tags.

315

> **Tip** To edit the text for HTML Text slices in the Slice Options dialog box, change the slice type to No Image. This breaks the link with the text object on the artboard. To ignore text formatting, you can enter <unformatted> as the first word in the text object.

Delete All Slices

Each time you draw a slice, it is numbered, and auto slices around it need to renumber to match. Sometimes, subslices overlap, which can get confusing if you don't keep track and the image requires many slices. If you ever need to clear the slices from the page and start over, select Object ➤ Slices ➤ Delete All, and begin to slice again.

Lock Slices

To lock slices, choose View ➤ Lock Slices. Alternatively using the layers panel you can lock or unlock the slice layer or sublayers. Only user slices are visible auto slices are hidden. Refer to Figure 13-30.

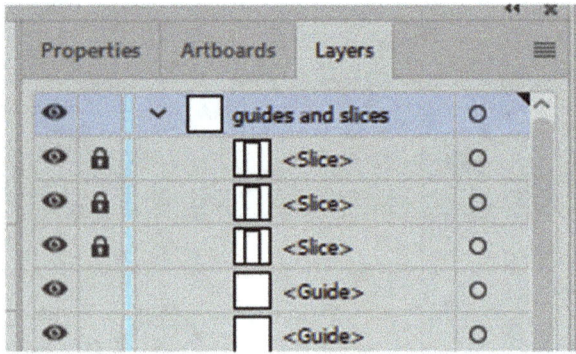

Figure 13-30. Lock slices in the Layers panel

Hide Slices

To Hide the slices, choose View ➤ Hide Slices.

Save Your Slices for the Web

As with Photoshop CC, to save slices, you go to File ➤ Export ➤ Save for Web (Legacy) and use the Slice Select tool (K). Use the Toggle Slice Visibility tool (Q) to select the slices and then adjust their settings in the preview on the right. Refer to Figure 13-31 for the tools.

CHAPTER 13 ■ ACTIONS TO SPEED UP FILE CONVERSION AND SLICING TOOLS

Figure 13-31. Save for Web (Legacy) dialog box tools

The background slice default is usually a GIF, but you can change each slice to a PNG or a JPEG file. At the bottom of the Preset panel is the option to export the slices, as seen in Figure 13-32.

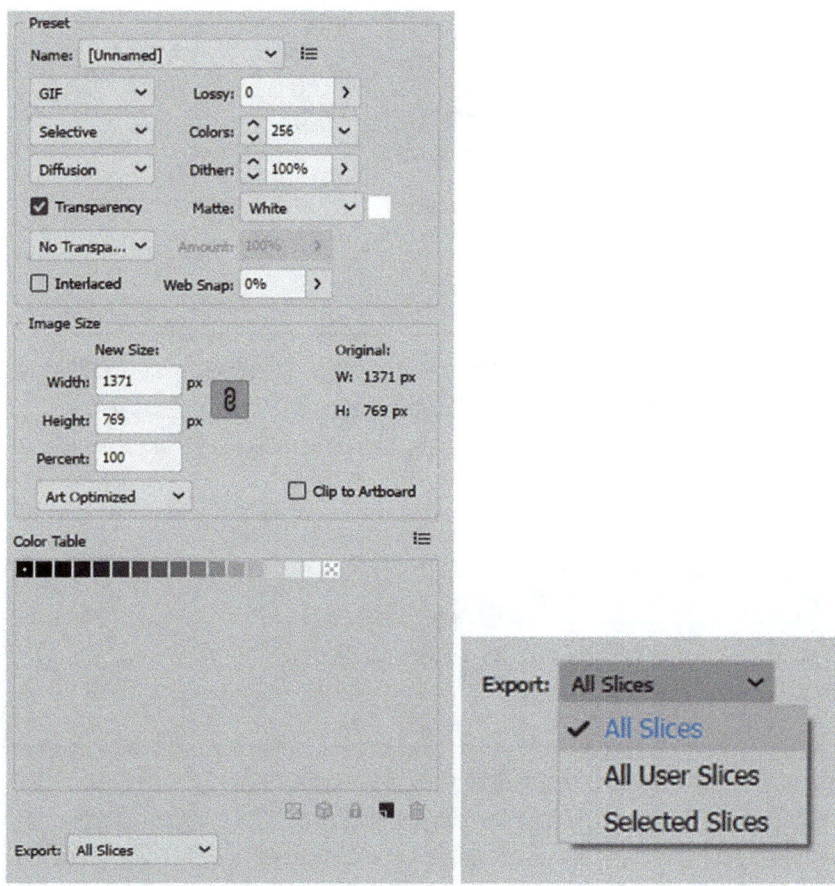

Figure 13-32. Choose how you want to export your slices

317

You can choose to export all the slices, all the user slices, or just the slices you have selected.

You can further optimize the size of the slices for the web in the Preset drop-down menu. Refer to Figure 13-33.

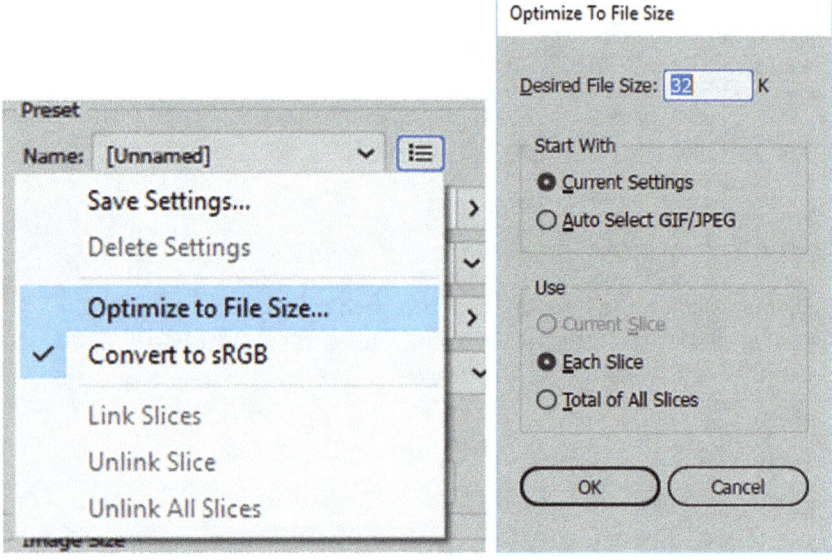

Figure 13-33. Choose Optimize to File Size to alter each slice's size

Remember to select more than one slice, use Shift+mouse-click.

■ **Tip** Another quick way to save the slices if you are not in the Save for Web (Legacy) dialog box as GIF only is from the main menu choose File ➤ Save Selected Slices (GIF). However unlike save for web, this option does not allow you to adjust your slice settings or set other file formats for the slices like JPEG or PNG. Refer to Figure 13-34.

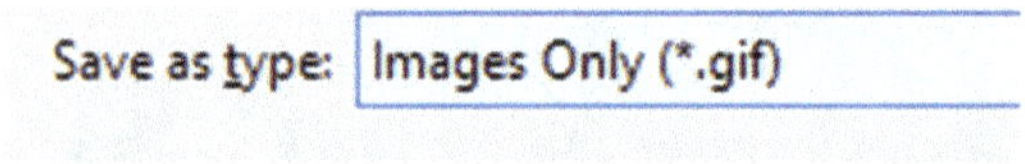

Figure 13-34. Save Select Slices only lets you save a GIF slice

■ **Note** When you click Save in the Save for Web (Legacy) dialog box (see Figure 13-35), you may discover that you can only save the GIF images and not the HTML, as you can in Photoshop CC. I'm not sure if this was something the Illustrator designers forgot to update, but do not despair. You can copy this code if you press the Preview button in the lower left. This opens the browser. The code for your slices is below the images. You can then copy this information into your HTML file and edit it in Dreamweaver CC.

CHAPTER 13 ACTIONS TO SPEED UP FILE CONVERSION AND SLICING TOOLS

Figure 13-35. *Click the Preview button if you want to see the HTML code*

The following is an example of some of the code.

```
<html>
<head>
<title>testing_page</title>
<meta http-equiv="Content-Type" content="text/html; charset=iso-8859-1">
</head>
<body bgcolor="#FFFFFF" leftmargin="0" topmargin="0" marginwidth="0" marginheight="0">
<div style="position:absolute; left:0px; top:0px; width:1996px; height:1482px;">
    <div style="background-image:url(slice_example_ill_01.gif); position:absolute; left:0px;
    top:0px; width:1996px; height:459px;" title="">
<!--more code here -->
    </div>
</body>
</html>
```

The code in your file will likely be different, but at least this is a decent work-around should you require HTML and CSS as a starting point for your site design.

Creating Image Maps

You can also create a hotspot or image map within a slice using the Attributes panel. Refer to my image_map example.ai file.

Image map links can take on other shapes, such as a polygon, while a slice can only have a rectangular URL link. Refer to Figure 13-36.

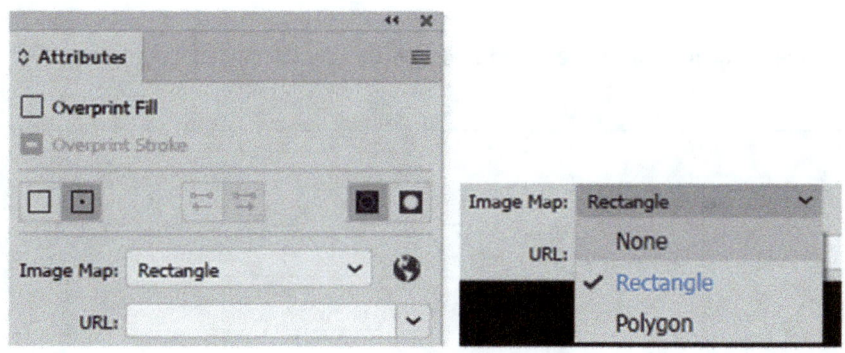

Figure 13-36. *Creating an image map with the Attributes panel*

319

You can enter a relative or full URL into the hotspot image map area. The Globe icon allows you to browse for the link, but beware that if the slice you are on already contains a URL in the Slice options, this could cause a conflict. Refer to Figure 13-37.

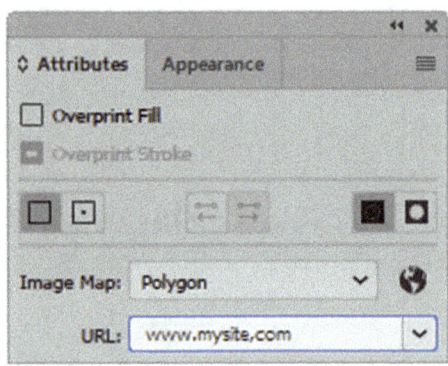

Figure 13-37. Creating an image map (star) with the Attributes panel

Complex objects do not produce image maps in Illustrator, so it is better to use Dreamweaver to draw complex shapes, as you will see in Part 6.

■ **Note** Style information for the image map can be retrieved when you go to Save for Web (Legacy) and click the Preview button.

```
<map name="image_map_example_02_Map">
<area shape="poly" alt="" coords="93,167, 76,165, 65,177, 62,161, 46,154, 61,146, 63,129, 75,141, 91,137, 84,153, 93,167" href="www.mysite.com">
</map>
```

Summary

In this chapter, you reviewed scripts, actions, batching actions, slicing tools, and image maps. You also saw how to retrieve important CSS and HTML information for your slices that you could later use in Dreamweaver to build your website.

Although you can't create animations or videos in Illustrator, in the next chapter, you learn that you can use some of its tools to create objects and layouts that could be used as frames in animations or for video. In addition, you discover a SVG file JavaScript interactivity secret.

CHAPTER 14

Tools for Animation and Video

In this chapter, you look at a few tools to enhance your drawings for scenes or frames in an animation or video that could be imported into either Photoshop CC or Animated CC as vector Smart Objects or library symbols. You also look at the SVG Interactivity panel, which you may not know much about.

> **Note** This chapter does not have any actual projects; however, you can use the files in the Chapter 14 folder to practice opening and viewing for this lesson. They are at `https://github.com/Apress/graphics-multimedia-web-adobe-creative-cloud`.

Tools for Animation

Unlike Photoshop CC, Illustrator CC does not have a Timeline panel for video or animation. As you noticed in Chapter 12, you cannot export a GIF animation, only static GIF images.

There are a few tools, however, that you can use to help you create parts for your animation. Later these shapes can be used in programs like Photoshop CC, Animate CC, and Dreamweaver CC. Let's look at a few to get you started on your animation.

SVG Interactivity Panel

As you saw when you created SVG files for the web, they are scalable or responsive, so they will not become pixilated like GIF, JPEG, or PNG images. Bitmap or raster files can be used to create graphic buttons or rollovers in Dreamweaver; however, in the SVG Interactivity panel, you can also create an SVG image that acts like a button when saved or exported for a webpage. Refer to Figure 14-1.

CHAPTER 14 ■ TOOLS FOR ANIMATION AND VIDEO

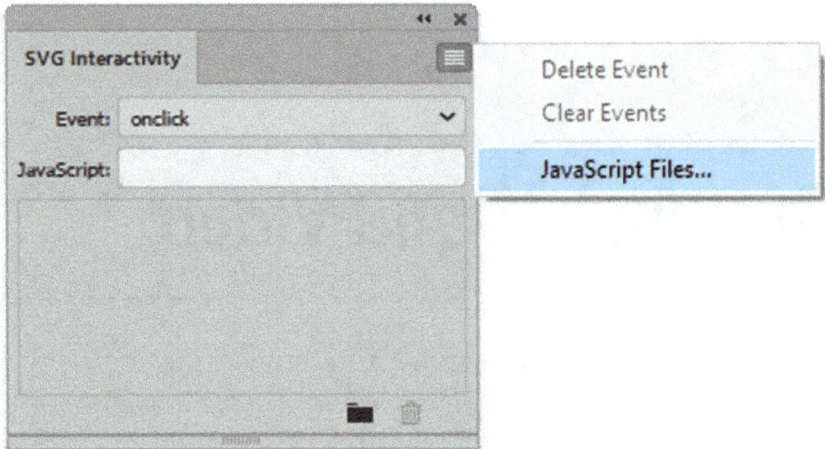

Figure 14-1. *The SVG Interactivity panel*

■ **Note** To use the SVG Interactivity panel correctly, you must first design your images in an AI or EPS file. Make sure to give each of the layers a distinct name because the JavaScript regards these layers or sublayers as an object with an ID. Look at the vases_orginal.ai in the SVG folder and Figure 14-2.

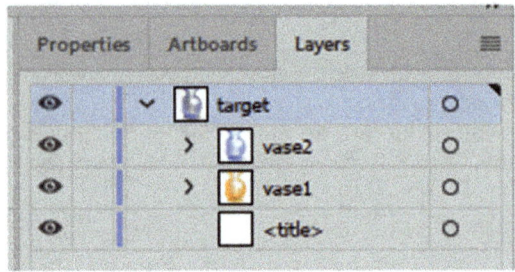

Figure 14-2. *Each layer that will interact must be named distinctly in the Layers panel*

Then you need to Save As or Export As an SVG, using one of the methods described in Chapter 12. Refer to Figure 14-3.

324

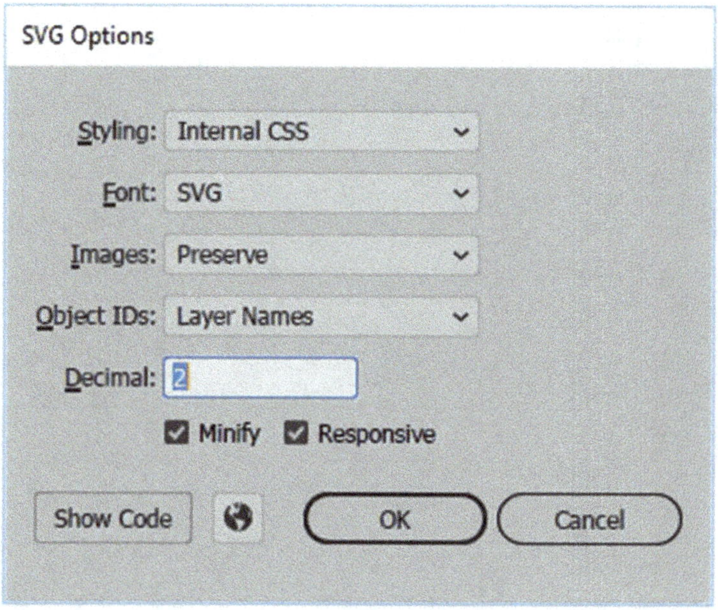

CHAPTER 14 ■ TOOLS FOR ANIMATION AND VIDEO

Figure 14-3. Save your SVG settings

Once done, click OK to save your new SVG file in a folder; make sure to give the file a name. You can look at my finished file, Asset_1.svg.

Once the file is in the SVG format, only then can you work with the SVG Interactivity panel. If you are in an AI or EPS file, JavaScript that you type in this panel does not always copy correctly into the SVG, so it is very crucial to follow these steps if you want interactivity in your SVGs. You can check this if you go to Show Code (see Figure 14-3); you will see no actions applied if you were to add any event to this panel in the original EPS or AI file.

Open the newly created SVG file in Illustrator to enter one or more event triggers and JavaScript into the panel. Make sure to select the top layer on the target, as I have in Figure 14-4.

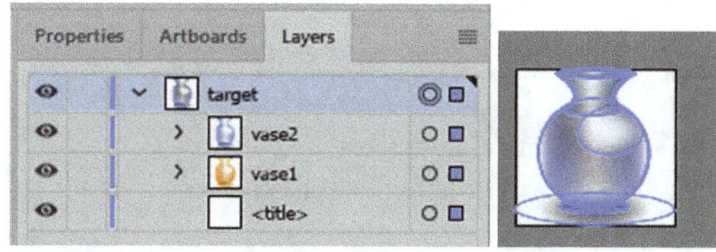

Figure 14-4. The target must be selected in the Layers panel before you can enter any JavaScript in the SVG Interactivity panel

With the target selected, you can start entering information in the SVG panel.

The following command or event triggers are available for SVG elements. Refer to Figure 14-5.

325

CHAPTER 14 ■ TOOLS FOR ANIMATION AND VIDEO

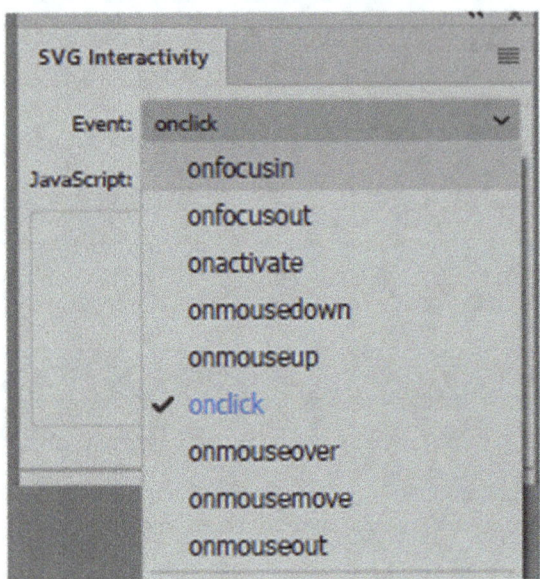

Figure 14-5. *Event triggers in the SVG Interactivity panel will only work when you are in an SVG file*

Elements

The following are JavaScript events that will effect elements or the shapes in the svg file when triggered.

- **onfocusin:** Triggers the JavaScript action when the element receives focus, such as selection by the pointer.
- **onfocusout:** Triggers the JavaScript action the SVG element loses focus (often when another element receives focus).
- **onactivate:** Triggers the JavaScript action with a mouse click or keypress, depending upon the element.
- **onmousedown:** Triggers the JavaScript action for when the mouse button is pressed down over an element.
- **onmouseup:** Triggers the JavaScript action when the mouse button is released over an element.
- **onclick:** Triggers the JavaScript action when the mouse is clicked over an element.
- **onmouseover:** Triggers the JavaScript action when the pointer is moved onto an element.
- **onmousemove:** Triggers the JavaScript action while the pointer is over an element.
- **onmouseout:** Triggers the JavaScript action when the pointer is moved away from an element.
- **onkeydown:** Triggers the JavaScript action when a key is pressed down.
- **onkeypress:** Triggers the JavaScript action while a key is pressed down.
- **onkeyup:** Triggers the JavaScript action when a key is released.

326

CHAPTER 14 ■ TOOLS FOR ANIMATION AND VIDEO

Document

The following are JavaScript events that will effect the entire SVG documents.

- **onload:** Triggers the JavaScript action after the SVG document has been completely parsed by the browser. Use this type of event to call one-time-only initialization functions.

- **onerror:** Triggers the JavaScript action when an element does not load properly, or another error occurs.

- **onabort:** Triggers the JavaScript action when the page loading is stopped before the element is completely loaded.

- **onunload:** Triggers the JavaScript action when the SVG document is removed from a window or frame.

- **onzoom:** Triggers the JavaScript action when the zoom level is changed for the document.

- **onresize:** Triggers the JavaScript action when the document view is resized.

- **onscroll:** Triggers the JavaScript action when the document view is scrolled or panned.

When the mouse or button is released, whatever action you applied will occur.

Each event must be entered one at a time into the SVG Interactivity panel, along with the JavaScript. Then click in the lower box to confirm it. Refer to Figure 14-6.

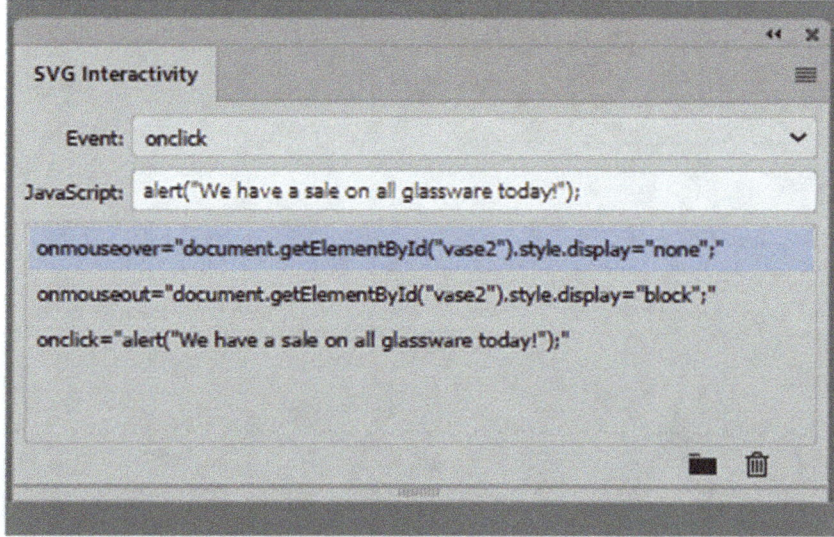

Figure 14-6. *Event triggers in the SVG Interactivity panel will only work when you are in an SVG file*

327

CHAPTER 14 ■ TOOLS FOR ANIMATION AND VIDEO

The following are some scripts that I added to my vase.

```
onmouseover="document.getElementById("vase2").style.display="none";"
onmouseout=="document.getElementById("vase2").style.display="block";"
onclick="alert("We have a sale on all glassware today!");"
```

The only part that you must write is the JavaScript without the outer quotes. Illustrator does the rest.

If, at any point, you need to make a change, select that line and alter the text, then click another line to confirm the change. To delete a script, click the Trash icon. The SVG Interactivity panel only allows you to enter one event per target so that you cannot enter an event twice.

Save your SVG in Illustrator at this point.

If you test the file in a browser, the preceding script allows you to hide and show the top vase when you move your mouse in and out of the browser area; and then when you click it, a message or alert is revealed. This testing is only possible in a browser, not in Illustrator. You may have to open your own SVG file a few times if you need to adjust before testing again in the browser. Refer to Figure 14-7.

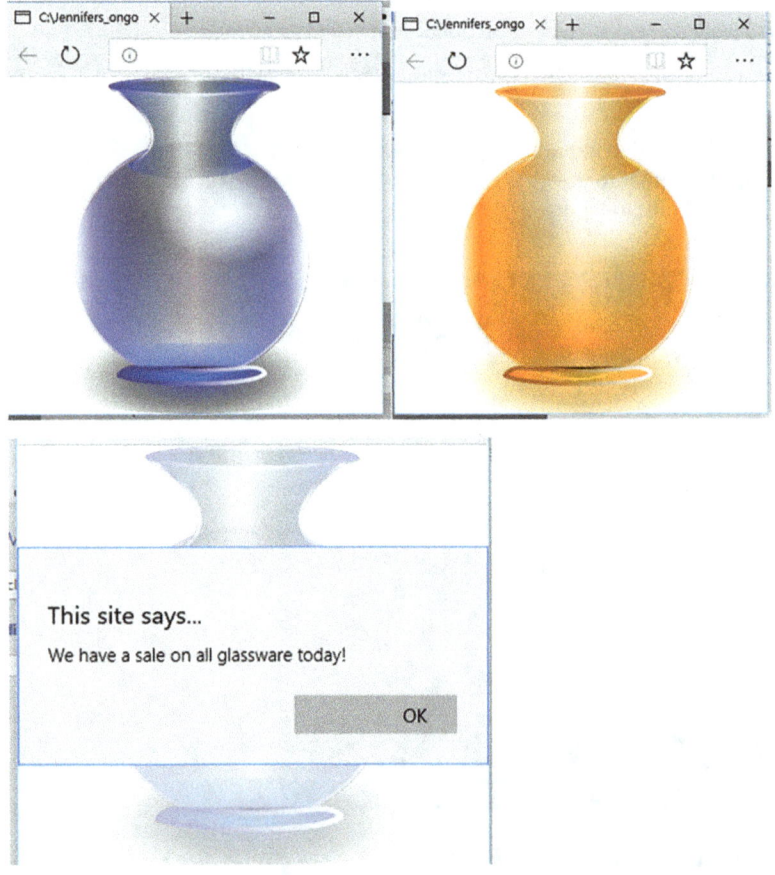

Figure 14-7. *The mouse can now interact with the SVG file in the browser*

Notice that if you scale your SVG in the browser, it never loses its shape. In Part 6, I show you an example of a slightly scaled SVG in Dreamweaver that does not take up a whole page.

CHAPTER 14 ■ TOOLS FOR ANIMATION AND VIDEO

Adding additional linked scripts

To add JavaScript to the panel that is linked to the events, click the folder in the lower right of the panel, or choose JavaScript files from the SVG Interactivity panel's menu. Refer to Figure 14-1.

This opens the JavaScript Files dialog box, as seen in Figure 14-8.

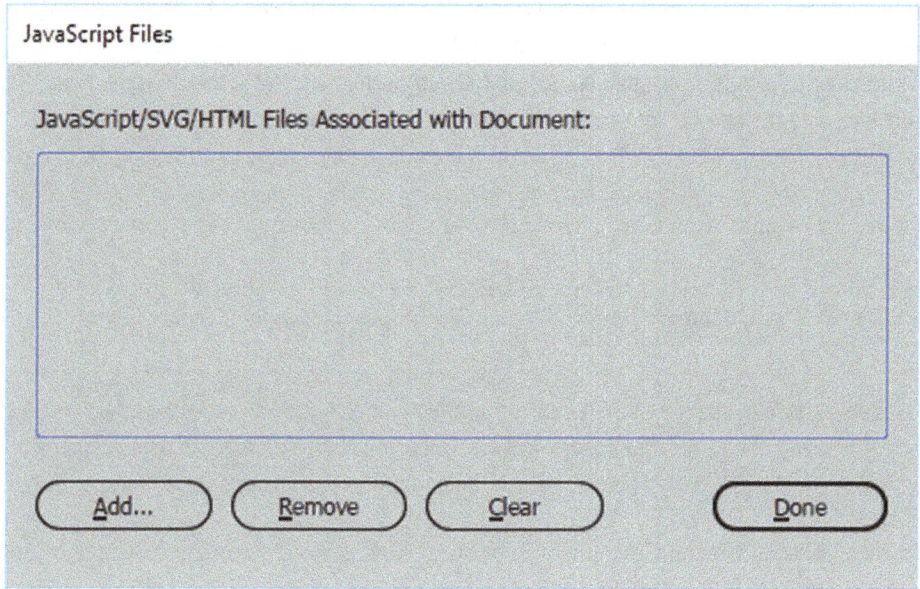

Figure 14-8. *The JavaScript Files dialog box*

The Add button allows you to add a URL to some external JavaScript that you might use for additional interaction that relates to the event in your file on your website. Refer to Figure 14-9.

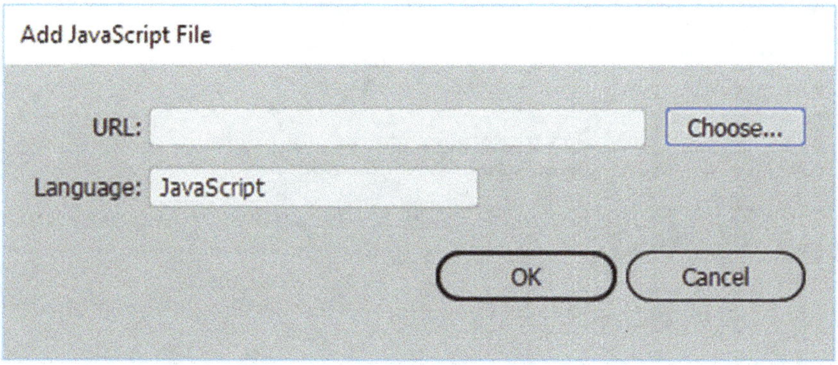

Figure 14-9. *Add a link to an external JavaScript file*

The Choose button allows you to search for and add a link to the associated JavaScript file that contains the JavaScript actions, and add that information to the file.

329

If you have a file to add to your project, click OK to complete the link. For this project, click Cancel.

For your own project, if you later want to unlink that file, press the Remove or Clear buttons (see Figure 14-8). Then click Done to exit.

Make sure to save your SVG file, as you will see it again on the Hot Glass Tango website in Part 6.

■ **Note** If you plan to insert your SVG file into an HTML file, be aware that if you insert it as an image <img>, the graphic will appear, but the interactivity will be unavailable. Although it appears as an image, SVG is more a set of codes that coordinates by simply projecting an image. To keep the interactivity of the SVG, you need to copy that file's code, including the actions, into the HTML file itself; or use an <object> tag instead. You see that in my example in Part 6. When an SVG is in an <img> tag, you can force the image to size using CSS and adjusting the width and height. This can get complicated, so we'll look this issue in more detail in Part 6.

The main thing to note in this section is that if you understand the rules of how the SVG Interactivity panel works, you can use JavaScript to interact with your shapes in simple or complex animations.

■ **Tip** If you want scalable shading, use the SVG filters. They are found in the main menu under Effect ➤ SVG Filters. They are great for creating effects like blurs and shadows. Once you apply a filter to an object, you can change it in the Appearance panel by clicking it and choosing a different filter from the menu while you preview it. Refer to Figure 14-10.

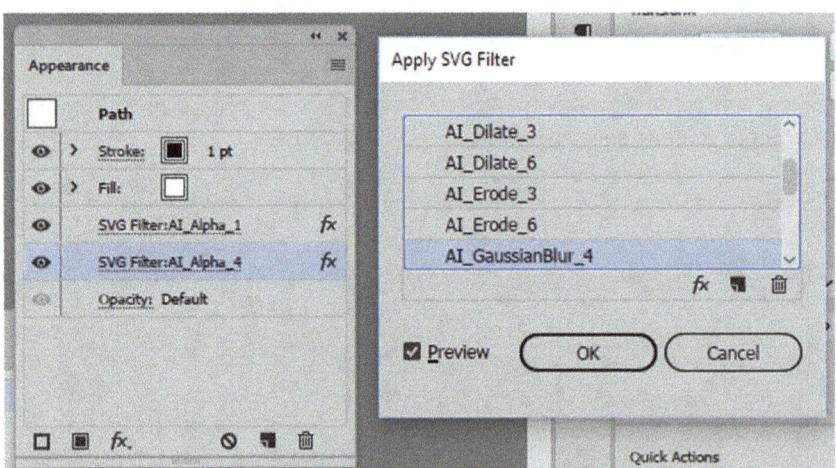

Figure 14-10. The Appearance panel allows you to alter your SVG filters

Copying Illustrations to Photoshop (Vector Smart Objects)

If you are creating graphics for the web or an animation, you can build your shapes or objects in Illustrator. Then you can select the whole object that you designed with the Selection tool (V) and choose Edit ➤ Copy from the menu. Refer to Figure 14-11 and the gif_images.ai file.

CHAPTER 14 ■ TOOLS FOR ANIMATION AND VIDEO

Figure 14-11. *A flower is designed in Illustrator and is selected so that it can be a Smart Object*

With Photoshop CC open, you can then open the document you want to paste the elements into. Select Edit ➤ Paste and choose Paste As: Smart Object. And then click OK, as seen in Figure 14-12.

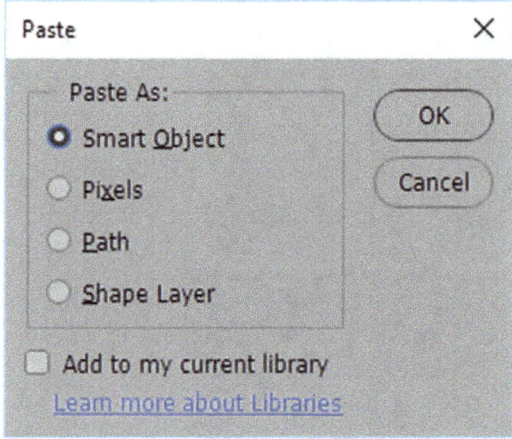

Figure 14-12. *Paste an image as a Smart Object*

Once scaled in Photoshop, make sure to hit the Enter or Return keys on your keyboard, or click another tool. Note if you are in Photoshop CC 2018, An alert will appear; click Place to confirm the Smart Object placement. Refer to Figure 14-13. Note that in CC 2019 hitting the Enter or Return keys will not produce an alert and the Smart Object is placed right away.

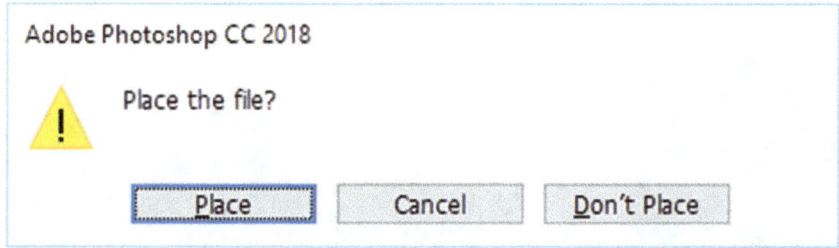

Figure 14-13. *Click Place to confirm the scale of a smart object*

Smart Objects, unlike pixel photos, remain scalable as a vector object in Photoshop. You can always double-click the Smart Object layer if you need to edit it in Illustrator CC. Upon closing, the image updates. These Smart Objects can be manipulated as you would manipulate a Smart Object you originally created in Photoshop. You can add vector masks and effects.

331

CHAPTER 14 ■ TOOLS FOR ANIMATION AND VIDEO

You can see in the gif_animation.psd file how these Smart Objects from Illustrator can be used in a GIF animations timeline. Likewise, you can use similar steps in Animate CC and use the same graphics in an animation there. You will explore that in Part 4; for now, refer to Figure 14-14.

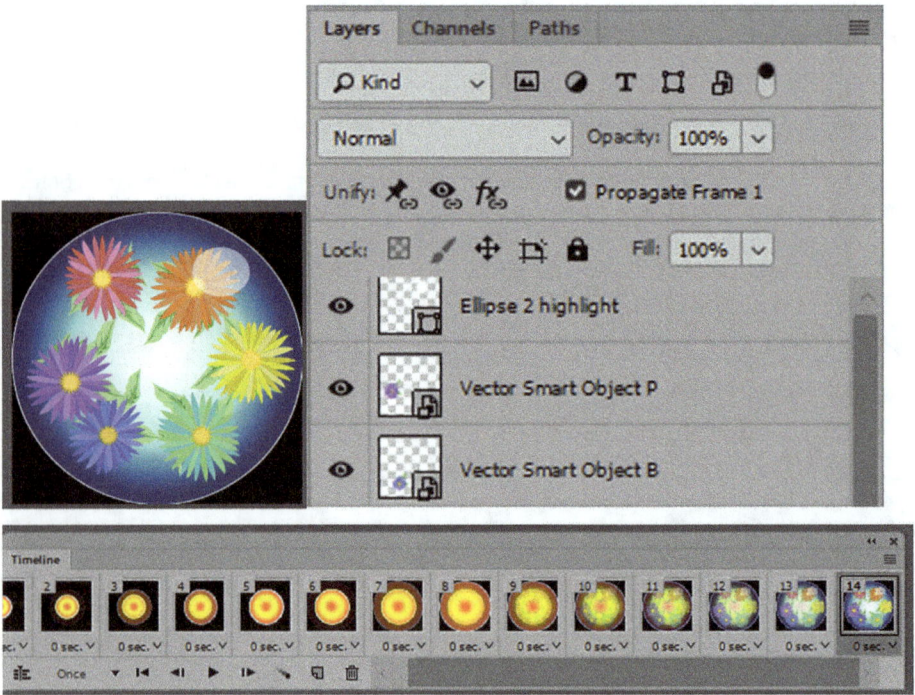

Figure 14-14. *Use Illustrator's vector Smart Objects in Photoshop to create GIF animations*

Rasterize Smart Objects

In Photoshop, if you want to rasterize a Smart Object, you can right-click the layer in the panel and choose Rasterize Layer, of go to Layer ➤ Smart Object ➤ Rasterize. Refer to Figure 14-15.

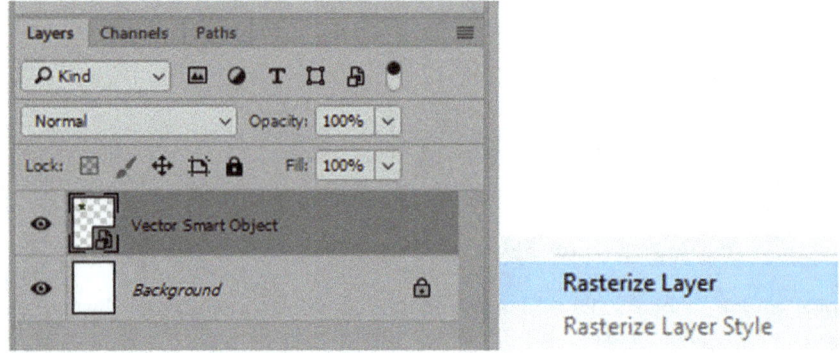

Figure 14-15. *Rasterize a smart object*

332

CHAPTER 14 ■ TOOLS FOR ANIMATION AND VIDEO

This causes the Smart Object to become pixilated, and you will no longer be able to scale it. Choose Edit ➤ Undo to undo the change right away.

■ **Note** You look at how to add Photoshop and Illustrator graphics to Adobe Animate CC in Part 4.

Puppet Warp Tool

The Puppet Warp tool creates parts of your animation for a program like Animate CC. It is found in the Web workspace in the Tools panel and is grouped with the Free Transform tool (E). Refer to Figure 14-16.

Figure 14-16. *Puppet Warp tool in the Tools panel*

It in many ways, when you click a shape (see pupper_warp_example.ai) it appears like the Gradient Mesh tool (U) for adding select gradients; however, the Puppet Warp tool creates a mesh when you click the pushpin cursor on it. You can temporarily manipulate parts of your shape, including the mesh, to bend and scale it, as seen in Figure 14-17.

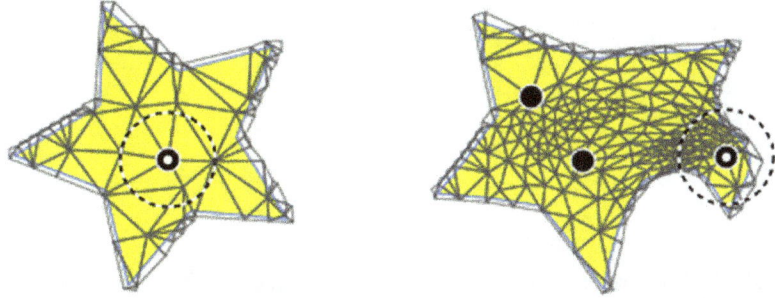

Figure 14-17. *A shape is altered with the Puppet Warp tool*

Adding three or more pins allows you to manipulate more areas. You can also rotate the pins to give a spin or a swirl to the shape.

333

The following are some other things that you can try.

- Shift-click the pins to select more than one pin, or choose Select All Pins from the Control panel. Refer to Figure 14-18.

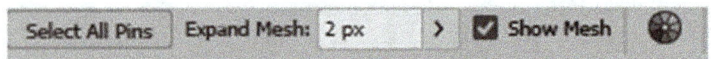

Figure 14-18. Setting for Puppet Warp tool in the Control panel

- To remove the selected pins, press the Delete key.
- To constrain the transformation of your artwork around the selected pin, press Alt while dragging it.
- When working with grouped objects, right-click the shape to undo the Puppet warp, or undo a newly added pin before you close the file. Refer to Figure 14-19.

Undo Puppet Warp	Undo Add Pin
Redo	Redo

Figure 14-19. Undo basic steps by right-clicking the puppet warped object while working on it

If you switch to Selection tool (V) in the Tools panel, and then back to the Puppet Warp tool, you can keep editing the shape; it retains the warp mesh. Refer to Figure 14-20.

Figure 14-20. Use the Selection tool (V) if you need to move your object that has been puppet warped and then continue working with the Puppet Warp tool

---

■ **Note** Make sure to save a copy of the original vector image within your file in the Symbols panel. The reason for doing this is, if you close and open the AI file, you cannot later undo the warps back to the original shape (even with a symbol on the artboard). This is why saving the shape as a symbol is important as you can always remove the symbol from the artboard and begin again with an unwarped symbol. Nevertheless when the file is opened and you select the symbol or shape, with the puppet warp tool, the shape of the warp is retained even if you delete the pins. You just can't revert back to the original shape of the symbol on the artboard. If you need to retain the original shape pre-warp for an animation a better option is to use Smart Objects in Photoshop, as you will see shortly.

CHAPTER 14 ■ TOOLS FOR ANIMATION AND VIDEO

With the Puppet Warp tool, you also have access to options in the Properties panel and Control panel. Refer to Figure 14-21.

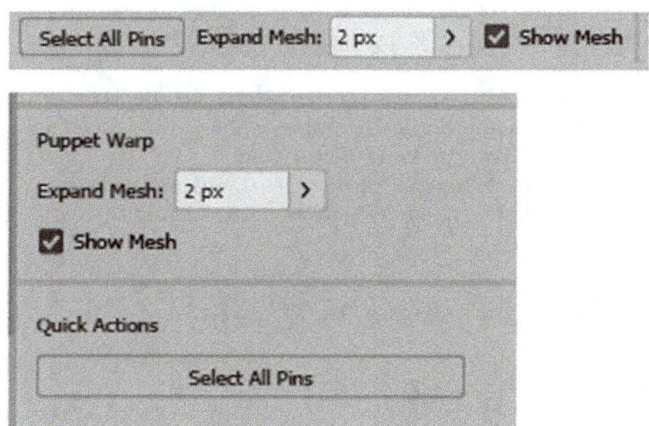

Figure 14-21. Puppet Warp tool settings found in the Control panel(upper) and Properties panel (lower)

- **Select All Pins:** Selects all the pins that you've plotted on the selected artwork.
- **Show Mesh:** Deselects to show only the adjustment pins, providing a clearer preview of your transformations.
- **Expand Mesh**: Adjust with the slider or enter a number to bring disjointed select objects together to transform them with the Puppet Warp tool, as seen in Figure 14-22.

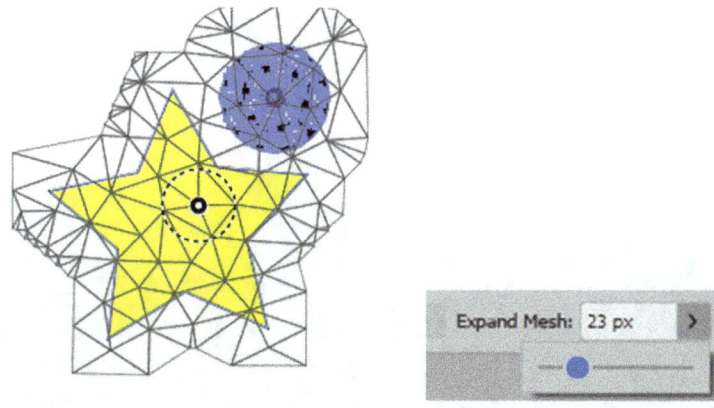

Figure 14-22. Expand the mesh so that you can adjust shapes together

■ **Note** Puppet warp does not work on shapes that have a gradient mesh applied.

335

Using Puppet Warp in Photoshop

Puppet warp in Illustrator is very similar to Edit ➤ Puppet Warp in Photoshop; it uses pins if you compare their Control panels; however, the warp used in Photoshop should be applied to Smart Objects that were either created in Photoshop or copied from Illustrator (refer to the "Copying Illustrations to Photoshop" section in this chapter).

Smart Object layers always work best with the puppet warp because you can always alter the layer. With regular rasterized layers, once the warp is created and applied with the Check icon in the Control panel, it cannot be undone, unless you go back in your steps in the History panel before saving.

As a vector Smart Object in Photoshop, it creates a smart filter that allows you to bend the shape or revert to the original if you later decide to delete the smart filter. Refer to Figure 14-23 and Figure 14-24.

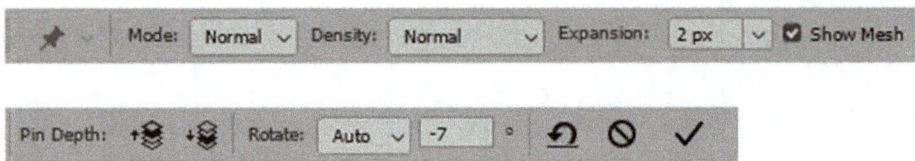

Figure 14-23. Edit ➤ Puppet Warp in Photoshop allows you to have access to similar features found in Illustrator, as seen in the Control panel

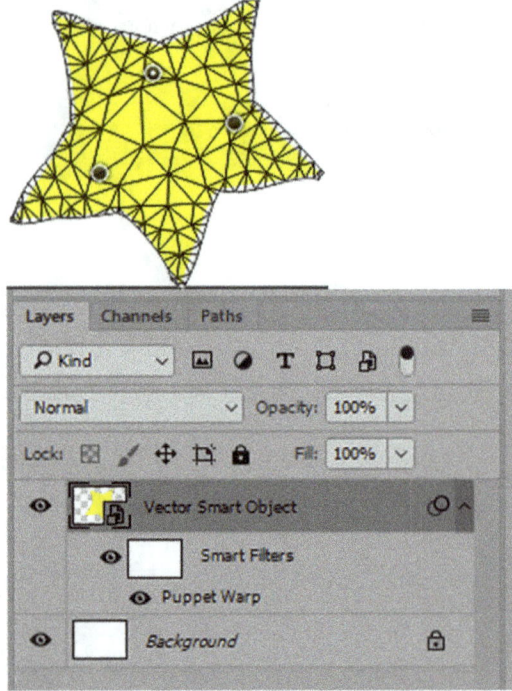

Figure 14-24. Using the smart filter in Photoshop for puppet warps allow you to revert to the original shape if you delete the filter

CHAPTER 14 ■ TOOLS FOR ANIMATION AND VIDEO

Rather than draw all of your movements by hand, the puppet warp is great tool if you need to create some Smart Objects that have a gradual shape change for your Photoshop or Animate Timeline Animation or in a video, frame by frame. Refer to Figure 14-25.

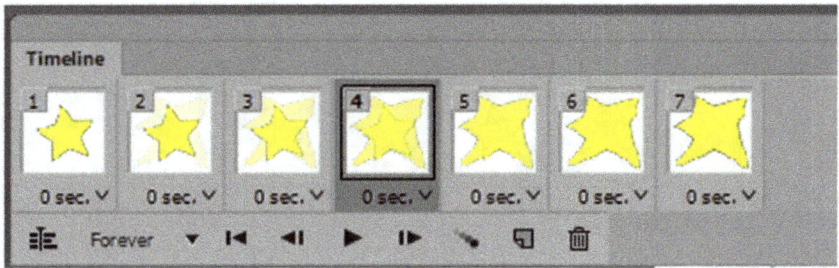

Figure 14-25. *In Photoshop, Smart Objects that have been warped with the Puppet tool can be used in a GIF animation*

For more information and examples on the Puppet Warp tool, visit the following.

- https://helpx.adobe.com/illustrator/using/puppet-warp.html
- https://helpx.adobe.com/illustrator/how-to/bend-shapes-warp-artwork.html

Tools for Video

Now let's discover what Illustrator CC has to offer for your video projects.

New Layout for Film and Video

While you can't create any videos in Illustrator CC as you would in Photoshop CC, Illustrator does allow you to create various document sizes and artboards at File ➤ New Film and the Video Layer tab. Refer to Figure 14-26.

CHAPTER 14 ■ TOOLS FOR ANIMATION AND VIDEO

Figure 14-26. *Illustrator allows you to set file sizes for illustrations that you might uses in a film or video*

Click Create to see the new layout.

You can use this layout to create single frames that could export as a JPEG and later used in Photoshop, Premiere Pro, or After Effects for various backgrounds or images for a scene. To view the video ruler, select View ➤ Rulers.

Adding 3D Images

Finally, I should mention Illustrator's ability to create basic 3D Shapes. You can add 3D effects to images in your frame by selecting Effects ➤ 3D to create some basic shapes that can be extruded, revolved, or rotated. There are also map art symbols for basic texture. Refer to 3D_example.ai and Figure 14-27.

CHAPTER 14 ■ TOOLS FOR ANIMATION AND VIDEO

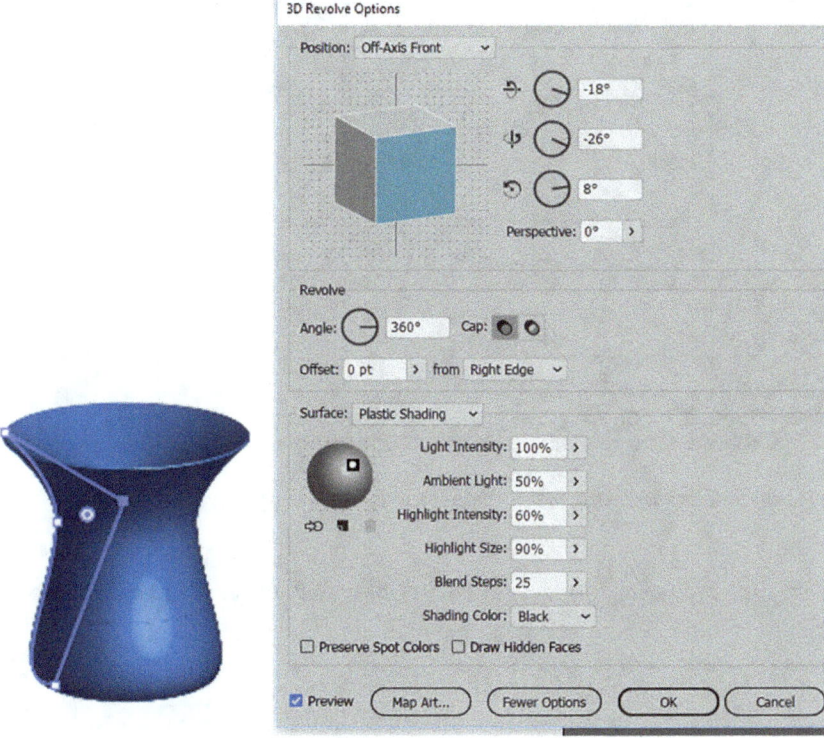

Figure 14-27. *Create a 3D rotated object for a video or animation*

You can continue to alter the shape after clicking OK. Use the Direct Selection tool (A) and the Appearance panel if you need to adjust to the original dialog box (in this case, 3D revolve). Refer to Figure 14-28.

CHAPTER 14 ■ TOOLS FOR ANIMATION AND VIDEO

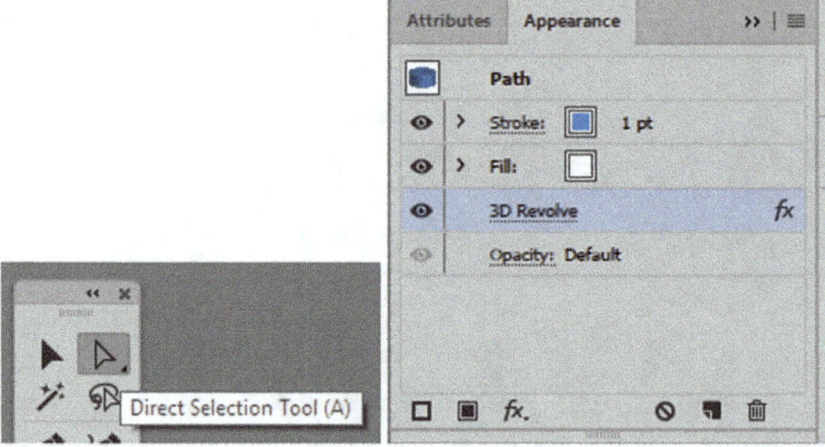

Figure 14-28. *The Direct Selection tool (A) and Appearance panel can be used to refine your 3D shape in Illustrator*

To make the object more realistic, you need to add it as a Smart Object in Photoshop and continue to style it there with other effects.

Summary

This chapter looked at some tools and panels that you can use for animation and video. You saw how SVG files can become interactive with JavaScript. You discovered that Smart Objects that come from Illustrator can be incorporated into animations and videos in Photoshop. In the next chapter, you take a quick look at a few miscellaneous tools in Illustrator that you can use for your web design projects.

CHAPTER 15

Other Miscellaneous Items in Illustrator That You Can Use for Web Design

In this chapter, you look at a few miscellaneous tools that might assist you in your web design project. Some are like the ones you saw in Photoshop in Chapter 8, and you can refer to those sections in that chapter for more details. One new feature that you will look at is Creating Swatch Patterns.

> **Note** This chapter does not have any actual projects; however, you can use the files in the Chapter 15 folder to practice opening and viewing for this lesson. They are at `https://github.com/Apress/graphics-multimedia-web-adobe-creative-cloud`.

Library CC

The Libraries panel is under the Window menu. Refer to Figure 15-1.

CHAPTER 15 ■ OTHER MISCELLANEOUS ITEMS IN ILLUSTRATOR THAT YOU CAN USE FOR WEB DESIGN

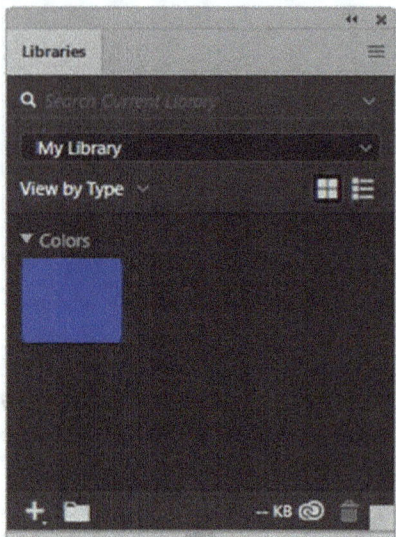

Figure 15-1. *The Libraries panel in Illustrator*

This panel was introduced with the Creative Cloud. In the library, you can store colors and images that you use in projects. You can then move over to a program like Photoshop or Dreamweaver, and the colors are stored there too, so that you can refer to them during your project.

Web Fonts and SVG Fonts

As in Photoshop, you have access to web fonts Adobe Fonts (Typekit) and SVG fonts. In Illustrator, there are at least four access points.

- The **Character panel**, as seen in Figure 15-2.

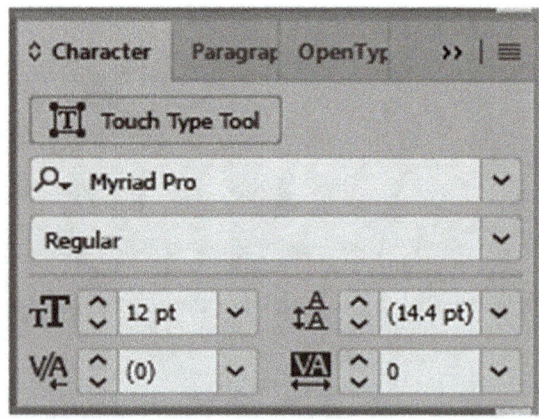

Figure 15-2. *Character panel where you have access to Adobe SVG fonts*

342

CHAPTER 15 ■ OTHER MISCELLANEOUS ITEMS IN ILLUSTRATOR THAT YOU CAN USE FOR WEB DESIGN

- The **Glyphs panel**, where you can view all the options and varieties of an SVG font. It's like having free clip art. Refer to Figure 15-3.

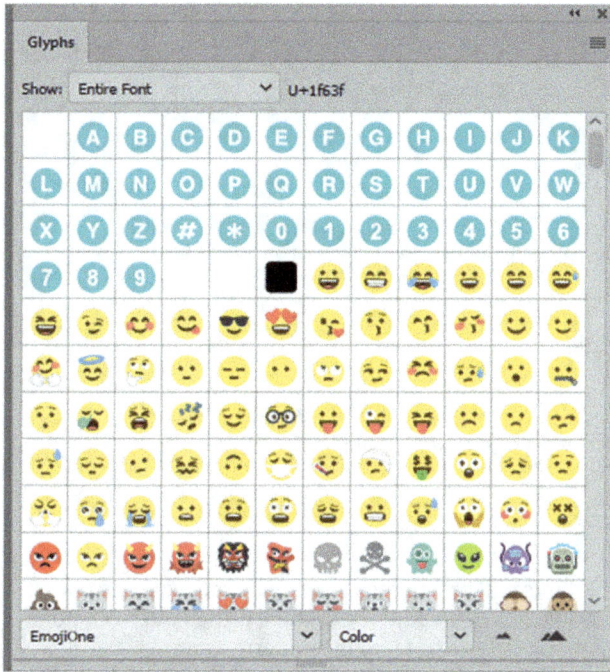

Figure 15-3. Glyphs where you have access to SVG fonts

- The **Control panel**, when the Type tool is selected. Refer to Figure 15-4. This area in CC 2019 was updated so that you can filter your current fonts and add new fonts from Adobe easily.

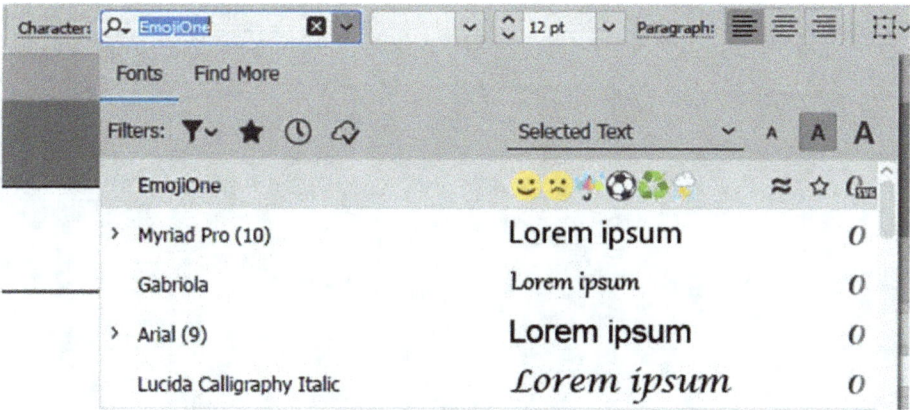

Figure 15-4. Control panel where you have access to SVG fonts and other Adobe Fonts

343

CHAPTER 15 ■ OTHER MISCELLANEOUS ITEMS IN ILLUSTRATOR THAT YOU CAN USE FOR WEB DESIGN

- The **Properties panel**, when the type tool is selected. Refer to Figure 15-5.

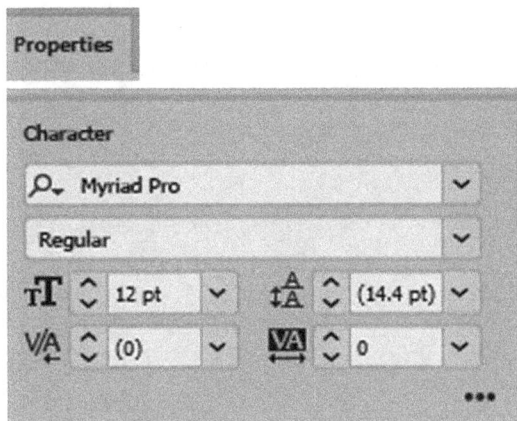

Figure 15-5. *Properties panel where you have access to SVG fonts and Typekit*

Creating Swatch Patterns

As you saw in Photoshop CC, you can use different filters and brushes to create repeating patterns for backgrounds. Whereas there are no filters or effects like this in Illustrator CC, there is the Pattern Options panel, which lets you design a pattern swatch from basic objects (refer to the pattern_example.ai file). Figure 15-6 shows the Pattern Options panel.

CHAPTER 15 ■ OTHER MISCELLANEOUS ITEMS IN ILLUSTRATOR THAT YOU CAN USE FOR WEB DESIGN

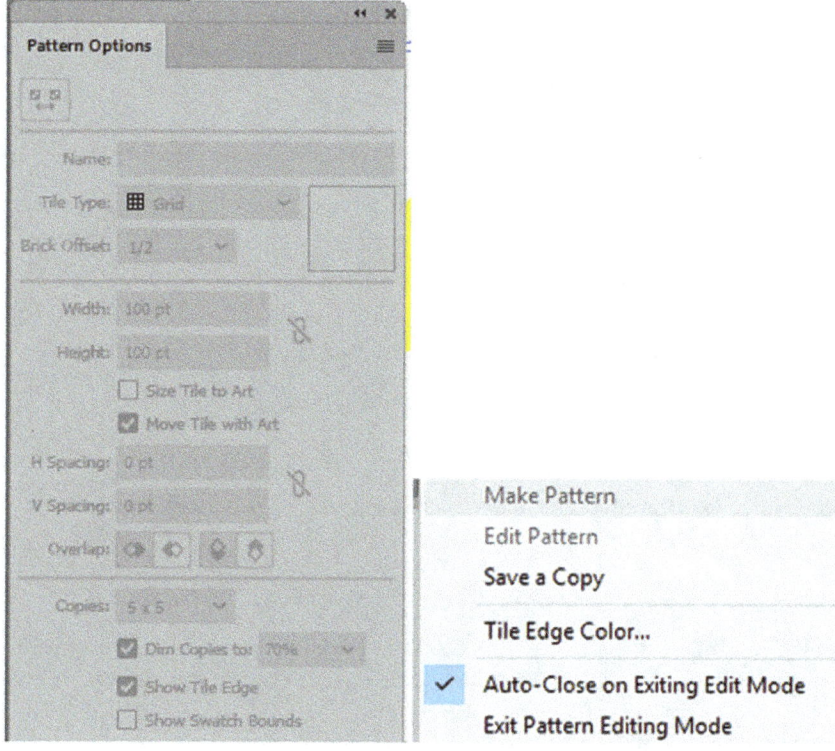

Figure 15-6. *The Pattern Options panel in the inactive state and its menu*

When no object or object group on the artboard is selected, the Pattern Options panel remains unavailable until you select vector objects (see Figure 15-8) with the Selection Tool (V) and choose Object ➤ Pattern ➤ Make from the main menu.

At this point, you get a message that the new pattern has been added to the swatch panel. Refer to Figure 15-7.

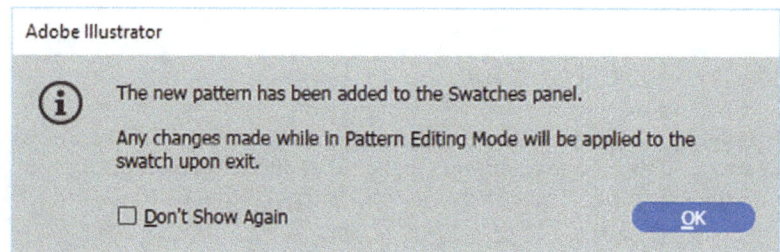

Figure 15-7. *A new pattern has been added to the Swatches panel*

345

CHAPTER 15 ■ OTHER MISCELLANEOUS ITEMS IN ILLUSTRATOR THAT YOU CAN USE FOR WEB DESIGN

Click OK. A new pattern will appear, as seen in Figure 15-8.

Figure 15-8. *A new pattern appears in preview*

The new pattern has been added to the Swatches panel, as seen in Figure 15-9, where you can see it in its base state.

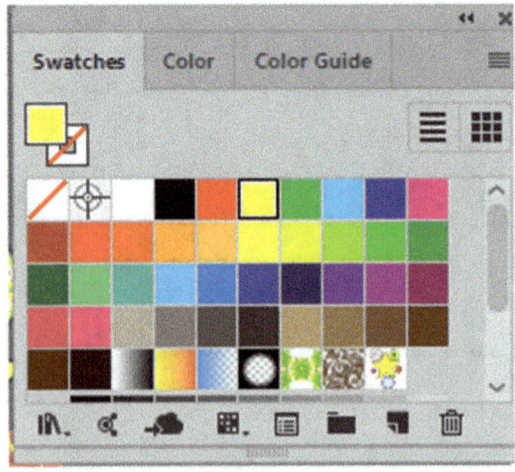

Figure 15-9. *The pattern in the Swatches panel in the lower right*

At this point, however, it is not yet a finished pattern. You need to start editing it in the panel.
You will know that you are in pattern-editing mode when you see the New Pattern icon in the upper-right corner of your artboard; your Layers panel reflects this, as well. Refer to Figure 15-10.

CHAPTER 15 ■ OTHER MISCELLANEOUS ITEMS IN ILLUSTRATOR THAT YOU CAN USE FOR WEB DESIGN

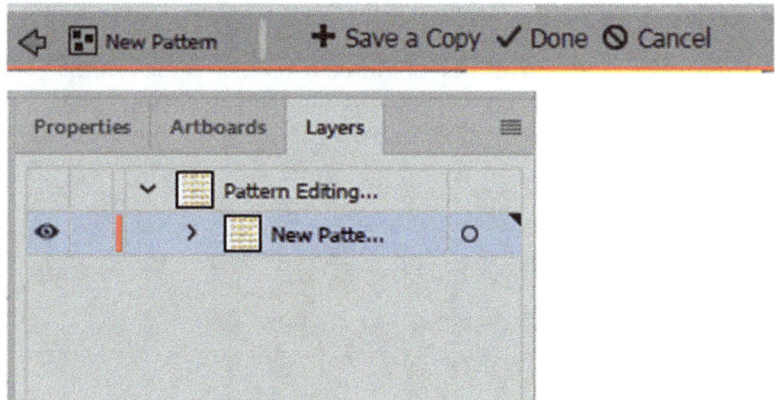

Figure 15-10. The artboard and the Layers panel inform you that you are in pattern-editing mode

You can save a copy of the pattern, or work on the original. When finished, click Done to confirm your pattern in the swatch, or click Cancel to exit and not create a pattern at all. For now, you will stay in pattern-editing mode.

At this point, the panel is available. Refer to Figure 15-11 for the next steps.

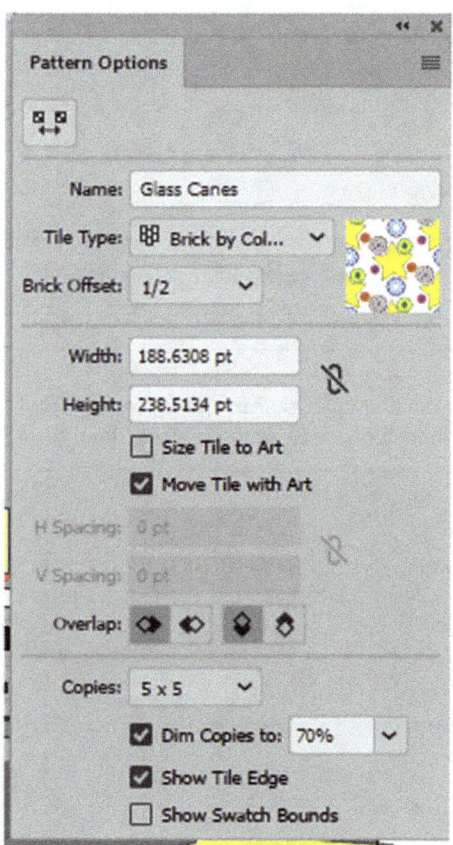

Figure 15-11. The Pattern Options panel while in pattern-editing mode

347

CHAPTER 15 ■ OTHER MISCELLANEOUS ITEMS IN ILLUSTRATOR THAT YOU CAN USE FOR WEB DESIGN

Start by giving the pattern a new name so that you can identify it in the Swatches panel. I called mine Glass Canes.

The first icon in the upper left of the panel is the Pattern Tile tool. You can click this button to turn the tile on or off so that you can drag, scale, and adjust the starting shape distance from other repeating shapes by using the handles. When you are done, turn it off so that you can make other adjustments. Refer to Figure 15-12.

Figure 15-12. Bring the grouped objects in closer using the pattern tile tool

---

■ **Note** To undo this move right away, chose Edit ➤ Undo if you need to revert backward. Holding the Shift key scales the spacing proportionately.

After the name change, the next alteration that you can set is the tile type. You can choose from several different grids or arrangements that adjust how the shapes fit together. I chose Brick by Column. Refer to Figure 15-13.

CHAPTER 15 ■ OTHER MISCELLANEOUS ITEMS IN ILLUSTRATOR THAT YOU CAN USE FOR WEB DESIGN

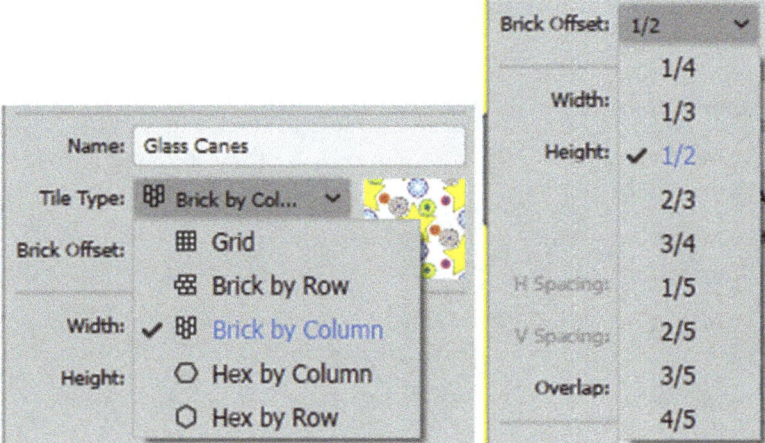

Figure 15-13. Choose Tile Type and Brick Offset

- **Grid**: The default. It provides evenly spaced squares; however, it does not make for a very compact pattern.

- **Brick by Row and Brick by Column**: Has a square tile and allows you to adjust the Brick Offset by degrees. The tiles are shifted vertically or horizontally, depending on what option you choose.

- **Hex by Column** and **Hex by Row**: Hexagonal tiles; it is the most compact of the patterns; however, you don't have access to Brick Offset.

- **Brick Offset** tiles are shifted either vertically or horizontally, depending on what option you chose in Tile Type. (I chose the 1/2 setting.)

- **Width** and **Height** are the same as the Pattern Tile Tool icon, except you can enter a number rather than using the handles. Clicking the Lock Icon lets you scale proportionately. This area is only accessible when the Size Tile to Art is unchecked. Refer to Figure 15-14.

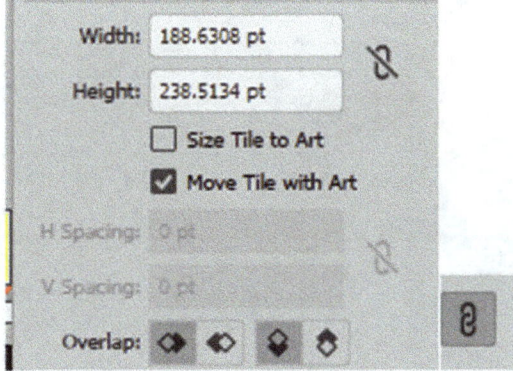

Figure 15-14. Setting the width and height of the pattern in points

349

CHAPTER 15 ▪ OTHER MISCELLANEOUS ITEMS IN ILLUSTRATOR THAT YOU CAN USE FOR WEB DESIGN

If you made a mistake when entering the width or height, and you want to revert, click Size to Tile Art, which resets the spacing. Refer to Figure 15-15.

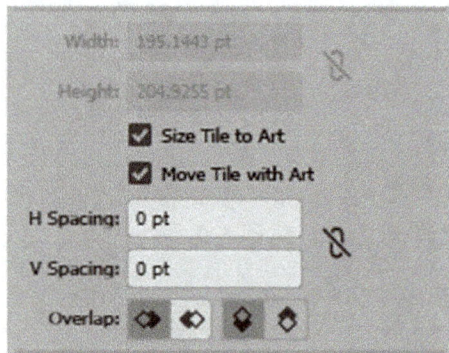

Figure 15-15. *Setting the H Spacing and V Spacing of the pattern in points*

- When **Size Tile to Art** is checked, you can use H Spacing or V Spacing, which add or remove spacing between each shape in the pattern. A positive number spreads the space, while a negative number shrinks the space. You can also link the spacing so that it is proportionate as you scale up or down.

- **Move Tile with Art** allows you to move the preview pattern tile with the art; if unchecked, the tile can be moved separately from the art. Refer to Figure 15-16. To undo, select Edit ➤ Undo right away.

Figure 15-16. *Move the preview tile separate from the art*

350

CHAPTER 15 ■ OTHER MISCELLANEOUS ITEMS IN ILLUSTRATOR THAT YOU CAN USE FOR WEB DESIGN

- **Overlap** is how the shape overlaps when they are compressed together. Refer to Figure 15-17.

Figure 15-17. *The Overlap pattern settings*

Overlap pattern settings can be

- left in front
- right in front
- top in front
- bottom in front

■ **Note** This type of overlapping may not be evident unless the shapes are touching.

- **Copies** has to do with preview or the number of copies that are on the screen while you edit the pattern. This does not affect the final pattern layout. The default is 5×5, but you can set it to any number of copies from the pop-up list, as seen in Figure 15-18.

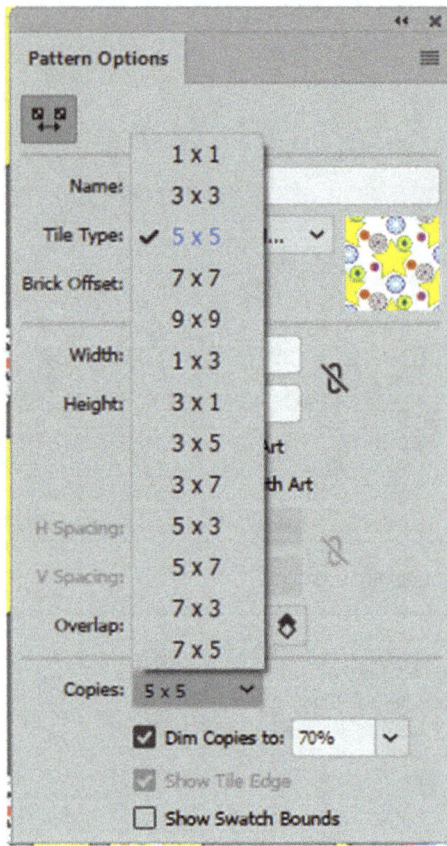

Figure 15-18. *Number of copies you can preview while in Pattern Editing mode*

- **Dim Copies to** allows you to dim the preview pattern so that you can distinguish it from the original shape. The range is 0%–100% and does not affect the final pattern outcome.

- **Show Tile Edge** lets you turn on or off the tile so that you can preview the pattern as one unit.

- **Show Swatch Bounds** shows which areas will or will not be repeated. Anything outside the bounds is not repeated, except in this preview. Along with the tile, the swatch bounds are saved as a transparent box guide within the pattern swatch.

Once the pattern is complete or closed, click Done to confirm. Then you can apply your pattern to an object on the artboard. Refer to Figure 15-19.

CHAPTER 15 ■ OTHER MISCELLANEOUS ITEMS IN ILLUSTRATOR THAT YOU CAN USE FOR WEB DESIGN

Figure 15-19. *Apply the pattern to an object or vector shape*

You can alter the pattern at Object ➤ Pattern ➤ Edit Pattern when you have the pattern swatch selected in the Swatches panel. Refer to Figure 15-20.

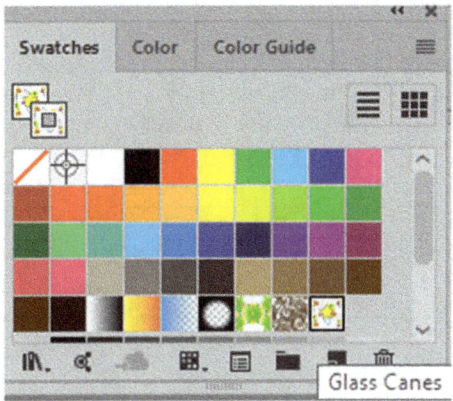

Figure 15-20. *Only when the swatch is selected can you edit the pattern*

■ **Note** Object ➤ Pattern ➤ Tile Edge Color refers to the color of the guide that appears when you are previewing the pattern. Refer to Figure 15-21.

353

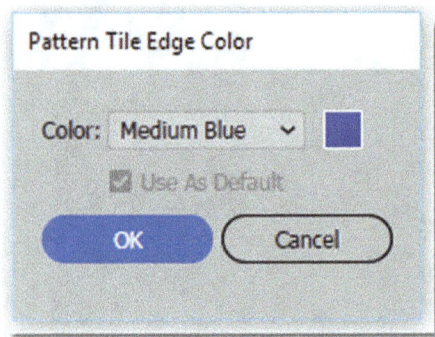

Figure 15-21. *Change Pattern Tile Edge color if blue is difficult to see for your pattern*

■ **Note** The default is blue, but you can change it to another color if you find it hard to see or it clashes with your pattern.

Once you have completed the pattern, you can add the pattern to a box shape of a specific size and export it as a GIF, JPEG, or PNG for your background. Or, as you did in Chapter 14, you can copy it as a Smart Object into Photoshop and do further editing or cropping there. The final image pattern, used in combination with CSS, allows you to make a background pattern in Dreamweaver CC. You look at how to add background patterns in Dreamweaver in Part 6 of this book.

■ **Note** If you do not want patterns to scale with the shape, in the Transform panel, choose Transform Object Only. Currently, it is set to Transform Both. Refer to Figure 15-22.

CHAPTER 15 ■ OTHER MISCELLANEOUS ITEMS IN ILLUSTRATOR THAT YOU CAN USE FOR WEB DESIGN

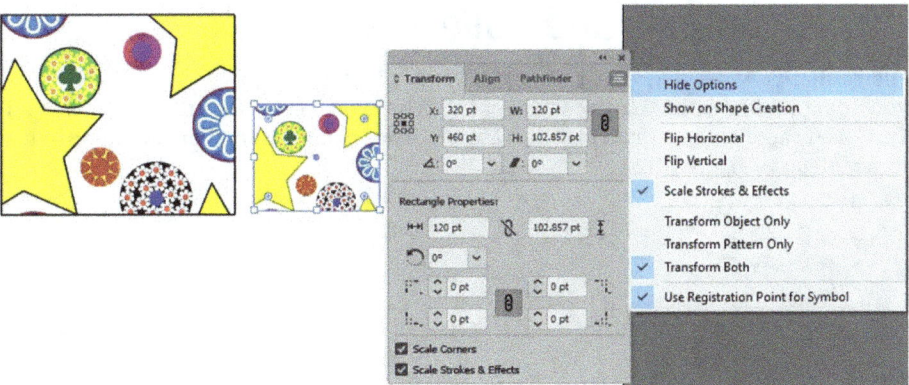

Figure 15-22. *Choose how the pattern will be transformed inside the object*

If you only want to transform the pattern, choose Transform Pattern Only; however, you may get a warning on the Transform panel about what the transformation will affect. To remove it, click the warning, which reverts the setting to Transform Both. Refer to Figure 15-23.

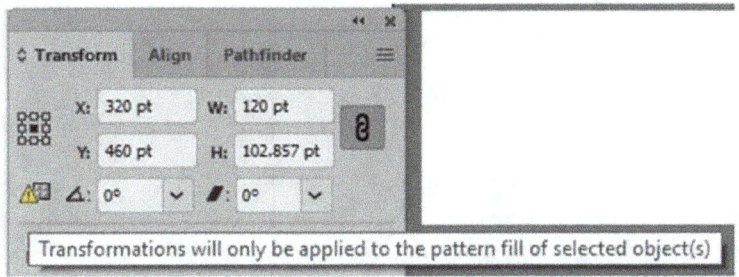

Figure 15-23. *Warning that appears if you only want to transform the pattern of an object*

These options allow you to scale your shape separately from the pattern swatch so that one or the other will not enlarge at the same time as you scale either the object or the pattern.

As you can see, you can create many unusual patterns in Illustrator for your next website project.

355

CHAPTER 15 ■ OTHER MISCELLANEOUS ITEMS IN ILLUSTRATOR THAT YOU CAN USE FOR WEB DESIGN

Graphic Styles for Buttons and Rollovers

Like Photoshop CC, Illustrator has styles that you can apply to buttons for the web.

In Chapter 11, you briefly looked at the Graphic Styles panel. When you create custom swatches and fill in the Appearance panel, you can then drag them into the Graphic Styles panel to save them in the current file or in their own library. Refer to Figure 15-24.

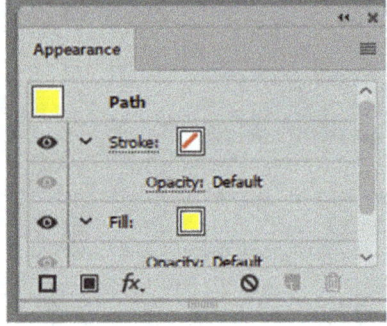

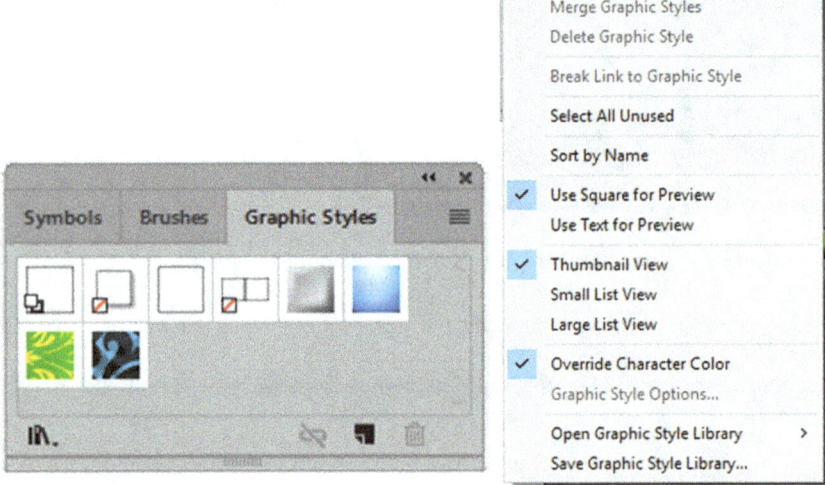

Figure 15-24. *The Appearance panel and Graphic Styles panel, where you can save your new styles*

In the Library icon (in the lower left of the panel), you can choose the Buttons and Rollovers panel. This opens those styles; you can add them to your current Graphic Styles panel by dragging them in or applying them to an object, such as a button, while it is selected (see Figure 15-25).

CHAPTER 15 ■ OTHER MISCELLANEOUS ITEMS IN ILLUSTRATOR THAT YOU CAN USE FOR WEB DESIGN

Figure 15-25. Add a graphic style to an object

Symbols Panel for Web Symbol Creation

Once an object has graphic styles applied, it can be stored in a library called the Symbols panel, which has many clip art symbols that you can use on your website. Refer to Figure 15-26.

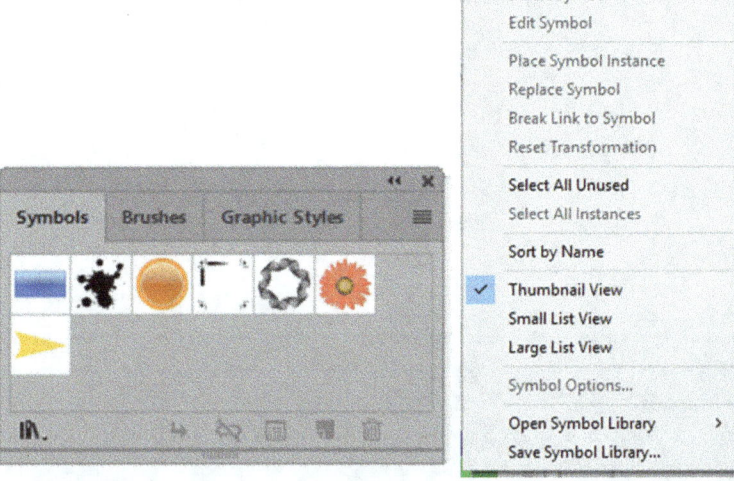

Figure 15-26. Add symbols to your Symbols panel

The following are some useful icons that you can access from the Library panel (see Figure 15-27):

- Mobile
- Web Buttons and Bars
- Web Icons

357

CHAPTER 15 ■ OTHER MISCELLANEOUS ITEMS IN ILLUSTRATOR THAT YOU CAN USE FOR WEB DESIGN

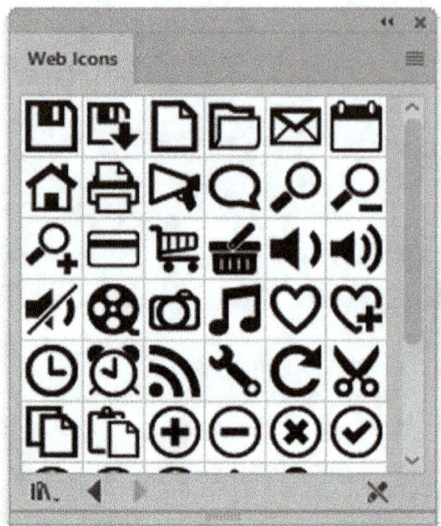

Figure 15-27. *Access some of the symbols found in the symbols library for web design*

Like the Graphic Styles panel, the Symbols panel allows you to add and remove your own custom symbols from selected objects on the artboard and to create your own library of icons. You can drag these symbols onto your board so that you do not have to create them again if you are building a website layout. Figure 15-28 shows the dialog box that appears when you add and name a new symbol. In Animate CC, you can decide if the export type is a movie clip or a graphic, but this makes no difference in Illustrator.

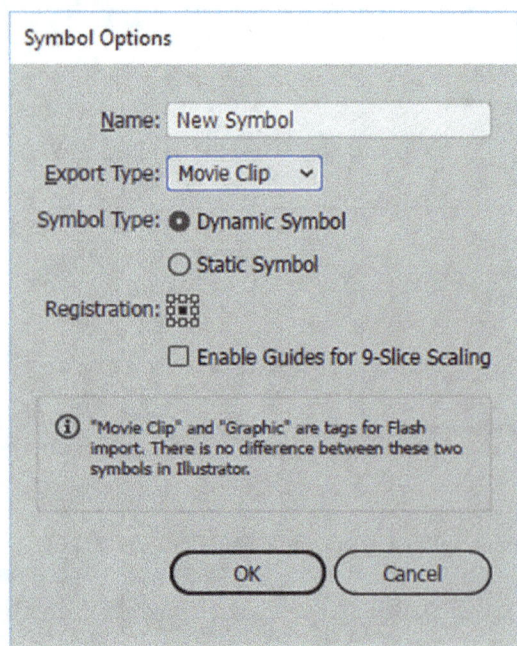

Figure 15-28. *Symbol Options dialog box. Note that the tip is referring to when importing into Animate.*

358

CHAPTER 15 ■ OTHER MISCELLANEOUS ITEMS IN ILLUSTRATOR THAT YOU CAN USE FOR WEB DESIGN

You can also choose a dynamic or static symbol, set the registration point, and enable guides for nine-slice scaling.

Double-clicking a symbol in the Symbol panel allows you to edit it in Symbol Editing mode, which is reflected in the Layers panel.

To exit, click the arrow in the upper left of the artboard. Refer to Figure 15-29.

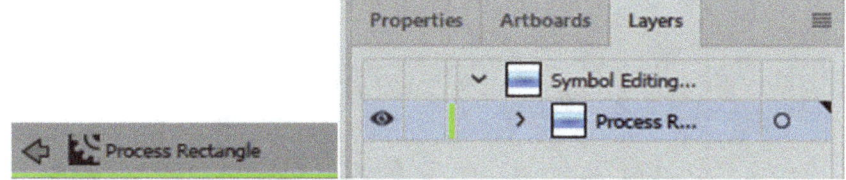

Figure 15-29. *Symbol Editing mode as seen on the artboard and Layers panel*

Only dynamic symbols appear with a plus beside them, as seen in Figure 15-30. If you need to unlink them, choose the Break Link to Symbol icon, also seen in Figure 15-30.

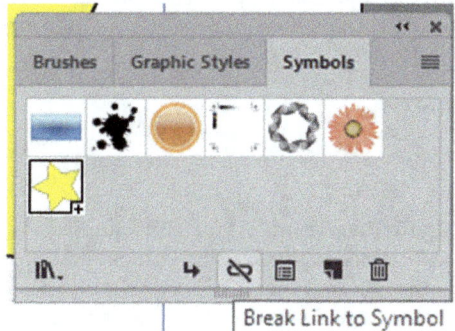

Figure 15-30. *To break a symbol, whether static or dynamic, from the Symbols panel choose the Break Link to Symbol icon*

This breaks the link with the symbol; the artboard object is no longer linked to the symbol.

For more information on symbols and dynamic features, refer to https://helpx.adobe.com/illustrator/using/symbols.html.

Color Blindness Proofs

There is a feature that most people might not know exists in Illustrator, but it has been around for several versions. If you want more information on color blindness proofs, refer to Chapter 8, which has settings for protanopia (red loss) and deuteranopia (green loss) that are similar to the ones in Illustrator. To find the settings, go to View ➤ Proof Setup. Refer to Figure 15-31.

359

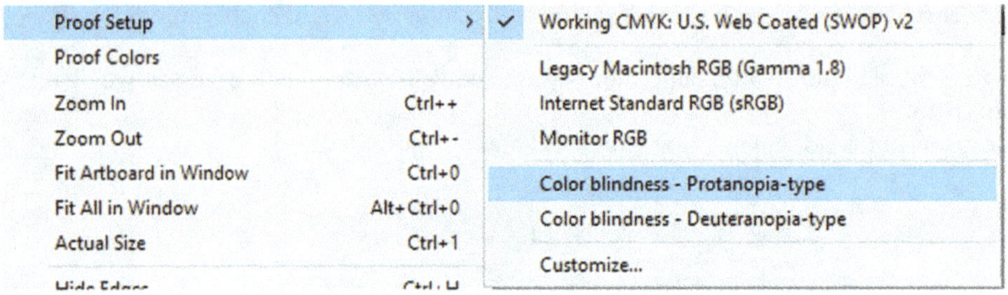

CHAPTER 15 ■ OTHER MISCELLANEOUS ITEMS IN ILLUSTRATOR THAT YOU CAN USE FOR WEB DESIGN

Figure 15-31. Access color blindness proofs if you need to check your colors

To return to normal settlings, choose View ➤ Proof Setup and choose the Working Proof; it can be RGB or CMYK, depending on the file that you have open.

■ **Note** Tritanopia (blue loss) and monochromacy (all color loss) are not very common among people with color blindness, so you won't find a proof for them here. If you need to check this type of proof, I recommend bringing the graphic as a Smart Object into Photoshop and use one of the adjustment layers, as shown in Chapter 8.

Summary

In this chapter, you looked at a few miscellaneous features in Illustrator that can assist you with your next web design project. Swatch Patterns are one of the best features, and I encourage you to experiment and create your own custom patterns.

In the last chapter of Part 3, you are going to put some of the knowledge that you learned into practice as you continue to work on the graphics for the Hot Glass Tango site.

CHAPTER 16

∎ ∎ ∎

Putting It into Practice with Illustrator CC

In this chapter, you review exporting images for a webpage site, and you look at a few more scripts to add to an SVG file to create an informational map.

> **Note** This chapter has actual projects that are in two folders. You can use the files in the Chapter 16 folder to practice opening and viewing for this lesson. They are at `https://github.com/Apress/graphics-multimedia-web-adobe-creative-cloud`.

In this chapter you will be export some images for a website known as Hot Glass Tango, which tells the story (through images, animation, video, and audio) of how handmade glass items are created. The multimedia items that you create in this chapter will be used to finish the final website in Part 6.

Exporting Images for an Instructional Webpage

The images that you are going to export for this project are in the domes.ai file. In Part 6, you are going to create a how-to page for the Hot Glass Tango website on creating a half-dome glass paperweight. When you open the file, you see the step-by-step illustrations on their own layers. Refer to Figure 16-1.

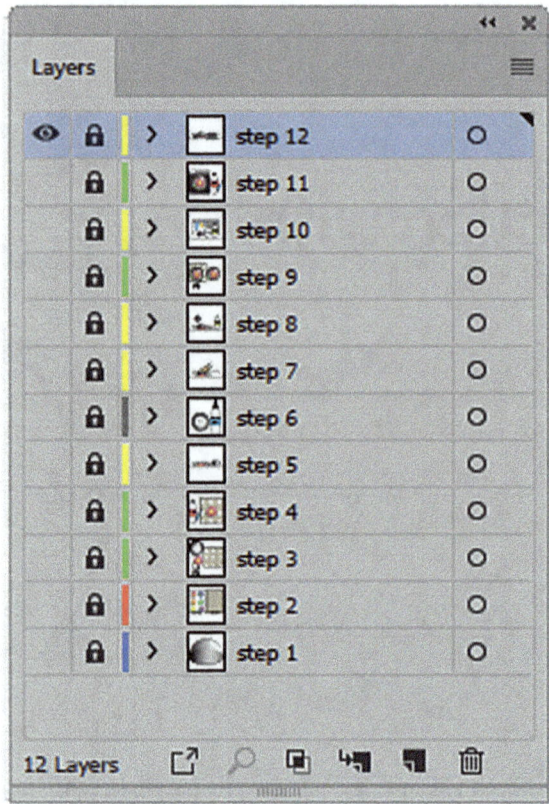

Figure 16-1. A layer for each step in the how-to project in the Layers panel

If you are designing a multistep illustration project, you may find this an effective way to keep all of your illustrations organized in one location rather than in multiple files. As I completed drawing each step, I locked the layer and turned off the visibility. The only layer that is visible is step 12, as seen in Figure 16-1 and Figure 16-2.

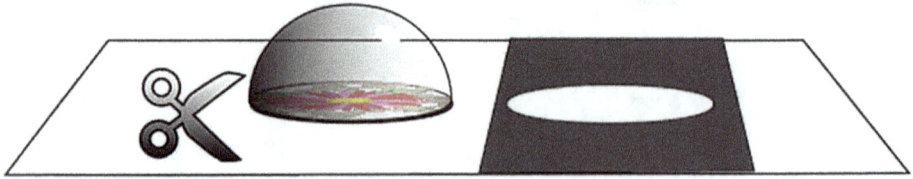

Figure 16-2. Step 12 is the visible layer on the artboard

Now I want to export each layer as a transparent GIF image.

The only way that you can create a GIF image in Illustrator is to use File ➤ Export ➤ Save for Web (Legacy). If you are going to create PNG or JPG files, use the Asset Export panel, as discussed in Chapter 12.

At this point, you could choose File ➤ Export ➤ Save for Web (Legacy) or instead use the prebuilt action found in the Actions panel (see Chapter 13) called Save For Web GIF 64 Dither. This might be too low res, so let's create a similar action, but with a slightly different setting. Refer to Figure 16-3.

CHAPTER 16 ■ PUTTING IT INTO PRACTICE WITH ILLUSTRATOR CC

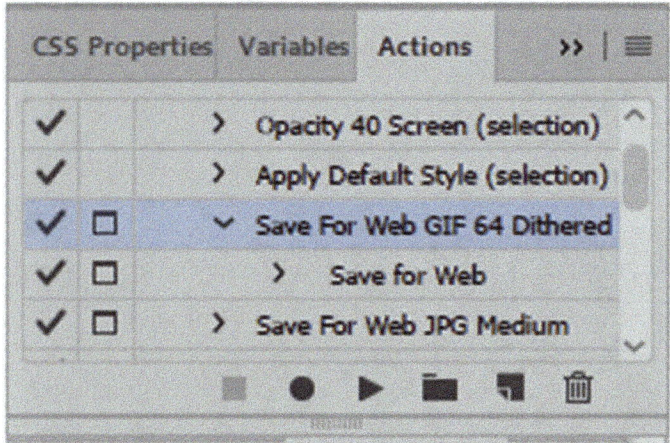

Figure 16-3. The prebuilt action maybe too low res, so you may need to create a custom action

Create a Custom Action

In your Actions panel, create a new action set called Save GIF Files, as seen in Figure 16-4.

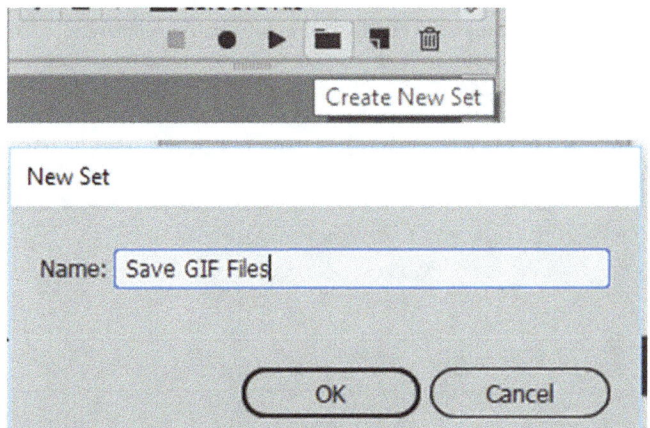

Figure 16-4. Create a new action set

Click OK to confirm, and it is added to the Actions panel.
In the folder set you just created, create a new action called GIF Selective Diffusion 256. Refer to Figure 16-5.

363

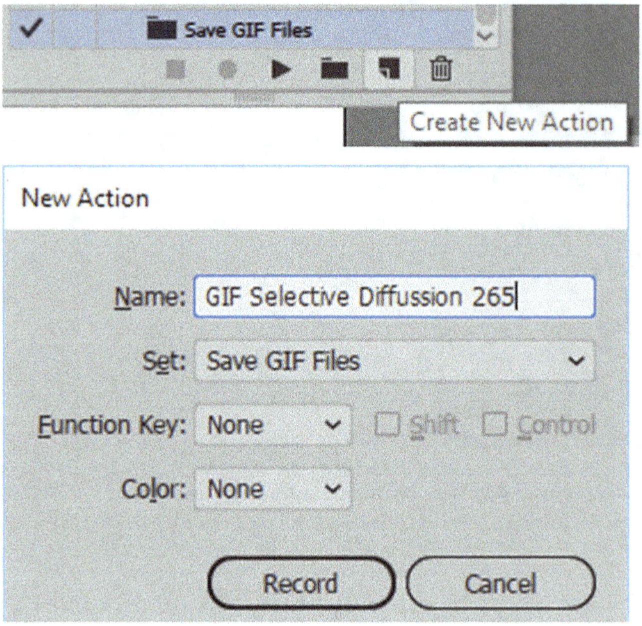

CHAPTER 16 ■ PUTTING IT INTO PRACTICE WITH ILLUSTRATOR CC

Figure 16-5. Create a new action for your GIF files

This should allow you to keep all the gradients looking clean and crisp and allow for transparency. This is a good option should you want to change the background in your website to another color later and not have a white box around your illustrations.

Click Record to start the action.

While recording in the Actions panel, go to File ➤ Export ➤ Save for Web. Refer to Figure 16-6.

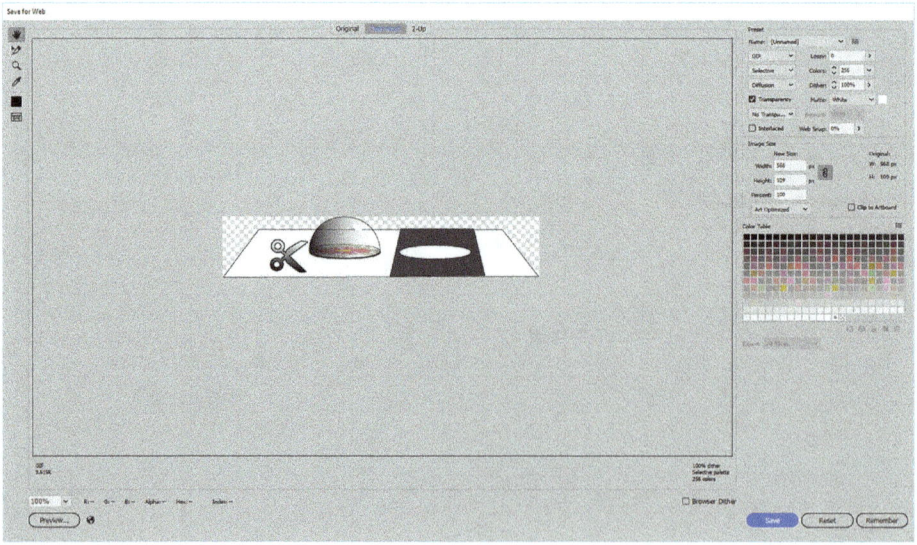

Figure 16-6. The image in the Save for Web (Legacy) dialog box

364

CHAPTER 16 ■ PUTTING IT INTO PRACTICE WITH ILLUSTRATOR CC

Set your settings as shown in Figure 16-7.

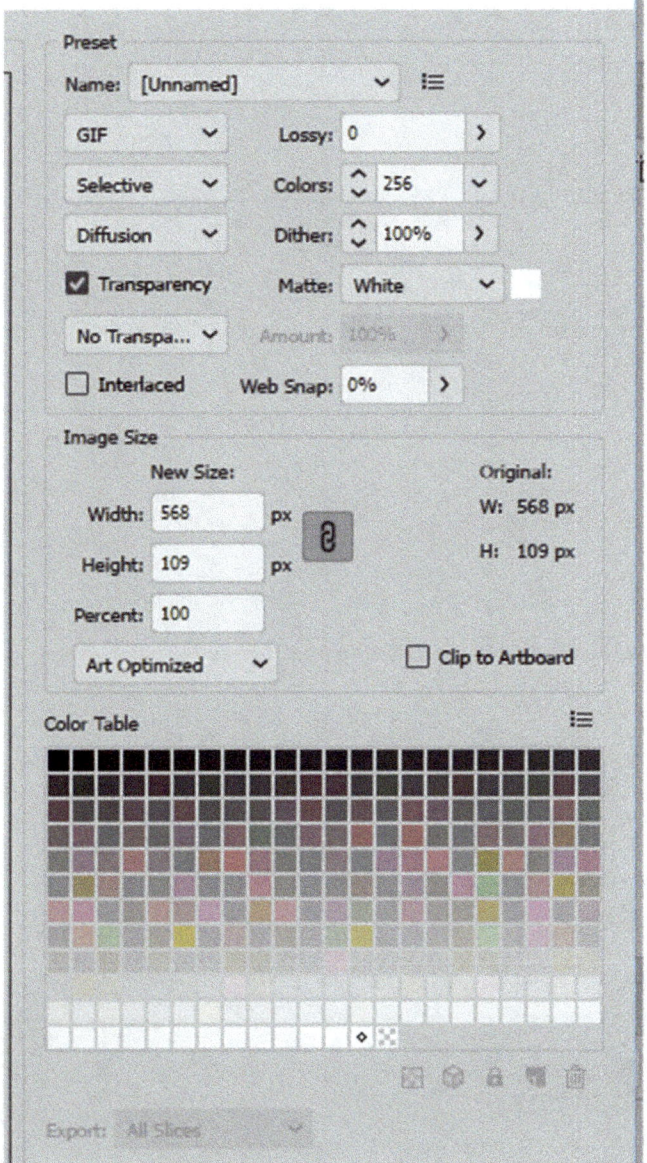

Figure 16-7. *GIF settings in the Save for Web (Legacy) dialog box*

- GIF Lossy: 0
- Selective Colors: 256
- Diffusion Dither: 100%
- Check: Transparency Matte: White

365

CHAPTER 16 PUTTING IT INTO PRACTICE WITH ILLUSTRATOR CC

- No Transparency Dither
- Uncheck: Interlaced
- Web Snap: 0%
- Leave Width and Height at the default
- Choose Art Optimized
- Clip to Artboard: uncheck

When done, save your first image (step12.gif) to your website's Images folder or whatever folder you choose. Refer to Figure 16-8.

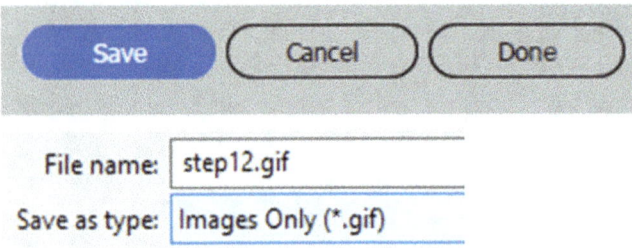

Figure 16-8. *Save your GIF file in a folder*

Once the Save for Web (Legacy) dialog box closes, click the Stop button on your Actions panel to stop the action. Refer to Figure 16-9.

Figure 16-9. *Stop recording your actions in the Actions panel*

You have now completed the action. Make sure that the Toggle dialog icon is on in the action so that the window will open.

Now you can go back to the Layers panel; this time, make step 11 visible so that you can export it next. Make sure to turn off the step 12 layer visibility because you do not need to export it again. Refer to Figure 16-10.

CHAPTER 16 ■ PUTTING IT INTO PRACTICE WITH ILLUSTRATOR CC

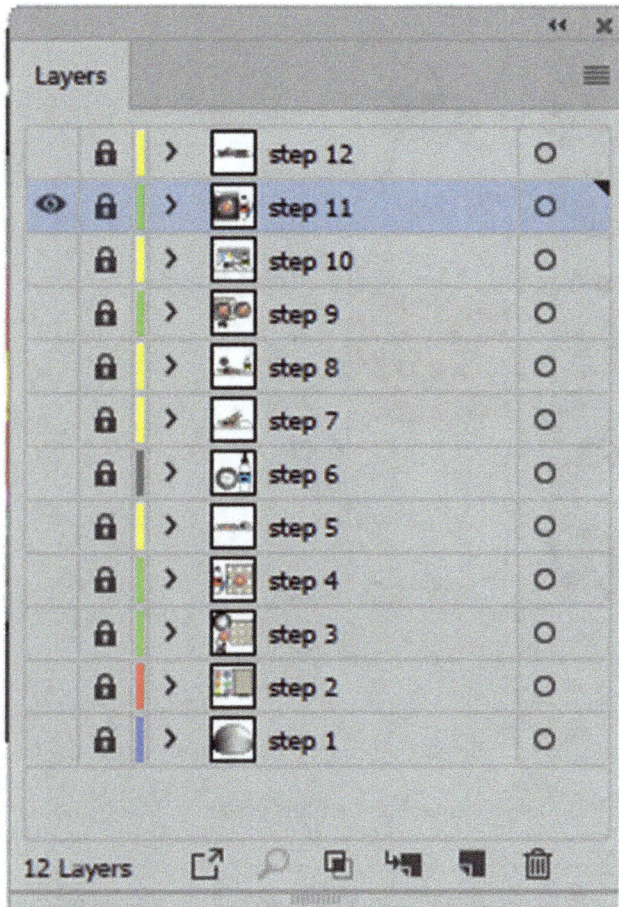

Figure 16-10. *Turn on the next layer's visibility in the Actions panel so that you can export only its artwork*

With the new layer selected, return to your Actions panel and play the GIF Selective Diffusion 256 action again.

This time, when the Save for Web (Legacy) dialog box opens, it sizes the GIF width and height to the new illustration. Refer to Figure 16-11.

367

CHAPTER 16 ■ PUTTING IT INTO PRACTICE WITH ILLUSTRATOR CC

Figure 16-11. *How the preview of the gif image appears om the Save for Web dialog box*

Click the Save button and save step11.gif in your folder.

Repeat these steps for the remaining 10 images. You should have 12 images in total that you can use for your website.

You can close the AI file without saving changes. You have completed the first project.

■ **Note** In Part 6, examples these gif files may have slightly different names, but you can always rename the file that you create in this lesson to match mine later.

Next, you look at how to create an informational map using SVG.

Exporting an SVG File

In Chapter 14, you looked at SVG interactivity to create a vase that changed color when your mouse hovered over it, and an alert message appeared when the vase was clicked. In Chapter 13, you took a brief look at image maps and saw how a shape can open a link. With SVG interactivity, you can create an informational image map so that when you hover over part of an illustration or shape, a message appears. Look at the map_test.ai file in the SVG folder. Then open the map_test.svg file in your browser and see how it interacts. Refer to Figure 16-12.

CHAPTER 16 ■ PUTTING IT INTO PRACTICE WITH ILLUSTRATOR CC

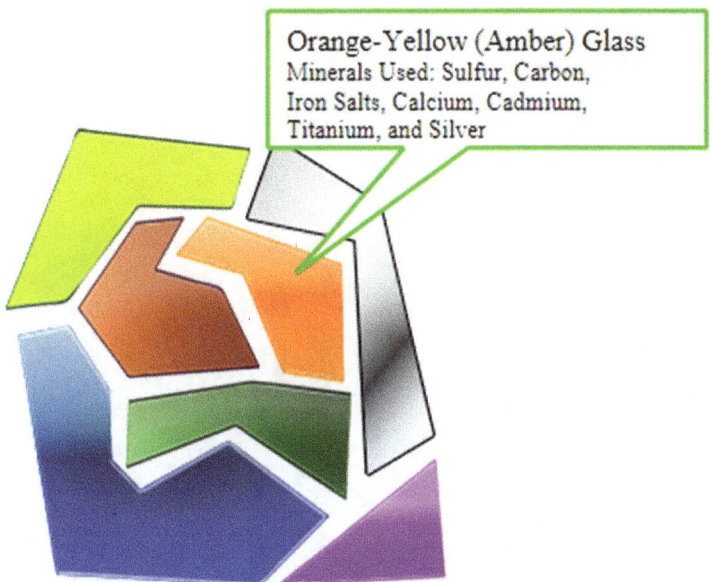

Figure 16-12. *When you hover over the broken glass shapes, you can determine what each piece is made of*

When you hover over each colored shape of glass, you discover what that color is composed of. This technique could be very useful for a project where you want information in distinct parts of a map to guide people, or parts of an organ, like an ear, or to dissect a flower. There are many possibilities.

In map_test.ai, I created 14 sublayers and named them. Seven of them are the broken glass shapes and the other seven are the grouped text messages that will be linked to the glass shapes; one for each. Refer to the Layers panel and Figures 16-13 and 16-14.

CHAPTER 16 ■ PUTTING IT INTO PRACTICE WITH ILLUSTRATOR CC

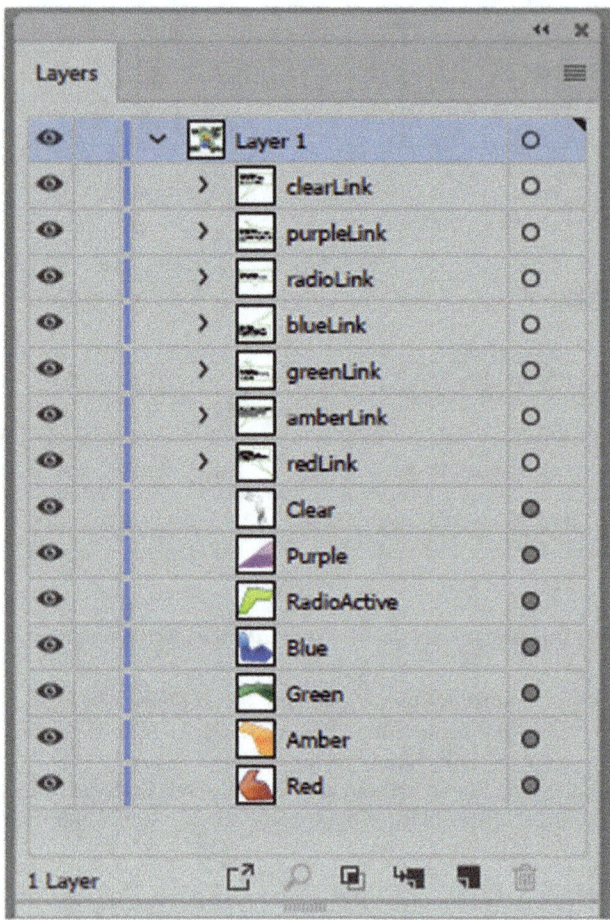

Figure 16-13. *The Layers panel with each sublayer named and organized*

Figure 16-14 looks rather cluttered on the artboard, but we will change that shortly.

370

CHAPTER 16 ■ PUTTING IT INTO PRACTICE WITH ILLUSTRATOR CC

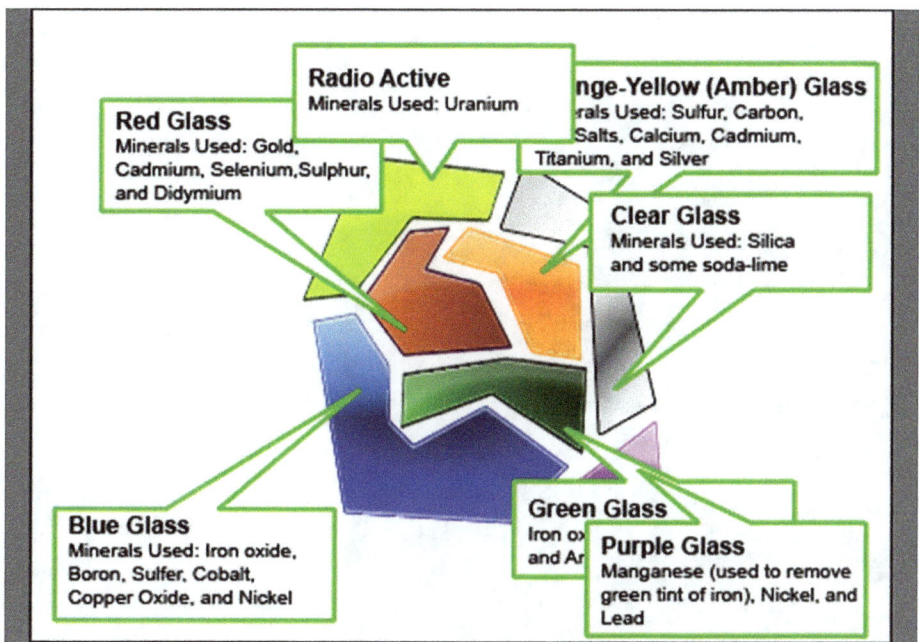

Figure 16-14. *How the sublayers currently appear on the artboard*

I gave my layers and sublayers one-word names, and I made sure that I knew which text link went with which colored glass piece. When you choose longer names, you can write them with letters and numbers (e.g., object1, object2) or with what scripters call camel code (e.g., redLink, greenLink), in which one letter is capitalized so that you see a break in the word. Do not use dashes (-), underscores (_), or spaces in your names because this causes the SVG interactivity links to fail.

Once you have reviewed the file, leave the layers as you see them in Figure 16-13. Next, choose File ➤ Save As or File ➤ Save A Copy (if you want the original file to remain open while working on the SVG file) and save as an SVG. Save your file as map_test2.svg so that you do not overwrite my example. Refer to Figure 16-15.

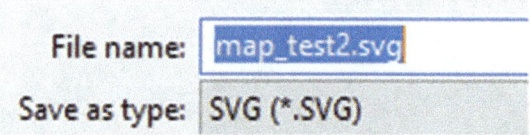

Figure 16-15. *Save your file as an SVG*

Now choose the SVG Options settings shown in Figure 16-16.

371

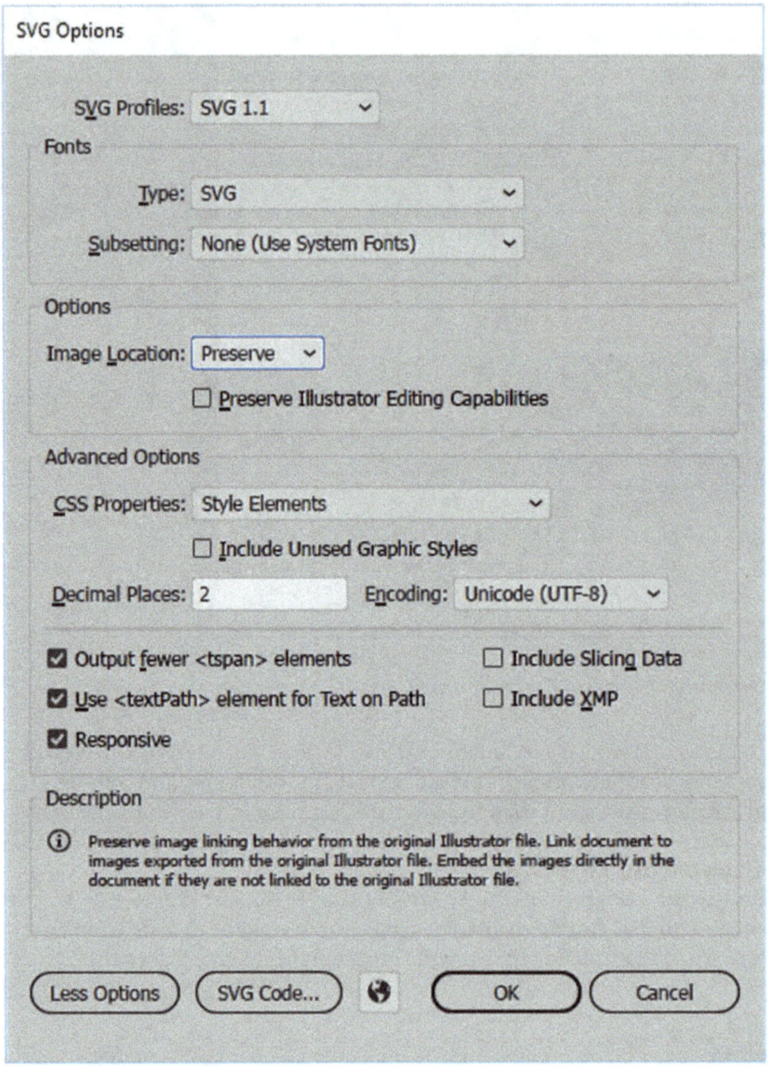

CHAPTER 16 ■ PUTTING IT INTO PRACTICE WITH ILLUSTRATOR CC

Figure 16-16. Settings in the SVG Options dialog box

- SVG Profiles: SVG 1.1
- Type: SVG
- Subsetting: None (Use System fonts)
- Image Location Choose either embed or preserve from the menu. In my original settings I chose embed.
- Preserve Illustrator Editing Capabilities: unchecked
- CSS Properties: Style Elements
- Uncheck Include Unused Graphic Styles

CHAPTER 16 ■ PUTTING IT INTO PRACTICE WITH ILLUSTRATOR CC

- Decimal Places: 2
- Encoding: Unicode (UTF-8)
- Output fewer <tspan> elements: check
- Use <textPath> element for Text on a Path: check
- Check: Responsive.

Leave the other two setting unchecked.
When done, click OK to save your file.
If the newly created SVG file map_test.svg is not in Illustrator, choose File ➤ Open and locate the file. You can close my original AI file without saving changes.
In the SVG file, look again at the Layers panel. It should look the same as the AI file. Refer to Figure 16-17.

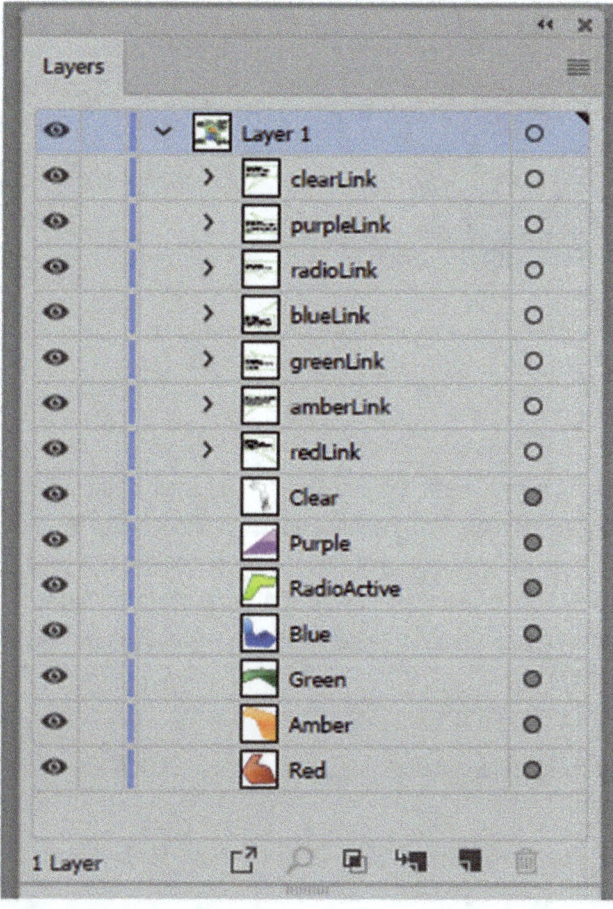

Figure 16-17. *The Layers panel as viewed in the SVG File*

Now turn off all the visibility eyes for the seven sublayers with the word *link* so that the information boxes are no longer visible, as seen in Figure 16-18. Now the artboard is less cluttered. Keep the main layer's (Layer 1) eye on.

373

CHAPTER 16 ■ PUTTING IT INTO PRACTICE WITH ILLUSTRATOR CC

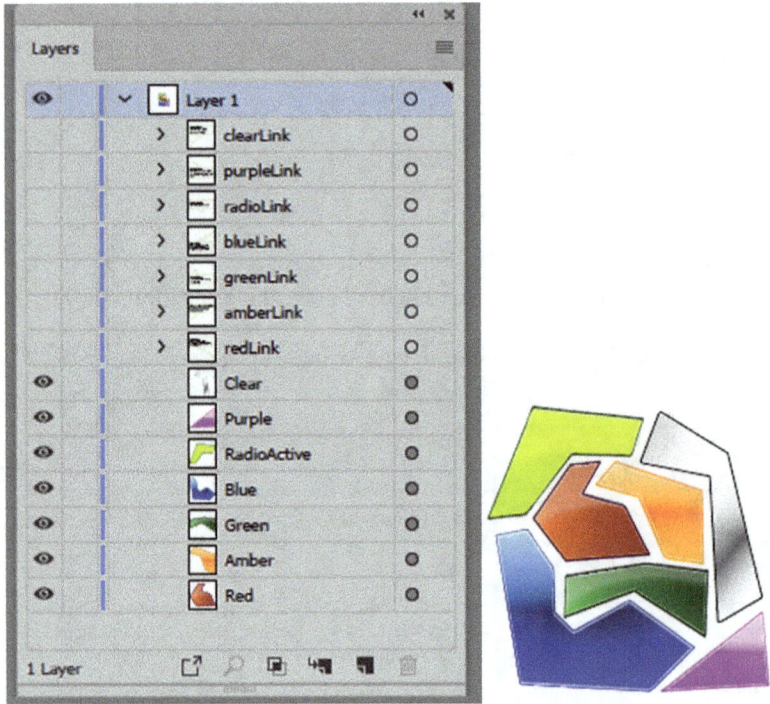

Figure 16-18. *The text link layers visibility is turned off and the artboard appears less cluttered*

Make sure to save the SVG file at this point.

■ **Note** When converted to an SVG, an AI file does not always retain the JavaScript if you enter it into the SVG Interactivity panel. Save the file as an SVG and then open the SVG. For my workflow, I find it better to enter the JavaScript only into the SVG file; that way, if I need to use the original AI file for other projects, the objects shapes are clean of extra code, which might be accidently copied into other AI files. Also, filters do not always convert correctly in the SVG file, so you may need to alter your graphics slightly if certain colors don't convert as expected.

In the Layers panel, select the layer called Clear and click the circle target on the right so that you know this object is fully selected. Refer to Figure 16-19.

374

CHAPTER 16 ■ PUTTING IT INTO PRACTICE WITH ILLUSTRATOR CC

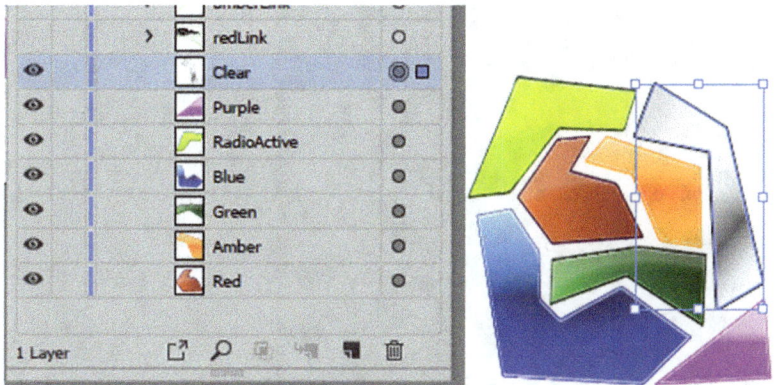

Figure 16-19. *With the clear sublayer targeted, you can now add SVG interactivity to the object*

Now go to the SVG Interactivity panel.

While the target is selected, choose Event: onmouseover from the drop-down menu and enter the following code into the JavaScript box, as seen in Figure 16-20.

```
document.getElementById("clearLink").style.display="block";
```

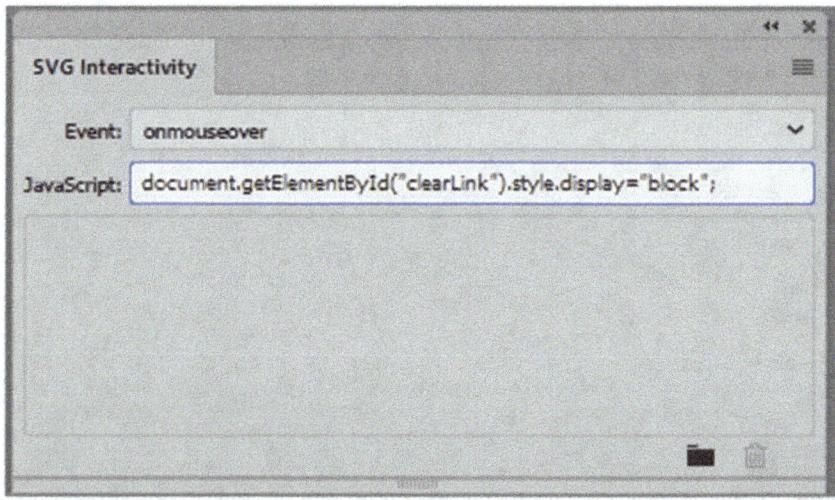

Figure 16-20. *Add your JavaScript code for an object to the SVG Interactivity panel*

Click in the lower box area to confirm the code and then choose Event: onmouseout and enter the following code into the JavaScript area, as seen in Figure 16-21.

```
document.getElementById("clearLink").style.display="none";
```

375

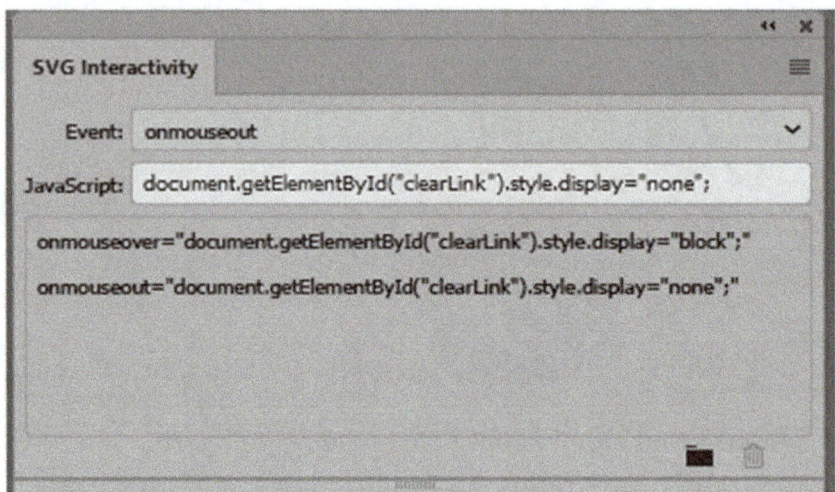

Figure 16-21. *Add your JavaScript code for an object to the SVG Interactivity panel*

Click in the lower gray area to confirm it into the SVG Interactivity panel, and save your SVG file.

When you changed the object's color to show or hide, you set the `"clearLink"` text to show when the mouse hovers over the `"block"` object. To hide this, it is set `"none"` when the mouse moves away from the object.

Open this file in your browser, and you see that when you hover over or move away from the clear glass shape, the text shows and hides. Refer to Figure 16-22.

Figure 16-22. *In the browser, when you hover over the clear glass, a message appears; it hides when you move away from the object*

You now want to create interactivity for all the other shapes. If you get confused, you can refer to my map_test.svg file. However, make sure that, for each object, you always select the layer and the target for that layer so that the entire object is selected. Refer to Figure 16-23.

CHAPTER 16 ■ PUTTING IT INTO PRACTICE WITH ILLUSTRATOR CC

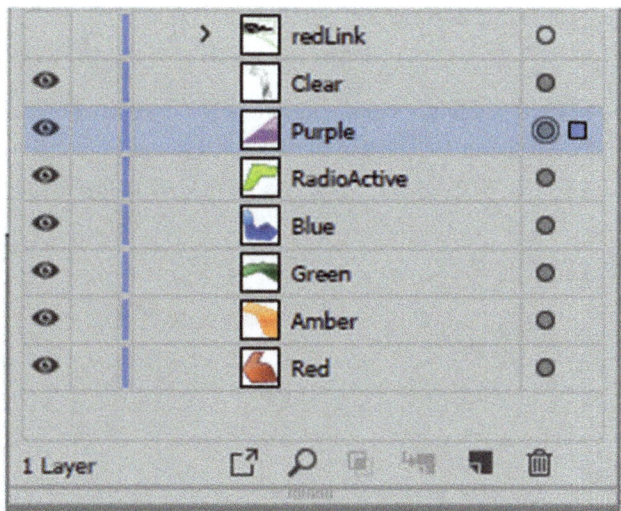

Figure 16-23. *Always select the target for a layer so that it will be linked correctly in the SVG Interactivity panel*

Only then should you start adding your JavaScript to the SVG Interactivity panel. Table 16-1 shows the remaining code.

Table 16-1. *The Remaining Code for Each Sublayer*

Target Color	Event	JavaScript
Purple	onmouseover onmouseout	document.getElementById("purpleLink").style.display="block"; document.getElementById("purpleLink").style.display="none";
RadioActive	onmouseover onmouseout	document.getElementById("radioLink").style.display="block"; document.getElementById("radioLink").style.display="none";
Blue	onmouseover onmouseout	document.getElementById("blueLink").style.display="block"; document.getElementById("blueLink").style.display="none";
Green	onmouseover onmouseout	document.getElementById("greenLink").style.display="block"; document.getElementById("greenLink").style.display="none";
Amber	onmouseover onmouseout	document.getElementById("amberLink").style.display="block"; document.getElementById("amberLink").style.display="none";
Red	onmouseover onmouseout	document.getElementById("redLink").style.display="block"; document.getElementById("redLink").style.display="none";

Once you have entered the code, make sure to save your file and test it in the browser. You may have to go back to Illustrator to make changes and save, and then refresh the browser.

As you can see, you don't have to know a lot of JavaScript to find creative ways to work with Illustrator's SVG Interactivity panel.

CHAPTER 16 ■ PUTTING IT INTO PRACTICE WITH ILLUSTRATOR CC

File ➤ Close any open files and then File ➤ Exit Illustrator. This concludes our Illustrator projects for Part 3.

■ **Note** If your own project has a lot of sublayers, and you find that some shapes are not hiding when the file opens in the browser and only disappear after being hovered over once, make sure to check your layer order in the SVG file. Sometimes a layer's eye needs to remain on and all of its sublayers' eyes need to be turned off, as seen in Figure 16-24.

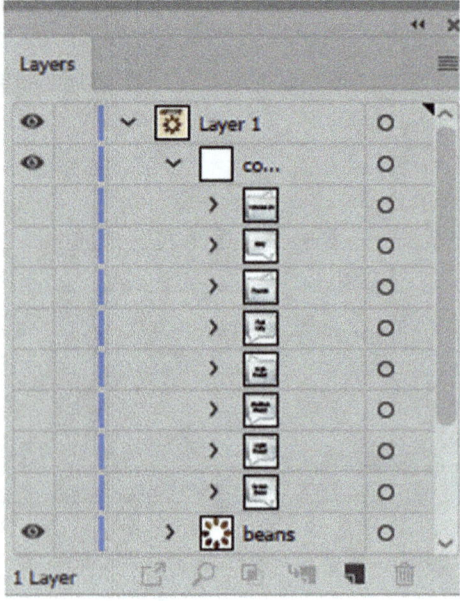

Figure 16-24. *Check your layer order if you notice that your SVG file does not respond correctly in the browser*

Summary

In this chapter, you reviewed how to create images for a webpage and work with an interactive informational map from an SVG file. This chapter concludes your study of Illustrator. Make sure to review any areas of Part 3 that you don't understand so that you feel comfortable working with your own graphics in Illustrator.

In Part 4, you journey to the next junction point in the software maze: Adobe Animate CC. You'll discover how it creates animations, movies, and HTML5 canvases.

PART IV

Working with Animate to Create Animations, Movies, and HTML5 Canvas

CHAPTER 17

Getting Started with Animate CC

In this chapter, you look at an Adobe software program called Animate CC, including some of its main tools and panels. You also look at HTML5 Canvas and some of its uses. Finally, you learn how to convert an ActionScript 3.0 FLA (.fla) to a new HTML5 Canvas FLA (.fla) file.

Note This chapter does not have any actual projects; however, you can use the files in the Chapter 17 folder to practice opening and viewing for this lesson. They are at https://github.com/Apress/graphics-multimedia-web-adobe-creative-cloud.

In Part 3, as you traveled through the symbolic maze of Photoshop and Illustrator to create graphics for the web. Now you are going to travel to the third junction or software point, Adobe Animate CC. (formerly Flash and Edge Animate).

Here you learn how to create animations, movies, and an HTML5 animated canvas. Refer to Figure 17-1.

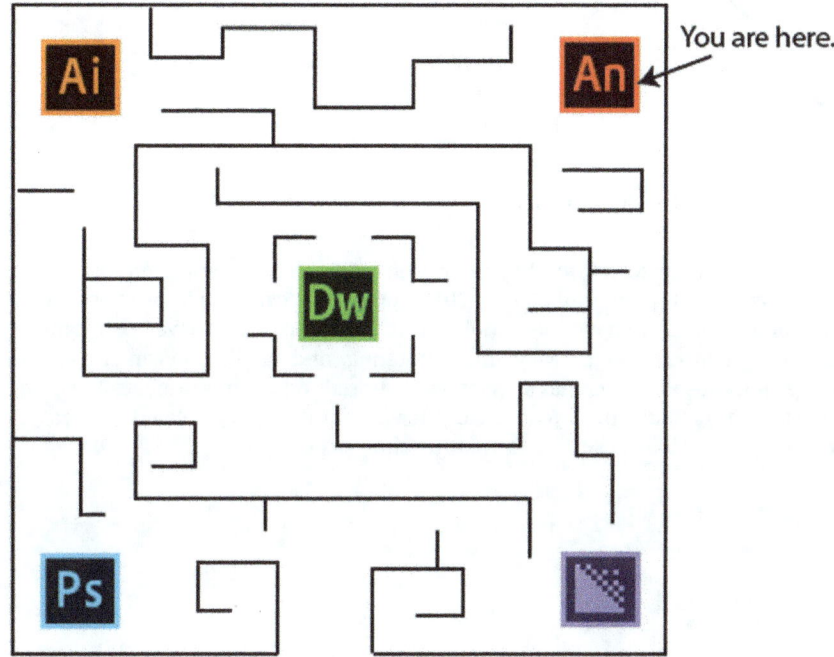

Figure 17-1. *You are now at the third junction point in the maze: Animate CC*

© Jennifer Harder 2018
J. Harder, *Graphics and Multimedia for the Web with Adobe Creative Cloud*,
https://doi.org/10.1007/978-1-4842-3823-3_17

When I think of Animate CC, I go back to when it was called Macromedia Flash. Before Flash was bought by Adobe in 2005, Adobe was developing its own version of an animation program called Adobe LiveMotion. Around this time, LiveMotion was removed from development and Adobe decided to continue with Flash instead. I remember being so excited that I could finally learn to create interactive animated graphics.

As a young child, I enjoyed drawing and thought it would be wonderful to bring my ideas to life. After graduating from college in 2002, I spent time creating some basic animations to show how various printing machinery operates so that it would help my clients understand printing jargon that they might not be familiar with. It's been said that "a picture is worth a thousand words." How much might an animation or video be worth if it moved at so many more "pictures" or frames per second? Many of the files I created were in Small Web Format (SWF) or Flash format, when Flash websites were popular; however, over the next few years, they were found to be processor intensive, and SWF files have slowly fallen out of favor in the web design community.

Luckily, Adobe has been moving forward with Animate CC and has improved what is known as HTML5 Canvas, which uses a combination of images, HTML, CSS, and JavaScript—similar to the SVG files that you looked at in Illustrator. You will look at it in more detail a shortly.

If you are not familiar with HTML5 Canvas in Animate, you have other export options, such as saving a video (via Media Encoder) or producing a GIF animation that you can use in Adobe Dreamweaver CC. You can see in Figure 17-2 that graphics from Photoshop and Illustrator can easily be imported into Animate and then later exported to other Adobe programs within the Creative Cloud.

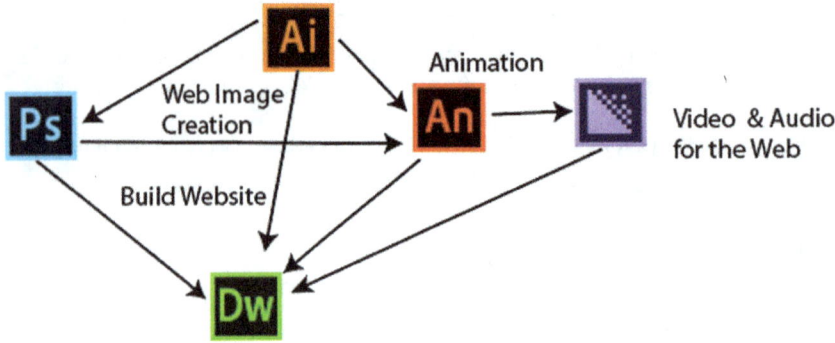

Figure 17-2. Adobe Animate works well with other Adobe software in the Creative Cloud

If you have never used Animate on a project or are a beginner user, I recommend reading *Adobe Animate CC Classroom in a Book* by Russell Chun Adobe Press, 2018), where you can get a basic overview of the program and many of its tools. Even if you have used Adobe Flash in the past, there have been some major changes to the program, so I encourage you to review the new settings and panels. You can also check out Animate's Help menu or opening console, which has step-by-step tutorials on various projects. In Part 4, you work with graphics that are already created and save them for the web or other video-related projects.

As you can see in Figure 17-3, you will look at several formatting choices for export.

CHAPTER 17 ■ GETTING STARTED WITH ANIMATE CC

Figure 17-3. *Adobe Animate has several different export options to choose from. Which one is right for your project?*

Getting Started

Let's begin by opening Animate CC. If you do not have it on your computer, but you do have the Creative Cloud console, click the Install button (see Figure 17-4) and follow the instructions on how to install the program. Currently, I am using Animate CC 2018.

Figure 17-4. *Click Install in the Creative Cloud beside the Adobe Animate icon to begin installing the software*

383

> **Note** Before you install an Adobe program, make sure that your computer meets the system requirements; otherwise, the install may fail. For more information, check https://helpx.adobe.com/animate/system-requirements.html.

If you already have Animate installed on your computer, double-click the icon or the Creative Cloud console; click Open to launch the program (see Figure 17-5).

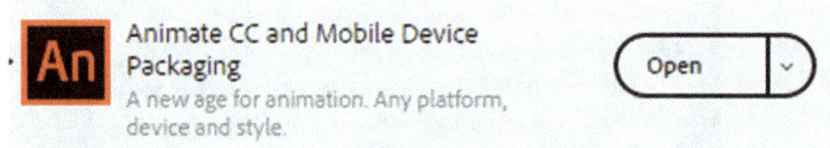

Figure 17-5. A graphic of how Animate CC appears in the Creative Cloud console with its open button

Differences and Similarities Between Animate and Character Animator CC

When in the Creative Cloud console, you may have come across another animation program known as Character Animator CC. If you want to learn more about it, can click the What's New button. Refer to Figure 17-6.

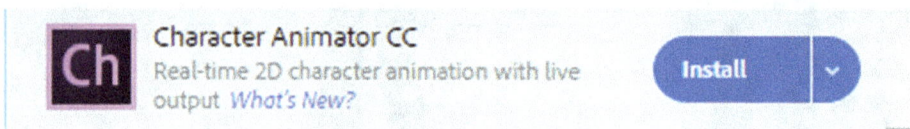

Figure 17-6. Character Animator is another program in the Creative Cloud console that is in many ways similar to Animate CC

If you check the larger map of software in Chapter 1, you see that this program is better suited for a workflow that focuses on professional video animation with Premiere Pro and After Effects for television and video, and not for animation directly in use for the web.

Having said that, you can use a video that you created in these programs on a website if the correct file format is rendered to MP4.

At present, other than using similar graphics created with Illustrator or Photoshop, there does not appear to be a direct link between Animate and Character Animator if you want to directly transfer FLA files between programs. One possible option is to export a sequence of PNG files. You'll look at that in Chapter 22. In Part 4, you focus on Animate CC.

Setting up the Workspace

Once Animate CC opens, set up your workspace so that you see the same workspace that I am using. Make the workspace similar to how it appears in Photoshop or Illustrator. Go to File ➤ New and choose HTML5 Canvas, and then click OK. (I'll talk more about File ➤ New in a moment.)

CHAPTER 17 ■ GETTING STARTED WITH ANIMATE CC

When a new document is open, chose the Essentials workspace from the Workspace icon in the upper right, as seen in Figure 17-7.

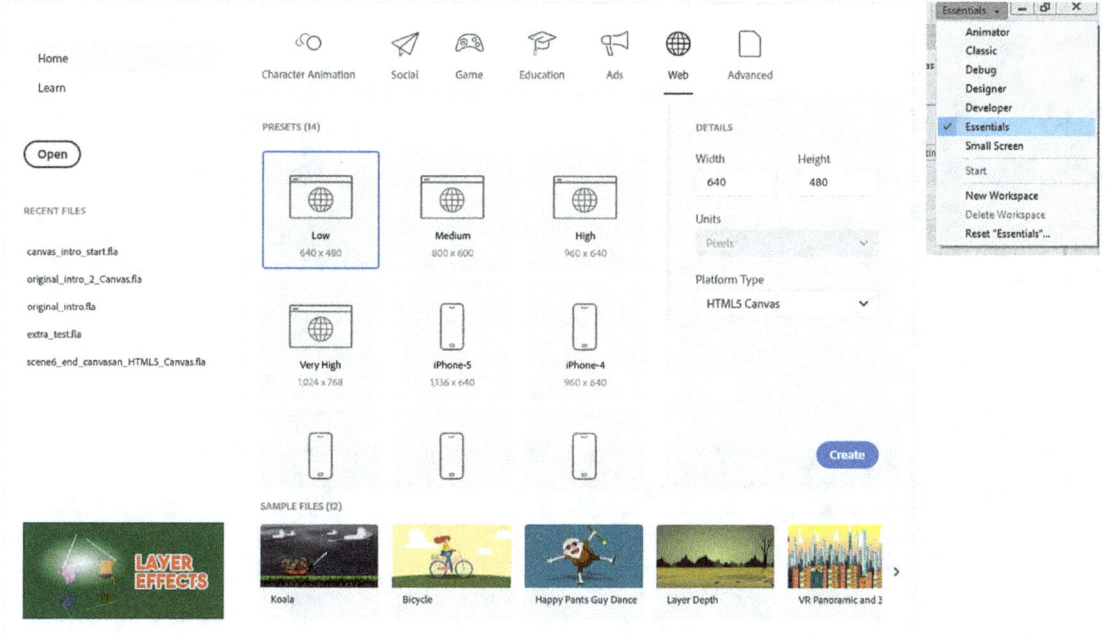

Figure 17-7. *Choose the Essentials workspace while working in Animate CC*

Drag your Tools panel to the left, and adjust it with the upper arrows and mouse cursor handles so that it is two columns. Your layout should look something like Figure 17-8.

385

CHAPTER 17 ■ GETTING STARTED WITH ANIMATE CC

Figure 17-8. *How the Essentials workspace appears with minor adjustments in layout*

I like this layout because it is like working in Photoshop and Illustrator. I think it is important to keep the layouts as similar as possible when you are working with a variety of Adobe software; that way, you can easily find the tools that you need.

If you prefer another workspace for your web design animations, you can always choose a different one or create your own custom workspace (New Workspace) as seen in Figure 17-7.

Create a New FLA Document

To create a new HTML5 Canvas file, you can use the opening console, which starts when Animate opens, or choose File ➤ New. Refer to Figure 17-9. This console and most of the layout has been updated in the CC 2019 version so that it integrates better with Photoshop and Illustrator.

CHAPTER 17 ■ GETTING STARTED WITH ANIMATE CC

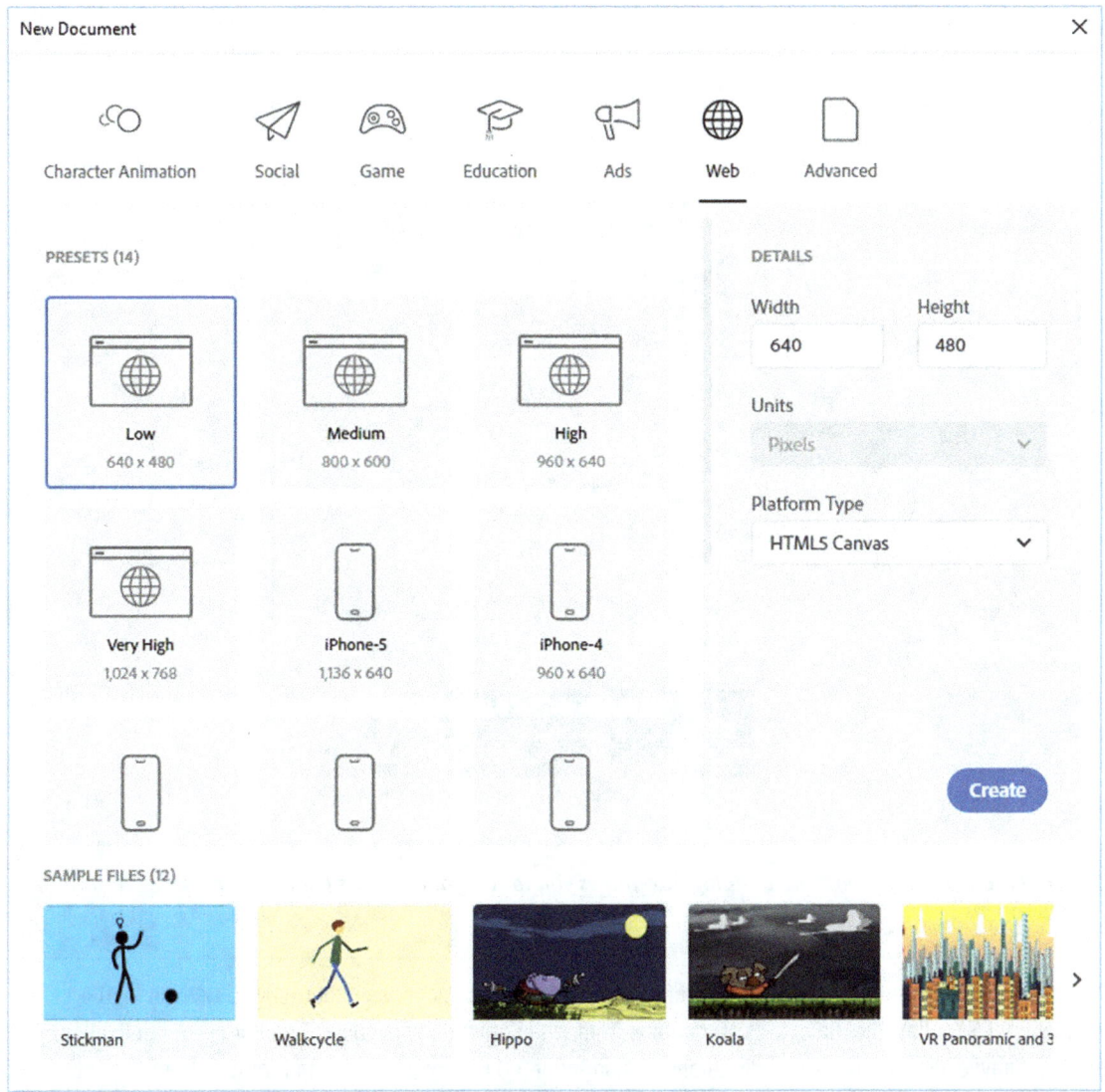

Figure 17-9. When Animate opens, this dialog box appears in the center of the screen so that you can begin a new project

File ➤ New lets you set the size (width and height) of your canvas or ActionScript 3.0 files. You can also set the grid ruler units (under Advanced tab). The frame rate, and your base background color now can only be set in the properties once you click create. You can change these settings in your document using various panels. For now, choose a preset from the Web or Advanced tab with a platform type of HTML5 Canvas or Action Script 3.0 and click the Create button. Refer to Figure 17-10.

387

CHAPTER 17 ■ GETTING STARTED WITH ANIMATE CC

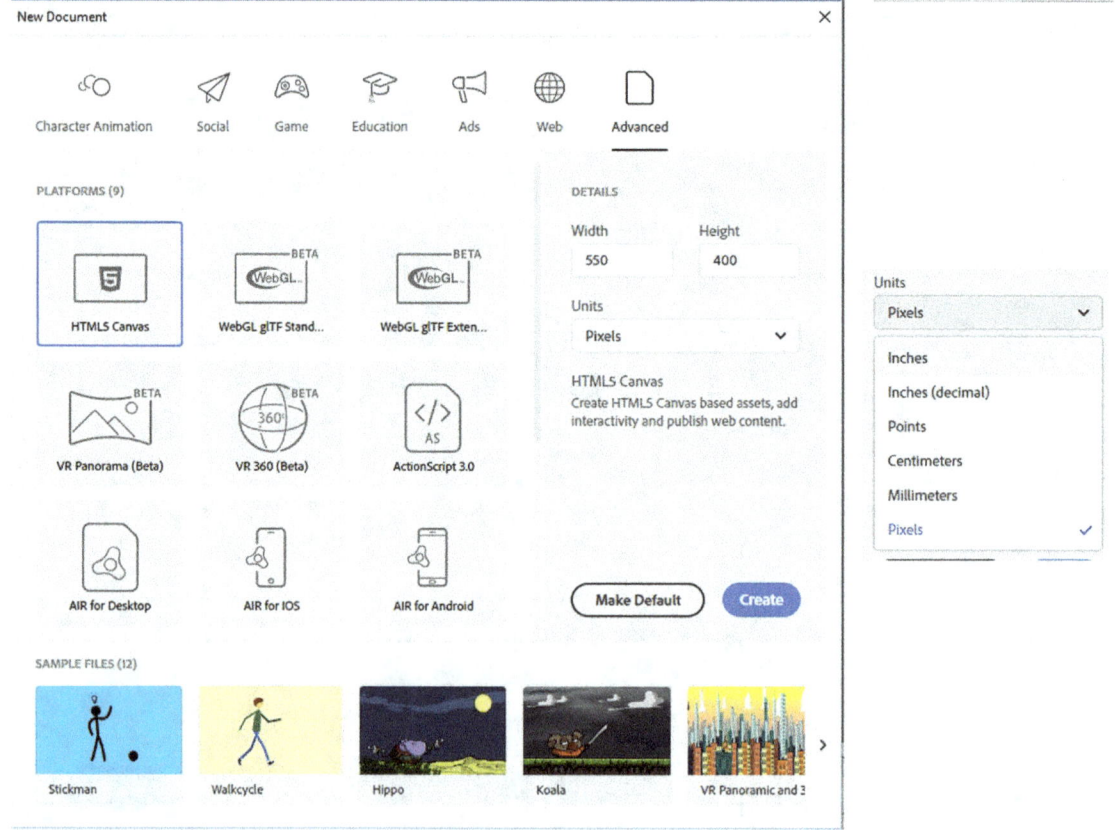

Figure 17-10. *The new Document dialog box allows you to edit your settings before you click Create and the new file opens*

■ **Note** When you start an Animate project for a website, you can choose either HTML5 Canvas (.fla) or ActionScript 3.0 (.fla). The .fla extension remains from when Animate was called Flash or Flash Application. HTML5 Canvas allows you create animations. ActionScript 3.0 is very slowly being removed from Animate and is generally used for creating files that are for SWF animations and gaming files; however, ActionScript 3.0 files have a lot more options than HTML5 Canvas, such as 3D and certain visual and audio effects because JavaScript has not yet advanced far enough in certain areas to compensate for all options. Nevertheless, Animate's HTML5 Canvas allows improved scaling and resizing (responsive), which is just as good as the older SWF files.

If you are planning to use your animation only for export as a video (.mov), I recommend using ActionScript 3.0 (FLA) because you will have access to a wider range of features.

If you have saved your file ActionScript 3.0 (FLA) or have some older files from past projects, you can still work with them in Animate CC. I show you how to make copies of that file and convert them the HTML5 Canvas (FLA) format shortly.

CHAPTER 17 ■ GETTING STARTED WITH ANIMATE CC

You will look at other formats, like WebGL and Air, when you export your Animate files in Chapter 21.

The other lower section in the New Document dialog box is for templates that are already created for you to use in a project, such as an HTML5 canvas, video (Media Playback), or simple games for your site. You can also access this area under File ➤ New from Template. Refer to Figure 17-11.

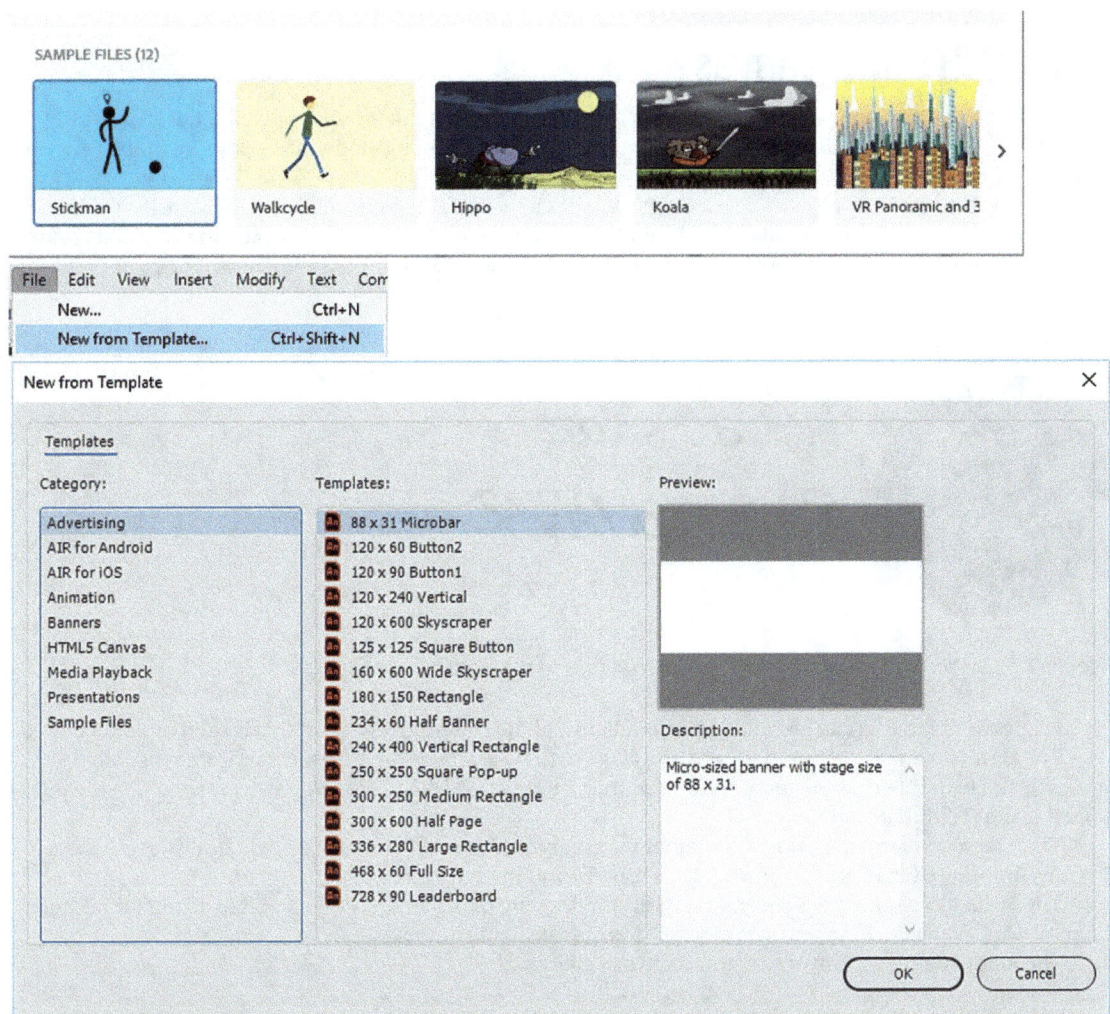

Figure 17-11. The Template tab in the New Document dialog box changes to New from Template when that dialog box is chosen

For now, stay in the Web or Advanced tab and click Create for an HTML5 Canvas (FLA) file.

■ **Note** You can tell you are in the HTML5 Canvas FLA because your files tab shows up when you click Create as Untitled -# (Canvas). A file that has been saved as an ActionScript 3.0 FLA shows up as Untitled-#, without the word *canvas*. Refer to Figure 17-12.

389

CHAPTER 17 ■ GETTING STARTED WITH ANIMATE CC

Figure 17-12. The differences in HTML5 Canvas (FLA) and ActionScript 3.0 (FLA) file types

What Is HTML5 Canvas?

At some point you are going export an HTML5 Canvas file. The (.fla) file is not a canvas yet; it is only a starting file used to output the dynamic animation in an HTML webpage for your responsive mobile site. You might be wondering what HTML5 Canvas is.

In a website, the HTML <canvas> element, which is new to HTML version 5, is used like an SVG file to draw graphics on a webpage. In this case, the graphic or animation is created within <canvas></canvas> tags. They act as a container. Code known as JavaScript draws and animates the graphics. Refer to Figure 17-13.

Figure 17-13. You can add still or animated drawings to the canvas as well as text

Shapes in the canvas can be solid colors, gradients, photographs, or even text that is solid or multicolored.

The HTML <canvas> element is used as a stage to draw graphics on the fly, via scripting (usually JavaScript). The JavaScript is usually added within the published HTML file and as an external (.js) file that is linked to the HTML file.

The <canvas> element is only a container for graphics. You must use JavaScript to draw the graphics. Luckily, Animate CC can create most of that script for you to save time.

The <canvas> element has several methods for drawing paths, boxes, circles, and text, and for adding images. Check out www.w3schools.com/graphics/canvas_intro.asp.

The following sections overview the <canvas> element.

HTML5 Canvas Can Draw Text

With HTML5 Canvas, you can draw colorful text with or without animation.

Low resolution text renders poorly so test text for clarity and at different sizes after the published canvas is output with the setting of responsive.

HTML5 Canvas Can Draw Graphics

Canvas has features for graphical data presentation with imagery, photos (.jpg, .gif, and .png), graphs, and charts.

- You can create linear and radial gradients.
- You can only draw in 2D using x and y coordinates. There is no 3D option yet.
- Resolution is dependent on canvas size.

HTML5 Canvas Can Be Animated

Canvas objects can move. Everything is possible—from simple bouncing balls to complex animations.

The animation is drawn pixel by pixel. As the object changes position in the scene, it is redrawn, including objects covered by other graphics.

Basic audio and video can be linked to the canvas, but these files remain external and must be included when uploading the HTML file.

HTML5 Canvas Can Be Interactive

Canvas can respond to JavaScript events that you programed into the Actions panel Animate. It can respond to any user action (key clicks, mouse clicks, button clicks, finger movement).

Event handlers offer some support, such as using `addEventListener()` and direct callbacks (e.g., `canvas.onclick =`).

> **Note** You should use the JavaScript language examples provided with Animate (CreateJS) so that your animations respond correctly. While you can use JavaScript that was not created using Animate, or JavaScript created in non-Adobe programs, the coding may not work as planned, so make sure to test often before uploading your file to the web.

HTML5 Canvas Can Be Used in Games

This book focuses on video and animation in Animate. Nevertheless, the canvas can also be used to create fun and interactive games.

Canvas methods for animations offer a lot of possibilities for HTML gaming applications; however, some work better if programed outside of Animate using other software or by being hand coded. If you are interested in 2D gaming specifically, I recommend reading one of the Apress books by Rex van der Spuy; he has written about this topic extensively in several books.

Working with RAW Files

The main RAW file that Animate works with is the FLA file, which essentially contains the entire Animate animation project, which includes layers, graphics, audio, video, and coding that make the animation appear as though it is moving.

CHAPTER 17 ■ GETTING STARTED WITH ANIMATE CC

Animate has some panels that you should find familiar and others that are foreign. You'll look at some of them briefly as you go through Part 4.

The two primary areas of any animation are the canvas or (artboard stage) and the timeline.

Properties Panel

There is only one artboard in the FLA file, which is called the *stage*, as seen in Figure 17-14.

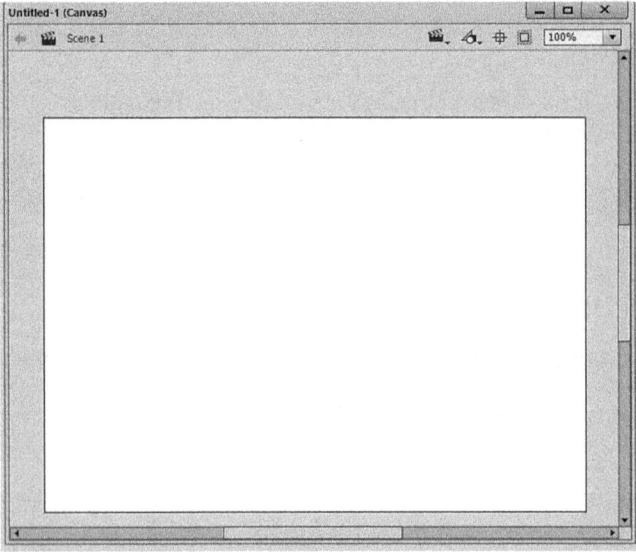

Figure 17-14. *The blank stage of a newly created HTML5 Canvas (FLA) file*

The canvas' size, frame rate, and color are set to a default preset when you create a new file. However, once the file is created, you can alter these settings using the Properties panel. Refer to Figure 17-15.

CHAPTER 17 ■ GETTING STARTED WITH ANIMATE CC

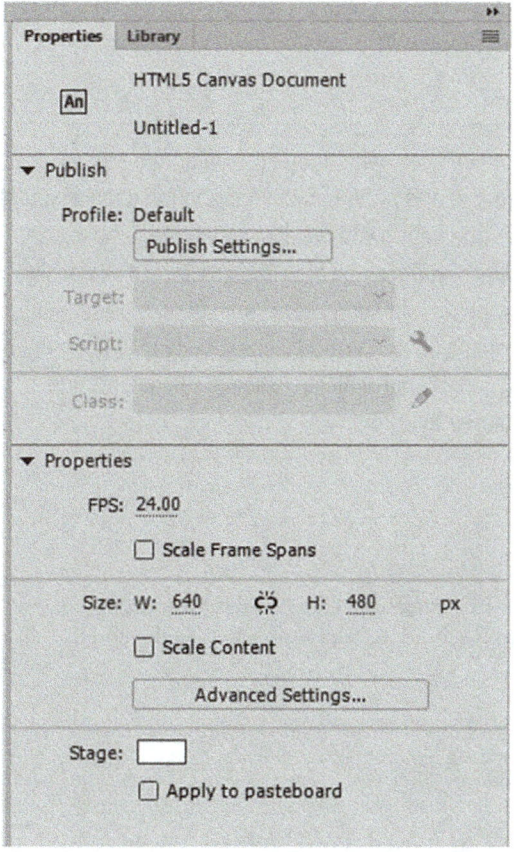

Figure 17-15. *Animate's Properties panel and its basic settings for a new HTML5 Canvas(FLA) file*

For example, if you remember that you need to increase the frames per second (fps) from 24 to 30, in the Properties tab, click the text field and enter 30, as seen in Figure 17-16.

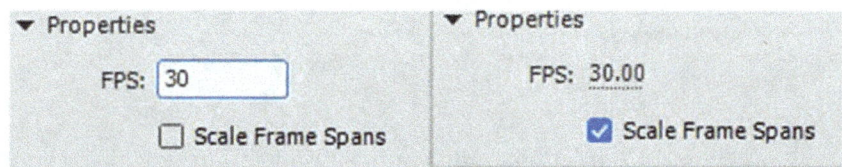

Figure 17-16. *Enter a new fps or frames per second setting. Sacle Frame Spans is checked to avoid time distortion in the Timeline panel*

393

CHAPTER 17 ■ GETTING STARTED WITH ANIMATE CC

Having said this, keep in mind that when you increase your frame rate in a completed animation, the animation may now move faster than expected. Also, a lower frame rate slows down the animation and causes it to move in a jerky or stilted manner.

■ **Note** If you decide to export your animation as a video (.mov), know what frame rate your other video footage will be running at. As you saw in Chapter 7, all the footage was at 30 fps. Keep this in mind when you're working with others on a group project; know the exact frame rate before you build an animation to be used as an intro or end credits with other footage. For short animations, you may be able to correct the issue easily by stretching a few frames in the timeline panel. However, for longer and complicated animations, adjustments could take several hours. You don't want to be wasting time when you are on a deadline. One way to get around this is to check Scale Frame Spans (see Figure 17-6) when you start your project. A second remains as one second on the timeline whether your animation is 24 fps or altered to 30 fps.

Timeline Panel

The Timeline panel looks quite similar to the video timeline in Photoshop. Like Photoshop, it uses keyframes, tweens, and folders to store the frames and graphics. Refer to the Canvas_test.fla file and to Figure 17-17.

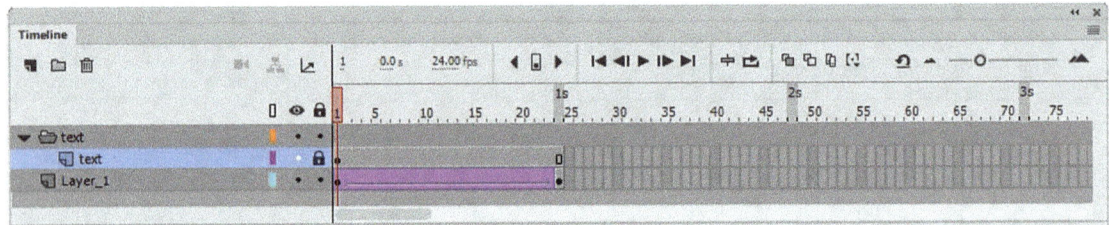

Figure 17-17. The Timeline panel

You will come back to the Timeline panel in Part 4.

Library Panel

Unlike Photoshop, there is no separate Layers panel. Media assets such as graphics (symbols), bitmaps, video, and audio are stored in the Library panel. These items can either be created in Animate or imported from other Adobe programs, as seen in Figure 17-18.

CHAPTER 17 ■ GETTING STARTED WITH ANIMATE CC

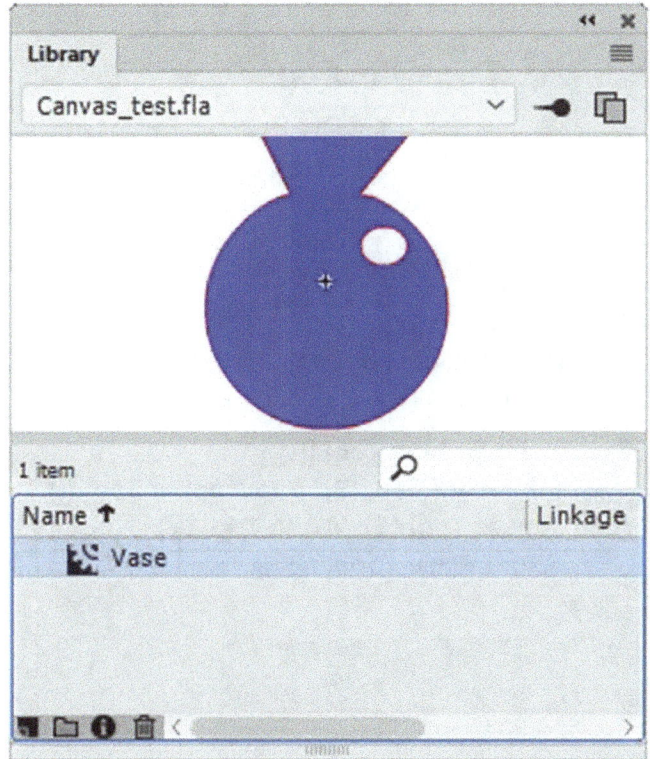

Figure 17-18. The Library panel is used to store the (.fla) files graphics

These library items (symbols, movie clips, graphics, buttons) can be dragged onto the stage and resued many times throughout the animation. You'll look at the Library panel again in Part 4.

■ **Note** This panel is not the same as the CC Libraries panel that we look at in Part 4.

Tools Panel

Another familiar panel is the Tools panel, which has many of the selection (V), subsection (A), pen, drawing, shape and text tools (T) found in Photoshop and Illustrator. Extra tool properties appear at the bottom of the Tools panel when a specific tool is selected.

There are a few tools that are only found in Animate, such as the Bone tool (M) and the Camera tool (C). If you have never worked with these tools, before you make the attempt, read *Animate CC Classroom in a Book* to learn more in detail. Refer to Figure 17-19 and hover over each of the tools with your mouse cursor so that you can see their names in the tool tips. You briefly look at the Bone and Camera tools in Chapter 21.

395

CHAPTER 17 ■ GETTING STARTED WITH ANIMATE CC

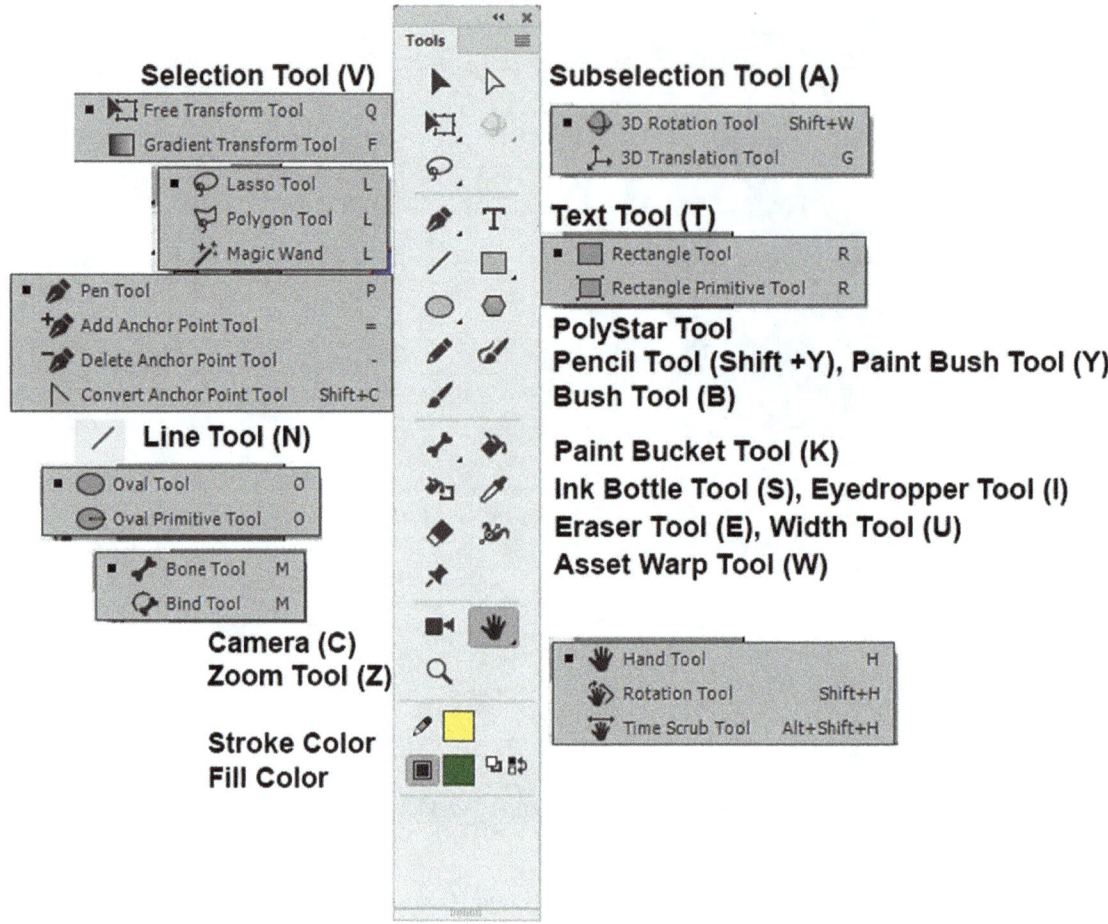

Figure 17-19. *The Tools panel, when dragged out and expanded to two columns so that it looks similar to tools panels of Photoshop and Illustrator. The Bone and Camera tools only appear in Animate.*

FLA Conversions ActionScript to HTML5

If you have older ActionScript 3.0 FLA files that you want to convert to HTML5 Canvas, I recommend that you first save copies of the original ActionScript files for backup. Open the AS3_file.fla file to practice with. ActionScript 3.0 FLA files can contain various effects and options that are not available in HTML5 Canvas FLAs. Refer to Figure 17-20.

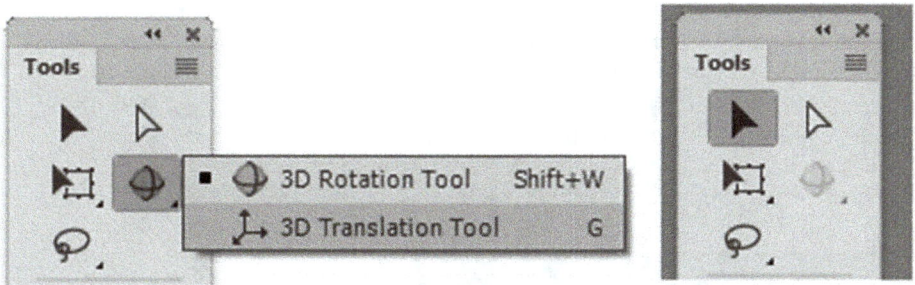

Figure 17-20. *In the Tools panel, the ActionScript 3.0 FLA has access to 3D tools; however for the HTML5 Canvas FLA, it is unavailable*

When you save your file as an ActionScript 3.0 FLA, you can access the 3D Rotation tool (W) and the 3D Translation tool (G). You can use them as part of your animation if you plan to output the file as a video file (.mov). You can also output a video file from an HTML5 Canvas FLA, but you will not have access to the 3D rotation tool.

To convert your ActionScript 3.0 to HTML5 Canvas, go to File ➤ Convert To ➤ HTML5 Canvas. Refer to Figure 17-21.

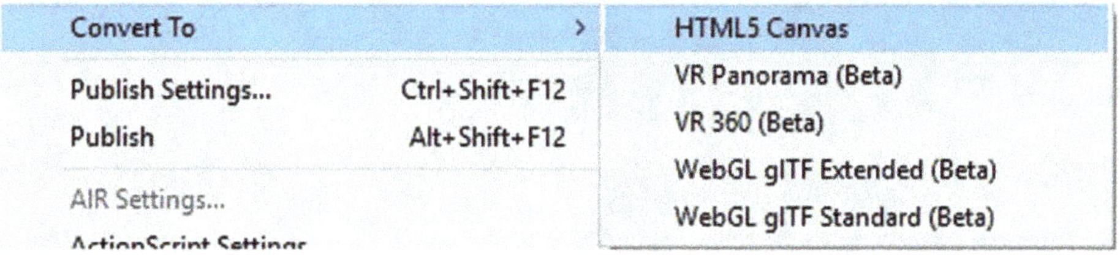

Figure 17-21. *Convert an ActionScript 3.0 file to HTML5 Canvas*

At this point, you can rename the file; add "canvas" to the end of the file name so that you know the difference between the older ActionScript and the newer canvas file. Refer to Figure 17-22.

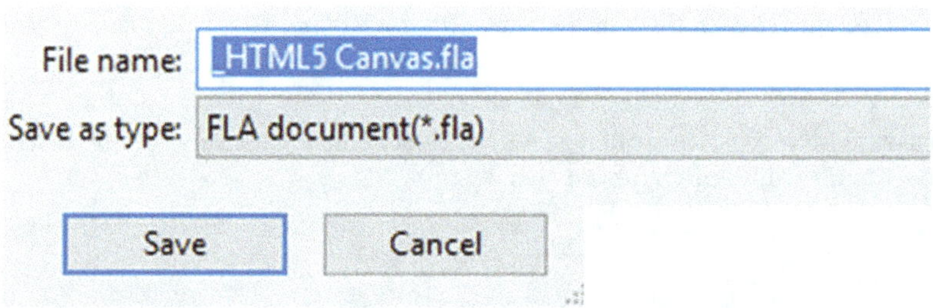

Figure 17-22. *Convert an ActionScript 3.0 file to an HTML5 Canvas file, and name the new file*

Find a location in your folder and then click Save to confirm. While doing so, you may run into a warning in the Output panel (docked with the Timeline panel). If your file could not convert some effects, it will list them. You may not be able to correct some errors because JavaScript will not allow for the conversion; however, for most basic conversions, you will only see minor difference in the canvas file.

CHAPTER 17 ■ GETTING STARTED WITH ANIMATE CC

If you do run into an error, I recommend going back to your orginal ActionScript 3.0 file and make a copy of the file to edit. The errors are listed in the Output panel; read this carefully. In some cases, perhaps it could not convert colors or filters; some of these errors can be ignored if the color shift is slight. In other cases, you may need to alter the type of tween or the layer order to correct the error. Then try converting the file to HTML5 Canvas again and see if the error disappers. You may need to repeat this a few times to get the result you want.

If there are no errors, the panel writes: New document generated successfully! Refer to Figure 17-23.

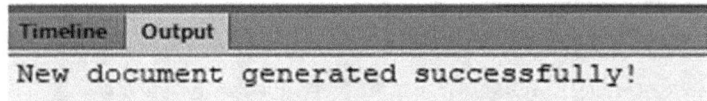

Figure 17-23. *The Output panel lets you know if there are any issues during the conversion process*

As you work with your Animate (FLA) files and publish them, always check the Output panel for errors or messages so that you know if your files are publishing correctly.

The new HTML5 Canvas file opens in a tab beside the older ActionScript 3.0 file, and you can spend time comparing them. Note the differences in conversion type in the Properties panel, as seen in Figure 17-24.

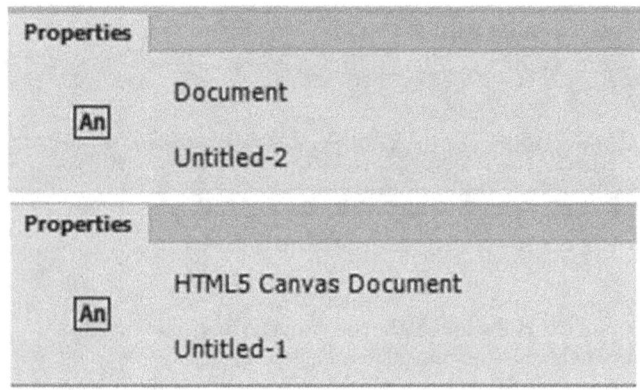

Figure 17-24. *The Propreties panel shows you which file type you are currently looking at—ActionScript 3.0 or an HTML5 Canvas document*

When you are done, you can save (File ➤ Save) any open FLA files. Select File ➤ Close and File ➤ Exit to exit Animate CC. Or keep Animate and the files open for the next chapter.

Summary

In this chapter, you looked at how to set up a workspace for Animate CC. You also saw some differences between the ActionScript 3.0 and HTML5 Canvas FLA file formats. You learned that, depending on your web project, you might want to use a specific format or convert it to a canvas.

You also looked at a few panels that should be familiar to you from Photoshop and Illustrator, including the Properties, Timeline, and Tools panels. Also, you looked at a new panel called the Library panel, which you will become more familiar with in Part 4. In the next chapter, you are going to look at Animate's color choices.

CHAPTER 18

Color Choices: RGB

In this chapter, you look at the color options available in Animate CC, and the tools and panels to assist you when working with color.

> **Note** This chapter does not have any actual projects; however, you can use the files in the Chapter 18 folder to practice opening and viewing for this lesson. They are at `https://github.com/Apress/graphics-multimedia-web-adobe-creative-cloud`.

In Photoshop CC and Illustrator CC, you have a variety of color modes, including CMYK, RGB, and Grayscale. Because Animate animations are specifically for the web, the only color mode that is available is RGB. CMYK is for print, and its color gamut or range is slightly different from what you see on your screen in RGB. While Animate CC can convert CMYK images to RGB during the import of files to the Library panel, for a more accurate conversion, it is better to have your files already in the RGB mode when they are created in Illustrator and Photoshop.

In Adobe programs, you can edit the color in your graphics by using the settings discussed in Chapter 3 and Chapter 11. Once in RGB mode, your color range will look similar across the devices in which you plan to view the animation.

Adding Color to the Stage

As you saw in Chapter 17, you can change the color of your stage by using the Properties panel. There are many web-safe RGB colors that you can choose from. Refer to Figure 18-1.

CHAPTER 18 ■ COLOR CHOICES: RGB

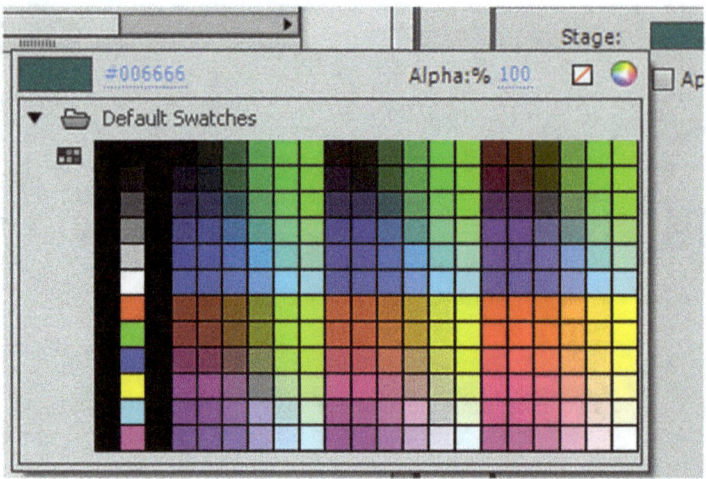

Figure 18-1. *Choose a color for the stage using the Properties panel*

You can choose a transparency or alpha setting, set to none (red slash on a white icon), or select the Color Picker icon in the upper right to open the dialog box. Refer to Figure 18-2.

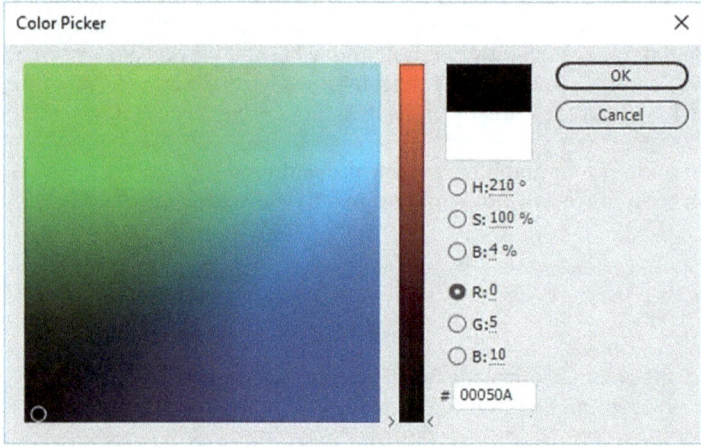

Figure 18-2. *The Color Picker dialog box*

The Color Picker dialog box should be familiar to you by now because you saw it in Photoshop and Illustrator. Note that in Animate, however, it offers fewer options, but you can still view color by HSB, RGB, and web hexadecimal color. After choosing a color, click OK. This will be the new color for the stage.

The Tools Panel Stroke and Fill

In the Tools panel, as in Illustrator, you can set the stroke and a fill color for your shape before you draw it on the stage, as seen in Figure 18-3.

CHAPTER 18 ■ COLOR CHOICES: RGB

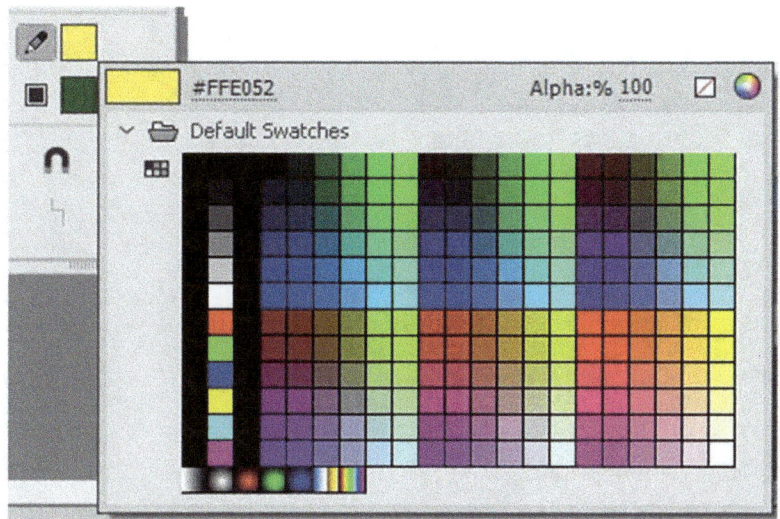

Figure 18-3. *Stroke (pencil icon) and Fill (square icon) color options can be changed and set to web-safe colors*

In this area, you have access to alpha (transparency), no fill, the color picker, and gradients and any imported bitmap patterned image that you want to use as a fill or stroke.

■ **Note** The Paint Bucket tool (K) allows you to add a fill color to a shape. The Ink Bottle tool (S) in the Tools panel allows you to add a stroke to a shape. Refer to Figure 18-4.

Figure 18-4. *The Paint Bucket tool (upper right) and the Ink Bottle tool (lower left) can add or alter the color of a shape's fill or stroke*

Properties Panel

When you select the entire shape with the Selection (V) or Subselection tool (A), you have the option to change the stoke or fill color in the Properties panel in the Fill and Stroke tab, as seen in Figure 18-5.

401

CHAPTER 18 ■ COLOR CHOICES: RGB

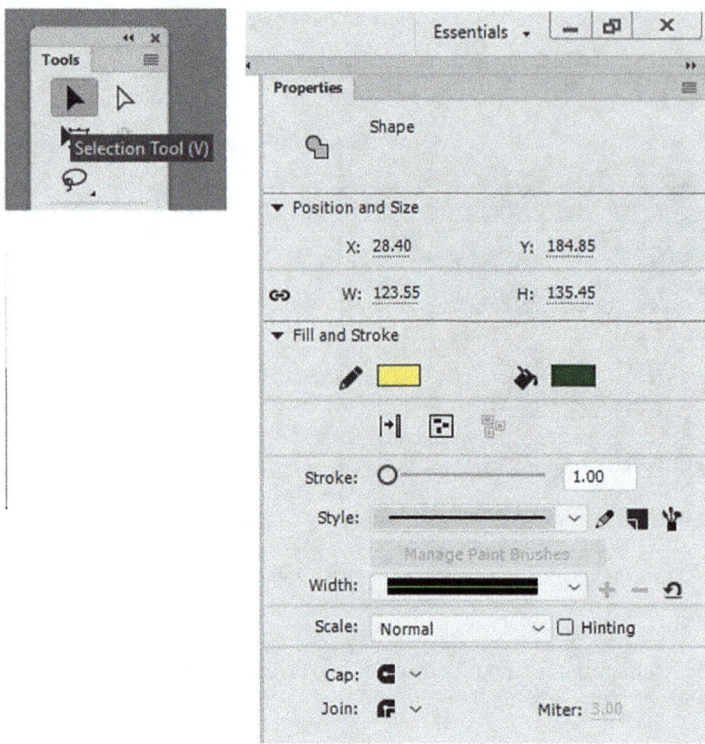

Figure 18-5. Fill and stroke options in the Properties panel for a shape when selected with one of the selection tools in the tools panel

Here you can also adjust the width and style of the stroke and alter the cap and join of a shape. You look at shapes and their properties in more detail throughout Part 4. For now, you will focus on color.

Animate has two other panels for working with color. Open the canvas_color.fla file.

Color Panel

The Color panel offers none (no color) solid color, gradient (linear and radial), and bitmap fill. Refer to Figure 18-6.

CHAPTER 18 ■ COLOR CHOICES: RGB

Figure 18-6. All types of color settings are in the Color panel

You can also use it to add new colors to your pallet and reverse or change the colors of the stroke and fill within the panel. Refer to Figure 18-7.

Figure 18-7. Reverse the stroke and fill colors of a shape

Gradient Fills

As you saw in Chapter 11, when you want to work with gradients, you need to use the Gradient panel and the Gradient tool in the Tools panel. In Animate, you first select whether you want to alter the stroke or the fill of an object, and then select a linear or radial gradient from the drop-down menu. Using the Gradient Transform tool (F), you can alter the gradient of the shape by dragging or rotating the gradient, as you did in Illustrator. Refer to Figure 18-8.

403

CHAPTER 18 ■ COLOR CHOICES: RGB

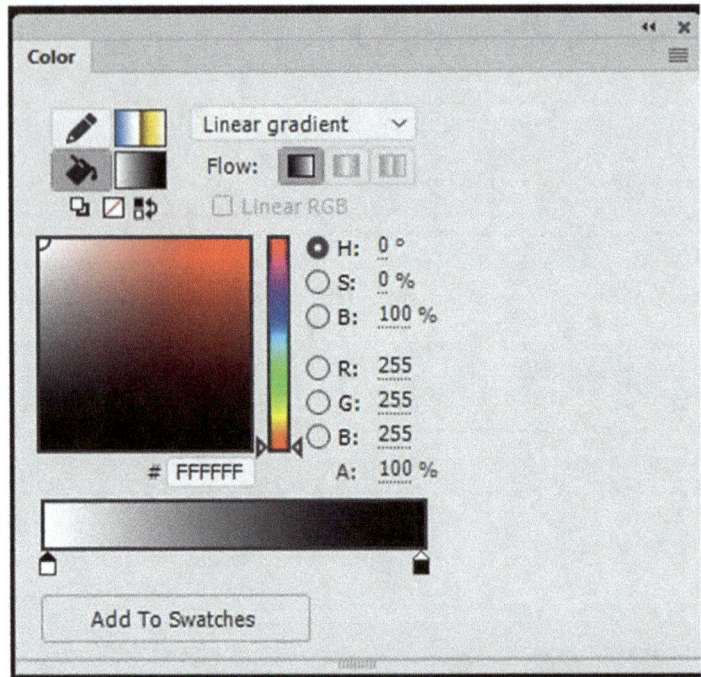

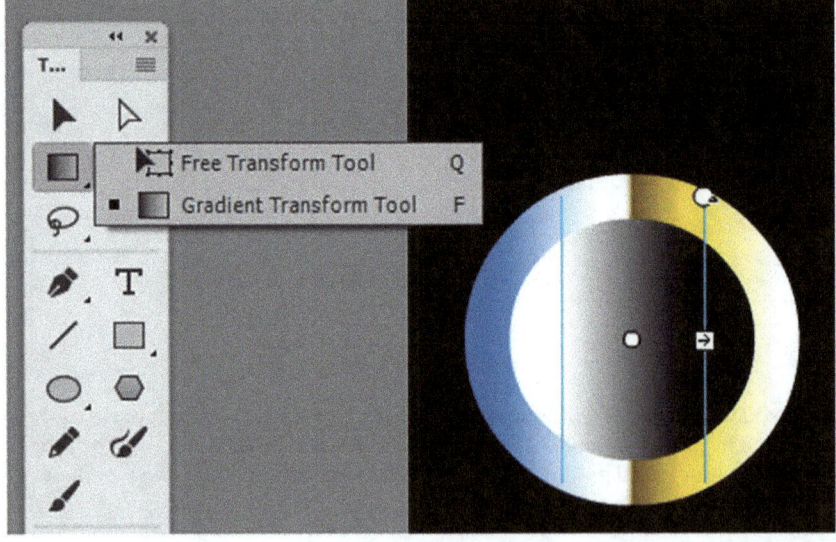

Figure 18-8. Alter the gradient further with the Color panel and Free Transform tool

Linear gradients produce a blend of colors that move on a linear path. Radial gradients are a blend of colors moving outward from the center point of a shape in a circular path.

CHAPTER 18 ■ COLOR CHOICES: RGB

■ **Note** You must work in an ActionScript3.0 FLA file to have access to certain gradient options, like reflect color, repeat color, and linear RGB, which creates an SVG-compliant gradient. With HTML5 Canvas, you can reflect or repeat a gradient, but you have to do that by hand—adding, adjusting, or dragging away color stops in the gradient area. Refer to Figure 18-9.

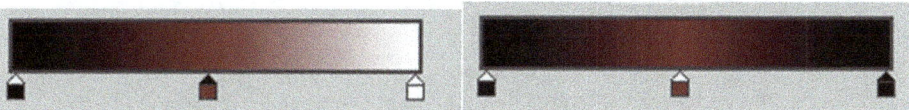

Figure 18-9. Alter the gradient further by adding more color stops

You can also set the alpha transparency for each stop when you select it, and then change the (A:) setting of the color stop.

Bitmap Fills

A bitmap fill is a bitmap file used as a patterned background that tiles or repeats. A bitmap file opens the Import to Library dialog box and allows you to use such file formats as PSD, JPEG, GIF, PNG, bitmap, and DIB (device-independent bitmap).

To add a bitmap to your Color panel, you must first choose Bitmap fill from the drop-down menu. Using the Import to Library dialog box, locate a low-res pattern and then click Open. This adds the fill to your Library panel and Color panel. Then, you can use either the fill or stroke to add it to your shape. Refer to Figure 18-10.

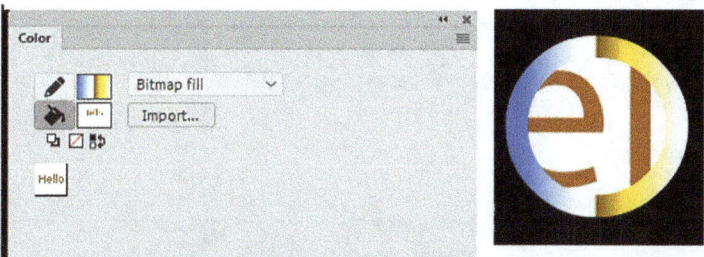

Figure 18-10. A bitmap fill is added to the fill of the shape

If you want to add any new swatches (solid color or gradient) to the Swatches panel, from the Color panel, click the Add to Swatches button, as seen in Figure 18-8.

405

> **Note** You only see the bitmap fill with the other swatches when you directly access it from the Fill or Stroke tools while in the Colors panel; if you go directly to the Swatch panel, it is not available to apply. Also, if your shape lacks a fill or stroke, first apply a solid color using either the Paint Bucket tool or the Ink Bottle tool, and then use the Color panel to apply the bitmap fill.

Swatches Panel

The Swatches panel is often docked with the Color panel. It is similar to the Swatches panels in Photoshop and Illustrator. When a panel opens for new file, it comes with default swatches, but you can also tag swatches, create your own set using the Empty Folder icon, and then add colors swatches (Create a New Swatch icon) or a new pallet within an empty folder. You can also delete swatches (Trash icon). Then you can save your new set using the panel's menu for another project, or add (load) more colors. These colors can be reused for other projects. Refer to Figure 18-11.

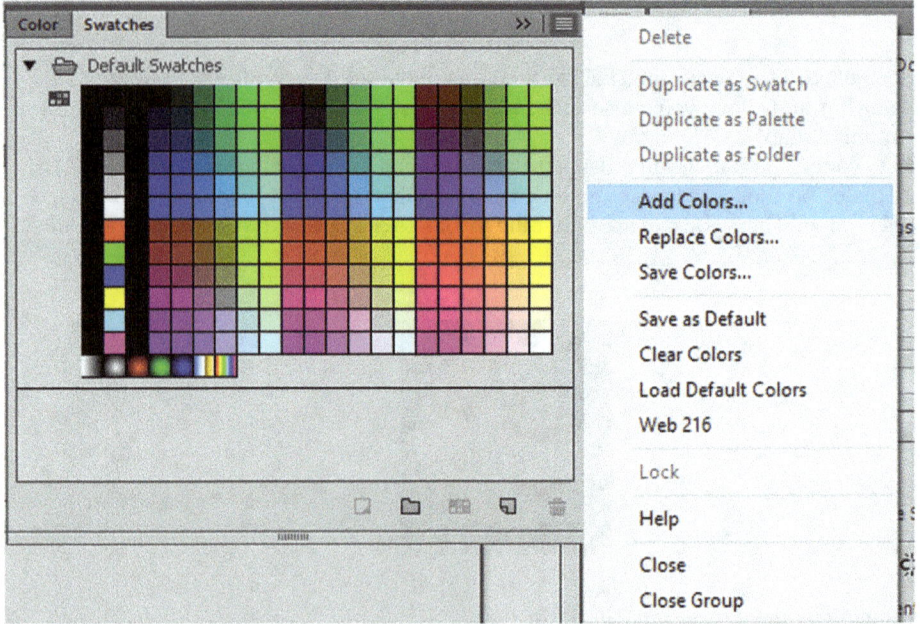

Figure 18-11. *The Swatches panel allows you to add or remove swatches from the current project*

You can acquire colors from an Animate color set (.clr), a color table (.act), or even a GIF file (.gif).
You cannot set the alpha transparency for a swatch to do that; use the Color panel when applying an alpha setting to a shape.

CHAPTER 18 ■ COLOR CHOICES: RGB

Info Panel

If you are unsure of which color is on the stage, use the Info panel. Using the Eyedropper (I) tool from the Tools panel, you can hover over a shape on the stage to determine the current color. Refer to Figure 18-12.

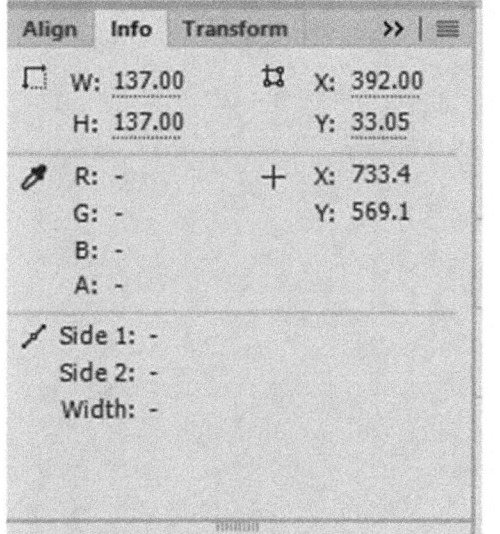

Figure 18-12. *You can find the RGB settings for a fill or stroke using the Info panel and the Eyedropper tool*

Summary

In this chapter, you looked at the color options in Animate CC, as well as tools and panels for working with solid colors, gradients and bitmap fills. In the next chapter, you discover how to import artwork from Adobe programs, such as Photoshop and Illustrator, into the Animate canvas.

CHAPTER 19

Importing Your Artwork

In this chapter, you look at how to import your graphics from Photoshop and Illustrator into Animate. You'll also look at how to edit the graphics within Animate if the import of certain effects is not as successful as you hoped.

Note This chapter does not have any actual projects; however, you can use the files in the Chapter 19 folder to practice opening and viewing for this lesson. They are at `https://github.com/Apress/graphics-multimedia-web-adobe-creative-cloud`.

As you saw in Chapter 18, a graphic could be imported into the Color panel via the Library panel. While it's easy to draw most basic shapes in Animate, I find that to create professional-looking shapes and human bodies, it's much easier to draw and organize them in Photoshop or Illustrator. For this reason, you may want to use these same objects for print or in other areas of your website; so keeping the originals in an (.ai) or (.psd) format is an innovative idea.

In the process of creating your objects, you may have added some effects to these objects that you want to visually retain after import, and in some cases, still be able to edit in Animate. Let's look at how you can import these files, along with their effects, into Animate.

Importing Files to the Stage or Library Panels

From the menu, you can choose File ➤ Import ➤ Import to Stage, or File ➤ Import ➤ Import to Library. With either option, you can add the following graphic file formats: AI, SVG, PSD, JPEG, GIF, PNG, and bitmap. Refer to Figure 19-1.

CHAPTER 19 ■ IMPORTING YOUR ARTWORK

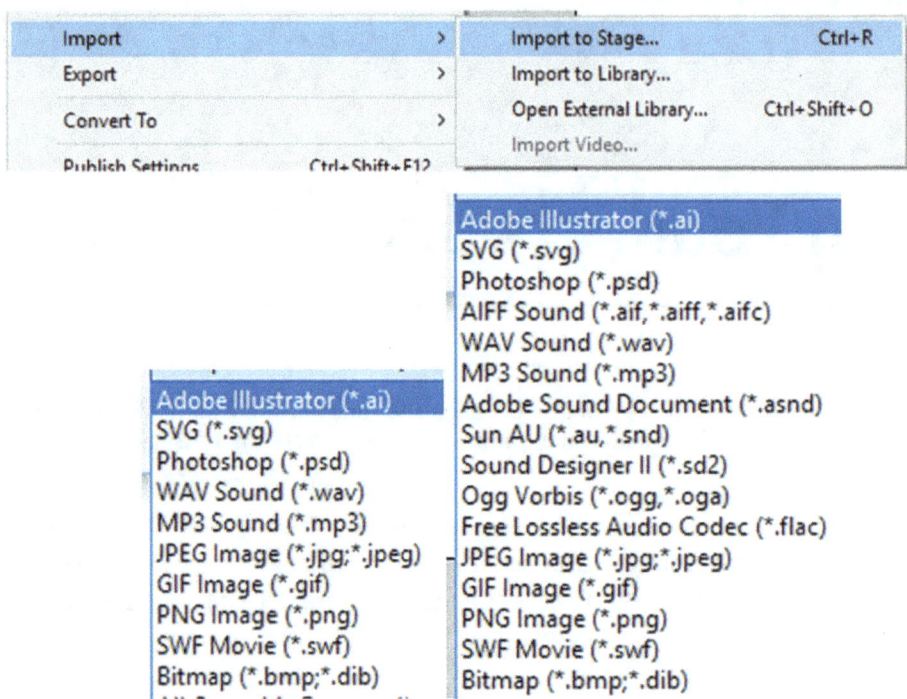

Figure 19-1. *Possible file formats you can import into Animate CC. You may have additional options depending on what software is installed on your computer.*

If you're not familiar with these file formats, review them in Chapter 1.

■ **Note** If you have QuickTime 4 or higher installed on your computer, you can also import TIFF files. More information on this is at `https://helpx.adobe.com/animate/using/placing-artwork.html`.

Import to Stage imports the artwork directly on the Canvas stage and the Library panel. Import to Library places the files into the Library panel only. If you don't plan to use your images right away on the stage in the current key frames, then Import to Library is the option to choose.

Import an Image Sequence

With Import to Stage, if the images within your folder are in sequence—img_1.jpg, img_2.jpg, img_3.jpg, and so on, Animate recognizes this and asks if you want to import all images at the same time, as seen in Figure 19-2.

CHAPTER 19 ■ IMPORTING YOUR ARTWORK

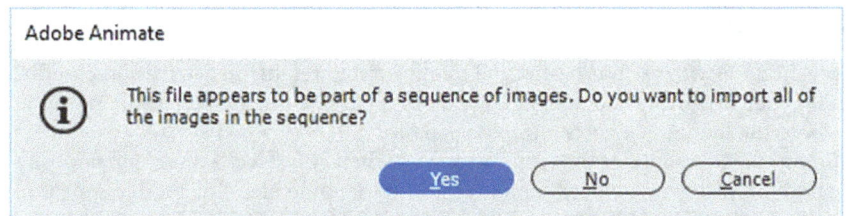

Figure 19-2. *An info alert will ask if you want to import all images in a sequence*

If yes, the images are imported as separate keyframes in the Timeline panel, as seen in Figure 19-3. This saves you the time of importing each image separately if you have created a frame-by-frame portion in your animation. If not, then only the image you selected from the sequence will import.

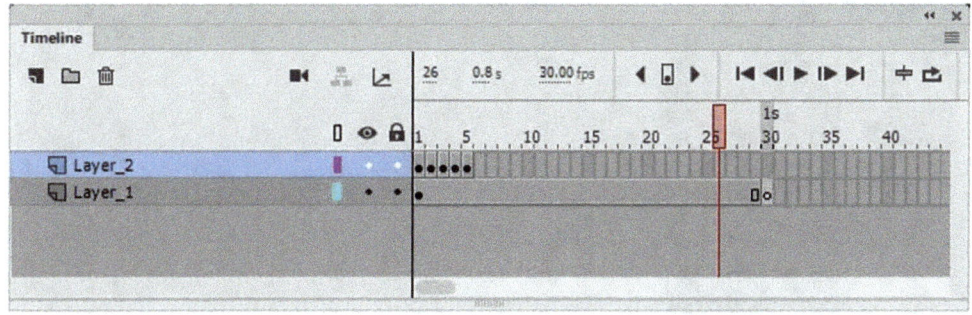

Figure 19-3. *Add your image sequence to the timeline on a layer*

Export Images from an External Library

Sometimes you may want to grab images from another FLA file's library. You can do this using File ➤ Import ➤ Open External Library.

■ **Note** With HTML5 Canvas, the Option to File ➤ Import ➤ Import Video is not available; only for ActionScript 3.0. While you can import WAV and MP3 audio via the Import to Stage or Import to Library, there is another way to add video to your HTML5 Canvas: the Components and Component parameters panels, which I discuss in Chapter 20.

Importing Illustrator and Photoshop Files with Their Elements or Effects Intact

Let's take a short detour back to Photoshop CC and Illustrator CC to talk about what kinds of effects might be applied to objects or layers in these programs and how it relates to Animate.

411

Photoshop CC Blending Modes

If you have built a file in Photoshop CC with various layers, you might want to retain or keep certain blending modes that you have applied to your layers and shapes so that you don't have to adjust them again in Animate. For this section, refer to the blending_effects_animate.psd file.

Photoshop offers 27 different blending modes that you can access when you select a layer, and choose the mode from the Layers panel's drop-down menu, as seen in Figure 19-4. Some blending modes appear differently or not at all, depending on if the object is on a white, black, or colored area.

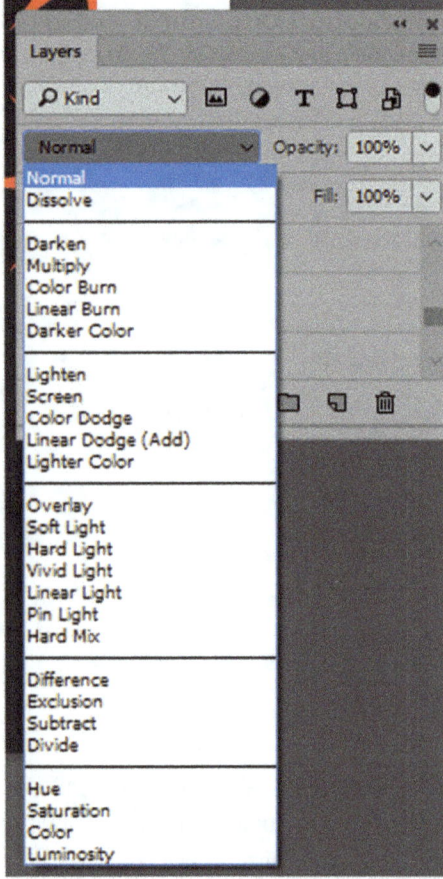

Figure 19-4. Blend modes in Photoshop CC

Blend modes affect four areas.

- **Blend color**: The color applied to the blend mode of the layer (normal, lighten, darken).
- **Opacity**: The degree of transparency or alpha applied to the blend mode.
- **Base color**: The color of pixels on the layer beneath the above blend's color layer.
- **Result color**: The result of the blend's effect on the base color layer when the colors are combined.

CHAPTER 19 ■ IMPORTING YOUR ARTWORK

Figure 19-5 shows how those blend modes appear in the Layers panel in Photoshop.

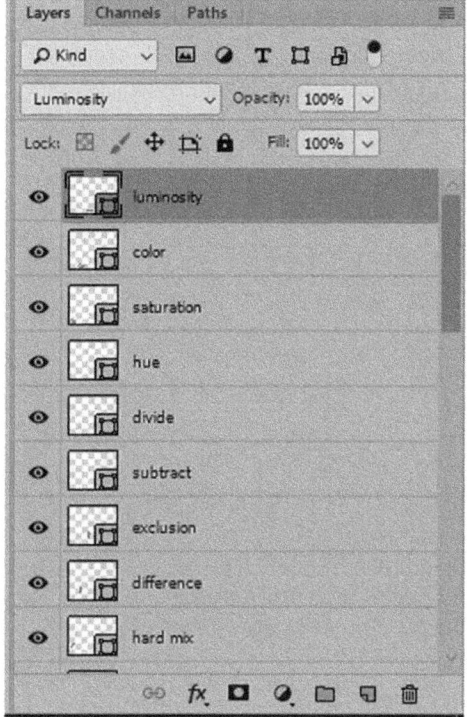

Figure 19-5. *Each layer has a different blending mode applied*

Table 19-1 lists the blends that are available.

Table 19-1. *Photoshop Blending Modes*

Normal -default	Color Dodge	Pin Light
Dissolve	Linear Dodge(Add)	Hard Mix
Darken	Lighter Color	Difference
Multiply	Overlay	Exclusion
Color Burn	Soft Light	Subtract
Linear Burn	Hard Light	Divide
Darker Color	Vivid Light	Hue
Lighten	Linear Light	Saturation
	Color	Luminosity

For more detailed information on these blending modes, visit https://helpx.adobe.com/photoshop/using/blending-modes.html.

413

If you are not sure how to use blending modes in Photoshop, make sure to read *Adobe Photoshop CC Classroom in a Book* by Andrew Faulkner and Conrad Chavez (Adobe Press, 2017) to review this area.

■ **Note** Two blends that are not in this list are Behind and Clear. These only appear as modes for painting tools and have nothing to do with the blending mode effects in the Layers panel. Refer to Figure 19-6.

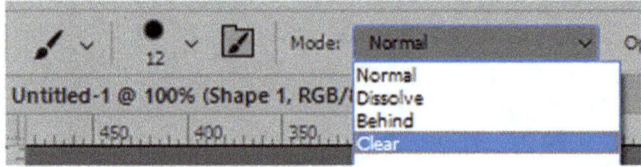

Figure 19-6. *Additional blending modes for paint brushes only*

- **Behind:** Edits or paints only on the transparent part of a layer. This mode works only in layers with Lock Transparency deselected. It is like painting on the back of transparent areas on a sheet of acetate.

- **Clear:** Edits or paints each pixel and makes it transparent. This mode is available for the Shape tools (when fill region is selected), Paint Bucket tool, Brush tool, Pencil tool, Fill command, and Stroke command. You must be in a layer with Lock Transparency deselected to use this mode.

The Photoshop file with the red suns on black and white stripes shows how the red interacts differently with the base color, depending on which effect is chosen. In Figure 19-7, note how the hue blending mode (the fourth row on the far right) will not appear unless a certain color is behind it.

CHAPTER 19 ■ IMPORTING YOUR ARTWORK

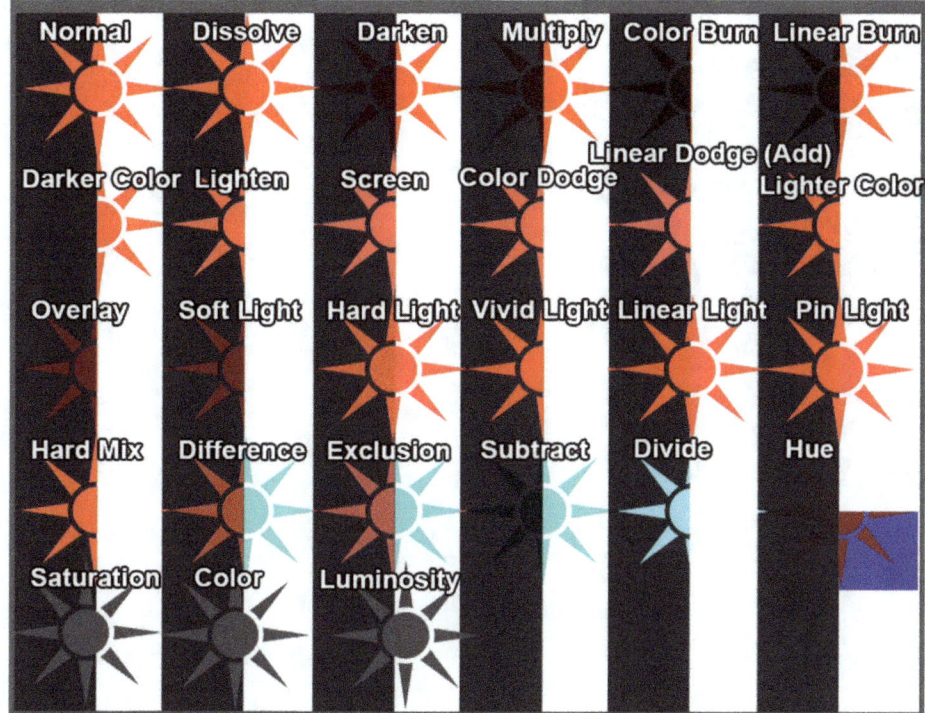

Figure 19-7. How the red suns appear in the Photoshop file

Photoshop CC Layer Styles FX

Other Layer styles are found via the Layers panel in the FX icon. Refer to the layerstyles_animate.psd file and Figure 19-8.

CHAPTER 19 ■ IMPORTING YOUR ARTWORK

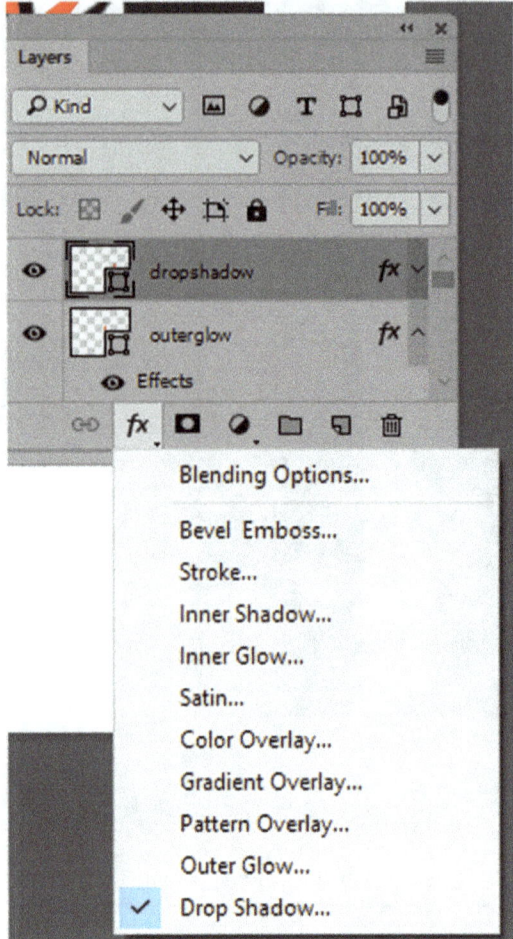

Figure 19-8. *Applying effects or FX to a layer in Photoshop*

In the dialog boxes for each layer, you can create any number of effects that you can apply to your shapes, such as a drop shadow, glow, or emboss. As mentioned in Chapter 8, many more prebuilt complex effects can be found in the Styles panel of Photoshop. Refer to Figure 19-9.

CHAPTER 19 ■ IMPORTING YOUR ARTWORK

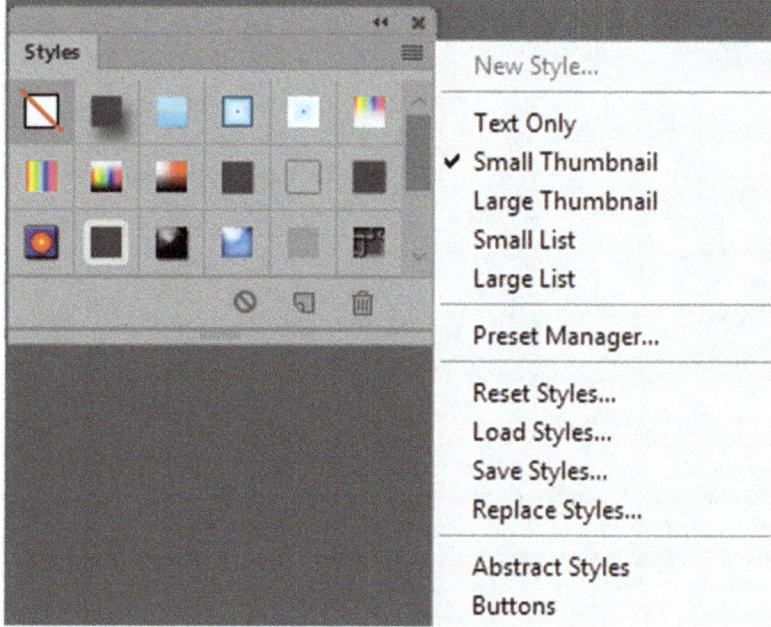

Figure 19-9. *The Styles panel has many prebuilt styles that you can apply to layers in Photoshop*

Figure 19-10 shows how the Base styles appear on the red sun in Photoshop.

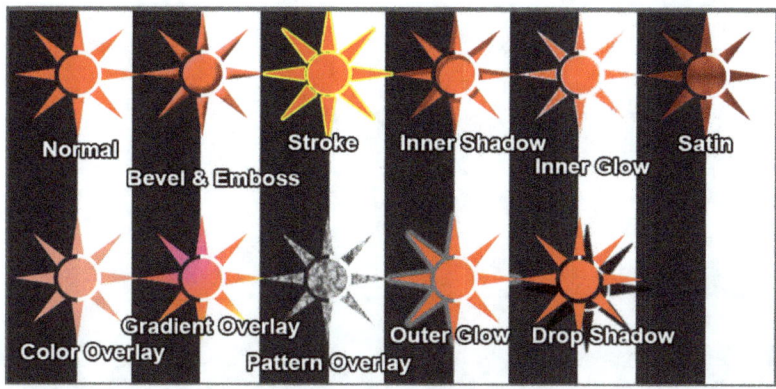

Figure 19-10. *Each shape as a different effect (FX) applied to it*

Illustrator CC Blending Modes

The same is true in Illustrator CC; various objects may have different blending effects applied to them. Unlike Photoshop, where you apply the effects to the layer, in Illustrator, you apply the effects to the object via the Transparency panel when the object is selected. Refer to Figure 19-11.

417

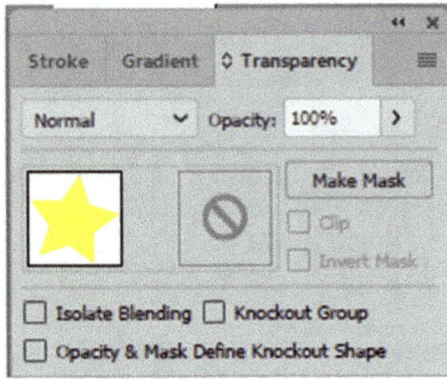

Figure 19-11. *Add a blend mode to an object in Illustrator*

There are only 16 blend options in Illustrator. This is due to how Illustrator handles the blending of vector images. If you need access to Photoshop's blending options, you can always copy your Illustrator vector object as a Smart Object into Photoshop and use those blending modes instead.

As with Photoshop CC, the resulting color change produced by the blend is a combination of blend color, opacity, and base color. Refer to Figure 19-12.

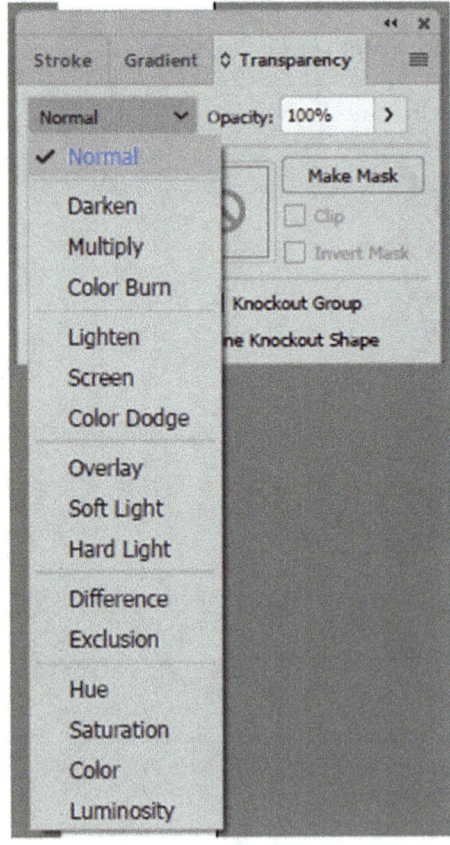

Figure 19-12. *The drop-down menu for the blend mode options*

Table 19-2 lists the blends that are available.

Table 19-2. Illustator Blending Modes

Normal -default	Soft Light
Darken	Hard Light
Multiply	Difference
Color Burn	Exclusion
Lighten	Hue
Screen	Saturation
Color Dodge	Color
Overlay	Luminosity

For more details on these Illustrator blending modes, visit https://helpx.adobe.com/illustrator/using/transparency-blending-modes.html.

Also refer to *Adobe Illustrator CC Classroom in a Book* by Brian Wood (Adobe Press, 2017) if you are unsure how to use these modes effectively.

Notice how the red star changes on the base colors, depending on the type of effect that is chosen. Refer to Figure 19-13.

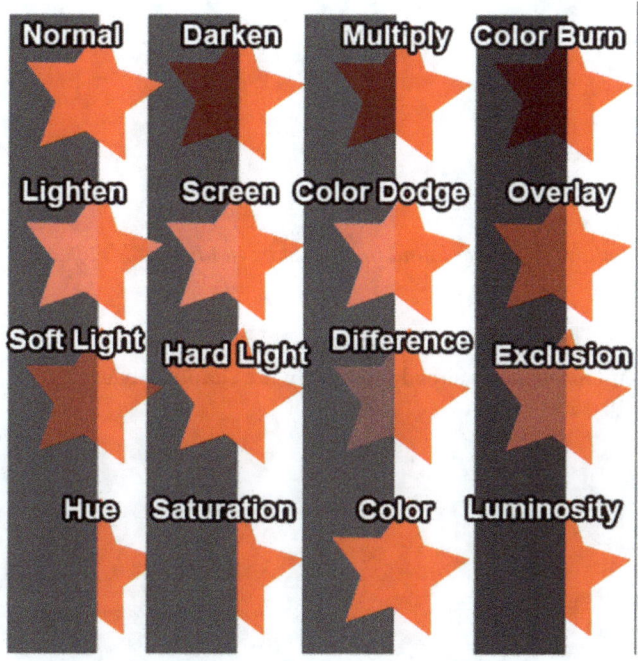

Figure 19-13. Different blend modes effect how each star appears on the background

CHAPTER 19 ■ IMPORTING YOUR ARTWORK

Illustrator CC Effects FX

In Illustrator, you can apply various effects or filters to your shapes. Look at the filter_stars.ai file. To access these effects, you can use filters such as Effect ➤ Stylize, SVG filters and other Photoshop-related effects in the lower half of the menu. Refer to Figure 19-14.

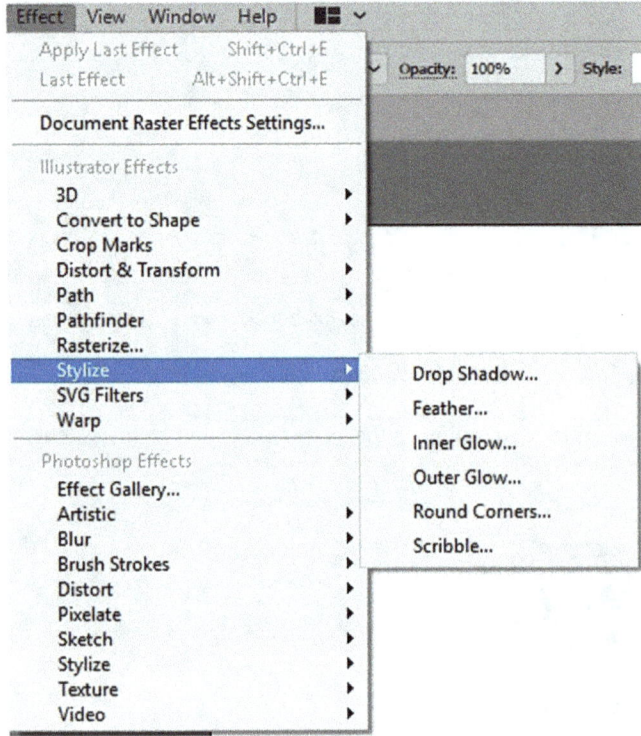

Figure 19-14. *There are many effects that are similar to the ones found in Photoshop in Illustrator's Effect menu*

You saw in Chapters 11 and 15 that these could be edited in the Appearance panel.

As mentioned in Chapter 15, you can find many of effects already created in the Graphic Styles panel and the Graphic Style libraries. Refer to Figure 19-15.

CHAPTER 19 ■ IMPORTING YOUR ARTWORK

Figure 19-15. *The Graphic Styles panel can store many prebuilt styles*

You can add your own effects using the Appearance panel in the FX icon, as seen in Chapter 15. Figure 19-16 shows how these filter effects appear on some star shapes in Illustrator.

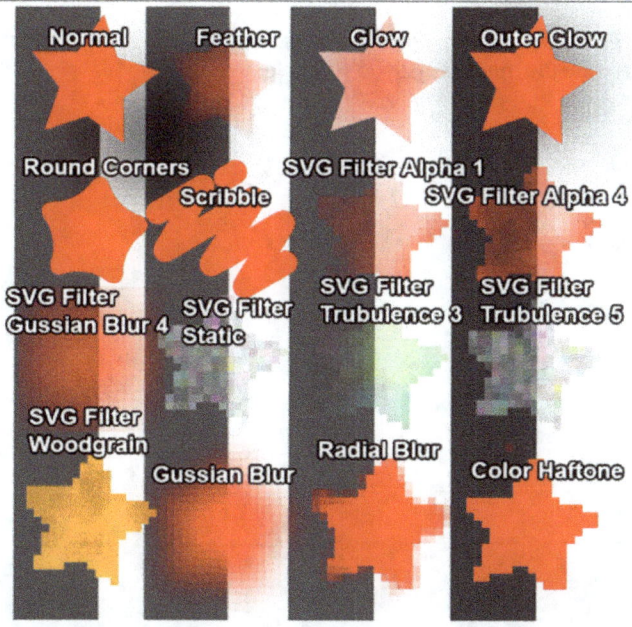

Figure 19-16. *Applying effects (FX) in Illustrator to shapes*

Importing into Adobe Animate

Now that you know more about blend modes and effects, let's import these effects and filter from a Photoshop (.psd) file and an Illustrator (.ai) file.

If you have Photoshop or Illustrator open after you saved the files, you can now close those programs and return to Adobe Animate to start importing.

421

CHAPTER 19 ■ IMPORTING YOUR ARTWORK

To test and add your filter and effects on the stage, Choose File ➤ Import ➤ Import to Stage, and select either a PSD or an AI file, and click Open. To make sure that you are seeing the same screenshot in your dialog box, click the Show Advanced Options button on the bottom left of the Import to Stage dialog box. Refer to Figure 19-17.

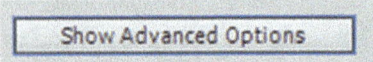

Figure 19-17. *Show Advanced Options button for import*

It then changes to Hide Advanced Options, as seen in Figure 19-18.

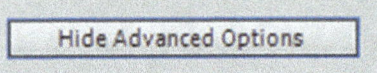

Figure 19-18. *Hide Advanced Options button for import*

If you plan to edit all of your images as one group rather than individually, use the Hide Advanced Options layout. When Advanced settings are hidden, these are the options that you see. Refer to Figure 19-19.

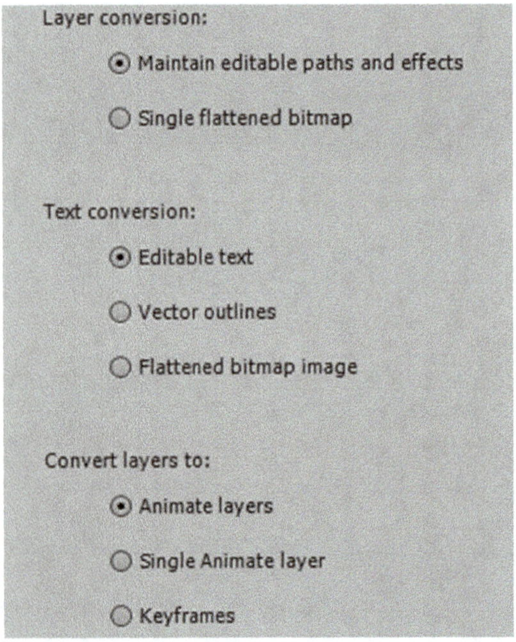

Figure 19-19. *Basic import setting for all imported layers*

422

No matter which option you use, for this lesson, you want to make sure that you maintain editable paths and effects, and do not flatten, that any text remains editable and does not become an outline or a bitmap image, and that each item is set to individual Animate layers rather than a single layer or keyframe for an image sequence.

For now, stay on the Advanced settings option.

Photoshop PSD Import of File

In Import to Stage advanced options, the top area of the dialog box has an option if your (.psd) file has Photoshop layer comps, which you read about in Chapter 4. If the file only has one layer comp, then this area menu is unavailable; if two, then you can select the layer comp from the drop-down menu. Use Blending_effects_animate.psd for this example. Refer to Figure 19-20.

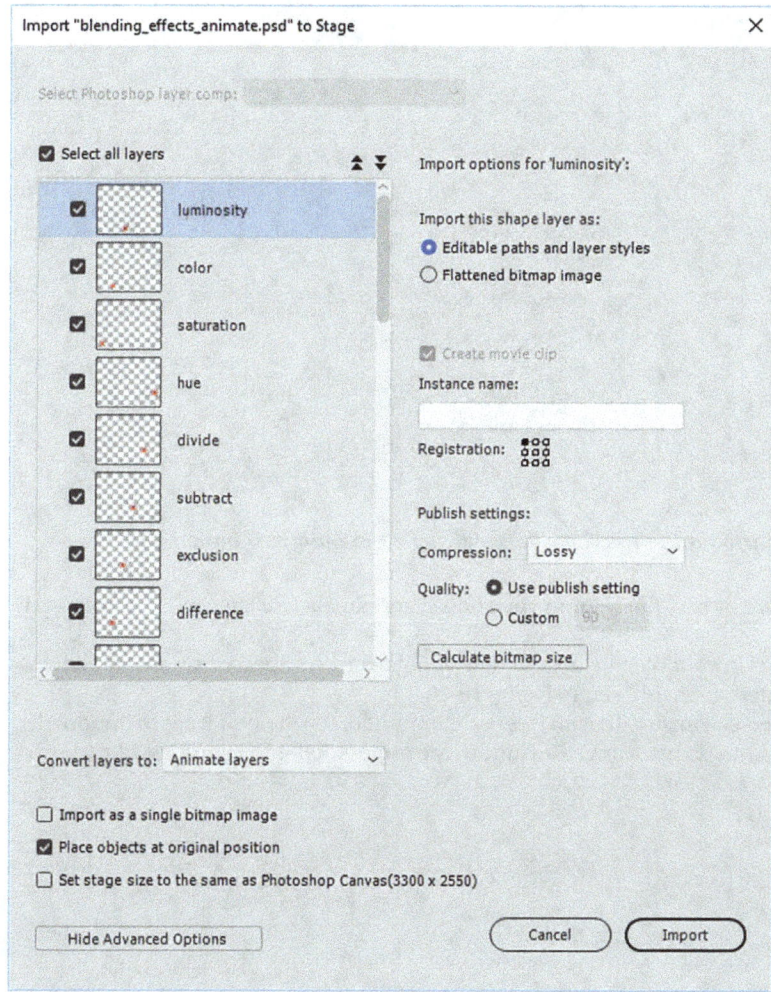

Figure 19-20. *When a Photoshop file only has one layer comp, then the layer comp option is unavailable*

CHAPTER 19 ■ IMPORTING YOUR ARTWORK

When working with several artboards, the preview layout appears with folders. You have to select artboards from the layers preview area on the left, as you would any other layer, as seen in Figure 19-21.

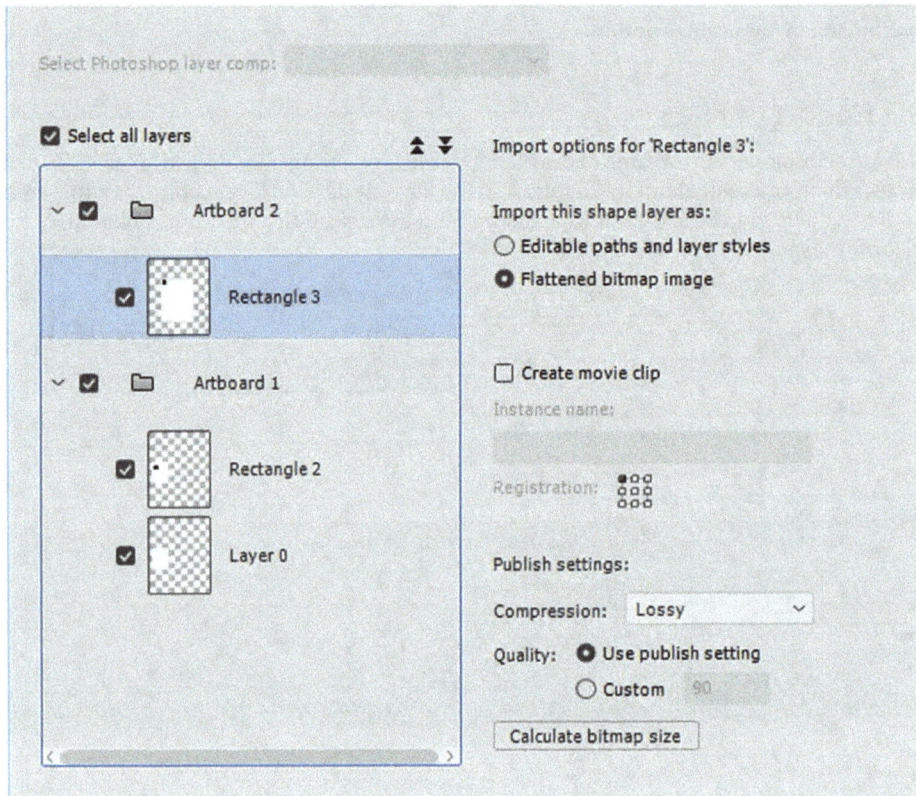

Figure 19-21. *If your file contains artboards, this is how they will appear in Animate's Import panel*

Whether you have one artboard or two, the settings you choose in Animate will affect which layers you plan to import.

If there are folders or artboards in your file, the up and down double arrows above the preview allow you to expand and collapse all folders at once. Refer to Figure 19-20.

By clicking Select all layers, you can ensure that all layers are imported. If you don't want to import all layers or folders, uncheck the ones you do not want to include in the import. Refer to Figure 19-22.

CHAPTER 19 ■ IMPORTING YOUR ARTWORK

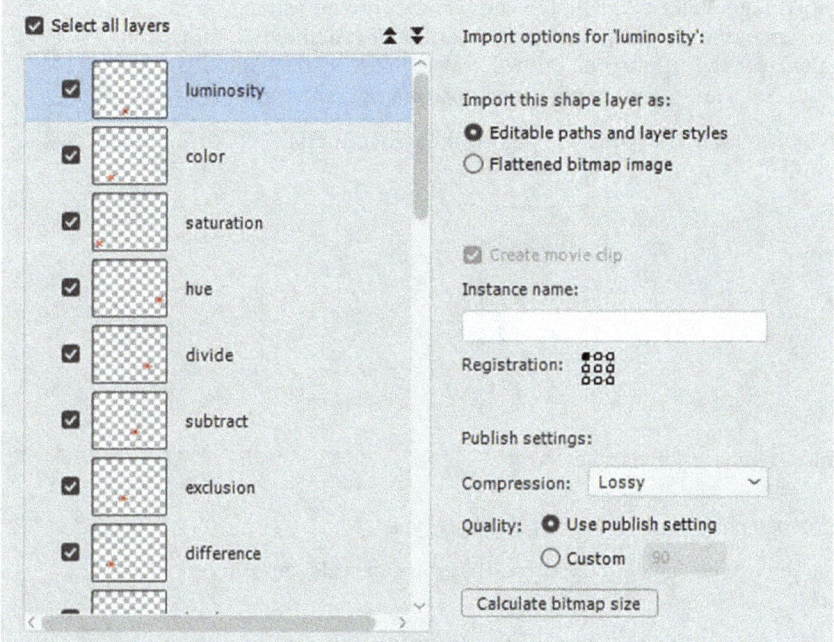

Figure 19-22. *All layers have been selected*

For example, you may have created a background in Photoshop that was only for testing how an object appeared on a certain color. You may not plan to use that background as part of the animation, so uncheck it.

Animate gives you two options on how to import a shape layer.

In advanced settings, you can set each layer individually. You will know which layer is selected by the change in the message in the upper right. Shift-click layers that you want to have the same setting and apply an import option.

- **Editable paths and layer styles:** This ensures that any paths (vector shapes drawn with the pen tool) or layer styles that you have created in Photoshop will import and you can still edit them within Animate. However, be aware that this is dependent on two conditions: the type of FLA format you chose (ActionScript 3.0 or HTML5 Canvas) and whether Animate supports that layer style. You'll look at this shortly.

■ **Note** Animate cannot import Photoshop Smart Objects as editable objects because they contain raster and vector elements. So, to retain the visual attributes of these Smart Objects, you must rasterize them and import them as bitmaps. You cannot import adjustment layers such as levels or invert and these must be applied and rasterize together with the layer you are altering in Photoshop. Also, HTML5 Canvas FLA can only import the first frame of a video's layers in a PSD file. If you need more frames of the video to be in your Animate file, you have to flatten the frames into clips in Photoshop or import the video into a video component, as you will see in Chapter 20.

425

- **Flattened bitmap image:** Rather than flatten your artwork in Photoshop, you can allow Animate to flatten the artwork. This is a good option if you find that Animate is not supporting the layer styles; however, this will cause that style to be uneditable in Animate, so always run a test to make sure you choose the right option.

If your (.psd) layer contains editable text, you have slightly different options. Refer to Figure 19-23.

Figure 19-23. *Choose the Import options for your text layer*

- **Editable text:** You can change or edit the text and retype it.
- **Vector outlines:** The text has an editable shape that you can scale, but you can't retype the letters.
- **Flatten bitmap image:** This option is removed in the 2019 version. The text becomes a bitmap graphic and can't be accurately altered, as you would a vector or editable text layer; however, the basic shape and any applied effect on the font are retained to preserve the way it appeared in Photoshop.

If you want your layer to be a movie clip symbol added to the Library panel, you can check the "Create a movie clip" box (it is already checked if "Editable paths and layer styles" is selected). Then give the movie clip a name and set its registration point. The registration point is useful when objects may spin or move along a motion path. Refer to Figure 19-24.

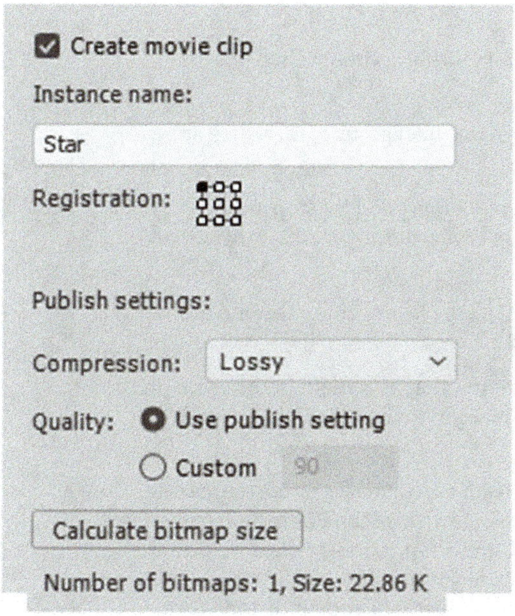

CHAPTER 19 ■ IMPORTING YOUR ARTWORK

Figure 19-24. You can set a name for each layer as a movie clip symbol for the stage

Like the exporting of a graphic, you can set the quality of the import or publish settings. Compression can be lossy (compression of JPEG format) or lossless (no compression or a GIF or PNG format), and you can set a custom quality for the size. If you are worried the graphic may be too large, click the Calculate Bitmap Size button, which gives the file size. By Shift-clicking two or more layers in the preview, you calculate the file size of these bitmap shapes or layers collectively. You can then decide how these layers are converted and distributed.

The next section in advanced setting deals with how the layers convert to the stage. Refer to Figure 19-25.

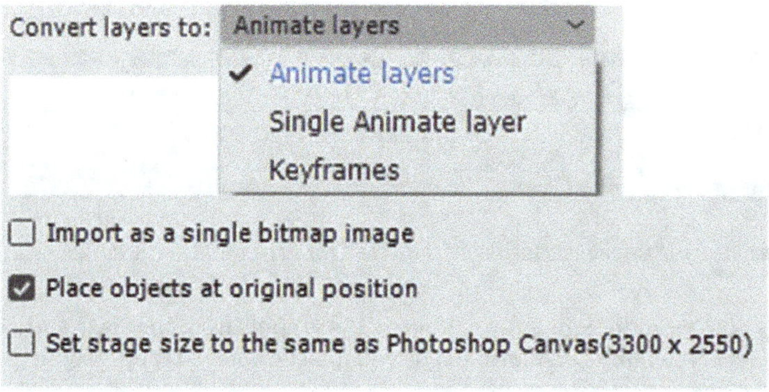

Figure 19-25. Decide how you want your Photoshop layers to convert

427

You can convert layers to the following.

- **Animate layers:** Puts each graphic on its own layer. This is good if each item is to move separately in the keyframes.

- **Single Animate layer:** If all the layers are part of one background, then they appear on one layer and not separately.

- **Keyframes:** Puts each layer on its own keyframe. This is good for stop-frame animations where one character needs multiple keyframes to create a movement, such as jumping or running.

- **Import as a single bitmap image:** Ensures that all the layers import as one bitmap. If you don't want this to happen, leave it unchecked.

- **Place objects at original position:** Ensures that the shapes remain in the same place or coordinates that they were in Photoshop in relation to the other layers, regardless of the size of the Animate stage.

- **Set stage size the same as Photoshop Canvas (# X #):** Increases or decreases the size of your Animate stage or canvas to match whatever size the Photoshop canvas is. With multiple artboards of varying sizes from Photoshop, Animate chooses one size for all the layers and not the different artboard sizes. If you don't want your Animate stage to change, leave this box unchecked; some shapes will appear outside the canvas until you drag them to a different location.

When you are done with your settings, click the Import button. Refer to Figure 19-26.

Figure 19-26. *Click the Import button so that the layers can import to the stage*

Upon clicking Import, you may discover a warning in the Output panel regarding some effects not being applied. Refer to Figure 19-27.

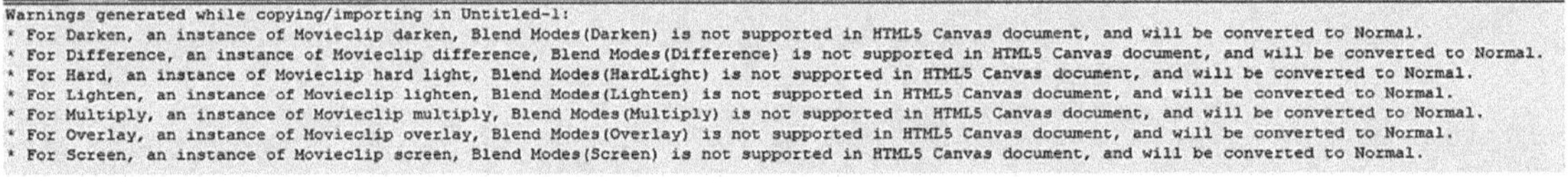

Figure 19-27. *The Output file gives a warning message if certain effects do not apply in the Animate file*

If these effects do not retain simply, Edit ➤ Undo right away to remove the graphic from the stage and Library panel, and then re-import those layers as bitmaps. Alternatively, you may be able to reapply some settings using Animate, as you will see shortly.

In HTML5 Canvas, you can import as a bitmap to retain the basic blend settings. In ActionScript 3.0 FLA, you may not have to set bitmap for all layers. Either way, the bitmaps (Assets folder) and movie clip symbols appear in the Library panel on the Stage and Timeline panels. Refer to my final file, animate_photo_blend.fla. For the most part, this is a retained the bitmap representation of the blend that cannot be altered. Refer to Figure 19-28.

CHAPTER 19 ■ IMPORTING YOUR ARTWORK

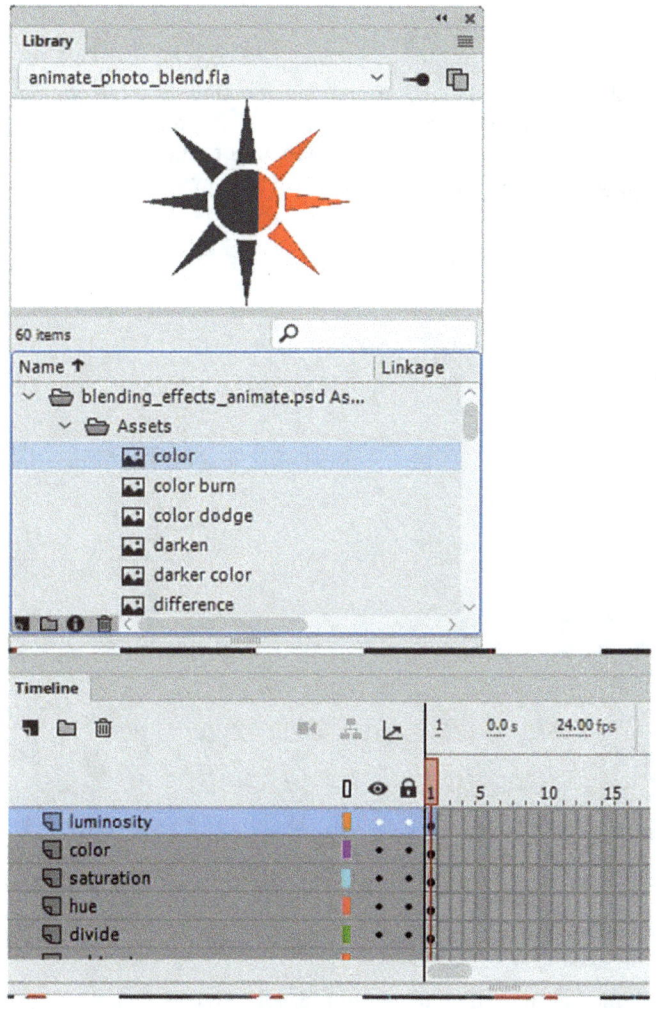

Figure 19-28. *Each of the layers were imported into the Library and Timeline panels appearing on the stage*

■ **Important Tip**   Photoshop CC does a better job of scaling your images than Animate, so if your images are too large on the stage, make sure to scale it to the correct size in Photoshop before you import.

CHAPTER 19 ■ IMPORTING YOUR ARTWORK

Illustrator AI Import

Importing an Illustrator (.ai) file to the stage is very similar to importing a Photoshop (.psd) file; however, there are a few key differences. Use the blendmode_stars.ai and blendmoded_stars2.ai files for this example.

Again, in a new HTML5 Canvas file, choose File ➤ Import ➤ Import to Stage. Make sure the settings are in Advanced Options so that you can follow along with me. As with Photoshop import, if you stay in the regular settings, it is assumed that you are editing all layers as a group, and you will not have the preview options, as seen in Figure 19-29.

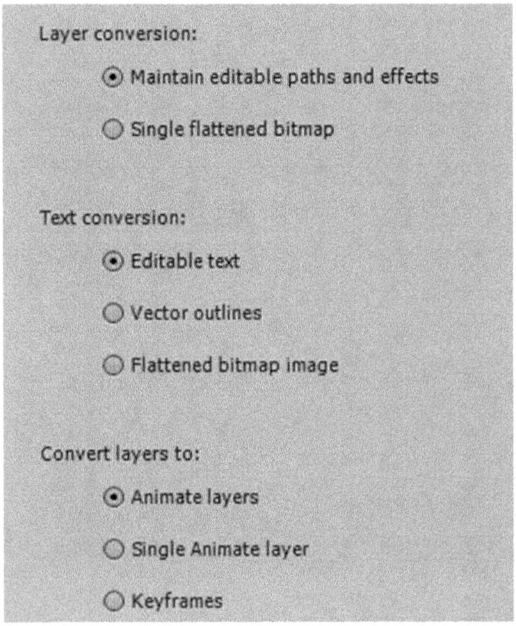

Layer conversion:
- ● Maintain editable paths and effects
- ○ Single flattened bitmap

Text conversion:
- ● Editable text
- ○ Vector outlines
- ○ Flattened bitmap image

Convert layers to:
- ● Animate layers
- ○ Single Animate layer
- ○ Keyframes

Figure 19-29. Basic import setting for all Illustrator layers

- **Select Illustrator Artboard:** If your file has more than one artboard, you can choose the artboard from the drop-down menu that you want to import the objects from. Refer to Figure 19-30.

CHAPTER 19 ■ IMPORTING YOUR ARTWORK

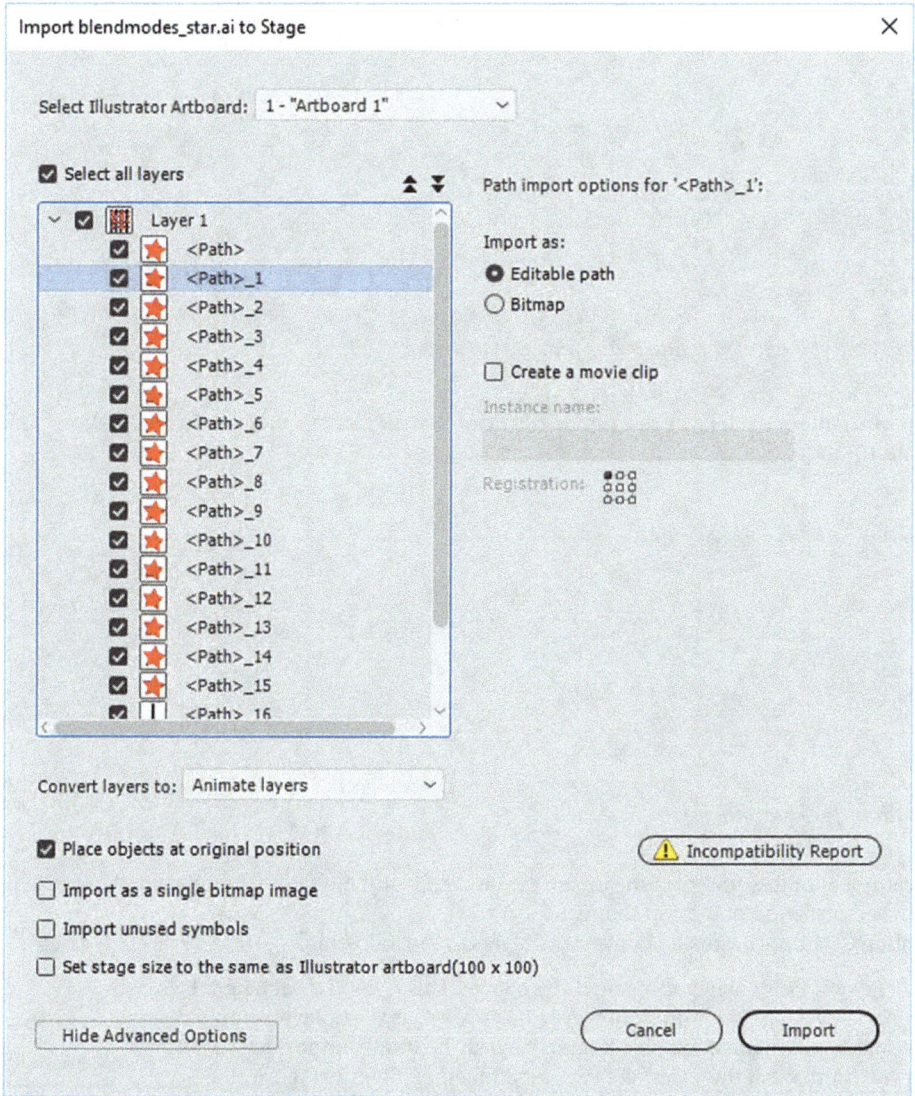

Figure 19-30. Import all layers and sublayers to the stage

As with Photoshop PSD import, you can select all layers or chose the layer that you want to alter. The double arrows on top of the preview allow you to collapse or expand to see the sublayers.

- **Import as**: Allows you to set the settings for each object you plan to import.

- **Editable Path:** The path or shape remains editable. Illustrator symbols import as Animate symbols if on a layer. Clipping masks, transparency, pattern strokes, and fills are preserved.

- **Bitmap:** The shape is changed to a bitmap image.

431

If the layer or sublayer contains text, as with the Photoshop (.psd) import, you can choose whether the text remains editable, is only vector outlines, or is a bitmap graphic. Refer to Figure 19-31.

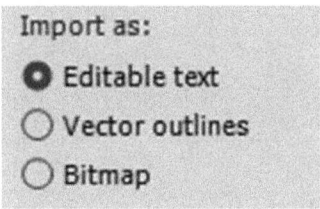

Figure 19-31. *Choose how you want you Illustrator files' text to import*

Like Photoshop, you can set each layer as a movie clip symbol with a name, along with registration points. Refer to Figure 19-32.

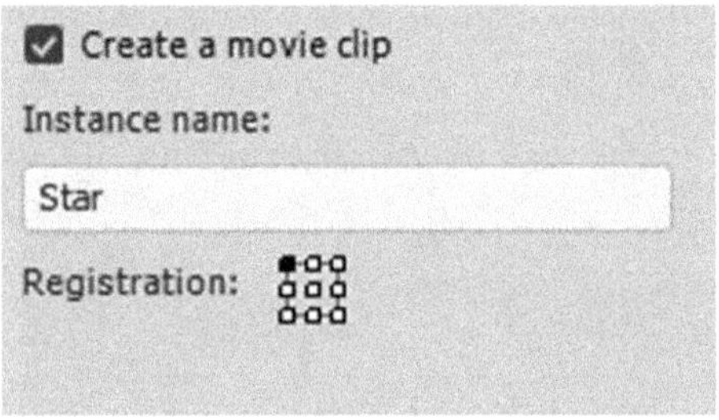

Figure 19-32. *Set a name for your movie clip*

However, you cannot alter the quality of the image as you could with the Photoshop (import) because you are working with vectors, and not bitmap shapes.

Like the Photoshop CC import, you can convert the layers to the following.

- **Animate layers:** Puts each graphic on its own layer. This is good if each item is to move separately in the keyframes; however, be aware that all sublayers import as one layer, so make sure to put each object on its own layer, or only import to the Library panel if you don't want the sublayers to appear together. Refer to Figure 19-33.

CHAPTER 19 ■ IMPORTING YOUR ARTWORK

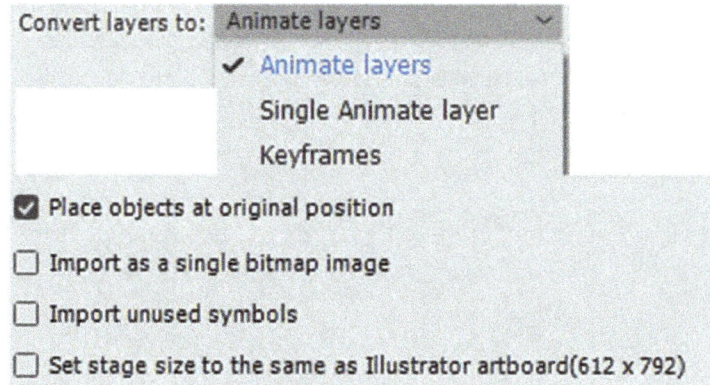

Figure 19-33. Convert Illustrator layers on import

- **Single Animate layer**: If all the layers are part of one background, then they appear on one layer, and not separately.

- **Keyframes:** Puts each layer on its own keyframe. This is good for stop-frame animations where one character needs multiple keyframes to create a movement, such as jumping or running.

- **Place objects at original position:** Ensures that the shapes remain in the same place in relation to the other Illustrator layers as they appeared in Illustrator regardless of the size of the Animate stage.

- **Import as a single bitmap image:** Ensures that all the layers import as one bitmap. If you don't want this to happen, leave it unchecked.

- **Import unused symbols:** Imports the unused symbols.

- **Set stage size the same as Illustrator Artboard (# X #):** Increases or decreases the size of your Animate stage or canvas to match the size of the Illustrator artboard. If you don't want your Animate stage to change, leave this box unchecked.

When you are done with your settings, click the Import button, as seen in Figure 19-34.

Figure 19-34. Choose Import to import your Illustrator layers

433

CHAPTER 19 ■ IMPORTING YOUR ARTWORK

■ **Note** Before import, the dialog box will generate an incompatibility report. You can review this for issues before you import your Illustrator layers or choose to ignore and import the layers. Check "apply recommended import settings" and Click OK to Exit and the warning will disappear. Refer to Figure 19-35.

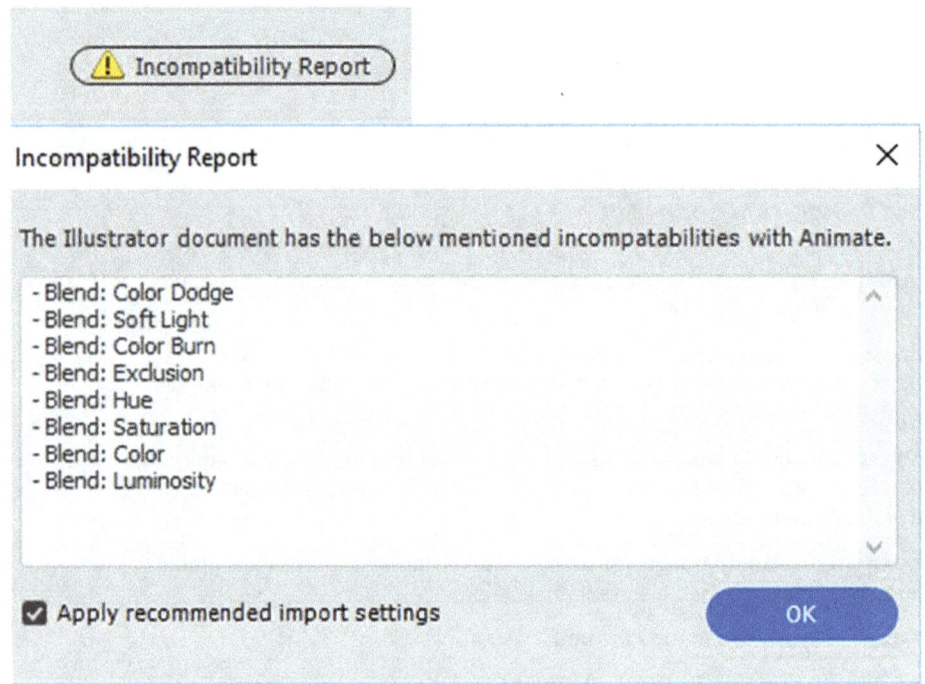

Figure 19-35. Review the Incompatibility Report for issues with blends or effects

As with Photoshop, upon clicking Import, you may discover a warning in the Output panel about some effects not being applied. If these effects do not retain, simply Edit ➤ Undo right away to remove the items from the stage and Library panel, and import these layers again as a bitmap. Alternatively, you may be able to reapply some settings using Animate, as you will see shortly.

For HTML5 Canvas animations, when you import your movie clips, I recommend importing the objects with effects as a bitmap; however, be aware that it may come in as low resolution. For ActionScript 3.0 FLA files, you may be able to retain some of the effects and not have to import all layers as bitmaps. Either way, the bitmaps and movie clip symbols appear in the Library panel, as well on the stage and timeline. Refer to Figure 19-36.

434

CHAPTER 19 ■ IMPORTING YOUR ARTWORK

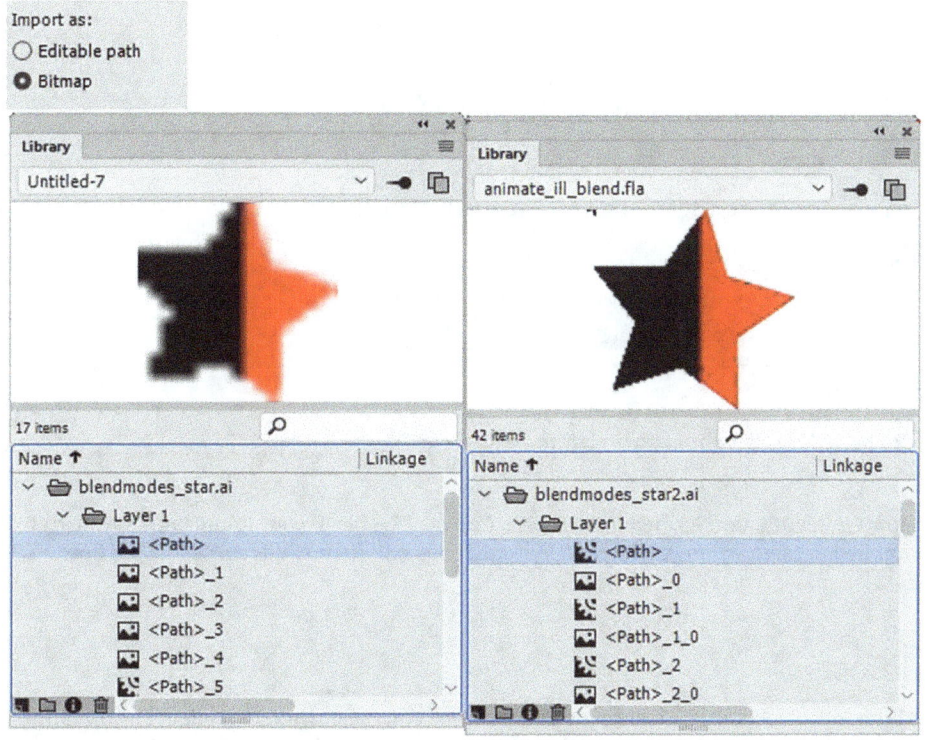

Figure 19-36. *If the Illstrator objects you import as a bitmap are too small in Illustrator, they may appear too low resolution*

In the HTML5 Canvas file, if you find that the resolution is too low upon import, make the shape a bit larger in a new Illustrator file. Illustrator imports at the size that the shape is on its artboard so if it is very small it may be very blurry. By increasing the size of the shape in a new file before importing, you get a better resolution of the effect that you are making into a bitmap. You can always scale the symbol down in Animate later without affecting the bitmaps quality. Refer to the animate_ill_blend.fla file.

■ **Note** If you only have one shape that you want to quickly paste into an Animate layer rather than import, while in Illustrator with a shape selected you can Edit ➤ Copy and then in Animate choose from the menu Edit ➤ Paste in Center, this will add the shape directly into an FLA file onto the stage into the current keyframe. In some cases, you may find that this method preserves some blend settings; however, you have the option to either import a shape or a grouped object as a bitmap or keep the AI Importer preferences; either way, you have to make the pasted object a symbol to add it to the Library panel. Refer to Figure 19-37.

CHAPTER 19 ■ IMPORTING YOUR ARTWORK

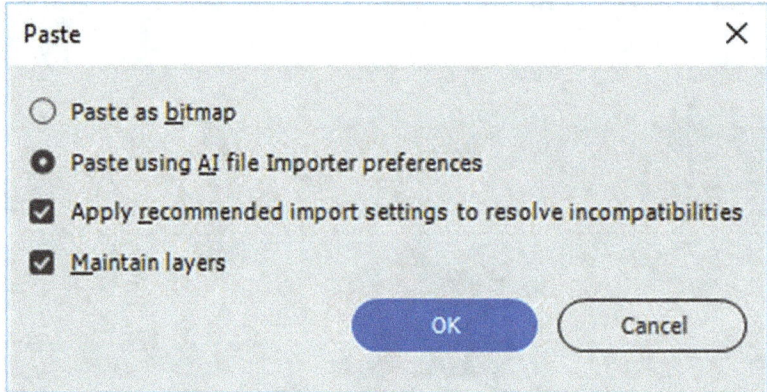

Figure 19-37. *You can paste Illustrator objects directly into Animate*

Whether you import into an ActionScript 3.0 or HTML5 Canvas FLA file, if your Photoshop or Illustrator files have no effects applied to them when you import, leave them as editable, as this preserves the best quality of that graphic.

Animate CC Effects

If you never applied blends or effects in Photoshop or Illustrator, or you need to alter an effect in Animate CC, you can still apply effects to your movie clips via the Properties panel via the Color Effect, Display, and Filters tabs. This does not affect the original movie clip symbol in the Library panel; only the one placed on the stage. Refer to Figure 19-38.

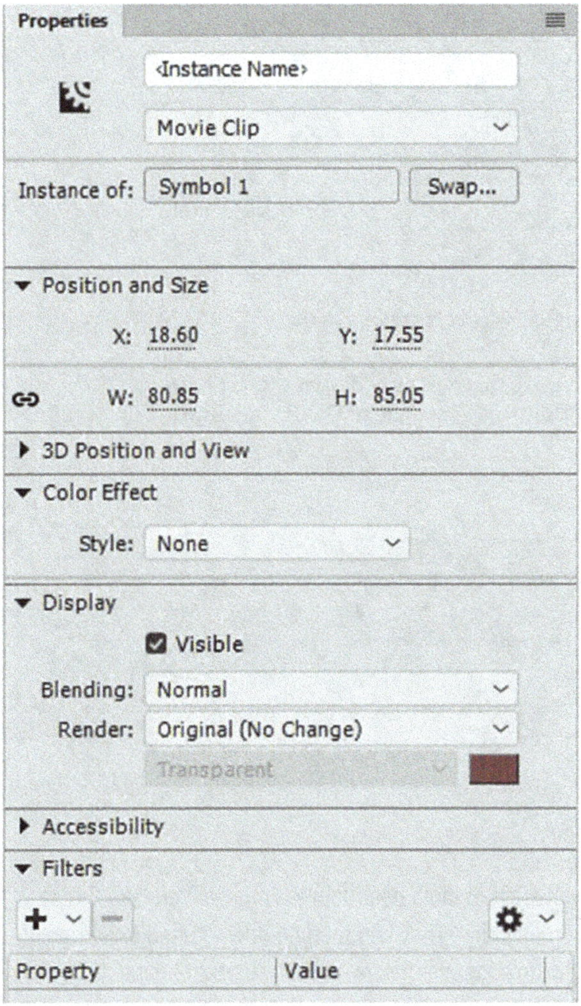

Figure 19-38. For movie clip symbols, the Properties panel allows you to adjust the effects of the symbol

■ **Note** If you are using an ActionScript 3.0 FLA file, you have access to all of these options; however, with an HTML5 Canvas FLA, some JavaScript has not caught up yet to some blending modes and filters, so they are not available in this format. If you need to retain these effects from your Photoshop or Illustrator files, make sure to rasterize the artwork as a bitmap as mentioned in the "Illustrator AI Import" section of this chapter.

Working with Symbols

The color effects can only be applied to symbols (created from shapes in Animate or added at import) and cannot be applied to imported shapes (single or grouped shapes), primitives, drawing objects, or bitmap images that are on the stage. Refer to Figure 19-39.

CHAPTER 19 ■ IMPORTING YOUR ARTWORK

Figure 19-39. These shapes or primiatives cannot have color effects applied to them

Symbols are created from a shape, object, or primitive that you have drawn with a Shape tool, Line tool (N), Rectangle tool (R), Oval tool (O), PolyStar tool, Primitive (Rectangle or Oval), or a drawing object after it was converted from a primitive. Refer to Figure 19-40.

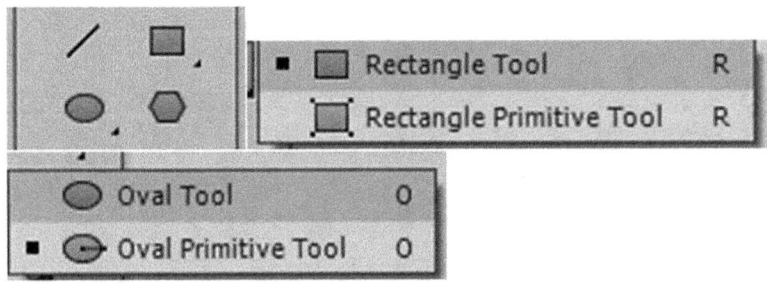

Figure 19-40. Tools used to create shapes and primitives

■ **Note** These shapes follow a type of edit hierarchy of least to most destructive. Primitives are like Smart Objects and maintain some editing options in the Properties panel. They can then be downgraded to a drawing object via the Properties panel (see Figure 19-41); this is how an object acts in Illustrator that keeps its stroke attached. The drawing object is then downgraded to a shape using break apart icon where parts or sections become detached. A shape can be upgraded to a drawing object, but not a primitive. Primitives, objects, and shapes can be grouped with Modify ➤ Group or Ungroup for easier movement on stage. Regardless, none of these are symbols.

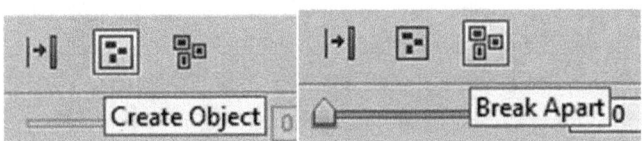

Figure 19-41. Primatives can become objects or broken appart using the Properties panel

Drag around the entire shape with the Selection tool (V) or Subselection tool (A) and right-click the shape, and choose Modify ➤ Convert to Symbol. Or from the Library panel, click the New Symbol icon (far lower left) in the lower left or in the panel's menu to create a new blank symbol. Refer to Figure 19-42.

438

CHAPTER 19 ■ IMPORTING YOUR ARTWORK

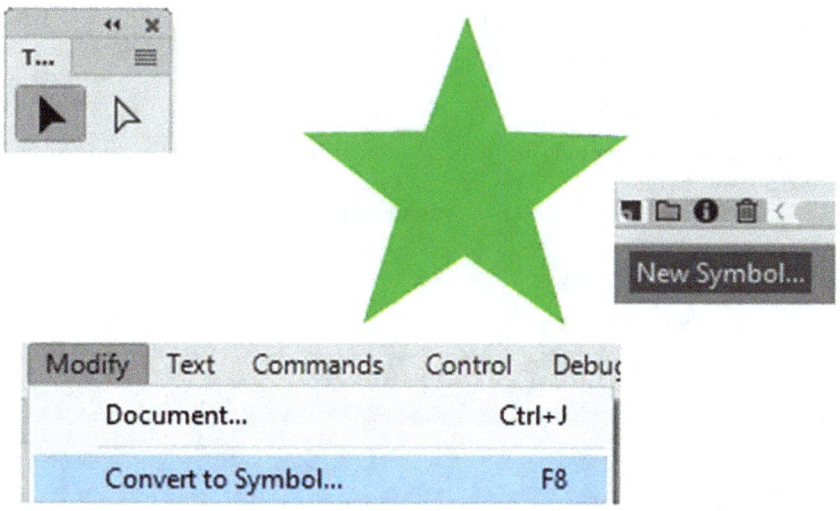

Figure 19-42. Convert a shape to a symbol or create a new blank symbol

■ **Tip**   If the Selection tool(V) touches the inside of the shape it will select only the fill and you can drag it away from the Stroke. The Subselection tool(A) can only select points on an object, but it will not separate the fill from the stroke, so they move together as fills and strokes do in Illustrator or like a drawing object.

You are presented with a dialog box in which you can enter a name and select the type of symbol. Refer to Figure 19-43.

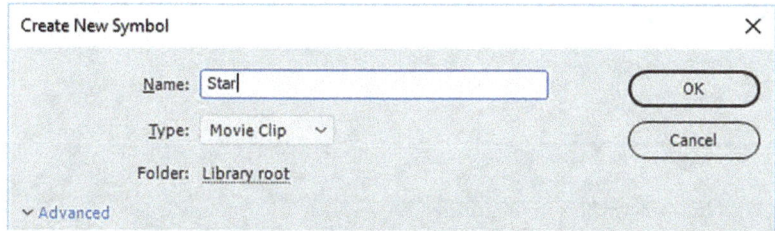

Figure 19-43. Give your symbol a name and a type

■ **Note**   The Advanced tab options are only available to ActionScript 3.0 FLA files, not HTML5 Canvas FLA files. We are using ActionScript 3.0 only for creating videos (.mov), not SWF files, so this Advanced area is not relevant to the chapter.

CHAPTER 19 ■ IMPORTING YOUR ARTWORK

There are three types of symbols available from the type drop-down menu.

- **Movie clip:** A graphic or contains nested animation.
- **Button:** Creates animated buttons.
- **Graphic:** Used for backgrounds or symbols that don't require movement on the stage. They can also be used in the Frame Picker panel, as you will see in Chapter 21. Refer to Figure 19-44 to see how the three different symbols appear in the library.

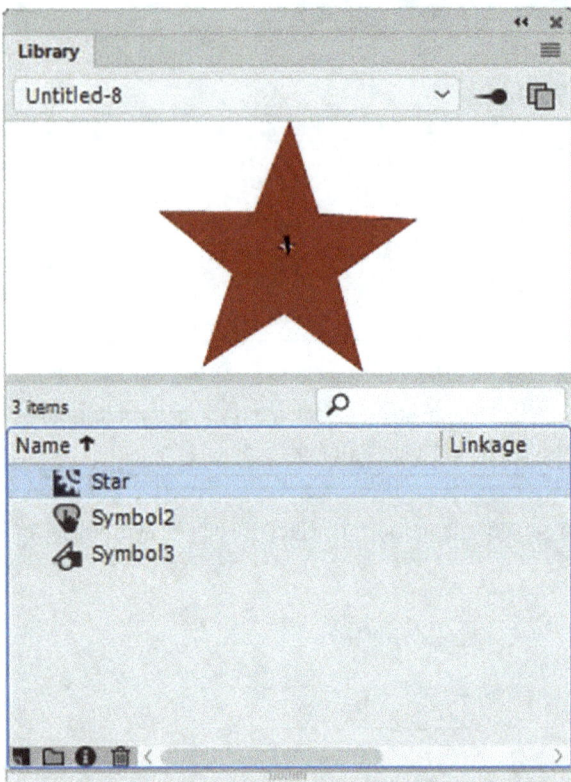

Figure 19-44. Movie clip, graphic, and button symbols in the library

Once you click OK in the Create New Symbol dialog box, the shape or graphic is wrapped in the symbol and added to the library. The shape can be added to the library only as a symbol. Refer to Figure 19-45.

CHAPTER 19 ■ IMPORTING YOUR ARTWORK

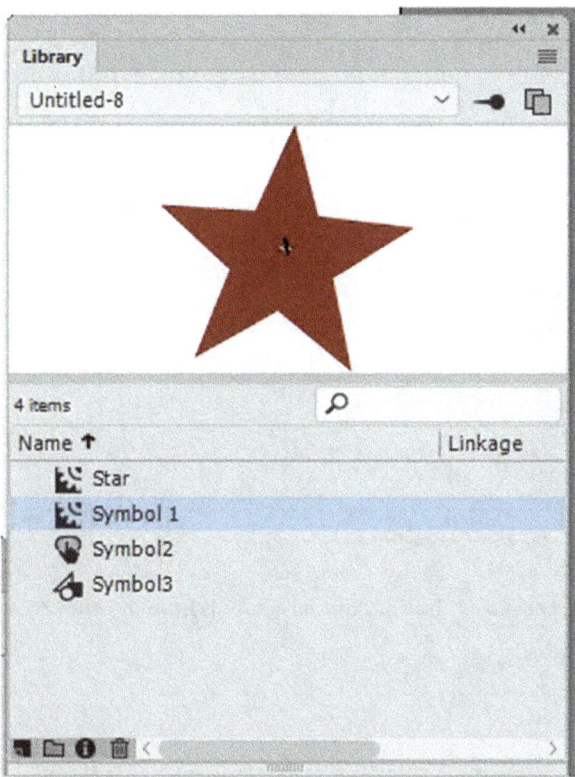

Figure 19-45. Adding another movie clip to the library

This protects the original shape from being altered or broken apart, such as its fill being separated from the outline stroke. You can now scale symbols and apply color effects to it without effecting the original shape. If you need to edit the original shape, simply double-click the symbol on the stage or library to enter the shape's editing mode. Begin editing the shape with tools or the Properties panel. Refer to Figure 19-46.

Figure 19-46. Entering shape editing mode

To exit the symbol editing mode and return to outside symbols, simply click the arrow on the left until you are back to the main stage.

If you need to edit the type of symbol, select it and click the (I) Properties icon in the Library panel. This allows you to rename the symbol or change its type of clip. If you need to alter a symbol on stage, use the Properties panel. You can click the symbol name in the Instance of: field to change the type, the change is reflected in the Library panel. Likewise, use the Properties panel to alter the instance behavior of the symbol and swap it without affecting any further settings in the Libabry panel. Refer to Figure 19-47.

441

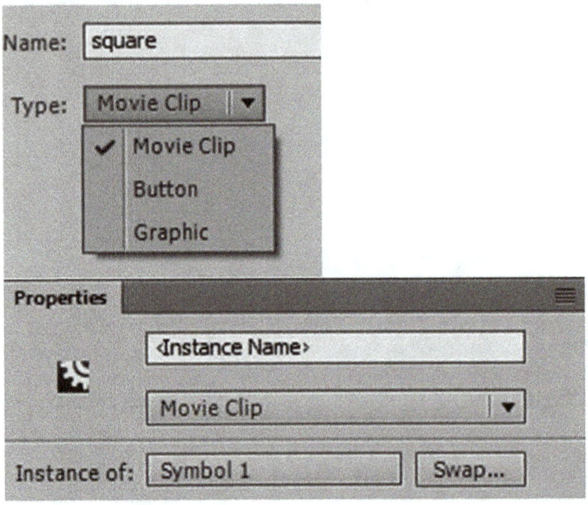

CHAPTER 19 ■ IMPORTING YOUR ARTWORK

Figure 19-47. Alter your symbols' properties either via the Library or Properties panels

With the symbol selected, you can apply the color effects or drag additional symbols from the Library panel onto the stage and alter them as well.

Color Effect Tab

These effects allow you to give your movie clip symbol some basic color effects that are available to both ActionScript 3.0 and HTML5 Canvas FLA files. Refer to the animate_color_effects.fla file and Figure 19-48.

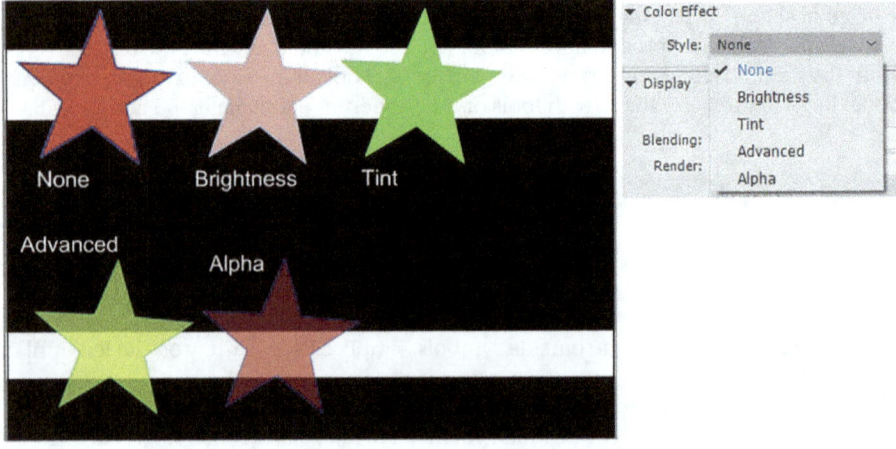

Figure 19-48. Color effects alter the color and opacity of a symbol

442

CHAPTER 19 ■ IMPORTING YOUR ARTWORK

- **None:** The default with no effect applied.
- **Brightness:** Allows you to alter how light or dark a clip appears. Darker colors are a negative percentage and lighter colors are a positive percentage. If you find the resultant color appears too white or black, keep your slider somewhere in the middle range and do not set to either extreme. This does not affect the movie clips transparency or alpha. Refer to Figure 19-49.

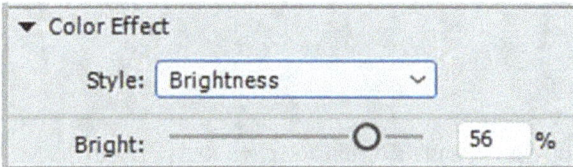

Figure 19-49. Alter the brightness of a symbol with color effect

- **Tint:** Allows you to adjust the color of the object and its red, green, and blue color channels. You can give the original color a slight tint or make it a totally new color by adjusting the sliders or choosing from the color pallet on the upper right. Refer to Figure 19-50.

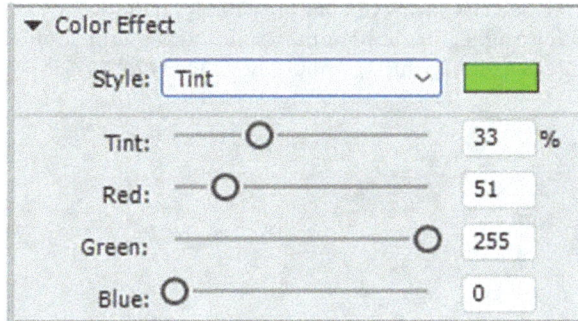

Figure 19-50. Alter the tint of a symbol with color effect

- **Advanced:** Allows you to adjust transparency (alpha) as well as the RGB color channels. By dragging and holding your mouse over the numbers, you can alter the range and color of the movie clip symbol. Refer to Figure 19-51.

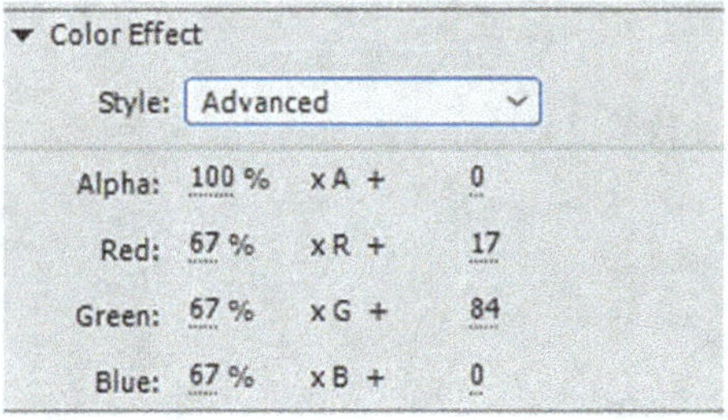

Figure 19-51. Alter the advanced color of a symbol with Color Effect

443

CHAPTER 19 ■ IMPORTING YOUR ARTWORK

- **Alpha:** Only affects the transparency of the movie clip symbol, but not its color, as seen in Figure 19-52.

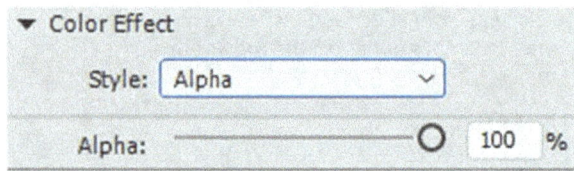

Figure 19-52. Alter the alpha of a symbol with color effect

You can apply these color effects by selecting your symbol and using the Selection tool (V) from the Tools panel to choose the blending mode from the drop-down menu.

Display Tab

The next section in the Properties menu is the Display tab. This area refers to how the blending effects are applied to the movie clip symbols and button symbols. It is not available for graphic symbols. If you imported these effects from a Photoshop (.psd) file or an Illustrator (.ai) file, many of them are preserved when you click the symbol in an ActionScript 3.0 FLA file. You can decide whether the object on stage is visible or not by clicking the Visible check box; however, because JavaScript has not caught up to some of these effects, the HTML5 Canvas FLA is limited. So if these effects are important to your Canvas animation, make sure to rasterize, merge layers, or make the graphics a bitmap during import. Refer to Figure 19-53.

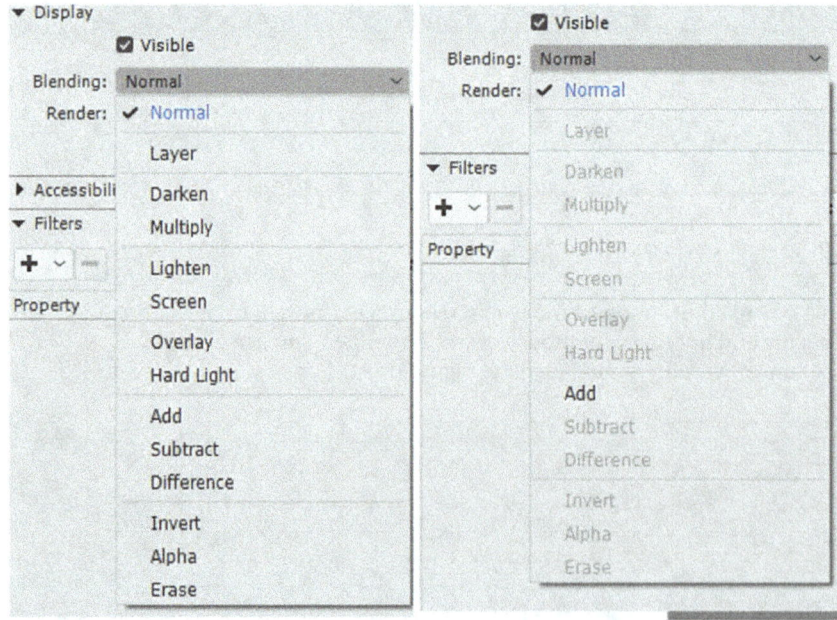

Figure 19-53. Blending options for AS3, on the right for HTML5 Canvas

CHAPTER 19 ■ IMPORTING YOUR ARTWORK

The final blending color change is a result of the blend color; it alters opacity or alpha and the base color. For example, if you have two movie clips, the lower movie clip is considered the base, and you would apply no blending to it (Normal). The upper movie clip symbol is the one you apply the blending to. Refer to File animate_blends.fla and Figure 19-54.

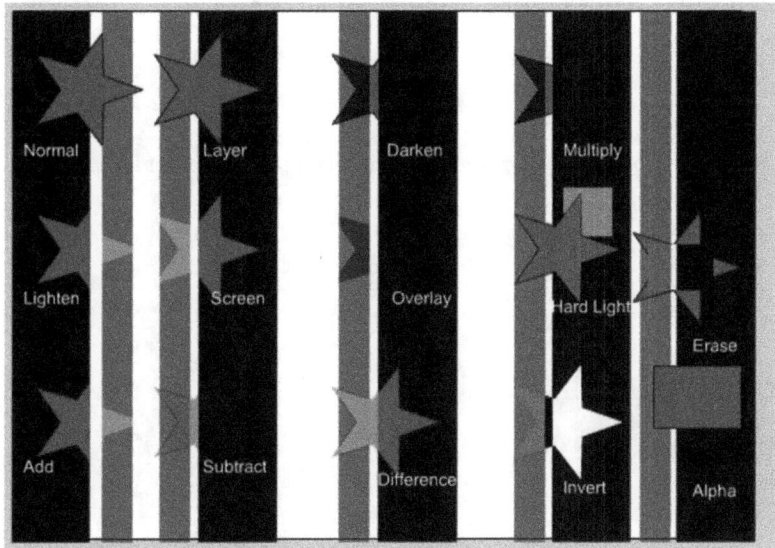

Figure 19-54. *The stars have different blend effects applied*

The following are the available blending options.

- **Normal:** Default values; no interaction with the base colors.
- **Layer:** Lets you stack movie clips on top of each other without affecting their color.
- **Darken:** Only areas lighter than the blend color are replaced. Darker areas do not change.
- **Multiply:** Multiplies base by blend color; this creates darker colors.
- **Lighten:** Only areas darker than the blend color are replaced. Lighter areas do not change.
- **Screen:** Multiplies the inverse of the blend color by the base color; this gives a bleached effect.
- **Overlay:** Depending on the base color, the effect multiplies or screens.
- **Hard Light:** Depending on the blend color, the effect, multiplies or screens; this gives a spotlight effect.
- **Add:** Creates an animated lightening dissolve or disappearance effect between two images.
- **Subtract:** Creates an animated darkening dissolve or effects disappearance between two images.

- **Difference:** Subtracts either the blend color from the base color or the base color from the blend color; it all depends on which has the greater brightness value. Like how a film color negative appears.
- **Invert:** Opposite of the base color; for example, black is white and white is black.

The final two blends are often confusing to most designers who first use them, because they rely on a parent and child setup.

Nested Movie Clips

To create these kinds of movie clips, you cannot place one movie clip symbol on top of another for it to work correctly. Refer to my drawing in Figure 19-55.

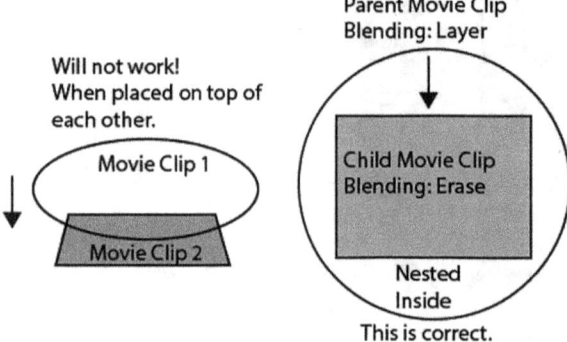

Figure 19-55. Working with nested movie clip symbols

The outer movie clip is called the *parent*, and for the following filters to work, rather than leaving it as the default blending of normal, you need to set the parent to layer. Then you need to double-click the "parent" movie clip to enter it. Inside this movie clip, you create another movie clip symbol, which becomes the "child." It is nested within the "parent" or rests upon the inner shape. Because this setup is based on hierarchy, any modifications made to the parent affects the child. You can apply either a blend of Alpha or Erase to the child movie clip. Since a child rests within the parent, it appears as though the filter is not working correctly. Only until you exit the parent movie clip will the blending appear correct with the child that is nested within. Refer to Figure 19-56.

- **Alpha:** Applies an alpha mask, making the object invisible although still on stage.
- **Erase:** Like alpha, removes all base color pixels, including those in the background image. Acts like a mask layer.

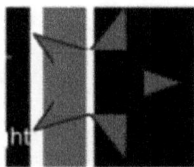

Figure 19-56. The movie clip symbol has a blend of layer applied to the outer parent. Erase is applied to the nested child within as it rests upon the inner shape.

> **Note** Only apply these blends to "child" or nested movie clips if you want them to operate correctly.

For more information on blending modes in animate, visit https://helpx.adobe.com/animate/using/applying-blend-modes.html.

Let's take a moment to compare the blending effects that Animate accepts from Photoshop CC and Illustrator CC. Refer to Table 19-3.

Table 19-3. Comparing the Blending Effects of Three Adobe Programs: Photoshop, Illustrator, and Animate

Blending Effect	Photoshop CC	Illustrator CC	Animate CC ActionScript 3.0	Animate CCHTML 5 Canvas
Normal	✓	✓	✓	✓
Layer			✓	
Darken	✓	✓	✓	
Multiply	✓	✓	✓	
Lighten	✓	✓	✓	
Screen	✓	✓	✓	
Overlay	✓	✓	✓	
Hard Light	✓	✓	✓	
Add (Linear Dodge)	✓*		✓	✓
Subtract	✓*		✓	
Difference	✓	✓	✓	
Invert	✓* as a separate adjustment layer which cannot be imported		✓	
Alpha			✓	
Erase			✓	
Dissolve	✓			
Color Burn	✓			
Linear Burn	✓			
Darker Color	✓			
Color Dodge	✓	✓		
Lighter Color	✓			
Soft Light	✓	✓		
Vivid Light	✓			
Linear Light	✓			

(continued)

CHAPTER 19 ■ IMPORTING YOUR ARTWORK

Table 19-3. (*continued*)

Blending Effect	Photoshop CC	Illustrator CC	Animate CC ActionScript 3.0	Animate CCHTML 5 Canvas
Pin Light	✓			
Hard Mix	✓			
Exclusion	✓	✓		
Divide	✓			
Hue	✓	✓		
Saturation	✓	✓		
Color	✓	✓		
Luminosity	✓	✓		

■ **Note** During import conversion of a PSD document to an ActionScript 3.0 FLA, I have noticed that Animate seems to have trouble recognizing Linear Dodge (Add) and Subtract, and outputs them either as Normal or some other filter. In the AI document, there is no equivalent to Linear Dodge (Add) or Subtract. If you find this happening to your file, you need to reset it using the Animate CC blending drop-down menu.

You can apply these blending modes by selecting your movie clip with the Selection tool (V) and choosing the blending mode from the drop-down menu.

Display Render

Depending on what you intend some of your graphics to do in an animation, they can become processor intensive. In that case, you may want to adjust your symbol's render options. Refer to Figure 19-57.

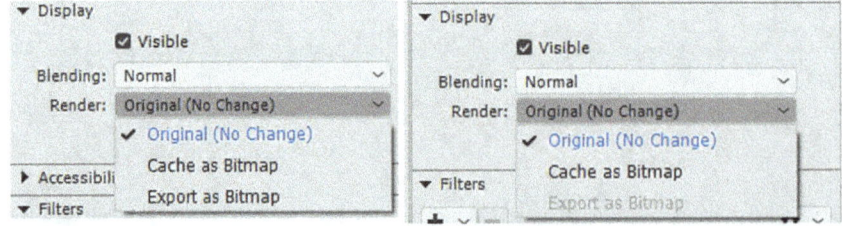

Figure 19-57. Alter the render setting of a symbol, HTML5 Canvas(right) has fewer options than ActionScript 3.0

CHAPTER 19 ■ IMPORTING YOUR ARTWORK

■ **Note** Unlike ActionScript 3.0 FLA, an HTML5 Canvas FLA can only render Cache as Bitmap, but not Export as Bitmap. Either one may help the animation run smoother because vector art is more processor intensive than a bitmap. As a rule, the setting should be applied to movie clip symbols that don't have an enteral timeline animation and don't size adjust or rotate frequently.

In the HTML5 Canvas FLA, you have no control over the smoothing or compression settings applied to the exported bitmap images.

You can set the bitmap background as either transparent or opaque (choose a color in the color picker); however, only the transparency option is available to HTML5 Canvas. Refer to Figure 19-58.

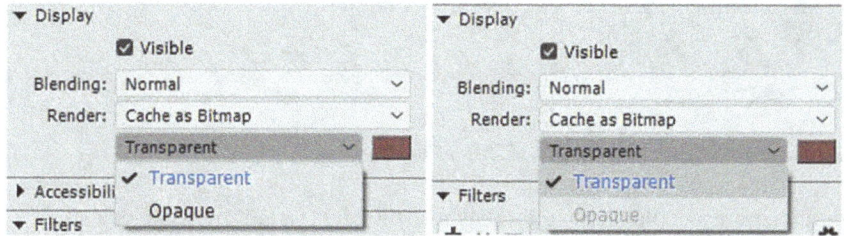

Figure 19-58. *Alter the color display settings of a symbol, HTML5 Canvas(right) has fewer options than ActionScript 3.0*

Filters Tab

Filters can be used in a variety of ways to enhance animated symbols on the stage along with the animation Timeline panel.

Like Photoshop CC and Illustrator CC. Animate CC has a few basic filters that you can apply to movie clip and button symbols. You cannot apply them to graphic symbols. You can access them all in an ActionScript 3.0 FLA file; however, for HTML5 Canvas, a few are not available because the JavaScript options have not caught up. Refer to Figure 19-59.

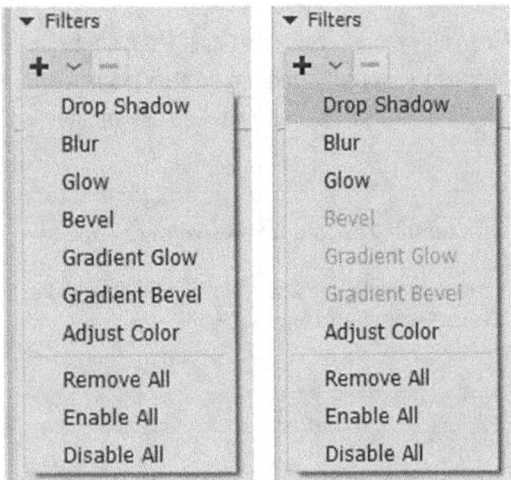

Figure 19-59. *Filter options for ActionScript 3.0(left) and HTML5 Canvas (right)*

Although Animate does not copy exact filters into this tab when you import a PSD or AI, it does maintain such things as the basic paths and blending modes within the movie clip symbol and tries to render them as accurately as possible. If you find that it is not rendering accurately, you can always import as a bitmap or apply these filters within Animate to a movie clip with no previous filters applied.

I will explain the settings for each filter and only point out new properties in subsequent filters. Refer to the animate_filters.fla file and Figure 19-60.

CHAPTER 19 ■ IMPORTING YOUR ARTWORK

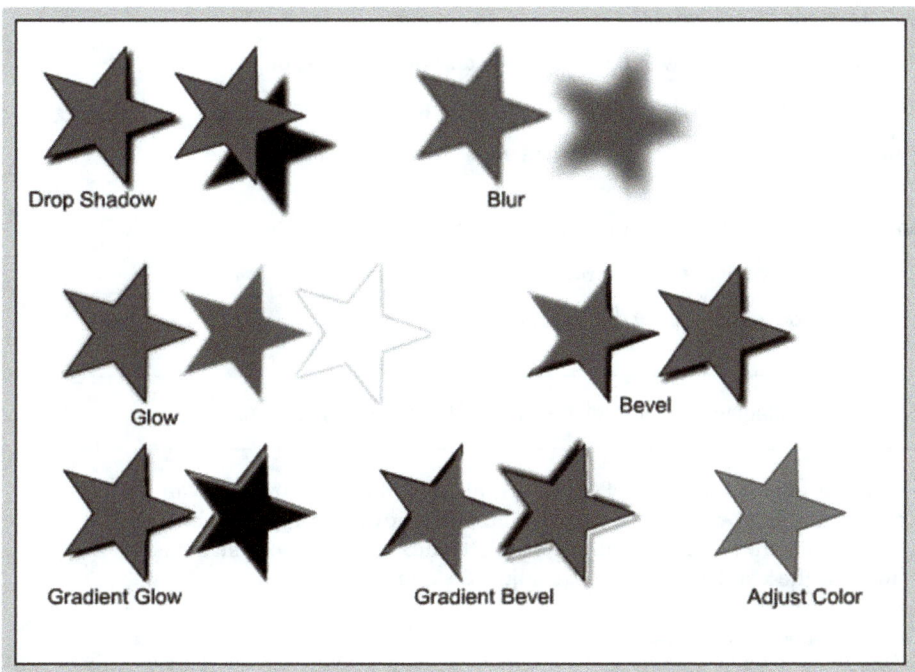

Figure 19-60. *Filters that you can apply in Animate to symbols*

- **Drop Shadow:** Simulates the look of a movie clip casting a shadow onto a surface. Refer to Figure 19-61 for settings.

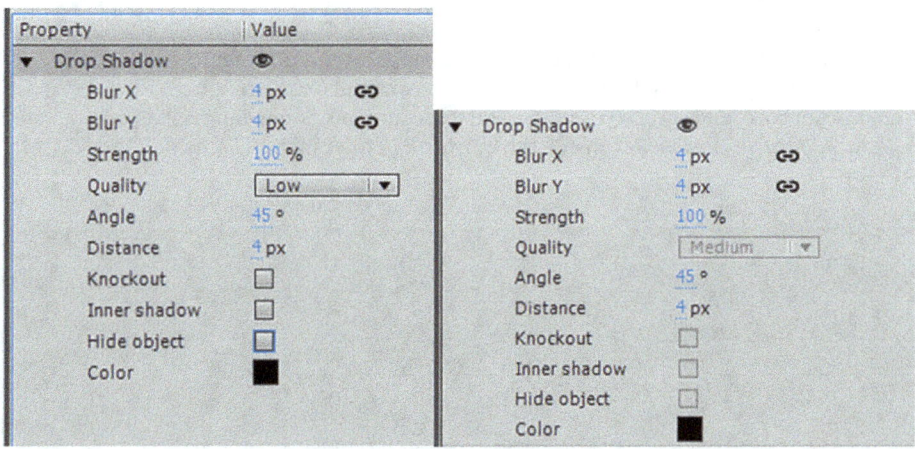

Figure 19-61. *Drop Shadow filter settings for AS3 and Canvas*

- **Blur X and Y:** Sets the coordinates of the blur shadow spread in pixels; they can be linked or unlinked.
- **Strength:** Sets the intensity of the shadow 0%–100%.

451

CHAPTER 19 ■ IMPORTING YOUR ARTWORK

- **Quality:** Low, medium or high; how accurately it appears.
- **Angle:** The angle or the shadow in degrees, or which side it appears on.
- **Distance:** The number of pixels it appears from the object.
- **Knockout:** Removes or masks the inner fill of the movie clip leaving only the shadow.
- **Inner shadow:** Puts the shadow within the movie clip, and not outside.
- **Hide object:** Reveals only the shadow behind, and not the movie clip
- **Color:** You can choose the color of the shadow.

■ **Note** Some options of drop shadow are not available for an HTML5 Canvas FLA file.

- **Blur:** Softens the edges and details of objects. Applying a blur to a movie clip can make it appear as if it is behind other objects or make a movie clip appear to be in motion. Refer to Figure 19-62 for settings. As with the drop shadow, you can adjust the spread using the x and y coordinates to adjust the quality.

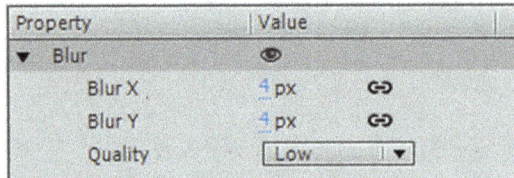

Figure 19-62. *Blur filter settings for AS3 and Canvas*

- **Glow:** Lets you apply a color around the edges of a movie clip symbol. Refer to Figure 19-63 for settings. As with the drop shadow, you can adjust the strength, quality, color, knockout, and spread with the x and y coordinates. Inner glow is like inner shadow in that the glow is now inside the movie clip rather than the outside.

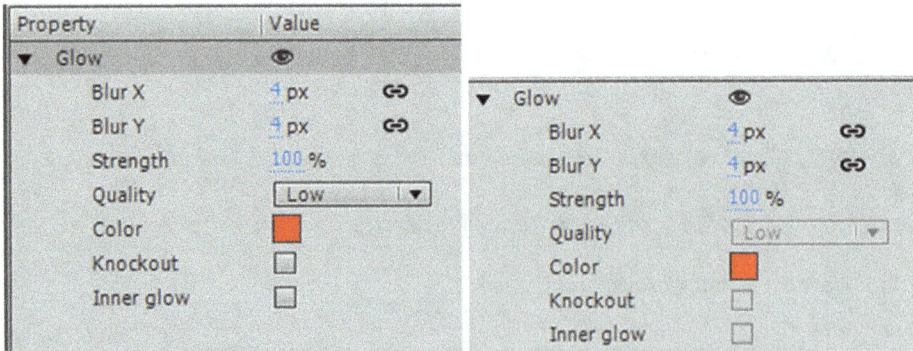

Figure 19-63. *Glow filter settings for AS3 and Canvas*

CHAPTER 19 ■ IMPORTING YOUR ARTWORK

■ **Note** Some options of glow are not available to HTML5 Canvas FLA file.

Bevel (Action Script 3.0 FLA only)

Applies a highlight to the object that makes it appear to be curved up above the background surface. It is like the bevel and emboss found in Photoshop CC. Refer to Figure 19-64 for settings.

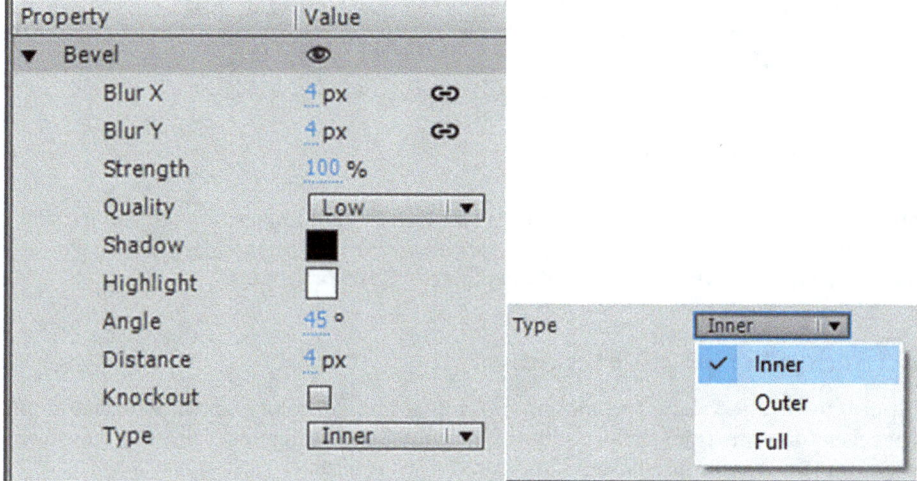

Figure 19-64. *Bevel filter settings for AS3 only*

As with the drop shadow, you can adjust the spread using the x and y coordinates, strength, quality, color (now divided into shadow and highlight), angle of bevel, distance of bevel, and knockout. Type is like inner shadow in that the bevel can be inside, outside, or fully on the movie clip.

Gradient Glow (Action Script 3.0 FLA only)

Produces a glow with a gradient color across the surface of the glow. The gradient glow requires one color at the beginning of the gradient with an alpha (transparency) value of 0. You can move the position of the color with the handles, and you can change the color by double-clicking the handle to access the color picker. You can also add more color handles by clicking below the gradient, or drag them off to remove them. Refer to Figure 19-65 for settings.

453

CHAPTER 19 ■ IMPORTING YOUR ARTWORK

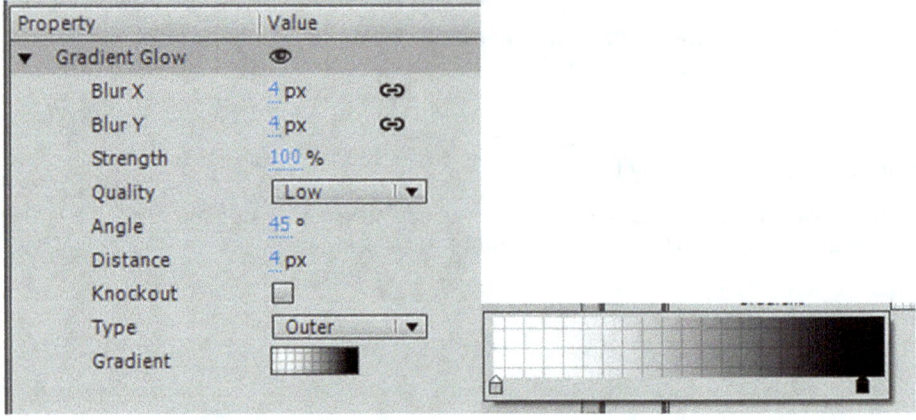

Figure 19-65. *Gradient glow filter settings for AS3 only*

As with the drop shadow, you can adjust the spread using the x and y coordinates, strength, adjust the quality, angle of glow, distance of bevel and knockout. Type is like inner shadow in that the gradient glow can be inside, outside or full on the movie clip. The gradient replaces the color property.

Gradient Bevel (Action Script 3.0 FLA only)

Makes a movie clip appear to be raised above the background, with a gradient color across the surface of the bevel. The gradient bevel requires one color in the middle of the gradient with an alpha value of 0; however, any gradient can have up to 15 color transitions. Refer to Figure 19-66 for settings.

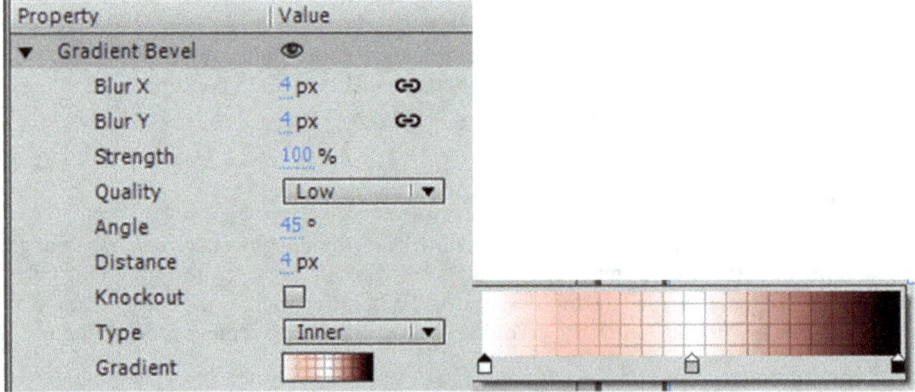

Figure 19-66. *Gradient Bevel filter settings for AS3 only*

As with the drop shadow you can adjust the spread using the x and y coordinates, strength, adjust the quality, angle of bevel, distance of bevel and knockout. Type is like inner shadow in that the bevel can be inside, outside or full on the movie clip. The gradient replaces the color property.

CHAPTER 19 ■ IMPORTING YOUR ARTWORK

Adjust Color

Allows you to finely control the color attributes of the selected movie clip, including contrast, brightness, saturation, and hue; it is very similar to the color effects area you looked at earlier. Refer to Figure 19-67 for settings.

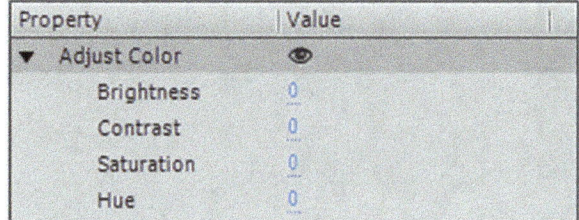

Figure 19-67. Adjust Color filter settings for AS3 and Canvas

As you would in Photoshop or Illustrator you can apply several filters to a movie clip symbol using the plus (+) icon. You can remove all from the drop-down menu or one by selecting it and using the minus (-) icon. Refer to Figure 19-68.

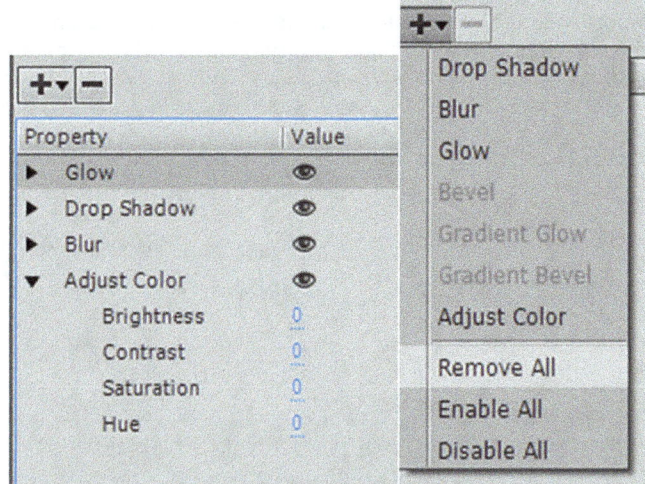

Figure 19-68. Add as many filters as you require to your symbol

You can enable or disable all filters from the plus (+) drop-down menu or use the Eye icon to turn them on or off one at a time.

The Widget icon lets you copy selected or all filters. You can paste, reset, or save the filters as a preset and edit the preset. Refer to Figure 19-69.

455

CHAPTER 19 ■ IMPORTING YOUR ARTWORK

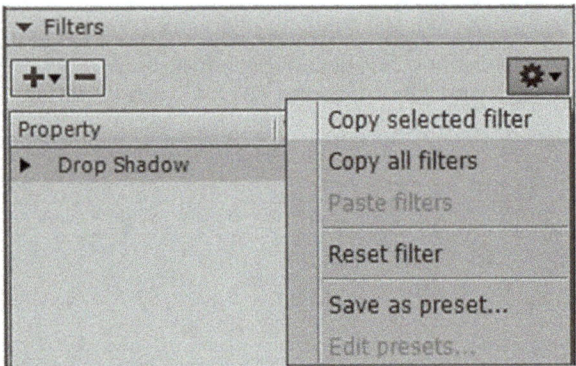

Figure 19-69. *Save settings for your filter for other projects as a preset or reset the current filter*

Import Other Graphic File Formats

It should be noted that BMP, JPG, PNG, and GIF files import directly to the stage and Library panel with no extra dialog boxes, so you do not need worry about any extra details regarding these formats for now, other than that you can apply the Animate effects to them when they are made into symbols, as you would with shapes.

With an SVG file, you have the option of importing graphics paths to the same layer and frame, each path on a different layer, or each path on a different keyframe. You also have the option to alter the size of the stage to match the SVG artwork. Refer to Figure 19-70.

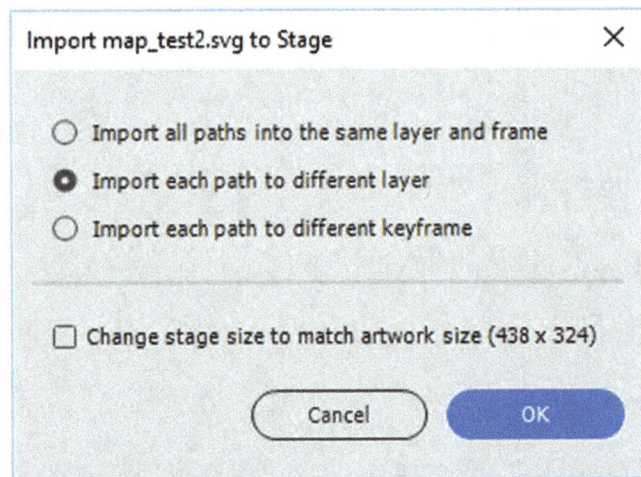

Figure 19-70. *The SVG Import options*

Once you have chosen your SVG import setting, click OK, and it is added to the stage; however, you still need to make the graphic into a symbol to add it to the Library panel.

Summary

In this chapter, you looked at several ways to import artwork that comes from Photoshop and Illustrator. You then compared the filters and effects that are retained by Animate, and saw how to keep the basic look of the properties that do not remain editable in HTML5 Canvas. Then you saw how to apply the filters that Animate offers when applied to symbols. Finally, you saw that graphics like JPG, PNG, and SVG could be imported into Animate as well.

In the next chapter, you look at how to import audio and video into your Animate FLA files.

CHAPTER 20

Import Your Audio and Video

In this chapter, you look at how to import audio and video into your ActionScript 3.0 file or HTML5 Canvas FLA files.

> **Note** This chapter does not have any actual projects; however, you can use the files in the Chapter 20 folder to practice opening and viewing for this lesson. They are at https://github.com/Apress/graphics-multimedia-web-adobe-creative-cloud.

Import Audio

The audio that you add or import into an FLA document may have been created or edited using a program like Adobe Audition CC, or extracted from a video file using Adobe Media Encoder CC. Refer to Figure 20-1.

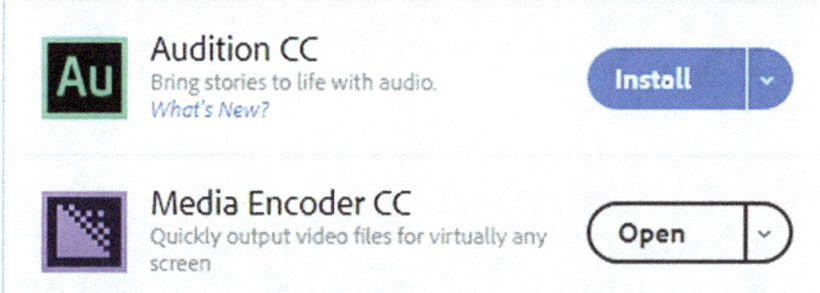

Figure 20-1. Possible Adobe programs used to edit or extract audio

Whatever the method or program used to create your audio, when you choose File ➤ Import ➤ Import to Stage, this adds the audio to the stage in a layer keyframes in the Timeline panel and the Library panel. File ➤ Import ➤ Import to Library adds audio only to the Library panel; you must drag the audio from the library into a keyframes in the Timeline panel if you want to add it to the stage. As you saw in Chapter 19, you can choose several audio options that are also used on the Internet. Refer to Table 20-1.

CHAPTER 20 ■ IMPORT YOUR AUDIO AND VIDEO

Table 20-1. *Audio that You Can Import into Your ActionScript 3.0 and HTML5 Canvas Files*

Audio Formats for the Web	ActionScript 3.0 FLA (.mov Video)	HTML5 Canvas FLA
MP3 Sound (.mp3)	✓	✓
WAV Sound (.wav)	✓	✓
Ogg Vorbis (.ogg, .oga)	✓	*
Other Audio Formats		
AIFF Sound(.aif, .aiff, .aifc)	✓	
Adobe Sound Document (.asnd). non-destructive and from legacy, Adobe Soundbooth	✓	
Sun AU (.au, .snd)	✓	
Sound Designer II (*.sd2)	✓	
Free Lossless Audio Codec (.flac)	✓	

■ **Note** While you cannot add Ogg Vorbis sound to your HTML5 Canvas file via Animate CC, there is another way to alter the sound files attached to your Canvas later in Dreamweaver CC in Part 6. I will show you how you can replace or swap the audio link outside of Animate in Dreamweaver's Code view. Having said that, MP3 and WAV audio are accepted by the most modern browsers, so if you don't have an Ogg Vorbis file option, it's not a deal breaker. You may also have access to audio formats not listed here if you have QuickTime 4 or higher installed on your computer.

Once the sound is added or imported into the Library panel, be aware that ActionScript 3.0 FLA has more sound options than the HTML5 Canvas FLA. These sound options can only be accessed when you click the layer and then the frame that contains the sounds. It is good practice to keep sounds on their own layers. Sound can also be added to button symbols.

CHAPTER 20 ■ IMPORT YOUR AUDIO AND VIDEO

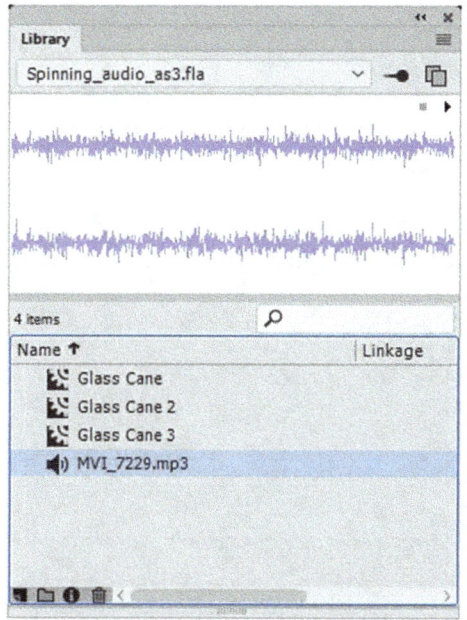

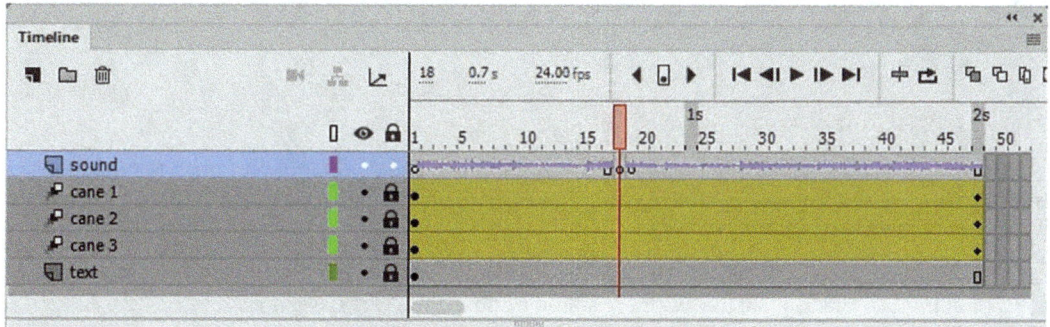

Figure 20-2. *The sound is in the Library panel and in the Timeline panel on its own layer that I named sound*

Refer to the Spinning_audio_as3.fla and Spinning_audio_canvas.fla files, and to Figure 20-2.

In the Properties panel, when the sound layer is selected, the Sound tab allows you to see the name of the sound file. To remove the sound, choose None, or a new sound, if you have another one in the Library panel, from the drop-down menu to replace it. Refer to Figure 20-3.

461

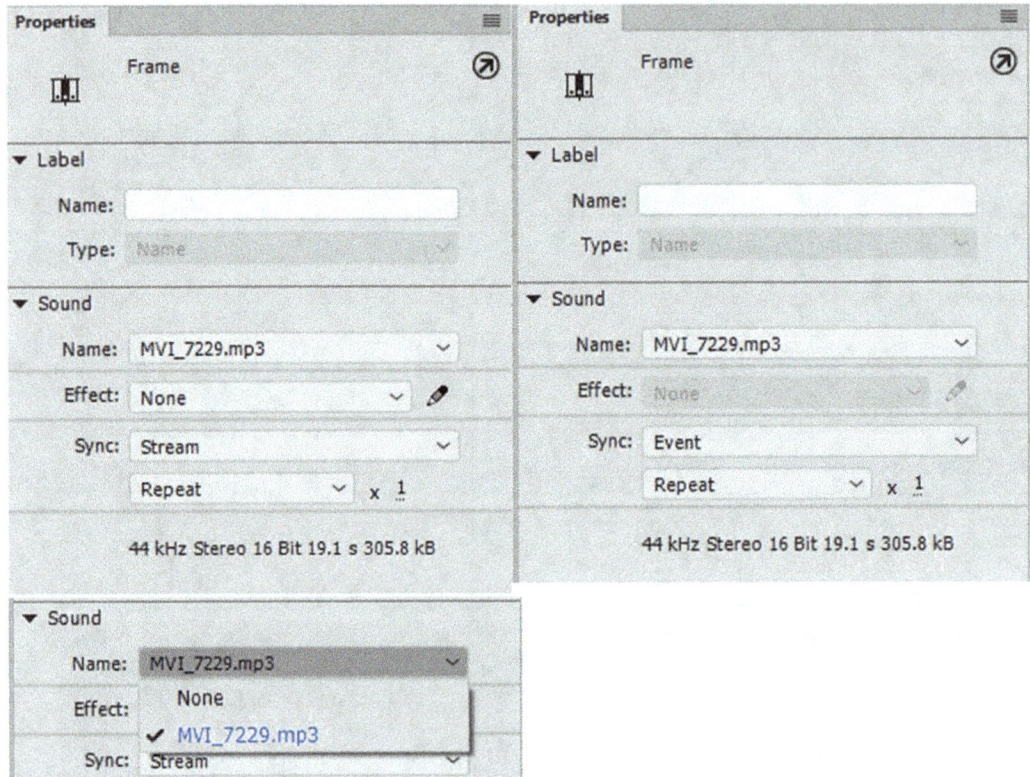

Figure 20-3. *The options for sound in the Properties panel for ActionScript 3.0 (left) and HTML5 Canvas (right). You can remove and replace a sound.*

Notice that the ActionScript 3.0 file has more sound options than HTML5 Canvas. When a sound is replaced, it updates in the Timeline panel as well.

Sound Effect Settings

The Sound Effect drop-down menu is only available for ActionScript 3.0 files, not HTML5 Canvas. Keep this in mind that if you are planning to create a video (.mov), it will become an MP4 file later. Effect allows you to control which audio channel the sound comes from, or if the sound will fade in or out. Refer to Figure 20-4.

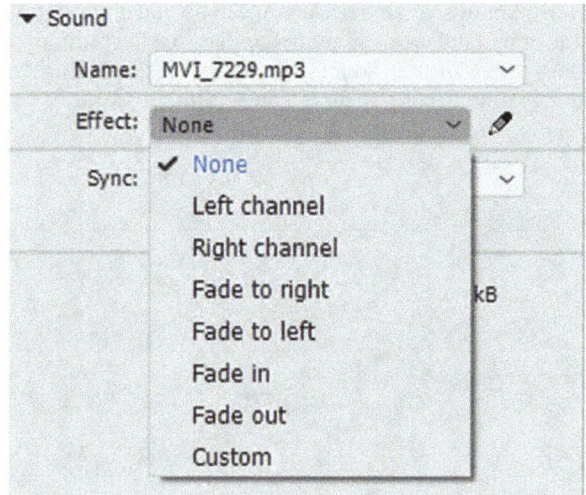

Figure 20-4. Adjust the sound channel in the Effect drop-down menu

You saw a setting similar to this in Photoshop when you created your video timeline in Chapter 7, so you should know a little bit about sound already.

You can alter the effect by choosing Custom or the Pencil icon on the right, which brings up the Edit Envelope dialog box. Refer to Figure 20-5.

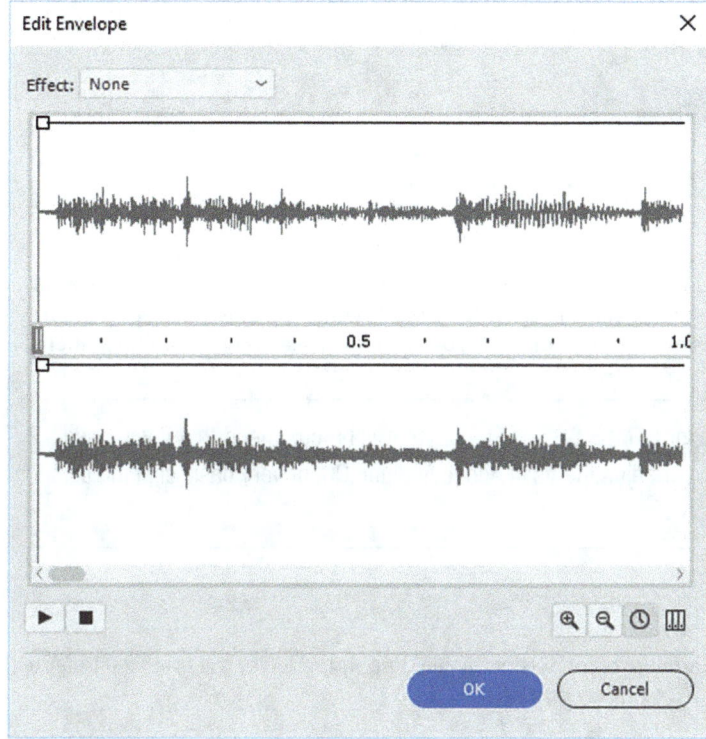

Figure 20-5. The Edit Envelope dialog box

CHAPTER 20 IMPORT YOUR AUDIO AND VIDEO

You can move the handles on the bars to edit how the sounds volume will change in the left and right channels, clip where it will begin or end by dragging the end handles or add more handles to adjust sound volume further. Drag them out of the envelope to remove them. You can zoom in or out on the timeline for micro adjustment either by seconds (clock icon) or frames (frame icon). Refer to Figure 20-6.

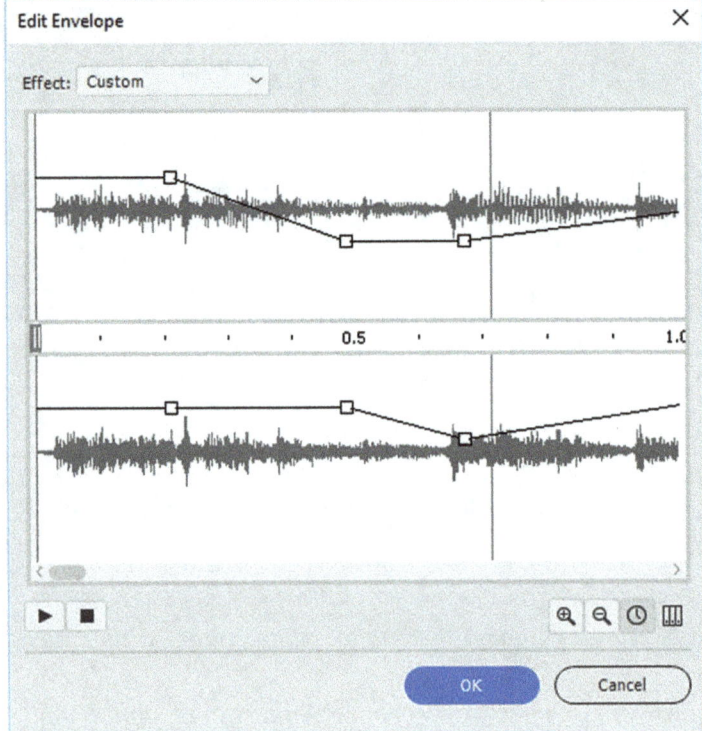

Figure 20-6. Edit the sounds

When you complete your edits, hit the Play button to preview your sound (the square stops the sound), and then click OK to exit and keep the changes. You can enter this area anytime to adjust your edits again. The original sound in the Library panel is not affected; only the sound on the stage in the Timeline panel.

■ **Note** This adjustment is not available for HTML5 Canvas FLA or WebGL. I recommend that if you need to clip your sound outside of Animate, do your adjustments in Adobe Audition CC, or very basic clipping using Media Encoder CC, as we will look at in Part 5.

Sync Setting

Sync affects how the sound plays in the timeline when it is published and uploaded to the Internet. Refer to Figure 20-7 for ActionScript 3.0 and HTML5 Canvas comparison.

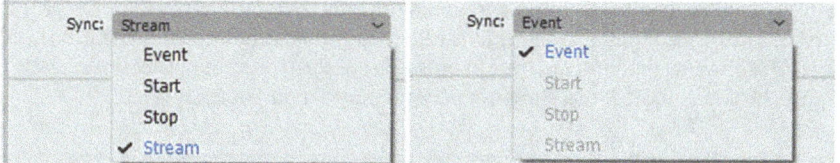

Figure 20-7. *Sync for ActionScript 3.0 (left) and HTML5 Canvas (right)*

For HTML5 Canvas, you only have the Event option.

Event

Synchronizes the sound to an event occurrence. An event sound plays when its starting keyframe first appears, and then plays in its entirety, independently of the playhead in the timeline, even if the Canvas file stops playing. Event sounds can overlap when you play your published Canvas file.

If an event sound is playing, and the sound is instantiated (for example, by the user clicking a button again, or the playhead passing the starting keyframe of the sound), the first instance of the sound continues to play, and another instance of the same sound begins to play simultaneously. Keep this in mind when using longer sounds, as they can potentially overlap and cause unintended audio effects that you may not want for your buttons or while playing a video component on the canvas.

Start

Start is the same as Event, except that if the sound is already playing, no new instance of the sound plays.

Stop

With Stop, the sound is muted. It silences the specified sound, which can be resumed on another frame when sync is changed. This is like when you cut your audio for the video in the Photoshop video timeline and then continued it at another point in the track.

Stream

Stream synchronizes sound to play on a website. Animate forces animation to keep pace with streaming sounds. If Animate CC can't draw animation frames quickly enough, it skips frames. Unlike event sounds, stream sounds stop if the video file or older SWF stops playing. Also, a stream sound can never play longer than the length of the frames it occupies or the video timeline. Stream sounds can overlap when you publish your video file.

An example of a stream sound is the voice of a character in an animation that plays in multiple frames.

These sound settings are remembered in the sync options in the Property inspector. If a sound is selected from the sound section of the Property inspector, then on trying to set another sound on a new keyframe from the Property inspector, Animate CC remembers the previous sound's stream or event sync options.

CHAPTER 20 ■ IMPORT YOUR AUDIO AND VIDEO

Stream also allows you to split the audio at one frame and then continue in another frame later. Right-click a frame that you want to split from, and then choose Split Audio (Modify ➤ Timeline ➤ Split Audio). Insert a blank keyframe (Insert ➤ Timeline ➤ Blank Keyframe) or frames before the split to provide space between them, as seen in Figure 20-8. You look at the Timeline panel in more detail in Chapter 21.

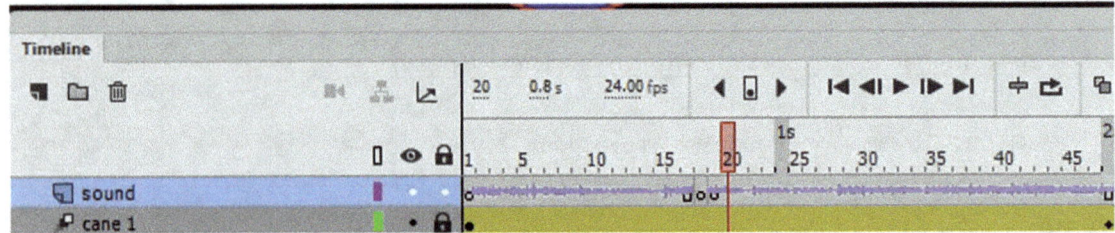

Figure 20-8. *Split the audio if you need to create a silent space of in the ActionScript 3.0 file*

Repeat Sound

For both ActionScript 3.0 and HTML5 Canvas FLA file formats, you can choose whether you want to repeat or loop the sound and then set the number of times. Loop is like setting "forever." Refer to Figure 20-9.

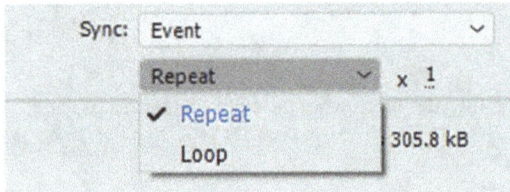

Figure 20-9. *Set the number of times the sound should repeat or a continuous loop*

In the next section, you look at the options available for importing video.

Import Video

The Import Video dialog box only works with ActionScript 3.0 FLA and certain embedded video formats, such as FLV, F4V, and MP4 (H264). Use this if your intent is to export later as a SWF file. In this book, however, our focus is to export either a MOV file or an HTML5 Canvas file. You may have access to additional video formats if you have QuickTime 4 or higher installed on your computer. Refer to Figure 20-10.

466

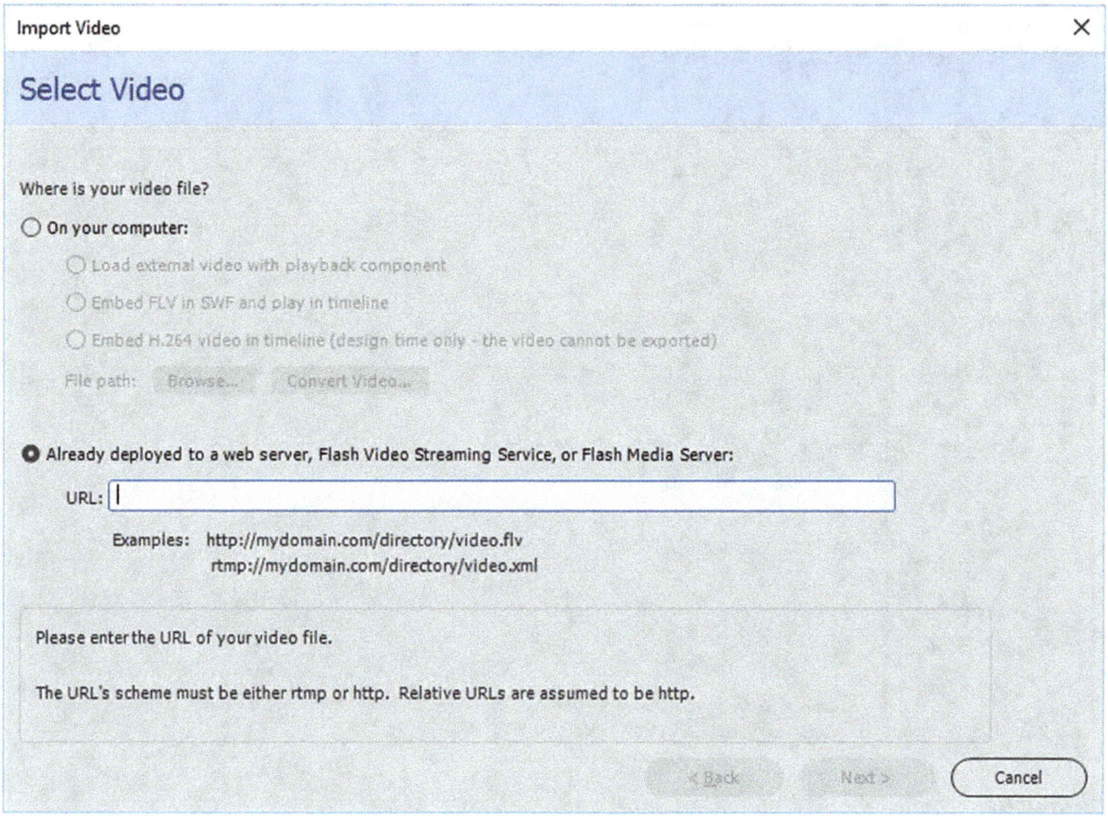

Figure 20-10. The Import Video dialog box works with SWF video

In this book, Animate CC's main purpose is to create an animation that could become a video, used in a Photoshop as part of a video, or used as an HTML5 Canvas. There may be times that you want to import a small video into HTML5 Canvas. For example, in my animation (video_canvas.fla), I created my characters appear to be watching a TV screen or in a theater. How was this accomplished?

Components and Component Parameters

Animate has a unique way of dealing with adding a video to the stage using the Components and Component Parameters panel. Refer to how it appears for HTML5 Canvas in Figure 20-11.

CHAPTER 20 ■ IMPORT YOUR AUDIO AND VIDEO

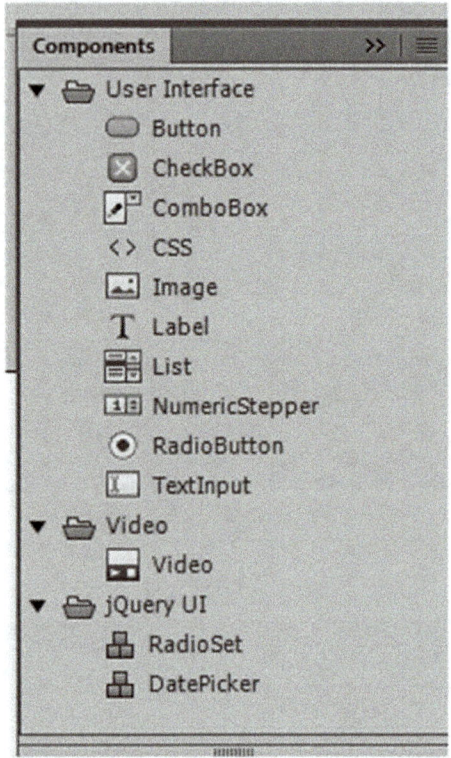

Figure 20-11. *Options for the Components panel*

While also containing form components in the Components panel, toward the bottom, there is also a video component available. Again, it is possible to add video to an ActionScript 3.0 file if you add images that were in a sequence or frame by frame.

If you want a small video to be part of your HTML5 Canvas, select the video component and drag it onto the stage. Refer to Figure 20-12.

Figure 20-12. *The video component is added to the stage*

468

CHAPTER 20 ■ IMPORT YOUR AUDIO AND VIDEO

It's also added to the Library panel, as seen in Figure 20-13.

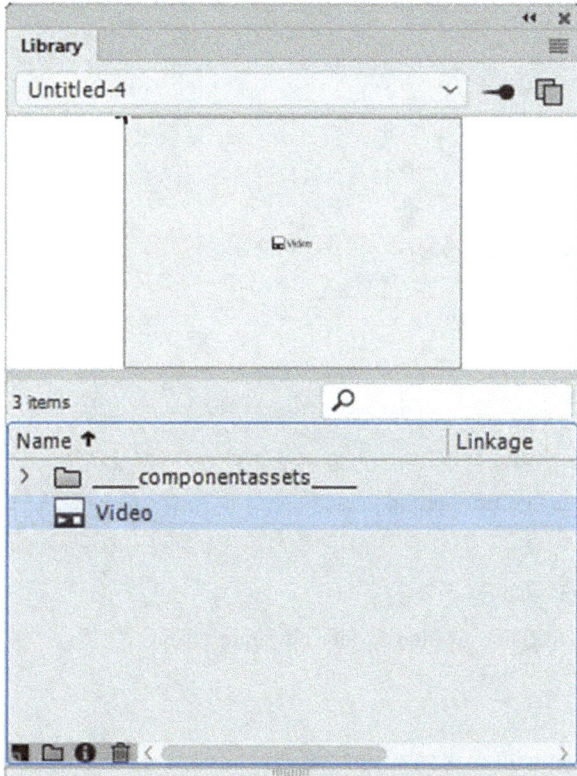

Figure 20-13. *The video component is added to the Library panel*

Once you add this to the stage, you can use the Component Parameters panel. Refer to Figure 20-14.

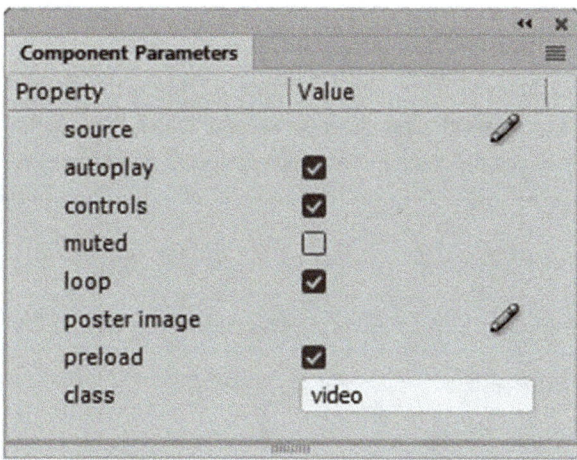

Figure 20-14. *The Video Component Parametes panel*

469

CHAPTER 20 ■ IMPORT YOUR AUDIO AND VIDEO

In the parameters, you can adjust the setting for the video as you would any HTML5 video.

Click the pencil (next to source) to link to a video, and the Folder icon to add a content path. Refer to Figure 20-15.

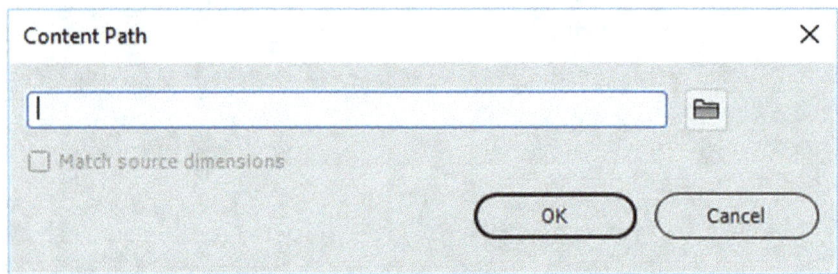

Figure 20-15. *Adding a Video Source content path*

The following are the formats that you can choose from: .mp4, .ogg, .ovg., and .webm.

- **Match source dimensions** causes the video component to scale.
- **Autoplay** ensures that the video plays at start.
- **Controls** makes the HTML5 video controls visible.
- **Muted** turns off or on sound, if there is sound in the video. It does not mute sound that is outside the video on another layer in the canvas.
- **Loop** determines whether the video loops.
- **Poster image** is an image that appears on the front of the video either before it plays or when it completes; it can be in JPEG, PNG, GIF, or bitmap format. It should be the same dimensions as your video to scale correctly.
- **Preload** determines how the video loads.
- **Class** effects how the video appears in the HTML5 file and how it reacts with the CSS class styling. Refer to Figure 20-16.

■ **Note** Until the file is published as an HTML5 Canvas, you will not be able to interact or preview the video; only animations around the video. Make sure that your timeline and fps (frames per second) match those in the video, or you could end up with some unusual results in which the video moves faster or slower than expected.

CHAPTER 20 ■ IMPORT YOUR AUDIO AND VIDEO

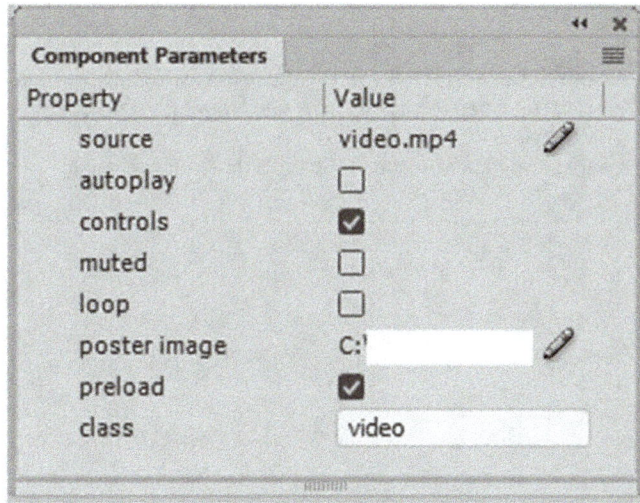

Figure 20-16. *The final component parameters*

You can look at the final canvas and the video_canvas.fla and video_canvas.html files to see the results. Refer to Figure 20-17.

Figure 20-17. *Adding a graphic below the video gives the effect that people are watching a video in a movie theater*

■ **Note** You cannot add a graphic over the top of the video component because it will always try to remain on top. You may need to make your canvas a little taller so that you can incorporate your cartoon animated audience below it.

471

Summary

In this chapter, you looked at how to add audio to your ActionScript 3.0 and HTML5 Canvas. You also added a small video component so that you could link an HTML5 video to your Canvas file. Hopefully, you are beginning to see where each FLA option has its unique uses.

In the next chapter, you review the Timeline panel and look at some of the tools that you can use to modify your animation before you export it.

CHAPTER 21

Working with the Timeline Panel

In this chapter, you review the Timeline panel and some old and new panels that work with the Timeline panel to assist you in creating and enhancing your animations before you export them.

> **Note** This chapter does not have any actual projects; however, you can use the files in the Chapter 21 folder to practice opening and viewing for this lesson. They are at https://github.com/Apress/graphics-multimedia-web-adobe-creative-cloud.

Working with the Timeline Panel

If you have worked with the Timeline panel in Flash or Animate CC, you see that it is an integral part of this software if you want to create movement in an animation. As you saw in Part 2 with Photoshop CC, when you stitch together a video, each section or movement is made of frames. The number of frames that run within a second (fps) is usually between 24 and 30, so that the movement does not appear choppy. The same is true for the Animate timeline. Refer to Figure 21-1.

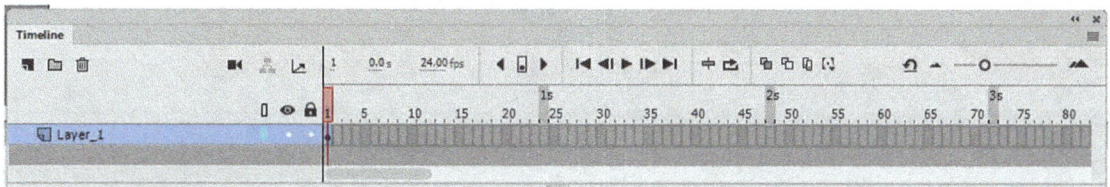

Figure 21-1. *The Timeline panel with one layer that currently has blank keyframes*

A Review of Layers

While the focus of this book is to learn how to get your files web-ready, let's take a moment to compare this Timeline panel and its frames with the video timeline presented in Photoshop CC.

Open the scene6_timeline_example.fla file to follow along. You will use similar files for the Hot Glass Tango website in Chapter 24.

© Jennifer Harder 2018
J. Harder, *Graphics and Multimedia for the Web with Adobe Creative Cloud*,
https://doi.org/10.1007/978-1-4842-3823-3_21

CHAPTER 21 ■ WORKING WITH THE TIMELINE PANEL

■ **Note** For a more in-depth review of layers, I recommend *Adobe Animate CC Classroom in a Book*, but this chapter presents a basic review.

The Animate timeline is a combination of the Timeline and Layers panels that you see in Photoshop, but they are not separate. They interact with whatever is on the stage. If you need to hide or store something off the stage, save it as a symbol (graphic, movie, button), audio, or component in the library, and only place it on the stage in the correct timeline frames when required.

Layers appear like stacks of filmstrips stacked on top of each other, which is to give the feeling of depth. They can also keep organized the sections that appear above or below.

Figure 21-2. *A scene from the intro of Hot Glass Tango*

For example, a character might be standing outdoors or, in Hot Glass Tango, inside a glass studio. In this case, the letters and his final project, the cobalt glass vase, are in the forefront; the male character is behind the letters holding the pipe that is attached to the glass that he is expanding. Behind him is a type of glass-heating furnace, also known as glory hole, and behind that is the colorful background. If you go in that order, you find the background to be the lowest visible layer. Refer to Figure 21-3. Note when you open this file you may receive a warning that it contains camera effects click OK to open the file.

CHAPTER 21 ■ WORKING WITH THE TIMELINE PANEL

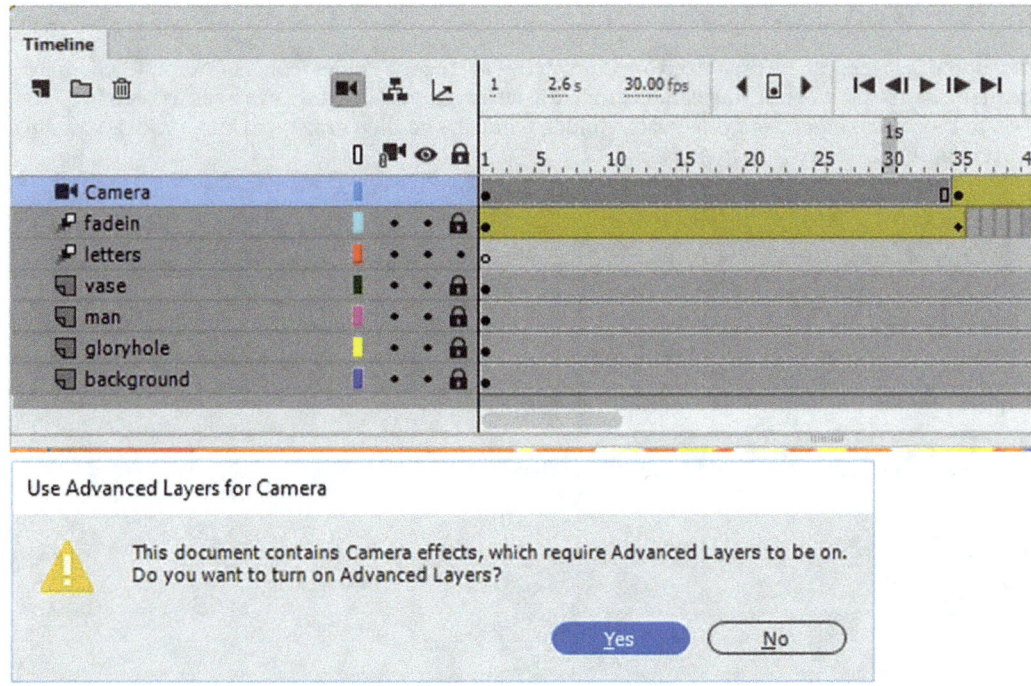

Figure 21-3. *The Timeline panel and layer order. The symbols in front are higher than the background. Advanced Camera layer is in use.*

■ **Note** In this case, sound is below all the layers. That is OK because the sound never appears on the stage and is only background noise. It could be above all layers, but it does not interact with the movement in anyway. In this case, I put it at the bottom of the layers so that it would look like you saw it in the Photoshop Video Timeline panel in Chapter 7, where the sound track is always at the bottom of the list.

New Layers

Layers can be created by selecting the layer and pressing the New Layer icon in the upper left of the Timeline panel. You can also remove a selected layer by clicking the Trash icon. Refer to Figure 21-4.

Figure 21-4. *Create a new layer in the Timeline panel*

475

CHAPTER 21 ■ WORKING WITH THE TIMELINE PANEL

Folders

As in Photoshop CC, layers can be organized into folders by clicking the Folder icon. For example, you may have more than one sound layer, or you want to group the letters and vase together as a set, as seen in Figure 21-5. To keep them organized, you create a folder, name it, and then drag them into a folder. You can expand and collapse that folder to save space.

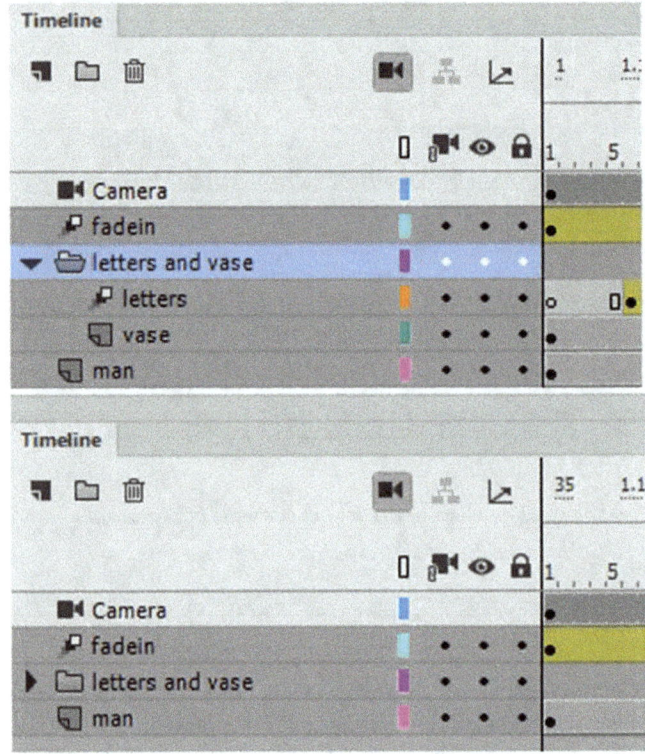

Figure 21-5. *A folder can store many layers if you want to keep them separate and organized*

For my example, I kept them separate because there are not a lot of layers in the file, but you can practice creating a folder, as seen in Figure 21-5. Just make sure to keep the layers in the folder in the same order as shown here. Then you can drag the files out of the folder and delete the folder. Just don't delete the layers.

Hide and Show Layers and Folder

As with Photoshop CC, you can hide or show layers and folders by turning the Eye icon off or on. When on, there is a dot under the Eye icon; and when off, it is an X, as seen in Figure 21-6.

CHAPTER 21 ■ WORKING WITH THE TIMELINE PANEL

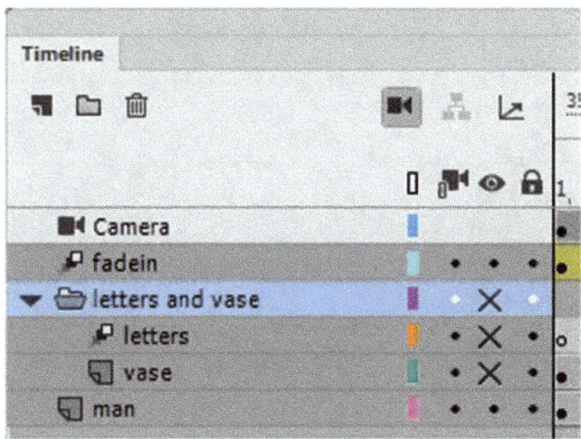

Figure 21-6. Turn a layer on or off

This is good when you are checking to see what kind of objects are behind the current layer or for scrubbing the timeline with the playhead to compare movements between two layers, as you will see shortly.

Lock Layers and Folders

You can also lock the layer using the Lock icon if you don't want the object on that layer to move while moving other objects on another layer. Lock can also affect the folder and all the layers within can be locked when a folder lock is selected. Refer to Figure 21-7.

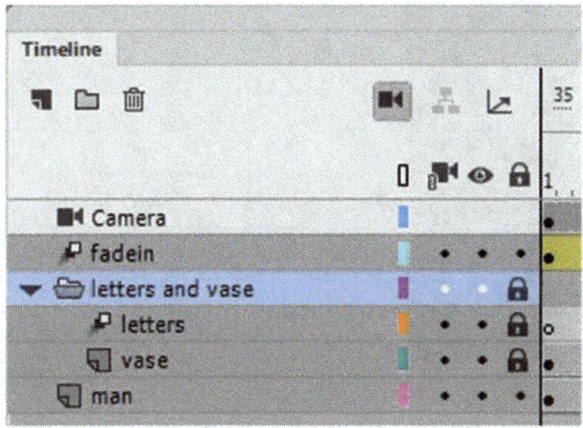

Figure 21-7. Lock a layer to prevent movement on the stage

Layer Outlines

The rectangular icon next to the Camera icon allows you to show all layers as outlines, or you can select a layer and only show it in outlines by clicking the colored square. This is only a preview so that you can view movement on all layers; it does not appear like this in the final animation. Refer to Figure 21-8.

477

CHAPTER 21 ■ WORKING WITH THE TIMELINE PANEL

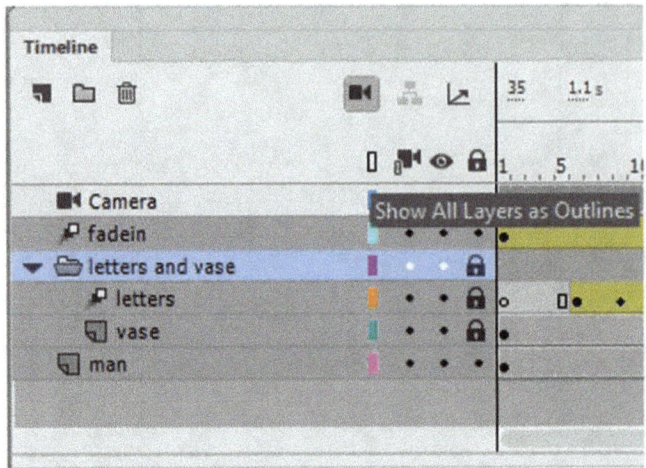

Figure 21-8. Click the regtangle so that the shapes on the stage will appear as outlines

The shapes show up in the outline color that matches their layer color. Refer to Figure 21-9.

Figure 21-9. The outline preview in Animate

478

Click the Outline icon in the layer again to remove the outline color and return it to the state shown in Figure 21-2.

Advanced Layer Settings

The icons in the upper left of the timeline are the new setting for Advanced layers in CC 2019 as seen in Figure 21-10 some are currently on, off or unavailable. This depends on if you are working with AS3 or HTML5 FLA file. Figure 21-10.

Figure 21-10. *Control the Advanced Layers setting by turning them on or off*

This is an advanced layer setting like camera, parenting and layer depth are used in certain types of animations where you are trying to create a camera zoom, a flying toward or away motion for 2D visuals, or locking on to a horizon point with the camera. As you approach different objects that are at varying distances, you arrive at some faster than others. You can see examples of this at https://helpx.adobe.com/ca/animate/using/timeline-layers.html and https://helpx.adobe.com/animate/using/working-with-camera-in-animate-cc.html#parallax-effect.

For this project, other than the camera layer, I left the layer depth setting off, but look at Spinning_advanced_layers.fla where layer depth has been added. In your own project, if you click the first time, you may receive the alert seen in Figure 21-11.

CHAPTER 21 ■ WORKING WITH THE TIMELINE PANEL

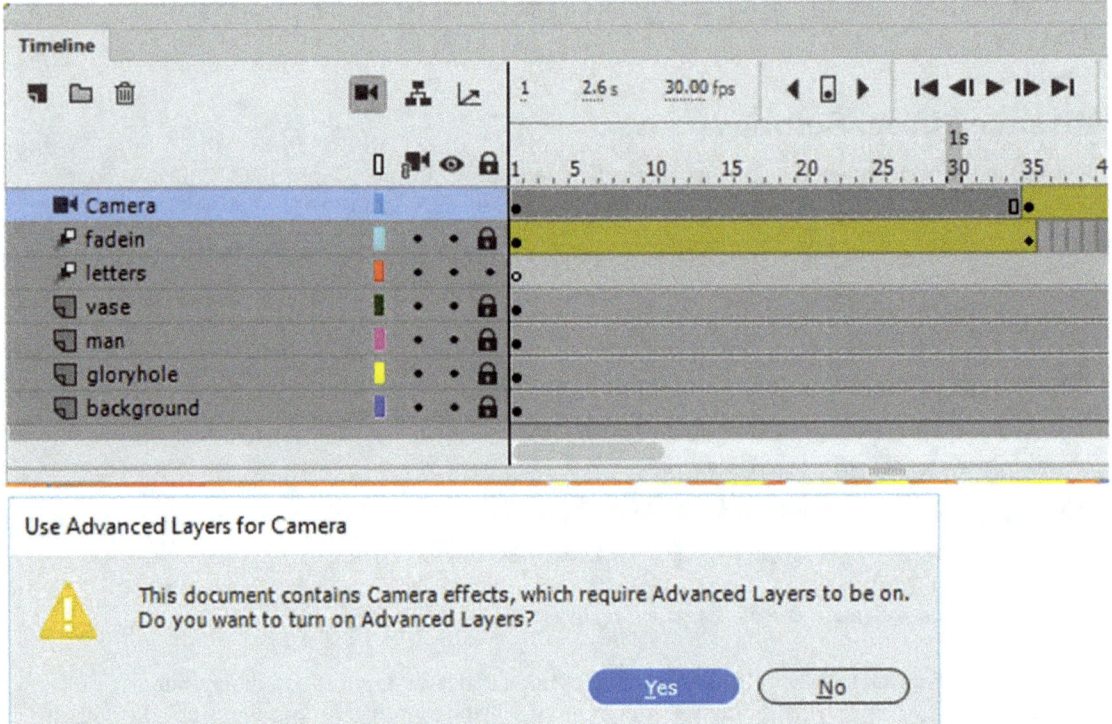

Figure 21-11. The Use Advanced Layers alert

If you do not want to use Advanced Layers, click NO. Click Yes to activate the advanced layers which includes camera effects for layers, layer parenting and the layer depth option. Note that your layer names in the Timeline panel may alter slightly with an added underscore (_) for names with a spaces so that they can work with the Layer Depth panel and other advanced settings.

Layer Depth Panel

Any shape that is on a layer turns into a symbol so that you can work with Z-depth or the camera layer, as you will look at later.

When you work with the Layer Depth panel, make sure your layers are unlocked in the Timeline panel so that you can move the selected layer depth up or down on the right preview. Refer to Figure 21-12.

CHAPTER 21 ■ WORKING WITH THE TIMELINE PANEL

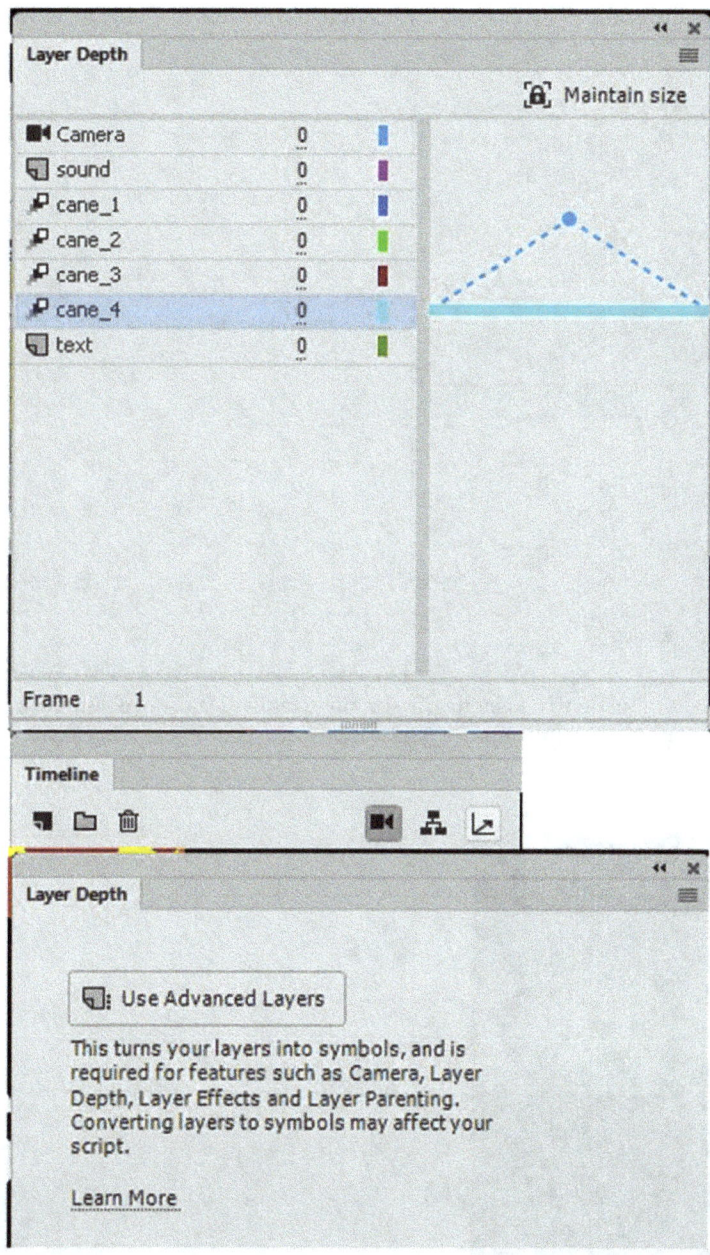

Figure 21-12. *The Layer Depth panel with no layer's depths altered in frame 1 (Below)The Layer depth panel when no advanced setting are on*

481

CHAPTER 21 ■ WORKING WITH THE TIMELINE PANEL

The depth can be adjusted for that frame or those frames collectively outside or within a folder. Refer to Figure 21-13.

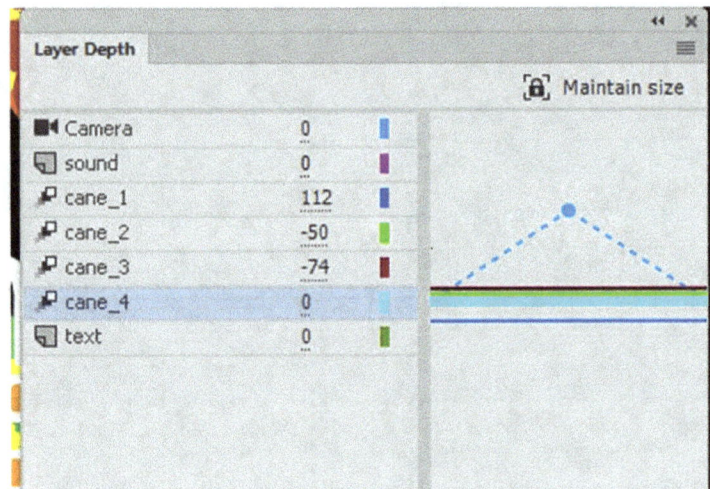

Figure 21-13. Adding depth to one or more layers

Moving the depth upward causes the symbol on that layer to grow or move forward (negative number); moving the depth downward causes the symbol to shrink or move backward (positive number) away from the viewer. Refer to Figure 21-14.

Figure 21-14. Symbols from a lower layer now overlap an upper layer

CHAPTER 21 ■ WORKING WITH THE TIMELINE PANEL

This adds keyframes to the motion tween, depending on where you are in the timeline. Depending on the depth at each keyframe, it will appear as though symbols that were once behind on one layer are now moving in front of another symbol on another layer.

If you find that you do not want to use this feature, on a specific layer's keyframe then while on that keyframe reset it back to 0. Refer to Figure 21-15.

Figure 21-15. *Deactivate Advanced Layers*

Doing this deactivates the layer depth and reverts some items back to symbols that no longer shrink, grow, and move behind and in front of one another (Z-depth), as well as those effects attached to the camera layer. You can activate them again, but be aware that some settings may have altered if you make changes after reactivating. Other advanced settings that can interact with Layer depth and camera in an Action Script 3.0 FLA include the new Layer parenting. While not included in the examples, Refer to Figure 21-16 to see what this advanced feature looks like. You can learn more at https://helpx.adobe.com/ca/animate/using/timeline-layers.html#Layerparenting.

483

CHAPTER 21 ■ WORKING WITH THE TIMELINE PANEL

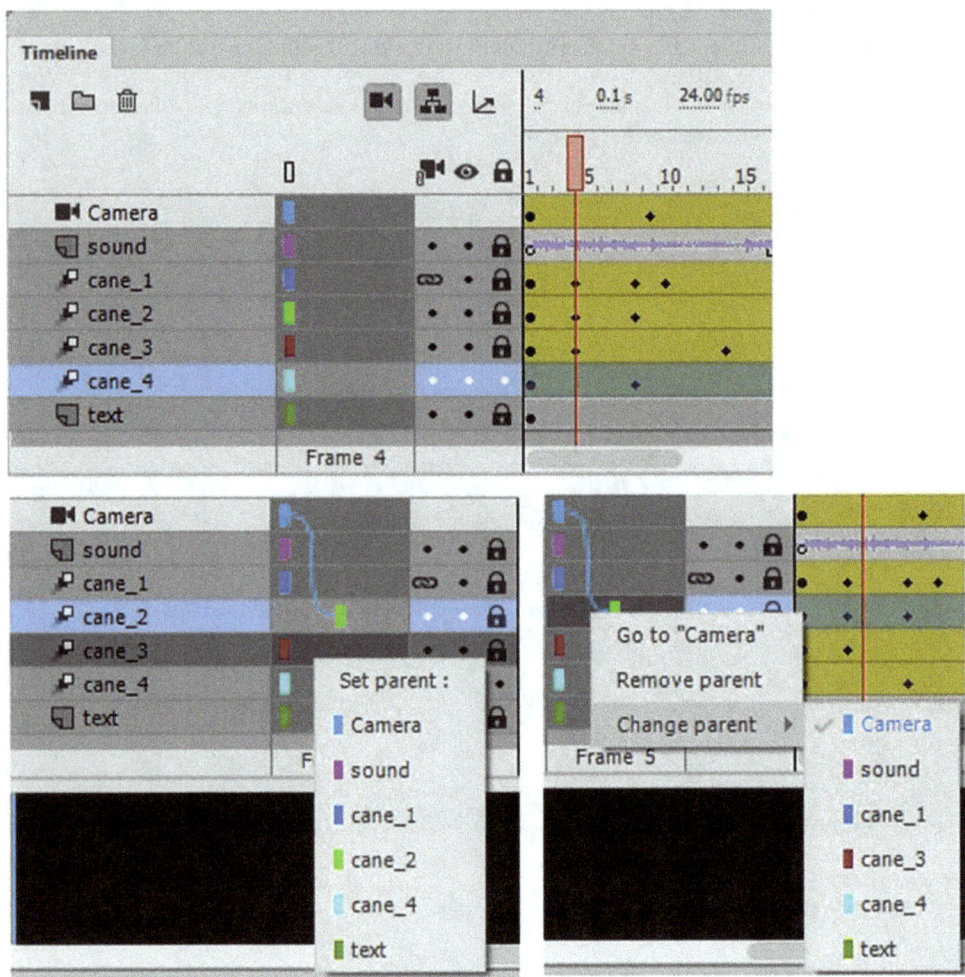

Figure 21-16. *Layer parenting as it acts with the Layer Depth panel*

Whether you plan to use advanced layers or not, make sure that you save you objects as symbols (as you saw in Chapter 20) before beginning your animation project.

■ **Note** When you work with layer depth, it is good practice to make sure each layer outline is a distinct color so that you can easily select it in the panel. Layers with the same color can be confusing to work with, and you might add a motion keyframe to the wrong layer. I show you how to adjust the outline color in the next section.

484

Layer Types

As in Photoshop CC, there are several types of layers.

You can adjust the type of layer by double-clicking the Layer icon or right-click the layer and choose Properties from the pop-up menu. For the Mac, Ctrl-click and select Properties. This brings up the Layer Properties dialog box for that layer. Refer to Figure 21-17.

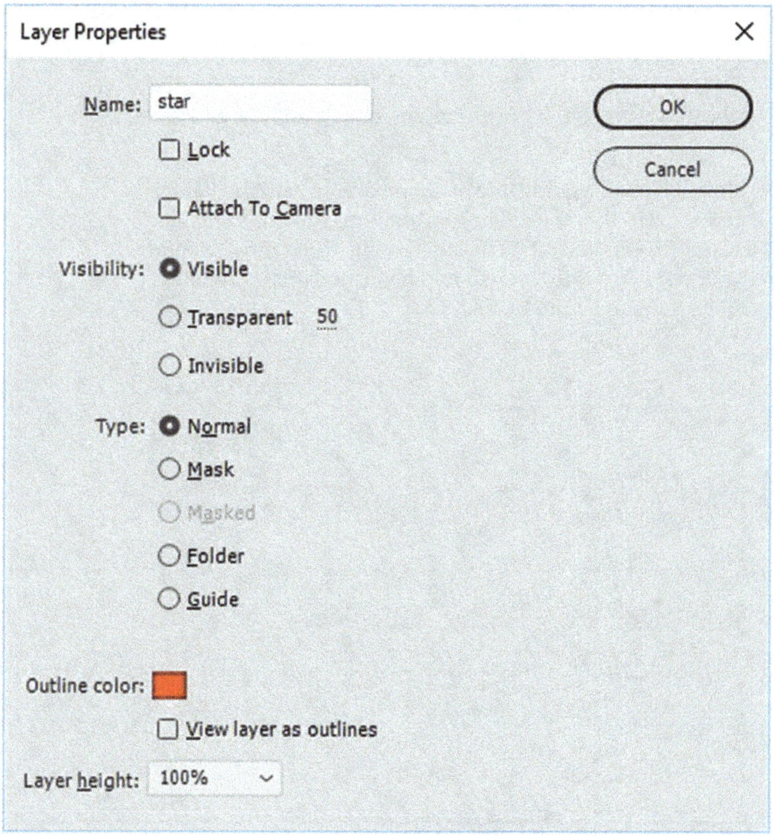

Figure 21-17. The Layer Properties dialog box

You can make most layer adjustments outside of the dialog box, such as renaming by double-clicking the name, locking the layer, or viewing the layer as (visible or invisible) or as outlines; however, if you want to make the visibility semitransparent, you need to set this in the Layers properties. By default, a layer type is normal. In the dialog box, there are at least four other options. Look at the Spinning_layer_types.fla file.

- **Mask:** As with a layer in Photoshop, a layer in Animate can have a linked mask. It can only be applied to it the layer that is linked to a mask layer and both layers are locked. The mask shape itself acts as a window to the masked layer below. Refer to Figure 21-18.

Figure 21-18. Creating a masked layer in the Timeline panel

- **Masked:** This is the layer below the mask; otherwise, it is a normal layer. Both mask and masked layers can have motion tweens applied to them; if they are symbols, the tween appears as part of the mask or masked icon. Shape and Classic tweens can appear with the Mask icon.

- **Folder:** You can change the newly created layer to a folder, or a new folder to a layer after you name it.

- **Guide:** The guide layer often contains a guide line or shape drawn with the Pencil tool (Shift-Y) or Paint Brush tool (B) that is used in combination with a symbol on another layer that has a classic tween to control its movement. The symbol on that layer is then considered guided. The guide layer should be turned off if you don't want the guide shape visible. Refer to Figure 21-19.

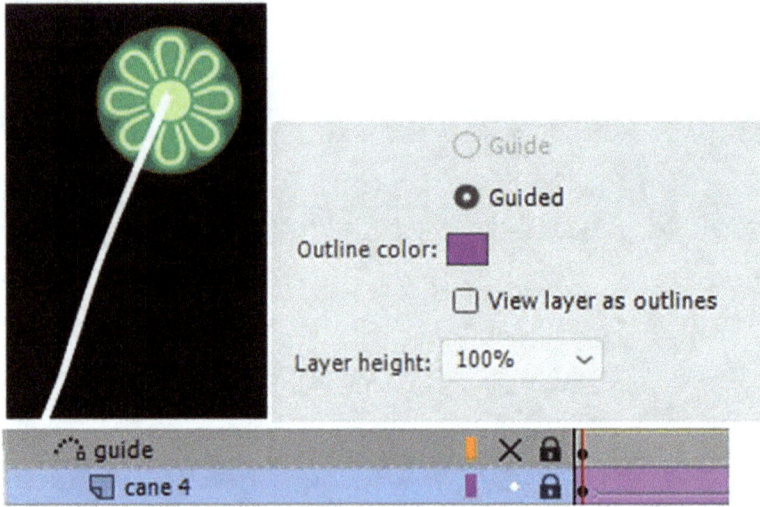

Figure 21-19. A created line acts as a guide to the symbol in a Classic tween

- **Guided**: Only appears as an option if the guide layer is connected and linked below.

You can also choose a different outline color and a layer height from the properties; this increases the size of the layer in the timeline by 100%, 200% or 300%, so it is easier to select, but it has nothing to do with layer order or how a symbol on the layer appears on the stage.

There are two other advanced layers types not shown.

- **Camera (for zoom and camera angles):** You can access this type of layer by clicking the Camera icon in the Timeline panel and then using the Camera tool (C) in the Tools panel. The same icon removes or hides the camera layer. Refer to the spinning_advanced_layers.fla file to see this layer in action as you move the playhead on the timeline. Refer to Figure 21-20.

CHAPTER 21 ■ WORKING WITH THE TIMELINE PANEL

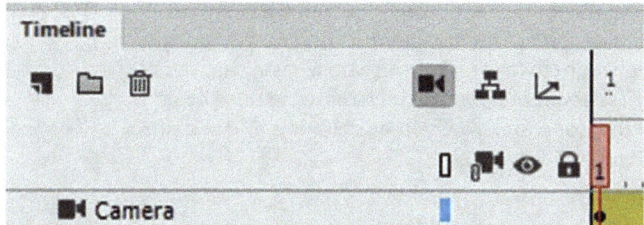

Figure 21-20. *Add or remove a camera layer*

You cannot choose this option in the Layer Properties dialog box by double-clicking it. You will find most options, including switching the layer type to normal, are inactive; however, if you have the advanced layers on, you can then attach the camera to it using a Link icon. Refer to Figures 21-21 and 21-22.

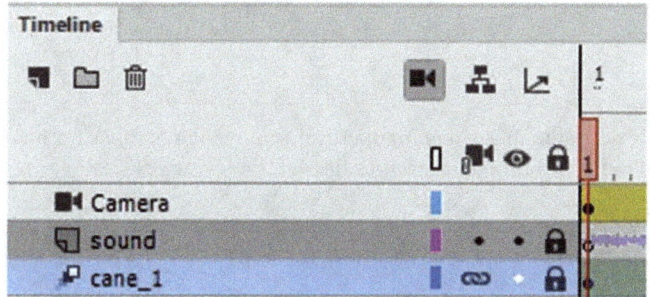

Figure 21-21. *A camera layer is added to the Timeline panel and a layer is linked to the camera*

This causes the camera and the objects to be more in sync with each other or locked on. The layer properties attached to the camera is checked. Refer to Figure 21-22.

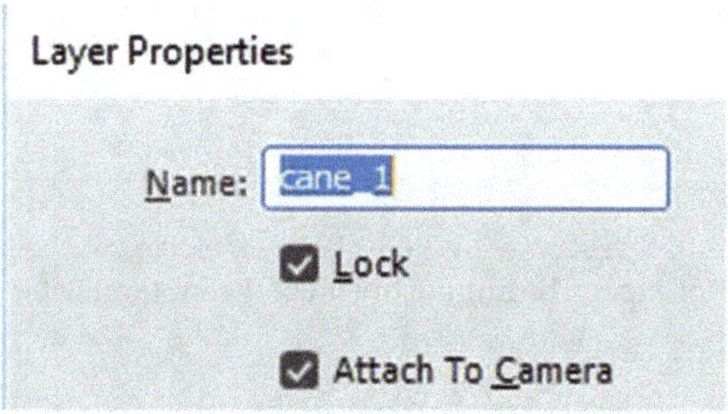

Figure 21-22. *Attach to Camera is checked in the Layer Properties dialog box*

487

- **Armature bone:** Used when creating movement with the Bone tool when two or more bones are attached. Armatures are great for character running movements, but they are difficult to master. If you want to learn how to create a basic character, I recommend *Adobe Animate CC Classroom in a Book*, which demonstrates basic walking movements. You'll look at the Bone tool briefly in this chapter and see some examples in Chapter 24. Refer to Figure 21-23.

Figure 21-23. The armature layer

- **Audio**: Unless used in a button symbols, audio should be stored on a normal layer or layers by itself so if it is accidently deleted, it does not disrupt the animation by removing parts of it.

The Parts of the Timeline

Now let's look at the parts of the timeline itself. A timeline has a rectangular frame, and each of those frames represent a moment that frame is on the stage. Refer to Spining_layertypes.fla. Refer to Figure 21-24.

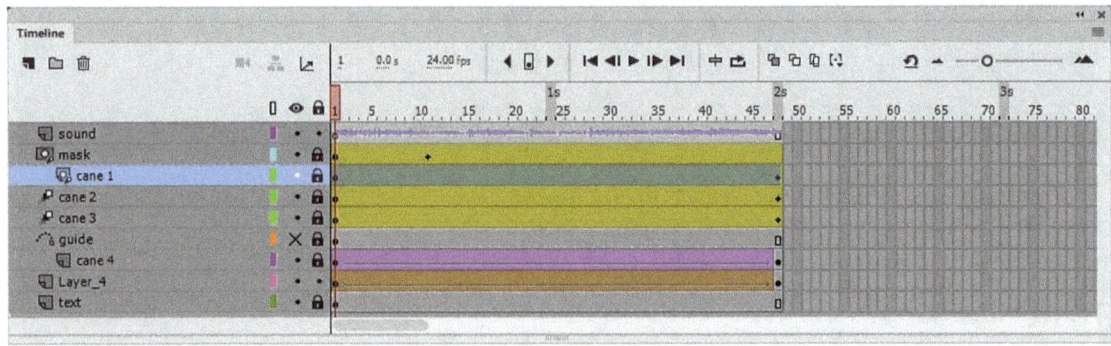

Figure 21-24. Parts in the Timeline panel

In Animate, you can navigate and preview these frames in several ways. When a layer is selected, you can use the keyframe arrows in the Timeline panel to move to the beginning or end of the motion. Refer to Figure 21-25.

Figure 21-25. Move to different keyframes in the timeline

CHAPTER 21 ■ WORKING WITH THE TIMELINE PANEL

You can use the red handle (playhead) with your mouse at the top of the timeline to scrub through the timeline one frame at a time. Refer to Figure 21-26.

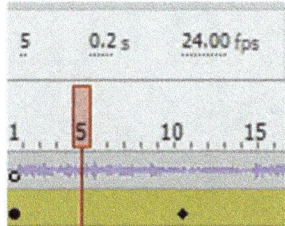

Figure 21-26. *Use the playhead to move along the timeline*

In the upper area of the Timeline panel, the preview features allow you to go to the first frame, move back one frame, play or stop the entire animation, move forward one frame, or move to the end of the animation. Refer to Figure 21-27.

Figure 21-27. *Preview the timeline*

The next upper section allows you to center all the frames on the stage, and then you can loop (Loop icon) a selected area (adjusted with the handles) while pressing the Play button. Refer to Figure 21-28.

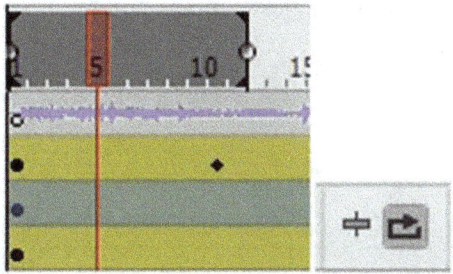

Figure 21-28. *Loop a section of frames to preview them*

489

CHAPTER 21 ■ WORKING WITH THE TIMELINE PANEL

The last section allows you to preview using onion skins and onion skin outlines. These only show a section of the animation and do not affect the actual animation. Refer to Figure 21-29.

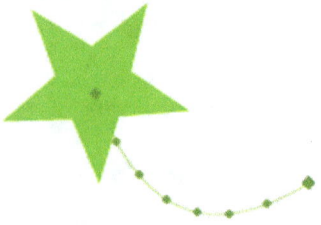

Figure 21-29. *Preview several frames' movements using onion skins and outlines*

The Edit Multiple Frames icon (the third icon) lets you edit multiple frames of motion within a range. Refer to Figure 21-30.

Figure 21-30. *Edit the motion of the frames*

The Modify Marker icon (the fourth icon) lets you set ranges of which areas to preview. Refer to Figure 21-31.

Figure 21-31. *Adjust the marker range in the Timeline panel*

490

The far left area in the timeline shows the current frame, the frames per second, the seconds or fractions of a second into the animation (where the playhead has stopped), and scroll handles at the bottom are for moving along the animation in the timeline. The upper right section allows you to reset the timeline, or to zoom in to the timeline frames, or out of the timeline to see it as one unit. Refer to Figure 21-32.

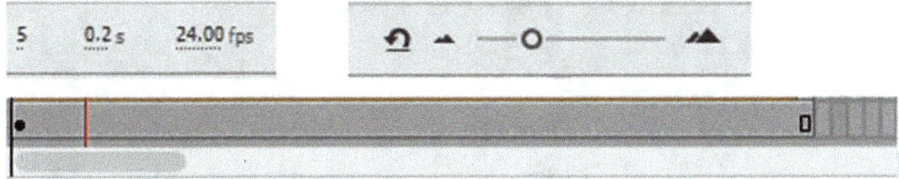

Figure 21-32. Use these areas of the Timeline panel to navigate the frames

■ **Note** Most web animations play at about 12 to 24 frames per second. Some developers recommend increasing your frame rate to 30 or 60 fps (video quality) to make the animation run smoother; however, this can put more strain on the CPU and browser, so run some tests first. Most Canvas animations can run at 24 fps. I recommend for the web a maximum of 30 if you are going to incorporate scenes into a video in Photoshop. If specifically for gaming, then 60 might be better for smother movements. Either way, before you start an animation, always set the rate first because with complex animation, this can be difficult to adjust once you have created many keyframes and layers.

Frames Types

There are several distinct types of animation frames that can be created within an animation. They often relate to the layer type that was chosen.

You can add frames by clicking the spot you want to insert the frame, and either choosing from the Insert ➤ Timeline and choosing a frame type, or right-clicking the spot and choosing from the pop-up menu. Refer to Figure 21-33.

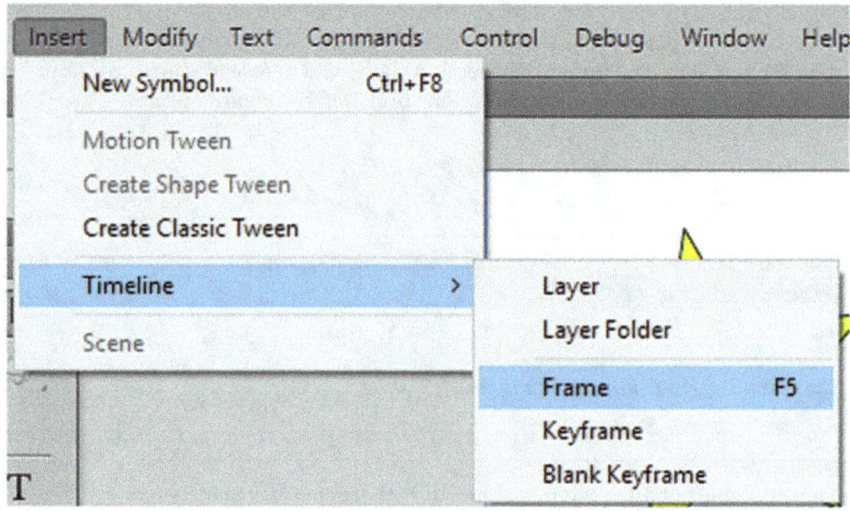

Figure 21-33. Choose a frame type

- **Blank keyframe:** A single frame that has no content on the stage. They are gray in color with an outline dot. Refer to Figure 21-34.

Figure 21-34. A blank keyframe

- **Blank frame:** If there are multiple frames in one section that contain no content, they are often gray and start with an outline dot and then end with an outline rectangle. Refer to Figure 21-35.

Figure 21-35. Blank frames

- **Keyframe with content:** Dark gray in color and have a filled dot because there is content on the stage for this frame in the layer. When multiple filled keyframes are beside each other, this is often a sign that this may be a stop-motion animation or multiple images from a video, such as an image sequence. Refer to Figure 21-36.

Figure 21-36. A keyframe with content

CHAPTER 21 ■ WORKING WITH THE TIMELINE PANEL

You can create a frame-by-frame animation by right-clicking a long frame and choosing to convert to Frame-By-Frame Animation and then an option from the side list. Refer to Figure 21-37.

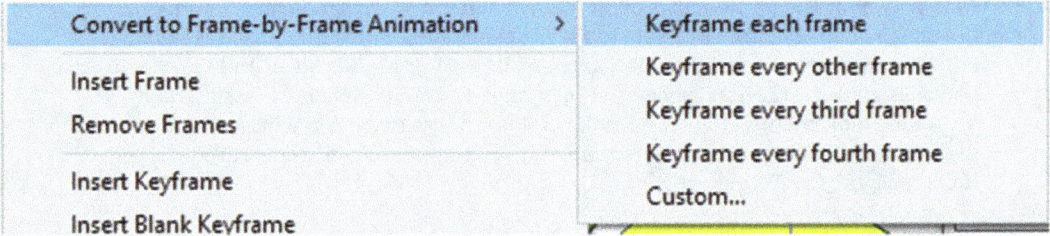

Figure 21-37. Split frames into frame-by frame animations

The Custom option allows you to choose your own divisions, such as every fifth frame. Refer to Figure 21-38.

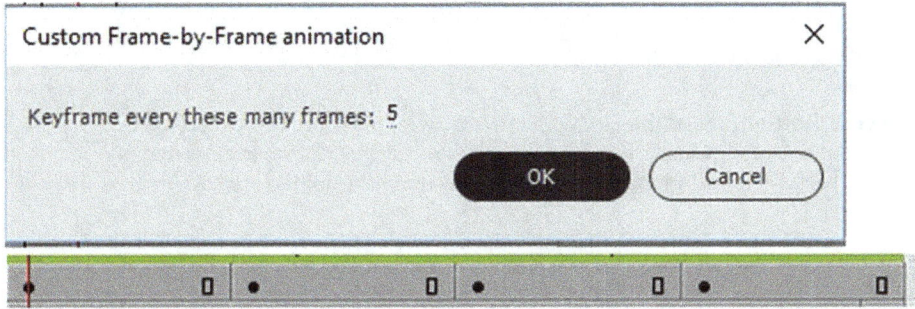

Figure 21-38. Frames spit with a keyyframe every five frames

- **Frames with content:** If there are multiple frames in one section that contain content and no movement, they are dark gray and start with a solid dot and end with a rectangular outline. It may be one long keyframe throughout the animation or broken by another keyframe that contains a different symbol on the stage. Refer to Figure 21-39.

Figure 21-39. Multiple keyframes with content

493

Tweens

The following describes the types of tweens.

- **Classic tween:** The frame shows up purple with an arrow. This indicates movement of a shape or symbol from one spot to the next keyframe, which in this case is static. For a Classic tween to act like a Motion tween it requires a guide layer. And the tween becomes guided. HTML5 Canvas's Output panel recommends using Classic tweens for simple movements, but at publication, it knows how to convert a basic Motion tween into a Classic tween when required for the animation to run smoothly. Refer to Figure 21-40.

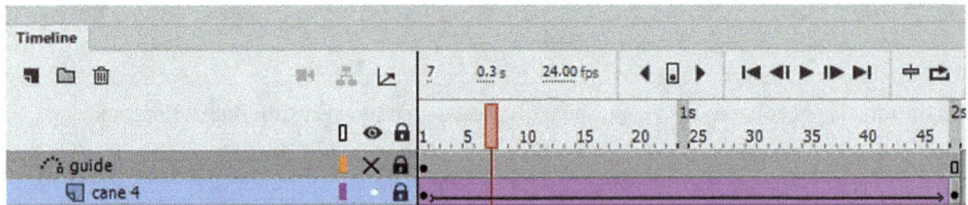

Figure 21-40. The classic tween in the timeline

- **Motion tween:** More advanced than a Classic tween. Symbols using this tween can transform and move along in a variety of ways across the stage. Motion tweens may have multiple keyframes within the motion that show up in the golden area. Refer to Figure 21-41.

Figure 21-41. The Motion tween

You can also use advanced layer settings with a motion tween.

- **Shape tween:** The morphing of a shape to another. A symbol cannot morph, but it can contain a shape tween. A orange bar with an arrow is used for this tween. While a symbol on a Motion tween can scale in size or rotate, its basic shape cannot alter as it does with a Shape tween. Refer to Figure 21-42.

CHAPTER 21 ■ WORKING WITH THE TIMELINE PANEL

Figure 21-42. *The Shape tween*

- **Camera tween:** A golden color and can contain the Motions tweens of zoom and moving left or right. Refer to Figure 21-43.

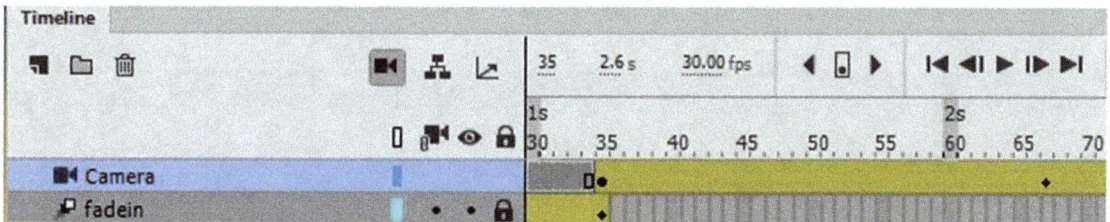

Figure 21-43. *The Camera tween*

- **Armature tweens:** They are green and contain the main points of movement, called *poses*. Refer to Figure 21-44.

Figure 21-44. *The Armature tween*

- **3D tween:** This can only be used in ActionScript 3.0 FLA files. With a Motion tween it allows you to work with the 3D tools. Crosshairs appear when you select a keyframe and chose 3D Tween. You'll look at 3D in Chapter 23 to morph your symbol in the Z-path. You can get out of a 3D tween by selecting the keyframe and unchecking 3D tween. Refer to Figure 21-45.

495

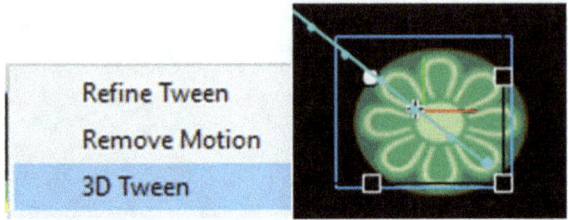

Figure 21-45. *Adding a 3D tween to the Motion tween*

With any layer that contains a tween, you can right-click it and choose to remove.

Other Frame Types

The following are other frame types.

- **Audio frames:** Show the audio previewed in the timeline with jagged lines representing the sound. Refer to Figure 21-46.

Figure 21-46. *The sound frame*

The sound stops when it reaches the end of the frame in ActionScript 3.0 video; however, in HTML5 Canvas, it may continue to play beyond the frame.

- **Comment frames:** Labeling frames that are blank frames keeps thoughts organized. For example, knowing which video, sound, or action is playing on the preceding frames. Also, you call a name rather than frame numbers when creating certain complex JavaScript actions on an HTML5 Canvas timeline. The comments can be added when a frame is selected, and then entered into the Frame Properties panel. Refer to Figure 21-47.

CHAPTER 21 ■ WORKING WITH THE TIMELINE PANEL

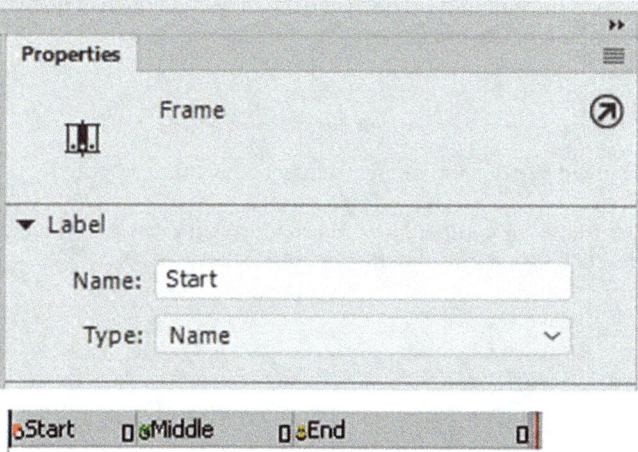

Figure 21-47. Adding comments to blank frames to keep your video or animation organized

- A little red flag appears when a frame is labeled as a name.
- A green // is a comment
- A yellow anchor is an anchor type.

Actions Panel

When a lower case "a" appears in a frame this indicates is there is an action on a frame it can be referenced in the Actions panel as seen in Figure 21-48.

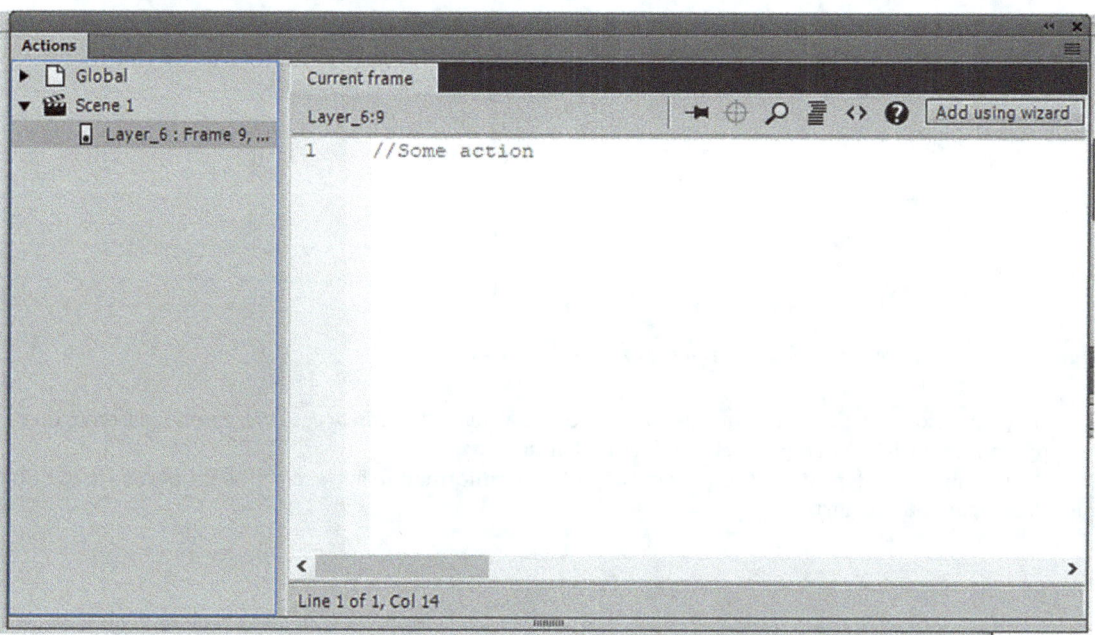

Figure 21-48. The Actions panel where you can add JavaScript

497

CHAPTER 21 ■ WORKING WITH THE TIMELINE PANEL

You don't have to label frames or actions for simple animations; however, the Output panel may report a warning if you do not label frames in certain JavaScript code instances.

Further Information on Frames

Any frame when selected in its entirety can be moved by dragging when the cursor changes to a double-sided arrow to shrink or expand the frame.

Frames can be copied and pasted into other frames or another layer. Alternatively they can be reversed or removed when you choose an option by right-clicking a frame. Refer to Figure 21-49.

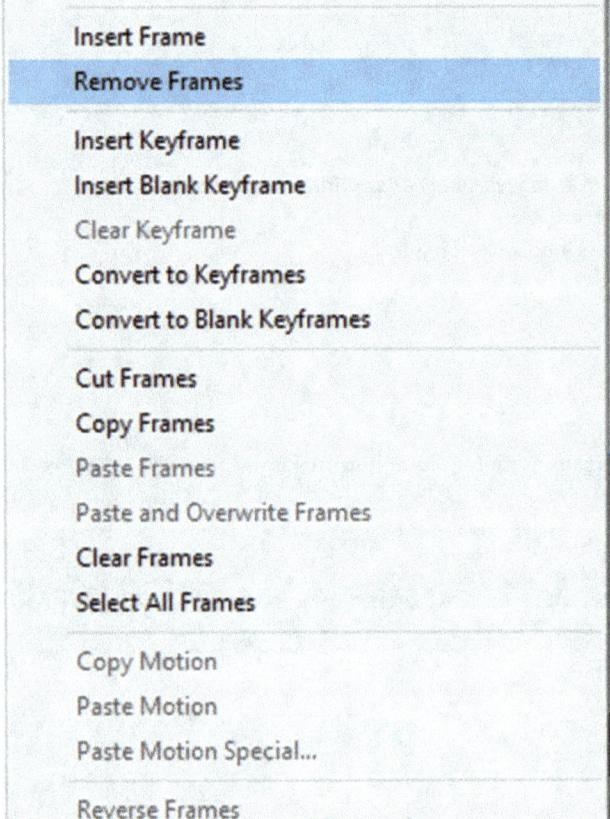

Figure 21-49. Options from the Frames pop-up menu

They can also be cleared without deletion of the actual layer. You can access these options from either the pop-up menu when you right-click a point in the frame.

Depending on the type of keyframe or tween, different information appears in the Properties menu that you can edit, as you see next.

More Information About Shape Tweening

Unlike Classic and Motion tweens, a Shape tween cannot be made up of symbols. It can be made of primitives, drawing objects, shapes, and grouped shapes, which you saw in Chapter 19.

Sometimes the shape does not morph as you would expect, so to control a complex shape, you need to use your Properties panel as well as Shape hints (Modify ➤ Shape ➤ Add Shape Hint).

You can have up to 26 shape hints, which range from A to Z. They appear as little circles, as seen in Figure 21-50.

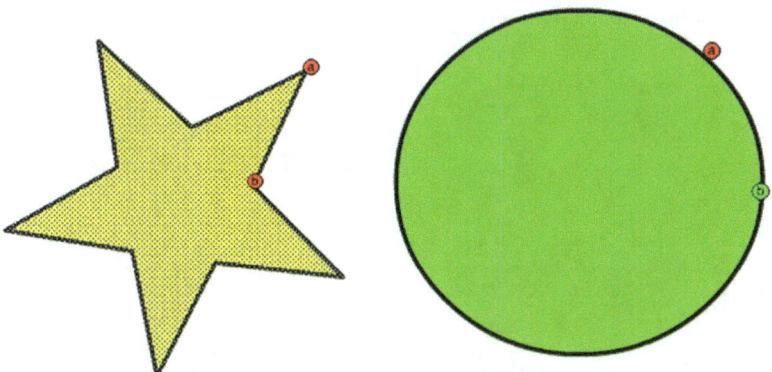

Figure 21-50. Adding shape hints to a Shape tween

The following are some tips about shape hints:

- Hints allow you to mark object points that you want to morph in a specific direction so that the shape tween does not appear as a tangled mess, and each transition remains smooth and recognizable.

- To view them, when you return to the shape, choose View ➤ Show Shape Hints.

- The hints must have a corresponding hint at the end of the tween.

- Shape hints are yellow in a starting keyframe, green in an ending keyframe, and red when not on a curve.

- For best results when tweening shapes, follow these guidelines: In complex shape tweening, create intermediate shapes and tween them instead of just defining a starting and ending shape. Shape tweening is a lot like using the blend tool in Illustrator CC, you can use this tool to create your transitory shapes and then break these symbols apart in animate to use as your transition shapes.

- Make sure that shape hints are logical; for example, if you're using three shape hints for a triangle, they must be in the same order on the original triangle and on the triangle shape to be tweened. The order cannot be ABC in the first keyframe and then ACB in the second.

- Shape hints work best if you place them beginning at the top-left corner of the shape and move counterclockwise.

- You can right-click a shape hint to remove it. Or choose Modify ➤ Shape ➤ Remove All Hints.

Easing for Classic, Shape, and Motion Tweens

For symbols and shapes to have realistic movements on the Timeline panel, you can use a type of timing known as easing. Easing can be applied to different types of tweens; however, the settings often appear different for each type in the Properties panel and Timeline panel. This next section shows how to locate and edit the easing for each type of tween.

Shape Tween Easing

You can create advanced tween movements in the Tweening tab in the Properties panel when a frame containing the Motion tween is selected. Refer to Figure 21-51.

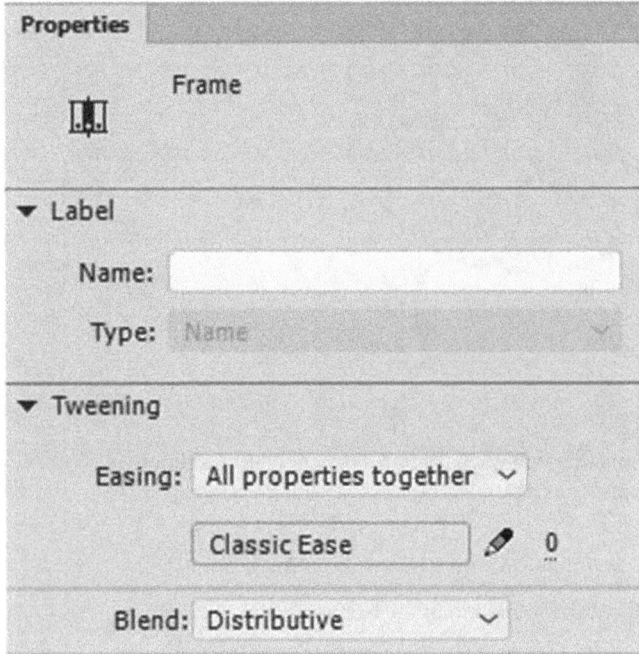

Figure 21-51. Properties panel for Shape tweening

- **Easing:** You can choose all properties together or each property separately from the drop-down menu.

Ease in (–) or Ease out (+)?

Easing adds a gradual speed up or slow down to an animation's beginning or end.

You can choose from several different preset eases. Then you must double-click in the middle box to apply it to your frame and Movie Clip symbol. Refer to Figure 21-52.

CHAPTER 21 ■ WORKING WITH THE TIMELINE PANEL

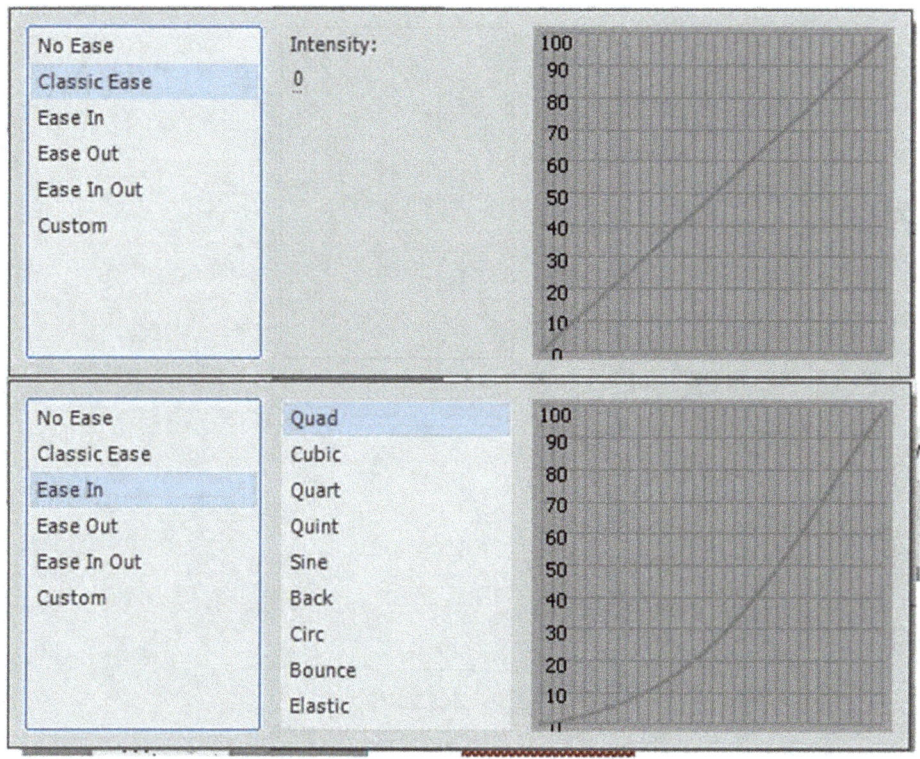

Figure 21-52. *Adding an ease to a shape*

- **Classic ease:** Allows you to set your own intensity, while ease in or out has other settings you can choose from when you double-click the options, as seen in Figure 21-52.

- **Custom ease:** Clicking the Word or Pencil icons allows you to create, save, and apply your own custom ease. You can preview it with the Play and Stop buttons. Refer to Figure 21-53.

501

CHAPTER 21 ■ WORKING WITH THE TIMELINE PANEL

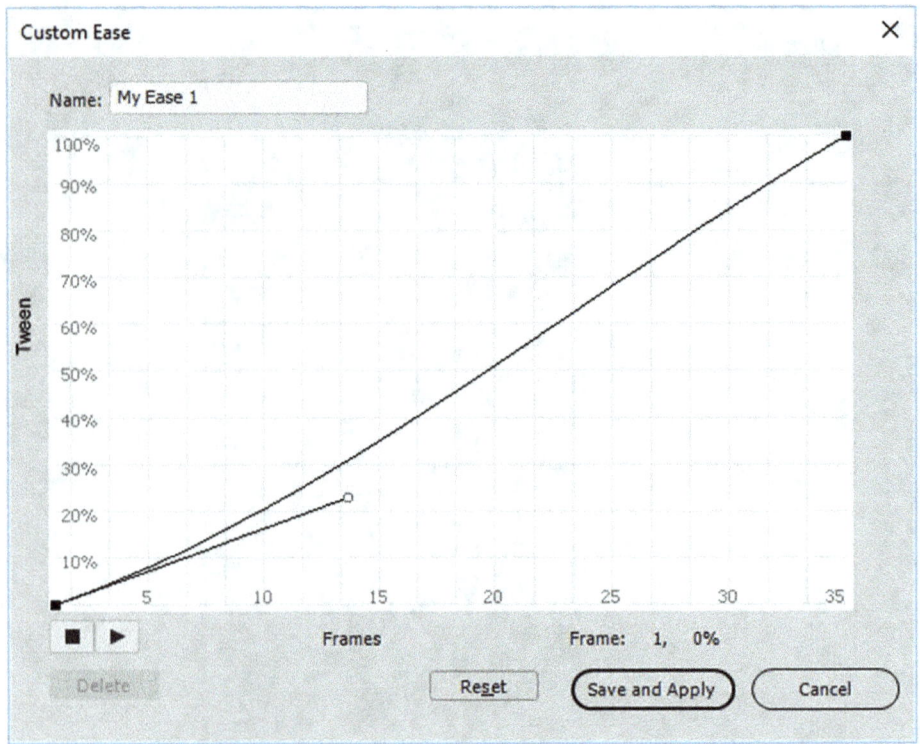

Figure 21-53. Creating a custom ease

- **Blend:** Set to distributive or angular using the drop-down menu in Figure 21-51.

Classic Tween Easing

Classic tweens have a similar layout to Shape tweens in the Properties menu; however, this time, you are working with a symbol and not a shape. Refer to Figure 21-54.

CHAPTER 21 ■ WORKING WITH THE TIMELINE PANEL

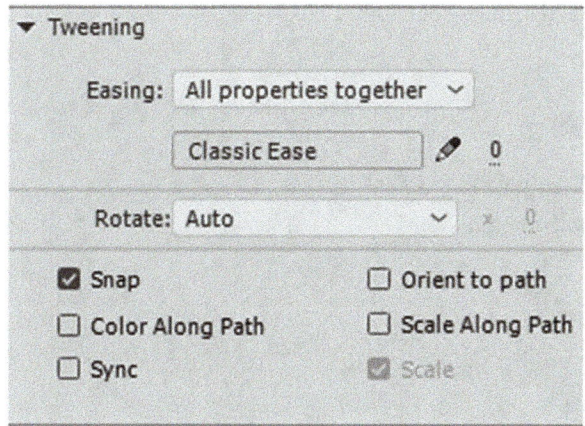

Figure 21-54. Clasic tweening ease tween in the Properties panel

Remember Classic tweens need a guide layer and a guided layer, or they'll just move in a straight direction. You are affecting the guided layer that the symbol is on.

As before with shape, you can choose all properties or each property separately. Each property separately allows you to add different easings to your symbol in the frames, such as the position, rotation, scale, color, and any filters that were applied. Refer to Figure 21-55.

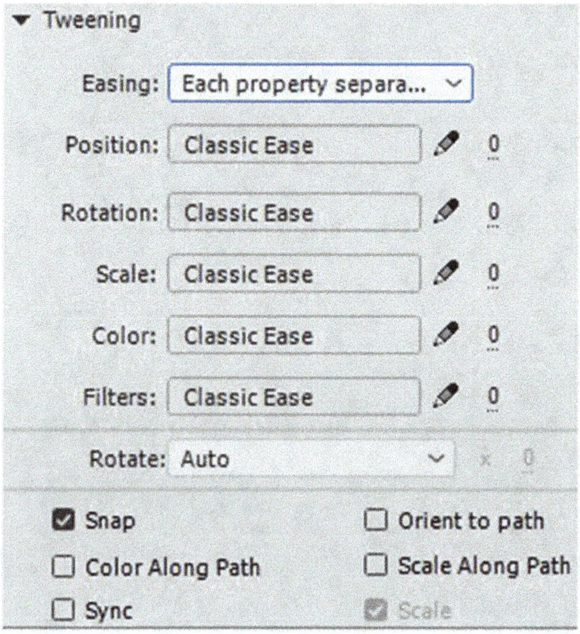

Figure 21-55. Tweening settings for the Classic tween in the Properties panel

503

CHAPTER 21 WORKING WITH THE TIMELINE PANEL

You can also choose the direction of rotation auto (clockwise or counter-clockwise) and the number of times it rotates in the specified direction.

- **Snap**: Snaps to guide
- **Orient to path**: Path rotation
- **Color Along Path**: Change color transformation as per path color
- **Scale Along Path**: Change scale as per with of path
- **Sync**: Sync Symbols
- **Scale**: Scale shape

Motion and Camera Tween Easing

The Motion tween and Camera tween both involve motion and can have varying Motion tweens settings that appear in the Properties menu. Refer to Figure 21-56.

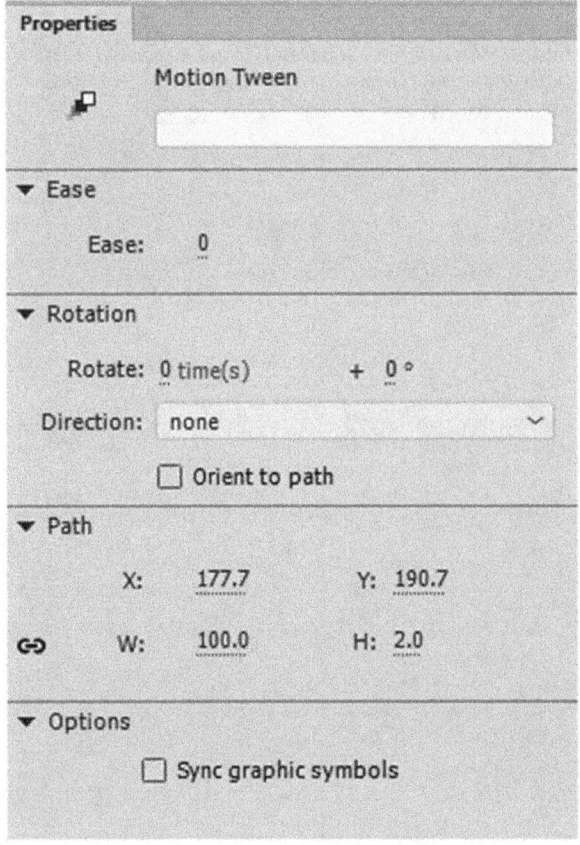

Figure 21-56. Motion tween settings in the Propreties panel

CHAPTER 21 ■ WORKING WITH THE TIMELINE PANEL

They allow you to create complex tween movements very easily. Both of their Property panels are identical, since both involve the movement of symbols.

As before, you can set the ease in the Properties menu; however, to set a custom or preset ease you need to look in a different location in the timeline, which you will in a moment.

Like with the Classic tween you can set the times of the rotation and the direction clockwise and counter-clockwise, but you can also additionally rotate in degrees. You also can orient to Path and Sync graphic symbols in the Options tab.

To adjust the easing, double-click the frame of any of these tweens motion or camera (or right-click and choose Refine tween) and you will see within the layer added settings that you can manipulate to create custom easing and symbol movement. Refer to Figures 21-57 and 21-58.

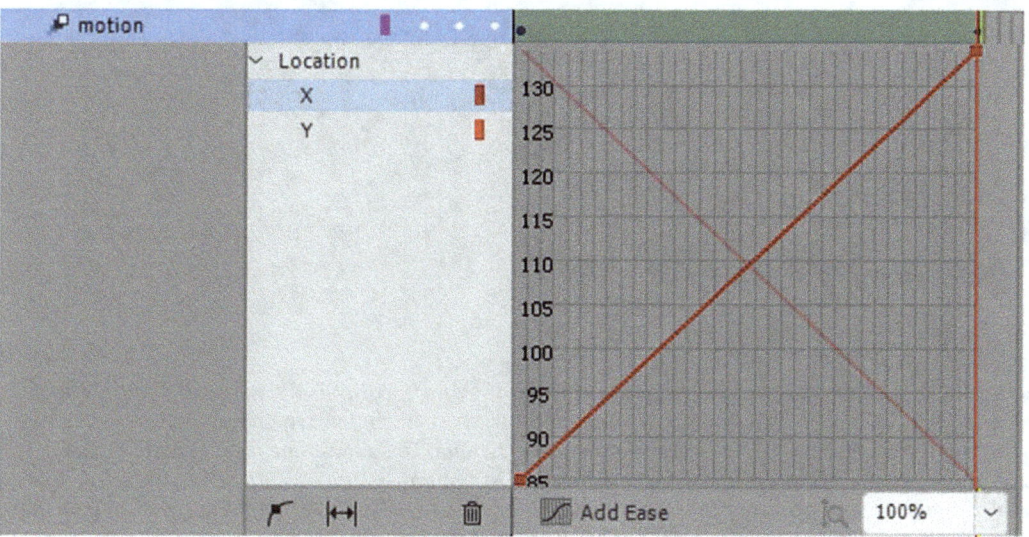

Figure 21-57. *Adjust the easing of a Motion tween*

505

CHAPTER 21 ■ WORKING WITH THE TIMELINE PANEL

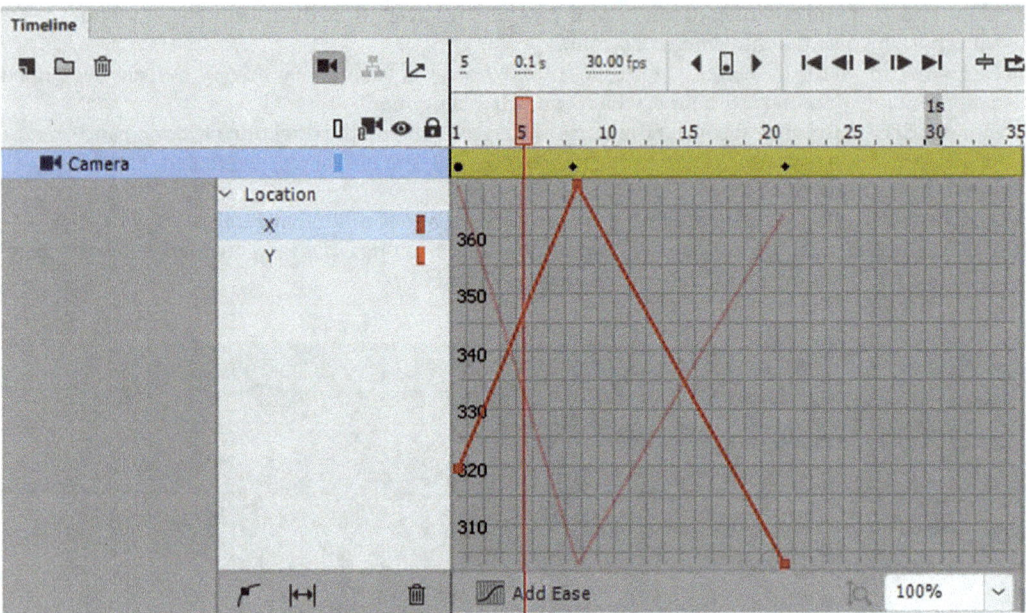

Figure 21-58. *Adjust the easing of a Camera tween*

The X and Y indicate where on the stage the symbol is moving. X controls the horizontal and Y the vertical movements. By moving the control or anchor points, you can change which frame the movements happen on, and isolate and keyframe movement you want to alter. To collapse the layer, double-click the frame or right-click and uncheck refine tween from the pop-up menu.

If you shrink or enlarge your symbol that can be controlled as well in the same manner in the Transform section. X controls the width and Y the height of the symbol. Refer to Figure 21-59.

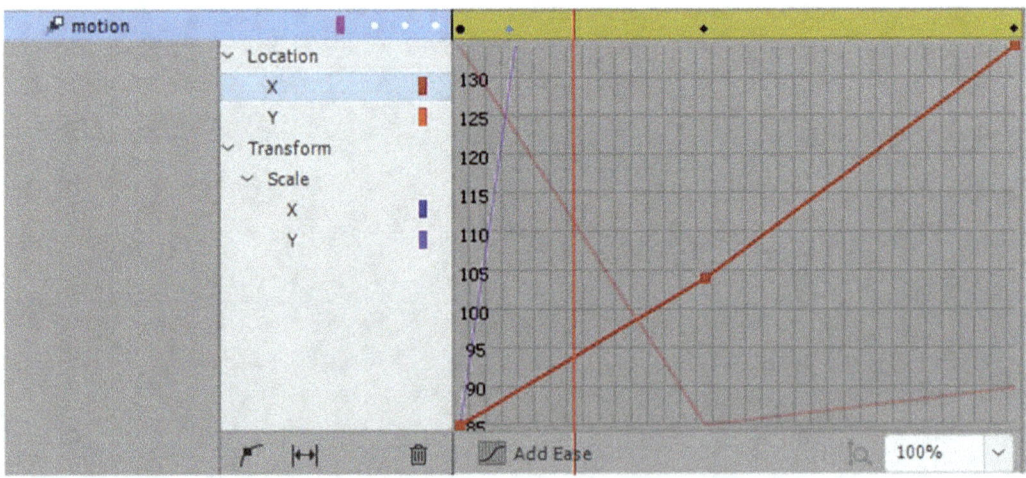

Figure 21-59. *Control the movent and scale of a tween*

You can also add additional points to the graph, trash/remove points, or expand the graph to view it better.

Clicking the Add Ease icon reveals many ease options to choose from, so make sure to experiment. Refer to Figure 21-60.

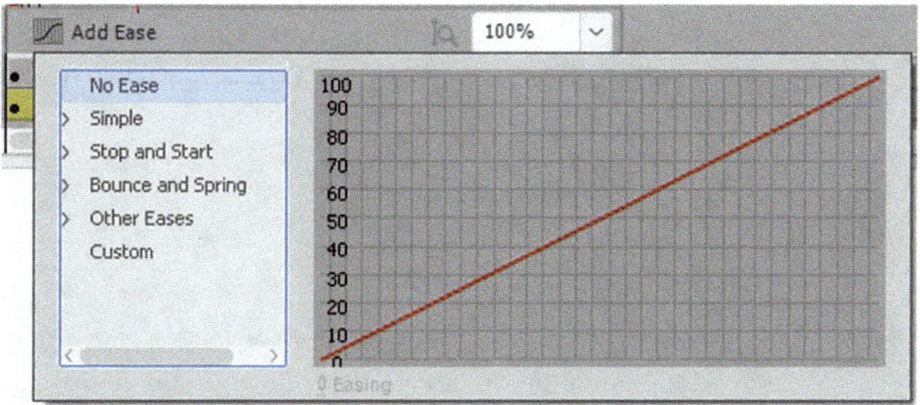

Figure 21-60. Add other custom eases from the list

Clicking the triangles reveals more suboptions.

Remember that if you add an ease here, it may affect or reset the ease that was added in the Properties panel.

Zoom in by percentage if you need to adjust the easing and direction more accurately. Refer to Figure 21-61.

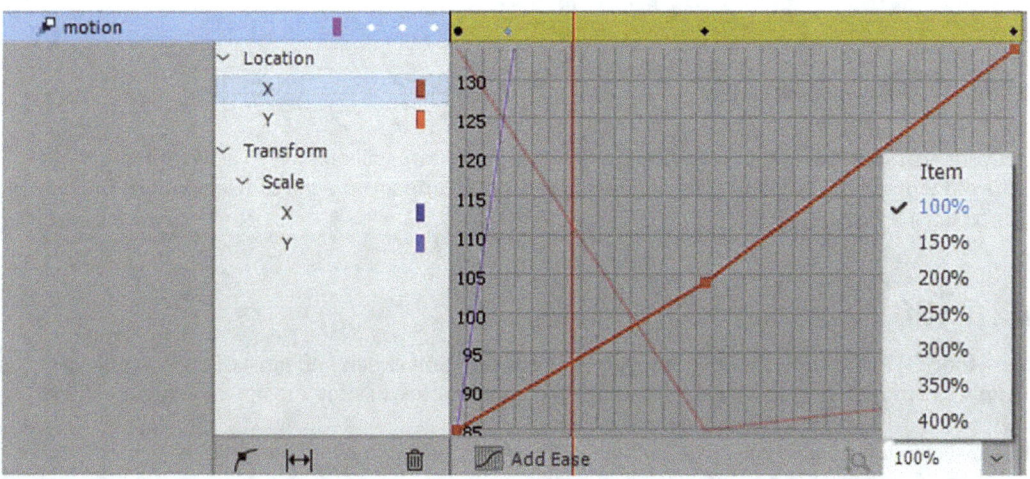

Figure 21-61. Adjusting an ease

Motion Presets Panel

If you don't like any of the motions of the symbols that you created on the stage, you can use the Motion Presets panel. You can use the choices that are provided by Animate CC (in the Default Presets folder), and then customize them to make your own custom presets. You can preview them in the Motion Presets panel. Refer to Figure 21-62.

Figure 21-62. *The Motion Presets panel*

Select your symbol on the stage and click Apply in the panel. You will receive a warning that this will override the old motions. Click OK to override the old setting. To undo, you need to select Edit ➤ Undo right away to revert to your original settings.

Camera Tool

The Camera tool (C) in the Tools menu acts very much like a motion tween and most of the custom easing that you apply to a motion tween you can also apply to camera frames to simulate the movement of a real camera.

In this case, the main scene layer can remain stationary or contain movement while the camera moves.

The camera layer zooms in and out rotates or moves around the scene; each new movement is a keyframe. Refer to Figure 21-63.

Figure 21-63. Camera tool and how it appears on the stage and in the Timeline panel

■ **Note** You do not have to have all Advanced Layers on to use the Camera tool only the camera tool icon in the Timeline panel. If you discover your camera controller disappears, go to the Workspace tab and choose Reset Essentials. This should bring it back on screen when using the Camera tool, though you may have to rearrange your other tools again, as you did in Chapter 17.

You can use most of the camera modes) in HTML5 Canvas and WebGL. Except for the Color Effects tab, which you can currently only access in an ActionScript 3.0 file that you can use to create a video. With either format, you can access these effects while you are using the Camera tool from the Tools panel. Refer to Figure 21-64.

CHAPTER 21 ■ WORKING WITH THE TIMELINE PANEL

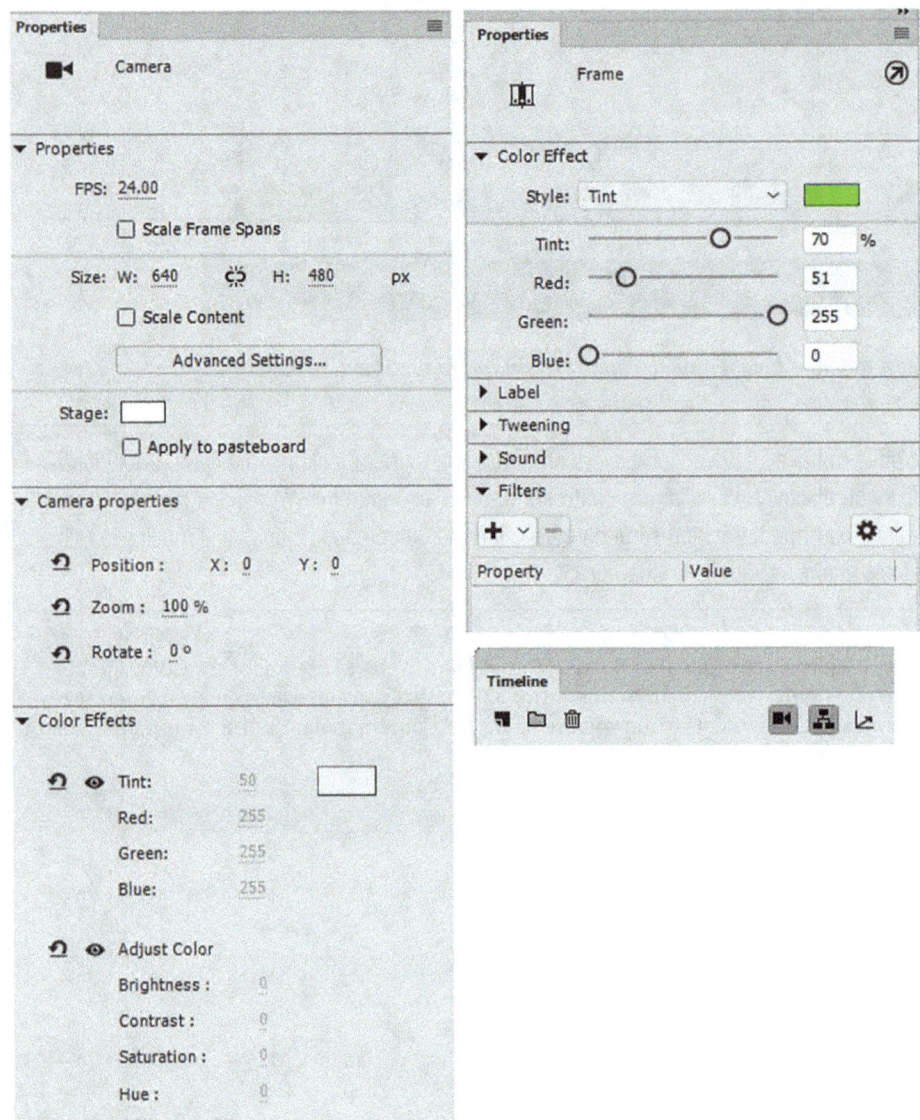

Figure 21-64. *Settings in the Properties menu) for the camera and new layer effects*

Camera properties can adjust the position (panning), zoom, and rotation of the camera.

Color Effects are like the color effects for working on individual symbols; however, in this case, the tint effects the whole screen. Also in regards to color, it should be noted that in version CC 2019 in ActionScript 3.0 file you can now add layer color effects and filters to non-tween, shape and classic tween frames that can interact with your Camera layer. If this is an effect, you want for an HTML5 Canvas animation, test it an ActionScript 3.0 FLA file to see what it does try to export the frames as individual GIFs or JPEGs, and then add them as keyframes into your HTML5 Canvas file; otherwise, you may need to do this work in Photoshop CC.

510

CHAPTER 21 ■ WORKING WITH THE TIMELINE PANEL

Another alternative is to create a layer that is covered by a black, white, or colored square Movie Clip symbol. If you adjust the alpha of this symbol and add a Motion tween, you can give similar effects of fading in or out. Refer to the scene6_timeline_example.fla file, which could be converted to HTML5 Canvas, and the symbol scene fade-in layer Motion tween effect would work similar to a camera color) effects.

Bone Tools
Bone Tool and Armature Easing

You will look at some examples of Bone tool movement in Chapter 24; for now, just review the figures in the book so that you get a basic idea of the tool that uses what is known as IK, or *inverse kinematics*, where joints or bones are chained in a parent-child relationship and move along with the connected bone as a puppet or a marionette moves. Refer to Figure 21-65.

Figure 21-65. *The animation of the glass worker uses the Bone tool to move his body*

This can be used to create natural movements for joints in the body. As you can see in Figure 21-66, when Bone tools are applied, a normal layer becomes an armature layer.

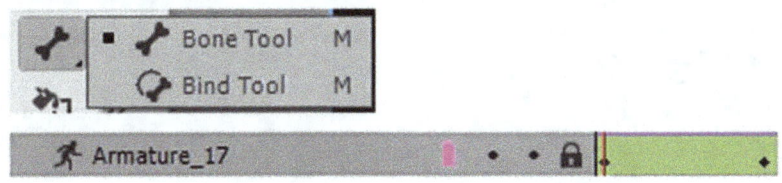

Figure 21-66. *The Bone and Armature tools*

511

It is like a Motion tween in some ways, but there are distinct differences.
Bones can be two symbols that move on common joints. Refer to Figure 21-67.

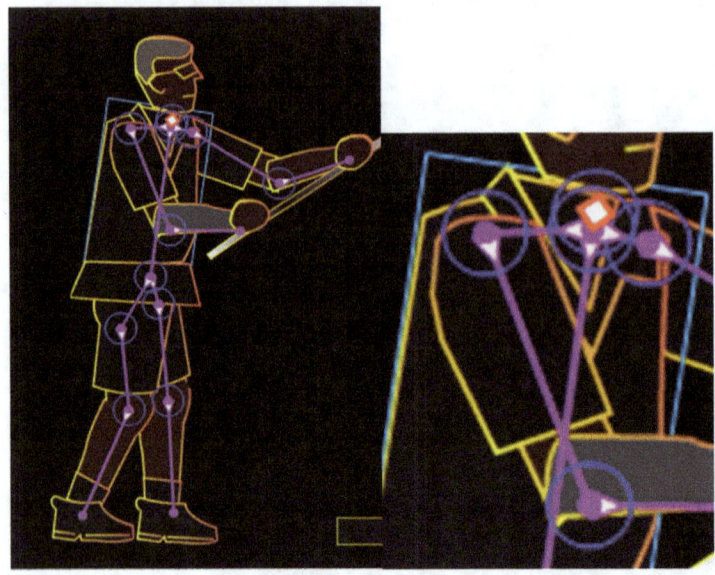

Figure 21-67. *Adding of armature points to a figure*

They can also be multiple joints added to a shape within a symbol.

■ **Tip** If you go into a symbol (nested armature) to adjust the bones make sure that it is broken apart as a shape within the symbol before using the Bone tool. Animate does not like to have the tool applied to a grouped shape (fill and stroke grouped); in some instances, this slows down or crashes the program. Outside the symbol, it is OK to apply the armature, even if it has a stroke.

The Bone tool is probably one of the most complicated tools in Animate CC. It requires many hours of practice to master.

To create your bones or body parts, you need to design them in Illustrator CC. Refer to Figure 21-68.

CHAPTER 21 ■ WORKING WITH THE TIMELINE PANEL

Figure 21-68. *Parts of the body that I designed in Illustrator*

At this point, you can in one of two ways export your shapes as symbols to Animate. Refer to Chapter 19 for more information on importing.

- In Illustrator, save each shape by dragging it into the Symbols panel, but make sure they are on their own layer while on stage. Then in Animate, you can select File ➤ Import ➤ Import to library; then, they are in the Library panel ready for you to drag onto the stage.

- Or select the shape in Illustrator and choose Edit ➤ Copy. In Animate, choose Edit ➤ Paste in Center and choose to paste as AI Importer preferences. Once the group or shape is on the stage, you can then convert to a movie clip or symbols and add it to the Library panel. Refer to Figure 21-69.

CHAPTER 21 ■ WORKING WITH THE TIMELINE PANEL

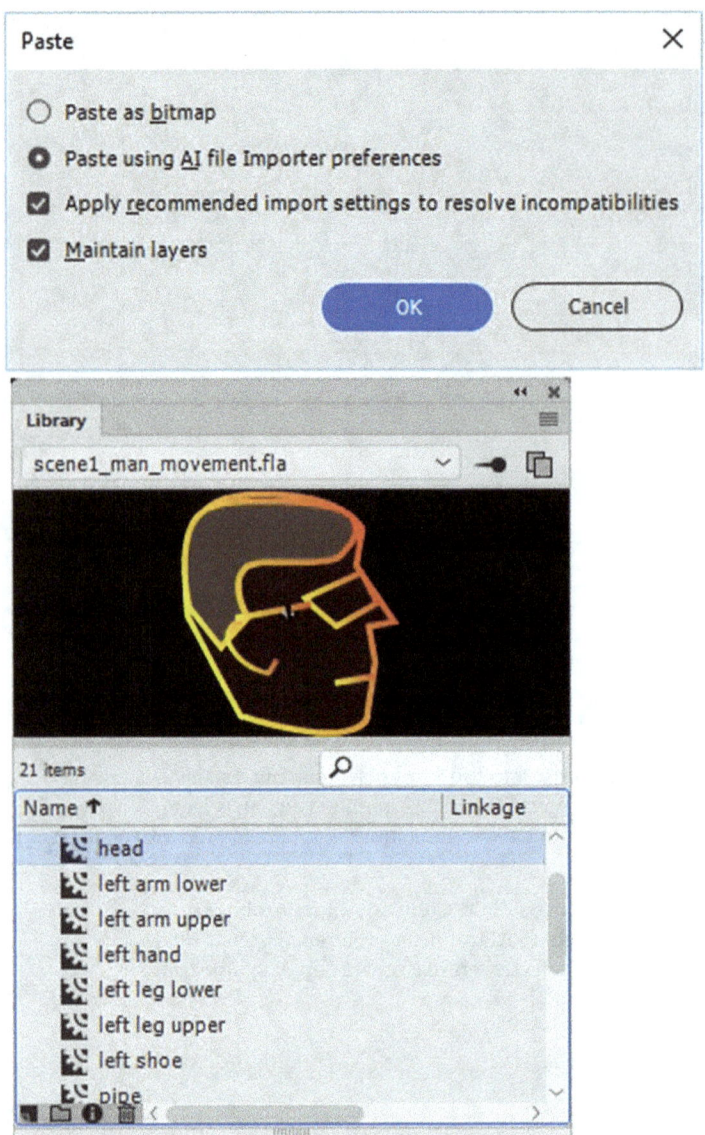

Figure 21-69. *Adding your shapes to the stage and then to the Library panel*

Then when all the symbols are on the stage use the Bone tool to drag and connect your joints. All the joints are on the one armature layer and not separate layers. Once you have joined all the armature symbols, you cannot add or paste additional symbols to the armature layer. You must add the new symbol to a new layer, and then use the Bone tool to connect it to become part of the armature layer.

Joints can be modified with the Selection tool (V) and mouse drag Alt/Option or Ctrl keys and Modify ➤ Arrange to move the armature symbols forwards and backwards so they overlap correctly.

Moving around the bones can be done using the parent/child arrows in the Properties menu. Refer to Figure 21-70.

CHAPTER 21 ■ WORKING WITH THE TIMELINE PANEL

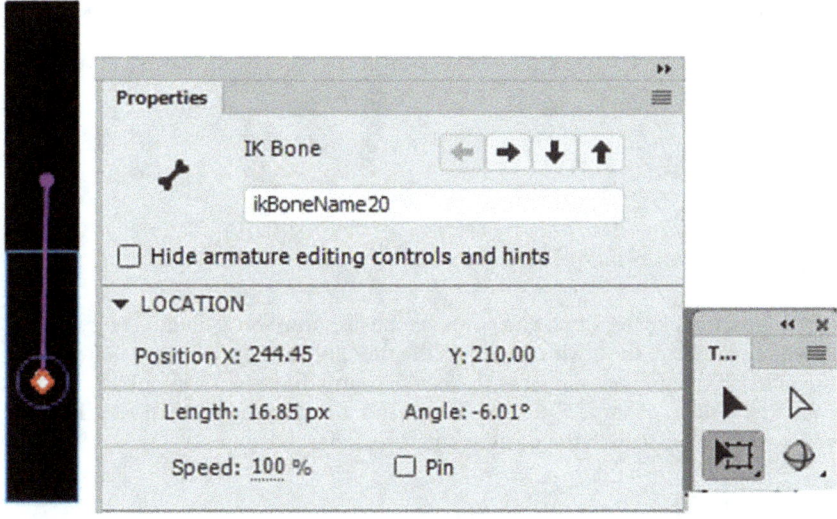

Figure 21-70. Move around the bones using the Properties panel and the Tools panel to control the movement and placement of joints

Joint movement can also be constrained at each point (IK Bone) so that the movement is more realistic, such as the knee or arm joint only moving in one direction, or pinned to the stage to keep the bone from moving. The Free Transform tool (Q) allows you to adjust the location points of the IK bones on each shape when you select the point on the symbol.

Not all shapes have to have joints. You can create your own joints in a straight or single bone-shape, like an animal tail, a snake, or a flower stalk. Refer to Figure 21-71 and the flower_stock.fla and flower_stock.html files.

Figure 21-71. The flower stock bends

515

CHAPTER 21 ■ WORKING WITH THE TIMELINE PANEL

On the timeline, you can copy and insert poses after keyframes are created when you right- click a frame. Refer to Figure 21-72.

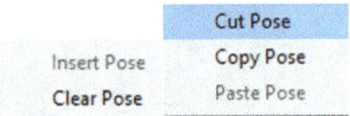

Figure 21-72. Copy and cut poses along the armature's timeline

When you create a nested animation like the stock that contains the armature on a shape. The symbol on the stage will not animate when you scrub the keyframe across the timeline. It is unfortunate that you can't preview nested animations to get the movements in sync. So, make sure that when you publish your HTML5 Canvas file or video the first time to observe where you may need to adjust the animation as I have done, so that each of my keyframes are in sync with the nested armature. Refer to Figure 21-73.

Figure 21-73. The nested armature and armature on the main stage

You see more about exporting in Chapter 22.

The Bind Tool

By default, the control points of a shape are connected to the bone that is nearest to them. You can use the Bind tool (M) to edit the connections between individual bones and the shape control points. Refer to Figure 21-74.

CHAPTER 21 ■ WORKING WITH THE TIMELINE PANEL

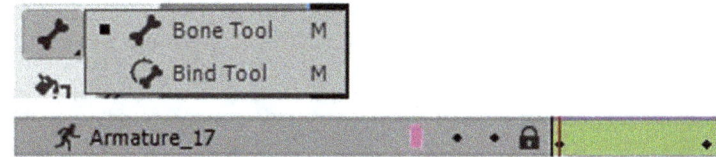

Figure 21-74. The Bind tool in the Tools panel can also be used with the armature layer in the Timeline panel

In this way, you can control how the stroke distorts when each bone moves for better results. This technique is useful when the stroke of a shape does not distort as you want when the armature moves, as you can see in the flower stock example.

The Spring and Damping easing in the Properties panel control how the bones will ease. Refer to Figure 21-75.

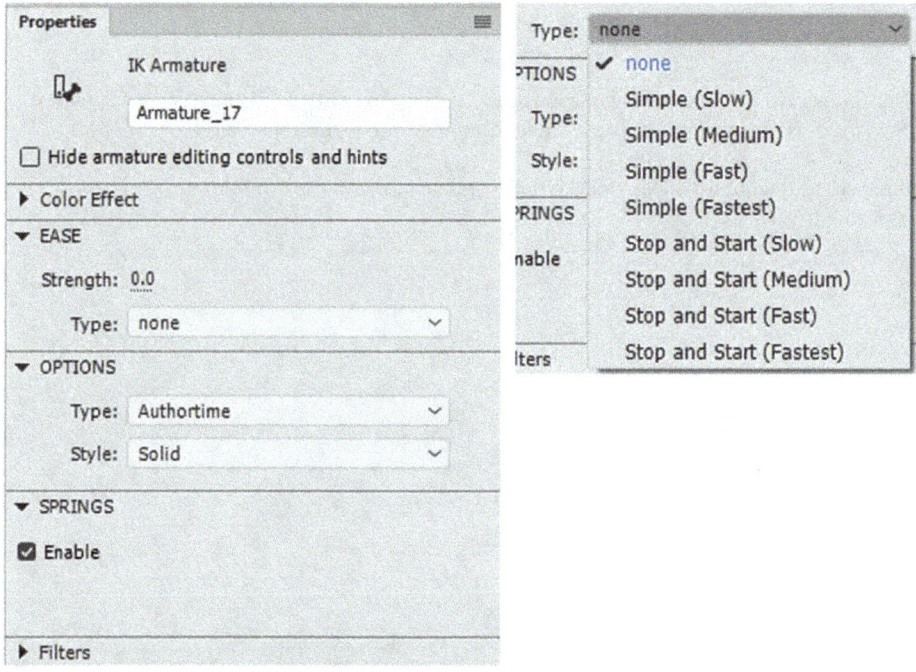

Figure 21-75. The Bone tool options for easing in the Properties panel

517

CHAPTER 21 ■ WORKING WITH THE TIMELINE PANEL

The easing options can be accessed in the Type drop-down menu. They range from slow to fastest.

In the Options tab, you can control the armature style to be wire, solid (default), line, or none. Refer to Figure 21-76.

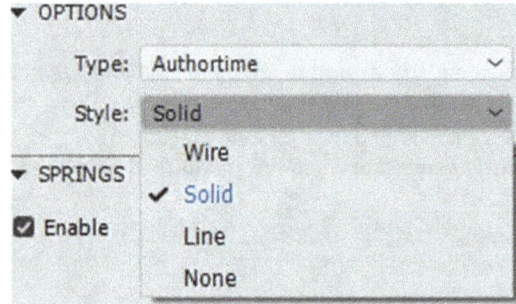

Figure 21-76. Armature styles for bones

Unlike other motion layers, the armature layer does not allow you to control advanced settings when you double-click it. So, you must control the settings for each bone in the Properties panel for location, rotation, and translation.

How the bone bounces and wobbles is controlled in the Spring tab with the Strength and Damping options. Refer to Figure 21-77.

CHAPTER 21 ■ WORKING WITH THE TIMELINE PANEL

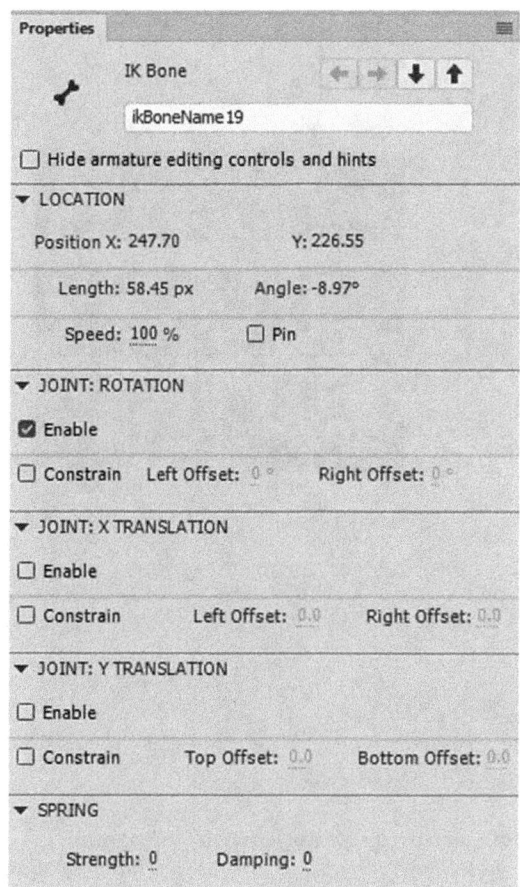

Figure 21-77. Set the spring for each bone joint

For more information on working on the Bone tool, make sure to review *Adobe Animate CC Classroom in a Book* by Russell Chum and to visit https://helpx.adobe.com/animate/using/bone-tool-animation.html. You might also find the short article, "Mysteries of the Bone Tool" by Joseph Labrecque to be helpful (see https://theblog.adobe.com/mysteries-of-the-bone-tool/).

Frame Picker Panel

The Frame Picker panel only works with graphic symbols that have nested frames and no nested tween frames. You can add multiple keyframes to them. You can then choose the order you want the frames to play by using the Properties panel and the Frame picker panel. While the graphic symbol is selected in the main timeline. Movie Clip and Button Symbols will not work in the Frame Picker and you must set them to Graphic in the Library Panel for them to appear in the Frame Picker panel. Refer to Figure 21-78. A new feature which as been added along with the Frame Picker in CC 2019 is Lip Syncing now you can use graphic symbols to control mouth movement as well for specific frames if your video will contain audio.

519

CHAPTER 21 ■ WORKING WITH THE TIMELINE PANEL

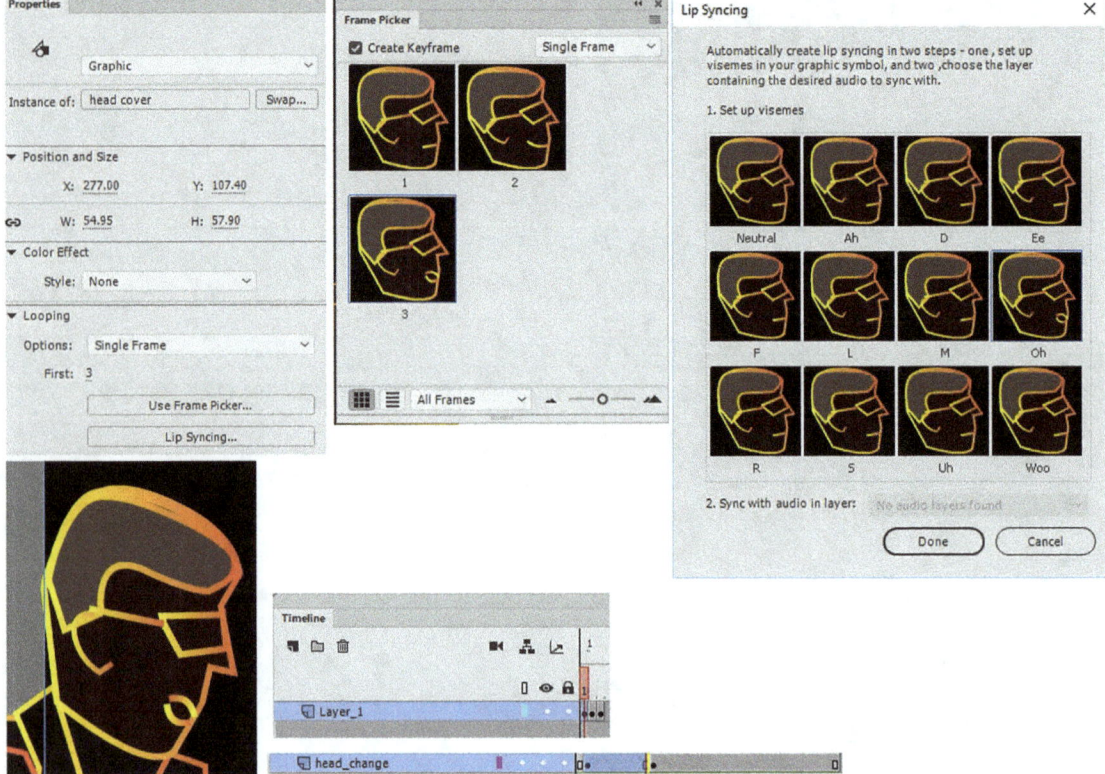

Figure 21-78. *Using the frame picker and the graphic symbol, you can change the face reactions of your character if the graphic contains different keyframes, mouth movements can also be controlled with lip syncing*

These are good for talking characters, where different frames switch during looping to create mouth movements for each syllable of a word.

Scene Panel

The Scene is grayed out if you create an HTML5 Canvas file. You will not have access to create multiple scenes, which are better suited to video. In this case, it is better to use an ActionScript 3.0 FLA to create your animation with scenes and export as a video, which you look at in Chapter 22. Refer to Figure 21-79.

520

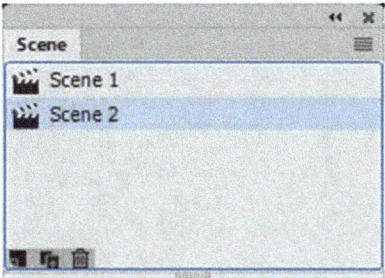

Figure 21-79. The Scene panel

Scenes basically are a new stage each time. A new scene is a blank stage each time; however, the items in the Library panel remain the same, so you can reuse symbols for new scenes.

Summary

In this chapter, you reviewed the Timeline panel and how layers and frames interact. You also looked at some of the tools (bone and camera) and related panels (frame picker and layer depth) that you can use to enhance your animation before it is exported. Remember, don't expect to master the Bone tool and armature layer overnight; keep experimenting with it and learn how it operates.

In the next chapter, you are going to look at several options for exporting part or all of your animations and video.

CHAPTER 22

Exporting Your Files to the Web

In this chapter, you look at how to export your image files (JPEG, PNG, GIF, SVG) and your animations (GIF, HTML5 Canvas, OAM), and video (MOV). You also discover some other related formats used for web design. The MOV file will be imported into Media Encoder CC in Part 5; you look at the web setting formats for this file then.

> **Note** This chapter does not have any actual projects; however, you can use the files in the Chapter 22 folder to practice opening and viewing for this lesson. They are at https://github.com/Apress/graphics-multimedia-web-adobe-creative-cloud.

Saving or Exporting Your Files for the Web

As you can see, there are many steps to creating an animation. There are some tools or properties that you might use more frequently than others depending upon your level of skill or the animation you are trying to accomplish. While it would be impossible to go through all possible animation options, I hope that the overview so far has given you some idea of how the basic tools and panels function. Now let's move on to exporting our finished graphics for the web.

As with Photoshop CC and Illustrator CC, there are many ways to Export the file in Animate CC; you can see this in Table 22-1.

Table 22-1. Possible Export Settings for Animate Files

File Format	Option 1: File ▶ Export ▶ Export Image	Option 2: File ▶ Export ▶ Export Image(Legacy)	Option 3: File ▶ Export ▶ Export Movie	Option 4: File ▶ Export ▶ Export Video	Option 5: File ▶ Export ▶ Export Animated GIF	Option 6: File ▶ Publish Settings HTML5 Canvas
JPEG (.jpg, .jpeg, .jpe)	✓	✓	✓ (sequence)			✓
PNG (8 and 24 .png)	✓	✓	✓ (sequence)			✓* only via ActionScript 3.0 FLA file
GIF (static and animated) (.gif)	✓ (static only)	✓ (static only)	✓ (sequence) (static only)		✓ (animated)	✓* only via ActionScript 3.0 FLA file
SVG (.svg)		✓				✓
OAM package						✓
SWF movie (.swf)		✓	✓			✓* only via ActionScript 3.0 FLA file
MOV (.mov)				✓		

Unlike Photoshop and Illustrator, when you choose File ➤ Save or File ➤ Save As in Animate, the only option you have are to save as an Animate Document (.fla) or an uncompressed version (.xfl). The only direct way to save for the web is via the File ➤ Export options or go to File ➤ Publish, as seen in Figure 22-1.

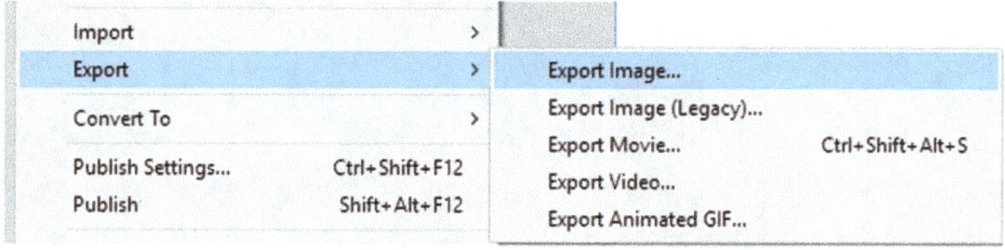

Figure 22-1. *The main menu allows you to export or publish your web files*

If you reviewed Parts 2 and 3, many of these formats should be familiar to you; however, if you are not sure, review Chapter 4 and Chapter 12 for clarification on file formats and import settings.

■ **Note** In recent versions, Animate CC has removed the ability to export a bitmap file; you can only import. Also, you cannot create a PDF directly from Animate. If creating a PDF document is important for your project, I recommend saving the frames you want as graphics or as image sequence JPEG files, and then placing them on pages in Adobe InDesign CC, and then Exporting from Adobe InDesign CC as a PDF. This is a bit more work but at least the layout looks professional.

As you move through each of the following options for export, I introduce some file formats that I have not discussed, such as OAM package, SWF movie, and the transition video file—the MOV.

Option 1: File ➤ Export ➤ Export Image

Use the flower_stock.fla file for this example.

File ➤ Export ➤ Export Image is in many ways like the Export for Web (Legacy) version that you have seen in Photoshop and Illustrator; however, Animate CC has its own legacy version that you look at in Option 2. It's uncertain why Adobe does not call this identical layout in Animate "Legacy"; however, the arrangement of the Export Image dialog box is like what you find in Illustrator's File ➤ Export ➤ Save For Web (Legacy) option. Refer to Figure 22-2.

CHAPTER 22 ■ EXPORTING YOUR FILES TO THE WEB

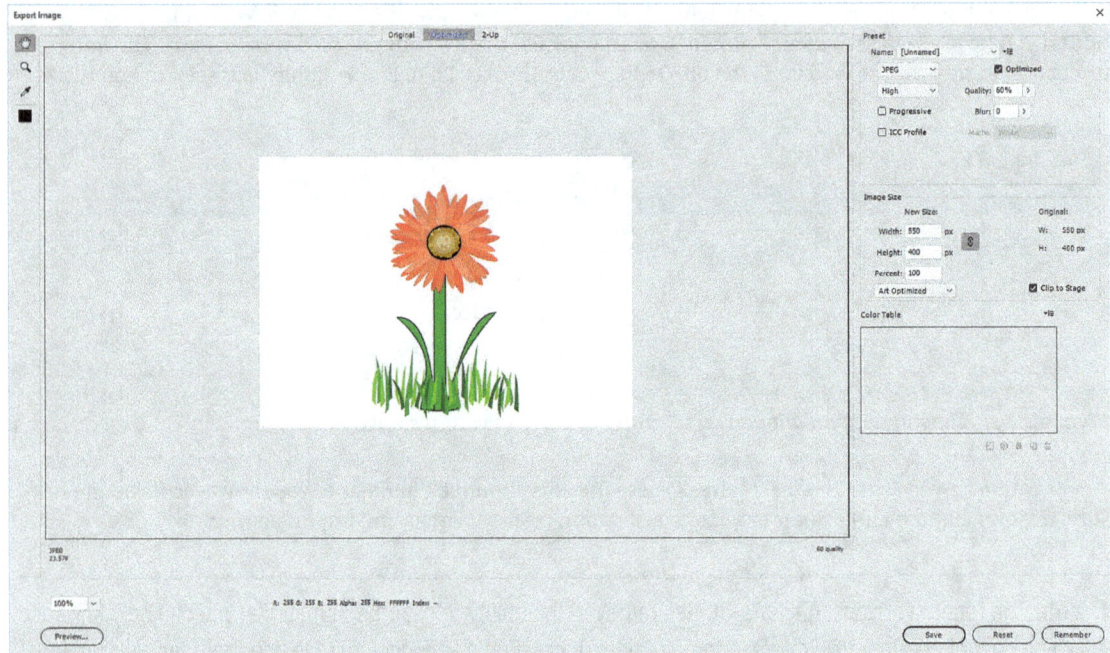

Figure 22-2. *Animate's Export Image dialog box is similar to Illustrator's and Photoshop's Save for Web dialog box*

The layout is very similar in that you have the ability to compare up to two images during preview and save the final preset; however, notice that on the upper left there are only four tools: Hand tool (H), Zoom tool (Z), Eyedropper tool (I) and Eyedropper Color tool. The Slice tools are missing because the purpose of program is to create single animation frames and not slices for a webpage, so there are no slicing options. Compare to Illustrator Option 4 in Chapter 12.

Ideally, if you have created a single background image in Animate CC for a static website, this is the best way to export it as a JPEG, GIF, or PNG (8 or 24). As with Illustrator, if you click the Preview button in the lower left, Animate, or even generate some HTML text, you can copy into an HTML file. You cannot save a separate HTML file here for export, only images of the current frame. Refer to Figure 22-3.

CHAPTER 22 ■ EXPORTING YOUR FILES TO THE WEB

```
Format: JPEG
Dimensions: 550w x 400h
Size: 23.21K
Settings: Quality is 60, Non-Progressive, Optimized on


<html>
<head>
<title>flower_stock</title>
<meta http-equiv="Content-Type" content="text/html; charset=iso-8859-1">
</head>
<body bgcolor="#FFFFFF" leftmargin="0" topmargin="0" marginwidth="0" marginheight="0">
<img src="flower_stock.jpg" width="550" height="400" alt="">
</body>
</html>
```

Figure 22-3. Animate generates some HTML that you can use for an exported image on your website

If extracting HTML information for your work is important, later in this chapter (see Option 6) there is a much better way to generate animated images for the canvas and HTML pages using the Publish Settings dialog box.

Coming back to the Export Image dialog box, whatever file format you choose (GIF, JPEG, or PNG), this option only lets you export the current image in the frame, not a sequence.

In the upper right of the Export Image dialog box, Animate CC has several setting presets that you can choose from, or you can create your own preset, as seen in Figure 22-4.

CHAPTER 22 ■ EXPORTING YOUR FILES TO THE WEB

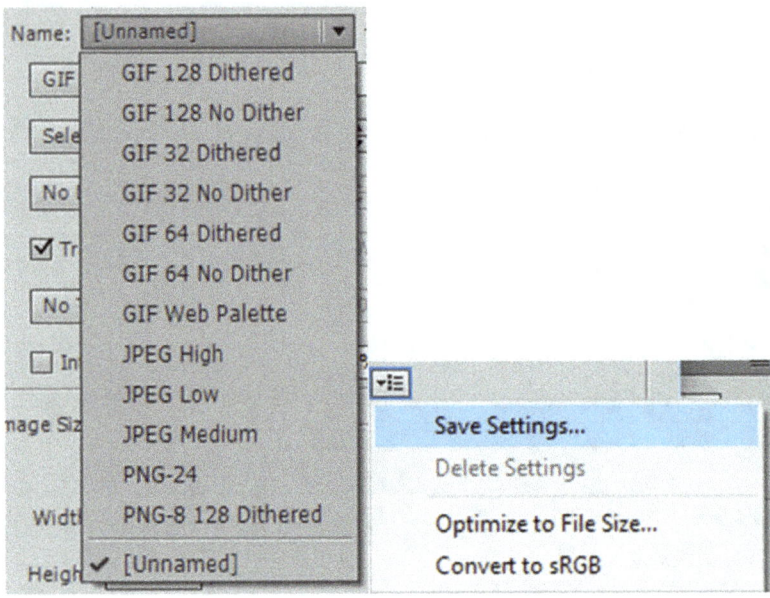

Figure 22-4. *Presets found in the Export Image dialog box*

You can save these settings and optimize your file size for raster images; however, if you want to save vector files, such as SVG, you need to look at either Option 2: Export Image (Legacy) or Option 6: Publish Settings for HTML5 Canvas. In Figure 22-4, Convert To sRGB ensures that all the colors are the correct web RGB format.

GIF

Using this dialog box only gives you one frame exported as a static GIF image; if you want to export an animated GIF, then look at Option 5: Export Animated GIF, which brings up specific options for this type of file format. For now, let's review the current settings in the Export Image dialog box. Refer to Figure 22-5.

528

CHAPTER 22 ■ EXPORTING YOUR FILES TO THE WEB

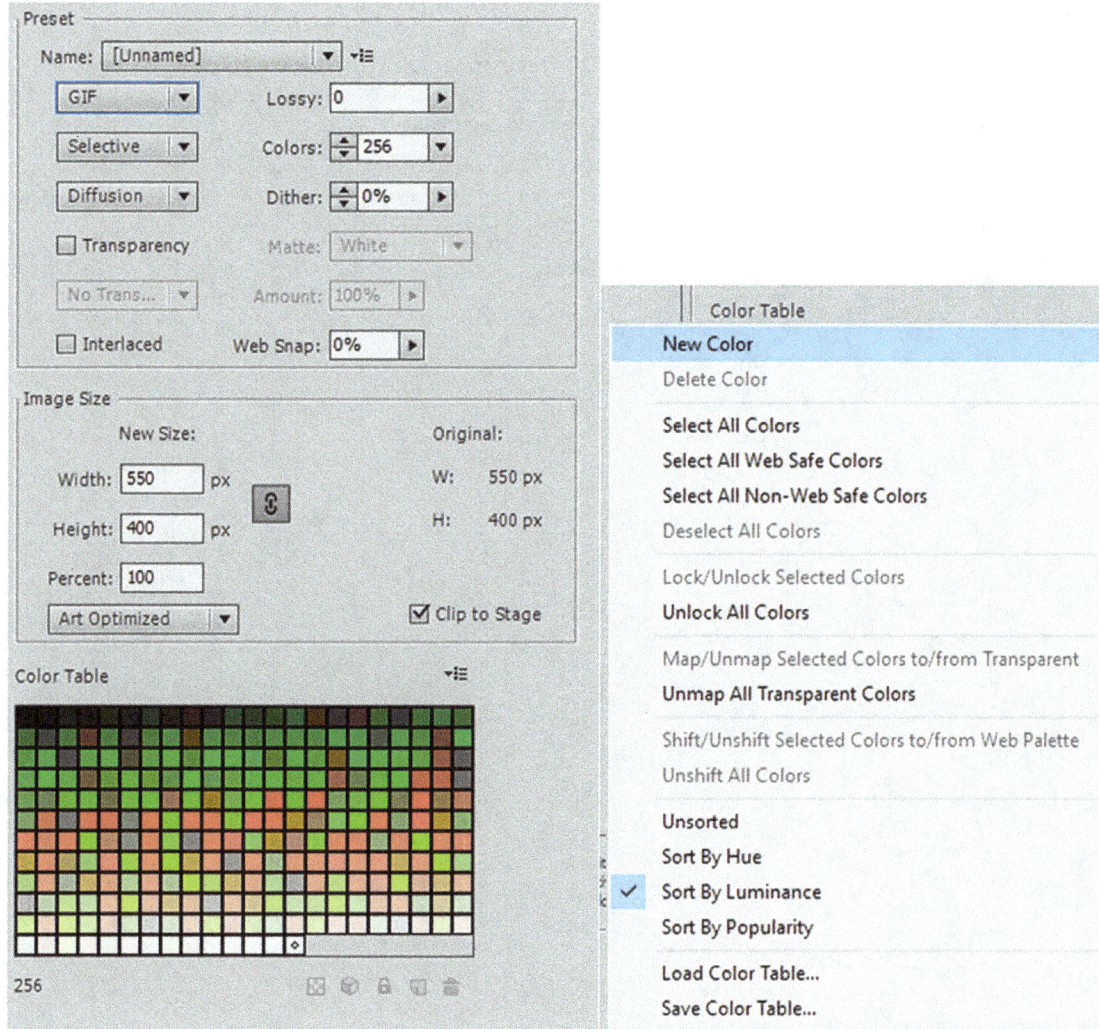

Figure 22-5. Settings for a static GIF image in the current frame

Most settings in the Preset area are the same as Photoshop CC and Illustrator CC's Save for Web (Legacy), so refer to Chapters 4 and 12 for a more detailed explanation of items such as lossy and dither. You can set image size and anti-aliasing to None, Art Optimized, or Text Optimized.

Clip To Stage sets the clipping boundary to the stage rather than the smallest enclosing box or clipping box.

Color Table for GIF has the same settings as the dialog box in Photoshop CC; however, in this section there is no option for animation, which you can only acquire if you export as an animated GIF. The color table menu has options for how to add, delete, and sort the colors. You can also save or load color tables from here.

529

JPEG

Most Preset settings are the same as in Photoshop CC or Illustrator CC's Save for Web (Legacy), so refer to Chapters 4 and 12 for a more detailed explanation on quality and blur. You can set image size and anti-aliasing to None, Art Optimized, or Text Optimized. Refer to Figure 22-6.

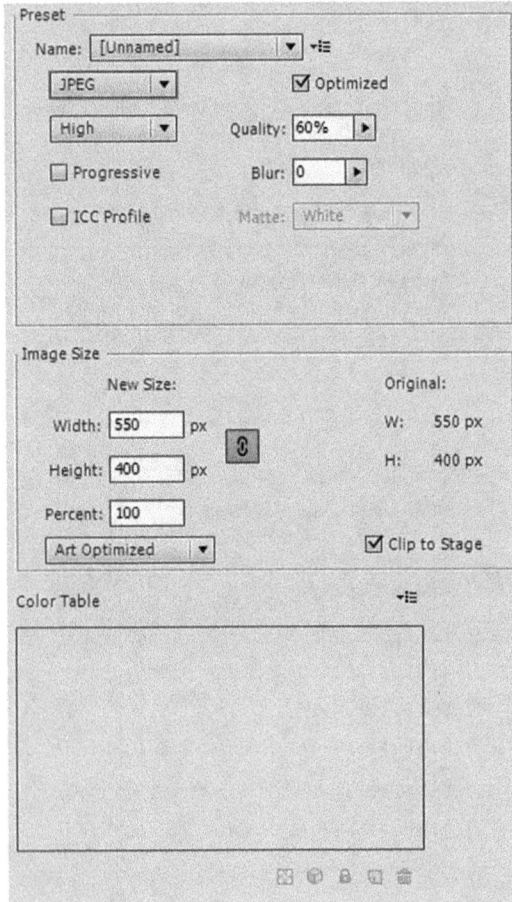

Figure 22-6. Settings for a JPEG image in the current frame

PNG-8 and PNG-24

Most settings are the same as Photoshop CC and Illustrator CC's Save for Web (Legacy), so refer to Chapters 4 and 12 for a more detailed explanation on color settings and dither. You can set image size and anti-aliasing to None, Art Optimized, or Text Optimized. Refer to Figure 22-7 for both options.

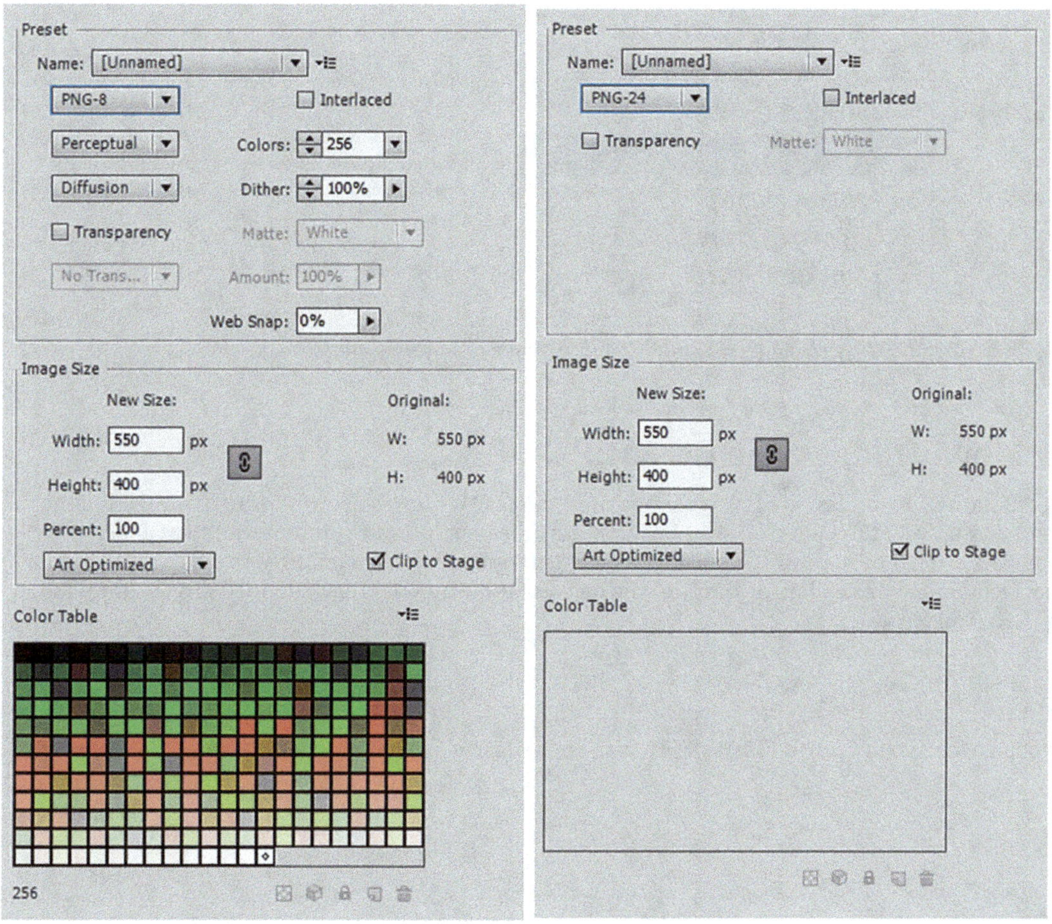

CHAPTER 22 ■ EXPORTING YOUR FILES TO THE WEB

Figure 22-7. PNG-8 and PNG-24 settings for the image in the current frame

In all cases, clicking Save allows you to save an image in the folder you choose. Refer to Figure 22-8.

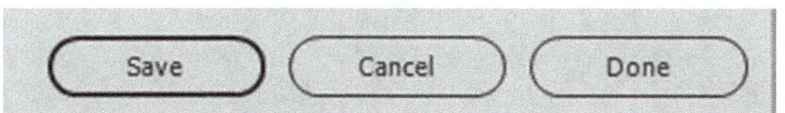

Figure 22-8. When you have chosen your setting for the current image, save your image

Option 2: File ➤ Export ➤ Export Image (Legacy)

Animate CC's version of Export Image (Legacy) is a bit different from what you find in Photoshop CC or Illustrator CC, so for a beginner who is trying to navigate to the correct export options, this can be a bit confusing.

When you choose File ➤ Export ➤ Export Image (Legacy), you are presented with file formats and the decision of where to save the file; this is like what you choose in Photoshop CC as File ➤ Save As. Refer to Figure 22-9.

531

CHAPTER 22 ■ EXPORTING YOUR FILES TO THE WEB

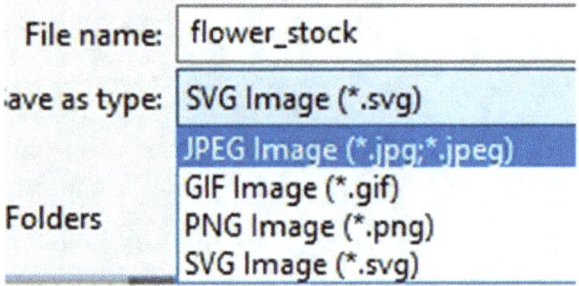

Figure 22-9. *Export Image (Legacy) is similar to File ➤ Save as in Photoshop*

SWF Movie (removed in CC 2019)

When Animate CC was called Flash, it was popular to create SWF movies; however, gradually the Internet has moved away from this option. SWF animations are processor intensive on some deceives, making SWF less popular, so it has been slowly falling out of favor. This option has been removed in the CC 2019 version, I do not recommend this option for your website because some browsers have stopped this file format from being viewed on the web.

JPEG

This option allows you to create a single JPEG image from the current frame. Refer to Figure 22-10 for settings.

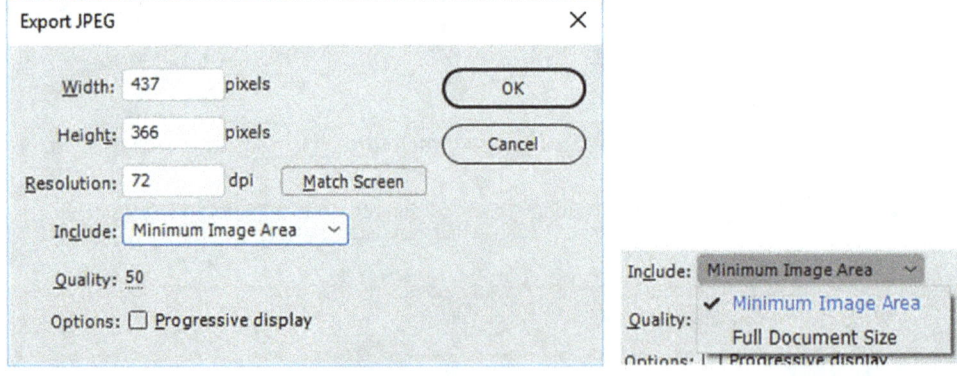

Figure 22-10. *Export JPEG dialog box*

If you need a resolution to be slightly higher for printed or PDF material in InDesign CC, you can adjust the resolution. For print work, 300 dpi is a good quality setting, although the file size is larger; however, in most cases for the Internet, you leave this at the default of 72 dpi. Doing so adjusts the width and the height as well. To reset, click Match Screen, which returns it to the default size.

In the Include drop-down menu, you can set the dimensions of the file to the minimum image area to decrease the size of the file or set to full document size. You can also adjust the quality from 0 to 100 and choose if you want a progressive display of the image as it loads. The default is to leave it unchecked.

GIF

As with the JPEG, you can create a single static GIF image from the current frame. Refer to Figure 22-11.

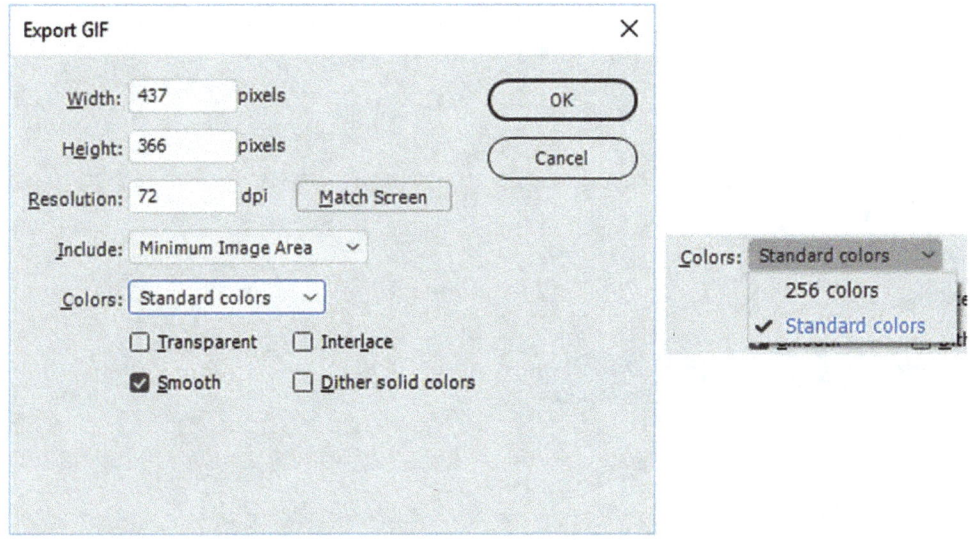

Figure 22-11. Export GIF dialog box

If you need a resolution to be slightly higher for some printed or PDF material in InDesign CC, you can adjust the resolution; this adjusts the width and the height as well. In most cases, however, a JPEG file is a better export option for print work. To reset the size, click Match Screen, which returns it to the default size. In the Include drop-down menu, you can set the dimensions of the file to either the minimum image area to decrease the size of the file or set to full document size. You can also adjust the colors to be standard or 256. Note in the Option 1 Export Image dialog box that you have greater control over the colors using the color table; however, you can still decide whether the background is transparent, interlace, or smooth, and whether to dither the solid colors in the image.

CHAPTER 22 ■ EXPORTING YOUR FILES TO THE WEB

PNG

As with the JPEG, you can create a single PNG image from the current frame. Refer to Figure 22-12.

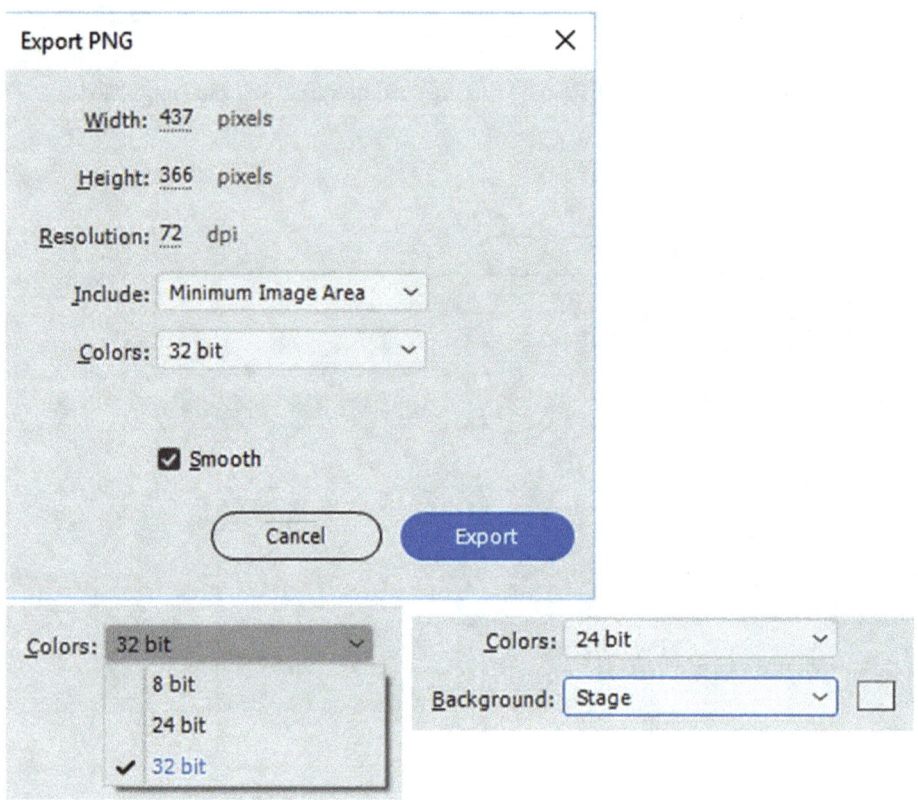

Figure 22-12. *Export PNG dialog box for 8, 24, and 32 bit*

If you need a resolution to be slightly higher for some printed or PDF material in InDesign CC, you can adjust the resolution; this adjusts the width and the height as well. JPEG is usually the best file format for print material, but you can achieve some good results with PNG as well. In the Include drop-down menu, you can set the dimensions of the file to either the minimum image area to decrease the size of the file or set to full document size. You can also adjust the colors to be 8, 24, or 32 bit. You can set the background to stage or opaque (a color chosen from the color picker) for 8 and 24 bits.

In Option 1: Export Image dialog box, you have greater control over the colors using the color table; however, you can still decide whether to smooth the graphics or not.

CHAPTER 22 ■ EXPORTING YOUR FILES TO THE WEB

SVG

As noted in Photoshop CC and Illustrator CC, an SVG, or Scalable Vector Graphic, can be displayed as an image but is code that you can manipulate in a text editing program (e.g., Notepad ++) or for the web using Dreamweaver CC. Refer to Figure 22-13 to review the dialog box settings.

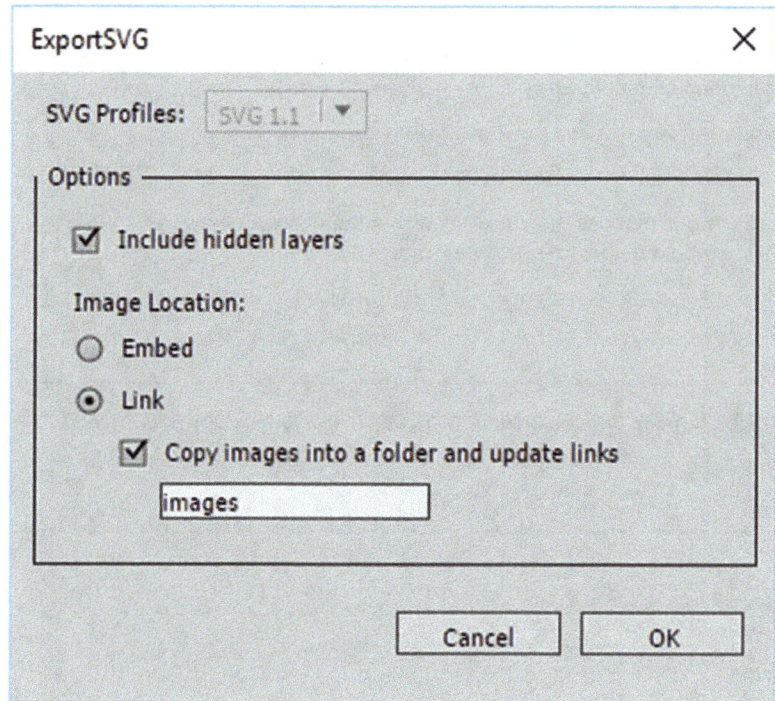

Figure 22-13. Export SVG dialog box

SVG defines vector-based graphics in XML format. In HTML5, you can embed SVG elements directly into your HTML pages. The code might look like this:

```
<svg width="400" height="180">
  <rect x="50" y="20" width="150" height="150"
  style="fill:blue;stroke:pink;stroke-width:5;fill-opacity:0.1;stroke-opacity:0.9" />
</svg>
```

In Figure 22-13, you see that when you export an SVG. You can include or exclude hidden or turned off layers from your FLA file. The image location (non-SVG graphics within the file) can either be embedded or linked and placed into an image folder, or whatever name you choose for your project.

535

The following are some things that SVG (XML) is good for.

- 2D graphics uses X and Y coordinates
- Can use JavaScript event handlers
- Shapes (objects) can be changed and re-rendered
- Not resolution dependent (scale and zoom in)
- Best suited to large rendering areas like Google Maps; however, the rendering is slow if a complex DOM (Document Object Model)
- Not for game applications, but can be used for some basic animations
- Can use CSS3, XML, and JavaScript to animate an SVG
- Like CSS3 animation transitions that use the <div> tag rather than <svg>, be aware that they may not always run in older browsers, so test first

For more information, visit https://en.wikipedia.org/wiki/SVG_animation and www.w3schools.com/graphics/svg_examples.asp.

■ **Note** In the main menu of Animate CC, there are some commands that allow you to copy, export, or import the motion as an XML. If you plan to use this option for export, you need to select the first frame that has content. Refer to Figure 22-14.

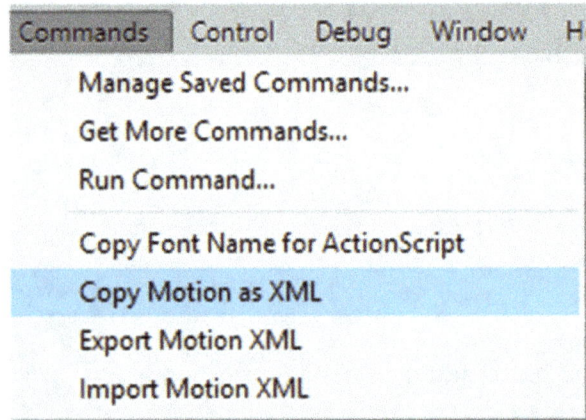

Figure 22-14. *There are a few commands in the main menu that allow you to work with XML*

This allows you to save that information as an XML file, which may be useful for SVG animations. You see what commands are in Chapter 23.

CHAPTER 22 ■ EXPORTING YOUR FILES TO THE WEB

Option 3: File ➤ Export ➤ Export Movie

If you are working with frames that you plan to use to create a sequence in Photoshop or Premiere Pro for a movie, you can use this option to Export your files: File ➤ Export ➤ Export Movie.

As you saw in Option 2, you are presented with the file format choices and a place to save the files. Refer to Figure 22-15.

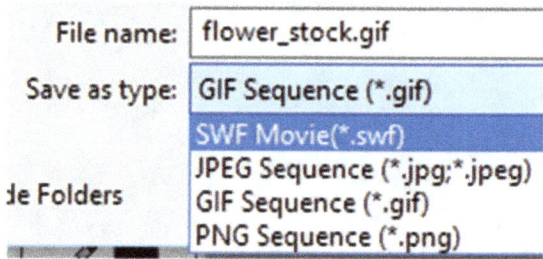

Figure 22-15. *File options for exporting image sequences for a movie*

■ **Note** There is no SVG sequence option.

SWF Movie

You can export a SWF movie if you plan to use it for a personal project on your computer; however, because some browsers no longer accept this format, I do not recommend using it for your website project.

JPEG

This brings up the same dialog box that you saw in Option 2, but without the Include drop-down option. Refer to Figure 22-16.

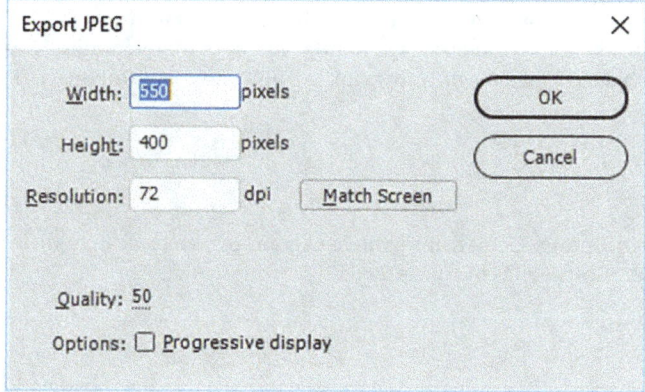

Figure 22-16. *Export JPEG options for a sequence*

537

CHAPTER 22 ■ EXPORTING YOUR FILES TO THE WEB

When you click OK, it creates a sequence of images based on the number of frames in your animation; for example, 20 frames is 20 images. So, if you have a lot of frames, consider whether you want to use this option because there is not a range option here. Files export with the name and then a sequence, such as 001.jpg, 002.jpg, and so forth.

GIF

This brings up the same dialog box that you saw in Option 2, but without the Include drop-down menu option. Refer to Figure 22-17.

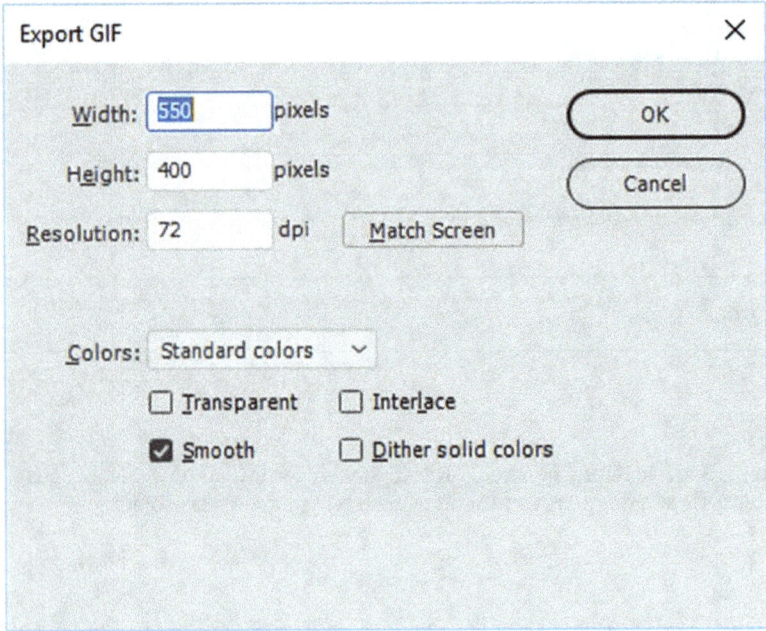

Figure 22-17. Export GIF options for a sequence

As with JPEG, clicking OK creates a sequence of images based on the number of frames in your animation. There is no setting for the range of the sequence; keep this in mind if you have many frames. Files export with the name and then a sequence such as 001.gif, 002.gif, and so forth. This is not the same as a GIF animation, as you see in Option 5.

PNG

This brings up the same dialog box as you saw in Option 2. You can set the background to stage or opaque (a color chosen from the color picker) for 8 and 24 bits. Refer to Figure 22-18.

CHAPTER 22 ■ EXPORTING YOUR FILES TO THE WEB

Figure 22-18. Export PNG options for a sequence as 8, 24 or 32 bit

Clicking Export creates a sequence of images based on the number of frames in your animation. As with GIF and JPEG, there is no option to set the frame range. Files export with the name and then a sequence such as 001.png, 002.png, and so forth.

Option 4: File ➤ Export ➤ Export Video

When you choose File ➤ Export ➤ Export Video, Animate only allows you to render your FLA file in a (.mov) file format. Refer to Figure 22-19.

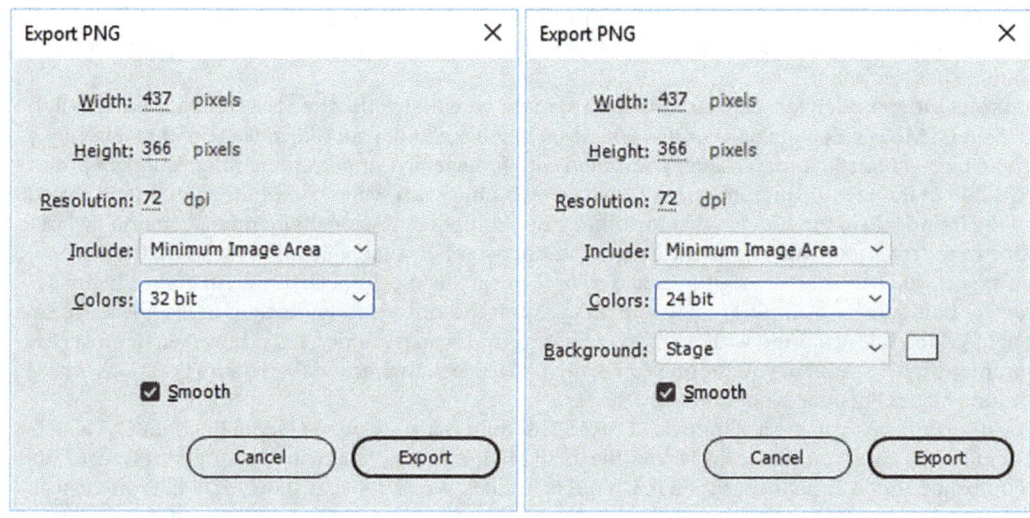

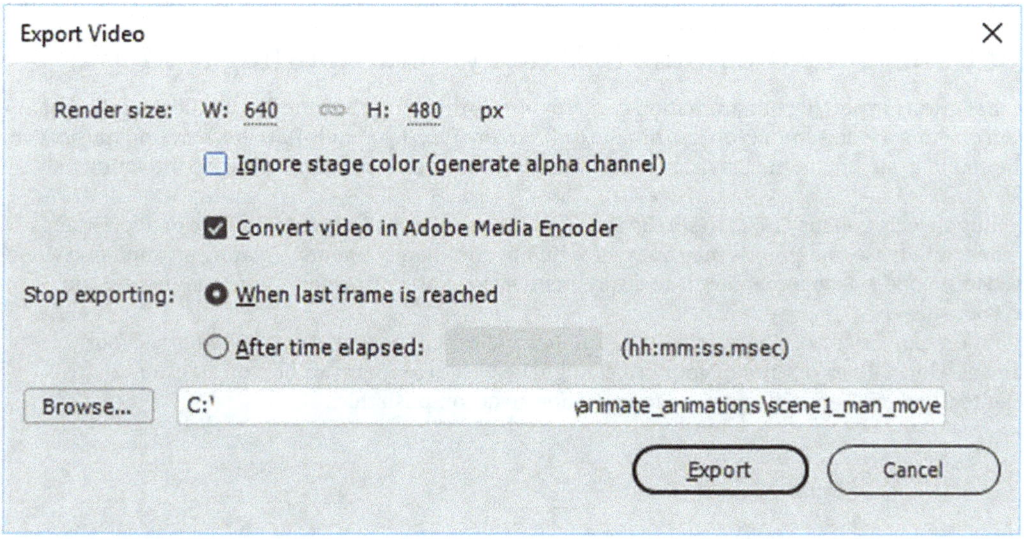

Figure 22-19. Export Video dialog box

539

This is great for Mac users who have the QuickTime viewer on their machines; however, if you're a Windows PC user, you might not have this program. If you want to preview the video after export, don't worry, Animate has a solution.

When you render a video for the web, you need to make sure that your video is a standard file size that is viewed in an HTML5 <video> tag. Secondly, when you begin creating your file, make sure that it is the correct frame rate—about 30 fps if it is later combined with footage of a similar frame rate. Your own projects may use a different frame rate, but remember consistency is important when combining files. In my project, I matched the frame rate of the FLA to what my other video camera files were. Remember, you don't want to be adjusting frame rates after you create the animation since it is a headache to adjust frames afterward.

Upon export, you can choose to ignore stage color if you are using alpha channel. An alpha channel (like a green or blue screen) is important if you plan to export the video into Photoshop or Premiere Pro so that part of the video is transparent with a different background scenery added later; however, in most cases, you may want the background of your animation's stage, so leave it unchecked. Make sure that Convert video in Adobe Media Encoder is checked.

This setting crucial if you are a Windows PC user. This automatically opens Media Encoder CC, which you look at in Part 5. Then you can convert your file to an MP4, which is what you want for your website and for your Photoshop Video Timeline, as seen in Chapters 7 and 9. While you can show MOV files on the web, it requires extra plug-ins. HTML5 video is a good option with modern browsers, so a video that is converted to MP4 is the clear choice. If the video is long and you only want to convert a section, you can set the Stop Export option to either when the last frame is reached (default) or after the time has elapsed.

Note This option might be better for getting a range of frames in a sequence than Option 3. You can then bring the movie into a program like Photoshop and choose Flatten Frames to clips in the Timeline Video panel, then select the layers you need for your project. Refer to Chapter 7 to review this option.

Finally, locate the folder you want to save the file in and click Export. Give Adobe Media Encoder CC time to open and do the rendering, and then you can adjust your final MP4 settings there. You look at this software in Part 5.

Tips for Controlling the Audio in Video When Exporting to MOV

Be aware that during export, if your animation contains audio, there may be times when the sound is not in sync. When creating a video animation in Animate or Premiere Pro, if you only have background music, you can set the sound to stream on the first frame. Do not use Event on the first frame because the sound may not copy.

In adding speech, you may need to set the sound as Event either on the second frame or a few frames into the video; otherwise, the sounds may not sync with the mouth movements. Creating an animated video takes practice. A good rule to remember is to always render then test your video a few times before you upload to your site.

While short animations of a few seconds are rather small when they render as MOV files, if your animation has a lot of filters or bitmap graphics, it might be best to render your files on an external drive. Please refer to Chapters 7 and 9 if you need to know how to accomplish this.

CHAPTER 22 ■ EXPORTING YOUR FILES TO THE WEB

Option 5: File ➤ Export ➤ Export Animated GIF

Refer to the flower_stock2.fla file.

The settings for File ➤ Export ➤ Export Animate GIF are identical to Option 1: File ➤ Export ➤ Export Image, except that they allow you to only export an animated GIF file. Notice the other preset settings in Figure 22-20; you have the animation option in the dialog box.

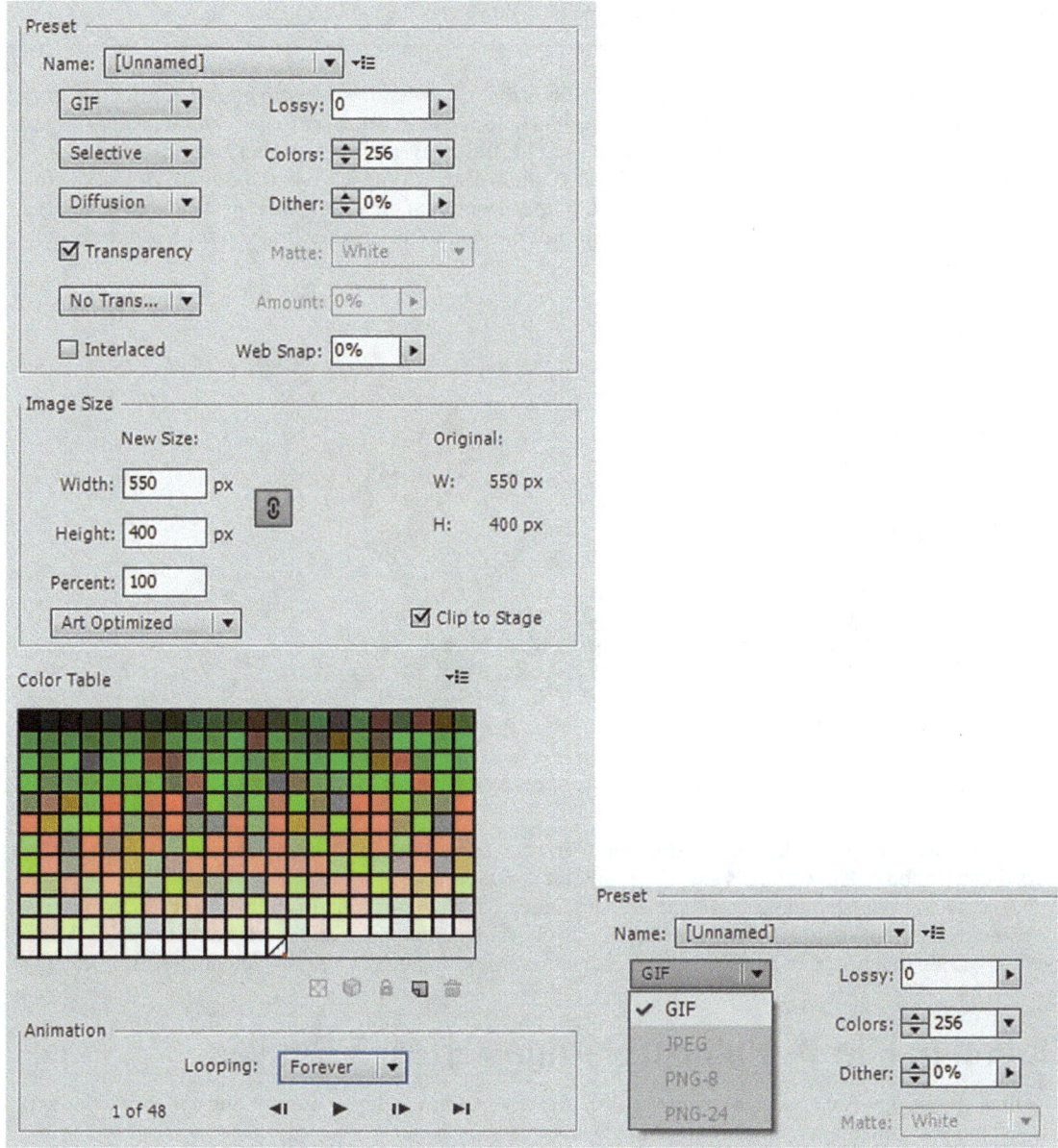

Figure 22-20. *When creating a GIF animation, you have the option of controlling the looping of the animation*

The Animation settings allow use to preview the animation before export using the previous frame, play/stop, next, and last frame controls. You can then set the looping to once or forever, and click Save to export your file.

■ **Note** You cannot set the loop to a certain number of times, as you can in Photoshop CC. If this is a concern, a work-around is to convert a copy of the FLA file to an ActionScript 3.0 and use the File ➤ Publish Settings to choose GIF Image from the list of possible published files, as you will see in Option 6.

Another thing to be aware of with animated GIFs is that they do not work with nested animations. If you look at the flower_stock.fla file, the stock originally had a nested animation symbol of the stock layer turned on, Armature_7. When you export the animation as a GIF, the stem remains stationary. At this point, you have a few options: export your animation as MOV (Option 4) or HTML5 Canvas (Option 6). Or work with a copy of the original and cut the nested animation shape layer out of the symbol and paste it onto the stage, as you can see in Armature _5 and Aramture_6 without the stem. This ensures that you see movement in the GIF animation. Refer to Figure 22-21.

Figure 22-21. *Graphic animation of moving stem; note how the nested stem animation on the left does not animate in the GIF however when the animation is placed on the main stage on the right then it animates*

Personally, I would work with Options 4 or 6 for a nested animation, so as to not destroy the original work; but it's good to know there is a work-around for GIF animations.

Regardless of which options you choose, an animated GIF does not contain audio, so any audio that your file contains does not copy over during the export. If you want to retain your audio, it is better to export your file as a MOV video that becomes an MP4 video file, or save your file as an HTML5 Canvas, which you look at next.

Option 6: File ➤ Publish Settings HTML5 Canvas

The final option that you look at is how to Publish an HTML5 Canvas. If you are working with an ActionScript 3.0 FLA file that you intend to make into a movie, then use Option 4.

Animate CC is about animation. It can save you the time and labor of plotting out the movements of each object. As a web designer and JavaScript programmer, while I like the analytical side of my work, I really like the design part more. I would rather use my imagination creating action and adventures for my characters than plotting out each point mathematically. So, if you like Animate, hopefully you feel the same way I do about design.

To create, work, and access the Publish Settings of an HTML5 Canvas file, you need to convert the ActionScript 3.0 FLA to an HTML5 Canvas FLA using File ➤ Convert to, or in File ➤ New choose an HTML5 Canvas FLA. Remember HTML5 Canvas does not have all the options as an ActionScript 3.0 FLA, because JavaScript has not caught up to all animation blending and sound options. Nevertheless, it can be a very powerful tool on the web for creating an intro page for your website with sound and interactivity that you can continue to edit in Dreamweaver CC.

In Chapter 17, you learned a bit about HTML5 Canvas; refer to that chapter if you need to review this information. You don't need to use Animate CC to create a canvas or a canvas animation; much of it you can do by hand if you have the skills in Dreamweaver. I show you how to create a basic static canvas in Part 6.

Having said that, once you have finished your masterpiece, you want to publish it. First, choose File ➤ Publish Settings to ensure that you are exporting the files in the formats and settings you want. Likewise, you can access this area in the Properties panel when you click off the stage. Refer to Figure 22-22.

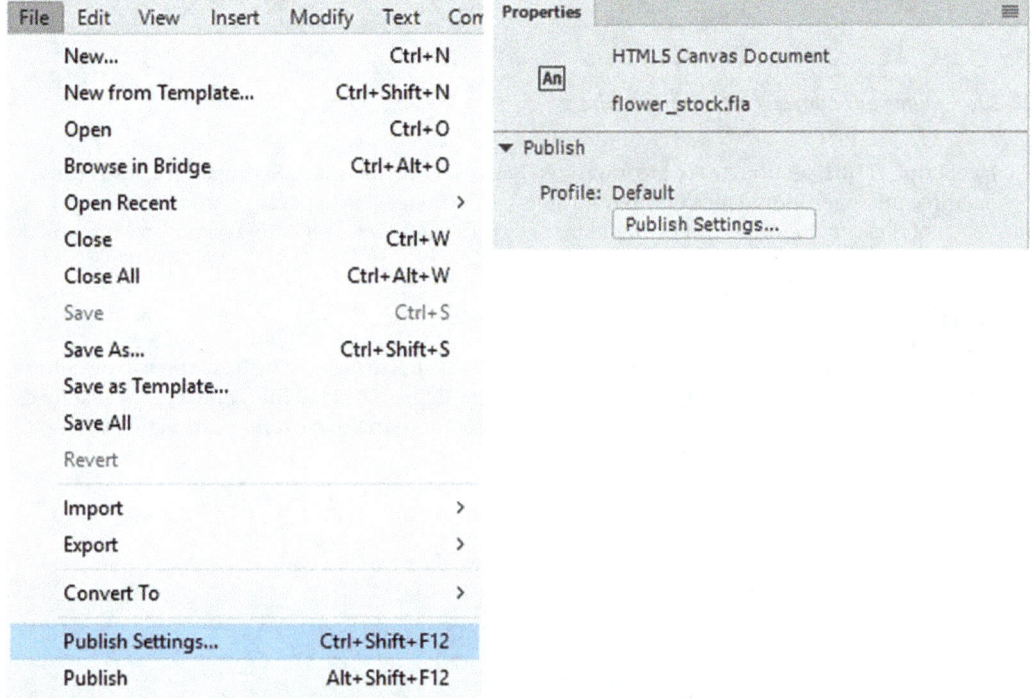

Figure 22-22. *Choose Publish Settings either from the File menu or the Properties panel*

Publish Settings

In the Publish Settings dialog box, you find several tabs in which you can adjust your settings before publishing the canvas.

Available to all tabs is the Profile option at the top of the dialog box; it is set to default, but with the Widget icon, you can create, duplicate, rename, import (.apr), export, or delete a profile after you have made changes to the default. Refer to Figure 22-23.

Figure 22-23. *Create your own custom profile settings*

In the JavaScript/HTML section, there are four tabs (Basic, HTML/JS, Image Settings, and Web Fonts). There are also three other additional tabs or other formats (JPEG image, OAM package, and SVG Image). Let's look at each of these in order. The following items only publish if their respective check box is enabled.

JavaScript/HTML Basic Tab

The Basic tab is where you make most of the changes in your Publish Settings dialog box. You can give the output file a different output name, or keep the current name, and then click the folder next to the text field to locate the folder you want to publish the files into (if it is different than the current location that your HTML5 Canvas FLA is located). Refer to Figure 22-24.

CHAPTER 22 ■ EXPORTING YOUR FILES TO THE WEB

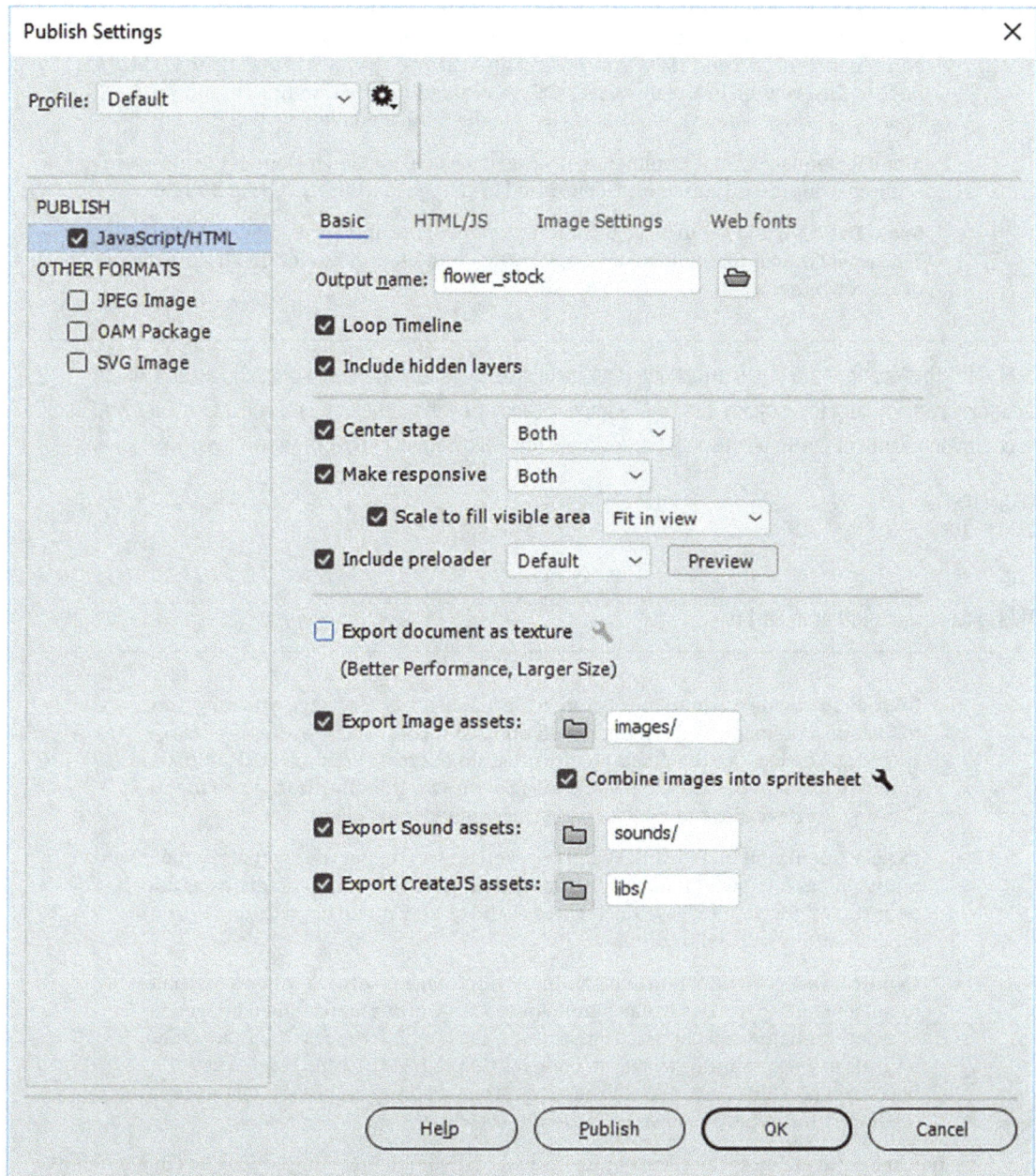

Figure 22-24. *Basic tab settings in the Publish Settings dialog box*

- **Loop Timeline:** If you don't want the timeline to loop and only play once, disable this checkbox; otherwise, leave it checked.
- **Include hidden layers:** If there are layers in your timeline that have the Eye icon turned off and are hidden because you don't want them published, then disable the check box. Doing this may reduce file size; otherwise, leave it checked.

- **Center Stage:** Position the animation in the center of the browser or the viewing area. Animation can be centered by height, width, or both. Publish Settings uses a combination of CSS and HTML to center your <canvas> </canvas> tag on the HTML page in the browser. In Dreamweaver CC, you can adjust these settings to suit your design, as I show when you look at dissecting the published file.

- **Make Responsive:** Set the animation to scale to change the dimensions of the browser or the viewing area. Animations can respond to change in width, height, or both.

- **Scale To Fit Visible Area:** Scale the animation to fill the entire available viewing area. The aspect ratio is maintained always. Choose Fit In View or Stretch To Fit from the drop-down menu.

> **Note** This is important if you are building a responsive website and plan to package as an OAM in Dreamweaver. Without this setting, the OAM's inner <canvas> will not become responsive, even if you use CSS to control the width of the <object> tag. For example, the following is in CSS Dreamweaver.

```
#EdgeID{
width:100%;
}
```

This is discussed further in Part 6.

- **Include Preloader:** Sometimes before a file loads, if it is very large, you may want to include a preloader animation; for example, showing a bar growing or circle spinning. You can use the default of the program or create your own GIF animation and then link it to the file when you choose to browse from the drop-down menu. Clicking Preview allows you to see what this preloader look like.

- **Export Document as Texture:** When checked this will export all symbols in the animation as one raster image or texture. If your file has a a lot of gradients as mine does you might want to leave unchecked as the quality might degrade and only use for animations with solid colors.

- **Export Image Assets:** When you combine your image assets, this allows Animate to put any files that it regards as bitmap or too large into a folder called images, or whatever name you choose. The <canvas> tag later references this folder when it needs to work with the JavaScript code inside the HTML (.html) and external JavaScript (.js) files that are published later. You can also combine small images in the library into what is known as *sprite sheets*.

You look at how to create sprite sheets independent of the Publish Settings dialog box in a moment. Essentially, sprite sheets are a combination of different frames combined into one image file. Accessing one image file rather than many makes the graphic appear faster. The published canvas then uses a combination of HTML, JavaScript, and CSS to reference parts of that sprite image when required. Figure 22-25 shows an example of how this could be used for button symbols.

CHAPTER 22 ■ EXPORTING YOUR FILES TO THE WEB

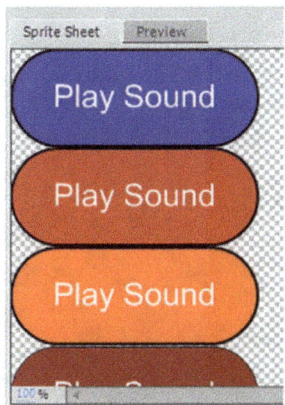

Figure 22-25. *Sprite sheet for a button rollover symbol*

- **Export Sound Assets:** If your file contains sounds or audio (.wav, mp3), they are stored in the sounds folder. Note that with HTML5 Canvas, you could not import an Ogg Vorbis file. Once the file is published, you can always go inside the file and alter this link on your own project in Dreamweaver CC and change the audio type or swap the audio file.
- **Export CreateJS Assets:** Exports a library of JavaScript code that comes from a company called CreateJS. you need this library for your animation to function You see how this library is connected when you open the file.

These folders can be toggled on or off; if toggled off, the assets are exported to the same folder as the output file. Refer to Figure 22-26.

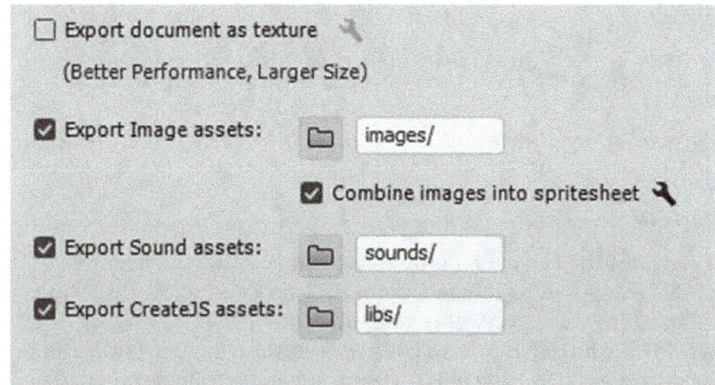

Figure 22-26. *Settings for the folders that your images, sounds, and CreateJS assets are added to*

■ **Note** In a linked video, there is no folder option, so there is no new folder created to store your video other than what you created when you linked the component earlier. If you do not like this final link location, you need to edit the code in a text editor like Dreamweaver CC after it is published.

JavaScript/HTML HTML/JS Settings Tab

The HTML/JS tab controls such things as the HTML template that is used to publish the HTML5 Canvas file. Unless you have advanced knowledge of how the internal structure of the canvas works, for now leave it at the default. If you plan to use a different template, you can import new or export the template for someone else to use in their project. Refer to Figure 22-27.

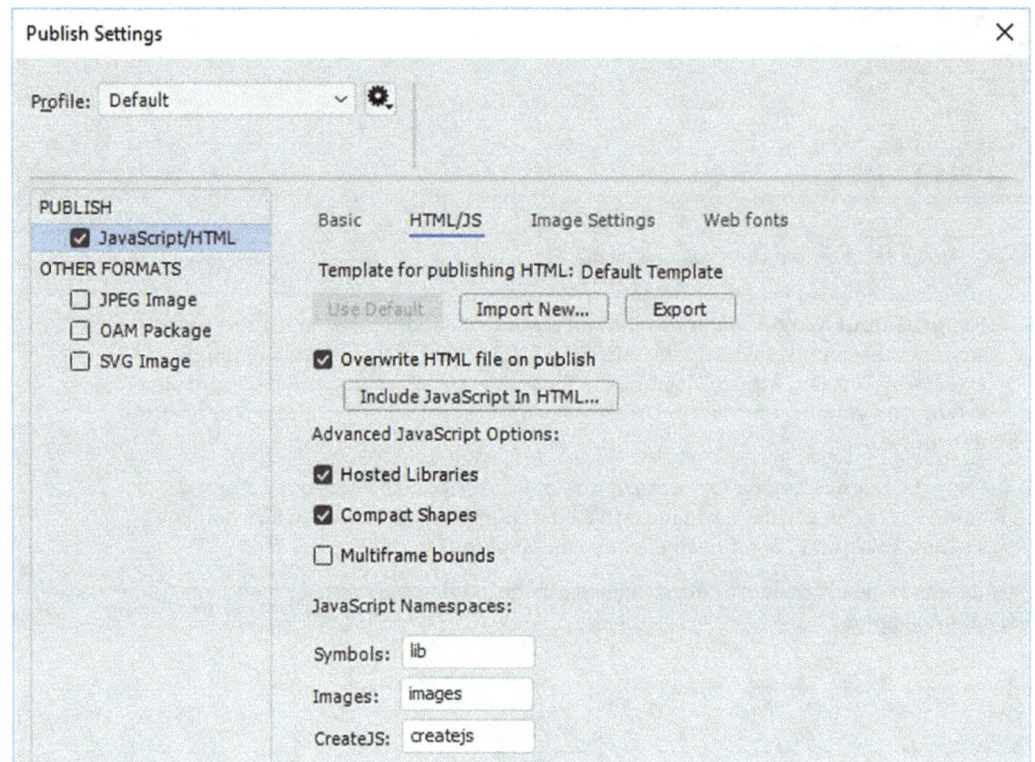

Figure 22-27. The HTML/JS tab in the Publish Settings dialog box

Overwrite HTML File On Publish

This overwrites the current HTML file, if you published an earlier one. To avoid this, either uncheck this setting or make sure that you give the next file you publish a different name: file_rev2 and so on. By default, this is checked so that you don't have multiple files made every time you publish.

This is good if you already have the HTML file linked in your website. You can also include JavaScript in HTML; this is the default. It includes JavaScript and JSON code in HTML and generates a single output file instead of a separate HTML and multiple JavaScript files. Click the button "Include JavaScript In HTML…" an alert message appears, as seen in Figure 22-28.

CHAPTER 22 ■ EXPORTING YOUR FILES TO THE WEB

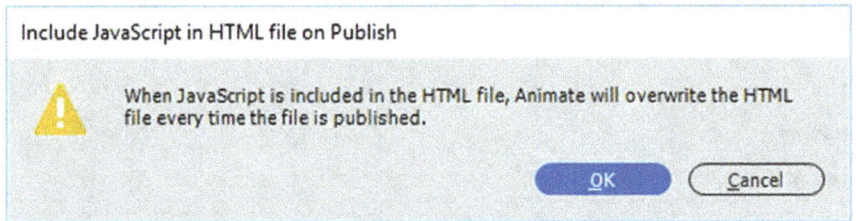

Figure 22-28. *An alert regarding how the HTML and JavaScript is handled*

Clicking OK alters the setting to stop including JavaScript in HTML. It generates separate JavaScript and HTML files. Animate CC needs to publish the document once for this to take effect. Refer to Figure 22-29.

Figure 22-29. *An alert regarding how the HTML and JavaScript is handled if you click the button again to reset*

If you do not want this setting, click Cancel and exit the Publish Settings dialog box so that you do not save the changes.

Advanced JavaScript Options

The following are the advanced JavaScript options.

- **Hosted Libraries:** When checked, uses copies of the libraries hosted on the CreateJS CND at code.createjs.com. It allows libraries to be cached and then shared between various sites.

- **Compact Shapes:** When checked, vector instructions are output in a compact form, and when deselected, the instructions are readable and verbose; this is useful if you need to debug or learn how the code operates.

- **Multiframe bounds:** When checked, the timeline symbols include a frameBounds property containing an array or rectangles corresponding to the bounds of each frame in the timeline. A multiframe bound significantly increases the publish time, so by default, it is unchecked.

549

CHAPTER 22 ■ EXPORTING YOUR FILES TO THE WEB

- **JavaScript Name Spaces:** These are the namespaces used in JavaScript to identify items.
  - Symbols: lib
  - Images: images
  - CreateJS: createJS

If you are an advanced user, you can alter these name spaces; however for now, leave as is.

JavaScript/HTML Image Settings Tab

With your HTML5 Canvas files, you can generate your spritesheets as PNG images, JPEG images, or both. Some settings are enabled or disabled. Alternatively you can also choose the option to export document as a texture. For now leave this setting unchecked. Refer to Figure 22-30.

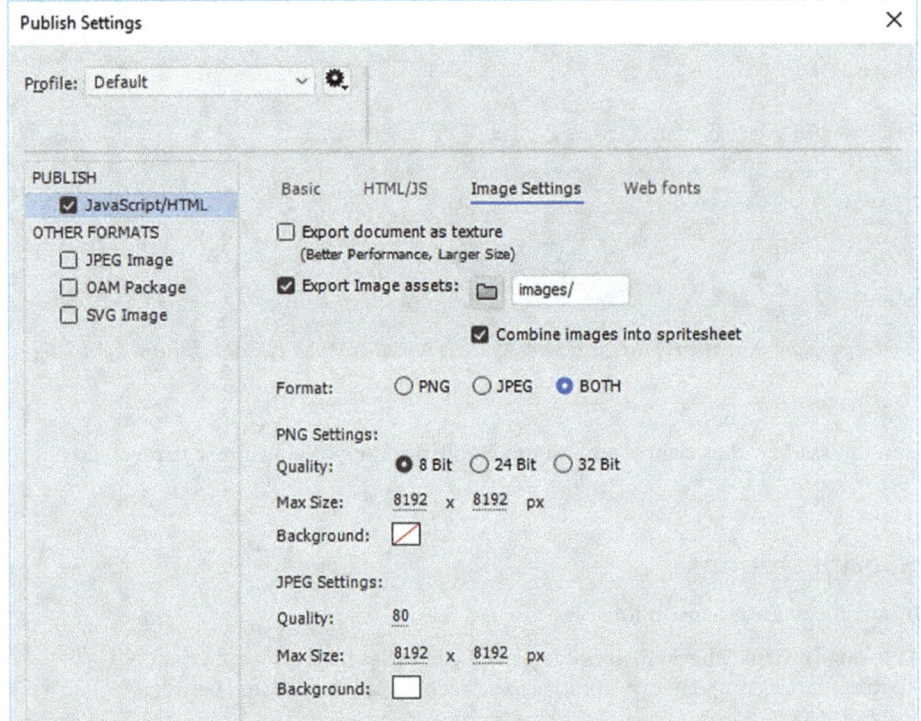

Figure 22-30. Spritesheet tab settings in the Publish Settings dialog box

By default, PNG is chosen since it can have transparency; however, if this is not an issue, you can use JPEG and give it a matte background. As you saw with other export options, you can adjust the quality and size of the image, or in this case, the sprite sheet file. Also, as you saw in the Basic tab section of this chapter, the spritesheet combines all the frames of a button symbol or bitmap graphics onto a one-page image. This improves the speed and performance of the canvas animation.

CHAPTER 22 ■ EXPORTING YOUR FILES TO THE WEB

JavaScript/HTML Web Fonts Tab

As with Photoshop CC and Illustrator CC, web fonts are available in Animate CC. You look at how to access them in more detail in Chapter 23. If you have a domain URL where your content is hosted, you can enter this URL domain link in the blank text area. Refer to Figure 22-31.

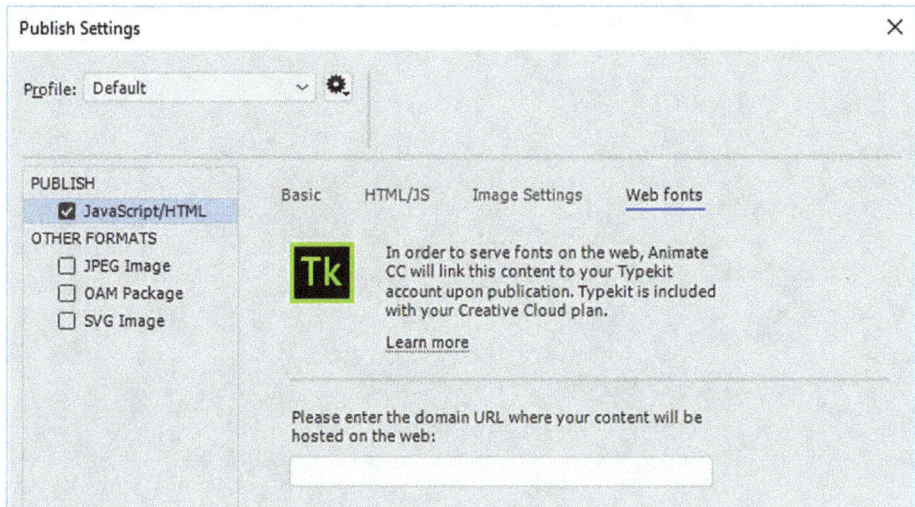

Figure 22-31. *Web Fonts tab settings in the Publish Settings dialog box*

■ **Note** You can leave this area blank, if you are using your own web fonts rather than ones found Typekit, the computer's default font using the static text or dynamic text (accessed via the Text tool(T) and Properties panel), or have no fonts in the file. Only a setting of dynamic text on a font allows you to access the Typekit (Adobe Fonts) and Google web fonts, as you see in Chapter 23.

After reviewing these four tabs, if you are not altering any other publish settings, you can either click OK at the bottom of the dialog box and continue working on your file with the saved settings, or click Publish and view the final files. Refer to Figure 22-32.

Figure 22-32. *Click Publish when you have completed adjusting your settings for the HTML5 Canvas*

However, before you do that, let's look at a few more settings in case you want to output other formats at the same time.

551

CHAPTER 22 ■ EXPORTING YOUR FILES TO THE WEB

Other Formats

On the left side of the Publish setting you can also choose to publish when checked other formats at the same time as the HTML5 Canvas. The following text explains those choices.

JPEG Image

This publishes a JPEG image of the current frame, but not a sequence. You can give the file a different name and output location. Refer to Figure 22-33.

Figure 22-33. Settings for JPEG image in the Publish Settings dialog box

You can adjust the size or match to movie's width, height, and quality, and choose to load as progressive.

OAM Package

Along with the package, this generates a PNG poster from the current frame; it can be transparent. You can give the file a different name and output location, or you can use another external file for the poster image (also a PNG) if you locate it in another folder. Refer to Figure 22-34.

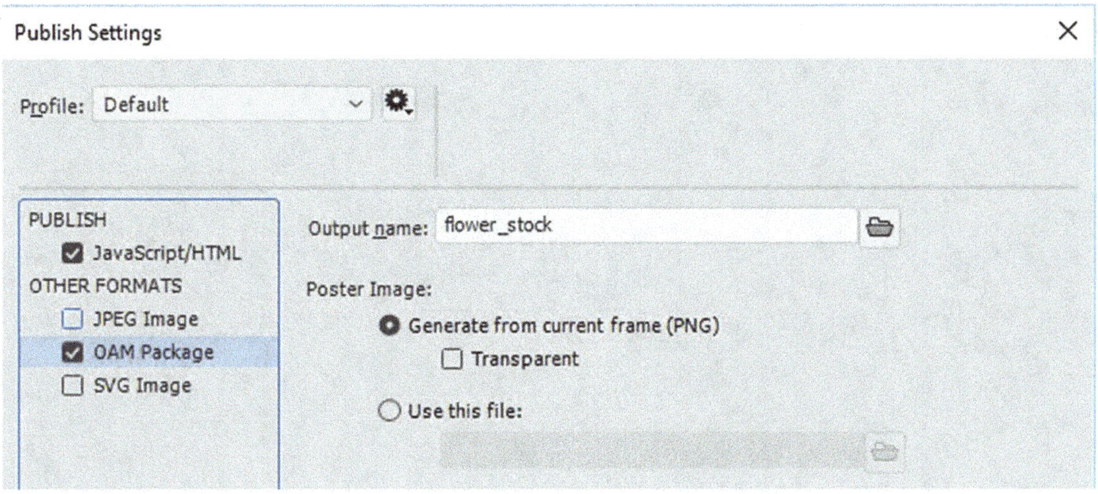

CHAPTER 22 ■ EXPORTING YOUR FILES TO THE WEB

Figure 22-34. Generate an OAM package in the Publish Settings dialog box

The OAM (.oam) files generated in Animate CC can be placed in other Adobe applications, such as Dreamweaver CC, Muse CC, and InDesign CC. An OAM package is an animated widget file, or OpenAjax Metadata.

An OAM file is like a ZIP file that packs all the necessary assets into an Assets folder and includes some configuration information in an XML document.

To look inside, you can try replacing the .oam extension to .zip, and review the content inside of it. It is sometimes called an Animate Deployment Package file.

In Dreamweaver CC, the same file is called Animated Composition because inserting it brings the Animate CC composition into Dreamweaver CC onto an area of a page. You look at how to insert this file in Dreamweaver CC in Part 6. Essentially, when the OAM file is inserted in a <div> tag on an HTML page, Dreamweaver CC unpacks the OAM and creates an Animation assets folder within the main or root site folder, which may include JavaScript, XML, and image files. These files link to that animation and are placed inside the HTML file in an <object> tag, that looks something like this:

```
<object id="EdgeID" type="text/html" width="570" height="420" data-dw-widget="Edge"
data="animation_assets/motion/Assets/flower_stock.html">
     </object>
```

The <object> tag has an ID of EdgeID, which is a throwback to before Adobe Edge Animate merged with Flash to become Animate. Like the <canvas> tag, the <object> tag becomes a window into what is going on inside the flower_stock.html file, which contains various JavaScript links controlling the movements within the <object> tag.

The OAM package publishes at the same time and separately when you publish the Canvas (JavaScript/HTML). Also, to ensure what is inside the OAM package and the HTML5 Canvas are responsive, set the basic tab of the JavaScript/HTML to the make responsive. As noted, This setting is also packaged into the OAM. This is the only way that you are able to scale the OAM successfully in Dreamweaver. Refer to Figure 22-35.

553

CHAPTER 22 ■ EXPORTING YOUR FILES TO THE WEB

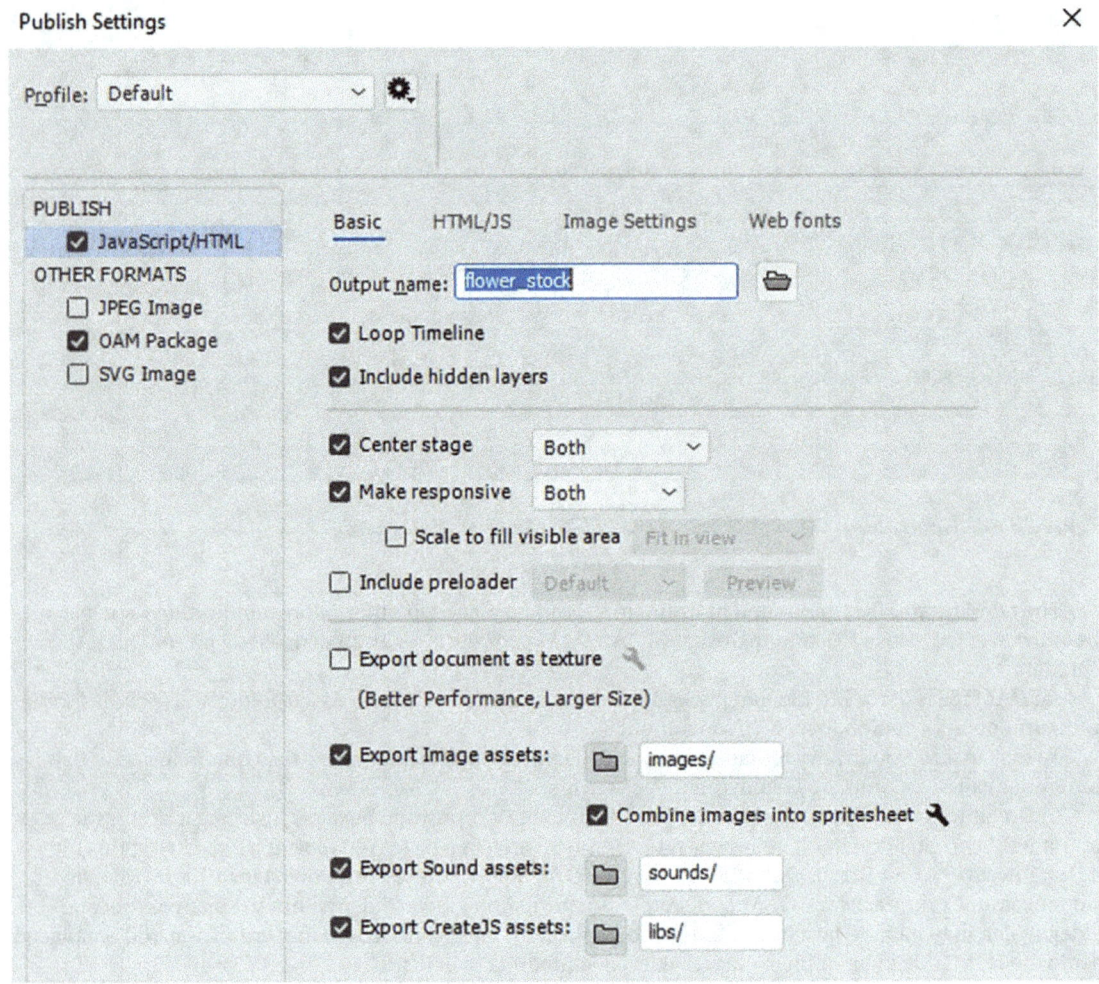

Figure 22-35. *With the OAM Package selected, make sure to check responsive in the Basic tab*

■ **Note** You can also publish an OAM file from an ActionScript 3.0 FLA file, but this relates to SWF files, which are not part of this chapter.

CHAPTER 22 ■ EXPORTING YOUR FILES TO THE WEB

SVG Image

Like Export Option 2, this generates an SVG image of the current frame. You can give the file a different name and output location. The SVG profile is SVG 1.1. You can include hidden layers, and the image location can be embedded or linked to the folder that the SVG image is saved in. The links update if you need to republish. Refer to Figure 22-36.

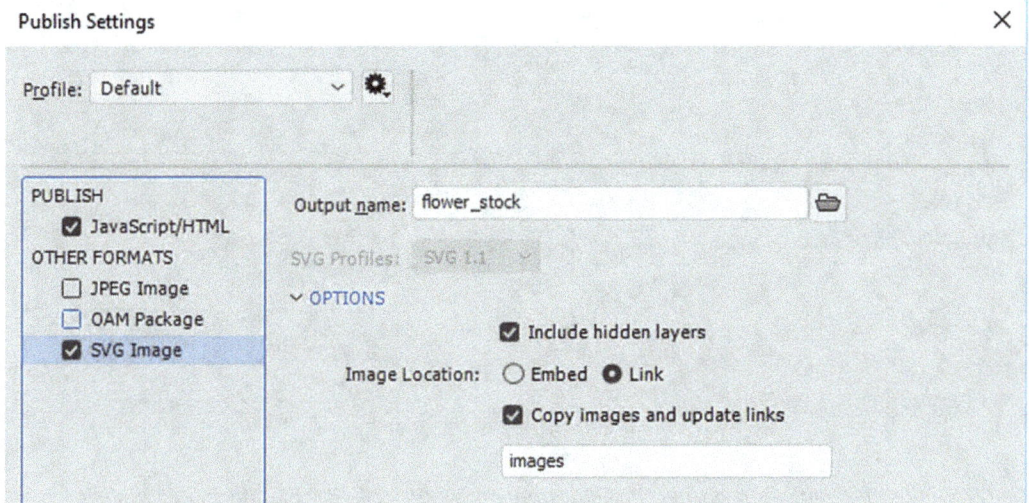

Figure 22-36. *Publish and SVG image using the Publish Settings dialog box*

Other Image Format Alternatives with ActionScript 3.0 FLA Files

While the HTML5 Canvas gives you quite a few format options that you can publish, there may be situations where where you need a few additional formats. The following formats are listed here.

PNG Image

If you need to just publish a single frame as PNG, you can do this only with an ActionScript 3.0 FLA file. Refer to Figure 22-37; otherwise, use Options 1 and 2.

555

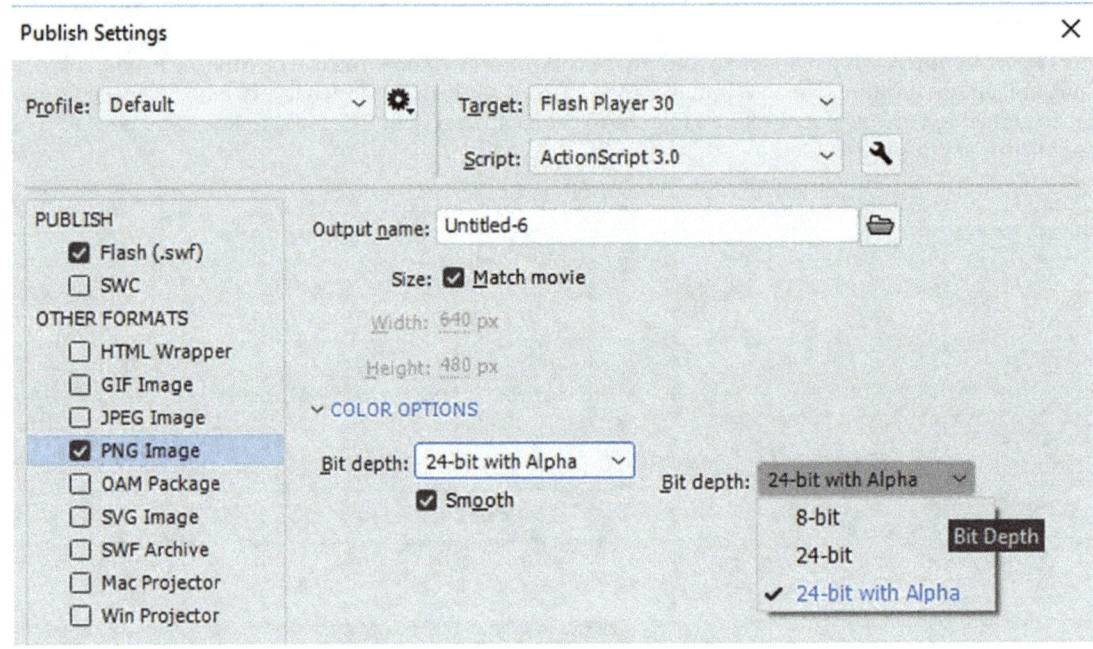

Figure 22-37. Options for publishing a single PNG file from an ActionScript 3.0 FLA file in the Publish Settings dialog box

GIF Image

If you need to just publish a single frame or an animation as a GIF, you can do this only with an ActionScript 3.0 FLA file; otherwise, use Option 2: File ➤ Export ➤ Export Image (Legacy), or Option 5: File ➤ Export ➤ Export Animated GIF. Refer to Figure 22-38.

CHAPTER 22 ■ EXPORTING YOUR FILES TO THE WEB

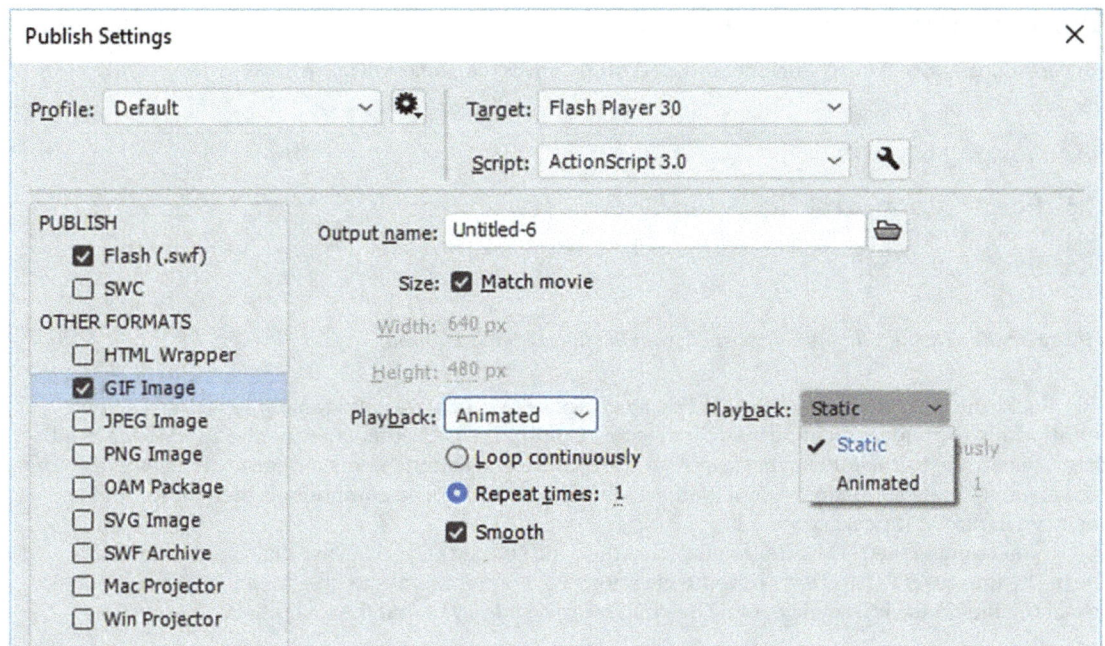

Figure 22-38. Options for publishing a single static GIF file or animated file from an ActionScript 3.0 FLA file in the Publish Settings dialog box

■ **Note** Unlike in Option 5, you can set the repeat times to a specific number, as you would in Photoshop CC.

For more advanced information on publishing HTML5 Canvas, visit `https://helpx.adobe.com/animate/using/creating-publishing-html5-canvas-document.html`.

Let's return to the newly HTML5 Canvas file and look at what it is made up of when the files are published.

557

Dissecting the Canvas HTML5 File

Now let's look inside flower_stock.html, the HTML5 Canvas file. Refer to Figure 22-39.

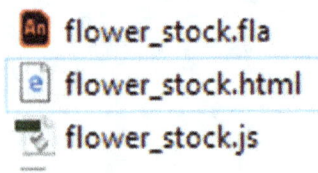

Figure 22-39. *The files that are published from the flower stock example*

Unlike the OAM file that was created as a package, HTML5 Canvas files remain separated (.js and .html) within the folder you published them to. Also, unlike the OAM there may not be an XML file in all cases. In both cases, the folders that are created are image and sound folders if there are images and sounds that required in the animation. And if there was a video file and linked components then these would be included in the OAM package as well.

Upon opening the HTML file, you find that the code contains the <canvas> tag. You can open this file in Dreamweaver CC and view how the file is formed. It also has links to internal and external CreateJS JavaScript files in the <head> tag area. The <body> tag is where you find the animation.

```
<body onload="init();" style="margin:0px;">
    <div id="animation_container" style="background-color:rgba(255, 255, 255, 1.00);
    width:550px; height:400px">
            <canvas id="canvas" width="550" height="400" style="position: absolute;
            display: block; background-color:rgba(255, 255, 255, 1.00);"></canvas>
            <div id="dom_overlay_container" style="pointer-events:none; overflow:hidden;
            width:550px; height:400px; position: absolute; left: 0px; top: 0px; display:
            block;">
            </div>
    </div>
</body>
```

You can copy the created code in the <head> and <body> sections into your own HTML page, and then add CSS to style it to match the theme of your site. Alternatively, you can use OAM package, which you may find easier to handle when you add it to a webpage. You look at that in more detail in Part 6.

Always make sure to test your new file and adjust the links (JavaScript, audio, and video) if they are in distinct folder locations on your own site. You look at this in more detail in Part 6. Personally, I find the HTML5 Canvas animation to be as great as the index or intro page on a site to welcome visitors and encourage them to visit other pages within the website. You create one in Chapter 24.

Other Export Options from the Symbols in the Library Panel

While working on your animation, you may not want to export the entire animation; just select items as images from the Library panel.

When you right-click an object in the Library panel, you can chose one of the following options.

Export PNG Sequence

This allows you to export all the frames within a Movie clip Symbol (nested) as a PNG sequence. The dialog box lists the total number of frames within the Movie Clip and you can set the size, resolution, color quality, and background color as either stage or opaque. Then decide whether to smooth the graphics or not. This is like Option 3 from earlier in the chapter, but you are only working with one symbol and not the whole animation. Refer to Figure 22-40.

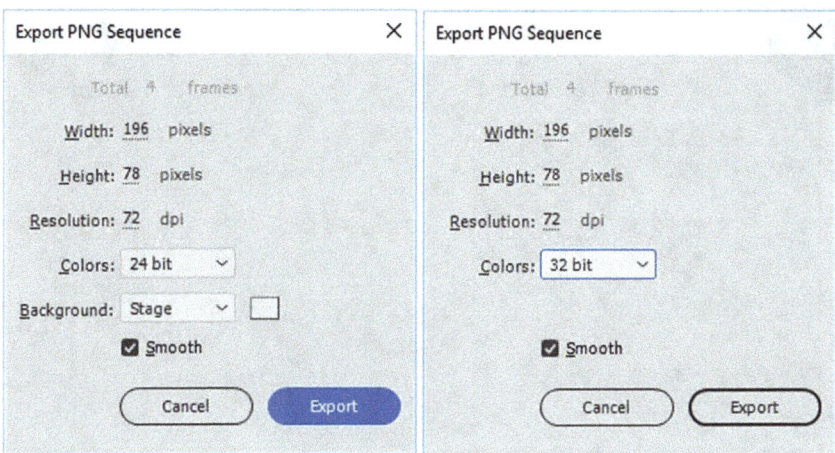

Figure 22-40. Export a PNG sequence for a symbol only

Generate Sprite Sheet

Rather than publish your entire animation, you can generate a sprite sheet (frames loaded on one sheet to save time for the program to find the images for the animation) for one or more of your symbols. You can publish it for more than one symbol by Shift-click selecting them and then right-clicking and choosing Generate Sprite Sheet from the pop-up menu. Refer to Figure 22-41 and button_example.fla.

CHAPTER 22 ■ EXPORTING YOUR FILES TO THE WEB

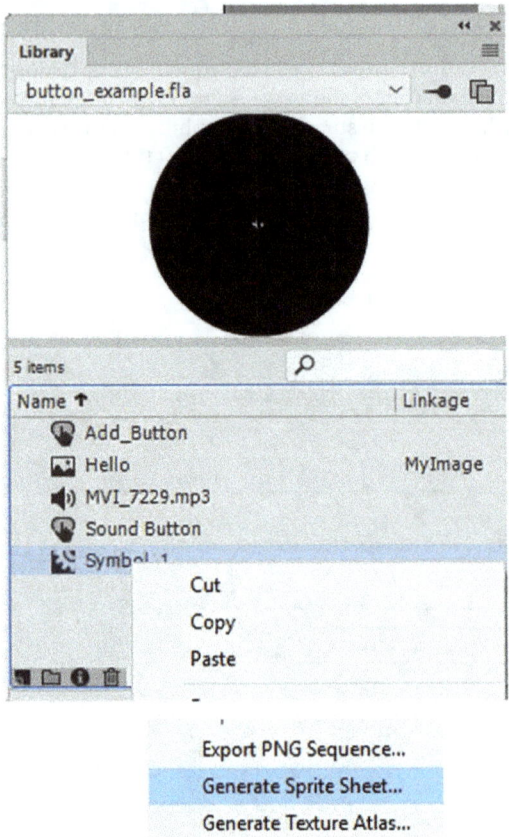

Figure 22-41. While selecting one or more symbols choose generate Sprite Sheet

They appear on the left side of the Generate Sprite Sheet dialog box. Refer to Figure 22-42.

CHAPTER 22 ■ EXPORTING YOUR FILES TO THE WEB

Figure 22-42. *A generated sprite sheet in the dialog box*

The Preview tab shows how the final sprite sheet appears before export.

Further settings allow you to control the image dimensions, which are by default set to autosize, and control the width and height; or choose custom options. The image formats are JPEG or PNG. Refer to Figure 22-43.

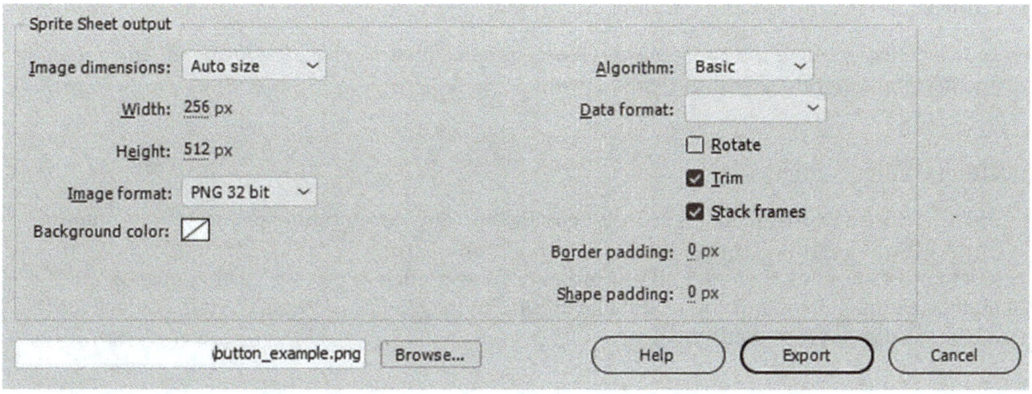

Figure 22-43. *Sprite sheet output options*

561

CHAPTER 22 ■ EXPORTING YOUR FILES TO THE WEB

PNG 8 or 32 can contain transparency, so it is usually 32 that is the default option. You can set the background color. JPEG must have a background color, but you can adjust the quality. Other settings on the right include

- **Algorithm:** How the packing is applied to the frames, Basic (default), or Max Rects; this alters which symbols appear and in what order.
- **Data format:** This outputs the internal format used for image data; if you're not sure

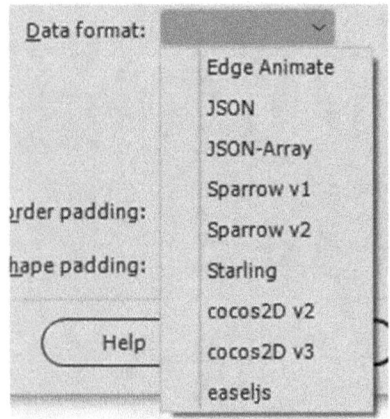

Figure 22-44. Data format options

what setting to use, leave this area blank. Refer to Figure 22-44.

- **Rotate:** Rotates the sprites 90°. This option is only available for some data formats.
- **Trim:** Saves space on the sprite sheet by trimming unused pixels from each symbol frame added to the sheet.
- **Stack frames:** Prevents duplicate frames within the selected symbols from being duplicated in the resulting sprite sheet.
- **Border and shape padding:** Adds extra padding around the sprites.

Then you can choose where the sprite sheet is saved by selecting browse in the lower left and choosing a location and clicking export to export the sprite sheet.

Generate Texture Atlas

The texture atlas is not for web design, but more for gaming and app development using an extra plug-in known as Unity, which binds objects together for the animation.

Since the topic of this book is about building animations and video for the web, I am not going into any detail on this feature; however, if you would like to learn more, check out `https://helpx.adobe.com/animate/using/create-sprite-sheet.html`.

CHAPTER 22 ■ EXPORTING YOUR FILES TO THE WEB

Other Web Export Options

So far, you have looked at the export options that are for images (GIF, JPEG, PNG, and SVG), video (MOV) formats, and two types of animation files (Animated GIF and HTML5 Canvas) and the Canvas' its related packaging OpenAjax Metadata (OAM).

In addition, there are a few other alternatives for various projects other than SWF files that you can use for various mobile and website projects. I list them briefly here.

AIR Options

When you choose File ➤ New, under the Advanced tab, you find three Adobe AIR options. Refer to Figure 22-45.

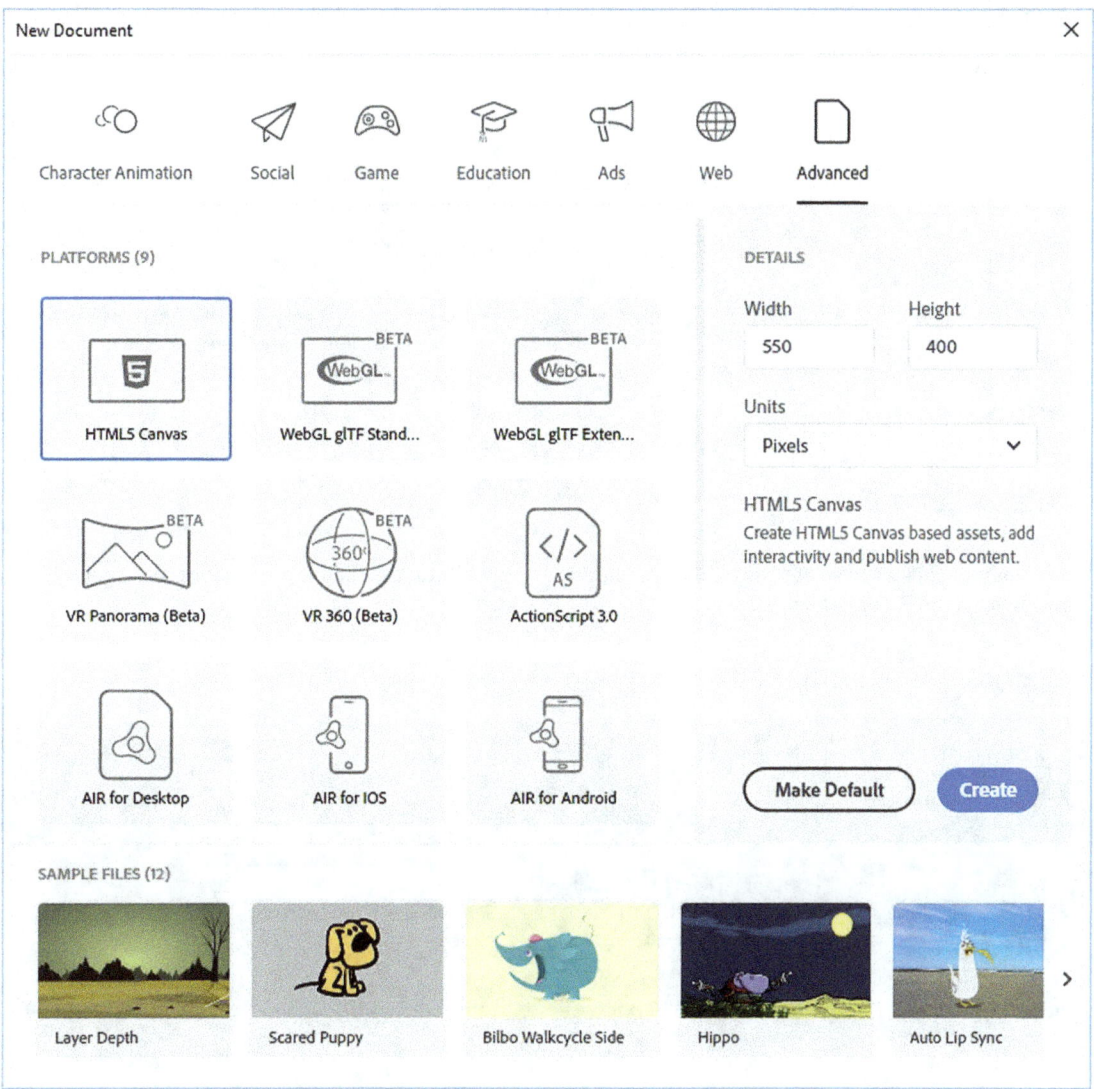

Figure 22-45. *Options for AIR in the New Document dialog box*

563

CHAPTER 22 ■ EXPORTING YOUR FILES TO THE WEB

AIR is for animated files that are geared toward mobile devices (Android and Apple iOS), but you can also make files for the desktop. They don't require a Flash player and can run without the browser. There are at least three options.

- Air for Desktop (.air)
- Air for Android (.apk)
- Air for iOS (.ipa)

Each of these files can be adjusted and set to a new setting in the Properties panel under the Publish tab. Refer to Figure 22-46.

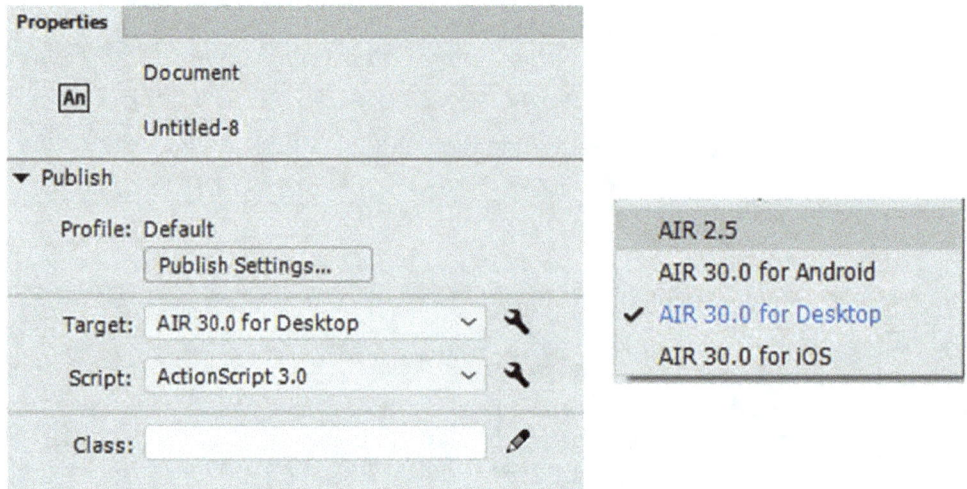

Figure 22-46. AIR Option settings

When you click Publish Settings, this information is carried into the dialog box under the Target drop-down menu. Refer to Figure 22-47.

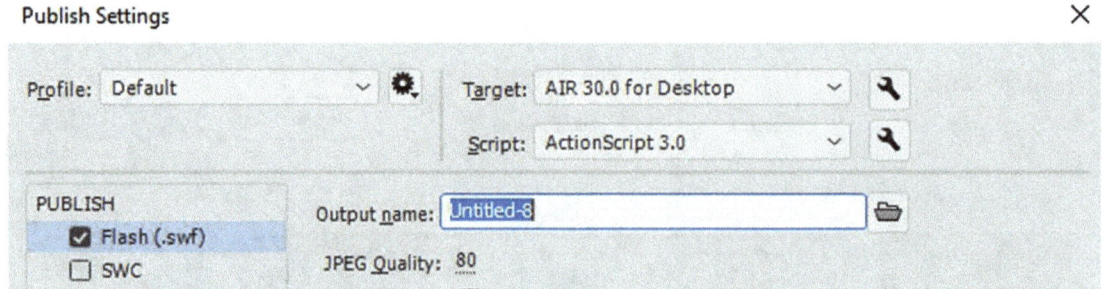

Figure 22-47. Target Publish Settings for AIR package

CHAPTER 22 ■ EXPORTING YOUR FILES TO THE WEB

While at first glance it might appear that you are creating a SWF file, if you click the little wrench (player settings) by the Target drop-down menu, you see that this is an AIR package. Refer to Figure 22-48.

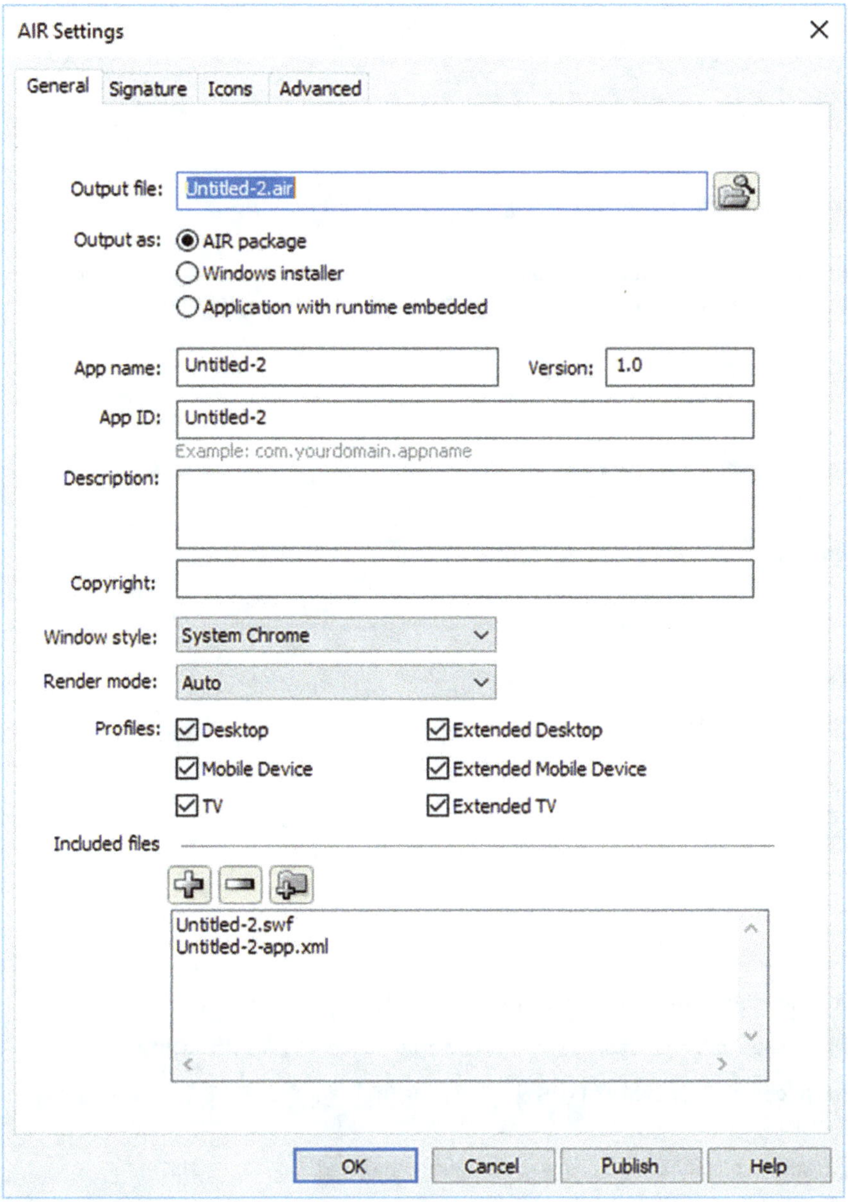

Figure 22-48. AIR Settings dialog box

CHAPTER 22 ■ EXPORTING YOUR FILES TO THE WEB

This setting is not available to Flash files. Refer to Figure 22-49.

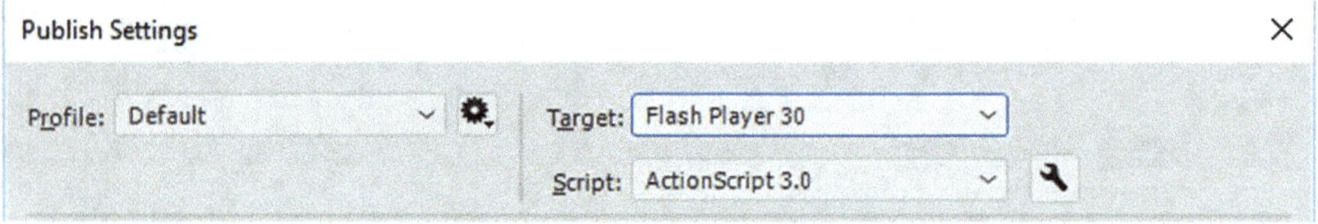

Figure 22-49. *When you target Flash Player, the AIR setting the upper wrench disappears*

For AIR packages to run and publish on the web, you are required to set up various signature certificate and security settings for those who sell and download the files; this keeps users safe. Refer to Figure 22-50.

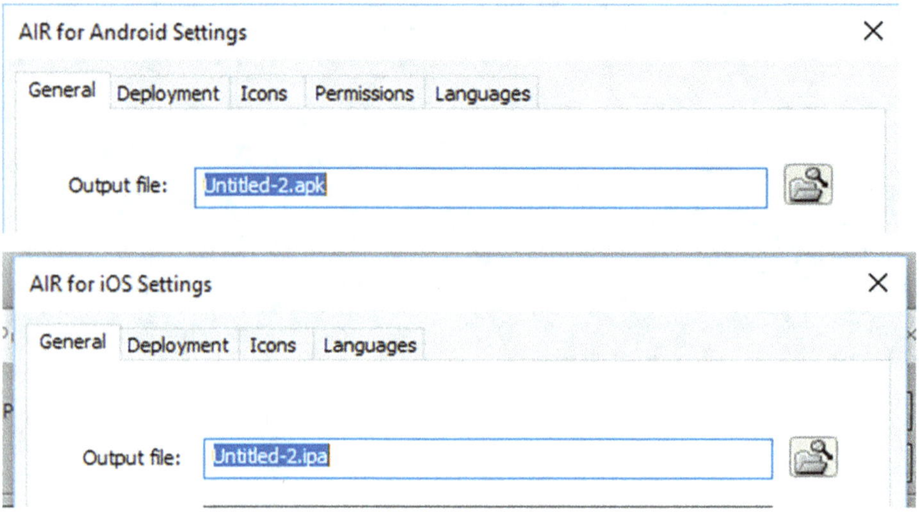

Figure 22-50. *AIR settings for Android and iOS*

For more information on working with AIR, visit the following:

- https://helpx.adobe.com/animate/using/publishing-adobe-air-desktop.html
- https://helpx.adobe.com/animate/using/publishing-air-android-applications.html
- https://helpx.adobe.com/animate/using/packaging-applications-air-ios.html
- https://helpx.adobe.com/animate/how-to/air-applications-ios-devices.html

Projector

Two other options found in the export settings are Mac Projector (.app) and Win Projector (.exe). Refer to Figure 22-51.

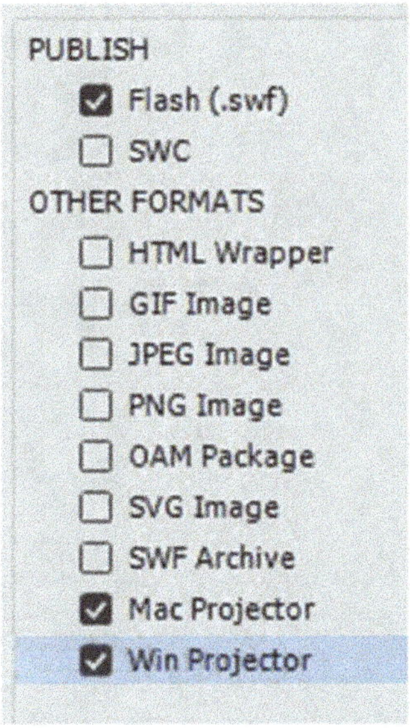

Figure 22-51. Mac and Win Projector options in the publish setting of an ActionScript 3.0 FLA file

A projector is a self-contained file that includes the Flash player runtime if your audience doesn't have a Flash player installed. These files play like an application, but don't require a web browser. It begins to run once you double-click the icon; however, unlike AIR, you don't have the same range of publishing options and settings.

WebGL

Found under File ➤ New under the Advanced Tab now has 4 WebGL options: gltf Standard, gltf Extended, VR 360, and VR Panorama. All are in Beta version. 360 and Panorama animations can be used for virtual reality and game environments. This Web Graphics Library is a JavaScript API for rendering 2D and 3D graphics within any compatible web browser without the use of plug-ins. Besides JavaScript, it uses JSON files (JavaScript Object Notation), which is like XML; both are for storing data to render complex graphics. For more information, visit https://en.wikipedia.org/wiki/WebGL.

However, when you choose any one of these WebGL options, be aware that Animate CC WebGL does not currently allow the use of the 3D tools, some text features, masks, and video, because they are not currently supported; however, as the technology improves, this is likely to change. Refer to Figure 22-52.

CHAPTER 22 ■ EXPORTING YOUR FILES TO THE WEB

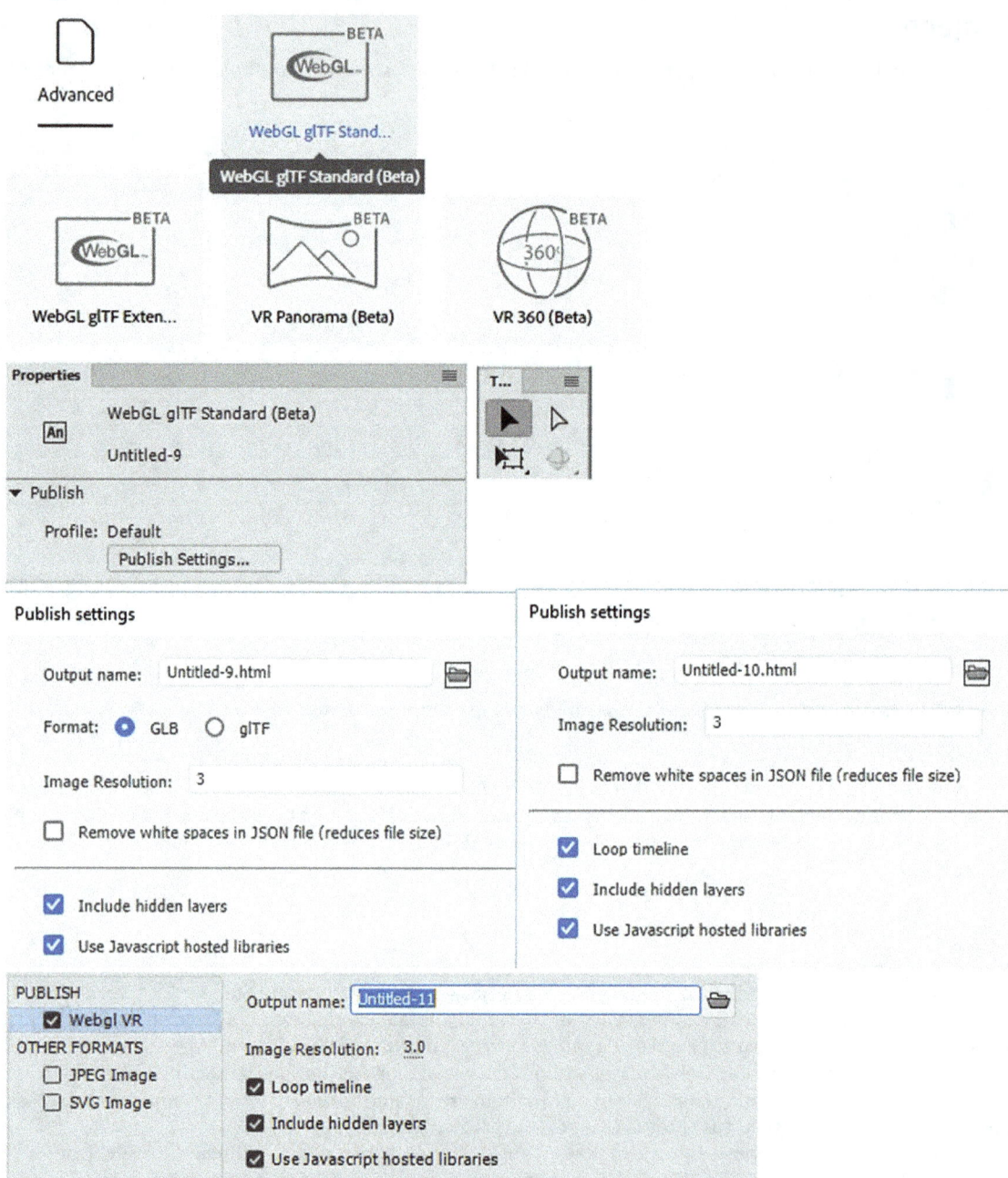

Figure 22-52. *Options for various WebGL file types*

As with HTML5 Canvas, you have the option to create along with certain WebGL files, JPEG images, and an SVG image.

For more information on WebGL publishing, visit
`https://helpx.adobe.com/animate/using/creating-publishing-webgl-document.html`.

Summary

This chapter covered a lot of options for exporting all or parts of the FLA files as images, animations, and video. You also looked at some file formats that you may not have been familiar with such as MOV and an OAM file. You also looked inside the HTML5 Canvas file (.html) and saw that it is linked to external JavaScript. It also has the options to be linked to sounds, external images, and video via components (e.g., video_canvas.html). Finally, you looked at other export options for the web.

In the next chapter, you look at a few miscellaneous tools that you can use in Animate for your own projects, and then you'll finish Part 4 by putting your knowledge into practice.

CHAPTER 23

Other Miscellaneous Items in Animate that You Can Use for Web Design

In this chapter, you look at a few final tools that you can use to enhance your designs in Animate.

> **Note** This chapter does not have any actual projects; however, you can use the files in the Chapter 23 folder to practice opening and viewing for this lesson. They are at https://github.com/Apress/graphics-multimedia-web-adobe-creative-cloud.

Edit ➤ Preferences

Although you do not design any actual JavaScript in the Actions panel, which you will look in a moment, make sure to look at the code editor if you plan to work with JavaScript within Animate.

You can leave most settings in Edit ➤ Preferences in Animate CC at the default; however, if you are planning to use the Actions panel to add JavaScript, you can change formatting in the code editor to Format Code ➤ Select Language JavaScript then you can edit the preferences further. Refer to Figure 23-1.

CHAPTER 23 ■ OTHER MISCELLANEOUS ITEMS IN ANIMATE THAT YOU CAN USE FOR WEB DESIGN

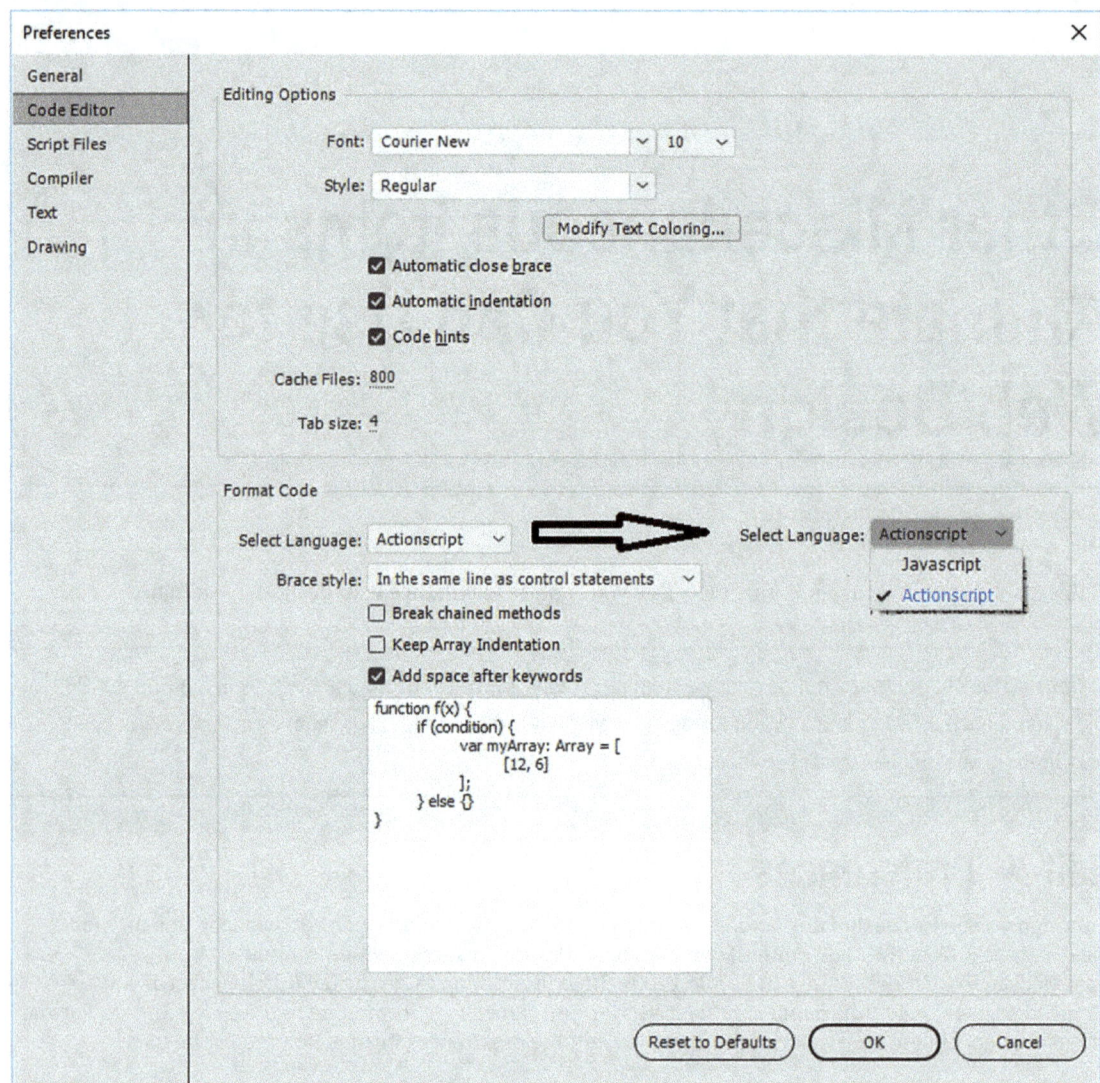

Figure 23-1. *The Preferences panel allows you to change from ActionScript to JavaScript settings*

Click OK to set changes, or you can reset to defaults if you need the original settings; however, in most cases, it is assumed that you are using JavaScript in an HTML5 Canvas, so you do not have to alter anything this area.

CHAPTER 23 ■ OTHER MISCELLANEOUS ITEMS IN ANIMATE THAT YOU CAN USE FOR WEB DESIGN

Actions, Code Snippets, and History Panels

As you have seen, Photoshop CC and Illustrator CC both have what is known as the Actions panel.

Actions Panel

In Animate CC, the Actions panel is very different from what you saw previously. In this case, it refers to the actions that are applied to the symbols on the stage for the HTML5 Canvas. From this panel, you can customize your code to alter the actions of your symbols on the stage. Movie clip and button symbols can have actions that are composed of JavaScript; however, in most basic animations, when you publish an HTML5 Canvas, the actions are automatically created as the file being exported, so you don't have to do a lot of programing work; however, if you want to make such things as responsive buttons that make an object move when clicked or cause an action to happen to a movie clip symbol within a game, then you need to use the Actions panel to make this happen. Refer to Figure 23-2.

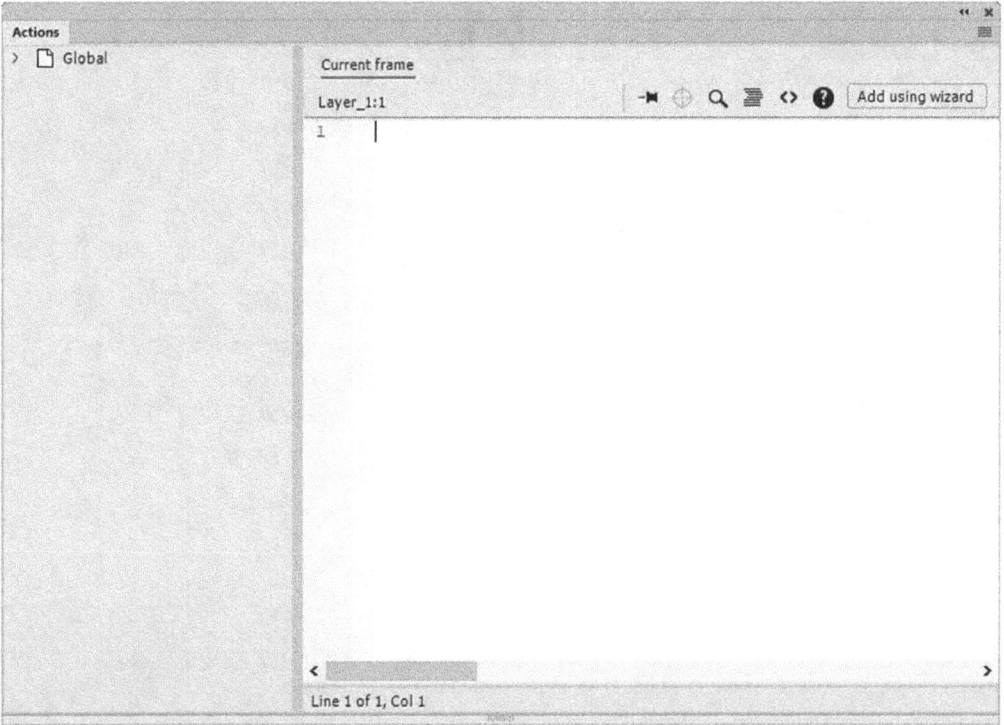

Figure 23-2. *When no symbol is selected in a current frame, the Action panel is blank*

573

CHAPTER 23 ■ OTHER MISCELLANEOUS ITEMS IN ANIMATE THAT YOU CAN USE FOR WEB DESIGN

This panel is where you can globally add your custom JavaScript to frames or symbols.

The Actions panel (in the upper right) allows you to pin code, search for keywords, find/replace, and format your code.

You can also access code snippets from there with the <> icon. Refer to Figure 23-3.

Figure 23-3. The Actions panel tools

Code Snippets Panel

When you create a code action that you want to use again for a symbol, you can store it or access it in the Code Snippet panel, which is found in the HTML5 Canvas folder. Refer to Figure 23-4.

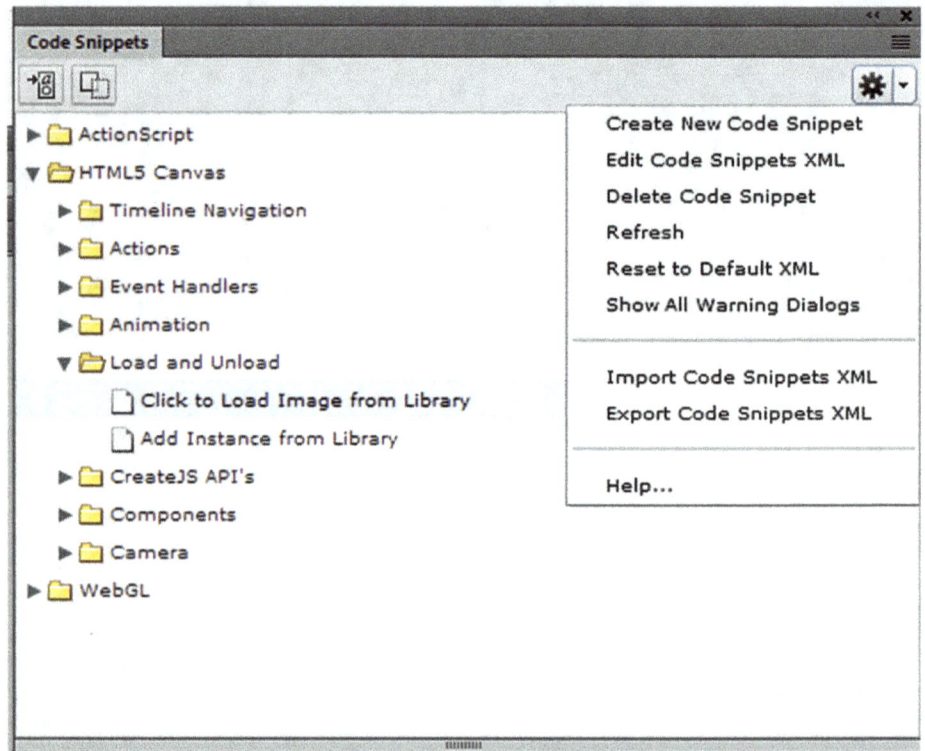

Figure 23-4. The Code Snippets panel

Animate has prebuilt code snippets that you can use on buttons, or you can create your own. These code snippets are a good starting point for non-programmers who want to easily learn JavaScript. Symbols that are used with the Actions panel require instance names that you set when you select the symbol and give it a name in the Properties panel. Refer to Figure 23-5.

574

CHAPTER 23 ■ OTHER MISCELLANEOUS ITEMS IN ANIMATE THAT YOU CAN USE FOR WEB DESIGN

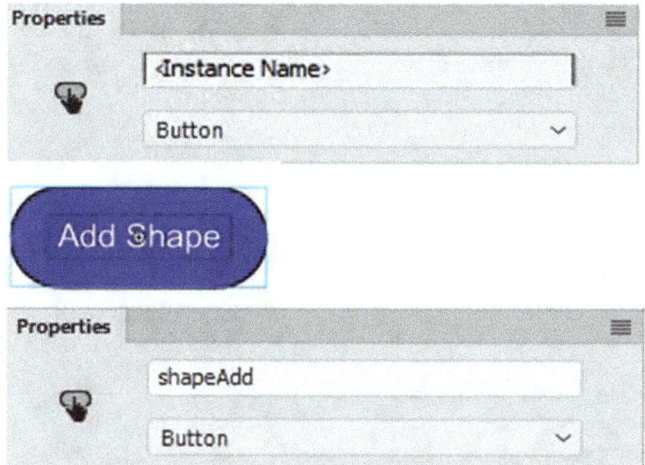

Figure 23-5. *The Properties panel: giving a button an instance name*

With the button symbol selected, when you add a code snippet to the current frame in the timeline, Animate creates its own actions layer ("a"), and then you fill in the data in the Actions panel, if required, to match the action with the symbol. Refer to Figure 23-6.

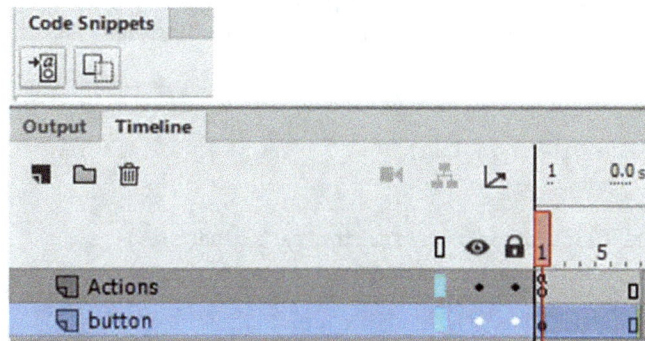

Figure 23-6. *An action layer is added to the Timeline*

In this case, I used the snippet example, HTML5 Canvas ➤ Load and Unload ➤ Click to Load Image from Library, as seen in Figure 23-7.

575

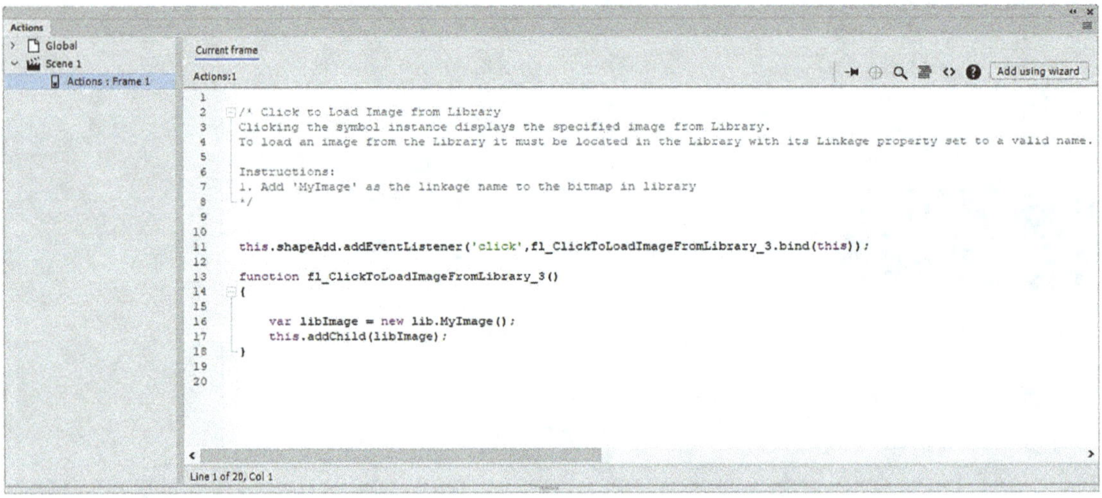

CHAPTER 23 ■ OTHER MISCELLANEOUS ITEMS IN ANIMATE THAT YOU CAN USE FOR WEB DESIGN

Figure 23-7. Code is automatically added to the Actions panel for the button action

The following is the code.

```
* Click to Load Image from Library
Clicking the symbol instance displays the specified image from Library.
To load an image from the Library it must be located in the Library with its Linkage
property set to a valid name.

Instructions:
1. Add 'MyImage' as the linkage name to the bitmap in library
*/

this.shapeAdd.addEventListener('click',fl_ClickToLoadImageFromLibrary_3.bind(this));

function fl_ClickToLoadImageFromLibrary_3()
{

        var libImage = new lib.MyImage();
        this.addChild(libImage);
}
```

Your code may have slightly different in numbering, but the key instruction to watch for is this:

```
Add 'MyImage' as the linkage name to the bitmap in library
```

This means that before you publish your HTML5 Canvas file, you need to go back to the Library panel and locate the bitmap file, and in the linkage column, enter **MyImage**. Refer to Figure 23-8.

576

CHAPTER 23 ■ OTHER MISCELLANEOUS ITEMS IN ANIMATE THAT YOU CAN USE FOR WEB DESIGN

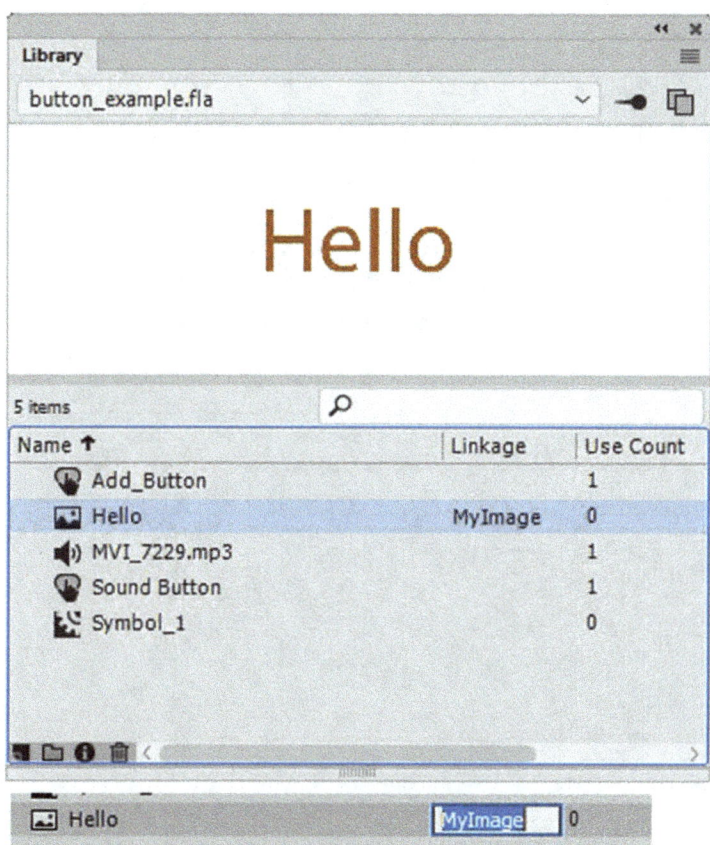

Figure 23-8. *Add the name MyImage to the linkage area of the image*

It may not appear as though there is a spot to enter under Linkage, but it when you double-click in this area, a white text area will appear.

If you do not add this linkage, the code will not work.

In this case, I have already completed the example for you in the button_example.fla file. You can see the result in the published button_example.html file.

You see the Code Snippets panel again in Part 6. In the meantime, try a few actions in your HTML5 Canvas file, but make sure to carefully follow the instructions regarding linkage to avoid errors.

■ **Note** For more code help for your own project, click the Add Using Wizard button. Refer to Figure 23-9.

577

CHAPTER 23 ■ OTHER MISCELLANEOUS ITEMS IN ANIMATE THAT YOU CAN USE FOR WEB DESIGN

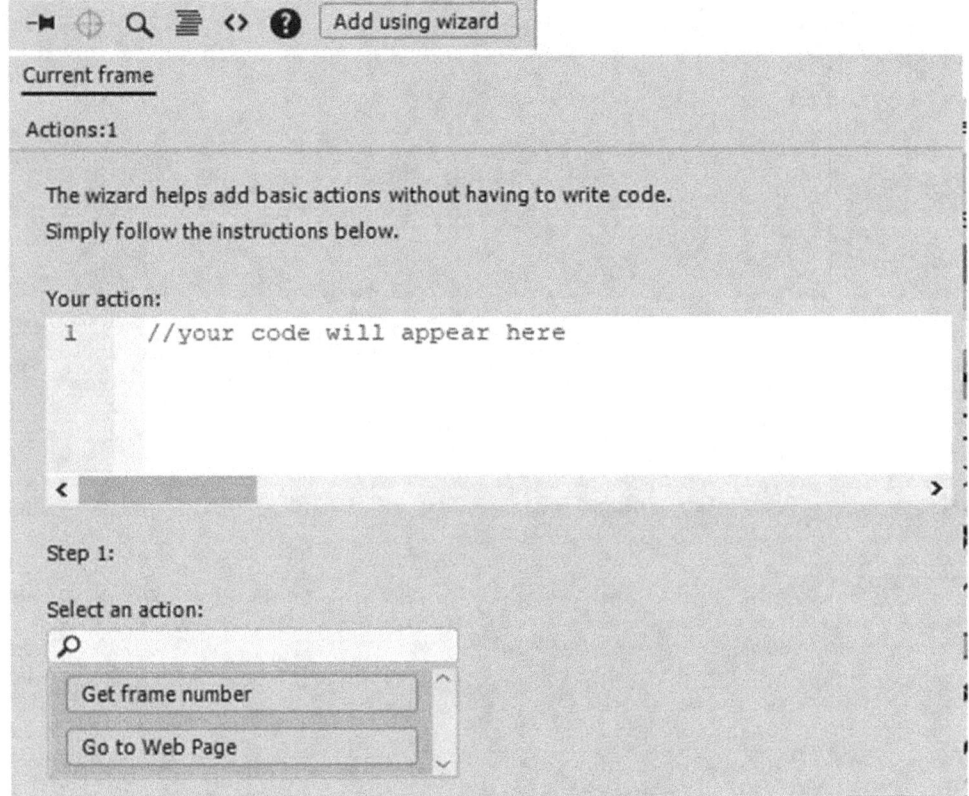

Figure 23-9. *The wizard can help you write basic code in Animate*

The wizard gives you step-by-step help by choosing from a list for writing basic code.

Click Next to continue to the next step until you reach Finish and Add; or click Cancel to get out of the wizard area of the Actions panel.

So now that you know a bit more about what the Actions panel does in Animate, how can you create "actions" or recorded steps in Animate like you did in Photoshop or Illustrator that you can save for other projects?

History Panel

Animate CC uses a different panel to create recorded steps: the History panel. Refer to Figure 23-10.

CHAPTER 23 ■ OTHER MISCELLANEOUS ITEMS IN ANIMATE THAT YOU CAN USE FOR WEB DESIGN

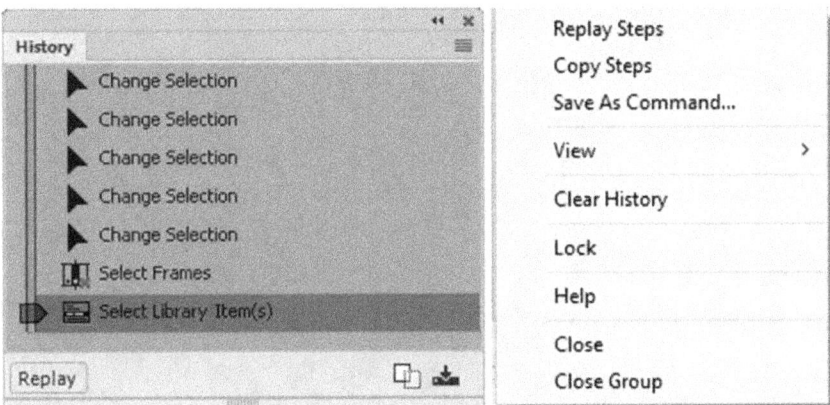

Figure 23-10. *The History panel can be used to create some basic commands*

The History panel looks like the one in Photoshop and shows the list of steps that have occurred since you opened the file. Using the slider on the left, you can go back or forward in your steps if you make a mistake. By default, Animate supports 100 levels of undo in the History panel. You can increase the amount under Edit ➤ Preferences ➤ General tab. If you record steps, you might draw a circle and then convert it to a symbol, and as you do, this each step is recorded. You can replay steps, copy steps to the clipboard, or save them as a command. Refer to Figure 23-11.

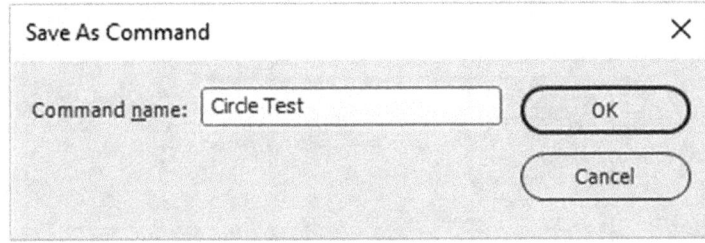

Figure 23-11. *Save As a Command dialog box*

A command is basically the same as an action in Photoshop or Illustrator.
Enter a command name and then click OK.
These steps can be replayed and then saved as commands in the Commands menu. You will find some commands already saved in the main menu. Refer to Figure 23-12.

579

CHAPTER 23 ■ OTHER MISCELLANEOUS ITEMS IN ANIMATE THAT YOU CAN USE FOR WEB DESIGN

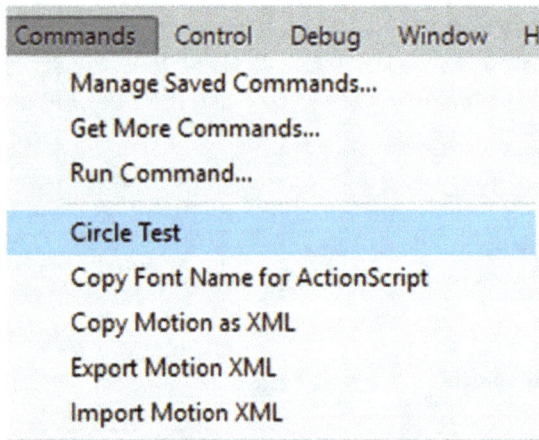

Figure 23-12. *Commands are added to the list*

Commands can be managed (renamed or removed), acquired, and run. Copying the steps to a clipboard and into a program like Notepad allows you to view things like coordinates and the size of a shape in relation to its placement on the stage.

If you plan to remove commands, in Manage Saved Commands, be aware of which ones come with Animate and should remain, so that you do not accidentally remove the wrong ones. Refer to Figure 23-13.

Figure 23-13. *Manage Saved Commands: remove ones that you created or rename them here*

CHAPTER 23 ■ OTHER MISCELLANEOUS ITEMS IN ANIMATE THAT YOU CAN USE FOR WEB DESIGN

CC Libraries

The CC Libraries panel is shown in Figure 23-14.

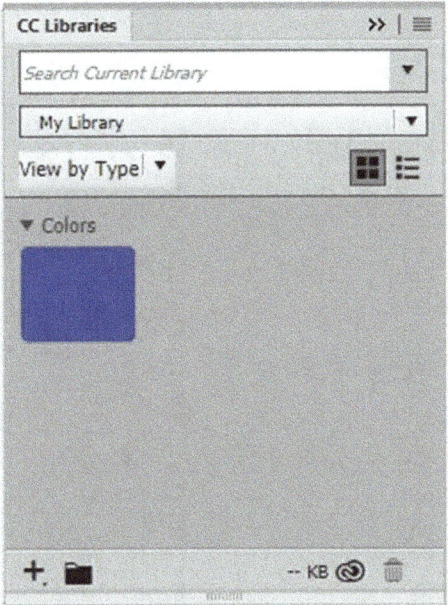

Figure 23-14. *The Libraries panel*

It was introduced with the Creative Cloud. With Animate CC Libraries, you can store colors and save media assets that you create to use in projects. You can then move over to a program like Dreamweaver, and the colors are stored there so that you can refer to them during your project. Notice that CC Libraries is the same as the Library panel in Photoshop, Illustrator, and Dreamweaver. The reason for the slight name change is that Animate already has a Library panel that it uses to store your project's symbols in. This can be a bit confusing when working between programs; however, use this panel if you want to move objects to the Creative Cloud and share between other Adobe programs.

581

CHAPTER 23 ■ OTHER MISCELLANEOUS ITEMS IN ANIMATE THAT YOU CAN USE FOR WEB DESIGN

Patterns for Paint Brush and Pen Tools

While Animate CC does not have any specific tool for creating patterns, many default presets of patterned brushes are available in the Brush Library panel when you use the Pen (P)or Paint Brush (Y) tools in the Tools panel. Editing or importing these pattern brushes allows you more flexibility in your animation, as seen in Figure 23-15.

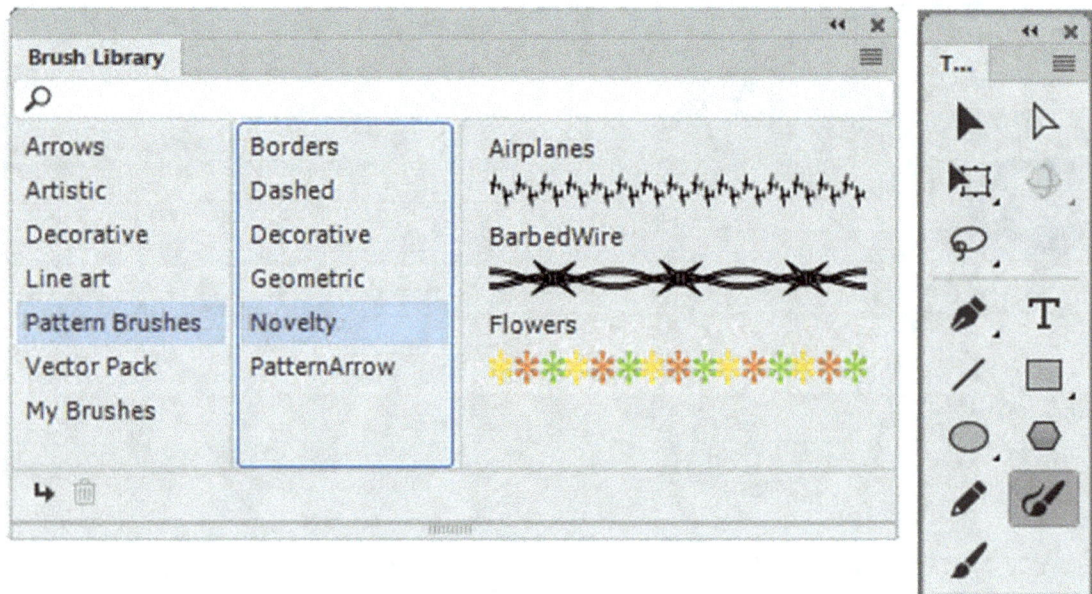

Figure 23-15. *The Brush Library panel and the Tools panel*

CHAPTER 23 ■ OTHER MISCELLANEOUS ITEMS IN ANIMATE THAT YOU CAN USE FOR WEB DESIGN

You can also access this area in the Properties panel when using the Paint Brush tool by clicking the Brush Library icon. Refer to Figure 23-16.

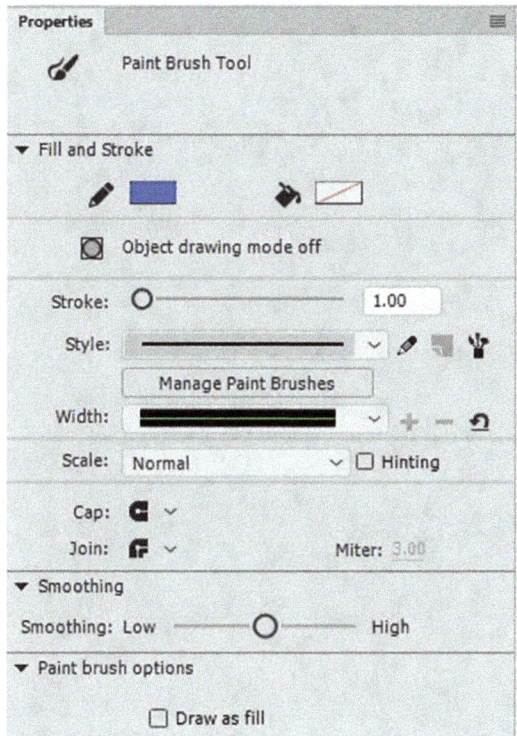

Figure 23-16. *The Properties panel when accessing the Paint Brush tool*

■ **Note** These types of brushes do not work for the Pencil (Shift+Y), Brush tool (B) or Eraser tool (E) in the Tools panel and properties. For these, you have to use the generic brushes that come in the Tools panel or Properties panel. Refer to Figures 23-17, 23-18, and 23-19.

CHAPTER 23 ■ OTHER MISCELLANEOUS ITEMS IN ANIMATE THAT YOU CAN USE FOR WEB DESIGN

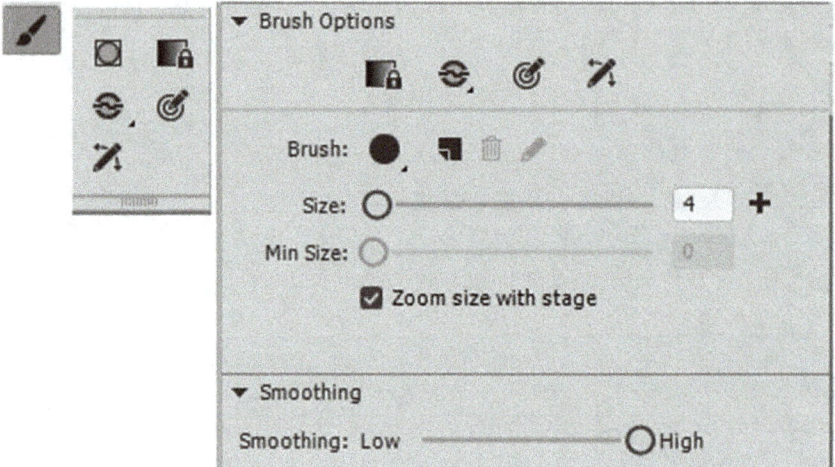

Figure 23-17. *The Brush tool and its options in the lower part of the Tools panel and Properties panel*

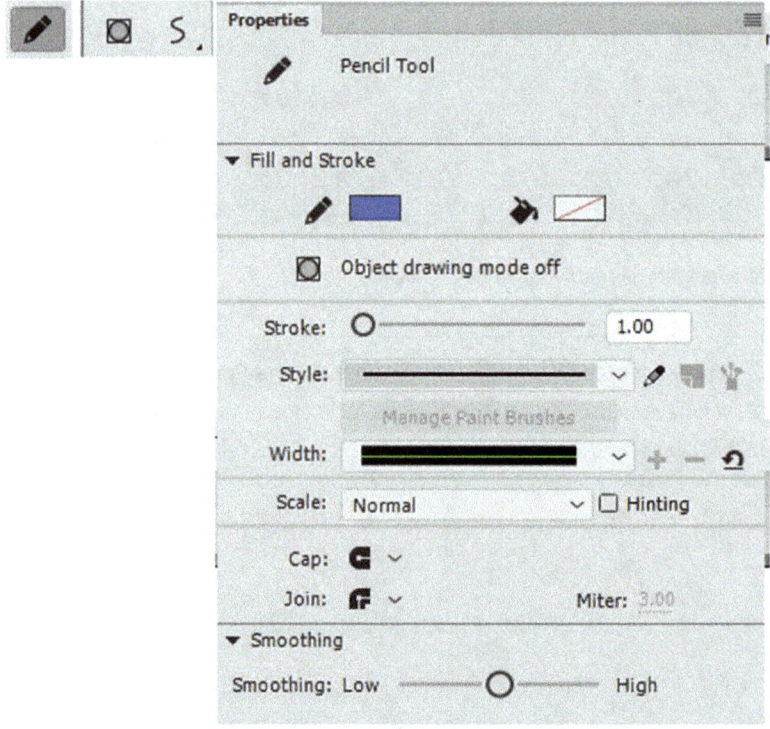

Figure 23-18. *The Pencil tool and its options in the lower part of the Tools panel and Properties panel*

584

CHAPTER 23 ■ OTHER MISCELLANEOUS ITEMS IN ANIMATE THAT YOU CAN USE FOR WEB DESIGN

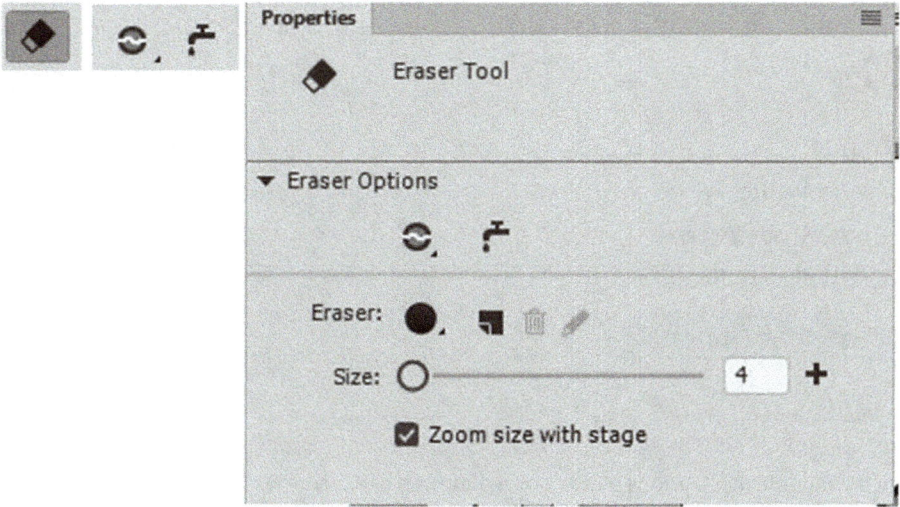

Figure 23-19. The Eraser tool and its options in the lower part of the Tools panel, and the Properties panel settings

You can also create your own brushes and store them in the My Brushes sections. Refer to Figure 23-20.

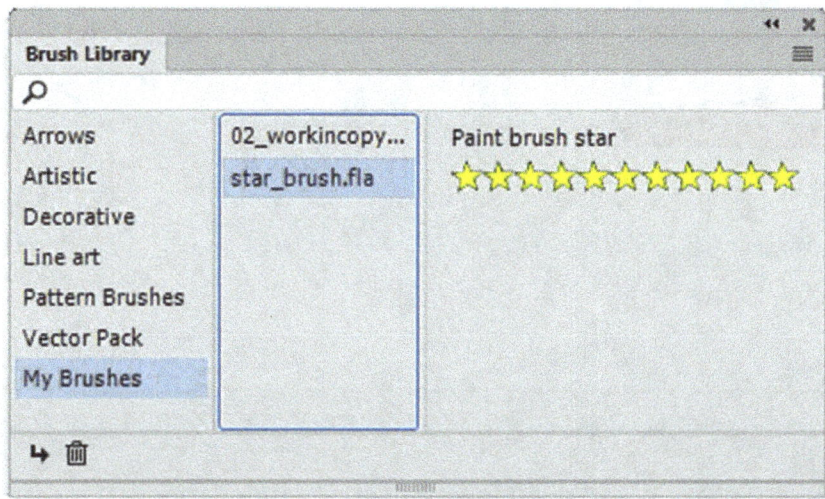

Figure 23-20. The My Brushes is where you can store your personal brushes in the Brush Library panel

You can create your own by selecting a shape (not a symbol), right-clicking it, and choosing Create Paint Brush. Refer to Figure 23-21.

585

CHAPTER 23 ■ OTHER MISCELLANEOUS ITEMS IN ANIMATE THAT YOU CAN USE FOR WEB DESIGN

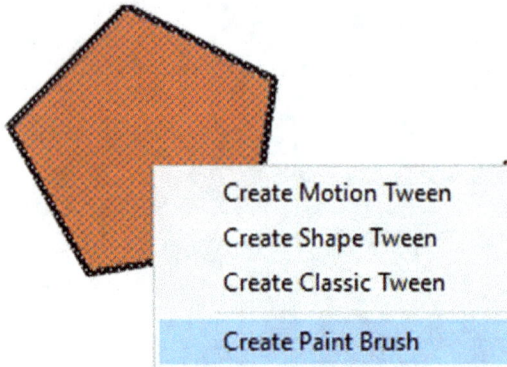

Figure 23-21. Create your own paint brush

This brings you to the Paint Brush Options dialog box, where you can create art brushes or patterned brushes. Refer to Figure 23-22.

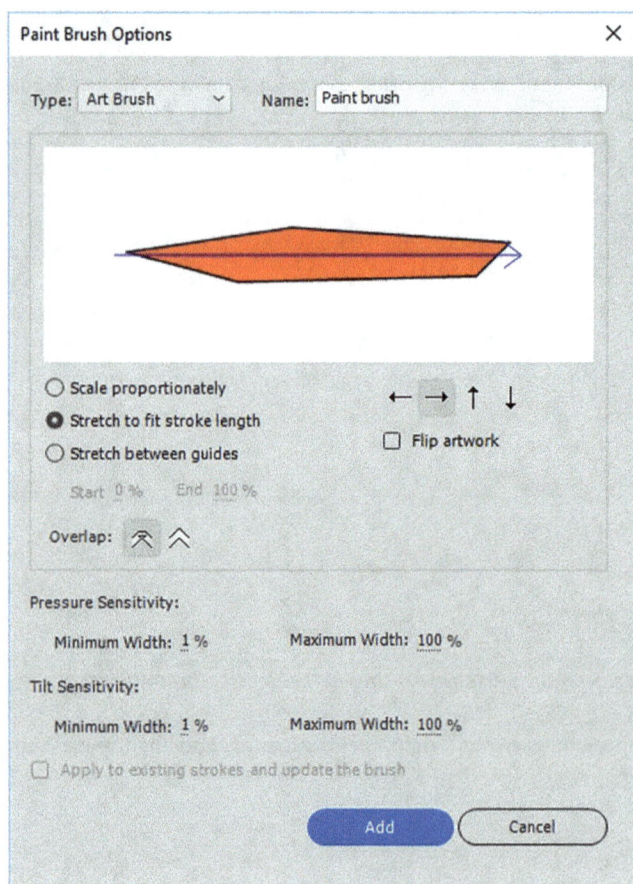

Figure 23-22. The Paint Brush Options dialog box

CHAPTER 23 ■ OTHER MISCELLANEOUS ITEMS IN ANIMATE THAT YOU CAN USE FOR WEB DESIGN

- **Art brush** allows you to scale proportionately or stretch (fit stroke length or between guides) one solid shape along a path. Flip the artwork using the arrows or Flip Artwork check box. Overlap parts of the shape. Adjust pressure and tilt sensitivity is useful if you are using a stylus rather than a mouse.
- **Pattern brush** repeats a pattern over the length of the stroke. You can scale, adjust spacing, and flip artwork. In addition, you can alter how the artwork appears at corners from the At Corners drop-down menu. Refer to Figure 23-23.

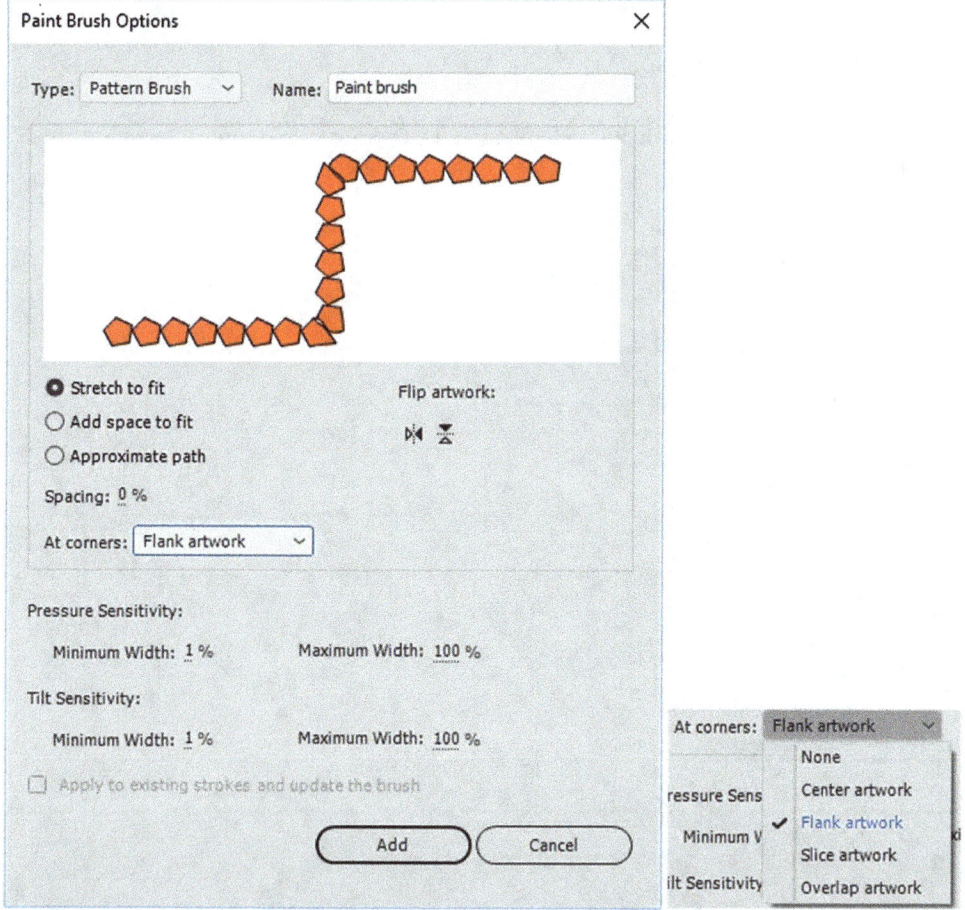

Figure 23-23. Adjust the corners of your brush with the None, Center, Flank, Slice, or Overlap settings

Pressure and tilt sensitivity is also available, as it was for the art brush.

Note that the "Apply to existing stokes and update the brush" option is not be available until you add the brush to your set.

To add to My Brushes, set the name of the brush and then click the add button on the lower right of the Paint Brush Options dialog box. Refer to Figure 23-24.

587

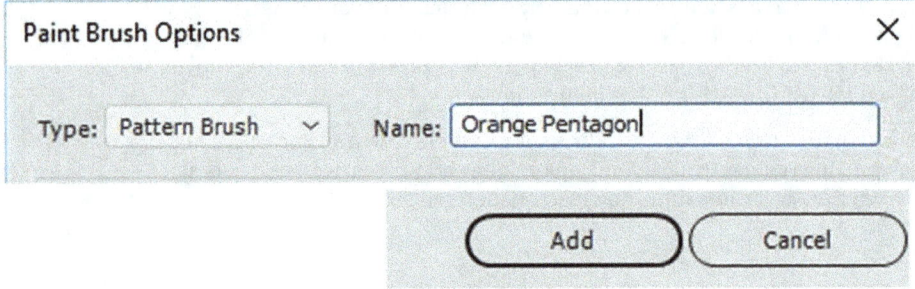

Figure 23-24. Add your Brush to the set in your file

While not as detailed as the pattern brush option in Illustrator CC, you can add some interesting brush designs to your brush library. Refer to Figure 23-25 and the Properties panel.

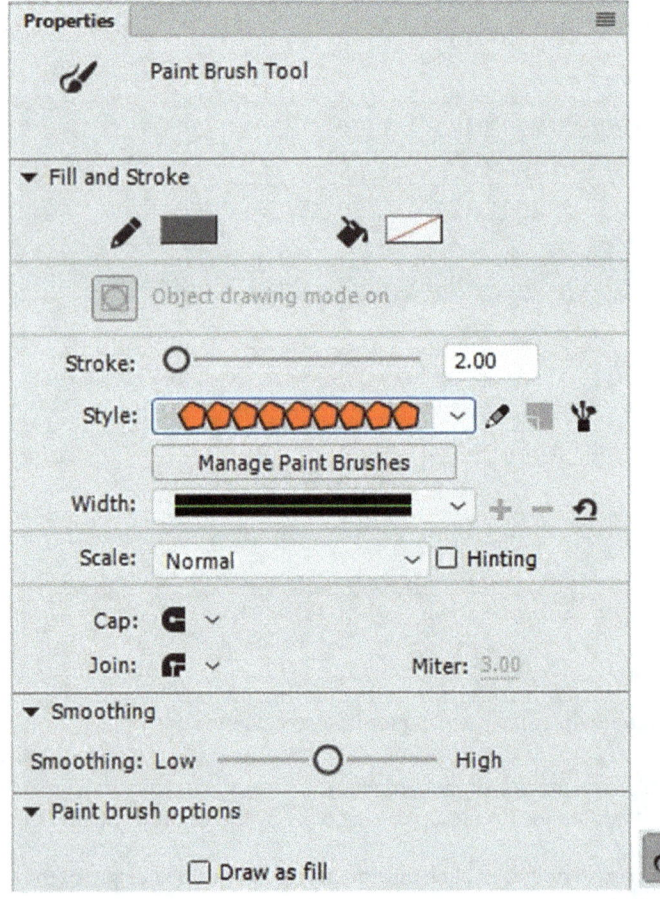

Figure 23-25. The brush appears in the Properties panel

CHAPTER 23 ■ OTHER MISCELLANEOUS ITEMS IN ANIMATE THAT YOU CAN USE FOR WEB DESIGN

Give your file a name, such as paint_brush.fla.

Now you need to do one more crucial step to complete the process of adding the paint brush to the Brush Library panel. If you do not, it will only be available for this file. Using the paint brush tool under the Manage Brushes button, you can choose if you want to save the pattern to the Brush Library. Refer to Figure 23-26.

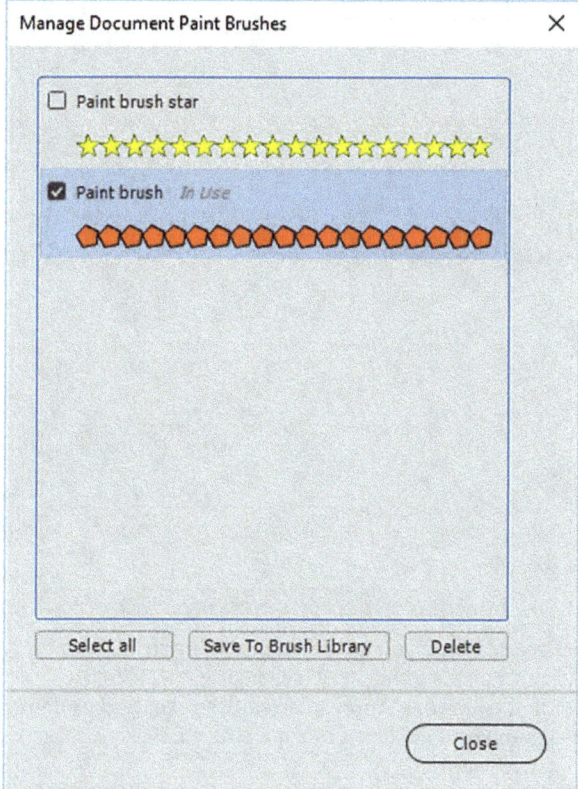

Figure 23-26. *Add your brush to the brush library*

Select your newly created brush in the dialog box, choose Save to Brush Library, and click the Close button.

In Figure 23-27, the new brush is saved in the Brush Library panel.

589

CHAPTER 23 ■ OTHER MISCELLANEOUS ITEMS IN ANIMATE THAT YOU CAN USE FOR WEB DESIGN

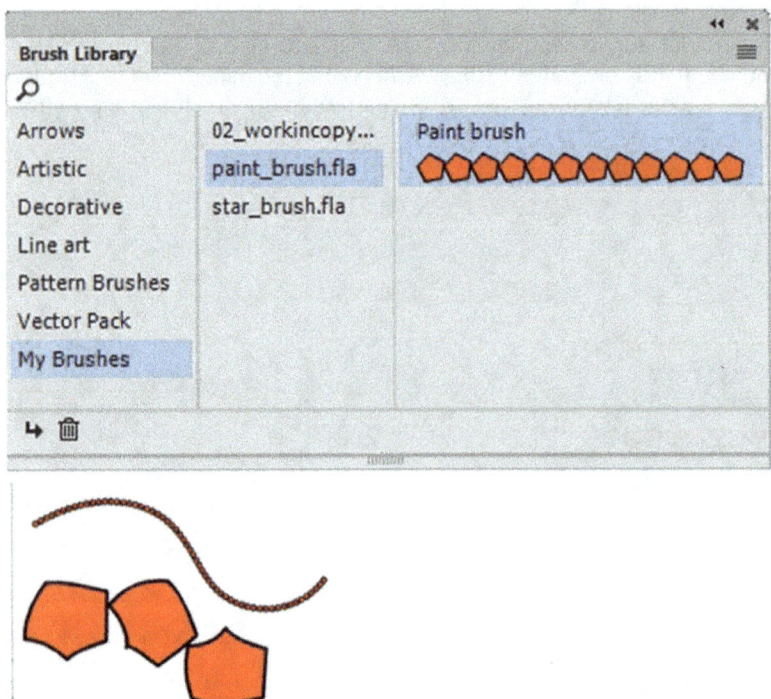

Figure 23-27. *The brush is added to the Library panel and you can use it on the stage*

You can now paint with it on the stage in various stroke sizes. If you need to delete a brush, click the Trash icon. If you need to edit the brush in the document, click the Pencil tool (see Figure 23-24) in the Properties panel to make alterations to the brush, and then check the "Apply to existing strokes and update the brush" box. The Add button changes to update and then you can click it to adjust the changes to your stroke on a shape. Refer to Figure 23-28.

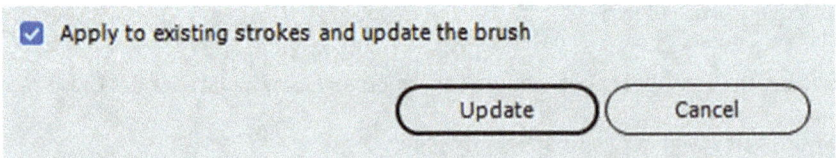

Figure 23-28. *Update the changes you made to the brush*

For more information on brushes, visit `https://helpx.adobe.com/animate/using/working-with-paint-brush.html` and `https://helpx.adobe.com/ca/animate/using/creating-paint-brushes.html`. Note: that in the new CC 2019 version you can now use the new Asset warp tool (W) pin in the tools panel to alter your brush pattern designs further on a shape. It operates in a similar manner to the Puppet warp tools in Photoshop and Illustrator as see in Chapter 14.

CHAPTER 23 ■ OTHER MISCELLANEOUS ITEMS IN ANIMATE THAT YOU CAN USE FOR WEB DESIGN

3D in Animations

Only ActionScript 3.0 FLA files allow you to use the 3D tools; so if you are planning to create a video with some symbols that contain 3D, make sure to use this format and not the HTML5 Canvas FLA. Refer to Figure 23-29.

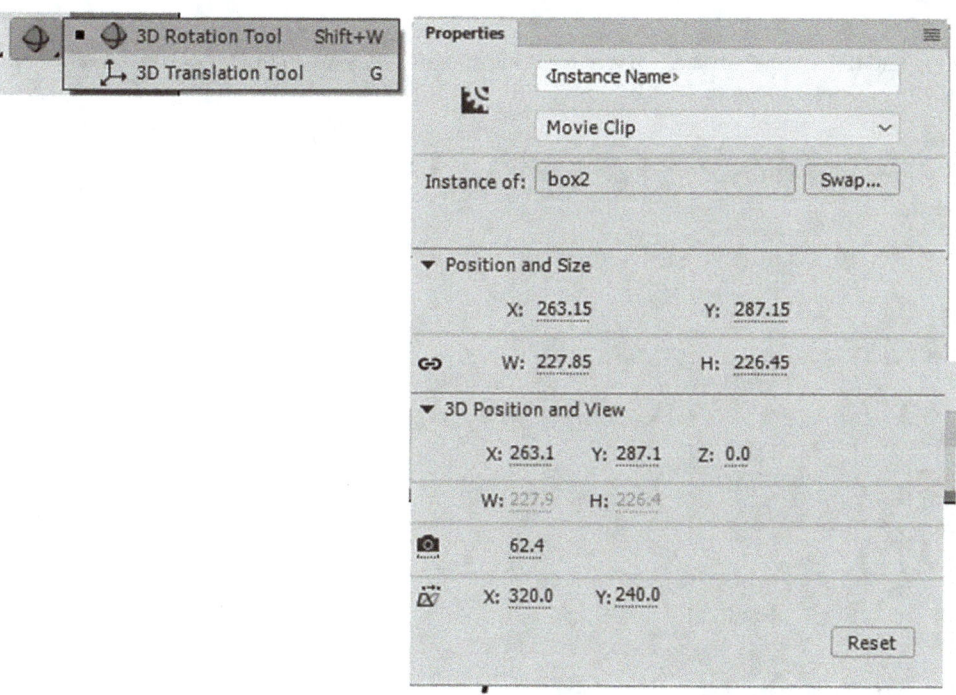

Figure 23-29. *The properties of a Movie Clip when using 3D tools*

Text must be in a symbol to work with the tool if you want a 3D scaling effect. Refer to 3DText.fla and Figure 23-30.

Figure 23-30. *Text symbol scaled in 3D using tools*

591

CHAPTER 23 ■ OTHER MISCELLANEOUS ITEMS IN ANIMATE THAT YOU CAN USE FOR WEB DESIGN

Having said that, you can trick the 3D to work with text in HTML5 Canvas. If you create the text in an ActionScript 3.0 file, make the 3D modifications to the movie-clip symbol and then right-click Convert to bitmap (F8). Copy and paste into the HTML5 Canvas file and resave as a symbol. The only drawback is that you cannot edit the text. You can export as a JPEG or publish as part of the animation.

Web Fonts

As with Photoshop and Illustrator, you can use web fonts in Animate. They are in the Properties panel when you use the Text tool (T). Refer to Figure 23-31.

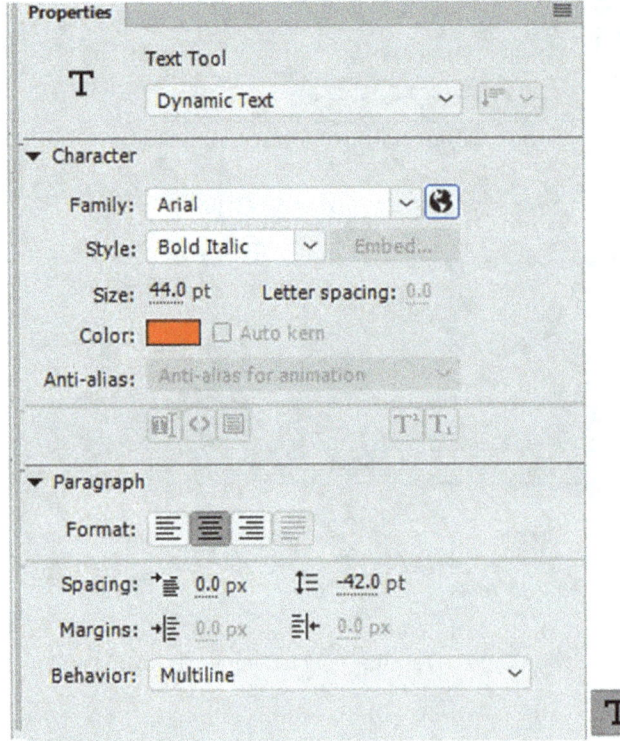

Figure 23-31. *The text tool has access to web fonts*

Static fonts are on your computer. They are not universal to all computers. In the Static setting, the font cannot update dynamically. So a viewer on the Internet who does not have your font, views the text in a font that their computer chooses as a replacement. For example, Arial might be replaced by Helvetica. Refer to Figure 23-32.

592

CHAPTER 23 ■ OTHER MISCELLANEOUS ITEMS IN ANIMATE THAT YOU CAN USE FOR WEB DESIGN

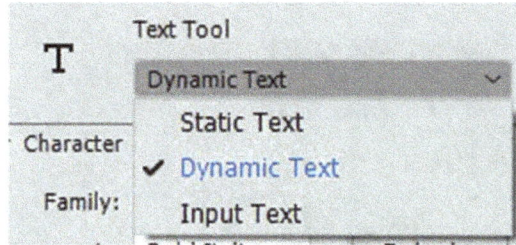

Figure 23-32. *Choosing the type of text to use in your HTML5 Canvas file*

While at first this may not see like a deal breaker, each font has different spacing and sizing, which may cause the parts of the font to appear the wrong size or to be chopped off in the animation.

For video, the font is rendered as it appears on your computer, and does not alter when viewed online. Using fonts from your computer is OK for when you are creating a HTML5 Canvas file that is viewed only on your computer; however, viewers with different fonts will notice styling changes if they see the HTML5 Canvas online. So you need to turn the font into a graphic or a dynamic web font, which is in the Properties panel under the Globe symbol. When you use the Type Tool Dynamic Fonts are also known as web fonts and are part of Adobe Fonts Typekit. Refer to Figure 23-33.

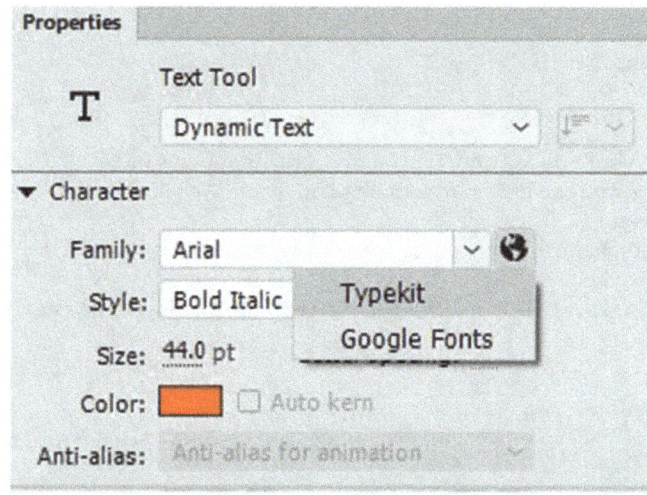

Figure 23-33. *Choose the type of web font you want to use*

You must be signed into a Creative Cloud account to use Adobe Fonts Typekit.

If you do not have it, you get the following error message when trying to select the font: "No user is signed in. Web fonts cannot be used."

If you are logged in, a Adobe Fonts Typekit font appears like what's shown in Figure 23-34.

593

CHAPTER 23 ■ OTHER MISCELLANEOUS ITEMS IN ANIMATE THAT YOU CAN USE FOR WEB DESIGN

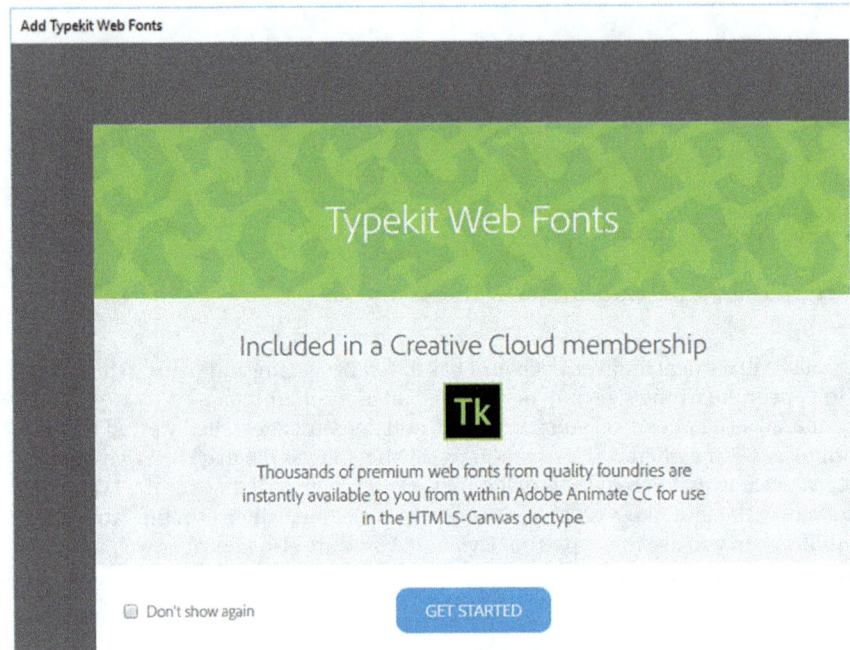

Figure 23-34. *Set up for Adobe Fonts Typekit web fonts*

Click Get Started to start viewing fonts.

The HTML/JavaScript Content is linked to your Adobe Fonts Typekit Account. As you saw in Chapter 22, with the Publish Settings dialog box, you can link your domain's URL in the Web Fonts tab. Adobe Fonts Typekit is also used in Dreamweaver CC.

You can link and unlink fonts as you require them. For help on how to do this, refer to `https://helpx.adobe.com/animate/using/typekit-web-fonts.html`.

Google Fonts are another dynamic option. Like Adobe Fonts Typekit, you can link or unlink fonts as required. Refer to Figure 23-35.

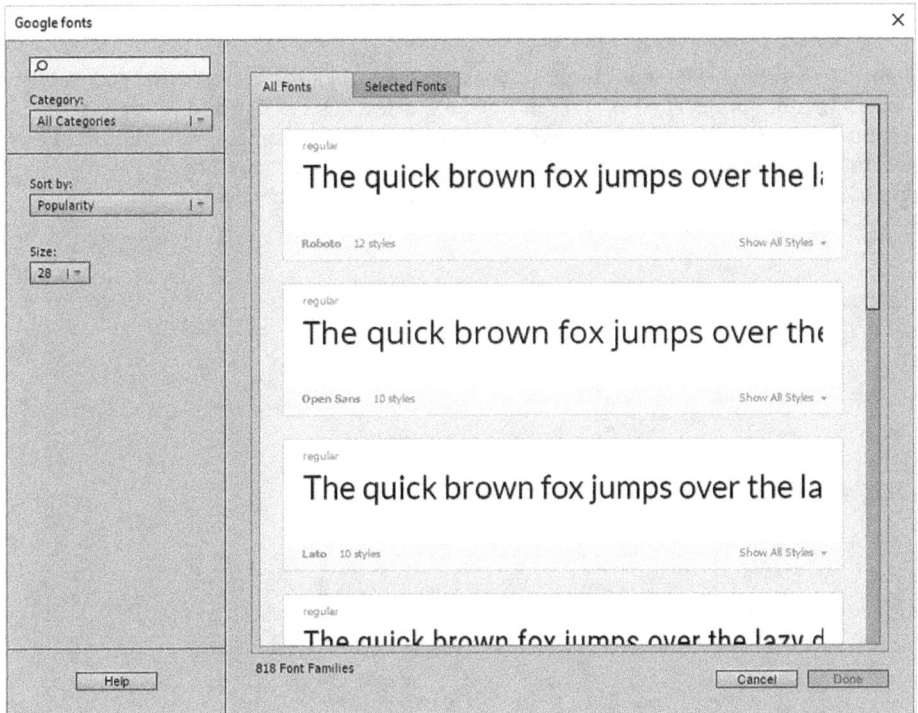

Figure 23-35. Google font options

For more information on Google fonts, visit https://helpx.adobe.com/animate/using/google-fonts.html.

The Dangers of Flashing Graphics

Animate CC, unfortunately, does not have a section on color blindness to view proofs of your animation. Alternatively, you could bring screenshots of selected frames into Photoshop CC to check how people with color blindness will interpret your animation.

There is another important mater that you need to consider when you are creating animations with frames and moving items: *the dangers of flashing graphics*. An animated graphic that pulsates on the screen can affect the vision and brain of the viewer. Some people have photosensitive epilepsy (PSE), which causes them to have seizures that are triggered by visual stimuli that form patterns in time or space, such as flashing lights and bold or regular fast pulsating moving patterns.

So as a web designer, you should be aware of this and avoid adding large areas of an animation that flash more than three times in any one second. For more information and the latest criteria, visit https://en.wikipedia.org/wiki/Photosensitive_epilepsy.

CHAPTER 23 ■ OTHER MISCELLANEOUS ITEMS IN ANIMATE THAT YOU CAN USE FOR WEB DESIGN

Summary

In this chapter, you looked at a few miscellaneous tools, such as brushes, 3D, and web fonts that you can use within Animate for your animation projects. Also, you saw how to create a basic action and where to find commands. You discovered that not everyone sees or experiences graphics the same way as you do, and as a designer, it is your responsibility to make your animations an enjoyable experience to watch.

In the last chapter of Part 4, you are going to put the knowledge that you learned in Animate into practice and create three projects that will be part of the Hot Glass Tango website.

CHAPTER 24

Putting It into Practice with Animate CC

In this chapter, you review how to export animations (GIF and HTML5 Canvas) and video clips for a website.

> **Note** This chapter has actual projects that are in three folders. You can use the files in the Chapter 24 folder if you do not have any file examples of your own to practice opening and viewing for this lesson. They are at https://github.com/Apress/graphics-multimedia-web-adobe-creative-cloud.

In this chapter, you will export animations for the Hot Glass Tango website, which tells the story (through images, animations, video, and audio) of how handmade glass items are created. Later, these multimedia items that you create will be used to finish the final website in Part 6.

Create an Animated GIF

In Chapters 6 and 9, where you were working in Photoshop to create a GIF animation, you used the Timeline panel with frames. As you saw in Chapter 22, Photoshop is not the only software that you can use to create these types of animations in a Timeline panel.

It really all depends on the workflow that you are presented with and how the images for the animation were acquired. For example, if you have a lot of photographs and are comfortable with Photoshop, you probably want to create the GIF Animation in that program. However, if you have a lot of illustrations from Illustrator, or have created the animation in Animate, then you likely would not want to import all your work back into Photoshop just to create an animate GIF.

One benefit is the Animate timeline, in which you have greater control over your shape and symbol movements. A drawback with Animate GIF animation is that sometimes the resolution is not as good as you get with exporting with Photoshop; if your animation has a lot of color photos, graphics, and gradients, you need to take a bit more time to adjust the settings in the Export Animated GIF dialog box to get the best quality.

In the Gif_Animation folder, you will find the original graphic—gif_images.ai, some completed GIF animation files, and the working gif_animation.fla file. Open the FLA file. Refer to Figure 24-1.

CHAPTER 24 ■ PUTTING IT INTO PRACTICE WITH ANIMATE CC

Figure 24-1. *The animation on the stage in the animate FLA file*

It is very similar to the paperweight graphic animation that you created in Photoshop in Chapter 6. The stage is currently 200×200 pixels.

However, this time, I used the Animate Timeline panel to create the object cooling effect. The Timeline panel uses a Classic tween and a Motion tween with two layers, and the duration lasts for about 4 seconds. Refer to Figure 24-2.

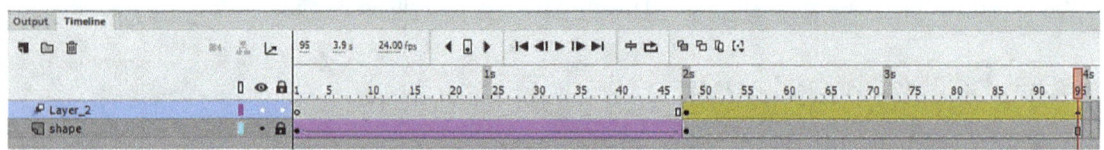

Figure 24-2. *The timeline for the GIF animation*

This time, all the images are converted to symbols and are stored in the Library panel as either movie clip symbols or graphic symbols, as seen to Figure 24-3.

CHAPTER 24 ■ PUTTING IT INTO PRACTICE WITH ANIMATE CC

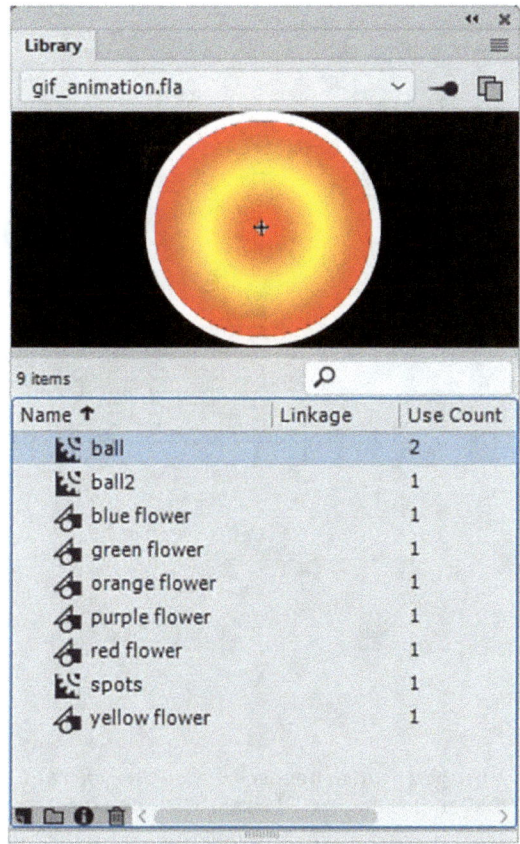

Figure 24-3. Symbols for the GIF animation are stored in the library

Because the flowers do not make a lot of movement, I left them as graphic symbols, but I could have made them all into movie clip symbols if I wanted to. I made sure not to have any nested animations in the symbols because they will not function correctly when I export an animated GIF. All animation is on the stage of the HTML5 Canvas FLA file.

Once you have reviewed the animation with the playhead, you can now Export the File.

Export your GIF Animation

Go to File ➤ Export ➤ Export Animated GIF. This opens the Export Image dialog box, but only for the animated GIF options. Refer to Figure 24-4.

CHAPTER 24 ■ PUTTING IT INTO PRACTICE WITH ANIMATE CC

Figure 24-4. *The animated GIF in the Export Image dialog box*

Currently, the default is a transparent background; however, you want to uncheck that so that you can keep the black area of the stage. Figure 24-5 is a close-up of the settings that I used for the GIF animation.

CHAPTER 24 ■ PUTTING IT INTO PRACTICE WITH ANIMATE CC

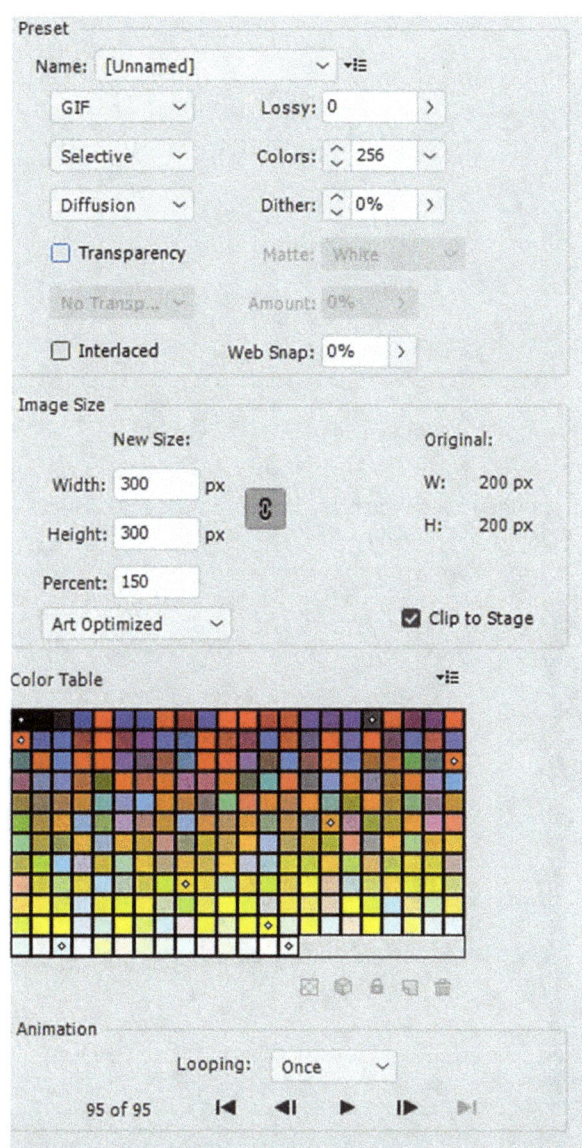

Figure 24-5. *The settings used for the GIF animation in the Export Image dialog box*

The following are the settings:

- GIF   Lossy: 0
- Selective
- Colors: 256
- Diffusion
- Dither: 0%
- Transparency: uncheck
- Interlaced: uncheck
- Web Snap: 0%
- Image Size: I increased the size to 300×300 px, or 150%, but you can leave at 200×200 px if you prefer the original size.

I chose Art Optimized and Clip to Stage because I wanted to keep the black background visible. Then I set the Animation looping to Once, and previewed it. Refer to Figure 24-6.

Figure 24-6. *The GIF animation preview*

Animate creates a more banned effect with its GIF animation when it comes to gradients; however, I find that this gives almost an effect like heat rising and rippling as the object cools: in this case, that is OK for me. If you want a less banned effect, you may have to create more subtle gradients or use solid colors. When done, click Save at the bottom of the dialog box, as seen in Figure 24-7.

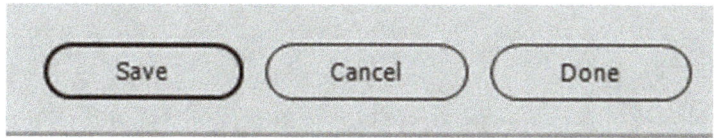

Figure 24-7. *Click Save to save your GIF animation*

Name it animation gif_animation_300.gif so that you know you increased the size of the animation to 300 pixels, as seen in Figure 24-8.

Figure 24-8. *Save a your GIF animation in your folder*

Save your new file in your Images folder or to the location of your choice, and then exit the Image Export dialog box. Close gif_animation.fla without saving any changes. You have now completed the first project. Next, you will create some video.

Create a Video (.mov) File

In Chapters 7 and 9, you looked at in Photoshop how to work with the Timeline panel to create and render your video for Hot Glass Tango. You may have noticed that several of the animated introduction clips and the closing credits were not created in Photoshop but imported as MP4 files into Photoshop later. That is because they were animated in Adobe Animate and then exported as video or MOV directly into Adobe Media Encoder, which you look at in Part 5. Animate uses this two-step process to preserve the original quality of the animation, should you want to use it for other non-web related projects in another program like Adobe Premiere Pro. However, for this book your goal is to create an MP4 file for the web or to use later in Photoshop to keep the file size small for rendering.

Open the Animated_movie_scenes folder, in which you will find eight ActionScript 3.0 FLA files. The reason that I used ActionScript 3.0 rather than HTML5 Canvas FLA is because I wanted to have all panel and tool options available to me so that I could create the video with no graphic restrictions. I already have the MOV created, should you want to compare what you do in this lesson to my settings. In Part 5, you look at the MP4 creation step.

The following are the ActionScript 3.0 FLA files:

- scene1_man_zoom_out_r2.fla
- scene1_man_movement.fla
- scene2_3_flame.fla
- scene4_5_swing.fla
- scene6_end.fa
- scene6_end_fade.fla
- scene7_credit.fla
- scene7_credit_fade.fla

The reason that I ordered the files in this manner was to keep a mental checklist of the order that I was planning for my storyboard for the video. The intro (scenes 1–6) and the end credits (scene 7) are like mini movies. They are only the last a few seconds, but they set and close the scenes for the entire Hot Glass Tango story.

Creating a Storyboard

If you're planning a lot of scenes for an animation, it's a clever idea to create a storyboard or a quick sketch so that you know what each scene is about. I usually start creating my scene with pencil and paper, and then I can scan my drawings into the computer and use Illustrator to draw the parts of the character or background. I usually review the stills at this point in Illustrator, and once the drawings are refined, I copy and paste the pieces or objects into an Animate file onto the stage. Then I convert them to symbols and begin the animation process. Refer to Figures 24-9 and 24-10 to see how the scenes could be part of a storyboard.

CHAPTER 24 ■ PUTTING IT INTO PRACTICE WITH ANIMATE CC

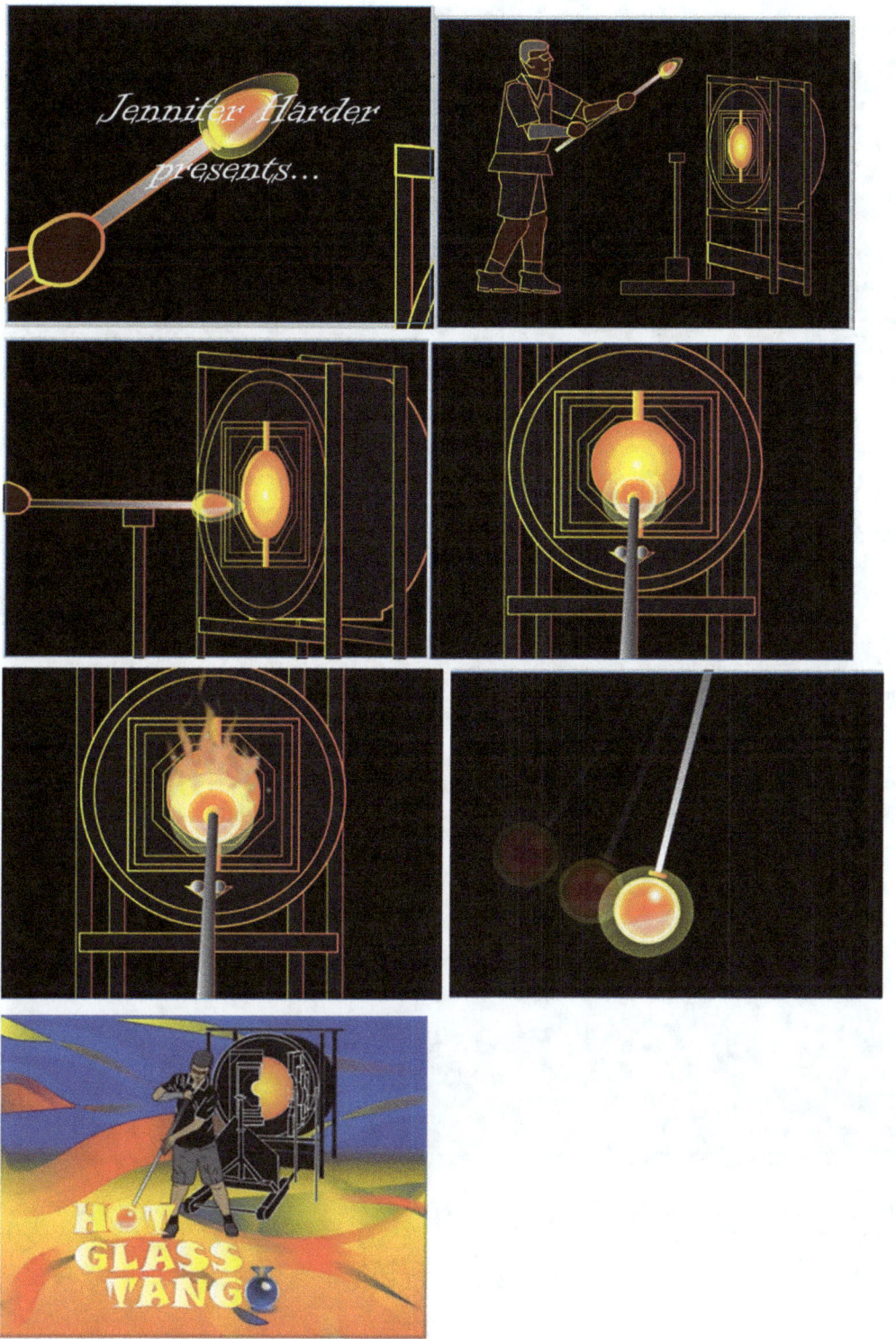

Figure 24-9. *Important scene changes that are part of the storyboard for the introduction*

CHAPTER 24 ■ PUTTING IT INTO PRACTICE WITH ANIMATE CC

Figure 24-10. Important scene changes that could be part of the storyboard for end credits

Pre-Plan Your Video Settings

Upon starting the animation, I made sure to match the frame rate (30 fps) and dimensions (e.g., 640×480) of the camera video footage that will be part of the full video in Photoshop.

Depending on the length of your project, animation takes time and a lot of pre-planning, sometimes even more that it takes to shoot video with a camera. If you are working with a team, make sure to take time to review the stills such as background and character colors with your group, because once your characters are animated, it takes time to undo or re-create long scenes that need to be reworked at the last moment before rendering your video.

Reviewing the Files

You can open my FLA files and take a moment to look at the stage, the timelines, and the Library panels to review the symbols and layers (camera, tweens, and armatures) that are used to create scenes. Refer to Figure 24-11.

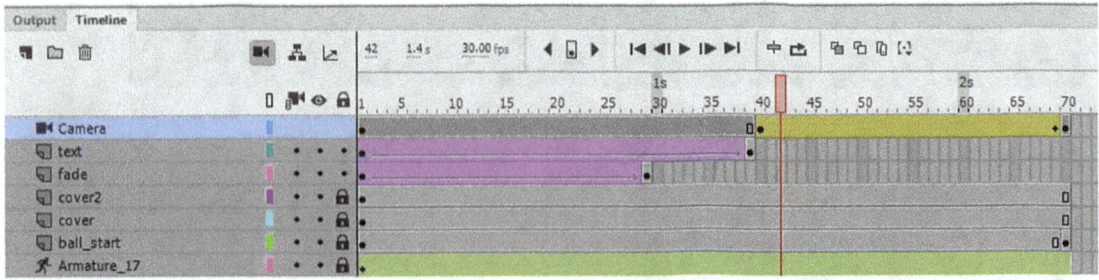

Figure 24-11. Example of how the timeline appears for one of scenes that contains camera angles a tweens and an armature for the main character

606

> **Note** I did not add any audio to these files because I planned to add that in Photoshop so that I could spread it over all the scenes, including the video footage with no major breaks. So, my files will render without sound. However, for your own projects, feel free to add audio sound effects and voices because they will be rendered as part of the video (.mov).

For this lesson, keep open the scene1_man_zoom_out_r2.fla file.

You can repeat the process that I show you with the other FLA files if you like afterward, since the steps are identical and you may want to practice this on your own a few times, if you don't have a project to work with.

> **Note** In Chapter 9, when you rendered the Photoshop video in MP4 files can be quite large. In this case, the largest (.mov) of the eight is about 75 MB. Depending on your computer's hard drive space, if you have longer animations that you plan to render, and you think the MOV will be over 500 MB, I recommend rendering them on an external drive (as you were instructed in Chapter 9) to avoid your program or computer crashing. However, my files are quite small so if you don't want to put these files on an external drive, it should be OK because you are only rendering one file at a time, and not collectively.

Exporting the Video

Go to File ➤ Export ➤ Export Video. Refer to Figure 24-12.

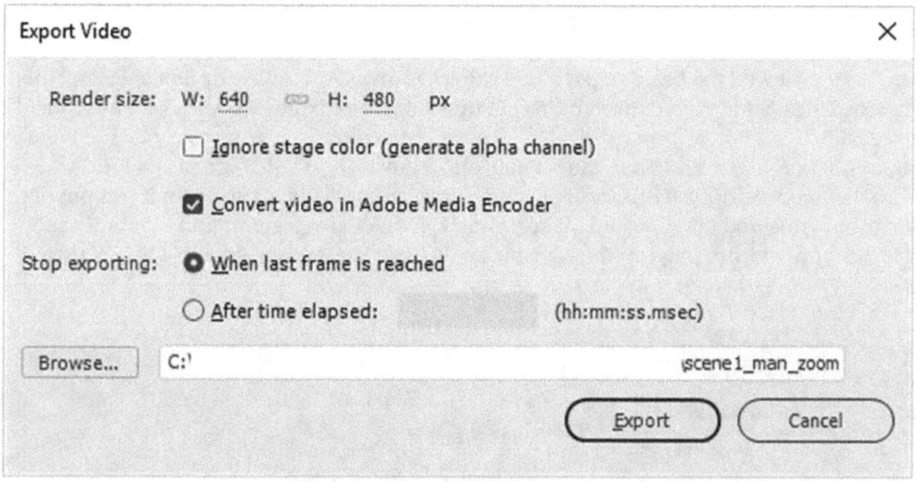

Figure 24-12. The Export Video dialog box

As in Chapter 22, make sure that Ignore Stage Color (generate alpha channel) is unchecked, and that Convert Video in Adobe Media Encoder is checked.

Choose Stop exporting ➤ When last frame is reached, and then browse for a location to save your file. In this case, create your own folder in a different location so that you do not override my files.

Or give the exported file a new name, such as scene1_man_zoom_out_final.mov.

Click the Export button.

Opening in Adobe Media Encoder

At this point, do not move on exporting the next FLA file yet, but let Adobe Media Encoder open. The MOV file is added to the Queue panel in Media Encoder. Refer to Figure 24-13.

Figure 24-13. Media Encoder opens and adds your file to the Queue panel

Do not do anything in Media Encoder yet because you deal with this next step in Part 5. Go back to Animate and export another FLA file to video; each time you do, this file is added to the Media Encoder Queue panel. When you are done, close your FLA file and then close Media Encoder. Media Encoder stores or remembers the linked names of the files in the Queue panel until you are ready to do the final rendering to an MP4 (H.264) format.

You have completed the second project. Now let's move to the final project, where you create an HTML5 Canvas animation for the website.

Create an HTML5 Canvas Animation

In Chapter 22, Option 6 you reviewed the basic steps to Exporting a Canvas Animation by first checking the File ➤ Publish Settings and the clicking the Publish button in the dialog box. Now let's work with a file for the Hot Glass Tango website.

Go to the canvas_animation folder and open the scene6_end_canvasan_HTML5_Canas.fla file. I converted this file from the ActionScript 3.0 FLA, scene6_end_canvasan.fla. This is a scene that was out of the original movie intro, but I decided that it would make a good HTML5 Canvas animation to modify and add sound to for my index.html or intro page on the website. So, I chose File ➤ Convert to HTML5 Canvas. Refer to Figure 24-14.

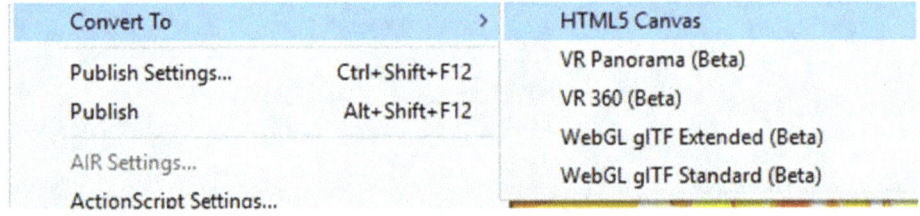

Figure 24-14. Convert your ActionScript 3.0 FLA to an HTML5 Canvas

I saved the file to scene6_end_canvasan_HTML5_Canas.fla, which is the file you should have open in Animate.

Take some time to review the file; you will notice that it has a sound layer and sound in the Library panel. Refer to Figures 24-15 and 24-16.

CHAPTER 24 ■ PUTTING IT INTO PRACTICE WITH ANIMATE CC

Figure 24-15. *The Hot Glass Tango HTML5 Canvas animation*

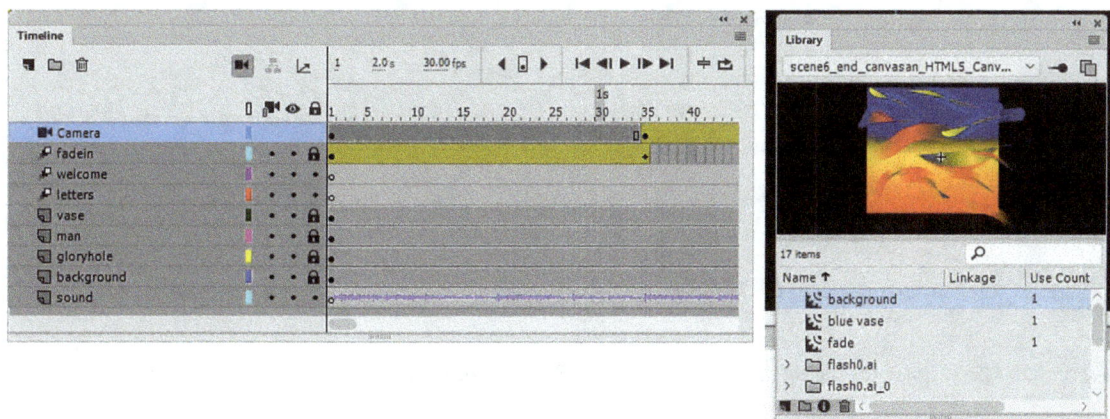

Figure 24-16. *How the Animation appears in the Timeline and Library panels with sound*

In Chapter 20, when you imported audio. You don't have a lot of control of the duration or volume that the audio plays at in an HTML5 Canvas file. The sound keeps on playing even if the animation has reached its conclusion. Unlike with video, only when the sound file has reached its conclusion will it stop. In some cases, this might be OK for your intro page, if you want some quiet music playing while the user decides which page to navigate to next. In most cases, make sure that the sound does not run more than 30 seconds to a minute after the animation has stopped, or this could become tedious and annoy the viewer. They might leave the page and not continue to the rest of the website. So, run some tests to determine the sound duration, and then clip it in Adobe Audition CC or Media Encoder CC to the appropriate length.

609

Publish HTML5 Canvas and OAM File

With your file open, go to File ➤ Publish Settings and use the Default settings. In the Publish Settings dialog box, go to the Basic tab and make sure that Publish JavaScript/HTML is checked. Refer to Figure 24-17.

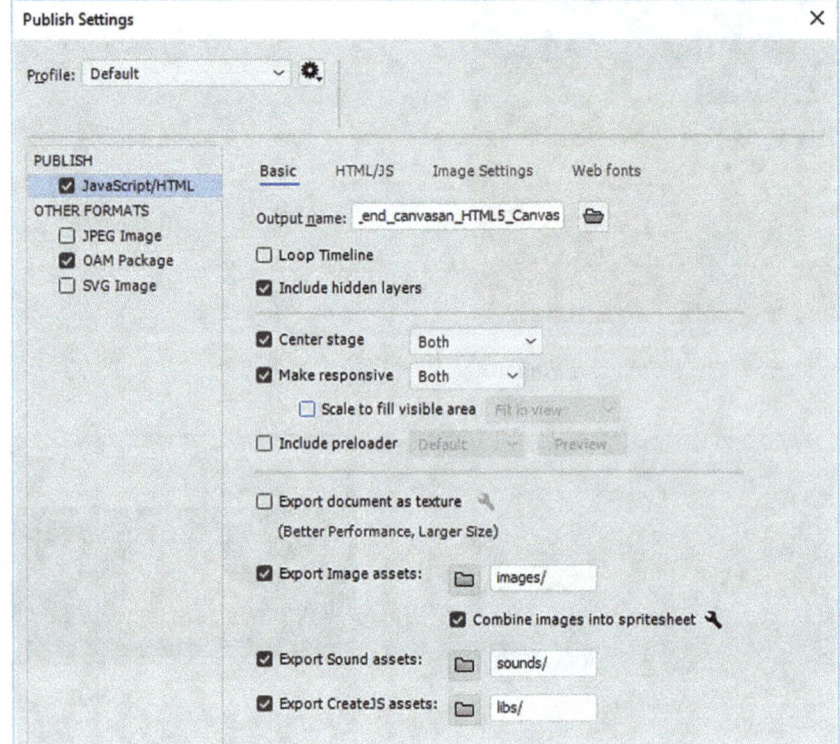

Figure 24-17. Settings for the Basic tab in the Publish Settings dialog box

Make sure to browse an output name and location for the file to output so that you do not overwrite my files in case you need to compare them later. Uncheck the Loop Timeline box so that the animation and sound will only play once.

- **Center stage:** Check the box and choose the Both setting (in some projects, you may want to leave this uncheck if the animation will not be at the center of the stage).
- **Make responsive:** Check the box and the Both setting for your responsive site.
- **Scale to fill visible area:** Keep the box unchecked.
- **Include preloader:** Keep the box unchecked.

Make sure that the Image, Sound, and CreateJS export settings are checked and have the same folder, as seen in Figure 24-17. Alternatively, you can try "export document as texture", but I found this made the gradients too raster so I left it unchecked.

You do not need to adjust any of the other tab settings for JavaScript/HTML in this project.

Next, check OAM Package under OTHER FORMATS. Select it so that you can see its options. Refer to Figure 24-18.

CHAPTER 24 ■ PUTTING IT INTO PRACTICE WITH ANIMATE CC

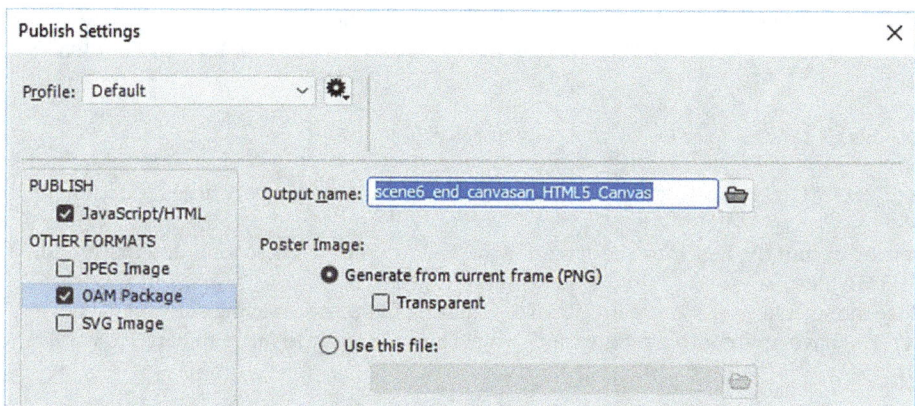

Figure 24-18. *OAM Package settings in the Publish settings dialog box*

Browse where the OAM file will output under. The Output name and location for the OAM and Canvas files should remain the same for now.

Under poster image, choose to generate from current frame a PNG file and transparent should remain in checked. In this case, you should have the playhead on the last frame in the Timeline panel. If you do not, click OK to exit the Publish Settings dialog box to correct this. Refer to Figure 24-19.

Figure 24-19. *Click OK to save and exit without publishing, or Publish and create the HTML5 Canvas and OAM package*

Then drag the playhead to the last frame in the Timeline panel and choose File ➤ Publish Settings. Refer to Figure 24-20.

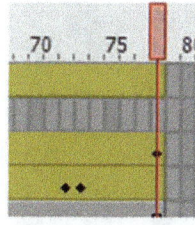

Figure 24-20. *Drag your playhead in the Timeline panel to the final frame if you want it to be the poster image in the OAM package*

If some settings in the basic tab change, make sure to reset it, as seen in Figure 24-17, and then click Publish to publish the HTML5 Canvas and its related OAM package, which you will insert later on the index.html web page for the Hot Glass Tango website.

611

CHAPTER 24 ▪ PUTTING IT INTO PRACTICE WITH ANIMATE CC

The Output panel may give a warning regarding colors if Animate cannot accurately reproduce the gradients because of the type of graphics that were imported Illustrator; but you can ignore the warning for this file.

```
Only circular (not oval) radial gradients are supported. (7)
```

If you compare this HTML5 Canvas scene to the video version, you will notice very little reduction in gradient quality.

In the folder that you output the files into, there is an OAM file, a sounds folder containing the sound, and external JS and HTML files.

You can now close the scene6_end_canvasan_HTML5_Canas.fla file without saving changes (File ➤ Exit Animate). You have now completed the third project and are ready to move to Part 5 to work with Media Encoder.

Summary

In this chapter, you reviewed how to create animations for webpages and video clips for the Hot Glass Tango website. This chapter concludes your study of Animate CC. Make sure to review any areas of Part 4 that you don't understand so that you feel comfortable working with your own graphics in Animate.

In Part 5, you journey to the next junction point in the software maze: Adobe Media Encoder CC. You'll discover how it can be used to create and export audio and video files.

PART V

Working with Media Encoder to Create Audio and Video Files

CHAPTER 25

Getting Started with Media Encoder

Getting Started

In Part 4, as you traveled through the symbolic maze, you worked with Animate to create graphics, video, and animation for the web. Now you are going to travel to the fourth and final junction point: Adobe Media Encoder CC. Here you discover how to export video and web graphics that are ready for your website when you reach Dreamweaver in Part 6. Refer to Figure 25-1 so that you can see where you are in the maze.

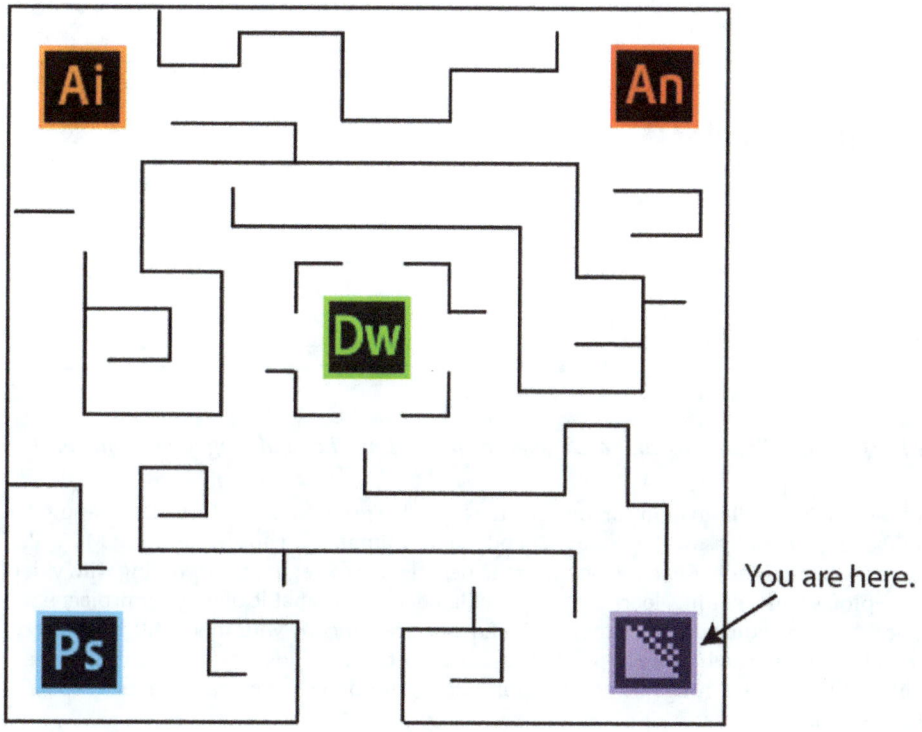

Figure 25-1. *In Part 5, you work with Adobe Media Encoder*

CHAPTER 25 ■ GETTING STARTED WITH MEDIA ENCODER

■ **Note** This chapter does not have any actual projects; however, you can use the files in the Chapter 25 folder to practice opening and viewing for this lesson. They are found at https://github.com/Apress/graphics-multimedia-web-adobe-creative-cloud.

Media Encoder CC is a program in the Adobe Creative Cloud collection that is often overlooked when designing audio and video artwork for the web. When I think of video rendering programs, the following five come to mind: Premiere Pro, Premiere Rush, After Effects, Character Animator, and Prelude. Refer to Figure 25-2.

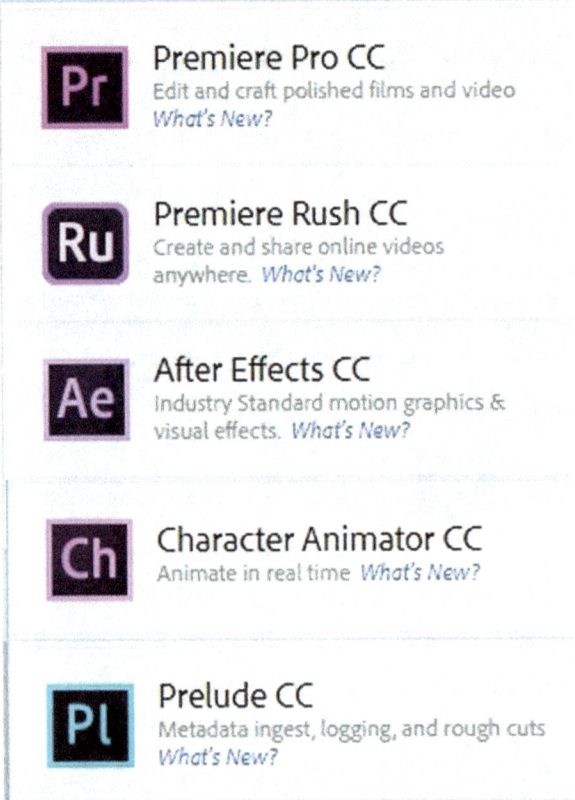

Figure 25-2. These five Creative Cloud programs are often used in creating and rendering professional video

However, as you saw in Part 2, Photoshop can be used to render basic video with effects that are suitable for a website. And in Part 4, you briefly saw that Media Encoder and Animate CC can also render a MOV file that you can work with further in Media Encoder. So, from the perspective of beginner in working with video, if you have never done professional editing, learning what Media Encoder is capable of for your project is a good place to start. Besides basic edits to your video, Media Encoder can encode your media file in a variety of formats that your audience can watch on multiple devices. In addition, if you just need to separate some audio from a video file, rather than learning how to do this in Adobe Audition CC, you can do this it Media Encoder. Refer to Figure 25-3.

616

CHAPTER 25 ■ GETTING STARTED WITH MEDIA ENCODER

Figure 25-3. *Audition can be used to assist you in working with audio files*

As you can see in the diagram shown in Figure 25-4, once the Animate video is rendered in Media Encoder, it can be used in a program like Dreamweaver for your website (you look at that in Part 6).

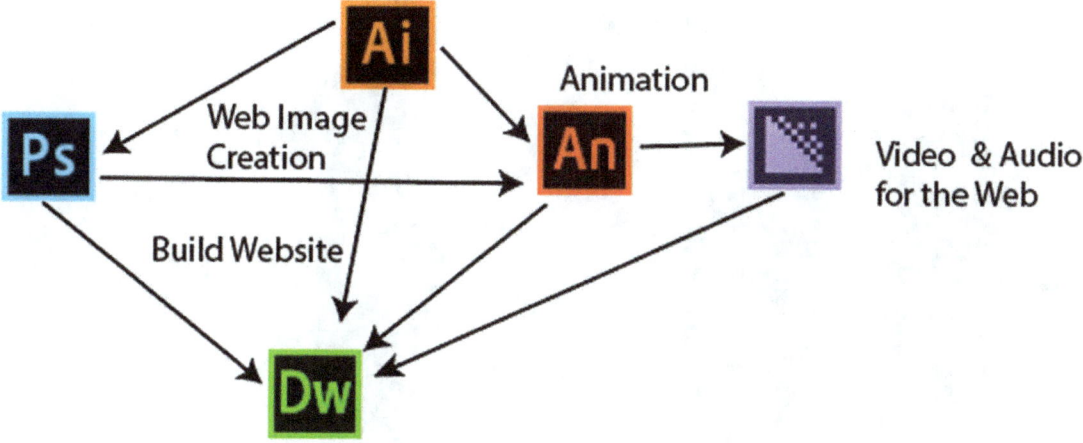

Figure 25-4. *Files rendered from Media Encoder are used in your website*

If you have never used Media Encoder before, it is not a difficult program to use. Unfortunately, since there is not a "Classroom in a Book" for beginners to this software, I recommend reading resources, such as the Adobe Help section (https://helpx.adobe.com/media-encoder/using/whats-new.html), as an overview of the program and many of its tools.

In Part 5, you are working with videos that have already been created and then saving them for the web in various formats. Refer to Figure 25-5 to see what sort of file formats you are working with throughout Part 5.

617

CHAPTER 25 ■ GETTING STARTED WITH MEDIA ENCODER

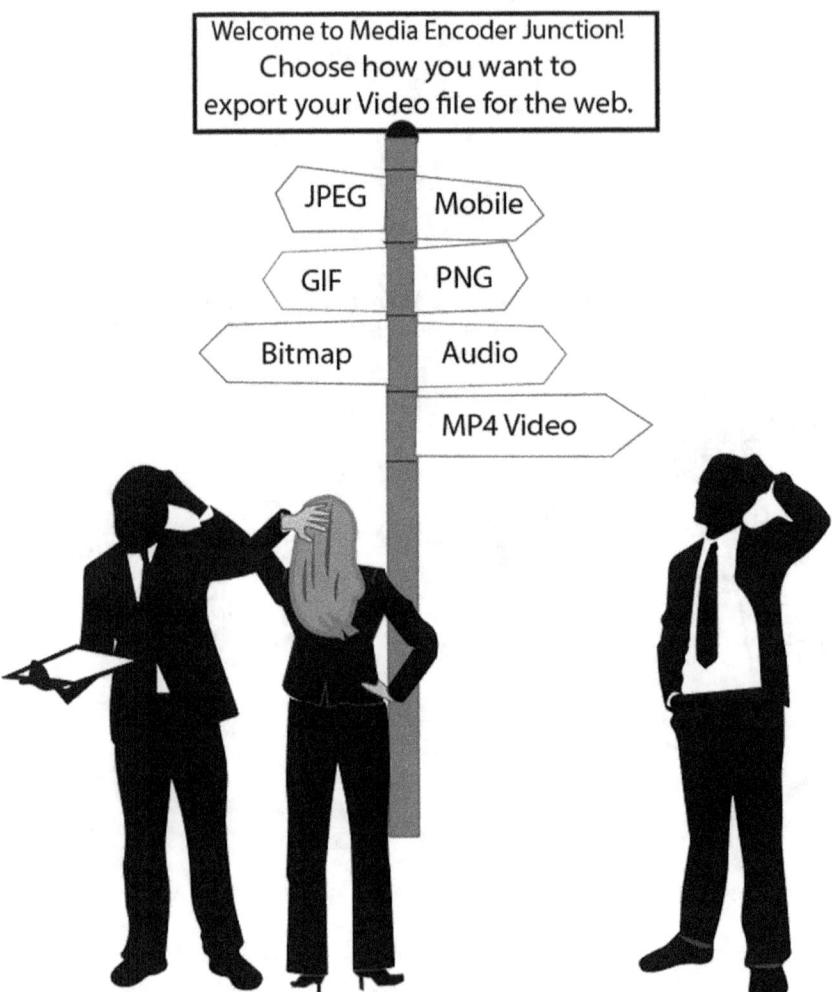

Figure 25-5. *As with other Adobe Creative Cloud programs, there are several web file formats that you can export to*

Let's begin by opening Media Encoder CC. If you do not have it on your computer, but you do have the Creative Cloud console, click the Install button (see Figure 25-6) and follow the instructions on how to install the program.

CHAPTER 25 ■ GETTING STARTED WITH MEDIA ENCODER

Figure 25-6. Click the Install button beside your Media Encoder icon if the program is not already installed

In older versions of Creative Cloud, Media Encoder automatically installs along with Flash (now Animate CC); however, since you can use Media Encoder with several other programs, Adobe now regards it as a separate program, so you can choose whether to install it now or later. If you are working with Animate or Photoshop, however, I recommend that you install it at the same time as these programs.

■ **Note** Before you install an Adobe program, make sure that your computer meets the system requirement; otherwise, the install may fail. For more information, check `https://helpx.adobe.com/media-encoder/system-requirements.html`.

Also, if you plan to render large files, make sure to have an external drive to render onto so that you do not crash your computer during the rendering.

If you already have Media Encoder CC installed on your computer, double-click the icon, or from the Creative Cloud console, click Open to launch the program, as seen in Figure 25-7.

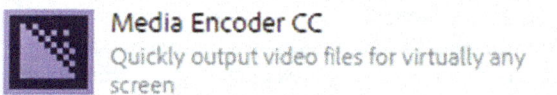 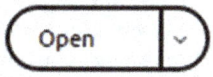

Figure 25-7. Open Media Encoder CC so that you can start working in the program

I am using the 2018 and 2019 version.

Upon opening Media Encoder CC, you find that its layout is very different than what you have encountered so far in Photoshop CC, Illustrator CC, and Animate CC. The workspace has been separated into four sections or panels, and there does not appear to be any Tools panel. So, you might be wondering how you should work with this layout to output video. Refer to Figure 25-8.

CHAPTER 25 ■ GETTING STARTED WITH MEDIA ENCODER

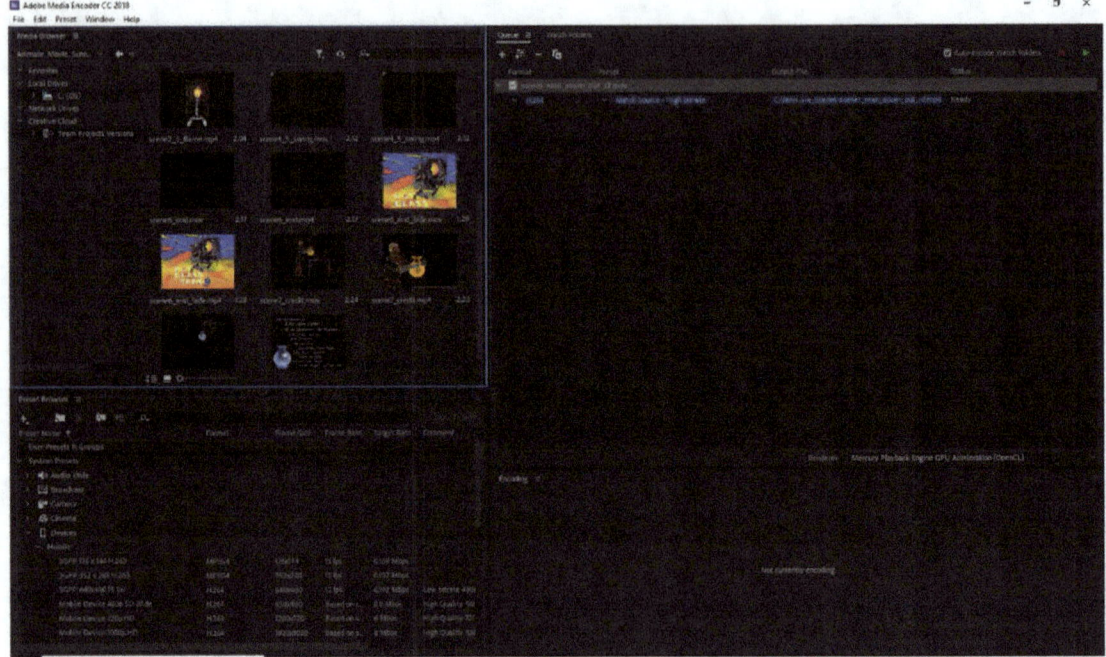

Figure 25-8. Inside the Adobe Media Encoder CC program

Looking at the Setup of Media Encoder CC and Queue

When you exported a video from Animate CC in Chapter 24, recall that there was a setting in the Convert the Video in Media Encoder dialog box. When the Export button was clicked, Media Encoder opened and the MOV file was in the Queue panel, so that you could adjust the setting for an MP4 (H.246) file format. Refer to Figure 25-9.

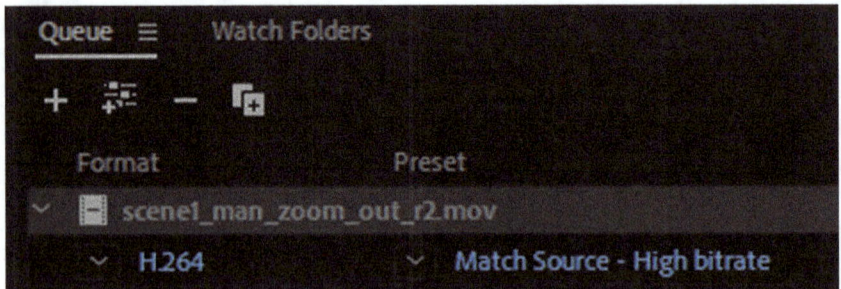

Figure 25-9. The MOV file was added to the Queue panel

You'll look at this panel in a moment, but first let's look at an overview of the entire program.

When you open Animate, there are no files or size options for creating a new file from scratch. You can only add files that are already created via File ➤ Add Source. This is kind of like File ➤ Open. Refer to Figure 25-10.

CHAPTER 25 ■ GETTING STARTED WITH MEDIA ENCODER

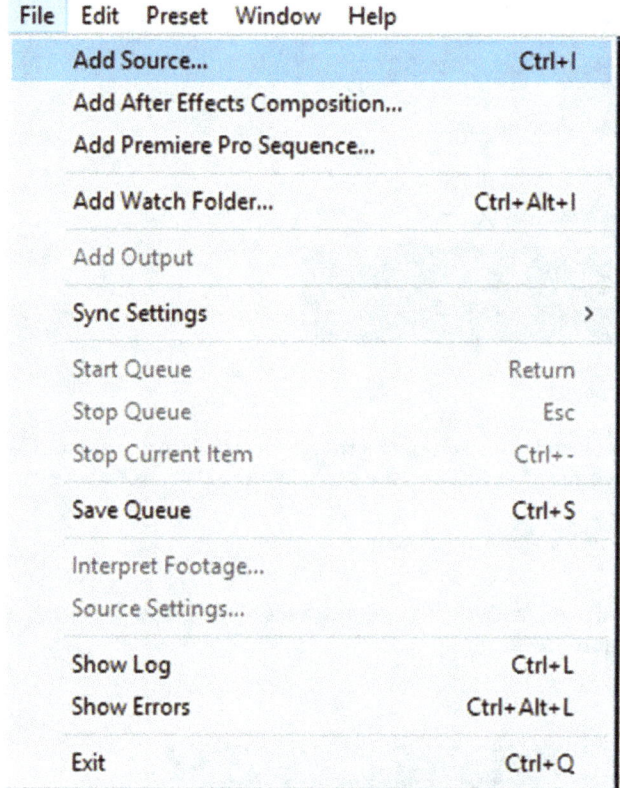

Figure 25-10. *The File drop-down menu*

If you had files that came from other Adobe programs, you could choose Add After Effects Composition or Add Premiere Pro Sequence. Any video from another source—Adobe program or not, you have to choose Add Source to add to the Queue panel.

Set up a Workspace

Unlike Photoshop, Illustrator, and Animate, there are no options for workspaces other than the default. This can be found in Workspaces ➤ Default Workspace. Refer to Figure 25-11.

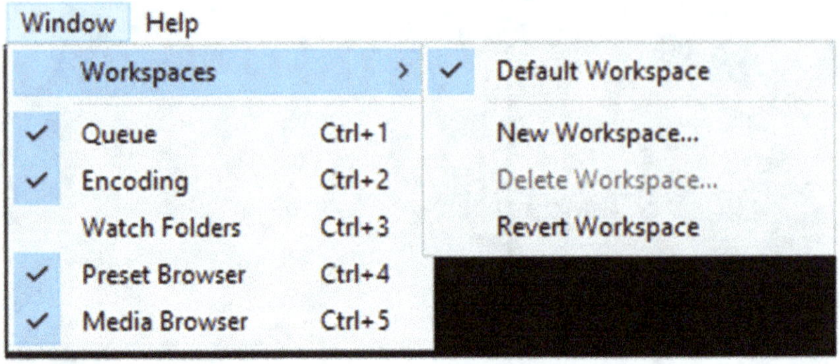

CHAPTER 25 ■ GETTING STARTED WITH MEDIA ENCODER

Figure 25-11. Choose a workspace or create your own

This may be because there are only five panels to work with. You can rearrange the panels in any order that works for your workflow and create a new workspace; however, for now, you stay with the default workspace.

Adjusting Your Preferences

If you do not like working in a black program layout, you can adjust the appearance of the program in the Edit ➤ Preferences Appearance tab, as seen in Figure 25-12.

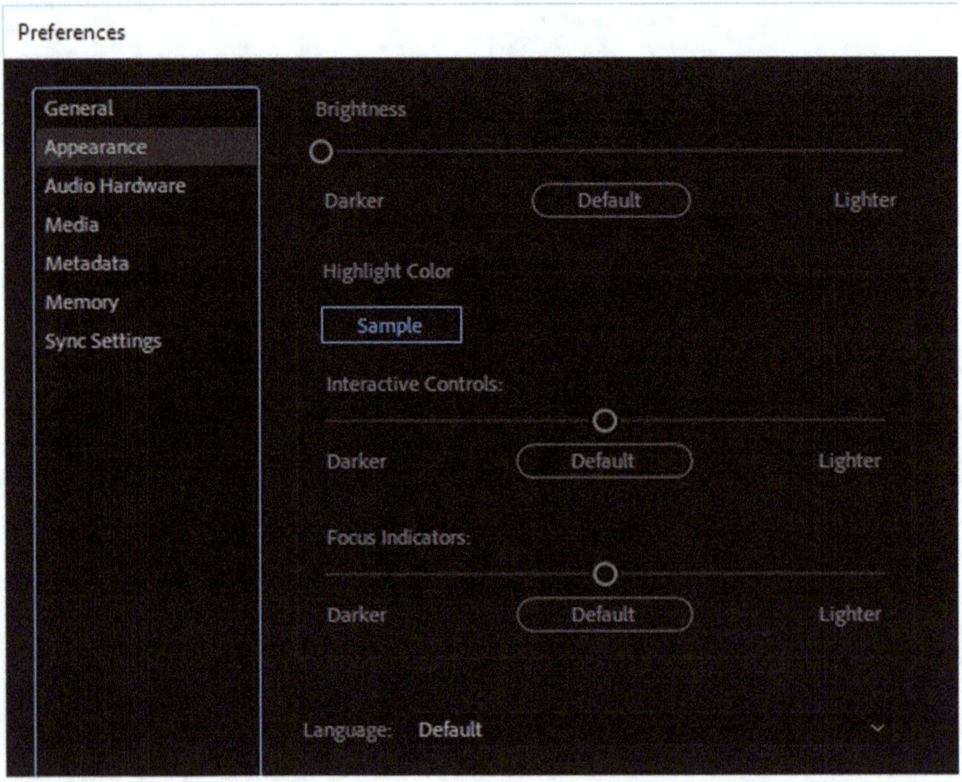

Figure 25-12. Setting the Appearance Preferences of the program

622

CHAPTER 25 ■ GETTING STARTED WITH MEDIA ENCODER

In the other Adobe programs, I prefer to work with a mid-gray background, but for video in Media Encoder, I prefer the brightness level to be set at darker. Feel free to adjust these settings while working on your projects; for now, just leave them at the default settings—including highlight color, interactive controls, focus indicators, and language—so that you can follow along.

Let's review the other tabs.

- **General**: Settings for the queue (how it handles the encoding and alerts you), importing Premiere Pro Files, output, video renderer and color management. The video rendering is the GPU engine that comes with your computer processor. On my computer, I use Mercury Playback Engine GPU Acceleration (Open CL); however, there may be a different one on your computer. Refer to Figure 25-13.

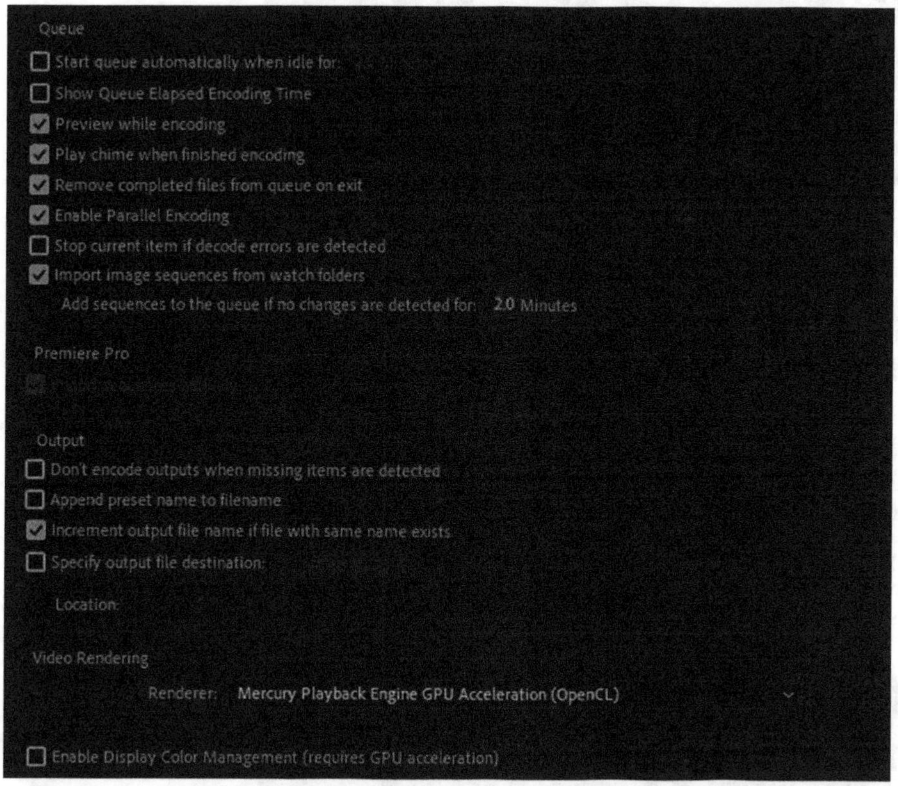

Figure 25-13. General tab settings

CHAPTER 25 ■ GETTING STARTED WITH MEDIA ENCODER

- **Audio Hardware**: Settings for the type of audio hardware that is being used. I am using Realtek Audio, which came with my computer, as the default output; but on your computer, it might be a different setting. Refer to Figure 25-14.

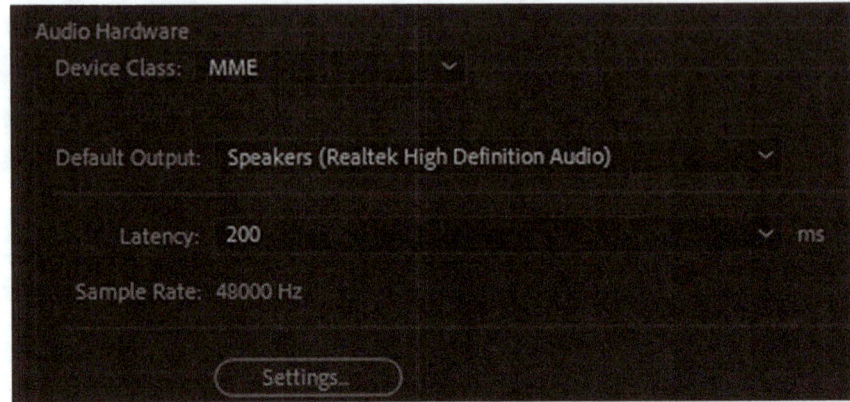

Figure 25-14. Audio Hardware tab settings

Sometimes your audio hardware settings or driver can affect whether you can extract audio out of certain video formats like AVI. Keep this in mind if you ever find that one of your imported video files does not extract the audio, and you are left with no sound after export.

- **Media**: Settings for media cache files and database, intermediate media timebase, captions on import, and accelerated decoding for H.264.
- **Metadata**: Writes a unique identifier to imported files that don't already contain one. Also, settings for source and output template metadata that was added to the file.
- **Memory**: You may have to adjust the RAM for programs such as After Effects, Premiere Pro, Prelude, Photoshop, SpeedGrade, or Audition; otherwise, leave at the default settings. Refer to Figure 25-15.

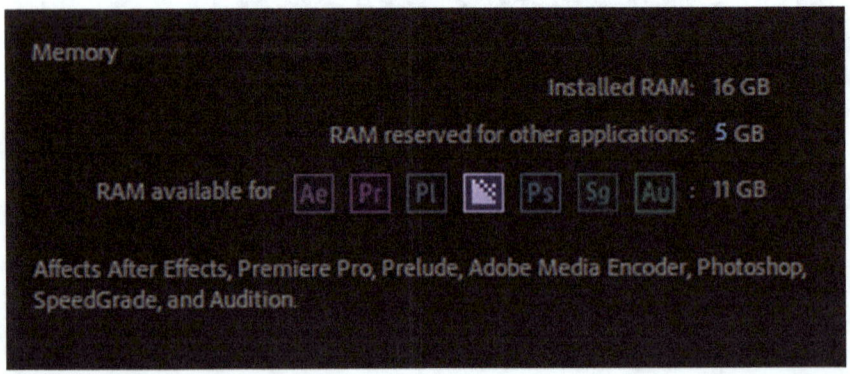

Figure 25-15. Memory tab settings

CHAPTER 25 ■ GETTING STARTED WITH MEDIA ENCODER

- **Sync Settings:** If certain settings must remain in sync or synchronized within the program, they can be enabled or disabled here. They can be synchronized across multiple machines. You can upload preferences related to your workspace layouts. Also, there are keyboard shortcuts and presets to your Creative Cloud account. These settings could be downloaded and uploaded to other machines within your company. Refer to Figure 25-16.

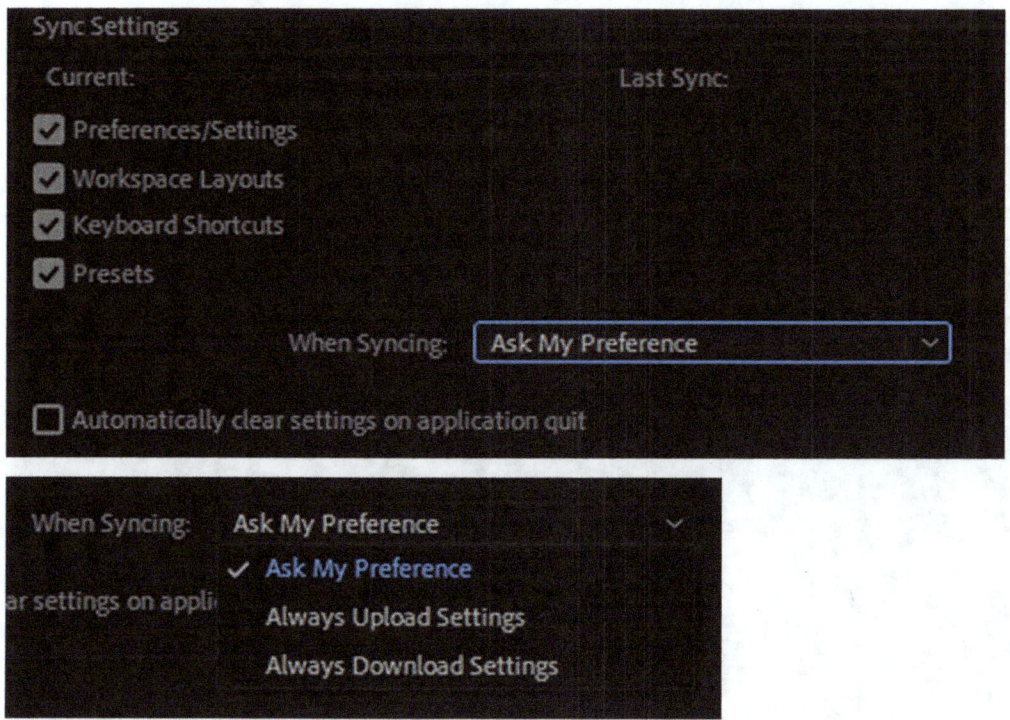

Figure 25-16. Sync Settings tab with settings

Sync Settings can be cleared when you quit the application.

When you are done reviewing the preferences, if you have made changes, click OK in the lower right of the Preferences dialog box; otherwise, click Cancel to leave the settings at the default. Refer to Figure 25-17.

Figure 25-17. Click OK or Cancel to exit the Preferences dialog box

Now let's look at each of the panels, moving clockwise within the default workspace.

625

Media Browser Panel

The Media Browser panel is much like choosing File ➤ Open or File ➤ Import as you would in Photoshop, Illustrator, or Animate. It allows you to preview the video and images that are within certain folders on your drive. As you navigate the media in your folders, you can easily select or drag-and-drop files into the Queue panel. Refer to Figure 25-18.

Figure 25-18. Inside the Media Browser panel

As with other panels, they possess menus that allow you to close, undock, or maximize panels if you need to move around. Refer to Figure 25-19.

CHAPTER 25 ■ GETTING STARTED WITH MEDIA ENCODER

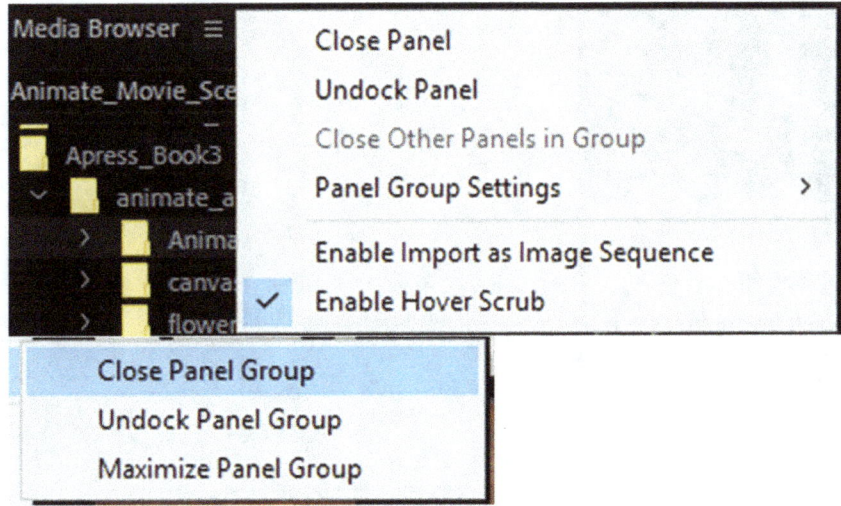

Figure 25-19. *Panel menu options*

Here you can look through various internal and external drives, including the Creative Cloud, and search for the folder that contains your media. If your media is several raster images (GIF, JPEG, or PNG), you can enable Import As Image Sequence. To revert panel settings, choose Window ➤ Workspaces ➤ Revert Workspace.

Clicking a video file in this panel lets you preview it. There is a hover scrub so that you can watch portions of the video when you hover over it or move the playhead when Enable Hover Scrub is checked (see Figures 25-19 and 25-20).

Figure 25-20. *Hover scrub allows you to preview the video before it is added to the Queue panel*

When you right-click the video, you can choose whether to import to the Queue panel, Stitch Clips Together (adds as group the queue), Add the Folder as a Watch Folder, Reveal in Explorer, or Add to Favorites. Refer to Figure 25-21.

627

CHAPTER 25 ■ GETTING STARTED WITH MEDIA ENCODER

Figure 25-21. Choose what you would like to do with the video before you import

The upper right area of the panel allows you to narrow the search of the files that you want to import into the queue. Refer to Figure 25-22.

Figure 25-22. Search options in the Media Browser panel

You can search by file type. Refer to Figure 25-23.

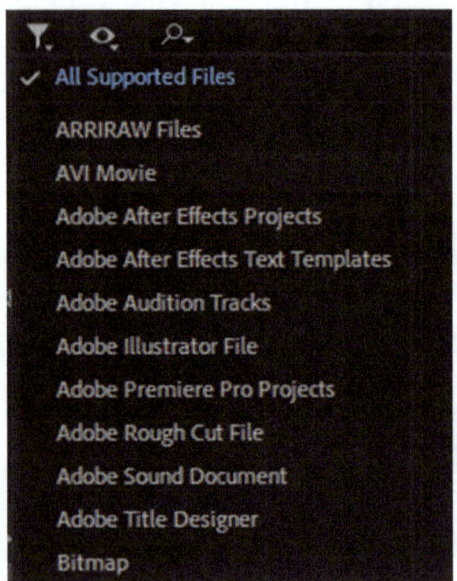

Figure 25-23. Search by file type. There are many more options than what are shown here.

CHAPTER 25 ■ GETTING STARTED WITH MEDIA ENCODER

By Directory viewers, depending upon your directory some of these locations may not be available to you. Refer to Figure 25-24.

Figure 25-24. *Search by directory viewers*

Enter the name of the file in the search text box. Refer to Figure 25-25.

Figure 25-25. *Search by name of file*

The lower half of the panel lets you alter your thumbnail view by image, list, or zoom. Refer to Figure 25-26.

Figure 25-26. *Navigate your files by thumbnail, list, or zooming in or out to see a better view*

629

Queue Panel

The Queue panel is where you set your export settings before you render and export. Refer to Figure 25-27.

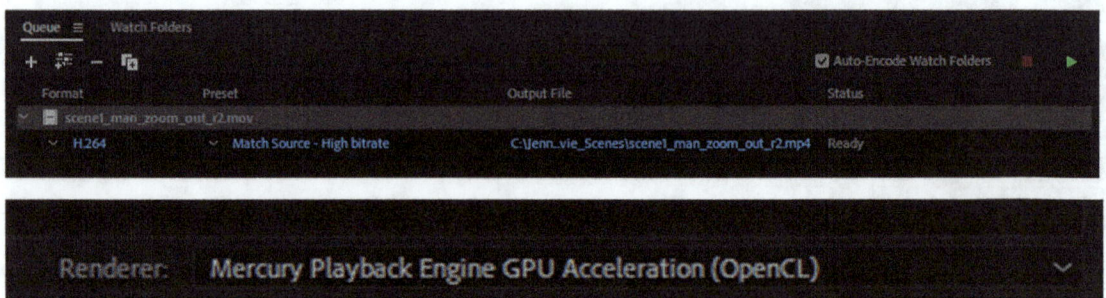

Figure 25-27. *The Queue panel lets you add all the files that you plan to export*

You can add media sources to the queue by using the plus (+) symbol and remove it using the minus (-) symbol, as seen in Figure 25-28.

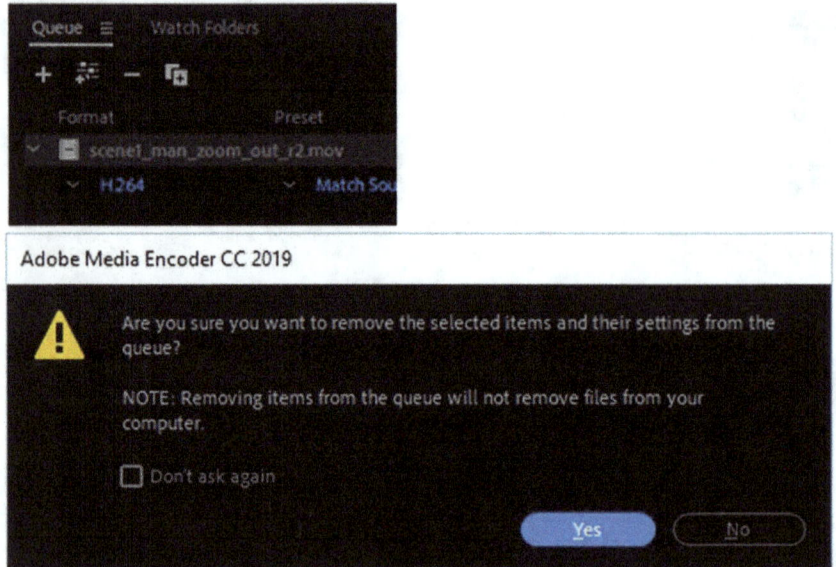

Figure 25-28. *The Queue panel adds or removes files from the queue*

CHAPTER 25 ■ GETTING STARTED WITH MEDIA ENCODER

When you click, yes this removes the file from the Queue panel it does not delete it from the drive. Choosing the No button in the alert leaves the file in the Queue.

When a file is selected, you can also use the Add Output icon (the second icon) to add output of the same file after the first or the Duplicate icon (the fourth icon) to add a duplicate of the presets for that file so that you can output the same file again in a different format. Refer to Figure 25-29.

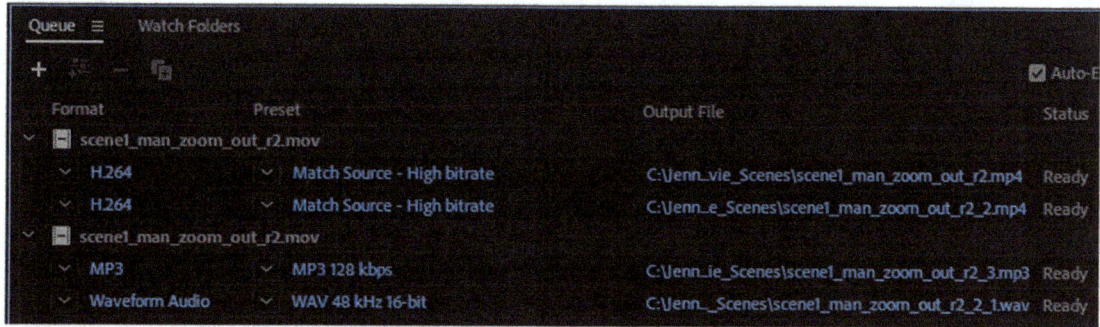

Figure 25-29. Adding various file settings to the Queue panel

Auto-Encode Watch Folders automatically encodes all watch folders from the Watch Folders panel, as seen in Figure 25-30.

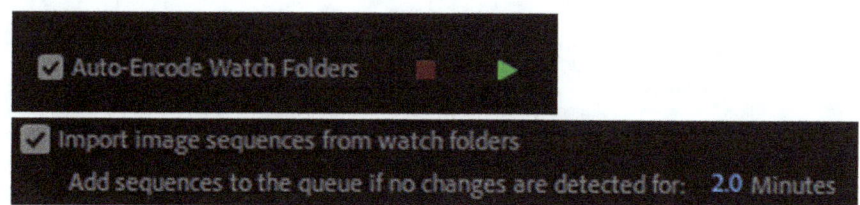

Figure 25-30. Audio-Encode Watch Folders setting: stop and start

A watch folder is a set folder that you can place media into, and Media Encoder detects these files after a few minutes, depending on what time detection preferences you set, and then adds them to the queue and automatically starts rendering. I explain how this speeds up your workflow in more detail shortly.

Next to the Auto-Encode check box you will see two more icons when you are ready to encode all files with the new format, preset and output folder file location, the green triangle Play button can be clicked. This begins the encoding and rendering export process of your imported file. If you realize that you made a mistake, press the red Stop button square to stop the process. Your video renderer is listed in the lower right of the panel (see Figure 25-27), and you can change it from the drop-down menu should you choose to. For now, leave it at whatever default the program is currently using for your computer.

631

Format Options

You look at the Format column in more detail later. It refers to files for the web and other video projects. You can change the format by clicking the drop-down menu next to the format name and choosing a new one from the list. Refer to Figure 25-31.

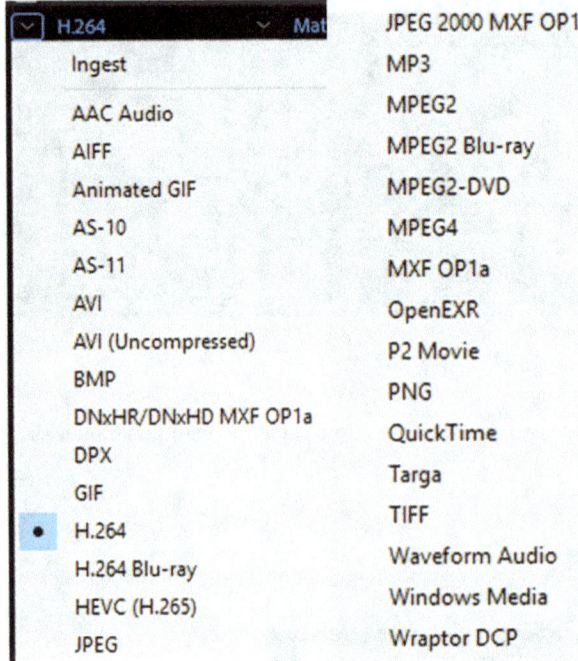

Figure 25-31. Options for the Format column in the Queue panel

When you click on the format name this opens the Export Settings dialog box. Refer to Figure 25-32.

CHAPTER 25 ■ GETTING STARTED WITH MEDIA ENCODER

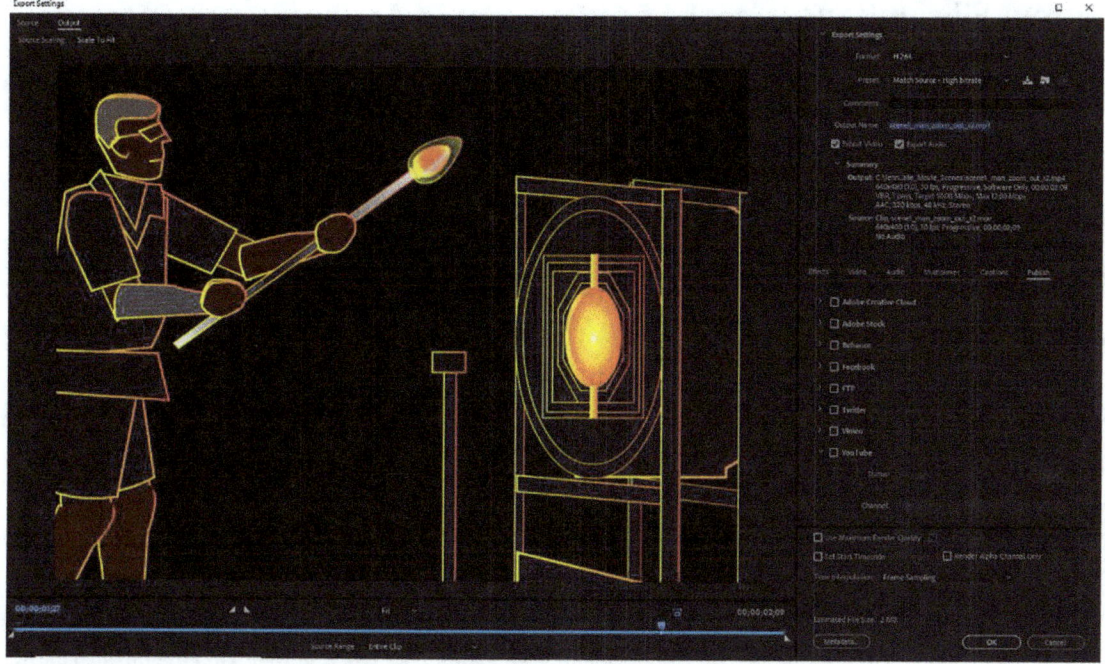

Figure 25-32. The Export Settings dialog box

This is a very advanced area that changes depending upon the format that is chosen. You look at it in more detail in Chapters 26, 27, and 28 when you export web formats.

For now, you can cancel to get out of this area and return to the Queue panel.

Preset Options

Preset type can be chosen when clicking the drop-down menu next to the name or by clicking the name and entering the Export Settings area. There are many options, depending on what format is chosen. You look at the ones related to the web in the next three chapters. Refer to Figure 25-33.

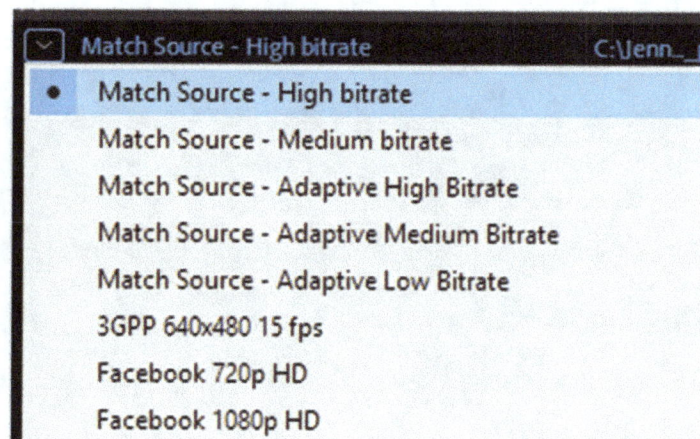

Figure 25-33. Preset options

633

Output File Options

The Output File column allows you to choose the location (Save As) that you wish to output the final rendered file. Refer to Figure 25-34.

Figure 25-34. Output options and Status

Status Options

The Status column states whether the file is ready to output or is done. If a file is missing from the original folder, or failed, a warning status and icon appear. Failed encoding often appears with a log explaining the error. If you have the sound on your computer enabled, you hear distinct types of alerts, like chimes.

Interpret Footage

When a file is selected in the Queue panel, choose File ➤ Interpret Footage. Right-clicking the file also allows you to adjust to the frame rate pixel aspect ratio, field order, and alpha channel. Refer to Figure 25-35.

CHAPTER 25 GETTING STARTED WITH MEDIA ENCODER

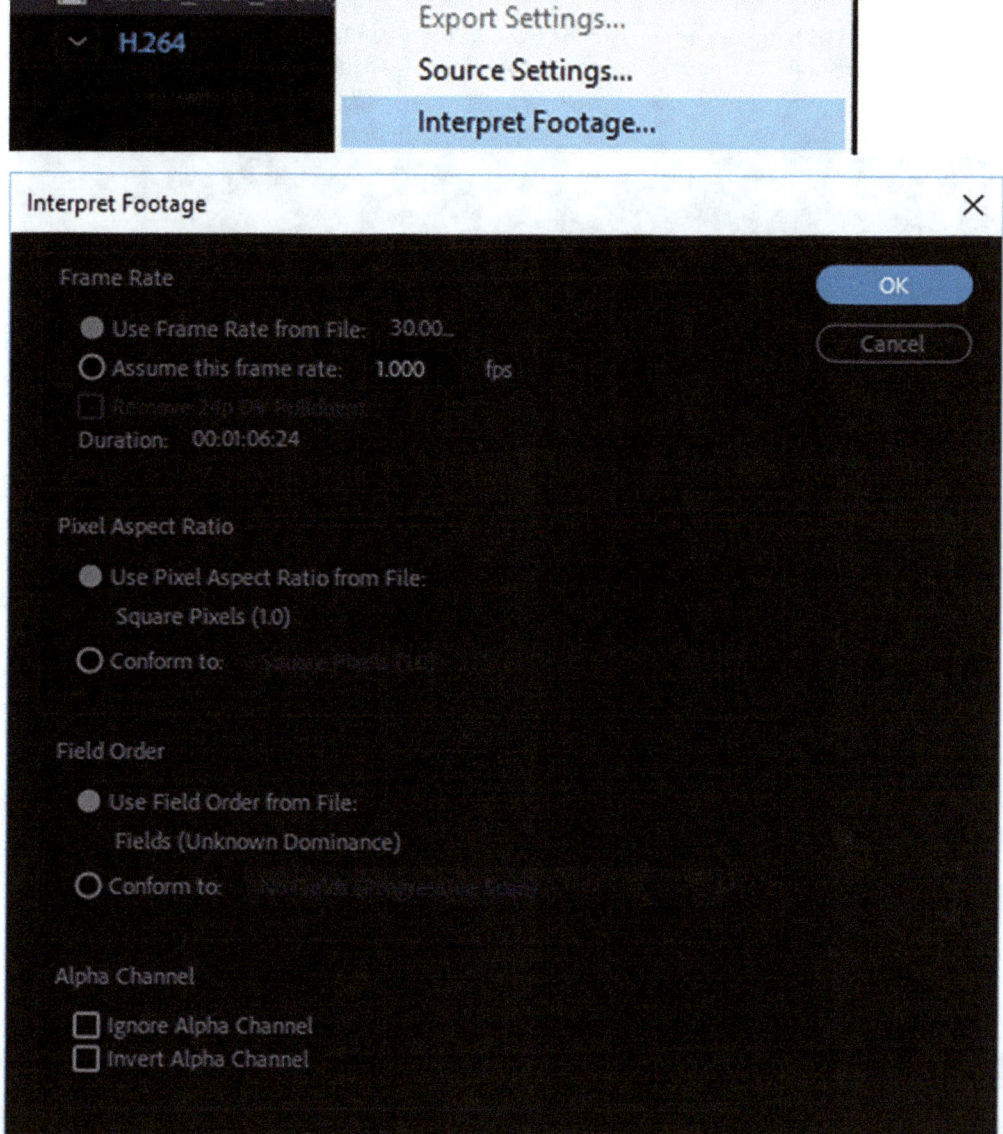

Figure 25-35. Interpret Footage dialog box

Much of this can be adjusted via the Export Settings dialog box for video, which you look at in more detail in Chapter 26. But if you need the footage to be interpreted differently because of alpha channels, you can adjust it here to match the setting of other files for your projects. Click Cancel to exit this dialog box.

Watch Folders Panel

This panel is found docked with the Queue panel to the right. It is very similar to adding a droplet/batch action, as you saw in Photoshop CC. Here you can add (+) or remove (-) a folder or add a final output folder. Refer to Figure 25-36.

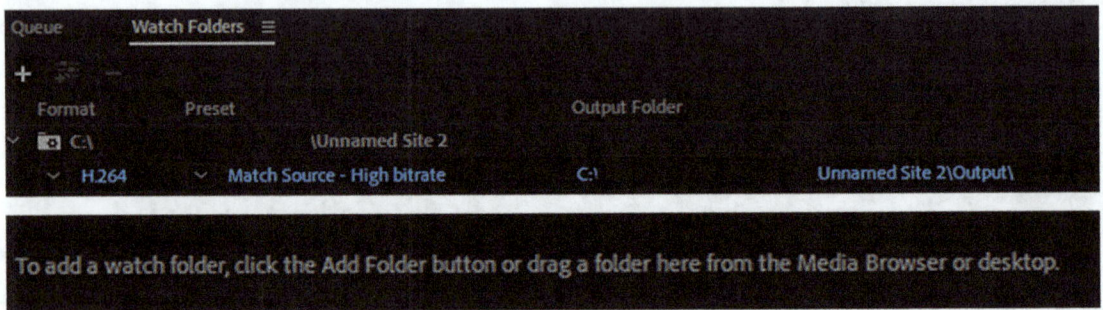

Figure 25-36. *Watch Folders panel*

Media Encoder detects the files present in the folder. Here files that appear within this watched folder alert Media Encoder that they need to be added to the queue and rendered based on format, preset, and output, which were set in the Watch Folders panel. If you have a lot of video that needs similar settings, this is a good option and allows you to speed up the rendering process; however, make sure to run a test with one file before you add more. In rendering image sequences, you may get more files than you expected.

Encoding Panel

The Encoding panel only has a preview of images in it when a file is being rendered; otherwise, it remains blank. For multiple outputs, the Encoding panel displays a thumbnail preview, progress bar, and the completion time estimate of each encoding output. When done, it moves on to the next file to encode until complete. Refer to Figure 25-37.

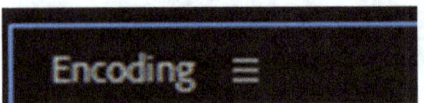

Figure 25-37. *The Encoding panel*

Preset Browser Panel

The Preset Browser panel lists all the presets that are currently available for Media encoder. There are many to choose from.

System Presets are organized into categories in a collapsible folder structure based on use and device. They are organized further by format, frame size, frame rate, target rate, and comments (notes on what to use the preset for). Refer to Figure 25-38.

CHAPTER 25 ■ GETTING STARTED WITH MEDIA ENCODER

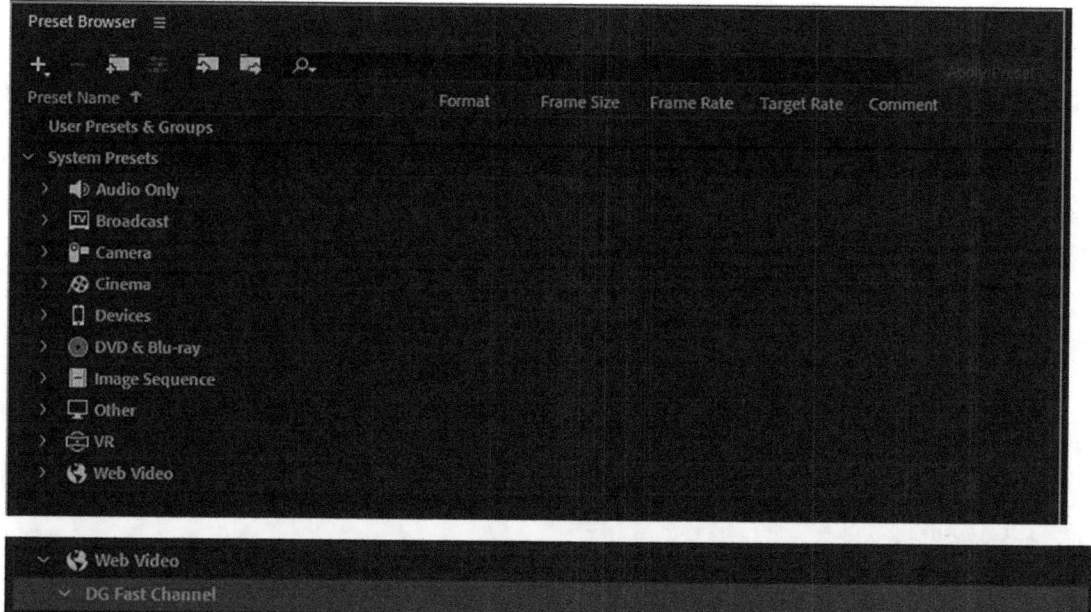

Figure 25-38. The Preset Browser panel

In this book, you focus on presets that relate to your web files. You can either expand or collapse the menus to find the correct preset you want to use, or use the search area to search by name.

If you want to edit presets, the icons in the upper left above the user presets and groups allow you to create custom presets. The icons from left to right are New Preset, Delete Preset, Create New Preset Group, Preset Settings, Import Presets, and Export Presets. Refer to Figure 25-39.

Figure 25-39. Adjusting the presets in the Preset Browser panel

Once created, then you can apply the presets by selecting and clicking the Apply button. This applies presets or groups to the files in the Queue panel, usually to a duplicate output. Alt+click allows you to apply to the watch folder. You can also access this area in Preset in the main menu. Settings are saved (exported) or imported as a video preset file (.epr).

637

Preset Menu Options

Many of these similar options can be accessed through the preset menu. Preset ➤ Settings... allows you to inspect the selected setting more in depth before adding it to the queue. Refer to Figures 25-40 and 25-41.

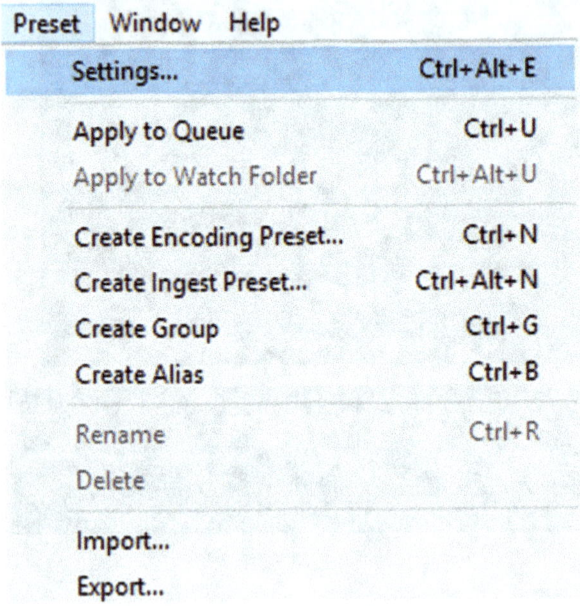

Preset	Window	Help	
Settings...			Ctrl+Alt+E
Apply to Queue			Ctrl+U
Apply to Watch Folder			Ctrl+Alt+U
Create Encoding Preset...			Ctrl+N
Create Ingest Preset...			Ctrl+Alt+N
Create Group			Ctrl+G
Create Alias			Ctrl+B
Rename			Ctrl+R
Delete			
Import...			
Export...			

Figure 25-40. *Viewing preset settings*

Figure 25-41 shows the detailed setting, but they vary by the format information.

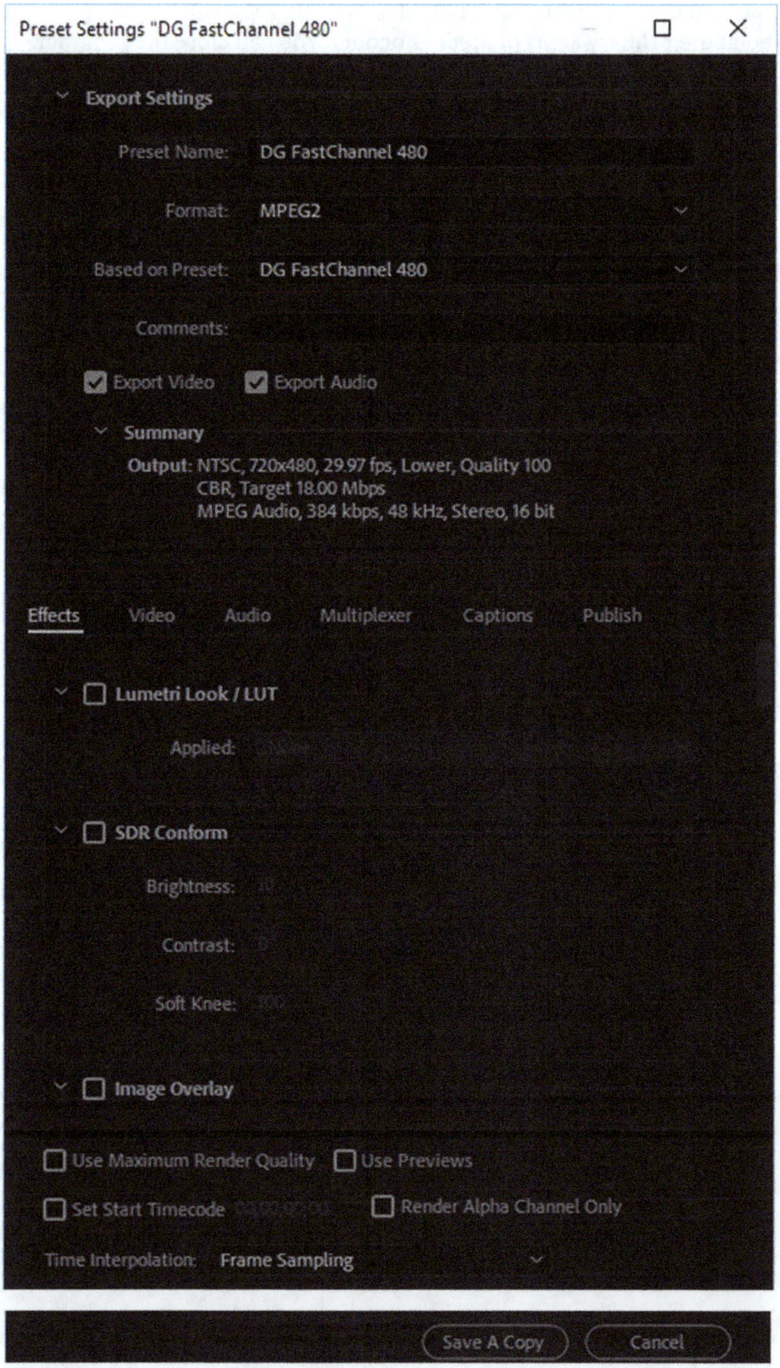

CHAPTER 25 ■ GETTING STARTED WITH MEDIA ENCODER

Figure 25-41. Preset Settings dialog box for a specific file format

CHAPTER 25 ■ GETTING STARTED WITH MEDIA ENCODER

To exit, click Save A Copy if you want to create a duplicate, or in this case, click Cancel.

At this point, you have looked at the primary areas of Media Encoder. You can close the program (File ➤ Exit) or keep it open for the next chapter, where you start working with the video files for export and render.

Summary

This chapter was an overview of the main panels in Media Encoder. You discovered that this program's appearance is different from Photoshop, Illustrator, and Animate, but it is still an important part of the process for getting video files ready for the web.

In the next chapter, you encode your video files (.mov and .avi) as MP4 (H.246) files and look at two other web formats.

CHAPTER 26

Working with Your RAW Video Files (AVI and MOV)

In this chapter, you review the AVI and MOV video formats, and then look at how they can be formatted as MP4 for the web with Media Encoder. You then learn how to stitch video clips together. Later you look at two other file formats for the web.

Note This chapter does not have any actual projects; however, you can use the files in the Chapter 26 folder to practice opening and viewing for this lesson. They are at https://github.com/Apress/graphics-multimedia-web-adobe-creative-cloud.

Working with Your RAW Files (AVI or MOV)

The quality and format of the digital video that you shoot largely depends on the device that it was shot from, or in an animation, the software it was produced in. In filming, you may have used your smartphone, camera, camcorder, or archived film that was converted to a digital format. Other video footage, as you saw in Part 4, might come from a program like Animate CC in the form of an animation or MOV. Regardless of how you acquired your video footage or still images, if you are planning on using the files for your website, you need to use Media Encoder CC to convert them to the correct file format that runs in an HTML5 <video> or <audio> tag when you insert the link into Dreamweaver CC.

Two common file formats that you encounter when working with RAW video are AVI (.avi) and MOV (.mov); they are uncompressed video, so their file size may be considerably large—up to a gigabyte or more depending on the length and quality of the video. So, if you're working with video that is more than a gigabyte, you should have an external drive to do your rendering and file storing to avoid a computer crash.

Note You may have your RAW video for a project in another file format other than .avi or .mov; if this is the case, refer to the Media Browser panel to see if your file type can be imported into Media Encoder CC. You look at a case where this is an issue in Chapter 27.

CHAPTER 26 ■ WORKING WITH YOUR RAW VIDEO FILES (AVI AND MOV)

Audio Video Interleave

Audio Video Interleave (AVI, .avi) is a multimedia container format introduced by Microsoft in November 1992 as part of its video for Windows software. AVI files can contain both audio and video data or moving image content in a file container. This container supports synchronous audio-with-picture playback. When these files are created with a digital camera (e.g., Canon) they are accompanied with a THM (.thm) file, which is a thumbnail image of the video file or a preview the first frame; it is like a JPEG file. While it is not necessary to keep the THM, it is quite small and it does allow a preview of the video to load faster.

For more information on AVI, visit https://en.wikipedia.org/wiki/Audio_Video_Interleave.

QuickTime File Format

QuickTime File Format (MOV, .mov) is a computer file format used natively by the QuickTime framework and was developed by Apple Inc. The format specifies a multimedia container file that contains one or more tracks, each of which stores a particular type of data: audio, video, or text (e.g., for subtitles), single still image, or timecode. Each track either contains a digitally-encoded media stream (using a specific format) or a data reference to the media stream located in another file.

The QuickTime Video Player is often found with Apple computers; it is not loaded onto Microsoft platforms, so it does not always work on alternate players like Windows Media Player. Thankfully, after the MOV is rendered (as in the video imported from Animate CC), you can use Media Encoder to preview the file and render it in a format that you can view in your media player.

Convert Video with Export Settings

Once you have imported your video files it is time to Export them to the correct formats for your website. There are three main formats that most desktop and mobile browsers recognize for the web.

MP4 (.mp4) is known as H.264 in Adobe Media Encoder. There are many presets that you can choose from in the Preset Browser panel in the Mobile and Web Video subsections; however, to see all the choices at once, you can find the settings in the Queue panel under the Preset drop-down menu. Refer to Figure 26-1 and Media Encoder to see the full range.

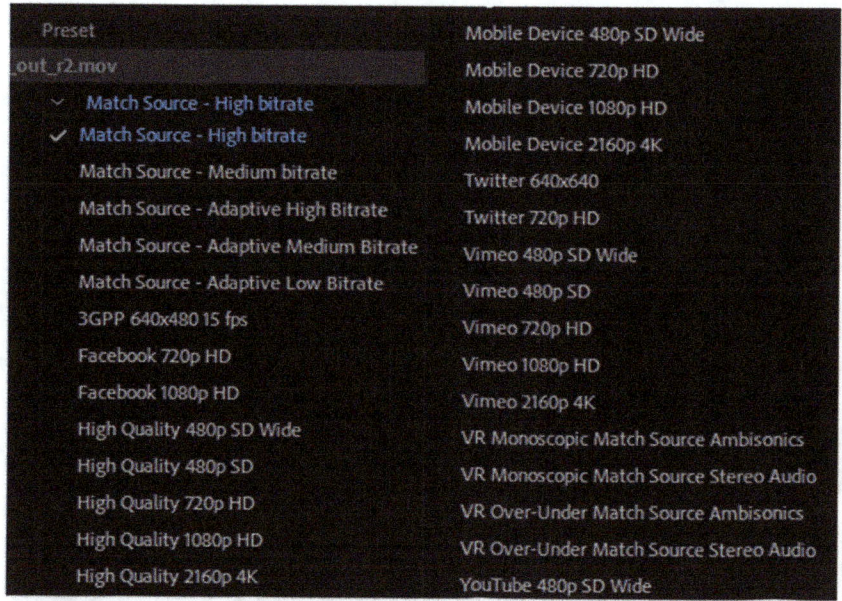

Figure 26-1. *Preset Options for an MP4 file. There are many to choose from*

Notice that there are settings for files specifically for Facebook, mobile devices, Twitter, Vimeo, and YouTube. If you are not sure what setting to choose and the video is relatively small, as a suggestion, I generally stick with the choice of Match Source – High Bitrate; however, you may want to render your video in several MP4 formats to check which has the smallest file size, dimensions, and optimum quality for your video.

In the Preset Browser panel, you may have noticed another similarly named preset under System Presets ➤ Devices ➤ Mobile ➤ MPEG4 (H.263). Refer to Figure 26-2.

This creates a small file size specifically for mobile devices with the .3gp extension. This file extension

Figure 26-2. *MPEG4 file format for mobiles*

may not play in all browsers and has a low frame rate, so it is better to use MP4 or H.264 for your website.

Having said that, a 3GP file can come in handy when working with audio conversion, as you discover in Chapter 27. For more information on MPEG4, visit https://en.wikipedia.org/wiki/MPEG-4.

Match Source (see Figure 26-1) matches the source and frame rate of whatever speed the video is shot at. As you saw in Animate CC, a good frame rate for the web is generally between 24 fps and 30 fps; however, there are higher frame rates up to 60 fps. Larger frame rates mean a larger file size, and if you alter the frame rate of your video animation, it can either slow down or speed up the action and effect the audio as well. Nevertheless for conversions where you need to increase the frame rate from 24 to 30 frames, Media Encoder can successfully create in between frames that can fill in the blanks for footage when required.

CHAPTER 26 WORKING WITH YOUR RAW VIDEO FILES (AVI AND MOV)

Export Settings Dialog Box

When you click the Format name in the Queue panel, you can alter the export settings even further. Refer to Figure 26-3.

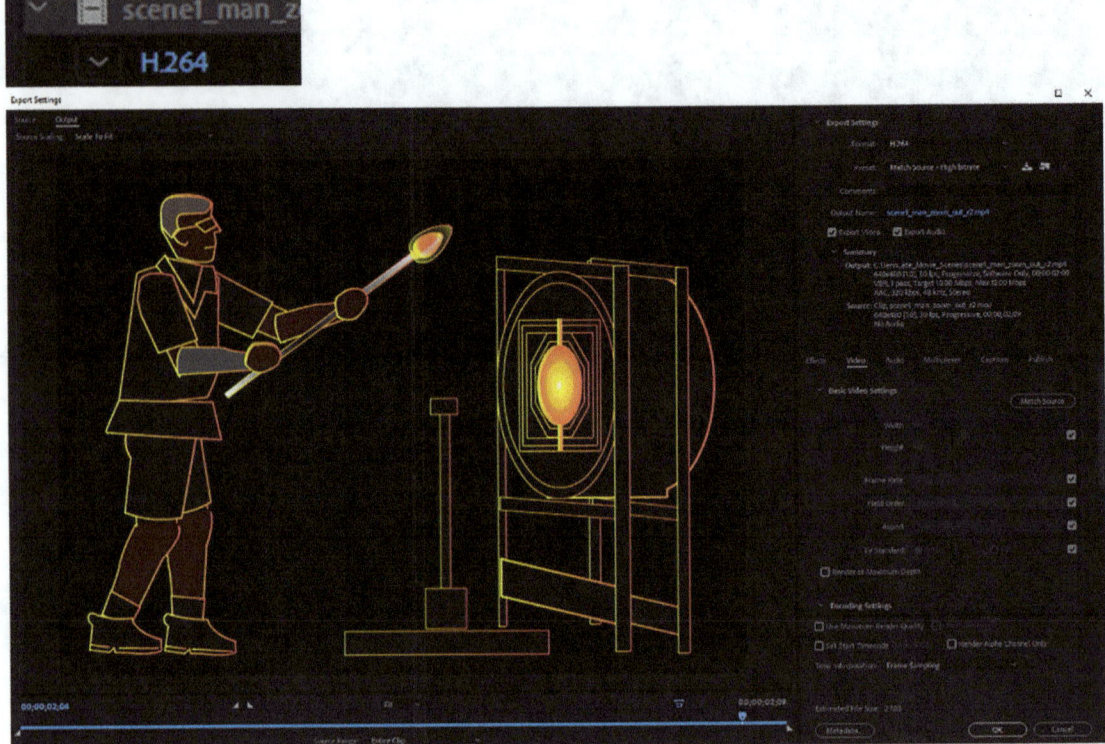

Figure 26-3. The Export Settings dialog box is revealed when you click the format name of the file

Now let's look at each part in the panel.

Source Tab

The Source tab allows you to crop or trim the output video when you click the Crop tool. This way, you can render only a portion of the video frame. It does not affect the original video. You can enter numbers into the left, top, right, and bottom. Refer to Figure 26-4.

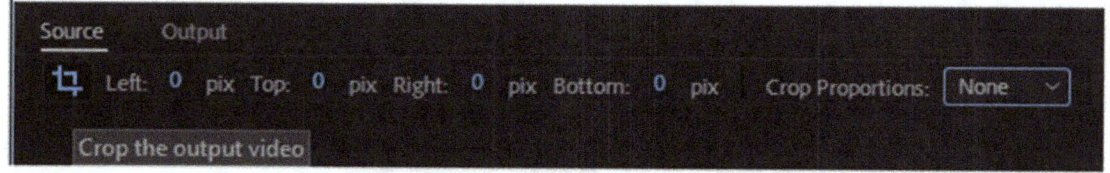

Figure 26-4. *Crop using the source image to determine the video final size*

Crop Proportions include various ratios so that the crop is proportionate. The default is none. You can see what a 4:3 ratio looks like in Figure 26-5; the outer area will not be in the scene.

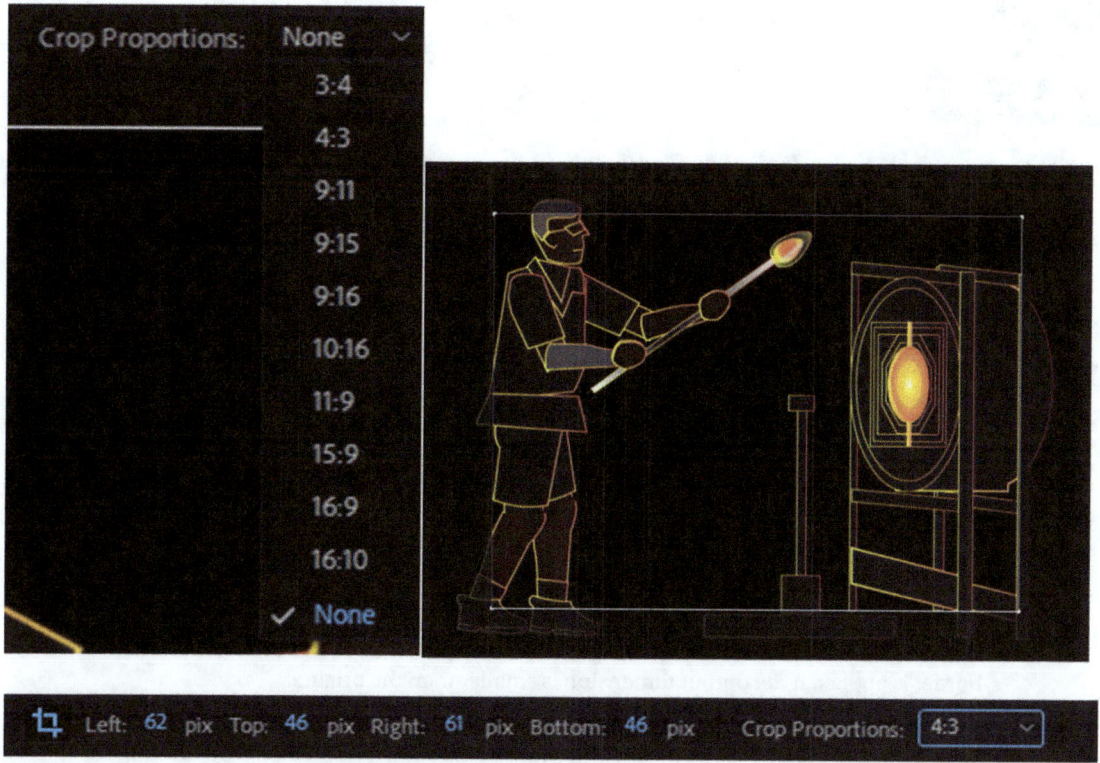

Figure 26-5. *Choosing a Crop proportions setting*

The handles of the Crop tool can be dragged to any custom size. In this animation, my plan was to bring it into Photoshop as part of the intro. I had already built it to the correct size, so no pre-cropping was required. Sometimes when you are working in Photoshop, it's good to leave some of the extra footage on the edges rather than crop because you can use that extra area to center your frame better for a scene; however, if the footage is going straight to the web, the Crop tool is very useful for editing tiny amounts of video quickly. For now, set all the crop points back to 0 pixels and crop proportions back to none, as seen in Figure 26-4, and unselect the Crop tool so that the options are not available.

Output Tab

The Output tab allows you to choose various Source Scaling options for the video frames. The Output tab is the area to look at after you have made adjustments in the Source Video tab area to the width and height.

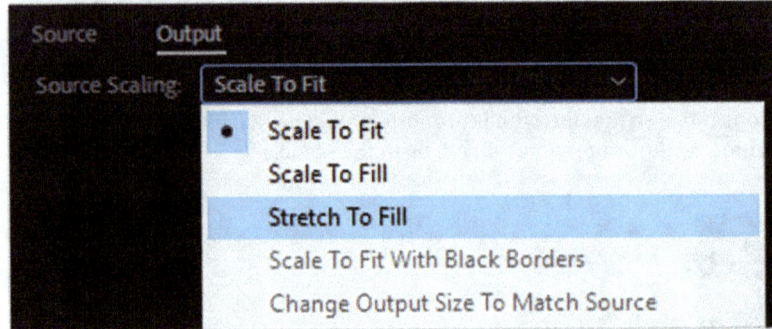

Figure 26-6. Output settings

Refer to Figure 26-6.
   The following are the options:

- **Scale To Fit** (default): Scales the source frames to fit within the output frame while maintaining pixel aspect ratio of the source. It trys to match the original video ratio that was set in the Source Video tab. If it does not match additional black side bars may be added to the footage.

- **Scale To Fill**: Scales the source frame to completely fill the output frame while cropping the source frame as necessary, but still maintains the pixel aspect ratio.

- **Stretch To Fill**: Resizes the source frame to completely fill the output frame. With this setting, distortions can occur because the pixel aspect ratio is not maintained and the output ratio might be different.

- **Scale To Fit With Black Borders**: The source frame, including the cropped area, is fit within the output frame. Even though the pixel aspect ratio is maintained, a black border is applied if the output dimension is smaller than the original.

- **Change Output Size To Match Source**: Automatically sets the height and width of the output video frame to the height and width of the source video frame, overriding the output frame size settings. This setting is not available to all export formats.

Options that are not available are grayed out in the drop-down list. In some cases, other options in Export Settings have to be altered for them to become available.
   Further details can be referenced at https://helpx.adobe.com/media-encoder/using/export-settings-reference.html.

Preview Settings

The lower center left below the video preview image is the timeline, which you can edit and scrub the blue playhead to preview. The start and end times (hours: minutes: seconds: frames) are listed on the left and right. Refer to Figure 26-7.

Figure 26-7. The video timeline and playhead

If you keep the entire timeline as the default, the source range reads the entire clip; however, if you drag the left and right set of point triangle to remove some unwanted footage in or outward, the source range changes to custom. Refer to Figure 26-8.

Figure 26-8. Setting points to clip in the video

You can set how much of the video you want to export. This is useful because sometimes after an animated video has been converted to a MOV in Animate, you have a few unwanted frames at the start of the video. You can clip those out by moving the points. Refer to Figure 26-9.

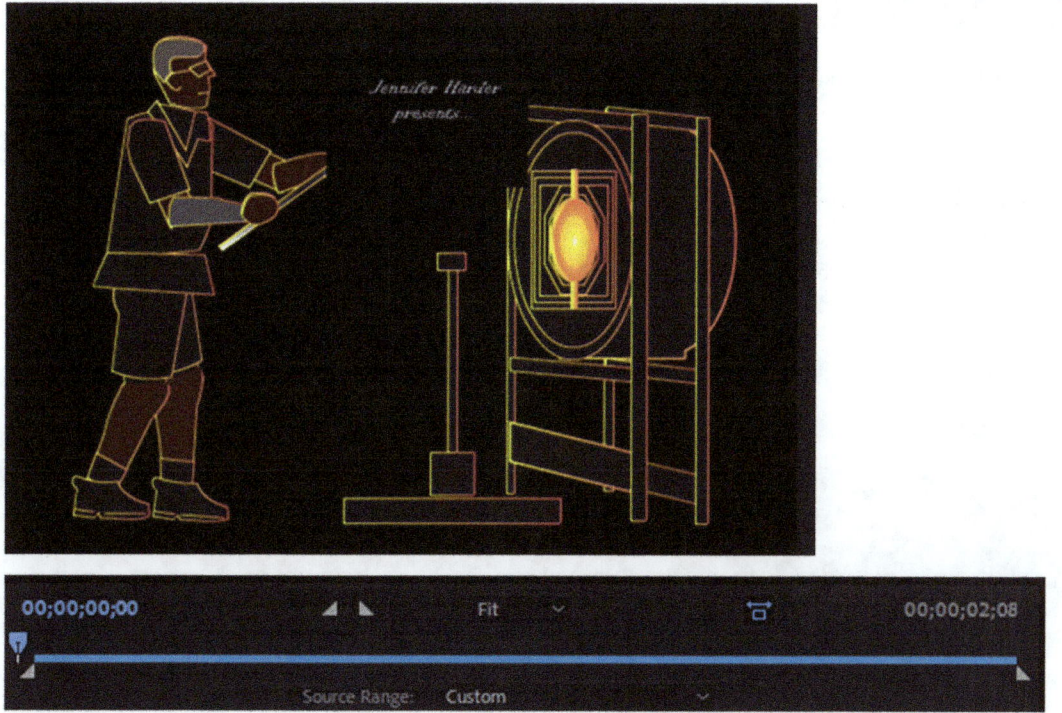

Figure 26-9. The first frame in this movie clip came in as a distorted camera angle, so I moved the point on the left in so that that frame is not part of the final rendering for the movie upon export

Alternatively, using the scrub in combination with the left and right set point buttons, you can accurately set where you want your video to begin and end. I find this very useful if I am doing a quick edit directly from the footage from my camera, and I want to chop out something at the end or beginning of my video. If you have several points to crop, it is better to make more duplicates in the Queue panel of the footage and then move the point marker to a different location for each.

The Fit drop-down menu allows you to zoom in and out of your preview to see the video at varying sizes. This does not affect the final output size of the video and is for viewing purposes only. The arrow box icon is enabled to Aspect Ratio Correction. Refer to Figure 26-10.

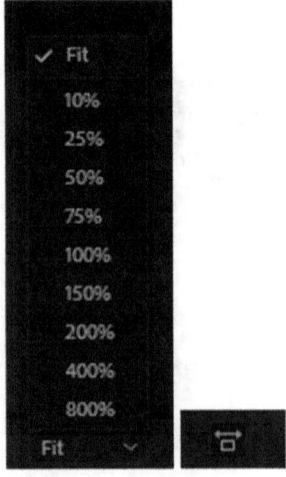

Figure 26-10. *The Fit drop-down and aspect ratio correction icon enabled*

Export Settings and Summary

Now let's move over to the Export Settings dialog box. Some options may not be available, depending on the format or preset that is chosen. Refer to Figure 26-11.

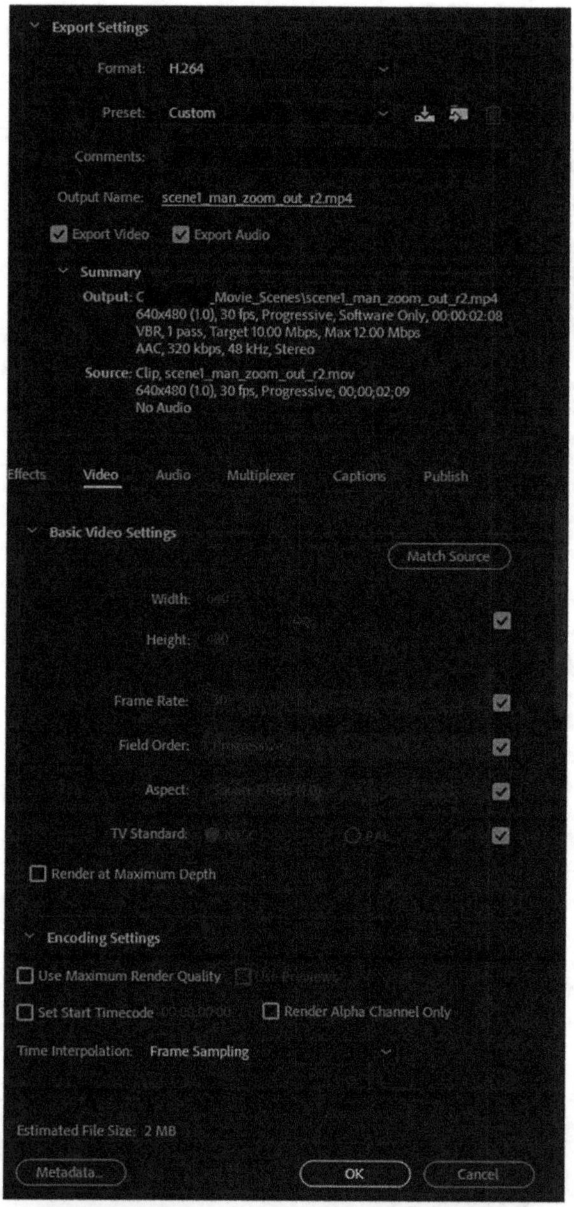

CHAPTER 26 ■ WORKING WITH YOUR RAW VIDEO FILES (AVI AND MOV)

Figure 26-11. Advanced format settings overview

Here you can change the format (H.264) and preset. When you make alterations to the video, instead of high-quality bitrate the preset becomes custom. To the right of the preset, you can also save, install, or delete presets. Refer to Figure 26-12.

CHAPTER 26 ■ WORKING WITH YOUR RAW VIDEO FILES (AVI AND MOV)

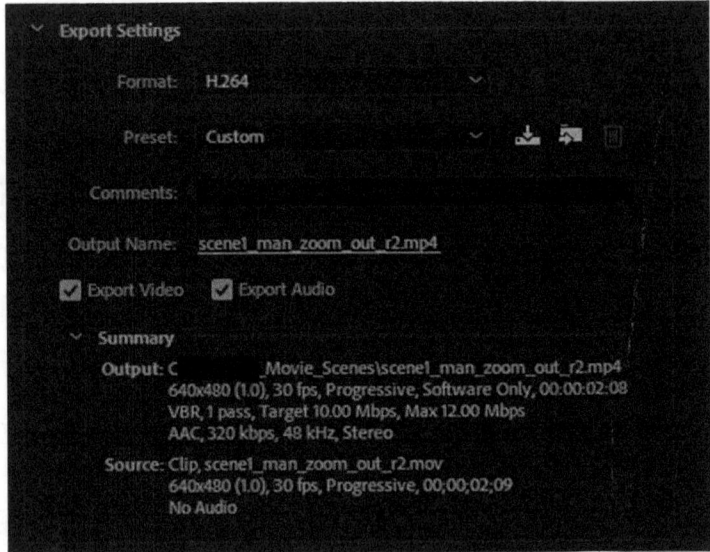

***Figure 26-12.** Advanced Export settings and summary*

You can add comments to your video if you are doing editing elsewhere, and you can review the output name.

If you want both the video and the audio to export, then both check boxes should be enabled; otherwise, only one or the other export. This is a good option if you only want to export the audio out of a video clip, as you see in Chapter 27. Or alternatively, only export the video if the audio does not relate to the story. This video had no audio to begin with, so that was detected for the output in the summary when the video was imported.

The summary lists the current setting to output and source file.

As you move down the right column, you see that there are other advanced edits that you can make to the video. Most of these (other than the Video or Audio tabs) you likely leave at default for your basic projects, but it is good to know what options are available. By clicking the arrow tabs, you can contract and expand the details of these tabs' settings. Checking them applies the settings. At default, most are unchecked or are autoenabled without the check box option.

You will now look at which settings are available when converting to MP4. Refer to Figure 26-13.

CHAPTER 26 ■ WORKING WITH YOUR RAW VIDEO FILES (AVI AND MOV)

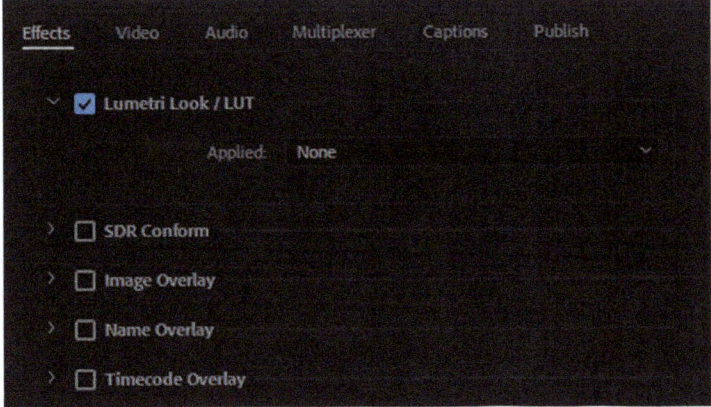

Figure 26-13. *Advanced Export settings tabs*

Effects Tab

The Effects tab controls several features, which you can view in more detail when you click the arrow to reveal the settings, as you saw in Figure 26-13 and Figure 26-14.

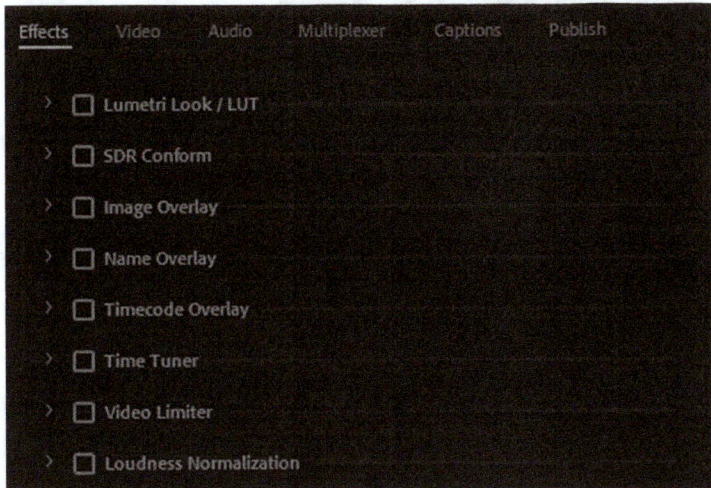

Figure 26-14. *Effects tab settings*

Lumetri Look/LUT

This controls the overall color or tint of the video. When disabled, the default is None or the original color that the video was shot in. You can give your video a black-and-white appearance or give it a vintage look, like older film in which the color has faded or dulled over time. This is a good option if you want to add this setting before importing to Photoshop. Some options could even make the video look better and improve the contrast. You can choose from the drop-down menu's many preset options. Or you can import your

CHAPTER 26 ■ WORKING WITH YOUR RAW VIDEO FILES (AVI AND MOV)

own options by selecting from the menu and locating the correct Look and LUT file formats, if you have additional options. Refer to Figure 26-15.

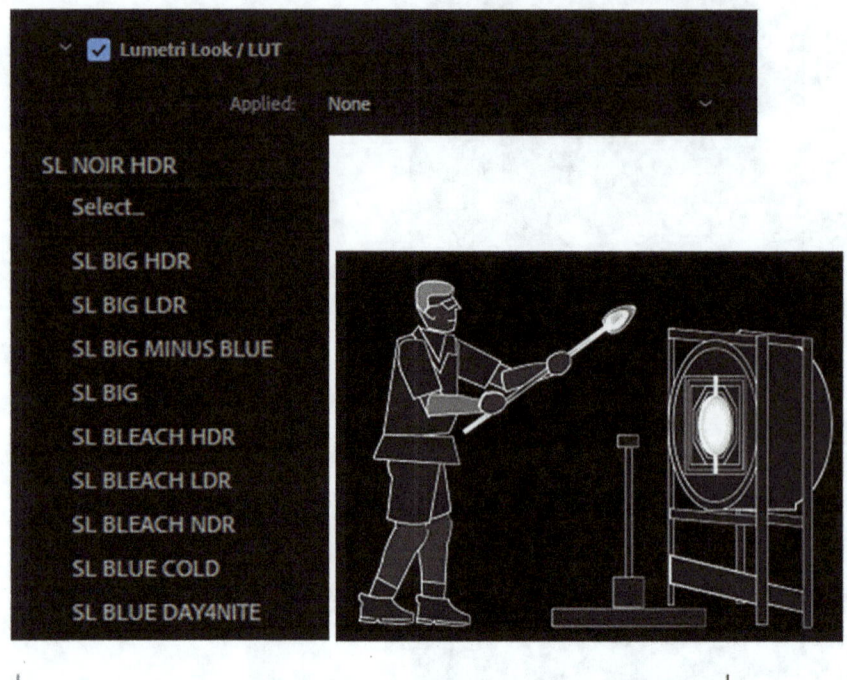

Figure 26-15. *Effects tab settings for Lumetri Look/LUT and select options*

When you want to preview, toggle the check box on or off to compare how the video looks before or after. While this may not be as robust as working in a program like After Effects or Photoshop, it is a good option if you want all of your video to have a consistent color grade in your video sequence.

SDR Conform

This controls the brightness, contrast, and soft knee of the video output overall. Refer to Figure 26-16.

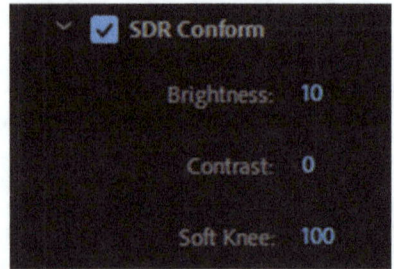

Figure 26-16. *Effects tab settings for SDR Conform*

652

CHAPTER 26 ■ WORKING WITH YOUR RAW VIDEO FILES (AVI AND MOV)

Soft knee refers to the transition to full compression mode; this can affect the graininess, shadows, or quality of the video. You can either enter a number or drag the number left or right to get a range. To compare before or after, enable and disable the checkbox. SDR Conform allows you to convert HDR (high dynamic range) video to the SDR (standard dynamic range) settings for playback on non-HRD devices.

Image Overlay

This allows you to overlay an image on top of your output video. Refer to Figure 26-17.

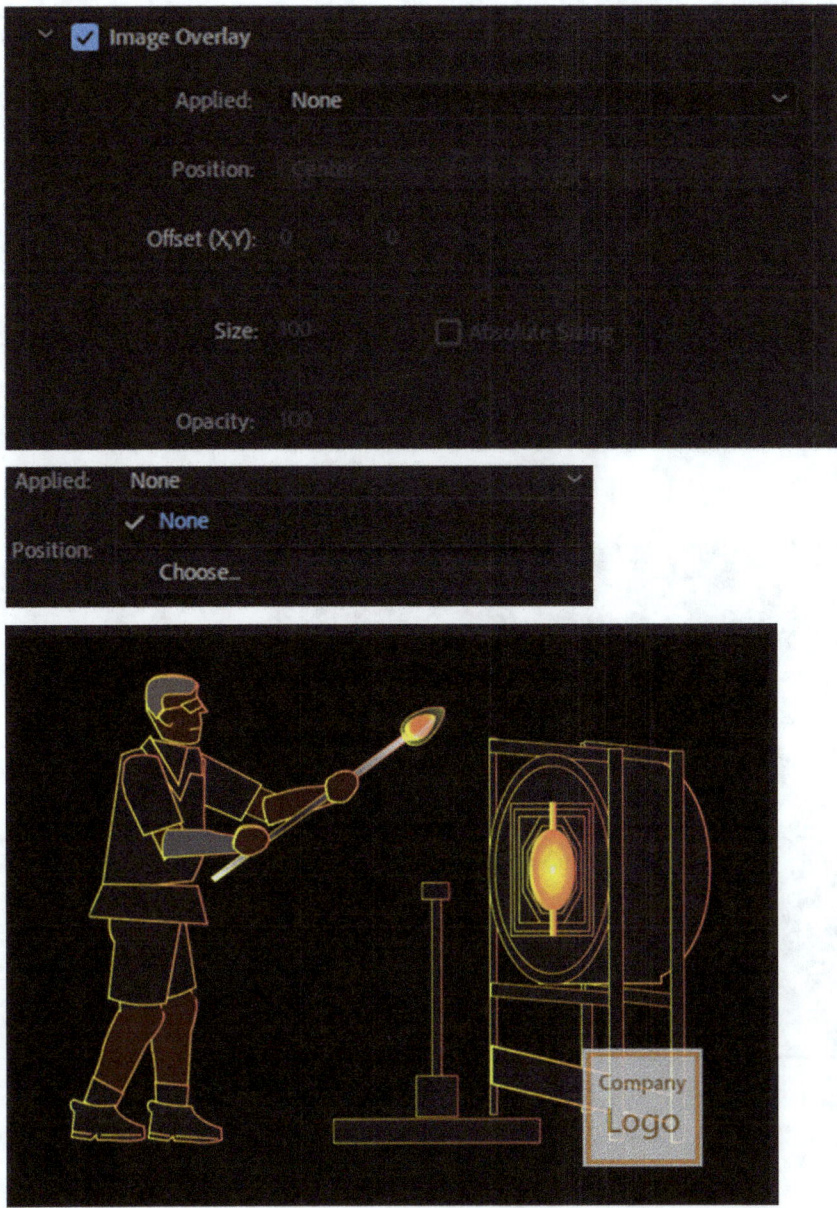

Figure 26-17. Effects tab settings for Image Overlay

CHAPTER 26 ■ WORKING WITH YOUR RAW VIDEO FILES (AVI AND MOV)

Once an image is chosen, you can adjust the position from the drop-down menu and use the offset (X, Y) for a custom position. Sizing and absolute sizing are based on video resolution. You can also set the opacity of this overlay image.

While this might make an interesting effect, another use for this is as a watermark to prevent piracy. For instance, on your site you might want to add your company logo to the video in the lower left or right. If someone downloads the video from your site, it is difficult for the viewer to remove that logo from every frame. If they want a clear video without the logo, they have to write to you and ask you for permission to use the video without the logo. If you decide to remove the overlay image, you can choose Clear from the Applied drop-down menu. Refer to Figure 26-18.

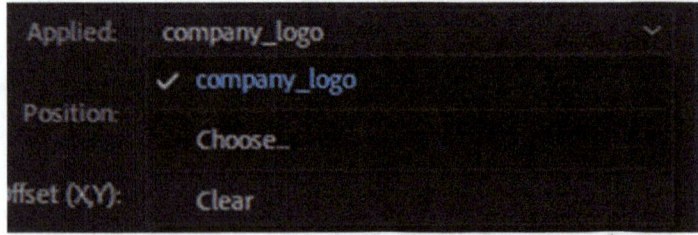

Figure 26-18. *Effects tab settings for Image Overlay remove overlay*

Name Overlay

This overlays the name of the file over the entire video. It can also act as a watermark for your video. Refer to Figure 26-19.

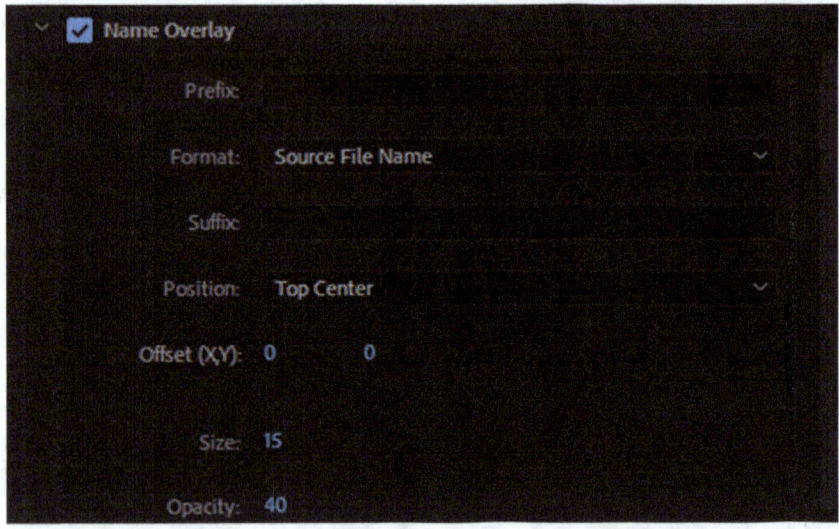

Figure 26-19. *Effects tab settings for Name Overlay*

654

CHAPTER 26 ■ WORKING WITH YOUR RAW VIDEO FILES (AVI AND MOV)

You can alter the following:

- **Prefix**: Text can be added to the beginning of the source file name.
- **Format**: Source File Name adds the current name of the file. Alternatively, you can have it without the file extension. It can also be the Output File Name with or without extension. Prefix and Suffix Only lets you enter your own text without file name or extensions that you can type into the prefix or suffix text field areas of this dialog box. Refer to Figure 26-20.

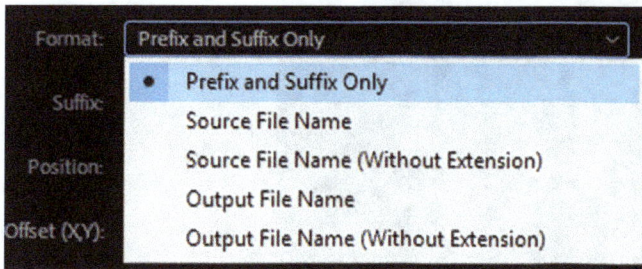

Figure 26-20. *Format options in Text Overlay*

- **Suffix**: Text can be added to the end of the source file name.
- **Position**: Sets a location or relative position of the text within the output frame using the drop-down menu.
- **Offset (X, Y)**: This is a custom position.
- **Size**: Adjusts the size of the text.
- **Opacity**: Sets from 0–100 to make transparent or visible, as seen in Figure 26-21.

Figure 26-21. *Format options in Text Overlay with name on image*

655

CHAPTER 26 WORKING WITH YOUR RAW VIDEO FILES (AVI AND MOV)

There does not appear to be a way to alter the color of the text (e.g., color picker) only white, so adding colored overlay text in Photoshop might be a better option in some cases. You can also remove the text by unchecking this option.

Timecode Overlay

This generates a time code on your video in a specific position, font size, and opacity. Refer to Figure 26-22.

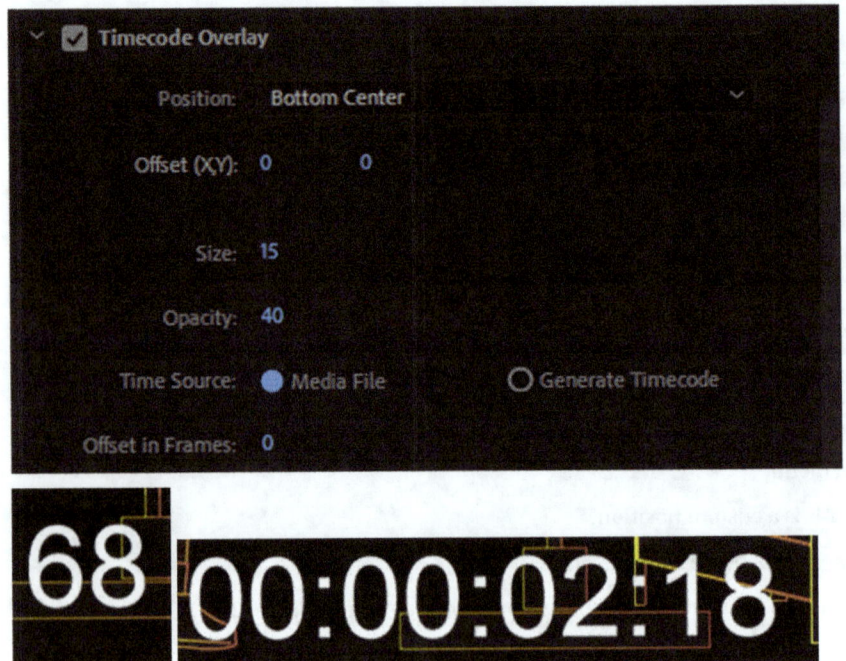

Figure 26-22. *Effects tab settings for Timecode Overlay as media file or generate timecode*

The time source can either be Media File or Generate Timecode. This affects or alters at what point the offset in frames starts, depending on the preview points. This is useful if you are trying to determine at what point the video should be cut. For Time Source, the media file default is set at 0 for offset in frames, and you can adjust the timecode by a given number of frames. For Generate Timecode, you can set the format; it starts at: 00:00:00:00 (hours: minutes: seconds: frames) for the overlay burn. Refer to Figure 26-23.

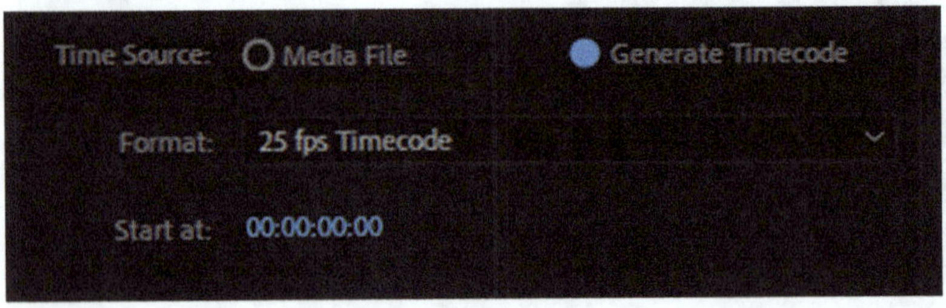

Figure 26-23. *Effects tab settings for Timecode Overlay generate timecode settings*

656

CHAPTER 26 ■ WORKING WITH YOUR RAW VIDEO FILES (AVI AND MOV)

Make sure that your format matches the current frame rate of the video or the timing may appear differently than the actual output frames. Refer to Figure 26-24.

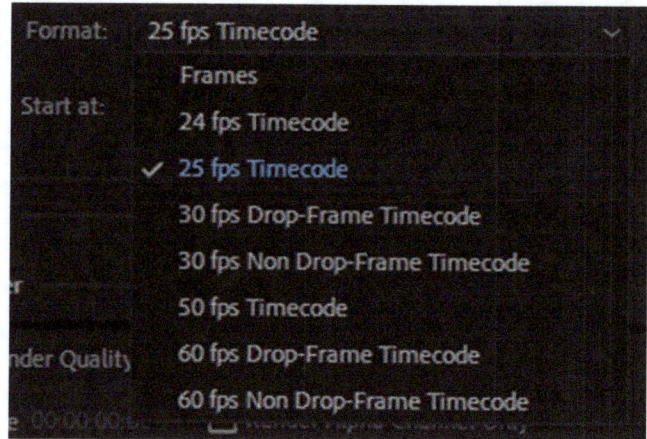

Figure 26-24. *Effects tab settings for Timecode Overlay generate timecode settings for format*

If you would like to learn more about timecode, refer to www.edithouse.com.au/information/about_timecode.html.

Time Tuner

If you want your video to complete within a certain time rather than cut out part of the video, you may want to alter the Target Duration within Time Tuner. This sets a new duration for the output file when it is enabled. Refer to Figure 26-25.

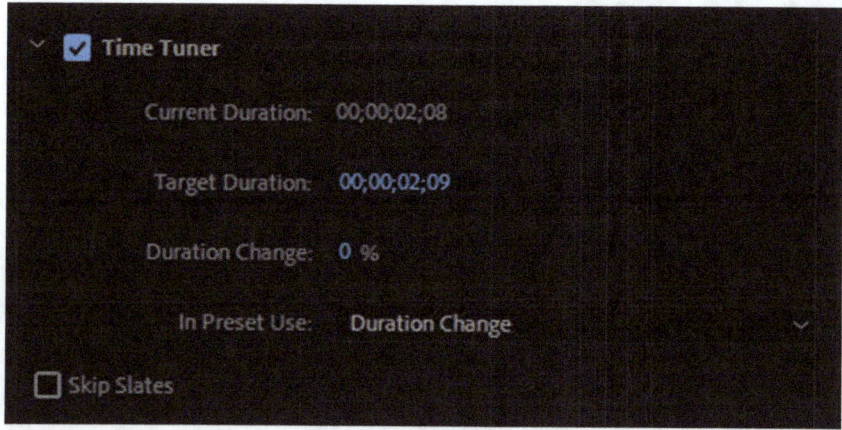

Figure 26-25. *Effects tab settings for Time Tuner*

657

This effects the duration change by percentage. In Preset Use: There are two choices: Target Duration adjust all outputs of a specific target duration, while Duration Change adjusts each as a percentage of the original source duration. You may need to run tests with each preset to help you decide which option to choose your your project.

Skip slates refers to a series of still images (slates) with a combined duration longer than 10 seconds. Checking this prevents the time tuner from being applied to them.

The time tuner may cause part of the video to drop or drag, and this may not be what you want. It could affect audio as well, so make sure to experiment with this setting if you plan to use it.

Video Limiter

Depending on the settings that you choose, it can affect or constrain the luminance and color of the output file so that the range is compressed within safe broadcasting limits.

Loudness Normalization

Also known as Automatic Loudness Correction, this affects how the audio is interpreted in the video. Refer to Figure 26-27.

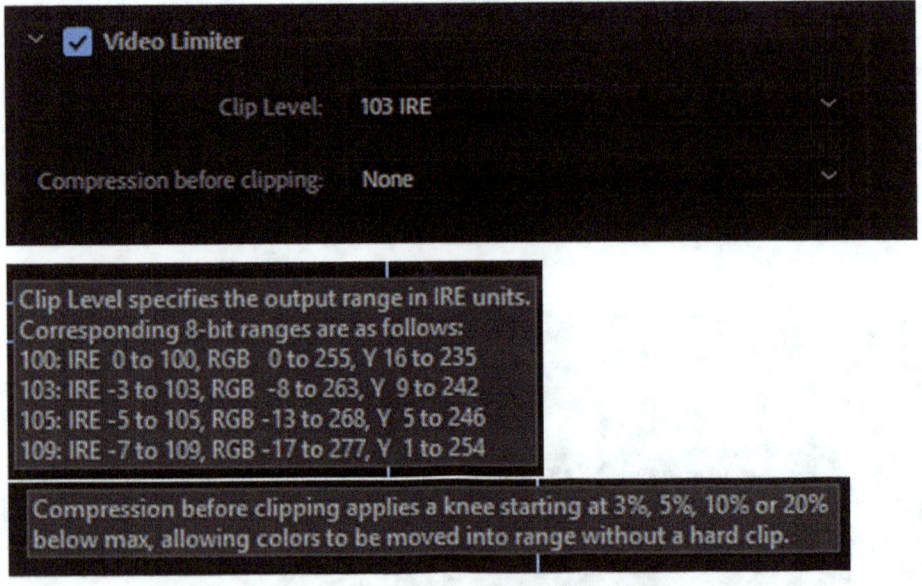

Figure 26-26. Effects tab settings for Video Limiter for clip level and compression

CHAPTER 26 ■ WORKING WITH YOUR RAW VIDEO FILES (AVI AND MOV)

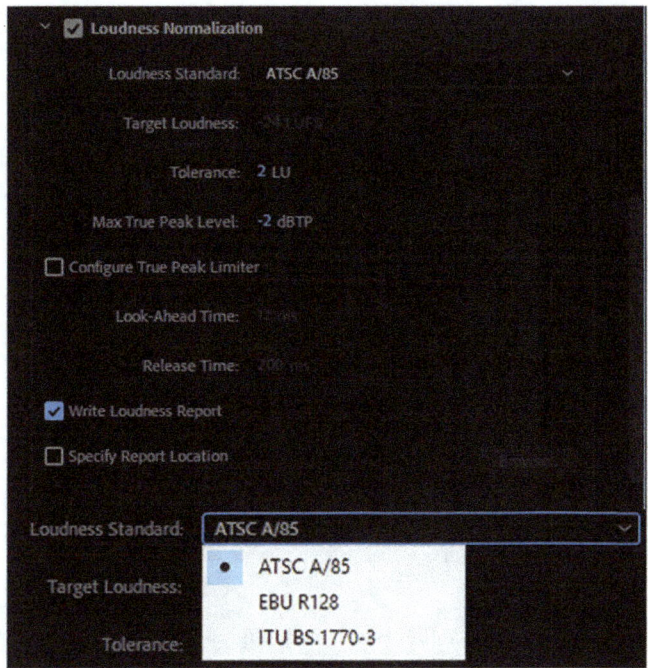

Figure 26-27. Effects tab settings for Loudness Normalization

You can ensure that your video and audio projects meet broadcast standards for loudness. You can also apply adjustments to the standards, such as target and tolerance, and maximum true peak level. Configure True Peak Limiter for Look ahead and Release time and view a written report of the loudness values. You can also specify where the report is published on your hard drive or external drive.

There are three loudness standards:

- ATSC A/85
- EBU R128
- ITU BS.1770-3: Only with this option can you alter the target loudness. The earlier noted standards do not allow you to alter the target loudness.

Adobe states that loudness normalization natively works with mono, stereo, and 5.1ch audio. If you use something other than those channel types (such as 4ch, 8ch, 16ch, and so on), the Channel Configuration screen appears.

Internet viewers may watch your video on their smartphones or websites. You can generally leave this area unchecked; however, if you plan to output the MP4 video for a use other than your website, you may want to experiment with these settings or check with your broadcaster. You can make other adjustments in the Audio tab.

659

CHAPTER 26 ■ WORKING WITH YOUR RAW VIDEO FILES (AVI AND MOV)

Video Tab

You can make further adjustments to the video in the Video tab. Refer to Figure 26-28.

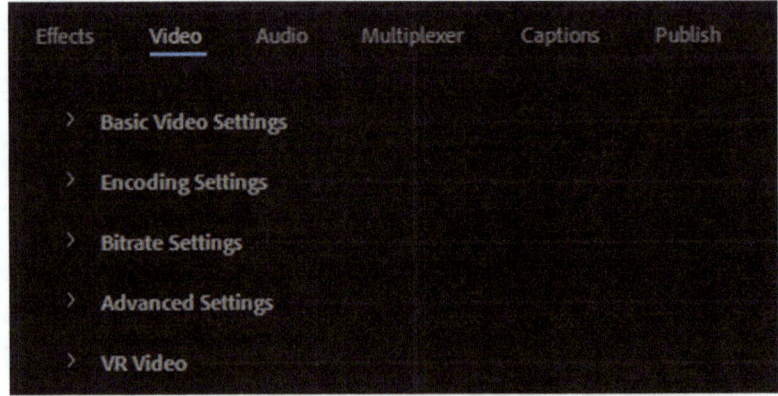

Figure 26-28. Video tab settings

- **Basic Video Settings:** Allows you to match the source files width and height, unlink to make disproportionate, adjust frame rate, field order, aspect ratio, and TV standard (NTSC or PAL). Refer to Figure 26-29.

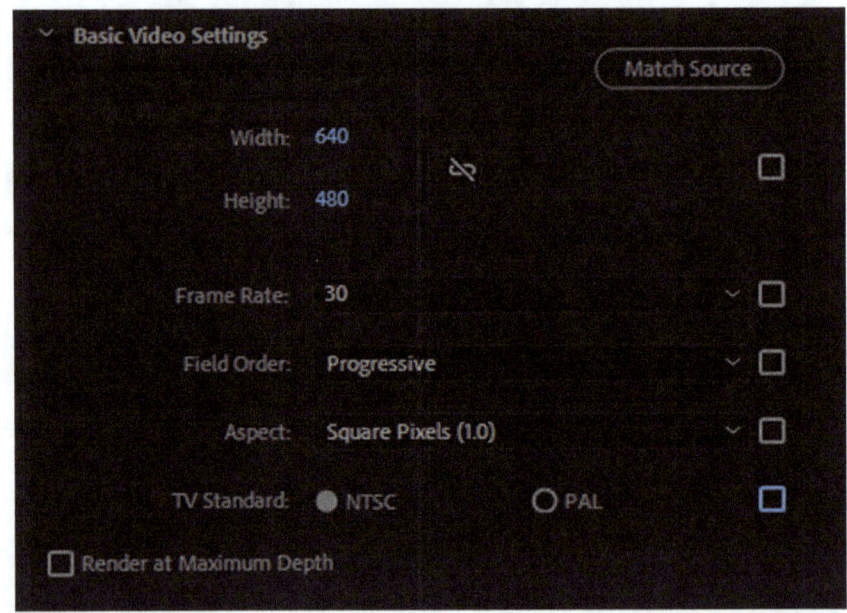

Figure 26-29. Video tab settings for Basic Video Settings

660

These setting are checked at default to match the source imported file. Unchecking them allows you to alter the settings and choose from a drop-down menu.

- **Match Source:** Resets all the setting back to original source.
- **Frame Rate:** Refers to the number of frames per second.
- **Field Order:** This has to do with interlacing; discussed in Part 2. The options are progressive, upper first, and lower first. Progressive is used for the computer screen and film.
- **Aspect:** The pixel aspect ratio of the video.
- **TV Standard:** NTSC is a format used by the USA, Canada, and Japan. Europe and Asia use PAL. Changing this area also alters the frame rate.
- **Render At Maximum Depth:** Improves the bit depth quality, but increases how long the encoding takes.
- **Encoding Settings:** This can affect other encoding information in the video. Refer to Figure 26-30.

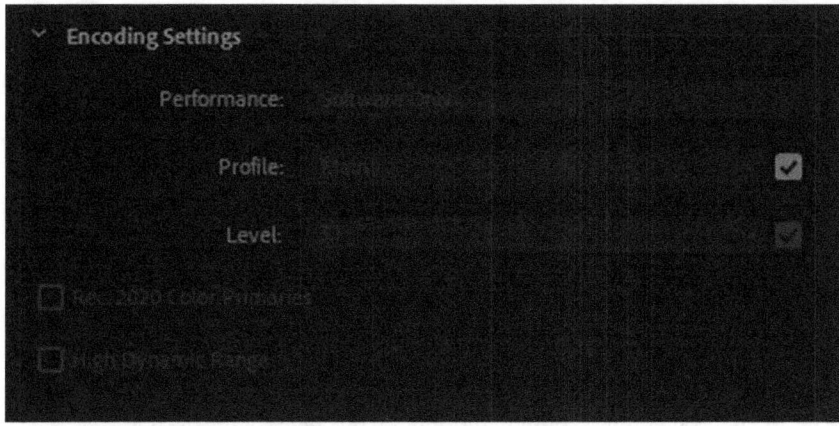

Figure 26-30. Video tab settings for Encoding Settings

Depending upon your computer setup, some setting here may be unavailable if certain hardware is not detected, such as performance, which in my case is set to software only.

- **Profile:** Constrains the bitrate range and controls other properties such as compression algorithm and Chroma format.
- **Level:** Constrains encoding parameters such as bit rate range and maximum frame size. This can only be accessed if you first unselect the profile
- **Rec. 2020 Color Primaries:** This can only be accessed when the profile of High 10 is chosen from the drop-down menu.
- **High Dynamic Range:** This can only be accessed when Rec. 2020 Color Primaries is selected.

- **Bitrate Settings:** This can control the rate or megabits per second (Mbps) of a video. Refer to Figure 26-31.

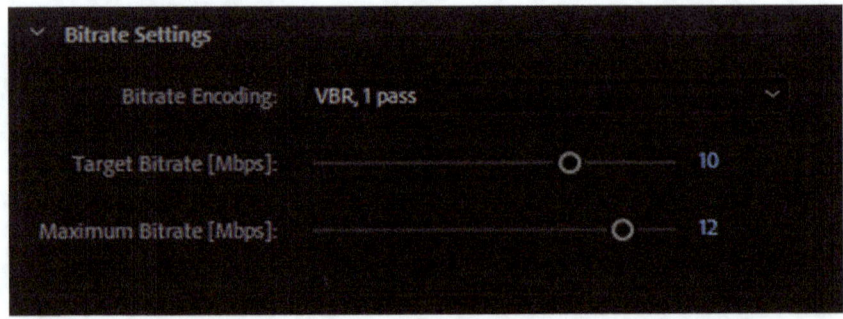

Figure 26-31. Video tab settings for Bitrate Settings

- **Bitrate Encoding:** There are three to choose from: CBR (constant bit rate), VBR (variable bit rate) 1 pass, and VBR 2 pass. *Pass* refers to the number of encoding passes.

- **Target Bitrate (Mbsp):** The target rate allowed by the encoder; you can set a range or type in a number (0.19–14)

- **Maximum Bitrate (Mbsp):** Higher values can improve maximum quality but increase decoder requirements. Like target bitrate, it ranges from (0.19–14) and is linked to the target so that when a number is selected from the target, it limits the range of the maximum bitrate. For example, if target is 14 then the maximum can only be 14.

- **Advanced Settings:** By default, this is unchecked and has a default of 72, which is determined by Media Encoder based on the frame rate of the video clip; however, when checked, you can chose from a range for the keyframe distance. *Keyframes* are complete video frames (or images) that are inserted at consistent intervals in a video clip. The frames between the keyframes contain information on changes that occurs between keyframes.

If your footage has a lot of scene changes or rapidly moving motion or animation, then the overall image quality may benefit from a lower keyframe distance. A lower keyframe distance corresponds to a larger output file. This sets the maximum number of frames between keyframes. If this number of frames without a keyframe occurs, the compressor inserts a keyframe regardless of whether the scene has changed. You can work with section in combination with Video Tab Bitrate Settings and it can affect the final file output size of your video. Refer to Figure 26-32.

Figure 26-32. Video tab settings for Advanced Settings

CHAPTER 26 ■ WORKING WITH YOUR RAW VIDEO FILES (AVI AND MOV)

- **Video is VR:** By default, this is unchecked. Once checked, you can adjust the frame layout for virtual reality. It adds video metadata. Refer to Figure 26-33.

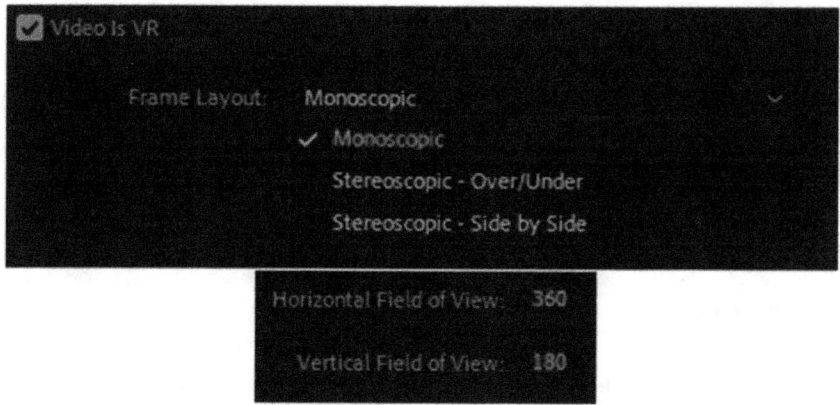

Figure 26-33. Video tab settings for Video is VR

When you hover over each option in the menu it describes how monoscopic and stereoscopic imagery is laid out in the frame. For each type you can now adjust the horizontal and vertical field of view.

Monoscopic means there is a single point of view in the recording, whereas *stereoscopic* means there is a separate recording for both eyes, adding more depth, such as in 3D or virtual reality video. This does not make the video one or the other, it only adds the information or metadata to the file.

To create 3D 360-degree view in monoscopic or stereoscopic video, you need a camera that can record in one of these formats. Then using professional video editing software like After Effects CC, you could stitch the final video together. A good article explaining monoscopic and stereoscopic is at www.onlinecmag.com/stereoscopic-videos-vs-monoscopic-360/.

Audio Tab

Besides video, you can control your audio settings. Refer to Figure 26-34.

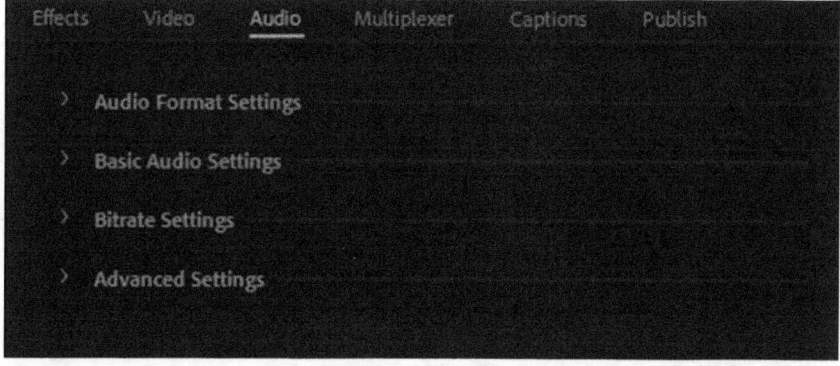

Figure 26-34. Audio tab settings

663

CHAPTER 26 ■ WORKING WITH YOUR RAW VIDEO FILES (AVI AND MOV)

- **Audio Format Settings:** Can be either ACC (advanced audio coding) or MPEG. Refer to Figure 26-35.

Figure 26-35. Audio tab settings for Audio Format Settings

Depending on the setting, different choices will be available in the other subsections below the Audio Format.

- **Basic Audio Settings:** Sets the parameters for the audio for either ACC or MPEG. Refer to Figure 26-36.

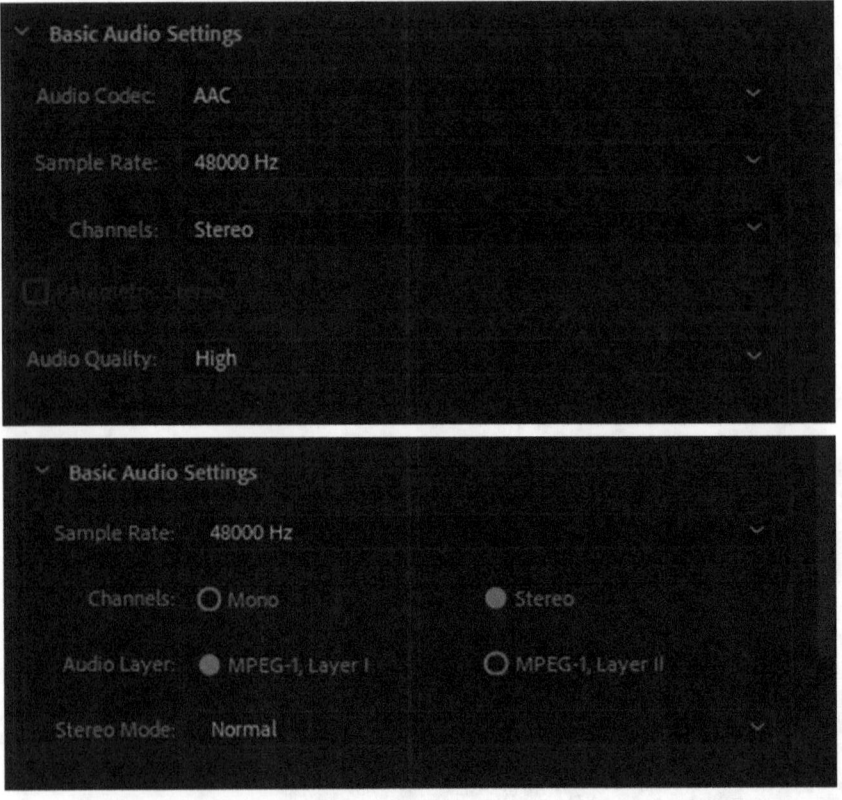

Figure 26-36. Audio tab settings for Basic Audio Settings ACC and MPEG

CHAPTER 26 ■ WORKING WITH YOUR RAW VIDEO FILES (AVI AND MOV)

- **Audio Codec:** This refers to the codec used to encode the audio stream. There are several ACC versions to choose from in the drop-down menu.

- **Sample Rate:** This is the sample rate of the audio in Hz (hertz).

- **Channels:** The number of channels in the output audio (mono, stereo, 5.1).

- **Parametric Stereo:** Recommended for stereo audio that has a bit rate below 40 kbsp (kilobytes per second). Only available for Audio Codec ACC+Version 2 when Channels is set to Stereo.

- **Audio Quality:** High, medium or low.

- **Audio Layer:** For MPEG-1 can be one or two layers: MPEG-1 Audio Layer I or MP1. It is a deliberately simplified version of MPEG-1 Audio Layer II and is created for applications where lower compression efficiency could be tolerated in return for a less complex algorithm that could be executed with simpler hardware requirements. While supported by most media players, the codec is considered largely obsolete, and replaced by MP2 or MP3. MPEG-1 Audio Layer II or MPEG-2 Audio Layer II (MP2) is a lossy audio compression format and is a standard for audio broadcasting. You can save the audio separately as an (.mp3) file, as you see in Chapter 27.

- **Stereo Mode:** For MPEGs can be normal, joint stereo, or dual channel. This is only available if the channel setting is stereo.

- **Bitrate Settings:** When you encode the audio, a higher bitrate means better quality. Refer to Figure 26-37.

Figure 26-37. *Audio tab settings for Bitrate Settings*

Keep in mind that your audio is only as good as the equipment or hardware that you use to record it. So in some cases, it may just mean a larger file size.

- **Advanced Settings:** Depending on if you choose ACC or MPEG, these settings differ. Refer to Figure 26-38.

CHAPTER 26 ■ WORKING WITH YOUR RAW VIDEO FILES (AVI AND MOV)

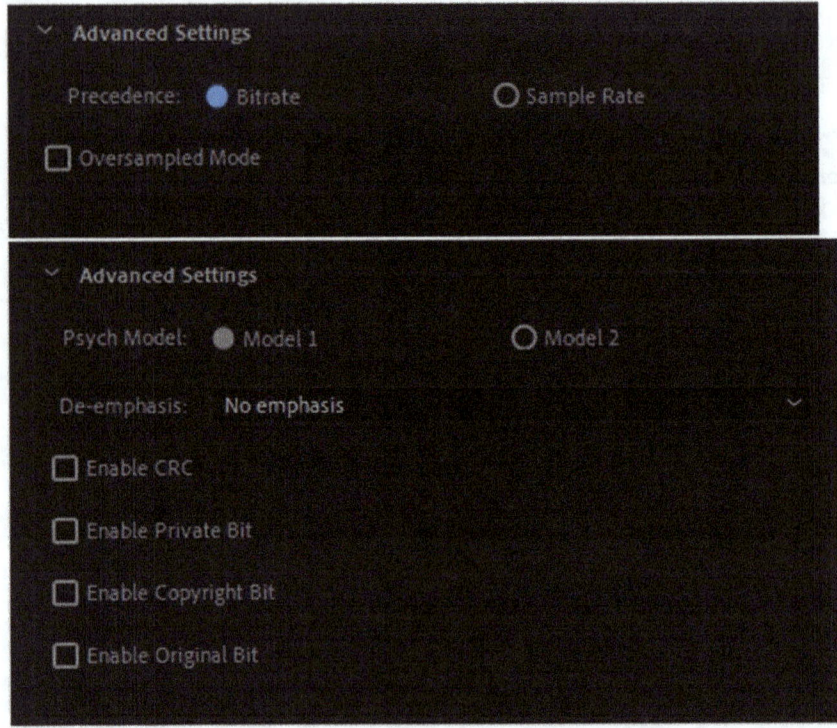

Figure 26-38. Audio tab settings for Advanced Settings ACC and MPEG

- **Precedence:** For ACC, bitrate constrains the sample rate based on the earlier chosen bitrate. Sample rate this constrains the bitmap values for the given sample rate. The option of Oversampled Mode may be available depending on what settings you changed earlier in the Audio tab.
- **Psych Model:** For MPEG, known as a Psychoacoustic model, it has to do with amplitude and noise level; you can choose either model 1 or 2.
- **De-emphasis:** Decreases the magnitude of some frequencies. By default, it is set to No emphasis. Refer to Figure 26-39 and see https://en.wikipedia.org/wiki/Emphasis_(telecommunications).

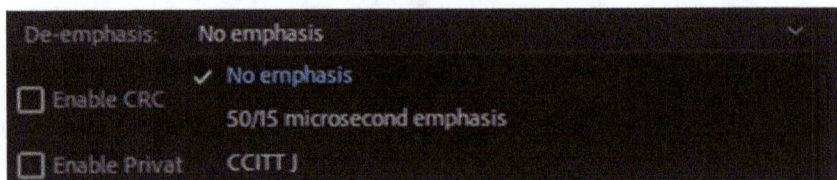

Figure 26-39. Audio tab settings for Advanced Settings MPEG de-emphasis

- **Enable CRC:** Cyclical Redundancy Code (CRC) to detect errors in the bitstream.
- **Enable Private Bit:** Available for private use.

CHAPTER 26 ■ WORKING WITH YOUR RAW VIDEO FILES (AVI AND MOV)

- **Enable Copyright Bit:** The copyright bit relates to what is called DRM (Digital Rights Management) and to whether it is legal or illegal to copy the audio.
- **Enable Original Bit:** This relates to the original bit stream, which can be recovered from audio using other software in certain cases.

Multiplexer Tab

The Multiplexer preset options (sometimes called Format) controls how MPEG video (mp4, 3GPP, none) and audio data are merged into a single stream. Refer to Figure 26-40.

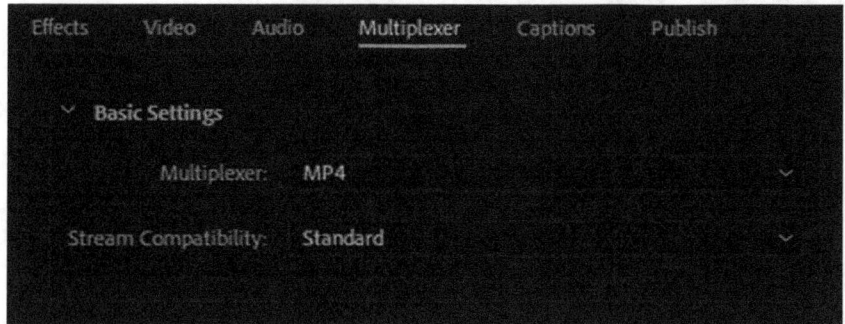

Figure 26-40. Multipexer tab settings for Basic Settings

Basic Settings is the default, in this case in MP4. You can choose different multiplexer options in the drop-down menu. When you choose MP4, different stream compatibility options are available such as standard, PSP, or iPod.

Captions Tab

Depending on the file format chosen for export (as in an MP4 (H.264) file), this area may not be accessible to edit if the original file did not have closed captioning (CC). If it was added to the RAW video in another program, like Premiere Pro, and then imported into Media Encoder, this area may have these options enabled. Refer to Figure 26-41.

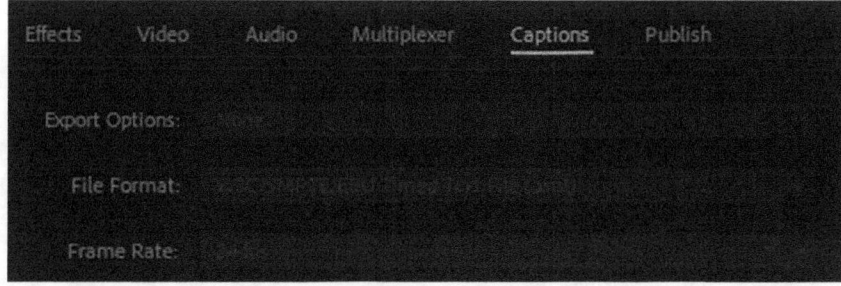

Figure 26-41. Captions tab settings for Basic Settings

CHAPTER 26 ■ WORKING WITH YOUR RAW VIDEO FILES (AVI AND MOV)

■ **Note** The Export options, file format, and frame rate relate to the captions, not to the frame rate of the video.

Publish Tab

Besides publishing your video file directly to your external hard drive, you may want to publish it to various websites or social media sites. Refer to Figure 26-42.

Figure 26-42. Publish tab settings

Media Encoder allows you to enable and enter login information for various sites and saves the information so that you don't have to do it each time for the same file.

Adobe Creative Cloud: Saves your file to a subfolder to later add to the Creative Cloud. Refer to Figure 26-43.

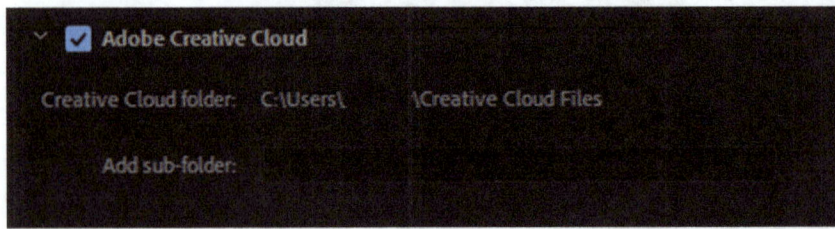

Figure 26-43. Publish tab settings for Adobe Creative Cloud

CHAPTER 26 ■ WORKING WITH YOUR RAW VIDEO FILES (AVI AND MOV)

- This is like having the Libraries CC panel as in the other Adobe programs where you can upload a file to the Creative Cloud.

- **Adobe Stock:** If you have an account with Adobe Stock, you can sign in. Refer to Figure 26-44.

Figure 26-44. *Publish tab settings for Adobe Stock*

- **Behance:** If you have an account with Behance, you can sign in and add a description and tag to the file. There is also the option to delete the local file after upload; leave this unchecked should you want to use the same file elsewhere. Refer to Figure 26-45.

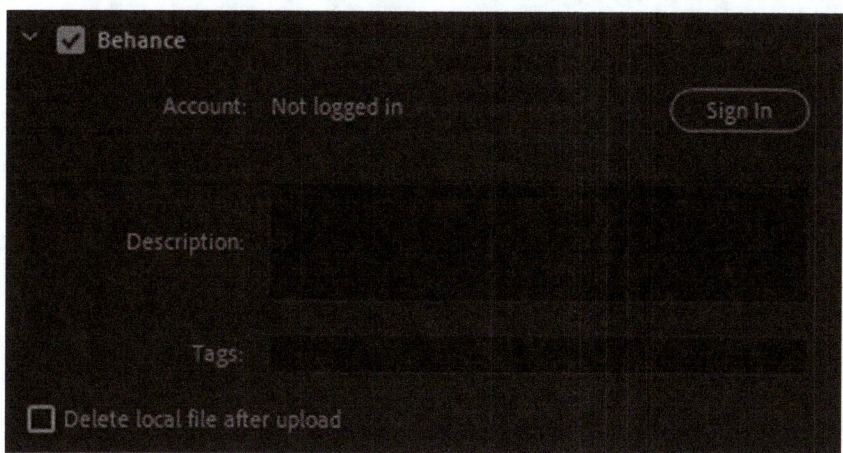

Figure 26-45. *Publish tab settings for Behance*

- **Facebook:** If you have a Facebook account, you can sign in and add a the page to upload to, the title, and description, before you upload the file. There is the option to delete the local file after upload; leave this unchecked should you want to use the same file elsewhere. Refer to Figure 26-46.

CHAPTER 26 ■ WORKING WITH YOUR RAW VIDEO FILES (AVI AND MOV)

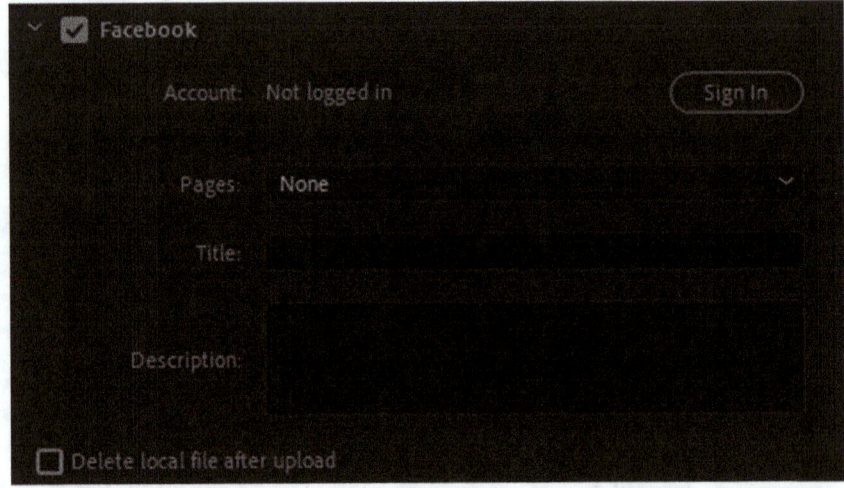

Figure 26-46. *Publish tab settings for Facebook*

- **FTP:** Also known as File Transfer Protocol, this is a good option if you have already set up your site using Dreamweaver CC and have an FTP account set up. Rather than going through Dreamweaver CC, you can upload the new file directly to the folder in the site if there is a last minute change to the video. Refer to Figure 26-47.

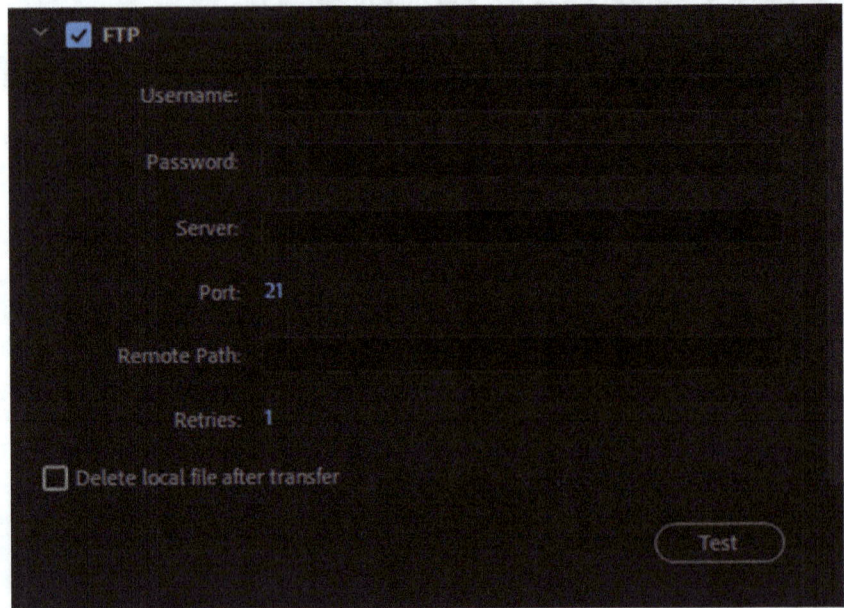

Figure 26-47. *Publish tab settings for FTP*

670

CHAPTER 26 ■ WORKING WITH YOUR RAW VIDEO FILES (AVI AND MOV)

Enter your username, password, and server, and set up the remote URL path. You look at this in more detail in Part 6. Leave port and retries at the default unless you have different settings within your company. Skype has been known to affect the port number, so this is something to check if you run into issues.

There is also the option to delete the local file after upload, leave this unchecked if you use the same file elsewhere.

- **Twitter:** If you have an account with Twitter, you can sign in and add status information. Refer to Figure 26-48. Like the previous publishing options, you can choose whether or not to delete the local file after upload.

Figure 26-48. Publish tab settings for Twitter

- **Vimeo:** If you have an account with Vimeo, you can sign in and add a channel to upload, the title, and a description of the file. You can also choose privacy settings (viewable by) and add tags. Like previous publishing options, you can choose whether or not to delete the local file after upload. Refer to Figure 26-49.

671

CHAPTER 26 ■ WORKING WITH YOUR RAW VIDEO FILES (AVI AND MOV)

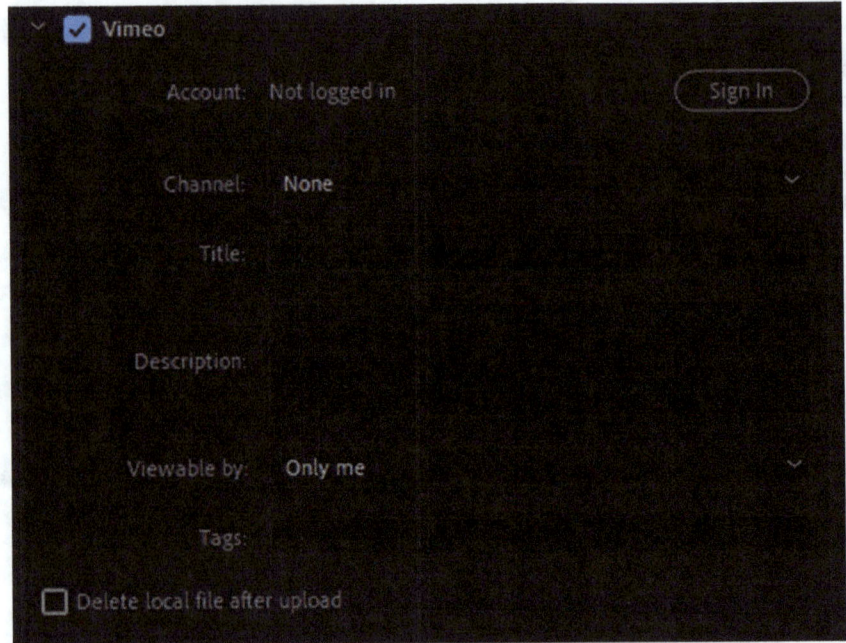

Figure 26-49. *Publish tab settings for Vimeo*

- **YouTube:** If you have an account with YouTube, you can sign in and add a channel and playlist to upload to as well as a, title and description to the file. You can then choose privacy settings and add tags. Custom Thumbnail is the cover or poster image, which could be none (default), from an image that you created, or a frame chosen from the video. Like previous publish options, you can choose whether or not to delete the local file after upload. Refer to Figure 26-50.

CHAPTER 26 ■ WORKING WITH YOUR RAW VIDEO FILES (AVI AND MOV)

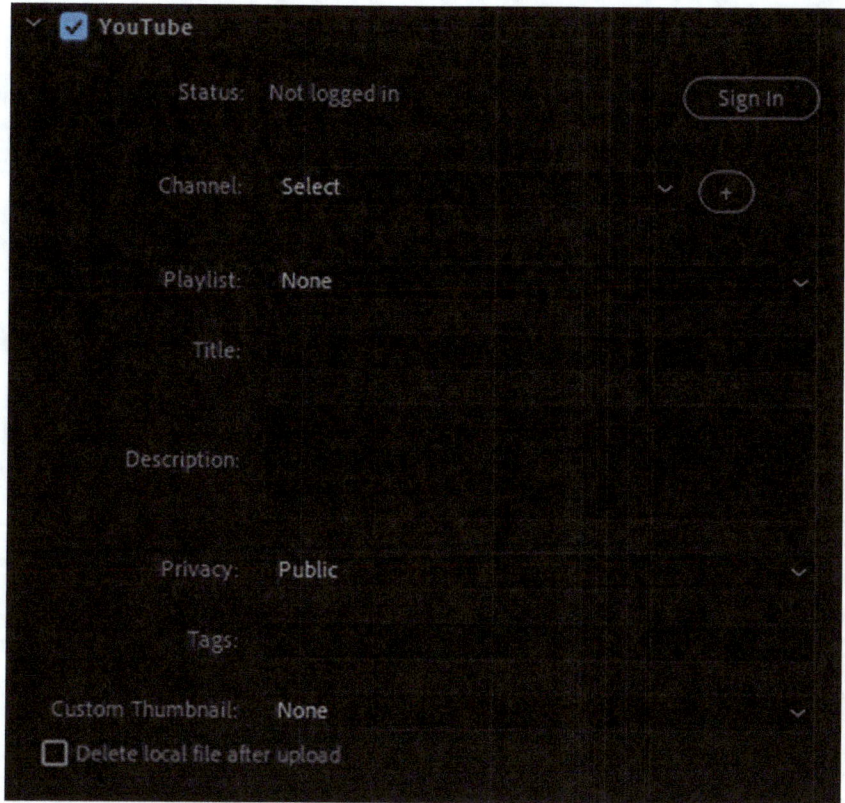

Figure 26-50. *Publish tab settings for Vimeo*

Render, Time Code, and Alpha and Output Size

The last section lets you enable or adjust the following settings.

- **Use Maximum Render Quality:** Increases encoding time if enabled.
- **Use Previews:** For sequence exports from Premier Pro; if these files are already created by Premiere Pro, then selecting this option selects those preview files making the rendering faster.
- **Set start time code:** This sets the start in the format of hh:mm:ss:ff.
- **Render Alpha Channel Only:** Use if the original video format has this channel.
- **Time Interpolation:** Depending on the setting from the drop-down menu, you can create smoother motion by blending adjacent frames when the input frame rate does not match the output frame rate. The default is Frame Sampling. Refer to Figure 26-51.

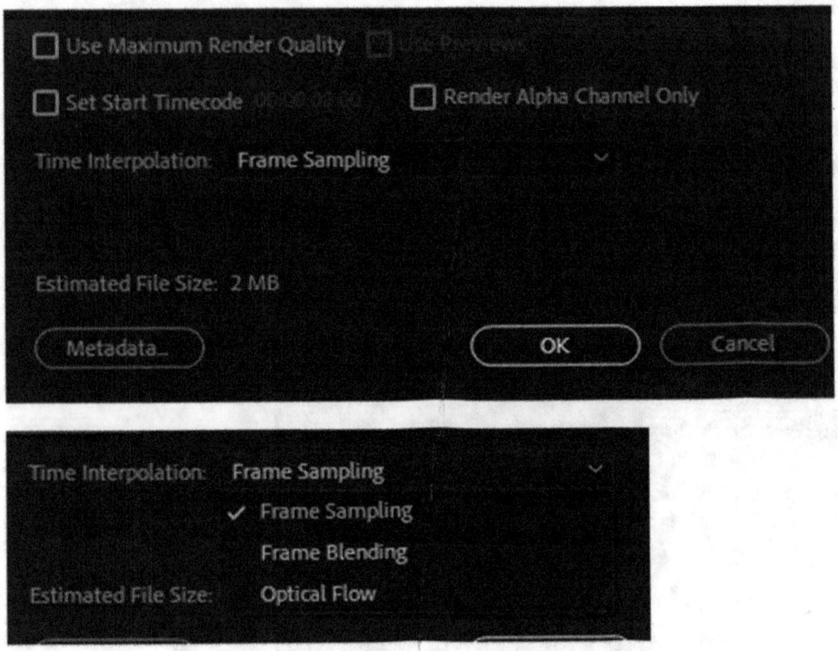

CHAPTER 26 ■ WORKING WITH YOUR RAW VIDEO FILES (AVI AND MOV)

Figure 26-51. Final export settings in the lower right

You can then see the estimated file size and check the metadata, as seen in Figure 26-52.

CHAPTER 26 ■ WORKING WITH YOUR RAW VIDEO FILES (AVI AND MOV)

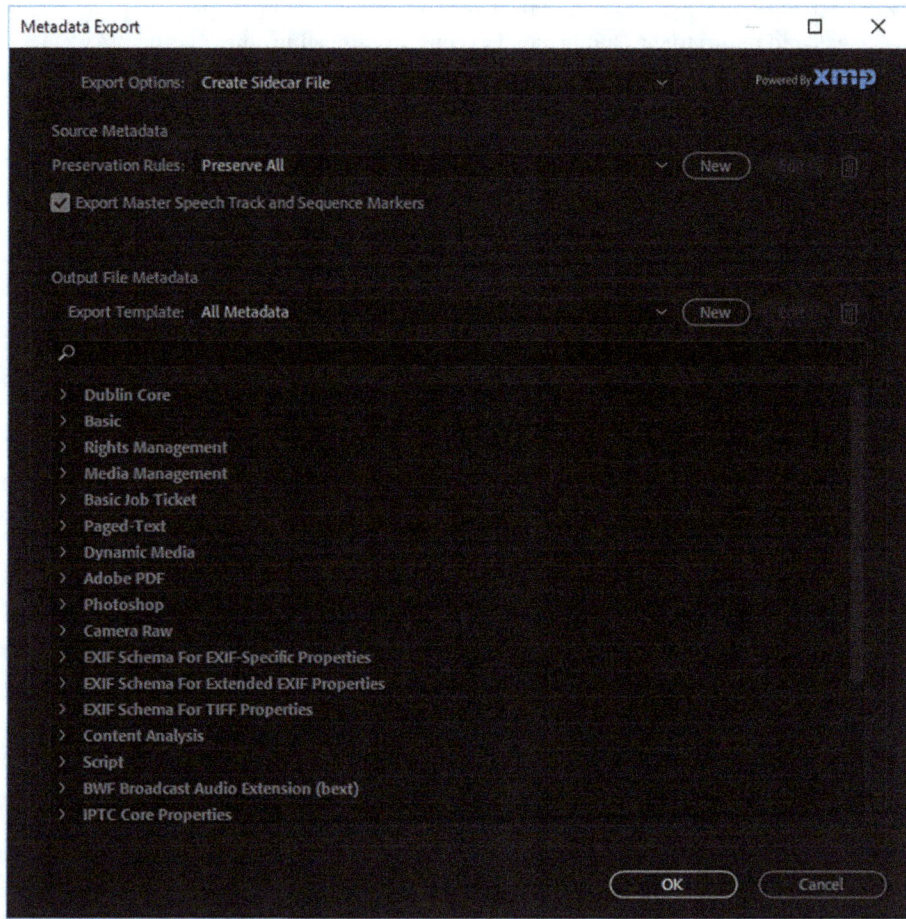

Figure 26-52. Metadata Export dialog box

The Metadata Export dialog box allows you to enter extra detailed information that may relate to rights management or media management. Depending on the type of file format you output, this information is included as data somewhere in or with the file as a sidecar (.xmp) file. Refer to Figure 26-53.

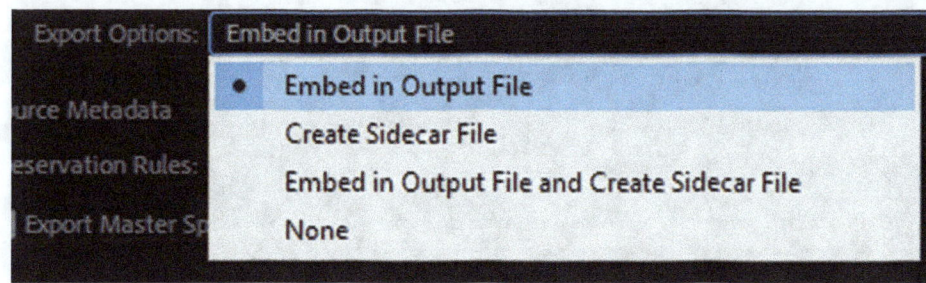

Figure 26-53. Metadata Export dialog box embed output settings

675

When done, click Cancel to exit the dialog box. And then in Export Settings, either click OK to confirm your settings or Cancel to exit and return to the Queue panel to continue adjusting other files before you export the MP4 file by pressing the green Play arrow.

Combine Video (Stitch Clips)

Back in the Queue panel, there is one final key area to look at. Video clips—whether still images, audio or video—can be combined as a single file from files that are Shift-clicked in the Media Browser panel; and then right-click and choose Stitch Clips Together. Refer to Figure 26-54.

Figure 26-54. Combining video clips

Like a single MP4 or WAV file, when selected in the Media Browser panel and then reordered in the Queue panel by dragging up or down to change the order. However, if a clear transition is not previously created between the two video files then the blend may appear choppy between transitions. A scene may break at the wrong location or the audio may not appear consistent upon reaching the stitch point. If video sources in a stitched clip do not have the same properties (for example, different frame sizes, frame rates, and so on), the properties of the first clip in the series determines the properties of the entire stitched clip.

Sources with differing frame sizes are scaled to fit the frame size of the first clip automatically. Though pixel aspect ratio is maintained, letter boxing and pillar boxing can occur, which may not be the effect you are trying to achieve. If this a concern, it is better to stitch your RAW video or animations together using Photoshop CC, Animate CC, or Premiere Pro CC, and then bring the file into Adobe Media Encoder for a final rendering. This way, you can control exactly where video or audio starts or stops and adjust frame sizes.

Regardless, like any file that is added to Media Encoder, they can be added or deleted from the Queue panel; they can also be reordered by dragging up or down in the list. You can also hide and show the source files. The stitch clip can also be renamed by clicking the source name in the Queue panel. Refer to Figure 26-55.

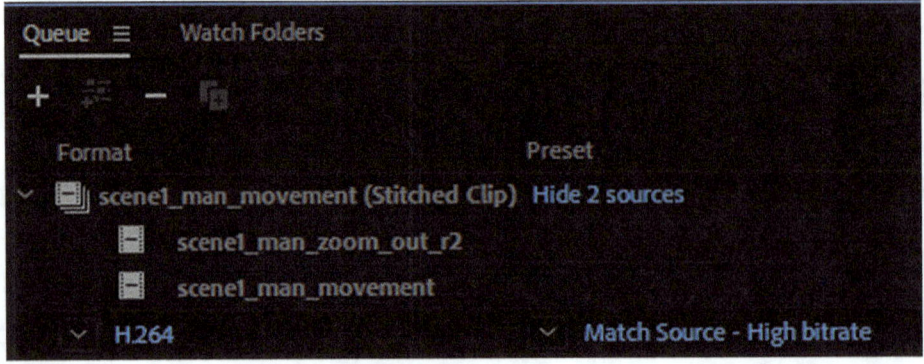

Figure 26-55. Combining video clips in Media Encoder

The combined files go into the selected output folder and render with their export settings when you click the green arrow to the right of the Queue panel.

Remember, if you need to export the same file again, you can always right-click the format and choose Reset Status in the Queue panel, and it is set back to Ready, as seen in Figure 26-56.

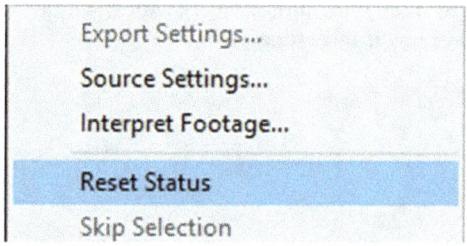

Figure 26-56. *Reset the status of a file back to ready in the Queue panel*

■ **Remember**   If you are not sure of the exact format size or preset to use for any of files that were discussed in this section, you can always refer to the Preset Browser panel and look at the Comment section to see what Adobe recommends.

WebM and Ogg

The other two formats that are supported by web browsers are WebM (.webm) and Theora (.ogg).

WebM is a media file format. It is primarily intended to offer a royalty-free alternative to use in the HTML5 video and the HTML5 audio tags.

Theora Ogg is a free lossy video compression format. It includes the Vorbis audio format and the Ogg container.

Media Encoder does not allow you to export as either of these formats without acquiring a third-party plugin. If you need these file formats for your project, you can download them from a company recommended on the Adobe forums that works with Adobe Media Encoder or Premier Pro (see www.fnordware.com/WebM/ and https://github.com/fnordware/AdobeOgg).

Another great option is a free program like Miro Video Converter is useful to download as well to convert to these formats. It is very simple to use, but you may not have all the codec setting which come in a program like Media Encoder and is best for small files. Larger files take longer to render and sometimes the quality is not always the greatest.

Since MP4 is viewed my most browsers, this may be the only file format you need for your video; however, if you are worried about browser compatibility WebM and Ogg are important backup source files for older browsers, as you see in Part 6.

For more information on these formats, visit https://en.wikipedia.org/wiki/WebM and https://en.wikipedia.org/wiki/Theora.

CHAPTER 26 ■ WORKING WITH YOUR RAW VIDEO FILES (AVI AND MOV)

Summary

In this chapter, you looked the RAW files—AVI and MOV, and available export settings for an MP4 (H.246) file for your website. You discovered that you can stitch multiple clips together in Media Encoder. Finally, you looked at two other video web formats: WebM and Ogg.

In the next chapter, you look at how to export the audio out of video files, and you work with an audio format that you cannot import into Media Encoder until you adjust its file format name.

CHAPTER 27

Working with Your RAW Video Files and Converting Them to Audio

In this chapter, you look at how to convert your video's audio to a sound file (.mp3 and .wav) for your website. You also look at the other web format (.ogg), as well as how to convert a specific audio file (.3ga) that is not accepted in Media Encoder.

> **Note** This chapter does not have any actual projects; however, you can use the files in the Chapter 27 folder to practice opening and viewing for this lesson. They are at https://github.com/Apress/graphics-multimedia-web-adobe-creative-cloud.

Convert Audio to (Export Settings)

As with the MP4 file that you created, you can extract only the audio from a video file for use on a website. Once you have imported your video file, it is time to export it to the correct audio formats. There are three main audio formats that most desktop and mobile browsers recognize for the web: MP3, WAV, and Ogg. You can use Media Encoder to extract your audio in at least two of these formats. You can view them in the Preset panel ➤ System Presets ➤ Audio Only. Refer to Figure 27-1.

CHAPTER 27 ■ WORKING WITH YOUR RAW VIDEO FILES AND CONVERTING THEM TO AUDIO

System Presets			
🔊 Audio Only			
AIFF 48 kHz	AIFF	-	48 kHz
Audio Only, 44.1 kHz 64 kbps	Windows Media	-	44.1 kHz
Audio Only, 48 kHz 128 kbps	Windows Media	-	48 kHz
MP3 128 kbps	MP3	-	44.1 kHz
MP3 192 kbps High Quality	MP3	-	44.1 kHz
MP3 256 kbps High Quality	MP3	-	44.1 kHz
Stereo AAC, 44.1 kHz 128 kbps	AAC Audio	-	44.1 kHz
Stereo AAC, 48 kHz 256 kbps	AAC Audio	-	48 kHz
WAV 48 kHz 16-bit	Waveform Audio	-	48 kHz

Figure 27-1. Audio Only drop-down tab in the Preset panel

MP3

MP3, or MPEG-3, has three different presets available in Media Encoder that run at different kilobytes per second (kbps); generally, the default is 128, but this depends upon the original source of the video file or original audio within the file. Refer to Figure 27-2.

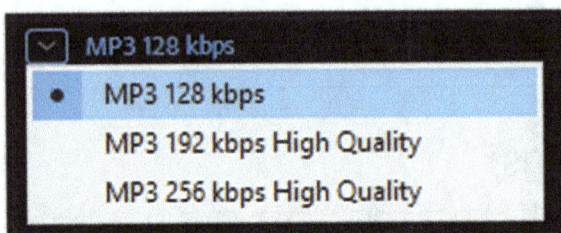

Figure 27-2. Preset options for MP3 in the Queue panel

Export Settings Dialog Box

When you enter the Export setting dialog box as you did with the MP4 file, this time, only Export Audio is enabled, and export video will be disabled as in Figure 27-3.

Figure 27-3. Only Export Audio can be accessed in the Export setting dialog box

CHAPTER 27 ■ WORKING WITH YOUR RAW VIDEO FILES AND CONVERTING THEM TO AUDIO

Preview Settings

The preview is blank because no video is occurring, as seen in Figure 27-4.

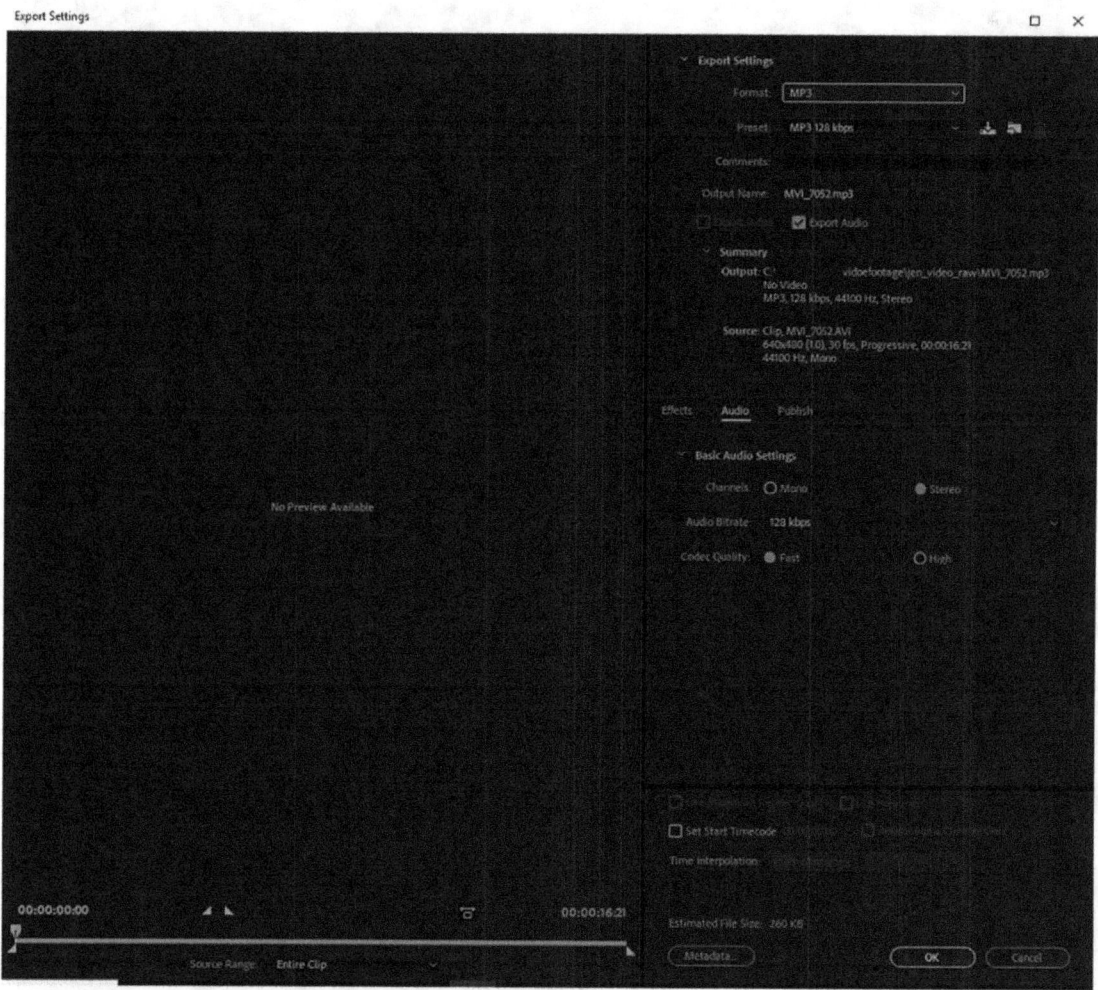

Figure 27-4. No video preview is available for audio only files

Note that Media Encoder does not preview the audio. So, you need to use your computer's media player initially to know at what point the sound occurs. However, once you know this, use the lower timeline in the Export Setting dialog box (hours: minutes: seconds: frames); you can then drag the lower triangles into position in Media Encoder and clip the area of audio to the few seconds or minutes that you require. Refer to Figure 27-5.

681

CHAPTER 27 ■ WORKING WITH YOUR RAW VIDEO FILES AND CONVERTING THEM TO AUDIO

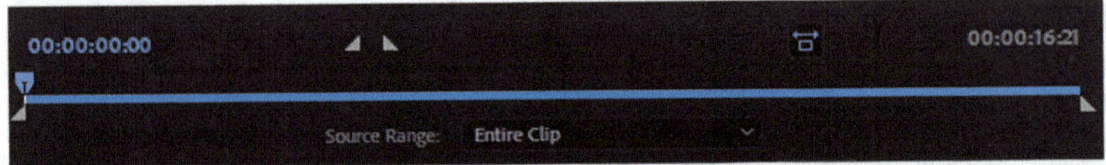

Figure 27-5. Audio preview of the entire clip in Export settings. Drag the triangles inward if you want to clip the audio.

Likewise, in Photoshop, you can trim your audio further, as seen in Chapters 7 and 9.

Export and Summary Settings

Many of the export settings and summary are like the MP4, as you saw in Chapter 26. You can adjust your preset import and export, trash a preset, add comments, change the output file name, change the export location, and review the summary before export. Refer to Figure 27-6.

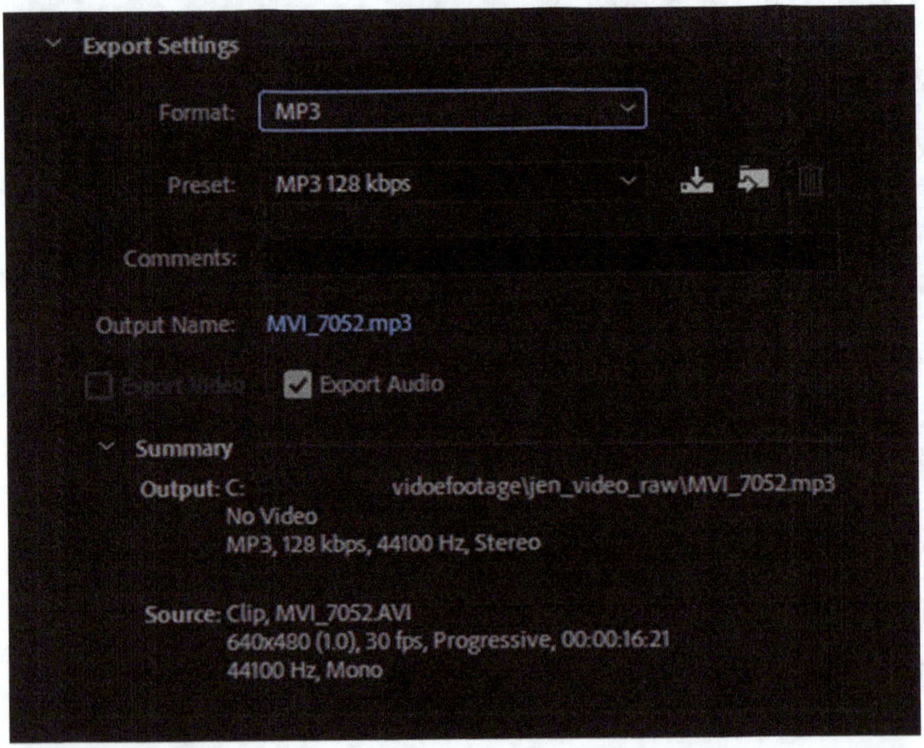

Figure 27-6. Export and Summary settings in the Export settings dialog box

However, with MP3, you are limited to the Effects, Audio, and Publish tabs. Refer to Figure 27-7.

CHAPTER 27 ■ WORKING WITH YOUR RAW VIDEO FILES AND CONVERTING THEM TO AUDIO

Figure 27-7. Effects tab in the Export settings dialog box

Effects Tab

The Effects tab allows you to control two areas: Time Tuner and Loudness Normalization.

These can only be adjusted when their check boxes are enabled; by default, they are unchecked.

Time Tuner

As with MP4, the Time Tuner feature sets the current and target duration, and shows the duration change as a percentage. (See Chapter 26 for more information).

Skip slates refers to a series of still images with a combined duration longer than 10 seconds. Checking this should prevent the time tuner from being applied to them; however, if there are no images visible in an audio clip, it may have no effect.

Be aware that the time tuner may cause part of the audio to drop or drag, which may not be what you want; so make sure to experiment with this setting if you plan to use it. Refer to Figure 27-8.

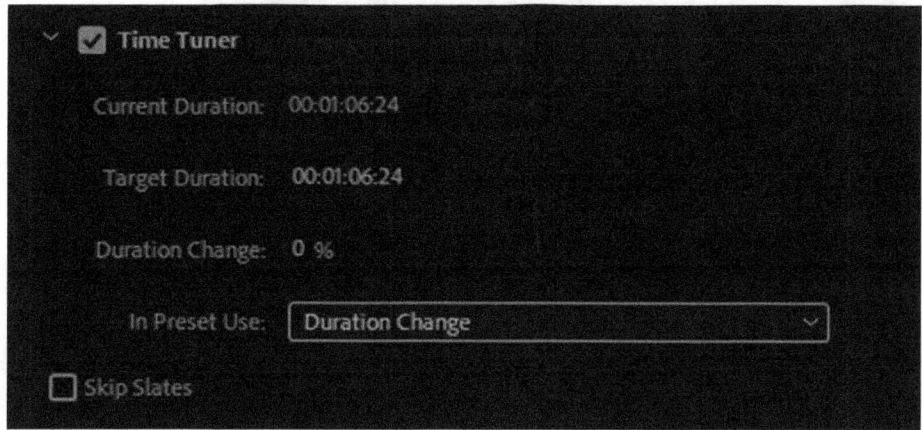

Figure 27-8. Effects tab in the Time Tuner settings

CHAPTER 27 ■ WORKING WITH YOUR RAW VIDEO FILES AND CONVERTING THEM TO AUDIO

Loudness Normalization

As with MP4 files, loudness can be adjusted. There are at least three loudness standards to choose from; for more information, refer to the MP4 settings in Chapter 26. Like MP4, the MP3 setting allows you to save a loudness report. This area assists you in making sure your audio does not reach excessive levels and meets the required broadcast specs. Refer to Figure 27-9.

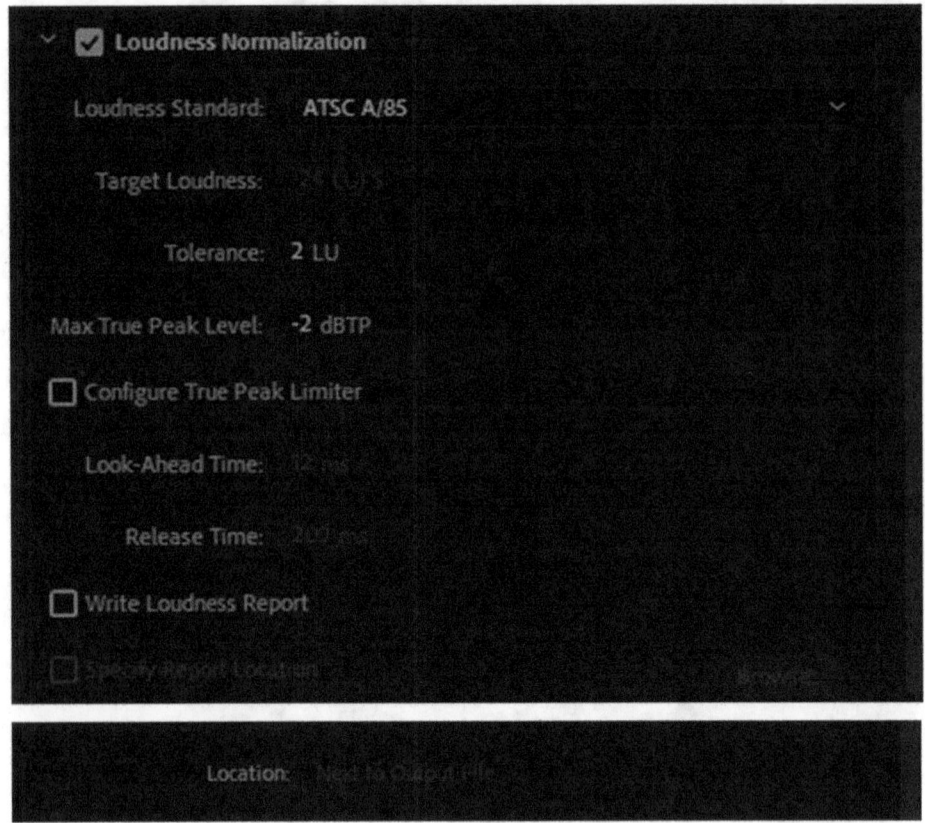

Figure 27-9. Effects tab in the Loudness Normalization settings

Audio Tab

Audio lets you adjust the Basic Audio Settings, such as whether the channels are mono or stereo; the audio bit rate, which may be a setting that is not one of the three main presets; and the codec quality (fast or high). Refer to Figure 27-10.

CHAPTER 27 ■ WORKING WITH YOUR RAW VIDEO FILES AND CONVERTING THEM TO AUDIO

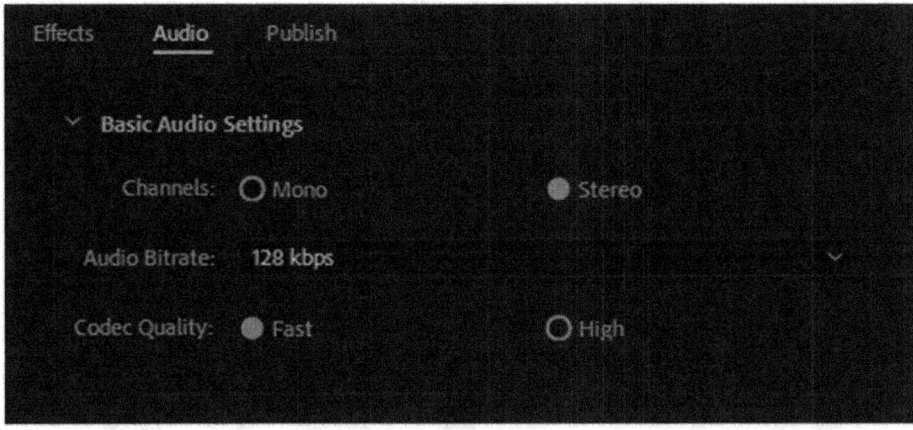

Figure 27-10. *Audio tab in the Basic Audio Settings*

Publish Tab

An audio MP3 file can be published either on your hard drive, external drive, to Adobe Creative Cloud, or directly to your website via FTP. Refer to Figure 27-11.

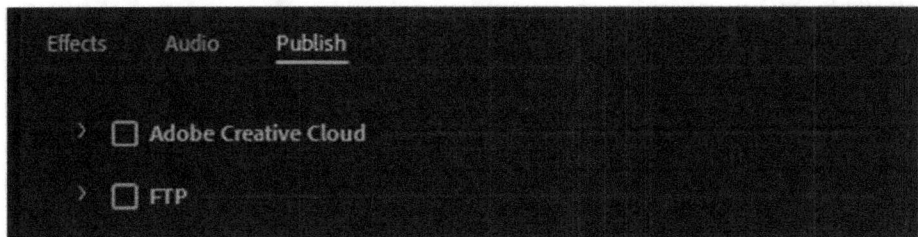

Figure 27-11. *Publish tab in Adobe Creative Cloud and FTP settings*

You cannot publish directly to other social media sites, such as Facebook, Twitter, or YouTube. Refer to Figure 27-11. This is likely because these social media sites are more video driven. If you're planning an audio file with no action, a better option to use in these platforms would be is to create a video file in Photoshop or Premiere Pro and add a single image to the background while the music plays, and then use Media Encoder to export the file as an MP4.

You can see more tips on this tab in Chapter 26.

Time Code Settings

As with MP4, the lower right area of the Time Code settings are the same, though some areas are unavailable since you are only working with audio. You can still set the start time code, view the estimated file size, and set the metadata. Refer to Figure 27-12.

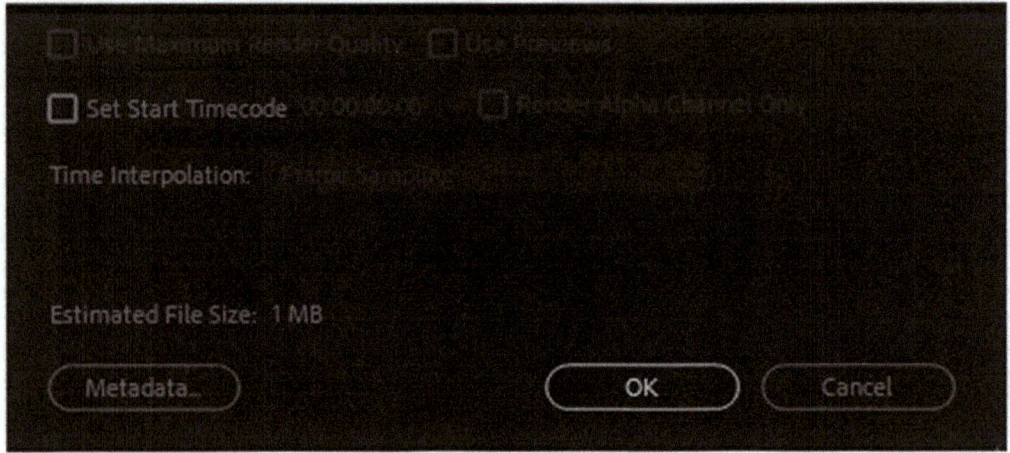

Figure 27-12. Time code settings in the Export setting dialog box

When done, click OK to exit the setting, or cancel if you don't want to apply changes to your MP3 output file.

Waveform Audio (.wav)

Waveform or WAV is the other audio file for the web. It is a Microsoft and IBM audio file format that is standard for storing audio bitstream on PC computers. It only has one preset (WAV 48 kHz 16 bit) in Media Encoder, and has many settings similar to the MP4 video and MP3 audio. Refer to Figure 27-13.

Figure 27-13. Format Preset settings in the Queue panel

> **Note** Only export audio is available in the Export setting dialog box because you are only dealing with sound as in Figure 27-14.

Export and Summary Settings

As you can see, like MP3, the WAV Export Settings and Summary Settings are basically the same; only the Preset setting is different. Refer to Figure 27-14.

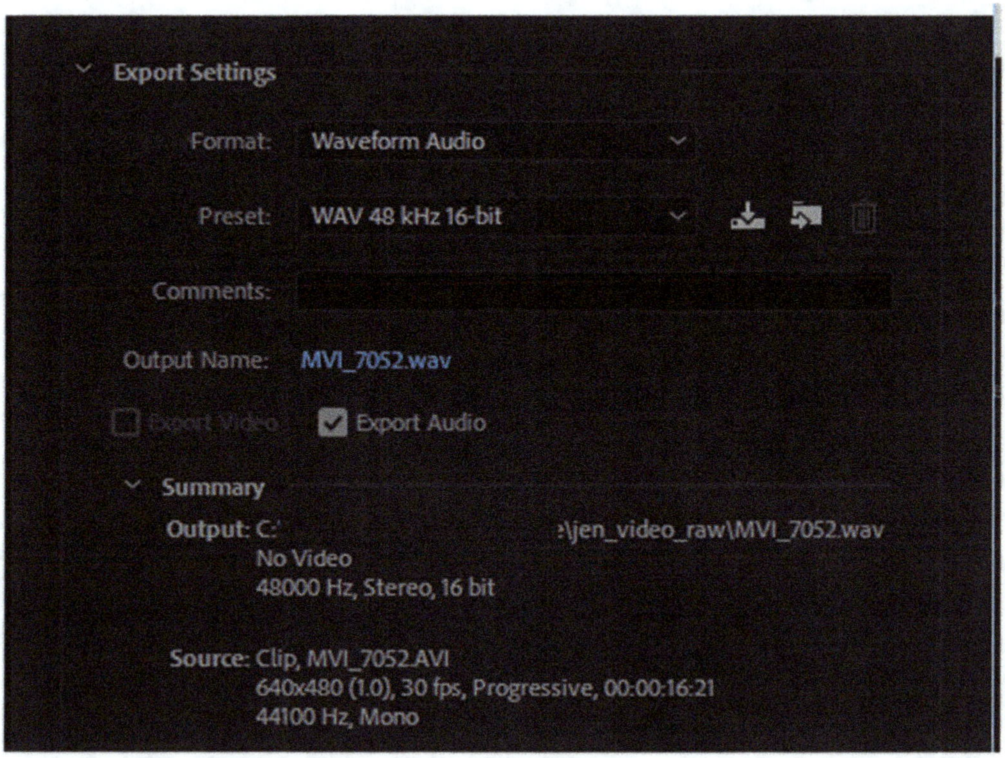

CHAPTER 27 ■ WORKING WITH YOUR RAW VIDEO FILES AND CONVERTING THEM TO AUDIO

Figure 27-14. Export Settings dialog box for WAV format

Effects Tab

As with MP3, the WAV file is limited to two effects: time tuner and loudness normalization. The settings can be activated and edited when the check boxes are enabled. Refer to the MP3 Effects tab section and Figure 27-15.

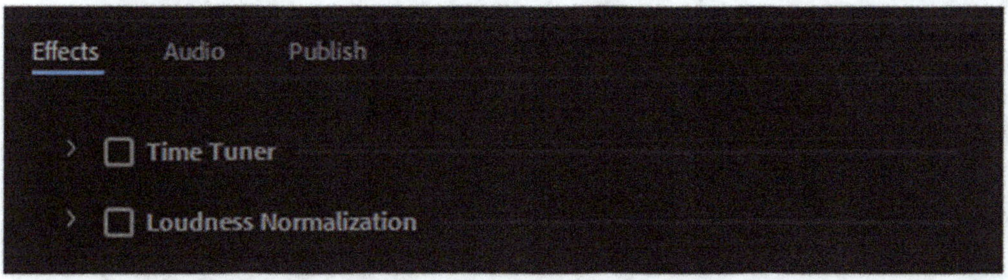

Figure 27-15. Export settings Effects tab

Audio Tab

In the Audio tab, you can set the Audio Codec setting to Uncompressed or several different compression states that encode the audio bitstream. Refer to Figure 27-16.

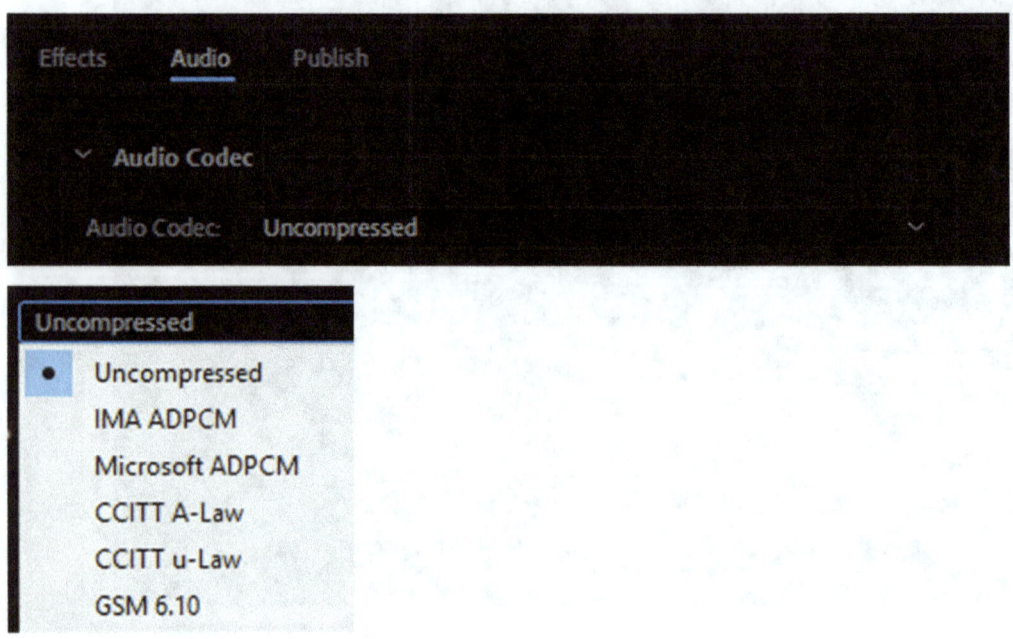

Figure 27-16. Audio tab Audio Codec setting

In the Basic Audio Settings, as with MP3, this area adjusts the sample rate in Hz, the channels (mono or stereo), and the sample size in bit-depth amount. Refer to Figure 27-17.

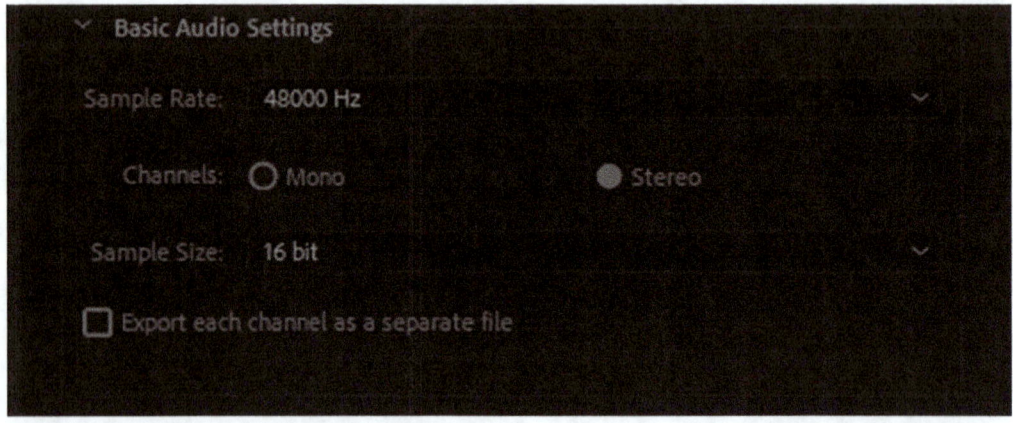

Figure 27-17. Audio tab for Basic Audio Settings

In addition, you can export each channel as a separate file.

CHAPTER 27 ■ WORKING WITH YOUR RAW VIDEO FILES AND CONVERTING THEM TO AUDIO

Publish Tab

As with MP3, files WAV files can be published on your hard drive, external drive, to Adobe Creative Cloud, or directly to your website via FTP. With the default settings, you cannot publish directly to other social media sites like Facebook, Twitter, or YouTube. I mention why this is and some tips for how to deal with this in the Publish tab earlier in this chapter and in Chapter 26. Refer to Figure 27-18.

Figure 27-18. *Publish tab for Adobe Creative Cloud and FTP*

However, for your work in this book, you want to leave the audio files you export either in the .mp3 or .wav format without any images.

Time Code Settings

As with MP3 files, the WAV files can have the Set Start Timecode and the Metadata settings adjusted. Refer to Figure 27-19.

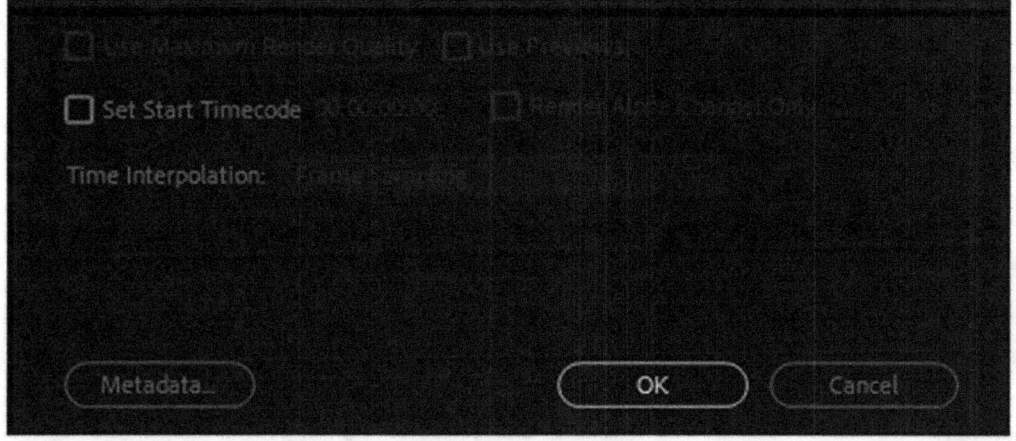

Figure 27-19. *Time Code settings in the Export Setting dialog box*

689

When done, you can click OK to confirm the settings, or cancel if you don't want to apply changes and return to the Queue panel.

■ **Note** As you saw in Chapter 26, you can stitch audio files together using Media Encoder. Refer to that section in the Chapter 26 if you need to know how to do this. Just remember to use an audio format for the stitched clips.

Theora Ogg (.ogg)

Theora Ogg is the third audio format used for the web. To convert a video to this format, I recommend using the third-party programs that Adobe recommends on its forums, or Miro Video Converter. Since WAV and MP3 are heard on most browsers, these may be the only file formats that you need for your audio. However, if you are worried about browser compatibility, Ogg is an important backup source file, as you will see in Part 6.

For information on other professional audio editing programs, refer to Adobe Audition CC and the Ogg export area at https://helpx.adobe.com/audition/using/saving-exporting-files1.html.

Working with Audio Files That Are Audio 3GA

While working on this chapter, I decided that I wanted to record some audio for the projects with my voice to give a dialog of what is going on in the Hot Glass Tango video. After writing a short script, I decided to use my smartphone to record the audio, and then I emailed the audio to myself so that I could convert the formats to MP3 or WAV in Media Encoder. However, at this point, I ran into a bit of a roadblock.

The file format for these audio files was 3GA, and Adobe Media Encoder and Photoshop do not allow you to import this format. I could not even play the audio in my computer's media player. So, knowing I was on a deadline and I needed the audio, I decided what to do.

After doing some research on the web, I discovered that 3GA files are basically the same type of multimedia container as 3GP. In Chapter 26, I mention 3GP and MPEG4 for video. 3GP contains audio and video, but 3GA only has audio. By simply making a copy of the 3GA file in your computer and changing the new file's format extension to 3GP, you can import the file into Media Encoder and convert it to an MP3 or WAV file, which you can then import into other projects. Refer to Figure 27-20.

Figure 27-20. *You can import a 3GP file into the Queue panel and convert it to another audio format*

Summary

In this chapter, you looked how to work with video files like AVI and MOV, and extract audio from the files. You then reviewed various export settings for each audio format: MP3 and WAV. You then looked at options on how to create an Ogg audio file. Finally, you discovered a way to convert an audio file that was not accepted by Media Encoder into a format that it recognized for import.

In the next chapter, you look at how to extract images in a sequence from Media Encoder.

CHAPTER 28

Working with Your RAW Video Files and Converting Them to an Image Sequence

In this chapter, you look at how to extract image sequences from your video file (.avi or .mov) for your projects in the bitmap, JPEG, PNG, and GIF (static and animated) formats.

> **Note** This chapter does not have any actual projects; however, you can use the files in the Chapter 28 folder to practice opening and viewing for this lesson. They are at https://github.com/Apress/graphics-multimedia-web-adobe-creative-cloud.

Convert to Other Web Formats (Image Sequence)

If you are just looking to export your video as an image sequence or animated GIF, Media Encoder allows you to do this as well. You can find them in the Preset Browser panel under System Presets ➤ Image Sequence, or in the Queue panel under the Format name. Let's look at the following options for the web. Refer to Figure 28-1.

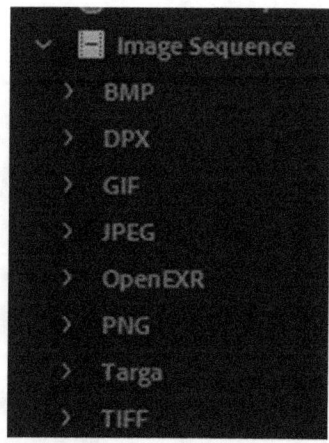

Figure 28-1. Image sequence choices in the Preset Browser panel

Remember that an image sequence can result in a lot of still images, depending on the number of frames per second the image is running. So unless you want a lot of stills, make sure to narrow or trim down your video to which images or frames (hours: minutes: seconds: frames) in the sequence you require. To work efficiently, only export a portion of your frames using the Export Settings dialog box's setpoint triangles and playhead. Also, doing the work on an external hard drive and saving the sequence on that drive ensures that your computer does not crash. Refer to Figure 28-2.

Figure 28-2. *Use your Export Settings dialog box preview area to narrow down the images that you want from a video*

The files are numbered, starting with 0; for example, file0.bmp, file1.bmp, and so on. Also, an XMP file that contains a log of the converted files is created.

■ **Note** Although Media Encoder cannot export certain file format settings, such as PDFs, it can open Illustrator EPS and AI files. Likewise, if your client gives you any older FLV files that were created in an older Adobe Flash program these can be opened and converted to an MP4 (H.264) video format or an image sequence.

As with MP4, you also have access in the Export Settings dialog box with the Source and Output tabs, which allow you to crop your images group. Use the Source Scaling or Cropping options so that you can refine the new dimensions of the files in the sequence that you want to want to output. Refer to Figure 28-3 and Chapter 26 for how to crop a section of video.

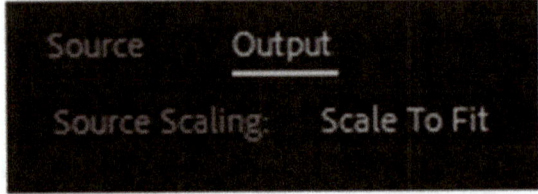

Figure 28-3. *Export Settings dialog crop images within a video sequence*

Bitmap Sequence Export settings

For the bitmap format in the Export Settings dialog box, notice that audio export is not available—only video; this is true for all image sequences. Bitmap only has one preset and its summary is like MP4. Refer to Figure 28-4.

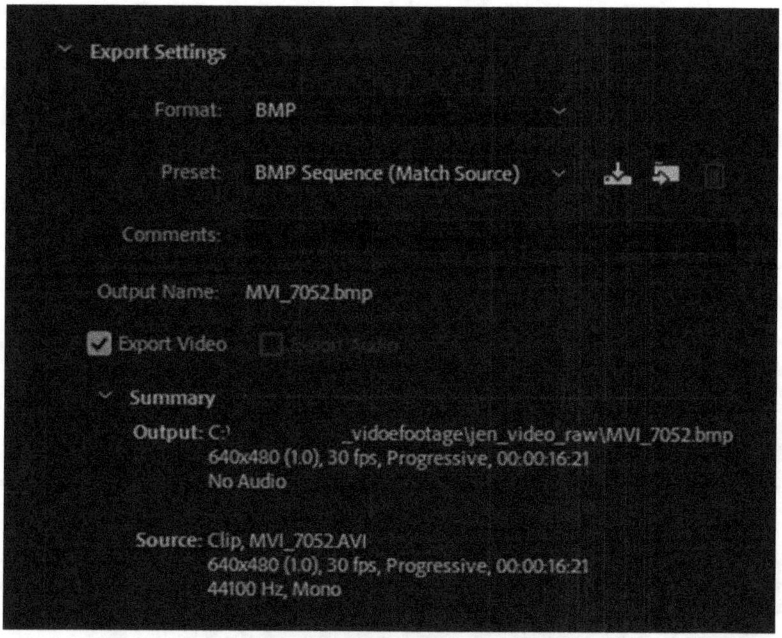

CHAPTER 28 ■ WORKING WITH YOUR RAW VIDEO FILES AND CONVERTING THEM TO AN IMAGE SEQUENCE

Figure 28-4. Export and Summary settings for a BMP Sequence

Effects Tab

These options are the same as the ones for MP4 files. Refer to the Effects tab in Chapter 26 for more information. Refer to Figure 28-5.

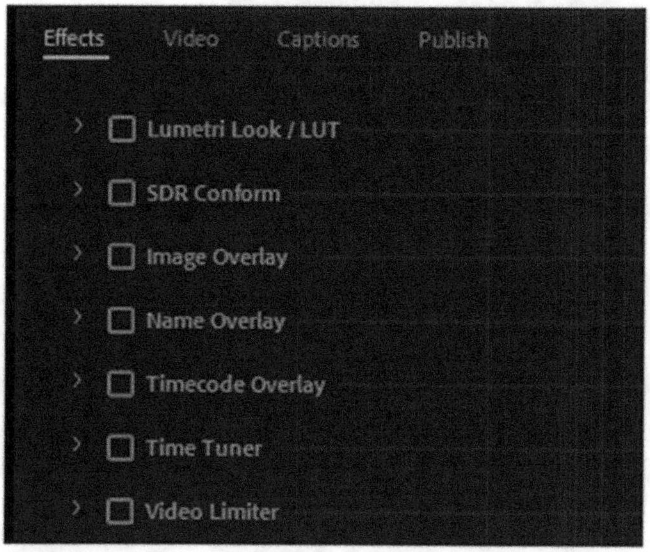

Figure 28-5. Export and Summary settings for a BMP Sequence

CHAPTER 28 ▪ WORKING WITH YOUR RAW VIDEO FILES AND CONVERTING THEM TO AN IMAGE SEQUENCE

Lumetri Look and SDR Conform are a fast way to give your images an overall color effect. You may have used this setting for other video files and want to keep the look of these images in the sequence consistent with the video if you plan to use them in the same project. Also, the Image Overlay and Name Overlay options can quickly watermark your images in the sequence.

Video Tab

In Basic Settings, you can match the source or set your own width and height for the image sequence; the Export As Sequence option ensures that a sequence of still files is written for each video frame. Refer to Figure 28-6.

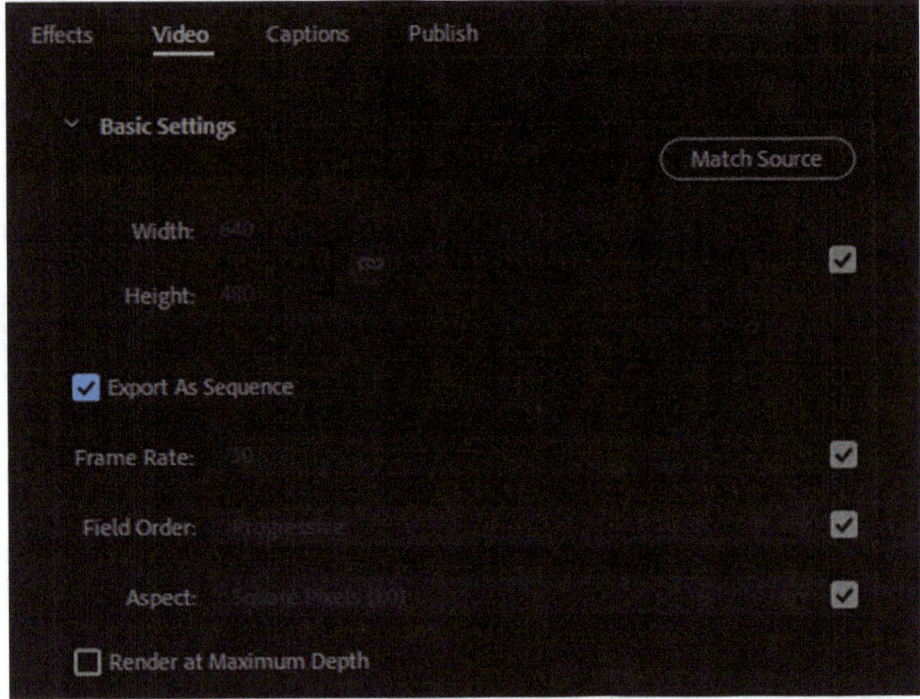

Figure 28-6. *Video tab for Basic Settings*

The settings on the right allow you to alter the frame rate, field order, and aspect ratio.

Render at Maximum depth may improve the image quality, but the rendering may be longer than expected and increase the file size.

Captions Tab

If the video contains close captions, they would be included; if not this area is left unavailable. It may also be unavailable because you are only exporting a sequence and not an actual video. Refer to Figure 28-7.

694

Figure 28-7. Captions tab, the settings are not available

Publish Tab

As with the audio files (MP3 and WAV), your options are to publish on your hard drive, external drive, to Adobe Creative Cloud, or directly to your website via FTP. You cannot publish directly to social media sites like Facebook, Twitter, or YouTube. This is because you are publishing a sequence of images and not a video. Refer to Figure 28-8.

Figure 28-8. Publish tab for Creative Cloud and FTP

Image sequences should be stored in a folder and then uploaded to a site for use in a gallery. If you plan to use them for another project they can be further edited using Photoshop or Animate for another MP4 video that will be used on your site or a social media site.

Render Time Code and Alpha Channel Settings

In the lower right of the Export Settings, you have access to the render quality, Set Start Timecode, Render Alpha Channel Only, Time Interpolation, and Metadata. Refer to Figure 28-9.

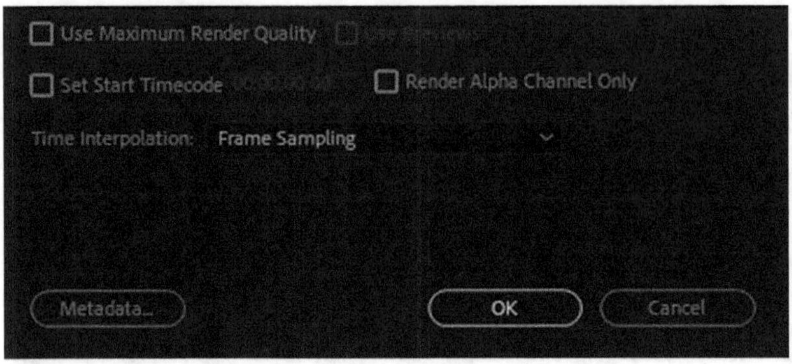

CHAPTER 28 ■ WORKING WITH YOUR RAW VIDEO FILES AND CONVERTING THEM TO AN IMAGE SEQUENCE

Figure 28-9. Final options for setting your render and metadata

At this point, you can either click OK to confirm your changes, or click Cancel to return to the Queue panel.

JPEG Sequence Export Settings

Not to be confused with JPEG 2000 MXF PO1a, which is not for our website, JPEG only has one preset for sequence; otherwise, Export Settings and Summary Settings are identical to the BMP. Refer to Figure 28-10.

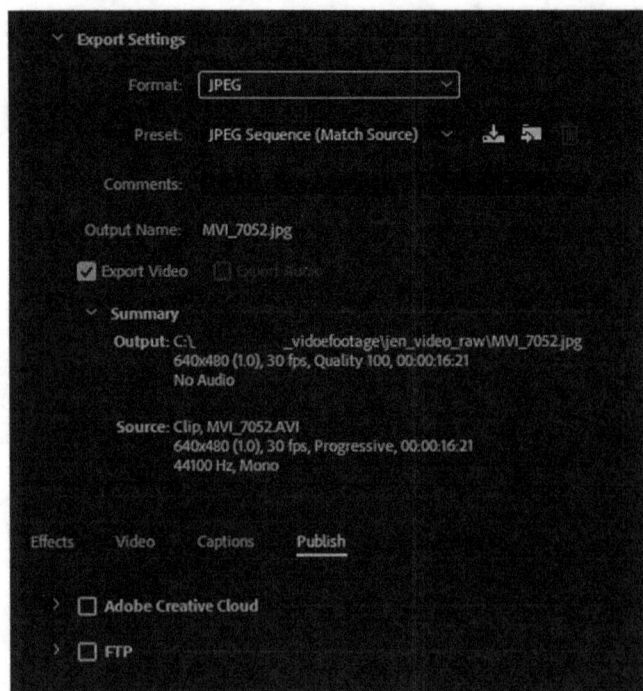

Figure 28-10. Export and Summary setting for JPEG image

The Effects, Caption, and Publish tabs are the same as BMP.

Video Tab

The only area of difference is the Video tab, where you can match the source or adjust your own quality. Refer to Figure 28-11.

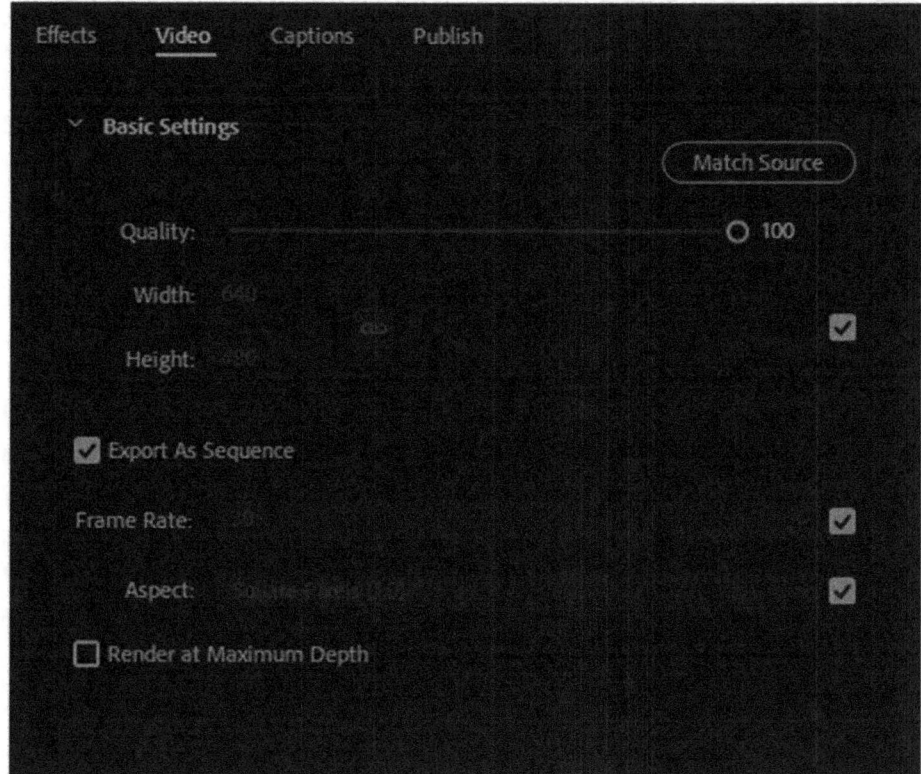

Figure 28-11. *Video tab for Basic Settings*

As with BMP, you can set the width and height, as well as check Export As Sequence to match the frame rate, aspect ratio, and render at maximum bit depth. You can alter the frame rate and choose an aspect from the drop-down menus when you uncheck them.

PNG Sequence Export Settings

PNG Sequence is set up like BMP; however, it has two presets: one with alpha or transparency and one without. Refer to Figure 28-12.

CHAPTER 28 ■ WORKING WITH YOUR RAW VIDEO FILES AND CONVERTING THEM TO AN IMAGE SEQUENCE

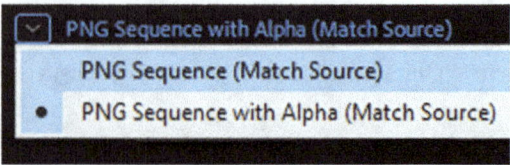

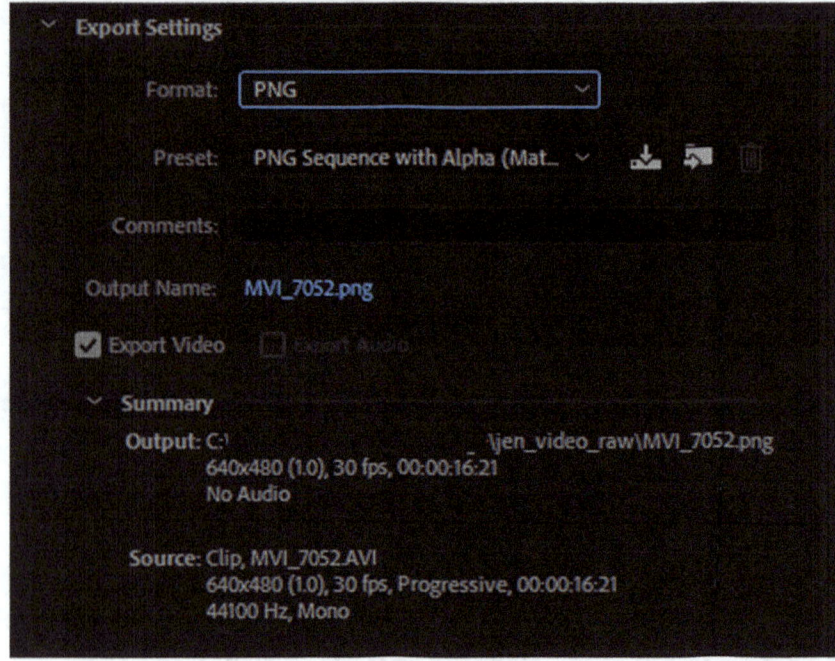

Figure 28-12. Preset, Export, and Summary settings for a PNG file

The Effects, Captions, and Publish tabs are the same as the BMP image sequence.

Video Tab

The main difference is in the Export Settings Video tab, where you can match the source settings or set your own for width and height. Check Export as a sequence to match the frame rate and aspect ratio, and you can choose to render at maximum bit depth. Refer to Figure 28-13.

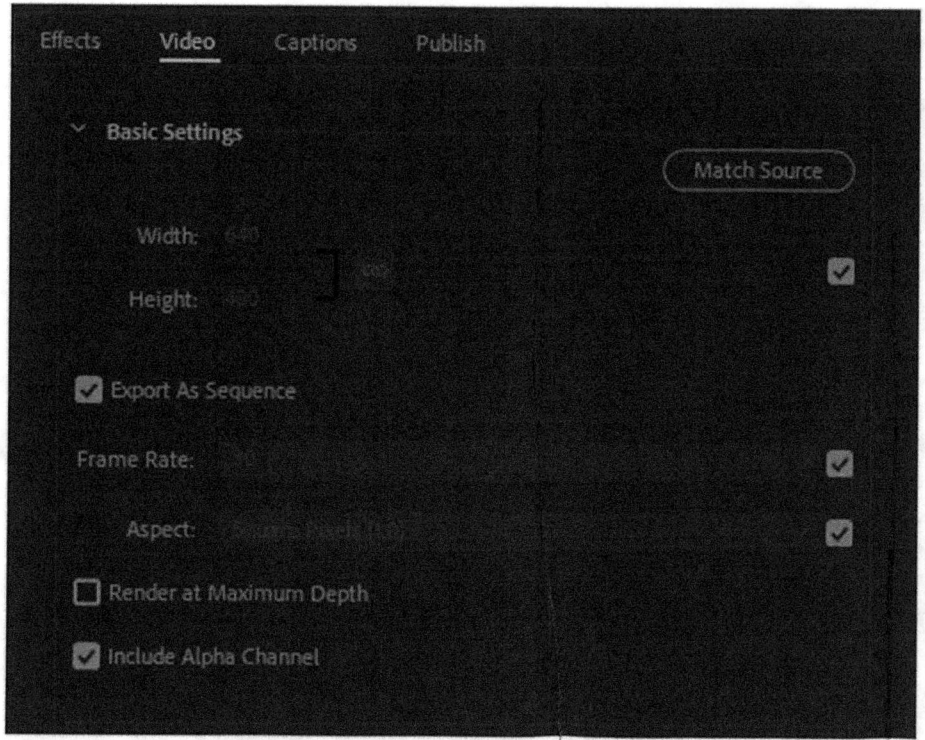

Figure 28-13. *Video tab for Basic Settings for a PNG sequence*

Enabling or disabling Include Alpha Channel alters the preset and determines whether the alpha channel or transparency is included or not.

GIF (Static) Image Sequence Export Settings

The GIF image sequence is the basically identical in Export Settings as the BMP file, and you cannot render any of the images transparent as you can in Photoshop CC. Refer to Figure 28-14.

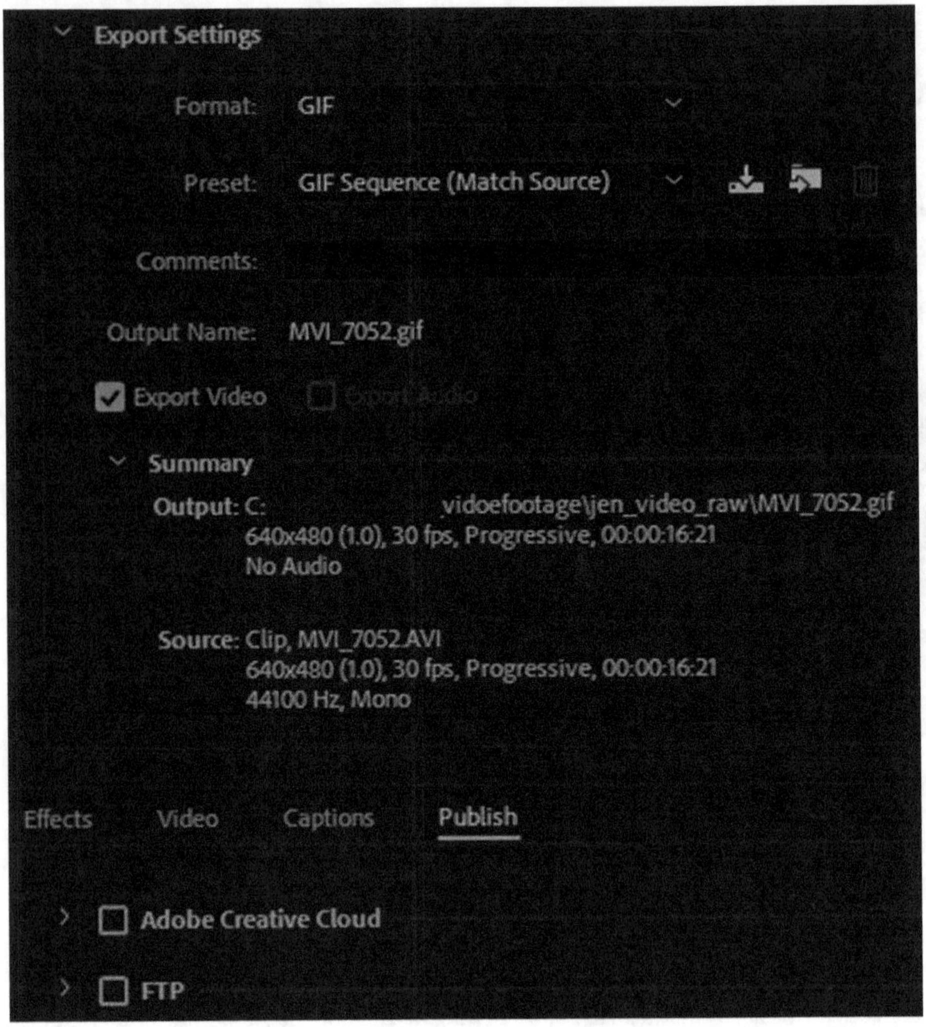

CHAPTER 28 ■ WORKING WITH YOUR RAW VIDEO FILES AND CONVERTING THEM TO AN IMAGE SEQUENCE

Figure 28-14. Export Settings for GIF sequence

Remember GIF images are best for logos or graphics with very little color like an animation. For full-color photos for the web, it is best to use a JPEG or PNG sequence. PNGs generally have a lower file size, but can retain their image quality.

Animated GIF

As a single animation file (not a sequence), this must be chosen from the Format option as Animated GIF. Refer to Figure 28-15.

CHAPTER 28 ■ WORKING WITH YOUR RAW VIDEO FILES AND CONVERTING THEM TO AN IMAGE SEQUENCE

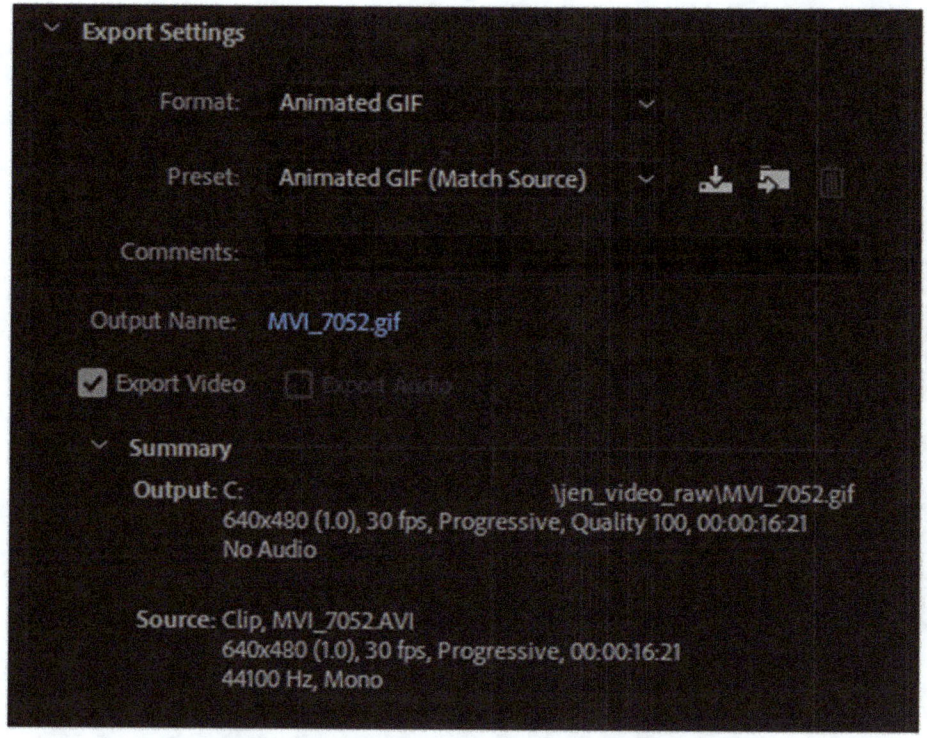

Figure 28-15. Export Settings and Summary for GIF animation

The Export Settings, Summary, Effects, and Captions and lower render settings tabs are the same as a BMP file. However, the Video and Publish tabs do have some slightly different settings.

Video Tab

The Video tab in Basic Settings allows you to either match source or adjust the quality, width, and height, frame rate, field order, aspect ratio, and render at maximum bit depth. Refer to Figure 28-16.

CHAPTER 28 ■ WORKING WITH YOUR RAW VIDEO FILES AND CONVERTING THEM TO AN IMAGE SEQUENCE

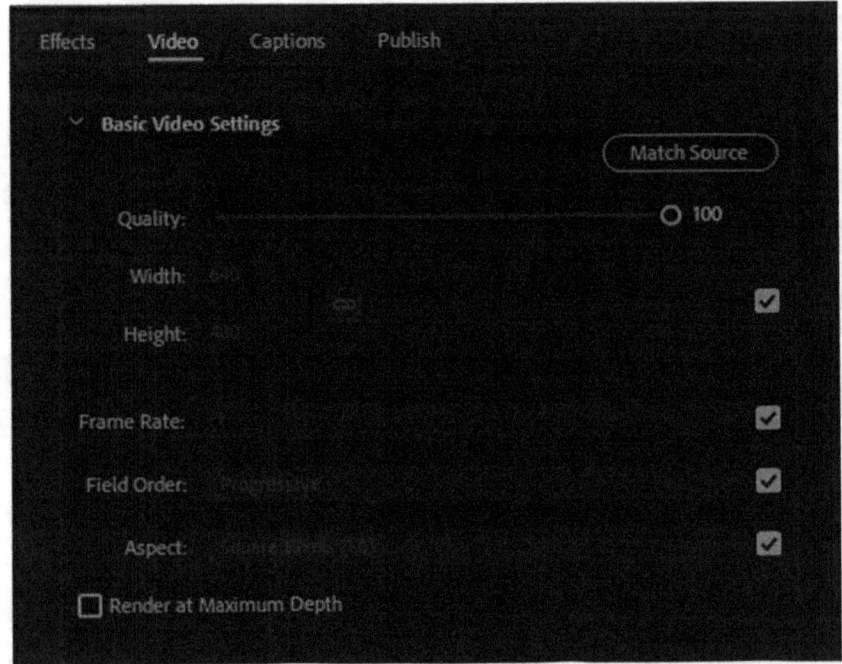

Figure 28-16. Video tab in Basic Video settings

Publish Tab

The Publish tab allows one extra option: you can upload your animation to Facebook. You can also publish on your hard drive, external drive, to Adobe Creative Cloud, or directly to your website via FTP, as seen in Figure 28-17.

Figure 28-17. Publish tab for Adobe Creative Cloud, Facebook, and FTP

You cannot publish directly to other social media sites, like Twitter or YouTube. This is because you are publishing GIF animations and not actual video.

> **Note** If you are planning using any of your images in your sequence for print or high-quality documents, TIFF Image Sequence is a good option to output the images. You can always place these in your InDesign CC file in the document layout and then export as a PDF file in Adobe Acrobat. Media Encoder cannot create PDF files, so this is a way to add images from your video to a document.

Summary

In this chapter, you looked at how to convert frames in your video into image sequences for other projects. You also saw that like Photoshop and Animate, you can use Media Encoder to create an animated GIF.

In the last chapter of Part 5, you put your knowledge into practice and work with some video and audio files to export media for the Hot Glass Tango site.

CHAPTER 29

Putting It into Practice with Media Encoder CC

In this chapter, you review how to export video files (AVI and MOV) and create an MP4 file. In the second project, you practice extracting sound from a video file and converting it to MP3 and WAV formats.

> **Note** This chapter has actual projects, which are in two folders. You can use the files in the Chapter 29 folder to practice opening and viewing for this lesson. They are at https://github.com/Apress/graphics-multimedia-web-adobe-creative-cloud.

In this "Putting it into Practice" chapter, you export video and audio for the Hot Glass Tango website, which tells the story (through images, animations, video, and audio) of how handmade glass items are created. The video and audio that you create in this chapter is used to complete the website in Part 6.

Create a Video MP4 File

Taking off from Chapter 24, you are working with the following ten MOV files:

- scene1_man_zoom_out_r2.mov
- scene1_man_movement.mov
- scene2_3_flame.mov
- scene4_5_swing.mov
- scene6_end.mov
- scene6_end_fade.mov
- scene7_credit.mov
- scene7_credit_fade.mov
- MVI_1361.mov is used later in another video project
- MVI_7052.avi is used later in another gallery project

These files are found in the ME_video folder. Remember to keep a backup copy of these originals if you need to practice with them again.

CHAPTER 29 ■ PUTTING IT INTO PRACTICE WITH MEDIA ENCODER CC

In Media Encoder, make sure to add these 10 files the Queue panel with the plus (+) icon, and make sure that their format settings are H.264. Refer to Figure 29-1.

Figure 29-1. Add your files one at a time using the add source icon

Likewise, if you have any other files from earlier chapters that are not part of this project, select them and use the minus (-) to remove them for now. When Adobe's alert asks if you are sure you want to remove the selected items and their settings from the Queue, choose Yes. Refer to Figure 29-2.

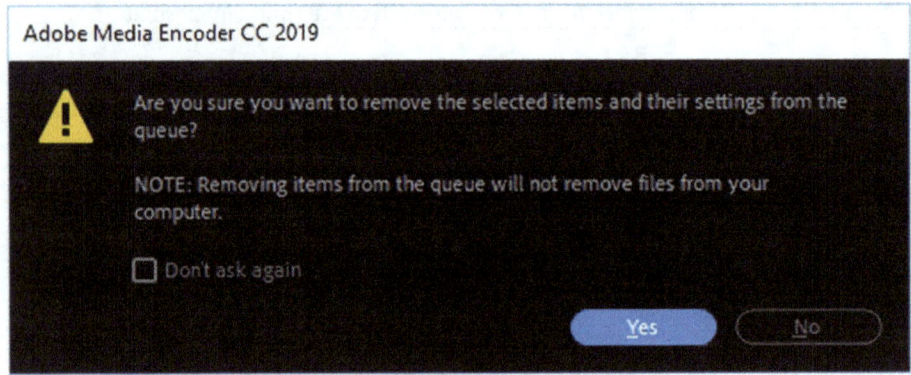

Figure 29-2. Remove your unwanted files from the Queue panel

Your Queue panel should look something like what's seen in Figure 29-3. None of the files is stitched together; however, your Output File column will probably be different from mine.

CHAPTER 29 ■ PUTTING IT INTO PRACTICE WITH MEDIA ENCODER CC

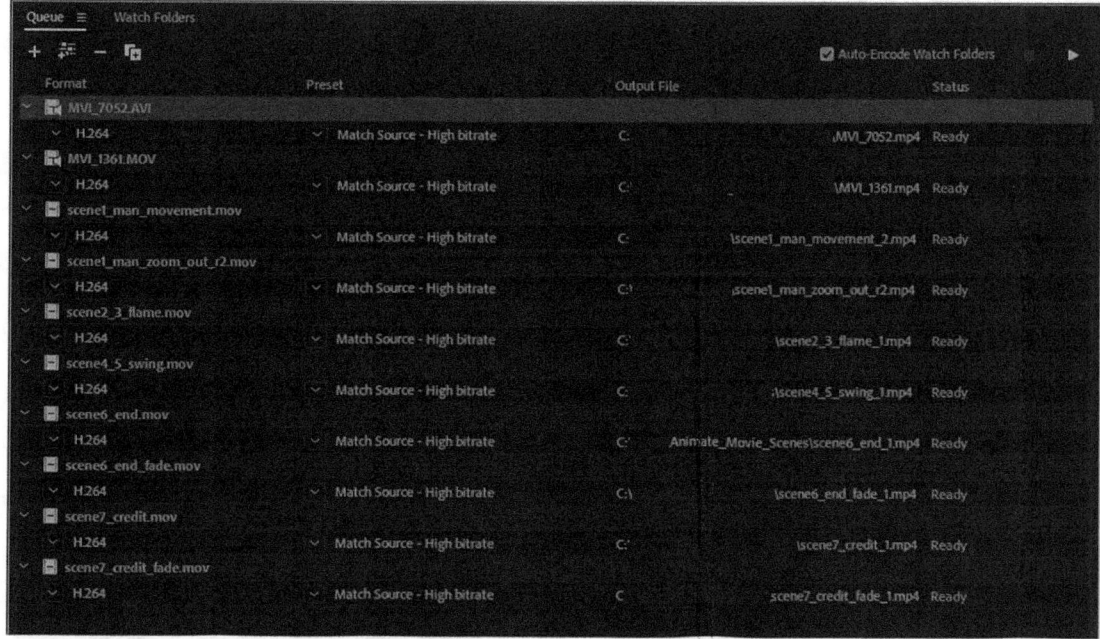

Figure 29-3. *Your ten files in the Queue panel*

Click each output link and find a folder that you would like to output the file to. Rendering a large number files on a drive can cause some computers to labor or crash. A good idea is to work with your files on an external drive. The files I have presented are relatively small, so they should be OK if you want to work off your own computer's drive; it's up to you.

In the scene1_man_zoom_out_r2.mov file, click the Format column's H.264 link to enter the Export Settings dialog box for that file. Refer to Figure 29-4.

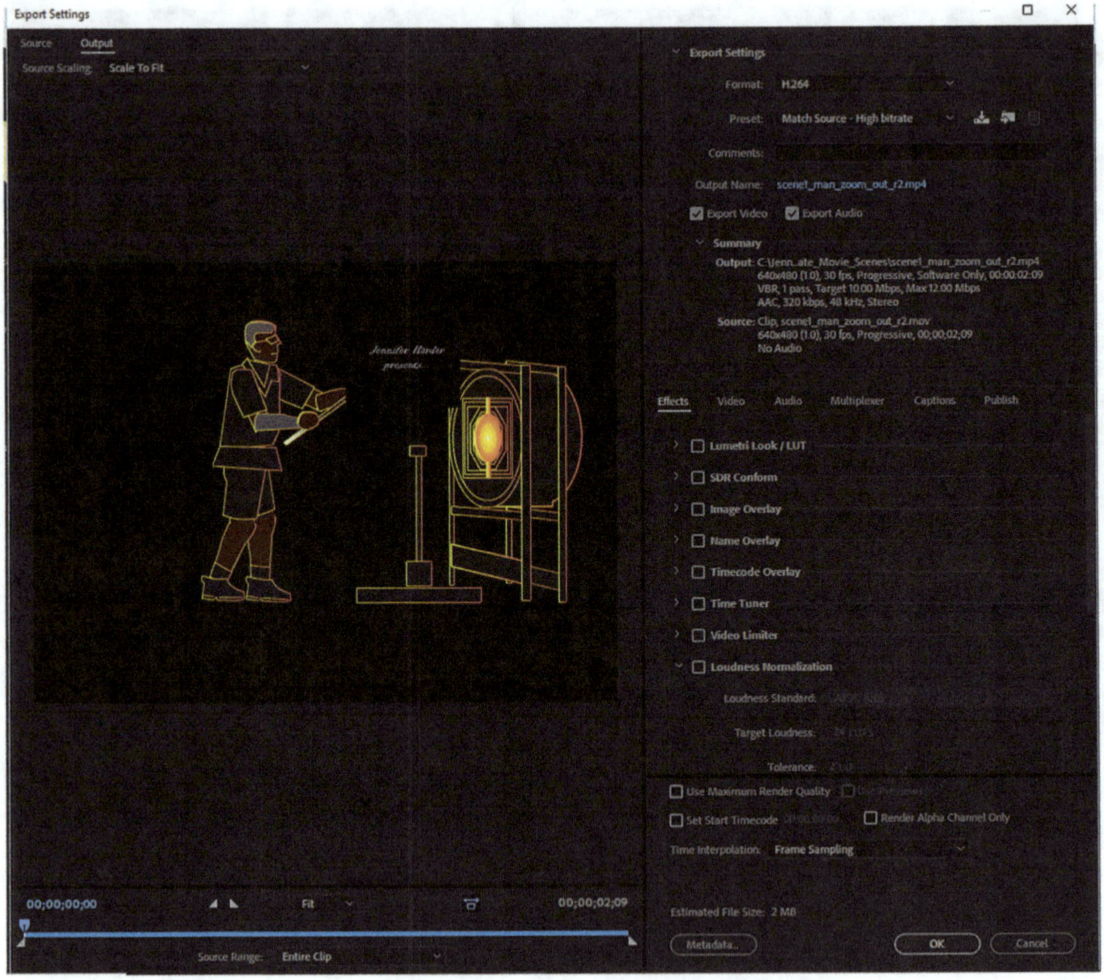

CHAPTER 29 ■ PUTTING IT INTO PRACTICE WITH MEDIA ENCODER CC

Figure 29-4. *Edit your output file in the Export Settings dialog box*

There is very little editing that needs to be done to this file. It is already set at preset Match Source - High bit rate. The correct dimensions are 640×480, and from the Source summary you can see it is running at 30 fps. That is because this animation will be part of the introduction for a Photoshop video called Hot Glass Tango. These animations never contained any audio, so you can uncheck Export Audio, but it will make a trivial difference to the final export size. Refer to Figure 29-5.

Figure 29-5. *Choose whether to export the audio or not*

CHAPTER 29 ■ PUTTING IT INTO PRACTICE WITH MEDIA ENCODER CC

The one area that you want to adjust is making a minor clip at the beginning of the video to remove an odd camera angle that remains when Animate converted the FLA file to a MOV file. Refer to Figure 29-6.

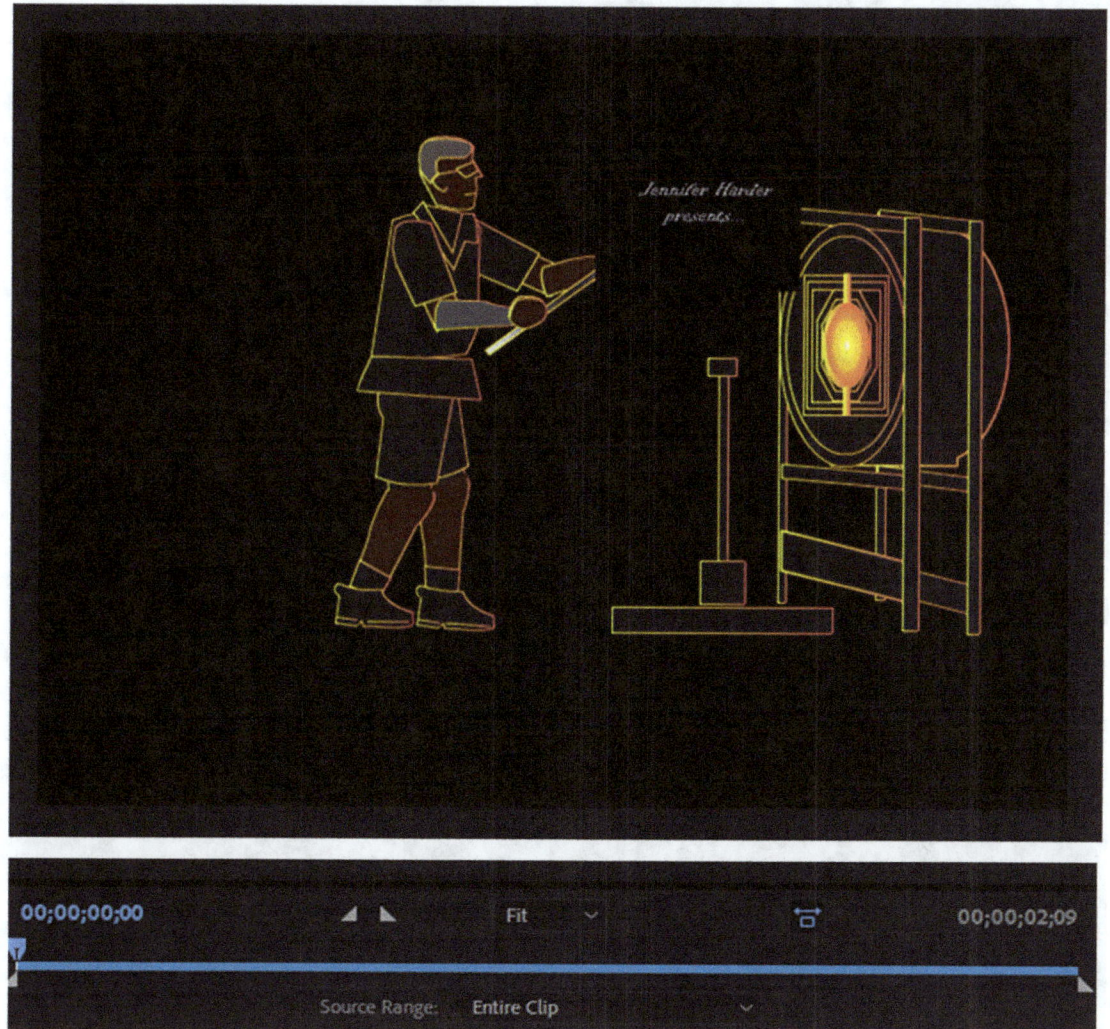

Figure 29-6. *The entire clip needs some editing before export*

The first frame looks rather odd. So, you need to move the left clip point inward by at least a fraction so that it does not register on the start time. To figure this out, move the blue playhead slowly toward the right until you see the frame seen in Figure 29-7.

Figure 29-7. Moving the playhead to find the correct starting point of the animation clip

Now drag the left set point to the same location to clip it from that point, and remove any footage beforehand. Refer to Figure 29-8.

Figure 29-8. Moving the left stop so that it cuts out the first frame

Remember to use the preview screen as your guide if you are unsure of the correct point. Your end time the on left has removed about a frame; 00:00:02:09 is now 00:00:02:08 (hours: minutes: seconds: frames). The Source Range changes from Entire Clip to Custom.

If you want, you can drag the playhead to the end, but you do not need to adjust the right set point because the frames for the rest of the animation are good.

When you are done, click OK to exit the Export Settings dialog box and confirm your changes. Refer to Figure 29-9.

CHAPTER 29 ■ PUTTING IT INTO PRACTICE WITH MEDIA ENCODER CC

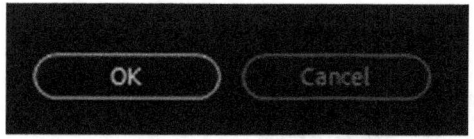

Figure 29-9. Click OK to confirm your changes

Media Encoder saves your changes, and you can go back to this area any time to adjust your set points before your export.

■ **Note** If you find that the right set point has moved, reset your point using Source Range and choosing Entire Clip, and then move your left point again. Refer to Figure 28-8.

Repeat the steps for the seven files (.mov) in the Queue panel, as listed in Table 29-1.

Table 29-1. Adjustments to MOV File Times

File	Original Time	New Export Time
scene1_man_movement.mov	00:00:03:29	00:00:03:28
scene2_3_flame.mov	00:00:02:04	00:00:02:04 less than frame
scene4_5_swing.mov	00:00:02:12	00:00:02:11
scene6_end.mov	00:00:02:17	00:00:02:17 no frame change
scene6_end_fade.mov	00:00:01:29	00:00:01:28
scene7_credit.mov	00:00:02:24	00:00:02:23
scene7_credit_fade.mov	00:00:01:29	00:00:01:28

In all cases, the main area you need to adjust is the left set point marker to fix the first camera angle. Usually, it is no more than a frame or less off the left. Use these images as your guides. Refer to Figure 29-10.

CHAPTER 29 ■ PUTTING IT INTO PRACTICE WITH MEDIA ENCODER CC

Figure 29-10. *Guide images on where to set the left clip; note that some clips start on a black background so what you are seeing is correct for those video clips.*

Now let's look at the MVI_7052.avi file. If you play this file in your computer's media player, you notice that it has audio in it. All the camera video footage files that I used in Part 2 were originally either MOV or AVI. They all contained audio. However, this audio was not relevant to the storyline, so rather than import directly into Photoshop, I first converted them to an MP4 file in Media Encoder and removed the audio before I exported them. This AVI file has audio that you are now going to remove before exporting. Click the H.264 under the name of the file to enter its Export Settings dialog box. Refer to Figure 29-11.

CHAPTER 29 ■ PUTTING IT INTO PRACTICE WITH MEDIA ENCODER CC

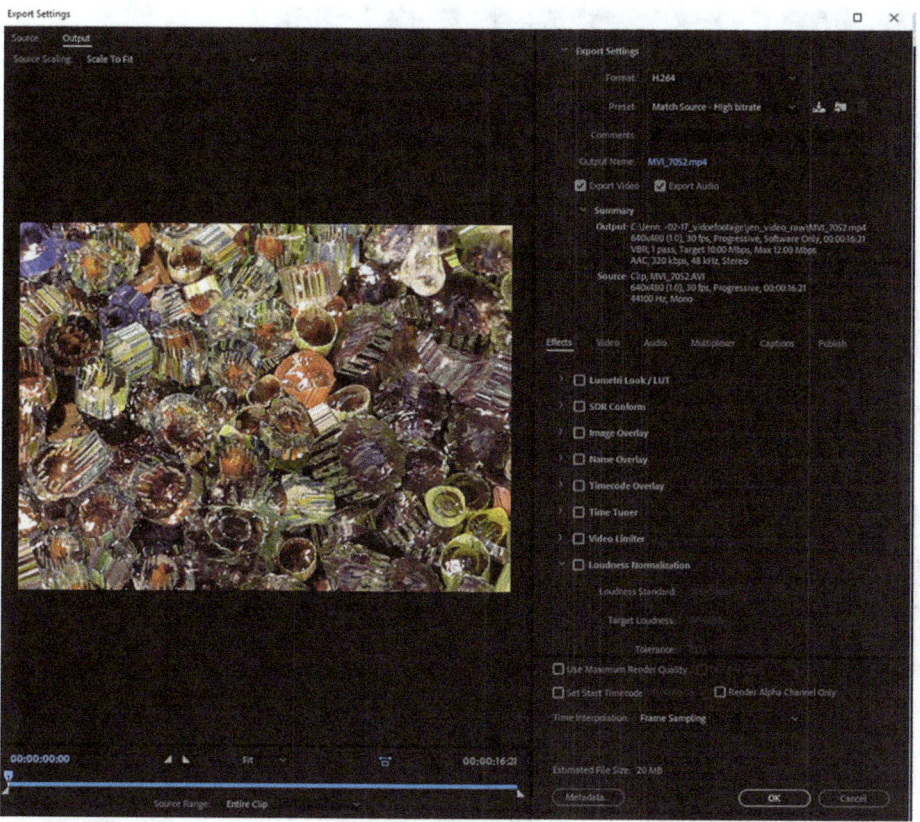

Figure 29-11. *Preview of an AVI video of glass canes*

The entire video clip is a little over 16 seconds long. For practice, you may want to clip this down to 5 seconds. I leave that decision to you.

The next setting you need to adjust is on the right of the preview; you need to uncheck Export Audio. This sets the preset to custom, but everything else remains the same. Refer to Figure 29-12.

CHAPTER 29 ■ PUTTING IT INTO PRACTICE WITH MEDIA ENCODER CC

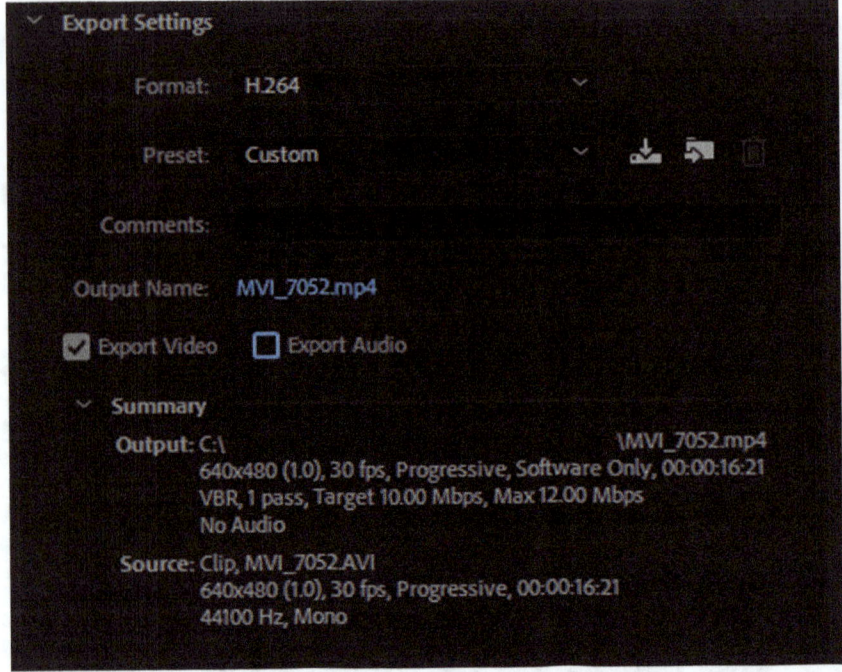

Figure 29-12. Settings for the current AVI file

This file is 640×480; it runs at 30 fps. With the removal of audio, any additional clipping made to the video reduces its file size further. Click OK to confirm changes and return to the Queue panel. Refer to Figure 29-13.

Figure 29-13. Click OK to confirm your settings

Finally, let's look at the MVI_1361.MOV file. This time, you are working with a MOV file that was shot using a Canon camera, and not created in Animate. When you click the H.264 icon to enter the Export Settings dialog box, the dimensions of the file are different than the others. You need to make some changes so that this file conforms with the size and frame rate of the others if you want to use them together for your project. I referred to this in Chapter 7. In an ideal set up, make sure that any cameras you shoot video with are running in the same frame rate and ratio dimensions. This introduces fewer issues into your workflow, especially when combining your film. Refer to Figure 29-14.

714

CHAPTER 29 ■ PUTTING IT INTO PRACTICE WITH MEDIA ENCODER CC

Figure 29-14. *Adjusting the formatting for the MOV video file*

As you may have discovered, however, you don't always get ideal footage from clients, so be prepared to find work-arounds.

The entire video clip is about 28 seconds, but if you want to make it about 15 seconds, I leave that up to you. On the right, uncheck Export Audio. This sets the preset to custom. as seen in Figure 29-15.

715

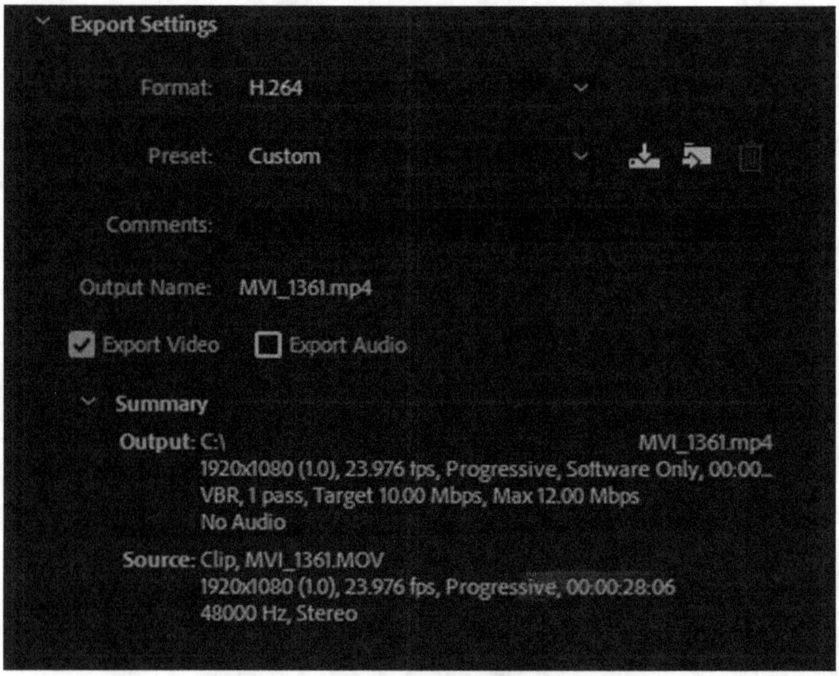

CHAPTER 29 ■ PUTTING IT INTO PRACTICE WITH MEDIA ENCODER CC

Figure 29-15. Export setings and summary for the file

Review the Summary settings. Two things stand out. The current dimensions are 1920×1080, and the frames rate is set at 23.976, which is close to 24 fps.

Your goal for this part of the project is to make sure the dimensions are 640×480 and that the video runs at 30 fps.

Click on the Video Tab, so that you can start adjusting the Basic Video Settings. Some of the areas you saw in Chapter 26 are grayed out for now. Refer to Figure 29-16.

CHAPTER 29 ■ PUTTING IT INTO PRACTICE WITH MEDIA ENCODER CC

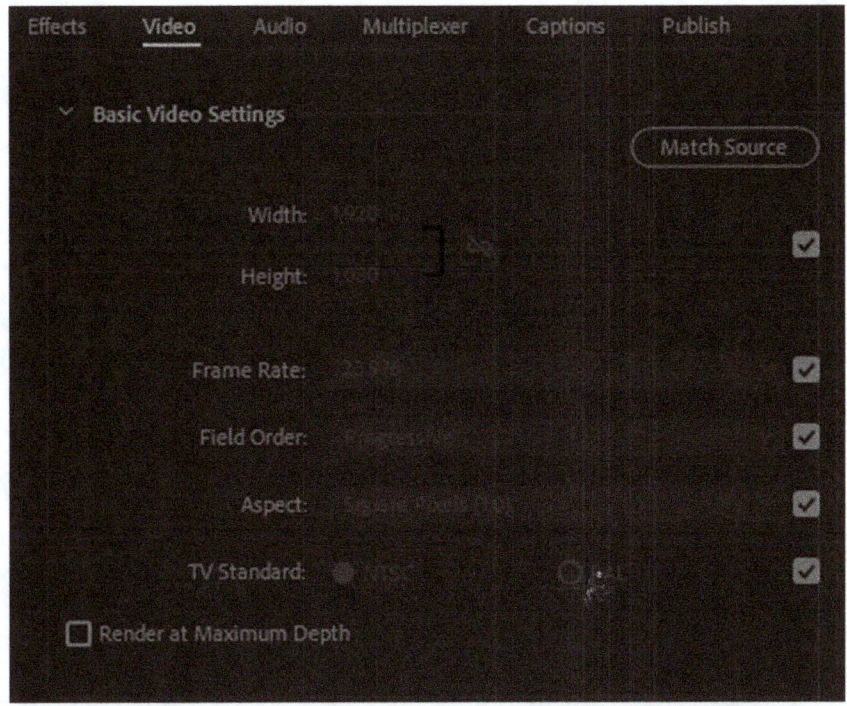

Figure 29-16. *Video Tab for Basic Video Settings*

First, uncheck width and height on the right so that you can access the numbers as seen in Figure 29-17.

Figure 29-17. *Width and Height settings*

Make sure to keep the width and height linked and enter 480 in the height. This keeps the ratio roughly at 4:3 standard aspect and makes the width 852. The video is not distorted. Refer to Figure 29-18.

Figure 29-18. *Width and Height settings are currently scaled and proportionate*

717

CHAPTER 29 ■ PUTTING IT INTO PRACTICE WITH MEDIA ENCODER CC

More information on aspect ratio and standard size is at https://en.wikipedia.org/wiki/Aspect_ratio_(image).

If you know that you are going to use this file in Photoshop (see Part 2), I recommend that you do not make any further changes to the width, because you can always use that extra width to move your video around and center it in the final 640×480 video. Likewise, for Photoshop, you could leave the video at its original size and make it a Smart Object that could be scaled to suit your needs.

This footage is going directly on to the web, so you need to make sure that its width is 640 to conform with the other AVI video. You'll adjust that in moment. For now, let's deal with the frame rate.

Uncheck the Frame Rate option. Refer to Figure 29-19.

Figure 29-19. Uncheck the Frame Rate to access this area

From the Frame Rate drop-down menu, choose 30, as seen in Figure 29-20.

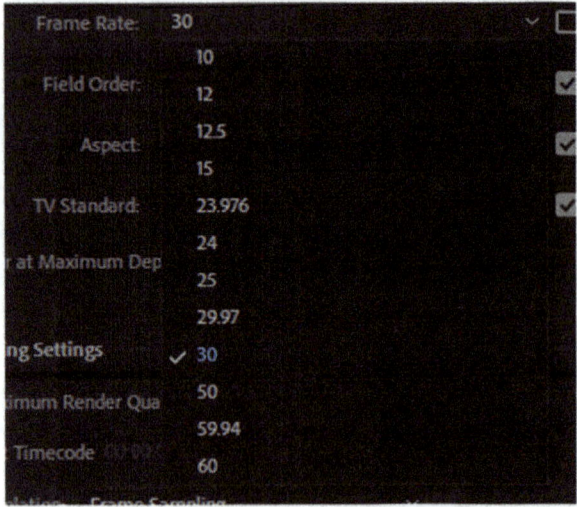

Figure 29-20. Set a new frame rate for this video

Now let's deal with the width dimension issue. Go back to Width and height in the Video tab and unlink them. Change the width to 640, which chops off some of the left and right sides of the video preview. Refer to Figure 29-21.

Figure 29-21. Unlink the width and height

CHAPTER 29 ■ PUTTING IT INTO PRACTICE WITH MEDIA ENCODER CC

This leaves a black edge at the top and bottom, which you don't want. Refer to Figure 29-22.

Figure 29-22. *Currently, the preview image as black area at the top and bottom*

So, in the output Tab on the upper left changes the source scaling from Scale To Fit to Scale To Fill. Refer to Figure 29-23.

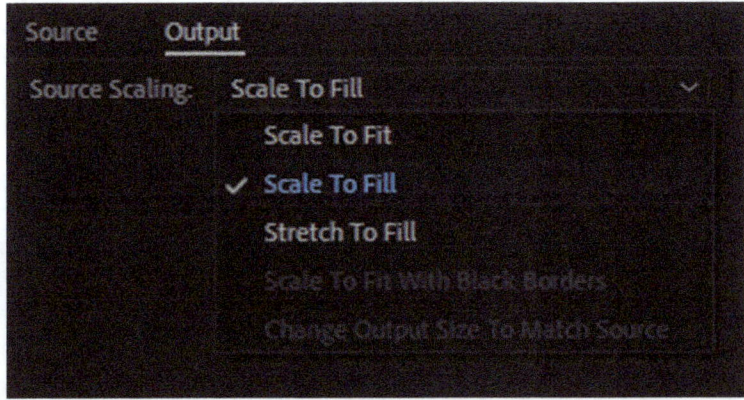

Figure 29-23. *Change your source scaling settings*

719

This looks much better. Refer to Figure 29-24.

Figure 29-24. *The final preview image with scaling adjusted*

In some video, this may cause a minor distortion, but this is a good work-around for a tight deadline. Do not use Stretch To Fill because it distorts the picture.

The Export Settings and Summary for output are now correct for this project, as seen in Figure 29-25.

CHAPTER 29 ■ PUTTING IT INTO PRACTICE WITH MEDIA ENCODER CC

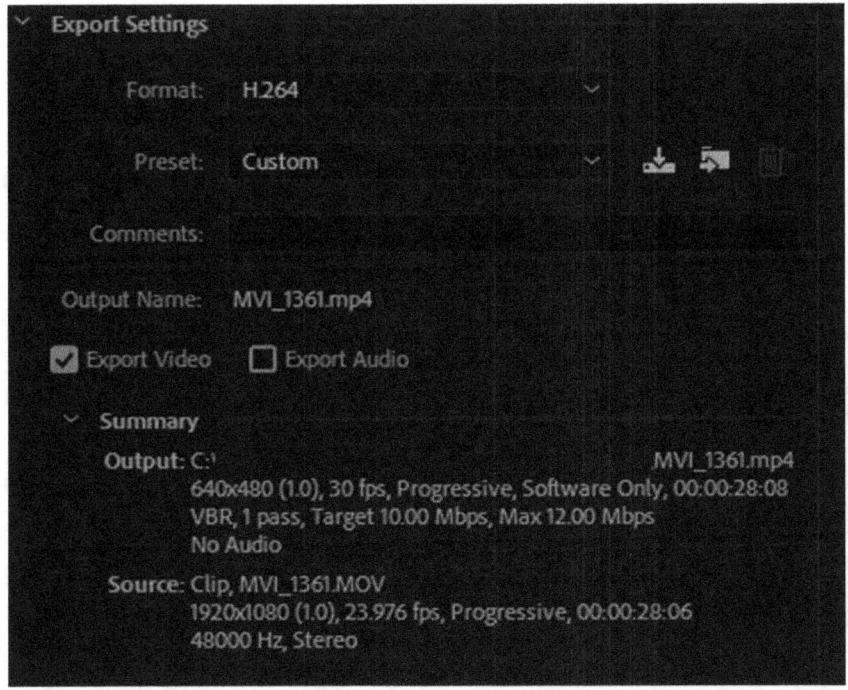

Figure 29-25. *New output settings in the Summary*

Keep these steps in mind if you ever receive a piece of footage that does not match the footage size dimension or frame rate of your other video file. It is best to scale down a high-definition video file. Avoid and never scale upward, as this reduces quality. Ideally, you want the best possible video display. Also, a minor adjustment of a few frames from 24 to 30 should not impact the quality of your file. Remember to always keep a copy of the original footage in case you need to reset the settings or use it in another program.

At this point, you can click OK to exit and confirm the Export Settings in the dialog box. Refer to Figure 29-26.

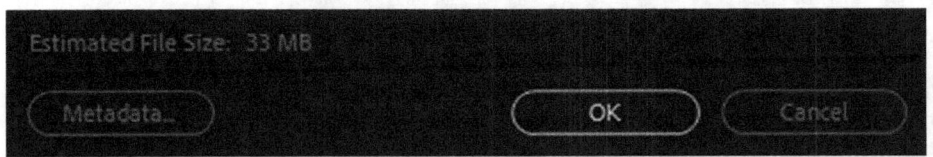

Figure 29-26. *Confirm the setting for your video*

You have no more adjustments to make; you are ready to export your files to MP4. If you have not already, make sure that you have set the correct Output File folder for each video.

When you are ready, click the green Start Queue button on the upper right of the Queue panel. Refer to Figure 29-27.

721

CHAPTER 29 ■ PUTTING IT INTO PRACTICE WITH MEDIA ENCODER CC

Figure 29-27. Start the Queue to begin export

Allow time for the files to render, as seen in Figure 29-28.

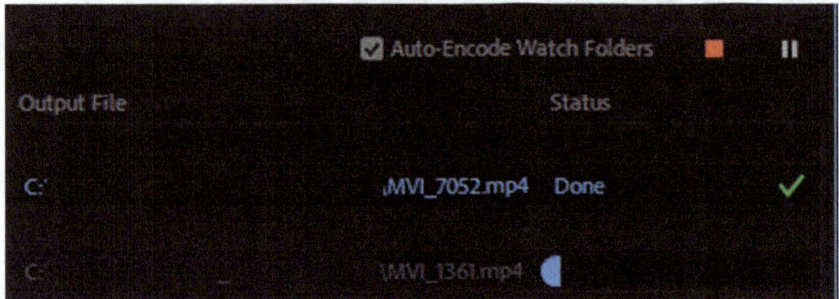

Figure 29-28. One file has completed rendering, and you are now seeing the second in progress

A green check appears when you are done, and a progress bar appears as each file is exporting and rendering. At the same time, you see some action in the Encoding panel as the file previews and completes. Refer to Figure 29-29.

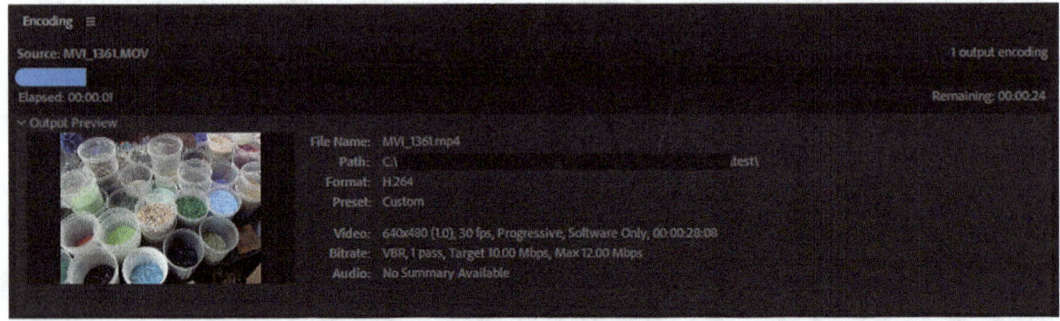

Figure 29-29. The Encoding panel is previewing through the file as it renders and exports

You can press the red Stop square if you need to stop the rendering and abort your projects.

Also, if you realize you made a mistake, after rendering, click the file format and choose Reset Status. Refer to Figure 29-30.

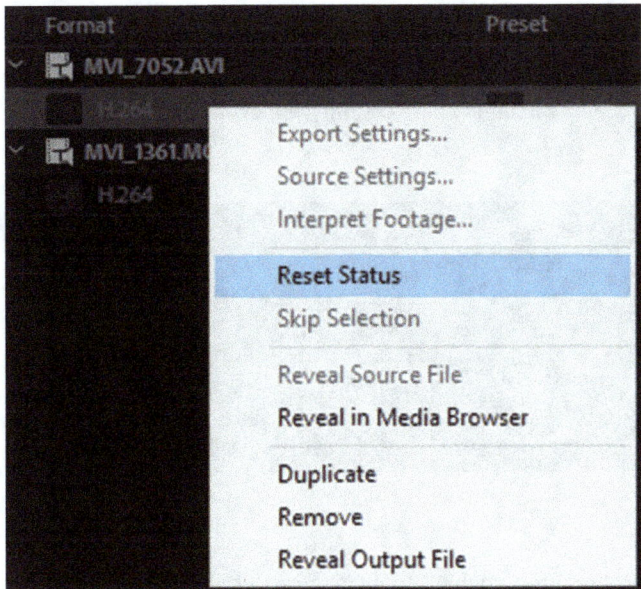

Figure 29-30. *Reset the status of your file to ready if you need to export it again*

Reset the file to ready so that you can render and overwrite the earlier MP4. If you don't want to overwrite, make sure to give the file a new name in the Output File column, such as mvi_7052_2.mp4.

There may be times when you want to export the audio with the video in your projects. Be aware that there are occasions where file formats even with the Export Audio checked and all indications that the render was successful, the audio does not play in the final MP4 file. This could be due to several factors.

- There was some sort of corruption in the original file (.mov or .avi). Discover if you can extract the audio separately or not.

- There could be a bug in a recent version of Media Encoder that mutes the audio tracks on output. You know this is the issue if a few days before an update you had no issues. Check the Adobe forums to see if anyone else is currently having this issue. For example, in the case of a file from Premiere Pro, sometimes a corrupt or empty audio track may have been left in the file. This can cause the problem in the audio in these tracks. A solution would be deleting older tracks, importing fresh audio tracks and outputting again into Media Encoder to see if the issue has been corrected.

- You are using the same version of Media Encoder as your colleagues, but the audio imports successfully on their machines, but not yours. This could be an issue if you are using different video or audio drivers on your machine than your colleagues (refer to Chapter 25). Media Encoder only uses what is available on your machine, so that driver may be fine converting an MOV's audio to MP4 but not an AVI's. If you run into this issue, check with your company's IT department to see what they might recommend, and continue to run tests on different platforms and computers.

You have completed the first project, and you are ready to move on to the second project. At this point, you can remove any files from the Queue panel (−).

CHAPTER 29 ■ PUTTING IT INTO PRACTICE WITH MEDIA ENCODER CC

Create an Audio MP3 File and a WAV File

In the empty source panel, add the AVI file from the ME_sounds_vid folder. You find MVI_7229.avi and (.THM), which does not and cannot export into Media Encoder. That's OK only work with the AVI. Refer to Figure 29-31.

Figure 29-31. *Add a new file to the Queue panel*

This is simply a video that is the duration of the sound, so that I could capture the audio. I put my camera microphone near the object creating the sound, and then pointed the camera near some cloth, since I was not intending to capture any actual action.

Alternatively, you may want to capture sound using your smartphone, as I did in Chapter 27, with the 3GA files. However, there may be times when you want to capture action and sound together, and then use the sound from that footage in another area of the video or for J-cuts and L-cuts, as you learned about in Part 2.

Change the format to MP3 from the drop-down menu. Refer to Figure 29-32.

Figure 29-32. *Changing the format of the video to MP3*

Now right-click the selected file and choose to duplicate, as seen in Figure 29-33.

CHAPTER 29 ■ PUTTING IT INTO PRACTICE WITH MEDIA ENCODER CC

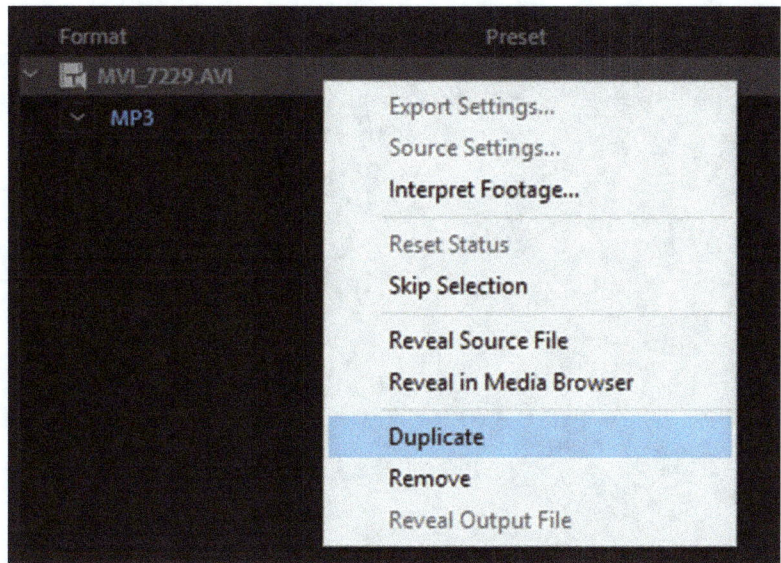

Figure 29-33. *Create a duplicate of the video whose format you want to change*

Change the duplicate to Waveform Audio, as seen in Figure 29-34.

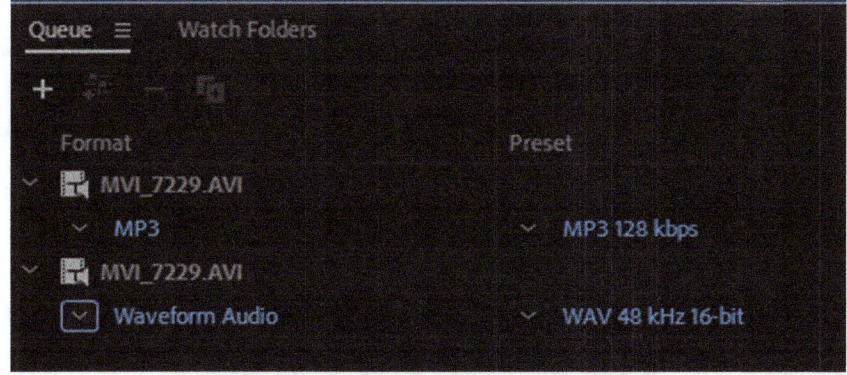

Figure 29-34. *There are now two formats of the same audio*

Set a location for the two output files. The files are quite small, so you may not need to render to an external drive; your own computer's drive should be OK.

Click on the MP3 icon to go into the Export Settings dialog box. Refer to Figure 29-35.

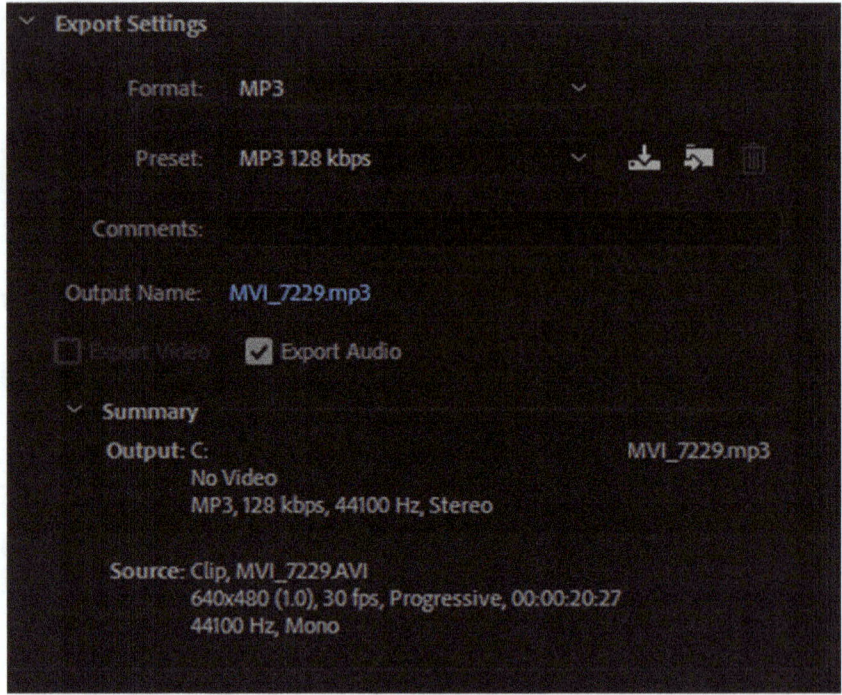

Figure 29-35. *Review the export settings for the MP3 file*

There you find that only Export Audio is available.

The duration of the audio is about 20 seconds.

Going down to the preview area, drag the left and right set point in by about a second (hours: minutes: seconds: frames) on each side. The sound does not start until at least a second in, and then trails off at the end. Unfortunately, you can't preview sound in Media Encoder, but you can use your computer's media player to give you an idea of where the sound starts and stops. Refer to Figure 29-36.

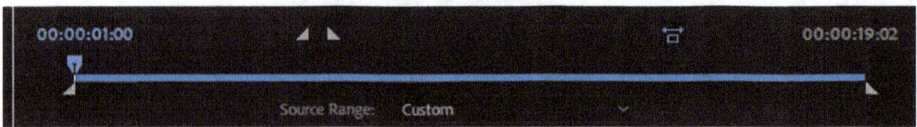

Figure 29-36. *Set the points as to what audio you want in the export*

When you are done, click OK to exit the Export Settings dialog box and return to the Queue panel. Refer to Figure 29-37.

CHAPTER 29 ■ PUTTING IT INTO PRACTICE WITH MEDIA ENCODER CC

Figure 29-37. Confirm the settings by clicking OK to return to the Queue panel

Then repeat these steps for the WAV file.

In the lower left of the Export Settings dialog box (see Figure 29-37), notice that the WAV file does not show the Estimated File Size. Nevertheless, the file is still small, but at least more than a megabyte larger than the MP3. Refer to Figure 29-38 for settings.

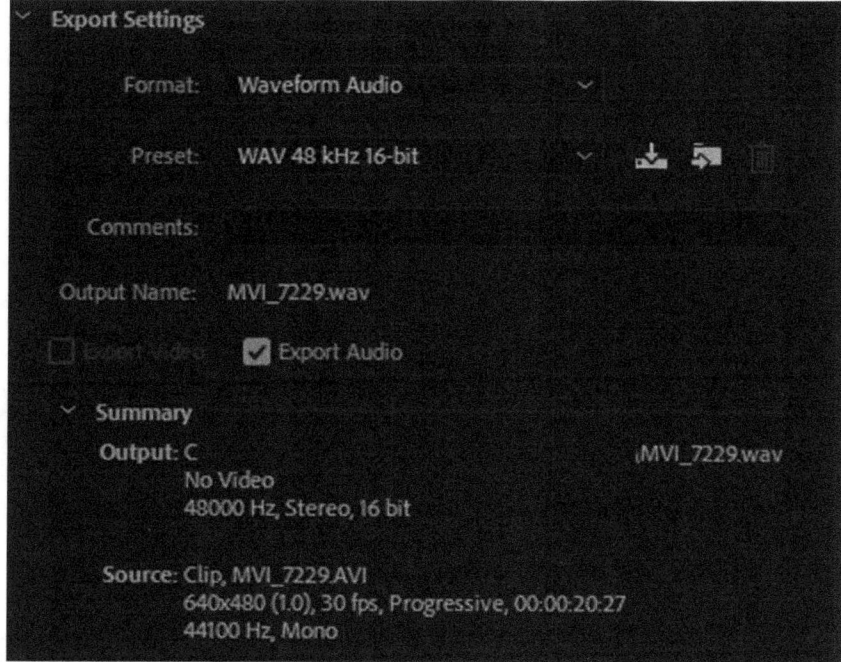

Figure 29-38. Settings for the Waveform Audio file

When done, click OK to return to the Queue panel.

When you are ready, click the green arrow to start the queue; each audio file should export to the selected output folder. Refer to Figure 29-39.

727

CHAPTER 29 ■ PUTTING IT INTO PRACTICE WITH MEDIA ENCODER CC

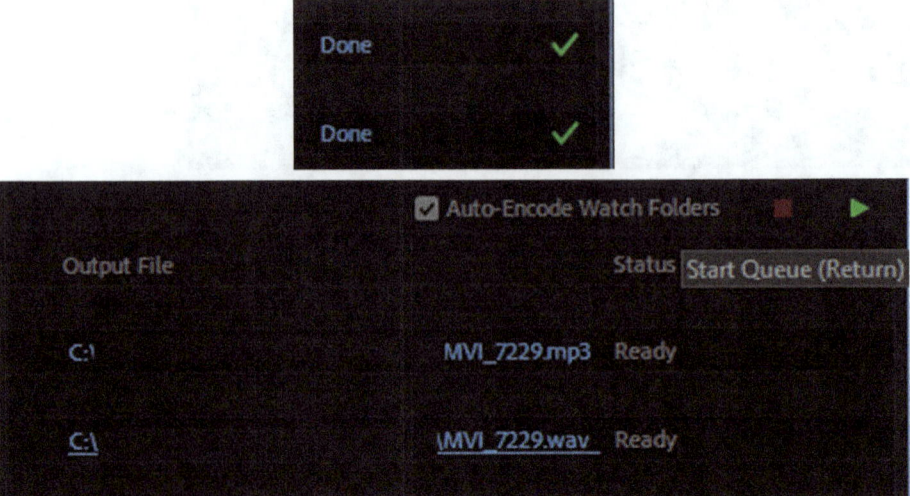

Figure 29-39. *When each file is rendered, the status is done*

Once complete, you can go to that folder and check the audio in your computer's media player to see if you extracted the correct amount of sound. If you discover that you made a mistake, right-click the selected file and choose Reset Status, and adjust before you export again. Refer to Figure 29-40.

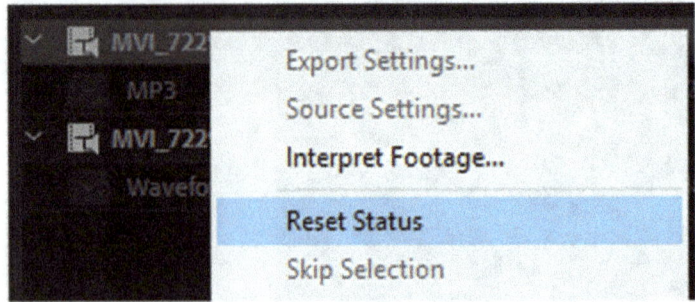

Figure 29-40. *Reset the status for those files you want to re-export in the Queue panel*

Remember, if you don't want to overwrite an audio file, give the file a new name in the Output File column before you export.

If you have an MOV file or another video format, you can try extracting the sound from that file. Also, if you have any audio files that you want to convert to either MP3 or WAV, try doing that now.

When you are done, if you have a lot of audio, organize your new files into folders on your drive, like MP3 or WAV.

You can now close Media Encoder without making any further changes and File ➤ Exit the program. You have completed the second project, and you are ready to move to Part 6 to work with Dreamweaver.

728

Summary

In this chapter, you reviewed how to create video and audio for the Hot Glass Tango website. This chapter concludes your study of Media Encoder CC. Make sure to review any areas of Part 5 that you don't understand so that you feel comfortable working with your own files in Media Encoder.

In Part 6, you journey to the center of the software maze: Adobe Dreamweaver CC. You'll discover how it can be used create a mobile website with your images, animations, audio, and video files.

PART VI

Working with Dreamweaver: Adding Images, Animations, and Multimedia to HTML5 Pages

CHAPTER 30

Getting Started with Dreamweaver CC

In this chapter, you look at how to set up your website to start working in Dreamweaver.

> **Note** This chapter does not have any actual projects; however, you can use the files in the Part 6 folder to practice opening and viewing for this lesson. They are at `https://github.com/Apress/graphics-multimedia-web-adobe-creative-cloud`.

Entering the Maze's Center

The purpose or endgame of a maze is to have a center or goal where you reach the destination or prize. So far, as you have seen in Adobe, you have come to different junction points (Photoshop CC, Illustrator CC, Animate CC, and Media Encoder CC) to create and assemble the graphics and media that are used for the final website.

There have been a few twists and turns along the way, but as you can see, most of your multimedia can be created or edited using the four core programs that you have looked at. Now you have reached the final and most crucial Adobe software for completing your web design goal: Dreamweaver CC. As you will discover, this program has a lot to offer and can assist you in the writing of HTML5, CSS (Cascading Style Sheets), and JavaScript code to create additional animations. Refer to Figure 30-1.

CHAPTER 30 ■ GETTING STARTED WITH DREAMWEAVER CC

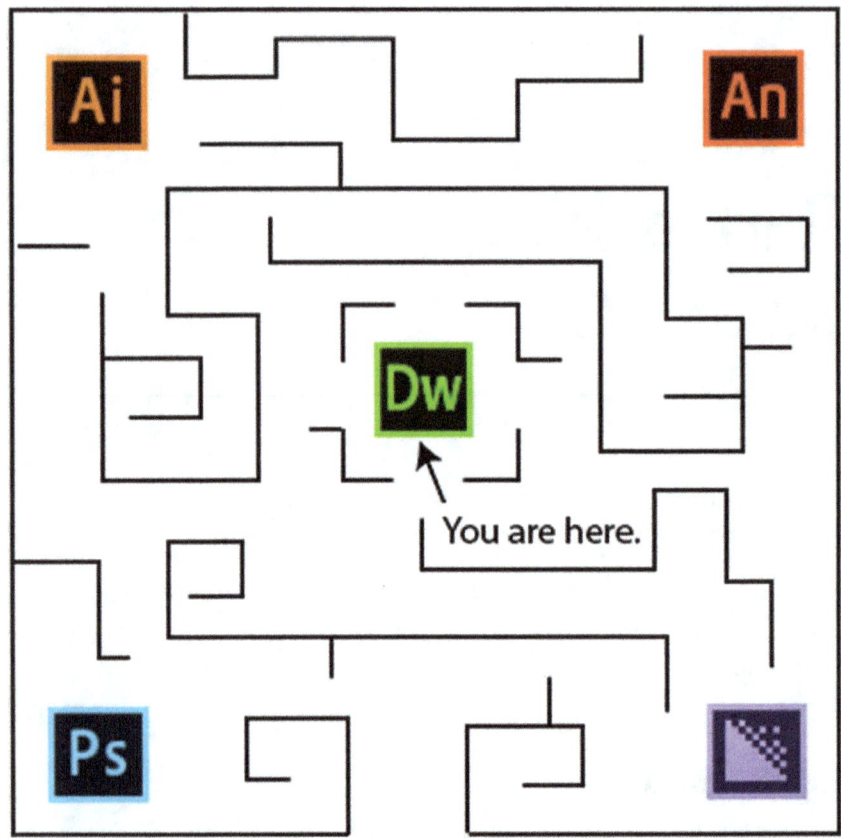

Figure 30-1. You are now in the center of the maze

Differences and Similarities Between Dreamweaver and Muse

Before you begin designing your website in Dreamweaver, or in this case, working with the HTML5 files for the Hot Glass Tango website, I would like to point out that Adobe Creative Cloud use to offer another website design program known as Muse CC. Refer to Figure 30-2.

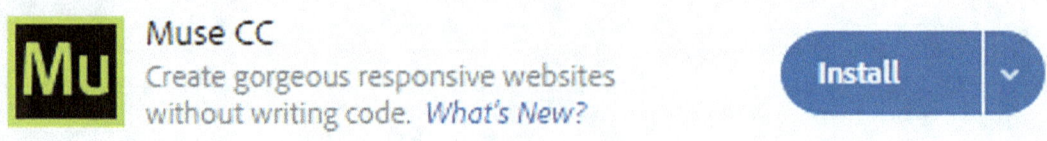

Figure 30-2. Adobe Muse was creating basic responsive websites

Muse CC was a great program for beginner web designers that did not want to learn coding just yet. You could use it to create some basic responsive websites using themes. You could also use your audio, video, and images as part of the design. As you progress as a designer and coder, however, you want to customize certain settings in your layout or themes, and your site may increase in size and complexity.

One main drawback to working with Muse was that if you're working with another person who uses Dreamweaver CC or any HTML complier to build your site, and you bring your Muse files for them to edit, once it's in Dreamweaver as HTML, you couldn't go back to Muse to continue designing. However, if you learn basic coding like HTML5, CSS, and JavaScript, there is no need for Muse and you can build your own responsive website using Dreamweaver.

Since not all settings in Muse were standardized, learning the code is the best web practice. Using Dreamweaver, you can still use HTML files from a client who may not have Dreamweaver or the four core Adobe programs mentioned earlier. Refer to Figure 30-3.

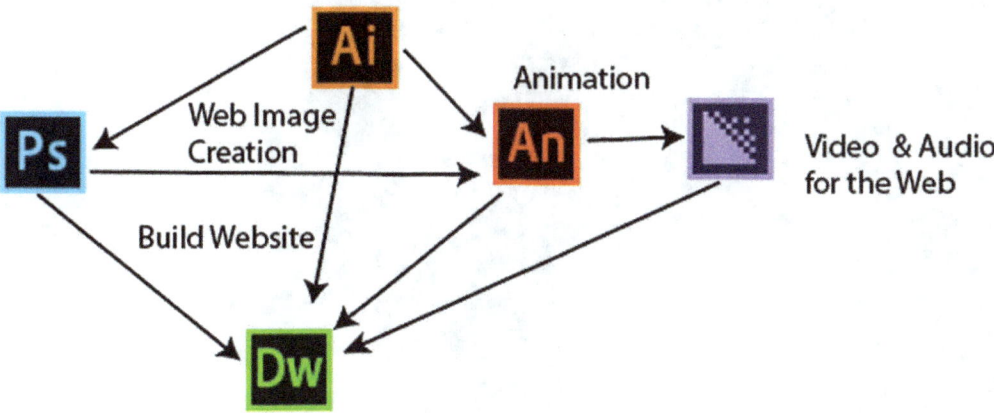

Figure 30-3. The Adobe programs that are used to build images for a website

In Part 7, you look at a few more programs that Adobe CC offers for web design for creating websites and related products, but for now, let's focus on using Dreamweaver to complete building your site. Refer to Figure 30-4.

Figure 30-4. Now that you have collected your multimedia, its time so start integrating it into your site

Setting up in Dreamweaver

My first complete website after college in 2003 was built using Adobe's first web development program, known as Adobe GoLive. I had read some books on basic web design but did not really understand what the purpose of the HTML coding and CSS formatting was. I was limited by what I could do with the layout because I could not manipulate the placement of the graphics and text to suit my requirements.

CHAPTER 30 ■ GETTING STARTED WITH DREAMWEAVER CC

Eventually, around 2006 or 2007, I became more serious about learning web design and started using Macromedia Dreamweaver (later bought by Adobe and replaced Adobe GoLive in 2007). I took some continuing studies courses for several years to continue my research into coding for work, and today besides building websites for clients, I work at the college as an instructor assisting students on the basics of web design with Adobe Dreamweaver CC.

If you have never used Dreamweaver before, I recommend reading a book like *Adobe Dreamweaver CC Classroom in a Book* by James J. Maivald (Adobe Press, 2017), where you get a basic overview of the program and many of its tools. You can also check out Dreamweaver's Help menu, which has step-by-step tutorials on various projects. Refer to Figure 30-5.

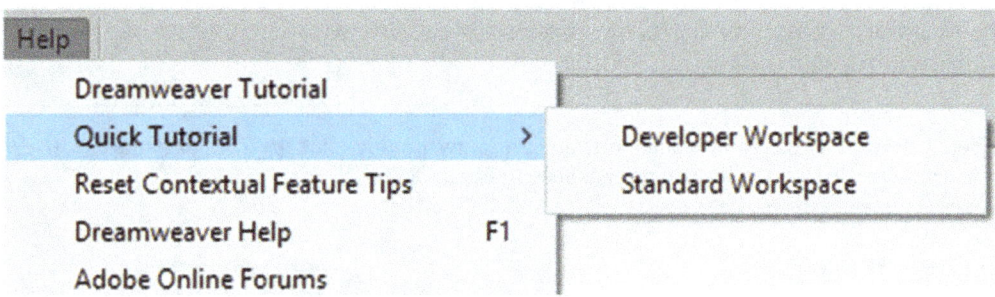

Figure 30-5. *Some tutorial information is available in the Help menu*

■ **Note** While working in Dreamweaver, you can do some dragging and dropping of files, but it is important to at least learn the basics of HTML5, CSS3, and some JavaScript or jQuery. You learn about these topics as you progress through the book and work with the Hot Glass Tango website that was built using Bootstrap. I recommend that if you want to see online tutorials and files that you can use in Dreamweaver, check out W3Schools where you can browse through the various lessons and examples at `www.w3schools.com`:

`www.w3schools.com/css/`

`www.w3schools.com/html/`

`www.w3schools.com/js/`

`www.w3schools.com/jquery/`

`www.w3schools.com/bootstrap/`

In this book, you work with some graphics that were already created. You will add them to various pages on the Hot Glass Tango website.

Let's begin by opening Dreamweaver CC. If you do not have it on your computer, but you do have the Creative Cloud software console, click the Install button (see Figure 30-6) and follow the instructions on how to install the program.

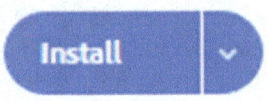

Figure 30-6. *Click the Install button to add Dreamweaver to your site*

■ **Note** Before you install any Adobe program, make sure that your computer meets the system requirements; otherwise the install may fail. For more information, check `https://helpx.adobe.com/dreamweaver/system-requirements.html`.

If you already have Dreamweaver installed on your computer, double-click the icon, or in the Creative Cloud console, click Open to launch the program as seen in Figure 30-7.

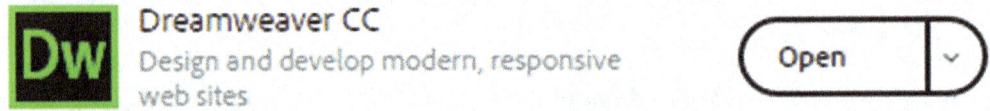

Figure 30-7. *Open Dreamweaver from the Creative Cloud console*

Once Dreamweaver CC opens, let's set up your workspace so that it is the same as mine.

Chose the Standard workspace from the Workspace icon in the upper right, as in Figure 30-8. This layout allows you to work with many visual tools, and a Split view gives you a preview of the layout while you code.

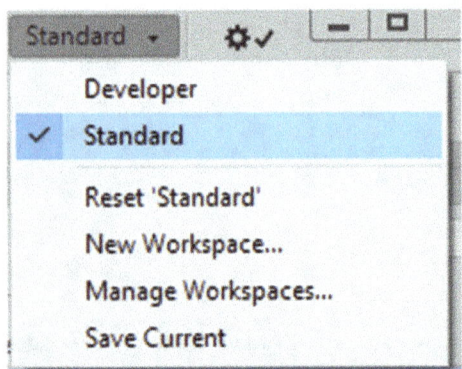

Figure 30-8. *Choose a workspace in Dreamweaver*

However, depending on your workflow, you may prefer the Developer workspace (a layout geared towards coding), or you may want to create a New Workspace, as you saw you could do with Photoshop (in Part 2), Illustrator (in Part 3), Animate (in Part 4), and Media Encoder (in Part 5). After saving your workspace, you can switch and manage your workspaces during your project while you edit your documents or panels.

Then I added the Properties panel (Window ➤ Properties). Refer to Figure 30-9.

CHAPTER 30 ■ GETTING STARTED WITH DREAMWEAVER CC

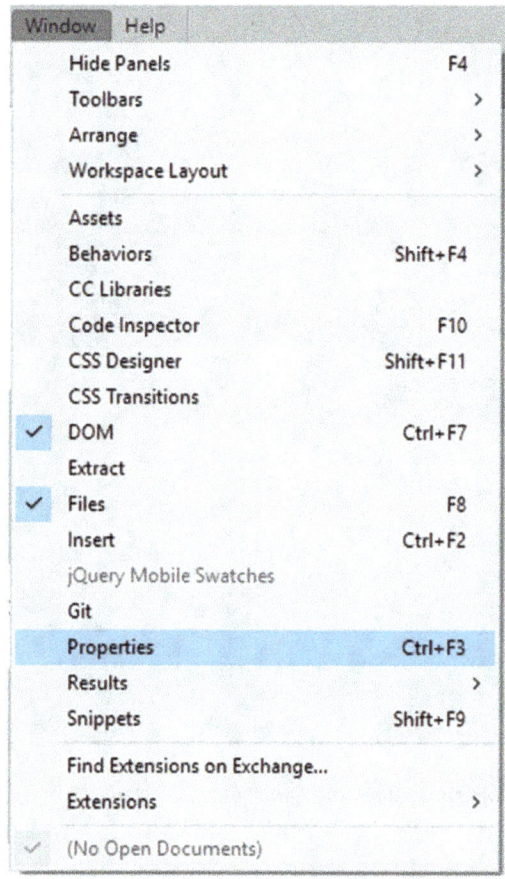

Figure 30-9. *Add the Properties panel to your workflow*

This way, you have the access to the Properties panel as you would with the other Adobe programs that you use, in case you need to make edits to your graphics and text. I usually drag this panel to the bottom of my screen so that it does not block the preview. Before you open and create a new file, the Properties panel is blank. Refer to Figure 30-10.

CHAPTER 30 ■ GETTING STARTED WITH DREAMWEAVER CC

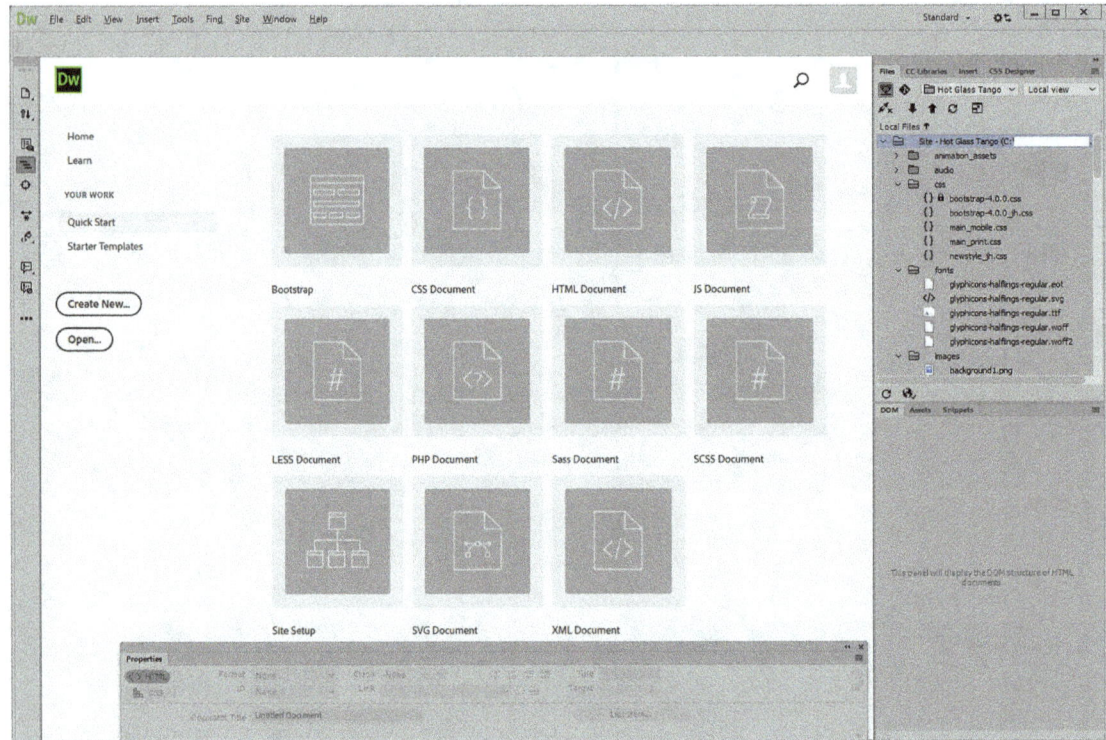

Figure 30-10. *Standard workspace in Dreamweaver with Properties panel and Quick Start selected*

Make sure to choose Quick Start; this option is found in the Start-up panel and the Work tab. This option allows you to quickly start building a preset file type without having to go through the File ➤ New dialog box.

Toolbar Overview

You will notice that, like Photoshop CC, Illustrator CC, and Animate CC, Dreamweaver CC has a toolbar that appears on the left (Windows ➤ Toolbars ➤ Common). However, the tools within it are very different than those in the other programs. Refer to Figure 30-11.

CHAPTER 30 ■ GETTING STARTED WITH DREAMWEAVER CC

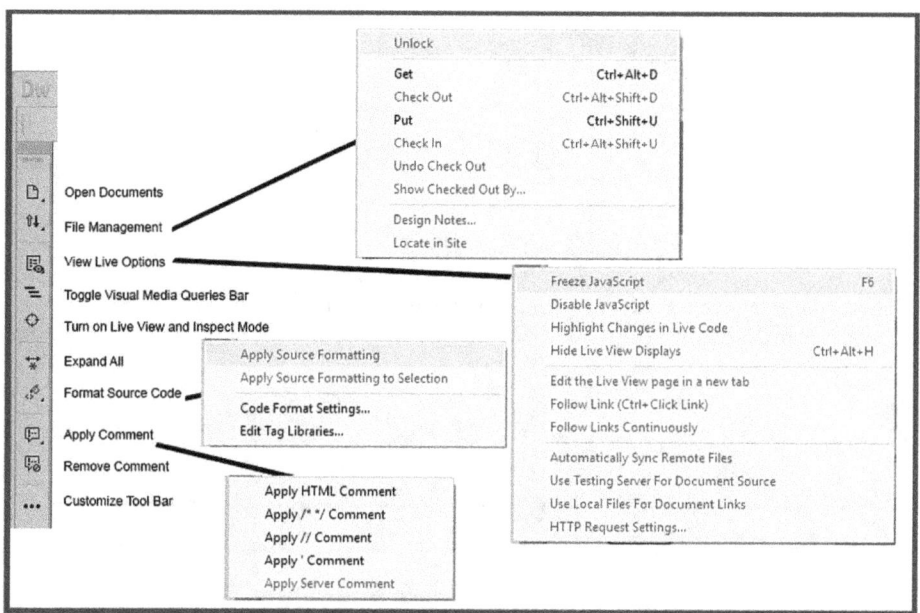

Figure 30-11. The Toolbar panel in Dreamweaver

Like Photoshop, you can customize the toolbar to suit your needs, by adding further menu options or removing unwanted tools from the toolbar. These settings can be saved as part of one of your customized workspaces.

- **Open Documents:** Allows you to open or review the currently opened documents, in a single window with the tabs. You can switch between the documents by selecting that file from the pop-out list.

- **File Management:** Allows you to get (download) and put (upload) a current file via FTP, providing you have this set-up, in Site ➤ Manage Sites, files can also be Check in or out if working with another group member or team, Design Notes allow you to add notes to a separate HTML file that team members can access as a reference. Locate in Site helps you locate the currently open file in your Files panel so that you can see where it is in the hierarchy of the site.

- **View Live Options:** This only appears in the toolbar if your Live option is enabled in Toolbars ➤ Document. Refer to Figure 30-12. It allows you to work with your JavaScript during testing to freeze or disable it. Highlight changes in the Live code, hide/show live view displays guides, edit the Live view page in a new tab, and follow links. You can also automatically synchronize with remote files and transfer the document you are viewing between your local and remote sites. Further options include the testing server for document source, local files for document links, and the HTTP Request settings.

741

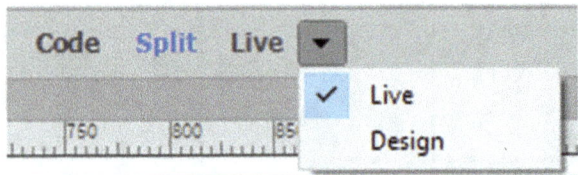

Figure 30-12. Choose whether to see your file in Live or Design view

- **Toggle Visual Media Queries Bar:** Allows this bar to show or hide when a file is open. Refer to Figure 30-13.

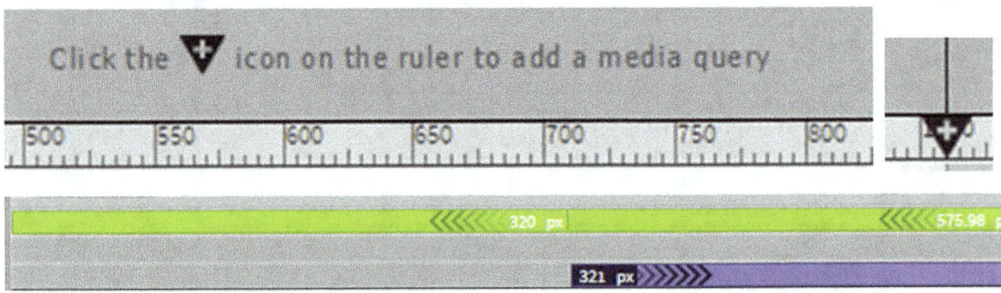

Figure 30-13. Review the media queries in your file

- Make a plus arrow appear on a ruler and you can set various change points or CSS media queries. This happens in various browser layouts; for example, your site may have three states: one for mobile, another for tablet, and a final for the desktop. This can ultimately be controlled using CSS. Media query refers to the type of media (mobile, tablet, or desktop) that you are viewing the website on. For now, leave this area hidden or in Design view. Design view displays a representation of the document, previewing how the user views a page in a web browser.

- **Turn on Live view and inspect mode:** Live view is an interactive preview of your website that is accurately rendering in real time. In this view, you can also edit your HTML elements. This tool also removes the rulers. You can add them back by clicking in the design and then the Live view in the Document toolbar. When this is on, you can click the menu area (triple horizontal lines) of the image and then the code appears in a pop-out dialog box that you can edit and it points out where the code can be found when you are in Split view. Refer to Figure 30-14.

CHAPTER 30 ■ GETTING STARTED WITH DREAMWEAVER CC

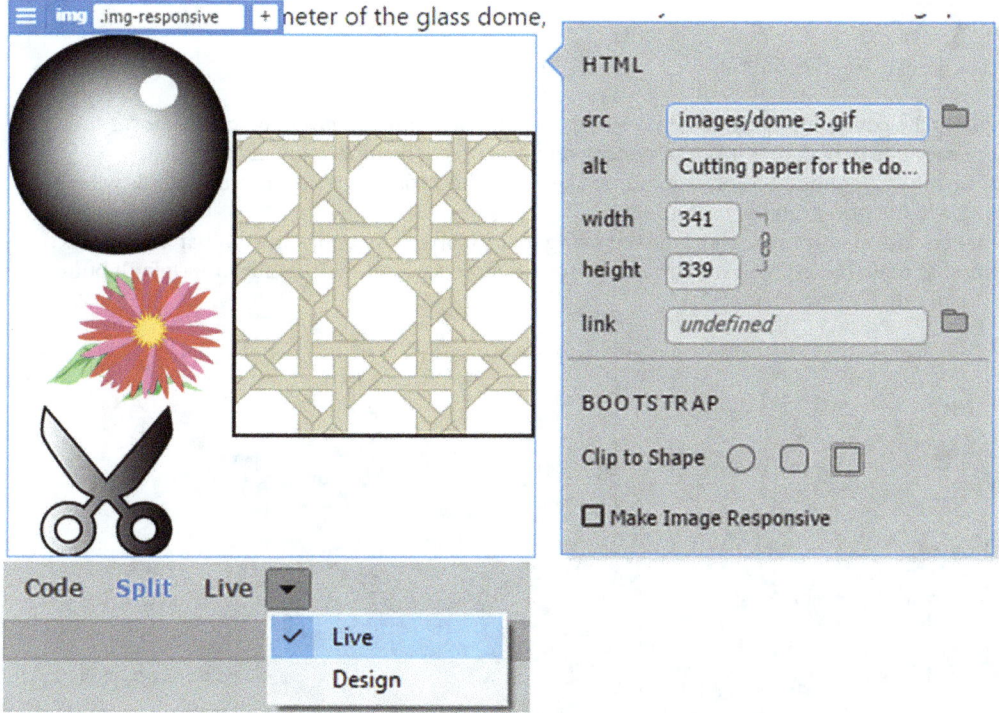

Figure 30-14. *Use inspect mode to check the sizes of images*

- **Expand All:** Refers to when you are working either in Code view or Split view, if part of the code is collapsed or hidden, Expand All restores all the code to the expanded or show state so that you can look at it all.

- **Format Source Code:** Allows you to apply formatting to a selection; it also allows you to view and edit code format settings and edit tag libraries, which are advanced settings that require knowledge of HTML and CSS. This tool is only visible when in Code view or Split view.

- **Apply Comment and Remove Comment:** Allows you to add or remove HTML, CSS, JavaScript, or server comments. Comments are lines of code that do not affect the operation of the code. They are just helpful reminders or hints while working on a project to you as the designer or other designers as to what the code does. In HTML you might write

```
<!-- This div will contain a video -->
```

This reminds you or the designer what goes in that <div> tag. In CSS or JavaScript, you might write for a large area of code:

```
/* This section is for navigation*/
```

CHAPTER 30 ■ GETTING STARTED WITH DREAMWEAVER CC

or for one line of code

```
//This is the width of the button.
```

   Highlighting the comment in the Code view and clicking the Remove Comment icon removes the comment symbols. It now becomes just a sentence which can affect the operation of the code.
   As with the other mentioned Adobe programs like Photoshop you can access more subtools when you click the triangle in the lower right of each tools.
   Also, you can add a few more tools to the bar using the ... icon to customize the toolbar and access the Customize Toolbar dialog box. If you want to remove or reset the toolbar, click the Restore Default button and then Done to exit. Refer to Figure 30-15.

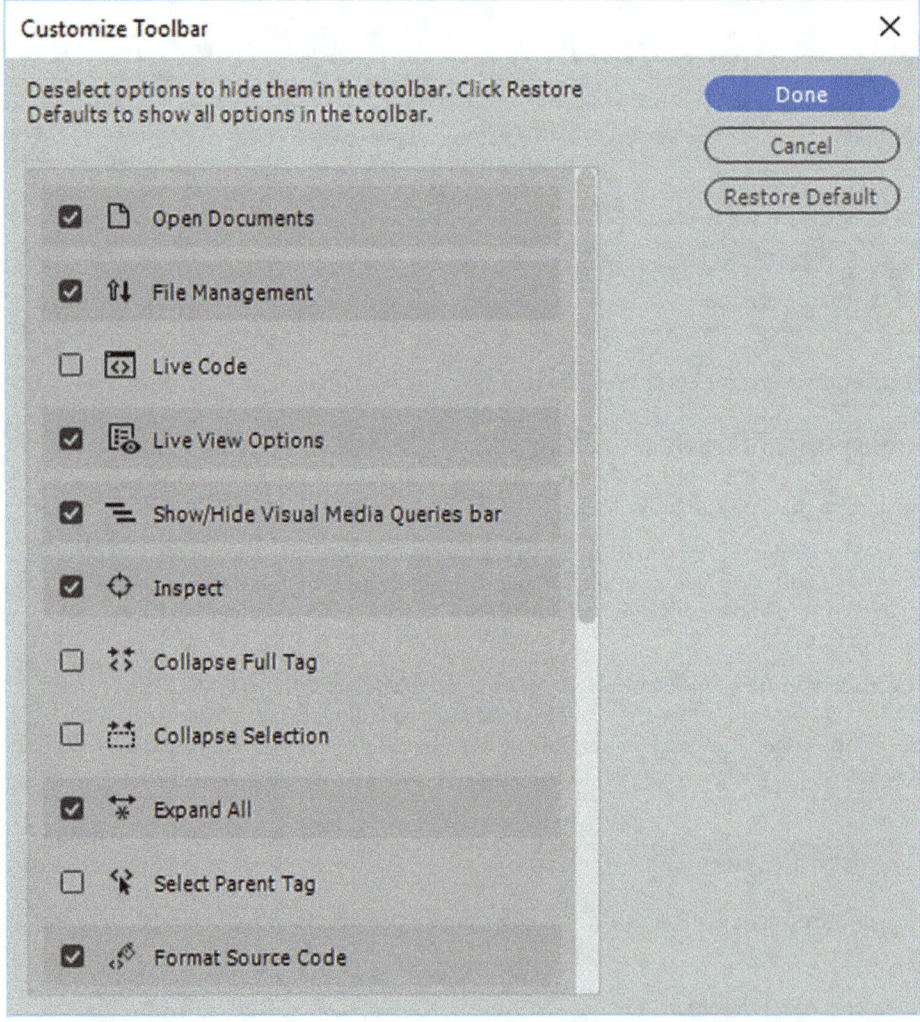

Figure 30-15. Scroll through the Customize Toolbar dialog box to see if there are any other tools you want to add to the toolbar

CHAPTER 30 ■ GETTING STARTED WITH DREAMWEAVER CC

However, most of the tools and settings that you need are found in the Properties panel and the Insert panel, which you look at in more detail shortly. Nevertheless, take some time to check out the extra tools and add them to your toolbar if required for your project.

There is also the Toolbars Standard panel, as seen in Figure 30-16.

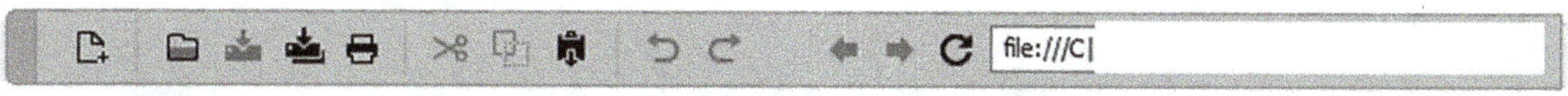

Figure 30-16. Toolbar Standards panel

This panel allows you to quickly access many of the settings you would find in the File or Edit menus.

You can create a new document, open a document in your site, save, save all files currently open, print the code of the file, cut, copy, paste, redo, undo, and refresh the current file.

■ **Note** If you would like to set your interface to the same color as mine, go to Edit ➤ Preferences and choose the Interface tab. Then choose an App Theme (third from the left) and code theme: light, and click Apply and close. Refer to Figure 30-17.

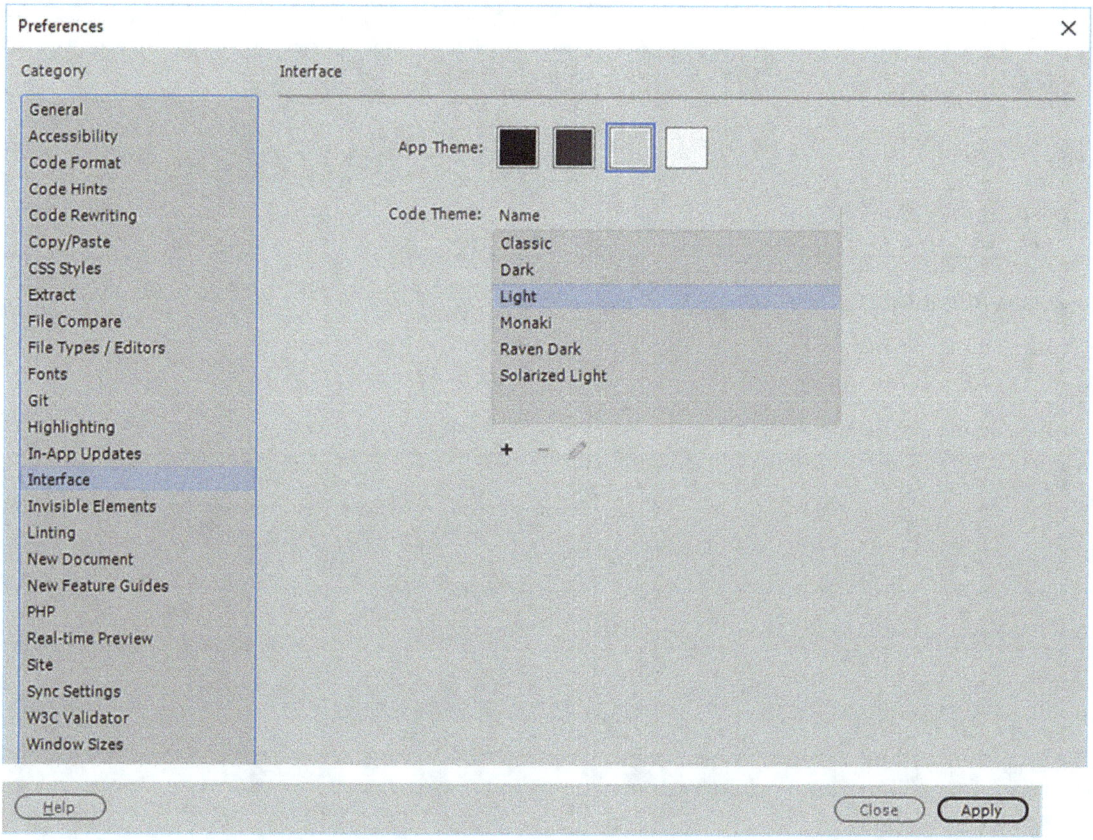

Figure 30-17. Preferences panel setting the interface color

745

CHAPTER 30 ■ GETTING STARTED WITH DREAMWEAVER CC

I prefer a medium gray and a light code theme, as I find it reduces eye strain, but you may prefer another setting.

To create a new HTML5 page, you can do it through the Opening Start-up console in the Quick Start tab, which appears when Dreamweaver opens, or File ➤ New. Refer to Figure 30-18.

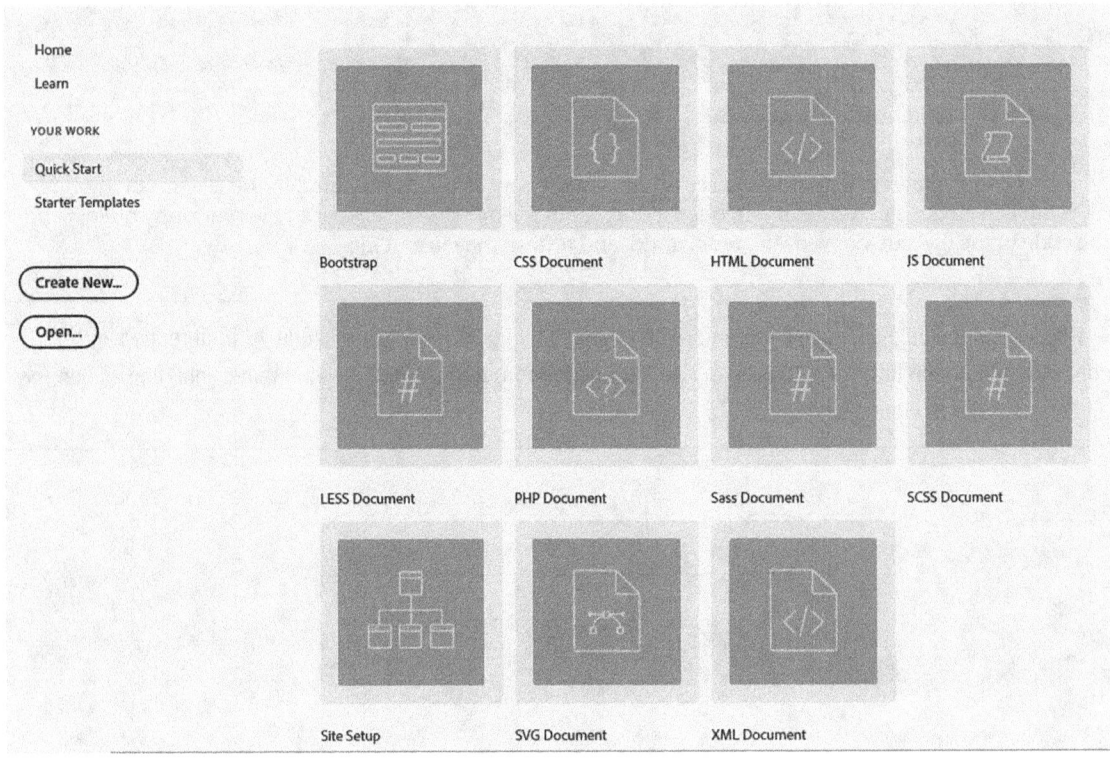

Figure 30-18. *The Quick Start file choice for Dreamweaver*

CHAPTER 30 ■ GETTING STARTED WITH DREAMWEAVER CC

File ➤ New Document lets you set the document type to HTML5. Refer to Figure 30-19.

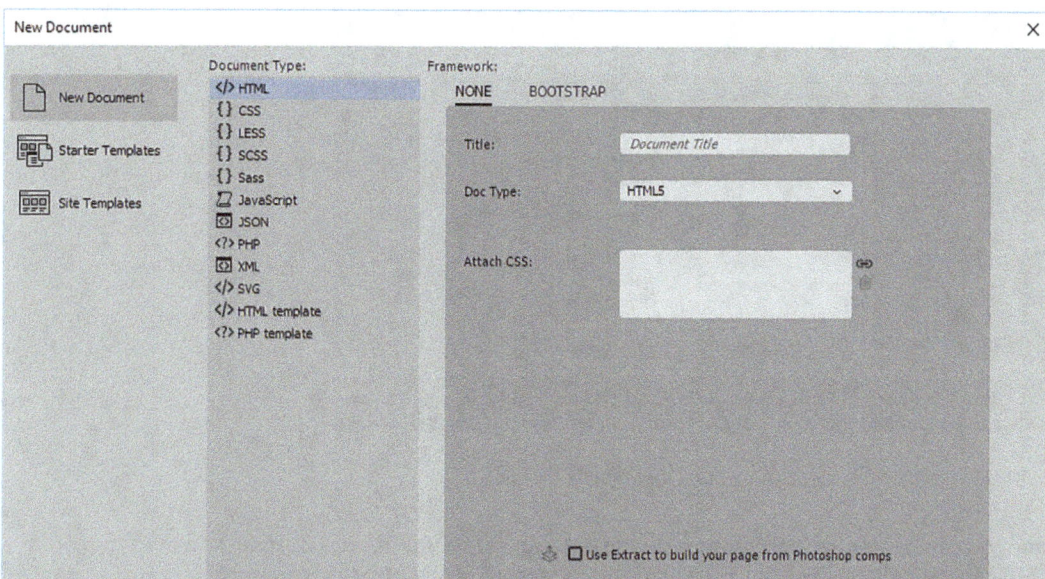

Figure 30-19. *New Document dialog box*

If you have been using the default of HTML4 in the past or need to revert to an older file version, you can choose it from the drop-down menu; however, do not keep the doc type as HTML5.

You can also work with a variety of other file formats, such as external CSS, external JavaScript, JSON, PHP, XML, and SVG. See Chapters 14 and 16 for more information on SVG files.

In addition, Dreamweaver allows you to create templates. Templates are in some ways like themes that you see on a website; you build one template background, and then all the HTML5 pages that you base on that template for your website is consistently similar. You can either create your own template, work with a starter template that Adobe has created, or a site template that a client has already created for you.

You look at templates in more detail in Chapter 35. Let's first discuss HTML5 files. Click the Create button in the New Document dialog box to create a new HTML5 document.

What is HTML5 (.html)?

When you first create an HTML document via File ➤ New, like any file, it is not in any folder or location until it is saved. For all your projects in this book, you should save it as the latest version of Hypertext Markup Language, or HTML version 5. Refer to Figure 30-20.

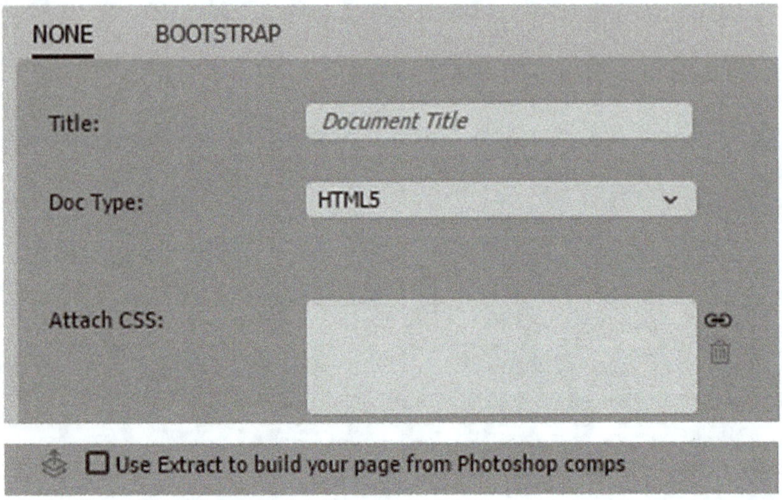

CHAPTER 30 ■ GETTING STARTED WITH DREAMWEAVER CC

Figure 30-20. New Document dialog box Doc Type HTML5

Here you can name give the document a title (this appears in the <title> tag), choose a doc type of HTML5. If you have already created an external file, attach a CSS file with the Link icon; you can also remove it using the Trash icon.

■ **Note** Use extract to build your page from Photoshop comps works if your RAW PSD file contained Photoshop layer comps. See Chapter 4 on how to export comps as seen in Figure 30-20.

Older client files that are in HTML may have been saved in HTML4 doc type format as either transitional or strict. Refer to Figure 30-21.

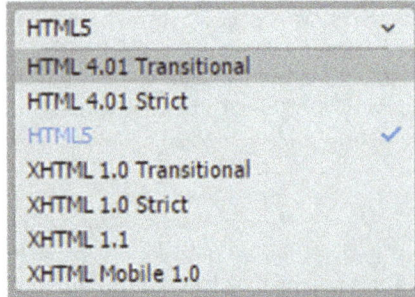

Figure 30-21. Choose from the Doc Type settings

It's hard to know what settings are inside of an HTML file until you view the code, since both HTML4 and HTML5 have the same .html file extension; however, there are differences between HTML4 and HTML5. Refer to Table 30-1.

Table 30-1. *HTML4 and HTML5 Formats*

HTML 4.01 Transitional (Allows some deprecated/obsolete tags)

<!DOCTYPE HTML PUBLIC "-//W3C//DTD HTML 4.01 Transitional//EN" "http://www.w3.org/TR/html4/loose.dtd">
<html>
<head>
<meta http-equiv="Content-Type" content="text/html; charset=utf-8">
<title>Untitled Document</title>
</head>

<body>
</body>
</html>

HTML 4.01 Strict (Does not allow deprecated/obsolete tags)

<!DOCTYPE HTML PUBLIC "-//W3C//DTD HTML 4.01//EN" "http://www.w3.org/TR/html4/strict.dtd">
<html>
<head>
<meta http-equiv="Content-Type" content="text/html; charset=utf-8">
<title>Untitled Document</title>
</head>

<body>
</body>
</html>

HTML5 (While this allows some older features, you cannot access the new audio and video features of HTML unless you use this format.)

<!doctype html>
<html>
<head>
<meta charset="utf-8">
<title>Untitled Document</title>
</head>

<body>
</body>
</html>

For more information on doc types, review the examples at www.w3schools.com/tags/tag_doctype.asp.

To access the full range of new HTML5 features and work with the latest CSS, you need to use the HTML5 doc type and click Create to create your new page.

Let's now take a moment to review the HTML5 settings. Make sure that you are either in Code view or Split view in Toolbars ➤ Document to look at the code. Your new blank document should look like Figure 30-22.

```
1    <!doctype html>
2 ▼  <html>
3 ▼  <head>
4    <meta charset="utf-8">
5    <title>Untitled Document</title>
6    </head>
7
8    <body>
9    </body>
10   </html>
11
```

Figure 30-22. A new HTML5 file open in Dreamweaver in Code view

Most tags or elements have opening and closing tags: <tag></tag>. However, not every tag has a closing tag partner, so it is important to review how to type each element; for example, an image tag is written as a self-closing tag.

<img src="image.gif" width="2" height="2" alt=""/>

Refer to www.w3schools.com/html/default.asp and www.w3schools.com/tags/default.asp.

- **<!doctype html>:** Defines the doc type.

- **<html> </html>:** Surrounds the head, meta, title, and body tags: It lets you know this is an HTML document. If one of these tags is altered incorrectly or removed, the document becomes corrupt, and you should fix it right away if you are working on the file in Dreamweaver CC. See how to do this in the "Fixing Errors" section. You also want to add the lang or language attribute of your site, like this: <html lang="en">. Refer to Figure 30-23.

```
1    <!doctype html>
2 ▼  <html lang="en">
3 ▼  <head>
4    <meta charset="utf-8">
5    <title>Untitled Document</title>
6    </head>
7
8    <body>
9    </body>
10   </html>
11
```

Figure 30-23. Add language to your HTML5 files

Dreamweaver CC does not add this attribute because it does not know what language your site is. If the language is English, then you use lang="en"; if French, lang="fr"; or Spanish, lang="es".

For a more complete reference, you can view this information at www.w3schools.com/tags/ref_language_codes.asp.

- **<head> </head>:** The head acts as container for all the head elements. The head tags in a new document contains the <meta>, and <title> tags, by default. However, once you start building the document, it can contain a lot more tags for the document, including reference to internal <style> or external <link> CSS, JavaScript <script>, <base> or <nonscript> tags. The viewers of your website never see what is in the head; however, the head tag is like your brain—it controls how much of the information is going to be presented or displayed. The viewer only sees what is in the <body> tag or what is figuratively external. Remember, what is going on in the "head" is displayed visually in the body "language" or code.

- **<meta charset="utf-8">:** An attribute of an element found within the head tag. Defines metadata about an HTML document. Metadata is often extra data that can be added to a file whether it be HTML or even audio or video, as you saw in Adobe Media Encoder CC. Metadata for the HTML5 document has a charset or character set attribute included, depending on the country of origin; with the text or symbol characters it may be different, but UTF-8 is common to North America. UTF-8 is character encoding for Unicode.

Other metadata that you may encounter that you must enter yourself refers to extra text for search engines or the view port if you are building a mobile site.

```
<meta name="description" content="Free Information">
<meta name="keywords" content="HTML5, CSS3, JavaScript">
<meta name="author" content="Jennifer Harder">
<meta name="viewport" content="width=device-width, initial-scale=1.0">
```

This information is optional depending on your project. Just be aware that if you do not enter a meta viewport, your mobile website may not function properly and will not be able to correctly expand on a smartphone or tablet.

- **<title>Untitled Document</title>:** Found in the head tag. Defines the title or name of the document page. While it is important to save the file with a file name, it also needs a title that appears in the browser. Without a title that is unique, viewers will not know what page in your website they are on when they look at the tabs in their browser. Adding a title improves the navigation on your site, as it is displayed in search engines for the purposes of optimization and usability.

- **<body></body>:** The final most important tag in your HTML file is the body. Viewers see in their browsers what you placed within this tag. It can contain tags such as text, images, tables, lists, and hyperlinks. It is to this area you are adding images or references to images that appear via CSS or JavaScript that is found in the head tag. You can add JavaScript to the body area, but this code is often referenced to JavaScript that appears somewhere in the head.

Import and Save Your File to Your Site

Once you have created a new file, it is time to save it with a name in your site folder. If you have not set up a site, you can save the file to any folder as you would a Photoshop or Illustrator file; however, if you are saving multiple HTML files, it is important to be able to save these files to the same folder repeatedly without getting mixed up. When building a website, organization is key. Saving a site makes Dreamweaver remember the same folder each time you save a new file.

Before saving your first HTML page in the main menu, go to Site ➤ New site.

***

■ **Note** If you have already created a site, skip down to the File ➤ Save area.

***

To set up a basic site, the two primary areas you need to look at are the Site and Servers tabs. If you don't have a remote website yet, that is OK. For now, you will just focus on the Site panel so that you can start building your local site for your project. In Chapter 38, you set up the remote area, but you need to make your own custom revisions, which depend on your FTP host site, the location of your domain name system (DNS), and what kind of server they use. Refer to Figure 30-24.

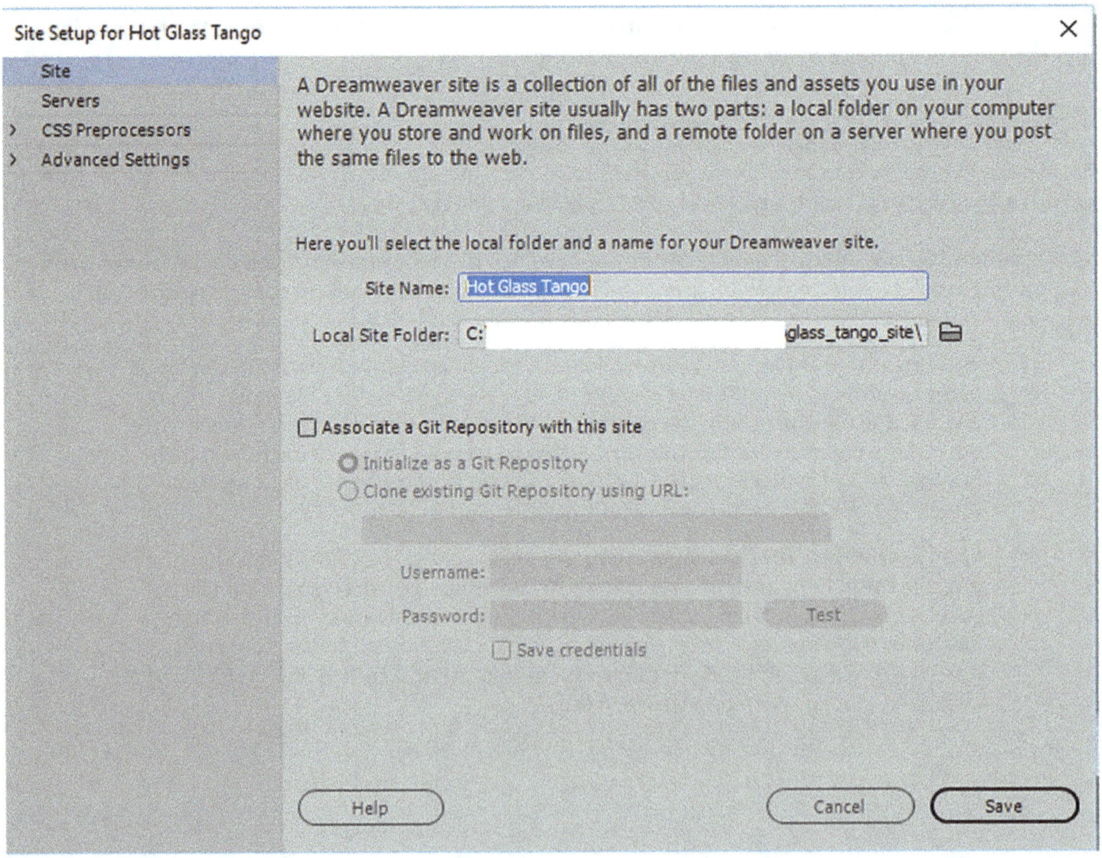

Figure 30-24. Site setup Site tab

CHAPTER 30 ■ GETTING STARTED WITH DREAMWEAVER CC

To follow along, Locate the "glass tango site" folder for this chapter you will be using it as a reference in Part 6.

In the site, add a site name: Hot Glass Tango. This is a reference point for you when you work in the Files panel, as you may have more than one site. Then use the Local Site Folder icon to locate where you want your local site folder to be, or in this case, the folder that is for this chapter; it may be on your local drive or your external drive. Ignore the area that refers to a Git repository because this has to do with uploading files to a GitHub site, which you are not doing in this book.

Now click the Servers tab. For now, this area should not have an added remote server. You look at this in more detail in Chapter 38. Refer to Figure 30-25.

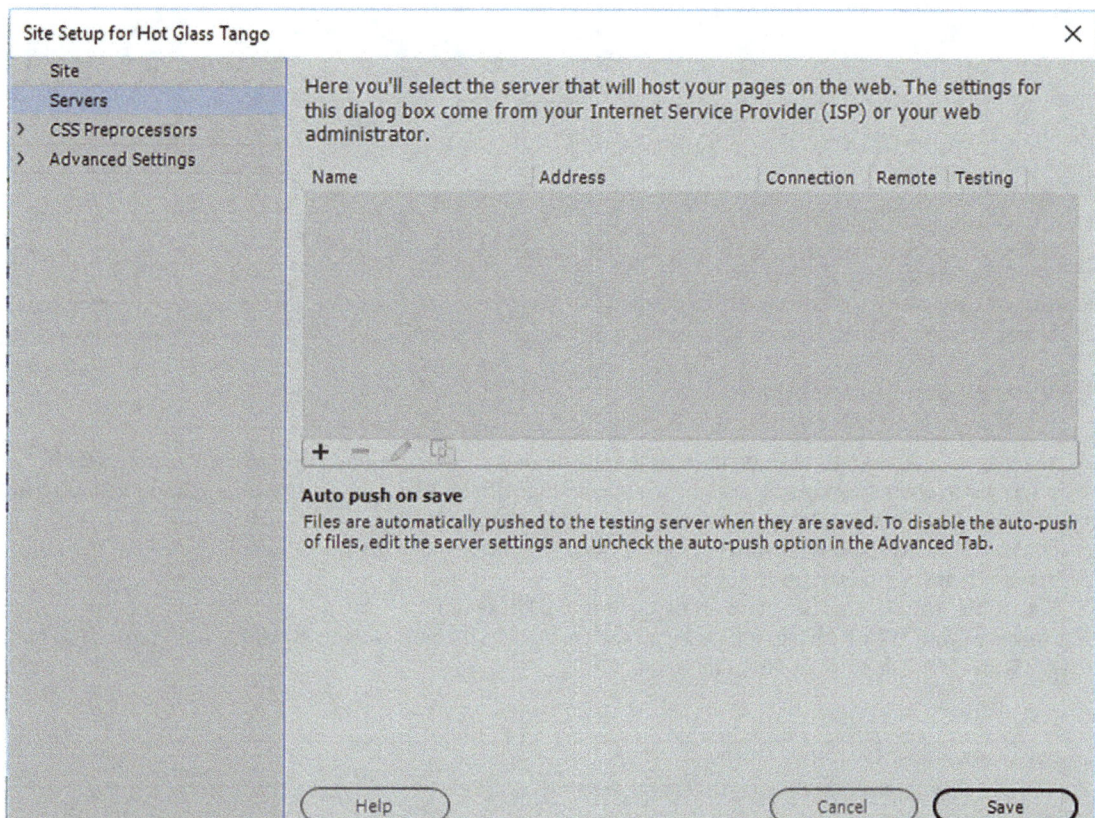

Figure 30-25. *Site Setup Servers tab*

CHAPTER 30 ■ GETTING STARTED WITH DREAMWEAVER CC

Now go to the Advanced Settings tab and choose from the Bootstrap drop-down; make sure that it is the 4.0.0 version setting. Refer to Figure 30-26.

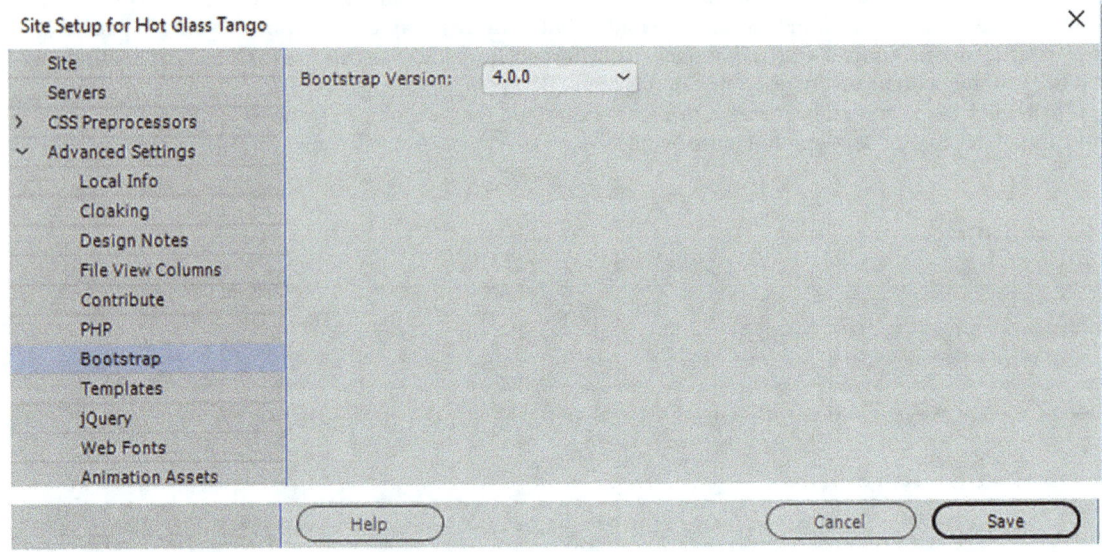

Figure 30-26. Advanced Settings tab

You learn a bit more about Bootstrap in Chapter 35. It is a free front-end framework that comes with Dreamweaver to create responsive designs while working with HTML, CSS, and various adaptable JavaScript (jQuery) plug-ins. Version 4.4.0 is supported by version IE 10 and higher.

You may want to visit the Advanced Settings tab if you must make further adjustments to your own site, but for now click Save to exit the dialog box.

Your folder should now be set up and appear in the Files panel.

Now save your HTML file; go to File ➤ Save, give it a distinct name like myfile.html, and make sure that the type is an HTML document. Refer to Figure 30-27.

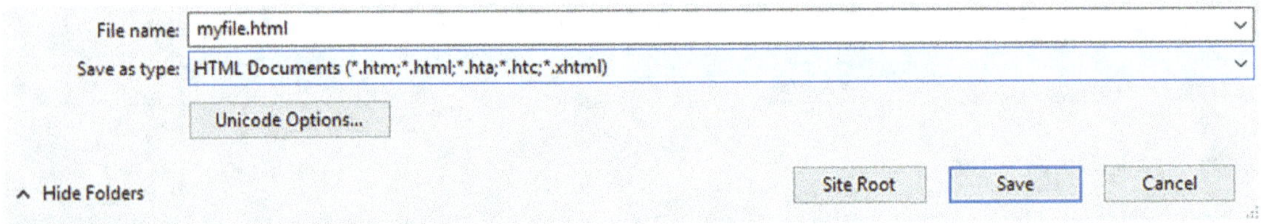

Figure 30-27. Save your file as an HTML document

If you are unsure if you are in the Site Root folder, click the Site Root button; otherwise, locate the folder within the site root that you want to save the file into.

Once done, click Save.

Files Panel

You see the new file appears in the Files panel and in your drive. Note that if you move the file outside of Dreamweaver CC, you may have to click the Refresh icon at the bottom of the panel to reflect that change. Refer to Figure 30-28.

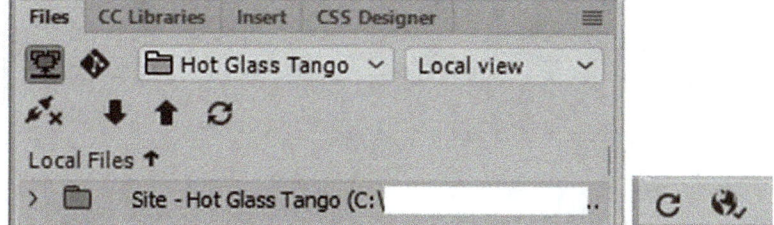

Figure 30-28. Files panel and Refresh icon to see alterations

However, if a file is moved outside of Dreamweaver, it may not update links if there are any changes. The best practice is to update links within Dreamweaver or move files within the Files panel rather than your computer's file folder. That way, Dreamweaver can keep track and alert you to changes to links.

The Files panel is very useful for navigation in your site because it lets you add or remove files using its panel menu rather than leaving Dreamweaver. Refer to Figure 30-29.

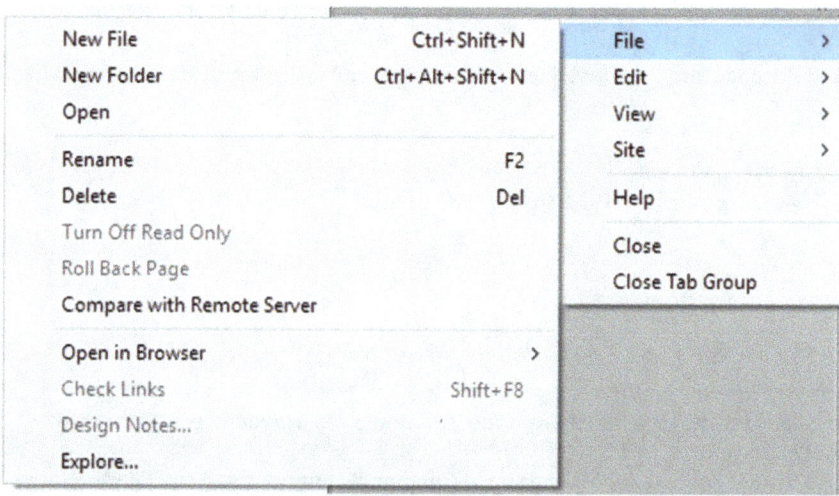

Figure 30-29. Options in the Files panel menu

Just remember that when you delete a file in the Files panel, it is permanently deleted outside of Dreamweaver as well.

Fixing Errors

While typing errors can occur within the HTML file, you can tell the file is corrupt or has an error by looking at the bottom left of your HTML page. If there is a green check, there are no errors to report. A red X means something is wrong in the code, and you need to correct it. Often, the errors won't appear until you have saved the file. Refer to Figure 30-30.

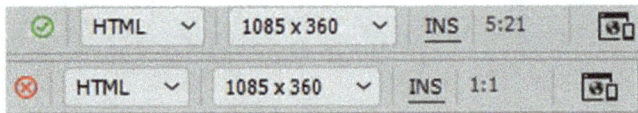

Figure 30-30. *Detecting errors in an HTML5 file*

Hovering over the X and clicking it opens the Output panel, which gives you a hint as to what the error, is as seen in Figure 30-31.

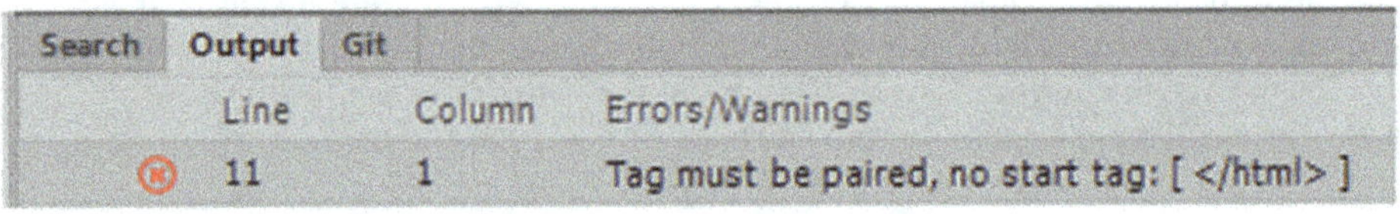

Figure 30-31. *Dreamweaver gives you a hint when in detects an HTML5 error within the open document*

Likewise, you can look at the code and see the red text line number. Hovering over it gives a similar message. Refer to Figure 30-32.

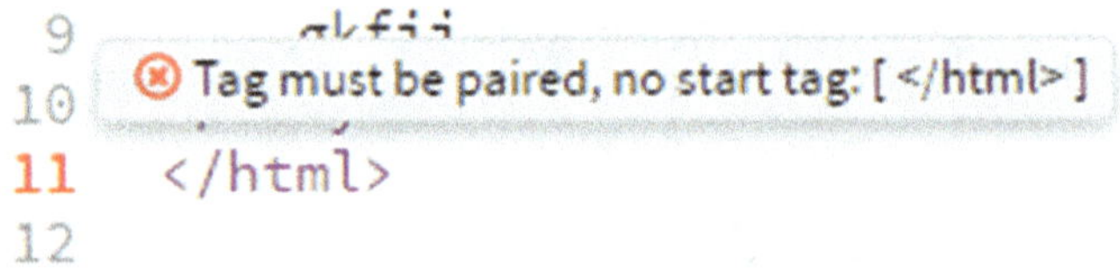

Figure 30-32. *In Code view, Dreamweaver shows where the error is located*

When you have corrected any errors, save the file, and the icon returns to a green check. Errors are removed from the Output panel as well.

You look at other ways to further validate files in the site in Chapter 38. For now, you can File ➤ Close this practice file. File ➤ Exit Dreamweaver or leave the program open for the next chapter.

Summary

In this chapter, you looked at some of the differences between Dreamweaver and the previously used Muse. You saw how different Adobe platforms or your clients' files can work with Dreamweaver. You then set up your workspace in Dreamweaver, created a basic HTML5 document, imported a site, and saved your file. You also saw how to use the Files panel to organize your work. Lastly, you looked at how Dreamweaver detects errors in a file and helps you correct them.

In the next chapter, you start adding graphics to the Hot Glass Tango site.

CHAPTER 31

Working with Images and Tags

In this chapter, you look at how to add images on a page and how to tag elements. You then discover how to add a logo to your browser's tab and how to use HTML5 resources in the Snippets panel.

> **Note** This chapter does not have any actual projects; however, you can use the files in the Part 6 folder to practice opening and viewing for this lesson. They are at `https://github.com/Apress/graphics-multimedia-web-adobe-creative-cloud`.

Now that you have saved your first HTML5 file, let's look at where you can insert images and how to interact with them on the page.

When you first create a new site in Dreamweaver CC, you need to make sure that you have a local site root folder into which you put all of your HTML pages. Along with pages, it is important to store all of your images within the root folder or root directory along with the index.html file.

Within the Hot Glass Tango root folder, you find a folder called images, which stores all the images that you have collected for the site. Refer to Figure 31-1.

CHAPTER 31 WORKING WITH IMAGES AND TAGS

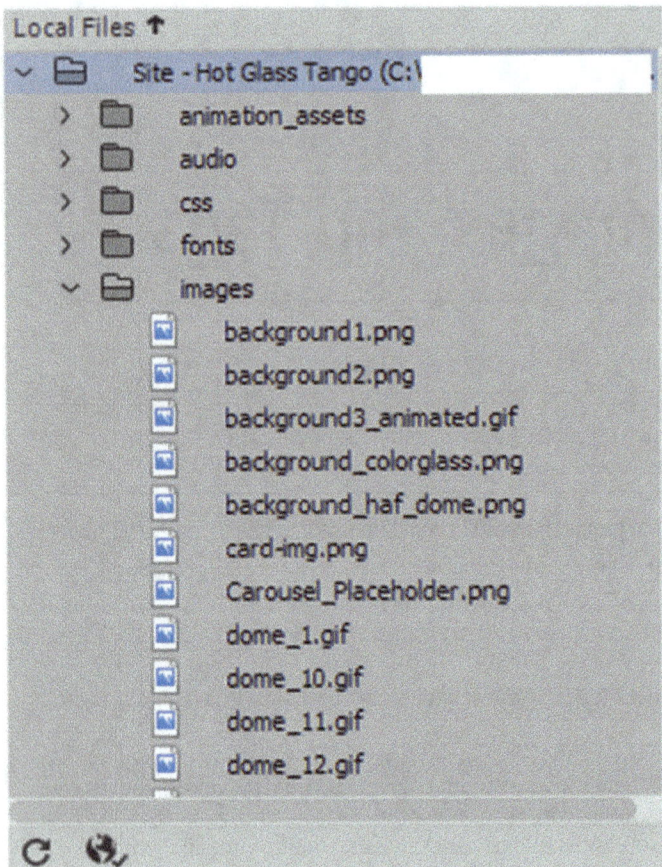

Figure 31-1. Images for the site are stored in the images folder

The following are the formats that you can include in this folder:

- Bitmap (.bmp)
- JPEG (.jpg)
- PNG (.png)
- GIF (static and animated) (.gif)
- SVG (vector) (.svg)

You could also include PDF files in the images folder if you want to; however, if you have any, I recommend saving them in their own folder (e.g., pdf_documents). Either way, make sure to keep the folder name lowercase because some servers do not like the folders to have uppercase letters.

If you have quite a few GIF animations, you may want to create a subfolder called gif_animations, just to keep things organized. Figure 31-2 shows how that might look in the files panel.

CHAPTER 31 ■ WORKING WITH IMAGES AND TAGS

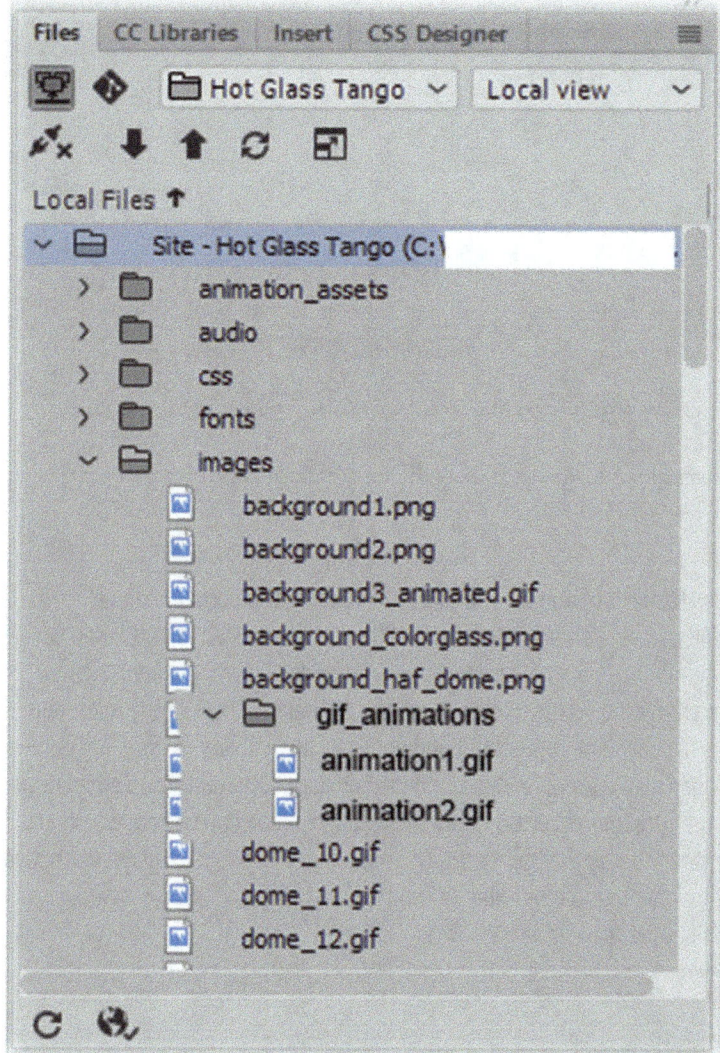

Figure 31-2. *You can create subfolders within your images folder to keep files separate and organized*

For your own project, if you have not already added an images folder to your root directory, you can do so by making sure that your site folder is selected in the Files panel, and then in its menu on the upper right, choose File ➤ New Folder, as seen in Figure 31-3.

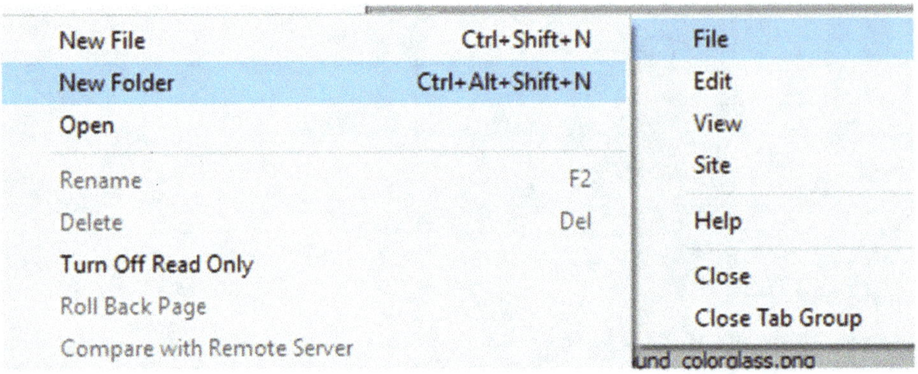

Figure 31-3. *You can create subfolders within your images folder to keep files separate and organized*

This creates a new folder that you can rename. You can select the images folder and choose File ➤ New folder to create a subfolder, like gif_animations or any name you choose.

■ **Note** When you create a folder or an HTML webpage for your site, you must follow certain naming conventions. Always name the folder or file with lowercase letters and without spaces. Start with a letter. Do not use special characters. You can use numbers, hyphens, underscores, and periods. For instance, you can use an underscore (_) if you require a space for the words. Finally, keep the file names short. Many operating systems are case sensitive. If you have a file called AboutMe.html and another called aboutme.html, the server might become confused about which to display. So proper naming conventions are important. The same is true for image links. There are some folders that Dreamweaver CC creates and allows to be capitalized, which you look at when you review templates and library items in Chapter 35. The names of those folders should not have lowercase letters because corruption of the folder and other files linked to them can occur. If Dreamweaver names or creates the folder, it's probably best to leave it as it is.

Adding More Images to the Folder

At this point in the Hot Glass Tango project, all the images are already in the images folder. If you want to add more images, use your computer's File Explorer feature to locate the images. Copy and paste these images into the site's images folder or subfolders, and then return to Dreamweaver. Click the lower Refresh icon in the Files panel so that you can see that they were added to images folder. Refer to Figure 31-4.

CHAPTER 31 ■ WORKING WITH IMAGES AND TAGS

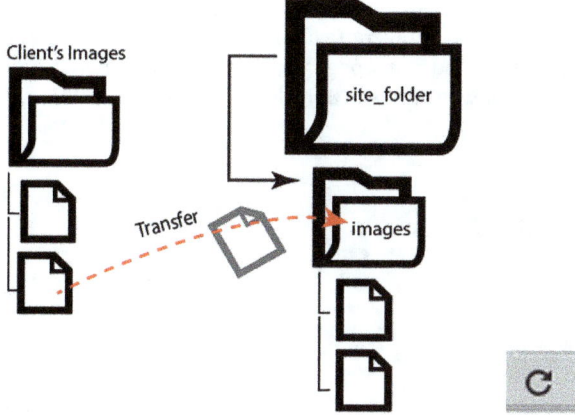

Figure 31-4. *Add images to your site, then use the refresh icon at the bottom on the files panel so that you can see them*

You can use the Files panel to move your images from one subfolder to the next. What you move or delete in the Files panel directly affects your files and their hierarchy, so when you delete an image file (File ➤ Delete), make sure that you have a backup in case you need to add that file again. Refer to Figure 31-5.

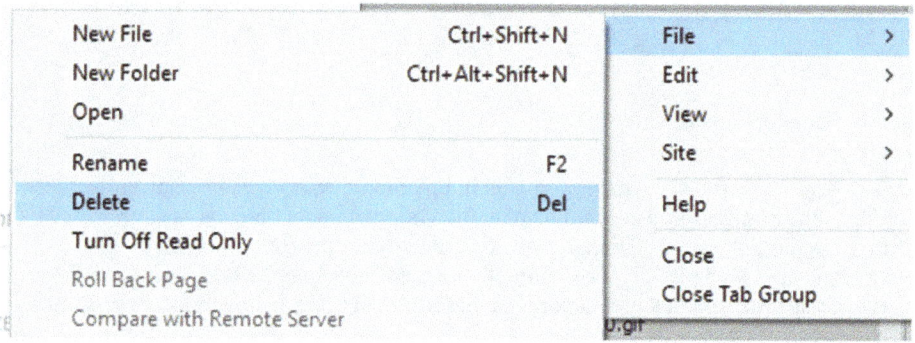

Figure 31-5. *The Files panel has options for editing and deleting files*

When you are creating a new site, your first HTML page or homepage, is index.html, which is a common name for sites on servers. This is known as your default page and all sites should have one. When a user types in www.mysite.com, this automatically takes them to the index.html page. Users do not have to type www.mysite.com/index.html.

This is because the browser knows that if it locates the index.html page, it is the website's homepage and that is the starting point. If you were to call your default page home.html instead of index.html, your browser would become confused and would not be able to locate the main page when www.mysite.com is typed in. The user might receive a message like "Cannot locate this page...", which is not what you want. The only way to access this page is to type www.mysite.com/home.html,; this just adds length to an already long name. The point is, whatever the first page of your site represents, it should be called index.html to avoid browser confusion. Having said that, any HTML page you create can contain images.

761

The pages in Hot Glass Tango use a template that I modified with a Bootstrap layout, which uses viewports and makes the site mobile-friendly. If you would like to know more about templates, I discuss them in more detail in Chapter 35. For now, you'll just focus on the blank page you created in Chapter 30. You can also read *Adobe Dreamweaver CC Classroom in a Book* by James J. Maivald for a more in-depth review of templates.

Inserting Images on an HTML Page

Figure 31-6 shows a new blank HTML5 webpage in Code view.

```
index.html  ×
 1     <!doctype html>
 2 ▼   <html lang="en">
 3 ▼   <head>
 4     <meta charset="utf-8">
 5     <title>Untitled Document</title>
 6     </head>
 7
 8     <body>
 9     </body>
10     </html>
11
```

Figure 31-6. *The HTML5 blank document*

In Dreamweaver's Design view, you see what is going on in the <body> </body> tags. Currently, there is no content between the <body> tags, so no content displays on your webpage; the page is white. The Hot Glass Tango about.html page has at least three images within various <div> tags.

To add images to a blank area on a page, you can point your cursor between the body tags (<body> </body>) or <div> tags in Code view, or click the cursor on a blank area of the page in Design view. Either way gets the same result.

Insert Panel

Now locate the Insert panel. Make sure that you're in the HTML tab in the upper left. Refer to Figure 31-7.

CHAPTER 31 ■ WORKING WITH IMAGES AND TAGS

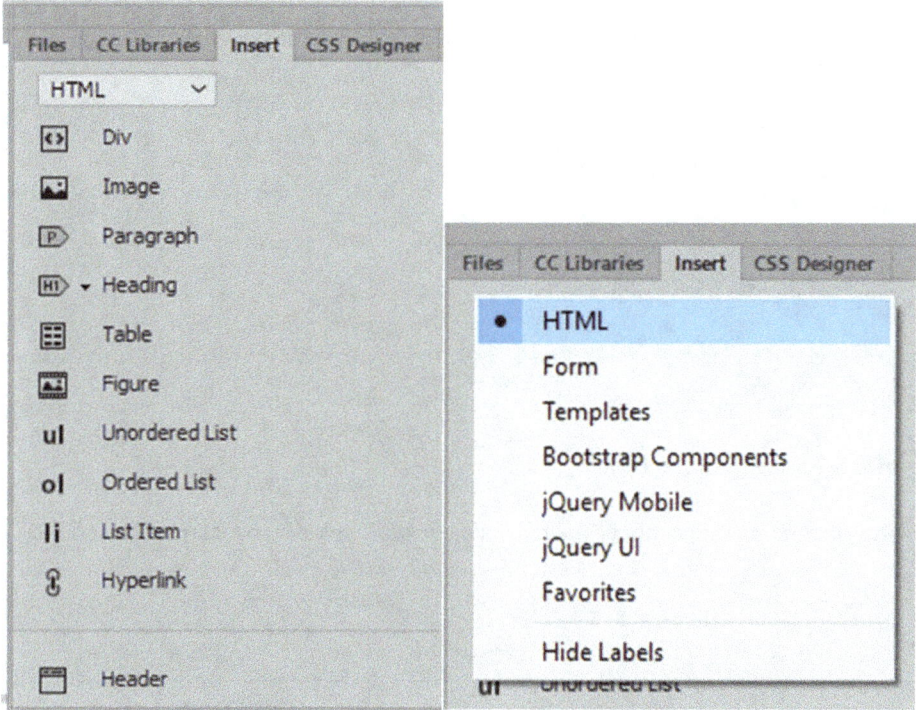

Figure 31-7. *The Insert panel with its tab to display various options*

The Insert panel is very much like the Tools panel in other Adobe programs in that houses many of the HTML tags and widgets that you require for designing your website. You can quickly insert short code for images or tables into your pages. Because there are so many, they have been organized in various tabs so that they are easier to locate. In this panel, you can create your own custom favorites to make the search easier. You can also find them in the main menu in the Insert area, should you prefer that workflow method instead. Many of the commonly used ones are at the top of the list. Refer to Figure 31-8.

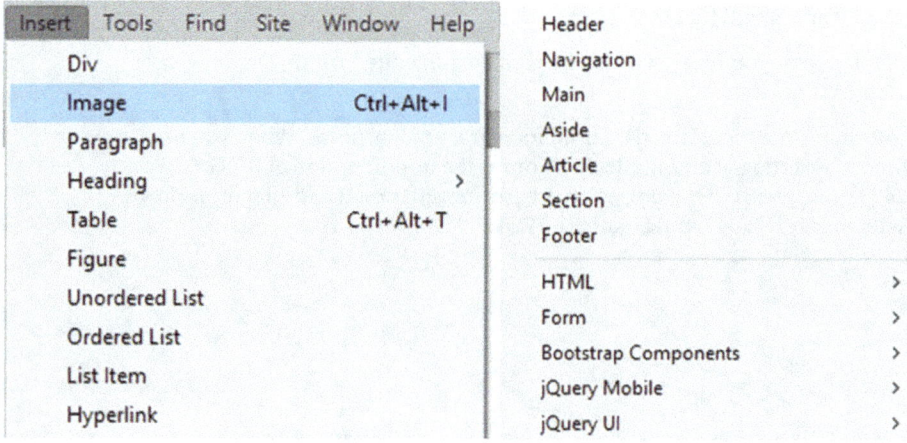

Figure 31-8. *All the items in the Insert panel are also in the main menu Insert drop-down*

763

CHAPTER 31 ■ WORKING WITH IMAGES AND TAGS

You choose how to access your images for insertion.

Back at the Insert panel, with your cursor still blinking on the page within the tag, click the Image icon. Refer to Figure 31-9.

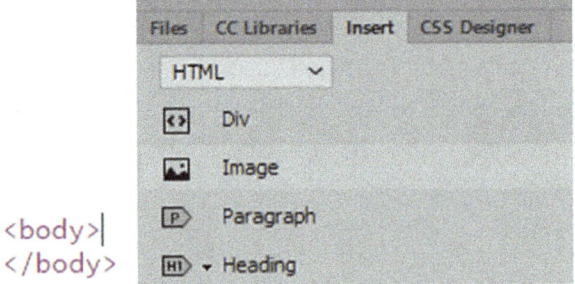

Figure 31-9. Insert an image using the Insert panel

This automatically brings up the Select Image Source dialog box, where you can locate and insert files. Refer to Figure 31-10.

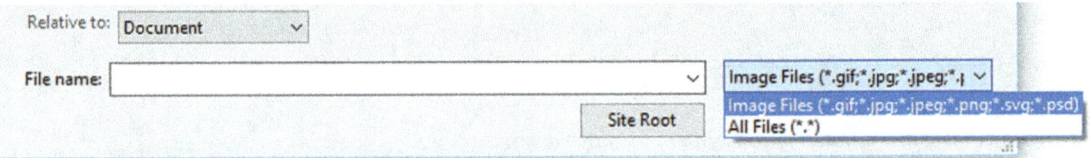

Figure 31-10. Locate the image file that you want to insert

The following files can be inserted:

- JPEG (.jpg, jpeg)
- PNG (.png)
- GIF (static and animated) (.gif)
- SVG (scalable vector graphic) (.svg) can be created and edited within Dreamweaver (File ➤ New SVG document).
- PSD (Photoshop Document) (.psd) is used for extraction purposes. When you use this method of inserting, it automatically chooses the import option of JPEG, GIF, or PNG 8, 24, 32; any preset in the preset list; or any format from the format drop-down menu. Refer to Figure 31-11 and Figure 31-12.

CHAPTER 31 ■ WORKING WITH IMAGES AND TAGS

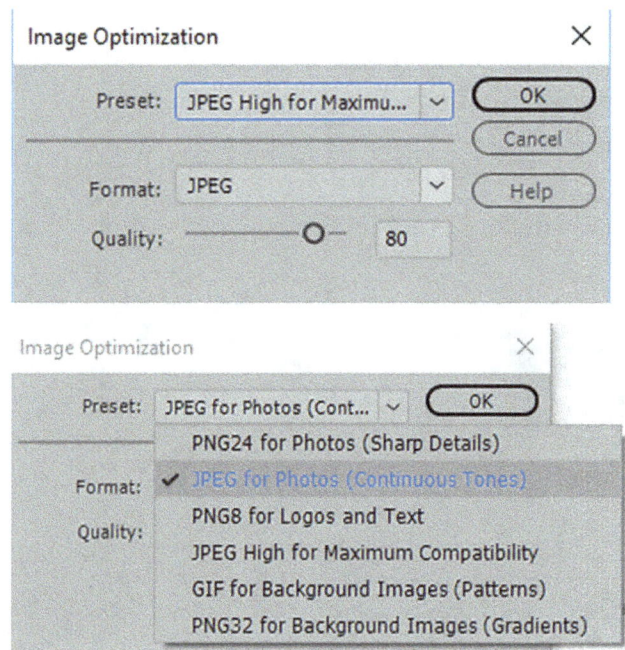

Figure 31-11. Image Optimization preset options for a JPEG file that was originally a PSD

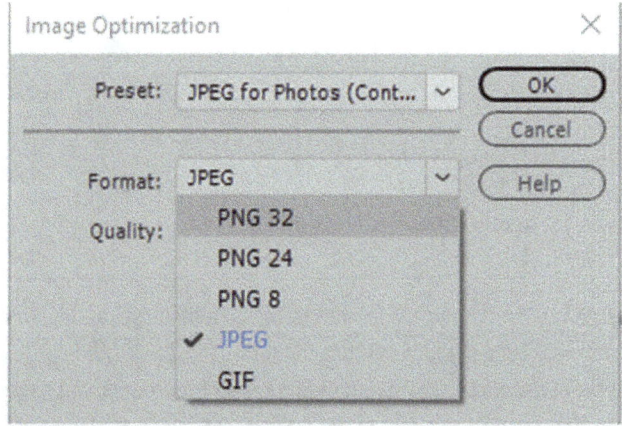

Figure 31-12. Image Optimization Format options for an image file that was a PSD

This is a wonderful way to quickly import a graphic without reverting to Photoshop; however, in most cases, it is better to work in your native program. To get the ideal setting and decrease load time for your image assets, use your export settings, like Save For Web in Photoshop, Illustrator, Animate, or Media Encoder. Many of these settings are referenced in Chapters 4, 12, 22, and 28.

Once you click OK to a PSD file, you can locate the images folder and save in that location. Refer to Figure 31-13.

765

CHAPTER 31 ■ WORKING WITH IMAGES AND TAGS

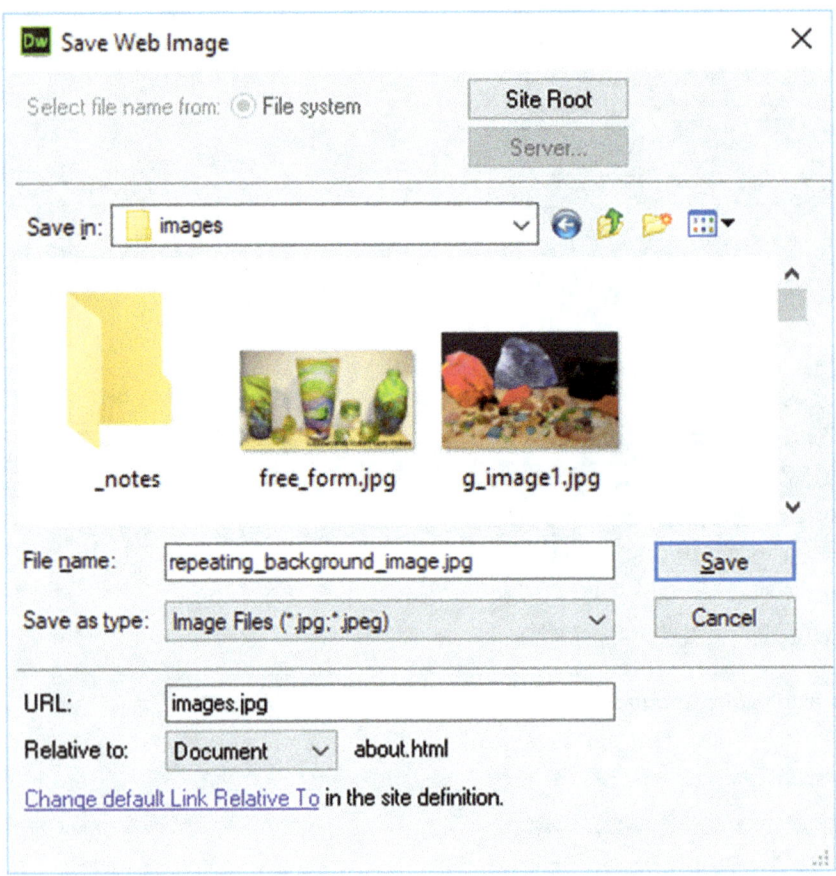

Figure 31-13. The newly created JPEG image is saved in the images folder

This image is added as a Sync image. If changes are made, Dreamweaver detects them.

■ **Note** The bitmap or (.bmp) is not included here as an insert option. The bitmap file is quite large, and it is better to use one of the other formats for your project. However, if you want to include this file, select All Files from the drop-down list so that it is viewable in your image search. Width and height are not recorded; you have to enter them manually in Code view or use the Properties panel. And you do not have access to certain image editing features that are available to other formats.

Once you have selected an image from your image folder, click OK to insert it onto the page. Refer to Figure 31-14.

CHAPTER 31 ■ WORKING WITH IMAGES AND TAGS

Figure 31-14. Click OK when you have selected the image you want to insert into the webpage

If you review the file in Split view, you see that the image tag <img/> is added to the page. Refer to Figure 31-15.

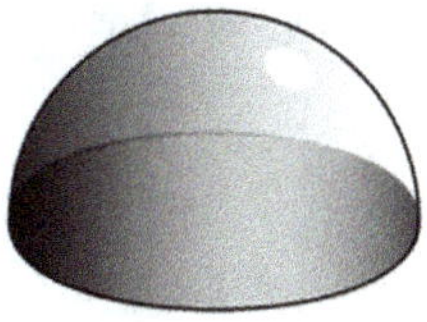

```
1    <!doctype html>
2  ▼ <html lang="en">
3  ▼ <head>
4    <meta charset="utf-8">
5        <meta name="viewport" content="width=device-width, initial-scale=1">
6    <title>Untitled Document</title>
7    </head>
8
9  ▼ <body>
10   <img src="images/dome_1.gif" width="195" height="138" alt=""/>
11   </body>
12   </html>
13
```

Figure 31-15. The image in Design view and the resulting code in Code view

```
<img src="images/dome_1.gif" width="195" height="138" alt=""/>
```

The image tag has no opening or closing tags; instead, it is self-closing or contained. When inserting an image, no matter what image type is chosen, there are generally four important attributes within the tag.

- **src:** The source link to the image in the images folder.
- **width:** The width of the image in pixels.
- **height:** The height of the image in pixels.
- **alt:** The alternate text. If the image does not load or people with visual disabilities need to read with a screen reader, this has the text that describes the image.

    Example: `<img src="images/dome_1.gif" width="195" height="138" alt="A clear glass dome paperweight."/>`

If you don't want to add any text, leave this attribute empty. However, do not delete or remove the alt attribute from your image tag or else you get a warning when you validate your page, as you see later. A good practice is to always have alt attributes for your images. Missing alts can affect your site's rank and make it difficult for search engines to locate keywords that would bring more viewers. You can do the same with a PNG or JPEG.

Working with SVG Images

When you insert SVG files, you do not see a width or height attribute because scalable vector graphics are meant to size to whatever area they are placed into without losing quality. If you have used the setting of responsive within the SVG, then your image is able to scale up or down to fill an area on your page. You cannot simply insert an <svg> tag on a page and expect it to display.

You could insert an SVG as an image, but it can only be viewed in Live view; otherwise, it appears as a broken image.

```
<img src="images/sale_asset_1.svg" alt=""/>
```

Refer to Figure 31-16.

Figure 31-16. *An SVG appear as a broken image in Design view on a webpage*

A better way to work with an SVG is to insert it into a <div> tag so that you can scale the width and height of the <div> with CSS, or to wrap it within an <object> tag, as you can see on the contact.html page in Live view.

```
<object id="EdgeID2" type="text/html" width="500" height="500" data-dw-widget="Edge" data="images/sale_asset_1.svg">
          </object>
```

The object tag allows you to keep the interactivity of the SVG. You can apply CSS to adjust scaling. Adding width and height constrains how much the object can scale.

■ **Note** You use the object tag again when you insert an OAM (animated composition) in an HTML5 Canvas file in Chapter 36.

Two other tag methods you could try are <embed>, which creates a container for external applications or plug-in content, and <iframes>, which creates an inline frame. Both of these allow you to keep your interactivity of your SVG; however, the iframe may require CSS to make it responsive. You can see the code here:

```
<embed src="images/sale_asset_1.svg ">
<iframe src="images/sale_asset_1.svg "></iframe>
```

Properties Panel

For the moment, let's focus on GIF, JPEG, and PNG image formats while working with the Properties panel. You can alter or add settings to your image tag in the Properties panel. Refer to Figure 31-17.

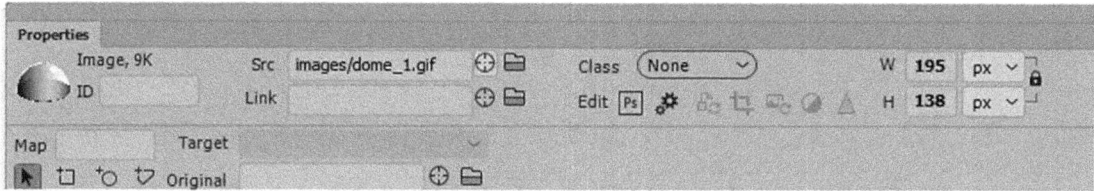

Figure 31-17. The Properties panel when an image is selected in Design view

The Properties panel shows a preview of the image and its file size. (SVG and bitmap do not show a preview image here).

- **ID attribute:** Useful for formatting with CSS and JavaScript, which you'll look at in Chapter 34.

- **src:** Browse for a new source file to replace the old one using the Folder icon or point to it by dragging the target to a file located in the Folder panel. If you are not careful, you could point to the wrong file. I personally like to browse via folder to save time.

- **Link:** Adds a URL to the current file; it can be internal, external, or even an email.

- **Class:** Allows you to format the image further with CSS classes, as you look at in Chapter 32.

- **Edit:** Allows you to edit the image in the program of your choice or do some basic edits using one of six tools. Be aware that not all tools are available to all images. You are editing the actual file and not a copy of it, so any changes made are permanent to that file. It is better to make changes to a copy or go back to the original RAW image (PSD, AI, EPS), and then save a new copy in the same format. That way, if you want to revert, you have not destroyed the original image. Refer to Figure 31-18.

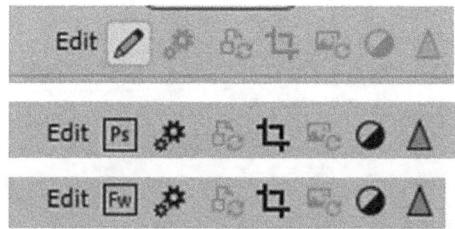

Figure 31-18. The Properties panel Quick Edit icons for various images

Some quick area tools include going back to the native program to work on the file. When you do this, make sure to keep your files in the correct folder; the editing program will show a warning if it can't locate the original file because the link was altered.

If Dreamweaver does not know which program to edit the file in, it shows a Pencil icon. If you want to set a program that Dreamweaver automatically opens, click the Pencil icon; this shows an alert that you can click OK to and then enter Edit ➤ Preferences ➤ File Types and Editors. Refer to Figure 31-19 and Figure 31-20.

CHAPTER 31 ■ WORKING WITH IMAGES AND TAGS

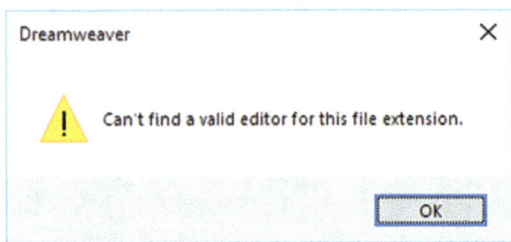

Figure 31-19. *A warning appears when you search for a valid editor and the file extension is not known by Dreamweaver*

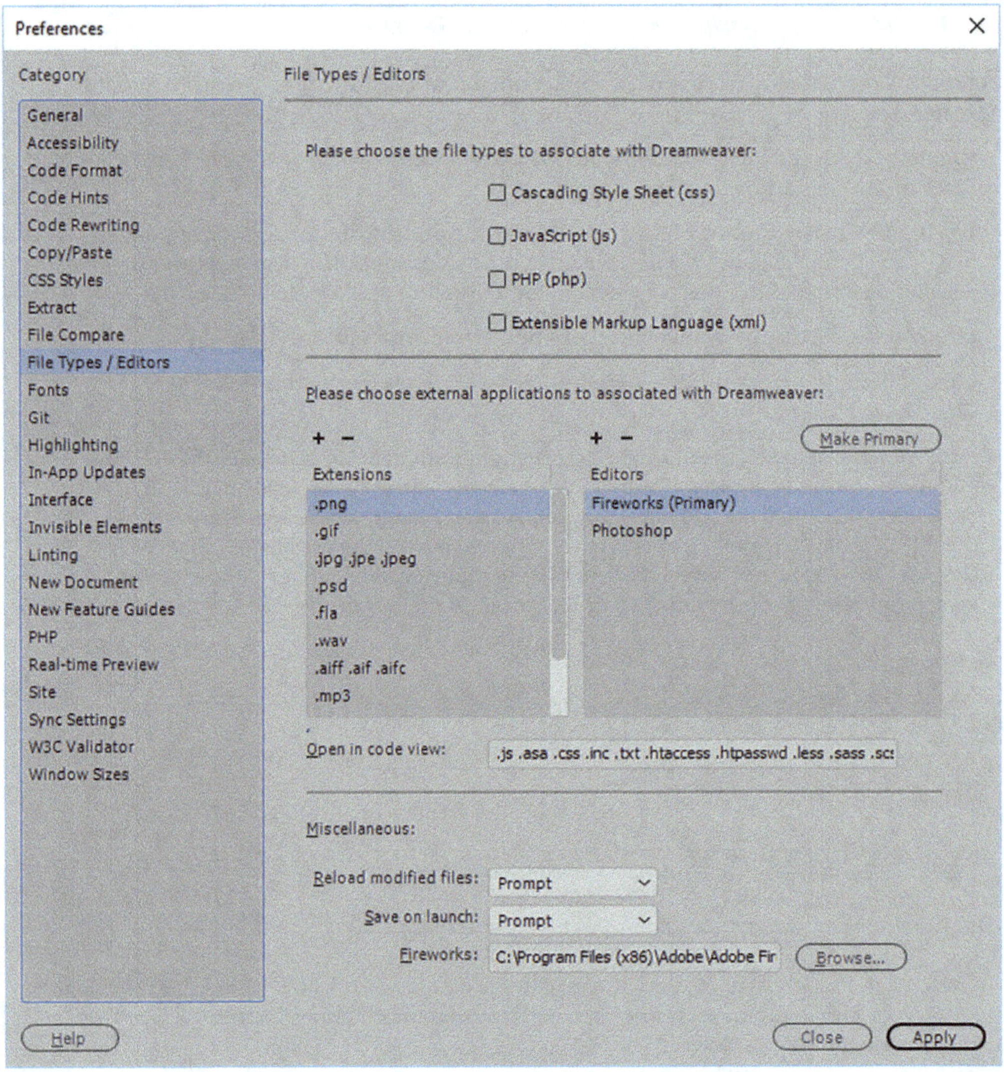

Figure 31-20. *The Preferences allow you to add a new extension and editor to the list or decide what should be the primary editor*

You can add extensions that are not listed in this area (using the plus icon) and set your editor for the file format by setting one in the list to Make Primary (editor) or adding a new editor using the plus symbol once done click Apply and then close. With GIFs or JPEGs, Photoshop is your primary editor. However, if you have an older version of Fireworks on your computer, a PNG file might show up instead. You can resolve this in Preferences by making Photoshop the primary editor. If there is no editor for an SVG file, you could add one.

You also have access to some Quick Edit options (rather than entering the original program). Refer to Figure 31-21.

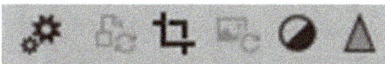

Figure 31-21. Quick Edit options in the Properties panel

Remember that Quick Edits alter your images permanently; make sure you have a backup of these images in another folder, should you need to revert to an original state.

Image Optimization

Here you can alter the image optimization settings to the current (.gif) image or change it to another format. Doing so may degrade the quality of the image. Refer to Figure 31-22.

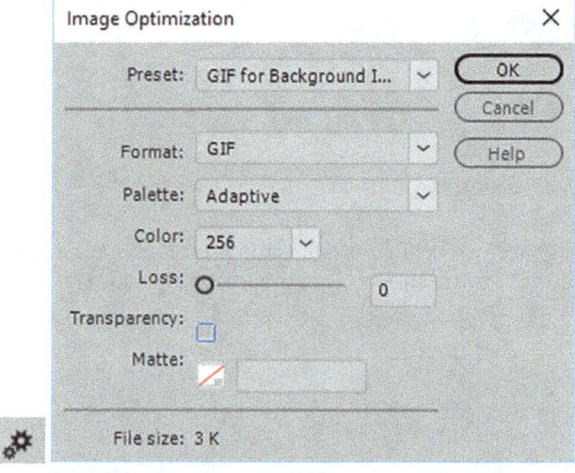

Figure 31-22. Image Optimization dialog box appears for the selected image from the Properties panel icon

Update From Original

When the image on the Dreamweaver page is out of sync with the original Photoshop file, Dreamweaver detects that the original file has been updated. The application displays one of the Smart Object icon's arrows in red. When you select the web image in Design view and click the Update from Original button in the Property Inspector, the image updates automatically. The updated image reflects the changes that you made to the original Photoshop file. Note that if your image was not synced with Photoshop, then this option is not available. You need to update the file manually by going back to the original image in Photoshop and relinking the updated image to the source. Refer to Figure 31-23.

Figure 31-23. *Image Sync icon*

Crop

Crop edits images by reducing the area of the image. You can use crop or remove unwanted aspects surrounding the center of interest. This can make the image stand out better, but it alters the dimensions of the image permanently, which you may not want. Refer to Figure 31-24.

Figure 31-24. *When Crop from the Quick Edits is clicked, a warning appears*

This draws a crop area around the image. In Design view, you can move the crop box around and then hit the Crop Mark icon in the Properties panel to confirm. If you realize you made a mistake, choose Edit ➤ Undo right way to undo your crop and restore and revert the image. Refer to Figure 31-25.

CHAPTER 31 ■ WORKING WITH IMAGES AND TAGS

Figure 31-25. *The Crop preview, to revert you must choose Edit ▶ Undo right away*

Resample

This setting adds or subtracts pixels from resized JPEG and GIF image files to match the appearance of the original image as closely as possible. Resampling an image reduces its file size and improves download performance, but not quality.

When you resize an image in Dreamweaver, you can resample it to accommodate its new dimensions. When a raster object is resampled, pixels are added to or removed from the image to make it larger or smaller. Resampling an image to a higher resolution typically causes a little loss of quality. Resampling to a lower resolution, however, always causes data loss and usually a drop in quality. When you select an image in Design view and move its handle to a smaller or larger size, it alters the width and height and makes the Resample icon available. Refer to Figure 31-26.

Figure 31-26. *Resample an image*

Clicking the Resample icon confirms the resample and sets the new setting. As with cropping, if you realize you made a mistake after you click OK, choose Edit ▶ Undo to restore and revert the image. Be aware that if you scale an image smaller, and then change your mind and make it larger again, the file is degraded, and you likely need to start a new copy of the original.

Brightness/Contrast

Modifies the contrast or brightness of pixels in an image. Brightness and contrast affect the highlights, shadows, and midtones of an image. You typically use the Brightness/Contrast option when correcting images that are too dark or too light. If you realize you made a mistake after you click OK, choose Edit ➤ Undo to restore and revert the image. Refer to Figure 31-27.

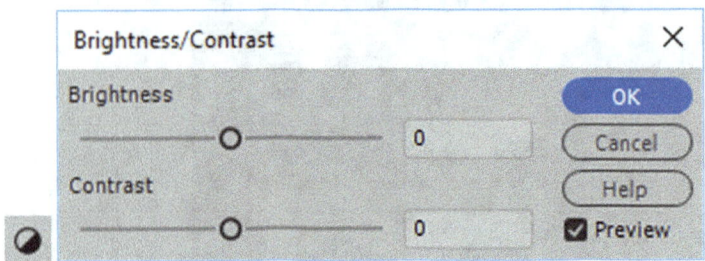

Figure 31-27. Adjust the brightness and contrast of an image

Sharpen

Adjusts the focus of an image by increasing the contrast of edges found within the image. When you scan an image or take a digital photo, the default action of most image capturing software is to soften the edges of the objects in the image. If softened too much, the image appears blurry. Ideally, the scanning prevents extremely minute details from becoming lost in the pixels from which digital images are composed.

To bring out the details in digital image files, it is often necessary to sharpen the image. The Sharpen option increases the edge contrast, making the image appear sharper. that too much sharpening can make your image appear overly pixilated which may not be what you want. For ideal images, always start your project with high-quality photos from the client.

If you realize you made a mistake after you click OK, choose Edit ➤ Undo to restore and revert the image. Refer to Figure 31-28.

Figure 31-28. Sharpen an image

Width and Height

This displays the current width and height of the image in pixels by default, but you can switch to percentage (%), which may be better for working with a mobile site via the drop-down menus. You can type in a new width and height which be scaled proportionately if the lock symbol remains in the lock state. If you do not click the check box to confirm this change, it does not affect the original image. You can revert by clicking the Reset To Original Size icon to restore the original width and height settings. Refer to Figure 31-29.

CHAPTER 31 ■ WORKING WITH IMAGES AND TAGS

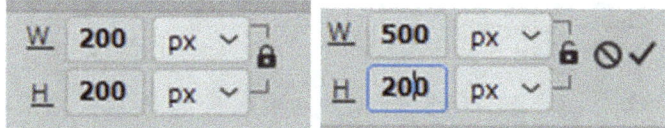

Figure 31-29. *Adjust the width and height of the image and then either revert back to the original size or click the check to confirm the changes*

In Part 6, you see how to use CSS to scale an image proportionally to various sizes and make it responsive for different devices in the browser without loss of quality.

Alternate Text

You can add alt image text and a title with this option. Alt (alternate text) adds context if your images for screen readers or if the images link is broken and does not appear. The title attribute acts in the same way. Some browsers prefer the title attribute over the alt attribute, so it is best practice add both. However, unlike the alt tag, the title may not appear if the image does not display. Figure 31-30.

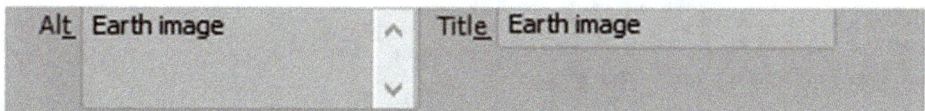

Figure 31-30. *Add alt and title attributes for your images*

The last area in the Properties panel deals with image maps, which you look at in a moment. This is like a URL link that is added over the top of an area in a photograph. This area in the Properties panel only displays when in Design view and the image that you plan to add the map to is selected. You looked at image maps briefly in Chapter 13. Refer to Figure 31-31.

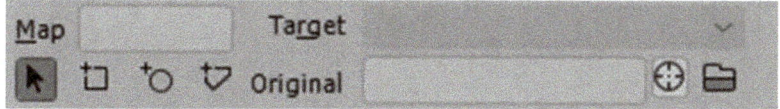

Figure 31-31. *Image map icons*

Before you look at that tag in detail, you need to continue exploring other tags that you can add your images to.

Adding Images Inside Various Tags

Within the <body> tags, you can add text (<h1><h2><h3><h4><h5><h6><p>) and images (<img/>) as many times as you want. Refer to Figure 31-32.

775

CHAPTER 31 ■ WORKING WITH IMAGES AND TAGS

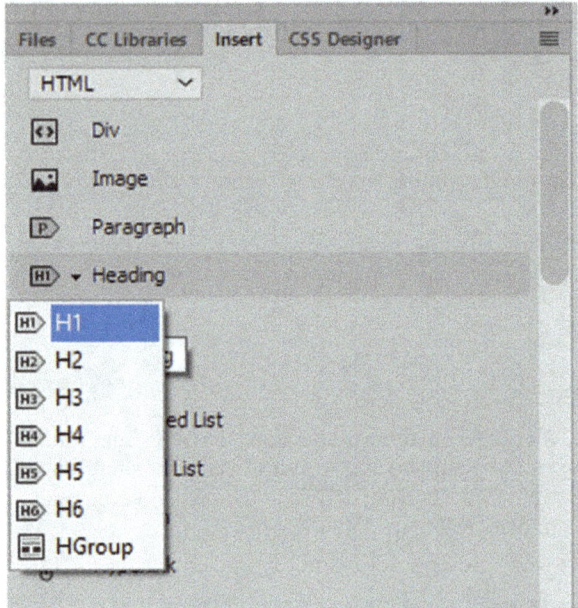

Figure 31-32. *The Insert panel had text and image tags*

You can do this manually by typing in Code view, or by placing your cursor somewhere on the page in Design view or Split view and using the Insert panel to add the tags. For information on whether to use an <hgroup> tag, refer to https://developer.mozilla.org/en-US/docs/Web/HTML/Element/hgroup.

Without basic structures to format where your images are placed, your images move freely and the website has no form. Even from a mobile design point of view, you need to be able to set a point of transition from one size to the next. There must be some way of controlling these points of the website's transition for various browsers as it expands and contracts. A human body needs bones, or just like the website, it flops around randomly.

In addition to older tags, HTML5 has tags. If you need to review older tags and examples, check out www.w3schools.com/tags/default.asp.

A Bit of HTML History

In the 1990s, when websites were first built, designers used <table> tags to create areas where content and images would go. You could put tables within tables or the other table's cells, which made the design more complex. At that time, most designers were creating sites for desktop computers only. You would use spacers or transparent GIF images to create space within the table. Most computer monitors were roughly the same size or ratio, and so flexibility was not crucial. When designers thought of *mobile*, it was a cellphone that was often large and bulky and had a small low-resolution screen that showed who was calling or paging you, and perhaps with some very basic text and ultralow resolution graphics. At that point, most work was done on desktop computers.

The problem with tables is they aren't flexible when it comes to varying monitor widths. To keep the basic content and structure looking the same, you have to create different webpages to conform to each monitor size.

Fast-forward to the 2000s, where the first modern tablets and smartphones arrived on the market. Instead or carrying a large laptop around, users wanted to see websites and information on smaller devices and be able to go to meetings and show their company's products on these devices. Tables increasingly became a problem, because websites were too small and barley readable, and their layouts did not format or sit like they should on the page. A solution had to be found. More flexible tags had to be created.

There are now various layout tags that you can add your images to and place the image <img/> tag within.

<div> Tags

The first element or tag that was used to replace the <table> for web layout was known as the <div> tag. div stand for *division*, an element that divides a section of a website. Like tables, you can place divs inside of divs to create more sections. And you can look that them in Live view. Refer to Figure 31-33.

Figure 31-33. *To create a structure, you can place divs inside of divs*

It is more flexible than tables. Divs can be more accurately scaled, moved and removed using CSS and its responsive media queries which you look at when get to Bootstrap in Chapter 35. Divs are used with CSS and are called upon using the tag's name, a unique ID, or classes to layout a webpage, which you'll look at in Chapter 32. They perform certain tasks when incorporated with JavaScript. Using the Insert panel, you can insert a <div> tag on an HTML page and then insert an image within. Refer to Figure 31-34.

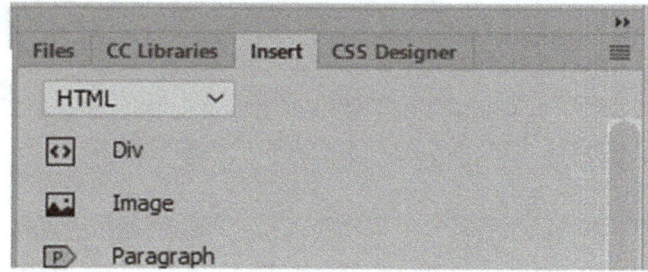

Figure 31-34. *Add a <div> tag using the Insert panel*

CHAPTER 31 ■ WORKING WITH IMAGES AND TAGS

When you insert a div, you are asked to choose a point to insert the it in the dialog box. The default is an insertion point, which is where you place the cursor; however, you can choose either after or before the start of the tag. Then you can give it a class, ID, or both. Refer to Figure 31-35.

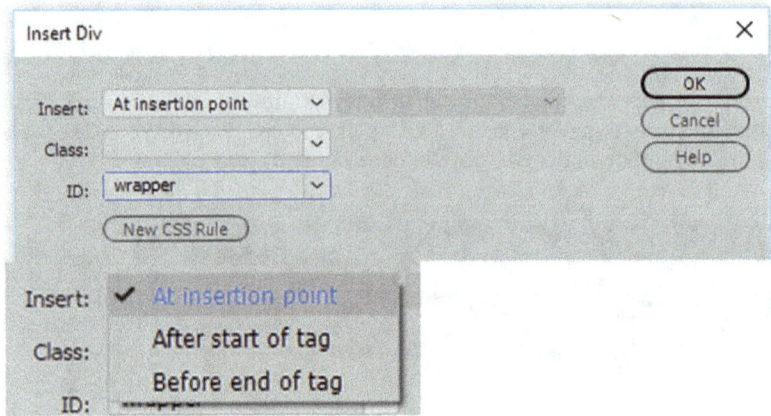

Figure 31-35. Insert a div and add an ID using the insert div dialog box

Then click OK to confirm the <div> tag in the code. A whole website could be built just using <div> tags. However, the most common <div> tag that goes around a website structure is given the unique ID of wrapper. Refer to Figure 31-36.

```
1   <!doctype html>
2   <html lang="en">
3   <head>
4       <meta charset="utf-8">
5       <title>Home Page</title>
6   </head>
7   <body>
8   <div id="wrapper">
9       Content for  id "wrapper" Goes Here
10      </div>
11  </body>
12  </html>
13
```

Figure 31-36. A div is inserted into Code view

■ **Note** There is no rule that you must use a wrapper. You can call the ID whatever you want or only wrap certain areas that you want to contain within the wrapper. However, giving it this name is an effective way to remember what the tag or element does.

CHAPTER 31 ■ WORKING WITH IMAGES AND TAGS

Dreamweaver places filler text between the <div> tags (dotted lines in Design view) that you can highlight and delete, leaving just the cursor blinking. And, you can add an image from the Insert panel. Refer to Figure 31-37.

Content for id "wrapper" Goes Here

Figure 31-37. A div in Design view

In the Properties panel, the tag appears with an icon, the div type and ID, and the option to add a class or create a class for the <div> tag (you look at this in Chapter 32). Refer to Figure 31-38.

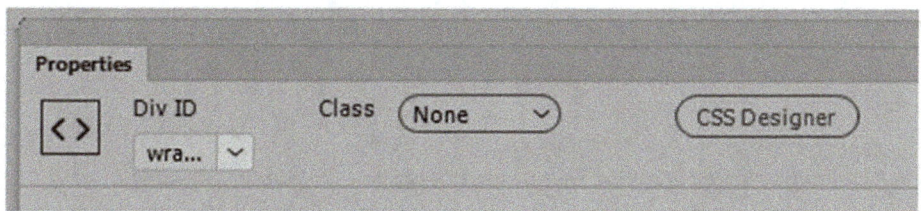

Figure 31-38. The Properties panel when a div is selected

You can locate the image in the images folder and click OK to insert. Refer to Figure 31-39.

Figure 31-39. Insert an image into the div using the Insert panel

Later, you look at how CSS is used to structure the size and placement any <div> tag.

```
<div id="wrapper"><img src="images/dome_1.gif" width="195" height="138" alt=""/></div>
```

Sematic Elements

When HTML4 began, most designers inserted one div inside another to create a structure for the website. And in combination with CSS, giving each div a unique ID or class, a site that was for desktop and mobile devices could be built. This structure and the viewport continued into HTML5. Refer to Figure 31-40.

779

```
 1    <!doctype html>
 2  ▼ <html lang="en">
 3  ▼ <head>
 4    <meta charset="utf-8">
 5        <meta name="viewport" content="width=device-width, initial-scale=1">
 6
 7    <title>Home Page</title>
 8    </head>
 9  ▼ <body>
10  ▼ <div id="wrapper">
11        <div id="header"></div>
12        <div id="nav"></div>
13  ▼     <div id="main">
14            <div id="section-a"></div>
15            <div id="section-b"></div>
16        </div>
17        <div id="footer"></div>
18    </div>
19    </body>
20    </html>
21
```

Figure 31-40. *How a beginning structure of a basic website could look; note a viewport was added*

If there are a lot of divs on a page, it becomes confusing as to where one starts or stops, especially if they are nested many times, because the closing tags are all the same.

Also, web designers are not always consistent with the names they give their IDs in the structure; some might be id=foot or id=footer, or id=base, and so on. This makes it difficult for people with visual impairments to navigate a site with their screen readers. The web is for everyone, and this is what accessibility is all about. There has to be some sort of consistency. So, HTML5 tags called *semantic elements* were created.

Semantic elements are scaled and create structure for a site. Unlike divs, their order has meaning to a screen reader. The <div> or <span> is non-semantic and has no meaning to the average viewer. But words like <table>, <form>, or <article> do have meaning to a user and are therefore semantic. Also, their placement is very important when a site is validated, so you cannot use them in any combination you want. You can find these elements in the Insert panel if you scroll within the HTML tab. Refer to Figure 31-41.

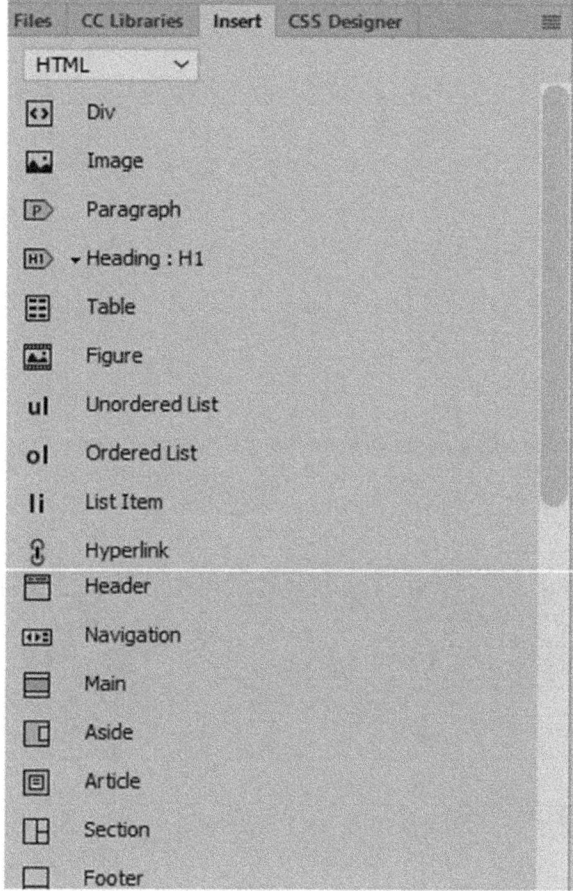

Figure 31-41. *Many of the new semantic elements appear in the Insert panel in the HTML tab*

Any of these can have an <img> tag placed inside of it. I briefly describe them next.

Figure and Figure Caption

The <figure> and <figcaption> tags are inserted at the same time. An image <img> can be placed within the figure. The nested figcaption is used to describe the figure. It is like the descriptive figure captions that are found below each of the images in this book.

```
<figure><img src="images/dome_1.gif" width="195" height="138" alt="A glass dome
paperweight"/>
<figcaption>Figure 1-2. A glass dome paperweight.</figcaption></figure>
```

The images could be illustrations, diagrams, photos, or code listings. The figure and its figcaption could be found nested within a <div> tag or some other semantic element. Refer to Figure 31-42.

CHAPTER 31 ■ WORKING WITH IMAGES AND TAGS

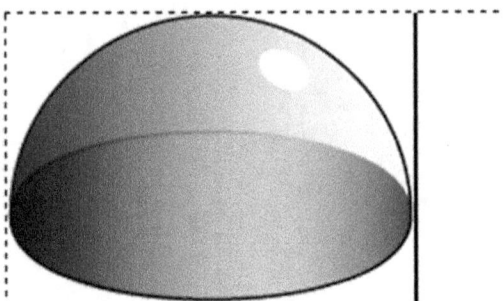

Figure 1-2. A glass dome paperweight.

Figure 31-42. *Adding a figure and figure captions around the image*

The <figcaption> can only be inside of a figure. Its text does not have to have any heading or paragraph tag within it, but like heading text, it is styled using CSS, which you look at later. The Properties panel does allow you to add an ID, CSS, and several types of formatting to the tags as required. Refer to Figure 31-43.

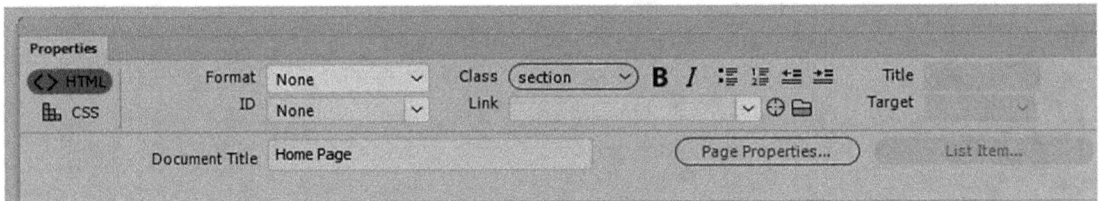

Figure 31-43. *The Properties panel when figcaption text is selected*

Header

The <header> tag is used for introductory content, or it contains navigation links. It could also be used as the banner area containing company logo on a webpage. It can also replace the <hgroup> tag or be a header of a <section> or <article> tag or used for authorship information. You can have more than one <header> tag within a section. <header> is not the same as the <head> tag and is found outside the body while the <header> is found inside the <body>, usually within the wrapper. You can give it an ID or class, but it's not a requirement. Refer to Figure 31-44.

CHAPTER 31 ■ WORKING WITH IMAGES AND TAGS

Figure 31-44. Insert Header dialog box with ID added

```
<header id="banner">Content for  id "banner" Goes Here</header>
```

Then you can insert your banner image <img> for the webpage. When selected, the Properties panel allows you to add CSS formatting. Refer to Figure 31-45.

Figure 31-45. How the Header appears in the Properties panel

■ **Note** A <header> cannot be placed within <footer>, <address>, or another <header> tag.

Navigation

The <nav> tag is useful for an area with navigation hyperlinks modified by CSS or a few images (rollovers). Not all links in a document should be used inside of a <nav> element. A <nav> should only be used for major blocks of navigation links.

This tag is very useful in browsers and in screen readers for disabled users. Browsers can use this element to determine whether to omit the initial rendering of the content.

783

You can give it an ID or class, but it's not a requirement. Refer to Figure 31-46.

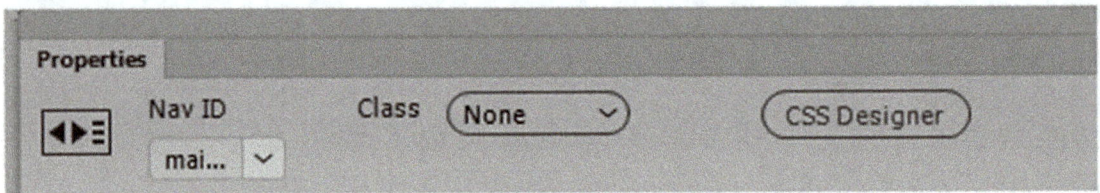

Figure 31-46. Insert Navigation dialog box with ID added

```
<nav id="navigation">Content for  id "navigation" Goes Here</nav>
```

You could insert your navigation images <img> using CSS or rollover links for the webpage to other webpages.

When selected, the Properties panel allows you to add CSS formatting. Refer to Figure 31-47.

Figure 31-47. How the nav appears in the Properties panel

Main

The <main> element refers to the main content of the document or the main story. The content inside of the <main> tag should be unique to the document and should not contain any content that is repeated across documents such as sidebars, navigation links, copyright information, site logos, and search forms. It should also be noted that there must not be more than one <main> element in a HTML document. The <main> element must NOT be a descendant or child of an <article>, <aside>, <footer>, <header>, or <nav> element, though it could be the container (parent) for these elements.

Figure 31-48 shows how this might look.

CHAPTER 31 ■ WORKING WITH IMAGES AND TAGS

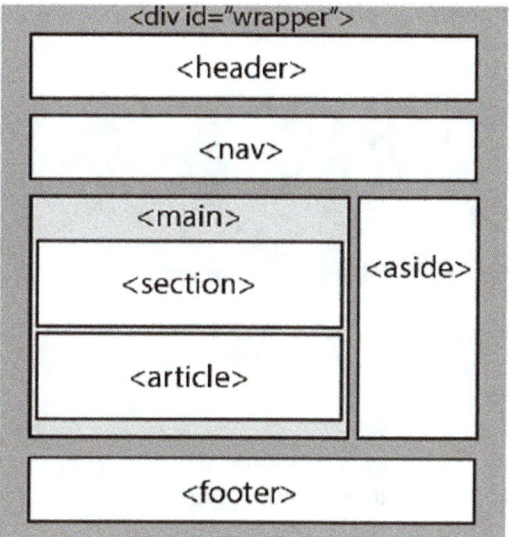

Figure 31-48. *A possible layout for a website using the main tag*

You can give it an ID or class, but it's not a requirement. Refer to Figure 31-49.

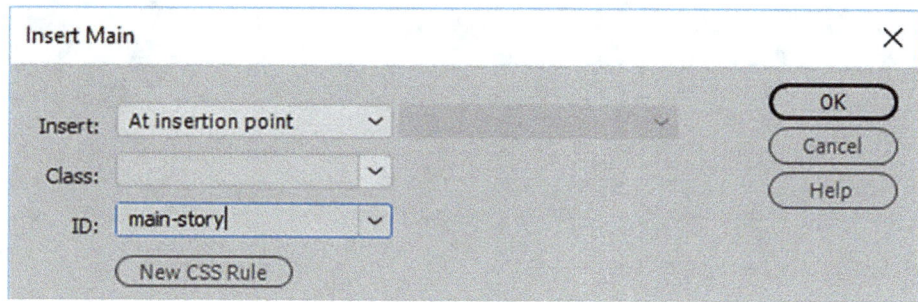

Figure 31-49. *Insert Navigation dialog box with ID added*

```
<main id="main-story">
   <div class="section1">
      <figure><img src="images/dome_1.gif" width="195" height="138" alt="A glass dome
      paperweight"/>
         <figcaption>Figure 1-2. A glass dome paperweight.</figcaption>
      </figure>
   </div>
   <div class="section2">Some text...
   </div>
</main>
```

CHAPTER 31 ■ WORKING WITH IMAGES AND TAGS

Then you can insert your images, text, or other semantic elements into the <main> tag. The Properties panel allows you to add CSS formatting. Refer to Figure 31-50.

Figure 31-50. How the main ID appears in the Properties panel

Aside

The <aside> tag defines content aside from the page content. The aside content should be related to the surrounding content. It is on its own or it could be placed as a sidebar in an <article>. You can give it an ID or class, but it's not a requirement. Refer to Figure 31-51.

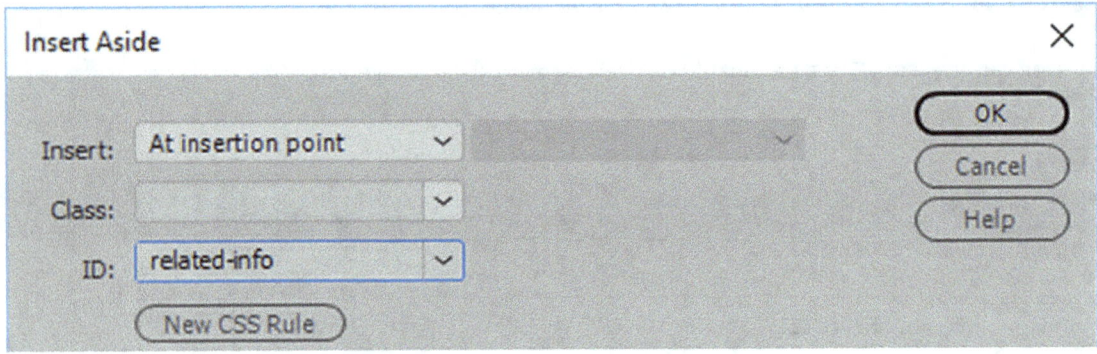

Figure 31-51. Insert Aside dialog box with ID added

```
<aside id="related-info">Content for  id "related-info" Goes Here</aside>
```

You can insert your images, text, or other semantic elements into the <aside> tag. When selected, the Properties panel allows you to add CSS formatting. Refer to Figure 31-52.

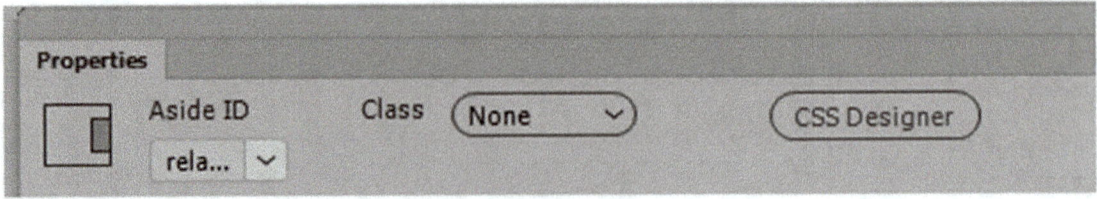

Figure 31-52. How the aside appears in the Properties panel

786

CHAPTER 31 ■ WORKING WITH IMAGES AND TAGS

Article

The <article> element defines an article. The <article> tag specifies independent, self-contained content. It should make sense on its own and it should be possible to distribute it independently from the rest of the site. The following are some of uses of the <article> element.

- Forum posts
- Blog posts
- News stories
- Comments

More than one article element can appear within the <main> tag. It is often confused with the <section> tag; in some cases they are interchangeable, depending on how your website is constructed. You can give it an ID or class, but it's not a requirement. Refer to Figure 31-53.

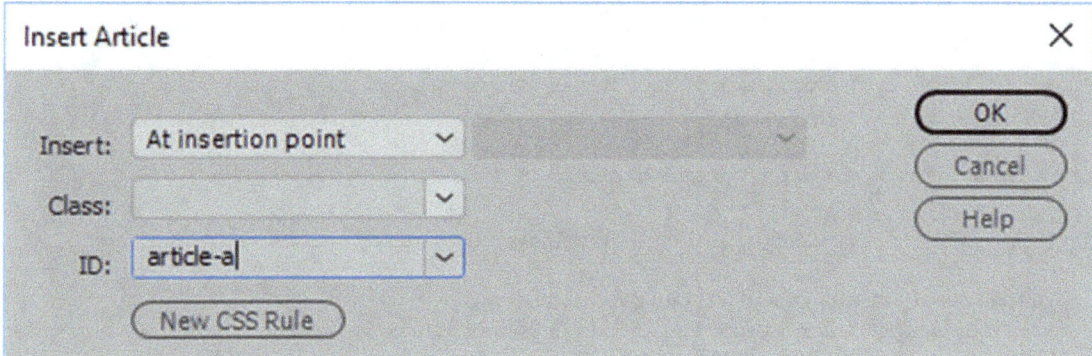

Figure 31-53. Insert Article dialog box with ID added

You can insert your images and text into the <article> tag.

<article id="article-a">Content for id "article-a" Goes Here</article>

When selected, the Properties panel allows you to add CSS formatting. Refer to Figure 31-54.

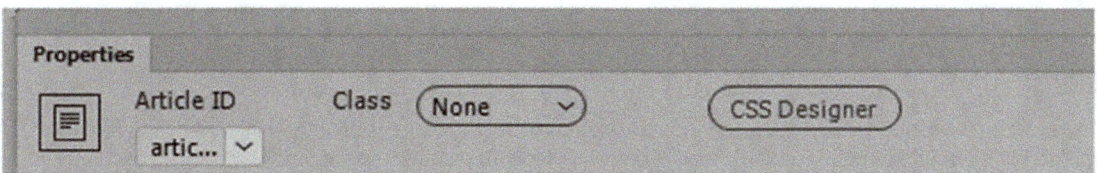

Figure 31-54. How the Article appears in the Properties panel

787

Section

The <section> tag defines a section of a document. It can be chapters, headers, footers, or any other section of a document. More than one section element can appear within the <main> tag. It is often confused with the <article> tag; in some cases, they are interchangeable, depending on how your website is constructed. Articles are inserted inside sections. You can give it an ID or class, but it's not a requirement. Refer to Figure 31-55.

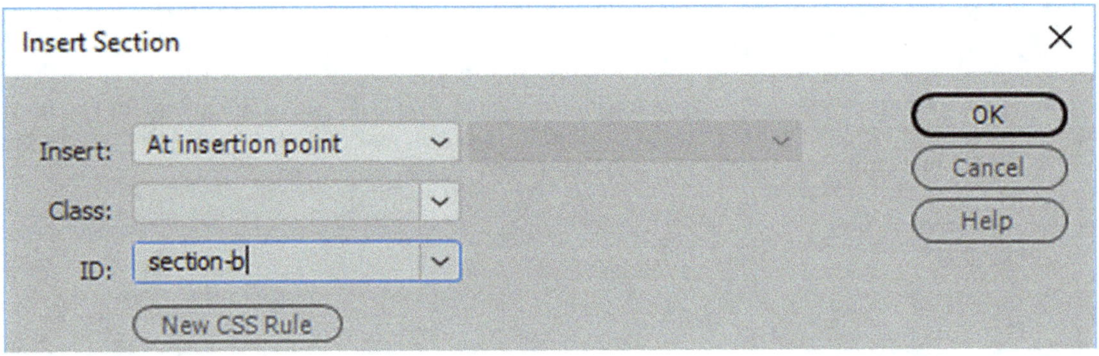

Figure 31-55. Insert Section dialog box with ID added

```
<section id="section-b">Content for  id "section-b" Goes Here</section>
```

You can insert your images and text into the <section> tag.
The Properties panel allows you to add CSS formatting. Refer to Figure 31-56.

Figure 31-56. How the section appears in the Properties panel

Footer

The <footer> element defines the footer of a document or section. A section can have more than one footer. A <footer> element should contain information about its containing element or tag.

A <footer> element typically contains the following:

- authorship information
- copyright information
- contact information (inside an <address> tag)

- sitemap
- back to top links
- related documents

When it appears at the bottom of a webpage, it can contain navigational images and links. Footers and headers are often used together. You can give it an ID or class, but it's not a requirement. Refer to Figure 31-57.

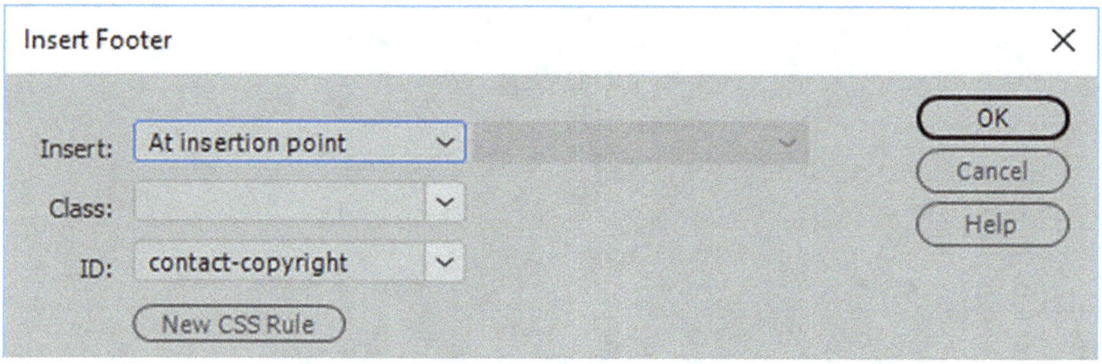

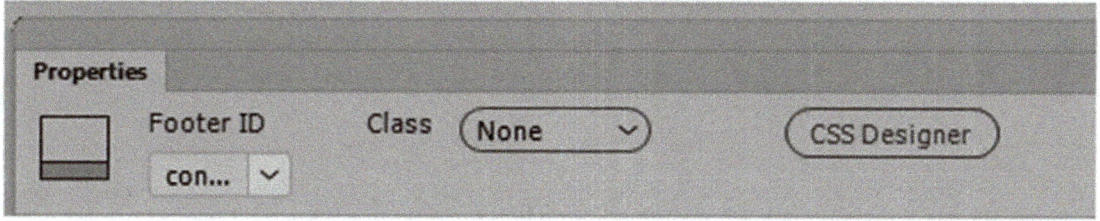

Figure 31-57. Insert Footer dialog box with ID added

`<footer id="contact-copyright">Content for  id "contact-copyright" Goes Here</footer>`

You can insert your images <img> and text into the <footer> tag.
When selected, the Properties panel allows you to add CSS formatting. Refer to Figure 31-58.

Figure 31-58. How the footer appears in the Properties panel

While semantic elements are good to use, there may be times when your content does not fall into any other category, or you need to add navigation somewhere else. In these cases, there is nothing wrong with using a <div> tag; perhaps in time, more semantic elements will become available. In the meantime, it is important to practice using them to build your website to make it more accessible to all users. in the next chapter, you look at how these tags can be altered further using CSS.

For more information, on semantic elements make sure to check out www.w3schools.com/html/html5_semantic_elements.asp.

Are Tables Obsolete in Web Design?

Developers have shifted from using tables to a div-based structure, which has made the responsive-based website cleaner with more reliable code and functionality. Nevertheless, tables are not gone for good. Tables and their cells are now used for their true purpose: to hold data and images like a Microsoft Excel spreadsheet. Do you want to show company profits or a product sheet? You can insert a table somewhere in your <main> tag and display the data. Refer to Figure 31-59.

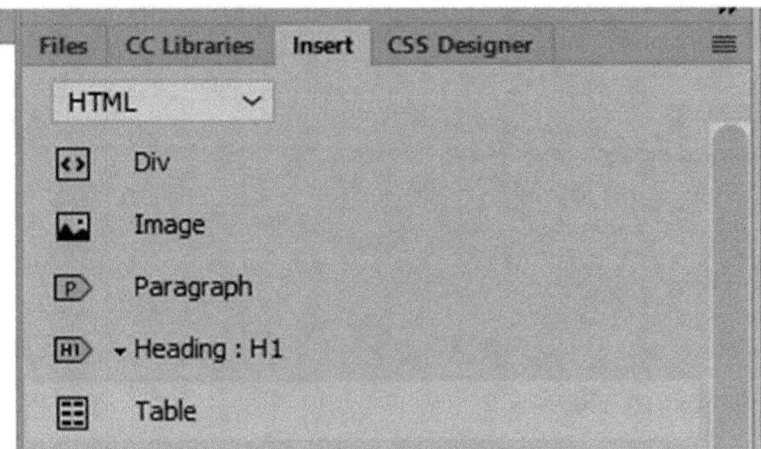

Figure 31-59. *Insert a table using the Insert panel*

Here you can set the rows <tr> and columns <td>. You can also add the attributes of width (pixel or percent), border thickness, cell padding or spacing. Be aware that these attributes are not supported by HTML5. After you create the table, you should alter it using CSS instead. Refer to Figure 31-60.

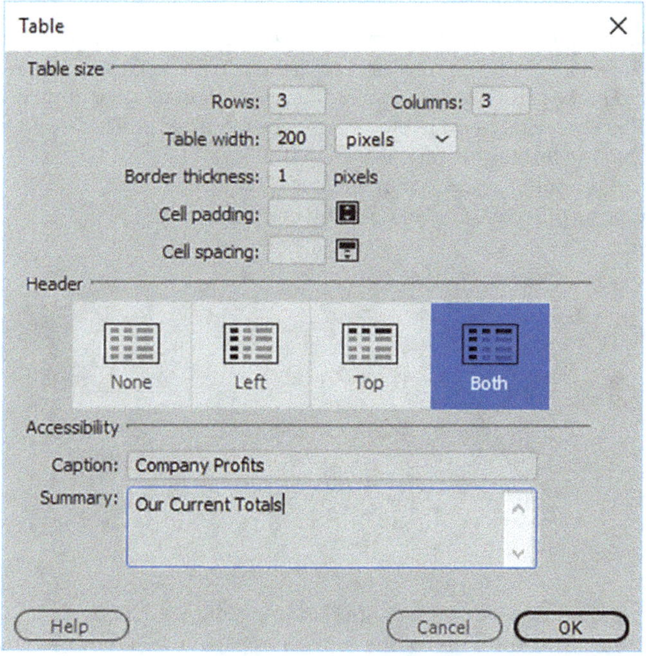

CHAPTER 31 ■ WORKING WITH IMAGES AND TAGS

Figure 31-60. Insert a table settings entered into the table dialog box

Lastly, you can add a table header to the left <th scope=row> and top <th scope=col> and then add a caption for accessibility. Note that the attribute summary is not supported by HTML5, so you may want to leave this blank. When done, click OK and add your text and images to the <td> cell tags.

```
<table width="200" border="1" summary="Our Current Totals">
  <caption>
    Company Profits
  </caption>
  <tbody>
    <tr>
      <th scope="col"> </th>
      <th scope="col"> </th>
      <th scope="col"> </th>
    </tr>
    <tr>
      <th scope="row"> </th>
      <td> </td>
      <td> </td>
    </tr>
    <tr>
      <th scope="row"> </th>
      <td> </td>
      <td> </td>
    </tr>
  </tbody>
</table>
```

Table tags are better manipulated using CSS for a mobile site. You can still run into formatting issues, depending on what is within the table, so you need to take this into account and test the pages for each device size that the table could be viewed on. For example, while rows and columns can get narrower, a row of data needs to be kept on the same row for it to make sense. At some point, the cells might wrap or appear broken. With CSS, you can modify this for smaller screens, but done incorrectly, the table can still look broken. So developers continue to struggle with table formatting for each unique site.

In the Properties panel, you can see many of the settings that are in the Insert Table dialog box, including icons that allow you to clear the column width, clear row height, and convert to either pixels or percentage. Refer to Figure 31-61.

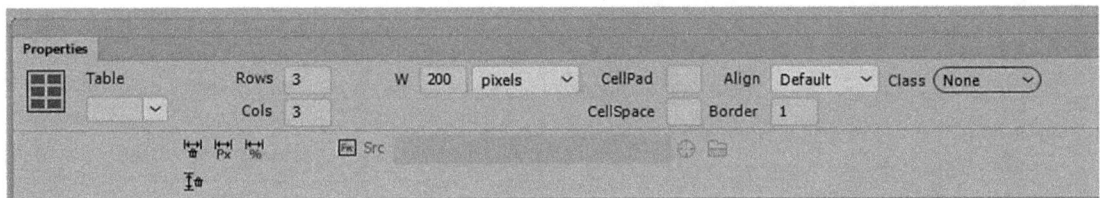

Figure 31-61. *The table settings in the Properties panel*

Settings like cellpad, cellspace alignment, and border are better controlled using classes in CSS.

The properties of rows and cells are accessed in the lower half of the Properties panel when they are selected. Alignment, width, height, and background color should be controlled with CSS rather than typed into the panel. You can still use the settings when two or more cells or rows are selected to split or merge, and you can determine whether a row or column is a header <th> or has the attribute of no wrap (nowrap=nowrap) to alter text wrap. Refer to Figure 31-62.

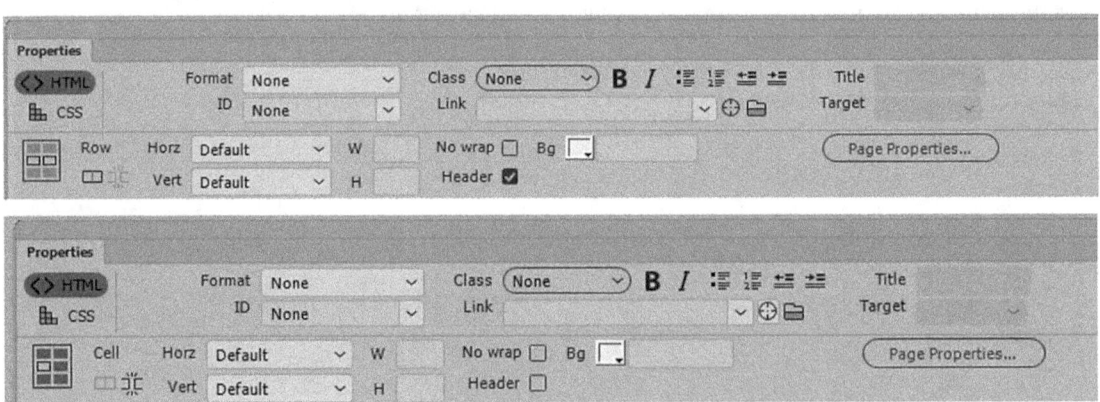

Figure 31-62. *The table row and cell settings in the Properties panel*

You can still add images to table cells, but a better idea is to add them to the background using CSS. Before you look at CSS, let's look at a few other tags that also work with images.

CHAPTER 31 ■ WORKING WITH IMAGES AND TAGS

Image Maps <area> and <map> Tags

If you have a large image on your site, such as a map of various countries, a chart of the constellations, or any elements that are collectively part of one picture, you can add an image with clickable areas, rather than make individual navigation buttons. Any JPEG, GIF, PNG, SVG, or BMP file can be the background for an image map. When you plan to create an image map to access the tools in the Properties panel, make sure that you are in Design view; otherwise, these properties are inaccessible. Refer to Figure 31-63.

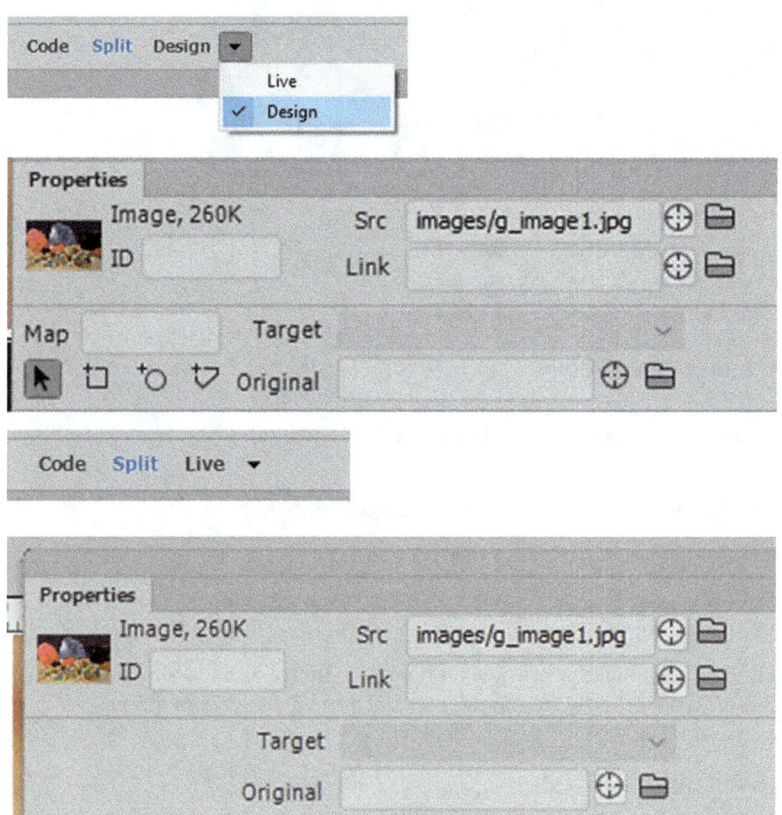

Figure 31-63. *Only in Design view do you have access to the Image map options in the Properties panel*

You need to select your image in Design view to access the tools. They allow you to draw a transparent hotspot or <area> on the map. This area can have a link and a target. An image can have many hotspots. Figure 31-64 shows an example.

793

CHAPTER 31 ■ WORKING WITH IMAGES AND TAGS

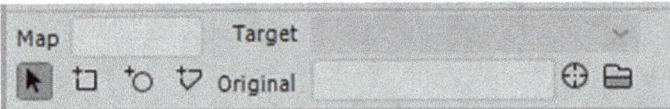

Figure 31-64. Various types of hotspots in Dreamweaver

- **Pointer Hotspot tool:** Allows you to select, size, and move the hotspot to a new location.
- **Rectangle Hotspot tool:** Lets you create a square or rectangular hotspot.
- **Circle Hotspot tool:** Lets you create a circular or oval hotspot.
- **Polygon Hotspot tool:** Lets you create a hotspot that can contain many points. This is useful if drawing the boundaries of a map.

Once the hotspots are drawn in Design view, they preview on top of the image as light-blue squares. In the actual browser, they are invisible, and only the cursor changes so that you know they are there.

The code may look something like this:

```
<img src="images/g_image1.jpg" alt="" width="600" height="400" usemap="#Map"/>
    <map name="Map">
        <area shape="rect" coords="30,105,133,211" href="#">
        <area shape="circle" coords="280,122,52" href="#">
        <area shape="poly" coords="406,100,428,148,433,219,531,240,567,217,591,223,
        597,97,440,82" href="#">
    </map>
```

When you select the <img> tag in Code view, you see that a name has automatically been added to the map and the image now has an attribute link: usemap=#Map. It is important that these remain the same name, or the link between them can become corrupt and fail to work. Refer to Figure 31-65.

CHAPTER 31 ■ WORKING WITH IMAGES AND TAGS

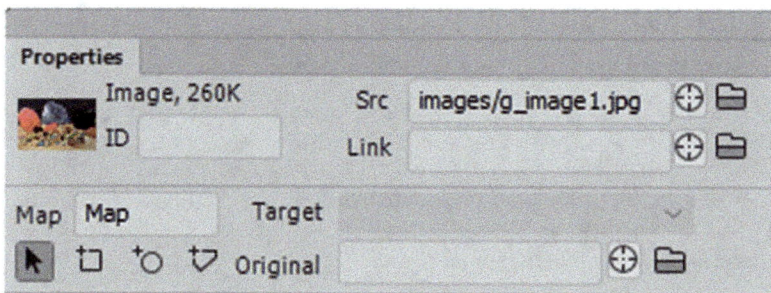

Figure 31-65. The selected image map with an ID

Notice that when you select an <area> tag in the Properties panel, the tool changes to a hotspot. This is the same for all hotpot types. Refer to Figure 31-66.

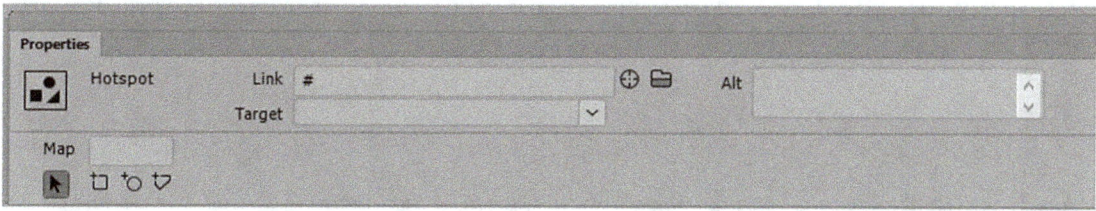

Figure 31-66. The selected hotspot in the Properties panel

Here you can add a link to another page on the site (local) and/or external site. Use the target or browse folders to locate a page.

As you saw when you made Photoshop slices in Chapter 5, a target can be any of the following.

- **_blank:** Opens a linked file in a new window or tab and leaves the original webpage open (this is the same as choosing New).

- **_self:** Opens the linked document in the same frame that it was clicked in (this is the same as default or leaving it blank).

- **_parent:** Displays the linked file in its own parent frameset. Do not use this option unless the file contains a frame. The link is considered a child and it appears in the parent frame.

- **_top:** Replaces the entire browser window with the linked file, removing all the current frames. The name must match a frame in the HTML file for this to work. When the link is clicked, the specified file appears in a new frame.

Besides a link, your image map should have an alt attribute that names what the hotspot links to; for example, alt=Information about Glass. Refer to Figure 31-67.

CHAPTER 31 ■ WORKING WITH IMAGES AND TAGS

Figure 31-67. *New information added to the hotspot in the Properties panel*

The following code in the area tag is added.

```
<area shape="rect" coords="30,105,133,211" href="glass.html" target="_blank" alt="Information about Glass">
```

If you do not add an alt attribute, Dreamweaver displays a warning symbol and a message appears in your Output panel to remind you to add this information in your code or via the Properties panel. Refer to Figure 31-68.

Figure 31-68. *Until all the hotspots are resolved, you may get this yellow warning in Dreamweaver; when resolved, it returns to a green check*

After you save the file, the warning disappears and returns to a green check.

■ **Note** you do not need a title attribute as this appear to corrupt the <area> tag.

Recently, HTML5 has added a few more attributes to the <area> tag; they currently do not show up in Dreamweaver's Properties panel but could be added via Code view. If you would like to look at the new settings for media, you can view them at www.w3schools.com/tags/tag_area.asp.

Be aware that not all new HTML5 features are available for older browsers or your current browser, always read the documentation on the W3Schools website to see if the HTML5 feature is supported by your target browsers.

Another good website to check is Can I Use (https://caniuse.com), which provides more information on tags.

Let's look a few more HTML5 tags you can add images to. Some are supported by most browsers and others are still experimental.

The <picture> and <source> Element

The <picture> tag gives web developers more flexibility in specifying image resources. The <source> is an empty element that can specify multiple media resources for the <picture> tag. For it to work correctly, you need to create media queries using either inline CSS or a class.

```
<picture>
  <source media="(min-width: 650px)" srcset="glass1.jpg">
  <source media="(min-width: 465px)" srcset="glass2.jpg">
  <img src="glass3.jpg" alt="Flowers" style="width:auto;">
</picture>
```

The most common use of the <picture> element is art direction in mobile-responsive designs. Instead of having one image that is scaled up or down based on the viewport width, multiple images can be designed to nicely fill the browser's viewport; for example, one size for a desktop, another size for a tablet, and a third size for a smartphone.

The <picture> element must hold two different tags: one or more <source> tags and one <img> tag. The <source> element has the following attributes:

- **srcset (required):** Defines the URL of the image.
- **media:** Accepts any valid media query that is normally defined in CSS.
- **sizes:** Defines a single width descriptor, a single media query with width descriptor, or a comma-delimited list of media queries with a width descriptor (min-width: 650px).
- **type (optional):** Defines the MIME type.

The browser uses the attribute values to load the most appropriate image. The browser uses the first <source> element with a matching hint and ignores any following <source> tags.

The <img> element is required as the last child tag of the <picture> declaration block. The <img> element is used to provide backward compatibility for browsers that do not support the <picture> element, or if none of the <source> tags matched.

The <picture> element works like the <video> and <audio> elements, which you look at in Chapter 36. In all cases, you set up various sources, and the first source that fits the preferences is the one being used by the browser.

The <details> and <summary> Elements

The <details> tag specifies additional information that the user can view or hide on demand.

```
<details>
  <summary>Book</summary>
  <p> Title of Book</p>
  <p>All content and graphics on this web site are the property of Jennifer</p>
</details>
```

The <details> tag is used to create an interactive widget that the user can open and close. Any sort of content can be put inside the <details> tag, including images. Normally, you have to use CSS and JavaScript to create this type of widget, but now you can do it with HTML5. It is currently supported by all modern browsers, except for Microsoft Edge and Internet Explorer.

The content of a <details> element should not be visible unless the open attribute is set; for example, <details open>. For the default closed option, remove the word *open*.

The <summary> tag is used to specify a visible heading for the details. The heading can be clicked to view or hide the details.

CHAPTER 31 ■ WORKING WITH IMAGES AND TAGS

The <dialog> Element

The <dialog> tag defines a dialog box or window.

The <dialog> element makes it easy to create pop-up dialogs and modals on a webpage. Note that this tag is still experimental. It is supported in most modern browsers, except Edge and Internet Explorer. Like the <details> tag, it can use the open attribute.

```
<dialog open>This is an open dialog window</dialog>
```

The <menu> and <menuitem> Elements

The menu item tag is still in the experimental stage for most browsers and has currently been removed from HTML5; it is only supported by Firefox for use in context menus. Its purpose is to define a command/menu item that the user can invoke from a pop-up menu using a combination of HTML and JavaScript.

The <menu> tag defines a list/menu of commands. It is used for context menus, toolbars, and listing form controls and commands.

Perhaps in the future menus will also include images.

Inserting Images Favicons into Your Browser's Tab

To finish this chapter, let's look at one last image format that you may not have noticed. If you want your website to have a company logo rather than the default browser icon in the tab, there is a way to alter this by adding an image to the in your <head> tag.

Yes, I know I said that images belong in the <body>, and most of the time, that is where these links should be. In most cases, unless JavaScript code is involved, or you are trying to affect the browser tab icon. With JavaScript, if you do not have references to the image in the <body>, those images never appear in the browser. The browser tab icon appears outside the window. In this case, you need to create a favicon.

So far, you have created images for the web in JPEG (.jpg), GIF (.gif), PNG (.png), SVG (.svg), and bitmap (.bmp) formats. So, what is a favicon and what is its format?

A favicon is generally a square that can range from 16×16 pixels, up to 32 or 64 pixels square. Sometimes designing with a larger square and compressing the final size helps you create a more detailed graphic. It is originally a JPEG, GIF, or PNG file. Refer to Figure 31-69.

Figure 31-69. *Adding a favicon to the browser tab*

The file format must end with .ico (e.g., favicon.ico) for the image to appear in the browser. None of the programs that you have looked at so far has allowed you to save a file in this format. You need to create a copy of your image and then rename it (e.g., company.gif to company.ico). Your computer may give you a warning message saying that it does not recognize this format; that's OK. Your browser will recognize it once you insert the link in the correct area of your webpage.

```
<link rel="shortcut icon" type="image/x-icon" href="images/favicon.ico" />
```

CHAPTER 31 ■ WORKING WITH IMAGES AND TAGS

You may have to adjust your link depending on where you put the image in your image folder. But it should be entered somewhere before the head tab closes. Refer to Figure 31-70.

```
7    <title>Home Page</title>
8        <link rel="shortcut icon" type="image/x-icon" href="images/favicon.ico" />
9    </head>
```

Figure 31-70. *Adding a favicon link in the head of a webpage*

Only until you upload the webpages will the image in favicon appear in the tab of your browser.

Some newer browsers support the original GIF, PNG, or SVG file formats. A few allow it to be an animated GIF, but not all older browsers. Also, some Macintosh browsers require a format called .icns. For more information on this file format, check out `https://en.wikipedia.org/wiki/Favicon`.

■ **Note** HTML5 developers are working on a way to display the favicon at assorted sizes for visual media, but this is not available to browsers yet. You can check out the information at `www.w3schools.com/tags/att_link_sizes.asp`.

HTML5 and the Snippets Panel

Dreamweaver CC also has snippets of code available in the Snippets panel (HTML_Snippets). Refer to Figure 31-71.

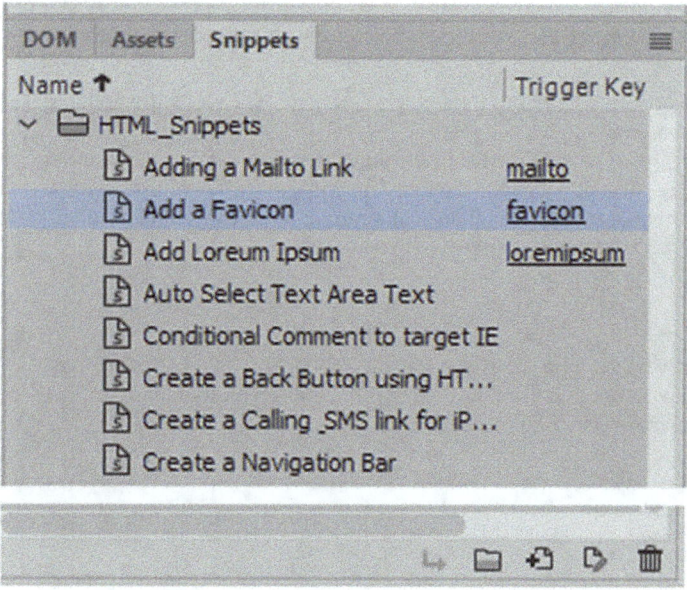

Figure 31-71. *Adding a favicon link using the Snippets panel*

799

CHAPTER 31 ■ WORKING WITH IMAGES AND TAGS

Snippets are a great library resource that you can use as shortcuts to code that you frequently use, or you can add your own to the list. If you don't have a file open, you can view the code by clicking the snippet and the Edit Snippet button (the paper-and-pencil icon next to the Trash icon) and check out the code. This opens the Snippet dialog box. In this case, I found the code for adding a favicon. Refer to Figure 31-72.

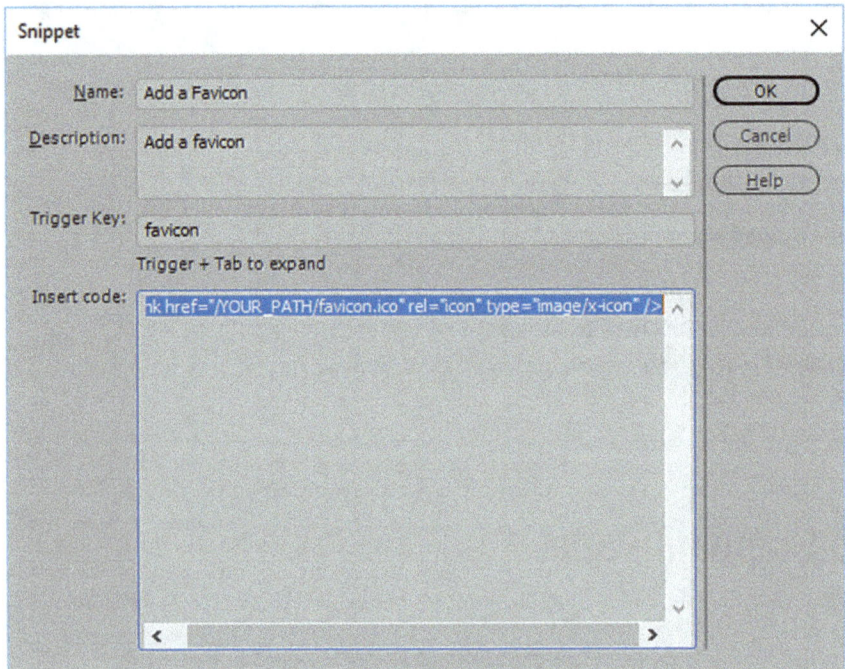

Figure 31-72. *You can review the code in the Snippet dialog box before you insert it using the Snippets panel*

Select and highlight the text in the Insert Code field and press Ctrl+C or Cmd+C to copy the text to paste later. Click Cancel so that you don't save changes.

Alternatively, you could use the arrow Insert icon in the Snippets panel to insert the text on your page. You could then add this link into the head section of your HTML5 file. The Snippets panel offers many options, such as meta tags for mobile and hand-held devices. You look at snippets throughout Part 6.

Summary

In this chapter, you looked at how to insert various types of image formats. You also looked at <div> tags, semantic elements, and some upcoming elements that are new to HTML5. Finally, you looked at favicons and learned how to use the Snippets panel to insert small pieces of text.

CHAPTER 32

Working with CSS

In this chapter, you look at how to work with CSS, linking CSS, and what you can use to enhance your images and turn them into animations using CSS.

> **Note** This chapter does not have any actual projects; however, you can use the files in the Part 6 folder to practice opening and viewing for this lesson. They are at https://github.com/Apress/graphics-multimedia-web-adobe-creative-cloud.

While in a file's <head> tag, you will look at another way to add images or color to the backgrounds of the tags (rather than directly into the <div> tag or semantic element). You can link to internal or external CSS (Cascading Style Sheet) to format and display the tags or "bones" in your HTML files body. Using media queries, these backgrounds are interchangeable when viewed on different browsers or mobile devices.

CSS Inline Internal or External Styles?

While a whole book could be written on CSS itself, and there are many good reference books available formatting properties, the focus of this section of the book is to look at how that formatting (or properties) can be applied to images that appear as a background or boarder within the tag itself.

A good reference to see how CSS works is W3Schools (www.w3schools.com/css/). They have many simple tutorials that you can observer and copy directly into Dreamweaver CC's Code view and edit yourself.

Let's briefly review three ways that CSS can be added or linked to an HTML5 webpage.

Inline CSS

The first way to add CSS is directly as an attribute of the tag or inline. Inline CSS downloads quickly because it is directly on the page viewed in the browser and it is not linked to an external CSS file. Inline has advantages and disadvantages. It can be used to apply a special style attribute to a single HTML element, such as <h1> or <body> tag. With code, you can see a background image and color added to the <body> tag.

```
<body bgcolor="#E4D5E9" background="images/background1.png">
Other conteent on the page...
</body>
```

Here the color is added as a fallback in case the image becomes unlinked or cannot display for some reason. The viewer at least sees some color. Also, background images do not require alt tags because their purpose is only to enhance the website, not to provide information.

CHAPTER 32 ■ WORKING WITH CSS

If you don't want to type in Code view, you can select the body tag and use the Properties panel to select the Page Properties button. Refer to Figure 32-1.

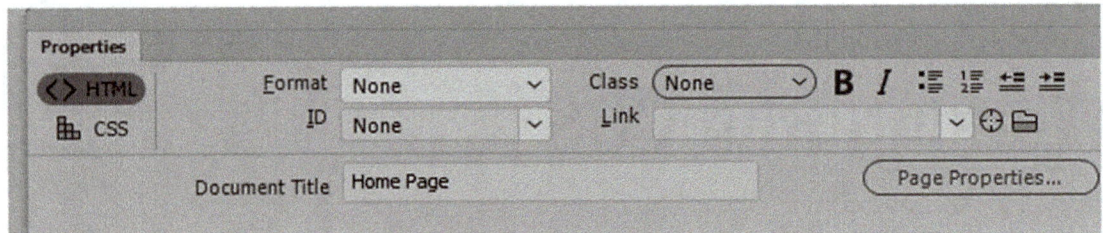

Figure 32-1. The page properties in the Properties panel allow you to edit some inline CSS

The Page Properties dialog box appears whether you are in the HTML tab or the CSS tab. Appearance (HTML) allows you to add a background image and a background color. Color can also be applied to text and links. You can adjust the margins on the left and the top. You can also adjust the width and height. Refer to Figure 32-2.

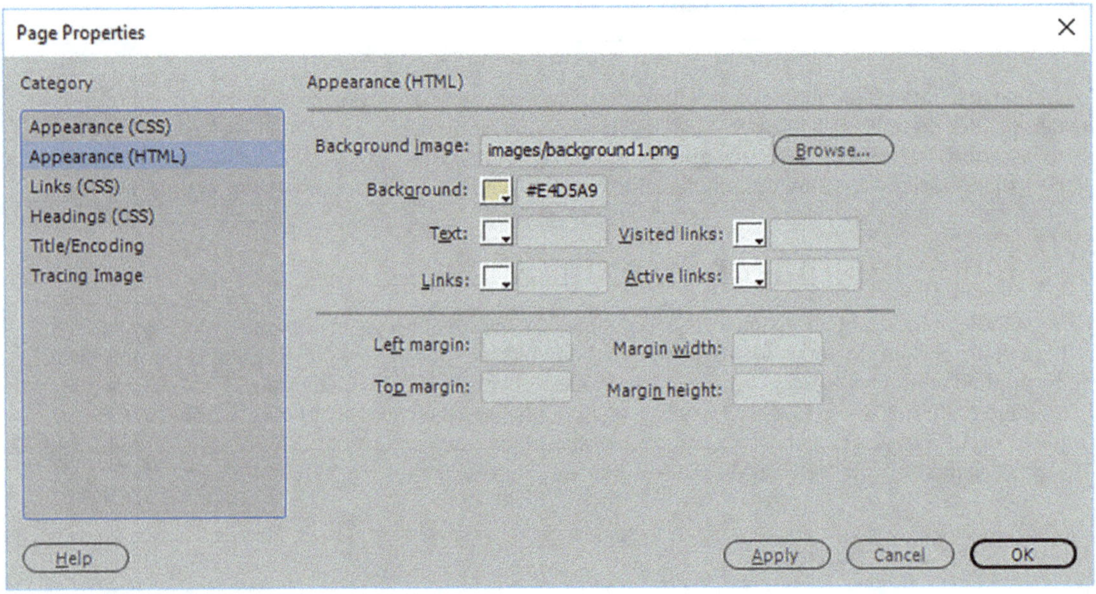

Figure 32-2. The page properties Appearance HTML dialog box area allows you to add inline CSS

Press OK to confirm these changes.

CHAPTER 32 ■ WORKING WITH CSS

■ **Note** Color in Dreamweaver can be written in three ways: RGBa, hex code, or HSLa, if you don't know the exact numbers you can use the color picker and eyedropper that appears in any of the color pullouts. Only hex code works with inline CSS; however hex does not allow for transparency or alpha filter (a) as the other color modes do. The other colors modes and hex work internal and external CSS which you look at shortly. Refer to Figure 32-3.

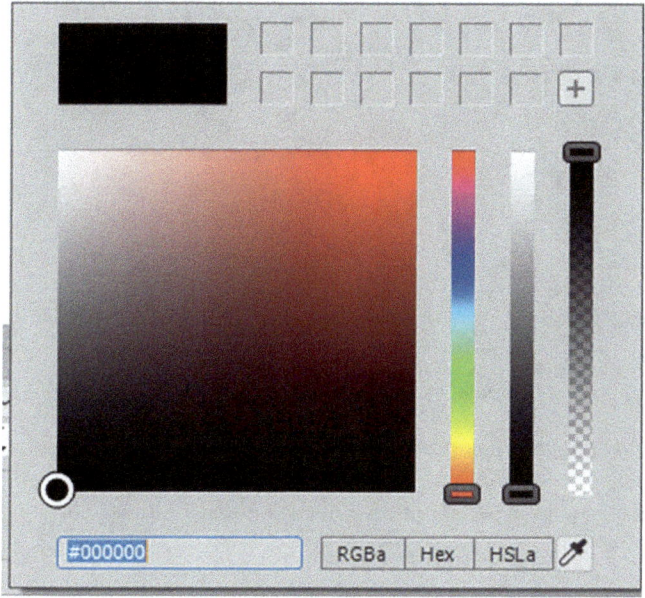

Figure 32-3. *The Color Picker in Dreamweaver is similar to what you saw in the other Adobe programs*

The choices are RGBa (red, green, blue and alpha transparency), hex or hex code (written with hashtag number sign (#)), and HSLa (hue, saturation, luminosity, alpha), which also has an alpha channel. You can also enter actual words, like red or green, to get a variety of colors. Most modern browsers accept alpha channels and transparency; however, if you find you're running into color issues on a browser, stick with hex code, which you can easily find using the color picker.

CSS is good for formatting each tag individually on a single HTML page, but there are several issues that you can run into using inline CSS.

- You must format each tag separately, which can lead to errors if you must type or copy and paste each formatting into each tag.
- The amount of formatting in each tag could become quite lengthy once you start adding font colors, margins, padding, or other styling.
- If you want to have similar styling on another HTML page, you must copy and paste it into the next document; this wastes time and can lead to errors.
- Another issue is scope, which refers to when one CSS style overrides another CSS style because it is closer to the tag itself. Anything inline is as close as you can get to the tag, so any CSS that comes before is overwritten.

803

CHAPTER 32 ■ WORKING WITH CSS

Use inline CSS sparingly and only if you plan to override some settings for just that page. Remove any inline CSS from your HTML5 page if you do not plan to use it. Most of it is located via the Properties panel ➤ Page Properties dialog box ➤ Appearance (HTML) tab, but you may have to scan through the code in Code view or use Tools ➤ Clean up HTML to remove obsolete tags if you are working from a client's files. Refer to Figure 32-4.

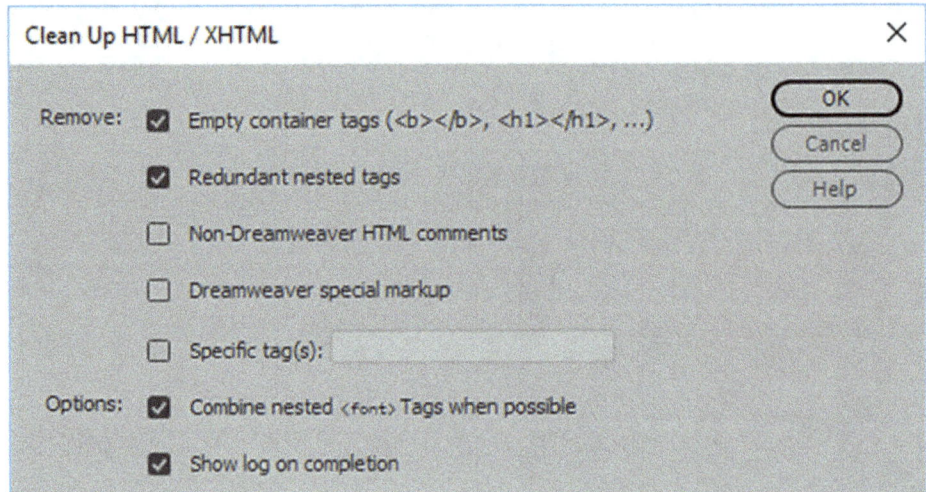

Figure 32-4. *Clean up your HTML or XHTML to remove inline styles or obsolete tags*

If you plan to use the CSS more than once on a page, a better option is to use internal or linked external CSS.

Internal CSS

In Dreamweaver CSS, there are several ways to apply CSS. The first example you saw was inline. The second being internal, which is used to define a style for a single page. Internal CSS always appears in the <head> tag of the document, usually in the <title>. All styles appear between the <styles> </styles> tags.

```
<!doctype html>
<html lang="en">
<head>
<meta charset="utf-8">
<meta name="viewport" content="width=device-width, initial-scale=1">

<title>Home Page</title>
        <link rel="shortcut icon" type="image/x-icon" href="images/favicon.ico" />
        <style type="text/css">
        body {
    background-color: #E4D5A9;
    background-image: url(images/background1.png);
}
```

```
</style>
</head>
<body>
Some Content Here...
</body>
```

One way to do this is to select the body tag and from the Properties panel, and then click the Page Properties button and select the Appearance CSS tab. Refer to Figure 32-5.

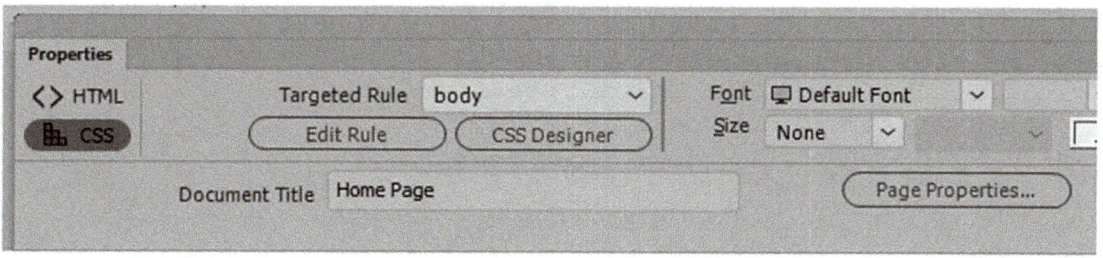

Figure 32-5. Add inline CSS to a page

This automatically creates some internal CSS in the head for the <body> tag. You can also alter the font, font size, text color, image repeat options (repeat, repeat-x, repeat-y, or no repeat), and the margins. Refer to Figure 32-6.

Figure 32-6. The page properties Appearance CSS dialog box area allows you to add inline CSS

Click OK to apply the changes.

Other CSS that you can affect is found in the Links (CSS) and Headings (CSS) tabs, where you can alter text style and color in the <body> tag.

CHAPTER 32 ■ WORKING WITH CSS

■ **Tip** For the background image, the url('images/image.jpg') can either have single, double or no quotes around the link, either way is OK to right in Code view, but make sure the link is correct or you will not see the image.

■ **Note** Trace image is an inline code that is used if you are designing a website and need to use a temporary background image to design or CSS layout over top. Once you are done, remove this information from the <body> tag, as it is only for design purposes. Refer to Figure 32-7.

```
<body tracingsrc="images/120x120.gif" tracingopacity="100">
```

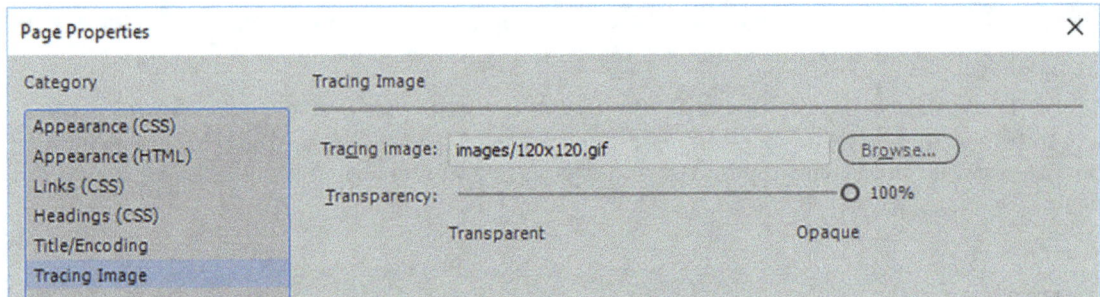

Figure 32-7. Page Properties allows you to temporarily add an image for tracing and design only while working on your website

CSS Designer Panel

Another way to add inline CSS is to use the CSS Designer panel. This panel allows you to create CSS styles, add a source internal or external linked file, and adjust the media queries along with their selectors and their properties, as seen in Figure 32-8.

CHAPTER 32 ■ WORKING WITH CSS

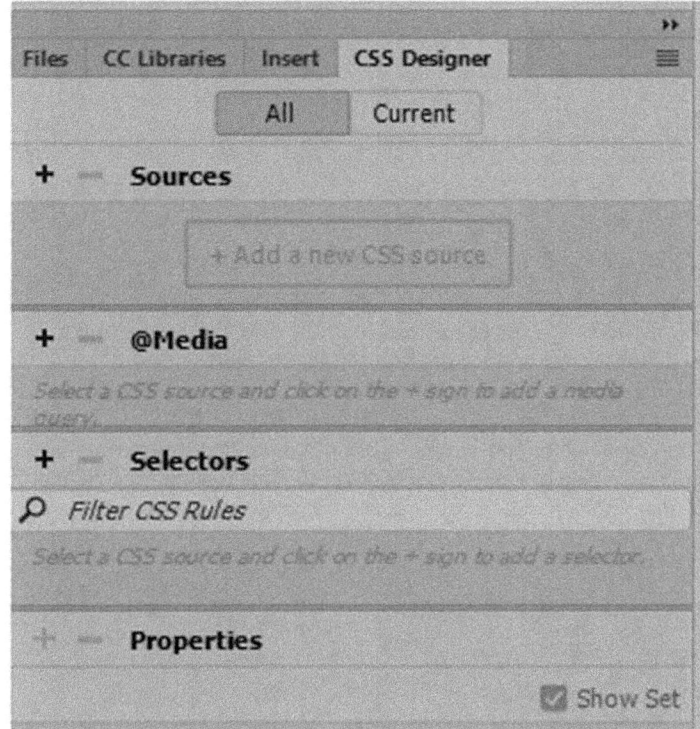

Figure 32-8. *CSS properties panel helps you link and edit the CSS that is attached to your webpages*

The first thing to do is to make sure that the panel is set to the All tab, since you want to see all CSS in the document; in the example shown in Figure 32-9, there is an internal CSS <style> but no external.

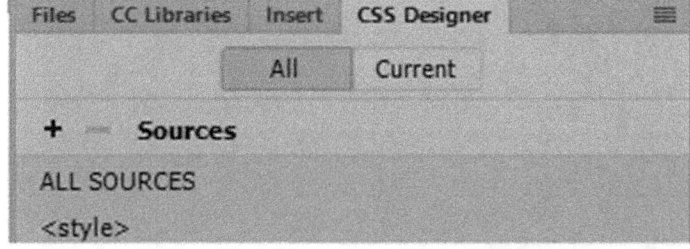

Figure 32-9. *An internal style sheet is found using the CSS Designer panel*

If you did not have an internal style sheet, click the plus (+) icon in the Sources tab. The minus (–) icon removes any unwanted internal CSS styles. Once the plus icon is clicked, you can choose from the drop-down menu to create a new or attach an existing CSS file (external), or define in a page (internal). Refer to Figure 32-10.

807

Figure 32-10. Adding an internal style sheet using Define in Page

Define in Page creates the <style> tags and adds it in the <head> tag in Code view. If there is already an internal style when you choose this option, it does nothing since the <style> tag is in place.

You can see in the CSS Designer panel in Figure 32-9 that a <style> has been added to the Sources section.

In the CSS Designer panel, skip over the Media Query tab since you are not designing for a mobile site yet. You look at this in more detail in Chapter 35. Move down to the Selectors tab. This is where you define your CSS selectors for your internal source that apply to tags in your current document. You can move the upper and lower handle in the tabs if you need more room. Refer to Figure 32-11.

Figure 32-11. Selectors tab in CSS Designer

Click the plus icon to add a selector. This could be <tag> ID or class. If you type in the word body, Dreamweaver gives you hints if you are not sure of the exact wording of the tag. As you type more letters, the choices narrow down to a few relevant rules. Refer to Figure 32-12.

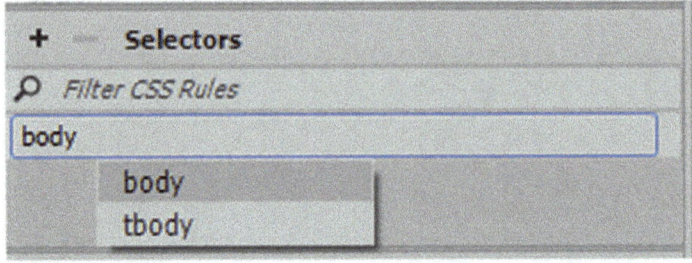

Figure 32-12. Type in a selector

Then select body from the list.
Later, you can filter through the list with the search text box if you have a lot of rules.

CHAPTER 32 ■ WORKING WITH CSS

The new body rule is now in the Selectors section; you find it in the Code view in the styles tag. If you realize you made a mistake, you can select it and click the minus (–) icon to remove it and type it in again. Refer to Figure 32-13.

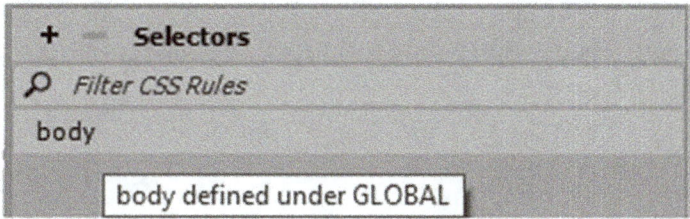

Figure 32-13. *The Selector rule now appear in the list and in the <styles> in Code view*

With the word or tag body rule selected in the list, move down to the Properties tab and click the plus (+) icon. Refer to Figure 32-14.

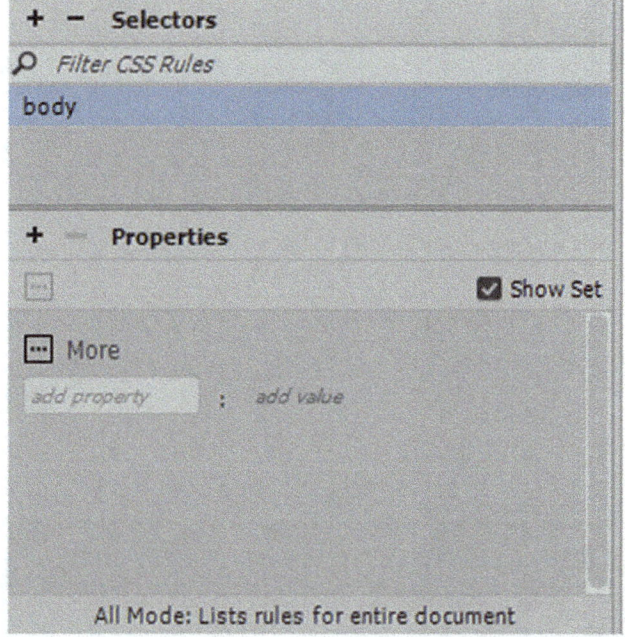

Figure 32-14. *Add properties to the selector in the CS Designer panel*

This adds a field for a property and value that you can enter. Dreamweaver helps you with a list of properties so that you can find the correct one, in this case, background color. Refer to Figure 32-15.

CHAPTER 32 ■ WORKING WITH CSS

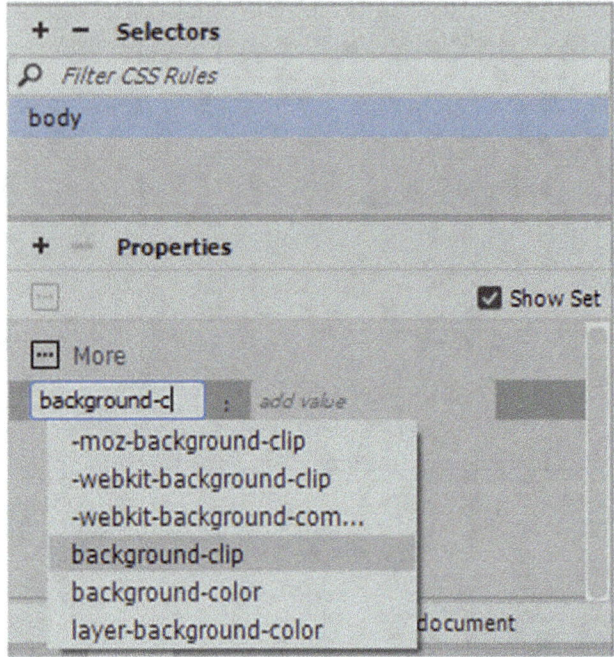

Figure 32-15. Find the correct properties to add to your body tag

When you find the correct one, "background-color", select it.
Then select the value text area and add hex code with a # symbol. Refer to Figure 32-16.

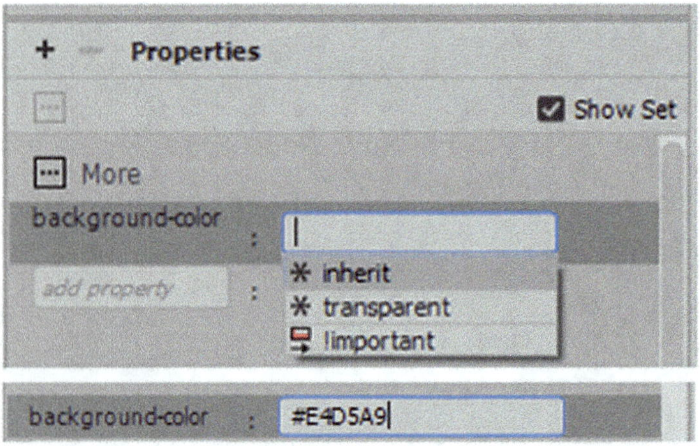

Figure 32-16. In the Properties tag add in a color for the background value

CHAPTER 32 ■ WORKING WITH CSS

■ **Note** Dreamweaver does not bring up the color picker at first in the CSS Designer panel, so make sure you know what the color code is before start typing. I find that a clever work-around is to instead type the color value in Code view rather than in the CSS Designer panel as this bring up the color picker and other helpful hints that CSS Designer does not always show. Refer to Figure 32-17.

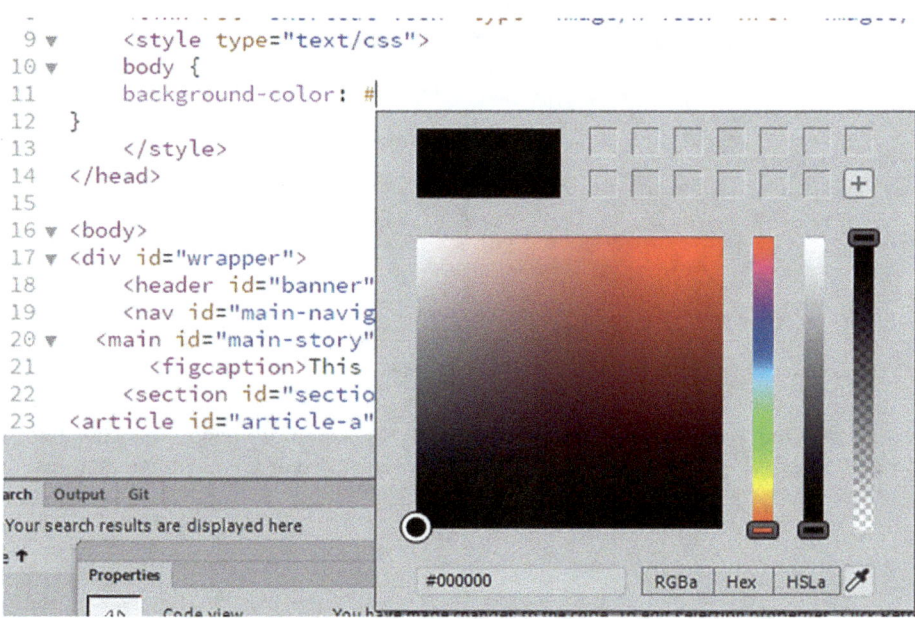

Figure 32-17. *Certain hints or dialog boxes do not always show up in CSS Designer so sometimes you may find it easier working in Code view*

If you use Code view after you have selected the color and pressed the Enter key to confirm it, Dreamweaver may not add a closing properties semicolon.

background-color: #E4D5A9;

You need to do this before you move on to the next property. The CSS Designer panel does, however, add the semicolon for you.

Only once the background color CSS is locked in after you create another tag or selector in CSS Designer Panel the Color Picker dialog box becomes available, and you can now alter it by selecting the tab. Refer to Figure 32-18.

811

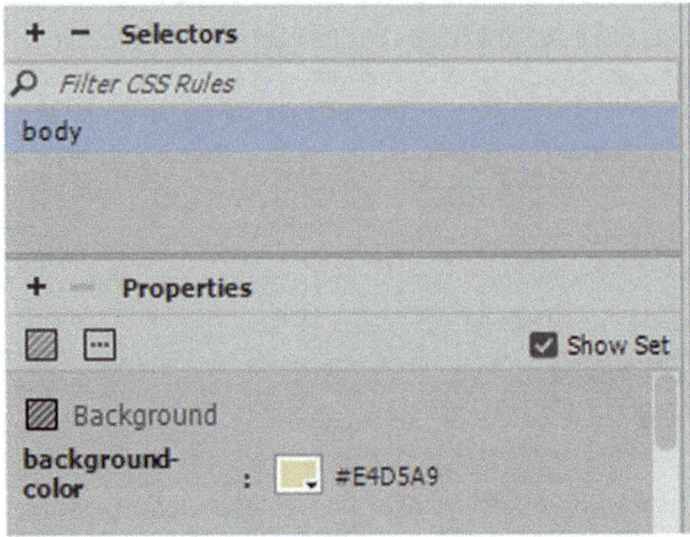

Figure 32-18. Only once another tag is created can access the color picker

While the body tag is selected, you can add properties such as the background-image by clicking the properties plus (+) icon; the minus (–) icon allows you to remove any unwanted properties when they are selected. Refer to Figure 32-19.

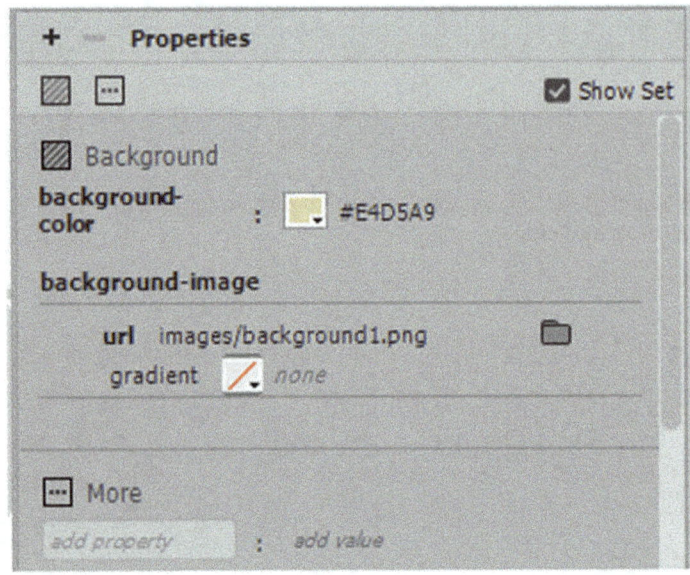

Figure 32-19. Add properties to the body tag

Finding the URL may be easier in Code view because you have the browse feature available right away if you cannot remember the exact link of the file. Refer to Figure 32-20.

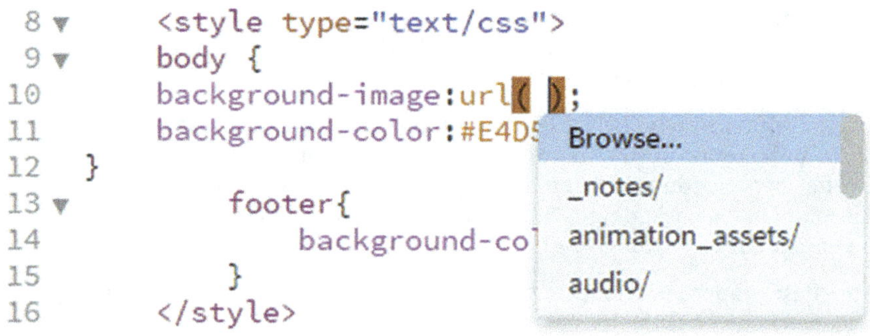

```
8 ▼        <style type="text/css">
9 ▼        body {
10            background-image:url( );
11            background-color:#E4D5
12        }
13 ▼        footer{
14                background-co
15            }
16        </style>
```

Figure 32-20. Add properties to the body tag

Once confirmed in the CSS Designer, you can then change the background images link as required. Refer to Figure 32-19.

```
body {
    background-image: url(images/background1.png);
    background-color:#E4D5A9;
}
```

Adding Other Background Properties

Clicking the More button (see Figure 32-19) in the CSS Designer Properties tab reveals more options or properties.

Background images have properties or values such as whether the images tile or repeat.

- **background-repeat: repeat;** This is the default and repeats vertically (y) and horizontally (x).
- **background-repeat: repeat-x;** This repeats the background along the x coordinate.
- **background-repeat: repeat-y;** This repeats the background along the y coordinate.
- **background-repeat: no-repeat;** This leaves only one image and it does not repeat.

The "space" and "round" properties affect how the background repeats. CSS background-images can have more than one image in the background.

```
body {
    background-image: url(images/backgroundimage1.png), url(images/backgroundimage2.gif);
    background-repeat: no-repeat, repeat;
    background-color: #cccccc;
}
```

The following properties are added when background-repeat: no-repeat; is used.

- **background-position: right top;** Other placement words are right, bottom, and center. You can also use pixels (2px 2px) or percentages(50% 50%) for placement. The first value is the vertical (x) and the second is the horizontal (y). A shorthand example of this is

    ```
    background: #ffffff url(images/glass.png) no-repeat right top;
    ```

- **background-attachment: fixed;** Specifies that the background image should be fixed (does not scroll with the rest of the page). Scroll is the default, and there is the local option that scrolls with the tag's contents.
- **background-origin: content-box;** The background-origin property specifies the origin position (the background positioning area) of a background image. This property has no effect if background-attachment is fixed. It is often used if one or more images are found in the background. One might be set to value of content box and the other to border box or padding-box.

For more information on these properties, refer to https://www.w3schools.com/cssref/css3_pr_background-origin.asp.

```
#wrapper {
    border: 10px double black;
    padding: 25px;
    background: url(images/background1.gif), url(images/background2.gif);
    background-repeat: no-repeat;
    background-origin: content-box, padding-box;
}
```

The following are CSS3 elements, so they are relatively new but work in some older browsers.

- **background-size: 300px 100px;** Specifies the size of a background image with "auto" and in pixels or percentages 50%, 50%. You can also set it to a value of contain to keep it visible within a boundary of the element. A value of cover allows the image to resize within the element to cover that area. It is often used when the background is set to no repeat, and it can be used with more than one image in the background. You may need to add vendor extensions to make these run correctly, which you can view at www.w3schools.com/cssref/css3_pr_background-size.asp.
- **background-blend-mode: lighten;** Defines the blending mode of each background layer (color, image, or both). It is like the blend filters you see in Photoshop, Illustrator, and Animate. These values are not supported by Internet Explorer or Edge. The following are the available options:
    - normal (the default)
    - multiply
    - screen
    - overlay
    - darken
    - lighten
    - color-dodge
    - saturation
    - color
    - luminosity

For more information, visit www.w3schools.com/cssref/pr_background-blend-mode.asp.

- **background-clip: padding-box;** Defines how far the background (color or image) should extend within an element.

Background Image Gradients

The CSS background-image property can also create gradients that are liner or radial and repeat by percentage in the background of your website. However, be aware that even though the word *image* is used, there may or may not be any actual image URLs (PNG, GIF, JPEG) within the parentheses, only colors that are being drawn by the CSS the browser. Images and gradients (linear and radial) can be combined, although they may not show up in every older browser; for example,

```
.background-main{
    background-image: url(../images/background2.png),url(../images/background1.png),
    -webkit-linear-gradient(270deg,rgba(255,0,0,0.00) 73.58%,rgba(255,110,0,1.00) 100%);

    background-image: url(../images/background2.png),url(../images/background1.png),
    linear-gradient(180deg,rgba(255,0,0,0.00) 73.58%,rgba(255,110,0,1.00) 100%);
    background-blend-mode: lighten, normal, normal;
    background-repeat: repeat-x;
}
```

Figure 32-21 shows an example of linear gradients in the CSS Designer panel. Notice how the color picker alters to add a gradient slider so that you can set color points.

CHAPTER 32 ■ WORKING WITH CSS

Figure 32-21. A gradient with opacity can be altered in the color picker

Radial gradients, although they appear in the Design view while editing, do not allow the same color picker choices, so you may have to edit by hand in Code view. Refer to Figure 32-22.

```
}
.container{
    background-color: rgba(255,241,215,0.75);/*0.75 opac
    background: radial-gradient(transparent, #FFF1D7);
    border-radius: 50px;
}
```

Figure 32-22. Edit radial gradients in Code view only

More information on gradients is at www.w3schools.com/css/css3_gradients.asp.

■ **Note** There are other settings: initial and inherit. The initial keyword is used to set a CSS property to its default value or override. The inherit keyword specifies that a property should inherit its value from its parent element. Elements are sometimes affected when one or more CSS properties are combined with inline styles in the tag (see reference to scope in Inline CSS section in this chapter) and how it inherits it styling. Initialvalue: is a new setting is CSS3 and this property may not work in older browsers.

Enabling or Disabling CSS Properties

With the property selected, you can enable or disable (turn on or off), or remove the property entirely with the Trash icon. A property that is disabled appears with CSS comment quotes around it.

/* [disabled]background-image: url(images/background1.png); */

This is like the way that you use layers or show/hide in Photoshop, Illustrator, and Animate. Refer to Figure 32-23.

Figure 32-23. Enable or disable layer properties

Clicking the disable symbol again enables it and returns the CSS onto the page in Design view.

Adding CSS to Other Tags and Elements

In this next section you will look at how CSS can be applied to various HTML tags and semantic elements.

Tags

There are many other CSS properties and values that you could add to the <body> tag that would affect the font or styling of links. However, the body tag is not the only tag that you can add CSS inline styles to.

Any tag selector can be added between the <style> tags in the head; refer to Chapter 31 if you need to review HTML5 elements. For example, if you wanted to target the <main> or <footer> elements, you could write

```
<style>
main {
    background-color: #111111;
    background-image: url(images/background1.png);
}
footer {
    background-color: #222222;
    background-image: url(images/background2.png);
}
</style>
```

Both would have a different background and default color. If you wanted both to have the same background and default color, then you could write

```
<style>
main, footer {
    background-color: #111111;
    background-image: url(images/background1.png);
}
</style>
```

Combining or separating styles is useful, and you can do this with all tags. In CSS, tags are always written with their full name. However, as you saw with semantic elements in Chapter 31, some tags, like <div>, can be used more than once on a page, like <header>, <footer>, <article>, or <section>.

IDs

You may only want to target a specific <div> or semantic element so you could use an ID instead. IDs are unique, and they can only be used once per page. In CSS, the ID always starts with a # symbol, but it is written without the # when referenced in the tag.

```
<style>
#wrapper {
    background-color: #111111;
    background-image: url(images/background1.png);
}
</style>
```

Now only that div or sematic element is affected.

```
<div id="wrapper"> </div>
```

You can see how this looks in the Properties panel where the ID was added. Refer to Figure 32-24.

Figure 32-24. *The Properties panel with div ID*

Class

When you want to target more than one tag with CSS, you can use a class. Unlike IDs, which can only style a single element, classes can be used as many times as you want on page. In CSS, a class always starts with a period (.), but it is written without the period when referenced in the tag.

```
<style>
.image-glass {
    background-color: #111111;
    background-image: url(images/background1.gif);
}
</style>
```

Now in the following <div> or semantic elements the class could be added:

```
<div class="image-water"> </div>
<section class="image-water"></section>
```

Those without the class are never altered by the CSS.

A class can be applied when a tag is selected in Code view; you can use the Properties panel to select the class from the list. Refer to Figure 32-25.

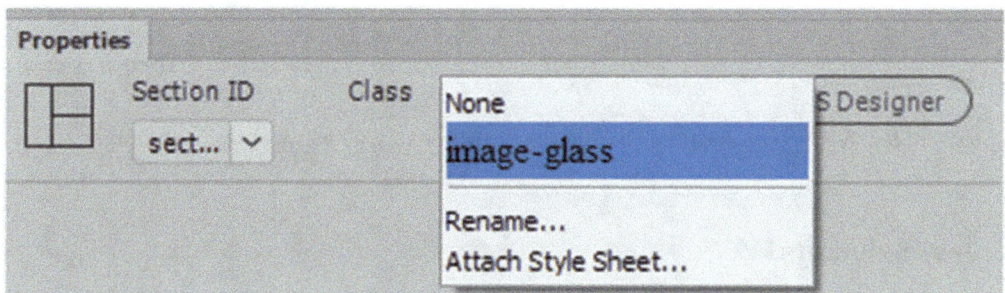

Figure 32-25. *The Properties panel add a class to a div or attach a style sheet*

The default is set to none. From here you can also rename your style. This changes both the style and tag. Refer to Figure 32-26.

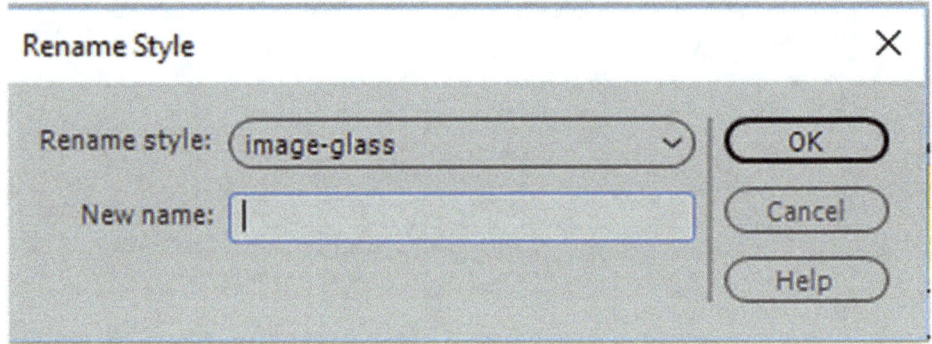

Figure 32-26. Rename the selected style

Also, you can attach an external style sheet from this area in the Properties panel.

Classes and tags can work together; for example, in your CSS, you can apply some styles to the tag and one or more classes as attributes.

```
<style>
section {
color: red;
}
.image-glass {
    background-color: #111111;
    background-image: url(images/water.gif);
}
.small-text {
font-size: 7px;
}
</style>
```

The CSS added to the body may look something like this:

```
<div class="image-water small-text"> </div>
<div> </div>
<section></section>
<section class="image-water"></section>
```

When text is added, it is sized and colored in different ways because of the way the classes target the link.

Pseudo Class Selectors

One final selector that you may come across is the pseudo class, which is a bit more complex or advanced to work with. Essentially, it defines a special state of an element that can be altered by adding a keyword to a selector.

For example, it can be used to style:

- an element when a user mouse hovers over a link, the color alters
- an element when it gets focus, like an input tag

While these elements may not all have background images, you may want to use them within a div that you want to change in some way when you hover, such as the color of a button or a div element.

```
<style>
.nav-box {
    background-color: green;
    background-image: url(images/background1.png);
    color: white;
    padding: 25px;
    text-align: center;
}
.nav-box:hover {
   background-image: url(images/background2.png);
   background-color: blue;
}
</style>
```

If you applied this class (.nav-box) to a <div> tag, when your mouse hovers over it, the image in the background changes. Pseudo classes can be used in some very creative way, which you'll look at again. For more information, visit www.w3schools.com/css/css_pseudo_classes.asp.

To access the base class or the pseudo class for a tag, use the Properties panel to select the base class first.

```
<div class="nav-box"> <div>
```

External CSS

So far you have looked at inline CSS and internal CSS. However, with internal, while it is much easier to work with because all the styling is in one location, you still have two issues.

- The more CSS you add to the page the more room it takes up. It takes the page longer to load.

- You want to use the CSS on other HTML pages, so you must copy and paste the CSS into those pages, which wastes time, and some of it you may not want to use on all pages so now you have to spend time removing those lines of code.

If you are going to use CSS in multiple pages, it is far better to create an external style sheet and link it to the page. External stylesheets can define the style for multiple pages on your site. When you edit one linked file, you can change the property values of all linked pages. Bear in mind, however, that any internal CSS left on the page overrides the external CSS because it is closer to the tag. If you do not remove the internal styling first you may wonder, why your new styles do not format correctly.

Use internal CSS only for pages that require a very specific styling, such as overriding the background or a link color just for that page; otherwise, it is best to keep all CSS in a main external file.

To create an external CSS file, you can use Dreamweaver's CSS Designer panel in the same way that you used it to create your internal style sheet and format it. However, there are some key differences. If you are worried about losing any CSS in the <styles> area, I recommend that you copy, paste, and save this text in a .txt file like Notepad++. Then if you remove the internal styling or need to copy it into the external file at another time, it is not lost.

CHAPTER 32 ■ WORKING WITH CSS

CSS Designer Panel

In the CSS Designer panel, select the <style> if it is still in your file and press the minus key in the Sources tab to remove it. Refer to Figure 32-27.

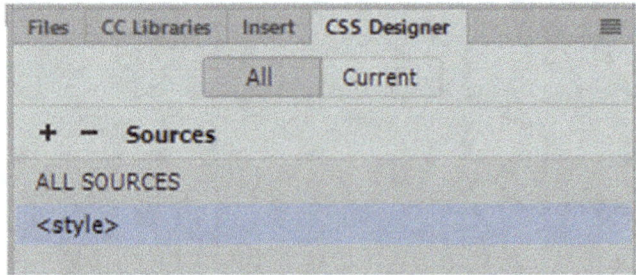

Figure 32-27. Remove internal styles

Your page goes back to base settings. If you saved a backup of the CSS you're OK; otherwise, Edit ➤ Undo should return it, so you can copy it into a temporary file.

With the internal CSS gone, in the Sources tab, click the plus (+) icon and choose Create A New CSS File, or Attach Existing CSS File, if you already have created one. Refer to Figure 32-28.

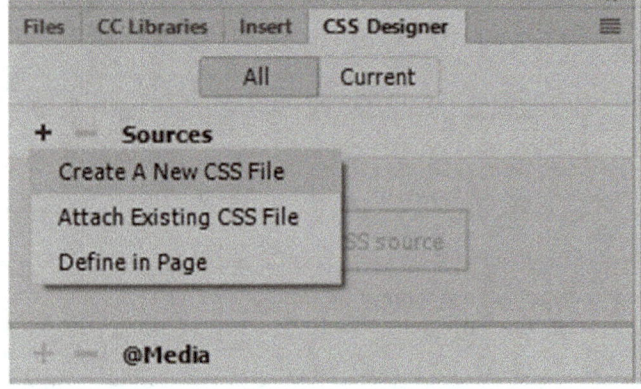

Figure 32-28. Create or add an existing style sheet

Create A New CSS File allows you to add a new file. Leave the setting at Link. Click Browse to locate a location for the new CSS file, as seen in Figure 32-29.

822

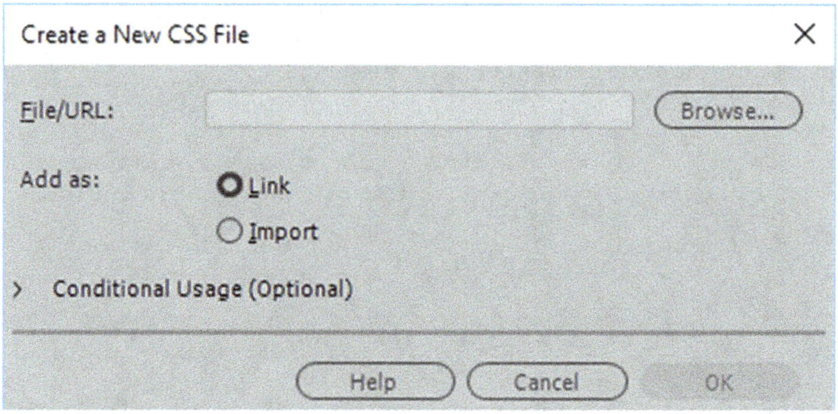

CHAPTER 32 ■ WORKING WITH CSS

Figure 32-29. *Create a New CSS File dialog box*

The Conditional Usage (Optional) tab refers to how you plan to use your CSS; besides different media types it can be used for screen and for print so that the client can print correctly formatted sheets when they print from your website. You'll look at this option later in more detail. For now, leave it unselected and click Browse. Give your CSS file a name and save it with your HTML files in the site root folder or in its own CSS folder. Refer to Figure 32-30.

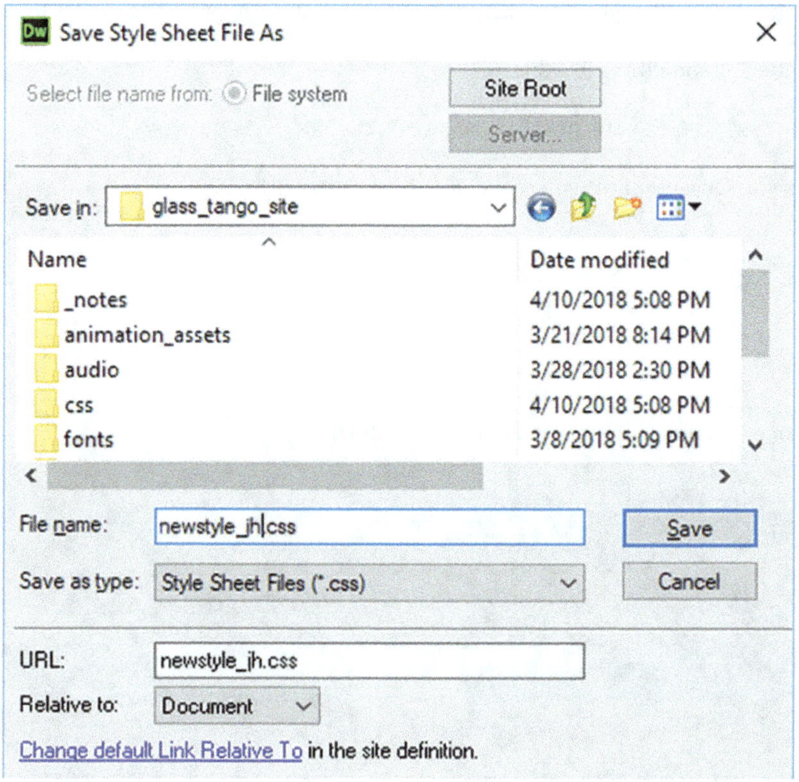

Figure 32-30. *Create a New CSS file and save it in the CSS folder to stay organized*

823

CHAPTER 32 ■ WORKING WITH CSS

When I built the Hot Glass Tango website, I found that as the CSS became more complicated, I needed to have more than one CSS file. To keep organized, I stored all the CSS in one folder.

When done, click Save to return to the original dialog box. Refer to Figure 32-31.

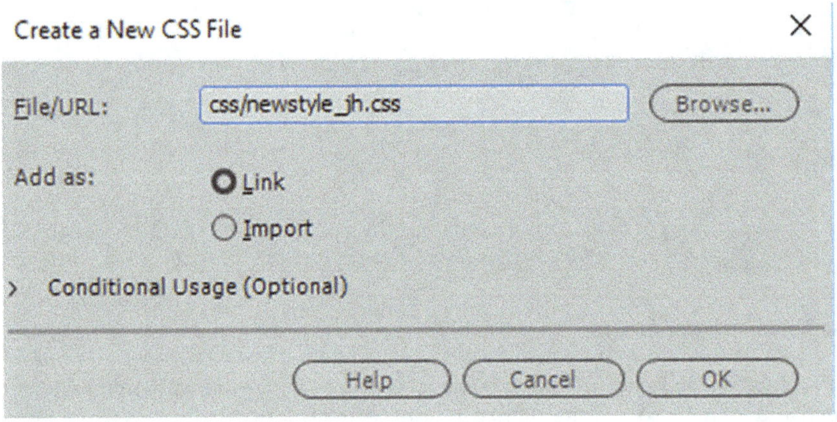

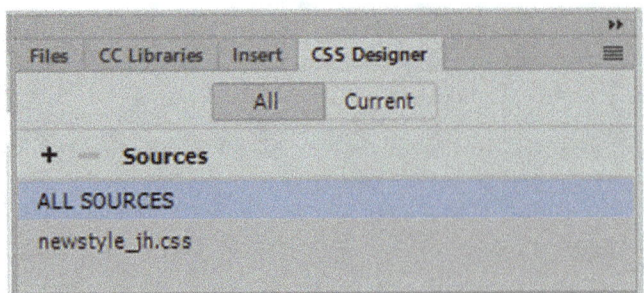

Figure 32-31. The new CSS file is linked

You now have a location that your new file is saved in a CSS folder. Click OK.

You not see the effects of the new CSS file right away since it is currently empty, however, you know that it linked to you HTML file with three indications.

In the <head> tag, you see the link something like this:

`<link href="css/newstyle_jh.css" rel="stylesheet" type="text/css">`

In the top of the document, you see a new link icon to that file. Refer to Figure 32-32.

Figure 32-32. Attaching an external CSS

In CSS Designer, a new source is added to the file. Refer to Figure 32-33.

Figure 32-33. Attached an external CSS in the CSS Designers panel

824

CHAPTER 32 ■ WORKING WITH CSS

To access the CSS external file, you can click the CSS icon file link at the top of your page. Or in the Files panel, locate the new CSS file and once you locate it here, double-click to open. Refer to Figure 32-34.

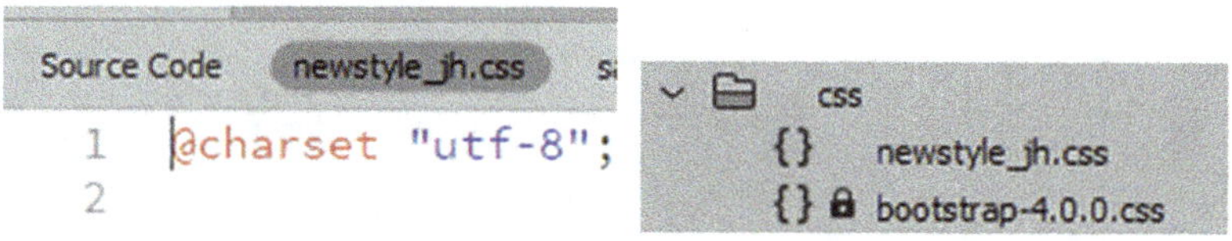

Figure 32-34. CSS is attached to a webpage as an external file

Either way the external CSS file is blank except for a charset rule.

Click line 2; this is the point where you add your CSS or what you have already created. If you want to practice adding the CSS for color and background images using CSS Designer, refer to the section on inline CSS as the process is basically the same except that now you are adding it to an externally linked file, so you do not require the CSS <style> tags anymore. The linking takes place through the <link> tag in the <head> of your document.

In my example, my copied text might look something like Figure 32-35.

Figure 32-35. Some CSS is added to an external style sheet

As you can see, there are no <style> tags because they are not required. Save the file after each change and then return to the Source Code tab, as seen in Figure 32-43.

You might notice that only the colors are only coming in. This is because you have placed the CSS in a folder rather than in the root site and so now the links are slightly different. You can make a correction by adding a (../) and this should resolve the issue and return the images. This is sending me into the correct folder, but you may have to adjust this differently, depending on how you set up your site. Refer to Figure 32-36.

825

CHAPTER 32 ■ WORKING WITH CSS

```
test.html ×
Source Code    newstyle_jh.css*    sale_asset_1.svg
  1    @charset "utf-8";
  2
  3 ▼      body {
  4           background-image: url(../images/background1.png);
  5           background-color: #E4D5A9;
  6      }
  7 ▼         footer{
  8              background-color:#E4D5A9;
  9          }
 10          .image-glass{
 11              background-image: url(../images/background1.png);
 12
```

Figure 32-36. *Altering the link of the background image file*

Save the CSS and return to the Source Code tab.

Now that you have created an external CSS file, you can create HTML5 pages and with CSS Designer choose Attach Existing CSS file. This follows the same process as Create A New CSS File, except this time, you browse and locate the existing file and attach it to your HTML document. Refer to Figure 32-37.

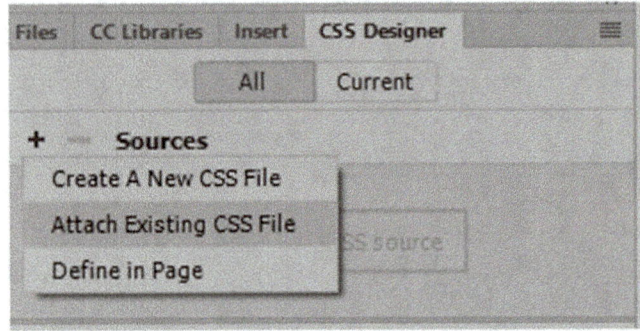

Figure 32-37. *Attach Existing CSS File dialog box*

CHAPTER 32 ■ WORKING WITH CSS

When done, make sure to add as Link and click OK, and the CSS that was created be linked.

You can continue to edit the CSS with Code view or CSS Designer and continue to add background images.

File ➤ New ➤ CSS

It should be noted that if you are a designer and you plan to create a new CSS file that you don't want to attach right away. You can choose File ➤ New ➤ CSS from the New Document dialog box and click Create, which brings up a new CSS file that you can save to the root directory or a folder, but it is not linked to any HTML file until you create a link in the <head> of a document. Refer to Figure 32-38.

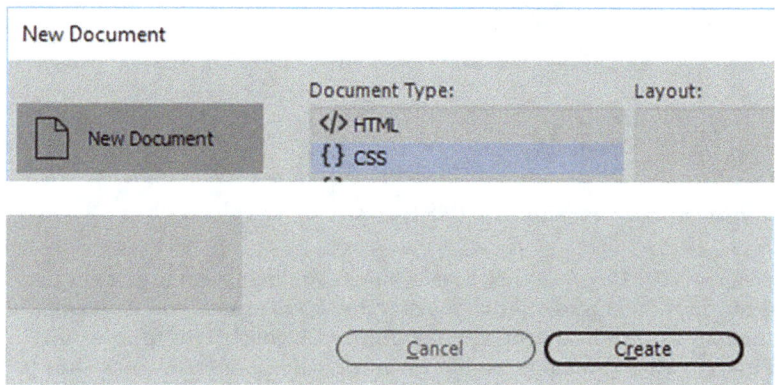

Figure 32-38. *Creating a blank CSS document for a new project without attaching it to a file*

What Is CSS3?

So far, you have looked at CSS and learned how to attach it to an HTML5 document, and to add background and color images to <div> and semantic elements. I've said that some CSS is CSS3, but what does that mean and what other features does CSS3 have to offer?

Like HTML5, the fifth version of HTML, CSS3 is the third version or revision of Cascading Style Sheets. As multimedia changes on the web for different viewing devices, new innovations like animations, transitions, color filters, gradients, and effects like rounded corners have been added. Like HTML5 not all older browsers support the new CSS3 standards, so before using a new feature or property, it is important to check whether it is compatible with the browsers that many of your viewers use. Refer to www.w3schools.com/cssref/css3_browsersupport.asp and https://caniuse.com.

There are also ways to add some backward compatibility to a website, such as an HTML5 shiv or JavaScript to emulate or compensate for how a CSS3 property or HTML5 tag behaves on a website and make it act like the modern version, or at the very least alert the user.

Refer to www.w3schools.com/html/html5_browsers.asp and https://modernizr.com.

It should be noted that within Dreamweaver CC in CSS Snippets, you can also find a few helpful resources, such as Eric Myers CSS Reset and HTML5 Stylesheet Reset.

Remember to click the Edit Snippets button and copy the insert code. Or with a new file, use the arrow insert key on the Snippets panel to add the code on a blank CSS or HTML5 page. Refer to Chapter 31, if you need to review this panel. Refer to Figure 32-39.

CHAPTER 32 ■ WORKING WITH CSS

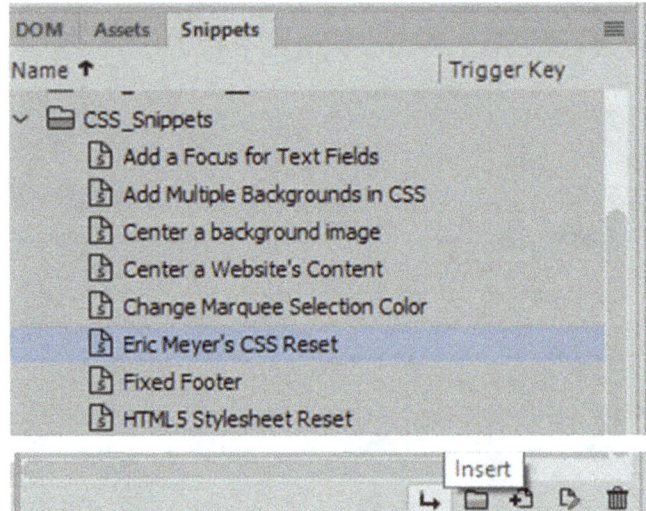

Figure 32-39. *Resources in the Snippets panel for working with CSS*

Just be aware that some of the snippets are a few years old, so take time to compare them to more recent versions online to see if you should add any other CSS to the file. You may then want to add code as an updated version of the snippet, calling it something like (YourName) CSS Reset. To do so, highlight only the code that you want to be part of your snippet and click the New Snippet button to add it to the library. Also make sure to save a backup elsewhere, in case Dreamweaver CC should every overwrite it during an upgrade.

For the Hot Glass Tango website, I used the built-in resets that came with the Bootstrap files in the CSS folder when I created my layout; you look at this in more detail in Chapter 35.

Having said that, I believe that in backward compatibility there is only so far back you can go, and at some point, you or your clients need to upgrade their browser to embrace the latest changes. From what I have noticed, Internet Explorer, or Edge, is usually the last to accept new CSS3 or HTML5 upgrades, so I would probably not design lower than Internet Explorer 9. Also, if you find that some of your clients' tablets and smartphones are not accepting some CSS3 when you design your site for responsive media, you may want to leave out CSS3 in that part of the media query and focus on the padding, margins, and text formatting rather than have all queries function the same. You look at media queries in more detail later.

Now let's continue to look at some CSS examples for working with images in Dreamweaver, some of which involve using CSS3.

Applying CSS to the <img> Tag

Whether you are working with an <img>, <div>, or any semantic element, they can all be placed and adjusted on the page using the CSS properties width, height, margin (the space outside), padding (the space inside), and border (edge of box). An example is the box model, as seen in the following code:

```
div {
width: 300px;
height:300px;
border: 10px solid green;
padding: 10px;
margin: 10px;
}
```

CHAPTER 32 ■ WORKING WITH CSS

These properties have been around for a long time for styling. You can further adjust each side of a border, padding, or margin by value as margin-bottom, margin-left, margin-right, or margin-top.

This order can be applied to padding and borders so that every side is a slightly different thickness, border color, or style.

You can see in the CSS Designer panel how you can easily adjust this; look at the Properties tab. Refer to Figure 32-40.

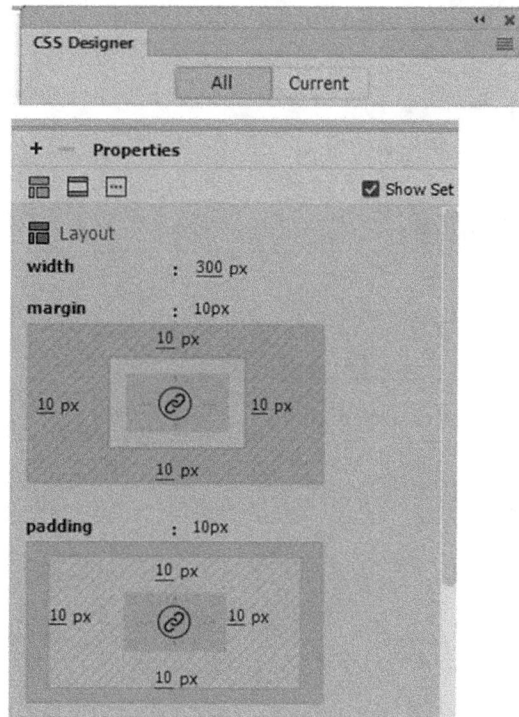

Figure 32-40. *Altering the width, margins and padding in CSS Designer*

You can alter the style of the border, and choose other styles and widths for each side. Refer to Figure 32-41.

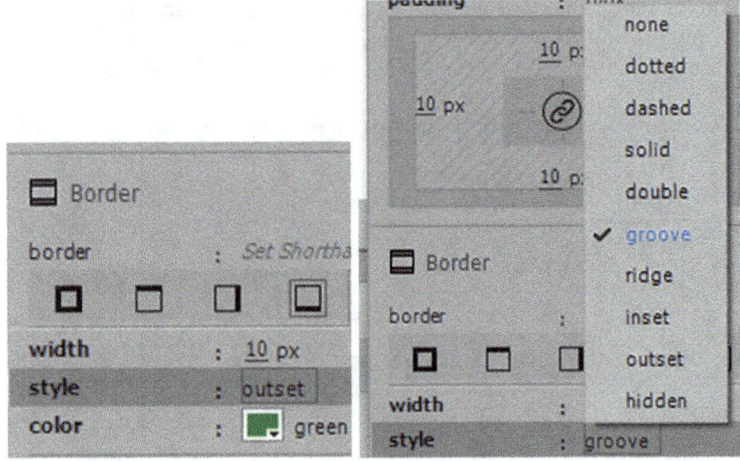

Figure 32-41. Border style for each side of and image

Should You Add Background Images to Form Elements?

If you add a background image, you can affect other tags, such as those used with the <form> </form> tag. You can find form elements in the Insert Form tab. Refer to Figure 32-42.

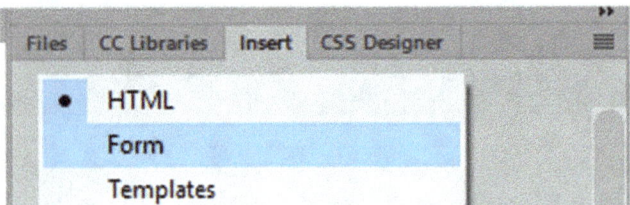

Figure 32-42. Alter other tags besides the <div>

These include, but are not limited to, text form fields, button types, and menus/list boxes. All can have a color or a background image added to them. I generally do not add background images (static or animated) to form elements other than maybe a button because with the filling of forms, text is often very detailed and serious work. Having a clashing pattern in an area where a person is trying to fill out text is very distracting and makes the text difficult to read for the viewer. If you do want a color in the background of your field to match your site, stick with solid colors and make sure that the hex code color does not clash with your text.

In Chapter 8 and Chapter 15, I talked about color blindness and how it makes some colors difficult to read. If you are not sure you can always make a screenshot of your form and then bring it into a program like Photoshop and use one of the Color Blindness View ➤ Proof Set Up to see what it looks like and make your CSS adjustments. A similar online example for inspecting color at www.toptal.com/designers/colorfilter.

For now, you focus on the Insert panel's HTML tab, since most of our work with images and CSS is done here.

CSS3 Borders

Whether you're working with a static (JPEG, PNG, GIF, SVG) or animated GIF within a <div> tag or as a CSS background, rather than having a solid-colored border, you can add a border image.

This is done by setting the border size, and then style to solid and the color to transparent (no color). In this situation you don't want to add a Hex color because the border image is that color. With graphics, the border may be quite thick, so padding is important for preventing the text from overlapping. Here is an example of how that could look:

```
#borderimg1 {
  border: 10px solid transparent;
  padding: 15px;
  -webkit-border-image: url(images/border_test.png) 30 round; /* Safari 3.1-5 */
  -o-border-image: url(images/border_test.png) 30 round; /* Opera 11-12.1 */
  border-image: url(images/border_test.png) 30 round;
}
```

■ **Note** That some older browsers may not support the property border-image, so you can add the vendor extensions -webkit- for safari and -o- for opera. You must add the same URL to each one. In the preceding code example, I used a PNG image in the URL because I found that a GIF did not stretch accurately for some reason. When working with images in CSS3, always run a test of the script in a separate file before adding to the main file. This saves you a lot of headaches if you test new or experimental settings away from the main design.

The border-image (short form) can be modified further in five main ways.

- **border-image-source:** The path to the image to be used as a border.
- **border-image-slice:** How to slice the border image.
- **border-image-width:** The width of the border image.
- **border-image-outset:** The amount by which the border image area extends beyond the border box or overlaps the actual tag.
- **border-image-repeat:** Whether the border image should be repeated, rounded or stretched (default).

For more information, visit www.w3schools.com/css/css3_border_images.asp.

Rounded CSS3 Borders

Since we are on the topic of borders, you can also round the edges of your tags and sematic elements.

```
div {

    border: 2px solid red;
    padding: 10px;
    border-radius: 25px;
}
```

For border radius, you can have a background image in your div. This does not appear to work with border-image, so you cannot round your image in the border.

But, you can set your radius to different pixel sizes for each corner, which can give you some very unusual border shapes.

```
border-top-left-radius: 5px;
border-top-right-radius: 10px;
```

CHAPTER 32 ■ WORKING WITH CSS

```
border-bottom-right-radius: 8px;
border-bottom-left-radius: 6px;
```

You can further edit the radius using the CSS Designer panel in the Properties tab. Refer to Figure 32-43.

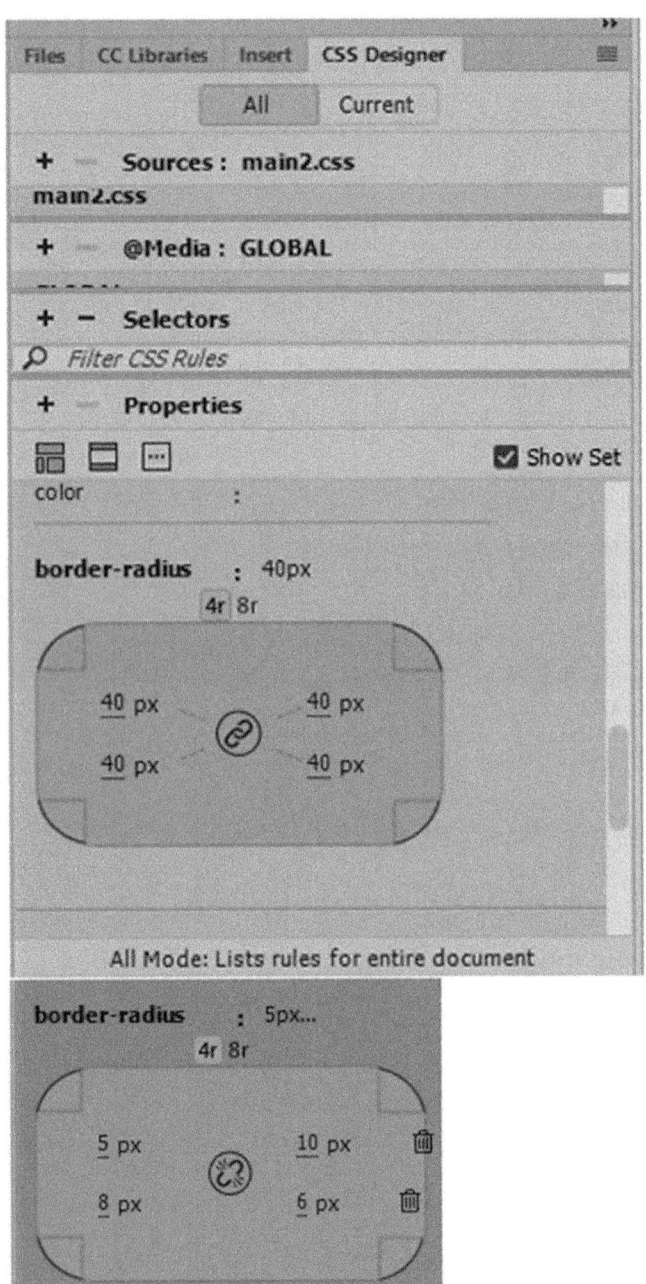

Figure 32-43. *Alter the border radius in CSS Designer*

By unlinking, you can set each radius differently.

Also, in the Snippets panel (CSS Effects), you find code similar to what is available on W3Schools. Refer to Figure 32-44.

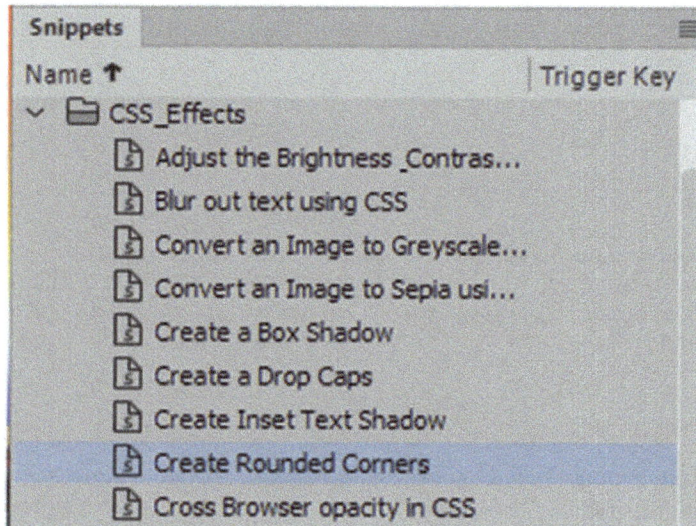

Figure 32-44. *The Snippets panel CSS Effects has further resources for editing your image and div elements*

Just make sure when you use this code to check it against the current vendor extensions that are being used.

You can see more examples at www.w3schools.com/cssref/css3_pr_border-radius.asp.

Outline CSS2

There is another way to add a fancy border. You can also add a second stroke, called an *outline*.

Outlines differ from borders in three ways:

- An outline is a line drawn around elements, outside the border edge to make the element stand out.
- An outline does not take up space.
- An outline is generally rectangular; you cannot adjust each side to be different. It does not allow you to adjust its edge radius independently.

The outline property is a shorthand property for setting the following individual outline properties:

- **outline-width:** by name(thick) or pixel number
- **outline-style:** sets the style, like solid or dotted
- **outline-color**

The outline property is specified as one, two, or three values. The order of the values does not matter. The outline is not a part of the element's dimensions; therefore, the element's width and height properties do not contain the width of the outline.

You can also add an outline offset. The outline-offset property adds space between an outline and the edge or border of an element. The space between an element and its outline is transparent. Here an example:

```
div {
    border: 2px solid black;
    outline: 2px solid red;
    outline-offset: 15px;
}
```

CSS3 box-decoration-break

The box-decoration-break property specifies how the background, padding, border, border-image, box-shadow, margin, and clip-path of an element are applied when the box for the element is fragmented. This is relatively new to CSS3 and is not currently support by Microsoft Edge. It has two settings: slice and clone. You can learn more about it at www.w3schools.com/cssref/css3_pr_box-decoration-break.asp.

Adding CSS3 Filters and Shadows

There are other effects that you can add to your <img> <div> or semantic elements, which don't have to be added using Photoshop or Illustrator. This makes simple changes easy when you are working with a client on a site.

As you saw in the Snippets panel, there are quite a few CSS3 effects that can be used. The following discusses the CSS that makes this possible.

box-shadow

The box-shadow property attaches one or more shadows to an element.

```
div {
    border: 1px solid;
    padding: 10px;
    box-shadow: 5px 10px;
}
```

This is an example of multiple shadows:

```
box-shadow: 7px 7px red, 10px 10px yellow, 15px 15px green;
```

The values that you can add include horizontal or vertical offset (h-offset and v-offset); this is required to offset the shadow to the right and bottom. This is the default use of the box-shadow property; negative numbers are set to the left and top.

You can also add a blur radius to make the shadow appear fuzzier. Spread increases the size of the shadow. You can alter the color of the shadow and set an inset to make the shadow inner rather than the default of outset or outer.

```
box-shadow: 6px 6px 14px 6px #ebebeb;
box-shadow: inset 5px 5px 15px #1abc9c;
```

You can modify your box shadow further using the CSS Designer panel in the Properties tab. Refer to Figure 32-45.

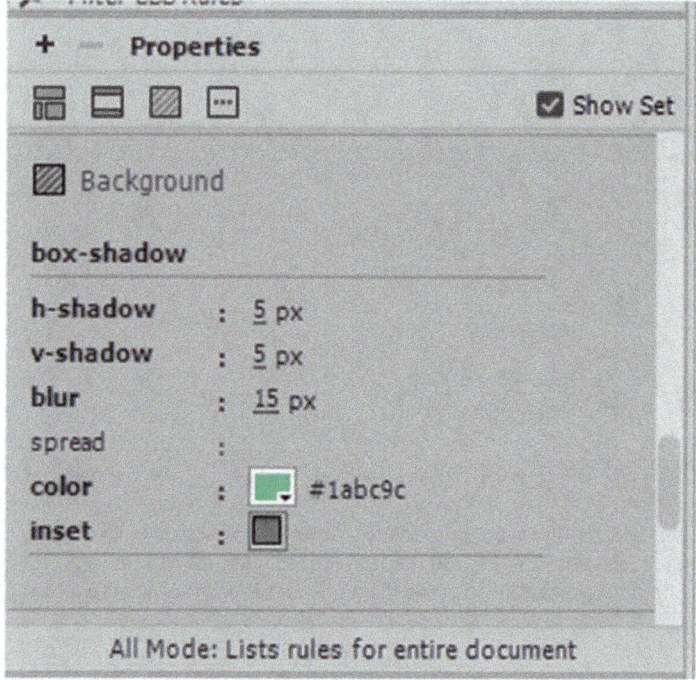

Figure 32-45. Modify the box shadow using CSS Designer panel's h-shadow and v-shadow

Box shadows can be used in combination with photos and CSS transform, which you look at in more detail later. For more information, refer to www.w3schools.com/cssref/css3_pr_box-shadow.asp.

text-shadow

You can also add a shadow to text using text-shadow.

```
div{
text-shadow: 2px 2px 3px #ff0000;
}
```

It basically has values similar to box-shadow (h-shadow, v-shadow, blur radius, and color), except that they are for adding shadow to text rather than a box. Shadows cannot be inner or inset, only outset. Refer to Figure 32-46.

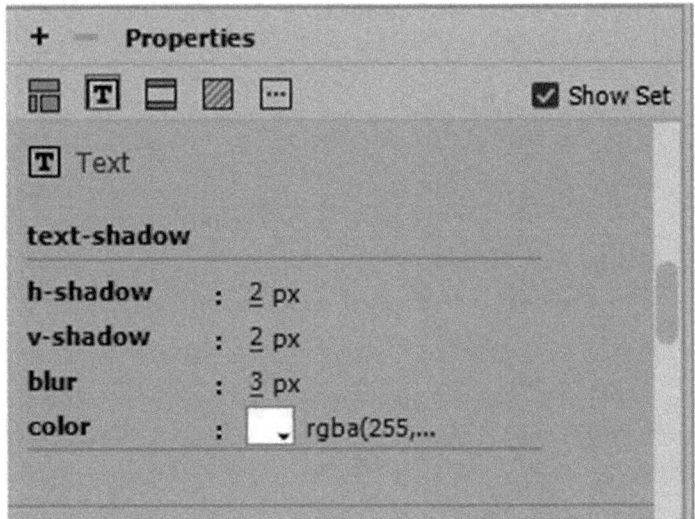

Figure 32-46. *Modify the box shadow using CSS Designer panel*

I find text shadow to be extremely useful when building a gallery, and I know the text is over a colorful image as a description or caption. I add a bit of shadow and blur to the text so that it stands out on the images (see gallery.html). As with the box shadow, you can add more than one shadow by separating them with commas.

```
div{
text-shadow: 2px 2px 3px #ff0000, 0 0 10px #0000ff;
}
```

CSS Filters

CSS Filters (filter) are similar to the blends that you can create in Photoshop and Illustrator. There are at least 11 filters that you can use on a photograph that are often applied to the <img> tag.

- **None:** This is default when no filter is applied
- **blur(px):** Applies a blur effect to the image. A larger value creates more blur. If no blur the value is 0.
- **brightness(%):** Adjusts the brightness of the image. 0% makes the image black while 100% (default of 1) is the original image, if you use a higher value over 100%, like 110% this make the image brighter.
- **contrast(%):** Adjusts the contrast of the image. 0% makes the image black while 100% (default of 1) is the original image, if you use a higher value over 100% this make the image less contrasted.
- **drop-shadow(h-shadow v-shadow blur spread color):** This filter is very similar to the CSS drop-shadow property; however, be aware that some browsers do not always support the spread values so make sure to compare and test this filter first; for example, filter: drop-shadow(8px 8px 10px gray);.

- **grayscale(%):** Converts the image to grayscale or a desaturation. 0% (0) is default and represents the original image. 100%(1) make the image completely gray (used for black and white images); however, negative values are not allowed.

- **hue-rotate(deg):** Applies a hue rotation shift on the image. The value defines the number of degrees around the color circle the image samples be adjusted. 0 deg is default, and represents the original image whereas the maximum value is 360 degrees.

- **invert(%):** Inverts the samples in the image. 0% (0) is default and represents the original image.100%(1) make the image completely inverted, but negative values are not allowed.

- **opacity(%):** Sets an opacity level for the image. The opacity-level describes the transparency-level (alpha), where: 0% is completely transparent. 100% (1) is default and represents the original image (no transparency or alpha).

Negative values are not allowed and an alternative to this filter is similar is the opacity property; for example, opacity: 0.5;. In some cases, if text is preset with the background this cause the text to fade as well in that case it is better to use a background-color of RGBa and just adjust the alpha so that the text is not affected.

- **saturate(%):** Saturates the image. 0% (0) make the image completely un-saturated. 100%(1) is default and represents the original image. Values over 100%, like 110% provides super-saturated results; however, negative values are not allowed.

- **sepia(%):** Converts the image to sepia tone. 0% (0) is default and represents the original image. 100% (1) make the image completely sepia; however, negative values are not allowed.

- **url():** This is a link to the location of an XML file that specifies an SVG filter and may include an anchor to a specific filter element. You saw SVG filters in Illustrator CC being used; for example, filter: url(svg-url#element-id).

You can use many of these filters either separately or in combination. Further examples can be found in Dreamweaver's Snippets panel (CSS Effects).

- Adjust the brightness and contrast of an image
- Convert an image to grayscale
- Convert an image to sepia
- Cross browser opacity
- Invert the colors of an image
- Rotate the hue of an image
- Saturate an image

Be aware the latest browser Microsoft Edge does allow you to view these filters. Internet Explorer does not. There are some JavaScript syntax alternatives you can insert, so make sure to check W3Schools (www.w3schools.com/cssref/css3_pr_filter.asp) if this is a concern.

Also make sure to add the correct vendor extensions for those browsers that require it; for example, -webkit-; otherwise, it would be best to do the blending in Photoshop or Illustrator so that your audience sees the correct image.

Image Masking in CSS3?

Another filter that in the future we might be able to look forward to is Mask this is still in the experimental stages, but allows you to mask an element. In addition, you may be able to work with gradients with the masking.

For more information, visit https://developer.mozilla.org/en-US/docs/Web/CSS/mask-image.

Adding Custom Images to Bullets

If you need bulleted lists for your site, you can add them via the Insert panel in the HTML tab as you did with the <div>, <img>, and other semantic elements. Refer to Figure 32-47.

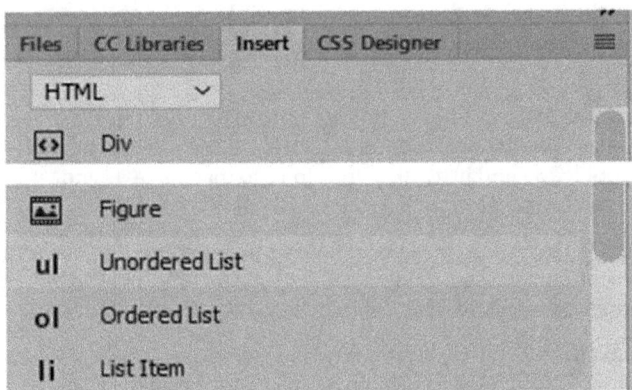

Figure 32-47. Add list item bullets

As a review, unorder lists <ul> use bullets each part of the list is a list item or <li>. There are about 3 default sets (disk, circle, square) and you have the option of setting the list to none, if you don't want bullet which can be useful if you are creating some form of navigation.

An ordered list <ol> uses list items <li> as well but rather than being the same bullet or bullet set they are a set of numbers (1,2,3) letters (a,b,c, or A,B,C) or roman numerals (i,ii,iii or I, II, III). These can be added via an attribute of type being added to the tag; for example type="A". For more information on lists, refer to www.w3schools.com/html/html_lists.asp.

However, what if you want custom bullets from an image that is static GIF or PNG, or a GIF animation? This can be altered in two ways; one is via the content property and using an unorder list.

```
ul {
    list-style: none; /* Remove HTML bullets */
    padding: 0;
    margin: 0;
}
li {
    padding-left: 16px;
}
li:before {
    content: "o"; /* Insert content that looks like bullets */
    padding-right: 8px;
    color: blue; /* Or a color you prefer */
}
```

Earlier you looked at pseudo class and pseudo elements. They can be used to target certain elements or the actions of a certain element such as hover. However, you can also target where a custom bullet start and stop. The first thing to do is remove the original default bullets of the unordered list, list-style: none;. Then in the <li>, add the new bullet using the :before content property (pseudo element) before the words of each bullet. The :after pseudo element adds them after each word. If you just plan to use symbols, W3Schools has an entire entity reference chart of choices at www.w3schools.com/cssref/css_entities.asp.

If you wanted an asterisk, you would write

```
content: " \ 002A";
```

This creates an asterisk bullet. There are many clip-art symbols to choose from in the list. And you can color to a separate color from the text.

However, our main goal here is to add an image not a symbol. To do this, you must make a small symbol 32×32 pixels or less with a transparent background; it can be a GIF or PNG.

Rather than using content, you can use the property list-style.

```
ul {
    list-style: square url(images/shape.gif);
}
```

This sets the list-style-type, list-style-position, list-style-image.

Now the type of list in this case does not really matter what style it is because you are overriding it with the new image.

```
ul {list-style-type: square;}
```

The position can either be on the outside or inside. You do not need to write outside as this is the default.

```
list-style-position: inside;
```

The image is the URL link. This link should match the location of where your image is located.

```
list-style-image: url(images/shape.gif);
```

Refer to Figure 32-48 to see how this appears in the CSS Designer panel in the Properties tab.

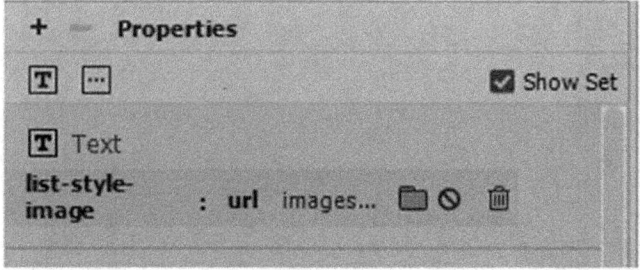

Figure 32-48. *Add an image or GIF animation to a replace a list item bullet using CSS and the CSS Designer panel*

CHAPTER 32 ■ WORKING WITH CSS

As with the content property, you can use pseudo elements (:before and :after) to target placement but you could go even further using [target attributes] and your content properties, as you look at in Chapter 37, for when you need to have thumbnail reference links for images that don't display.

Creating CSS Animation Transitions and Transforms

So far with CSS, you have looked at some ways to enhance your images and tags using CSS. You also saw that many of these examples are stored in Dreamweaver's Snippets panel, and you can add your own examples to the Snippet panel library. As you explore the Snippets panel, you may come across a few more CSS3 items that you have never used that relate to animation.

Refer to the folders CSS Animations, Transitions, and CSS Effects (Rotate and Element 3D Transform). Refer to Figure 32-49.

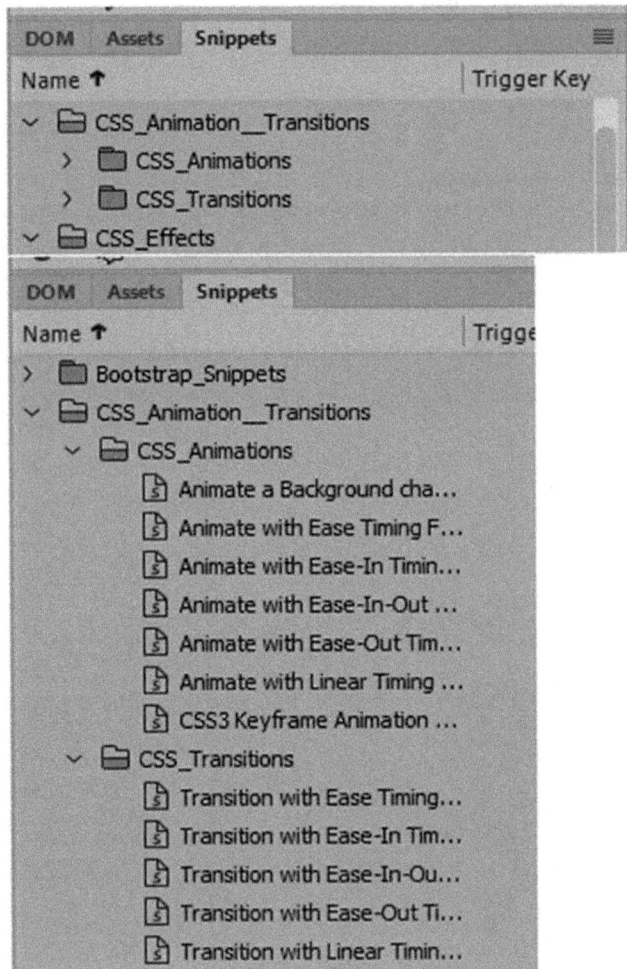

Figure 32-49. Examples of animation and transitions can be found in the Snippets panel

840

Before CSS3, you had to rely on scripts like JavaScript or ActionScript Flash to create animations for the web. While Adobe Animate CC is a wonderful program for creating complex animations, sometimes you just want to create a simple movement of a <div> tag with a background image or color transition. These transitions allow you to alter property values with ease from one value to another. As you can see, Dreamweaver offers several good examples for you to test. And if you require more, you can find quite a few at W3Schools, such as the following:

- www.w3schools.com/css/css3_animations.asp
- www.w3schools.com/css/css3_transitions.asp
- www.w3schools.com/css/css3_2dtransforms.asp
- www.w3schools.com/css/css3_3dtransforms.asp

Let's look at the main properties of each CSS type of CSS.

Note While the examples in the Snippets panel do work, I have noticed that in some older version of Dreamweaver CC 2017 the vendor prefixes for the Opera browser show up as a zero rather than a lowercase o; for example, -O-animation should be -o-animation. I did not encounter this in the CC 2018 version, so from what I can see, the Adobe designers have corrected this error in the latest version. Also note that in most cases of backward compatibility, the vendor prefixes that are currently used are -moz- or -webkit-. The most modern browsers, however, don't require this extension in the properties. Nevertheless, this is useful information to keep in mind depending on what audience you are design for or if you are working with CSS that a client designed a few years ago.

CSS3 Animations

As you saw in Photoshop CC and Animate CC, animations are made up of keyframes and properties that control the direction and duration of the moving object. The same is true with CSS3 in the form of code.

An animation in CSS3 lets an element such as a <div> tag gradually change from one style to another. This can be done using the selectors and properties of To - From or by percentage and their respective values. You can change as many CSS properties as you want for as many times as you want.

To use CSS animation, you must first specify some keyframes for the animation. Other properties can be applied to the <div> tag, such as width or height, and these can be altered by the animation properties and keyframe that are linked to it. To get an animation to work, you must bind the animation to an element.

```
div {
    width: 100px;
    height: 100px;
    background-color: blue;
    -webkit-animation-name: colorchange; /* Safari 4.0 - 8.0 */
    -webkit-animation-duration: 4s; /* Safari 4.0 - 8.0 */
    animation-name: colorchange;
animation-duration: 4s;
animation-delay:2s;
}
```

```css
/* Safari 4.0 - 8.0 */
@-webkit-keyframes colorchange {
    from {background-color: blue;}
    to {background-color: yellow;}
}

/* Standard syntax */
@keyframes colorchange {
    from {background-color: blue;}
    to {background-color: yellow;}
}
```

Keyframes hold the styles the element has at certain times. The following are the main properties.

- **@keyframes:** Specifies the animation code. Animation happens when the CSS styles change gradually from one to another; during this time you can the set of CSS styles many times. Properties can be found within the brackets {} of the key frame. Examples are: from{starting property: value;), to{ending property: value;} or percent, which lets you be more accurate in your animation changes.

```css
@keyframes colorchange {
    0%   {background-color: red;}
    25%  {background-color: yellow;}
    50%  {background-color: orange;}
    100% {background-color: purple;}
}
```

Movement can also be added within the brackets and you could return to your starting point.

```css
@keyframes colorchange {
    0%   {background-color:red; left:0px; top:0px;}
    25%  {background-color:yellow; left:100px; top:0px;}
    50%  {background-color:blue; left:100px; top:100px;}
    75%  {background-color:orange; left:0px; top:100px;}
    100% {background-color:purple; left:0px; top:0px;}
}
```

Here you can see points of change at 25% then again at 50% and the final ending color at 100%.

- **animation:** A shorthand property for setting all the animation properties.
- **animation-delay:** Specifies a delay for the start of an animation if you don't want it to start right away such as animation-delay:2s; which means 2 seconds of delay. Then the animation-duration can begin. Negative duration can be used as well such as animation-delay:-2s; This moves the animation 2 seconds into the animation duration or as if it had already been playing for 2 seconds. It can also be defined in milli-seconds (ms).
- **animation-direction:** Specifies whether an animation should be played forward, backward, or in alternate cycles. The default is animation-direction: normal; This runs the animation in the original order set up. A reverse setting plays the animation backward. Other options include alternate (plays forward then backward) and alternate-reverse (plays backward then forward). In alternate and alternate-reverse, you need to set the animation-iteration-count: 2; otherwise, it does not play both the forward and reverse movements, only one way.

- **animation-duration:** Specifies the time that an animation should take to complete one cycle; for example, 4s means 4 seconds. The default is 0 seconds (0s) if this property is not added. It can also be defined in milliseconds (ms).
- **animation-fill-mode:** Specifies a style for the element when the animation is not playing. It can be before it starts, after it ends, or both times; for example, animation-fill-mode: both;.
- **none:** This is the default value. Animation does not apply any styles to the element before or after it is executing.
- **forward:** The <div> element retains the style values set by the last keyframe (depends on animation-direction and animation-iteration-count).
- **backward:** The <div> element gets the style values set by the first keyframe (depends on animation-direction) and retains this during the animation-delay period.
- **both:** The animation follows the rules for forward and backward, extending the animation properties in both directions or times in the keyframe. (from and to).
- **animation-iteration-count:** Specifies the number of times an animation should be played. You can play as many times as you like. For example, animation-iteration-count:3; means three times, but if you wanted an infinite loop, you could set it to animation-iteration-count: infinite;.
- **animation-name:** Specifies the name of the @keyframes animation. This is the name that is tied to the animation; for example, see how colorchange is referenced as the animation.

```
div {
   /*Some CSS properties*/
   animation-name: colorchange;
}
@keyframes colorchange {
    from {background-color: blue;}
    to {background-color: yellow;}
}
```

- **animation-play-state:** Specifies whether the animation is running (default) or paused; for example, animation-play-state: paused;.
- **animation-timing-function:** Specifies the speed curve of the animation. This effects the movements as to whether they speed up or slow down within the animation, this can make movements fluid and smooth. You saw examples of this in Animate CC in Part 4 and the same concept can be applied to animation of CSS3.
- **ease:** An animation starts slowly start, speeds up, and then ends slowly (this is default setting).
- **linear:** An animation with the same speed from start to end.
- **ease-in:** An animation with a slow start.
- **ease-out:** An animation with a slow end.
- **ease-in-out:** An animation with a slow start and end.
- **step-start:** Equivalent to steps(1, start).

- **step-end:** Equivalent to steps(1, end).
- **steps(int,start|end):** A stepping function with two parameters. The first parameter specifies the number of intervals in the function. It must be a positive integer (greater than 0). The second parameter is optional; the value "start" or "end", and specifies the point at which the change of values occurs within the interval. If the second parameter is omitted, it is given the value "end".
- **cubic-bezier(n,n,n,n):** Lets you define your own values in a cubic-bezier function. The values are numeric values from 0 to 1; for example,

    ```
    #div1 {animation-timing-function: cubic-bezier(0,0,1,1);}
    #div2 {animation-timing-function: cubic-bezier(0.25,0.42,0.25,1);}
    ```

Animation can be written in shorthand.

```
div {
    animation: colorchange 5s linear 2s infinite alternate;
}
@keyframes colorchange {
    0%   {background-color:red; left:0px; top:0px;}
    25%  {background-color:yellow; left:100px; top:0px;}
    50%  {background-color:blue; left:100px; top:100px;}
    75%  {background-color:orange; left:0px; top:100px;}
    100% {background-color:purple; left:0px; top:0px;}
}
```

Also, like all other CSS, you can apply it to an ID or to a class (.easeinAnimObj) within a tag. In Dreamweaver, the Snippets panel gives you hints when you insert the snippet as to what to name the class so that your animation animates correctly.

```
<div class="easeinAnimObj">
/*
Define this in your CSS
.easeAnimation = Replace it by the name you want to give your animation
.easeAnimObj = Assign this class to elements to which you intend to apply the animation
*/
```

If you find additional animations that you like, save them in a file as a backup and add them to the Snippets panel for later use.

CSS Transitions and Transitions Panel

Transitions are in the Snippets panel. Refer to Figure 32-57. Since they are found in the same folder, are they the same as CSS animations?

Transitions allow you to change property values smoothly (from one value to another) over a given duration. For example, when you hover over a <div> tag element, the CSS of transition effect causes the element to grow or shrink.

To create a transition effect, you must specify at least two things:

- the CSS property that you want to add an effect to
- the duration or time of the effect

CHAPTER 32 ■ WORKING WITH CSS

If no duration is specified, the transition does not work because it is at zero; for example,

```
div {
    width: 100px;
    height: 100px;
    background: red;
    -webkit-transition: width 2s; /* Safari */
    transition: width 2s;
}
```

Then add a :hover pseudo class.

```
div:hover {
    width: 300px;
}
```

This the element changes on the hover state. Its width grows to 300px;. You could also add a height and even a color change for the hover. When the mouse is removed, the shape gradually changes back to its original size.

Like animation, many of the properties are similar except that they have the word transition before instead of animation. For example, animation-delay is now transition-delay.

The following are the transition properties.

- **transition:** A shorthand property for setting the four transition properties into a single property; for example,

```
div {
    transition: width 2s linear 1s;
}
```

- **transition-delay:** Specifies a delay in seconds (s) or milliseconds(ms) for the transition effect before starting; for example, transition-delay: 1s;. The default value is 0s.

- **transition-duration:** Specifies the number of many or milliseconds a transition effect takes to complete.

- **transition-property:** Specifies the name of the CSS property the transition effect is for; for example, transition-property: width;. This target the width. If you want to target the height, change it to transition-property: height;.

- **transition-timing-function:** Specifies the speed curve of the transition effect; this is like the animation properties.

- **ease:** A transition effect with a slow start, then speeds up, and then ends slowly (default setting).

- **linear:** A transition effect with the same speed from start to end.

- **ease-in:** A transition effect with a slow start.

- **ease-out:** A transition effect with a slow end.

- **ease-in-out:** A transition effect with a slow start and end.

- **step-start:** Equivalent to steps(1, start).

- **step-end:** Equivalent to steps(1, end).

- **steps(int,start|end):** This is a stepping function with two parameters. The first parameter specifies the number of intervals in the function. It must be a positive integer (greater than 0). The second parameter, which is optional, is either the value "start" or "end", and specifies the point at which the change of values occurs within the interval. If the second parameter is omitted, it is given the value "end".

- **cubic-bezier(n,n,n,n):** This lets you define your own values in a cubic-bezier function. The values are from 0 to 1; for example,

```
#div1 {transition-timing-function: cubic-bezier(0,0,1,1;}
#div2 {transition-timing-function: cubic-bezier(0.25,0.1,0.25,1);}
```

Transition can also be combined with transformation. You look at 2D and 3D transforms in a moment. You can see it in this example:

```
div {
    width: 100px;
    height: 100px;
    background: red;
    -webkit-transition: width 2s, height 2s, -webkit-transform 2s; /* Safari */
    transition: width 2s, height 2s, transform 2s;
}
div:hover {
    width: 300px;
    height: 300px;
    -webkit-transform: rotate(180deg); /* Safari */
    transform: rotate(180deg);
}
```

Also, like all other CSS, you can apply it to an ID or to a class (.linearTransition) within a tag. In Dreamweaver, the Snippets panel gives you hints when you insert the Snippet as to what to name the class so that your transition animate correctly.

```
<div class=".linearTransition">
/*
  Define this in your CSS
  .linearTransition = Replace it by the name you want to give your transition
*/
```

You would also change your :hover state to something like .linearTransition:hover or whatever name in the CSS.

Unlike the CSS3 animation, Dreamweaver CC has a special panel for transitions called the CSS Transition panel.

CSS Transition Panel

If your website's CSS currently contains no transition examples that are linked to tag, ID, or class, the CSS Transition panel appears blank. However, if you have already created a CSS Transition panel, it displays a basic preview of the available transitions. Refer to Figure 32-50.

CHAPTER 32 ■ WORKING WITH CSS

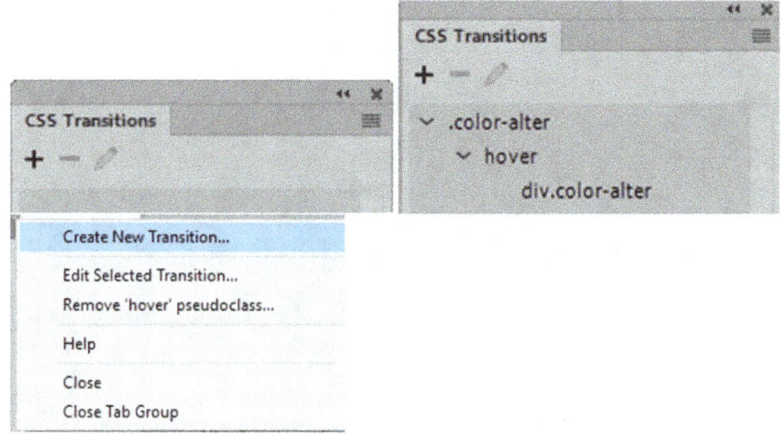

Figure 32-50. *The CSS Transitions panel*

To add or apply a new transition to an element, make sure that you select the <div> tag that you want to apply the new transition to, click the plus (+) icon, to remove the code select the transition in the panel and click the minus (-) icon. To edit, select the transition in the panel and then click the Pencil icon. You can also use the submenu to access the same icons found on the panel or by right-clicking the transition in the panel.

■ **Note** For this transition to be viewable in your browser, you need to add the class to a <div> tag either before or after you create the transition with a starting width, height, and background color or background image; otherwise, the animation may not be visible. You can use the CSS Designer panel or enter the information in Code view in your external CSS file as seen in the following code example.

```
Example:
.color-alter{
width: 50px;
    height: 30px;
    background-color: aqua;
/*transition and its vendor prefixes be added below this once you enter your information in the dialog box*/
}
```

In the HTML document, this is how the class for the transition should be added.

```
<div class="color-alter"> </div>
```

If you are creating a new transition rather than entering it yourself in your CSS file, you can use the New Transition dialog box to help set it up. Click the plus (+) icon to enter the dialog box. Refer to Figure 32-51.

847

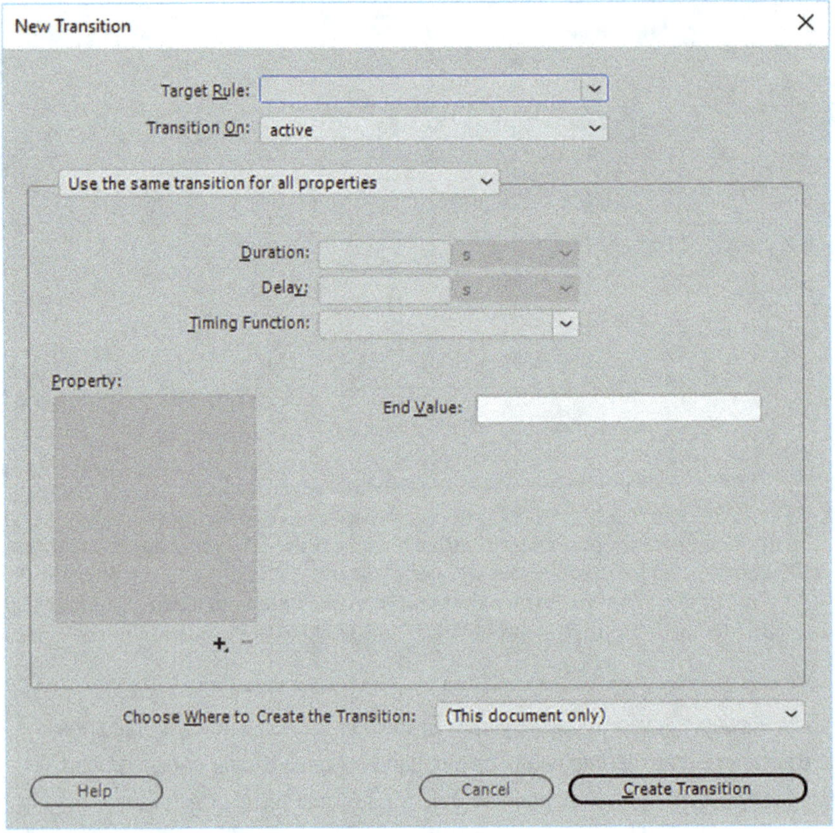

CHAPTER 32 ■ WORKING WITH CSS

Figure 32-51. The New Transition dialog box

- **Target Rule:** This is a current class or rule that you have created and can select from the drop-down menu. If there is no current target, then you can enter your own. In this case I chose the class ".color-alter". Refer to Figure 32-52.

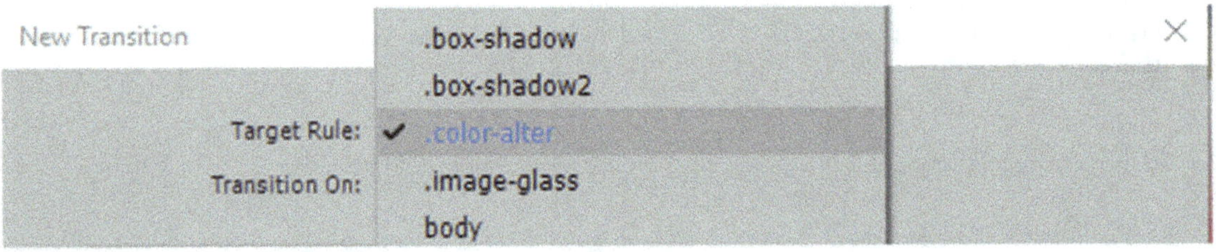

Figure 32-52. Set a Target rule

CHAPTER 32 ■ WORKING WITH CSS

- **Transition On:** Allows the user to choose the state the transition is triggered on. There are several pseudo classes to choose from. Active are used with a link like an a:link. Checked, disabled, enabled, focus, and indeterminate are used with various <input> form elements. Hover is used when hovering over a <div> tag element, but it might be used for a link as you would :target with an anchor; for example, #news:target. This area does not allow you to apply the same transition in the same class again. For example, if you already used the :hover pseudo class, when you try to apply it again, it is gone from the list. Only a new class with a different name that never used :hover allows this option to be available again. Refer to Figure 32-53.

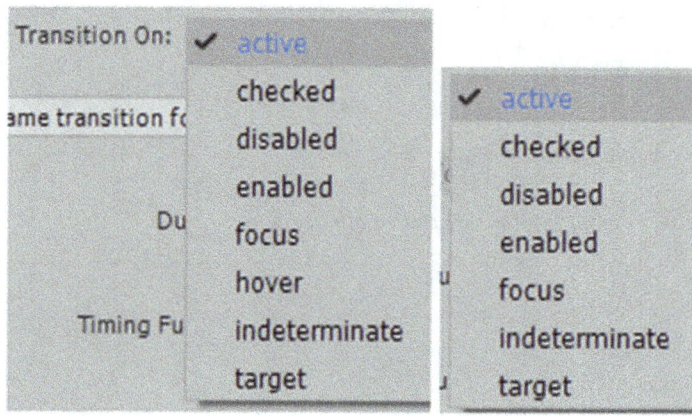

Figure 32-53. Transition states once used are not available in the list for the current class

From the next drop-down menu, you can choose to use the same transition for all properties that you enter next or a different transition for each property. This depends on the complexity of the transition you plan. In Edit mode, it is the second option when you click the Pencil icon. Refer to Figure 32-54.

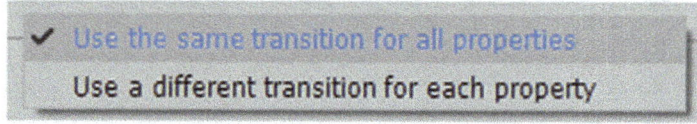

Figure 32-54. Alter how you want the transition to be applied

You can set the transition duration (either in seconds or milliseconds). You can set the transition delay and the timing function. This sets the speed for the ease in and out. For a detailed list of what each function means, refers to the transition-timing-function section earlier in this chapter on the topic of CC transitions. Refer to Figure 32-55.

CHAPTER 32 ■ WORKING WITH CSS

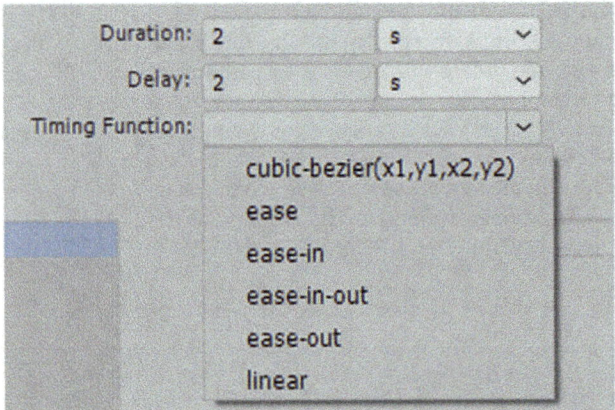

Figure 32-55. Set duration, delay, and timing function

Next, you look at the properties that affect the end value. Refer to Figure 32-56.

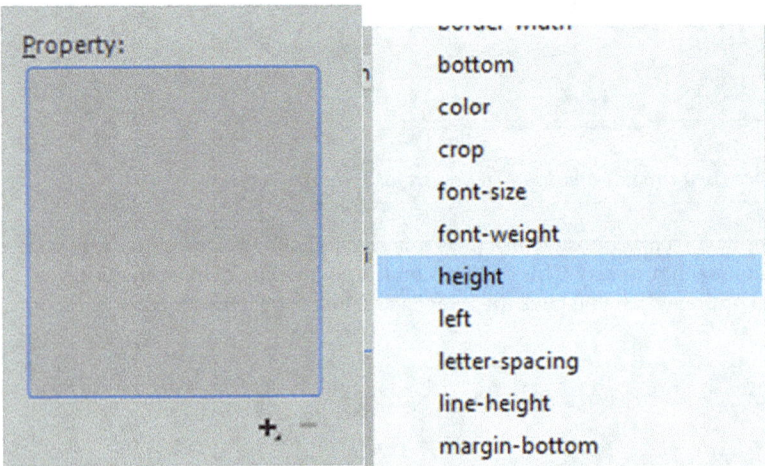

Figure 32-56. Set the end value properties

You can add one or more transition-properties to the list by clicking the plus (+) icon and choosing one at a time from the list. This would be the equivalent of writing height; or background color. Minus (–) removes properties. Refer to Figure 32-57.

850

CHAPTER 32 ■ WORKING WITH CSS

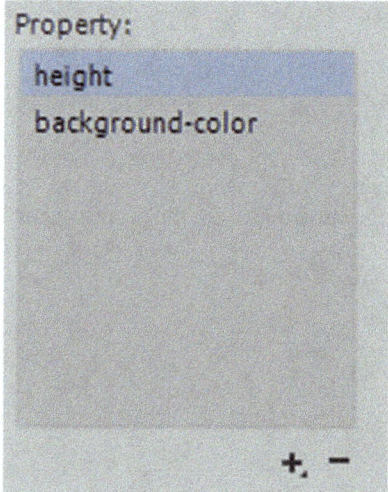

Figure 32-57. Properties added to the list

Depending on what property value you choose, the end value may be different. In width or height, it could be auto or 100px, or whatever setting you are using, such as em or %. Refer to Figure 32-58.

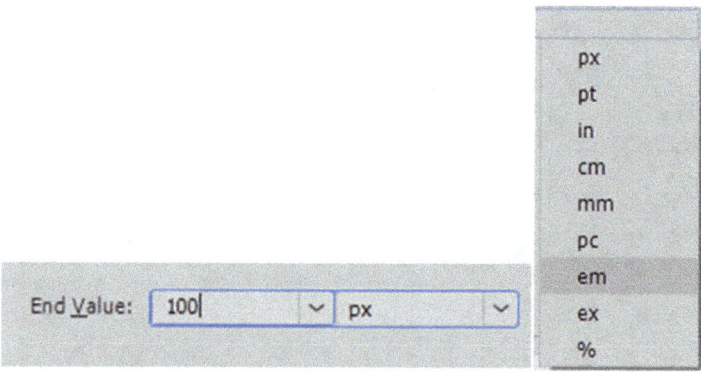

Figure 32-58. Set the end value

Once the end value is entered, press Enter or Return on your keyboard to confirm it.

Lastly, you want to determine where the CSS transition is placed: in this document or a new style sheet file. Refer to Figure 32-59.

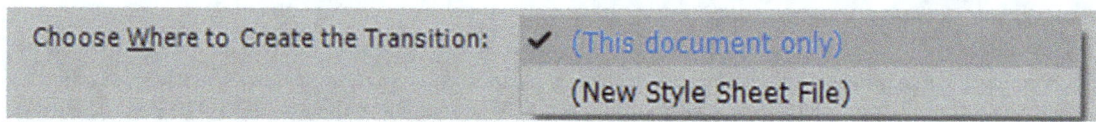

Figure 32-59. Determine where you want the CSS to appear internal or external

851

CHAPTER 32 ■ WORKING WITH CSS

If you are experimenting, I recommend keeping your transition in a new style sheet file. After you have perfected it, copy it into your final CSS file with your other CSS.

You may want to keep all your CSS transitions in a separate CSS file to keep them organized and separate from other CSS; the choice is up to you. Just make sure that the external file links correctly to your document.

It is much easier to type or select these options in Dreamweaver rather than type everything by hand in Code view. When you are done, click the Create Transition button. If you receive a warning, it may be because you did not add something to a text field, so follow the instructions and then click the button again. Refer to Figure 32-60.

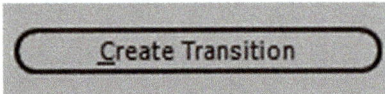

Figure 32-60. Click the Create Transition button to confirm the transition settings

Once you exit the dialog box, Dreamweaver generates your CSS transition in (short form) based on the setting you provided in the current document or in a new CSS file.

To remove a transition from the panel, when selected, use the minus (–) icon. You have options for what you want to remove. You can remove the whole transition or the class for the <div> tags or elements. Refer to Figure 32-61.

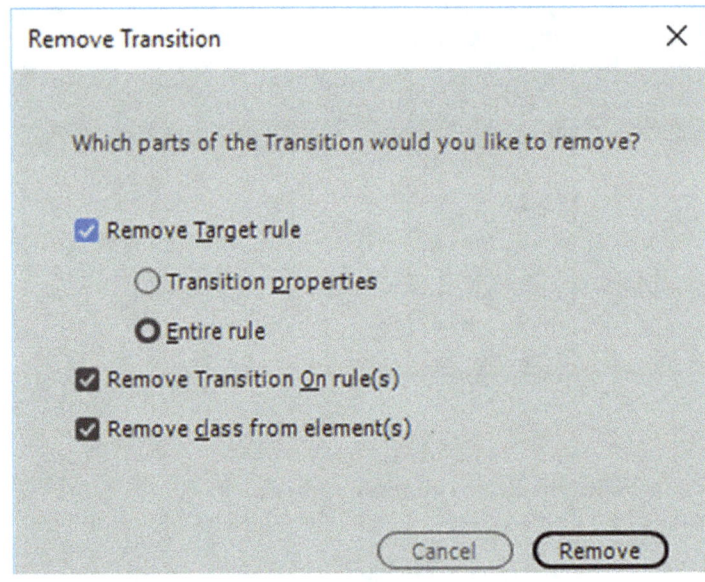

Figure 32-61. Remove Transition dialog box

When a rule like :hover is selected in the Transitions panel, you can then use the Pencil icon to edit it further. The Edit transition dialog box is very similar to the New Transition dialog box, but its default setting is "Use a different transition for each property" if there are multiple properties. Refer to Figure 32-62.

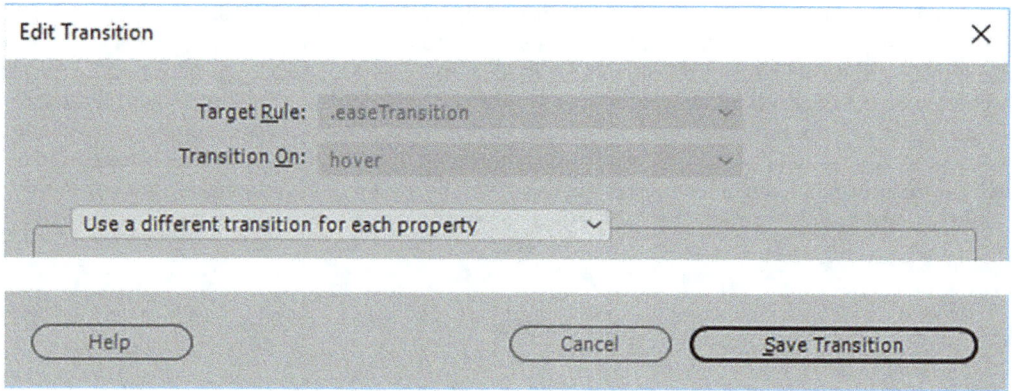

Figure 32-62. *Edit Transition dialog box*

When done editing, click Save Transitions to save the changes. When you switch to Live view, the new content should be functioning automatically.

■ **Note** If you noticed that you applied the class to the wrong tag, for instance <body>, you can delete it in Code view. Then select the correct tag, and using the Properties panel, apply the class to the correct <div> tag.

The final code might look like this:

```
.color-alter{
    width: 50px;
    height: 30px;
    background-color: aqua;
    -webkit-transition: all 2s linear 2s;
    -o-transition: all 2s linear 2s;
    transition: all 2s linear 2s;
}
.color-alter:hover {
    height: 200px;
background-color:#FF0004;
}
```

Next, you look at the third type of CSS3 animation: transforms.

CSS Transforms 2D and 3D: It's All About Perspective

Transforms let us do some amazing things with <div> and semantic elements. In combination with CSS animations (from, to) or CSS transitions that use the :hover pseudo class, you can translate, rotate, scale, and skew elements in two dimensions (x and y) or in three dimensions (x, y and z). The <div> or element changes shape, size, and position. Unfortunately, there are not a lot of examples available in the Snippets panel other than Reverse Text Using CSS and Rotate and Element (3D transform).

You can find more examples on the W3Schools website at www.w3schools.com/css/css3_2dtransforms.asp and www.w3schools.com/css/css3_3dtransforms.asp.

Because transforms are newer, they rely on vendor prefixes for older browsers, such as -webkit-, -ms-, or -o-. Always check which prefixes should be added for any new CSS3 elements to reach the largest audience; for example, as -ms-transform: translate(50px, 100px); for Microsoft Edge users. At some point, when all the modern browsers agree, you just have to write transform: translate(50px, 100px); without the vendor prefix.

To begin a transform, you need to have a starting width and height for your class that is attached to the <div> tag. Then below that, add the transform properties; for example,

```
.shape {
    width: 200px;
    height: 100px;
    background-color: yellow;
    /*transforms below*/
    -ms-transform: scale(0.5,0.5); /* IE 9 */
    -webkit-transform: scale(0.5,0.5); /* Safari */
    transform: scale(0.5,0.5); /* Standard syntax */
}
```

2D Transform

Let's look at the properties of the 2D transform.

- **transform:** Applies a 2D or 3D transformation to an element or <div>.
- **transform-origin(x%,y%):** Allows you to change the position on transformed elements. It must be used with the transform property. You can use negative and positive presents or values, 0% is the default; for example,

```
div {
    transform: rotate(45deg);
    transform-origin: 20% 40%;
}
```

Other values are x (left, center, right and length) and y (top, center, bottom and length). Each property can then have functions applied to it.

- **matrix(n,n,n,n,n,n):** A 2D transformation, using a matrix of six values, combines the 2D transform methods into one; for example, matrix(scaleX(),skewY(),skewX(),scaleY(),translateX(),translateY())looks something like transform: matrix(1, -0.3, 0, 1, 0, 0);. Note that rotation appears as a separate property.
- **translate(x,y):** A 2D translation, moving the element from its current position along the x axis and the y axis; for example, transform: translate(20px, 100px);. Moves 20 pixels right and 100 pixels down.
- **translateX(n):** A 2D translation moving the element along the x axis.
- **translateY(n):** A 2D translation moving the element along the y axis.

- **scale(x,y):** A 2D scale transformation changing the elements width and height or making the <div> larger or smaller; for example, transform: scale(3, 4);. This would make the <div> three times the original width and four times the original height. To decrease a <div> to a quarter of its size you could write, transform: scale(0.25, 0.25);.

- **scaleX(n):** A 2D scale transformation changing the element's width.

- **scaleY(n):** A 2D scale transformation changing the element's height.

- **rotate(angle):** A 2D rotation; the angle is specified in the parameter as clockwise or counter-clockwise; for example, transform: rotate(20deg);. If you change to –20deg, this rotates it in a counter-clockwise direction.

- **skew(x-angle,y-angle):** A 2D skew transformation along the x axis and the y axis; for example, transform: skew(30deg, 10deg);. When a second parameter is not written, it is assumed to be 0 degrees. A negative degree skew the X or Y – axis of the <div> in the opposite direction.

- **skewX(angle):** A 2D skew transformation along the x axis.

- **skewY(angle):** A 2D skew transformation along the y axis.

You can add any of these functions in one transform property, such as

```
transform: rotate(20deg) scale(3,4);
```

When a transform is added to a CSS Transition panel and you select edit or new, it is added as another property that appears in the hover area of the class. Refer to Figure 32-63.

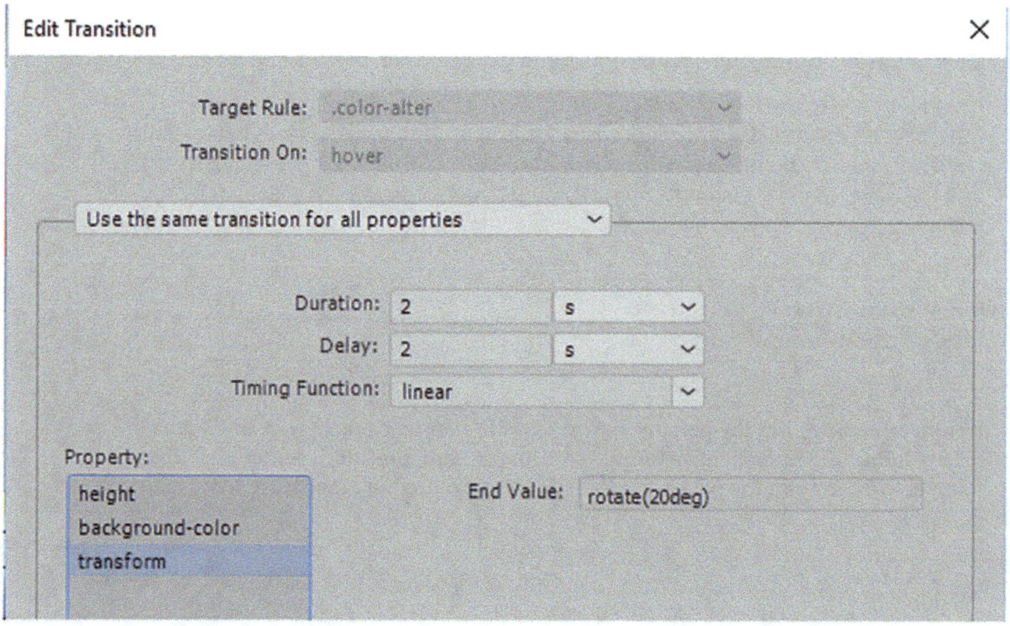

Figure 32-63. The Transition dialog box

The :hover pseudo class in Code view may look like this:

```
.color-alter:hover {
    height: 200px;
        background-color:#FF0004;
        transform: matrix(1, -0.3, 0, 1, 0, 0);
        transform: rotate(20deg);
}
```

3D Transform

Much of the same properties work with 3D transforms, except you are adding the z axis, or a third dimension. CSS3 makes the transform appear that it has changed in 3D space, and if you apply it to a transition, it makes the <div> element appear as if it is moving in a 3D way. 3D transform works with all modern browsers, but you may need to add vendor prefixes to the properties.

Let's look at the properties of the 3D transform.

- **transform:** Applies a 2D or 3D transformation to an element or <div>.
- **transform-origin(x%,y%,z):** Allows you to change the position on transformed elements. It must be used with the transform property. You can use negative and positive presents or values, 0% is the default; for example,

```
div {
    transform: rotate(45deg);
     transform-origin: 20% 40% 0;
}
```

Other values are x (left, center, right, and length), and y (top, center, bottom and length); z is just length.

- **transform-style:** The way nested elements are rendered in 3D space. This property must be with the transform to work correctly. The two main options are flat (default: child elements do not preserve the 3D position but are against the parent element) and preserve-3d(child elements preserve 3D position in their own space); for example,

```
div {
    transform: rotateY(60deg);
    transform-style: preserve-3d;
}
```

- **perspective:** Specifies the perspective on how 3D elements are viewed, and alters it. When defining the perspective property for an element, the child elements get the perspective view, not the parent element. For example, add perspective: 150px; :

```
.class1 {
    position: relative;
    height: 150px;
    width: 150px;
    margin: 50px;
    padding: 10px;
```

856

```
        border: 1px solid black;
        -webkit-perspective: 150px; /* Safari 4-8  */
        perspective: 150px;
}
.class2 {
        padding: 50px;
        position: absolute;
        border: 1px solid black;
        background-color: red;
        -webkit-transform: rotateX(45deg); /* Safari 3-8  */
        transform: rotateX(45deg);
}
```

Then apply it to the <div> tags.

```
<div class="class1">
  <div class="class2">WELCOME</div>
</div>
```

It is the inner class (class2) or child that receives the perspective and not (class1), which in this case is the parent.

The perspective property only affects 3D transformed elements. You can use this property with the perspective-origin property, which allows you to change the bottom position of 3D elements. Length (pixels) and none are the two values.

- **perspective-origin(x%,y%):** The bottom position of 3D elements for the x and y axis. The child elements get the positioning, not the parent element. This element must be used with the perspective property and can only be used on 3D transform elements; for example,

```
perspective: 150px;
perspective-origin: 10% 10%;
```

Other values are x (left, center, right and length) and y (top, center, bottom and length). In both cases, 50% is the default.

- **backface-visibility:** Defines whether or not an element should be visible when not facing the screen. This is an interesting effect that allow you to rotate or reverse an image. You can also determine whether the back be visible or hidden.

This property is useful when an element is rotated. An example is playing cards that flip. Each side has an image and uses functions such as rotate or rotate3d.

```
#div1 {
    backface-visibility: hidden;
}
#div2 {
    backface-visibility: visible;
}
```

3D transform has several functions that are used with the transform property, some of which are similar, but now have the z axis.

- **matrix3d(n,n,n,n,n,n,n,n,n,n,n,n,n,n,n,n):** Defines a 3D transformation, using a 4x4 matrix of 16 values. This one requires a bit of experimentation to figure out what numbers relate to which functions, but it essentially follows the same order as the 2D transform except that now you have added a z axis. I recommend using the separate functions if you are not sure what each one is for.
- **translate3d(x,y,z):** A 3D translation or movement of the element from its current position along the x, y and z axis; for example, transform: translate3d(10px, 0, 100px). Positive values move down, right and forward while negative values move up, left and backward or smaller;
- **translateX(x):** A 3D translation using only the value for the x axis.
- **translateY(y):** A 3D translation using only the value for the y axis
- **translateZ(z):** A 3D translation using only the value for the z axis (does not allow a percentage value.)
- **scale3d(x,y,z):** A 3D scale transformation; for example, transform: scale3d(2, 0.7, 0.2);. One would be the default, but 2 would be twice the size and 0.5 would be equivalent to 50% of the size of any axis. Positive and negative numbers can be used to move the element in a different axis.
- **scaleX(x):** A 3D scale transformation giving a value for the x axis.
- **scaleY(y):** A 3D scale transformation giving a value for the y axis.
- **scaleZ(z):** A 3D scale transformation giving a value for the z axis.
- **rotate3d(x,y,z,angle):** A 3D rotation. The numbers of x, y, and z could be a coordinate of the vector shape describing an axis of rotation. Positive numbers rotate clockwise. Negative numbers are also used of you are rotating counter-clockwise; for example, transform: rotate3d(0, 1, 0, 60deg);.
- **rotateX(angle):** A 3D rotation along the x axis.
- **rotateY(angle):** A 3D rotation along the y axis.
- **rotateZ(angle):** A 3D rotation along the z axis.
- **perspective(n):** Defines a perspective view for a 3D transformed element or elements depth. Zero or lower value give a pronounced perspective while higher value creates a foreshortening; for example,

```
perspective(500px);
```

You can add any of these functions in one transform property, such as

```
transform: rotate3d(0, 1, 0, 60deg) scale(3,4,2);
```

3D transforms can be edited in the CSS Transitions panel. Refer to Figure 32-64.

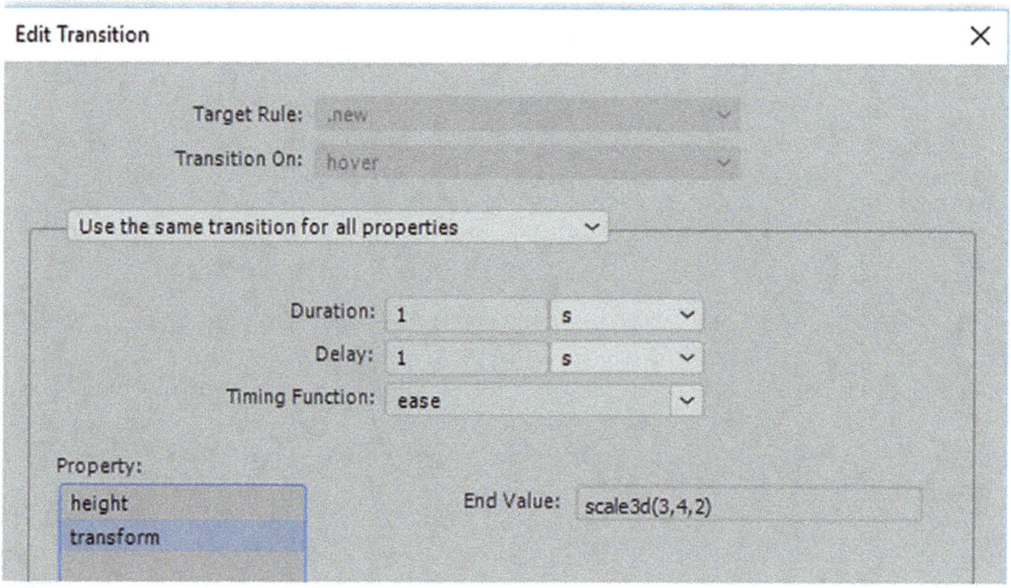

Figure 32-64. The Transition dialog box

Summary

In this chapter, you looked at how CSS can affect tags and elements. You looked at various CSS3 properties and learned how they can be edited in various panels in Dreamweaver. You also looked at animations, transitions and transforms.

In the next chapter, you look at how to enhance your site further for mobile web design.

CHAPTER 33

Working with Images for Mobile Web Design

In this chapter, you look at how to work with CSS that allows you to make your site more mobile and allows pages to float or stretch on the page, depending on what device you are viewing your website on.

> **Note** This chapter does not have any actual projects; however, you can use the files in the Part 6 folder to practice opening and viewing for this lesson. They are at https://github.com/Apress/graphics-multimedia-web-adobe-creative-cloud.

This last section on working with images <img> or the background images in CSS concerns how to work with images that may be viewed in other browser devices, like a tablet or smartphone, or even printed by the viewer. CSS and CSS3 have a variety of options that you can use to improve your layout for these situations. In Chapter 35, you look at using a library called Bootstrap, a front-end framework that is free and open source, which allows you to easily construct a mobile site and uses much of the CSS that has been discussed so far in Part 6.

CSS Floats

Sometimes you want images or a group of images to appear to float over the top of the text. This could be when you click over an image and you want to see it as a larger size (also called a *light box* or *modal image*). Or maybe a menu bar that has thumbnails with links that float along the side as you scroll down the page. There are many combinations that you can create; some of the more advanced ones may use JavaScript or jQuery along with the CSS and HTML to accomplish this. You look at JavaScript in Chapter 34; for now let's see how CSS can help with a float.

The *float* is a property that specifies an element's placement alongside its container; it allows text and inline elements to wrap around it.

Like Photoshop CC and its layers, for a <div> or semantic element to float, it needs to be above the other <div> elements.

You can move an element like a div that has a class applied to around using margin-left:auto; and margin-right:auto; to center.

```
.some-class{
margin-left: auto;
marging-right:auto;
}
```

CHAPTER 33 ■ WORKING WITH IMAGES FOR MOBILE WEB DESIGN

Or use the CSS float to move it left, right, or none.

```
.some-class{
float:left;
}
```

But none of these properties moves the element above the other elements.

The only way to do this is to use the position in conjunction with properties: top, left, bottom, right, and z-index. Figure 33-1 shows how this might look in CSS Designer panel and Code view.

Figure 33-1. Properties to position a div so that it floats above other divs in the CSS Designer panel when applied to a class

```
.float-above{
/*some other properties here*/
position: fixed;
top:200px;
left:10px;
z-index: 100;
}
```

- **Position:** A position can have a value of static, relative, fixed, absolute, or sticky.
- **Static:** Elements are static by default and they are not affected by top, left, bottom, or right properties, so the element moves to the normal flow of the page in the browser if it is made larger or smaller.
- **Relative:** Positioned normal to its relative position. If you add top, left, bottom, or right properties, it moves away from its relative position in whatever offset direction you set. And other elements may not fill the gap that is left unless they have additional CSS properties of their own.
- **Fixed:** As you see in the previous code example, it is positioned relative to the viewport of your browser. *Viewport* is important in mobile design, as you see in the next section of this chapter. *Fixed* means it always stays in the same place, even if the page is scrolled. The top, right, bottom, and left properties are used to position the element. Also, unlike relative, it does not leave a gap in the page where it normally would be located. In most cases, you do not need to add a z-index when you work with fixed, but you will see why that property is useful.
- **Absolute:** Positioned relative to the nearest positioned ancestor or parent element. If there are no parent elements, the <body> tag becomes the default and moves along with the scrolling page.
- **Sticky:** A relatively new CSS3 value that only the most modern browsers support. And it is positioned based on the user's scroll position. A sticky element could be relative or fixed, depending on the position of the scroll. It is positioned relative until a given offset position is met in the viewport—then it "sticks" into that place (like position:fixed). You must also specify at least one top, right, bottom, or left property for it to work.

Note In Dreamweaver's CSS Designer version 2019, sticky does not show up in the options; however, if you type in Code view, then it appears. Refer to Figure 33-2.

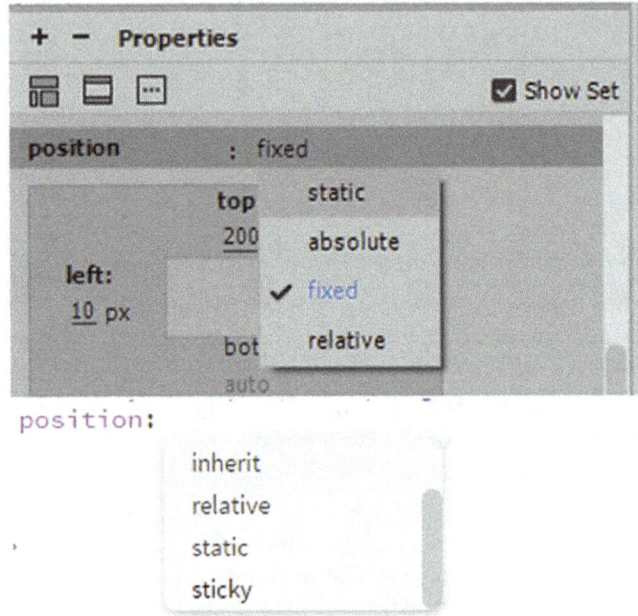

Figure 33-2. *Properties to position a div so that it floats above other divs in the CSS Designer panel when applied to a class, from the list you can choose fixed or change to another value. You can also type in Code view to get the option of sticky.*

Just remember that not all older browsers support the sticky value; make sure to check out the current vendor prefixes on W3Schools.

To learn more about positioning margins with top, bottom, left, and right check out www.w3schools.com/css/css_positioning.asp.

z-index

If you want to ensure that an element overlaps whether you are using the fixed, absolute, or relative position, use a z-index. The z-index only works with positioned elements. The z-index property specifies the stack order of an element (which element should be placed in front of, or behind, the others), just like layers in Photoshop CC or Illustrator CC.

An element can have a positive or negative stack order; a –1 places the <div> tag or element in the back, while a value of 1 places it in front. Be aware that because your website may have many elements, you may need to set a relatively high number, like 100. I find this ensures that the element is in the foreground.

One other item that is useful for cropping the image is the clip property.

Clip

Trims parts of an absolutely positioned element that contains an image in the top, right, bottom, and left; for example, clip: rect(20px,60px,200px,0px);

Other than fixed or absolute, it does not work with other position values or if an overflow property is set to visible.

Using the four rectangle coordinates, you can decide which areas of your image appear or do not appear. This is helpful when an image is larger than the containing element. The cropping of the image is nondestructive and is a better alternative than using Dreamweaver's Quick Edit tool in the Properties panel, as you saw in Chapter 31.

■ **Note** With model images or light boxes, an image that floats is often initially hidden, so it may require an additional property of display none. Also, to call up the image, you need to use additional JavaScript or jQuery. You can see many easy-to-create examples on W3Schools:

www.w3schools.com/howto/howto_js_lightbox.asp

www.w3schools.com/howto/howto_css_modal_images.asp

www.w3schools.com/howto/howto_css_modals.asp.

Later, on the Hot Glass Tango website, you see how you can use jQuery with Bootstrap to create a basic gallery.

Responsive Media Queries and the View Port

The viewport is an important part of creating websites for mobile devices. It allows you to control the user's visible area of the webpage. You can find the code for the viewport in the Insert panel in the HTML tab. Refer to Figure 33-3.

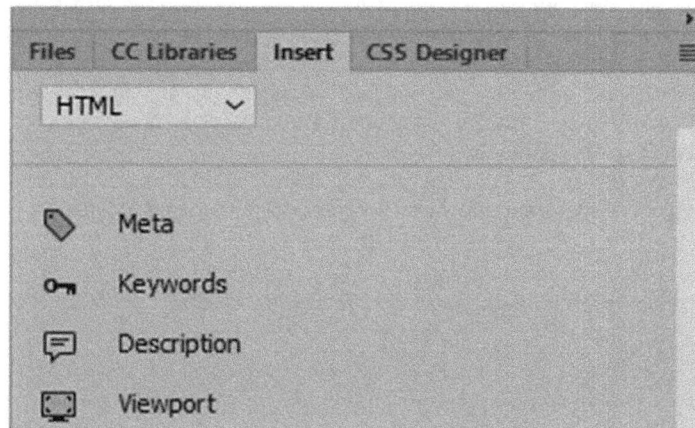

Figure 33-3. Use the Insert panel to add metadata and viewport tags

The code looks like this:

```
<meta name="viewport" content="width=device-width, initial-scale=1">
```

It is found within the <head> section of the document. This ensures that when the HTML5 pages are viewed on a tablet or smartphone, the pages scale correctly to match the device; otherwise, they may appear shrunken, and you may have difficulty zooming in and reading them.

- **Meta:** Gives the browser instructions on how to control the page's dimensions and scaling. In this case, its name attribute is viewport.
- **Content:** Sets the width of the page to follow the screen-width of the device. This can vary based on devices, but the setting to use is width=device-width.
- **Initial-scale=1:** Sets the initial zoom level when the page is first loaded by the browser. It can also be written as initial-scale=1.0; either way is OK. Figure 33-4 shows how it appears in the Properties panel.

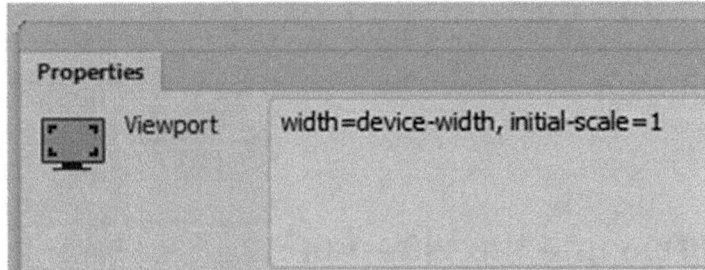

Figure 33-4. *The viewport tag in the Properties panel*

Whether you are using a laptop, tablet, or smartphone, and regardless of the screen orientation, users prefer to scroll vertically on a webpage. So, you want your pages to neatly fit and match within the screen size. While the viewport is helpful, you still need to take time to create CSS media queries for several devices. To explore media queries thoroughly requires a totally separate book. In Chapter 35, you see how to add media queries quickly using Bootstrap. In the following section you will find basics of how you can link your CSS media queries in Dreamweaver. You can also look at the Hot Glass Tango site to help you further your research for your own site, which likely has many similar media queries.

To begin, if you are starting with a new or existing HTML5 page that you intend to add external CSS to, the first thing that you need to do is go to your CSS Designer panel and add the New or Existing CSS file, as you saw in Chapter 32. Refer to Figure 33-5.

CHAPTER 33 ■ WORKING WITH IMAGES FOR MOBILE WEB DESIGN

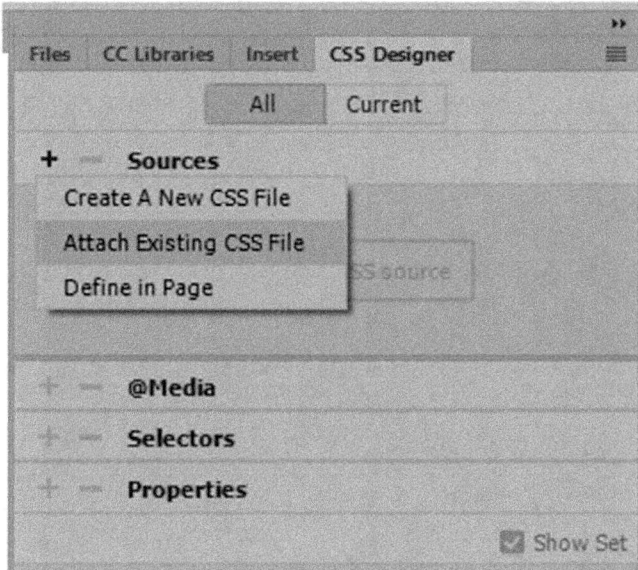

Figure 33-5. *Use the CSS Designer panel to add CSS and media queries*

You can see how to locate these files and attach them in Chapter 32.

However, this time, you want to ensure that the CSS is specifically for the screen. By default, it was originally set to all types of media, including print. In the optional section, turn down the Conditional Usage (Optional) tab to see this area. Refer to Figure 33-6.

867

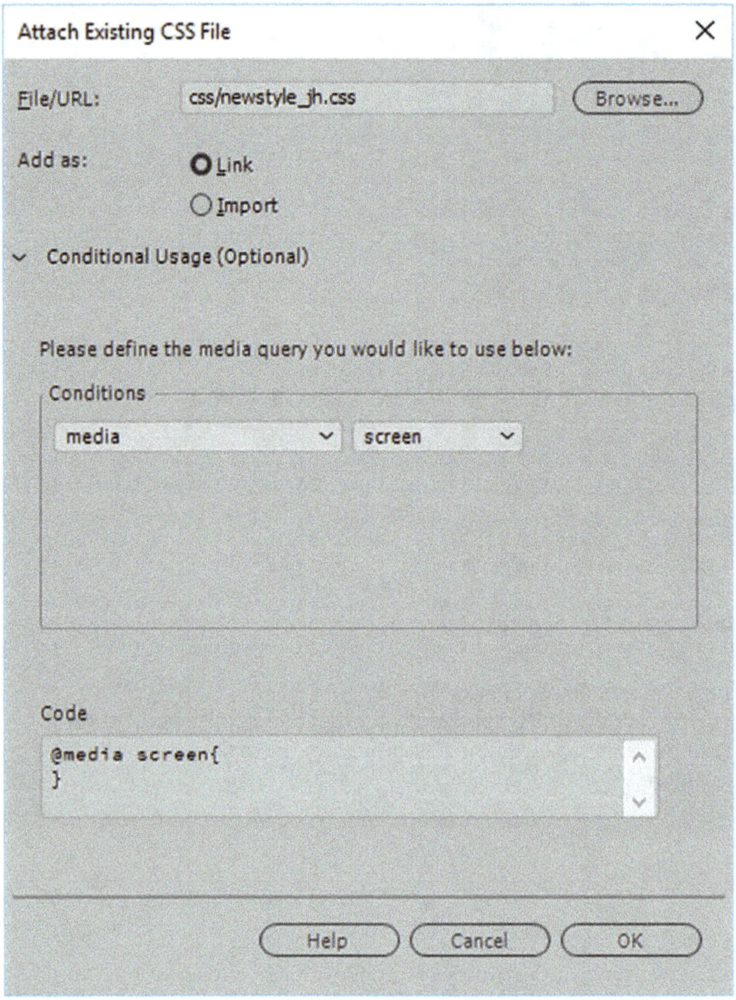

Figure 33-6. Set how you use the CSS for your website

The media is now set to screen from the drop-down menu. You could add more conditions for orientation, such as portrait or landscape by clicking the plus or minus icons. But you do not need to. Later in the chapter, you see how CSS takes care of this within the external file . Refer to Figure 33-7.

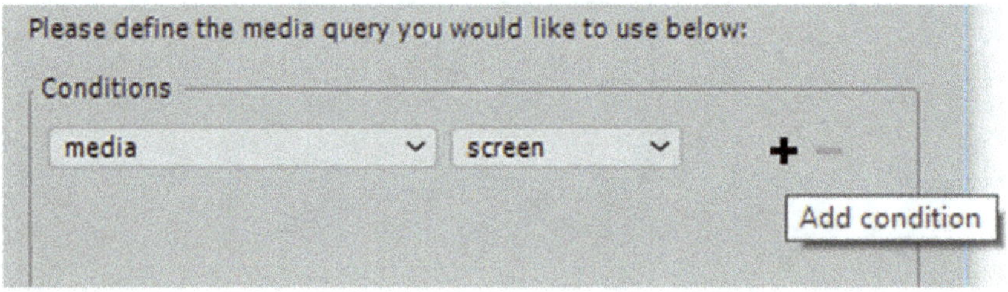

Figure 33-7. Set the CSS to be used only for screen

When you click OK, you have code in your CSS like this:

```
<link href="css/newstyle_jh.css" rel="stylesheet" type="text/css" media="screen">
```

Notice how an attribute of media="screen" was added to the <link> tag in the <head> section.

So why would you do this? Is not all CSS already for the screen? No, some CSS can be used for printers as well, just as you would print a Microsoft Word or a PDF document, you can use CSS to print HTML pages so that they format neatly. Originally many online catalogs and archived manuscripts were not meant to be published on the web, but for research purposes, viewers may want to print them. CSS with HTML can be a reliable way to keep your documents in a standard format for the viewer to print. You look at this briefly at the end of this chapter, but essentially, you can set separate CSS that is only used for printing devices so that all or certain pages can print correctly when you choose Print or Print Preview. Refer to Figure 33-8.

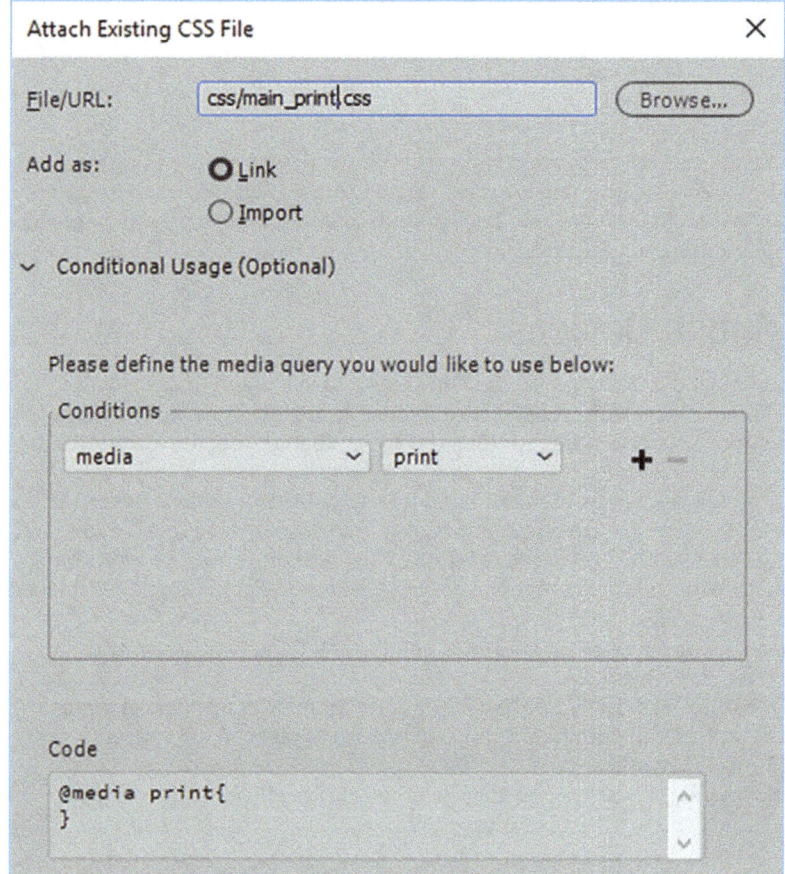

Figure 33-8. *Set the CSS to be used only for print and not for screen*

You then have two lines in the <head>, like this:

```
<link href="css/newstyle_jh.css" rel="stylesheet" type="text/css" media="screen">

<link href="css/ main_print.css" rel="stylesheet" type="text/css" media="print">
```

You can see how this appears in the CSS Designer panel, and on links on the page. Refer to Figure 33-9.

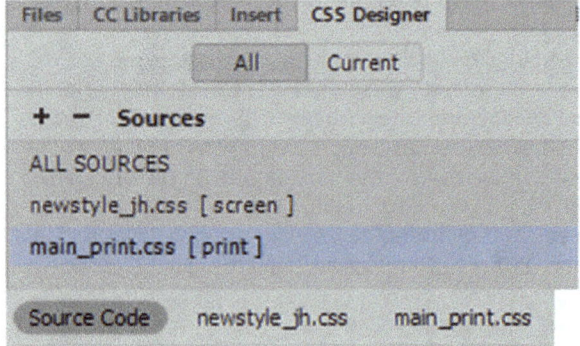

Figure 33-9. Adding print and screen CSS to a page

For the moment, you focus on the screen CSS.

Before you begin adding media queries, it's important that you take time in the early planning stages to decide what types of devices and browsers you are going to target. You may not want the exact same layout for each device. This can become apparent in files that have backgrounds or slices. Suddenly, you'll notice items don't fit correctly in the same location for each device.

Image Slices and Mobile Devices

As we saw in Photoshop (Part2) and Illustrator (Part3), you can add slices as background images to divs. While this may be OK for images viewed on desktop computers, you must scale in the browser for a tablet or smartphone the images can get really jumbled because the <div> order may change and move around in the device's browser.

In designing a website, it is critical to see how your background images perform in different browser sizes. For tablets and smartphones, it is better to have repeatable background patterns or a solid color rather than have photographic background images scale accurately at all sizes. In addition, it uses less processing power for those devices and your site loads quicker. For mobile devices, a better use of photographic images is for a gallery or an informational how-to page.

So regardless of whether you are using background images or not, the first thing to do is use grids or columns to show how your basic layout is going to flow.

W3Schools (www.w3schools.com/css/css_rwd_grid.asp) has a good example of this type of layout. Another good program to work with is the Gridulator (www.gridulator.com) if you need a background to work with in your Photoshop or Illustrator layouts.

Grid view works with box-sizing when you use the *, which covers all tags or elements; for example:

```
* {
    box-sizing: border-box;
}
.header {
    border: 1px solid red;
    padding: 15px;
}
.menu {
    width: 25%;
    float: left;
```

```
    padding: 15px;
    border: 1px solid red;
}
```

box-sizing: border-box; makes sure that the padding and border are included in the total width and height of the elements when you work with percentages of width.

However, depending on the number of columns, you may want to write it in a more intuitive way. With different classes controlling the layout of each column division; for example, you may write a 12-column layout like this:

```
* {
    box-sizing: border-box;
}
.header {
    border: 1px solid red;
    padding: 15px;
}
.row::after {
    content: "";
    clear: both;
    display: table;
}
[class*="col-"] {
    float: left;
    padding: 15px;
    border: 1px solid red;
}
.col-1 {width: 8.33%;}
.col-2 {width: 16.66%;}
.col-3 {width: 25%;}
.col-4 {width: 33.33%;}
.col-5 {width: 41.66%;}
.col-6 {width: 50%;}
.col-7 {width: 58.33%;}
.col-8 {width: 66.66%;}
.col-9 {width: 75%;}
.col-10 {width: 83.33%;}
.col-11 {width: 91.66%;}
.col-12 {width: 100%;}
```

It is a common practice to use a 12-column grid layout; each column is 8.33% of the total. The total width of the document is 12, or 100%. Depending on your target audience, the largest size of the site may be 1600 pixels or larger. You then apply different column classes to specific <div> tags to move the page around. This affects how each shifts.

```
<div class=col-3"></div>
```

In the Hot Glass Tango website, the CSS uses a similar kind of layout:

```
<div class="col-lg-6 offset-lg-3">
```

CHAPTER 33 ■ WORKING WITH IMAGES FOR MOBILE WEB DESIGN

Bootstrap has much of this layout predesigned in the CSS, so all you need to do is make modifications to the layout, which you look at in more detail in Chapter 35.

Once you have designed a rough idea of what you want each layout to look like, the next step is to add media queries.

Media Queries (Mobile-First)

Media queries are useful when modifying your site for a device that has specific screen resolution parameters. They are very similar to the conditions media="screen" that you set up in the HTML page, except that you can set multiple ones inside one external CSS rather than have to write alternate conditions and attach several external CSS files for the screen.

If you are building for desktops, tablets, and smartphones, depending on the dimensions, you create three media queries.

```
body {
    background-color: green;
/* other base properties*/
}

@media only screen and (max-width: 500px) {
    body {
        background-color: blue;
/* other properties for this size*/

    }
}
```

The @media only screen and (max-width: 500px) could be considered a break point; if you use this code, the background suddenly changes color when a max-width or maximum width reaches 500 pixels. In this case, there the default or base and the breakpoint which is within its own brackets. Using one media query works OK for two changes; however, you want to design for three. When working with mobile design, it is better to think about the mobile-first approach and then work your way down in the CSS to larger sizes.

Figure 33-10 shows how it can appear in the CSS Designer panel.

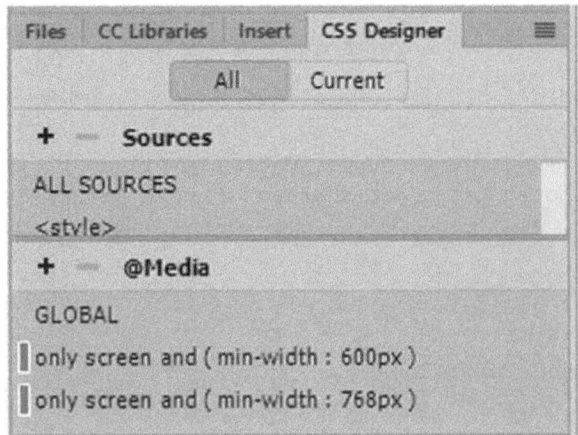

Figure 33-10. *View and add media queries to CSS Designer*

Figure 33-11 show how a page appears in Live mode; you can clearly see the breakpoints.

Figure 33-11. *How media queries appear in the Preview panel*

```
body {
    background-color: green;
/*other mobile and default properties for all*/
}

@media only screen and (min-width: 600px) {
    body {
        background-color: blue;
/*other tablet properties*/
    }
}

@media only screen and (min-width: 768px) {
 body {
        background-color: red;
/*other  desktop computer properties*/
    }
}
```

This time I used min-width or minimum width to alert at what breakpoint the changes occur.

You do this because rather than changing styles when the width gets smaller than 768 pixels (max-width), you should change the design when the width gets larger than 768 pixels (min-width). This makes it a mobile-first design.

You can add as many breakpoints as you require for each device. Sometimes your layout may need some intermediate breaks, but most times, four or five media queries may be all you need, depending on your target audience.

You can also have a set of CSS properties that only apply when the browser window is wider than its height, also called *landscape orientation*.

```
@media only screen and (orientation: landscape) {
    body {
/*other properties*/
        background-color: lightblue;
    }
}
```

This might be an option if the tablet or smartphone is turned horizontally.

As you saw in the earlier CSS of this section class columns can be added this time to each of the media queries.

```css
* {
    box-sizing: border-box;
}
.row::after {
    content: "";
    clear: both;
    display: table;
}
[class*="col-"] {
    float: left;
    padding: 15px;
}
html {
    font-family: "Arial", sans-serif;
}
.header {
    background-color: #9933cc;
    color: #ffffff;
    padding: 15px;
}
.menu ul {
    list-style-type: none;
    margin: 0;
    padding: 0;
}
.menu li {
    padding: 8px;
    margin-bottom: 7px;
    background-color: #33b5e5;
    color: #ffffff;
    box-shadow: 0 1px 3px rgba(0,0,0,0.12), 0 1px 2px rgba(0,0,0,0.24);
}
.menu li:hover {
    background-color: #0099cc;
}
.aside {
    background-color: #33b5e5;
    padding: 15px;
    color: #ffffff;
    text-align: center;
    font-size: 1em;
    box-shadow: 0 1px 3px rgba(0,0,0,0.12), 0 1px 2px rgba(0,0,0,0.24);
}
.footer {
    background-color: #0099cc;
    color: #ffffff;
    text-align: center;
    font-size: 0.5em;
    padding: 16px;
}
```

```css
/* For mobile and smartphones: */
[class*="col-"] {
    width: 100%;
}
@media only screen and (min-width: 600px) {
    /* For tablets: */
    .col-tb-1 {width: 8.33%;}
    .col-tb-2 {width: 16.66%;}
    .col-tb-3 {width: 25%;}
    .col-tb-4 {width: 33.33%;}
    .col-tb-5 {width: 41.66%;}
    .col-tb-6 {width: 50%;}
    .col-tb-7 {width: 58.33%;}
    .col-tb-8 {width: 66.66%;}
    .col-tb-9 {width: 75%;}
    .col-tb-10 {width: 83.33%;}
    .col-tb-11 {width: 91.66%;}
    .col-tb-12 {width: 100%;}
}
@media only screen and (min-width: 768px) {
    /* For desktop: */
    .col-1 {width: 8.33%;}
    .col-2 {width: 16.66%;}
    .col-3 {width: 25%;}
    .col-4 {width: 33.33%;}
    .col-5 {width: 41.66%;}
    .col-6 {width: 50%;}
    .col-7 {width: 58.33%;}
    .col-8 {width: 66.66%;}
    .col-9 {width: 75%;}
    .col-10 {width: 83.33%;}
    .col-11 {width: 91.66%;}
    .col-12 {width: 100%;}
}
```

Again, the base (global) and mobile settings are taken care of first; followed by the tablet, which is the next largest; and finally, the desktop computer.

Using media queries, you can see how a webpage on the Hot Glass Tango site changes when the browser window is compressed and expanded. With Bootstrap, additional sizes of even larger screens were added.

For more information, visit www.w3schools.com/css/css_rwd_mediaqueries.asp.

Scaling Images

Once you have worked out each of your layouts for each breakpoint and added colors or background images to your elements and <div> tags, the next step is to add images to your page. Unlike a static desktop site where images may remain roughly the same size, images for a mobile site need to shrink and/or grow as the browser changes for each device. In some cases, such as the tablet and smartphone, you may want to exclude or have low-res background images to speed download to the browser. You may still want your viewers to see the product images. You can scale your images using CSS. An <img> tag can be set in CSS to

```css
img {
width:100%;
height: auto;
}
```

This way, the image scales up or down and the height scales proportionately along with it. If it scales upward too much, the image loses its quality, which is not what you want.

So, the best choice is to change it to the property max-width with a value of 100%.

```css
img {
max-width:100%;
height: auto;
}
```

Max-width stops the image from scaling beyond 100%, but it can be scaled down, which is OK when it comes to quality.

Scaling a div with a Background Image

A background image can also be scaled. In a <div> or semantic element, you can use properties such as background-repeat and background-size to control how the image expands and contracts. This is good if you want to use it with CSS animation.

```css
div {
    width: 100%;
    height: 400px;
    background-image: url(images/img-name.jpg);
    background-repeat: no-repeat;
    background-size: contain;
    border: 1px solid red;
}
```

Setting the size to "contain" lets the background image scale and tries to fit the content area while maintaining the aspect ratio.

Remember, a setting of no repeat stops the image from repeating in the background and constrains its size, keeping it always visible. If you want the background to fill the area and are not worried about distortion or cropping, then background-size: cover; is a good option; however, part of your image may be clipped with this setting. If you have more than one image in the background, you can use them together.

```css
background: url(images/img_one.gif), url(images/image_two.jpg);
    background-repeat: no-repeat;
    background-size: contain, cover;
```

Loading a Different Image Based on Media Queries

Regardless of whether the image is in the background or an <img> tag, sometimes you don't want to load the same image on a smartphone or a tablet due to how the image flows on the page. You can add different backgrounds to your media queries depending on what device you are targeting; for example:

```
body {
    background-repeat: no-repeat;
    background-image: url(images/img_small.jpg);
/* default and mobile*/
}

/* For width 400px and larger: */
@media only screen and (min-width: 400px) {
    body {
        background-image: url(images/img_large.jpg);
    }
}
```

Remember to keep using the mobile-first method and test your images in different browsers and devices to make sure that they are changing and shifting correctly.

■ **Note** Another option is to use min-device-width, which checks the width of the actual device rather than the width of the browser (min-width). Keep in mind that if you are doing testing on your desktop computer, min-width shows you the changes as you expand and contract your browser; but with min-device-width, you not see the contraction unless you are testing on specific devices of that size.

```
@media only screen and (min-device-width: 400px) {
    body {
        background-image: url(images/img_large.jpg);
    }
}
```

This is optional; for now, just stick with min-width as I did for Hot Glass Tango.

Another option with mobile design is the <picture> element, which was discussed in Chapter 31. See www.w3schools.com/css/css_rwd_images.asp.

As with images, you can scale video using a similar process; you look at this in Chapter 36.

Dreamweaver offers Bootstrap, a CSS library, so you do not have to create your entire mobile-first web design from scratch. Dreamweaver offers some helpful examples that you can use in the File ➤ New and Insert panel, which takes away a lot of the labor of building a new layout each time and speeds up the design process. You'll look at how you can access the Bootstrap framework in Chapter 35.

If you don't want to use Bootstrap, you can use some of the responsive design snippets in the Snippets panel. Refer to Figure 33-12.

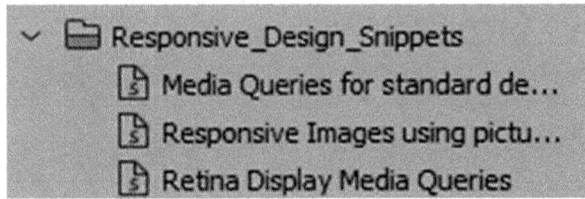

Figure 33-12. *The Snippets panel offers some responsive snippets for the design of mobile sites*

In addition, you can use Dreamweaver's templates to speed up the process of working with mobile design; you look at those in Chapter 35, but first let's finish up with the CSS.

Column Count

Another CSS3 feature that you can add to a <div> or semantic element is *column count*. As with any tag, you can add images to flow along with the text or as a background. Columns can be adjusted by their count or the number of columns they have. This can be altered each time you set a new media query. You might style your text in a laptop to have a column count of 3, a tablet a column count of 2, and a smartphone a column count of 1, and then the images flow with the text to fit that layout. Note that the other properties of the columns are fill, gap rule, span, and width.

```
div{
column-count: 3;
}
```

For more information, visit www.w3schools.com/cssref/css3_pr_column-count.asp.

CSS for Print with CSS Designer Panel

As with mobile devices, it is a clever idea to design some CSS so that most people could successfully print your webpages with their home printer on a letter-sized sheet (8.5×11).

As you saw in Figure 33-8, with the CSS Designer panel, you can add another external CSS file to your head section for print, in the Conditions section of the Attach new or existing CSS file dialog box as seen earlier in Figure 33-5.

With print, you don't have to add various sized media queries; however, make sure that the pages neatly format so that they print successfully on a portrait letter-sized page.

You can look at the example of the CSS in the Hot Glass Tango website's colorsglass.html and main_print.css. Because it is set to a print media, you never see its effects in the screen or browsers. The only time you preview it is when you choose File ➤ Print Preview in the browser. This gives you an idea of how the layout appears. Now you might think that in a paperless society, web designers should only focus on the mobile design. There may be important records, tables, and even images a person may want to print out from a specific page on a website in color or black and white.

When working with webpages, in a variety of viewport sizes, none of these may be suitable when you print the page on many sheets of paper. In this case, you need to create a fixed width since paper is not fluid. In some cases, Bootstrap has some prebuilt media widths set like a min-width of 576 pixels with various properties applied. But you may need to adjust this in your own CSS file, depending on the printer and margins you require. If you only want to print out certain areas of a page, you can exclude those <div> tags or elements with an additional class, such as

```
div{
display:none;
}
```

Now that element is completely removed from the page. This might be good for removing banners and navigation that the viewer does not want to print.

As an added feature, if you want some background images to only print in black and white, you could change the image source to the linked image that is black and white or a simplified line drawing that takes up less toner.

```
.banner{
background-image: url('img_bw.gif');
}
```

One other formatting tip is to use the *page break*.

```
page-break-after: always;
```

I find this property useful if I am concerned about text breaking from the heading or after a specified element. Other related properties are page-break-before:always; (before a specified element) and page-break-inside:avoid; (if possible avoid a break inside of the element).

Choose File ➤ Print Preview from your browser if you need to see if your pages are formatting correctly.

Now that we have finished our main discussion on CSS and images as they relate to mobile design, let's see how images interact with the third type of coding, known as JavaScript, along with Dreamweaver CC and its panels.

Summary

In this chapter, you looked at mobile-first design and some CSS, such as floats, media queries, and column counts that allow you to scale your images, <div> tags, and semantic elements for the screen. You also saw that CSS can be used for print media so that your images look their best no matter which media queries you use.

In the next chapter, you take a brief look at JavaScript and how it interacts with images in Dreamweaver.

CHAPTER 34

What Is JavaScript?

In this chapter, you look at how JavaScript is used with images and <div> tags to add further movement to some elements where CSS may not be enough.

> **Note** This chapter does not have any actual projects; however, you can use the files in the Part 6 folder to practice opening and viewing for this lesson. They are at https://github.com/Apress/graphics-multimedia-web-adobe-creative-cloud.

As you have seen, you can create action and movement with the new CSS3 features, such as animation. CSS can't do everything just yet—for some things you need JavaScript, especially if you must target older browsers that do not accept CSS3. JavaScript is used to compensate for some types of movement or styling that older browsers may not recognize.

In combination with HTML, it is one of the easiest programming languages to learn, and it can range in skill level from basic to complex. JavaScript code should not be confused with Java code, which is for programmers of applications. JavaScript only requires the browser to operate, while Java requires both the browser and a virtual machine (software and hardware) to compile.

JavaScript is an event-driven language, which means that it responds to actions taken by the user. It programs the behavior of webpages.

Object + Event = Action

Like CSS, it is written

- Inline within a tag in the <body>

    ```
    <button type="button" onclick="myFunction()">Try it</button>
    ```

- As separate section within the <body>

    ```
    <script>
    document.getElementById("demo").innerHTML = "My First JavaScript";
    </script>
    ```

- Into the <head> tag as internal JavaScript

    ```
    <script>
    function myFunction() {
        document.getElementById("demo").innerHTML = "Paragraph changed.";
    }
    </script>
    ```

- An external file (myfile.js) that is linked in the <head> with a link to a script within your site or on someone else's site if you are using their JavaScript Library.

```
<script src="myScript.js"></script>
<script src="https://www.somesite.com/javacsripts/myScript.js"></script>
```

■ **Note** The script within the external JavaScript file does not reside inside <script> tags. Also, you should not link to someone else's external script from a website, unless you have permission to do so.

JavaScript code is often linked to a

- tag: (getElementsByTagName)
- ID: (document.getElementById)
- class: (getElementsByClassName)

If the JavaScript is going to be used multiple times, it is better to write it as an external file and save it with your other JavaScript files in a folder so that you can easily access it. You can see how this might look in the Files panel. Refer to Figure 34-1.

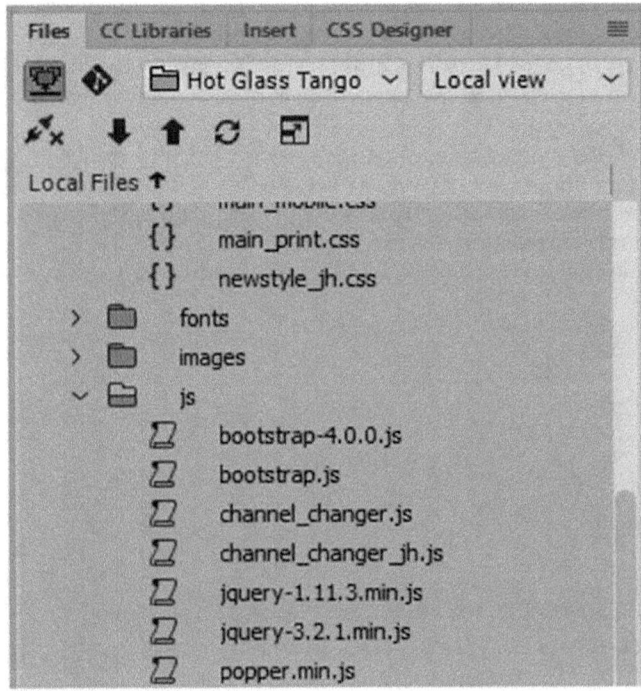

Figure 34-1. Adding JavaScript to your root folder

Regardless, you have to add some connecting JavaScript into the <body> area of the file. Since JavaScript is difficult to learn at first, it is good to look at examples of how others write the code, and then if you find a feature you like, try to replicate the order of where the <scripts> tags are placed. Overtime, as you practice, you learn to modify your own code and create your own <scripts> to suit your needs.

As with CSS, you can find many great starting examples at W3Schools (www.w3schools.com/js/default.asp), which you can copy into Dreamweaver's code editor to modify.

It takes time to learn JavaScript and all its features. If you are new to JavaScript, don't expect to learn it all in one day. Reading the tutorials or finding a book on the basics is very useful in getting started.

In this book, I point out a few basic settings for working with images, which you can use in Dreamweaver to get started.

Creating a New JavaScript File

You can create your first external JavaScript file via File ➤ New. Refer to Figure 34-2.

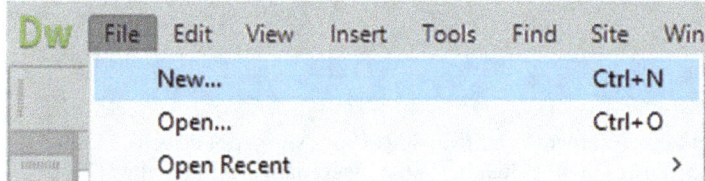

Figure 34-2. *Create a new external JavaScript file*

In the New Document window, choose JavaScript as the document type. Refer to Figure 34-3.

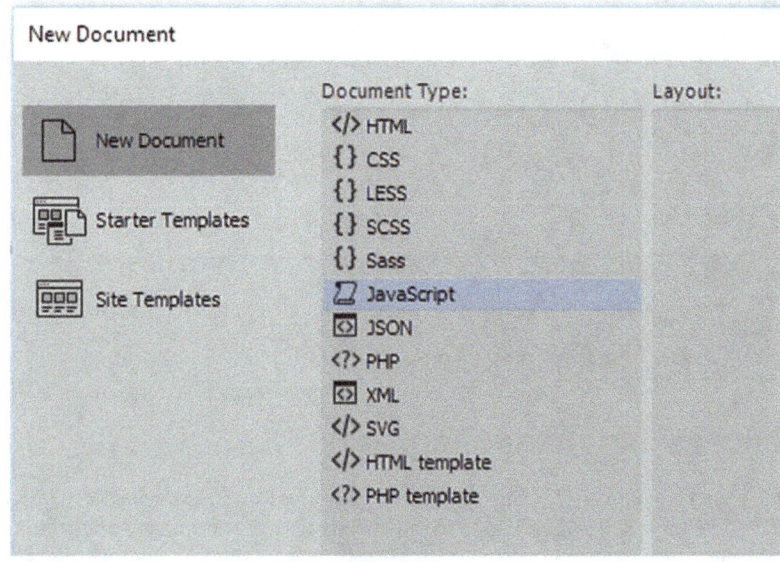

Figure 34-3. *Create a new JavaScript file*

JavaScript is code and there are no additional preview or feature settings. Once selected, click the Create button in the bottom right of the New Document dialog box. Refer to Figure 34-4.

Figure 34-4. *Click Create to create a new JavaScript file*

This creates a JS file. There is nothing within this file other than a comment line that starts with //. For longer comment lines, you can write a comment like this: /* This is a longer comment*/. Refer to Figure 34-5.

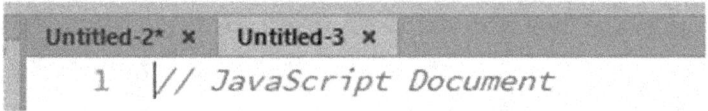

Figure 34-5. *A new external JavaScript file*

You would then copy your JavaScript here and save your file inside of your site's root directory folder.

For JavaScript, you can add a <script> tag link in the <head> via the Insert panel found in the HTML tab. Refer to Figure 34-6. In Code view of your HTML page, place the cursor in the location that you want the script to appear, and click the Script icon in the Insert panel.

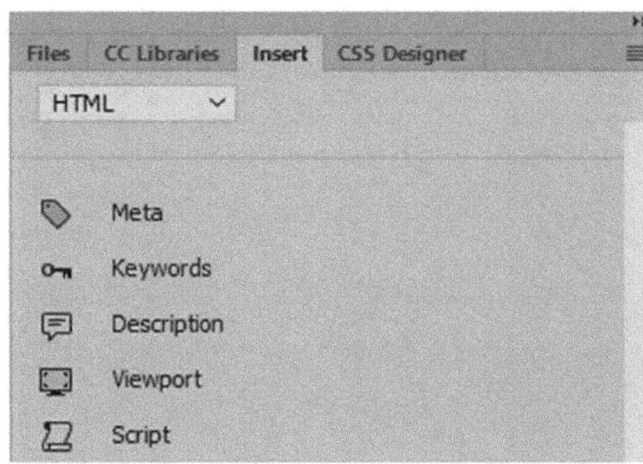

Figure 34-6. *Add a Script to your <head> area*

The Select File dialog box opens, and you can search in your JavaScript folder for the external file.

Once you locate the file, select it and click OK; it is then added to the <head> with the script tag and the link.

```
<head>
<meta charset="utf-8">
<meta name="viewport" content="width=device-width, initial-scale=1">
```

CHAPTER 34 ■ WHAT IS JAVASCRIPT?

```
<title>Home Page</title>
        <script type="text/javascript" src="js/somescript.js"></script>
</head>
```

■ **Note** An extra attribute of type="text/javascript" is sometimes added to the <script> tag; this helps older browsers identify that this is JavaScript, but it is optional to add this in HTML5.

It also appears linked in the upper area of the document. Here you can click the icon to access it for easy editing. When done, you can then return to the Source Code icon to return to your HTML5 code. Refer to Figure 34-7.

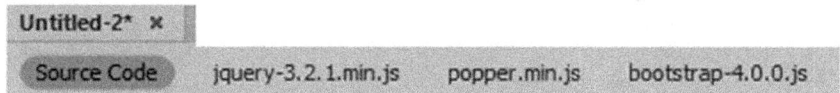

Figure 34-7. *JavaScript and jQuery files linked to the top of the file*

For the code to work correctly, ensure that the code is referenced to the correct tags, IDs, and classes in the <body> of the document.

Insert Rollover Images

You can see a basic example of working with images and JavaScript in the Insert panel in the HTML5 tab. A *rollover image* is also known as a mouseover and mouseout event. Refer to Figure 34-8.

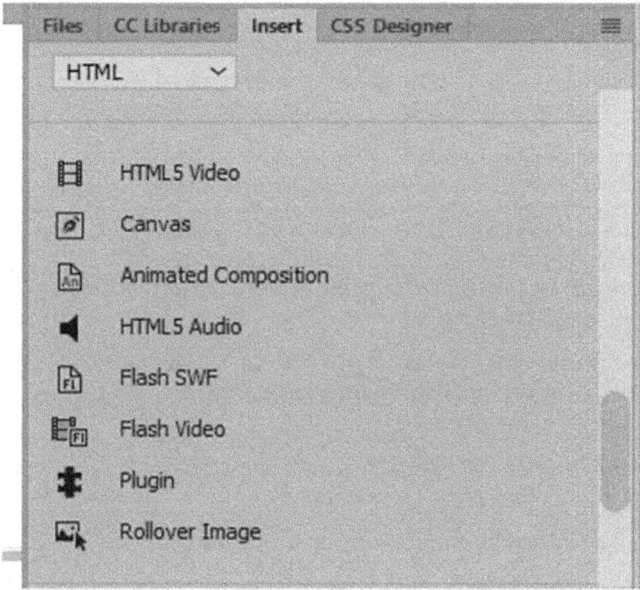

Figure 34-8. *Choose Rollover Image from the Insert panel*

885

CHAPTER 34 ■ WHAT IS JAVASCRIPT?

You can find this same command at Insert ➤ HTML ➤ Rollover Image.

You saw some examples of images that change when you add a pseudo-class or hover over them in CSS3. For a more interactive feel, you want some images to behave like buttons for navigation, or a printer button to change appearance, so a rollover image is a good option. Rollover images have two states: one when you are not hovering over them and one when you are. To add a rollover image, place the cursor somewhere inside of your HTML5 pages body in Code view and then click the Rollover Image icon in the Insert panel.

■ **Note** This rollover creation does not work by highlighting an image in Design view or Code view. You need to start with a fresh rollover image.

This brings up the Insert Rollover Image dialog box. A lot of this should look familiar from Part 2. Refer to Figure 34-9.

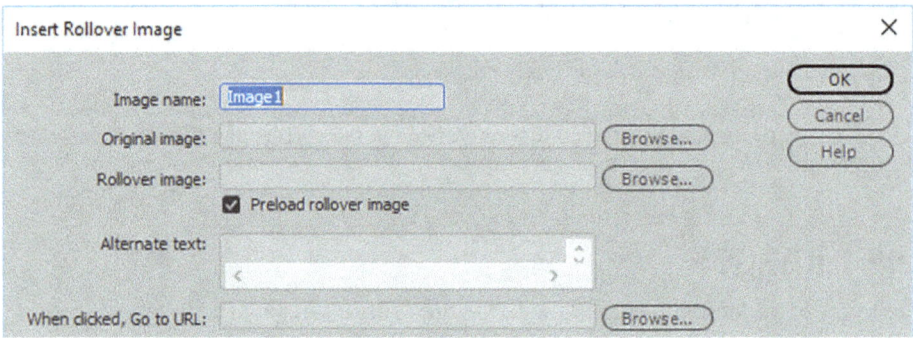

Figure 34-9. *The Insert Rollover Image dialog box*

- **Image name:** You can give the button a meaningful one word name with no spaces; this links it to the JavaScript that Dreamweaver is going to generate once you fill out each text field.

- **Original image:** The URL or location of the image you see when you are not hovering over it with your mouse. You can browse in your images file for the correct image.

- **Rollover image:** The URL or location of the image you see when you are hovering over it with your mouse. You can browse in your images file for the correct image. Notice that to keep organized, I added to the name_over or name_hover so that I know which file to match to the correct text field here.

- **Preload rollover image:** Make sure this remains checked so that it loads. This option is selected by default; it helps the images appear more quickly by preloading the rollover image. The browser then stores it in cache until the user hovers.

- **Alt text:** As with any image button, it is good to add alternate text so that screen readers for the visually disabled know what the button represents.

- **URL:** Here you can add a URL and browse within your root site or an outside site. Refer to Figure 34-10.

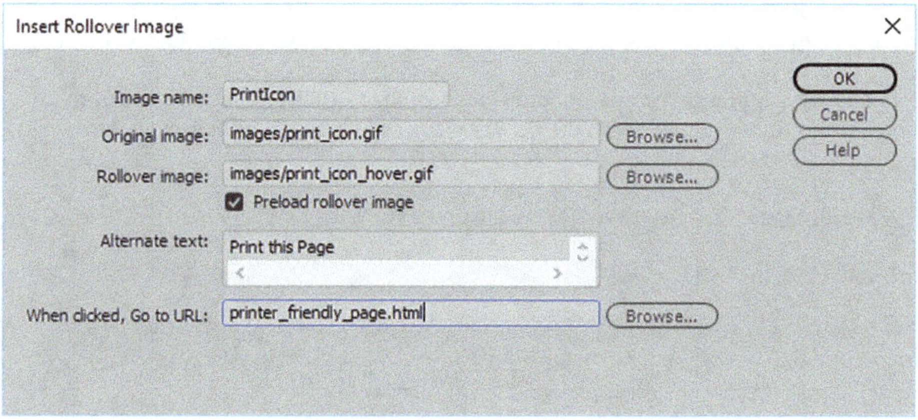

Figure 34-10. An example of how a rollover button is added to a site

Many people navigate to clickable URLs, so make sure that this links to the correct page or URL by using the Browse button. In this case, I am only using this link as dummy text to eventually replace with JavaScript, as you see shortly.

When done, click OK.

Dreamweaver generates the JavaScript for the Rollover button in the <head> and <body> sections. This is quite a bit of code in the <head>, and if you think this is taking up too much space, you could move it to an external JavaScript file. Just make sure to test that it is linked and still operating if you do. Note that the script within the <script> tags would go into the external file. Either way, it only needs to be written into the <head> once, even if you need to add two or more Rollover buttons.

```
<script type="text/javascript">
function MM_swapImgRestore() { //v3.0
  var i,x,a=document.MM_sr; for(i=0;a&&i<a.length&&(x=a[i])&&x.oSrc;i++) x.src=x.oSrc;
}
function MM_preloadImages() { //v3.0
  var d=document; if(d.images){ if(!d.MM_p) d.MM_p=new Array();
    var i,j=d.MM_p.length,a=MM_preloadImages.arguments; for(i=0; i<a.length; i++)
    if (a[i].indexOf("#")!=0){ d.MM_p[j]=new Image; d.MM_p[j++].src=a[i];}}
}

function MM_findObj(n, d) { //v4.01
  var p,i,x;  if(!d) d=document; if((p=n.indexOf("?"))>0&&parent.frames.length) {
    d=parent.frames[n.substring(p+1)].document; n=n.substring(0,p);}
  if(!(x=d[n])&&d.all) x=d.all[n]; for (i=0;!x&&i<d.forms.length;i++) x=d.forms[i][n];
  for(i=0;!x&&d.layers&&i<d.layers.length;i++) x=MM_findObj(n,d.layers[i].document);
  if(!x && d.getElementById) x=d.getElementById(n); return x;
}

function MM_swapImage() { //v3.0
  var i,j=0,x,a=MM_swapImage.arguments; document.MM_sr=new Array;
  for(i=0;i<(a.length-2);i+=3)
   if ((x=MM_findObj(a[i]))!=null){document.MM_sr[j++]=x; if(!x.oSrc)
   x.oSrc=x.src; x.src=a[i+2];}
}
    </script>
```

CHAPTER 34 ■ WHAT IS JAVASCRIPT?

This code is a collection of variables (var), conditions (if), and loops (for); each is inside of four functions (functions) that swap and restore the images as you hover and move away from them within the document.

The body tag contains some inline JavaScript that then loads (onload) rollover images. Within the body tags there is more inline JavaScript that swaps the images using events called onMouseOut and onMouseOver.

```
<body onLoad="MM_preloadImages('images/print_icon_hover.gif')">
```

Inside the body is the rest of the code.

```
<a href="printer_friendly_page.html" onMouseOut="MM_swapImgRestore()" onMouseOver="MM_swapImage('PrintIcon','','images/print_icon_hover.gif',1)"><img src="images/print_icon.gif" alt="Print this Page" width="150" height="70" id="PrintIcon"></a>
</body>
```

As you can see, Dreamweaver has added the HTML for the rollover and the URL. Since the preload setting was chosen, the preload script was added to the body so that the hover image would load faster.

As you add more rollover images or want to replace them, this can get tricky, so Dreamweaver has the Behaviors panel that makes working with JavaScript and linking images a bit easier.

Behaviors Panel

This panel is found by selecting Window ➤ Behaviors. As you work in Code view, you can click various tags or elements to reveal the behaviors that they possess. You can also add or remove behaviors by selecting and clicking the plus (+) or minus (–) icons. If you remove one by mistake, make sure to select Edit ➤ Undo right away because your rollover might stop working if you remove the code. You can also use the up and down arrows to order the behaviors. Refer to Figure 34-11.

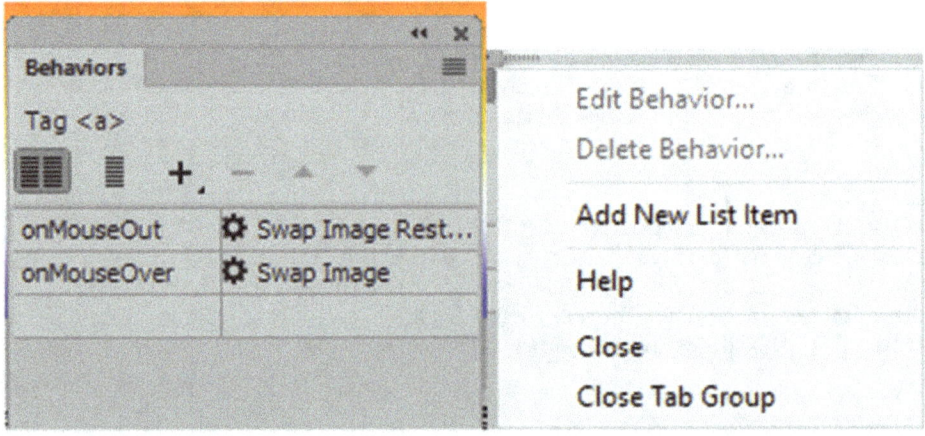

Figure 34-11. The Behavior panel and its menu when the rollover button is selected

CHAPTER 34 ■ WHAT IS JAVASCRIPT?

There are many events that you can choose from if you plan to add new ones using the drop-down menu, as seen in Figure 34-12.

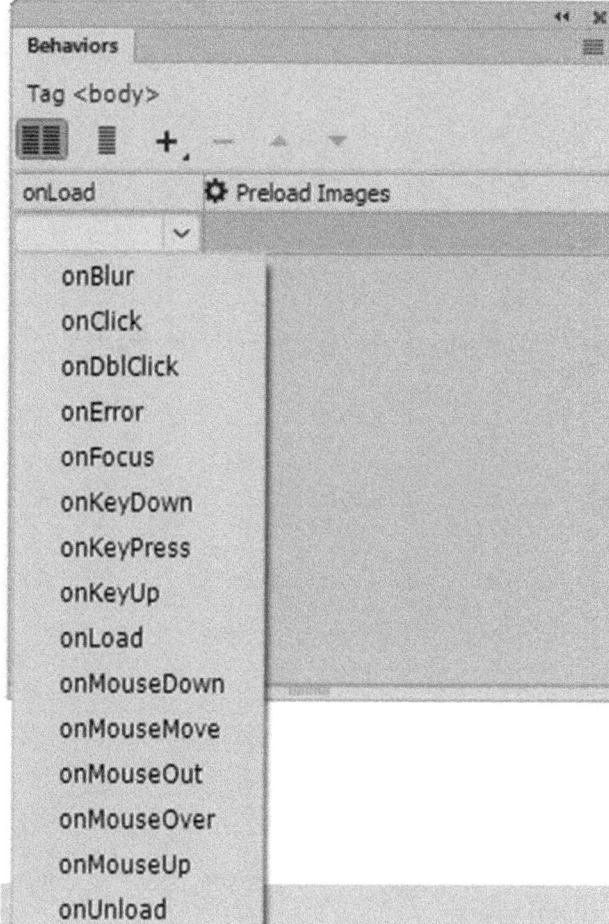

Figure 34-12. *Add an event from the Behaviors panel*

These can also be reviewed using the Show All and Set Events icons in the upper left of the panel. Refer to Figure 34-13.

CHAPTER 34 ■ WHAT IS JAVASCRIPT?

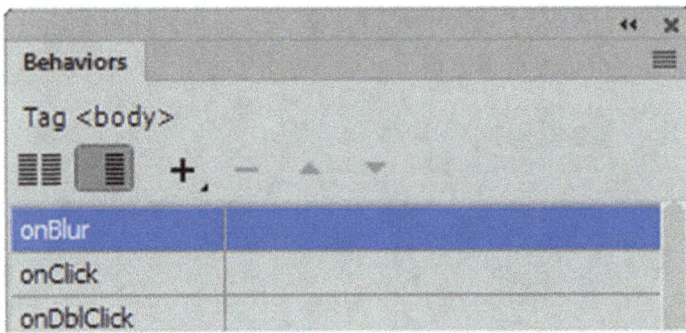

Figure 34-13. Review your events in the Behaviors panel

Once you have chosen an event, you can then add an action, or you can click the plus icon and choose from behaviors that were already created. Refer to Figure 34-14.

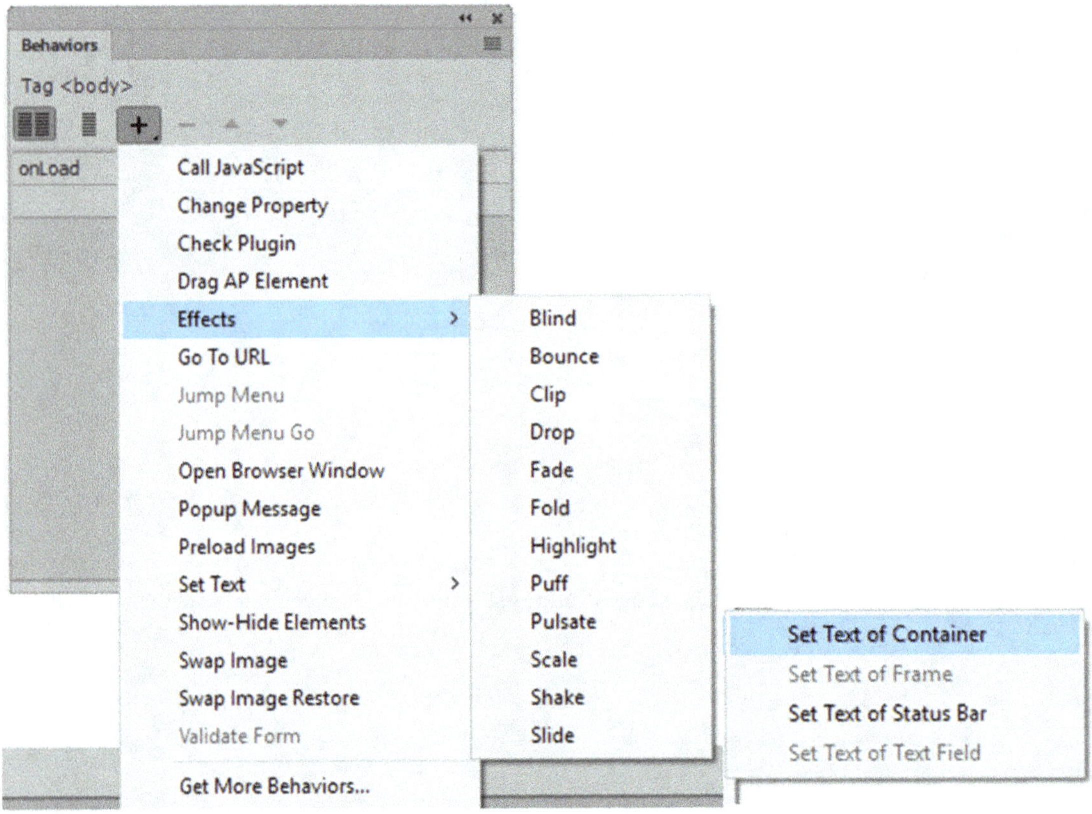

Figure 34-14. Possible actions added to events

CHAPTER 34 ■ WHAT IS JAVASCRIPT?

There are many to choose from in the drop-down list, and you can get more online. Some are very similar to the ones found in CSS Effects. They are applied to <div> elements that contain background images as well. Behavior Effects require a JavaScript library known as jQuery, which is loaded into a jQuery Assets folder. You'll look at jQuery in more detail in Chapter 35; for now let's continue with the print rollover example, which if we review the code is currently using two behaviors. First, the preload images and then second, the combination of swap image and swap image restore.

Without adding any more events, if you click the rollover's <a> tag in Code view, you get to the area where the two images are located. In the Behaviors panel you can change the swap image event to a different image if you made a mistake when linking the image in the dialog box. Refer to Figure 34-15.

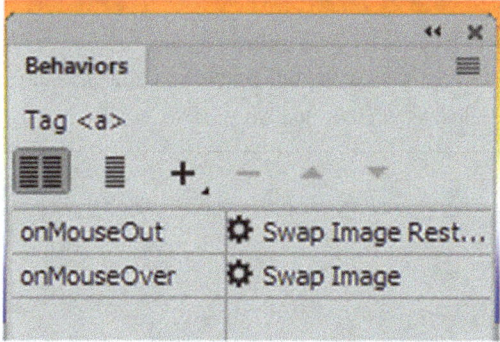

Figure 34-15. *Possible actions added to events*

By double-clicking the onMouseOver behavior, Swap Image in the Behaviors panel, you open the Swap Image dialog box. Refer to Figure 34-16.

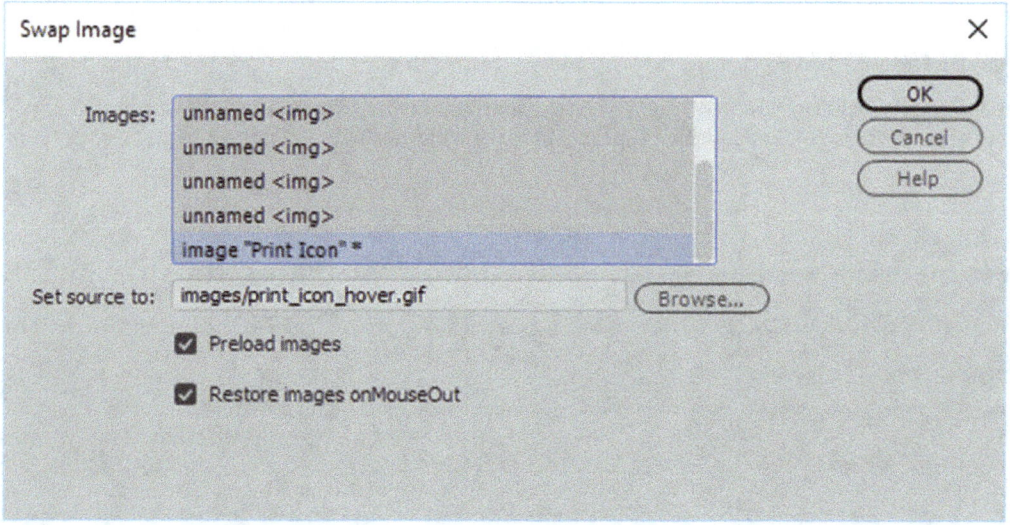

Figure 34-16. *Swap Image dialog box*

891

CHAPTER 34 ■ WHAT IS JAVASCRIPT?

Select the image you are changing, and change the source by browsing; make sure that both preload images and restore onMouseOut are checked. Click OK.

This reloads the hover image state in both the <body> tag and the <a> tag at once. Using this panel is especially important if you are working with single template-based pages (see Chapter 35), because your <body> tag might be locked, and this is the only way that you can edit the code properly. For example, if you change the code in the <a> only by hand and it does not update in the <body>, a linkage corruption could occur. In most cases, it is better to add these types of buttons to only the template so that you can access the <body> rather than separate template-based pages. You can check this swap using Live view or your HTML5 page in a browser. Try hovering over the image.

In a moment, you apply another behavior to this element.

■ **Note** If you need to swap the original image (onmouseOut) rather than using the Behaviors panel, use the Properties panel when you click the <img> tag in Code view or Split view. Refer to Figure 34-17.

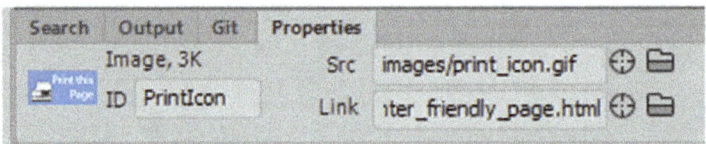

Figure 34-17. *Use the Properties menu to swap the non-hovering image onMouseOut in the image rollover*

In the src attribute, you can search for a new image in your images folder by clicking the folder to replace the old image.

Additional Behaviors

Another image-related behavior that you might want to experiment with is Open Browser Window, which allows you to open an image or webpage in a separate browser window. Refer to Figure 34-18.

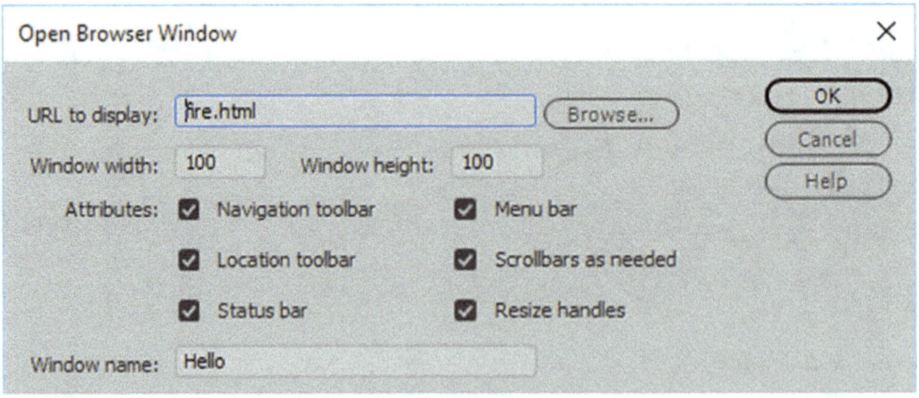

Figure 34-18. *The Open Browser Window dialog box*

CHAPTER 34 ■ WHAT IS JAVASCRIPT?

You can add this to an onClick event in the Behaviors panel.

The Show-Hide Elements also use onMouseOut and onMouseOver events, which allow you to show and hide <div> tags. Refer to Figure 34-19.

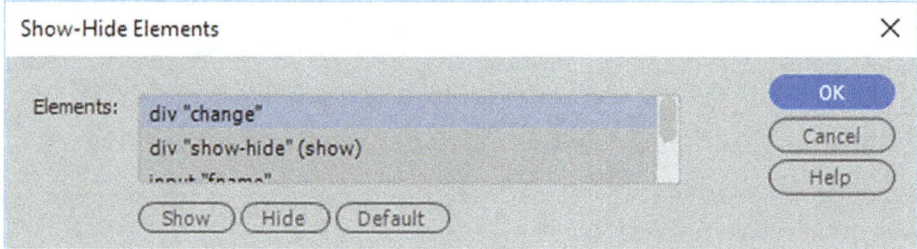

Figure 34-19. *Show-Hide Elements dialog box*

You can set a state for show and hide on the same <div> element. When you double click to reveal the show-hide elements dialog box click show for onMouseOut and hide for onMouseOver as seen in Figure 34-19. Refer to Figure 34-20 to see how the Behaviors should appear in the panel wen complete.

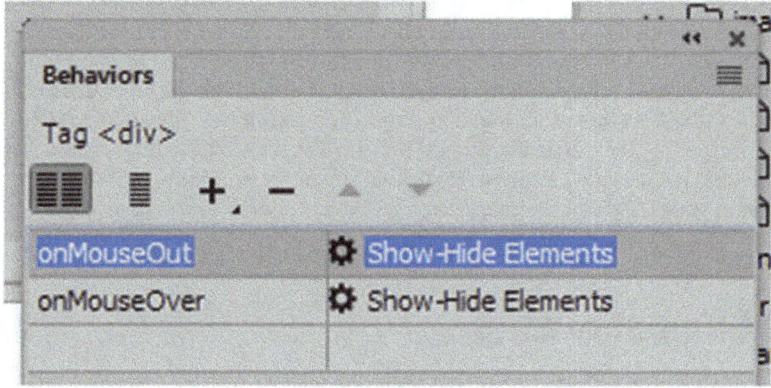

Figure 34-20. *Show-Hide Elements in the Behaviors panel*

Notice that in all of these examples, the new JavaScript goes into the <head> section. You could put the code into an external JS file if you find that it is taking up too much room, or you want to only use it on select pages.

With Show and Hide, not all JavaScript must go into the head (depending on who wrote it). The following is a variation I edited from W3Schools. You could use a button to hide and show a <div> that might contain an image or image background.

Show hide images simplified example:

First you write the CSS code in your linked external CSS file:

```
#myDIV {
    width: 100%;
    padding: 50px 0;
    text-align: center;
    background-color: lightblue;
    margin-top: 20px;
}
```

893

Then you add the following HTML to your page within the <body> tags:

```
<button onclick="myFunction()">Click Me</button>
<div id="myDIV">
This is a DIV element.
</div>
```

Then you add the following JavaScript within the <body> tag of your document, just below the HTML you just wrote:

```
<script>
function myFunction() {
    var x = document.getElementById("myDIV");
    if (x.style.display === "none") {
        x.style.display = "block";
    } else {
        x.style.display = "none";
    }
}
</script>
```

This time, the JavaScript is in the lower area of the <body> right below the </div> closing tag. It uses a function, conditions, and a combination of CSS to display and show. Therefore, it is important to make sure that if you have not built the JavaScript yourself, always follow the order of placement that the code designer has used. First, test your new code in a blank HTML5 document, and then add it your new file and test right away to make sure it is functioning correctly. CSS and JavaScript are very similar in the sense that if there is a naming conflict, you can get unexpected results, such as incorrect formatting or the animation fails to work. So, if you are adding something new to your HTML page, make sure that all IDs and, in some cases, classes are distinctly named.

JavaScript and the Snippets Panel

Dreamweaver also has a few JavaScript examples in its Snippet library in the JavaScript folder. Refer to this panel and Figure 34-21.

CHAPTER 34 ■ WHAT IS JAVASCRIPT?

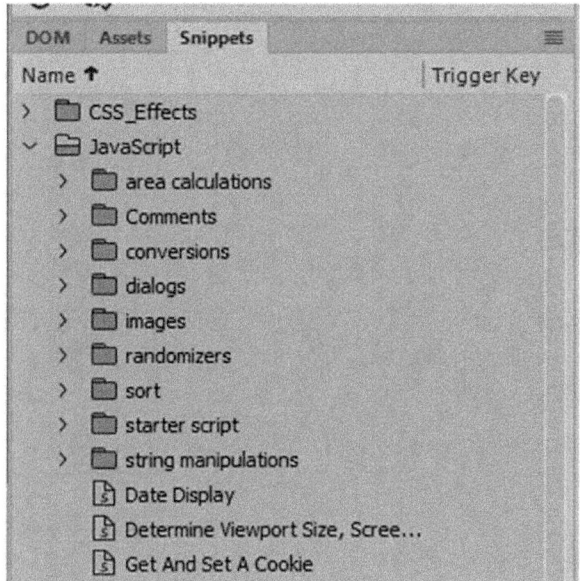

Figure 34-21. JavaScript resources in the Snippets panel

Most are for working with different conversions of forms; there are few specifically for working with images found in the images folder. Refer to Figure 34-22.

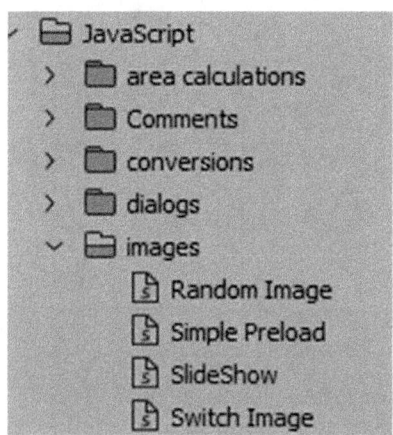

Figure 34-22. JavaScript image examples in the Snippets panel

- **Random Image:** Allows you to display a banner with random images. It requires at least one other snippet script called random number (randomizers folder) to work. You can click the Edit Snippet icon in the Snippets panel to review the code before you insert it and learn which other /*Dependencies*/ or additional snippet scripts are required. Refer to Figure 34-23.

895

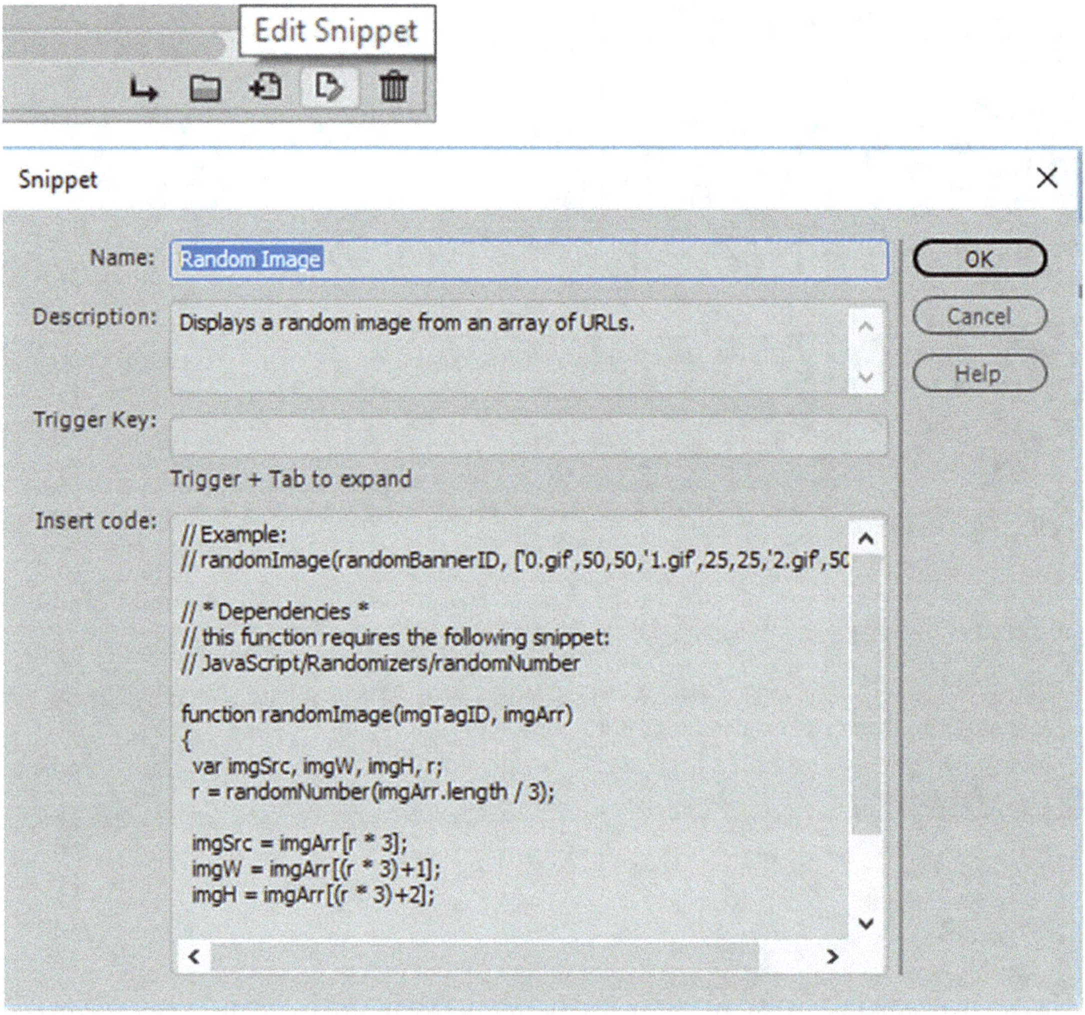

CHAPTER 34 ■ WHAT IS JAVASCRIPT?

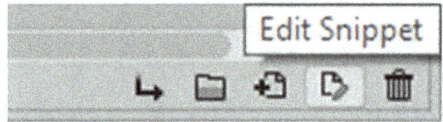

Figure 34-23. JavaScript snippets, reviewing the snippet before inserting it

- **Simple Preload:** This is like the preload image example you looked at in rollovers.
- **Slide Show:** Allows you to create a basic slide show. In this case, the snippet example tells you where each piece of code should be placed. The instructions lets you know that it requires another snippet known as a *switch image*, which you need to insert to complete the script.

■ **Note** The jQuery and Bootstrap examples use a JavaScript library that has many excellent galleries that you can modify in Dreamweaver. You look at this in Chapter 35.

As with any script, you can add snippets of your own to the panel as you increase your knowledge in JavaScript.

Print Preview

One JavaScript code example that you might want to add to the Snippets panel is how to change the printer button so that instead of going to a URL the code takes you to the browser's print dialog box. I think a "Print Script" would come in handy. In Chapter 33, you read about the importance of adding CSS for your printer. Once you have your media queries for print set up, you could add a <button></button> tag somewhere on your page; or in this case, to the image rollover that you created.

In the <head>, add this JavaScript.

```
<script language="javascript">
    function printpage(){
        window.print();
    }
</script>
```

Then in the <body>, apply this to a button.

```
<button type="button" onClick="printpage();">Print Page</button>
```

Or alternatively in your code that you created earlier for your rollover button within the <a> tag, as seen here.

```
<a href="#" onClick="printpage();" onMouseOver="MM_swapImage('PrintIcon',",'images/
print_icon_hover.gif',1)" onMouseOut="MM_swapImgRestore()"><img src="images/print_icon.gif"
alt="Print this Page" width="150" height="70" id="PrintIcon"></a>
```

I removed the URL in the href and changed it to a "#". This is so that the link never actually goes to a page; it only allows the Print Preview dialog box to open.

Figure 34-24 shows how it appears in the Behaviors panel.

Figure 34-24. *A JavaScript added event in the Behaviors panel and the final button*

When the button is clicked, the browser's Print dialog box opens and the viewer can choose what printer they want to print to. This saves the viewer time in that they don't have to go to the browser's main menu and choose File ➤ Print.

Summary

In this chapter, you briefly looked at how JavaScript is used with images so that the viewer can interact with objects on a page, such as a rollover image and the print dialog box. You also saw that Dreamweaver has some resources in the Snippets panel for other projects. You can use the Behaviors panel and the Properties panel to continue editing your JavaScript after you have added it to a webpage.

In the next chapter, you look at Bootstrap and how it incorporates with two of Dreamweaver's key features: the template and library items.

CHAPTER 35

Working with Bootstrap, Templates, Library Items, and the Assets Panel

In this chapter, you look at Bootstrap components and jQuery, and learn how they can work with templates and library items to create HTML5 pages in a website that has a theme.

> **Note** This chapter does not have any actual projects; however, you can use the files in the Part 6 folder to practice opening and viewing for this lesson. They are at https://github.com/Apress/graphics-multimedia-web-adobe-creative-cloud.

Bootstrap

Beyond the ways of working with JavaScript that were mentioned in Chapter 34, Dreamweaver CC allows you to work with code libraries and themes to further modify your galleries and multimedia projects. For example, in the Insert menu, there are tabs such as Bootstrap Components, jQuery UI, and jQuery Mobile (for mobile sites) that contain additional jQuery (JavaScript library) codes that allow you to enhance the layout of your images, such as collapsible dividers, tabs for organization, or galleries. Refer to Figure 35-1.

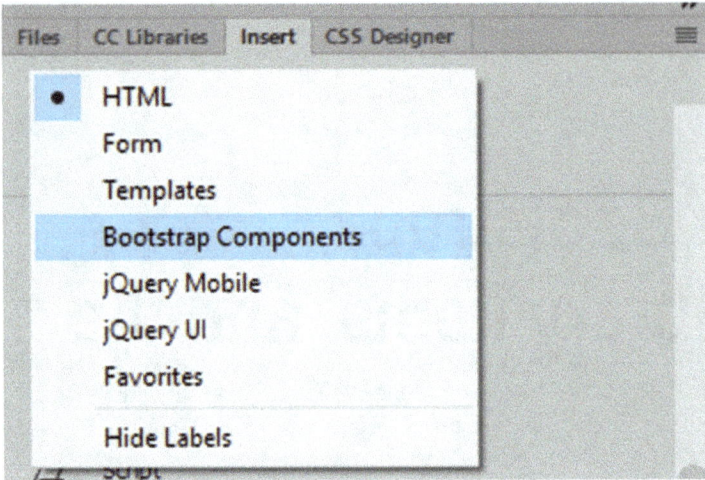

Figure 35-1. *The Insert panel has many more widgets included within Dreamweaver that you can use to enhance your site*

Check out each of these tabs to discover what they have to offer.

The Behaviors panel has several jQuery effects that can be applied to images if you are not using the CSS animation features. This adds a jQuery assets folder to your site root. Refer to Figure 35-2.

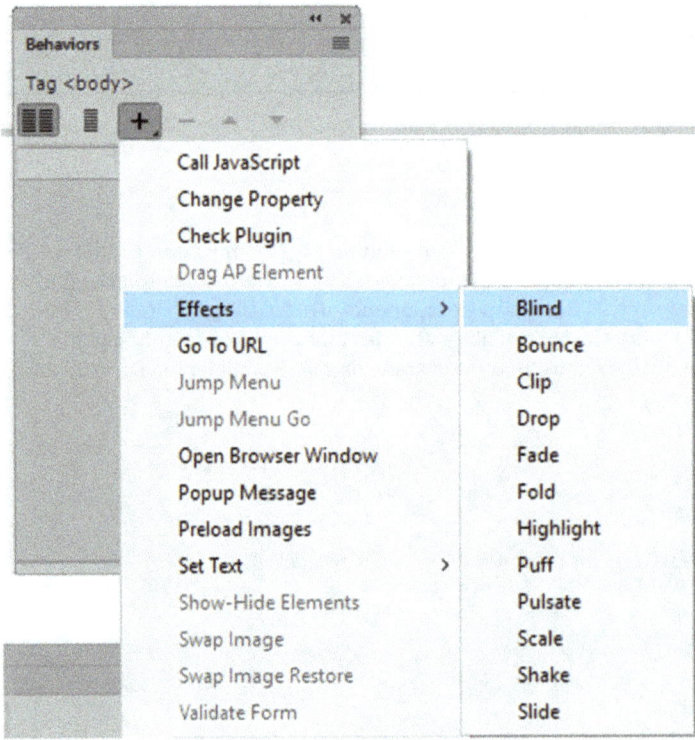

Figure 35-2. *jQuery Effects that you can add to a div via the Behaviors panel*

If you are new to jQuery, you can learn how to use these features and similar features from the following sites, all of which can be used in Dreamweaver and edited further to continue building a responsive website.

- W3Schools jQuery:

    www.w3schools.com/jquery/default.asp

- jQuery Official Site:
    - https://jquery.com
    - https://jqueryui.com
    - https://jquerymobile.com

Note The jQuery library does not regularly update in Dreamweaver CC, so if you want the most recent library, you can copy the code or use the external link from the jQuery site. Be aware that by using a newer jQuery version, the Properties panel may not work with the more modern library as expected; also make sure to use only one jQuery library link per page, or use a template-based page because using two versions of a jQuery library may cause a conflict.

Bootstrap is another powerful Dreamweaver tool. This front-end framework is used for ease of web development; it contains many prebuilt components that are composed of HTML, CSS, and jQuery. You can add these components to your own responsive site or to a Bootstrap layout that Dreamweaver generates based on the parameters you set. To use the Bootstrap components successfully from the Insert panel, take the time to understand how they operate.

- W3Schools Bootstrap: www.w3schools.com/bootstrap/default.asp
- Official Bootstrap Site: https://getbootstrap.com

In addition, you can find some Bootstrap examples for images in the Snippets panel. Refer to Figure 35-3.

CHAPTER 35 ■ WORKING WITH BOOTSTRAP, TEMPLATES, LIBRARY ITEMS, AND THE ASSETS PANEL

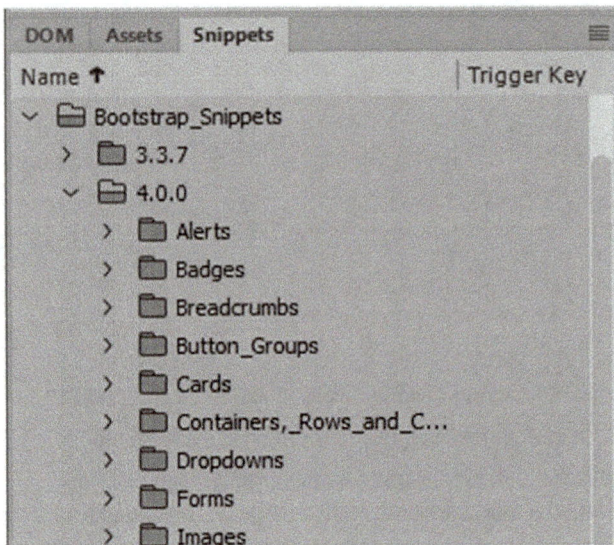

Figure 35-3. Bootstrap components are in the Snippets panel

The latest version of found in Dreamweaver is 4.0.0, but you can go back one legacy version to 3.3.7 if necessary. Also, if you need the latest updates, go to the official site to download the files. While you can add any of these Bootstrap snippets to your site, a far better way to work with them is to start with a fresh website. Before you start your project, make sure that your site in the Site ➤ Manage site setup is set to Bootstrap 4.0.0; otherwise, your site may not add the latest version of Bootstrap files when you create new pages or components. Refer to Figure 35-4.

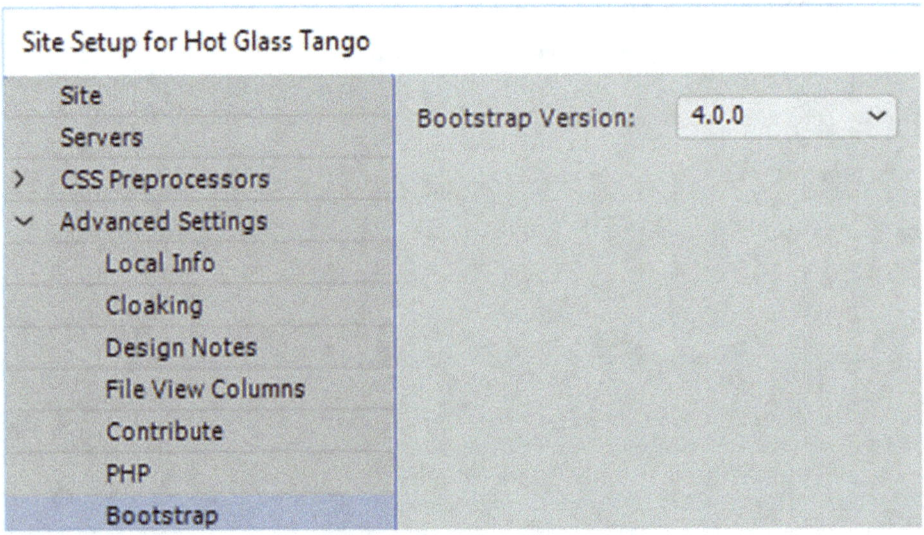

Figure 35-4. Make sure that your new site is using the latest version of Bootstrap in the Site Setup dialog box

CHAPTER 35 ■ WORKING WITH BOOTSTRAP, TEMPLATES, LIBRARY ITEMS, AND THE ASSETS PANEL

Bootstrap uses HTML elements and CSS that requires that you use HTML5.

Once saved, go to File ➤ New and start with a fresh site, as I did with my Hot Glass Tango site. Refer to Figure 35-5.

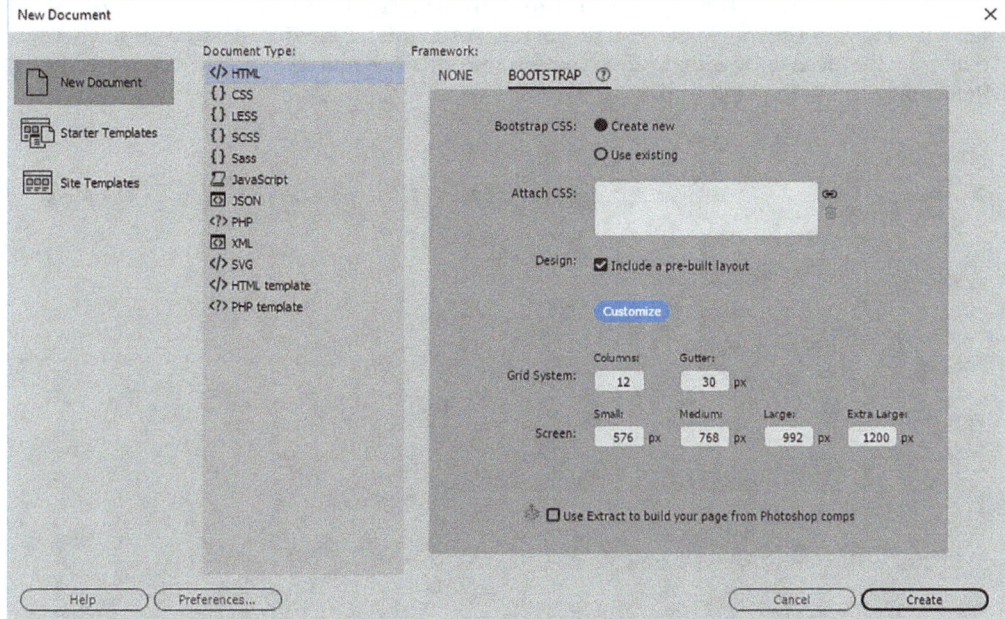

Figure 35-5. Choose the Bootstrap tap to quickly create your first mobile site

To start, I chose the Bootstrap tab and then chose to create new CSS. I then chose to include a prebuilt layout. This is helpful for beginners to Bootstrap so that they have a starting point. I then clicked the Customize button to see what the default grid, gutter system, and screen options are. Refer to Figure 35-6.

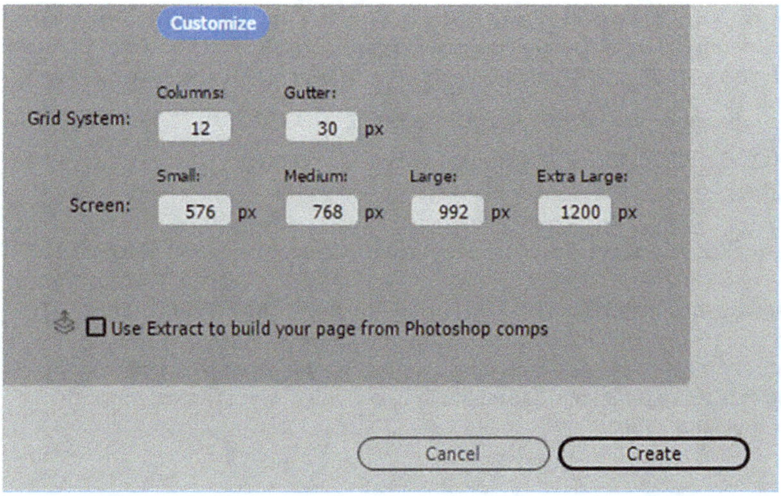

Figure 35-6. Choose the Bootstrap tab to quickly create your first mobile site

903

CHAPTER 35 ■ WORKING WITH BOOTSTRAP, TEMPLATES, LIBRARY ITEMS, AND THE ASSETS PANEL

You could alter any of these settings. Bootstrap's core framework is designed to be responsive and mobile-first. In my project, however, I left them at the default of a 12-column grid system and with a gutter of 30 pixels; the screen sizes are 576, 768, 922, and 1200. You can compare them to my files.

I left the Photoshop comps extract option unchecked; you look at that in Chapter 37.

After you click Create and save your page, you find that additional files, such as jQuery and Bootstrap CSS, have been added to your site root folder. You do not need to do this for the Hot Glass Tango site because you are just reviewing the files. Along with my CSS, you can see other CSS and jQuery that was created in the Files panel. Refer to Figure 35-7.

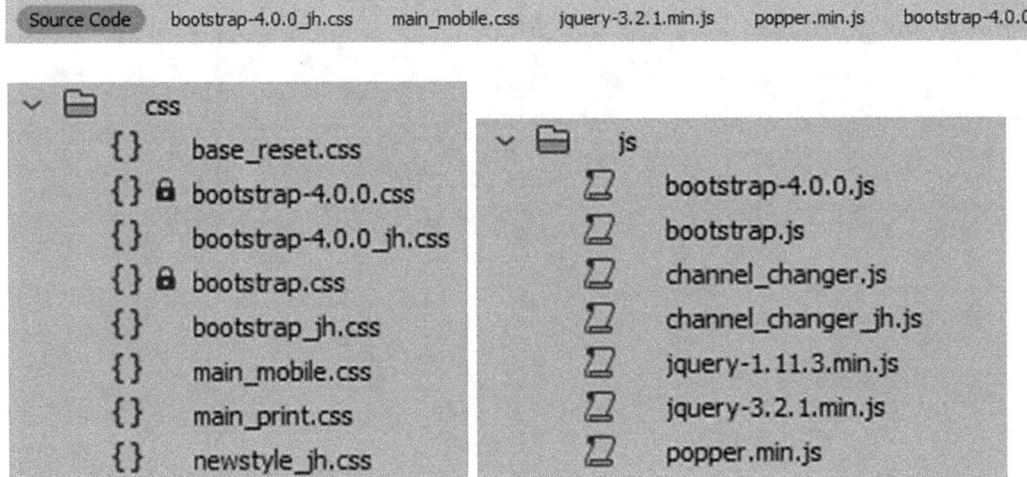

Figure 35-7. *Linked Bootstrap CSS, JavaScript, and jQuery files are added to your own CSS and JavaScript files in the folders in the File panel*

Some of the CSS for Bootstrap is added as locked. If you want to alter the CSS in some way, you can do one of two things as I did. You can create a new CSS file with additional media queries and place it below the current Bootstrap CSS in your HTML file, since it is closer to the attributes in the HTML file; it should override some of the CSS from bootstrap-4.0.0.css. Or you can create a copy of the locked boostrap-4.0.0.css file, add your initials to the copy (see Figure 35-7), and then link the copy to your HTML file instead. Here is the code in the <head>:

```
<link href="../css/bootstrap-4.0.0_jh.css" rel="stylesheet">
<link href="../css/main_mobile.css" rel="stylesheet">
```

Never try to alter the original locked Bootstrap file. It is best practice to keep the original as a backup in case you make an error or need to revert. I find this the best way to work if you are new to Bootstrap, and you are not sure what some classes are for. I also keep a backup copy of the Bootstrap CSS in another folder outside the site, if for some reason it becomes unlocked accidentally, and I need to add a new file.

I generally do not alter the jquery.js files unless I've added a carousel via the Insert panel, as on my gallery.html page, which you look at in more detail in Chapter 39. In it, you might want to slow down the speed of the moving image. Refer to Figure 35-8.

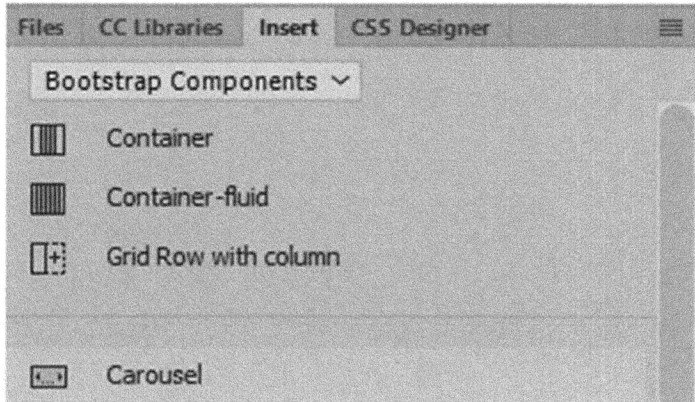

Figure 35-8. *After you have designed a basic layout you can use the Bootstrap components to add more interactivity for your images*

Other items that can be added by Bootstrap include blank dummy images for placement and fonts in the fonts folder. These are all things that you can keep or remove and replace with your own images and fonts as you build your site. You look at web fonts one more time in Chapter 37.

Regardless of how you build your site with or without Bootstrap, one thing that you may find tedious is that once you build one page, you may want to keep the navigation or banner and footer graphics of your site the same for many of your pages. Rather than go to each page and adjust a link every time, you can update all similar areas using templates and library items. You look at this next and how they can be incorporated into your design.

Working with Templates, Library Items, and the Assets Panel

It is important that before you do a lot of work on your site, you are familiar with templates, library items, and the Asset panel and how they relate to inserting HTML, CSS, and JavaScript(jQuery) on to your page.

Templates

A template allows the designer to add further conformity to the website. Dreamweaver has its own set of templates that end in a .dwt file format. The viewer never sees the template, yet it needs to be uploaded to the site with all its linked HTML5 pages so that it can operate correctly.

When most of my students start using templates in Dreamweaver, they are confused as to what its purpose is. Why not just create all of your HTML pages one at a time and make them distinct and different? From a design perspective, a website needs to have a theme or color scheme. If every page is vastly different on a website, the viewer starts to become confused as to where they are. Are they in the same site anymore, or are they somewhere else? Even sites created in programs like WordPress use themes and base a new page off of a common page. This is what a template is.

I find that a template saves time. I can keep common elements locked in the template, and I don't have to retype or update that area each time I want to create a variation on a new page. You can see from my template in the Files panel Templates folder that after I created a new template (main_v2.dwt), I was able to incorporate the Bootstrap links and code it by copying and pasting into various locations. Refer to Figure 35-9.

CHAPTER 35 WORKING WITH BOOTSTRAP, TEMPLATES, LIBRARY ITEMS, AND THE ASSETS PANEL

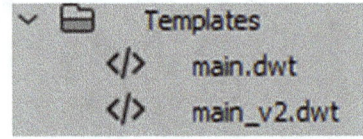

```
1   <!doctype html>
2 ▼ <html lang="en">
3 ▼ <head>
4   <meta charset="utf-8">
5       <meta http-equiv="X-UA-Compatible" content="IE=edge">
6       <meta name="viewport" content="width=device-width, initial-scale=1">
7   <!-- TemplateBeginEditable name="doctitle" -->
8   <title>Untitled Document</title>
9   <!-- TemplateEndEditable -->
10      <link href="../css/bootstrap-4.0.0_jh.css" rel="stylesheet">
11      <link href="../css/main_mobile.css" rel="stylesheet">
12  <!-- TemplateBeginEditable name="head" -->
13  <!-- TemplateEndEditable -->
14  </head>
15
16 ▼ <body class="background-main">
17 ▼ <nav class="navbar navbar-expand-lg navbar-dark bg-dark">
18          <a class="navbar-brand" href="index.html">Home</a>
```

Figure 35-9. *You can add Bootstrap links and HTML5 to your template comments*

To start creating a new template page for your project, go to File ➤ New and choose </> HTML template near the bottom of the Document Type column. Refer to Figure 35-10.

CHAPTER 35 ■ WORKING WITH BOOTSTRAP, TEMPLATES, LIBRARY ITEMS, AND THE ASSETS PANEL

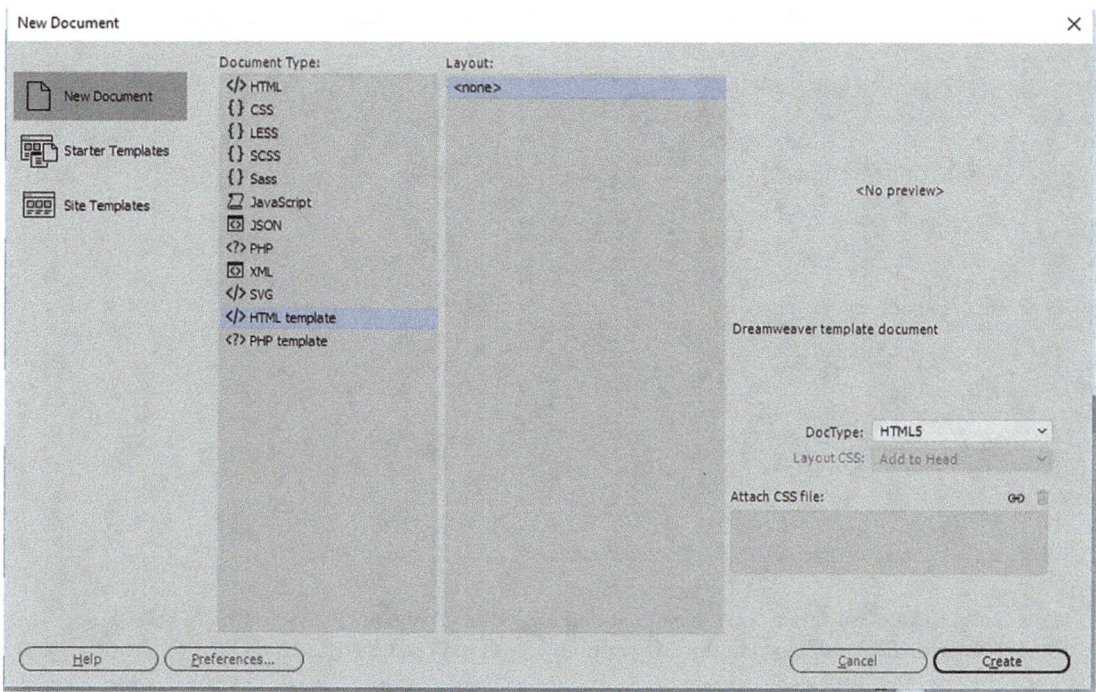

Figure 35-10. *Create a new HTML5 template using the New Document dialog box*

Choose HTML template from the New Document List; make sure that it is HTML5 doctype so that it works successfully with Bootstrap, and click Create. This is the same as creating an HTML file except that is has template comment areas; in this example, the comment is green in the <head> tag. Refer to Figure 35-11.

```
about.html ×    <<Template>> Untitled-1 ×
 1    <!doctype html>
 2  ▼ <html>
 3  ▼ <head>
 4    <meta charset="utf-8">
 5    <!-- TemplateBeginEditable name="doctitle" -->
 6    <title>Untitled Document</title>
 7    <!-- TemplateEndEditable -->
 8    <!-- TemplateBeginEditable name="head" -->
 9    <!-- TemplateEndEditable -->
10    </head>
11
12    <body>
13    </body>
14    </html>
15
```

Figure 35-11. *The new template*

Once you save the DWT file, it is added to a new folder called Templates. Refer to Figure 35-12.

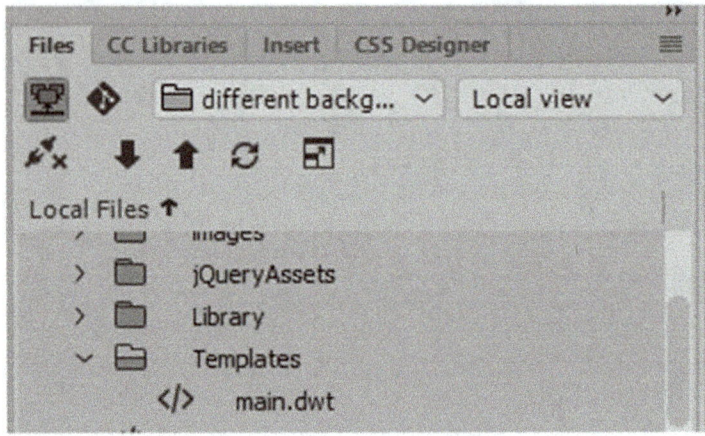

Figure 35-12. A template is added to the Templates folder

You may receive a warning if you have not added any editable regions to the <body>. Click OK to continue to save the file. You'll look at this in a moment. Refer to Figure 35-13.

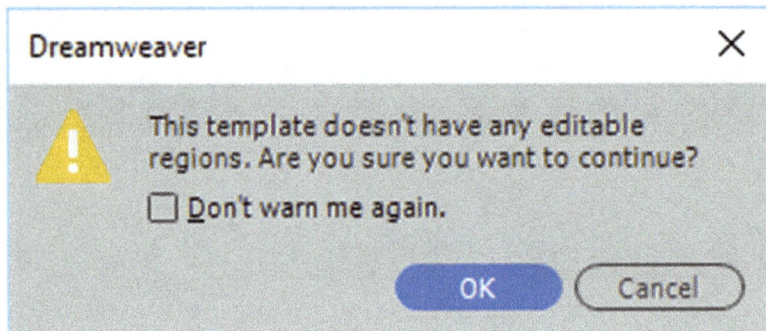

Figure 35-13. Until editable regions are added to the <body> you see this warning alert

If you are designing a mobile site, you can also use one of the templates from Starter Templates in the Responsive Starters or Bootstrap Templates folders. You can inspect the samples. Refer to Figure 35-14.

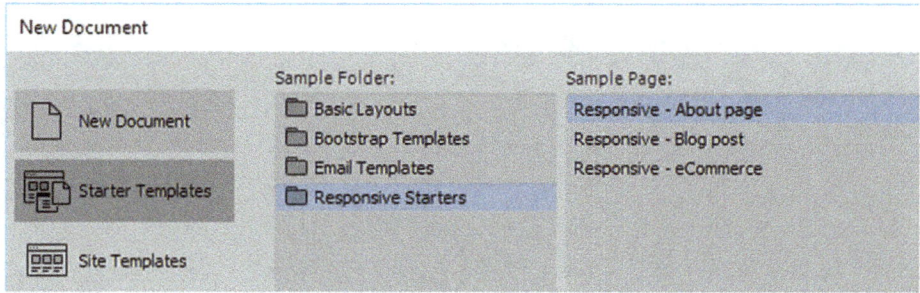

Figure 35-14. *Work with starter templates if you choose not to start with a blank template*

In this case, I started with a blank template for Hot Glass Tango; for your project, a new template opens and is saved in your site root Templates folder with the .dwt file extension.

Adobe Dreamweaver CC Classroom in a Book, by Jim Maivald, provides more information about working with templates. Like Bootstrap, templates are simple to use, but as a beginner, you can make some very subtle mistakes and files can become easily corrupted. The following are few important notes about HTML5 templates:

- Do not move the template (.dwt) file out of the Templates folder. This causes the links within to break and may cause it to stop working.

- Do not rename the Templates folder, leave the folder name with a capital letter.

- Within template file in code view do not change the text within the <title>Untitled Document</title> tags, you only change the text here when inside of the template-based pages.

- Do not remove or alter the template comments that are in the template file.

```
<!-- TemplateBeginEditable name="doctitle" -->
<title>Untitled Document</title>
<!-- TemplateEndEditable -->
<!-- TemplateBeginEditable name="head" -->
<!-- TemplateEndEditable -->
```

Doing any of these things corrupt the template and cause it not to work correctly.

The template behaves like any other HTML5 page. The main difference is that it has areas that are set and do not change. To have areas that change on your template-based pages, you need to create editable areas or regions. When a template is first created, it has a few editable areas in the <head>.

```
<!-- TemplateBeginEditable name="doctitle" -->
<title>Untitled Document</title>
<!-- TemplateEndEditable -->
```

They are set within comment tags. Dreamweaver recognizes these editable areas by the attribute name; in this case "doctitle" or "head". While working in the template <head>, you do not add or alter anything inside of this editable area. This area is only edited inside the template-based page. If you want to add JavaScript or CSS to your <head> in the template, you need to add it outside of the editable area.

```
<!-- TemplateBeginEditable name="doctitle" -->
<title>Untitled Document</title>
<!-- TemplateEndEditable -->
```

CHAPTER 35 ■ WORKING WITH BOOTSTRAP, TEMPLATES, LIBRARY ITEMS, AND THE ASSETS PANEL

```
<script>Add a script here</script>
<link href="../main.css" rel="stylesheet" type="text/css">

<!-- TemplateBeginEditable name="head" -->
<!-- TemplateEndEditable -->
<script></script>
</head>
```

Adding Editable Areas

In Figure 35-13, when you first started adding designs to your template <body> area, it contains no editable regions. After working on the layout, if you save the template, you get an alert stating that there are no editable regions. The purpose of editable regions is to control which area of the template's base design you can edit on your template-based pages.

Until you are ready to add an editable region, you need to press OK in the alert; otherwise, you can check the Don't Warn Me Again button, if you find this too repetitive.

To add an editable area, make sure that you are in the <body> in the <div> or element that you want to make editable. From the Insert panel ➤ Templates tab, choose Editable Region. Refer to Figure 35-15.

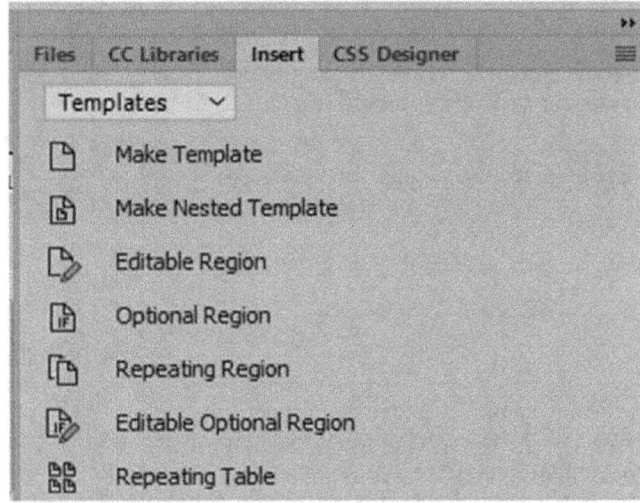

Figure 35-15. *In the Insert panel in the Templates tab choose Editable Region*

You are asked to give that editable region a meaningful name; when you are done, click OK. Refer to Figure 35-16.

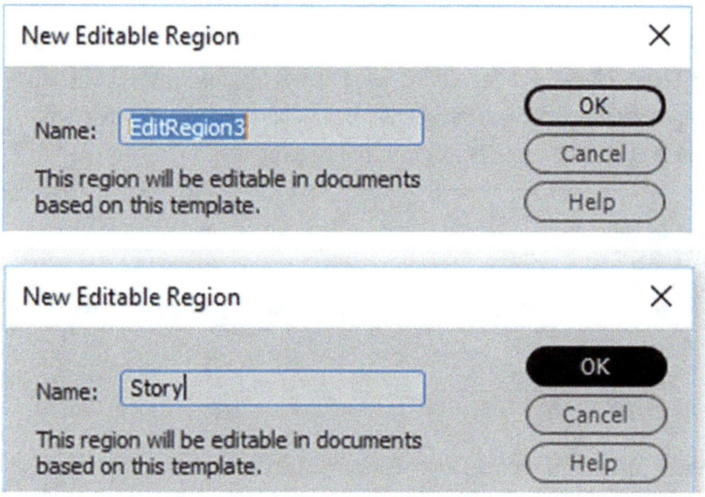

CHAPTER 35 ■ WORKING WITH BOOTSTRAP, TEMPLATES, LIBRARY ITEMS, AND THE ASSETS PANEL

Figure 35-16. Adding a new editable region to your page

This adds a template comment to that area in the <tag> element.

```
<body>
<div>
<header></header>
<main>
<!-- TemplateBeginEditable name="Story" -->Add Editable Content here<!-- TemplateEndEditable -->
<main>
</div>
</body>
```

Figure 35-17 shows how it appears in Design view.

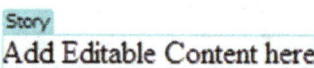

Figure 35-17. A template editable region is added and this is how it appears in Design view

Once you start creating template-based pages, this is the area that is available to you to add new graphics and video; all the other areas outside of this editable area remain locked unless you go back into the template and edit.

You can add as many editable areas as you want to your template. Hot Glass Tango template has two.

```
<!-- InstanceBeginEditable name="Subtitle" -->
<!-- InstanceEndEditable -->
<!-- InstanceBeginEditable name="main-story" -->
<!-- InstanceEndEditable -->
```

911

> **Note** You can also have a "hidden" editable region if additional JavaScript or jQuery needs to be added to an area at the bottom of the page before the </body> closes. The reason for doing this, is because some JavaScripts require this order. Not all template-based pages require the same JavaScript. Doing this is an alternative to putting the JavaScript into the template so that it loads everytime each template-based page opens.

Additional Editable Region Options

Here are some other template features you may want to explore further on your own. They are found in Insert panel ➤ Template tab.

Make Template

This makes a template out of a current file or another template. Just be aware that sometimes corruption can occur, so it is always best to start with a new blank template (see https://helpx.adobe.com/dreamweaver/using/dreamweaver-templates.html).

Make Nested Template

A nested template's design and editable regions are based on another template. Nested templates are useful for controlling content in pages on a site that share many design elements but have a few variations. For example, a base template might contain broader design areas and be usable by many content contributors for a site, while a nested template might further define the editable regions in pages for a specific section in a site.

Editable Region

These areas in a base template are passed through to the template or nested template and remain editable in pages created from a template unless new template regions are inserted in these regions. Changes to a base template are automatically updated in template-based pages, and in all template-based documents that are based on the main and nested templates. For more details on this topic visit these links:
   https://helpx.adobe.com/dreamweaver/using/creating-nested-template.html
   https://helpx.adobe.com/dreamweaver/using/creating-editable-regions-templates.html
   https://helpx.adobe.com/dreamweaver/using/editing-content-template-based-document.html
   Be aware that adding or altering editable regions while inside the template after the template-based pages have been created, these changes may not appear in the template-based pages.

Optional Region

An optional region is where users can set to show or hide in a template-based document. Use an optional region when you want to set conditions for displaying content in a document. When you insert an optional region, you can either set specific values for a template parameter or define conditional statements (If… else statements) for template regions. Use simple true/false operations or define more complex conditional statements and expressions. You can modify the optional region if necessary. Based on the conditions you define, template users can edit the parameters in template-based documents they create and control whether the optional region is displayed. You can link multiple optional regions to a named parameter. In the template-based page, both regions show or hide as a unit. For example, you can show a "closeout" image and sales price text area for a sale item. For more information, visit https://helpx.adobe.com/dreamweaver/using/using-optional-regions-templates.html.

CHAPTER 35 ■ WORKING WITH BOOTSTRAP, TEMPLATES, LIBRARY ITEMS, AND THE ASSETS PANEL

Repeating Region

A repeating region is a section of a template that can be duplicated many times in a template-based page. Typically, repeating regions are used with tables, but you can define a repeating region for other page elements. Repeating regions enable you to control your page layout by repeating certain items, such as a catalog item and description layout, or for data such as a list of items. There are two repeating region template objects that you can use: repeating region and repeating table. For more information, visit https://helpx.adobe.com/dreamweaver/using/creating-repeating-regions-templates.html.

Editable Optional Region

An optional region is non-editable but editable optional region is.
   For more information, visit https://helpx.adobe.com/dreamweaver/using/using-optional-regions-templates.html.

Repeating Table

See Repeating Region for more information. Refer to Figure 35-18. The Insert Repeating Table dialog box appears when this selection is made. It is similar to the insert table dialog box. Here you can set various setting such as rows, columns, cell padding, cell spacing, width, border, the rows of the table that will repeat and the region name.

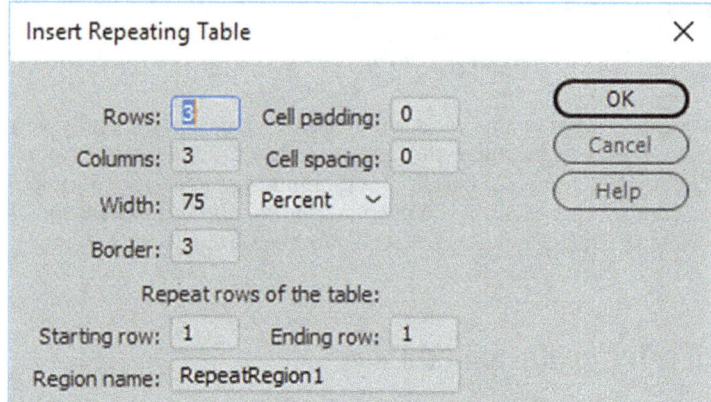

Figure 35-18. *The Insert Repeating Table dialog box*

Creating a Template-based Page

Once you have created and saved your template in the Templates folder with its editable regions, it is time to create a template-based page.
   Go to File ➤ New ➤ Site Template. Refer to Figure 35-19.

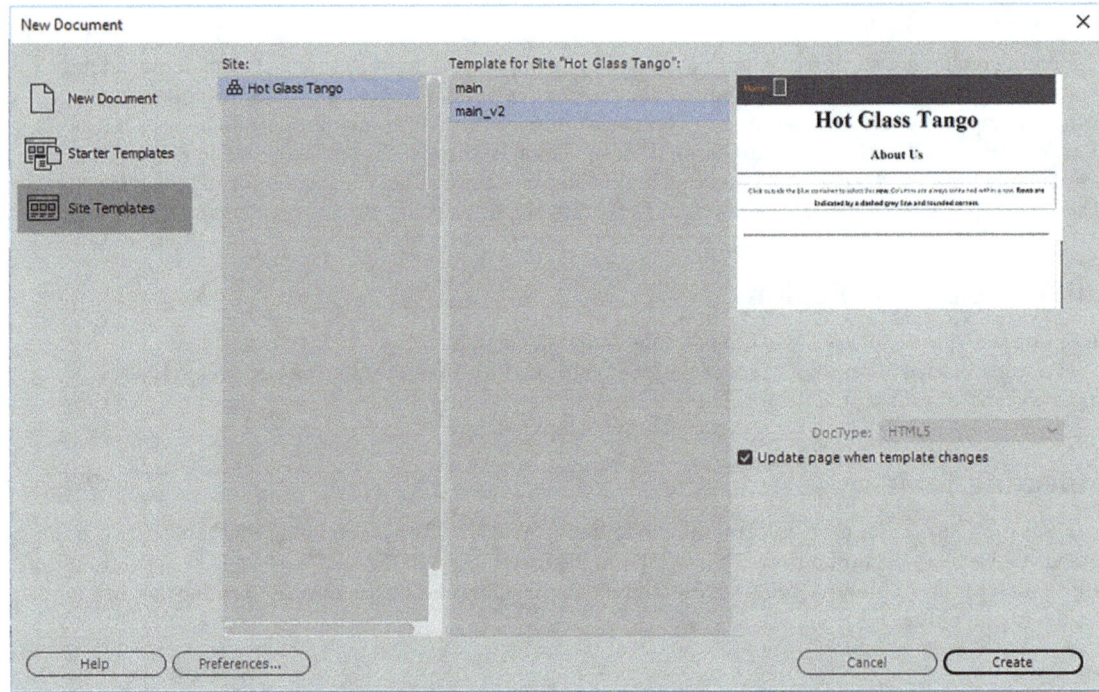

Figure 35-19. *Creating a template-based page from the New Document dialog box*

Here you locate your site and then select the template that you want to base the page on. Generally, you only have one template per site, but there may be cases in which you need more than one, depending upon your layout. I created index.html but did not make it template-based. This is important to consider during the layout and planning stages of building your site, especially if you need to keep your links updated. You then see a preview of the layout. Before you click Create, make sure that Update Page is checked when the template changes.

Hidden Area in <head> Tag of a Template-based Page

When you create the template, you add <script> tags for JavaScript and external CSS outside of the editable areas if you want to affect all template-based pages. If you want to affect only one template-based page, then you add the JavaScript or CSS inside of the editable area called *head* in the <head> tag of that template-based page.

```
<!-- TemplateBeginEditable name="head" -->

Add Scripts or CSS internal or external here

<!-- TemplateEndEditable -->
```

When adding CSS or JavaScript in this area, if it is above or below other CSS or JavaScript in the template, or if there is class or ID naming conflicts, it may affect the way the code behaves. So, keep this in mind as you add your code to this area.

CHAPTER 35 ■ WORKING WITH BOOTSTRAP, TEMPLATES, LIBRARY ITEMS, AND THE ASSETS PANEL

Templates Are Updateable

The wonderful thing about templates (.dwt) is that if you make an update to a graphic or text in a non-editable area, and then save the template, Dreamweaver makes that change globally to all pages that are based on that template. You can ensure that this is happening when the Update Template Files dialog box appears. Refer to Figure 35-20.

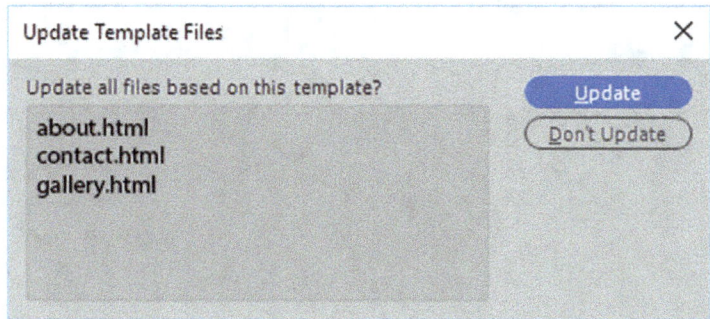

Figure 35-20. *Update the template-based pages when the template is altered and then saved*

In this example, you can see how many pages are affected.

If this is not the same number of pages that you know are template-based to that specific template, then there might be an issue of corruption with that HTML5 page or it may have become detached.

Click Update to update all the files.

This brings up another dialog box called Update Pages. Dreamweaver looks in the files (template-based pages) that use this template and updates them. Alternatively, you can choose to update the entire site. When complete, the Done icon is available and the log shows Done at the bottom of the report. If there any errors during the update, they are logged as well. Refer to Figure 35-21.

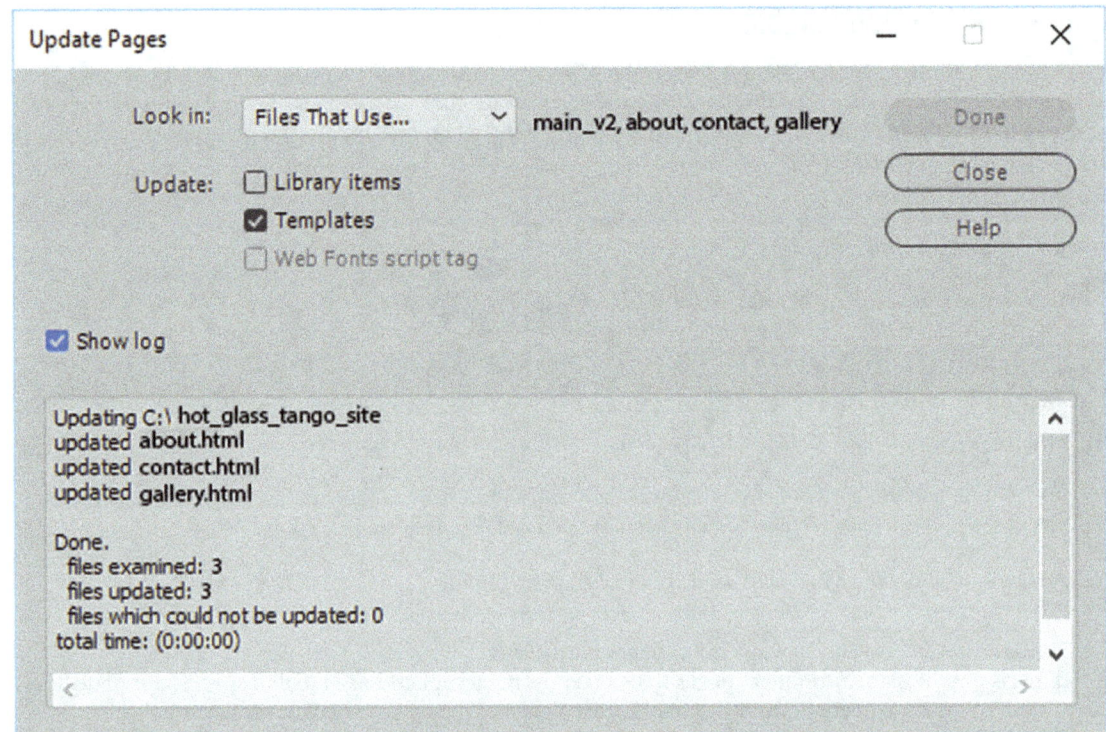

Figure 35-21. *Update Page dialog box logs all files that were examined and updated*

If you change the setting here, the Done button changes to a Start button, and you can run the update again.

When done, click the Close button, and you can close your template file. When you open a template-based file, you see that the change to template has happened to it and all your template-based pages.

Troubleshooting Templates

■ **Note** While you are working in the template, it is best to close all your template-based HTML pages because when you save the template changes, Dreamweaver makes the changes to the open template-based page, but it won't save it right-away. You then have to save the file upon closing, which is just an extra step in the work flow.

Sometimes when working with templates (at least on Microsoft computers), Dreamweaver appears to slow down. If you notice that not all of your template-based pages are showing up, it could mean one of two things. You were working with too many open files in Dreamweaver. With large sites, it is best to work with your project on an external drive. Close Dreamweaver, then open the program again and retry the update; this should correct the issue. If it does not, check if your template or the template-based page has become corrupted. In that case, you may need to re-create your template and try again.

CHAPTER 35 ■ WORKING WITH BOOTSTRAP, TEMPLATES, LIBRARY ITEMS, AND THE ASSETS PANEL

Alternatively, new templates can be attached to template-based files in Tools ➤ Templates ➤ Apply Template to Page. If the editable regions and layout are relatively the same, you can switch your template to a new one. Test a copy of one page to make sure that the transition is possible for other template-based pages. Refer to Figure 35-22.

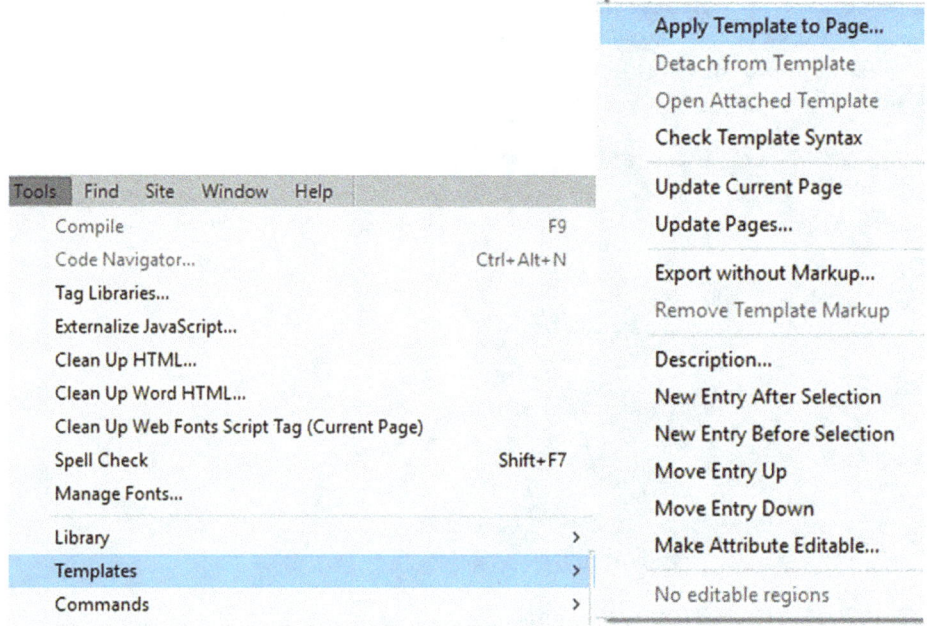

Figure 35-22. Additional template options in the Tools drop-down menu

Other options allow you to detach a template, check that its syntax is correct, makes an attribute editable that allows you to make advanced edits to a specific page, and reviews any editable regions. Refer to Figure 35-23.

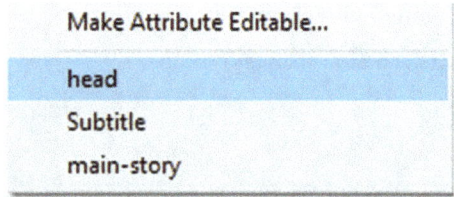

Figure 35-23. review the editable regions in your template

Library Items

Library items are actual files that can contain individual links to assets that you can place in your template-based webpages. The smaller pieces of code that they contain should be added to the editable areas of your template-based pages. You saw an example of library type items in Animate CC, where movie-clip symbols were stored. Library items (.lbi) are repeating pieces that you may want to use more than once on your site,

917

CHAPTER 35 ■ WORKING WITH BOOTSTRAP, TEMPLATES, LIBRARY ITEMS, AND THE ASSETS PANEL

but not on all pages. If you want to use pieces of code on every page, then add that code to the template, not as a library item to every page. If you want to code only on a few pages, or more than once on a page, like a button or link, then used a library item. Refer to Figure 35-24, which shows the Files panel.

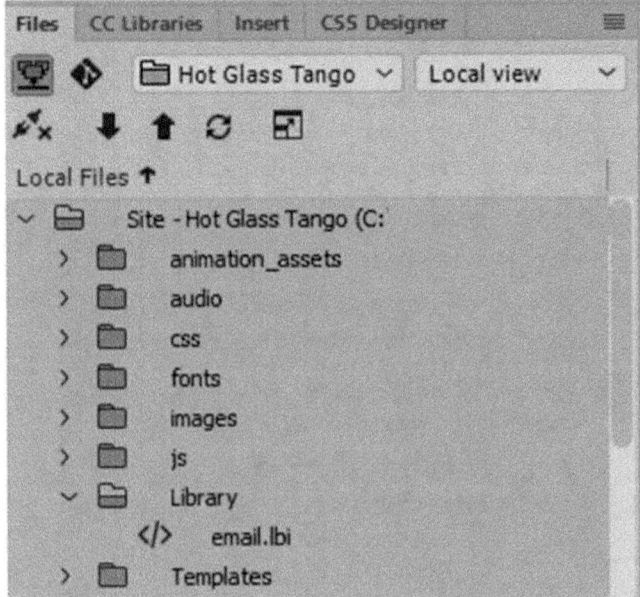

Figure 35-24. *Library items folder with a library item inside*

The following are a few important notes about library items:

- Dreamweaver stores library items in a single library folder in the root directory of each site.
- Like templates, do not move the library items (.lbi) file out of the library folder. This causes the links within to break and may cause it to stop working.
- Do not rename the library folder and leave the folder name with a capital letter.
- Like templates, library items can be updated after saving, and the changes cascade throughout the site. Refer to Figure 35-25.

CHAPTER 35 ■ WORKING WITH BOOTSTRAP, TEMPLATES, LIBRARY ITEMS, AND THE ASSETS PANEL

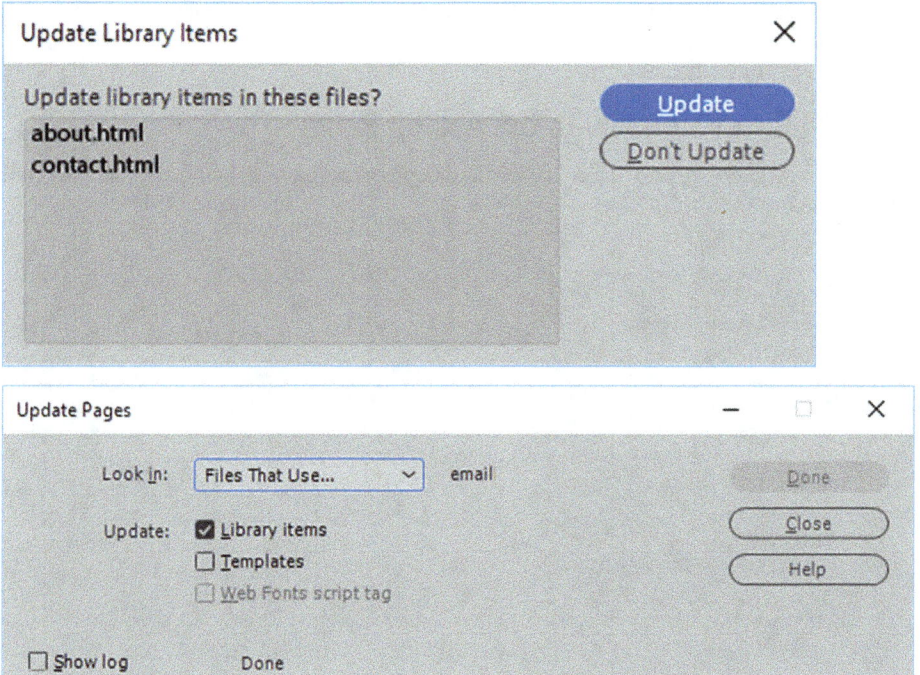

Figure 35-25. *Update the library items on their pages once a change is made*

The Tools menu allows you to update or add an object to the library folder. Refer to Figure 35-26.

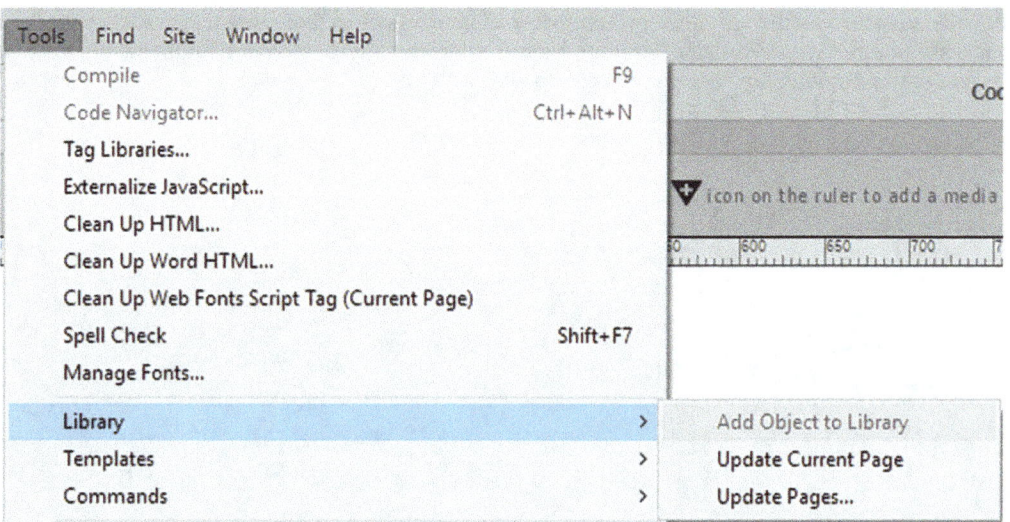

Figure 35-26. *The Tools drop-down panel allows you to update the library items*

919

CHAPTER 35 ■ WORKING WITH BOOTSTRAP, TEMPLATES, LIBRARY ITEMS, AND THE ASSETS PANEL

However, creating and inserting a library items is a bit different than creating a template page. To do that, you need to the Assets panel.

Creating and Adding Library Items with the Assets Panel

The Assets panel is the main way to create and insert library items onto a template-based page. See the open book icon at the bottom of the list on the left. Refer to Figure 35-27.

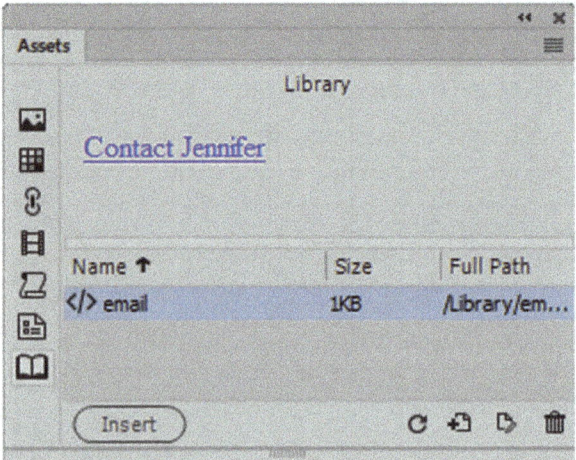

Figure 35-27. *The Assets panel allows you to review items such as how many library items you have and then preview them*

Additionally, the icons on the left side let you preview all images, colors, links, media, JavaScript, and templates. It is just another way to see all of your media and colors in your root folder without having to open an HTML File or search through the Files panel. Refer to Figure 35-28.

CHAPTER 35 ■ WORKING WITH BOOTSTRAP, TEMPLATES, LIBRARY ITEMS, AND THE ASSETS PANEL

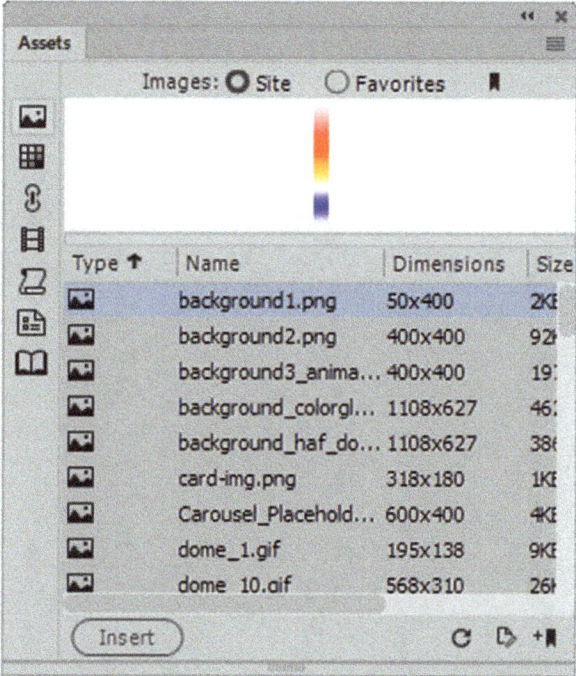

Figure 35-28. *Previewing Images using the Assets panel*

To create a library item, whether it is text, a graphic, or a combination of both, open the Assets panel. Click the Library tab and click the New Library Item button. Refer to Figure 35-29.

CHAPTER 35 ■ WORKING WITH BOOTSTRAP, TEMPLATES, LIBRARY ITEMS, AND THE ASSETS PANEL

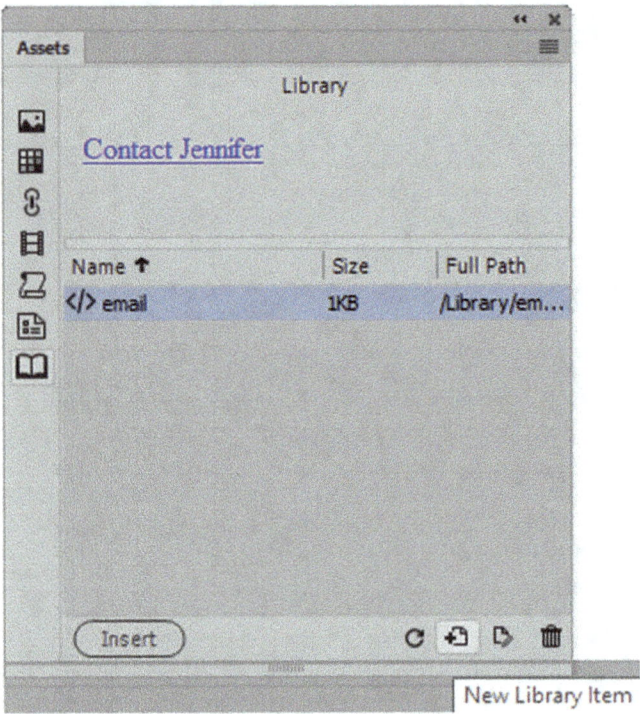

Figure 35-29. Add a new library item

This adds a new library item to the list and to your library folder, as seen in Figure 35-29. Dreamweaver gives you steps as to what to do next. First, you name the library item and then you click the Edit button and start adding your content. Refer to Figure 35-30.

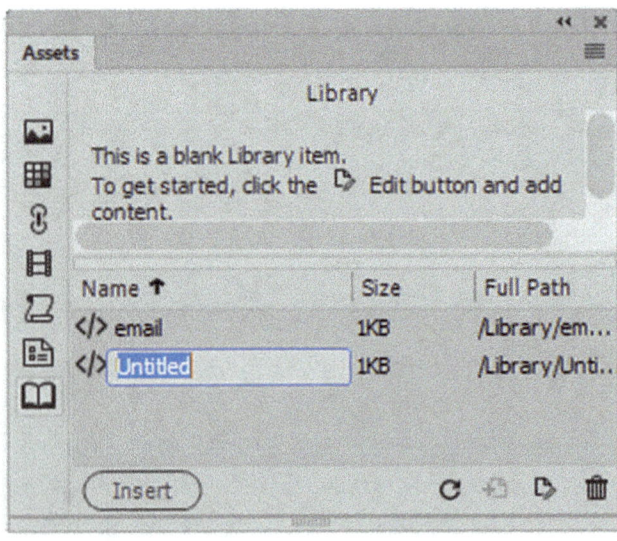

Figure 35-30. Adding a library item

CHAPTER 35 ■ WORKING WITH BOOTSTRAP, TEMPLATES, LIBRARY ITEMS, AND THE ASSETS PANEL

Or you can double-click the library item's name to open it. Refer to Figure 35-31.

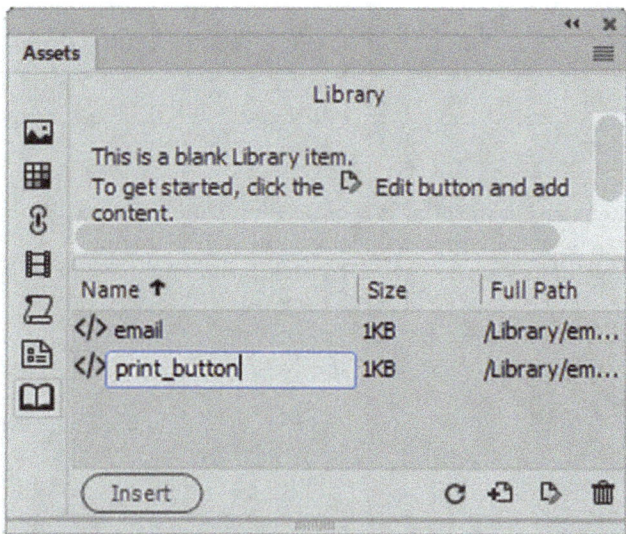

Figure 35-31. Rename and open the library item by double-clicking on it

The library item can be viewed in Code view, Split view, Design view, or Live view. Refer to Figure 35-32.

Figure 35-32. View a library item as you would an HTML page or template

However, be aware that you are only adding a line of code. A library item is only a part of a webpage, not the whole webpage. So, you only add an image or a few lines of code. You only reference the class in the tag, but you do not add the actual CSS external link to the library item.

```
<meta http-equiv="Content-Type" content="text/html; charset=utf-8">
<p class="bold-text">
   <a class="one"  href="mailto:your_email@gmail.com">Contact Jennifer</a>
</p>
```

If you're just looking at the library item, and it still is not linked or inserted to an actual page, then the formatting of the text appears different than what you expect. Even in Design view it appears unformatted, but this is OK. Once it is on a page with a CSS internal or external link, it references the class or ID and appears correctly styled.

CHAPTER 35 ■ WORKING WITH BOOTSTRAP, TEMPLATES, LIBRARY ITEMS, AND THE ASSETS PANEL

The following is an example of the CSS in an external style sheet.

```
.bold-text{
font-weight:bold;
}
.one{
color:green;
}
```

When you are finished creating the library item, save it and close it.

Now open the template-based page, and in Code or Design view, find the location in a <div> or sematic element that you want to insert your library item. With it selected, click the Insert button. Refer to Figure 35-33.

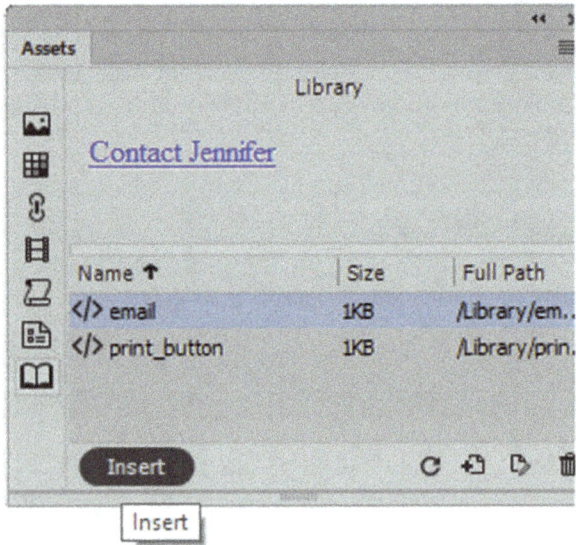

***Figure 35-33.** Insert a library item onto a template-based page*

This inserts your library item and its line of code and library comment tags has a yellow border.

```
<!-- #BeginLibraryItem "/Library/emaillink.lbi" -->
        <p class="bold-text"><a class="one"  href=" mailto:your_email@gmail.com ">Contact
        Jennifer</a></p>
        <!-- #EndLibraryItem -->
```

This area of code is locked on the HTML page, and you cannot edit it. To edit, you must go back to the Assets panel or the Files panel and double-click to open. Make changes and save it so that it updates in all locations, and then close the library item.

Detach Library Item

You may want to detach a library item to edit or create a new example.

If you want to detach the library item, you need to select it on a page, and in the Properties panel, you have the following options.

- **Open:** This opens the library item.

- **Detach from original:** To alter the selected library item on a page, this button allows you to detach and break the link to the original item, so that the code on the page is not part of the library link anymore. Refer to Figure 35-34. If you detach, the link is no longer linked to library item and therefore does not automatically update with the other library items.

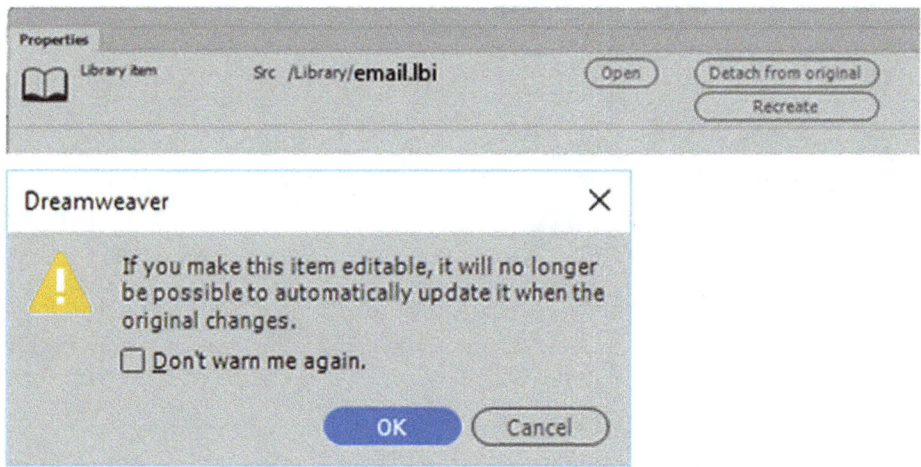

Figure 35-34. Detach a library item

- **Recreate:** Allows you to override the library item. Refer to Figure 35-35.

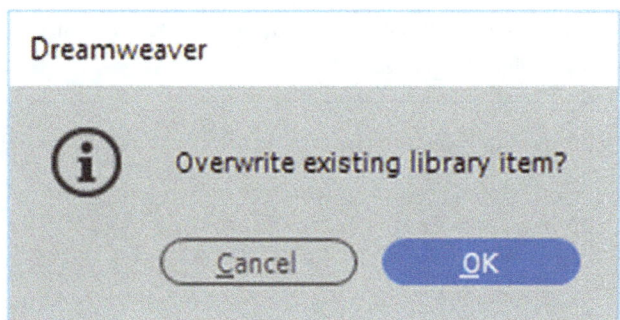

Figure 35-35. You are asked if you want to overwrite the library item

CHAPTER 35 ■ WORKING WITH BOOTSTRAP, TEMPLATES, LIBRARY ITEMS, AND THE ASSETS PANEL

Likewise, you can highlight text or an image in your <body> and in the Assets panel, click New Library Item. This speed up the process. If you don't like the results, click the Trash icon to remove it entirely from your root folder. Just keep in mind that this is a permanent change and affect any area on pages you added the library items to and the link becomes missing. Refer to Figure 35-36.

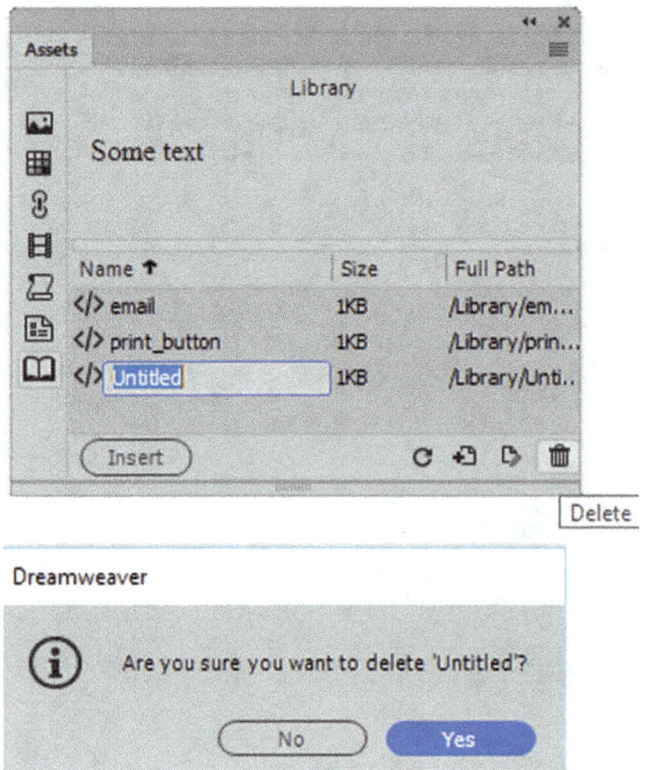

Figure 35-36. *When you delete a library item, it is permanently removed*

■ **Note** Regarding the Asset panel, if you are in Live or Design view, some tabs may be missing, so to ensure that you see all the tabs while working, use Design view. Refer to Figure 35-37.

926

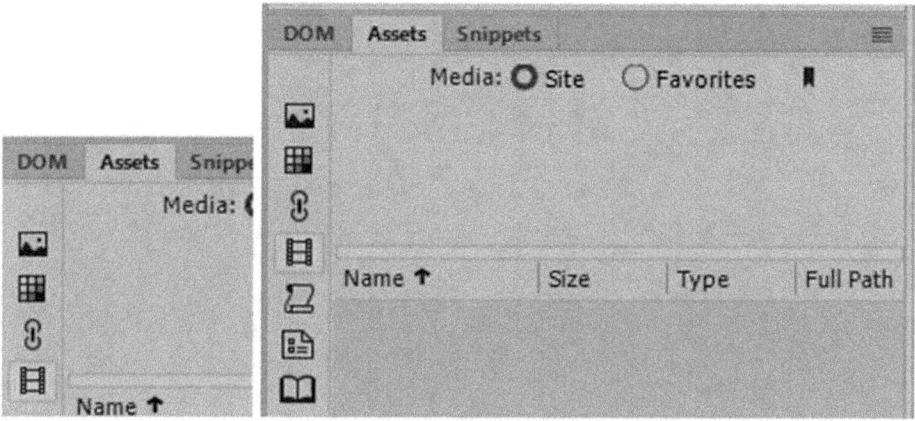

Figure 35-37. *The Asset panel changes from Live to Design view*

Summary

In this chapter, you looked at how Bootstrap is added to a template and how templates are useful so that your website has a theme and looks consistent. You also looked at library items and how they can be added to a website for select pages, but not to every page. Finally, you looked at the Assets panel and how you can use it to view images, templates, and library items that are inside your site's root directory folder.

In the next chapter, you look at how to add audio, video, and animations to your site.

CHAPTER 36

Working with Video, Audio, and Animations

In this chapter, you look at how to add your HTML5 video, audio, and canvas animations as an animated composition or OAM file. You'll also briefly look at a few other options that Dreamweaver has available for adding related multimedia.

> **Note** This chapter does not have any actual projects; however, you can use the files in the Part 6 folder to practice opening and viewing for this lesson. They are at `https://github.com/Apress/graphics-multimedia-web-adobe-creative-cloud`.

Whether or not your site contains templates and library items is up to you. At some point, you may want to add some animation, audio, or video files to your template-based or non-template-based pages. In this chapter, you deal with working with these types of files. You are interacting with the Files panel, Insert panel, and Properties panel when adjusting the code. Refer to Figure 36-1 to see how the Insert panel in the HTML tab contains all the media tags that you look at in this chapter.

CHAPTER 36 ■ WORKING WITH VIDEO, AUDIO, AND ANIMATIONS

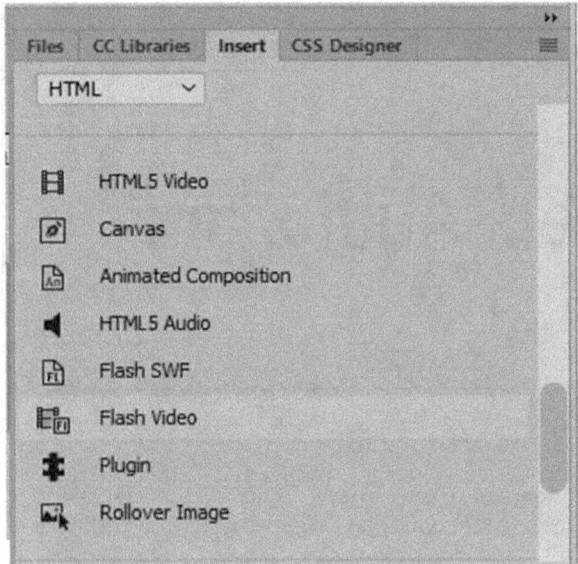

Figure 36-1. The Insert panel contains various multimedia tags

Inserting HTML5 Video

As you saw in earlier chapters, Photoshop CC, Animate CC, and Media Encoder CC can be used separately or in combination to create video for the web. The following are the type of video formats that are acceptable for HTML5:

- MP4 (.mp4)
- WebM (.webm)
- Ogg Theora (.ovg)

In Part 5, you learned about these three formats and how to use Media Encoder to create an MP4, also known as H.264. It is the most commonly used format for video on the Internet. To create the other two formats Webm and Ogg, you need to acquire an additional plug-in for Media Encoder from a third-party provider or find a freeware software (the Miro Video Converter) to create these formats. Refer to Part5 for this information. In most cases, MP4 video is sufficient for your website; however, if you are concerned with backward compatibility, then you want to make sure you have the additional formats.

Streaming and Embedded Video or Have The Video On Your Own Site?

For a website developer who is building a website for a client, the question is whether or not to upload to a site like Vimeo or YouTube with Media Encoder, or keep the HTML video files on their own site. When you upload your video to YouTube, you can utilize its fast streaming quality on your site. You can then embed the video using an <iframe> and a link on your page (src) to keep the site fast and play the video seamlessly; for example,

```
<iframe width="420" height="345" src="https://www.youtube.com/embed/tgbNymZ7vqY">
</iframe>
```

The final code (ID) from W3schools is the link code to the uploaded video on YouTube; in this case, the width and height are defined in the <iframe>.

If you would like to learn how to utilize the autoplay, playlist, loop, and control features within the link, check out www.w3schools.com/html/html_youtube.asp.

If your clients have a powerful enough server, it is better to use HTML5 and set up the video on their site, as you see in a moment. With large videos that run over 5 minutes or more, make sure to run tests; otherwise, you may experience slow load times or broken streaming. Learning how to insert HTML5 video on your own site gives you a better understanding of how video works.

Setup and Testing

If you have not created the video for you own site, you may want to review the video chapters for Photoshop, Illustrator, Animate, and Media Encoder. Once you have rendered your video, make a folder called video or videos in your site's root directory folder, and put your video files in there. In addition to keeping them organized, you may want to create subfolders, such as mp4, webm, and ogg, if you plan to have a lot of footage in theses formats. Also remember to give your video distinct names that are meaningful to you. This way, you can easily locate a video file if you need to replace it. Figure 36-2 shows how this looks in Dreamweaver's Files panel in the root folder.

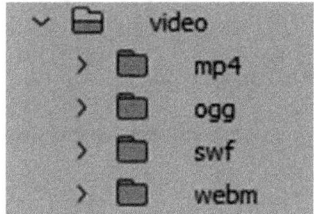

Figure 36-2. *In the Files panel there is a video folder that has all the formats organized*

▮ **Note** You may have older Flash files (.swf) for older browser compatibility; they are not a requirement because the Internet is moving away from this format. Some browsers do not support streaming these files. In the Hot Glass Tango, there is no SWF folder.

Besides the video files, you want to make sure that you have a JPG poster image, also known as a *splash screen design*. This is the image that the audience sees when the HTML5 video is not playing as the file first loads. Make sure that the image has the same dimensions as the video file; in this case, 640×480.

To insert the video, go to the Insert menu's HTML tab and locate the HTML5 video icon.

Find the place on your webpage that you want to insert the video links, place the cursor in that spot in Code view or Design view, and click the HTML5 video icon in the Insert menu. Refer to Figure 36-3.

931

CHAPTER 36 ■ WORKING WITH VIDEO, AUDIO, AND ANIMATIONS

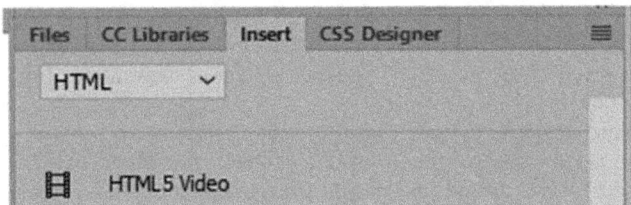

Figure 36-3. In the Insert panel you can scroll down and locate the tag for inserting HTML5 video

This inserts the HTML5 video tag.

`<video controls></video>`

If you select this tag in the Properties panel, you can see which links and settings you need to start adding to your video. Refer to Figure 36-4.

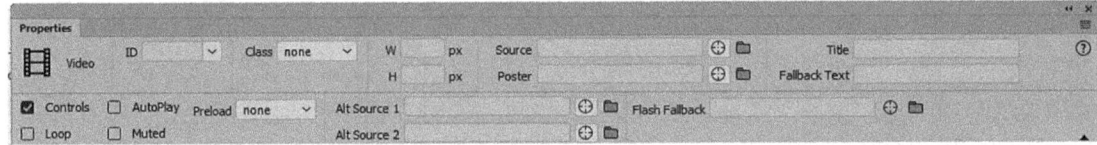

Figure 36-4. In the Properties panel, when you select the video tag, you can see there are many setting options for attributes

- **ID:** The same as ID for all other tags. Add a name for your video here. Accessed by CSS or JavaScript.

- **Class:** You can add a class to your video. Note that you are not able to alter some settings of the video's design, but you can add a border around the video or center the tag.

- **W and H:** This is the width and height of the video in pixels that you set in Media Encoder or whatever video editor you chose to export your file for the web. Remember, if you are using more than one source of the same video or a poster image, make sure that they are all the same width and height to prevent distortion in your layout.

- **Source:** This refers to the link to the main video that displays, in this case it is the MP4 video; if you do not have an MP4, you might make one of your other formats the source, but I recommend MP4 as the primary link.

- **Poster:** This is the link to an image that displays when your video is first downloaded, and the Play button has not yet been pressed. If you do not create a poster, the first frame of the video is used instead. Usually, a poster is a JPG file that you design as a title page in Photoshop. You find the poster in your images folder and then link it with the Folder icon in the Properties panel.

- **Title:** Refers to the title attribute of the video tag.

- **Fallback text:** If none of your video formats play in an older browser, you can add text here to let your clients know that they have to upgrade. You can add a message, such as "Your browser does not support HTML5 video."

- **Controls:** This is for the video's player area, to see the controls check the check box; it is the default setting so that the user can control when to start or pause the video or move to a different point with the sider. It also hides or shows the volume controls and screen size settings. By unchecking this option, the controls for the user may be unavailable when they view the video in their browser.

- **Loop:** This allows the video to loop and play many times. This is generally left unchecked by default.

- **AutoPlay:** This allows the video to start playing as soon as the page loads. The attribute does not work on all mobile devices. It is generally left unchecked by default.

- **Muted:** The sound is initially turned off when the video loads. This is generally left unchecked by default. If you don't want audio in your video, then make sure to remove it when you render your file.

- **Preload:** Specifies the method used to cache the video when it loads. Its default is set to none, but you can also choose auto (load the entire video when the page loads) or metadata (load only metadata when the page loads) from the drop-down menu. If AutoPlay is selected, this area is ignored. Refer to Figure 36-5.

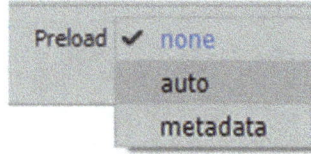

Figure 36-5. *Preload options for video in the Properties panel*

- **Alt Source 1:** This is the next available video source after the main source link. In this case, you locate a WebM video, as this is the next popular setting for browser compatibility. If you do not have a video in this setting, you can leave this link blank.

- **Alt Source 2:** This is the next available video source after the Alt source 1 link. In this case, you would locate a OVG video, as this is the third popular setting for browser compatibility. If you do not have a video in this setting, you can leave this link blank.

- **Flash Fallback:** You can add a flash fallback link to a SWF file here; however, if your video does not have this source option, or if you are not using SWF files, you can leave this link blank.

Once you are done, your Properties panel for the <video> tag should look something like this. You can see this in the video.html file and Figure 36-6.

CHAPTER 36 ■ WORKING WITH VIDEO, AUDIO, AND ANIMATIONS

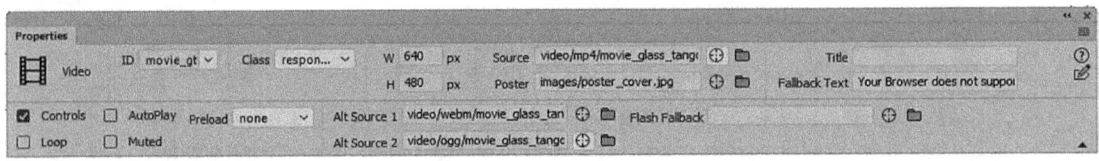

Figure 36-6. *The set up for the video tag*

The code looks something like this:

```
<video width="640" height="480" id="movie_gt" class="responsive-video" title="Hot Glass
Tango" poster="images/poster_cover.jpg" controls="controls">
  <source src="video/mp4/movie_glass_tango_part2.mp4"type="video/mp4">
  <source src ="video/webm/movie_glass_tango_part2.webmhd.webm" type="video/webm">
  <source src= "video/ogg/movie_glass_tango_part2.oggtheora.ogv" type="video/ogg">
  <p>Your Browswer does not Support HTML 5</p>
</video>
```

Within the <video> tag, first the poster attribute and then each video <source> is listed in order of compatibility; if none work, use the fallback text in a paragraph or <p> tag.

Additionally, you may want to edit this code further for each <source> tag. In Code view, click a source tag. In the Properties panel, you can look at each source separately. You can add an ID to each source, as well as a class, or alter the link just for that video source. Refer to Figure 36-7.

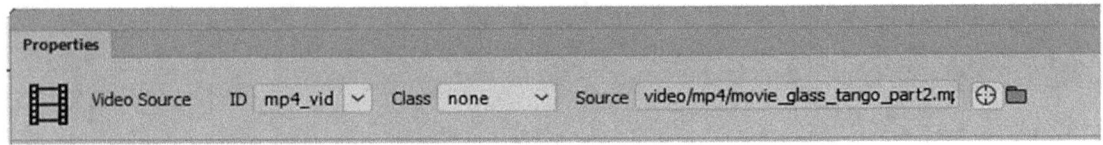

Figure 36-7. *Add an ID to each video source in the Properties panel*

The <source> tags look like this:

```
<video width="640" height="480" id="movie_gt" class="responsive-video" title="Hot Glass
Tango"  poster="images/poster_cover.jpg" controls="controls" >
<source id="mp4_vid"   src="video/mp4/movie_glass_tango_part2.mp4 type="video/mp4">
  <source id="webm_vid"   src="video/webm/movie_glass_tango_part2.webmhd.webm" type="video/webm">
  <source id="ogg_vid"   src="video/ogg/movie_glass_tango_part2.oggtheora.ogv"type="video/ogg">
  <p>Your Browswer does not Support HTML 5</p>
</video>
```

Adding IDs are useful if you need to call up some additional JavaScript, as you see in Chapter 39.

The final thing that you can do is add a codec to the type attribute. It is important to add at least the type and codecs. These help the browser determine whether it can decode the files.

Here in Code view, I have altered the code slightly with the codec for each source.

```
<video width="640" height="480" id="movie_gt" class="responsive-video" title="Hot Glass
Tango" poster="images/poster_cover.jpg" controls="controls" >
<source  id="mp4_vid"  src="video/mp4/movie_glass_tango_part2.mp4"  type='video/mp4;
codecs="avc1.42E01E,mp4a.40.2"' >
<source  id="webm_vid"  src="video/webm/movie_glass_tango_part2.webmhd.webm"  type='video/
webm; codecs="vp8,vorbis"' >
<source  id="ogg_vid"  src="video/ogg/movie_glass_tango_part2.oggtheora.ogv" type='video/
ogg; codecs="theora,vorbis"' >
        <p>Your Browser does not support HTML5 video.</p>
    </video>
```

■ **Note** You may get an error message after adding these codecs in Dreamweaver's Output panel, but in this case, you can ignore it because this is the standard way of setting up the codec. Refer to Figure 36-8.

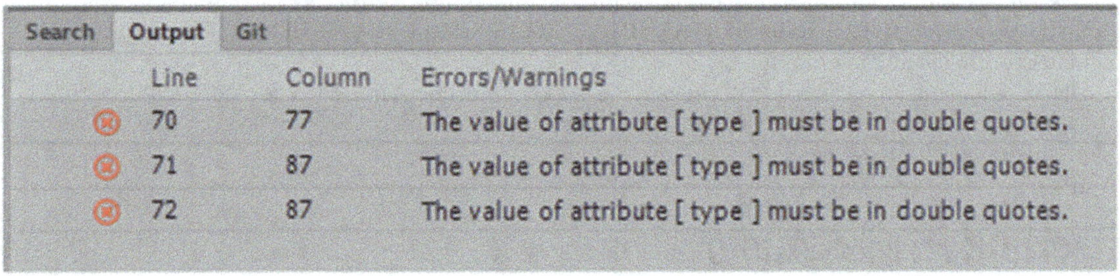

Figure 36-8. Dreamweaver may throw a warning on how the quotes are used, but you can ignore the warning

If there are any changes in this setting, you can check https://en.wikipedia.org/wiki/HTML5_video.

The Track Tag

One further tag that you may encounter within your video tag is the <track> tag for media elements. It is new to HTML5 and is not yet listed in the Properties panel. However, you can add it manually in Code view. Track is used for specifying subtitles, caption files, or other files containing text that should be visible when the media is playing. This setting is not required for your video and audio to run; it is an optional setting. Here is an example:

```
<track src="subtitles_en.vtt" kind="subtitles" srclang="en" label="French">
```

At this point, you might want to test your video and links in various browsers to make sure the media is playing correctly.

CHAPTER 36 ■ WORKING WITH VIDEO, AUDIO, AND ANIMATIONS

Mobile and Video Scaling

As with image <img>, videos are scaled or optimized for mobile devices and large monitors. You can add a width or a max-width (so it does not scale beyond a certain resolution) and a height of auto so that the video scales proportionately.

```
.responsive-video {
    max-width: 100%;
    height: auto;
}
```

You can learn more about this at www.w3schools.com/css/css_rwd_videos.asp.

Can You Insert Video into a Background Using CSS?

Like an image, you can insert video into a background using CSS, but it is simply behind other <div> and not using in the CSS property background image. This could be useful on an intro or index page, where the movie is behind a small amount of text that overlays the video while it plays with the controls removed. Objects moving in the background can be distracting. A better option is to use a GIF animation (no audio) within the background-image property. Or use a <canvas> animation from Animate CC because elements are better controlled and maintained.

If you're looking for an example of video in the background, check out www.w3schools.com/howto/howto_css_fullscreen_video.asp, which uses a combination of HTML, CSS, and JavaScript to control the video with a single button.

Inserting HTML5 Audio

As with video, you can add an HTML5 audio player to your website. Before HTML5 audio, sound files could only be played with plug-ins like Flash, so audio on websites is a relatively new idea. As you saw in with Media Encoder, HTML5 accepts three formats:

- MP3 (.mp3)
- WAV (.wav)
- Theora Ogg (.ogg)

In Media Encoder, you can create MP3 files and WAV sound files, but for Ogg, you need to acquire a third-party plug-in or use a free program like Miro Video Converter. Safari and Internet Explorer do not support Ogg, but Chrome, Firefox, and Opera do. In most cases, MP3 and WAV audio are sufficient for your website; however, if you are concerned with backward compatibility, then you want to make sure that you have the other formats.

Setup and Testing

If you have not created the audio for you own site, you may want to review the audio section for Media Encoder in Part 4. Once you have your audio, make a folder called audio or sounds in your site's root directory folder and put your audio files in there. In addition, to keep them organized, you may want to create subfolders, such as mp3, wav and ogg, if you plan to have a lot of audio in these formats. As with video, give the files a distinct name. This way, you can easily locate an audio file if you need to replace it. Figure 36-9 shows how this could look in Dreamweaver's Files panel.

CHAPTER 36 ■ WORKING WITH VIDEO, AUDIO, AND ANIMATIONS

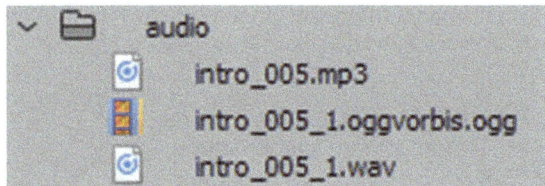

Figure 36-9. *The audio files added to an audio folder in the Site Root folder in the Files panel*

To insert the audio, go to the Insert menu's HTML tab and locate the HTML5 audio icon. Refer to Figure 36-10.

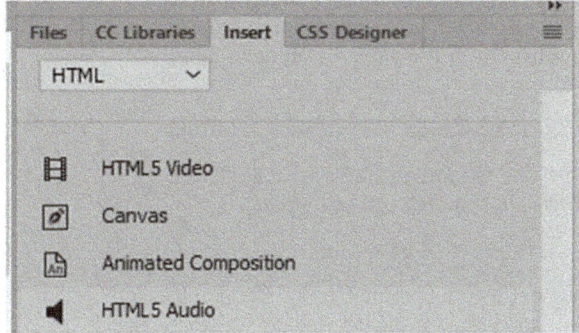

Figure 36-10. *In the Insert panel, locate the HTML5 audio tag to insert audio into your webpage*

Find the place on your webpage that you want to insert the audio links; place the cursor in that spot in Code view or Design view, and click the icon in the Insert menu.

This inserts the HTML5 video tag.

```
<audio controls></audio>
```

If you select this tag in the Properties menu, you can see which links and settings you need to start adding. Refer to Figure 36-11.

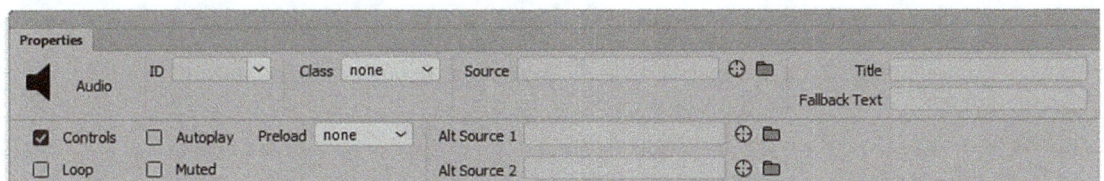

Figure 36-11. *The Properties panel with audio tag selected*

- **ID:** This is the same as ID for all other tags; add a name for your audio here. It is accessed by CSS or JavaScript.

937

- **Class:** You can add a class to your audio. Note that some settings you are not able to alter such as the default browser audio's design, but you can add a border around the audio area or center it.

- **Source:** This refers to the link to the main audio that displays; in this case, it is the MP3 audio. If you do not have MP3, you might make one of your other formats the source, but I recommend MP3 as the primary link.

- **Title:** Refers to the title attribute of the audio tag.

- **Fallback Text:** If none of your audio plays in a browser, you can add some text here to let your clients know that they may have to upgrade. You could add a message such as "Your Browser does not support HTML5 audio."

- **Controls:** This is for the audio's player area to see the Controls check the check box, it is the default setting so that the user can control when to start or pause the audio or move to a different point with the sider. It also affects the appearance of volume controls. If unchecked, the user cannot control the audio while listening to it in the browser.

- **Loop:** This allows the audio to loop and play many times. It is unchecked by default.

- **AutoPlay:** This allows the audio to start playing as soon as the page loads. This attribute does not work on all mobile devices. It is unchecked by default.

- **Muted:** The sound is initially turned off. It is unchecked by default.

- **Preload:** Specifies the method used to cache the audio when it loads. Its default is set to none, but you can also choose auto (load the entire audio when the page loads) or metadata (load only metadata when the page loads) from the drop-down menu. If AutoPlay is selected, this area is ignored. Refer to Figure 36-12.

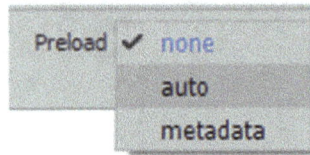

Figure 36-12. *Choose a preload property from the properties menu*

- **Alt Source 1:** This is the next available audio source after the main source link. In this case, you locate a WAV audio as this is the next popular setting for browser compatibility. If you do not have an audio in this setting, you can leave this link blank.

- **Alt Source 2:** This is the next available audio source after the Alt source 1 link. In this case, you locate a Ogg audio as this is the third popular setting for browser compatibility. If you do not have an audio in this setting, you can leave this link blank.

Once you are done, your Properties panel for the <audio> tag should look something like Figure 36-13.

Figure 36-13. *The audio settings have been added to the Properties panel*

The code looks something like this:

```
<audio id="audio_gt" title="Sound File" controls="controls" >
  <source   src="audio/intro_005.mp3"  type="audio/mp3" >
  <source   src="audio/intro_005_1.wav"  type="audio/wav" >
  <source   src="audio/intro_005_1.oggvorbis.ogg"  type="audio/ogg" >
        <p>Your Browser does not support HTML5 audio.</p>
     </audio>
```

Within the <audio> tag, which defines the sound content, each audio <source> that defines the media resource is listed in order of compatibility and finally if none of these sources work the Fallback Text in a paragraph or <p> tag is displayed.

You may want to edit this code further for each <source> tag. In code as with the <video> tag view click a source tag within the <audio>. In the Properties panel, you can look at each source separately. You can add an ID to each source as well as a class, or alter the link just for that audio source. Refer to Figure 36-14.

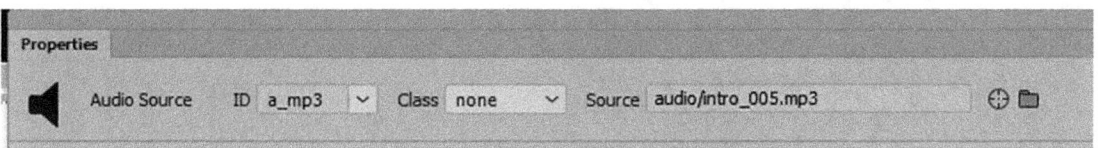

Figure 36-14. *Add an ID for each audio source using the Properties panel*

The <source> tags then look like this:

```
<audio id="audio_gt" title="Sound File" controls="controls" >
    <source   id="a_mp3"   src="audio/intro_005.mp3"   type="audio/mp3" >
    <source   id="a_wav"   src="audio/intro_005_1.wav"   type="audio/wav" >
    <source   id="a_ogg"   src="audio/intro_005_1.oggvorbis.ogg"   type="audio/ogg" >
        <p>Your Browser does not support HTML5 audio.</p>
     </audio>
```

Now the browser can detect which audio or alternate audio files it wants to choose.

IDs are useful if you need to reference additional JavaScript.

Unlike <video> sources, you do not need to add an attribute codec for audio. For more information, refer to https://en.wikipedia.org/wiki/HTML5_Audio.

At this point, you might want to test your audio and links in various browsers to make sure that the media is playing correctly.

Can You Insert Audio into a Background Using CSS?

Like video, you can hide the audio controls so that the sound cannot be turned off by the user. Keep in mind that this might be annoying to some users if the sound is very loud or they don't like music. This is not a good practice. It is generally better to provide users some control options, like a button to mute, lower the volume, or turn on the sound by choice.

You can apply sound to <div> elements with CSS background images that can alter or change using CSS3 transitions and transforms or make a sound using JavaScript when they are hovered over (mouse-enter) or clicked. Sound can have many uses on a website that user's can interact with. However make sure they have the option of turning off the sound as well.

Audio CSS Aural

A CSS feature for audio that you might not be aware of is *aural style sheets*. These style sheets convert text into audio for people who are visually impaired and require a screen reader or a speech synthesizer. The Internet should be for everyone, so if you want more information on how to add an aural style sheet, check out www.w3schools.com/cssref/css_ref_aural.asp.

Using CSS Designer panel when you create an external style sheet as in Chapter 33. You can instead under conditional usage (optional) choose a for media a setting of aural, instead of screen or print. Refer to Figure 36-15.

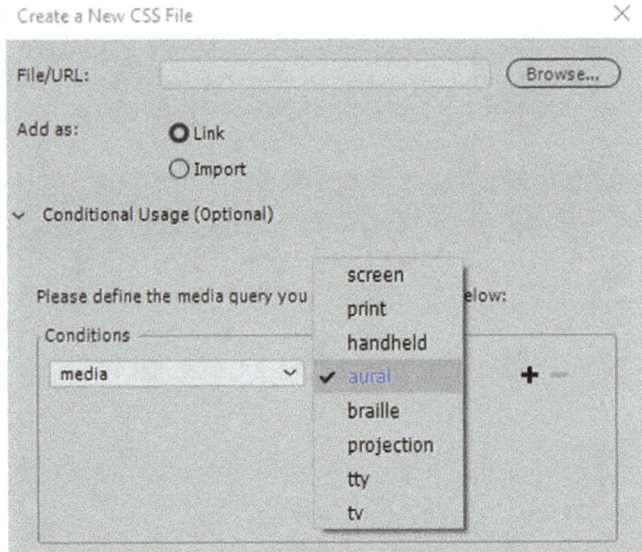

Figure 36-15. *Rather than create a style sheet for screen or print, you can create one just for aural*

Insert a Canvas Element

In Part 4, you were introduced to the HTML5 Canvas. I compared it to ActionScript 3.0 and all its features. A canvas or <canvas> element draws or animates graphics quickly via scripting like JavaScript. An HTML5 Canvas FLA file was exported along with a compressed OAM file, and the result was a generated group of files:

- a folder called images containing images
- a folder called sounds containing audio, generally MP3 or WAV files

CHAPTER 36 ■ WORKING WITH VIDEO, AUDIO, AND ANIMATIONS

- a JavaScript file (.js)that is linked and interacts with the HTML5(.html) file that is created

- an HTML5 file (.html) that contains the <canvas> element that contains the animation. When you looked inside this file you found internal inline CSS, internal JavaScript and a link to JavaScript on an external library site (Create JS) that helps control the animation.

- If you opened the generated OAM package, besides the above mentioned, you would also find XML files that control setting and the generated a poster image(.png).

You can also have a small video (MP4) inside the <canvas> that is part of the animation; this is created using the components panel. This appears as a separate linked file along with the aforementioned files.

Importing Animate Canvas into Dreamweaver

Once you have exported these files from Animate CC and brought them into Dreamweaver CC, you see that it contains many of the HTML5 tags that you reviewed in Chapter 31. At this point, it is up to you how you want to work with the <canvas> in the HTML file and incorporate it into your website.

Option 1

If you are planning for it to be an index or intro page that is not part of the template, you may just make a copy of this file with the new name and then continue to edit it with minor alterations, such as using CSS to center the <canvas> element, alter the background, add some text, add navigation links, or anything else that makes this page match your theme for your website.

At this point, make sure that you add your external JavaScript, images, and sounds to the correct folders in your root directory site. For your canvas animation you may want to keep a separate folder "sounds" from the one called "audio" if you have different sounds from different programs or alter this folder name during the Animate CC export. Publish in the Basic tab. It is more difficult to alter this folder link outside Animate; however, the link to the MP3 audio file is found in the generated external JS file in a section called lib.properties. Open this file and look for the manifest; and there you find the path to the sounds. If you have trouble locating this line, use Dreamweaver CC and select Find ➤ Find in Current Document. Refer to Figure 36-16.

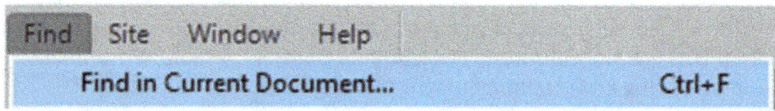

Figure 36-16. Locate a line of code within a current document

Enter the word **sounds**, as in Figure 36-17.

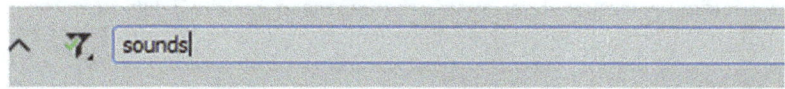

Figure 36-17. While in the external JavaScript file, you can use the search text box to find a line of code

Then find the path that you want to alter. Your file should look slightly different from Figure 36-18.

```
▼ lib.properties = {
      width: 640,
      height: 480,
      fps: 24,
      color: "#FFFFFF",
      opacity: 1.00,
      webfonts: {},
      manifest: [
          {src:"images/Bitmap3.jpg", id:"Bitmap3"},
   ▼      {src:"sounds/MVI_6393.mp3", id:"MVI_6393"}
      ],
      preloads: []
  };
```

Figure 36-18. *The line of code where the link to the audio of the canvas is found*

If you plan to alter the name of the file or replace it, use the Find tool to make sure that the parts of the file name match the new name throughout the JavaScript; make the changes carefully. Whatever audio alterations you make, always test that the sound still works correctly.

Option 2

When working with an HTML5 canvas from Animate, if you are planning on adding it to a template-based page, make sure to copy each part of the code from the original file into the corresponding point in your new page. In Code view, for example, JavaScript code and <meta> tags that were in the <head> of the original now go into the <head> editable area of the template-based page. You may need to add the JavaScript onload="init();to your template. If you already have JavaScript using this function, you don't have to add it again.

<body onload="init();>

Then add the other code in the <body>, including the <canvas>, into a specific <div> element on your page. Make sure to save and test the file links and JavaScript. You may need to adjust the CSS because it may not align the way you want it to at first. This is a laborious task. For template-based pages, there is a much cleaner way of working with the code—by using an OAM or animated composition.

Canvas Element Created Without Animate

You don't need to use Animate CC to create all of your <canvas> elements. If you are creating still images on a <canvas> element, you can use Dreamweaver to do the work.

In your document (in either Code view or Design view), choose the Canvas in the HTML tab. Refer to Figure 36-19.

CHAPTER 36 ■ WORKING WITH VIDEO, AUDIO, AND ANIMATIONS

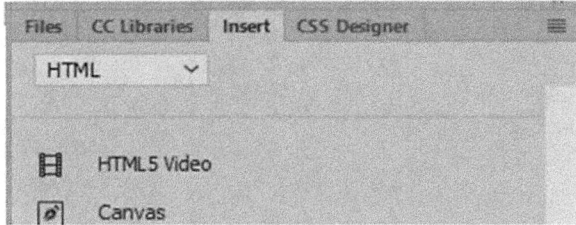

Figure 36-19. Use the Insert panel to create a canvas tag

This creates the <canvas> tag with a canvas ID.

```
<canvas id="canvas"></canvas>
```

Figure 36-20 shows how it appears in the Properties panel.

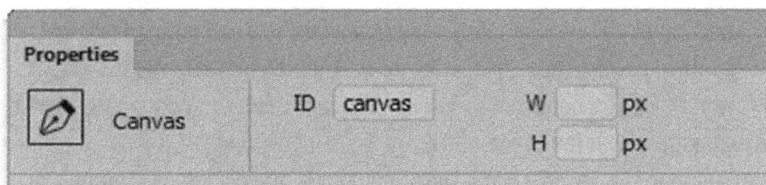

Figure 36-20. In the Properties panel you can view the canvas tag

You can set the width and height as you would in Animate for the stage. Refer to Figure 36-21.

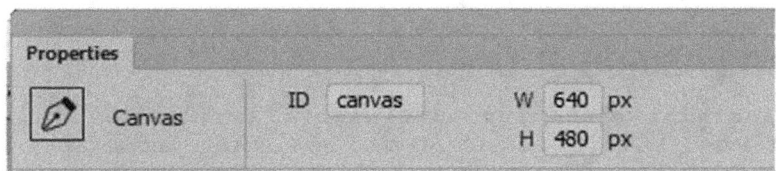

Figure 36-21. In the Properties panel, set the width and height of the canvas tag

As you saw in Animate CC, this program makes it quite easy to create graphics for the <canvas> element container. The canvas is used to quickly draw graphics (with color and gradients) with JavaScript formatting. If you aren't familiar with JavaScript formatting, this could be a challenging task, so Animate is an excellent choice for complex animations.

There are resources if you want to draw basic shapes or words on a canvas and copy this code into Dreamweaver's Code view to edit further.

- www.w3schools.com/html/html5_canvas.asp
- www.w3schools.com/graphics/canvas_intro.asp
- www.w3schools.com/graphics/canvas_reference.asp

Here is an example of how some code could be written:

```
<canvas id="myCanvas" width="200" height="100"
style="border:1px solid #d3d3d3;">
Your browser does not support the HTML5 canvas tag.</canvas>
<script>
var c = document.getElementById("myCanvas");
var ctx = c.getContext("2d");
// Create gradient
var grd = ctx.createLinearGradient(0,0,200,0);
grd.addColorStop(0,"blue");
grd.addColorStop(1,"red");
// Fill with gradient
ctx.fillStyle = grd;
ctx.fillRect(10,10,150,80);
</script>
```

Note The <canvas> element is interactive and responds to JavaScript events. You can program for user actions, such as click buttons and finger movements. These elements are used for gaming. Do not mix the game code you create in Animate CC with those you hand code yourself in Dreamweaver. I find that you should only use the JavaScript code that is compatible with the CreateJS library while in Animate CC, because it works with the frames per second feature of Animate CC. Trying to copy JavaScript code directly into an Animate HTML5 Canvas (.fla) Action panel from a site like W3Schools might work for a still image, but usually ends in animated graphics not functioning or having a jerky motion.

Insert Animated Composition or OAM

In Animate CC, when you export an HTML5 Canvas file, you also have the option of exporting an OAM file, also known as an animated composition. OAM and the canvas file are the same in that they both can contain animations, but the OAM's construction is slightly different in that you now must extract and import the HTML5 Canvas animation to insert it into Dreamweaver. From the OAM files, a folder called "animation assets" is created in the root directory, which you'll look at more closely in a moment.

After you have exported or published an OAM file from Animate, you notice that it is one single file and not separate parts. This is because the OAM is merely a package, like how you would create a ZIP file. Animate CC has put the files into one folder, and you need Dreamweaver CC to unpack it.

To do this, place your cursor either in code view or design view somewhere in a <div> or A semantic element on your webpage, and in the Insert panel's HTML tab, click the Animated Composition icon. Refer to Figure 36-22.

CHAPTER 36 ■ WORKING WITH VIDEO, AUDIO, AND ANIMATIONS

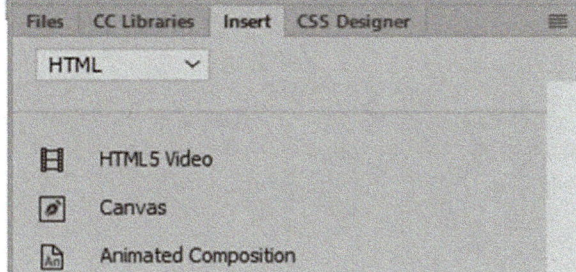

Figure 36-22. *Use the Insert panel to unpack and insert the animated composition HTML5 canvas*

If you have not saved the HTML page, Dreamweaver ask you to do so. Refer to Figure 36-23.

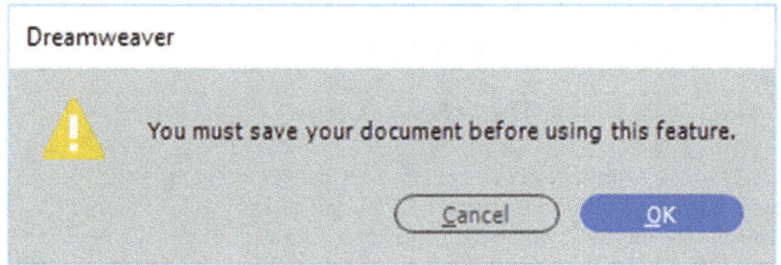

Figure 36-23. *Make sure you have saved your HTML file before you insert the animated composition*

Click OK and save the HTML file in the root directory folder. At this point, select the Animated Composition dialog box. You are asked to locate the OAM file. Make sure that it is saved in your sites root directory folder. Select it and click OK. It then begins to unpack the file and insert it. The unpacked OAMs are placed on individual pages and related files are linked via the data attribute. If the OAM has already been unpacked, you may get this warning. You can click OK to override, or click Cancel and copy the generated code from another document in your site if it has been unpacked once. Refer to Figure 36-24.

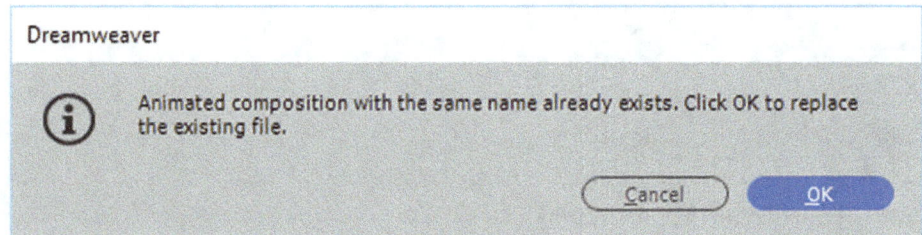

Figure 36-24. *If the animated composition has already been unpacked you may receive this warning*

945

CHAPTER 36 ■ WORKING WITH VIDEO, AUDIO, AND ANIMATIONS

The OAM then unpacks and creates code with an <object> tag. You can see an example of this on the Hot Glass Tango index.html file.

```
<div class="center-canvas">
    <object id="EdgeID" type="text/html" width="660" height="500" data-dw-widget="Edge"
    data="animation_assets/scene6_end_canvasan_HTML5_Canvas_res/Assets/ scene6_end_
    canvasan_HTML5_Canvas_res.html">
    </object>
</div>
```

Figure 36-25 shows how it appears in the Properties panel.

Figure 36-25. The unpacked animated composition contains the HTML5 Canvas file

The <object> ID tells you that it is an Edge file. As you saw in Part 4, Animate CC was once called Flash, and then it merged with Adobe Edge Animate to become Animate CC. You can add a class for a border or centering. As with the canvas, you can see the width and height and other data attributes that give a description and the link to another HTML file that contains the actual animation. The <object> is essentially acting as a linked object window to look inside another HTML page. This link is the unpackaged OAM file. All related files are found inside the animation assets folder. Refer to Figure 36-26.

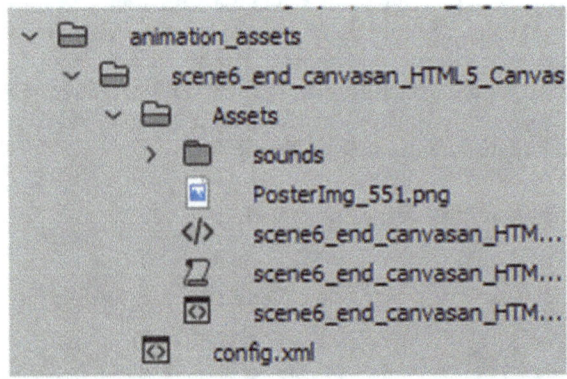

Figure 36-26. The unpacked animated assets as seen in the Files panel

Within the folder are:

- XML files to control order
- External JavaScript to control movement
- A graphic PNG file that is a poster image

CHAPTER 36 ■ WORKING WITH VIDEO, AUDIO, AND ANIMATIONS

- An HTML file that is linked to your new HTML page
- A folder that contain the audio sounds for the canvas file

The internal structure of this file is the same as the canvas file that you saw earlier, so if your plan is to add an animation from Animate CC to a template-based page, this is a cleaner and faster option. The <object> tag acts as a "window," and this is far better than trying to copy and paste your code from your HTML5 Canvas file directly into the template-based page. If you need to adjust your animation assets folder path, it is found in Site ➤ Manage Site in the Advanced Settings tab ➤ Animation Assets.

Inserting Flash SWF and Flash Video

I do not go into any detail regarding the steps for inserting Flash SWF (.swf) or Flash video (.flv) because most web designers are moving away from these formats due to the processing power and runtime strain it puts on mobile devices.

You can still use Dreamweaver to insert these formats if your client requests it, however. Refer to Figure 36-27.

Figure 36-27. You can still use the Insert panel to insert Flash SWF and Flash video files

■ **Note** If you are reviewing a client's older site and you are not sure if it contains Flash SWF or Flash video files, you can check in the Assets panel in the Media tab. Refer to Figure 36-28.

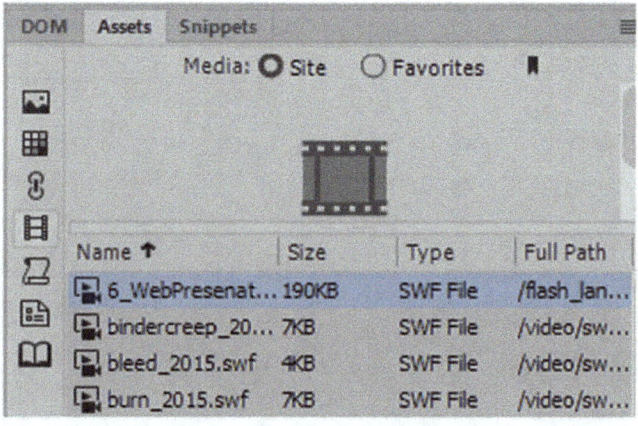

Figure 36-28. The Asset panel is a useful tool if you are trying to locate older flash files in a client's root folder

You can then locate the folders that they are stored in and remove the files that are old or outdated. Media in the Assets panel does not help you locate MP4 files or audio files.

947

Insert Plug-in

Dreamweaver lets you add other plug-ins to your website, including RealPlayer and QuickTime movies. For more information, refer to https://helpx.adobe.com/dreamweaver/using/adding-media-objects.html. Refer to Figure 36-29.

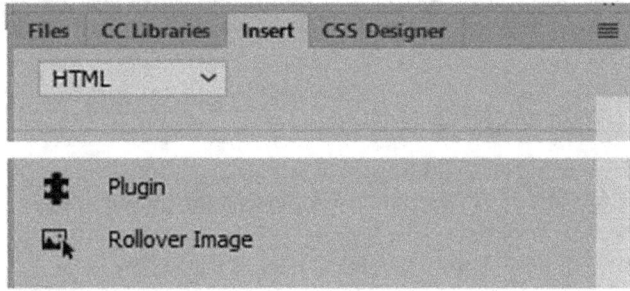

Figure 36-29. *Use the plugin tag to insert third-party media*

This concludes inserting various media into our HTML5 webpages by using the Insert HTML tab.

Summary

In this chapter, you looked at how to insert several types of multimedia, such as video, audio, HTML5 Canvas, and animated composition OAM. You looked at older multimedia options that Dreamweaver still offers.

In the next chapter, before you finish reviewing the site, you'll look at a few additional options and panels that you can use in Dreamweaver to enhance the look of your site.

CHAPTER 37

Additional Options to Apply Images in Dreamweaver

In this chapter, you look at a few other options that you may not have considered while working in Dreamweaver to apply images to your site.

> **Note** This chapter does not have any actual projects; however, you can use the files in the Part 6 folder to practice opening and viewing for this lesson. They are at https://github.com/Apress/graphics-multimedia-web-adobe-creative-cloud.

Target Attributes

Target attributes in HTML allow you to specify where to open a linked document, like a PDF, but with CSS selectors, they are a useful way you can display linked files that do not have an image preview or thumbnail, such as PDF files.

So far in in Part 6, you have not dealt with how to work with file types such as PDFs that don't show up as a graphic unless you click the link. CSS has a snippet that uses target attributes to get around this issue, so that you can at least see a thumbnail of the type of file type you are looking at if you have a lengthy list.

You can find this example under Snippets Panel CSS Snippets ➤ Style Links based on file type. Figure 37-1 shows a preview of the code and css_target_test.html.

CHAPTER 37 ■ ADDITIONAL OPTIONS TO APPLY IMAGES IN DREAMWEAVER

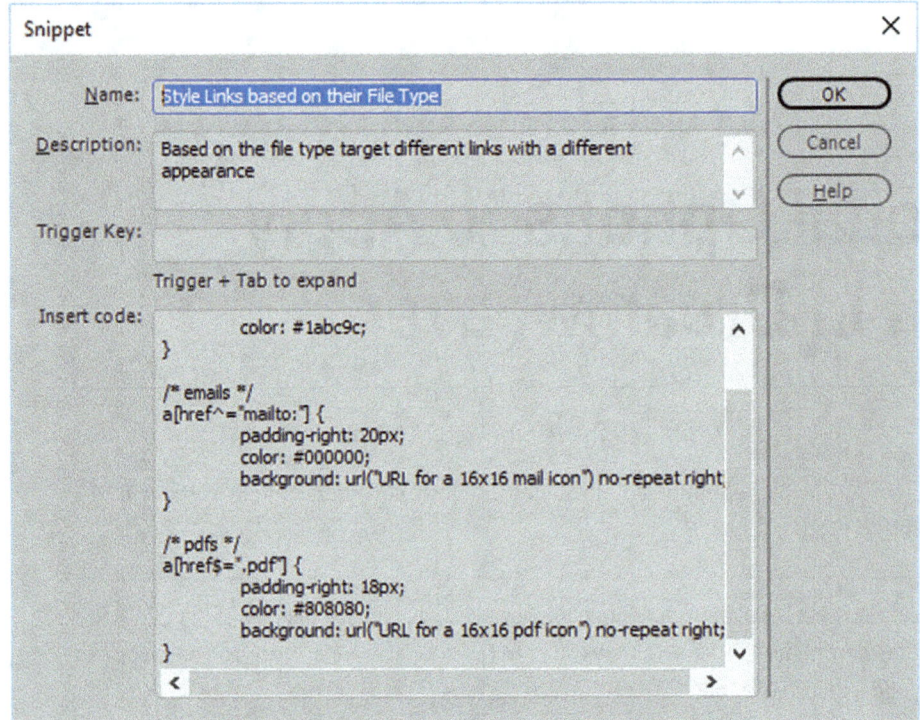

Figure 37-1. Modifying some snippet code for targets

I made some modifications to the CSS code that you can see here.

```
/* external links */
/* external links */
ul li{
        list-style: none;
        display:inline-block;
}
ul a{
        display:block;
        min-height: 15px;
        padding-left: 20px;
        background-repeat: no-repeat;
        background-position: 0 3px;
}
a[href^="http://"] {
        padding-right: 13px;
        color: #1abc9c;
}
```

```
/* emails */
a[href^="mailto:"] {
        padding-right: 20px;
        color: #000000;
        background: url(../images/icon_mail.gif) no-repeat left;
}

/* pdfs */
a[href$=".pdf"] {
        padding-right: 18px;
        color: #808080;
        background: url(../images/icon_pdf.gif) no-repeat left;
}
```

By targeting the <a> tag and the href attribute, you can target file extensions such as .pdf or the "mailto" link, and add a helpful graphic beside the link. You can see an example in Figure 37-2.

Figure 37-2. Add an icon beside files that need a small thumbnail preview

The HTML code looks like this:

```
<ul>
<li> <a href="file1.pdf" target="_blank">PDF File 1</a></li>
<li> <a href="file2.pdf" target="_blank">PDF File 2</a></li>
<li> <a href="mailto:your_email@gmail.com">Email Me</a></li>
<li> <a href="http://www.your_site.com">Some Site</a></li>
</ul>
```

Note that these are just temporary links for testing; there are no actual PDF files currently linked in my site. You can replace the links with your own file to test further. When adding a document like a PDF, always remember to add a "_blank" value to open the linked document in a new window or tab. This is a best practice when you open a PDF or are directing your user to a resource link that is not a page on your site.

Graphs and Charts

Other JavaScript libraries included with jQuery also allow you to create live pie charts and graphs that you can further edit in Dreamweaver using the <canvas> element. Just bear in mind that these might be in the form of third-party plug-ins (not created by Dreamweaver), so read the documentation carefully to understand how to set it up (see https://canvasjs.com/jquery-charts/).

Google Charts is free. You can learn how to edit and use it on W3Schools (www.w3schools.com/howto/howto_google_charts.asp) and then apply it to your page in Dreamweaver in Code view. Examples are at https://developers.google.com/chart/.

CHAPTER 37 ■ ADDITIONAL OPTIONS TO APPLY IMAGES IN DREAMWEAVER

Web Fonts

Like Photoshop, Illustrator, and Animate, Dreamweaver allows you to add web fonts. If possible, work with web fonts so that your site appears consistent for as many users as possible. Rather than embedding fonts, Google Fonts and Adobe Edge Web Fonts (formerly Typekit) are two examples.

Using two or three fonts for your site is usually enough. These fonts allow you to add creative headers to your webpages, even if your viewers' computers do not have those fonts installed. In the past, if you wanted a fancy script heading, you had to either make sure that you had a generic backup font family referenced in the CSS file in case your viewer did not have your font (New Times Roman or Helvetica), or you had to put a graphic in place of the font. However, this led to formatting issues, and it was difficult to update the graphic. When web fonts came along, it solved the issue.

In most cases, you use the fonts that are supplied by Adobe, but you can also use Google Fonts, which are considered the most compatible, as well if you add the correct external links to the <head> section of your HTML5 web page.

```
<link href='https://fonts.googleapis.com/css?family=Sofia' rel='stylesheet'>
```

There are many Google web fonts, and they are free and easy to use.

If you want to use the Adobe web fonts on your website, you can access them at Properties panel ➤ Font ➤ Manage Fonts. Refer to Figure 37-3.

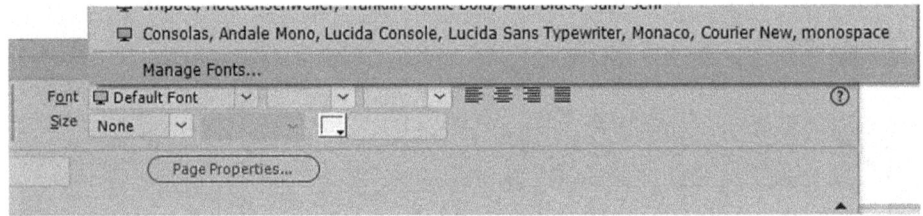

Figure 37-3. *Use the Properties panel to access and manage web fonts*

Or via the Tools ➤ Manage Fonts from the main menu.

This brings up all the available fonts that you can use, and you can apply them to your sites. Refer to Figure 37-4.

CHAPTER 37 ADDITIONAL OPTIONS TO APPLY IMAGES IN DREAMWEAVER

Figure 37-4. You can search through many available Adobe Edge Web Fonts

Not all web fonts are free. Choosing the right font takes time and research if you want to create a professional user experience. When selecting a web font, you must, consider such things as licensing, and whether you need to pay once or if there is another agreement, such as a Creative Cloud subscription. If you are on a budget, you might gravitate toward a free font; however, consider Table 37-1.

Table 37-1. Advantages and Disadvantages of Free and Paid Web Fonts

Free Fonts	Paid Fonts
They are free to use	They can be expensive
If overused by others, they can dilute your brand's image	Can make you stand out from your competition
Often only found in one weight and may be difficult to italicize or bold accurately	Come in more font weights, but you may need to pay more for extra ones
May or may not be a high quality font	If they are a higher quality, there may be support for multi-language symbols, and the typography creators will get paid

953

CHAPTER 37 ■ ADDITIONAL OPTIONS TO APPLY IMAGES IN DREAMWEAVER

When downloading them from a site, you may want to host them on your own site rather than use Adobe Edge or Google's hosting services. You add them in the Local Web Fonts tab. Refer to Figure 37-5.

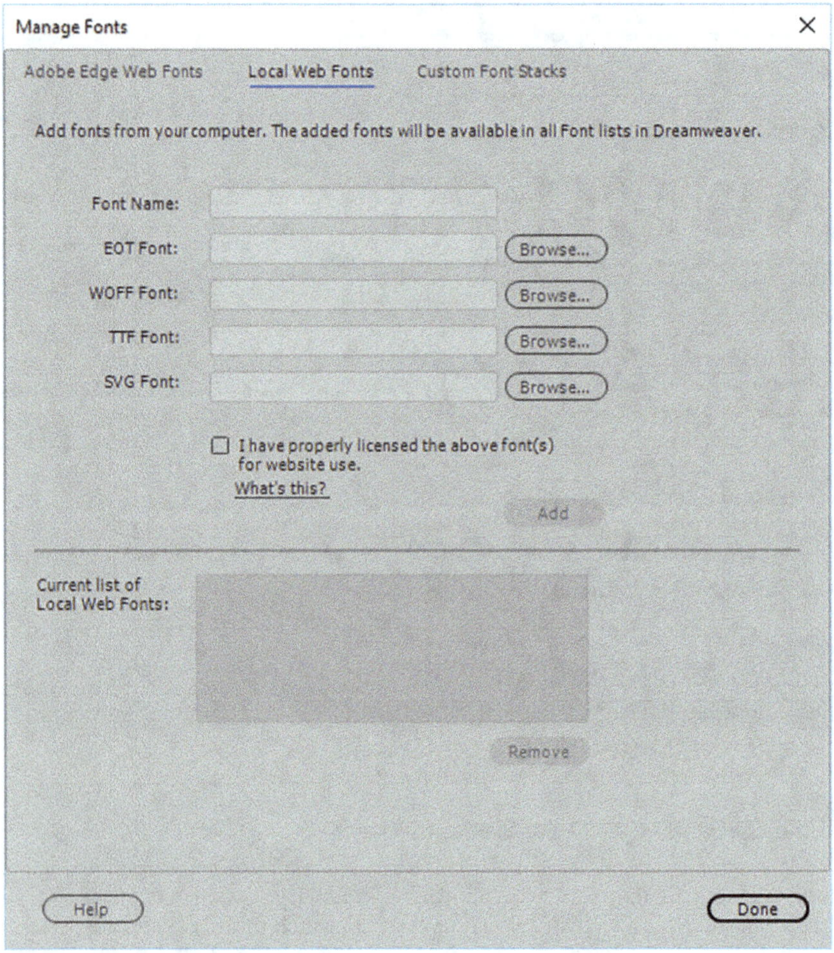

Figure 37-5. You can add fonts that are on your computer to your site if you have them properly licensed

When you add a web font, you need to make sure that first you list the font name and that it is available in at least four formats.

- **Embedded OpenType Fonts (EOT):** Designed by Microsoft and for use as embedded fonts on all webpages. You may see it as OpenType Fonts (OTF), which is used by Mac and Window computers.

- **The Web Open Font Format (WOFF or WOFF 2.0):** This font was added as a recommendation by W3C. It is OpenType or TrueType with extra metadata and added compression to support a variety of bandwidths. WOFF 2.0 is the next version and provides better compression, which is useful when working with mobile devices.

- **TrueType Fonts (TTF):** These are for both Mac and Windows computers. They are the most common format found on both operating systems. This format allows basic digital rights management and is supported by all major browsers. A lesser known format is the TrueType Collection(TTC), which allows many fonts in a single file to save space or fonts where many glyphs are common.
- **SVG Fonts/Shapes:** SVG is used to display various glyph shapes. Being in an uncompressed format, the size can be large, and there is no provision for font-hinting (lines up with a rasterized grid so that it can be legible at low-res sizes).

To learn which browsers support which fonts, go to www.w3schools.com/css/css3_fonts.asp.

Once you have a collection of custom web fonts to store in your root site, you can store them in a fonts folder. For example, depending on the version of Bootstrap if you use a widget from the Insert Panel Bootstrap tab, Dreamweaver automatically creates a fonts folder and then stores the fonts for that widget or other Bootstrap widgets in that location. Likewise, you can store your own web fonts there too. Refer to Figure 37-6.

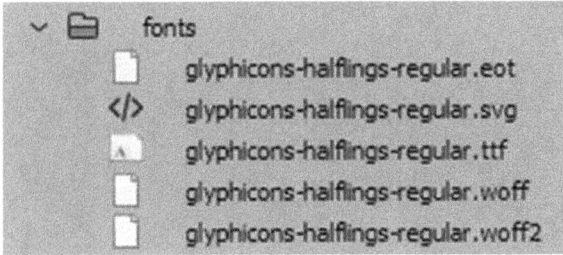

Figure 37-6. *Web fonts are added to the fonts folder*

You apply them within your external CSS file using the @font-face rule. First, define a name for the font (e.g., myFirstFont) and then point to the font file.

```
@font-face {
    font-family: myFirstFonts;
    src: url(somefont.woff);
}
@font-face {
    font-family: myFirstFont;
    src: url(somefont_bold.woff);
    font-weight: bold;
}
 div {
    font-family: myFirstFonts;
}
```

Note Keep the font name in the URL in lowercase to avoid conflicts in the browser.

CHAPTER 37 ADDITIONAL OPTIONS TO APPLY IMAGES IN DREAMWEAVER

In addition, you can add a @font-face when you want to apply bold or italic styles.

If you have different formats for the same font, they are separated by commas. You can see how this might appear with the Bootstrap font.

```
@font-face {
  font-family: 'Glyphicons Halflings';

  src: url('../fonts/glyphicons-halflings-regular.eot');
  src: url('../fonts/glyphicons-halflings-regular.eot?#iefix') format('embedded-opentype'),
    url('../fonts/glyphicons-halflings-regular.woff2') format('woff2'), url('../fonts/
    glyphicons-halflings-regular.woff') format('woff'), url('../fonts/glyphicons-halflings-
    regular.ttf') format('truetype'), url('../fonts/glyphicons-halflings-regular.
    svg#glyphicons_halflingsregular') format('svg');
}
```

You can see how this appears in the CSS Designer panel in the Properties section, where two sources show each separated by a semicolon; both are connected to the same font family. Refer to Figure 37-7.

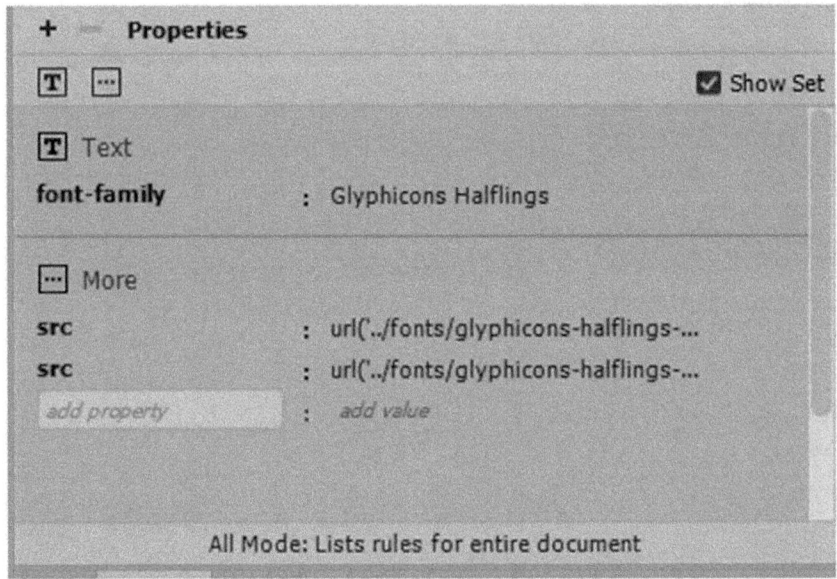

Figure 37-7. The CSS Designer panel with the fonts src listed

---

■ **Note** To view web fonts in Dreamweaver correctly, you need to set the viewing to Live view. Also, some newer versions of Bootstrap CSS rely on system fonts, so if you are using the web fonts I supplied for practice, make sure to add the @font-face to your own external CSS file and follow the earlier code examples.

Returning to the Manage Fonts dialog box, you can also organize your fonts further for a font family in Custom Font Stacks to determine which fonts on your desktop you want to preview for text, or use as alternatives if older browsers do not support the CSS3 @font-face web font. You can add or remove fonts using the double arrows in the dialog box, as well as add or remove the Font List stack using the plus or minus icons. Refer to Figure 37-8.

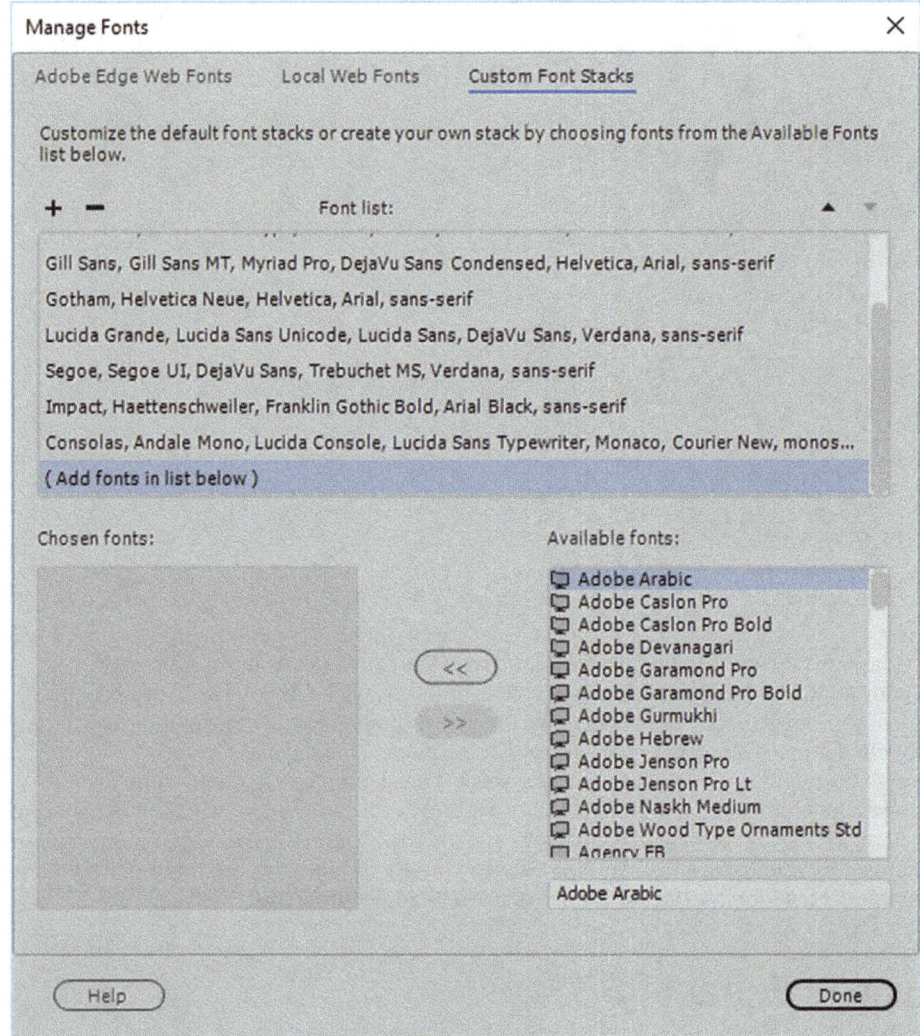

Figure 37-8. Manage Fonts in the Custom Font Stacks tab

When complete, click Done to exit this area. You can use these new families with your CSS.

CHAPTER 37 ADDITIONAL OPTIONS TO APPLY IMAGES IN DREAMWEAVER

CC Libraries Panel

This CC Libraries panel is shown in Figure 37-9.

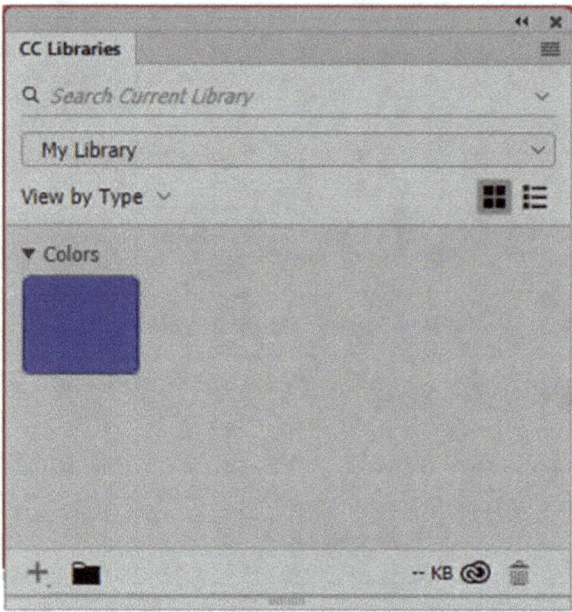

Figure 37-9. CC Libraries panel

It is a panel that was introduced with the Creative Cloud with Dreamweaver. You can store in the CC Libraries your most commonly used assets, like images, colors, and text styles that you use in projects. To increase your workflow, you can go back to a program like Photoshop, and the colors and graphics are stored there so that you can refer to them during your project upon returning to Dreamweaver.

By working through the cloud, you can insert linked assets to keep your pages updated. Note that Library CC is the same as the Library panel found in Photoshop, Illustrator, and Animate (CC Libraries). The reason for the slight name change is because Dreamweaver already has a Library Item folder that stores your library items. This can be a bit confusing when working between programs; however, use this panel if you want to move objects to the creative cloud and share between other adobe programs.

Dreamweaver ➤ Extract PSD

There is a final panel that Dreamweaver offers for working with your images, the Extract PSD panel. This is a great resource if you have Photoshop images (PSD) that allow you to extract CSS, images, fonts, colors, gradients, and measurements into your site. You don't have to have Photoshop open at the time because files are uploaded to the Creative Cloud console in a collaborative folder. You can work on them in that environment to get the information that you need. There is also drag-and-drop support to create image tags from PSD layers. And you can paste styles directly into Live view and the work with the CSS Designer panel. Refer to Figure 37-10.

CHAPTER 37 ■ ADDITIONAL OPTIONS TO APPLY IMAGES IN DREAMWEAVER

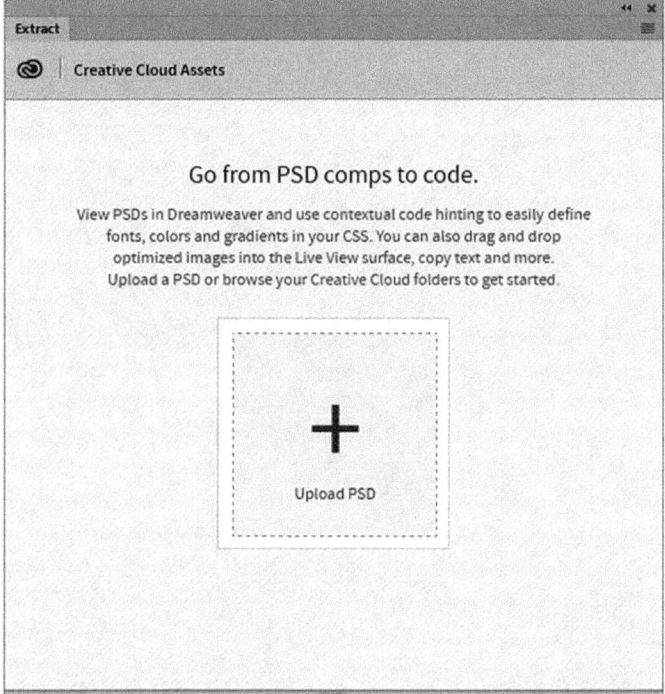

Figure 37-10. *Extract panel*

For more information, visit https://helpx.adobe.com/ca/dreamweaver/using/dreamweaver-integration-extract.html.

If you uploaded a PSD that you want to remove from Creative Cloud, under Assets ➤ Files. Under Open Folder click View on Web. Once inside this area you need to move the files found in the Files section to the Deleted folder; only this area can you permanently delete the file from the Creative Cloud. Refer to Figure 37-11 to see the View on Web folder link so that you can view your Creative Cloud files stored on-line.

959

CHAPTER 37 ■ ADDITIONAL OPTIONS TO APPLY IMAGES IN DREAMWEAVER

Figure 37-11. The Adobe Creative Cloud panel allows you to access uploaded images that you may want to delete later

In Dreamweaver, you can further adjust how your images will be extracted by going to Edit ➤ Preferences Extract tab. They can be extracted as PNG or JPEG. Refer to Figure 37-12.

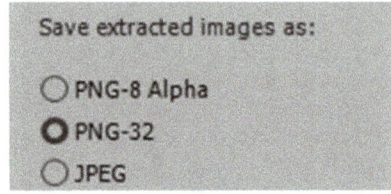

Figure 37-12. Preferences setting for extracting images

Summary

In this chapter, you looked at a few code resources and panels—such Web Fonts, CC Libraries, and Extract—that can be used to work with images in Dreamweaver.

In the next chapter, you adjust and validate the settings in your files before uploading your site.

CHAPTER 38

Final Testing, Getting Ready to Upload Your Site

In this chapter, you make the final adjustments to your site and upload your files to your server, as you see with the Hot Glass Tango site.

Note This chapter does not have any actual projects; however, you can use the files in the Part 6 folder to practice opening and viewing for this lesson. They are at `https://github.com/Apress/graphics-multimedia-web-adobe-creative-cloud`.

Once you have organized your HTML files, images, and media, it's time to finish your site with some prelaunch tasks: site maintenance, site testing, and quality control. Once you have finished building your site, knowing that it will run efficiently is important. Here are a few areas to look at before upload.

Edit ➤ Preferences of Browsers

As you continue to work with your files on your desktop, you can also set up which browsers you want to do a real-time preview in. Dreamweaver is not sufficient in its rendering or browser compatibility for testing. Under Edit ➤ Preferences, go to the Real-time Preview tab and set up the browser that you want as your primary, and secondary if you have more than one. Click Apply to confirm and exit. Refer to Figure 38-1.

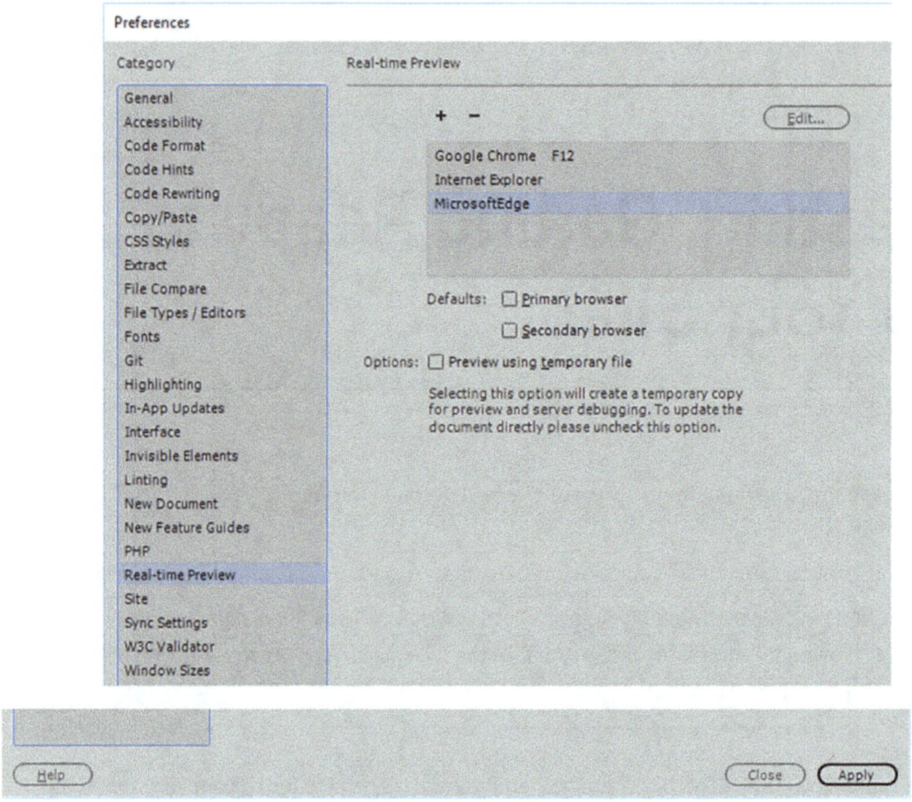

CHAPTER 38 ■ FINAL TESTING, GETTING READY TO UPLOAD YOUR SITE

Figure 38-1. Choose which browsers you want to preview your web pages in

Then the next time you test (File ➤ Real-time Preview), those browsers will be available in the list. You may want to add other browsers, such as Safari, Firefox, and Opera, and their versions to your testing computer. Refer to Figure 38-2.

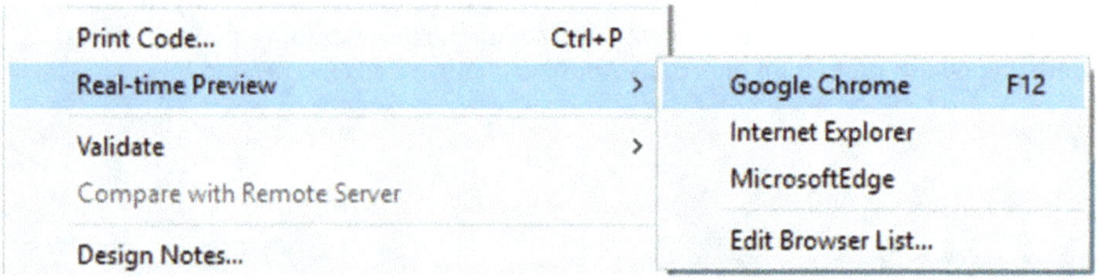

Figure 38-2. You can now choose which browser from the list you want to preview a webpage in

Solely testing your site on the machine it was developed on isn't best practice, because you cannot know whether or not it is compatible with other devices. Having multiple users test your site on their devices, as well as having a strategy for mobile testing, should be part of your project's development plan. For example, testing on several desktop operating systems, such as Windows 7, 8, or 10, or versions of Mac 10, as well as a variety of tablet and mobile smartphone devices. With testing, it really all comes down to time and the budget.

CHAPTER 38 ■ FINAL TESTING, GETTING READY TO UPLOAD YOUR SITE

Validation Options and Uploading Site

Before your site goes live, take the time to make sure that you have eliminated as many HTML5, CSS, and JavaScript errors as possible. Catching errors prelaunch saves time and money. If you don't correct such things such as broken links or missing images now, this can affect the user's ability to navigate through your site. For the user, this can cause frustration or cause them to miss important information; as a result, they may not return to your site. In turn, the quality of your website impacts the brand that you are trying to exhibit.

While there are many quality assurance tests available online, most errors you see in the Window ➤ Results ➤ Output panel if the red X appears at the bottom of the page. But you can always find a few more errors using Site ➤ Reports. Refer to Figure 38-3.

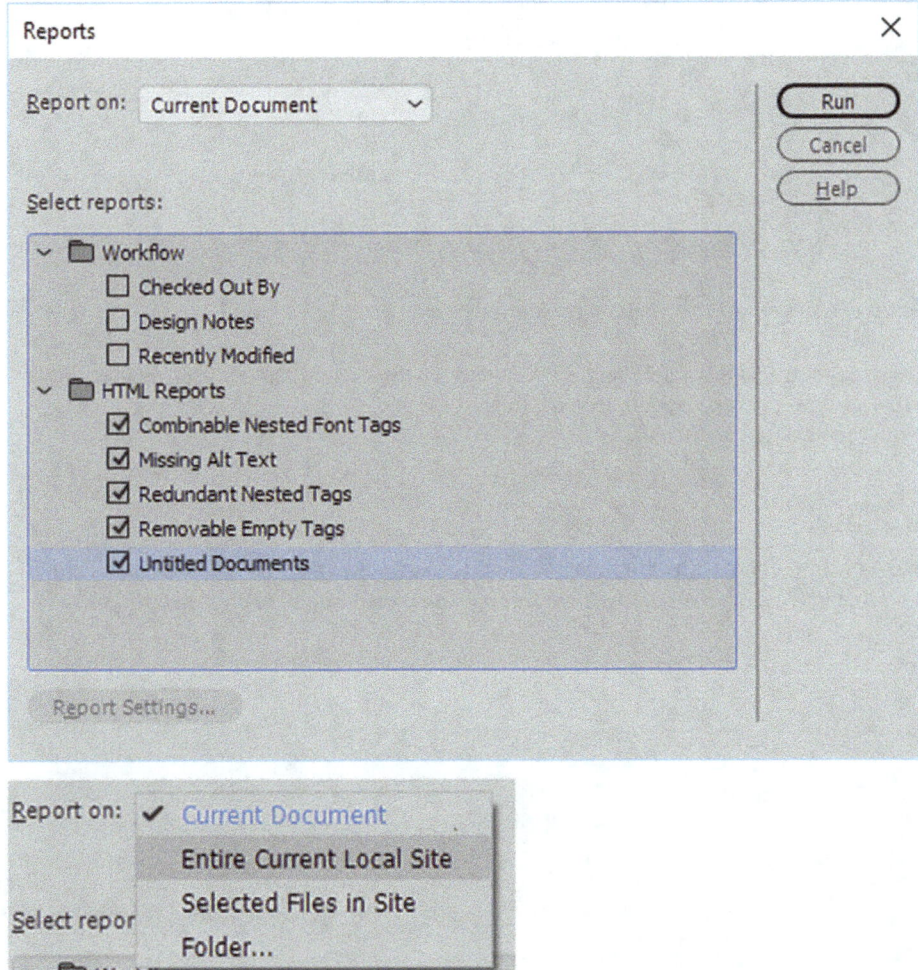

Figure 38-3. *Running a report usually brings up hidden errors that you may not have noticed before*

Reports can be run on the current document, selected files, or on the entire current local site. I generally only check off the boxes under the HTML Reports tab. This is great for discovering if any of my images are missing alt tags.

963

CHAPTER 38 ■ FINAL TESTING, GETTING READY TO UPLOAD YOUR SITE

Site Reports Panel

Warnings and errors appear in the Window ➤ Results ➤ Site reports panel. Refer to Figure 38-4.

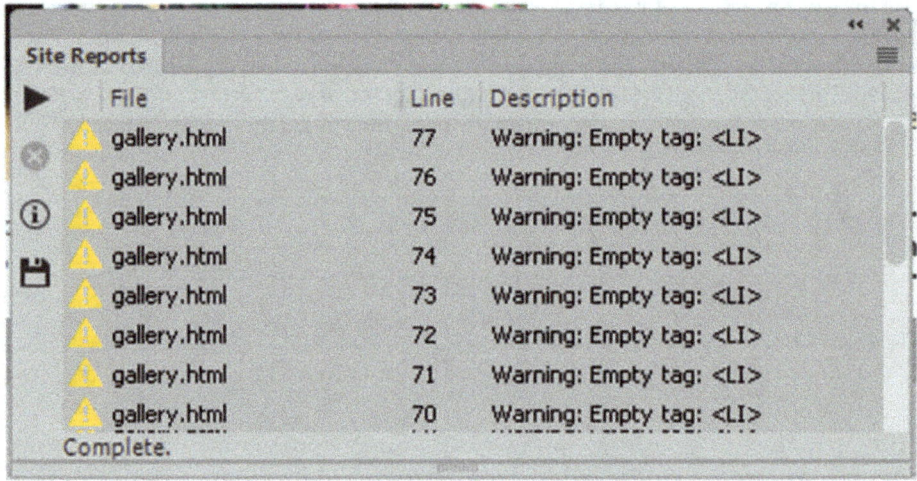

Figure 38-4. *The results of a site report can often reveal hidden errors*

You can open these pages by double-clicking the error. Find the lines where the error occurs, make the changes, resave the file, and run the report again to see if the error is gone.

Next, I discuss other panels that are useful.

Link Checker Panel

The Link Checker panel (Window ➤ Results ➤ Link Checker) checks for broken links, external links, and files in your root folder that may be orphaned. Right-click or use the panel's menu to choose options. Refer to Figure 38-5.

CHAPTER 38 ■ FINAL TESTING, GETTING READY TO UPLOAD YOUR SITE

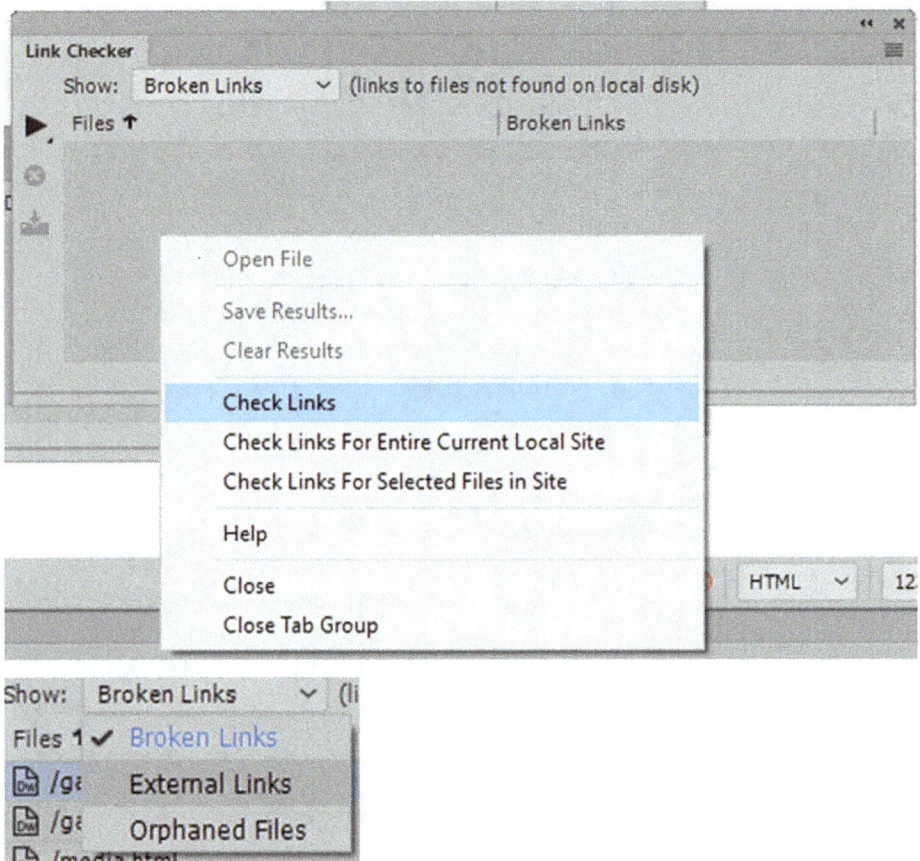

Figure 38-5. *The Link Checker panel reveals errors*

When no files are selected, you can choose from the panel's menu, Check links for entire Current Local site as seen in Figure 38-5.

If you have any linked PDF document on your site, make sure to manually check for the PDF using Find ➤ Find in Current Document and enter **.pdf**. Then check if those links are opening appropriately with the "_blank" targets attribute; correct if missing. Likewise, repeat these steps for external navigation.

Validation Panel

The Validation panel (Window ➤ Results ➤ Validation) brings up CSS and HTML validation issues. Right-click or use the panel's menu to choose options. Refer to Figure 38-6.

CHAPTER 38 ■ FINAL TESTING, GETTING READY TO UPLOAD YOUR SITE

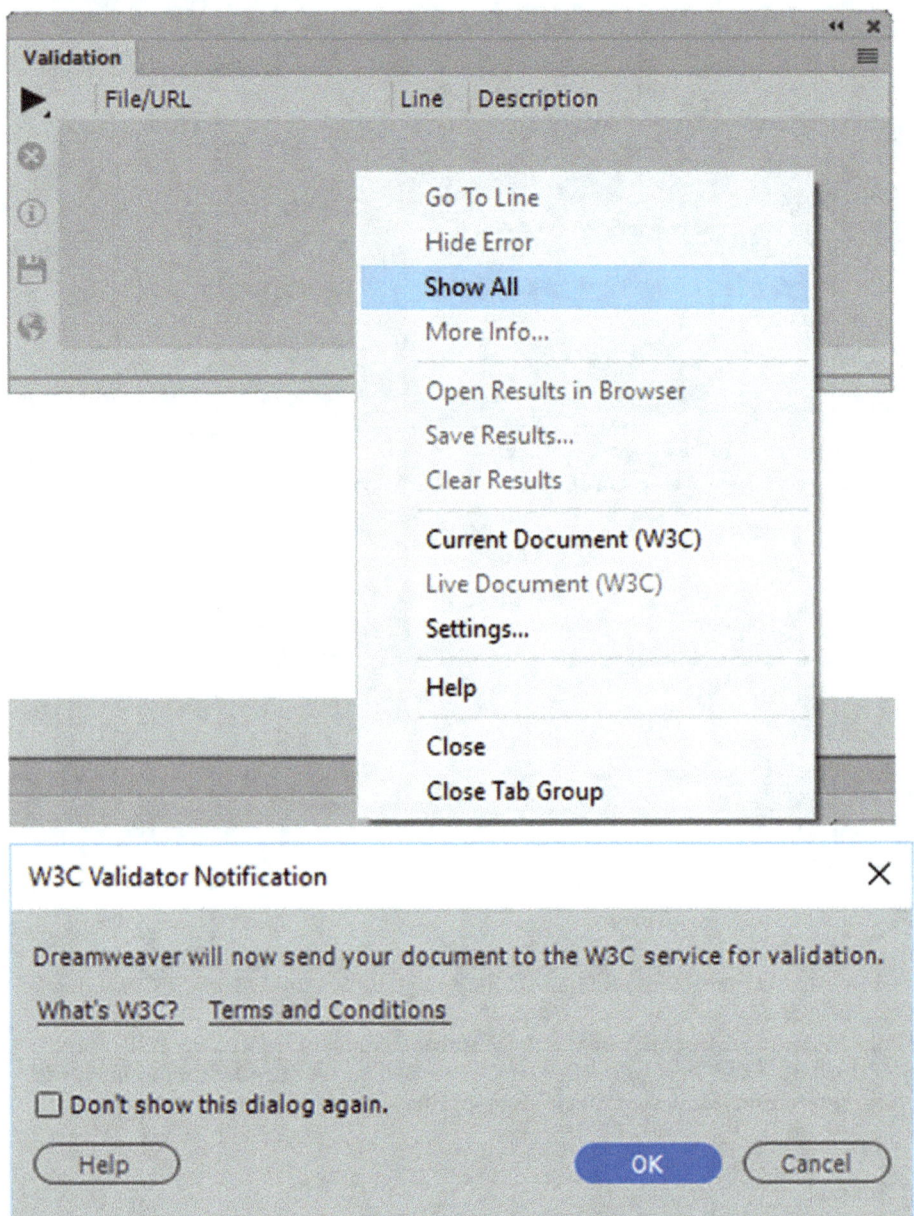

Figure 38-6. The Validation panel reveals errors that may be in your HTML and CSS files

Choosing Current Document W3C brings up a note that it will send the file to the W3C service for validation.

CHAPTER 38 ■ FINAL TESTING, GETTING READY TO UPLOAD YOUR SITE

■ **Note** Once your site is no longer local and is remote (uploaded) the alternative is to use the following links to do further testing:

For HTML, W3C validator: https://validator.w3.org/

For CSS: https://jigsaw.w3.org/css-validator/

Either way, you will find additional errors that you should correct on the local site and then upload the file again.

Output Panel

The other way to validate without uploading files is to rely on your Output panel (Window ➤ Results ➤ Output), which catches most HTML5 errors. Refer to Figure 38-7.

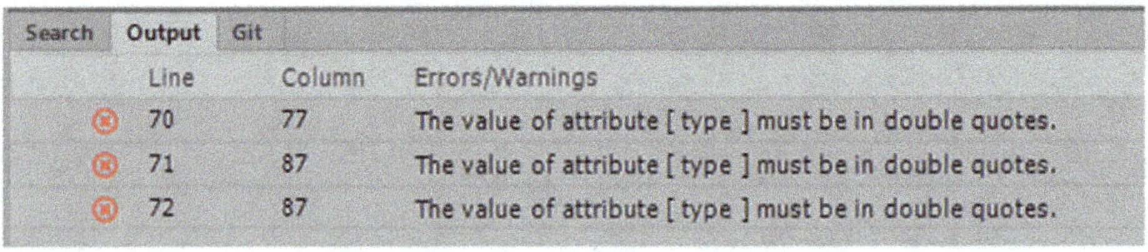

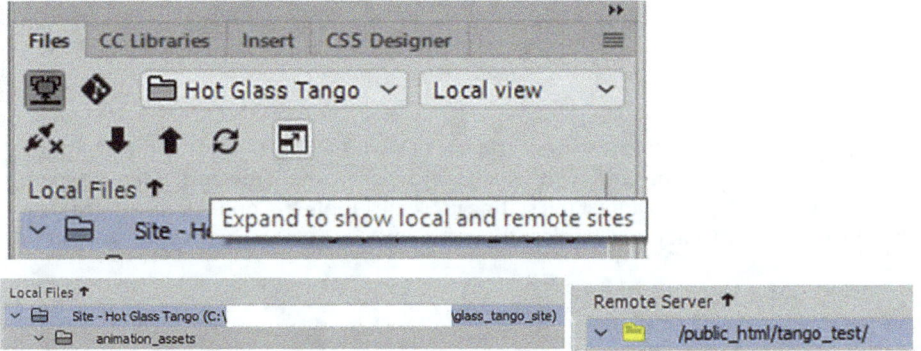

Figure 38-7. *Most basic HTML5 errors can be caught using the Output panel*

Local and Remote Sites

Before you enter the Local and Remote dialog box area found in your Files panel, it important to decide which side you want to see your local files on, the right or the left. Refer to Figure 38-8.

Figure 38-8. *Choose how you want to view uploaded files*

■ **Note** If you have not set up your Remote Server area in the Site dialog box, you may not see this button. Follow along with the screenshots for now.

967

CHAPTER 38 ■ FINAL TESTING, GETTING READY TO UPLOAD YOUR SITE

I prefer seeing my local files on the left and my remote files on the right; this is a common workflow. So go into Edit ➤ Preferences ➤ Site tab and change Always show Local Files on the Left and click Apply. Now when you go back to the Local and Remote dialog box, the local files are on the left and the remote files are on the right, as seen in Figures 38-8 and 38-9.

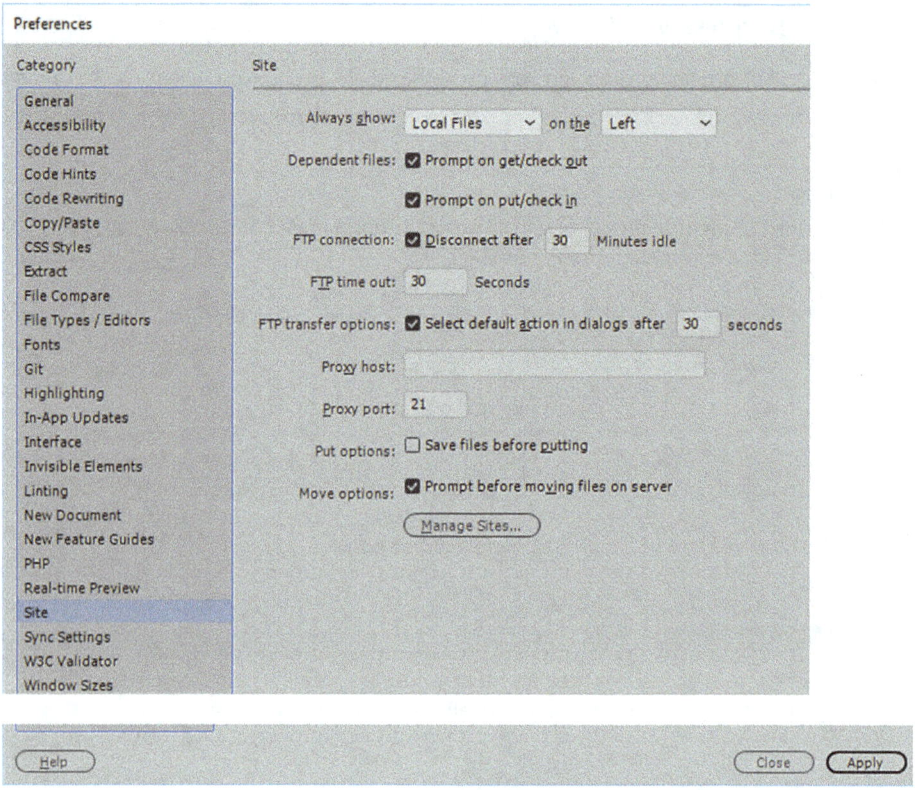

Figure 38-9. *Preferences ➤ Site tab*

You don't have to change most of the other settings in this tab. However, be aware of the proxy port 21. In some cases, it can interact with a program like Skype, which may be using the same port. If that happens, there may be a conflict, and you may need to adjust the setting in Skype (Tools ➤ Connection options) to a different port. For Dreamweaver, leave it at port 21 unless the company that manages your site has different settings.

Manage Site

Earlier, you set up your local site (Site ➤ New Site) and saved it. This area is where you manage the transfer and sync between the local and remote sites. Now you will go to Site ➤ Manage Sites, locate the site, select it, and then click the Pencil icon to edit the currently selected site. Refer to Figure 38-10.

CHAPTER 38 ■ FINAL TESTING, GETTING READY TO UPLOAD YOUR SITE

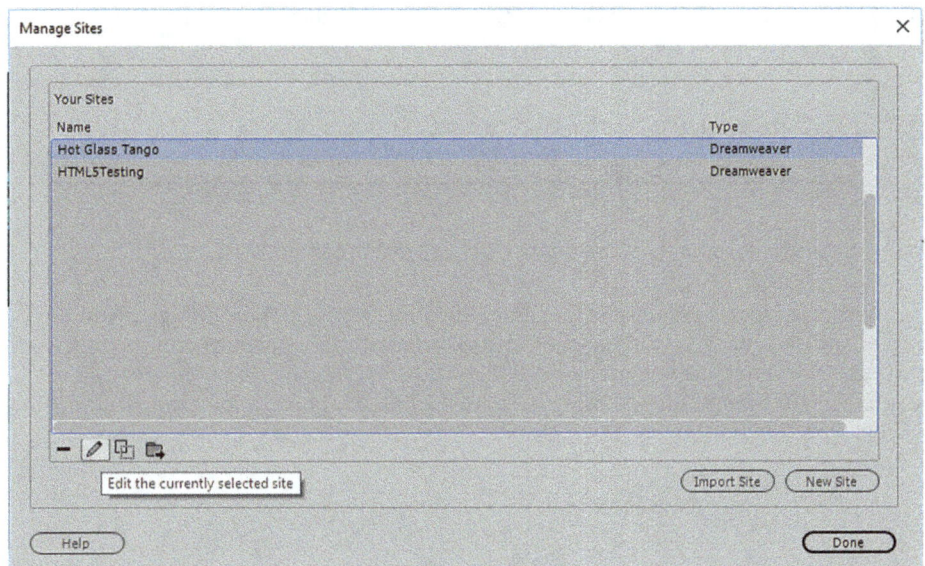

Figure 38-10. *Manage your site to set up a remote server*

Then proceed down to the Severs tab in the Site Setup dialog box, as seen in Figure 38-11.

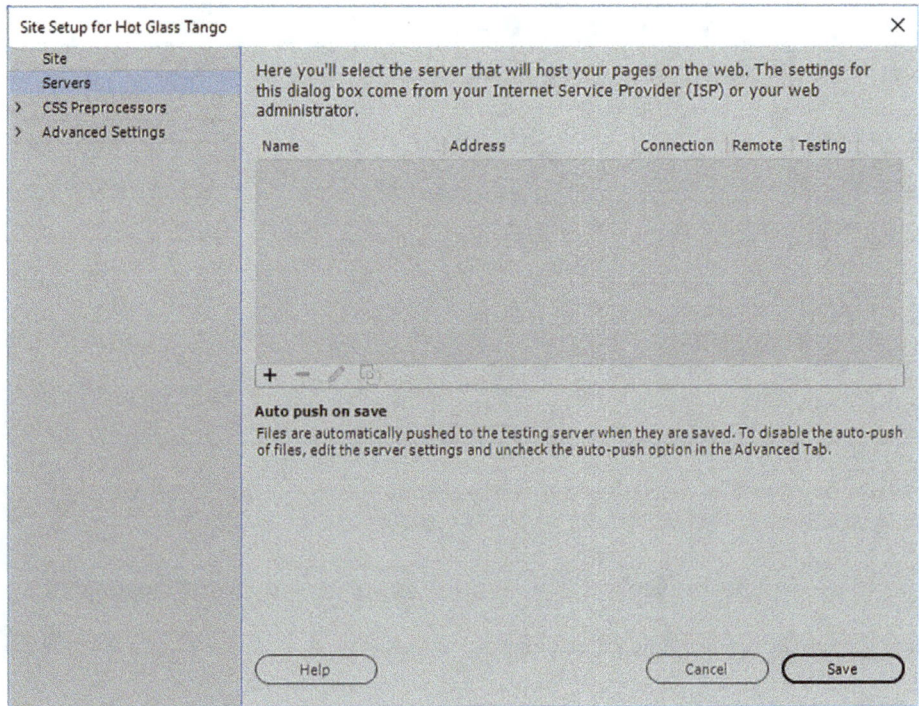

Figure 38-11. *Manage your site to set up a remote server*

969

CHAPTER 38 ■ FINAL TESTING, GETTING READY TO UPLOAD YOUR SITE

Currently, you may have no servers if you haven't set this up; otherwise, they appear here. Refer to Figure 38-12.

Name	Address	Connection	Remote	Testing
HostSite	mysite.com	FTP	●	○

Figure 38-12. If you have created a remote site connection, it appears in the Servers tab

If not, click the plus icon, as seen in Figure 38-11, to enter the server settings. Your settings are different from mine; in most cases, the Basic tab is all you need to set up. Check with your hosting site if you are not sure. Get the server name. The connection is generally FTP (File Transfer Protocol). Next, you need an FTP address or (IP address), a username, and a password. Leave the port at 21 unless you are instructed otherwise. Refer to Figure 38-13.

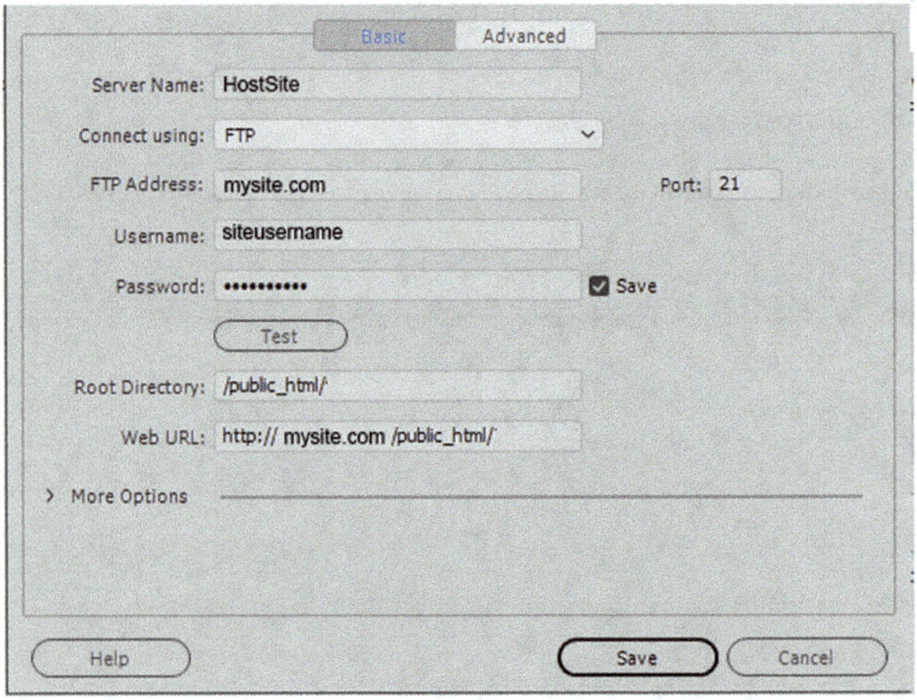

Figure 38-13. In the Basic tab, set the remote setting given by your hosting company so that you can FTP your files to the server

At this point, click test to see if you can connect. Make sure that your password and username are correct.

Your root directory should be in the public_html folder.

CHAPTER 38 ■ FINAL TESTING, GETTING READY TO UPLOAD YOUR SITE

Then set up your web URL for your index. If your site folder is not on the remote yet, you have to add this later and then alter the root directory and web URL in this dialog box and test again; for example

/public_html/mysitefolder/
http://mysite.com/public_html/mysitefolder/

Further options can be found in the More Options and Advanced tabs, but generally, you don't need to make adjustments here unless you are working with a testing server. So, you can leave this area at the default settings as with the Advanced Tab. Refer to Figure 38-14.

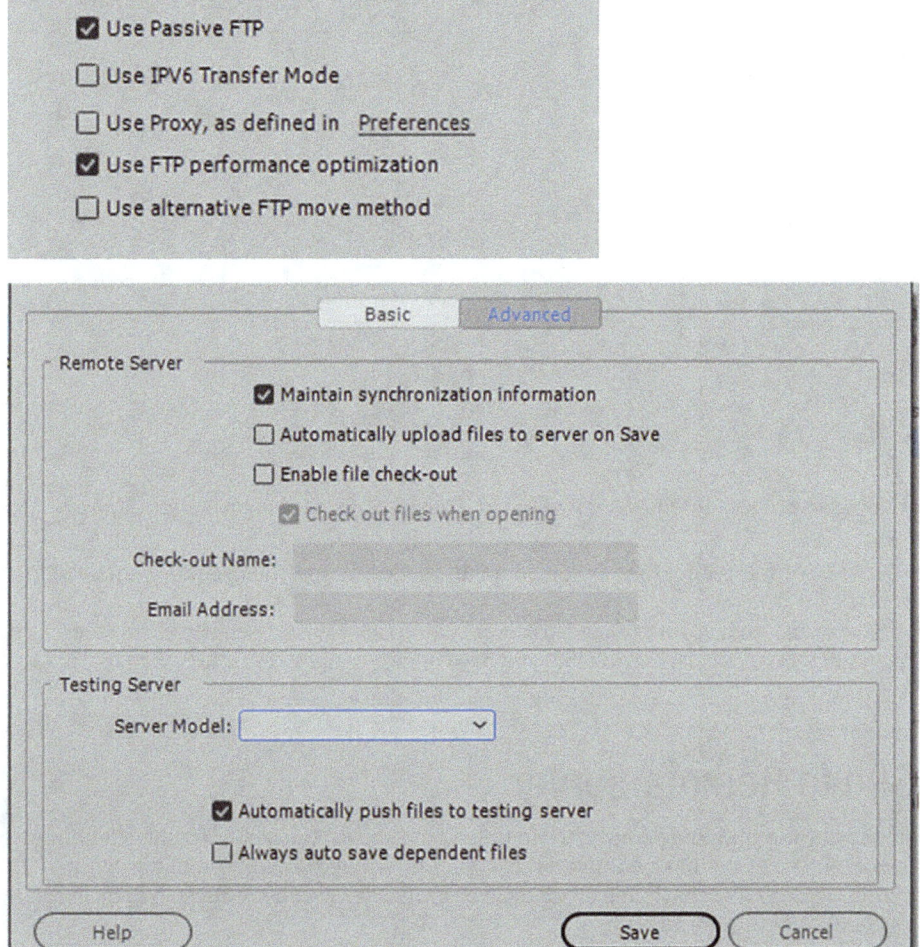

Figure 38-14. *Additional advanced settings you can leave at the default unless your hosing company advises otherwise*

When done, click Save to save your sever connection settings. You should now be linked to the remote, as seen in Figure 38-12.

971

Check Advanced Settings…

Before you leave the Site Setup dialog box and click its Save button to exit the site setup, take a moment to check the Advanced Settings tab on the left. Check the subtabs (jQuery, Web Fonts, and Animations Assets) to make sure that your links are pointing to the correct folder. Refer to Figure 38-15.

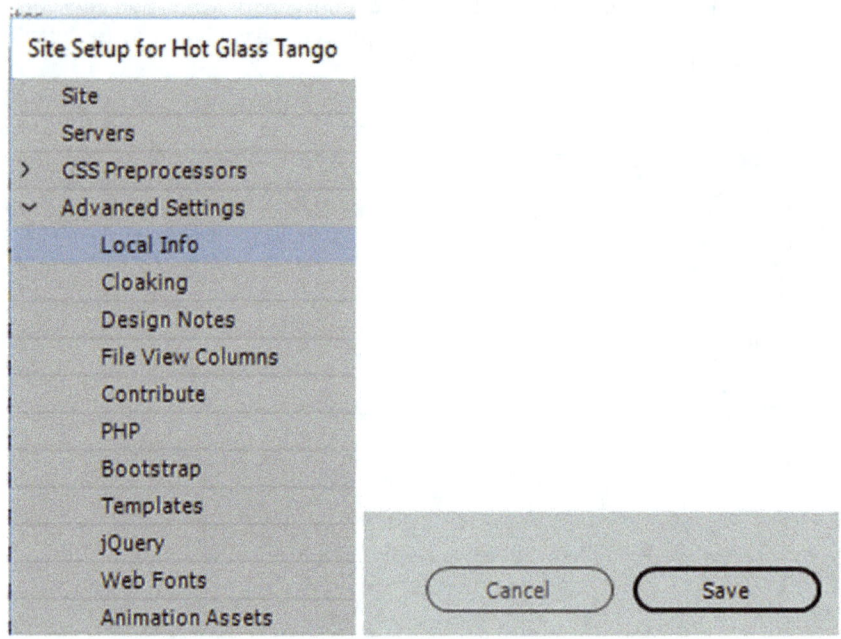

Figure 38-15. *Check through your advanced settings tab to see if any subtabs need their settings adjusted*

If you find your site to be running smoothly, or you do not have these items, then you may not need to adjust here; but it's good to check anyway.

Once done, click Save to ensure that your managed server settings are saved. Then click Done to exit the Manage Site area. You might receive an alert saying that you have made changes, if so click OK to return to your project.

Uploading Site to Remote Server

Once you have finished reviewing your Site Setup, you can upload the site to your server via the Files panel Local and Remote Sites dialog box icon that looks like a rectangle with a diagonal arrow. Make sure the remote server connection is enabled so that it appears plugged in with a yellow check mark and you can see the files on the remote side. Refer to Figure 38-16.

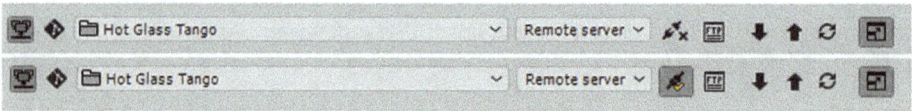

Figure 38-16. *Make sure to connect to the server with the plug-in checked so that you can upload your files*

CHAPTER 38 ■ FINAL TESTING, GETTING READY TO UPLOAD YOUR SITE

From the menu, choose Site ➤ Synchronize. Refer to Figure 38-17.

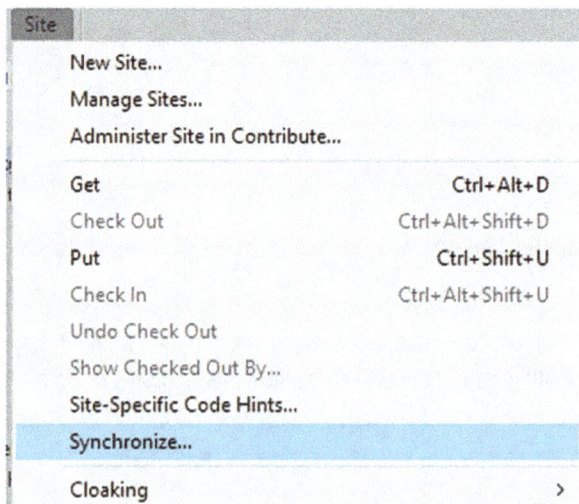

Figure 38-17. Choosing Site ➤ Synchronize allows you to start the upload process

From the Synchronize with Remote Server dialog box, choose the entire site for the first upload. In subsequent uploads, you can choose Selected Local Files Only, if you have uploaded before. Refer to Figure 38-18.

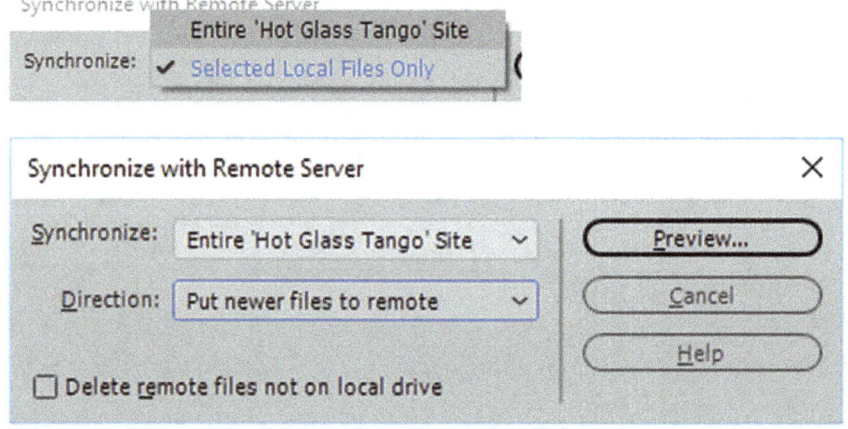

Figure 38-18. Upload files to remote server

973

- **Direction:** Select "Put newer files to remote" to upload them. Refer to Figure 38-19.

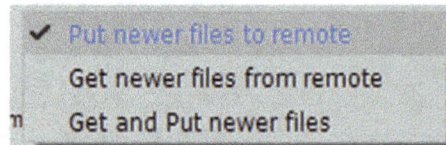

Figure 38-19. *Choose a direction for your files to go*

- **Delete remote files not on local drive:** unchecked.

■ **Note** I do not recommend getting newer files from remote (download) unless you are working on an older site and that is the only way to access them. Clients should give you the older files either as a ZIP file or on a USB or DVD if you are updating them for your site.

Lastly, click the Preview button, as seen in Figure 38-18.

Dreamweaver goes through the files to see what is newer than what is on the server. If it finds files that are newer, it asks if you want to upload them. Refer to Figure 38-20.

CHAPTER 38 ■ FINAL TESTING, GETTING READY TO UPLOAD YOUR SITE

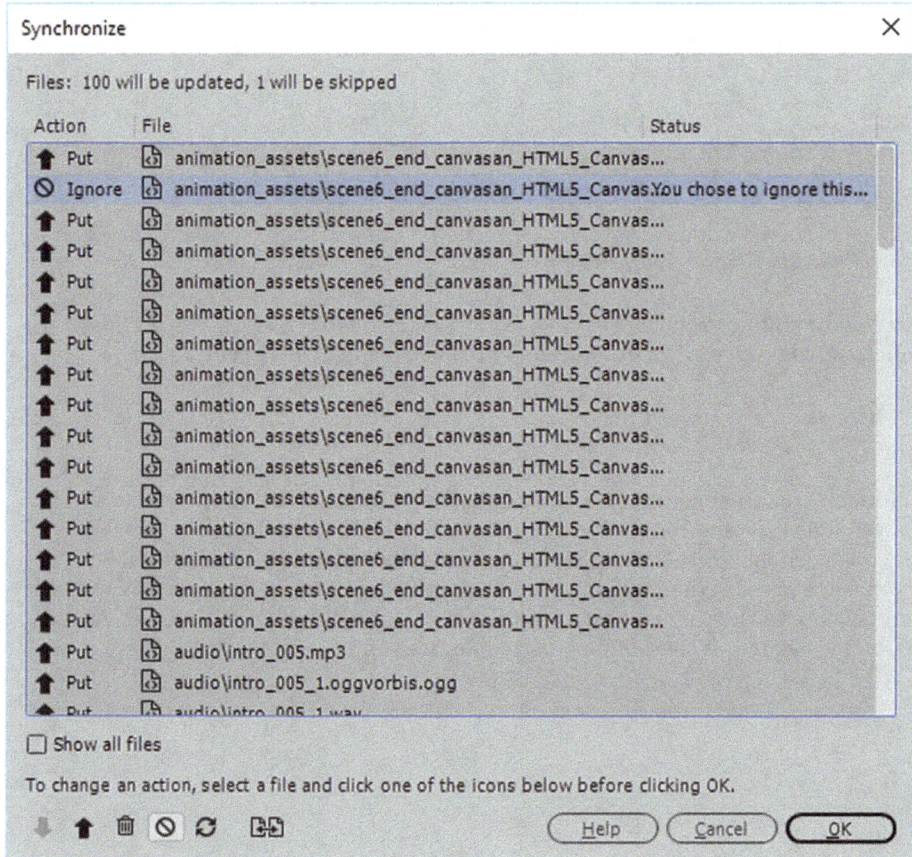

Figure 38-20. The Synchronize Preview dialog box

In the Preview dialog box, you can choose not to upload by clicking the crossed-out circle button in the lower left to ignore when that file name is selected. Or you can force the upload using the up arrow when the file is name is selected.

Once you have set which files you want to upload, click the OK button. Give it some time if you have a lot of files; the new files will appear in the Remote side.

During this process, Dreamweaver creates a log that includes file activity during the transfer, which you can view and save. It also records all FTP activity so if an error occurs, you can use the log to determine and troubleshoot the issue.

Later, outside Dreamweaver, you can type the URL into your browser to see if the files are online.

■ **Note** Your files must be inside the hosting server's public_html folder, or you (and the public) will not be able to see them.

Once done, you can click the local and remote button to exit this area and return to the main area of Dreamweaver which includes all the panels. Refer to Figure 38-21.

Figure 38-21. *Return to the main Dreamweaver interface*

At this point, you could continue to edit and upload, or close all files and File ➤ Close and File ➤ Exit Dreamweaver CC. You have achieved your goal of working with images and media to build a site.

Summary

In this chapter, you did some basic maintenance on your site before you uploaded it to the remote server. You also looked at how to adjust server settings so that your links to the remote server are correct. Finally, you synchronized and uploaded the site to the remote server. While there may be many more quality assurance tests that you may want to perform, this gives you a basic idea of how site maintenance works.

In the concluding chapter, you look at three final projects created in the Hot Glass Tango site. As you review these projects, take some time to consider how you could apply these ideas to your own projects.

CHAPTER 39

Putting It into Practice with Dreamweaver CC

In this chapter, you review three parts of the Hot Glass Tango website. First, you review how to insert images. You then look at how an image gallery carousel is added using Bootstrap. Finally, you look at a unique way of using JavaScript in which you can change which video is currently displayed in the <video> tag.

> **Note** This chapter does have any actual projects that you can review; however, you can copy the HTML files in the Part 6 folder called chapter_39_html_practice into the glass_tango_site folder. The completed files are already in this folder. Use them to practice opening and viewing for this lesson. They are at https://github.com/Apress/graphics-multimedia-web-adobe-creative-cloud.

So far in Chapters 9, 16, 24, and 29 you Put into Practice what you learned in four Adobe Programs. Throughout Part 6, you've seen how Dreamweaver can integrate images into a site and the site with the help of a Bootstrap Library and a Template can be Mobile friendly and responsive for more than one sized device. Let's take a moment to look more in depth look at a few key pages on the website in regards to the upcoming projects.

Adding Images to Web Pages Review

This section is more of a review of inserting images than an actual project; however, as you review the Hot Glass Tango howtomake.html webpage, take the time to explore how the colorful graphics were added to the page and review past chapters to compare. If you want to practice adding images to this page, use the howtomake_practice39.html file copy add it to the glass tango site folder and look for the HTML comment lines in Table 39-1.

Table 39-1. Insert These Images

Code Line	HTML Comment	Image	Alt/ Title Tag
95	<!--Insert DomeImage1-->	dome_1.gif	Glass Half Dome
96	<!--Insert DomeImage2-->	dome_2.gif	Scrapbooking paper
97	<!--Insert DomeImage3-->	dome_3.gif	Cutting paper for the dome
98	<!--Insert DomeImage4-->	dome_4.gif	Gluing an image onto the backing paper
99	<!--Insert DomeImage5-->	dome_5.gif	The composite image and the dome
100	<!--Insert DomeImage6-->	dome_6.gif	Spreading Diamond Glaze on bottom of dome
101	<!--Insert DomeImage7-->	dome_7.gif	Holding the dome down to allow it to dry
102	<!--Insert DomeImage8-->	dome_8.gif	Drying time and using nail polish remover for clean up
103	<!--Insert DomeImage9-->	dome_9.gif	Trim paper around the dome
104	<!--Insert DomeImage10-->	dome_10.gif	Nail polish remover final clean up
105	<!--Insert DomeImage11-->	dome_11.gif	Gluing velour paper to back of paperweight
106	<!--Insert DomeImage12-->	dome_12.gif	Cut away excess velour paper
108	<!--Insert Half DomeImageJPG-->	halfdoome_image.jpg	Side view of half dome paperweight

Use the Insert panel to practice adding images. When you highlight a comment, refer to the table. Afterward, you can delete the comment. Make sure to add an `img-responsive` class to each one, either in Code view or by using the Properties panel, like so:

`<img class="img-responsive" src="images/dome_1.gif" width="195" height="138" alt="Glass Half Dome"/>`

Also use the table to reference the text for your alt attributes that you need to add for each image. If you get stuck, refer to the original howtomake.html file.

In Chapter 31, I discussed how to add an image to a webpage using the <img> tag and the Insert and Properties panels, or via Insert ➤ Image from the main menu. Refer to that chapter while reviewing howtomake.html. As a review, the following images can be added to a webpage using this method.

- JPEG
- GIF (Static and Animated)
- PNG
- SVG

CHAPTER 39 ■ PUTTING IT INTO PRACTICE WITH DREAMWEAVER CC

Remember that while you can add an SVG file using this insert method, any form of interactivity will be lost; refer to contact.html. The best way to deal with this issue is to insert the SVG within an <object> tag, as seen on the contact.html and colorsglass.html pages. The object tag was used when you uncompressed your OAM file and extracted the HTML5 Canvas file into the image assets folder on the index.html page, as seen in Chapter 36.

As seen in the howtomake.html file at the bottom of the page, if you want to add a figure caption to your image, you need to wrap the <img> in a figure tag, as seen in Chapter 31 when you looked at sematic elements.

All these image formats can be added as backgrounds to the <div> tag or semantic element using external CSS, as in Chapter 32, using the background property, Code view and the CSS Designer panel.

The following are tips to remember while viewing this page.

- Some formats have better quality and respond better to compression and expansion.

- Background images should add interest and beauty to the site, as in the broken glass colors in the template-based page; however, they should not detract from the readability of the text. Remember to keep this in mind when dealing with viewers who experience color blindness.

- Using CSS effects such as opacity or RGBA to overlay an image can sometimes blur the image and make it easier for the viewer to read the text.

- When creating with media queries, keep in mind that complex graphics may be too processor intensive for some devices, so at that point, you may need to switch to a lower resolution graphic or just use a colored background.

- If adding CSS for print, decide which graphics you think your viewers should print and which ones should be excluded.

Now that you have reviewed the how to make and contact pages, try applying some of these tips to your own project. For now, let's move on to the second project.

Carousel Gallery (Bootstrap)

Let's look at the gallery.html webpage. If you would like to insert the gallery, use the gallery_practice39.html file copy it to the glass tango site folder and look for the <!--Insert Bootstrap Carousel Gallery Here--> HTML comment, so that you know where the gallery should go on the page. If you get stuck at any point, refer to the completed gallery.html file. After I designed my mobile-friendly responsive site in Chapter 35, I found a location that I wanted to add the carousel(sideshow component for images) using the Insert panel. Refer to Figure 39-1.

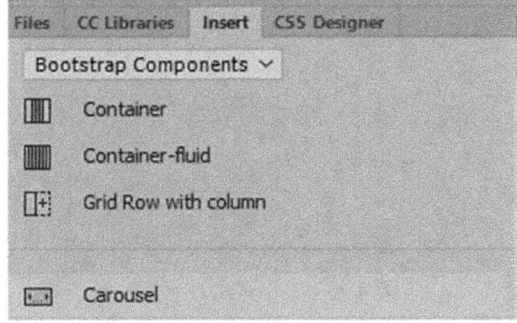

Figure 39-1. *Adding a carousel gallery to a website*

With or without a Bootstrap website, you can add a carousel to your project; just keep in mind that you may have to adjust the CSS for your project so that the colors and layout fit your theme. I always work on a blank page to test the layout before I insert it into a template-based page. Create a blank HTML page if you want to practice. Refer to Figure 39-2.

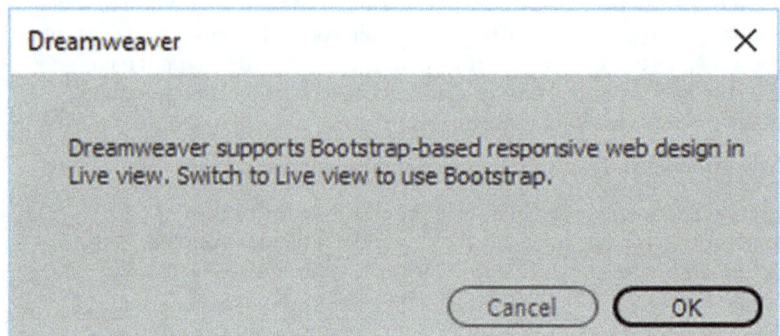

Figure 39-2. *The Bootstrap component*

This type of gallery can have at between three and twenty images in it. Based on the layout, more than twenty would be too difficult to maintain, and less than three does not add visual interest to the viewer. Just make sure to work with it in Live view so that you can see the results.

The following JavaScript and CSS are added to your site folder. In this case, it was already added; however, if these files are already in your folders from other components, only the additional items will be added. Refer to Figure 39-3.

Figure 39-3. *Bootstrap and jQuery files may be added as links to your file*

When you File ➤ Save the blank HTML file in your root folder, you are asked if you want to copy the dependent files seen in Figure 39-4.

CHAPTER 39 ■ PUTTING IT INTO PRACTICE WITH DREAMWEAVER CC

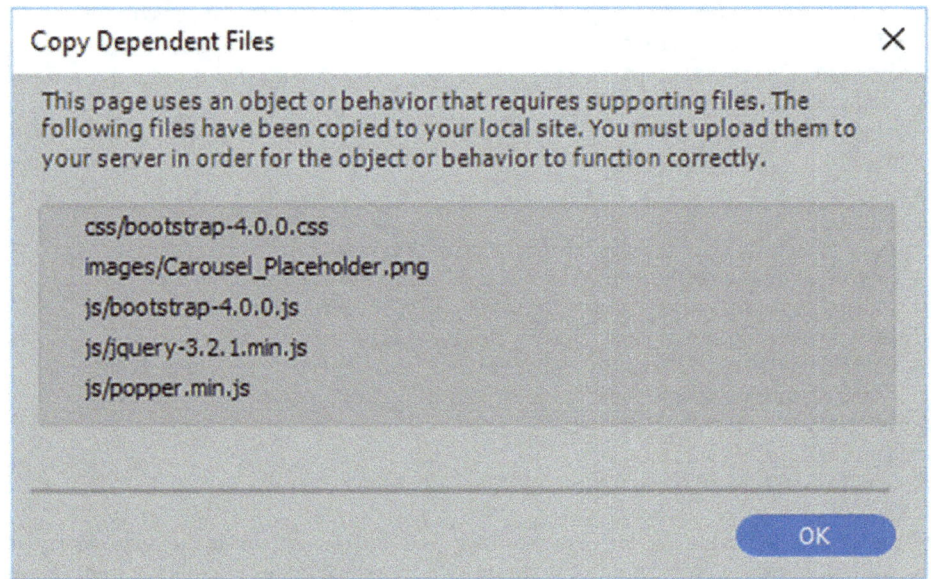

Figure 39-4. Copy Dependent Files

In this case, they are already present.

Besides the JavaScript and CSS, you also have a temporary placeholder image added to your image folder. You can replace this in the links with your actual images.

The inserted carousel code looks something like this for version 4.0.0. in the <body>:

```
<div id="carouselExampleIndicators1" class="carousel slide" data-ride="carousel"
style="background-color: grey">
    <ol class="carousel-indicators">
        <li data-target="#carouselExampleIndicators1" data-slide-to="0"
        class="active"></li>
        <li data-target="#carouselExampleIndicators1" data-slide-to="1"></li>
        <li data-target="#carouselExampleIndicators1" data-slide-to="2"></li>
    </ol>
    <div class="carousel-inner" role="listbox">
        <div class="carousel-item active"> <img class="d-block mx-auto"
        src="images/Carousel_Placeholder.png" alt="First slide">
            <div class="carousel-caption">
                <h5>First slide Heading</h5>
                <p>First slide Caption</p>
            </div>
        </div>
        <div class="carousel-item"> <img class="d-block mx-auto" src="images/Carousel_
        Placeholder.png" alt="Second slide">
            <div class="carousel-caption">
                <h5>Second slide Heading</h5>
                <p>Second slide Caption</p>
            </div>
        </div>
```

```
            <div class="carousel-item"> <img class="d-block mx-auto" src="images/Carousel_
        Placeholder.png" alt="Third slide">
            <div class="carousel-caption">
                <h5>Third slide Heading</h5>
                <p>Third slide Caption</p>
            </div>
        </div>
    </div>
        <a class="carousel-control-prev" href="#carouselExampleIndicators1"
        role="button" data-slide="prev"> <span class="carousel-control-prev-icon"
        aria-hidden="true"></span> <span class="sr-only">Previous</span> </a>
        <a class="carousel-control-next" href="#carouselExampleIndicators1"
        role="button" data-slide="next"> <span class="carousel-control-next-icon"
        aria-hidden="true"></span> <span class="sr-only">Next</span> </a> </div>
<script src="js/jquery-3.2.1.min.js"></script>
<script src="js/popper.min.js"></script>
<script src="js/bootstrap-4.0.0.js"></script>
```

See that the JavaScript is added to the bottom of the carousel, but the CSS remains in the head. Always keep this order if you want the carousel to run correctly. Figure 39-5 shows what the default looks like.

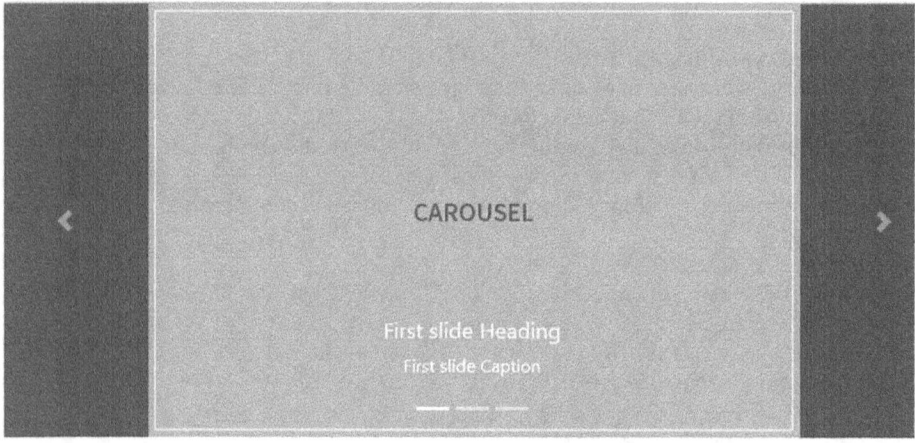

Figure 39-5. *The default carousel*

Now all you need to do is find the first instance of the placeholder image and alter the image link, alt tag, heading <h5>, and caption <p>. See the areas that I highlighted in bold in the code example below.

```
<div class="carousel-item active"> <img class="d-block mx-auto"
src="images/Carousel_Placeholder.png" alt="First slide">
    <div class="carousel-caption">
        <h5>First slide Heading</h5>
        <p>First slide Caption</p>
    </div>
```

I did this for each of the three images. Also, I added at least eight more images. Refer to gallery.html if you need to see the completed code. To do this, I made sure to copy in order the following text. Note that the carousel always starts at 0 as the first image, and moves to 1, which is the second image, and 2 is the third image. This relates to arrays in JavaScript. Never start the data-slide-to numbering of a Bootstrap carousel at 1 because this causes it to function incorrectly. JavaScript code expects the array to start at 0 because it is zero-based and this the first number it indexes. So, the fourth image is number 3 as seen in the following code.

```
<li data-target="#carouselExampleIndicators1" data-slide-to="3"></li>
```

And image 11 would be

```
<li data-target="#carouselExampleIndicators1" data-slide-to="10"></li>
```

Then I would add another div, such as

```
<div class="carousel-item"> <img class="d-block mx-auto" src="images/Carousel_Placeholder.png" alt="Fourth slide">
    <div class="carousel-caption">
        <h5>Fourth slide Heading</h5>
        <p>Fourth slide Caption</p>
    </div>
</div>
```

To keep organized, I often use the words *fourth* or *slide 4* (whatever slide it is) as part of the alt tag so that I don't get confused. This type of gallery is best with no more than 20 images. If you need a gallery with more images, I recommend checking out other Bootstrap options on the W3Schools website or the Bootstrap website. If you are concerned about accessibility standards, nested carousels do not always accurately support this. Nevertheless, they are responsive on your site, and each image should contain an alt attribute.

I also did some modifications to the bootstrap-4.0.0.css file. It was locked, as you saw in Chapter 35, so I made a copy called bootstrap-4.0.0_jh.css. I altered the background and I made my slide buttons more visible and easier to touch with the mouse. I made the text easier to read over top of the photos. To do this, I located that area of the CSS in my new copy of the Bootstrap file. I then searched for the classes in the text (Find ➤ Find in Current document) that matched the classes that are in the tags or elements of the carousel. The following are some classes or class collections to search within my copy of the bootstrap-4.0.0_jh.css file. In my file, it starts at line 5857 and ends 6057.

- carousel slide background-gallery
- carousel-indicators
- carousel-inner
- carousel-item active
- carousel-caption
- carousel-item
- carousel-caption
- d-block mx-auto
- carousel-control-prev
- carousel-control-prev-icon

- carousel-control-next
- carousel-control-next-icon

If you want to compare any changes in my CSS the original Bootstrap file, when you double-click the file bootstrap-4.0.0_jh.css file to style the CSS. I made minor edits to color properties to match my theme in the Files panel. To keep it locked choose only view to enter it. Refer to Figure 39-6.

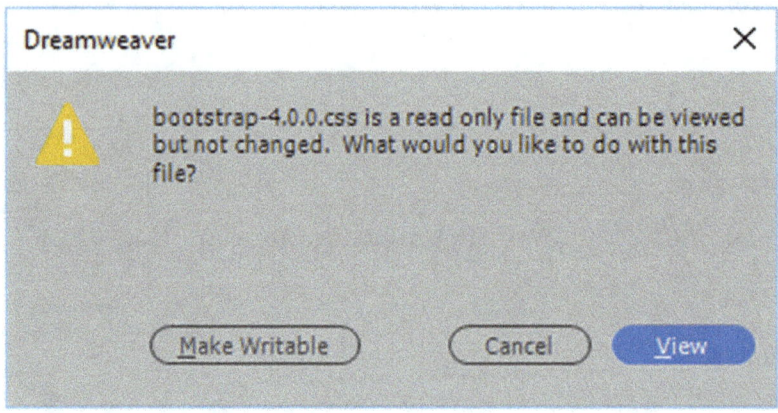

Figure 39-6. *When you enter the locked CSS file, you see this message*

If you compare the code, you see that I made very few changes to those lines. Though in other areas of my bootstrap, I made minor edits as well.

Likewise, I further overwrote some of the CSS in my gallery using my own external CSS file, called main_mobile.css; you can see these changes in line 81 of that file. I altered things like text shadow so that the lettering stood out better against the graphics; font size so that the lettering was easier to read; and the border of the <li> indicators circles so that they stood out too. This is to show you that you can override Bootstrap settings when you include another external CSS file below the Bootstrap CSS file. Refer to the <head> area of gallery.html if you need to compare.

Making any changes to the layout and CSS properties of a carousel takes time, so it may take a few hours of testing in a new CSS file to get the layout and colors to suit your needs. Alternatively, using your browser's Inspect Element feature may help you find the CSS you want to alter more quickly so that you can continue to edit the code in Dreamweaver.

You can adjust the speed of the carousel movement so that the viewers have more time to look at each picture in the bootstrap-4.0.0.js file. Look for line 557 in the carousel section. Refer to Figure 39-7.

CHAPTER 39 ■ PUTTING IT INTO PRACTICE WITH DREAMWEAVER CC

```
530    /**
531     * --------------------------------------------------------------------
532     * Bootstrap (v4.0.0): carousel.js
533     * Licensed under MIT (https://github.com/twbs/bootstrap/blob/master/LICENSE)
534     * --------------------------------------------------------------------
535     */
536
537    var Carousel = function ($$$1) {
538      /**
539       * --------------------------------------------------------------------
540       * Constants
541       * --------------------------------------------------------------------
542       */
543      var NAME                  = 'carousel';
544      var VERSION               = '4.0.0';
545      var DATA_KEY              = 'bs.carousel';
546      var EVENT_KEY             = "." + DATA_KEY;
547      var DATA_API_KEY          = '.data-api';
548      var JQUERY_NO_CONFLICT    = $$$1.fn[NAME];
549      var TRANSITION_DURATION   = 600;
550      var ARROW_LEFT_KEYCODE    = 37; // KeyboardEvent.which value for left arrow key
551
552      var ARROW_RIGHT_KEYCODE   = 39; // KeyboardEvent.which value for right arrow key
553
554      var TOUCHEVENT_COMPAT_WAIT = 500; // Time for mouse compat events to fire after touch
555
556      var Default = {
557        interval: 5000,
558        keyboard: true,
```

Figure 39-7. *Find the line that alters the speed of the carousel*

Look for: interval: 5000.

5000 is the default of 5 seconds, so if you want the gallery to move more slowly, let's say 10 seconds, then you would change the number to 10000. If you wanted it to move faster, then you might set it to 3000, or three seconds. However, most times, your audience will not appreciate a continuously fast-moving slider; no matter how great your images, this can be annoying and frustrate the viewer. In most cases, the viewer wants to have a bit of time to look at an image. I recommend either leaving it at the default interval or slowing it down to a speed that your audience is comfortable with.

Other than that, I made no other changes to the other JavaScript files.

When you are done, copy the carousel HTML from your blank HTML page into the HTML comment area in gallery_practice39.html.

Figure 39-8 shows how my gallery turned out in gallery.html.

Figure 39-8. *The final gallery in the Hot Glass Tango site*

CHAPTER 39 ■ PUTTING IT INTO PRACTICE WITH DREAMWEAVER CC

If you expand and contract your browser, you see that it is responsive.

One gallery on a site is often enough; you don't need to overload your site with a gallery on every page. Likewise, if this gallery does not suit your project's needs, there are many other similar galleries available online and in W3Schools that use similar HTML5, CSS, and JavaScript styling that you can incorporate into Dreamweaver. Examples include lightboxes and modal images, which are also found at W3Schools.

This concludes our look at the second project. Next, you look at the third and final project on the site.

Video with Channel Changer

In Chapter 36, you looked at how to add HTML5 video to a page using the <video> tag (see the media.html page). If you would like to practice, use the media2_practice39.html file copy it to the glass tango site folder and locate the following HTML comments.

```
<!--Insert Table Here for Buttons-->
       <!--Insert HTML5 Video Here-->
```

This is where you insert your code. Refer to media2.html to see the final result if you get stuck.

While having one video on the page is very useful, sometimes you may want to display more than one on a page. When you're trying to make a mobile site more compact, it seems kind of redundant to add five or more videos on a page, and viewers must keep scrolling down to see each one. What if the video has steps to follow? What if you are doing a whole series of short stories? How will your viewers feel if they must scroll down the page to see the next episode?

A few years ago, I did some research on this very topic. After modifying JavaScript code, I found a way to use JavaScript to change which video I wanted to view simply by clicking a button. Refer to the media2.html file and Figure 39-9.

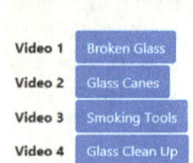

Figure 39-9. *The final gallery in the Hot Glass Tango site*

Each time you click a button, you change the poster image and the video.

Here is how the code works. I use only four videos to keep this example easy to understand, but you could expand this concept if you want to.

On the left, I created a <table> to keep my buttons organized. If you want to practice, use the media2_practice39.html file and add the following HTML under the comment.

```html
<!--Insert Table Here for Buttons-->
<table class ="channelTable">
  <tbody>
    <tr>
      <th scope="row">Video 1</th>
      <td><button onclick="Video1()" type="button" class="btn btn-primary">Broken Glass
      </button></td>
    </tr>
    <tr>
      <th scope="row">Video 2</th>
      <td><button onclick="Video2()" type="button" class="btn btn-primary">Glass Canes
      </button></td>
    </tr>
    <tr>
      <th scope="row">Video 3</th>
      <td><button onclick="Video3()" type="button" class="btn btn-primary">Smoking Tools
      </button></td>
    </tr>
    <tr>
      <th scope="row">Video 4</th>
      <td><button onclick="Video4()" type="button" class="btn btn-primary">Glass Clean Up
      </button></td>
    </tr>
  </tbody>
</table>
```

Each of the buttons has JavaScript tied to them onclick(). Refer to Chapter 34 if you need a review of JavaScript and events. This type of <button> tag is for buttons that are not used in forms.

On the right, I have my <video> tag. Add the following HTML under the comment.

```html
        <!--Insert HTML5 Video Here-->
        <video width="640" height="480" id="myVideoJH" poster="images/poster_cover_es1.jpg"
        preload="metadata" controls="controls" class="responsive-video" >
            <source id="mp4_src" src="video/mp4/MVI_1361_shardscolors.mp4" type='video/mp4; co
            decs="avc1.42E01E,mp4a.40.2"'>
            <source id="ogg_src" src="video/ogg/MVI_1361_shardscolors.oggtheora.ogv"
            type='video/ogg; codecs="theora,vorbis"'>
            <source id="webm_src" src="video/webm/MVI_1361_shardscolors.webmhd.webm"
            type='video/webm; codecs="vp8,vorbis"'>
              <embed id="swf_src" name="swf_src" src="video/swf/shardscolors.swf"
              type="application/x-shockwave-flash" width="640" height="480" />
            <!--<p> Your Browser does not support this video</p>-->
            <a href="video/mp4/MVI_1361_shardscolors.mp4"
  style="display:block;width:640px;height:480px;"
  id="player"> </a></video>
```

Note that the JavaScript link has already been added for you.

```html
<script src="js/channel_changer_jh.js" type="text/javascript"></script>
```

CHAPTER 39 ■ PUTTING IT INTO PRACTICE WITH DREAMWEAVER CC

This code is very much like what you saw in Chapter 36. However, in this case, I left the option of adding SWF files for older browsers; otherwise, you can leave the SWF area blank. The ID links to important code inside the external JavaScript, which has been added as a link below the <video> tag. Take some time to look at the channel_changer_jh.js JavaScript file.

I show one section here since other than links and names, the reset repeats.

```
var vid = document.getElementById("myVideoJH");
var play = document.getElementById("player");
//Video 1 Broken Glass
function Video1() {
vid.poster = "images/poster_cover_es1.jpg";
play.href = "video/mp4/MVI_1361_shardscolors.mp4";
    isSupp = vid.canPlayType("video/mp4");
    if (isSupp == "") {
        //video/ogg
        vid.src = "video/ogg/MVI_1361_shardscolors.oggtheora.ogv";
    } else if (isSupp == "") {
        //video/webm
        vid.src = "video/webm/MVI_1361_shardscolors.webmhd.webm";
    } else if (isSupp == "") {
        //flash backup
        vid.src = "video/swf/MVI_1361_shardscolors.swf";
    } else {
        vid.src = "video/mp4/MVI_1361_shardscolors.mp4";
    }
    vid.load();
}

//Video 2 Glass Canes
function Video2() {
}

//Video 3 Smoking Tools
function Video3() {
}

//Video 4 Glass Clean Up
function Video4() {
}
```

The code is tied to myVideoJH, which is the video's ID. It then looks for the player ID to play the video. There are four functions, one for each button. When the Video 1 button is clicked, this loads the first video (vid.poster) and any backup options in case the browser does not like the MP4 file. The same happens for Video 2, and so on.

The conditional statements if, else if, and else separate these options. As you can see, this method can be modified by adding more videos and file formats, and keeps them all in one compact location rather than scrolling down the page to see them one at a time. If you are not using SWF files, the else if condition could be removed from each function; it is optional.

```
else if (isSupp == "") {
        //flash backup
        vid.src = "video/swf/MVI_1361_shardscolors.swf";
```

With some modifications, this idea could be applied to buttons and audio files; although you would need to have some sort of visual clue, such as the button being a distinct color, so that the viewer knows which audio file they are listening to.

This concludes our discussion of Dreamweaver. You can continue to review the files or close the program, as this ends my coverage of the five core programs.

Summary

In this chapter, you reviewed how to add your images to a page and a Bootstrap carousel gallery. Then you created a way to change the video using JavaScript and the <video> tag for the Hot Glass Tango website. This chapter concludes your study of Dreamweaver CC. You should be proud of your accomplishments as you made the long journey through many of the twists and turns of working with multimedia. Come back to Part 6 any time to review areas that you don't fully understand. Ultimately, you want to feel comfortable working with your own files in Dreamweaver.

In Part 7, you take a brief look at some other programs that you can use for web design besides Dreamweaver, but they are part of the Adobe Creative Cloud. Then you have a quiz to test your knowledge.

PART VII

Further Dreamweaver Integration with Other Adobe Products for Websites

CHAPTER 40

What Other Programs That Are Part of Adobe Creative Cloud Can I Use to Display My Graphics or Multimedia Online?

In this last chapter, you look at some alternative multimedia programs that you can use instead of Dreamweaver. There is also a final quiz at the end to test your knowledge.

> **Note** This chapter does not have any projects.

Additional Creative Cloud Software for Your Projects

In Parts 2 through 6, you looked at the five core Adobe products (Photoshop CC, Illustrator CC, Animate CC, Media Encoder CC, and Dreamweaver CC). You can use these products to build a website with graphics, animations, video, and audio. Refer to Figure 40-1.

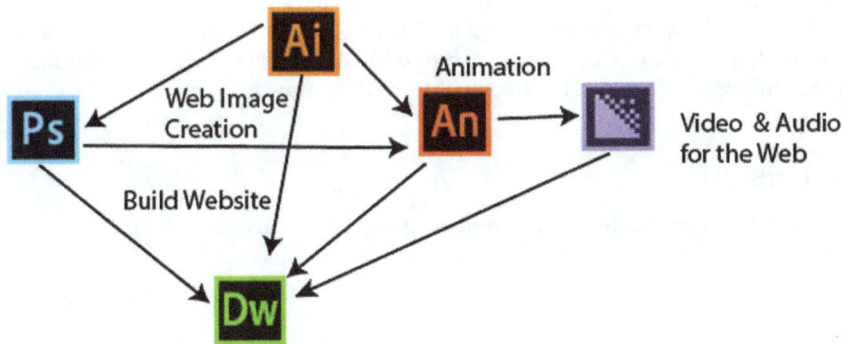

Figure 40-1. *The five core Adobe programs you reviewed*

© Jennifer Harder 2018
J. Harder, *Graphics and Multimedia for the Web with Adobe Creative Cloud*,
https://doi.org/10.1007/978-1-4842-3823-3_40

Other than a digital camera to capture video and images, and a microphone to capture sound or audio, you don't need a lot of high-tech equipment to build your own website on a small budget. However, it's great if the other members of your team have Adobe knowledge, such as

- For sound: Audition CC
- For additional video effects: Premiere Pro CC, After Effects CC, Prelude CC
- For images: Lightroom CC
- For 3D and animations: Character Animator, Dimension CC, and Fuse CC

All the resultant graphics or video that you export from these programs can be incorporated into a website that is designed using Dreamweaver CC.

Having said that, Adobe Creative Cloud has a few new programs for creating an image-driven website. Some of these may be useful to your company or clients, and you may want to research them further for your next project.

What Additional Adobe Creative Cloud Software Can You Use to Display Graphics or Multimedia Online?

Open your Creative Cloud console and scroll down the list to look at the following software icons.

Adobe InDesign CC

Adobe InDesign CC is mostly known for its page layout for print and PDFs. Refer to Figure 40-2.

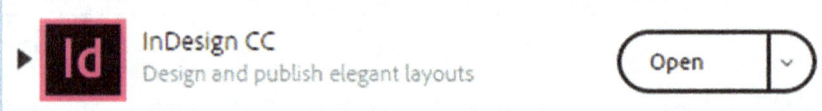

Figure 40-2. *Adobe InDesign CC*

However, did you know that besides exporting interactive PDFs (forms and transitions), you can also create EPUB documents? EPUBs are like mini-websites in digital book form that you can read on an e-reader like Adobe Digital Editions or any other e-reader application on your tablet or smartphone. Like a website, an EPUB can contain images, video, audio, animation in the form of an OAM file, or animations created within InDesign. EPUBs are another wonderful way to create a simple self-published magazine, book, or catalog for your clients to read on their mobile device. Apress has books on this topic if you want to learn more.

Adobe Experience Design

Adobe Experience Design is a new program for simple web/mobile apps and interactive click-through prototypes. Refer to Figure 40-3.

CHAPTER 40 ■ WHAT OTHER PROGRAMS THAT ARE PART OF ADOBE CREATIVE CLOUD CAN I USE TO DISPLAY MY GRAPHICS OR MULTIMEDIA ONLINE?

Figure 40-3. Adobe Experience Design or XD CC

Afterward, you can export your files in the form of PNG, SVG, JPG, and interactive PDF, which could be viewed by a client before the images are added to Dreamweaver CC.

The following are resources:

- https://en.wikipedia.org/wiki/Adobe_XD
- https://helpx.adobe.com/xd/help/whats-new.html
- https://helpx.adobe.com/ca/xd/help/share-embed-designs-prototypes.html
- https://helpx.adobe.com/xd/help/export-design-assets.html

Remember that this program is for creating prototypes, not the final website. So, to finish the website, you need to take the information from the prototype and ultimately lay out the whole website. Hopefully, at some point there will be an integration where HTML pages from the prototypes are published to Portfolio or Dreamweaver so that designers and developers can interact with these HTML files after export.

■ **Note** Adobe Acrobat Pro DC has the ability to export a file as HTML. This may be a feasible way to extract some further information (however limited) out of an interactive PDF for your website, but it's certainly not a perfect solution.

Adobe Portfolio

Adobe Portfolio can work Lightroom CC or Photoshop CC along with RAW images to create graphics driven (galleries) with pre-created template-based layouts. Refer to Figure 40-4.

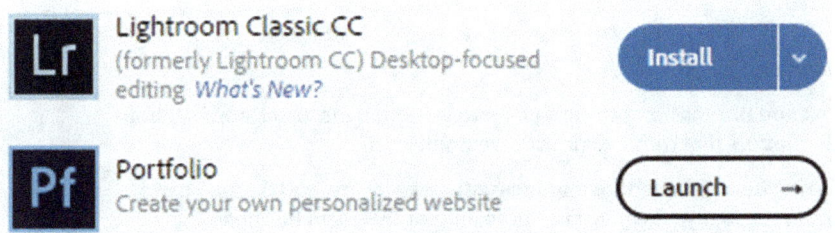

Figure 40-4. Lightroom Classic and Portfolio

If you are an artist and plan to create a website that is mainly about your artwork (photos, illustrations, video, and audio) with very little text, rather than create a large complicated website, Portfolio might be all you need.

995

CHAPTER 40 ■ WHAT OTHER PROGRAMS THAT ARE PART OF ADOBE CREATIVE CLOUD CAN I USE TO DISPLAY MY GRAPHICS OR MULTIMEDIA ONLINE?

Here are some resources:

- www.myportfolio.com
- https://helpx.adobe.com/creative-cloud/how-to/create-portfolio-website.html
- https://helpx.adobe.com/creative-cloud/how-to/create-online-portfolio.html

You can host on your own site or use your Creative Cloud Behance account along with Portfolio. Refer to Figure 40-5.

Figure 40-5. *The Behance account link*

The important thing about Portfolio is the template is already mobile-friendly, and you can use all your knowledge from the Photoshop, Illustrator, Animate, and Media Encoder chapters of this book. The one main drawback is that you may feel limited by the amount of customization you can do. These are all things to consider when designing a project for a client when it concerns designing and then later who oversees the future maintenance and updating of the site.

Adobe Spark: Storytelling with Audio and Video

If you like to do storytelling with your graphics and on your mobile apps, Spark is an interesting new product. Refer to Figure 40-6.

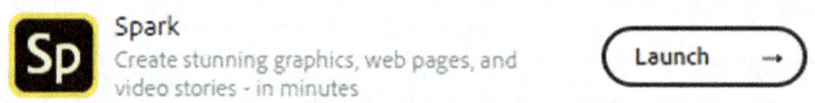

Figure 40-6. *Spark for storytelling*

It is made up of three features.

- **Spark Page:** Text and photos for crafting web stories. Is good for travel stories, photo albums, and newsletters that require some movement.
- **Spark Post:** Allows the adjustment of graphics with, text, layers, and filters. The process that would normally take place in Photoshop or InDesign has been simplified in Post for beginning users who tap buttons to control settings.

- **Spark Video:** Allows you to work with audio to tell a story. As with After Effects or Animate, you can also add effects like panning and zooming. However, this is not the same as editing film content, more like an animation that you create in Animate CC. In this instance, text, images, icons, and themes are combined into a presentation. Afterward, you speak your voice audio over the story to create the video. Later, you can export as an MP4 (H.264) video file that you can add to your website or social media site. For more information, refer to `https://spark.adobe.com`.

Exporting to Phone GAP Build

Adobe Phone GAP Build enables software programmers to build applications for mobile devices using CSS3, HTML5, and JavaScript, instead of relying on platform-specific APIs like those in Android, iOS, or Windows Phone. So, you could design the structure of an app in Dreamweaver and then use Phone GAP to complete the work.

You will not find it as part of the Creative Cloud; however, you can use this information from the following resources if you want to work with this product.

- `http://phonegap.com`
- `https://en.wikipedia.org/wiki/Apache_Cordova`
- `https://helpx.adobe.com/dreamweaver/kb/phonegap-build-cc-2014-update.html`

Test Your Knowledge Quiz

As a review, here are a few multiple-choice and true/false questions on topics that were covered in the book.

1. In Photoshop, which two panels are used to create a video?
    a. Properties and Channels
    b. Layers and Styles
    c. Layers and Timeline

2. To create a GIF animation in Photoshop, which export method must be used?
    a. Export As
    b. Save for Web (Legacy)
    c. Quick Export As

3. Which of the following file formats cannot contain transparency?
    a. GIF
    b. PNG
    c. JPEG

CHAPTER 40 ■ WHAT OTHER PROGRAMS THAT ARE PART OF ADOBE CREATIVE CLOUD CAN I USE TO DISPLAY MY GRAPHICS OR MULTIMEDIA ONLINE?

4. Which panel in Photoshop is useful for creating a set of steps that you can use many times?

   a. Layers

   b. Actions

   c. Styles

5. You can use Illustrator to export video and animations.

   a. True

   b. False

6. What coding language is used with the SVG Interactivity panel?

   a. JavaScript

   b. CSS

   c. HTML

7. Which color mode should you convert your files to before you export them for the web?

   a. CMYK

   b. RGB

8. Illustrator Objects are

   a. vector

   b. raster

9. In Animate, which format do you export a video as?

   a. MP4

   b. MOV

   c. AVI

10. Animate GIF animations can contain audio.

    a. True

    b. False

11. Which of the following tweens can you not create with a library symbol?

    a. Motion tween

    b. Classic tween

    c. Shape tween

12. By default, in which folder does HTML5 Canvas stores its audio files?

    a. Sounds

    b. Audio

    c. Music

13. Which two video formats for the web does Media Encoder not export?

    a. MP4

    b. WebM

    c. Ogg

14. Media Encoder allows you to export a WAV file.

    a. True

    b. False

15. If you want a range of frames from a video, which three formats can you export from Media Encoder to get an image sequence?

    a. PNG

    b. JPEG

    c. MP3

    d. GIF

16. In Media Encoder, which Export Setting allows you to colorize your entire video?

    a. Lumetri Look /LUT

    b. Image Overlay

    c. Time Tuner

17. In Dreamweaver, which tag should you use to keep your SVG files interactive?

    a. <img>

    b. <div>

    c. <object>

18. To insert your compressed HTML5 Canvas in a template-based webpage, which icon from the Insert panel would you choose?

    a. HTML5 Video

    b. Animated Composition

    c. Plugin

19. Which coding would you use to display your image in the background of a <div> tag?

    a. HTML

    b. CSS

    c. JavaScript

20. Which panel in Dreamweaver allows you to edit the attribute of your <video> and <audio> tags?

    a. CSS Designer

    b. Assets

    c. Properties

CHAPTER 40 ■ WHAT OTHER PROGRAMS THAT ARE PART OF ADOBE CREATIVE CLOUD CAN I USE TO DISPLAY MY GRAPHICS OR MULTIMEDIA ONLINE?

Answers:

1. c
2. b
3. c
4. b
5. b
6. a
7. b
8. a
9. b
10. b
11. c
12. a
13. b, c
14. a
15. a, b, d
16. a
17. c
18. b
19. b
20. c

Summary

In this chapter, you looked at a few other Adobe programs that are part of the Creative Cloud that you may want to use for your own projects. You also took a quiz to test your knowledge. I hope that you enjoyed this book, and that you are able to apply the knowledge that you acquired from building the Hot Glass Tango site for your future multimedia projects.

Index

A

ActionScript 3.0
    import audio, 460
        Library panel, 460–461
        Properties panel, 462
        repeat sound, 466
        Sound Effect settings, 463–464
        Sync Setting, 465–466
Adobe Audition CC, 185
Adobe Creative Cloud
    console software apps, 4
    definition, 3
    five core programs, 6
    maze, representation, 3
    simplified maze, 8
    software maze, 9
    software programs, 6–7
    web file formats (*see* Web file formats)
    website creation, 5
Adobe Creative Cloud panel, 960
Adobe Creative Cloud Software
    Adobe Experience Design, 994–995
    Adobe InDesign CC, 994
    Adobe knowledge, 994
    Adobe Portfolio, 995–996
    five core Adobe programs, 993
    Phone GAP Build, 997
    quiz, 997–1000
    Spark for storytelling, 996–997
Adobe Dreamweaver, 5
Adobe Experience Design, 994–995
Adobe Illustrator (.ai, .ait), 236
Adobe InDesign CC, 994
Adobe LiveMotion, 382
Adobe Media Encoder, 147, 160, 186, 459, 676
Adobe PDF (.pdf), 236
    Advanced tab, 257
    Bleeds tab, 256
    Compression tab, 256
    General tab, 255
    Marks tab, 256
    Output tab, 257
    Security tab, 258
    Summary tab, 259
Adobe Phone GAP Build, 997
Adobe Portfolio, 995–996
Adobe programs, 28
Adobe Spark, 996–997
Advanced export settings, 650
Animate CC
    actions panel, 573–574
    blending effects, 447–448
    Character Animator CC, 384
    code (*see* Code snippet panel)
    Creative Cloud, 382–384
    Display Render, 448–449
    Display Tab, blending options, 444–446
    effects
        color, 442–444
        properties panel, 437
        symbols, 438–442
    export options, 383
    External library, 411
    Filters
        Adjust Color filter settings, 455
        Bevel filter settings, 453–454
        options, 450
        save settings, 456
        settings, 450–452
    FLA file
        opening, 386–387
        settings, 388
        templates, 389
    flashing graphics, 595
    History panel
        create basic commands, 579
        Manage Saved Commands, 579–580
    HTML5 Canvas file (*see* HTML5 Canvas)
    import file formats, 410
    import images, 411
    Libraries panel, 581
    Macromedia Flash, 382

Animate CC (*cont.*)
    Preferences panel, 571–572
    RAW files
        FLA conversions ActionScript to HTML5, 396–398
        Library panel, 394–395
        Properties panel, 392–394
        Timeline panel, 394
        Tools panel, 395–396
    RGB
        adding color, 399
        Color panel, 403
        Color Picker, 400
        gradient, 404, 405
        Info panel, 407
        Properties panel, 401–402
        Swatches, 406
        Tools panel, 400–401
    workspace, setting, 384–386
Animated GIF
    publish tab, 702
    video tab, 701
Animate timeline, 473–474
Animations, CSS3
    animation-delay, 842
    animation-direction, 842
    animation-duration, 843
    animation-fill-mode, 843
    animation-iteration-count, 843
    animation-name, 843
    animation-play-state, 843
    animation-timing-function, 843
    backward, 843
    both, 843
    class (.easeinAnimObj), 844
    cubic-bezier(n,n,n,n), 844
    <div> tag, 841
    ease-in, 843
    ease-in-out, 843
    ease-out, 843
    forward, 843
    @keyframes, 842
    linear, 843
    none, 843
    step-end, 844
    steps(int,start|end), 844
    step-start, 843
    transitions and CSS effects, 840
    W3Schools, 841
Animation tools
    GIF animation, 127
    static GIF images, 323
    SVG interactivity panel (*see* SVG interactivity panel)
    timeline panel (*see* Timeline panel)

Appearance panel, 250
Artboards, 88–90
    choose number of, 265
    export sizes, 269
    mode, 267
    panel, 267
    PDF, 275
    screens dialog box, 268
    thumbnail buttons, 268
    two in one file, 266
Art brush, 587
Artwork
    Illustrator CC
        blending modes, 417–419
        effects FX, 420–421
    import Adobe Animate
        button option, 422
        layers, 422–427
        output, 428
        Timeline panels, 429
    import Illustrator AI
        bitmap, 435
        files, 432
        incompatibility report, 434
        layers, 430–431, 433
        objects, 436
    Photoshop CC
        blending modes, 412–414
        layer, 416–417
Assets tab
    export for screens, 276
    export layers panel, 281–282
    export panel, 276–281
Audio convertion to export settings
    MP3
        audio tab, 685
        effects tab (*see* Effects tab settings)
        export setting dialog box, 680
        options, 680
        preview settings, 681–682
        publish tab, 685
        summary settings, 682
        time code settings, 685–686
    Waveform Audio (.wav)
        audio tab, 688
        effects tab, 687
        export and summary settings, 686–687
        publish tab, 689
        time code settings, 689
Audio CSS aural, 940
Audio files (MP3, WAV, Ogg), 10
Audio frames, 496
Audio MP3 File
    factors, 723

media encoder CC
 add queue panel, 724
 add source icon, 706
 animation clip, 710
 AVI file, 714
 encoding panel, 722
 export audio, 708, 715, 726
 export settings, 708, 710–711, 714, 716, 721–722, 726–727
 FLA TO MOV file, 709
 frame rate, 718–719
 glass canes, 713
 guide images, 711–712
 MOV video file, 715
 output file, 707
 remove files, queue panel, 706
 reset status, 722–723
 source scaling, 719–720
 video duplication, 725
 video tab, 717
 video to MP3, 724
 waveform audio, 725
Audio tab settings
 ACC and MPEG
  advanced settings, 666
  basic audio settings, 664
 advanced settings MPEG de-emphasis, 666
 audio format settings, 664
 bitrate, 665
Audio Video Interleave (AVI), 642
Auto slices, 307

B

Bind tool, 516, 518–519
Bit depth, 32
Bitmap (.bmp), 32, 50, 52, 233, 283
 defined, 9
 sequence export settings
  caption tab, 694–695
  color effect, 693–694
  FTP, 695
  time code, 695
  video frame, 694
Bitmap fill, 405
Blank frame, 492
Blank keyframe, 492
Bone tool
 armature
  add points, 512
  IK, 511
  layer, 488
 Illustrator CC
  add shapes to stage, 513
  copy and cut poses, 516

 create, 512–513
 flower stock bends, 515
 joint movement, 514–515
 nested animations, 516
Bootstrap
 Behaviors panel, jQuery effects, 900
 components
  Insert panel, 904–905
  Snippets panel, 901–902
 create mobile site, 903–904
 CSS, JavaScript and jQuery files, 904
 front-end framework, 901
 HTML elements, 903
 images and fonts, 905
 Insert panel, 899–900
 Site Setup dialog box, 902
Box-shadow, 834–835

C

Camera tool
 color effects, 510
 layer properties dialog box, 486–487
 modes, 509
 motion tween and, 495, 504–507
 properties menu, 510
 Reset Essentials, 509
Canvas, 10
Captions tab settings, 667
Carousel gallery
 bootstrap-4.0.0.css file, 983
 Bootstrap and jQuery files, 980
 Bootstrap component, 980
 copy dependent files, 980–981
 create HTML page, 980
 default, 982
 font size, 984
 gallery.html, 985
 image link, alt tag, heading <h5>, and caption <p>, 982
 inserted carousel code, 981–982
 JavaScript code, 983
 JavaScript files, 985
 layout and CSS properties, 984
 lightboxes and modal images, 986
 Live view, 980
 locked CSS file, 984
 speed of, 984–985
 website, adding, 979
 W3Schools, 983
Cascading Style Sheets (CSS), 110, 286–287
 column count, 878
 export options, 286–287
 image slices and mobile devices, 870–871
 media queries (*see* Media queries)

1003

Cascading Style Sheets (CSS) (cont.)
   print, CSS Designer Panel, 878–879
   properties panel, 288–290
   viewport
      content, 866
      initial-scale=1, 866
      Insert panel, HTML tab, 865
      meta, 866
      Properties panel, 866
CC Libraries panel, 958
Character Animator CC, 384
Classic tween, 494, 502–504
Closed captioning (CC), 667
CMYK (cyan magenta, yellow, black), 11, 32
Code snippet panel
   bitmap file, 576
   button symbol, 575–576
   HTML5 Canvas, 574
   properties panel, 574
   wizard, 577–578
Color blindness proofs, 359–360
   deuteranopia (green loss), 197
   monochromacy (all color loss), 199
   protanopia (red loss), 197
Color dialog box, 38
Color effects, 510
Color Guide panel, 247
Color mode
   assign profile, 34, 242
   Bitmap, 32
   CMYK to RGB, 242–243
   display file name, 242
   Duotone, 36
   grayscale, 32
   HEX color, 37–38
   Index Color, 36–37
   Lab, 32
   Multichannel, 36
   pixel aspect ratio, 34
   RGB, 32, 34
      selection tool, 242
      web images, 239
   settings, 241
Color panel
   color picker, 244–245
   mode change, 243–244
   RGB setting, 244
Color Themes panel, 248
Column count, 878
Combining video clips, 676
Comment frames, 496–497
CompuServe GIF
   color picker, 58
   color table's eyedropper tool, 58
   indexed color, 55–56
      amount, 61
      dither, 60
      matte background option, 59–60
      palette drop-down menu, 56–58
         forcing colors, 58–59
   transparency option, 59
CSS3
   animations (see Animations, CSS3)
   background images, 830
   Bootstrap files, 828
   borders, 830–831
   box-decoration-break, 834
   box-shadow, 834–835
   custom bullets
      content property, 838
      GIF animation, 839
      list item bullets, 838
      property list-style, 839
      pseudo class, 839
      W3Schools, 839
   description, 827
   HTML5 shiv, 827
   image masking, 838
   <img> tag, 828–830
   Internet Explorer/Edge, 828
   outline CSS2, 833–834
   resources, CSS Snippets, 827–828
   rounded borders, 831–833
   text-shadow, 835–836
CSS Designer panel
   access color picker, 812
   background-color, 809–811
   body tag, add properties, 812–813
   color picker and helpful hints, 811
   internal style sheet, 807–808
   Selectors tab, 808
      add properties, 809
      selector rule, 809
      type in, 808
   source, media, selectors and properties, 806–807
CSS Filters
   blur(px), 836
   brightness(%), 836
   contrast(%), 836
   Dreamweaver's Snippets panel (CSS Effects), 837
   drop-shadow(h-shadow v-shadow blur spread color), 836
   grayscale(%), 837
   hue-rotate(deg), 837
   invert(%), 837
   None, 836
   opacity(%), 837

saturate(%), 837
sepia(%), 837
url(), 837
W3Schools, 837
CSS floats
   clip, 864–865
   light box/modal image, 861
   Photoshop CC and layers, 861
   position properties
      absolute, 863
      CSS Designer panel, 862
      fixed, 863
      position, 863
      relative, 863
      static, 863
      sticky, 863–864
   property, 861
   z-index, 864
CSS Transitions panel, 846–847
   Edit Transition dialog box, 852–853
   HTML document, 847
   New Transition dialog box, 847–848
      document/new style sheet file, 851
      drop-down menu, 849
      Edit mode, 849
      end value, 851
      end value properties, 850
      height/background color, 850–851
      set duration, delay, and timing function, 849–850
      Target Rule, 848
      Transition On, 849
   remove transition dialog box, 852
   save transitions, 853
   transition button, creation, 852

D

Dimensions (Dn), 7
2D transform
   Code view, 856
   matrix(n,n,n,n,n,n), 854
   rotate(angle), 855
   scaleX(n), 855
   scale(x,y), 855
   scaleY(n), 855
   skewX(angle), 855
   skew(x-angle,y-angle), 855
   skewY(angle), 855
   transform, 854
   transform-origin(x%,y%), 854
   Transition dialog box, 855
   translateX(n), 854
   translate(x,y), 854
   translateY(n), 854
3D transform
   backface-visibility, 857
   matrix3d(n,n,n,n,n,n,n,n,n,n,n,n,n,n,n,n), 858
   perspective, 856
   perspective(n), 858
   perspective-origin(x%,y%), 857
   rotate3d(x,y,z,angle), 858
   rotateX(angle), 858
   rotateY(angle), 858
   rotateZ(angle), 858
   scale3d(x,y,z), 858
   scaleX(x), 858
   scaleY(y), 858
   scaleZ(z), 858
   transform, 856
   transform-origin(x%,y%,z), 856
   transform-style, 856
   Transition dialog box, 858–859
   translate3d(x,y,z), 858
   translateX(x), 858
   translateY(y), 858
   translateZ(z), 858
2.5D Parallax Effect, 171
3D tools, Animate CC, 591–592
3D tweening, 495
<div> tag, 777
   code view, 778
   creating structure, 777
   design view, 779
   Properties panel, 779
   using insert div dialog box, 778
   using insert panel, 777, 779
Dreamweaver CC (Dw), 7, 961
   Adobe GoLive, 736
   Advanced Settings tab, 754
   Files panel, 755
   fixing errors, 756
   Help menu, 737
   Hot Glass Tango, 737, 753
   HTML5 (see HTML5)
   Install button, 737–738
   maze center, 733–734
   and Muse CC, 734–736
   open, Creative Cloud console, 738
   Properties panel, 738–740
   save file, HTML document, 754
   Servers tab, 753
   Site setup Site tab, 752
   templates, 747
   toolbar, 740–741
      apply comment and remove comment, 743
      Customize Toolbar dialog box, 744
      expand all, 743
      file formats, 747
      File Management, 741

Dreamweaver CC (Dw) (cont.)
    Format Source Code, 743
    new document, 747
    open documents, 741
    Preferences panel, 745
    Quick Start tab, 746
    Toggle Visual Media Queries Bar, 742
    Toolbars Standard panel, 745
    Turn on Live view and inspect mode, 742-743
    View Live Options, 741-742
    workspace, 738
Duotone, 36

E

Effects tab settings
    image overlay, 653-654
    loudness normalization, 659
    Lumetri Look/LUT, 651-652
    MP3
        loudness normalization, 684
        time tuner, 683
    name overlay, 654-655
    SDR Conform, 652
    text overlay, 655
    timecode overlay, 656-657
    time tuner, 657
    video limiter, 658
Embedded OpenType Fonts (EOT), 954
Encapsulated Postscript (EPS), 236
Encoding panel, 636
Enhanced metafile (.emf), 236
EPUB (.epub), 10
Event, 465
Export files
    animated files, 523-524
    Animated GIF
        audio, 542
        flower_stock.fla file, 542
        graphic, 542
        options, 541-542
        settings, 541, 542
    File ➤ Publish option, 525
    HTML5 Canvas (see HTML5 Canvas)
    Movie (see Movie)
    options, library panel (see Library panel, export files)
    Video (see Video)
    Web export options (see Web export options)
Export Image
    Image (Legacy)
        GIF, 533
        JPEG, 532
        photoshop, 532
        PNG, 534
        SVG, 535-536
        SWF movies, 532
    Web (Legacy) option
        Animate CC, 525
        GIF image, 528-529
        file size, 528
        HTML file, 526-527
        JPEG image, 530
        layout, 526
        PNG-8 and PNG-24 settings, 530-531
        presets, 528
        tools, 526
        Web dialog box, 526
Export settings dialog box. See also Audio tab settings
    advanced format settings, 649
    advanced settings, 651
    captions tab, 667
    effects tab (see Effects tab settings)
    format name, 644
    metadata, 674-675
    multipexer tab settings, 667
    output tab, 646
    preview settings, 646
    publish tab (see Publish tab settings)
    render alpha channel, 673
    render quality, 673
    source tab, 644-645
    time interpolation, 673
    video tab (see Video tab settings)
External CSS
    CSS Designer panel
        attached to webpage, 825
        Attach Existing CSS file, 826
        attaching, 824
        color and background images, 825
        create/add existing style sheet, 822
        create new CSS file and save, 822-823
        link of background image, 825-826
        new CSS file, 824
        remove internal styles, 822
    File ➤ New ➤ CSS, 827
    issues, 821
    overriding background/link color, 821
Extraction of code from layers
    CSS information, 190
    SVG data, 190
Extract PSD panel, 958-960

F

File conversion process
    Actions panel
        image size, 101, 105
        JPEG option, 103-104

mode conversion, 106
new action set, 96-98
recording, 98-100
Automate Batch Actions, 106-107
Automate Droplet Actions, 107-109
Illustrator CC
    action recording, 301
    action set creation, 300-303
    actions panel, 298-299
    SVG options dialog box, 301-302
Flash/Flash Application, 388
Flashing graphics, dangers of, 595
Flash SWF and Flash video, 947
Frame Picker panel, 519-520
Frames per second (fps), 178
Free fonts, 953

G

GIF files, 127
GIF (static) image sequence export settings, 699-700
Glyphs panel, 343
Google Charts, 951
Gradient fills, 403-404
Gradient panel, 248-249
Graphic file formats, 456
Graphic interchange format (GIF) animation
    Adobe Animate CC, 129
    benefit, 597
    color reduction algorithm, 79-80
    dither algorithm, 80-81
    drawback, 597
    export, 72
        open, 599-600
        preview, 602
        save, 603
        settings, 601-602
    FLA file, 597-598
    layers, creation, 127-128
    movie clip symbols, 598
    Photoshop CC
        Layers panel, 206-207
        save animation, 208
        settings, 208
        timeline, 207
    quick export format, 67
    resampling method, 81
    static and animated, 10
    timeline, 598
    web (legacy) dialog box, 78-79
Graphs and charts, 951
Grayscale, 32
Grid tile, 349

H

Hexagonal tile, 349
HEX color, 37-38
Hot Glass Tango, 361, 708
    action panel
        AI file, 368
        GIF files, 363
        GIF selective diffusion 256, 363-364, 367
        GIF settings, 365-366
        image preview, 368
        recording, 364, 366
        visibility, 366-367
        web (legacy), 364
    carousel gallery (Bootstrap) (see Carousel gallery)
    gallery image
        average size, 201-202
        exporting, 202-206
        GIF, 201
        PNG and JPEG, 201
        PSD file, 202
    GIF (see Graphic interchange format (GIF) animation)
    GIF 64 Dither, 362-363
    GIF animation
        Layers panel, 206-207
        save animation, 208
        settings, 208
        timeline, 207
    GIF image, 362
    HTML5 Canvas (see HTML5 Canvas animation)
    HTML5 video
        <button> tag, 987
        channel_changer_jh.js, 988
        comments, 986
        conditional statements, 988
        final gallery, 986
        links and names, 988
        media2.html file, 986
        media2_practice39.html file, 987
        mobile site, 986
        player ID, 988
    inserting images, 977-979
    JPEG poster image
        Layers panel, 210
        Movie Poster folder, 209
        save, 211
    layers panel, 361-362
    PNG/JPG files, 362
    video (see Video rendering)
    video file
        ActionScript 3.0 FLA files, 603
        Adobe Media Encoder, 608

INDEX

Hot Glass Tango (*cont.*)
    create storyboard, 604, 606
    exporting, 607
    pre-plan settings, 606
    review, 606-607
    visible layer, 362
Hot Glass Tango (*see* Timeline panel)
HTML5
    add language, 750
    <body></body>, 751
    Code view, 749-750
    CSS file, 748
    <!doctype html>, 750
    doc type settings, 748
    <head> </head>, 751
    <html> </html>, 750
    and HTML4 formats, 748-749
    image tag, 750
    <meta charset="utf-8">, 751
    metadata, 751
    New Document dialog box, 747-748
    opening and closing tags, 750
    <title>Untitled Document</title>, 751
HTML5 audio
    CSS aural, 940
    Files panel, 936-937
    formats, 936
    Insert panel, 937
    Media Encoder, 936
    Properties panel
        Alt Source 1, 938
        Alt Source 2, 938
        <audio> tag, 937-939
        AutoPlay, 938
        background using CSS, 940
        Class, 938
        Controls, 938
        Fallback Text, 938
        ID, 937, 939
        Loop, 938
        Muted, 938
        Preload, 938
        Source, 938, 939
        Title, 938
HTML5 Canvas
    ActionScript 3.0 FLA, 543
    Animate CC, 542
        alterations, 941
        code view, 942
        Find in Current Document, 941
        sounds, 941-942
        template-based pages, 942
    animated composition/OAM file
        animation assets, 944
        code, creation, 946
        Dreamweaver, 945
        HTML file, 945
        Insert panel, 944-945
        <object> tag, 947
        Properties panel, 946
        unpackaged, 945-946
        ZIP file, 944
    animation, 391
    creation, code, 558
    custom profile settings, 544
    definition, 390
    drawing graphics, 391
    drawing text, 390
    Dreamweaver's Code
        view, 943-944
    element, 390
    event handlers, 391
    FLA file, 940
    flower_stock.html, 558
    in games, 391
    Insert panel, 942-943
    JavaScript, 391, 943
    OAM file, 558, 940
    Properties panel, 543, 943
    publish settings
        ActionScript 3.0 FLA Files, 555-557
        JavaScript/HTML (*see* JavaScript/HTML options)
        JPEG image, 552
        OAM package, 552-554
        SVG image, 555
    shapes, 390
HTML5 Canvas animation
    convert ActionScript 3.0 FLA, 608
    Library panel, 608-609
    OAM file, 610-612
    publish settings dialog box, 610-612
HTML5 Canvas file
    import video
        added components, 468
        Component Parametes, 469
        components panel, 468
        final component parameters, 471
        formats, 470
        Library panel, 469
        results, 471
        Source content path, 470
        with SWF, 467
HTML5 video
    background using CSS, 936
    Files panel, 931
    formats, 930
    Insert panel, 931-932
    Media Encoder, 930
    mobile and video scaling, 936

Properties panel
    Alt Source 1, 933
    Alt Source 2, 933
    AutoPlay, 933
    Class, 932
    Code view, 935
    Controls, 933
    Fallback text, 933
    Flash Fallback, 933
    ID, 932, 934
    Loop, 933
    Muted, 933
    Poster, 932
    Preload, 933
    setting options, attributes, 932
    <source> tags, 932, 934
    Title, 932
    <video> tag, 933-934
    W and H, 932
    warning, 935
splash screen design, 931
streaming and embedded, 930-931
track tag, 935

I

Illustrator CC
    batch action process, 303-305
    buttons, 356-357
    color blindness proof, 359-360
    export settings, 253
    export web files
        export As, 283
        GIF, 292
        JPEG, 293
        preset setting, 291
        PNG-8, 293-294
        PNG-24, 293-294
        save a copy, 254
        screens, 264-265
        Web (Legacy), 290
    file conversion (see File conversion process)
    file creation
        raster effects, 231
        RGB Color, 229-230
        templates, 232
    graphics, 224
    graphic styles, 356-357
    Hot Glass Tango, image exporting (see Hot Glass Tango)
    import photoshop options, 235
    Libraries panel, 341-342
    raster graphics, 233
    raster images, 233-234
    RAW file types, 233

rollovers, 356-357
scripts, 297
slices (see Slicing tools)
smart object, 28
SVG file exporting
    camel code, 371
    clear layer, 374-375
    informational image map, 368
    JavaScript, 375-377
    layer order, 378
    layer's eye, 378
    layers panel, 369-370, 373
    onmouseover, 375
    sublayers, 369
    SVG interactivity panel, 375
    SVG options, 371-373
    target, 376-377
    visibility eyes, 373-374
Symbols panel, 357-359
vector formats, 236-237
video tool
    3D images, 338-340
    video layout, 337-338
web fonts and SVG fonts
    character panel, 342
    control panel, 343
    glyphs panel, 343
    properties panel, 344
workspace
    open program, 226
    tool options, 227
    web workspace, 226, 228
Images
    favicons to browser tab, 798-799
    formats, 758
    on HTML page, 762
        Insert panel (see Insert panel, HTML page)
        Properties panel (see Properties panel, HTML page)
        working with SVG images, 768
    HTML5 and Snippets panel, 799-800
    inside tags
        <details> and <summary> elements, 797
        <dialog> element, 798
        <div> tags, 777-779
        HTML history, 776-777
        Insert panel, 776
        maps <area> and <map> tags, 793-796
        <menu> and <menuitem> elements, 798
        <picture> and <source> element, 796-797
        semantic elements (see Semantic elements, tags)
        web design, tables, 790-792
    site, 758
    subfolders, 759-762

Image sequence
    animated GIF, 700-702
    bitmap, 692, 694-695
    crop images, 692
    export dialog box, setting, 692
    GIF (static), 699-700
    JPEG, 696-697
    PNG, 697-699
    preset browser panel, 691
Image size and resolution
    Canvas Size, 44-45
    Image Size dialog box, 42-44
Index Color, 36
Inline CSS
    <body> tag, 801
    Clean up HTML/XHTML, 804
    Color in Dreamweaver, 803
    <body> tag, 801
    <h1> tag, 801
    issues, 803
    page properties, Properties panel, 802
Insert panel, HTML page, 762
    Image Optimization Format options, 765
    Image Optimization preset options, 765
    inserting image, 764
    JPEG image, 766
    main menu, 763
    in Split view, 767
    as Sync image, 766
    tag attributes, 767
    Tools panel, 763
Interactive PDF, 10
Interlacing, 172
Internal CSS
    background-image property
        background-attachment: fixed, 814
        background-blend-mode: lighten, 814
        background-clip: padding-box, 815
        background-origin: content-box, 814
        background-position: right top, 813
        background-size: 300px 100px, 814
        gradients, 815-816
        information, 814
        radial gradients, 816-817
        repeat, 813
    <body> tag, 805
    CSS Designer panel (*see* CSS Designer panel)
    Enable/disable layer properties, 817
    <head> tag, 804
    Links (CSS) and Headings (CSS) tabs, 805
    page properties
        appearance CSS, 805
        image for tracing and design, 806
    Properties panel, 805
        class, 819-820
        IDs, 818-819
        pseudo class selectors, 820-821
        tags, 818
Interpolation, 153
Interpret Footage dialog box, 635
Inverse kinematics (IK), 511

J, K

JavaScript
    behavior panel
        <a> tag, 891
        actions, 890
        browser window, 892
        CSS, 894
        <div> elements, 891
        events, 889
        external JS file, 893
        HTML5, 894
        jQuery, 891
        linkage corruption, 892
        menu, 888
        onMouseOut, 892
        properties menu, 892
        review, 890
        show-hide elements, 893
        show hide images, 893-894
        swap image, 891
    code, 882
    CSS3, 881
    defined, 881-882
    Dreamweaver's code editor, 883
    file creation
        document type, 883
        external, 883
        JS file, 884
        <script> tag, 884
        source code icon, 885
    files panel, 882
    HTML, 881
    print preview, 897
    rollover image
        CSS3, 886
        defined, 885
        Dreamweaver, 887
        external file, 887
        HTML, 888
        HTML5, 886
        inline JavaScript, 888
        insert panel, 885
        insert rollover image dialog box, 886
        rollover button, 887
        URL, 888
    <scripts> tags, 883
    snippets panel
        images, 895
        random image, 895-896

      resources, 895
      simple preload, 896
      slide show, 896
      switch image, 896
JavaScript/HTML options
    Basic tab settings
      assets, 547
      center stage, 546
      changes, 546
      Choose Fit In View, 546
      CreateJS, 547
      export image assets, 546
      hidden layers, 545
      loop timeline, 545
      output file, 544
      preloader animation, 546
      Sprite sheet, 547
    HTML/JS Settings tab
      alert message, 548
      controls, 548
      HTML file on publish, 548
      options, 549–550
      reset, 549
    Image Settings tab, 550
    web fonts tab, 551
Joint Photographic Experts Group
      (JPEG), 272–273, 284
    color options, 52–53
    color picker window, 53
    defined, 9
    export as, 71
    format options, 54
    image options, 53–54
    matte background, 52
    options, 52
    quality control, 83
    quick export format, 66–67
    save, 11
    sequence export settings, 696–697
    web (legacy) dialog box, 82
jQuery, 891

L

Lab color, 32
Layer comps, 90–92
Layers, 92–93
Library items
    Animate CC, 917
    Assets panel
      adding, 922
      comment tags, 924
      CSS internal/external link, 923–924
      insert, template-based page, 924
      New Library Item button, 921–922
      previewing images, 920–921

      rename and open, 923
      review items, 920
      view, 923
    detach, 925–927
    folder, 918
    notes, 918
    tools menu, 919
    update, 918–919
Library panel, export options
    generation, sprite sheet
      Data format, 562
      location, 562
      output options, 561
      sprite sheet dialog box, 560, 561
      symbols, 559–560
      transparency, PNG 8/32, 562
    generation, texture atlas, 562
    PNG sequence, 559

M

Mac and Win Projector, 567
Media Browser panel
    enable hover scrub, 627
    menu options, 626–627
    navigation, 629
    search options, 628–629
Media Encoder CC, 6, 148, 642–643
    and Animate CC, 616–617
    appearance preferences
      audio hardware, 624
      general, 623
      media cache files, 624
      memory, 624
      metadata, 624
      settings, 622
      sync settings, 625
    audio (*see* Audio MP3 File)
    Creative Cloud console, 618–619
    Creative Cloud program, 616
    file formats, 617–618
    MOV file, 620
    Queue panel (*see* Queue panel)
    video (*see* Video MP4 File)
    workspaces, 621–622
Media queries, 874–875
    background image, <div>, 876
    Bootstrap, 866, 877
    browsers and devices, 877
    Conditional Usage (Optional) tab, 867
    conditions, 868
    CSS Designer panel, 866–867
    different backgrounds, 877
    dimensions, 872
    Hot Glass Tango, 875
    landscape orientation, 873

INDEX

Media queries (*cont.*)
    max-width, 872
    Preview panel, 873
    print, 869–870
    scaling images, 875–876
    screen, 868
    screen resolution parameters, 872
    Snippets panel, 877–878
    view and add, 872
Metadata Export dialog box, 675
Mobile Device Packaging (An), 6
Monoscopic, 663
Motion tweens
    Armature, 495
    camera, 495
    and Camera tween, 504–507
    3D tween, 495–496
    Motion Presets panel, 508
    shape, 494–495
Movie
    creation, sequence, 537
    File options, 537
    GIF options, 538
    JPEG options, 537
    PNG options, 538–539
    SWF movie, 537
Movie Clips, 446
MP4 (.mp4), 642
MPEG4 file format, 643
Multimedia tags, Insert panel, 929–930
Multipexer tab settings, 667
Muse CC, 734–736

N

Nudge, 134

O

OAM Package, 552–554
Ogg, 677
Outline CSS2, 833–834
Output tab, 646

P

Paid fonts, 953
Paint Brush tool
    editing, 582
    paint_brush.fla
        add design, 588
        create, 585
        Manage Brushes button, 589
        Options dialog box, 586–587
        save, 589

Properties panel, 583
    Eraser tool, 585
    options, 584
    Pencil tool, 584
    store, 585
    update, 590
Paint Bucket tool (K), 401
Pattern brush, 587
Pencil tool, 583–584, 590
Photoshop CC (Ps), 6, 128
    Creative Cloud application, 17–18
    export options, 47
    export web files
        artboards, 88–90
        layer comps, 90–92
        layers, 92–93
    file creation
        artboard, 23
        camera raw option, 27
        create button, 24–25
        file formats, 25–27
        layers panel, 25
        photo tab options, 23
        RGB color, 23
        video formats, 26
    file exporting
        save as option, 48–50
        save for web (legacy), 75
        web (legacy) option (*see* Web (legacy) option)
    graphic and web workspace
        edit toolbar icon, 20
        vs. essentials workspace, 19
        group tools, 20–21
        layout, 22
    Hot Glass Tango (*see* Hot Glass Tango)
    image format, 16
    learn panel, 16
    Media Encoder, 216
    timeline (*see* Timeline panel)
Photoshop PSD (.psd, .pdd), 233
Pixels/inch (PPI), 230
Plug-ins, 948
PNG 8, 83–84, 270–272
PNG-24, 85
Portable Document Format (PDF)
    Adobe InDesign CC, 61
    defined, 10
    photoshop alert, 62
    save Adobe PDF settings, 62–65
Portable Network Graphics (PNG), 10, 270, 285
    export as, 69–70
    format options, 55
    quick export format, 65–66
    sequence export settings, 697–699
    transparency, 55

Premiere Pro CC, 216
Project Felix (Fe), 7
Properties panel, HTML page
    alternate text, 775
    brightness/contrast, 774
    crop, 772-773
    design view, 769
    image optimization, 771
    Pencil icon, 769
    Preferences, 770-771
    preview of image, 769
    Quick Edit icons, 769
    Quick Edit options, 771
    resampling, 773
    sharpening, 774
    updating from original, 771
    width and height, 774
Publish tab settings
    Adobe Creative Cloud, 668
    Adobe Stock, 669
    Behance, 669
    Facebook, 670
    FTP, 670
    Twitter, 671
    Vimeo, 672-673
Puppet warp tool
    animate CC, 333
    bend/scale, 333
    control panel, 334
    expand mesh, 335
    gradient mesh tool, 333
    Photoshop
        animate timeline animation, 337
        control panels, 336
        smart filter, 336
        smart object layers, 336
    properties panel, 335
    select all pins, 335
    selection tool (V), 334
    settings, 335
    show mesh, 335
    spin/swirl, 333
    symbols panel, 334
    tools panel, 333
    wrap mesh, 334

Q

Queue panel
    add/removal files, 630-631
    drop-down menu, 621
    Encoding panel, 636
    export settings, 630, 632
    format options, 632
    Interpret Footage, 634-635
    MOV file, 620
    output options, 634
    Preset Browser panel, 636-637
    Preset menu options, 638-640
    Preset options, 633
    status options, 634
    watch folder, 631, 636
QuickTime File Format (MOV), 642

R

RAW files
    AVI, 642
    MOV, 642
RGB (red, green, blue), 11, 239-240

S

Scalable Vector Graphics (SVG), 274
    defined, 10
    export as, 73-74
    Options dialog box
        Advanced settings, 262-263
        font settings, 261
        lower buttons, 263
        options button, 259
        option settings, 262
        profile settings, 261
    quick export format, 68
Scene panel, 520-521
Semantic elements, tags
    <article> element, 787
    aside tag, 786
    <figure> and <figcaption> tags, 781-782
    <footer> element, 788-789
    <header> tag, 782-783
    Insert panel, 781
    <main> element, 784-786
    navigation, 783-784
    <section> tag, 788
Shape tweening, 494-495
    blend, 502
    classic ease, 501
    custom ease, 501-502
    properties panel, 500
    shape hints, 499
Show tile edge, 352
Site, uploading
    Advanced Settings tab, checking, 972
    Edit> Preferences, 961-962
    to remote server, 972-976
    validation options, 963
        Link Checker panel, 964-965
        local and remote sites, 967-968
        managing site, 968, 970-971

Site, uploading (*cont.*)
    Output panel, 967
    Site reports panel, 964
    Validation panel, 965-966
Slice Select tool (C), 114, 117
Slicing tools
    auto slices, 112-113
    badges, 113
    exporting
        file formats, 120
        generating CSS, 120-124
    Illustrator CC
        Align panel, 311
        auto/layer-based slicing, 308
        colors, 309
        creation, 307
        custom layout, 306
        deletion, 316
        divide slice dialog box, 310-311
        export, 317-318
        file size, 318
        forward/backward, 312
        hide, 316
        HTML code, 319
        HTML text, 315
        image, 312-313
        image maps, 319-320
        lines, 308
        lock, 316
        no image, 314-315
        none/color background, 313-314
        numbers, 309
        options, 310, 312
        principles, 306
        Save For Web (Legacy) dialog box, 309
        saving, 316-319
        user and auto slices, 307-308
        webpage, 306-307
    layer-based slice, 119
    Options panel, 114
    Slice Select tool (C)
        Options panel, 115
        Slice Options, 116-119
    user slice, 111, 113
Small Web Format (SWF), 382
Source tab, 644-645
Square tile, 349
Stitch clips, 676
Subslices, 307
SVG interactivity panel
    AI/EPS, 325
    appearance panel, 330
    documents
        event, 327
        event per target, 328

        JavaScript, 327
        onabort, 327
        onerror, 327
        onload, 327
        onresize, 327
        onscroll, 327
        onunload, 327
        onzoom, 327
        SVG file, 327
        testing, 328
    elements
        onactivate, 326
        onclick, 326
        onfocusin, 326
        onfocusout, 326
        onkeydown, 326
        onkeypress, 326
        onkeyup, 326
        onmousedown, 326
        onmousemove, 326
        onmouseover, 326
        onmouseup, 326
    JavaScript, 325, 329-330
    layer panel, 324
    save/export webpage, 323-325
    show code, 325
    SVG filters, 330
    SVG setting, 325
    triggers, 325-326
Swatches color panel, 40-41, 245-246
Swatches panel, 406
Swatches pattern
    altering, 353
    apply pattern, 352-353
    dreamweaver CC, 354
    message, 345
    new pattern, 346
    options panel, 344-345
    pattern-editing
        mode, 346-347
    tile tool, 348-349
        bounds, 352
        brick offset, 349
        copies, 351-352
        edge color, 354
        grid, 349
        hexagonal, 349
        H/V spacing, 350
        move art, 350
        overlap, 351
        show edge, 352
        square, 349
        width and height, 349
    transform pattern, 355
SWF animations, 532

T, U

Target attributes, 949–951
Templates
    added to Templates folder, 908
    Bootstrap links and HTML5, 905–906
    creation, 906–907
    Editable Region
        Design view, 911
        Hot Glass Tango, 911
        Insert panel, 910
        new editable region, 910–911
        purpose, 910
        <tag> element, 911
    Editable Region Options, 912–913
        Make Nested Template, 912
        Make Template, 912
        Optional Region, 912
        Repeating Region, 913
        Repeating Table, 913
    editable regions, 908
    Hot Glass Tango, 909
    HTML5, 909
    HTML pages, 905
    new, 907
    starter, 908–909
    template-based page
        creating, 913–914
        <head> tag, 914
    troubleshooting, 916–917
    Update Pages, 915–916
    WordPress, 905
Text-shadow, 835–836
Themes panel, 248
Theora Ogg, 690
TIFF (.tif,.tiff), 233
Timecode overlay, 656–657
Timeline panel, 129
    adding frame
        delete animation, 133
        duplicate selected frames icon, 131, 133
        layer eye, 132
        repeating frames, 133
    Animate timeline, 474
    bone (see Bone tool)
    Camera tool (C), 508–511
    classic tween (see Classic tween)
    Edit Multiple Frames icon, 490
    frame animation, 129
        layers, 129–130
        menu, 131
    frames
        Actions panel, 497–498
        audio, 496
        choosing, 491
        comment, 496–497
        keyframes, 493
        picker panel, 519–520
        pop-up menu, 498
        split frames, animations, 493
        tweens, 494–496
        types, 492
    GIF animation, 143
    Hot Glass Tango, 474
    keyframes, 473, 488
    layer
        advanced setting, 479–480
        armature, 488
        camera, 486–487
        create new, 475
        Depth panel, 480, 482–484
        hide/show layers and folder, 476–477
        lock layers and folders, 477
        order, 474–475
        outlines, 477, 479
        properties dialog box, 485–486
        storage, folders, 476
    layer style effects
        animation, 136–137
        effects(fx)layer, 135
        flattening frames, 140
        layer fill/adjustment layers, 136
        match layer, 139
        pattern overlay, 136
        reverse frames, 138–139
    make frames, 133
    marker range, 490
    Motion and Camera tween, 504–508
    new position, 135
    parts, 488–489
    playhead, 489
    preview, 489
    Scene panel, 520
    shapetweening (see Shape tweening))
    timeline animation, 134
    tweening layers, 140
        GIF animation, 141–143
        tween animation frames icon, 140
        tween effects, 141
    video timeline, 129
Time tuner, 658
Transforms
    2D (see 2D transform)
    3D (see 3D transform)
    Snippets panel, 853
    W3Schools, 854
    width and height, 854
Transitions, CSS
    class (.linearTransition), 846
    cubic-bezier(n,n,n,n), 846

■ INDEX

Transitions, CSS (*cont.*)
    2D and 3D transforms, 846
    <div> tag, 844
    ease, 845
    ease-in, 845
    ease-in-out, 845
    ease-out, 845
    linear, 845
    pseudo class, 845
    step-end, 846
    steps(int,start|end), 846
    step-start, 845
    transition, 845
    transition-delay, 845
    transition-duration, 845
    transition-property, 845
    transition-timing-function, 845
Transparency panel, 249–250
TrueType Fonts (TTF), 955
Tweening, 140
Tweens
    classic, 494
    motion, 494–496

■ **V**

Vector smart objects
    GIF animations, 332
    Puppet warp tool (*see* Puppet warp tool)
    rasterize smart object, 332
    selection tool (V), 330
    smart object layer, 331
    smart object placement, 331
    vector masks, 331
Video
    alpha channel, 540
    control audio, MOV export, 540
    creation, 146–147
    Export Video dialog box, 539
    file size, 146
    footage area, 148
    GIF animation, 145
    HTML5 <video> tag, 540
    Mac users, 540
    Media Encoder CC, 148, 540
    MP4 settings, 540
    Photoshop CC, 145
    RAW footage, 146
    video formats, 147
    video timeline menu (*see* Video timeline)
    web video, 147
Video convertion. *See* Export settings dialog box
Video files (MP4, WebM, Ogg/Ogv), 10
Video rendering
    audio tracks, 215–217
    dialog box, 218
    keyframes, 213–214
    organizing, 214
    preset options, 218–219
    process, 219
    save, 219
    split edit, 217
    text layer, 214–215
    timeline, 212–213
Video tab settings
    advanced, 662
    basic video settings, 660
    bitrate, 662
    encoding, 661
    Video is VR, 663
Video timeline
    after effects program, 178
    animation panel options, 183–184
    audio track, 184–185
    auto grouping, 182
    blend mode, 183
    close tab group, 187
    comments track, 179–180
    create, 149
    delete frame, 177
    3D tracks, 183
    duplicate frame, 177
    edit timeline comment, 178–179
    extract work area, 176
    frame animation, 151
    frame rate, 174, 178
    frame spacing, 183
    global lighting, 150
    insert blank frame, 177
    interpret footage, 171
        alpha channel, 172
        color profile, 174
        de-interlace, 172–173
        frame rate, 173
    layers, 149, 151–152
        clock icon, 154
        hold interpolation, 154
        keyframes, 152–155
        linear interpolation, 153
        type layer, 156–157
        vector mask, 155–156
    layers panel, 150–151
    lift work area, 176
    menu, 149
    motion option, 164
    onion skin count, 183
    onion skin options, 183
    Photoshop image sequence option, 187
    play feature, 174
    playhead, 176–177
    preview, 175
    PSD, 187

render video, 186-187
replace footage option, 161
scissor icon, 168
settings, 182
show/hide track, 180-181
smart object layers, 157
smart object's play icon, 164
timeline shortcut keys, 182
video layers, 158
    audio option, 160
    clone or brush tools, 160
    convert frames, 170-171
    convert smart objects, 163-165
    3D effects, 171
    delete timeline, 166
    delete track, 166
    duration, 159-160
    moving video, 162-163
    non-video layer, 159
    properties, 160
    restore frame, 161
    smart object, 161
    speed, 159
    split video, 168-169
    tracks, 158
    transition, 166-168
    trim, 169-170
    video groups, 161-162
widget icon, 175
zoom in or out, 178

W, X, Y

W3Schools, 801, 870, 983
Watch Folders panel, 636
WAV File
    media encoder CC
        queue panel, 728
        re-export queue panel, 728
        waveform audio file, 727
WBMP/Wireless Bitmap, 48, 86
    image options, 87
    web (legacy) dialog box, 86
Web design workflow
    color blindness proofs, 197-200
    extraction of code from layers, 190
    libraries CC, 189-190
    paint symmetry, 194-196
    repeating backgrounds
        creation, 192-194
    SVG fonts, 191-192
    web fonts, 191-192
    web styles, 196-197
Web export options
    AIR
        Android and iOS, 566
        Flash files, 566
        New Document dialog box, 563
        Settings dialog box, 564, 565
        target drop-down menu, 564
    Projector, 567
    WebGL, 568
Web file formats
    audio files, 10
    Bitmap, 9
    canvas, 10
    EPUB, 10
    GIF, 10
    Interactive PDF (.pdf), 10
    JPEG, 9
    PDF, 10
    PNG, 10
    Scalable Vector Graphics (.svg), 10
    video files, 10
Web fonts
    adding, Local Web Fonts, 954
    Adobe Edge Web Fonts, 953
    Adobe Typekit, 593-594
    Bootstrap widgets, 955
    browsers support, 955
    CSS Designer panel, 956
    CSS file, 952
    embedding, 952
    EOT, 954
    @font-face, 955-956
    free and paid, 953
    Google fonts, 594-595, 952
    Manage Fonts dialog box, 957
    Properties panel, 952
    SVG Fonts/Shapes, 955
    text tool, 592
    TTF, 955
    WOFF/WOFF 2.0, 954
WebGL files, 568
Web (legacy) option, 74
    color table, 75, 78
    dailog box, 75
    layouts compare, 75-76
    SVG, 77
    tools, 76-77
WebM, 677
Web Open Font Format (WOFF/WOFF 2.0), 954
Web-safe color, 39-40
Web symbol, 357-359
Windows metafile (.wmf), 236

Z

z-index, 864
Zoomify, 124-126

GPSR Compliance

The European Union's (EU) General Product Safety Regulation (GPSR) is a set of rules that requires consumer products to be safe and our obligations to ensure this.

If you have any concerns about our products, you can contact us on

ProductSafety@springernature.com

In case Publisher is established outside the EU, the EU authorized representative is:

Springer Nature Customer Service Center GmbH
Europaplatz 3
69115 Heidelberg, Germany

www.ingramcontent.com/pod-product-compliance
Lightning Source LLC
LaVergne TN
LVHW080308260326
834688LV00038B/1007